A Genealogical
Gazetteer of England

A Genealogical
Gazetteer of England

AN ALPHABETICAL DICTIONARY OF PLACES

With Their Location, Ecclesiastical Jurisdiction, Population,
and the Date of the Earliest Entry In the Registers of
Every Ancient Parish in England

Compiled by

FRANK SMITH
Co-Author

Genealogical Research in England and Wales, etc.

DEDICATED

to a simpler way

of performing genealogical research

in English records

PREFACE

The only work of its kind, this newly compiled volume contains all the genealogical information necessary to know before searching in English records for data about a family living in a particular locality. The information supplied is as follows:

(1) A description of each parish, chapelry, hamlet, etc., as it was in 1831.

(2) The date of commencement of all Church of England parish registers before 1813.

(3) The name of the county in which the place was situated in 1831.

(4) The distance in miles from the next largest place.

(5) The population of each place as of 1831.

(6) The ecclesiastical jurisdiction of each parish.

(7) Nonconformist groups as listed in the 1831 edition of Lewis' Topographical Dictionary.

(8) Corrections and additions to the above information as found in reference books and based on more than twenty years of research.

Although the value of this information is already known to those who have had considerable experience in research into English records, a word to the inexperienced researcher will no doubt be welcome about the especial value of a handy one-volume genealogical gazetteer as opposed to the modern gazetteers and atlases, on the one hand, or the older out-of-print works, on the other hand.

Before enquiring about the records of an English ancestor the researcher needs to study the locality where the family resided. Of course, the best sources for information on the topographical and geographical features of a region are those printed about the time in which the ancestor lived or those, in the case of England, at least one hundred years old. Modern gazetteers and atlases are for this purpose near useless since the changes in names, populations, etc., have been too great during this period; also, modern gazetteers and atlases generally list only the larger places.

Then too the modern works do not have the appropriate details of ecclesiastical divisions and the areas of probate jurisdiction which have to be known to search English records, since the early records such as ancient parish registers were for the most part kept by the officially recognized Church of England (Protestant). For example, before the 1st of July, 1837, when Civil Registration, or the keeping of vital records and statistics by the government, was established, the main source of genealogical data is the ecclesiastical parish of the Church of England and its divisions of rural deaneries, archdeaconries, dioceses, and provinces. Hence, the ecclesiastical jurisdiction within which towns, parishes, chapelries, townships, etc., are situated must be known when searching for parish registers of baptisms, marriages, and deaths from their date of commencement in 1538 until 1st of July, 1837.

It is important to remember, too, that many printed parish registers stop at 1812. As there had to be a stopping point somewhere, this year was chosen because beginning the 1st of January, 1813, it was required that every parish commence new registers which were composed of ruled forms for separate books of baptisms, marriages, and burials, and hence the transcription and printing of the registers largely ceased.

Similarly, before the 11th of January, 1858, most probates were granted in ecclesiastical courts by officials appointed by the Church of England, the exception being the few manorial and honor courts. The areas covered by probate courts were based for the most part on the various types of ecclesiastical divisions, although they did bear the names of existing towns, cities, and counties in some cases. Hence, the ecclesiastical jurisdiction of the probate courts must be known when searching for early wills, administrations, and inventories.

Likewise, the earliest English census records of genealogical value, having been taken in 1841 and 1851, are arranged by parishes and sub-districts and districts, and hence it is necessary to know the place and parish before beginning a search into these records.

Finally, the size of the population within a parish affected the size and arrangement of the registers, and hence it is necessary to have statistics and a description of the extent of the parish as it existed when the early records were kept.

Before the present work was compiled, the best work for consulting county maps along with the relevant geographical, historical, and statistical data was Samuel Lewis' multi-volume Topographical Dictionary of England, the best editions of which for genealogical purposes were published in 1831 and 1833. Lewis not only gave an account of every place of importance including counties, cities, boroughs, corporate and market towns, parishes, townships, chapelries, hamlets, and tythings, but gave as well the ecclesiastical jurisdiction of each place, its location, its population then, topographical and historical features, and other information.

In addition, to supplement the information found in Lewis' work, other works had to be consulted before beginning researches into early English records could be made, since the date when the parish register began and other information, could only be found in works now out of print.

In all, it would be necessary to look into several books before the correct information could be found, not to mention the unlikelihood of the average researcher knowing all these sources of information. Even the professional researcher would be frequently in difficulty, since these reference works, being out-of-print and especially scarce in the United States, are seldom readily available. Finally, the cost of compiling the necessary reference collection for searching into early English records would be nearly prohibitive for the average researcher and for many libraries. Thus, this present work is of inestimable value.

For details about the value and extent of the early English records, we refer you to the first two volumes of David E. Gardner and Frank Smith's Genealogical Research in England and Wales (Salt Lake City; Bookcraft Publishers, 1956-   ), a third volume of which is devoted to interpreting English handwriting and research procedures, and a fourth volume is forthcoming.

We strongly suggest the researcher first consult the information on locality and ecclesiastical jurisdiction contained in this volume — for this one-volume compilation makes available all the necessary data in a single alphabet. Since in the past many of the records to which this work gives access were little understood and rarely used, the availability of the present work will open new avenues of research for the experienced, as well as the beginning, researcher.

* * * * * * *

This work is based on Lewis' Topographical Dictionary of England (Samuel Lewis & Co.) London (1831 and 1833 editions); Parish Register Abstract, 1831 (H. M. Stationery Office, London, 1833); Key to the Ancient Parish Registers of England and Wales, Arthur M. Burke, (London, 1908). To these have been added corrections and additions found over the past twenty years as the original records were handled.

* * * * * * *

The compiler moved from the field of mining engineering into the field of genealogy in 1945 on a full-time professional basis. He supervised the Research Department of the British Mission Genealogical Department of the Church of Jesus Christ of Latter-day Saints before emigrating to the United States in 1953, to take a position in the Research Department at the Genealogical Society in Salt Lake City. Since 1961 he has supervised that department. He is co-author of Genealogical Research in England and Wales (three volumes with a fourth in progress) and co-compiler of Genealogical Atlases of England and Wales;

Scotland and Ireland. The present work is the result of six years of spare time work in this area because he believes that it is essential that as much reference material as possible be placed in the hands of the amateur so that he can plan his work in his own home and use his time in the library to the full.

INTRODUCTION

The purposes for the preparation of this Gazetteer are:

1. To avoid the dependence on several rare reference books now out of print and difficult to obtain.

2. To avoid having to refer to more than one of these books for the information required.

3. To save time by extracting from these rare reference books the information of genealogical value only.

4. To correct, as far as possible, the errors and inconsistencies contained in these reference books.

5. To add places and other genealogical information not found in the above books.

Information is listed in the following order:

1. Place (See details below.)

2. A description of the place as it was in 1831 (i.e. parish, chapelry, hamlet, etc.)

3. The date of commencement of the parish registers if the place is an ancient parish of the Church of England.

4. The county in which the place was situated in 1831.

5. The distance in miles from a larger place.

6. Its population in 1831.

7. The ecclesiastical jurisdiction in 1831 if the place is a parish.

8. Nonconformist groups as reported in the 1831 edition of Lewis' Topographical Dictionary.

PLACES

These appear in the same alphabetical order as they are listed in Lewis' Topographical Dictionary. Many of the spellings of places have been changed and standardized since these dictionaries were printed. The spellings appearing here have either been changed or cross-referenced. It is an asset for the genealogist to know what the old spellings were. Most of these have been preserved, and there should be no difficulty in locating them because of the cross references used.

There will be other local dialectic spellings found in records. A useful reference book to determine the correct spelling of these places is <u>Dialectic Nomenclature</u>. (Genealogical Society call no. Ref. 914.2 H776g).

There are many very small places that do not appear in the list. These may be located in modern gazetteers, directories or ordnance survey maps or might be located through contact with the local librarian or county archivist who usually have good references to their own localities.

Some examples of slight spelling differences which have affected the alphabetical listing of a place are Areley (Arley); Ashfordby (Asfordby); Aislaby (Aysleby); and Bassingthorpe (Basingthorpe).

There are more serious spelling differences which could cause problems such as Ash, also called Esh. Places beginning with Kirby will often be found under Kirkby and vice versa.

Several places now spelled as one word were once spelled as two words, alphabetized under the second word. For instance, Minchinhampton is listed as Hampton, Minchin. Levenshulme is listed as Hulme, Levens and Felixkirk as Kirk, Felix.

All places except extra-parochial districts are connected to a parish. The term parish used in this gazetteer refers to an ecclesiastical parish of the Church of England. If a place is a hamlet, a chapelry, a tything, etc., it is described as being part of an ecclesiastical parish and the details of that parish can be referred to for searches planned in church and probate records.

Persons living in extra-parochial districts could attend any church in the area. Searches for ancestors living in those places would need to be made in the records of all surrounding parishes and the appropriate probate jurisdictions.

Parishes or towns described as "boroughs" and "separate jurisdictions" have their own civil records.

Townships have their own Poor Law Records. Chapels with no registers may have had their own burial grounds.

PARISH REGISTERS

Those places recorded as parishes usually have listed the date of commencement of the parish registers as listed in <u>Key to the Ancient Parish Registers of England and Wales</u>, by Arthur M. Burke.

There are no Church of England parish registers before 1538. Where the beginning date is later than that, there may have been early registers dating back to 1538 at one time. On the other hand, a place might have been created a parish later than that.

Bishop's Transcripts exist for most counties back to 1598 and for some counties back to 1568. If the date of commencement of the parish registers is more recent than that, there may be Bishop's Transcripts for earlier dates and it would be worth checking for such information. See the chapters on parish registers and Bishop's Transcripts in Volume I of Genealogical Research in England and Wales by Smith and Gardner, for a description of these sources, and Chapter 9 of Volume II in Genealogical Research in England and Wales by Smith and Gardner, for the general condition of Bishop's Transcripts of each county.

Modern parishes created after 1812 have not been listed except those mentioned in Lewis' Topographical Dictionary. New parishes were created in growing towns after 1812. Where Lewis' Topographical Dictionaries do not provide such help, commercial directories and local county record office may help.

Some chapelries had registers and others did not. This is indicated in each case.

The Society of Genealogists of London have prepared a list of copies of parish registers they have, and are engaged in preparing a list of those available in other libraries in England and Wales.

Some places stated to be parishes have no registers. These are ancient parishes where the church was ruinated before 1538 and are marked "no registers." The inhabitants would attend a parish church nearby.

DISTANCE IN MILES

Lewis' Topographical Dictionaries gave a more precise direction such as ne by e. This is abbreviated to ne, etc., in all cases. Mileage varies slightly in different issues of Lewis' but this does not present a problem.

POPULATION

The population is as of 1831. There will, no doubt, be slight differences if comparison is made with other population tables of the same year. These differences are not serious. The value of the figure lies in presenting an idea as to what is involved in searching the records of the locality. Obviously the records of a parish having 10,000 people will be much larger than a parish having 100 people.

Where no population is given, it is included in the parish in which that small place is situated.

ECCLESIASTICAL JURISDICTIONS

The ecclesiastical jurisdiction is given for each parish and occasionally for other places. Usually other places within the parish will have the same ecclesiastical jurisdiction.

This jurisdiction is given so that it can be determined in which ecclesiastical court probate records are likely to have been granted. The ecclesiastical jurisdictions are generally, but not always, the same as the probate jurisdictions.

Where the parish is a Peculiar, it should be remembered that whereas the larger probate courts existed until 1858, most Peculiar courts closed before that time and probate jurisdiction was carried on in the larger courts. Details of the dates of closing of these courts can be found in a book called Wills and Their Whereabouts by B. G. Bouwens (revised by Anthony Camp).

Some parishes are described in Lewis' Topographical Dictionaries as donatives. Where these are not Peculiars they have been listed in their local archdeaconry and diocese. See Volume II of Genealogical Research in England and Wales for details of probate records.

Material being prepared by the Genealogical Society of the Church of Jesus Christ of Latter-day Saints, Inc., as Research Papers will greatly clarify the probate jurisdictional problem.

NONCONFORMIST GROUPS

These are listed in Lewis' Topographical Dictionary. Their listings are not complete.

Abbreviations have been used and refer to denominations such as General Baptists, Particular Baptists, Baptists, Methodists New Connexion, Wesleyan Methodists, Primitive Methodists, Lady Huntingdon's Connexion, Congregationalist, Unitarians, Independents, Calvinistic Methodists, etc.

See Volume I of Genealogical Research in England and Wales for details of the value of records kept by these nonconformist groups.

ABBREVIATIONS

arch	archdeaconry	pec	peculiar jurisdiction (of)
co	county of	pop	population
comp	comprising	regs	registers
dioc	diocese	sep juris	separate jurisdiction
incl	included		

Counties or Shires

Beds	Bedfordshire	Leics	Leicestershire
Bucks	Buckinghamshire	Lincs	Lincolnshire
Cambs	Cambridgeshire	Notts	Nottinghamshire
Gloucs	Gloucestershire	Staffs	Staffordshire
Herefs	Herefordshire	Warws	Warwickshire
Herts	Hertfordshire	Westm	Westmorland
Lancs	Lancashire	Worcs	Worcestershire

Places

N R	North Riding (of the county of)	W R	West Riding (of the county of)
E R	East Riding (of the county of)		

Directions

e	east	s	south
n	north	se	southeast
ne	northeast	sw	southwest
nw	northwest	w	west

Nonconformist Groups

Bapt	Baptists
Indep	Independents
Part Bapt	Particular Baptists
Prim Meth	Primitive Methodists
Soc of Friends	Society of Friends or Quakers
Unit	Unitarians
Wesl Meth	Wesleyan Methodists

ADDITIONS AND CORRECTIONS

for

A Genealogical Gazetteer of England

by FRANK SMITH

Baltimore, Genealogical Publishing Co., 1968 and 1969

* *

ALDINGHAM -- Change Glaston to Gleaston
ALDWARK -- Change to: ALDWARD
AUDENSHAW -- Change Aston to Ashton
AUGHTON -- Change Hatton to Halton
BERWICK BASSET -- add, after Wilts: 6-1/2 m nw Marlboro pop 160
    Pec Treasurer of Sarum
BIRKDALE -- Ormskirk now to be changed to North Meols
BONDS -- Change Garstand to Garstang
BOSSALL - Change Eaxton on the Moor to Flaxton on the Moor
BROCKLESBY -- Change 1672 to 1538
CATTERALL -- Change Garstand to Garstang
COCKERHAM -- Change Elle to Ellel
COLTON -- Change Waverthwaite to Haverthwaite
DUNNEDALE -- Change to: DUNNERDALE
HACKERSALL -- Change to: HACKENSALL
HATFIELD GREAT -- Change to: HATFIELD GREAT and LITTLE
HATTON hamlet parish -- Change Dover to Dove
HELEN'S ST -- After HELEN'S ST parish 1653, insert an additional
    entry: HELEN'S, ST chapelry 1713 parish Prescot Lancs 4 m ne
    Prescot archd and dioc Chester Indep Wesl Meth Roman Cath
HEYWOOD -- Change dioc Oxford to dioc Chester
HULL -- Change KINSTON to KINGSTON
HUYTON -- Change Robby to Roby
IREBY township -- Change Tatham to Thornton
KELLASNERGH -- Change to: KELLAMERGH
KIRKHAM -- Change Kellasnergh to Kellamergh and Weston to Weeton
LANCASTER -- Change Oycliffe to Oxcliffe and Hackersall to
    Hackensall
LEA -- Change Freston to Preston
LEVER, DARCH -- Change to: DARCY
LIVESLEY -- Change to: LIVESEY
LONDON -- Change in second paragraph, Bloosbury to Bloomsbury
MALTON, NEW -- Change W R York to N R York
MANTON -- Change Leeatham to Leatham
MAPPLETON parish 1682 -- After Beverly, insert: township Mapple-

ton pop 327 Pec archd East Riding dioc York

MELLING -- Change Wratton to Wrayton

MIDDLETON -- Change Ainswirth to Ainsworth

NEWCHURCH chapelry parish Winwick -- Change to: NEWCHURCH (or NEWCHURCH CALCETH or NEWCHURCH KENYON) chapelry 1599 parish Winwick Lancs

NEWCHURCH KENYON 1599 Lancs -- Delete

OLDHAM CUM -- Change entire first line to: OLDHAM borough chapelry St Mary 1558 St Peter 1765 parish Prestwich Lancs 7 m ne

ORMSBY parish 1675 -- Change to: ORMSBY ST MARGARET parish 1675

ORMSBY parish 1568 -- Change to: ORMSBY ST MICHAEL parish 1568

PIPEWELL -- Change Oakey to Oakley

PRESCOT -- Change Widdle to Windle

RASTRICK chapelry 1614 -- Change to 1719

RIBBESFORD -- add at end: also involved with dioc Hereford

ROCHDALE -- Change W R York to Lancs

ROTHWELL parish 1538 -- Change Otton to Oulton

SIGGLESTHORNE Little Hatfield -- Change to: SIGGLESTHORNE Great and Little Hatfield

SKIPSEA -- Change Bringhoe to Dringhoe

STANDISH -- Change Chanrock to Charnock

STIRCHLEY -- Change Lincoln to Lichfield

SYDENHAM chapelry -- Change Lewiston to Lewisham

TAVY parish 1560 -- Change to: TAVY ST MARY parish 1560

TAVY parish 1614 -- Change to: TAVY ST PETER parish 1614

TREVENTHAN -- Change to: TREVETHAN

TUNSTALL -- Between TUNSTALL parish 1568, and TUNSTALL township, insert an additional entry: TUNSTALL parish 1626 Lancs comp chapelry Leck, townships Burrow with Burrow, Cantsfield, Tunstall 3-3/4 m s Kirkby Lonsdale pop 757 archd Richmond dioc Chester

ULVERSTON -- Change Slawwith to Blawith

WADWOTTH -- Change to: WADWORTH

WALTON ON THE HILL parish 1586 -- Change Wesl to West; change Faxakerley to Fazakerley

WARRINGTON -- Change Roston to Rixton

WELLINGTON parish 1683 -- Change 24 m sw Somerset to 24 m sw Somerton

WHALLEY -- Change Clivinger to Cliviger; change Habergham, Eves to Habergham Eaves

WIGAN -- Change Uplolland to Upholland; insert comma (,) between Abram and Billings; delete Derbys

Between ECCLESTON and EDGBOLTON an entire page
of manuscript was omitted. The 26 entries follow below.

ECCLESTON parish 1603 Lancs 5 miles w Chorley comp townships
    Eccleston, Hisken, Parbold, Wrightington pop 3,068 archd and
    dioc Chester
ECCLESTON township parish Prescott Lancs pop 3,259
ECCLESTON, GREAT township parish St. Michael Lancs pop 624
ECCLESTON, LITTLE joint township with Larbrick parish Kirkham
    Lancs pop 230
ECCLESWELL hamlet parish Linton Herefs
ECCUP joint township with Addle parish Addle W R York pop 703
ECKINGTON parish 1558 Derbys 7 miles ne Chesterfield comp town-
    ships Eckington, Mosborough, Renishaw, Troway pop 3,948
    archd Derby dioc Lichfield Wesl Meth, Roman Cath
ECKINGTON parish 1678 Worcs 4 miles sw Pershore pop 700 archd
    and dioc Worcester
ECTON parish 1559 co Northampton 5 miles sw Wellingborough pop
    570 archd Northampton dioc Peterborough Wesl Meth
EDALE chapelry 1642 parish Castleton Derbys pop 333 archd Derby
    dioc Lichfield Wesl Meth
EDBURTON parish 1558 Sussex 4 miles e Steyning comp hamlet
    Fulking pop 267 pec Archbishop of Canterbury
EDDINGTON tything parish Hungerford Berks pop 479
EDDINSHALL township parish St. Oswald, Chester Ches pop 24
EDDISBURY township parish Delamere Ches pop 178
EDDLESBOROUGH parish 1567 Bucks 3 miles ne Ivinghoe, comp
    chapelry Dagnell, hamlets Rudnall, Northall pop 1,490 archd
    Buckingham dioc Lincoln
EDDLESTON township parish Acton Ches pop 104
EDDLETHORP township parish Westow E R York pop 53
EDECLIFT township parish Clun Shrops pop 460
EDENBRIDGE parish 1538 Kent 5-1/2 miles s Westerham pop 1,432
    archd and dioc Rochester
EDEN, CASTLE parish 1720 co Durham 10-1/2 miles se Durham pop
    260 archd and dioc Durham
EDENFIELD chapelry 1728 parish Bury Lancs archd and dioc Chester
EDENGALE Staffs See EDINGHALL
EDENHALL parish 1558 Cumberland 3-1/2 miles ne Penrith comp
    chapelry Langwathby, township Edenhall pop 544 archd and dioc
    Carlisle
EDENHAM parish 1654 Lincs 3-1/4 miles nw Bourne pop 777 archd
    and dioc Lincoln
EDENSOR parish 1539 Derbys 2-1/4 miles ne Bakewell pop 703
    archd Derby dioc Lichfield
EDGBASTON parish 1635 Warws 1-1/2 miles sw Birmingham pop
    3,954 pec Dean and Chapter of Lichfield

A GENEALOGICAL GAZETTEER

OF ENGLAND

ABBAS COMBE parish 1563 Somerset 4-1/2 miles sw Wincanton pop 448 archd Wells dioc Bath and Wells

ABBERBURY See ALBERBURY

ABBERLEY parish 1559 Worcs 4-3/4 miles sw Stourport pop 560 archd Salop dioc Hereford

ABBERTON parish 1703 Essex 4-1/2 miles s Colchester pop 202 archd Colchester dioc London Wesl Meth

ABBERTON parish 1661 Worcs 7 miles ne Pershore pop 90 archd and dioc Worcester

ABBERWICK township parish Edlingham Northumberland

ABBEY DORE See DORE, ABBEY

ABBOT'S ANN parish 1562 Hamps 2-1/4 miles sw Andover pop 562 archd and dioc Winchester

ABBOT'S ASTLEY See ASTLEY ABBOT'S

ABBOTS BICKINGTON See BICKINGTON, ABBOTS

ABBOTS BROMLEY See BROMLEY, ABBOTS

ABBOTSBURY parish 1574 Dorset 8-1/4 miles sw Dorchester pop 874 archd Dorset dioc Bristol

ABBOTSHAM parish 1653 Devon 2 miles w Bideford pop 387 archd Barnstaple dioc Exeter

ABBOTS KERSWELL See KERSWELL, ABBOTS

ABBOTS LANGLEY See LANGLEY ABBOTS

ABBOTS LEIGH See LEIGH, ABBOTS

ABBOT SIDE, HIGH township parish Aysgarth N R Yorks pop 589

ABBOT SIDE, LOW township parish Aysgarth N R York pop 173

ABBOTSLEY parish 1754 Hunts 4-1/4 miles se St. Neots pop 369 archd Huntingdon dioc Lincoln

ABBOTS MORTON See MORTON, ABBOTS

ABBOTSTON parish Hamps 2-3/4 miles nw New Airesford archd and dioc Winchester incl regs of Itchin Stoke

ABDON parish 1554 Shrops 9-3/4 miles ne Ludlow pop 170 archd Salop dioc Hereford

ABENHALL or ABINGHALL parish 1596 Gloucs 4-1/2 miles nw Newnham pop 767 archd Hereford dioc Gloucester

ABERFORD parish 1540 W R Yorks comp part township Aberford, townships Barlington, Sturton Grange pop 925 archd and dioc

York Wesl Meth

ABERGAVENNY parish 1653 co Monmouth 16 miles nw Monmouth pop 4, 230 archd and dioc Llandaff Bapt, Indep, Wesl Meth, Roman Cath

ABERYSTWITH (ABERYSTRUTH) parish 1736 co Monmouth 8 miles sw Abergavenny pop 5, 992 archd and dioc Llandaff

ABINGDON town, borough sep. juris. Berks 6 miles s Oxford comp parishes St. Helen 1538, St. Nicholas 1538 archd Berks dioc Salisbury incl parts or all townships Shippon, Norcott, Sandford, Barton, Pumney, Bapt, Indep, Wesl Meth

ABINGER parish 1559 Surrey 4-1/2 miles sw Dorking pop 767 archd Surrey dioc Winchester

ABINGHALL See ABENHALL

ABINGTON parish 1637 co Northampton 1-1/2 miles ne Northampton pop 155 archd Northampton dioc Peterborough

ABINGTON, GREAT parish 1664 Cambs 2-1/4 miles nw Linton pop 382 archd and dioc Ely

ABINGTON IN THE CLAY or ABINGTON PIGOTS parish 1653 Cambs 5-1/2 miles nw Royston pop 259 archd and dioc Ely

ABINGTON, LITTLE parish 1687 Cambs 2-3/4 miles nw Linton pop 253 archd and dioc Ely

AB KETTLEBY parish 1580 Leics 3-1/2 miles ne Melton Mowbray pop 331 archd Leicester dioc Lincoln

ABLINGTON tything parish Bibury Gloucs pop 103

ABNEY hamlet parish Hope Derbys pop 112

ABRAM township parish Wigan Lancs pop 511

ABSON or ABSTON parish (see WICK) Gloucs 7-1/4 miles ne Bristol pop 824 archd and dioc Gloucester

ABTHORPE parish 1737 co Northampton 3 miles sw Towcester archd Northampton dioc Peterborough

ABY parish (See BELLEAU) Lincs 3 miles nw Alford pop 204 archd and dioc Lincoln

ACASTER MALBIS parish 1693 E R Yorks 4-1/2 miles sw York pop 707 archd and dioc York

ACCONBURY or ACORNBURY parish (See regs of CALLOW) Herefs 4-1/2 miles s Hereford pop 163 pec Dean of Hereford

ACCRINGTON parish 1766 Lancs 5-1/2 miles se Blackburn pop 6, 283 archd and dioc Chester Bapt, Wesl Meth, Swedenborgians

ACHURCH See THORPE ACHURCH

ACKLAM, EAST parish 1716 E R Yorks comp townships Acklam with Barthorpe, Leavening pop 827 7-1/4 miles s New Malton pec Chancellor of Cathedral Church of York, Wesl, Prim Meth

ACKLAM, WEST parish 1732 N R York 2-3/4 miles se Stockton on Tees pop 102 archd Cleveland dioc York

ACKLINGTON township parish Warkworth Northumberland pop 285

ACKLINGTON PARK township parish Warkworth Northumberland pop 107

ACKTON township parish Featherstone N R York pop 51

ACKWORTH parish 1558 W R Yorks 3-1/4 miles sw Pontefract pop 1,660 archd and dioc York Wesl Meth

ACLE parish 1664 Norfolk 11 miles e Norwich pop 820 archd and dioc Norwich

ACOMB parish 1635 Ainsty and E R Yorks pop 882 pec of the Incumbent 2-1/4 miles w York Wesl Meth

ACOMB, EAST township parish Bywell St. Peter Northumberland pop 36

ACOMB, WEST township parish St. John Lee Northumberland pop 523

ACRISE parish 1561 Kent 5 miles nw Folkestone pop 194 archd and dioc Canterbury

ACTON township parish Weaverham Ches pop 335

ACTON parish 1653 Ches comp townships Acton, Aston juxta Mondrum, Austerson, Baddington, Brindley, Burland, Cholmondstone, Cool Pilate, Eddleston, Faddiley, Henhull, Hurlestone, Newhall, Poole, Stoke, Worleston pop 3,928 1-1/4 miles nw Nantwich archd and dioc Chester

ACTON parish 1539 Middlesex 5 miles w London pop 2,453 archd Middlesex dioc London Indep, Roman Cath

ACTON joint township with Old Felton parish Felton Northumberland pop 101

ACTON parish 1564 Suffolk 3 miles ne Sudbury pop 564 archd Sudbury dioc Norwich

ACTON BEAUCHAMP parish 1539 Worcs 4-3/4 miles sw Bromyard pop 239 archd and dioc Worcester

ACTON BURNELL parish 1568 Shrops 7-1/2 miles nw Much Wenlock pop 381 archd Salop dioc Lichfield

ACTON GRANGE township parish Runcorn Ches pop 149

ACTON, ILGAR tything parish Iron Acton Gloucs

ACTON, IRON parish 1570 Gloucs 3-1/2 miles nw Chipping Sodbury pop 1,372 Wesl Meth

ACTON PIGOT chapelry parish Acton Burnell Shrops

ACTON REYNALD township parish Shawbury Shrops pop 173

ACTON ROUND parish 1651 Shrops 3-3/4 miles se Wenlock pop 203 archd Salop dioc Hereford

ACTON SCOTT parish 1690 Shrops 3-1/4 miles se Church Stretton pop 204 archd Salop dioc Hereford

ACTON TRUSSELL chapelry 1571 Staffs 3 miles ne Penkridge pop 551 pec Prebendary of Whittington and Baswich

ACTON TURVILLE chapelry 1665 parish Tormarton Gloucs 5-3/4 miles e Chipping Sodbury pop 236

ADBASTON parish 1600 Staffs comp townships Adbaston, Bishop's Offlow, Flashbrook, Tunstall pop 601 4-3/4 miles sw Eccleshall pec Dean of Lichfield

ADBEER hamlet parish Trent Somerset

ADBOLTON hamlet parish Holme Pierrepoint Notts formerly parish consolidated in 1707 with Holme Pierrepoint

ADDERBURY, EAST parish 1598 co Oxford comp chapelries Barford
St. John, Bodicott, Milton, township West Adderbury 2-3/4 miles
ne Deddington pop 2, 473 archd and dioc Oxford Wesl Meth
ADDERBURY, WEST township parish East Adderbury co Oxford pop
397
ADDERLEY See ALTHERLEY
ADDERSTONE township parish Bamborough Northumberland pop 322
ADDINGHAM parish 1604 Cumberland 1-1/2 miles se Kirk Oswald
comp townships Gamblesby, Glassonby, Hunsonby with Winskill,
Little Salkeld pop 719 archd and dioc Carlisle Wesl Meth, Indep
ADDINGHAM parish 1612 comp township Addingham, part of Beams-
ley W R Yorks pop 2, 251 archd and dioc York Wesl Meth, Soc of
Friends
ADDINGTON parish 1558 Bucks 1-3/4 miles nw Winslow pop 72
archd Buckingham dioc Lincoln
ADDINGTON parish 1562 Kent 7 miles nw Maidstone pop 206 archd
and dioc Rochester
ADDINGTON parish 1559 Surrey 3-1/2 miles se Croydon pop 463
archd Surrey dioc Winchester
ADDINGTON, GREAT parish 1692 co Northampton 4-1/2 miles sw
Thrapston pop 282 archd Northampton dioc Peterborough
ADDINGTON, LITTLE parish 1588 co Northampton 3-1/4 miles n
Higham Ferrers pop 264 archd Northampton dioc Peterborough
ADDLE See ADEL
ADDLETHORPE parish 1564 Lincs 9-1/2 miles se Alford pop 175
archd and dioc Lincoln
ADEL parish 1606 W R Yorks 5-3/4 miles nw Leeds pop 1,063 archd
and dioc York
ADFORTON joint township with Payton and Grange parish Leintwar-
dine Herefs pop 218
ADGARLEY township parish Urswick Lancs
ADISHAM parish 1539 Kent 2-3/4 miles sw Wingham pop 390 pec
Archbishop of Canterbury
ADLESTROP chapelry 1538 parish Broadwell Gloucs 3-3/4 miles ne
Stow on the Wold pop 193
ADLINGFLEET parish 1684 W R Yorks comp townships Adlingfleet,
Fockerby, Haldenby with Eastoft pop 478 9-1/2 miles se Howden
archd and dioc York
ADLINGTON township parish Prestbury Ches pop 1,066
ADLINGTON township parish Standish Lancs pop 1,082
ADMARSH chapelry parish Lancaster Lancs
ADMINGTON hamlet parish Quinton Gloucs pop 177
ADMISTON or ATHELHAMPTON parish 1692 Dorset 6 miles ne
Dorchester pop 67 archd Dorset dioc Bristol
ADSTOCK parish 1538 Bucks 3 miles nw Winslow pop 445 archd
Buckingham dioc Lincoln
ADSTONE chapelry 1671 parish Canons Ashby co Northampton 6-3/4
miles nw Towcester pop 166

ADVENT parish 1709 Cornwall 1-3/4 miles s Damelford pop 244
archd Cornwall dioc Exeter
ADWALTON hamlet chapelry Drighlington parish Birstall W R Yorks
ADWELL parish 1539 co Oxford 1-3/4 miles se Tetsworth pop 48
archd and dioc Oxford
ADWICK LE STREET parish 1547 W R Yorks pop 536 4 miles nw
Doncaster archd and dioc York
ADWICK UPON DEARNE parish 1690 W R Yorks 6-3/4 miles ne
Rotherham pop 145 archd and dioc York
AFF PIDDLE or PUDDLE parish 1722 Dorset 9 miles ne Dorchester
pop 442 archd Dorset dioc Bristol
AGDEN township parish Malpas Ches pop 104
AGDEN township partly in parish Rosthern chiefly in Bowden Ches
pop 99
AGELTHORPE township parish Coverhan N R Yorks pop 145
AGLIONBY township parish Warwick Cumberland pop 107
AGNES ST parish 1653 Cornwall 8-1/2 miles nw Truro pop 6,642
pec Dean and Chapter of Exeter Bryanites, Indep, Wesl Meth
AIGHTON joint township with Bailey and Chaigley parish Mitton
Lancs pop 1,980
AIKE township partly in St John Beverley chiefly in Lockington E R
Yorks pop 86
AIKTON parish 1694 Cumberland comp townships Aikton, Biglands
with Gamelsby, Wampol, Wiggonby pop 755 archd and dioc
Carlisle
AILESWORTH hamlet parish Castor co Northampton pop 289
AINDERBY MYERS joint township with Holtby parish Hornby N R
Yorks pop 90
AINDERBY QUERNHOW township parish Pickhill N R Yorks pop 107
AINDERBY STEEPLE parish 1668 N R Yorks comp townships Ain-
derby Steeple, Morton, Thirntoft, Warlaby 2-3/4 miles sw North-
allerton pop 806 archd Richmond dioc Chester
AINSTABLE parish 1664 Cumberland 4-1/2 miles nw Kirk Oswald
pop 580 archd and dioc Carlisle
AINSWORTH chapelry 1727 parish Middleton Lancs 3 miles ne Bolton
le Moors pop 1,584
AINTREE township parish Sephton Lancs pop 247
AIRMYN W R Yorks See ARMIN
AIRTON township parish Kirkby in Malhamdale W R Yroks pop 179
AISHOLT or ASHOLT parish 1645 Somerset 7-1/4 miles sw Bridge-
water pop 228 archd Taunton dioc Bath and Wells
AISHOLT, LOWER hamlet parish Aisholt Somerset
AISKEW township parish Bedale N R Yorks pop 586 Anabapt, Roman
Cath
AISLABY township parish Eaglescliffe co Durham pop 143
AISLABY or ASLEYBY chapelry parish Whitby N R Yorks pop 277
AISLABY township parish Middleton N R Yorks pop 126
AISMUNDERBY joint township with Bondgate parish Ripon W R

Yorks pop 655

AISTHORPE parish 1594 Lincs 6 miles nw Lincoln pop 89 archd
Stow dioc Lincoln

AKEBAR township parish Fingall N R Yorks pop 53

AKELD township parish Kirk Newton Northumberland pop 171

AKELY parish 1682 Bucks 2-1/2 miles ne Buckingham pop 291 archd
Buckingham dioc Lincoln

AKENHAM parish 1583 Suffolk 4-1/2 miles nw Ipswich pop 119 archd
Suffolk dioc Norwich

ALBANS, ST. town, borough sep juris Herts 12-1/2 miles sw Hert-
ford pop 4,772 comp parishes St. Alban (the Abbey) 1558, St.
Michael 1649, St. Peter 1558 archd St. Albans dioc London Part
Bapt, Indep, Wesl Meth, Unit

ALBERBURY or ABBERBURY parish 1564 Shrops comp townships
Cruggion, Middleton, Uppington, Bauseley, Alberbury, Benthal
with Shrawardine, Eyton, Rowton with Amaston, chapelry Wollaston 8-1/4 miles w Shrewsbury pop 1,799 archd Salop dioc Hereford

ALBOURNE parish 1553 Sussex 2-1/2 miles nw Hurst Pierrepoint
pop 362 archd Lewes dioc Chichester

ALBRIGHTON near WOLVERHAMPTON parish 1649 Shrops 6 miles
se Shiffnal pop 1,054 pec Dean of Lichfield

ALBRIGHTON near SHREWSBURY parish 1555 Shrops 4 miles n
Shrewsbury pop 98 royal pec St. Mary's, Shrewsbury

ALBURGH parish 1541 Norfolk 3-1/4 miles ne Harleston pop 586
archd Norfolk dioc Norwich

ALBURY parish 1558 Herts 4-1/2 miles ne Bishop Stortford pop 631
pec Dean and Chapter of St. Paul, London

ALBURY parish 1653 co Oxford 3-1/4 miles sw Thame pop 929 archd
and dioc Oxford

ALBURY parish 1559 Surrey 4 miles se Guildford pop 929 archd
Surrey dioc Winchester

ALBY parish 1558 Norfolk 4-3/4 miles ne Aylsham pop 346 archd
and dioc Norwich

ALCESTER parish 1560 Warws 15 miles sw Warwick archd and dioc
Worcester Bapt, Indep, Wesl Meth, Unit

ALCISTON parish 1701 Sussex 4-3/4 miles ne Seaford pop 266
archd Lewes dioc Chichester

ALCONBURY parish 1559 Hunts 4-1/2 miles nw Huntingdon pop 765
archd Huntingdon dioc Lincoln Wesl Meth

ALCUMLOW joint township with Morston parish Astbury Ches

ALDBOROUGH parish 1539 Norfolk 2 miles sw Aylsham pop 275
archd and dioc Norwich

ALDBOROUGH or ALDEBURGH parish, borough 1558 sep juris
Suffolk 25 miles ne Ipswich pop 1,341 archd Suffolk dioc Norwich
Part Bapt, Indep, Wesl Meth

ALDBOROUGH parish 1538 W R Yorks comp chapelry Lower Dunsforth, townships Upper Dunsforth with Branton Green, Minskep,
Rowcliff, part of Humberton with Milby, boroughs Aldborough,

Boroughbridge pop 2,447 16-1/2 miles nw York pec Dean and
Chapter of York
ALDBOURNE parish 1637 Wilts 6 miles ne Marlborough pop 1,418
archd Wilts dioc Salisbury Wesl Meth
ALDBROUGH parish 1653 E R Yorks comp townships Aldbrough, East
Newton, West Newton, part of Cowdons pop 1,015 11-1/2 miles ne
Kingston on Hull archd East Riding dioc York Wesl Meth
ALDBROUGH township parish Stanwick St. John N R Yorks pop 522
Wesl Meth
ALDBURY parish 1693 Herts 3 miles ne Tring pop 695 archd Hunting-
don dioc Lincoln
ALDCLIFFE township parish Lancaster Lancs pop 96
ALDEBURGH See ALDBOROUGH
ALDEBY parish 1558 Norfolk 2-3/4 miles ne Beccles pop 530 archd
Norfolk dioc Norwich
ALDENHAM parish 1559 Herts 2-3/4 miles ne Watford pop 1,454
archd Huntingdon dioc Lincoln
ALDERBURY parish 1673 Wilts 3 miles se Salisbury comp chapelries
Farley, Pitton pop 1,323 pec Treasurer in Cathedral Church of
Salisbury Wesl Meth
ALDERBURY Shrops See ALBERBURY
ALDERFORD parish 1723 Norfolk 3-1/4 miles se Reepham pop 40
archd Norfolk dioc Norwich
ALDERLEY parish 1629 Ches comp townships Upper and Lower Al-
derley, Great Warford pop 1,338 4-3/4 miles nw Macclesfield
archd and dioc Chester Bapt
ALDERLEY parish 1559 Gloucs 2 miles se Wootton under Edge pop
200 archd and dioc Gloucester
ALDERMASTON parish 1558 Berks 10 miles sw Reading pop 636
archd Berks dioc Salisbury but incumbent has peculiar authority
ALDERMINSTER parish 1628 Worcs and Warws 5 miles se Stratford
on Avon pop 454 archd and dioc Worcester
ALDERSEY township parish Coddington Ches pop 153
ALDERSHOT parish 1571 Hamps 3-3/4 miles ne Farnham pop 665
archd and dioc Winchester
ALDERTON parish 1596 Gloucs 4-1/4 miles nw Winchcomb pop 330
archd and dioc Gloucester
ALDERTON parish 1597 co Northampton 3-3/4 miles se Towcester
pop 162 archd Northampton dioc Peterborough
ALDERTON parish 1676 Suffolk 7-1/2 miles se Woodbridge pop 575
archd Suffolk dioc Norwich
ALDERTON parish 1603 Wilts 7-1/2 miles sw Malmesbury pop 213
archd and dioc Salisbury
ALDERWASLEY chapelry parish Wirksworth Derbys pop 424
ALDFIELD chapelry parish Ripon W R Yorks pop 146
ALDFORD parish 1639 Ches comp townships Aldford, Churton, Great
Boughton, Buerton, Edgerley, chapelry Churton Heath or Bruera
pop 1,710 5-1/2 miles se Chester archd and dioc Chester

ALDHAM parish 1559 Essex 4-1/2 miles ne Great Coggeshall pop 407 archd Colchester dioc London

ALDHAM parish 1666 Suffolk 2 miles ne Hadleigh pop 318 archd Sudbury dioc Norwich

ALDINGBOURN parish 1558 Sussex 4-1/4 miles ne Chichester pop 833 archd and dioc Chichester

ALDINGHAM parish 1539 Lancs 5-3/4 miles s Ulverstone comp chapelry Dendron, townships Upper and Lower Aldingham, Glaston, Leece pop 844 archd Richmond dioc Chester

ALDINGTON parish 1558 Kent 5-1/2 miles nw Hythe pop 732 pec Archbishop of Canterbury

ALDINGTON hamlet parish Badsey Worcs pop 104

ALDRIDGE parish 1660 Staffs 3 miles ne Walsall pop 1,804 archd Stafford dioc Lichfield

ALDRINGHAM parish 1538 Suffolk 2-1/2 miles nw Aldborough pop 362 archd Suffolk dioc Norwich Part Bapt

ALDRINGTON Sussex See ATHERINGTON

ALDSTONE Cumberland See ALSTON

ALDSWORTH parish 1683 Gloucs 3-1/2 miles se Northleach pop 353 pec Vicar of Bibury, Consistorial Court of Bishop of Gloucester

ALDWARK township parish Ecclesfield W R Yorks

ALDWARK township parish Bradborne Derbys pop 97

ALDWINKLE ALL SAINTS parish 1653 co Northampton 4 miles n Thrapston pop 247 archd Northampton dioc Peterborough

ALDWINKLE ST PETER parish 1563 co Northampton 3-3/4 miles ne Thrapston pop 171 archd Northampton dioc Peterborough Part Bapt

ALDWORK township parish Alne N R Yorks 6-1/2 miles se Aldborough pop 190

ALDWORTH parish 1556 Berks 4-1/2 miles se East Ilsley pop 288 archd Berks dioc Salisbury

ALEMOUTH or ALNMOUTH township parish Lesbury Northumberland pop 415 Wesl Meth

ALETHORPE hamlet parish Fakenham Norfolk

ALEXTON See ALLEXTON

ALFOLD parish 1658 Surrey 8-1/2 miles se Godalming pop 514 archd Surrey dioc Winchester

ALFORD parish 1538 Lincs 34 miles e Lincoln pop 1,784 archd and dioc Lincoln Indep, Wesl Meth

ALFORD parish 1763 Somerset 1-3/4 miles nw Castle Cary pop 137 archd Wells dioc Bath and Wells

ALFRETON parish 1706 Derbys 14 miles ne Derby pop 5,691 archd Derby dioc Lichfield Wesl Meth

ALFRICK chapelry 1656 parish Suckley Worcs 7 miles sw Worcester pop 493

ALFRISTON parish 1538 Sussex 3-1/2 miles ne Seaford pop 694 archd Lewes dioc Chichester

ALGARKIRK parish 1678 Lincs 7-3/4 miles nw Holbeach pop 651

archd and dioc Lincoln

ALHAMPTON tything parish Ditcheat Somerset

ALKBORO parish 1538 Lincs 7 miles n Scunthorpe archd Stow dioc Lincoln

ALKERTON tything parish Eastington Gloucs pop 1,055

ALKERTON parish 1545 co Oxford 6 miles nw Banbury pop 192 archd and dioc Oxford

ALKHAM parish 1558 Kent 4 miles nw Dover pop 542 archd and dioc Canterbury

ALKINGTON tything parish Berkeley Gloucs pop 1,167

ALKINGTON township parish Whitchurch Shrops

ALKMONTON township parish Longford Derbys pop 79

ALKRINGTON township parish Oldham Lancs pop 367

ALLARTHORP joint township with Swainby parish Pickhill N R Yorks

ALLCANNINGS parish 1579 Wilts 5-3/4 miles e Devizes pop 811 archd Wilts dioc Salisbury

ALLEN, ST. parish 1680 Cornwall 4 miles nw Truro pop 637 archd Cornwall dioc Exeter

ALLEN, WEST See NINEBANKS

ALLENDALE parish 1662 Northumberland 9-3/4 miles sw Hexham comp Allendale, townships West Allendale, Broadside, Cotton, Keenty, Forest pop 5,540 pec Hexhamshire Soc of Friends, Wesl Meth

ALLENHEAD hamlet 1807 parish Allendale Northumberland 14 miles sw Hexham

ALLENSMORE parish 1698 Herefs 4 miles sw Hereford pop 592 Consistorial Court of Dean of Hereford

ALLENTON or ALLWINTON parish 1719 Northumberland comp townships Allenton, Biddlesdon, Borrowdon, Clennell, Fairhaugh, Linbriggs, Netheron North and South Side, Peals, Sharperton pop 822 19 miles sw Alnwick archd Northumberland dioc Durham

ALLER parish 1560 Somerset 6-1/4 miles w Somerton pop 490 archd Wells dioc Wells and Bath

ALLERBY or ALWARDBY joint township with Outerside parish Aspatria Cumberland

ALLERSTON parish 1680 N R Yorks 4-3/4 miles se Pickering pop 385 pec Dean of York

ALLERTHORPE parish 1620 E R Yorks 1-1/2 miles sw Pocklington pop 185 pec Dean of York

ALLERTON township parish Childwall Lancs pop 374

ALLERTON township parish Bradford W R Yorks pop 1,733

ALLERTON BYWATER township parish Kippax W R Yorks pop 375

ALLERTON, CHAPEL parish 1692 Somerset 4-1/4 miles sw Axbridge pop 313 pec Dean of Wells

ALLERTON, CHAPEL chapelry 1789 parish St. Peter, Leeds W R Yorks 2-1/2 miles ne Leeds pop 1934 archd and dioc York

ALLERTON MAULEVERER parish 1562 W R Yorks 5-3/4 miles ne Knaresborough comp townships Allerton Mauleverer with

Hopperton, Clareton pop 251 archd Richmond dioc Chester

ALLERTON, NORTH parish 1593 N R Yorks comp township North Allerton, Chapelries Brompton, Deighton, High Worsall, Romanby pop 4,118 32 miles nw York pec Dean and Chapter of Durham Indep, Wesl Meth

ALLESLEY parish 1562 Warws 2-1/2 miles nw Coventry pop 875 archd Coventry dioc Lichfield

ALLESTREY or ALLESTREE parish 1594 Derbys 2 miles n Derby pop 501 archd Derby dioc Lichfield Wesl Meth

ALLEXTON parish 1638 Leics 4 miles nw Uppingham pop 68 archd Leicester dioc Lincoln

ALLHALLOWS parish 1666 Cumberland 6-3/4 miles sw Wigton pop 205 anciently chapelry parish Aspatria archd and dioc Carlisle

ALLHALLOWS HOO parish 1629 Kent 9 miles ne Rochester pop 263 archd and dioc Rochester

ALLINGTON parish 1570 Dorset 3/4 miles nw Bridport pop 1,300 archd Dorset dioc Bristol

ALLINGTON parish 1630 Kent 1-3/4 miles nw Maidstone pop 37 archd and dioc Rochester

ALLINGTON tything parish South Stoneham Hamps pop 389

ALLINGTON parish 1623 Wilts 3-1/2 miles se Amesbury pop 80 archd and dioc Salisbury

ALLINGTON tything parish Chippenham Wilts

ALLINGTON tything parish Allcannings Wilts pop 162 Part Bapt

ALLINGTON, EAST parish 1554 Devon 3-1/2 miles ne Kingsbridge pop 677 archd Totnes dioc Exeter

ALLINGTON, EAST chapelry 1559 parish Sedgebrook Lincs

ALLINGTON, WEST parish 1559 Lincs 4-1/2 miles nw Grantham pop 357 archd and dioc Lincoln

ALLITHWAITE, LOWER township parish Cartmel Lancs pop 838

ALLITHWAITE, UPPER township parish Cartmel Lancs pop 759

ALLONBY chapelry 1759 parish Bromfield Cumberland pop 783 archd and dioc Carlisle

ALLOSTOCK township parish Great Budworth Ches pop 448 Unit

ALLSTONEFIELD parish 1538 Staffs 7-1/4 miles nw Ashbourn comp chapelries Upper Elkstone, Longnor, Quarnford, Warslow, townships Lower Elkstone, Fairfield Head, Heathy Lee, Hollingsclough pop 4,757 archd Stafford dioc Lichfield

ALLTON joint township with Idridgehay parish Wirksworth Derbys

ALLWINTON See ALLENTON

ALMELEY parish 1595 Herefs 5-1/4 miles w Weobley pop 670 archd and dioc Hereford

ALMER parish 1538 Dorset 5-3/4 miles se Blandford pop 176 archd Dorset dioc Bristol

ALMINGTON township parish Drayton in Hales Staffs pop 340

ALMINGTON joint township with Stone Delph parish Tamworth Warws pop 264

ALMODINGTON hamlet parish Earnley Sussex

ALMONDBURY parish 1557 W R Yorks comp chapelries South Cross-
land, Farnley Tyas, Honley, Linthwaite, Lockwood, Meltham, part
of Marsden, townships Almondbury, Austonley, Holme, Lingarths,
Nether Thong, Upper Thong 1-3/4 miles se Huddersfield pop
30,606 pec Lord of the manor Wesl Meth
ALMONDSBURY parish 1696 Gloucs comp tythings Almondsbury,
Earthcotigaunts, Hampton with Patchway, Over and Lower Tock-
ington 4-1/4 miles sw Thornbury pop 1,492 pec Bishop of
Bristol Wesl Meth
ALMSFORD or ANSFORD parish 1554 Somerset 3/4 miles n Castle
Cary pop 304 archd Wells dioc Bath and Wells
ALNE parish 1561 N R Yorks comp townships Aldwork, Alne, Flawith,
Tholthorp, Youlton 4-3/4 miles sw Easingwould pop 1,552 pec
Alne and Tollerton Wesl Meth
ALNE, GREAT chapelry 1605 parish Kinwarton Warws 2-3/4 miles
ne Alcester pop 343
ALNHAM parish 1688 Northumberland comp townships Alnham,
Prendick, Screnwood, Unthank pop 278 14 miles w Alnwick archd
Northumberland dioc Durham
ALNMOUTH See ALEMOUTH
ALNWICK parish, borough 1646 Northumberland 33 miles nw New-
castle upon Tyne pop 6,788 archd Northumberland dioc Durham
Burghers, Indep, Prim and Wesl Meth, Presb, Unit, Roman Cath
ALPHAMSTONE parish 1705 Essex 6 miles ne Halstead pop 277
archd Middlesex dioc London
ALPHETON parish 1571 Suffolk 6-3/4 miles ne Sudbury pop 309
archd Sudbury dioc Norwich
ALPHINGTON parish 1602 Devon 1-1/2 miles s Exeter pop 1,236
archd and dioc Exeter
ALPINGTON parish (regs with Yelverton) Norfolk 6 miles se Nor-
wich pop 197 archd Norfolk dioc Norwich
ALPRAHAM township parish Bunbury Ches pop 418 Wesl Meth
ALRESFORD parish 1742 Essex 6-1/2 miles se Colchester pop 297
archd Colchester dioc London
ALRESFORD, NEW parish 1698 Hamps 6 miles ne Winchester pop
1,437 pec of Incumbent Indep
ALRESFORD, OLD parish 1556 Hamps 3/4 miles n New Alresford
pop 459 pec of Incumbent
ALREWAS parish 1547 Staffs 5 miles ne Lichfield pop 1,607 pec
Prebendary of Alrewas and Weeford Wesl Meth
ALREWAS HAYES Extra parochial liberty Staffs 5-1/2 miles ne
Lichfield pop 77
ALSAGER chapelry 1789 parish Barthomley Ches 5-3/4 miles se
Sandbach pop 446 archd and dioc Chester Wesl Meth
ALSOP LE DALE chapelry 1640 parish Ashbourn Derbys 5-1/2
miles nw Ashbourn archd and dioc Chester Wesl Meth
ALSTON or ALSTON MOOR parish 1700 Cumberland 29 miles se
Carlisle pop 658 juris Consistorial Court of Bishop of Durham
Soc Friends, Indep, Prim and Wesl Meth

ALSTON joint township with Hothersall parish Ribchester Lancs
pop 1,030
ALSTONFIELD See ALLSTONEFIELD
ALSTONE hamlet parish Cheltenham Gloucs
ALSTONE chapelry 1550 parish Overbury Worcs 6-1/2 miles se
Tewkesbury pop 78
ALTCAR parish 1664 Lanes 7 miles sw Ormskirk pop 505 archd and
dioc Chester
ALTERNON parish 1688 Cornwall 7-3/4 miles sw Launceston pop
1,069 archd Cornwall dioc Exeter Wesl Meth
ALTHAM chapelry 1596 parish Whalley Lancs 5 miles w Burnley
pop 413 archd and dioc Chester
ALTHORNE parish 1734 Essex 4 miles nw Burnham pop 352 archd
Essex dioc London
ALTHORPE parish 1670 Lincs 11 miles nw Glandford Bridge comp
chapelry Amcotts, township Keadby pop 981 archd Stow dioc
Lincoln
ALTOFTS township parish Normanton W R Yorks pop 502
ALTON parish 1615 Hamps 17 miles ne Winchester pop 2,742 archd
and dioc Winchester Soc of Friends, Indep, Presb
ALTON BARNES parish 1592 Wilts 7 miles e Devizes pop 138 archd
Wilts dioc Salisbury
ALTON PANCRAS parish 1674 Dorset 8-1/4 miles n Dorchester pop
210 pec Dean of Salisbury
ALTON PRIORS chapelry 1664 parish Overton Wilts 7 miles ne
Devizes pop 205
ALTRINCHAM chapelry, borough 1799 parish Bowden Ches 7 miles
ne Nether Knutsford pop 2,708 archd and dioc Chester Meth, Unit
ALVANLEY chapelry 1791 parish Frodsham Ches 3 miles sw Frod-
sham pop 346 archd and dioc Chester
ALVASTON township parish Nantwich Ches pop 41
ALVASTON chapelry 1614 parish St. Michael, Derby Derbys pop 439
3-1/2 miles se Derby archd Derby dioc Lichfield Wesl Meth
ALVECHURCH parish 1545 Worcs 4-1/2 miles ne Bromsgrove pop
1,548 pec of Incumbent
ALVEDISTON parish 1592 Wilts 7-3/4 miles ne Shaftesbury pop 239
archd and dioc Salisbury
ALVELEY parish 1561 comp liberty Bridgenorth, township King's
Nordley Shrops 6-1/2 miles se Bridgenorth pop 949 royal pec
Bridgenorth
ALVERDISCOTT parish 1602 Devon 6 miles sw Barnstaple pop 339
archd Barnstaple dioc Exeter
ALVERSTOKE parish 1559 Hamps comp Gosport and Forton 1-1/2
miles sw Gosport pop 12,637 pec of Incumbent
ALVERTHORPE chapelry parish Wakefield W R Yorks pop 4,859
ALVERTON hamlet parish Kilvington Notts pop 16
ALVESCOTT parish 1663 co Oxford 5 miles se Burford pop 361
archd and dioc Oxford

ALVESTON parish 1742 Gloucs 3 miles se Thornbury pop 800 pec
    Bishop of Bristol Wesl Meth
ALVESTON parish 1539 Warws 2-1/2 miles ne Stratford pop 650
    archd and dioc Worcester
ALVETON parish 1660 comp chapelry Cotton, townships Denston, Far-
    ley Staffs 4-1/2 miles se Cheadle pop 2,391 archd Stafford dioc
    Lichfield Calv and Wesl Meth
ALVINGHAM parish 1579 Lincs 4 miles ne Louth pop 292 archd and
    dioc Lincoln
ALVINGTON parish 1668 Gloucs 5-1/2 miles sw Blakeney pop 281
    archd Hereford dioc Gloucester
ALVINGTON, WEST parish 1558 Devon 1 mile sw Kingsbridge pop
    872 archd Totnes dioc Exeter
ALWALTON parish 1572 Hunts 5 miles nw Stilton pop 294 archd Hunt-
    ingdon dioc Lincoln
ALWINGTON parish 1555 Devon 4-1/2 miles sw Bideford pop 486
    archd Barnstaple dioc Exeter
ALWINTON See ALLENTON
ALWOODLEY township parish Harewood W R Yorks pop 142
AMASTON joint township with Rowton parish Alberbury Shrops
AMBERLEY chapelry parish Marden Herefs pop 25
AMBERLEY parish 1560 Sussex 5 miles ne Arundel pop 637 archd
    and dioc Chichester
AMBERSHAM, NORTH tything parish Steep Hamps pop 121
AMBERSHAM, SOUTH tything parish Steep Hamps pop 183
AMBLE township parish Warkworth Northumberland pop 247
AMBLECOAT hamlet parish Old Swinford Staffs pop 1,236
AMBLESIDE chapelry 1642 parish Grasmere Westm 26 miles sw
    Appleby pop 1,095 archd Richmond dioc Chester
AMBROSDEN parish 1611 co Oxford 2-1/2 miles se Bicester comp
    chapelries Arncott, Blackthorn pop 194 archd and dioc Oxford
AMCOTTS chapelry parish Althorp Lincs pop 359
AMERSHAM or AGMONDESHAM parish, borough 1561 Bucks 33 miles
    se Buckingham pop 2,816 archd Buckingham dioc Lincoln Part
    Bapt, Soc of Friends
AMESBURY parish 1579 Wilts 7 miles n Salisbury pop 944 archd
    Wilts dioc Salisbury Wesl Meth
AMOTHERBY chapelry parish Appleton le Street N R Yorks pop 246
AMPLEFORTH or AMPLEFORD parish 1646 N R Yorks 4-1/2 miles
    sw Helmsley pop 623 pec Prebendary of Ampleforth Wesl Meth
AMPNEY or ASHBROOK parish 1602 Gloucs 3-1/2 miles e Ciren-
    cester pop 115 archd and dioc Gloucester
AMPNEY or EASINGTON parish 1620 Gloucs 4-1/2 miles se Ciren-
    cester pop 180 archd and dioc Gloucester
AMPNEY CRUCIS parish 1566 Gloucs 3-1/2 miles e Cirencester
    pop 590 archd and dioc Gloucester
AMPNEY DOWN parish 1603 Gloucs 4 miles sw Fairford pop 463
    archd and dioc Gloucester

AMPORT parish 1665 Hamps 4-1/4 miles sw Andover pop 713 archd and dioc Winchester

AMPTHILL parish 1605 Beds 7 miles sw Bedford pop 1,688 archd Bedford dioc Lincoln Soc of Friends, Wesl Meth

AMPTON parish 1559 Suffolk 5-1/4 miles ne Bury St. Edmunds pop 110 archd Sudbury dioc Norwich

AMWELL, GREAT parish 1558 Herts 1-1/2 miles se Ware pop 1,321 archd Middlesex dioc London

AMWELL, LITTLE liberty parish All Saints, Hertford Herts pop 368

ANCASTER parish 1722 Lincs 6-3/4 miles ne Grantham pop 491 archd and dioc Lincoln

ANCROFT chapelry 1742 co Durham locally in Northumberland adj Berwick on Tweed pop 1,384 archd and dioc Durham

ANDERBY parish 1565 Lincs 4-1/4 miles se Alford pop 217 archd and dioc Lincoln

ANDERSTON or ANDERSON WINTERBOURNE parish 1763 Dorset 6 miles s Blandford pop 54 pec Dean of Salisbury

ANDERTON township parish Great Budworth Ches pop 327

ANDERTON township parish Standish Lancs pop 343

ANDOVER parish, borough 1587 sep juris Hamps 26 miles nw Southampton pop 4,843 archd and dioc Winchester Bapt, Soc of Friends, Indep, Wesl Meth

ANDERSLEIGH parish 1678 Somerset 4-3/4 miles sw Taunton pop 54 archd Taunton dioc Bath and Wells

ANGERTOM, HIGH township parish Hartburn Northumberland pop 64

ANGERTON, LOW township parish Hartburn Northumberland pop 55

ANGLESEY parish Alverstoke Hamps

ANGLEZARKE township parish Bolton Lancs pop 168

ANGMERING parish 1563 Sussex 3-3/4 miles ne Little Hampton pop 928 archd and dioc Chichester

ANGRAM township parish Long Marston E R Yorks pop 67

ANGRAM GRANGE township parish Coxwold N R Yorks pop 29

ANICK township parish St. John Lee Northumberland pop 163

ANICK GRANGE township parish St. John Lee Northumberland pop 36

ANLABY township chiefly in parish Kirk Ella E R Yorks pop 398 Wesl Meth

ANMER parish 1578 Norfolk 5-3/4 miles ne Castle Rising pop 132 archd and dioc Norwich

ANN ABBOTS See ABBOTS ANN

ANNE, ST. or BRIERS chapelry parish Halifax N R Yorks

ANNESLEY parish 1599 Notts 6-1/2 miles sw Mansfield pop 403 archd Nottingham dioc York Wesl Meth

ANSFORD See ALMSFORD

ANSLEY parish 1639 Warws 5-1/2 miles nw Nuneaton pop 773 archd Coventry dioc Lichfield

ANSLOW or ANNESLEY township parish Rolleston Staffs pop 302 Wesl Meth

ANSTEY parish 1589 Warws 5-1/2 miles ne Coventry pop 268 archd

Coventry dioc Lichfield

ANSTEY parish 1541 Herts 3 miles se Barkway pop 417 archd Middlesex dioc London

ANSTEY chapelry 1556 parish Thurcaston Leics 3-3/4 miles nw Leicester Wesl Meth

ANSTEY parish 1686 Wilts 6-1/4 miles se Hindon pop 348 archd and dioc Salisbury

ANSTEY, EAST parish 1596 Devon 3 miles sw Dulverton pop 166 archd Barnstaple dioc Exeter

ANSTEY PASTURES extra parochial liberty Leics 3-3/4 miles nw Leicester pop 19

ANSTEY, WEST parish 1653 Devon 3-1/2 miles w Dulverton pop 226 archd Barnstaple dioc Exeter

ANSTON parish 1550 W R Yorks 6-1/2 miles nw Worksop pop 840 pec Chancellor in the Cathedral Church of York

ANTHONY, ST. IN MENEAGE parish 1602 Cornwall 6 miles sw Falmouth pop 300 archd Cornwall dioc Exeter Bapt

ANTHONY, ST. IN ROSELAND parish 1660 Cornwall 9-1/4 miles sw Tregony pop 144 archd Cornwall dioc Exeter

ANTHONY, EAST or ST. JACOB parish 1569 Cornwall 5-1/2 miles se St. Germans pop 3,099 archd Cornwall dioc Exeter Wesl Meth

ANTHORN township parish Bowness Cumberland pop 230

ANTINGHAM parish 1679 Norfolk 2-1/2 miles nw North Walsham pop 248 archd Norfolk dioc Norwich

ANTROBUS township parish Great Budworth Ches pop 476

ANWICK parish 1573 Lincs 4-3/4 miles ne Seaford pop 235 archd and dioc Lincoln

APESTHORPE See APPLESTHORPE

APETHORPE parish 1676 co Northampton 4-1/4 miles sw Wansford pop 297 pec Prebendary of Nassington

APETON township parish Gnosall Staffs

APLEY parish 1561 Lincs 2 miles sw Wragby pop 152 archd and dioc Lincoln

APPERLEY joint hamlet with Whitefield parish Deerhurst Gloucs Wesl Meth

APPLEBY parish 1572 Leics 5-3/4 miles sw Ashby de la Zouch pop 1,150 archd and dioc Leicester

APPLEBY parish 1576 Lincs 7 miles nw Glandford Bridge pop 517 archd Stow dioc Lincoln

APPLEBY town, borough sep juris comp parishes St. Lawrence 1694; St. Michael 1582, Westm 14 miles se Penrith pop 851 archd and dioc Carlisle Wesl Meth

APPLEDORE sea port parish Northam Devon Indep, Roman Cath

APPLEDORE parish 1700 Kent 6 miles se Tenterden pop 568 archd and dioc Canterbury

APPLEDRAM parish 1661 Sussex 1-3/4 miles sw Chichester pop 188 archd and dioc Chichester

APPLEFORD chapelry 1563 parish Sutton Courtney Berks 3-1/2

miles se Abingdon

APPLESHAW parish 1744 (see Amport Regs) Hamps 3 miles se Ludgershall pop 356 archd and dioc Winchester

APPLESTHORPE or APESTHORPE parish 1707 Notts pop 95 pec Prebendary of Apesthorpe

APPLETHWAITE township parish Windermere Westm pop 429

APPLETON parish 1569 Berks 5-1/2 miles nw Abingdon pop 441 archd Berks dioc Salisbury

APPLETON joint township with Hull parish Great Budworth Ches

APPLETON joint township with Widnes parish Prescot Lancs Wesl Meth

APPLETON parish Norfolk 3-1/2 miles ne Castle Rising archd and dioc Norwich no regs

APPLETON township parish Lastingham N R Yorks pop 269 Wesl Meth

APPLETON LE MOORS township parish Lastingham N R Yorks pop 269

APPLETON LE STREET parish 1715 N R Yorks comp chapelry Swinton, townships Amotherby, Appleton le Street, Broughton, Hildenley pop 860 3-3/4 miles nw New Malton archd Cleveland dioc York

APPLETON ROEBUCK township parish Bolton Percy E R Yorks pop 538 Wesl Meth

APPLETON UPON WISK parish 1629 N R Yorks 7-1/4 miles sw Yarm pop 553 archd Cleveland dioc York Wesl Meth

APPLETREE hamlet parish Aston le Walls co Northampton pop 83

APPLETREE WICK township parish Burnsall W R Yorks pop 425

APULDRAM See APPLEDRAM

ARBORFIELD parish 1705 Berks 5 miles se Reading pop 268 pec Dean of Salisbury

ARBURY joint township with Houghton and Middleton parish Winwick Lancs

ARCLEBY hamlet parish Plumbland Cumberland

ARCLID township parish Sandbach Ches pop 79

ARDELEY See YARDLEY

ARDEN joint township with Ardenside parish Hawnby N R Yorks pop 161

ARDINGLEY parish 1558 Sussex 4-1/2 miles ne Cuckfield pop 587 archd Lewes dioc Chichester

ARDINGTON parish 1674 Berks 2-3/4 miles e Wantage pop 404 archd Berks dioc Salisbury

ARDLEIGH parish 1555 Essex 4-3/4 miles ne Colchester pop 1,545 archd Colchester dioc London Wesl Meth

ARDLEY parish 1758 co Oxford 4 miles nw Bicester pop 170 archd and dioc Oxford

ARDSLEY township parish Darfield W R Yorks pop 1,029 Wesl Meth

ARDSLEY, EAST parish 1654 W R Yorks 3-1/2 miles nw Wakefield pop 853 archd and dioc York

ARDSLEY, WEST parish 1652 W R Yorks 4-1/2 miles nw Wakefield

pop 1,450 (anciently called Woodkirk) archd and dioc York
ARDWICK chapelry 1740 parish Manchester Lancs 1 mile se Manchester pop 5,524 archd and dioc Chester Wesl Meth
ARELY KINGS or LOWER ARELY parish 1539 Worcs 3/4 mile sw Stourport pop 372 archd and dioc Worcester
ARELY, UPPER parish 1564 Staffs 5-1/2 miles nw Kidderminster pop 735 pec Dean and Chapter of Lichfield
ARGAM parish (see Bridlington) E R Yorks 5-1/2 miles nw Bridlington archd East Riding dioc York
ARKENDALE chapelry 1780 parish Knaresborough W R Yorks 4 miles ne Knaresborough pop 260 pec honour of Knaresborough Wesl Meth
ARKENGARTHDALE parish 1659 N R Yorks 12 miles nw Richmond pop 1,446 pec manorial court of Arkengarthdale, New Forest, and Hope
ARKESDEN parish 1690 Essex 5-1/4 miles sw Saffron Walden pop 490 archd Colchester dioc London
ARKHOLME chapelry 1626 parish Melling Lancs 5-1/4 miles sw Kirkby Lonsdale pop 349 archd Richmond dioc Chester
ARKSEY parish 1557 W R Yorks 3 miles ne Doncaster pop 114 archd and dioc York
ARLECDON parish 1730 Cumberland 5-1/2 miles ne Whitehaven incl townships High and low Frizington, Whillymoor pop 475 pec Bishop of Chester
ARLESCOTE township parish Warmington Warws
ARLESTON joint liberty with Synfin parish Barrow Derbys
ARLEY parish 1557 Warws 6 miles ne Coleshill pop 270 pec Dean and Chapter of Lichfield
ARLINGHAM parish 1539 Gloucs 1-1/2 miles se Newnham pop 744 archd and dioc Gloucester Wesl Meth
ARLINGTON parish 1598 Devon 6-1/4 miles ne Barnstaple pop 235 archd and dioc Exeter
ARLINGTON tything parish Bibury Gloucs pop 333
ARLINGTON parish 1607 Sussex 3-3/4 miles sw Hailsham pop 727 archd Lewes dioc Chichester
ARLSEY parish 1538 Beds 4-3/4 miles nw Baldock pop 685 archd Bedford dioc Lincoln
ARMATHWAITE chapelry 1759 parish Hesket in the Forest Cumberland 5 miles nw Kirk Oswald archd and dioc Carlisle
ARMIN chapelry 1726 parish Snaith W R Yorks 3 miles ws Howden pop 567 pec court of Snaith
ARMINGHALL parish 1571 Norfolk 3-1/2 miles se Norwich pop 88 pec Dean and Chapter of Norwich
ARMITAGE joint parish with Handsacre 1673 Staffs 2-1/4 miles se Rugeley pop 977 pec Prebendary of Handsacre and Armitage, Cathedral Church of Lichfield Calv Meth
ARMLEY chapelry 1722 parish St. Peter, Leeds W R Yorks 2-1/2 miles nw Leeds pop 5,159 archd and dioc York Wesl Meth

ARMSCOTT hamlet parish Tredington Worcs pop 130

ARMSTON hamlet parish Polebrook co Northampton pop 25

ARMTHORPE parish 1653 W R Yorks 4 miles ne Doncaster pop 368 archd and dioc York

ARNCLIFFE parish 1669 W R Yorks comp chapelry Haltengill, townships Arncliffe, Buckden, West Halton, Hawkswith, Litton 10-1/2 miles ne Settle archd and dioc York

ARNCLIFFE, INGLEBY parish 1654 N R Yorks 7 miles sw Stokesley pop 335 archd Cleveland dioc York

ARNCOTT chapelry parish Ambrosden co Oxford pop 417

ARNE chapelry 1762 parish Holy Trinity, Wareham Dorset 4 miles ne Wareham pop 171 archd Dorset dioc Bristol

ARNESBY parish 1602 Leics 8-1/2 miles se Leicester pop 442 archd Leicester dioc Lincoln Part Bapt

ARNOLD parish 1544 Notts 3-1/2 miles ne Nottingham pop 4,054 archd Nottingham dioc York Gen and Part Bapt, Prim and Wesl Meth

ARRAM joint township with Atwick and Skirlington parish Atwick E R Yorks

ARRAS hamlet parish Market Weighton E R Yorks

ARRETON parish 1656 Isle of Wight Hamps 3 miles se Newport pop 1,864 archd and dioc Winchester

ARRINGTON parish 1538 Cambs 5-1/4 miles se Caxton pop 254 archd and dioc Ely

ARROW township parish Woodchurch Ches pop 91

ARROW parish 1588 Warws comp hamlets Ragley, Oversley 1 mile sw Alcester pop 466 archd and dioc Worcester

ARROWTHORNE township parishes Hornby and Brompton Patrick N R Yorks pop 59

ARTHINGTON township parish Addle W R Yorks pop 360

ARTHINGWORTH parish 1650 co Northampton 4-1/2 miles se Market Harborough pop 225 archd Northampton dioc Peterborough

ARTHURET parish 1610 Cumberland 3/4 mile s Longtown comp townships Brackenhill, Lineside, Longtown, Netherby pop 2,903 archd and dioc Carlisle

ARTILLERY GROUND, OLD liberty Middlesex pop 1,411

ARTINGTON tything parish St. Nicholas, Guildford pop 511

ARUNDEL parish, borough 1560 sep juris Sussex 10 miles ne Chichester pop 2,803 archd and dioc Chichester

ARVANS, ST. parish 1686 co Monmouth 2-1/4 miles nw Chopstow pop 304 archd and dioc Llandaff

ARYHOLME joint township with Hawthorpe parish Hovingham N R Yorks pop 42

ASBY parish 1657 Westm 4-1/4 miles sw Appleby comp townships Asby Coatsforth, Little Asby, Asby Winderwath pop 436 archd and dioc Carlisle

ASCOTE, CHAPEL extra parochial liberty Warws 2 miles nw Southam pop 15

ASCOTT UNDER WYCHWOOD parish 1569 co Oxford 5-3/4 miles ne
Burford pop 419 archd and dioc Oxford Part Bapt, Wesl Meth
ASCOTT hamlet parish Great Milton co Oxford pop 97
ASCOTT hamlet parish Whichford Warws
ASENBY township parish Topcliffe N R Yorks pop 238
ASFORDBY See ASHFORDBY
ASGARBY SLEAFORD parish 1676 Lincs 2-3/4 miles e Sleaford pop
55 archd and dioc Lincoln
ASGARBY Lincs 5-1/4 miles nw Spilsby pop 140 pec Dean and Chap-
ter of Lincoln
ASH hamlet parish Sutton on the Hill Derbys pop 50
ASH hamlet parish Throwley Devon pop 47
ASH co Durham (See Esh)
ASH parish 1553 Kent 3-3/4 miles nw Wrotham pop 505 archd and
dioc Rochester
ASH parish 1549 Surrey 5 miles ne Farnham pop 2,001 archd Surrey
dioc Winchester
ASH BOCKING parish 1555 Suffolk 6 miles se Needham Market pop
234 archd Suffolk dioc Norwich
ASH, GREAT township parish Whitchurch Shrops
ASH, LITTLE township parish Whitchurch Shrops
ASH NEAR SANDWICH parish 1558 Kent 3-1/4 miles nw Sandwich
pop 2,140 archd and dioc Canterbury
ASH PRIORS parish 1700 Somerset 6 miles nw Taunton pop 210 archd
Taunton dioc Bath and Wells
ASHAMSTEAD chapelry 1686 parish Basildon Berks 6 miles se East
Ilsey pop 346
ASHAMSTEAD chapelry parish Lewknor co Oxford
ASHBOURN parish 1547 Derbys comp town Ashbourne, chapelry Alsop
le Dale, townships Eaton, Hulland Ward Intacks, liberties Newton
Grange, Offcoat with Underwood, hamlets Hulland Ward, Sturston,
Yeldersley, Compton, chapelry Clifton 13-1/2 miles nw Derby
pop 4,884 archd Derby dioc Lichfield
ASHBRITTLE parish 1563 Somerset 6-3/4 miles w Wellington pop
625 archd Taunton dioc Bath and Wells
ASHBROOK, Gloucs (see Ampney)
ASHBURNHAM parish 1656 Sussex 4-1/2 miles sw Battle pop 721
archd Lewes dioc Chichester
ASHBURTON parish, borough 1603 Devon 19 miles sw Exeter pec
Dean and Chapter of Exeter Part Bapt, Indep, Wesl Meth
ASHBURY parish 1653 Berks 6-1/4 miles nw Lambourn pop 698
archd Berks dioc Salisbury
ASHBURY parish 1615 Devon 5-1/4 miles sw Hatherleigh pop 74
archd Totnes dioc Exeter
ASHBY parish 1723 Lincs 6-1/4 miles sw Grimsby pop 179 archd
and dioc Lincoln
ASHBY BY PARTNEY parish 1552 Lincs 2-1/4 miles ne Spilsby pop
170 archd and dioc Lincoln

ASHBY township parish Bottesford Lincs pop 378
ASHBY parish 1559 Norfolk 2-1/2 miles n Acle pop 82 archd Norfolk dioc Norwich
ASHBY parish 1620 Norfolk 8 miles se Norwich pop 218 archd Norfolk dioc Norwich
ASHBY parish 1553 Suffolk 6 miles nw Lowestoft pop 42 archd Suffolk dioc Norwich
ASHBY, CANONS parish 1708 co Northampton 8 miles nw Towcester pop 197 archd Northampton dioc Peterborough
ASHBY, CASTLE parish 1564 co Northampton 7-3/4 miles se Northampton pop 150 archd Northampton dioc Peterborough
ASHBY, COLD parish 1560 co Northampton 11-1/2 miles nw Northampton pop 385 archd Northampton dioc Peterborough
ASHBY DE LA LAUNDE parish 1695 Lincs 6-1/4 miles nw Sleaford pop 178 archd and dioc Lincoln
ASHBY DE LA ZOUCH parish 1561 Leics 18 miles nw Leicester pop 4,727 archd Leicester dioc Lincoln Bapt, Countess of Huntingdons, Indep, Wesl Meth
ASHBY FOLVILLE parish 1653 Leics 6 miles sw Melton Mowbry pop 391 archd Leicester dioc Lincoln
ASHBY ST. LEDGERS parish 1554 co Northampton 3-1/2 miles n Daventry pop 257 archd Northampton dioc Peterborough
ASHBY MAGNA parish 1586 Leics 4 miles ne Lutterworth pop 330 archd Leicester dioc Lincoln
ASHBY MEARS parish 1670 co Northampton 3-3/4 miles sw Wellingboro pop 466 archd Northampton dioc Peterborough
ASHBY PARVA parish 1585 Leics 3 miles nw Lutterworth pop 169 archd Leicester dioc Lincoln
ASHBY PUERORUM parish 1657 Lincs 4-1/4 miles ne Horncastle pop 391 archd and dioc Lincoln
ASHBY, WEST parish 1561 Lincs 1-3/4 miles n Horncastle pop 391 archd and dioc Lincoln
ASHCHURCH parish 1556 Gloucs 2-1/4 miles ne Tewkesbury comp tythings Aston upon Carron, Fiddlington with Natton, Northway with Newton, Pamington pop 649 archd and dioc Gloucester
ASHCOMBE parish 1583 Devon 3 miles e Chudleigh pop 320 archd and dioc Exeter
ASHCOTT parish 1678 Somerset 5 miles sw Glastonbury pop 834 archd Wells dioc Bath and Wells Wesl Meth
Ashdon parish 1553 Essex 3-3/4 miles ne Saffrom Walden pop 1,103 archd Colchester dioc London
ASHE parish 1606 Hamps 5-1/4 miles ne Whitchurch pop 146 archd and dioc Winchester
ASHELDAM parish 1721 Essex 5 miles sw Bradwell pop 144 archd Essex dioc London
ASHELWORTH parish 1566 Gloucs 5-1/2 miles nw Gloucester pop 540 archd and dioc Gloucester
ASHEN parish 1558 Essex 2-1/2 miles sw Clare pop 373 archd

Middlesex dioc London
ASHENDON parish 1670 Bucks 6-1/2 miles nw Thame pop 368 archd
Buckingham dioc Lincoln
ASHFIELD joint township with Ruthell parish Priors Ditton Shrops
ASHFIELD parish 1693 Suffolk 6 miles sw Framlingham pop 375
archd Suffolk dioc Norwich
ASHFIELD, GREAT parish 1678 Suffolk 5 miles se Ixworth pop 408
archd Suffolk dioc Norwich
ASHFORD chapelry 1687 parish Bakewell Derbys pop 782 pec Dean
and Chapter of Lichfield Gen Bapt
ASHFORD parish 1700 Devon 2 miles nw Barnstaple pop 99 archd
Barnstaple dioc Exeter
ASHFORD parish 1570 Kent 20 miles se Maidstone pop 2,809 archd
and dioc Canterbury Part Bapt, Soc of Friends, Countess of Hunt-
ingdons, Wesl Meth
ASHFORD parish 1699 Middlesex 3 miles e Staines pop 458 archd
Middlesex dioc London
ASHFORD BOWDLER parish 1609 Shrops 2-3/4 miles se Ludlow pop
99 archd Salop dioc Hereford
ASHFORD CARBONEL parish 1721 Shrops 3-1/4 miles se Ludlow
pop 289 pec Chancellor, Cathedral Church of Hereford
ASHFORDBY or ASFORDBY parish 1564 Leics 3 miles w Melton
Mowbray pop 467 archd Leicester dioc Lincoln
ASH HOLM township Parish Lambley Northumberland
ASHILL parish 1538 Norfolk 3-1/4 miles nw Watton pop 700 archd
and dioc Norwich
ASHILL parish 1558 Somerset 3-1/2 miles nw Ilminster pop 403 pec
Prebendary of Ashill
ASHINGDON parish 1564 Essex 2-1/4 miles nw Rochford pop 98
archd Essex dioc London
ASHINGTON township parish Bothall Northumberland
ASHINGTON parish 1567 Somerset 2-3/4 miles ne Ilchester pop 74
archd Wells dioc Bath and Wells
ASHINGTON parish 1736 Sussex 5-1/2 miles nw Steyning pop 285
archd and dioc Chichester
ASHLEY parish 1746 Cambs 3-1/4 miles se Newmarket pop 361
archd Sudbury dioc Norwich
ASHLEY township parish Bowdon Ches pop 379
ASHLEY parish 1588 co Northampton 5 miles sw Rockingham pop
304 archd Northampton dioc Peterborough
ASHLEY parish 1725 Hamps 3 miles se Stockbridge pop 93 archd
and dioc Winchester
ASHLEY parish 1551 Staffs 7 miles nw Eccleshall pop 825 archd
Stafford dioc Lichfield
ASHLEY parish 1658 Wilts 5 miles nw Malmesbury pop 99 archd
Wilts dioc Salisbury
ASHLEY HAY township parish Wirksworth Derbys pop 241
ASHMANHAUGH parish 1562 Norfolk 2-3/4 miles ne Coltishall pop

21

154 archd Norfolk dioc Norwich

ASHMANSWORTH parish 1811 Hamps 7-1/2 miles nw Whitchurch pop 222 pec Bishop of Winchester

ASHMORE parish 1651 Dorset 5 miles se Shaftesbury pop 191 archd Dorset dioc Bristol

ASHOLT Hamps (See Aisholt)

ASHORN township parish Newbold Pacey Warws

ASHOVER parish 1622 Derbys 7-1/2 miles nw Alfreton pop 3,179 archd Derby dioc Lichfield Prim and Wesl Meth

ASHOW parish 1733 Warws 2-1/2 miles se Kenilworth pop 176 archd Coventry dioc Lichfield

ASHPERTON parish 1538 Herefs 5-1/4 miles nw Ledbury pop 429 archd and dioc Hereford

ASHPRINGTON parish 1607 Devon 3 miles se Totnes pop 549 archd Totnes dioc Exeter

ASHREIGNEY or RINGS ASH parish 1653 Devon 4 miles sw Chumleigh pop 1,038 archd Barnstaple dioc Exeter

ASHTEAD parish 1662 Surrey 2-1/4 miles sw Epsom pop 607 archd Surrey dioc Winchester

ASHTON township parish Tarvin Ches pop 405

ASHTON parish 1541 Devon 3-3/4 miles nw Chudleigh pop 333 archd and dioc Exeter

ASHTON township Eye Herefs pop 299

ASHTON joint township with Lea, Cottam and Ingol parish Preston Lancs

ASHTON joint township with Stodday parish Lancaster Lancs pop 213

ASHTON parish 1778 co Northampton 7 miles se Northampton pop 380 archd Northampton dioc Peterborough

ASHTON hamlet parish Ufford co Northampton pop 126

ASHTON chapelry parish Oundle co Northampton pop 142

ASHTON BY BUDWORTH chapelry parish Great Budworth Ches pop 409

ASHTON, COLD parish 1734 Gloucs 10-1/4 miles se Bristol pop 322 archd and dioc Gloucester

ASHTON GIFFORD township parish Codford St. Peter Wilts

ASHTON IN MAKERFIELD chapelry 1698 parish Winwick Lancs 2-1/2 miles nw Newton in Makerfield pop 5,912 archd and dioc Chester Soc of Friends, Wesl Meth, Roman Cath

ASHTON KEYNES parish 1582 Wilts 4-1/2 miles w Cricklade pop 1,182 archd Wilts dioc Salisbury

ASHTON, LONG parish 1691 Somerset 2-3/4 miles sw Bristol pop 1,423 archd Bath dioc Bath and Wells

ASHTON, STEEPLE parish 1538 Wilts comp chapelries Littleton, Semington, tythings West Ashton, Great Hinton 3-1/4 miles se Trowbridge archd and dioc Salisbury

ASHTON UNDER HILL parish 1586 Gloucs 8 miles ne Tewkesbury pop 291 archd and dioc Gloucester

ASHTON UNDER LYNE parish 1594 Lancs 60 miles se Lancaster

archd and dioc Chester Indep, Prim and Wesl Meth

ASHTON UPON MERSEY parish 1636 Ches comp townships Ashton
upon Mersey, Sale pop 2,078 6-3/4 miles n Altrincham archd
and dioc Chester Calv, Meth, Unit

ASHTON, WEST tything parish Steeple Ashton Wilts pop 374

ASHURST parish 1692 Kent 4-3/4 miles w Tunbridge Wells pop 206
archd and dioc Rochester

ASHURST parish 1560 Sussex 3-3/4 miles n Steyning pop 423 archd
and dioc Chichester

ASHWATER parish 1558 Devon 7 miles se Holsworthy pop 862 archd
Totnes dioc Exeter

ASHWELL parish 1678 Herts 4-1/4 miles ne Baldock pop 1,072
archd Huntingdon dioc Lincoln

ASHWELL parish 1595 co Rutland 3 miles nw Oakham pop 209 archd
Northampton dioc Peterborough

ASHWELLTHORPE parish 1558 Norfolk 3-1/2 miles se Wymondham
pop 471 archd Norfolk dioc Norwich

ASHWICK parish 1701 Somerset 3-3/4 miles ne Shepton Mallet pop
995 archd Wells dioc Bath and Wells Meth, Presb

ASHWICKEN parish 1717 Norfolk 5-1/2 miles se Lynn Regis pop 80
archd and dioc Norwich

ASHWORTH chapelry 1741 parish Middleton Lancs 3-1/2 miles w
Rochdale pop 294 archd and dioc Chester

ASKE township parish Easby N R Yorks pop 105

ASKERN township parish Campsall W R Yorks pop 256

ASKERSWELL parish 1558 Dorset 4 miles e Bridport pop 228 archd
Dorset dioc Bristol

ASKERTON township parish Lanercost Abbey Cumberland pop 476

ASKHAM chapelry 1538 parish East Drayton Notts 2-3/4 miles n
Tuxford pop 329 pec Dean and Chapter of York

ASKHAM parish 1568 Westm pop 587 4-3/4 miles s Penrith archd
and dioc Carlisle

ASKHAM BRYAN parish 1695 E R Yorks 4 miles sw York pec lord of
the Manor Wesl Meth

ASKHAM RICHARD parish 1579 E R Yorks 5-3/4 miles sw York pop
234 archd and dioc York Wesl Meth

ASKRIGG chapelry 1701 parish Aysgarth N R Yorks 57 miles nw Yorks
pop 737 archd Richmond dioc Chester Wesl Meth

ASKWITH township parish Weston W R Yorks pop 400

ASLACKBY parish 1558 Lincs 2-1/2 miles se Folkingham pop 455
archd and dioc Lincoln

ASLACTON parish 1556 Norfolk 3-1/2 miles sw St. Mary Stratton pop
359 archd Norfolk dioc Norwich

ASLACTON township parish Whatton, Notts pop 389

ASPALL parish 1558 Suffolk 1-1/4 miles ne Debanham pop 126 archd
Sudbury dioc Norwich

ASPALL STONHAM see STONHAM ASPALL

ASPATRIA parish 1660 Cumberland comp townships Aspatria with

Brayton, Hayton with Melay, Outerside with Allerby pop 1,395
8 miles ne Cockermouth archd and dioc Carlisle Indep
ASPEDEN parish 1559 Herts 3/4 mile s Buntingford pop 560 archd
Huntingdon dioc Lincoln
ASPLEY township parish Eccleshall Staffs pop 26
ASPLEY joint hamlet with Fordhall parish Wootten Wawen Warws
ASPLEY GUISE parish 1563 Beds 2-1/4 miles nw Woburn pop 1,014
archd Bedford dioc Lincoln Wesl Meth
ASPULL township parish Wigan Lancs pop 2,426
ASSELBY township parish Howden E R Yorks pop 297 Wesl Meth
ASSENDON hamlet parish Pirton co Oxford
ASSINGTON parish 1598 Suffolk 2-1/4 miles sw Boxford pop 641
archd Sudbury dioc Norwich
ASTBURY parish 1572 Ches 1-1/2 miles sw Congleton pop 14,673
comp market town Congleton, townships Astbury Newbold, Bug-
lawton, Davenport, Hulme Walfield, Moreton with Alcumlow, Od-
drode, Radnor, Smallwood, Summerford archd and dioc Chester
ASTBURY, NEWBOLD township parish Astbury Ches pop 598
ASTERBY parish 1698 Lincs 7 miles n Horncastle pop 231 archd and
dioc Lincoln
ASTHALL parish 1684 co Oxford 3 miles se Burford pop 352 archd
and dioc Oxford
ASTLEY chapelry 1760 parish Leigh Lancs 3 miles e Leigh pop 1,832
archd and dioc Chester Wesl Meth
ASTLEY chapelry 1579 parish St. Mary, Shrewsbury Shrops 5 miles
ne Shrewsbury pop 239 pec St. Mary, Shrewsbury
ASTLEY parish 1670 Warws 4-1/2 miles sw Nuneaton pop 340 archd
Coventry dioc Lichfield
ASTLEY parish 1539 Worcs 3 miles sw Stourport pop 849 archd and
dioc Worcester
ASTLEY ABBOTS parish 1561 Shrops 2 miles n Bridgenorth pop 666
ASTON hamlet parish Invinghoe Bucks pop 406
ASTON joint hamlet with Thornton parish Hope Derbys pop 104
ASTON parish 1685 Herefs 4 miles sw Ludlow pop 56 archd Salop
dioc Hereford
ASTON parish 1558 Herts 3-1/4 miles se Stevenage pop 494 archd
Huntingdon dioc Lincoln
ASTON joint hamlet with Cote parish Bampton co Oxford pop 718
ASTON township parish Wem Shrops pop 250 Wesl Meth
ASTON township parish Muckleston Staffs pop 283
ASTON parish 1544 Warws, 2-1/4 miles ne Birmingham pop 32,986
comp chapelries Bordesley, Castle Bromwich, Deritend, Erding-
ton archd Coventry dioc Lichfield
ASTON parish 1567 W R Yorks 5-1/2 miles se Rotherham pop 564
archd and dioc York
ASTON ABBOTS parish 1559 Bucks 5-1/2 miles ne Aylesbury pop
303 archd St. Albans dioc London
ASTON BLANK parish 1724 Gloucs 4-1/4 miles ne Northleach pop

295 also called Cold Aston archd and dioc Gloucester
ASTON BOTTERELL parish 1559 Shrops 7-3/4 miles nw Cleobury
Mortimer pop 260 archd Salop dioc Hereford
ASTON BY SUTTON chapelry 1635 parish Runcorn Ches pop 166
archd and dioc Chester 3 miles ne Frodsham
ASTON CANTLOW parish 1578 Warws 4 miles ne Alcester pop 940
archd and dioc Worcester
ASTON, CHETWYND township parish Edgmond Shrops pop 246
ASTON, CHURCH chapelry 1621 parish Edgmond Shrops pop 451
ASTON CLINTON parish 1560 Bucks 2-3/4 miles nw Tring pop 1,001
archd Buckingham dioc Lincoln
ASTON EYRE chapelry parish Morvill pop 120 Shrops
ASTON FLAMVILLE parish 1579 Leics 2-1/2 miles se Hinckley pop
1,703 archd Leicester dioc Lincoln
ASTON GRANGE township parish Runcorn Ches pop 36
ASTON INGHAM parish 1633 Herefs 5-3/4 miles e Ross pop 591
archd and dioc Hereford
ASTON JUXTA MONDRUM township parish Acton Ches pop 152
ASTON LE WALLS parish 1540 co Northampton 8-1/2 miles ne Ban-
bury pop 240 archd Northampton dioc Peterborough
ASTON MAGNA hamlet parish Blockley Worcs
ASTON MIDDLE township parish Steeple Aston co Oxford pop 121
ASTON MOLLINS hamlet parish Dinton Bucks
ASTON, NORTH parish 1598 co Oxford 2-1/2 miles se Deddington
pop 305 archd and dioc Oxford Wesl Meth
ASTON ROWANT parish 1554 co Oxford 3-1/2 miles se Tetsworth
pop 946 archd and dioc Oxford
ASTON SANDFORD parish 1615 Bucks 4 miles ne Thame pop 82 archd
Buckingham dioc Lincoln
ASTON SOMERVILLE parish 1568 Gloucs 7-1/4 miles ne Winchcombe
pop 103 archd and dioc Gloucester
ASTON, STEEPLE parish 1538 co Oxford 4 miles se Deddington pop
562 archd and dioc Oxford
ASTON SUB EDGE parish 1539 Gloucs 1-1/4 miles nw Chipping
Campden pop 103 archd and dioc Gloucester
ASTON TIRROLD parish 1726 Berks 3-1/2 miles sw Wallingford pop
343 archd Berks dioc Salisbury
ASTON UPON CARRANT tything parish Ashchurch Gloucs pop 172
ASTON UPON TRENT parish 1667 Derbys 6-1/2 miles se Derby pop
620 archd Derby dioc Lichfield
ASTON UPTHORP chapelry parish Blewberry Berks pop 172
ASTON, WHITE LADIES parish 1558 Worcs 5 miles se Worcester
pop 381 pec Bishop of Worcester
ASTROP hamlet parish Kings Sutton co Northampton
ASTWELL hamlet parish Wappenham co Northampton pop 110
ASTWICK parish 1718 Beds 3-3/4 miles nw Baldock pop 97 archd
Bedford dioc Lincoln
ASTWOOD parish 1666 Bucks 5-3/4 miles ne Newport Pagnell pop

268 archd Buckingham dioc Lincoln

ASWARBY parish 1754 Lincs 4 miles nw Folkingham pop 113 archd and dioc Lincoln

ASWARDBY parish 1713 Lincs 4 miles nw Spilsby pop 80 archd and dioc Lincoln Wesl Meth

ATCHAM parish 1619 Shrops 4 miles se Shrewsbury pop 463 archd Salop dioc Lichfield

ATHELHAMPTON See ADMISTON

ATHELINGTON parish 1694 Suffolk 5 miles se Eye pop 129 archd Suffolk dioc Norwich

ATHERINGTON parish 1538 Devon 7 miles se Barnstaple pop 592 archd Barnstaple dioc Exeter

ATHERINGTON or ALDRINGTON formerly a parish Sussex 2-1/2 miles nw Brighton archd Lewes dioc Chichester Village depopulated No regs

ATHERLEY parish 1692 Shrops 4 miles nw Drayton in Hales pop 468 archd Salop dioc Lichfield

ATHERSTONE chapelry parish Mancetter Warws pop 3,870 Wesl Meth, Unit

ATHERSTONE UPON STOUR parish 1611 Warws 3 miles s Stratford upon Avon pop 87 archd and dioc Worcester

ATHERTON chapelry parish Leigh Lancs pop 4,145

ATLOW parish 1685 Derbys 5 miles ne Ashbourn pop 157 archd Derby dioc Lichfield

ATTENBOROUGH parish 1560 Notts 6 miles sw Nottingham pop 1,094 archd Nottingham dioc York

ATTERBY township parish Bishops Norton Lincs 10-1/4 miles nw Market Rasen pop 112

ATTERCLIFFE chapelry 1719 parish Sheffield W R Yorks pop 3,741 archd and dioc York Calv and Wesl Meth

ATTERTON hamlet parish Witherley Leics pop 76

ATTINGTON extra parochial liberty co Oxford 1 mile ne Testworth pop 7

ATTLEBRIDGE parish 1714 Norfolk 4-1/2 miles se Reepham pop 117 archd and dioc Norwich

ATTLEBURGH or ATTLEBOROUGH parish 1552 Norfolk 15 miles sw Norwich pop 1,939 archd Norfolk dioc Norwich Bapt, Wesl Meth

ATWICK parish 1538 E R Yorks 2-1/4 miles nw Hornsea pop 285 archd East Riding dioc York Wesl Meth

ATWORTH chapelry 1658 parish Great Bradford Wilts 4 miles ne Bradford pop 705

AUBORN parish 1749 Lincs 6-1/4 miles sw Lincoln pop 356 archd and dioc Lincoln Wesl Meth

AUCKLAND ST. ANDREW parish 1558 co Durham 1 mile s Bishop Auckland comp townships Byers Green, Counden Grange, Eldon, Middlestone, Midridge Grange, Old Park, Sunderland Bridge, Westerton, Windleston, St. Andrew Auckland, West Auckland, North Bedburn, South Bedburn, Barony, Binchester, Counden, Evenwood,

Hunwick with Helmington, Lynesack with Softley, Newfield, Newton Cap, Pollard's Lands, Shildon, East Thickley, chapelries St. Helen Auckland, Hamsterley town, Bishop Auckland pop 11,137 archd and dioc Durham

AUCKLAND ST. HELEN chapelry 1593 parish St. Andrew Auckland co Durham 3 miles sw Bishop Auckland pop 410 archd and dioc Durham

AUCKLAND, BISHOP chapelry parish St. Andrew Auckland co Durham pop 2,859 Soc of Friends, Indep, Wesl Meth

AUCKLAND, WEST township parish St. Andrew Auckland co Durham pop 1,529 Wesl Meth

AUDENSHAW township parish Aston under Lyne Lancs New Connexion Meth pop 3,781

AUDLEM parish 1557 Ches 7 miles s Nantwich comp townships Audlem, Buerton, Dodcot with Wilkesley, Hankelow, Tittenley pop 2,795 archd and dioc Chester Part Bapt

AUDLEY parish 1538 Staffs 5 miles nw Newcastle under Lyne comp chapelry Talk o' the' Hill, townships Audley, Bignall End, Eardley End, Knowle End, Park End, Liberty Halmer End pop 3,617 archd Stafford dioc Lichfield Wesl Meth

AUGHTON chapelry parish Hatton Lancs

AUGHTON parish 1541 Lancs 2-1/2 miles sw Ormskirk pop 1,462 archd and dioc Chester

AUGHTON parish 1611 E R Yorks comp chapelry East Cottingwith, townships Aughton, Laytham pop 665 E R Yorks archd and dioc York

AUGHTON township parish Aston W R Yorks

AUKBOROUGH parish Lincs 10-1/2 miles w Barton upon Humber pop 467 archd Stow dioc Lincoln Wesl Meth

AUKLEY township parish Finningley Notts pop 362

AULT HUCKNALL parish 1660 Derbys 5-1/2 miles nw Mansfield pop 618 archd Derby dioc Lichfield

AULTON See ALLTON

AUNSBY parish 1681 Lincs 4-1/2 miles nw Folkingham pop 117 archd and dioc Lincoln

AUST chapelry 1538 parish Henbury Gloucs pop 203

AUSTELL, ST. Parish 1565 Cornwall 34 miles sw Launceston pop 8,758 archd Cornwall dioc Exeter Bapt, Bryanites, Calv, Soc of Friends, Prim and Wesl Meth

AUSTERFIELD chapelry 1559 parish Blyth W R Yorks 1-1/4 miles ne Bawtry pop 280

AUSTERSON township parish Whitkirk W R Yorks pop 169

AUSTHWAITE joint township with Birker parish Millom Cumberland

AUSTONLEY township parish Almondbury W R Yorks pop 1,420

AUSTREY parish 1558 Warws 6 miles ne Tamworth pop 540 archd Coventry dioc Lichfield

AUSTWICK township parish Clapham W R Yorks pop 614

AUTHORPE parish 1561 Lincs 6-3/4 miles nw Alford pop 121 archd

and dioc Lincoln

AVEBURY parish 1696 Wilts 6-3/4 miles sw Marlborough pop 747 archd Wilts dioc Salisbury

AVELEY parish 1563 Essex 1-3/4 miles ne Purfleet pop 758 archd Essex dioc London

AVENBURY parish 1661 Herefs 1-1/2 miles se Bromyard pop 344 archd and dioc Hereford

AVENING parish 1557 Gloucs 3 miles n Tetbury pop 2,396 archd and dioc Gloucester

AVERHAM parish 1538 Notts 3-1/4 miles nw Newark pop 182 archd Nottingham dioc York

AVETON GIFFORD parish 1603 Devon 3-1/4 miles se Modbury pop 939 archd Totnes dioc Exeter

AVINGTON parish 1725 Berks 3 miles se Hungerford pop 94 archd Berks dioc Salisbury

AVINGTON parish 1609 Hamps 4-1/4 miles ne Winchester pop 191 archd and dioc Winchester

AVON chapelry parish Christian Malford Wilts pop 26

AVON DASSETT See DASSETT AVON

AWBRIDGE hamlet parish Mitchelmarsh Hamps

AWBURN chapelry parish Fraisthorn E R Yorks 5 miles sw of Bridlington

AWLISCOMBE parish 1559 Devon 2 miles nw Honiton pop 598 archd and dioc Exeter

AWNBY joint chapelry with Holywell parish Bytham Castle Lincs

AWRE parish 1538 Gloucs 2-1/2 miles ne Blakeney comp chapelry Blakeney, tythings Blidesloe, Etloe Duchy, Haglow pop 1,309 archd Hereford dioc Gloucester

AWSWORTH chapelry 1756 parish Nuthall Notts 7-1/2 miles nw Nottingham archd Nottingham dioc York

AXBRIDGE parish 1562 Somerset 18 miles sw Bristol pop 998 archd Wells dioc Bath and Wells Part Bapt, Wesl Meth

AXFORD tything parish Ramsbury Wilts pop 450

AXMINSTER parish 1559 sep juris Devon 25 miles ne Exeter comp town Axminster, tythings Beerhall, Westwater, Wyke pop 2,719 archd and dioc Exeter Indep, Wesl Meth, Roman Cath

AXMOUTH parish 1603 Devon 2-3/4 miles se Colyton pop 646 archd and dioc Exeter

AYCLIFFE parish 1560 co Durham 6 miles n Darlington comp townships Great Aycliffe, Brafferton, Preston le Skerne, Woodham pop 1,564 archd and dioc Durham Wesl Meth

AYDON township parish Corbridge Northumberland pop 99

AYDON CASTLE township parish Corbridge Northumberland pop 29

AYLBURTON chapelry parish Lidney Gloucs pop 388

AYLESBEAR parish 1580 Devon 4-1/2 miles sw Ottery St. Mary pop 1,025 archd and dioc Exeter

AYLESBURY parish, borough, 1564 Bucks 16-1/2 miles se Buckingham pop 4,907 pec Aylesbury Soc of Friends, Indep, Wesl Meth,

Part Bapt
AYLESBY parish 1561 Lincs 5-1/2 miles sw Great Grimsby pop 144
archd and dioc Lincoln
AYLESFORD parish 1653 Kent 3-1/2 miles nw Maidstone pop 1,301
archd and dioc Rochester Wesl Meth
AYLESTONE parish 1561 Leics 2-1/2 miles sw Leicester pop 758
archd Leicester dioc Lincoln
AYLMERTON parish 1696 Norfolk 2-3/4 miles sw Cromer pop 284
archd Norfolk dioc Norwich
AYLSHAM parish 1653 Norfolk 12-1/4 miles nw Norwich pop 2,334
archd and dioc Norwich Part Bapt, Meth
AYLTON parish 1748 Herefs 4-1/4 miles w Ledbury pop 126 archd
and dioc Hereford
AYLWORTH hamlet parish Naunton Gloucs
AYMESTREY parish 1568 Herefs 8 miles nw Leominster pop 1,006
archd and dioc Hereford
AYNHOE parish 1562 co Northampton 2-3/4 miles ne Deddington pop
664 archd Northampton dioc Peterborough
AYOTT ST. LAWRENCE parish 1566 Herts 3-1/4 miles nw Welwyn
pop 134 archd Huntingdon dioc Lincoln
AYOTT ST. PETER parish 1686 Herts 1-1/4 miles sw Welwyn pop
271 archd Huntingdon dioc Lincoln
AYSGARTH parish 1709 N R Yorks 8-1/2 miles w Middleham comp
chapelries Askrigg, Hawes, townships High Abbotside, Low Ab-
botside, Aysgarth, Bainbridge, Bishop Dale, Burton with Walden,
Capperby, Newbiggin, Thoralby, Thornton Rust pop 5,796 archd
Richmond dioc Chester Soc of Friends, Wesl Meth
AYSTON parish 1656 co Rutland 1-1/4 miles nw Uppingham pop 101
archd Northampton dioc Peterborough
AYTHORPE ROOTHING See ROOTHING, AYTHORPE
AYTON, GREAT parish 1666 N R Yorks 3 miles ne Stokesley pop
1,296 archd Cleveland dioc York Soc of Friends, Indep, Prim
and Wesl Meth
AYTON, EAST chapelry parish Seamer N R Yorks pop 360 Wesl
Meth
AYTON, LITTLE township parish Great Ayton N R Yorks pop 68
AYTON, WEST township parish Hutton Bushell N R Yorks pop 256
BABBICOMBE hamlet parish St. Mary church Devon
BABCARY parish 1704 Somerset 4-3/4 miles e Somerton pop 453
archd Wells dioc Bath and Wells
BABLINGLEY parish 1662 Norfolk 1-3/4 miles n Castle Rising pop
38 archd and dioc Norwich
BABINGTON parish 1725 Somerset 5-1/2 miles nw Frome pop 206
archd Wells dioc Bath and Wells Wesl Meth
BABRAHAM parish 1561 Cambs 4-1/2 miles nw Linton pop 273
archd and dioc Ely
BABWORTH parish 1622 Notts 1-1/4 miles w East Retford pop 449
archd Nottingham dioc York

BACH township parish St. Oswald Chester Ches pop 34
BACKFORD parish 1562 Ches 4 miles n Chester comp townships
Backford, Chorlton, Lea, Conghall, Great Mollington pop 487
archd and dioc Chester
BACKSHAW hamlet parish Holwell Somerset
BACKWELL parish 1693 Somerset 7-1/4 miles sw Bristol pop 1,038
archd Bath dioc Bath and Wells
BACKWORTH township parish Earsdon Northumberland pop 412
BACONSTHORPE parish 1692 Norfolk 3-1/4 miles se Holt pop 333
archd and dioc Norwich
BACTON parish 1724 Herefs 11-1/2 miles sw Hereford pop 178
archd and dioc Hereford
BACTON parish 1558 Norfolk 4-1/4 miles ne North Walsham pop 498
archd Norfolk dioc Norwich Part Bapt
BACTON parish 1558 Suffolk 6-1/2 miles n Stow Market pop 758
archd Sudbury dioc Norwich
BACUP chapelry 1788 parish Whalley 6 miles se Haslingden Lancs
archd and dioc Chester Part Bapt, Wesl Meth
BADBY parish 1559 co Northampton 2-1/4 miles sw Daventry pop
583 archd Northampton dioc Peterborough
BADDESLEY,CLINTON parish 1747 Warws 7 miles nw Warwick
pop 110 pec lord of the manor
BADDESLEY,ENSOR parish 1688 Warws 3-1/4 miles nw Atherstone
pop 568 archd and dioc Lichfield
BADDESLEY, NORTH parish 1682 Hamps 3-1/2 miles se Romsey
pop 297 donative pec with archd and dioc Winchester
BADDILEY parish 1579 Ches 3 miles sw Nantwich pop 267 archd and
dioc Chester
BADDINGTON township parish Acton Ches pop 132
BADDOW, GREAT parish 1538 Essex 1-3/4 miles se Chelmsford
pop 1,719 archd Essex dioc London
BADDOW, LITTLE parish 1561 Essex 2-1/2 miles nw Danbury pop
548 archd Essex dioc London
BADGER parish 1662 Shrops 5-3/4 miles ne Bridgenorth pop 142
archd Salop dioc Hereford
BADGEWORTH parish 1559 Gloucs 4 miles sw Cheltenham pop 858
archd and dioc Gloucester
BADDINGTON parish 1630 Gloucs 3-1/4 miles n Cirencester pop 167
archd and dioc Gloucester
BADGEWORTH parish 1671 Somerset 2-1/2 miles sw Axbridge pop
352 archd Wells dioc Bath and Wells
BADINGHAM parish 1538 Suffolk 4 miles ne Framlingham pop 866
archd Suffolk dioc Norwich
BADLESMERE parish 1558 Kent 4-1/4 miles s Faversham pop 135
archd and dioc Canterbury
BADLEY parish 1593 Suffolk 2 miles nw Needham pop 82 archd Suffolk dioc Norwich
BADMINTON, GREAT parish 1538 Gloucs 6-1/2 miles ne Chipping

Sodbury pop 529 archd and dioc Gloucester

BADMINTON, LITTLE tything parish Hawkesbury Gloucs pop 116

BADSEY parish 1538 Worcs 2-1/4 miles se Evesham pop 463 pec Bishop of Worcester

BADSHOT tything parish Farnham Surrey pop 1,173

BADSWORTH parish 1680 W R York 5 miles s Pontefract comp townships Badsworth,Thorp Audling, Upton pop 782 archd and dioc York Wesl Meth

BADWELL ASH parish 1559 Suffolk 8 miles nw Stow Market pop 490 archd Suffolk dioc Norwich

BAGBOROUGH, WEST parish 1558 Somerset 8-1/4 miles nw Taunton pop 453 archd Taunton dioc Bath and Wells

BAGBY chapelry 1556 parish Kirby Knowles N R Yorks 2-1/4 miles se Thirsk pop 289 Wesl Meth

BAGENDON See BADDINGTON

BAGGRAVE liberty parish Hungerton Leics pop 16

BAGINGTON parish 1628 Warws 3-1/2 miles se Coventry pop 257 archd Coventry dioc Lichfield

BAGLEY WOOD extra parochial liberty Berks 3-1/4 miles ne Abingdon pop 21

BAGNALL joint parish with Bucknall Staffs 3-3/4 miles ne Hanley archd Staffs dioc Lichfield

BAGNOR joint township with Wood Speen parish Speen Berks

BAGSHOT chapelry parish Windlesham Surrey

BAGTHORPE parish 1562 Norfolk 7 miles sw Burnham Westgate pop 73 archd Norfolk dioc Norwich

BAGULEY township parish Bowdon Ches pop 468

BAGWORTH chapelry 1559 parish Thornton Leics 5 miles ne Market Bosworth pop 328

BAGWORTH PARK extra parochial liberty Leics 5 miles ne Market Bosworth

BAILDON chapelry 1621 parish Otley W R Yorks 4-1/2 miles nw Bradford archd and dioc York

BAILEY joint township with Aighton and Chaigley parish Mitton Lancs

BAILIE township parish Bewcastle Cumberland pop 454

BAINBRIDGE township parish Aysgarth N R York pop 881

BAINTON chapelry 1713 parish Ufford co Northampton 5 miles ne Wansford pop 171

BAINTON hamlet parish Stoke Lyne co Oxford pop 27

BAINTON parish 1561 E R Yorks 5-3/4 miles sw Great Driffield pop 358 archd East Riding dioc York Wesl Meth

BAITHLEY See BALE

BAKEWELL parish 1614 Derbys comp markettown Bakewell, chapelries Ashford, Baslow, Beeley, Blackwell, Buxton, Chelmerton, Great Longstone, Monyash, Sheldon, Taddington, townships Brushfield, Bubnell, Flagg, Froggatt, Over Haddon, Harthill, Holme, Priestcliffe, Rowland, Great Rowsley, Wardlow, hamlets Calver, Curbar, Hassop, Little Longstone with Monsal Dale pop 9,503 pec Dean

and Chapter of Lichfield Indep, Wesl Meth
BALBY joint township with Hexthorp parish Doncaster W R Yorks
pop 420
BALCOMBE parish 1539 Sussex 4-1/2 miles n Cuckfield pop 641
archd Lewes dioc Chichester
BALDERSBY township parish Topcliffe N R York pop 267
BALDERSTONE chapelry 1767 parish Blackburn Lancs 5-1/2 miles
ne Preston pop 658 archd and dioc Chester
BALDERTON parish 1538 Notts 2 miles se Newark pop 830 archd
Notts dioc York
BALDOCK parish 1558 Herts 18 miles nw Hertford pop 1,704 archd
Huntingdon dioc Lincoln Soc of Friends, Indep, Wesl Meth
BALDON MARSH parish 1559 co Oxford 6 miles se Oxford pop 318
pec Dorchester
BALDON TOOT parish 1579 co Oxford 5-1/4 miles se Oxford pop
272 pec Dorchester
BALE or BAITHLEY parish 1538 Norfolk 4-3/4 miles sw Holt pop
275 archd and dioc Norwich
BALK township parish Kirby Knowle N R York pop 172
BALKHOLME township parish Howden E R York pop 117
BALLIDON chapelry parish Bradborne Derbys pop 105
BALLINGDON anciently BRUNDON parish 1564 Essex 1/2 mile sw
Sudbury pop 283 No church Regs at All Saints, Sudbury archd
Middlesex and dioc London
BALLINGHAM parish 1588 Herefs 7 miles nw Ross pop 147 archd
and dioc Hereford
BALNE township parish Snaith W R York pop 343
BALSALL TEMPLE chapelry 1679 parish Hampton in Arden Warws
pop 1,038 pec manorial court of Balsall Temple
BALSCOTT hamlet parish Wroxton co Oxford pop 213
BALSHAM parish 1558 Cambs 4 miles ne Linton pop 1,074 pec
Charterhouse, London
BALTONSBOROUGH parish 1538 Somerset 5 miles se Glastonbury
pop 675 archd Wells dioc Bath and Wells
BAMBROUGH parish 1638 Northumberland 4-3/4 miles ne Belford
comp chapelries Beadnell, Lucker, townships Alderstone, Bam-
brough, Bambrough Castle, Bradford, Budle, Burton, Elford, Fleet-
ham, Glororum, Hoppen, Mouson, Newham, Newstead, Outchester,
Ratwood, Shoston, Spindleston, North Sunderland, Swinhoe, Tuggal,
Warrenton, Warnford pop 3,949 archd Northumberland dioc
Durham
BAMBROUGH CASTLE township parish Bambrough Northumberland
pop 61
BAMBURGH See BAUMBER
BAMFORD hamlet parish Mathersage Derbys pop 238
BAMFORD joint township with Birtle parish Middleton Lancs
BAMPTON parish 1653 Devon 21 miles ne Exeter pop 1,961 archd
and dioc Exeter Part Bapt, Indep

BAMPTON parish 1538 co Oxford 16 miles sw Oxford comp chapelry
Shifford, hamlets Aston with Cote, Chimney, part of Bright Hamp-
ton pop 2,514 archd and dioc Oxford
BAMPTON parish 1637 Westm 9-3/4 miles nw Orton pop 636 archd
and dioc Carlisle
BAMPTON, KIRK parish Cumberland 6-1/2 miles w Carlisle comp
townships Kirk Bampton, Little Bampton, Oughterby pop 523
archd and dioc Carlisle
BAMPTON, LITTLE township parish Kirk Bampton Cumberland pop
213
BANBURY parish, borough 1558 sep juris co Oxford 22 miles n Oxford
pop 5906 pec court of Banbury Soc of Friends, Indep, Wesl Meth,
Unit
BANHAM parish 1558 Norfolk 5-1/4 miles ne East Harling pop 1,297
archd Norfolk dioc Norwich Wesl Meth
BANKFEE or SOUTH FIELD hamlet parish Longborough Gloucs
BANKS township parish Lanercost Abbey Cumberland pop 296
BANNINGHAM parish 1709 Norfolk 2 miles ne Aylesham pop 360
archd and dioc Norwich
BANSTEAD parish 1547 Surrey 3-1/2 miles se Ewell pop 991 archd
Surrey dioc Winchester
BANWELL parish 1570 Somerset 5 miles nw Axbridge pop 1,623 pec
Banwell at Wells Wesl Meth
BAPCHILD parish 1562 Kent 1-1/4 miles se Sittingbourne pop 319
archd and dioc Canterbury
BAPTON tything parish Fisherton de la Mere Wilts
BARBON chapelry parish Kirby Lonsdale Westm pop 318
BARBY parish 1748 co Northampton 5-1/4 miles nw Daventry pop
637 archd Northampton dioc Peterborough
BARCHESTON parish 1559 Warws 1/2 mile se Shipston upon Stour
pop 198 archd and dioc Worcester
BARCOMBE parish 1580 Sussex 3 miles ne Lewes pop 931 archd
Lewes dioc Chichester
BARDEN chapelry parish of Skipton W R York pop 214
BARDFIELD, GREAT parish 1662 Essex 4-1/2 miles se Thaxted
pop 1,029 archd Colchester dioc London
BARDFIELD, LITTLE parish 1539 Essex 3 miles e Thaxted pop 295
archd Colchester dioc London
BARDFIELD SAILING parish 1561 Essex 5-3/4 miles ne Great Dun-
mow pop 359 archd Essex dioc London
BARDNEY parish 1653 Lincs 10 miles w Horncastle pop 1,098 archd
and dioc Lincoln Wesl Meth
BARDON PARK extra parochial liberty Leics 9-1/2 miles nw Leices-
ter pop 65
BARDSEA township parish Urswick Lancs
BARDSEY parish 1538 W R York 4-1/2 miles sw Wetherby comp
townships Bardsey with Rigton, Wothersome pop 352 archd and
dioc York

33

BARDWELL parish 1538 Suffolk 2-1/4 miles ne Ixworth pop 799
arrchd Sudbury dioc Norwich Part Bapt
BARE township parish Lancaster Lancs pop 110
BARFORD parish 1700 Norfolk 4-3/4 miles n Wymondham pop 420
arrchd Norfolk dioc Norwich
BARFORD extra parochial liberty parish Arthingworth co Northampton
ton
BARFORD chapelry parish East Adderbury 1598 co Oxford 2-3/4
miles ne Deddington pop 131
BARFORD parish 1538 Warws 3 miles sw Warwick pop 748 archd
and dioc Worcester
BARFORD parish 1653 Wilts 2-1/2 miles w Wilton pop 570 archd
and dioc Salisbury Indep
BARFORD, GREAT parish 1564 Beds 6 miles ne Bedford pop 731
archd Bedford dioc Lincoln Wesl Meth
BARFORD, GREAT parish 1643 co Oxford 2-1/2 miles nw Deddington pop 350 archd and dioc Oxford
ton pop 350 archd and dioc Oxford
BARFORD, LITTLE parish 1653 Beds 2-1/2 miles sw St. Neots pop
176 archd Bedford dioc Lincoln
BARFORTH township parish Forcett N R York pop 128
BARFRESTON parish 1572 Kent 6 miles se Wingham pop 114 archd
and dioc Canterbury
BARHAM parish 1688 Hunts 6 miles ne Kimbolton pop 73 pec Prebendary of Longstow Cathedral Church of Lincoln
bendary of Longstow Cathedral Church of Lincoln
BARHAM parish 1558 Kent 6-1/4 miles se Canterbury pop 1,053
archd and dioc Canterbury
BARNHAM parish 1563 Suffolk 4 miles nw Ipswich pop 825 archd
Suffolk dioc Norwich
BARHOLME parish 1726 Lincs 3-3/4 miles nw Market Deeping pop
155 archd and dioc Lincoln
BARKBY parish 1586 Leics 5 miles ne Leicester pop 806 archd
Leics dioc Lincoln
BARKBY THORPE chapelry parish Barkby Leics pop 72
BARKHAM parish 1538 Berks 2-3/4 miles sw Wokingham pop 247
archd Berks dioc Salisbury
BARKING parish 1558 Essex 23 miles sw Chelmsford comp market
town Barking, Wards of Chadwell, Ilford and Ripple pop 8,036
archd Essex dioc London Wesl Meth
BARKING parish 1538 Suffolk 1-1/4 miles sw Needham Market pop
1,884 archd Suffolk dioc Norwich
BARKISLAND township parish Halifax W R York pop 2,292
BARKSTON parish 1561 Lincs 3-3/4 miles ne Grantham pop 430 pec
Prebendary of North Grantham in the Cathedral Church of Salisbury
bury
BARKSTON township parish Sherburn W R York pop 265
BARKSTONE parish 1569 Leics 6-1/2 miles se Bingham pop 297
archd Leicester dioc Lincoln
BARKWAY parish 1538 Herefs 13-3/4 miles ne Hereford pop 1,108

archd Middlesex dioc London Indep

BARKWITH, EAST parish 1695 Lincs 3-1/2 miles ne Wragby pop 187 archd and dioc Lincoln

BARKWITH, WEST parish 1685 Lincs 2-1/2 miles ne Wragby pop 113 archd and dioc Lincoln

BARLASTON parish 1573 Staffs 4-1/2 miles nw Stone pop 514 archd Stafford dioc Lichfield

BARLAVINGTON parish 1656 Sussex 4-1/2 miles s Petworth pop 111 archd and dioc Chichester

BARLBOROUGH parish 1648 Derbys 8 miles ne Chesterfield pop 713 archd Derby dioc Lichfield

BARLBY chapelry 1780 parish Hemingbrough E R York pop 348 pec of Howdenshire

BARLESTON chapelry 1655 parish Market Bosworth Leics pop 582

BARLEY parish 1559 Herts 2-1/4 miles ne Barkway pop 704 archd Middlesex dioc London

BARLEY joint township with Whitley Booths parish Whalley Lancs pop 707

BARLEYTHORPE chapelry parish Oakham Deanshold co Rutland

BARLING parish 1555 Essex 4-1/4 miles ne Prittlewell pop 317 pec of Dean and Chapter of St. Paul's London

BARLINGS parish 1627 Lincs 6-1/2 miles ne Lincoln pop 280 archd Stow dioc Lincoln

BARLOW, GREAT chapelry 1573 parish Staveley Derbys pop 581

BARLOW chapelry parish Brayton W R York pop 225

BARLOW, LITTLE township parish Dronfield Derbys pop 58

BARMBY ON THE MARSH chapelry 1782 parish Howden E R York pop 473 pec of Howdenshire Wesl Meth

BARMBY ON THE MOOR parish 1683 E R York 1-3/4 miles w Pocklington pop 452 pec of Dean of York Wesl Meth

BARMER parish Norfolk 5-3/5 miles sw Burnham Westage pop 43 archd Norfolk dioc Norwich

BARMING parish 1540 Kent 2-1/2 miles sw Maidstone pop 565 archd and dioc Rochester

BARMING, WEST hamlet parish Nettlestead Kent

BARMOOR township parish Lowick Northumberland

BARMSTON township parish Washington co Durham pop 73

BARMPTON township parish Haughton le Skerne co Durham pop 90

BARMSTON parish 1571 E R York 6-1/2 miles sw Bridlington pop 223 archd East Riding dioc York

BARNACK parish 1696 co Northampton 4 miles n Wansford pop 812 archd Northampton dioc Peterborough

BARNACLE hamlet parish Bulkington Warws

BARNACRE joint township with Bonds parish Garstang Lancs pop 519

BARNARD CASTLE chapelry 1609 parish Gainford co Durham pop 4,430 Indep and Prim and Wesl Meth

BARNARDISTON parish 1540 Suffolk 4-1/2 miles nw Clare pop 206 archd Sudbury dioc Norwich

BARNBOW township parish Barwick in Elmett W R York pop 1608
BARNBROUGH parish 1558 W R York 6-1/4 miles w Doncaster pop
520 archd and dioc York Wesl Meth
BARNBY parish 1701 Suffolk 3-3/4 miles se Beccles pop 303 archd
Suffolk dioc Norwich
BARNBY township parish Lythe N R York pop 224
BARNBY IN THE WILLOWS parish 1593 Notts 4-1/2 miles se Newark
pop 237 archd Notts dioc York
BARNBY MOOR joint township with Bilby parish Blyth Notts pop 205
BARNBY UPON DON parish 1600 W R York 5-3/4 miles ne Doncaster
incl Thorpe in Balne pop 561 archd and dioc York Wesl Meth
BARNES parish 1538 Surrey 5 miles sw London pop 1,417 pec of
Archbishop of Canterbury
BARNET BY THE WOLD parish 1753 Lincs 5 miles ne Glandford -
bridge pop 352 archd and dioc Lincoln
BARNET, CHIPPING parish 1678 Herts 14 miles sw Hertford pop
2,369 archd St. Albans dioc London
BARNET, EAST parish 1553 Herts 10-1/4 miles n London pop 547
archd St. Albans dioc London
BARNET, FRYERN parish 1674 Middlesex 8-3/4 miles nw London
pop 615 pec of Dean and Chapter of St. Paul's London
BARNEY parish 1538 Norfolk 5 miles ne Fakenham pop 263 archd
and dioc Norwich
BARNHAM village 1775 Suffolk comp parishes St. Gregory, St. Martin
archd Sudbury dioc Norwich
BARNHAM parish 1675 Sussex 5-1/2 miles sw Arundel pop 148 archd
and dioc Chichester
BARNHAM BROOM parish 1630 Norfolk 4-3/4 miles nw Wymondham
pop 463 archd Norfolk dioc Norwich
BARNHILL hamlet parish Malpas Ches
BARNINGHAM parish 1538 Suffolk 5-1/2 miles ne Ixworth pop 514
archd Sudbury dioc Norwich Wesl Meth
BARNINGHAM parish 1581 N R York 2 miles sw Greta Bridge comp
townships Barningham, Hope, Scargill pop 550 archd Richmond
dioc Chester Wesl Meth
BARNINGHAM, LITTLE parish 1538 Norfolk 6 miles nw Aylsham
pop 227 archd and dioc Norwich
BARNINGHAM NORWOOD parish 1538 Norfolk 5-1/4 miles se Holt
pop 42 archd Norfolk dioc Norwich
BARNINGHAM WINTER parish 1703 Norfolk 5-1/2 miles se Holt pop
114 archd Norfolk dioc Norwich
BARNOLBY LE BECK parish 1572 Lincs 5-1/4 miles sw Grimsby
pop 232 archd and dioc Lincoln
BARNOLDWICK parish 1587 W R York 9 miles sw Skipton comp townships Barnoldwick, Coates, Salterforth pop 2,724 pec Lord of
the Manor Part Bapt, Wesl Meth
BARNSHAW chapelry parish Sandbach Ches
BARNSLEY parish 1574 Gloucs 4-1/4 miles ne Cirencester pop 318

pec Vicar of Bibury

BARNSLEY chapelry 1568 parish Silkstone W R York pop 10,230 16
miles n Sheffield Soc of Friends, Indep, Prim Meth, Wesl Meth,
Roman Cath

BARNSTAPLE parish borough 1538 Devon 40 miles nw Exeter pop
6,840 archd Barnstaple dioc Exeter Bapt, Soc of Friends, Indep,
Wesl Meth

BARNSTON township parish Woodchurch Ches pop 123

BARNSTON parish 1539 Essex 2-1/4 miles se Great Dunmow pop
215 archd Middlesex dioc London

BARNSTONE chapelry 1596 parish Langar Notts

BARNTON township parish Great Budworth Ches pop 730

BARNWELL, ALL SAINTS parish 1558 co Northampton 2-1/4 miles
se Oundle pop 126 archd Northampton dioc Peterborough

BARNWELL, ST. ANDREW parish co Northampton 2 miles se Oundle
pop 284 regs with Barnwell All Saints, archd Northampton dioc
Peterborough

BARNWOOD parish 1651 Gloucs 1-1/2 miles se Gloucester pop 419
archd and dioc Gloucester

BARONY joint township with Evenwood parish St. Andrew Auckland
co Durham

BARR, GREAT chapelry 1654 parish Aldridge Staffs 3-1/4 miles se
Walsall pop 859 archd Stafford dioc Lichfield

BARR, PERRY Staffs See HANDSWORTH

BARRASFORD township parish Chollerton Northumberland pop 232

BARRAWAY chapelry parish Soham Cambs

BARRINGTON parish 1699 Cambs 6-3/4 miles sw Cambridge pop
485 archd and dioc Ely

BARRINGTON parish 1653 Somerset 3-3/4 miles ne Ilminster pop
468 archd Taunton dioc Bath and Wells

BARRINGTON, GREAT 1547 Gloucs 3-1/4 miles nw Burford pop
532 archd and dioc Gloucester

BARRINGTON, LITTLE parish 1640 Gloucs 3 miles nw Burford pop
162 archd and dioc Gloucester

BARRON'S PARK hamlet parish Desford Leics pop 19

BARROW parish 1571 Ches 5 miles ne Chester comp townships Great
Barrow, Little Barrow pop 678 archd and dioc Chester

BARROW ON TRENT parish 1662 Derbys 5-3/4 miles s Derby comp
chapelry Twyford, townships Stenson, liberty Synfin with Arleston
pop 584 archd Derby dioc Lichfield

BARROW township parish Hallystone Northumberland pop 14

BARROW chapelry parish Cottesmore co Rutland pop 144

BARROW parish 1727 Shrops 3-1/2 miles se Much Wenlock pop 351
archd Salop dioc Hereford

BARROW tything parish Kingsbury Espiscopi Somerset

BARROW parish 1542 Suffolk 6-3/4 miles w Bury St. Edmunds pop
856 archd Sudbury dioc Norwich

BARROW GURNEY parish 1590 Somerset 5-1/2 miles sw Bristol

pop 279 a donative archd Bath dioc Bath and Wells
BARROW, LITTLE township parish Barrow Ches pop 242
BARROW, NORTH parish 1568 Somerset 2-3/4 miles sw Castle Cary
pop 150 archd Wells dioc Bath and Wells
BARROW, SOUTH parish 1679 Somerset 3-3/4 miles sw Castle Cary
pop 139 pec of Dean and Chapter of Wells
BARROW UPON HUMBER parish 1561 Lincs 2-1/4 miles e Barton
upon Humber pop 1,334 archd and dioc Lincoln Part Bapt, Wesl
Meth
BARROW UPON SOAR parish 1563 Leics 2 miles w Mountsorrel
comp chapelries Mountsorrell, Quorndon, Woodhouse pop 6,254
archd Leicester dioc Lincoln Wesl Meth
BARROWBY parish 1538 Lincs 2 miles w Grantham pop 697 archd
and dioc Lincoln
BARROWDEN parish 1603 co Rutland 5-1/4 miles e Uppingham pop
485 archd Northampton dioc Peterborough
BARROWFORD township parish Whalley Lancs pop 2,633 Wesl Meth
BARSBY chapelry parish Ashby Folville Leics pop 230
BARSHAM parish 1558 Suffolk 1-3/4 miles sw Beccles pop 182
archd Suffolk dioc Norwich
BARSHAM, EAST parish 1646 Norfolk 2-1/4 miles n Fakenham pop
219 archd Norfolk dioc Norwich
BARSHAM, NORTH parish 1557 Norfolk 2 miles sw Little Walsing-
ham pop 84 archd Norfolk dioc Norwich
BARSHAM, WEST parish 1756 Norfolk 2-3/4 miles nw Fakenham
pop 101 archd Norfolk dioc Norwich
BARSTON parish 1598 Warws 4-1/2 miles se Solihill pop 342 pec
juris of lord of the manor
BARTESTREE chapelry parish Dormington Herefs pop 50
BATHERTON township parish Wybunbury Ches pop 34
BARTHOLOMEW HOSPITAL extra parochial liberty Kent 3/4 mile
s Sandwich pop 52
BARTHOMLEY parish 1563 Staffs 6-1/2 miles se Sandbach comp
township Batterley Staffs, chapelries Alsager and Haslington
townships of Barthomley and Crewe Ches pop 2,523 archd and
dioc Chester
BARTHORPE joint township with Acklam parish Acklam E R York
BARTINGTON township parish Great Budworth Ches pop 76
BARTLOW parish 1573 Cambs 1-3/4 miles se Linton pop 106 archd
and dioc Ely
BARTLOW END hamlet parish Ashdon Essex pop 205
BARTON parish 1688 Cambs 3-3/4 miles sw Cambridge pop 284
archd and dioc Ely
BARTON township parish Farndon Ches pop 168
BARTON joint township with Bradnor and Rustrock parish Kington
Herefs pop 424
BARTON township parish Preston Lancs pop 422
BARTON IN FABIS parish 1558 Notts 6-3/4 miles sw Nottingham

pop 379 archd Nottingham dioc York

BARTON parish 1714 Somerset 5 miles ne Somerton pop 410 pec of Prebendary of Barton Cathedral Church of Wells

BARTON parish 1676 Westm 4 miles sw Penrith comp chapelries Hartsop with Patterdale, Martindale, townships High Barton, Low Winder, Sockbridge, Yanwath with Eamont Bridge pop 346 archd and dioc Carlisle

BARTON parish 1724 N R York 5 miles sw Darlington comp chapelries Barton St. Cuthbert and Barton St. Mary which form township of Newton Morrell pop 499 archd Richmond dioc Chester

BARTON township parish Haukswell 1581 N R York pop 104

BARTON BENDISH village 1726 Norfolk 4 miles n Stoke Ferry formerly comp St. Andrew 1695, St. Mary, All Saints pop 459 archd Norfolk dioc Norwich

BARTON BLOUNT parish 1763 Derbys 11 miles w Derby pop 60 archd Derby dioc Lichfield

BARTON, EARLS parish 1558 co Northampton 3-3/4 miles sw Wellingborough pop 977 archd Northampton dioc Peterborough Part Bapt, Wesl Meth

BARTON, GREAT parish 1563 Suffolk 2-1/2 miles ne Bury St. Edmunds pop 778 archd Sudbury dioc Norwich

BARTON HARTSHORN parish 1582 Bucks 4-1/4 miles se Buckingham pop 145 archd Bedford dioc Lincoln

BARTON IN THE BEANS township partly in parish Shackerstone partly in Nailstone, chiefly in Market Bosworth Leics pop 163

BARTON IN THE CLAY parish 1558 Beds 3-1/4 miles s Silsoe pop 720 archd Bedford dioc Lincoln

BARTON LE STREET parish 1751 N R York 4-3/4 miles nw New Malton comp townships Coneysthorpe, Barton le Street, Butterwick pop 436 archd Cleveland dioc York Wesl Meth

BARTON LE WILLOWS township parish Crambe N R York pop 202

BARTON, ST. MARY hamlet parish St. Mary de Lode Gloucs pop 786

BARTON, ST. MICHAEL'S hamlet parish St. Michael Gloucs pop 676

BARTON MILLS parish 1663 Suffolk 1-1/2 miles se Mildenhall pop 591 archd Sudbury dioc Norwich Bapt

BARTON SEAGRAVE parish 1609 co Northampton 1-3/4 miles se Kettering pop 203 archd Northampton dioc Peterborough

BARTON STACEY parish 1713 Hamps 5 miles sw Whitchurch comp tythings Barton Stacey, Bransbury, Drayton, Newton Stacey pop 623 archd and dioc Winchester

BARTON ON HEATH or BARTON ON DUNSMORE parish 1575 Warws 5-1/2 miles s Shipton on Stour pop 201 archd and dioc Worcester

BARTON, STEEPLE parish 1678 co Oxford 4-3/4 miles sw Deddington pop 606 archd and dioc Oxford Wesl Meth

BARTON ST ANDREWS See BARTON BENDISH

BARTON TURF parish 1558 Norfolk 5 miles ne Coltishall pop 391 archd Norfolk dioc Norwich

BARTON ON DUNSMORE See BARTON ON HEATH

BARTON UNDERNEEDWOOD chapelry 1571 6 miles sw Burton on Trent, Staffs pop 1,344 archd Stafford dioc Lichfield
BARTON UPON HUMBER market town, borough St. Peter 1566 St. Mary 1570 Lincs 34 miles n Lincoln pop 3,233 archd and dioc Lincoln Indep, Prim, Wesl Meth
BARTON UPON IRWELL township parish Eccles Lancs pop 8,976 Wesl Meth
BARTON WESTCOTT parish 1559 co Oxford 4-1/4 miles e Neat Enstone pop 258 archd and dioc Oxford
BARUGH township parish Darton W R York pop 946
BARUGH AMBE township parish Kirby Misperton N R York pop 294 Wesl Meth
BARWELL parish 1652 Leics 1-3/4 miles ne Hinckley pop 1,505 archd Leicester dioc Lincoln Wesl Meth
BARWICK hamlet parish Abbot's Roothing Essex
BARWICK parish Norfolk 4-3/4 miles sw Burnham Westgage pop 35 archd Norfolk dioc Norwich
BARWICK parish 1560 Somerset 1-3/4 miles se Yeovil pop 415 archd Wells dioc Bath and Wells
BARWICK BASSETT parish 1674 Wilts 7-1/4 miles ne Calne pop 164 pec of Prebendal Court of Calne Archd Wilts dioc Salisbury
BARWICK IN ELMETT parish 1653 W R York 8 miles ne Leeds comp townships Barnbow, Barwick, Kiddal with Potterton, Morwick with Scholes, Roundhay pop 1,922 archd and dioc York
BASCHURCH parish 1600 Shrops 8 miles nw Shrewsbury pop 1,321 archd Salop dioc Lichfield
BASFORD township parish Wybunbury Ches pop 85
BASFORD parish 1561 Notts 2-1/2 miles nw Nottingham pop 6,325 archd Nottingham dioc York Wesl Meth, Meth of New Connection, Bapt
BASFORD township parish Cheddleton Staffs pop 300
BASHALL EAVES township parish Mitton W R York pop 324 Wesl Meth
BASILDON See BASSILDON
BASILDON chapelry 1653 parish Laindon Essex pop 124
BASING parish 1665 Hamps 2 miles ne Basingstoke pop 1,103 archd and dioc Winchester
BASINGSTOKE parish 1638 Hamps 18 miles ne Winchester sep juris archd and dioc Winchester Soc of Friends, Indep, Wesl Meth
BASINGTHORPE parish 1542 Lincs 3-3/4 miles nw Corby pop 122 archd and dioc Lincoln
BASLOW chapelry 1569 parish Bakewell Derbys 3 miles se Stoney Middleton pop 863 pec of Dean and Chapter of Lichfield Wesl Meth
BASSALEG parish 1754 co Monmouth 2-3/4 miles w Newport comp hamlets Duffrin, Craig, Rotherstone pop 1,664 archd and dioc Llandaff Bapt
BASSENTHWAITE parish 1573 Cumberland 5 miles nw Keswick pop

549 archd and dioc Carlisle

BASSETT HOUSE extra parochial liberty Leics 6 miles ne Hinckley pop 23

BASSILDON parish 1540 Berks 7-1/2 miles nw Reading pop 780 archd Berks dioc Salisbury

BASSINGBOURNE parish 1558 Cambs 3-1/4 miles nw Royston pop 1,446 archd and dioc Ely

BASSINGHAM parish 1572 Lincs 9 miles sw Lincoln pop 704 archd and dioc Lincoln Wesl Meth

BASSINGTON township parish Eglingham Northumberland

BASTON parish 1558 Lincs 3-1/4 miles nw Market Deeping pop 709 archd and dioc Lincoln

BASTWICK hamlet parish Repps Norfolk

BASWICH parish 1601 Staffs 2-1/4 miles se Stafford comp chapelries Acton Trussel, Bednall, townships Brockton, Milford, Walton pop 1,329 pec of Prebendary of Whittington and Baswich in the Cathedral church of Lichfield

BATCOMBE parish 1783 Dorset 10 miles sw Sherborne pop 178 archd Dorset dioc Bristol

BATCOMBE parish 1642 Somerset 2-3/4 miles ne Bruton pop 839 archd Wells dioc Bath and Wells Wesl Meth

BATCOMBE tything parish Nyland Somerset

BATH town Somerset 12 miles se Bristol comp parish Abbey 1569, St. James 1569, St. Michael 1569 archd Bath dioc Bath and Wells Soc of Friends, Bapt, Indep, Meth, Moravians, Unit, Roman Cath

BATHAMPTON parish 1754 Somerset 1-3/4 miles ne Bath pop 314 archd Bath dioc Bath and Wells

BATHEALTON parish 1712 Somerset 2-1/2 miles s Wiveliscombe pop 98 archd Bath dioc Bath and Wells

BATH EASTON parish 1634 Somerset 3 miles ne Bath pop 1,783 archd Bath dioc Bath and Wells Wesl Meth

BATHFORD parish 1727 Somerset 3-1/4 miles ne Bath pop 870 archd Bath dioc Bath and Wells

BATHLEY township parish Norton Muskham Notts pop 197

BATHWICK parish 1668 Somerset 1/2 mile ne Bath pop 4,035 archd Bath dioc Bath and Wells

BATLEY parish 1559 W R York 7 miles nw Wakefield comp chapelry Morley township Batley, chapelry Gildersome township Churwell pop 11,335 archd and dioc York Wesl Meth

BATSFORD parish 1562 Gloucs 2 miles nw Moreton in the Marsh pop 107 archd and dioc Gloucester

BATTERLEY township parish Barthomley Staffs pop 305

BATTERSBY township parish Ingleby Greenhow N R York pop 77

BATTERSEA parish 1539 Surrey 4 miles s London pop 5,540 archd Surrey dioc Winchester Bapt, Wesl Meth

BATTISFORD parish 1711 Suffolk 2-1/2 miles sw Needham Market pop 436 archd Suffolk dioc Norwich

BATTLE or BATTEL parish 1610 Sussex 7 miles nw Hastings pop

2,999 pec of Battle dioc Chichester

BATTLEFIELD parish 1663 Shrops 3-1/2 miles ne Shrewsbury pop 70 archd Salop dioc Lichfield

BATTLESDEN parish 1807 Beds 3 miles se Woburn pop 145 archd Bedford dioc Lincoln

BAUGHURST parish 1678 Hamps 7 miles nw Basingstoke pop 491 pec of Incumbent

BAULKING chapelry parish Uffington Berks pop 185 Incl in Regs Uffington

BAUMBER or BAMBURGH parish 1691 Lincs 4 miles nw Horncastle pop 356 archd and dioc Lincoln

BAUNTON parish 1625 Gloucs 1-3/4 miles ne Cirencester pop 144 archd and dioc Gloucester

BAVANT, NORTON Wilts See NORTON BAVANT

BAVERSTOCK parish 1559 Wilts 4 miles w Wilton pop 166 archd and dioc Salisbury

BAVINGTON, GREAT township parish Kirk Whelpington Northumberland pop 70 Scotch Presb

BAVINGTON, LITTLE township parish Throckrington Northumberland pop 72

BAWBURGH parish 1555 Norfolk 4-3/4 miles w Norwich pop 440 archd Norfolk dioc Norwich

BAWDESWELL parish 1557 Norfolk 4 miles sw Reepham pop 587 archd Norfolk dioc Norwich

BAWDRIP parish 1748 Somerset 3-1/4 miles ne Bridgewater pop 373 archd Wells dioc Bath and Wells

BAWDSEY parish 1744 Suffolk 8-1/2 miles se Woodbridge pop 454 archd Suffolk dioc Norwich Wesl Meth

BAWSEY parish 1540 Norfolk 3 miles ne Lynn Regis pop 39 archd and dioc Norwich

BAWTRY chapelry 1653 parish Blyth W R York pop 1,149 Indep, Wesl Meth

BAXTERLEY parish 1654 Warws 4 miles sw Atherstone pop 189 archd Coventry dioc Lichfield

BAYDON or BAYTON parish 1695 Wilts 4-1/4 miles n Ramsbury pop 358 pec of Dean of Salisbury Wesl Meth

BAYFIELD parish Norfolk 2-3/4 miles nw Holt archd and dioc Norwich

BAYFORD parish 1538 Herts 3 miles sw Hertford pop 332 archd Huntingdon dioc Lincoln

BAYFORD hamlet parish Stoke Trister Somerset

BAYHAM hamlet parish Frant Sussex

BAYLEHAM parish 1661 Suffolk 2-1/2 miles se Needham Market pop 238 archd Suffolk dioc Norwich

BAYNTON joint tything with West Coulston parish Edington Wilts

BAYSWATER hamlet parish Paddington Middlesex

BAYTON or BAYDON parish 1564 Worces 1-3/4 miles se Cleobury Mortimer pop 445 archd Salop dioc Hereford

BAYWORTH hamlet parish Sunningwell Berks
BEACHAMPTON parish 1628 Bucks 5-1/2 miles ne Buckingham pop
254 archd Buckingham dioc London
BEACHAMWELL Norfolk See BEECHAMWELL
BEACONSFIELD parish 1631 Bucks 31 miles se Buckingham pop
1,763 archd Buckingham dioc Lincoln
BEADLAM township parish Kirkdale N R York pop 151
BEADNELL chapelry 1766 parish Bambrough Northumberland 10-1/2
miles se Belford pop 251 archd Northumberland dioc Durham
BEAFORD parish 1653 Devon 5 miles se Great Torrington pop 624
archd Barnstaple dioc Exeter
BEAGHALL township parish Kellington W R York pop 563
BEAKSBOURNE parish 1558 Kent 3-1/2 miles se Canterbury pop
351 archd and dioc Canterbury
BEALINGS, GREAT parish 1539 Suffolk 2-1/2 miles w Woodbridge
pop 367 archd Suffolk dioc Norwich
BEALINGS, LITTLE parish 1558 Suffolk 2-3/4 miles sw Woodbridge
pop 272 archd Suffolk dioc Norwich
BEAMINSTER chapelry 1684 parish Netherbury Dorset 17-1/2 miles
nw Dorchester pop 1,968 Indep
BEAMISH township parish Chester le Street co Durham pop 1,848
BEAMSLEY township partly Parish of Addingham chiefly parish of
Skipton W R York pop 279
BEANLEY township parish Eglingham Northumberland pop 169
BEARD hamlet parish Glossop Derbys pop 283
BEARL township parish Bywell St. Andrew Northumberland pop 70
BEARLEY parish 1546 Warws 4-1/4 miles nw Stratford upon Avon
pop 230 archd and dioc Worcester
BEARSTEAD parish 1659 Kent 2-1/2 miles e Maidstone pop 594
archd and dioc Canterbury
BEARSTON township parish Muckleston Shrops pop 95
BEARWARD COTE township parish Etwall Derbys
BEAUCHAMP ROOTHING or RODING, Essex See ROOTHING, BEAU-
CHAMP
BEAUCHAMP STOKE Wilts See BEECHING
BEAUCHIEF ABBEY extra parochial liberty 1768 Derbys pop 88
a donative
BEAUDESERT parish 1661 Warws 1/2 mile e Henley in Arden pop
199 archd and dioc Worcester
BEAULIEU liberty 1654 Hamps pop 1,298 a donative Bapt
BEAU MANOR extra parochial liberty Leics pop 98
BEAUMONT parish 1692 Cumberland 4-1/2 miles nw Carlisle pop
276 archd and dioc Carlisle
BEAUMONT parish 1565 Essex 7-3/4 miles se Manningtree pop 452
archd Colchester dioc London Wesl Meth
BEAUMONT LEYS extra parochial liberty Leics pop 26
BEAUSALL chapelry parish Hatton Warws pop 249
BEAWORTH tything parish Cheriton Hamps pop 156

BEAWORTHY parish 1758 Devon 7-1/2 miles sw Hatherleigh pop 339 archd Totnes dioc Exeter

BEBBINGTON parish 1558 Ches 5-3/4 miles ne Great Neston comp townships Higher Bebbington, Lower Bebbington, Poulton with Spittle, Storeton and Tranmore pop 2,193 archd and dioc Chester

BEBSIDE township parish Norton Northumberland pop 100

BECCLES parish 1586 Suffolk 44 miles ne Bury St. Edmunds pop 3,862 archd Suffolk dioc Norwich Bapt, Indep, Meth

BECCONSALL joint chapelry with Hesketh parish Croston 1745 Lancs pop 523 archd and dioc Chester

BECHTON township parish Sandbach Ches pop 818

BECKBURY parish 1738 Shrops 7 miles ne Bridgenorth pop 307 archd Salop dioc Hereford

BECKENHAM parish 1538 Kent 1-3/4 miles w Bromley pop 1,288 archd and dioc Rochester

BECKERING Lincs See BICKERING

BECKERMET ST. BRIDGET parish 1675 Cumberland 2-1/2 miles s Egremont pop 574 archd Richmond dioc Chester

BECKERMET ST. JOHN parish 1680 Cumberland 2-1/2 miles s Egremont pop 397 archd Richmond dioc Chester

BECKETT tything parish Shrivenham Berks

BECKFORD parish 1549 Gloucs 6 miles ne Tewkesbury pop 433 archd and dioc Gloucester

BECKHAM, EAST no regs parish Norfolk 4-1/2 miles sw Cromer pop 50

BECKHAM, WEST parish 1689 Norfolk 4 miles e Holt pop 154 pec of Dean and Chapter of Norwich

BECKHAMPTON tything parish Avebury Wilts

BECKINGHAM parish 1573 Lincs 5 miles e Newark pop 401 archd and dioc Lincoln

BECKINGHAM parish 1619 Notts 3-1/4 miles nw Gainsborough pop 481 pec Chapter of Collegiate Church of Southwell Wesl Meth

BECKINGTON parish 1559 Somerset 3 miles ne Frome pop 1,340 archd Wells dioc Bath and Wells Bapt, Wesl Meth

BECKLEY parish 1703 co Oxford 4-3/4 miles ne Oxford pop 776 archd and dioc Oxford

BECKLEY parish 1597 Sussex 5-1/2 miles nw Rye pop 1,477 archd Lewes dioc Chichester Wesl Meth

BEDALE parish 1560 N R York 33-1/2 miles nw York comp market town Bedale, townships Aiskew, Burrel with Cowling, Crakenhall and Firby, hamlet of Rands Grange township Langthorne pop 2,707 archd Richmond dioc Chester Meth, Bapt, Roman Cath

BEDBURN, NORTH township parish St. Andrews Auckland co Durham pop 387

BEDBURN, SOUTH township parish St Andrews Auckland co Durham pop 296

BEDDINGHAM parish 1685 Sussex 2-1/4 miles se Lewes pop 264 archd Lewes dioc Chichester

BEDDINGTON parish 1538 Surrey 2 miles w Croydon pop 1,429 archd
Surrey dioc Winchester
BEDFIELD parish 1538 Suffolk 4-3/4 miles nw Framlingham pop 323
archd Suffolk dioc Norwich
BEDFONT, EAST parish 1678 Middlesex 3-3/4 miles sw Hounslow
pop 968 archd Middlesex dioc London
BEDFORD market town 1607, borough, Beds 50 miles nw London pop
6,959 comp parishes St Cuthbert 1607, St John 1609, St Mary 1544,
St Paul 1565, St. Peter 1572 sep juris Bapt, Indep, Wesl Meth,
Moravians, Prim Episcopal, Reformed Church of England
BEDFORD township parish Leigh Lancs pop 3,087 Wesl Meth
BEDHAMPTON parish 1688 Hamps 3/4 mile w Havant pop 537 archd
and dioc Winchester
BEDINGFIELD parish 1538 Suffolk 4 miles se Eye pop 322 archd
Suffolk dioc Norwich
BEDINGHAM parish 1555 Norfolk 4-1/4 miles nw Bungay pop 380
archd Norfolk dioc Norwich
BEDLINGTON parish 1654 co Durham 5-1/2 miles se Morpeth comp
townships Bedlington, North Blyth, with Cambois, Chopington,
Netherton, East Sleckburn and West Sleckburn pop 2,120 archd
Northumberland dioc Durham
BEDMINSTER parish 1690 Somerset 1-1/2 miles sw Bristol pop
13,130 archd Bath dioc Bath and Wells Bapt, Indep, Meth
BEDNALL joint chapelry and township with Acton Trussell parish
Baswich 1571 Staffs pec of Whittington and Baswich in the Cathe-
dral Church of Lichfield
BEDSTONE parish 1719 Shrops 4-1/2 miles ne Knighton pop 159
archd and dioc Hereford
BEDWARDINE parish 1558 Worcs 1 mile sw Worcester comp town-
ships St John Bedwardine Bishop's Wick pop 2,661 archd and
dioc Worcester
BEDWARDINE, ST MICHAEL Worcs See MICHAEL ST BEDWARDINE
BEDWAS parish 1653 co Monmouth 9 miles nw Newport pop 756 archd
and dioc Llandaff
BEDWELTY parish 1624 co Monmouth 16 miles nw Newport pop
10,637 archd and dioc Llandaff
BEDWIN, GREAT parish 1538 Wilts 5-1/2 miles sw Hungerford pop
2,191 pec of the Marquess of Aylesbury Wesl Meth
BEDWIN, LITTLE parish 1722 Wilts 4-1/4 miles sw Hungerford pop
587 pec of Marquess of Aylesbury
BEDWORTH parish 1653 Warws 3-1/2 miles s Nuneaton pop 3,980
archd Coventry dioc Lichfield Bapt
BEEBY parish 1538 Leics 6 miles ne Leicester pop 120 archd Lei-
cester dioc Lincoln
BEECH liberty parish Stone Staffs
BEECHAMWELL parish 1558 Norfolk 5-1/2 miles sw Swaffham pop
263 archd Norfolk dioc Norwich
BEECH HILL tything parish Stratfield Saye Berks pop 249 Part Bapt

BEECHING or BEAUCHAMP STOKE parish 1566 Wilts 5-1/4 miles se
Davizes pop 187 archd Wilts dioc Salisbury
BEEDING parish 1544 Sussex 1-1/2 miles se Steying pop 1,122 archd
Lewes dioc Chichester
BEEDON parish 1732 earlier regs destroyed by fire Berks 2-1/4
miles sw Easto Ilsley pop 306 archd Berks dioc Salisbury
BEEFORD parish 1564 E R York 9 miles se Great Driffield comp
chapelry Lissett, townships Beeford, Dunnington pop 894 pec of
manor court of Beeford Indep, Wesl Meth
BEELEY chapelry 1651 parish Bakewell Derbys pop 441 Wesl Meth
BEELSBY parish 1560 Lincs 5-3/4 miles e Caistor pop 158 archd
and dioc Lincoln
BEENHAM VALENCE parish 1561 Berks 8-3/4 miles sw Reading
pop 360 archd Berks dioc Salisbury
BEER chapelry parish Seaton Devon
BEER ALSTON parish, borough, Devon 14 miles n Plymouth Indep,
Wesl Meth
BEER CROCOMBE parish 1542 Somerset 6 miles nw Ilminster pop
182 archd Taunton dioc Bath and Wells
BEER FERRIS parish 1539 Devon 7-1/2 miles sw Tavistock pop
1,876 archd Totnes dioc Exeter
BEER HACKET parish 1549 Dorset 5 miles sw Sherborne pop 110
pec of Dean of Salisbury
BEER REGIS parish 1592 Dorset 7 miles nw Wareham pop 1,170 pec
Dean of Salisbury Indep, Wesl Meth
BEERHALL tything parish Axminster Devon
BEES, ST parish 1538 Cumberland 2-3/4 miles n Egremont comp
market town Whitehaven, chapelries Ennerdale, Eskdale with Was-
dale, Hensingham and Netherwasdale, townships St Bees, Kinney-
side, Downside Quarter, Preston Quarter, Rottington, Sandwith and
Wheddicar pop 19,203 archd Richmond dioc Chester
BEESBY parish united to Hawerby Lincs 8-1/4 miles nw Louth
BEESBY IN THE MARSH parish 1561 Lincs 2-1/2 miles ne Alford
pop 159 archd and dioc Lincoln
BEESTON hamlet parish Northill partly in parish Sandy Beds pop 238
BEESTON township parish Bunbury Ches pop 433
BEESTON parish 1538 Norfolk 4-1/2 miles ne Norwich pop 49 archd
and dioc Norwich
BEESTON parish 1558 Norfolk 4-1/4 miles ne Coltishall pop 52
archd and dioc Norwich
BEESTON parish 1538 Norfolk 7 miles ne Swaffham pop 702 archd
and dioc Norwich
BEESTON parish 1558 Notts 3-3/4 miles sw Nottingham pop 2,530
archd Nottingham dioc York
BEESTON chapelry 1720 parish St Peter, Leeds, W R York comp
townships Beeston Shaw, Cottingley Hall, New Hall, Parkside,
Royds and Snickells pop 2,128 archd and dioc York Wesl Meth
BEESTON REGIS parish 1743 Norfolk 3 miles nw Cromer pop 246

archd Norfolk dioc Norwich

BEETHAM parish 1608 Westm 3 miles nw Burton in Kendal comp chapelry Witherslack, townships Beetham, Farleton Haverbrack, Methop with Ulpha pop 2,639 archd Richmond dioc Chester

BEETLEY parish 1539 Norfolk 3-3/4 miles nw East Dereham pop 381 archd and dioc Norwich

BEGBROOKE parish 1664 co Oxford 2-3/4 miles se Woodstock pop 102 archd and dioc Oxford

BEIGHTON parish 1653 Derbys 7-1/4 miles se Sheffield pop 980 archd Derby dioc Lichfield

BEIGHTON parish 1589 Norfolk 2 miles sw Acle pop 262 archd and dioc Norwich

BEIGHTON Suffolk See BEYTON

BEILBY chapelry parish Haton E R York pop 248

BEKESBORNE see BEAKSBOURNE

BELAUGH parish 1539 Norfolk 1-3/4 miles se Coltishall pop 151 archd and dioc Norwich

BELBANK township parish Bewcastle Cumberland pop 485

BELBANK township parish Stapleton Cumberland pop 127

BELBROUGHTON parish 1539 Worcs 5 miles nw Bromsgrove pop 1,489 archd and dioc Worcester

BELBY township parish Howden E R York pop 44

BELCHAMP, ST PAUL'S parish 1538 Essex 2 miles se Clare pop 808 pec Dean and Chapter of St Paul's London

BELCHAMP, OTTEN parish 1578 Essex 5-1/4 miles ne Castle Hedingham pop 397 archd Middlesex dioc London

BELCHAMP, WALTER parish 1559 Essex 3 miles w Sudbury pop 670 archd Middlesex dioc London

BELFORD parish 1661 partly co Durham chiefly Northumberland 49 miles nw Newcastle upon Tyne comp market town Belford, townships Detchant, Easington, Easington Grange, Elwick, Middleton and Ross pop 2,030 archd Northumberland dioc Durham Wesl Meth, Presb

BELGRAVE parish 1653 Leics 1-3/4 miles ne Leicester chapelry South Thurmaston and Birstall pop 2,329 archd Leicester dioc Lincoln

BELLASIS township parish Stannington Northumberland

BELLASIZE township parish Eastrington E R York pop 189

BELLCHALWELL parish 1660 Dorset 6 miles nw Blandford Forum pop 205 archd Dorset dioc Bristol

BELLEAU parish 1650 Lincs 5 miles nw Alford pop 107 archd and dioc Lincoln

BELLERBY chapelry parish Spenninthorn N R York pop 417

BELLESTER township parish Northumberland pop 120

BELLINGHAM parish 1684 Northumberland 30 miles nw Newcastle upon Tyne comp townships East Charlton, West Charlton, Leemailing, the Nook and Tarretburn pop 1,460 archd Northumberland dioc Durham Seceders from Scottish church, Roman Cath

BELMISTHORPE or BELMSTHORP hamlet parish Ryall co Rutland
BELPER chapelry 1783 parish Duffield Derbys pop 7,890 Bapt, Indep,
   Wesl Meth, Unit
BELSAY township parish Bolam Northumberland pop 334
BELSHFORD parish 1698 Lincs 4-1/2 miles ne Horncastle pop 517
   archd and dioc Lincoln
BELSTEAD parish 1539 Suffolk 3-3/4 miles sw Ipswich pop 248
   archd Suffolk dioc Norwich
BELSTONE parish 1552 Devon 3 miles se Oakhampton pop 206 archd
   Totnes dioc Exeter
BELTON parish 1538 Leics 5 miles sw Kegworth pop 735 archd Lei-
   cester dioc Lincoln Wesl Meth
BELTON parish 1538 Lincs 2-1/4 miles ne Grantham pop 160 archd
   and dioc Lincoln
BELTON parish 1568 Lincs 1-3/4 miles n Epworth pop 1,597 archd
   Stow dioc Lincoln Wesl Meth
BELTON parish 1577 co Rutland 4 miles nw Uppingham pop 404
   archd Northampton dioc Peterborough
BELTON parish 1560 Suffolk 4-1/2 miles sw Great Yarmouth pop 425
   archd Suffolk dioc Norwich
BELVOIR extra parochial liberty partly in Lincs chiefly in Leics 7
   miles sw Grantham pop 105
BEMERTON parish Wilts 2 miles nw Salisbury incl regs Fugglestone
   archd and dioc Salisbury
BEMPTON parish 1597 E R York 3-1/4 miles ne Bridlington pop 287
   archd East Riding dioc York Wesl Meth
BENACRE Suffolk See BINACRE
BENAGER Somerset See BINEGAR
BENEFIELD parish 1570 Northampton 3-1/2 miles w Oundle pop 519
   archd Northampton dioc Peterborough
BENENDEN parish 1653 Kent 3-1/4 miles se Cranbrooke pop 1,663
   archd and dioc Canterbury
BENFIELD SIDE township parish Lanchester co Durham pop 534
BENFLEET, NORTH parish 1647 Essex 3-3/4 miles w Rayleigh pop
   303 archd Essex dioc London
BENFLEET, SOUTH parish 1582 Essex 4 miles sw Rayleigh pop 533
   archd Essex dioc London
BENGEO parish 1539 Herts 1 mile ne Hertford pop 855 archd Hunt-
   ingdon dioc Lincoln
BENGWORTH parish 1538 Worcs 1/2 mile se Evesham pop 965 pec
   of Bishop of Worcester
BENHALL parish 1562 Suffolk 2 miles sw Saxmundham pop 668 archd
   Suffolk dioc Norwich
BENHAM tything parish Speen Berks
BENNINGBROUGH township parish Newton upon Ouze N R York pop
   93
BENNINGHOLME joint township with Grange parish Swine E R York
   pop 105

BENNINGTON parish 1538 Herts 5-1/2 miles se Stevenage pop 631
    archd Huntingdon dioc Lincoln Wesl Meth
BENNINGTON parish 1560 Lincs 5 miles ne Boston pop 500 archd
    and dioc Lincoln
BENNINGTON, LONG parish 1560 Lincs 7 miles nw Grantham pop
    982 archd and dioc Lincoln Wesl Meth
BENNIWORTH parish 1691 Lincs 6-1/2 miles ne Wragby pop 373
    archd and dioc Lincoln
BENRIDGE joint township with Kirkby and Cartermoor parish Ponte-
    land Northumberland
BENRIDGE township parish Mitford Northumberland pop 53
BENSINGTON or BENSON parish 1566 co Oxford 11 miles nw Henley
    upon Thames pop 1,266 pec court of Dorchester
BENTFIELD hamlet parish Stansted Mountfitchet Essex pop 505
BENTHAL township parish Aberbury Shrops
BENTHALL parish 1558 Shrops 2-1/2 miles ne Much Wenlock pop
    525 archd Salop dioc Hereford
BENTHAM parish 1662 W R York 12 miles nw Settle pop 3,957 archd
    Richmond dioc Chester
BENTLEY parish 1539 Hamps 4 miles sw Farnham pop 728 archd
    and dioc Winchester
BENTLEY liberty parish Aldridge Staffs pop 104
BENTLEY parish 1539 Suffolk 6-1/2 miles sw Ipswich pop 363 archd
    Suffolk dioc Norwich
BENTLEY chapelry parish Shustock Warws pop 270
BENTLEY township parish Arksey W R York Wesl Meth
BENTLEY, FENNY parish 1604 Derbys 2-1/2 miles nw Ashbourn
    pop 308 archd Derby dioc Lincoln
BENTLEY, GREAT parish 1558 Essex 8 miles se Colchester pop
    978 archd Colchester dioc London Wesl Meth
BENTLEY, HUNGRY liberty parish Longford Derbys pop 92
BENTLEY, LITTLE parish 1558 Essex 5-1/2 miles se Manningtree
    pop 438 archd Colchester dioc London Wesl Meth
BENTON, LONG parish 1669 Northumberland 3-3/4 miles ne New-
    castle upon Tyne comp townships Long Benton, Killingworth,
    Walker and Weetsted pop 6,612 archd Northumberland dioc
    Durham
BENTWORTH parish 1604 Hamps 3-3/4 miles w Alton pop 592 archd
    and dioc Winchester
BENWELL township parish St John Northumberland pop 1,278
BENWICK chapelry parish Doddington Cambs pop 526
BEOLEY parish 1558 Worcs 7-1/2 miles se Bromsgrove pop 673
    archd and dioc Worcester
BEPTON parish 1723 Sussex 2-3/4 miles sw Midhurst pop 166 archd
    and dioc Chichester
BERDON parish 1715 Essex 5-1/2 miles nw Stansted Mountfitchet
    pop 342 archd Colchester dioc London
BERE CHURCH parish 1664 Essex 2-1/4 miles sw Colchester pop

142 archd Colchester dioc London

BERE REGIS See BEER REGIS

BERGHOLT, EAST parish 1653 Suffolk 3-1/2 miles nw Manningtree pop 1,360 archd Suffolk dioc Norwich Indep

BERGHOLT, WEST parish 1598 Essex 3-1/2 miles nw Colchester pop 786 archd Colchester dioc London Wesl Meth

BERKELEY parish 1653 borough Gloucs 17 miles sw Gloucester comp chapelry of Stone, tythings Alkington Hinton and Ham, hamlets Bradstone pop 3,899 archd and dioc Gloucester Wesl Meth

BERKELEY parish 1546 Somerset 2-3/4 miles ne Frome pop 531 archd Wells dioc Bath and Wells

BERKESWELL parish 1653 Warws 6-1/4 miles nw Coventry pop 1,450 archd Coventry dioc Lichfield

BERKHAMSTEAD or NORTH CHURCH parish 1655 Herts 1-1/4 miles nw Great Berkhamstead pop 1,156 archd Huntingdon dioc Lincoln

BERKHAMSTEAD, GREAT parish 1538 Herts 25-1/2 miles sw Hertford pop 2,369 archd Huntingdon dioc Lincoln Bapt, Soc of Friends, Indep

BERKHAMSTEAD, LITTLE parish 1646 Herts 4-3/4 miles sw Hertford pop 450 archd Huntingdon dioc Lincoln Wesl Meth

BERMERSLEY township parish Norton on the Moors Staffs pop 244

BERMONDSEY parish 1548 Surrey 1-1/2 miles se London pop 29,741 archd Surrey dioc Winchester

BERNERS ROOTHING or RODING Essex See ROOTHING, BERNERS

BERRICK PRIOR liberty parish Newington co Oxford

BERRICK SALOME chapelry 1609 parish Chalgrove co Oxford pop 134

BERRIER township parish Greystock Cumberland pop 113

BERRINGTON hamlet parish Chipping Campden Gloucs pop 129

BERRINGTON township parish Eye Herefs

BERRINGTON parish 1559 Shrops 5-1/2 miles se Shrewsbury pop 684 archd Salop dioc Lichfield

BERRINGTON hamlet parish Tenbury Worcs pop 165

BERROW parish 1699 Somerset 9-1/2 miles sw Axbridge pop 496 archd Wells dioc Bath and Wells Wesl Meth

BERROW parish 1698 Worcs 6 miles sw Upton upon Severn pop 507 pec of Dean and Chapter of Worcester

BERRY POMEROY parish 1662 Devon 1-3/4 miles ne Totnes pop 1,186 archd Totnes dioc Exeter

BERRYN ARBOR parish 1540 Devon 2-3/4 miles se Ilfracombe pop 794 archd Barnstaple dioc Exeter

BERSTED, SOUTH parish 1564 Sussex 6 miles se Chichester pop 2,190 pec of Archbishop of Canterbury

BERWICK parish 1609 Sussex 4-3/4 miles ne Seaford pop 203 archd Lewes dioc Chichester

BERWICK parish 1731 Wilts 5-3/4 miles sw Amesbury pop 232 pec of Bishop of Salisbury

BERWICK parish 1556 Wilts 5-1/4 miles se Shaftesbury pop 425 archd and dioc Salisbury

BERWICK parish 1759 Wilts 1 mile e Hindon pop 51 archd and dioc Salisbury

BERWICK BASSET parish 1674 Wilts

BERWICK HILL township parish Ponteland Northumberland pop 105

BERWICK SALOME co Oxford See BERRICK SALOME

BERWICK UPON TWEED parish 1572 borough co Durham 64 miles nw Newcastle upon Tyne pop 8,920 Consistorial Court of Durham Scottish Kirk, Bapt, Burghers, Anti-Burghers, Scottish relief, Wesl Meth

BESFORD township parish Shawbury Shrops pop 158

BESFORD parish 1539 Worcs 3 miles sw Pershore pop 146 archd and dioc Worcester

BESKABY hamlet parish Croxton Kerrial Liecs pop 9

BESSELSLEIGH parish 1689 Berks 5 miles nw Abingdon pop 124 archd Berks dioc Salisbury

BESSINGBY parish 1690 E R York 2-1/4 miles sw Bridlington pop 83 archd and dioc York

BESSINGHAM parish 1538 Norfolk 5-1/4 miles sw Cromer pop 137 archd Norfolk dioc Norwich

BESTHORPE parish 1558 Norfolk 1-1/4 miles se Attleburgh pop 542 archd Norfolk dioc Norwich

BESTHORPE chapelry parish South Scarle Notts pop 322 Wesl Meth

BESWICK extra parochial district near Manchester pop 248 Lancs

BESWICK chapelry 1657 parish Kilnwick E R York pop 205

BETCHWORTH parish 1558 Surrey 3-1/4 miles sw Reigate pop 1,100 archd Surrey dioc Winchester

BETHERSDEN parish 1556 Kent 6 miles sw Ashford pop 973 archd and dioc Canterbury

BETHNAL GREEN parish 1746 Middlesex 2-1/2 miles ne St Paul's pop 62,018 pec of the Commissary of London concurrently with the Consistorial Court of the Bishop Bapt, Indep, Meth, Episcopal Chapel

BETLEY parish 1538 Staffs 7-1/2 miles nw Newcastle under Line pop 870 archd Stafford dioc Lichfield Wesl Meth

BETTERTON tything parish Lockinge Berks

BETTESHANGER parish 1562 Kent 4 miles sw Sandwich pop 20 archd and dioc Canterbury

BETTISCOMBE parish 1746 Dorset 6 miles sw Beaminster pop 65 archd Dorset dioc Bristol

BETTUS parish 1624 Shrops 6 miles nw Knighton pop 389 archd Salop dioc Hereford

BETTWS parish 1696 co Monmouth 2-3/4 miles nw Newport pop 95 archd and dioc Llandaff

BETTWS NEWYDD parish 1734 co Monmouth 4 miles ne Usk pop 108 archd and dioc Llandaff

BETTWS Y CRUEN Shrops See BETTUS

BEVERCOATES parish Notts 2-1/2 miles nw Tuxford pop 51 archd

Nottingham dioc York

BEVERIDGE Dorset See BOVERIDGE

BEVERLEY Market town, Borough 1561 E R York 9 miles ne Kingston upon Hull pop 8,032 comp St John or Beverley Minster with St Martin 1558, St Mary with St Nicholas 1561 sep juris archd and dioc York Pec and exempt jurisdiction under Provost of the collegiate church Bapt, Soc of Friends, Prim, Wesl Meth

BEVERSTONE parish 1563 Gloucs 2 miles nw Tetbury pop 174 archd and dioc Gloucester

BEWALDETH joint township with Snittlegarth parish Torpenhow Cumberland pop 72

BEWCASTLE parish 1737 Cumberland 19 miles ne Carlisle comp townships Bailie, Belbank, Bewcastle and Nixons pop 1,335 archd and dioc Carlisle Presb

BEWDLEY chapelry parish Ribbesford incl in regs of Ribbesford borough Worcs 14 miles nw Worcester pop 3,908 sep juris archd Salop dioc Hereford Bapt, Soc of Friends, Wesl Meth, Unit

BEWERLEY township parish Ripon W R York pop 1,310

BEWHOLME township parish Nunkeeling E R York

BEWICK, NEW township parish Eglingham Northumberland pop 106

BEWICK, OLD township parish Eglingham Northumberland pop 227

BEXHILL parish 1558 Sussex 5-1/4 miles sw Hastings pop 1,931 archd Lewes dioc Chichester

BEXINGTON hamlet parish Abbotsbury Dorset

BEXLEY parish 1565 Kent 3 miles w Dartford pop 3,206 pec of Archbishop of Canterbury

BEXTON township parish Knutsford Ches pop 76

BEXWELL parish 1558 Norfolk 1 mile e Downham Market pop 53 archd Norfolk dioc Norwich

BEYTON otherwise BEIGHTON parish 1539 Suffolk 5-1/2 miles se Bury St Edmunds pop 330 archd Sudbury dioc Norwich

BIBURY parish 1551 Gloucs 3-3/4 miles sw Fairford comp chapelry Winson, tythings Ablington and Arlington pop 950 pec of Bibury

BICESTER parish 1558 co Oxford 12-1/2 miles ne Oxford pop 2,868 archd and dioc Oxford Wesl Meth

BICKENHALL parish 1682 Somerset 5-1/2 miles se Taunton pop 270 archd Taunton dioc Bath and Wells

BICKENHILL, CHURCH parish 1558 Warws 4 miles ne Solihill pop 725 archd Coventry dioc Lichfield

BICKER parish 1561 Lincs 1-3/4 miles ne Donington pop 627 archd and dioc Lincoln Wesl Meth

BICKERING hamlet parish Holton Lincs

BICKERSTAFFE township parish Ormskirk Lancs pop 1,309

BICKERSTON Norfolk See BIXTON

BICKERTON township parish Malpas Ches pop 373

BICKERTON township parish Rothbury Northumberland pop 26

BICKERTON township parish Bilton E R York pop 150

BICKINGTON parish 1603 Devon 3-1/4 miles ne Ashburton pop 351 pec of Dean and Chapter of Exeter Wesl Meth

BICKINGTON, ABBOT'S parish 1717 Devon 9 miles sw Great Torrington pop 77 archd Totnes dioc Exeter

BICKINGTON, HIGH parish 1707 Devon 7-1/4 miles ne Great Torrington pop 853 archd Barnstaple dioc Exeter

BICKLEIGH parish 1538 Devon 4-1/4 miles sw Tiverton pop 323 archd and dioc Exeter

BICKLEIGH parish 1694 Devon 7 miles ne Plymouth pop 466 archd Totnes dioc Exeter

BICKLEY township parish Malpas Ches pop 451 Wesl Meth

BICKMERSH hamlet parish Welford Warws pop 65

BICKNELL Somerset See BICKENHALL

BICKNOLLER parish 1558 Somerset 13-1/2 miles nw Bridgewater pop 285 archd Taunton dioc Bath and Wells

BICKNOR parish 1571 Kent 4-1/2 miles sw Milton pop 44 archd and dioc Canterbury

BICKNOR, ENGLISH parish 1561 Gloucs 3-3/4 miles n Coleford pop 598 archd and dioc Gloucester

BICKNOR, WELSH parish 1699 Herefs 7 miles sw Ross pop 91 archd and dioc Hereford Roman Cath

BICKTON chapelry parish St Chad Shrops

BICTON parish 1557 Devon 3-3/4 miles sw Sidmouth pop 213 archd and dioc Exeter

BIDBOROUGH parish 1632 Kent 3 miles sw Tonbridge pop 237 archd and dioc Rochester

BIDDENDEN parish 1538 Kent 5 miles ne Cranbrooke pop 1,658 archd and dioc Canterbury

BIDDENHAM parish 1663 Beds 2-3/4 miles nw Bedford pop 369 archd Bedford dioc Lincoln

BIDDESCOTE township parish Tamworth Staffs pop 11

BIDDESHAM parish 1621 Somerset 3 miles sw Axbridge pop 158 pec of Dean of Wells

BIDDESTONE parish 1688 Wilts 4-1/4 miles w Chippenham pop 45 archd Wilts dioc Salisbury

BIDDLESDON parish 1686 Bucks 3-1/2 miles ne Brackley pop 184 archd Buckingham dioc Lincoln

BIDDLESTON township parish Allenton Northumberland pop 156

BIDDULPH parish 1558 Staffs 3-1/4 miles se Congleton pop 1,987 archd Stafford dioc Lichfield Wesl Meth

BIDEFORD parish 1561 Devon 39 miles nw Exeter pop 4,846 sep juris archd Barnstaple dioc Exeter Bapt, Indep, Wesl Meth

BIDFORD parish 1664 Warws 4 miles se Alcester comp hamlets Barton, Broom, Marlclift pop 1,268 archd and dioc Worcester

BIDICK, SOUTH township parish Houghton le Spring co Durham pop 199

BIDSTONE parish 1581 Ches 9-1/2 miles n Great Neston comp chapelry Birkenhead, townships Bidstone with Ford, Claughton with Grange, Moreton and Saughall Massey pop 3,434 archd and dioc

Chester

BIERLEY, NORTH chapelry parish Bradford incl in regs of Hayton
pop 7,254 W R York

BIERTON parish 1560 Bucks 1-1/2 miles ne Aylesbury pop 605 pec
of Dean and Chapter of Lincoln

BIGBURY parish 1678 Devon 3-1/2 miles s Modbury pop 578 archd
Totnes dioc Exeter

BIGBY parish 1696 Lincs 4-1/2 miles e Glandford Bridge pop 190
archd and dioc Lincoln

BIGGE'S or CARLISLE'S QUARTER township parish Long Horsley
Northumberland pop 238

BIGGIN township parish Wirksworth Derbys pop 161

BIGGIN joint hamlet with Newton parish Clifton upon Dunsmoor Warws

BIGGIN township parish Kirk Fenton W R York pop 141

BIGGLESWADE parish 1697 Beds 10-1/2 miles se Bedford pop 3,226
pec of Prebendary of Biggleswade Cathedral church of Lincoln
Bapt, Wesl Meth

BIGHTON parish 1573 Hamps 1-3/4 miles ne New Alresford pop 290
archd and dioc Winchester

BIGLANDS joint township with Gamelsby parish Aikton Cumberland
pop 192

BIGNALL END township parish Audley Staffs pop 432

BIGNOR parish 1556 Sussex 5-1/2 miles se Petworth pop 130 archd
and dioc Chichester

BILBOROUGH parish 1569 Notts 4 miles nw Nottingham pop 330
archd Nottingham dioc York

BILBROUGH parish 1695 E R York 4-1/4 miles ne Tadcaster pop
238 archd and dioc York

BILBY joint township with Barnby Moor parish Blyth Notts

BILDESTON or BILSON parish 1558 Suffolk 14-1/2 miles nw Ipswich
pop 836 archd Sudbury dioc Norwich Bapt

BILHAM township parish Hooton Pagnell W R York pop 76

BILLERICAY chapelry parish Great Burstead Essex Bapt, Soc of
Friends, Indep

BILLESDON parish 1599 Leics 8-1/2 miles se Leicester pop 908
archd Leicester dioc Lincoln

BILLESLEY parish 1717 Warws 3-3/4 miles nw Stratford upon Avon
pop 24 archd and dioc Worcester

BILLING, GREAT parish 1662 co Northampton 4 miles se Northampton pop 372 archd Northampton dioc Peterborough

BILLING, LITTLE parish 1635 Northampton 3-1/4 miles ne Northampton pop 86 archd Northampton dioc Peterborough

BILLINGBOROUGH parish 1561 Lincs 3 miles e Folkingham pop 831
archd and dioc Lincoln

BILLINGE chapelry 1696 parish Wigan Lancs pop 1,279

BILLINGE, HIGHER END township parish Wigan Lancs pop 676

BILLINGFORD parish 1640 Norfolk 1-1/2 miles e Scole pop 313
archd Norfolk dioc Norwich

BILLINGFORD parish 1744 Norfolk 3-1/2 miles sw Foulsham pop 205 archd Norfolk dioc Norwich

BILLINGHAM parish 1570 co Durham 2-1/2 miles ne Stockton upon Tees comp chapelry Wolviston, townships Billingham, Cowpen Bewlay, Newton Bewlay pop 1,212 archd and dioc Durham

BILLINGHAY parish 1627 Lincs 9-1/2 miles ne Sleaford pop 1,787 archd and dioc Lincoln

BILLINGLEY township parish Darfield W R York pop 217

BILLINGSHURST parish 1630 Sussex 6-3/4 miles sw Horsham pop 1,540 archd and dioc Chichester Unit

BILLINGSIDE township parish Lanchester co Durham pop 18

BILLINGSLEY parish 1625 Shrops 5-1/2 miles sw Bridgenorth pop 161 archd Salop dioc Hereford

BILLINGTON chapelry 1651 parish Leighton Buzzard Beds pop 271 pec of Prebendary of Leighton Buzzard in Cathedral Church of Lincoln

BILLINGTON chapelry parish Blackburn Lancs pop 1,089

BILLISBORROW township parish Garstang Lancs pop 199 Wesl Meth

BILLOCKBY parish 1560 Norfolk 2-1/2 miles ne Acle pop 67 archd and dioc Norwich

BILL QUAY village chapelry Nether Heworth parish Jarrow co Durham

BILLY ROW joint township with Crook parish Brancepeth co Durham

BILNEY, EAST parish 1713 Norfolk 5 miles nw East Dereham pop 166 archd and dioc Norwich

BILNEY, WEST parish 1562 Norfolk 7 miles se Lynn Regis pop 236 archd and dioc Norwich

BILSBY parish 1679 Lincs 3/4 mile ne Alford pop 453 archd and dioc Lincoln

BILSDALE, WEST SIDE township parish Hawnby N R York pop 149

BILSDALE MIDCABLE chapelry 1588 parish Helmsley N R York pop 759 Soc of Friends

BILSINGTON parish 1562 Kent 6-1/2 miles se Ashford pop 332 archd and dioc Canterbury

BILSON Suffolk See BILDESTON

BILSTHORPE parish 1654 Notts 5 miles s Ollerton pop 217 archd Nottingham dioc York

BILSTON chapelry 1684 parish Wolverhampton Staffs pop 14,492 Bapt, Indep, Prim, Wesl Meth

BILSTONE chapelry parish Norton Juxta Twycross Leics pop 136

BILTON parish 1650 Warws 1-1/2 miles sw Rugby pop 463 archd Coventry dioc Lichfield

BILTON chapelry parish Swine E R York pop 91

BILTON parish 1571 E R York 5 miles ne Wetherby comp townships Bickerton, Bilton and Tockwith pop 894 pec of Prebendary of Bilton Cathedral Church of York

BILTON joint township with Harrogate parish Knaresborough W R York

BINACRE or BENACRE parish 1727 Suffolk 6 miles ne Southwold
   pop 208 archd Suffolk dioc Norwich
BINBROOKE village comp parishes St Gabriel 1688, St Mary 1694,
   Lincs pec of Dean and Chapter of Lincoln pop 1,030 archd and
   dioc Lincoln Wesl Meth
BINCHESTER township parish St Andrew Auckland co Durham pop 37
BINCOMBE parish 1657 Dorset 5 miles sw Dorchester pop 177 archd
   Dorset dioc Bristol
BINDERTON chapelry parish West Dean Sussex pop 89
BINEGAR parish 1717 Somerset 4 miles n Shepton Mallet pop 376
   pec of Dean of Wells
BINFIELD parish 1538 Berks 3-1/2 miles ne Wokingham pop 1,045
   archd Berks dioc Salisbury
BINFIELD chapelry parish St John Lee Northumberland pop 98
BINGHAM parish 1598 Notts 10 miles e Nottingham pop 1,738 archd
   Nottingham dioc York Prim, Wesl Meth
BINGLEY parish 1597 W R York 37 miles sw York comp market town
   Bingley, township East and West Moreton pop 9,256 pec of Court
   of the manors of Crossley, Bingley and Pudsey Bapt, Indep, Meth
BING WESTON quarter parish Worthen Shrops
BINHAM parish 1702 Norfolk 4 miles ne Little Walsingham pop 493
   archd and dioc Norwich
BINLEY parish 1660 Warws 2-1/4 miles se Coventry pop 212 archd
   Coventry dioc Lichfield
BINNINGTON township parish Willerby E R York pop 58
BINSEY parish 1591 co Oxford 2 miles nw Oxford pop 74 archd and
   dioc Oxford
BINSTEAD parish 1710 Hamps 5-1/2 miles ne Newport pop 258
   archd and dioc Winchester
BINSTEAD parish 1590 Hamps 3-3/4 miles ne Alton pop 960 archd
   and dioc Winchester
BINSTEAD parish 1638 Sussex 3-1/2 miles sw Arundel pop 114 archd
   and dioc Chichester
BINTON parish 1539 Warws 3-3/4 miles sw Stratford upon Avon pop
   227 archd and dioc Worcester
BINTREE parish 1686 Norfolk 1-1/4 miles sw Foulsham pop 412
   archd Norfolk dioc Norwich
BIRBECK FELLS hamlet parish Orton Westm
BIRCH chapelry 1752 parish Middleton Lancs
BIRCH chapelry Parish Warrington Lancs
BIRCH, GREAT parish 1560 Essex 5 miles sw Colchester pop 764
   archd Colchester dioc London
BIRCH, LITTLE parish Essex 4-1/4 miles sw Colchester pop and
   regs with Great Birch archd Colchester dioc London
BIRCH, LITTLE parish 1560 Herefs 6-3/4 miles s Hereford pop 351
   archd and dioc Hereford
BIRCH, MUCH parish 1599 Herefs 4-1/4 miles sw Hereford pop 489
   archd and dioc Hereford

BIRCHAM, GREAT parish 1668 Norfolk 7-1/2 miles sw Burnham Westgate pop 451 archd Norfolk dioc Norwich
BIRCHAM NEWTON parish 1562 Norfolk 7-1/4 miles sw Burnham Westgate pop 95 archd Norfolk dioc Norwich
BIRCHAM TOFTS parish 1715 Norfolk 7-1/4 miles sw Burnham Westgate pop 130 archd Norfolk dioc Norwich
BIRCHANGER parish 1689 Essex 1-3/4 miles sw Stansted Mountfitchet pop 360 archd Colchester dioc London
BIRCHER township parish Yarpole Herefs
BIRCHES township parish Great Budworth Ches pop 9
BIRCHINGTON parish 1539 Kent 3-1/2 miles sw Margate pop 843 pec of Archbishop of Canterbury
BIRCHOLT parish Kent 4 miles se Ashford pop 45 archd and dioc Canterbury
BIRCHOVER chapelry parish Youlgrave Derbys pop 101
BIRDALL joint township with Raisthorpe parish Warram Percy E R York
BIRDBROOK parish 1633 Essex 7 miles nw Castle Hedingham pop 515 archd Middlesex dioc London
BIRDFORTH chapelry 1616 parish Coxwold N R York pop 35
BIRDHAM parish 1538 Sussex 4 miles sw Chichester pop 486 archd and dioc Chichester
BIRDINBURY parish 1559 Warws 4-3/4 miles ne Southam pop 212 archd Coventry dioc Lichfield
BIRDSALL parish 1593 E R York 6 miles se New Malton pop 244 archd East Riding dioc York
BIRKBY township parish Cross Cannonby, Allerdale Cumberland pop 110
BIRKBY township parish Muncaster Allerdale Cumberland
BIRKBY parish 1721 N R York 6 miles nw North Allerton comp chapelry Hutton Bonville, townships Birkby and Little Smeaton pop 275 pec of Allerton and Allertonshire
BIRKDALE township parish Ormskirk Lancs pop 518
BIRKENHEAD chapelry 1719 Ches pop 2,569 archd and dioc Chester
BIRKENSHAW hamlet parish Birstall W R York
BIRKER joint township with Austhwaite parish Millom, Allerdale Cumberland pop 102
BIRKIN parish 1684 W R York 3-1/2 miles ne Ferrybridge comp chapelry Chapel Haddlesey, townships Birkin West Haddlesey, Courtney Hurst, Temple Hurst pop 873 archd and dioc York
BIRKSCEUGH Cumberland See BRISCO
BIRLEY parish 1754 Herefs 4 miles ne Weobley pop 147 archd and dioc Hereford
BIRLING parish 1558 Kent 6-3/4 miles nw Maidstone pop 502 archd and dioc Rochester
BIRLING township parish Warkworth Northumberland pop 85
BIRLINGHAM parish 1566 Worcs 3 miles sw Pershore pop 360 archd and dioc Worcester

BIRMINGHAM town borough Warws 18 miles nw Coventry pop 142,251 comp parishes St Philip 1715, St Martin 1754, St Mary 1774, St Paul 1779 and after 1812, St George, St Thomas, Christ Church, St Bartholomew, St Peter, St James archd Coventry dioc Lichfield Bapt, Soc of Friends, Indep, Prim and Wesl Meth, Swedenborgians, Unit, Scotch Church, Roman Cath, Jewish Synagogue

BIRSTALL chapelry 1574 parish Belgrave Leics

BIRSTALL parish 1558 W R York 7-1/2 miles sw Leeds comp chapelries Clackheaton, Drighlington, Heckmondwike, Liversedge and Tong, townships Great and Little Comersall, Hunsworth and Wike pop 24,103 archd East Riding dioc York Wesl Meth

BIRSTWICH township parish Hamsthwaite W R York pop 747

BIRTHORPE chapelry parish Semperingham Lincs pop 54

BIRTLE joint township with Bamford parish Middleton Lancs pop 1,650

BIRTLES township parish Prestbury Ches pop 54

BIRTLEY township parish Chester le Street co Durham pop 1,520

BIRTLEY chapelry 1728 Northumberland pop 447 archd Northumberland dioc Durham

BIRTS MORTON parish 1539 Worcs 5-1/4 miles nw Upton upon Severn pop 311 archd and dioc Worcester

BISBROOKE parish 1665 co Rutland 1-3/4 miles e Uppingham pop 177 archd Northampton dioc Peterborough

BISCATHORPE parish 1700 Lincs 8 miles ne Wragby pop 45 archd and dioc Lincoln

BISCOTT hamlet parish Luton Beds

BISHAM parish 1560 Berks 4-1/2 miles nw Maidenhead pop 771 archd Berks dioc Salisbury

BISHAMPTON parish 1599 Worcs 5-1/2 miles ne Pershore pop 393 archd and dioc Worcester

BISHOP AUCKLAND co Durham See AUCKLAND, BISHOP

BISHOP'S BOURNE parish 1558 Kent 4 miles se Canterbury archd and dioc Canterbury

BISHOP BURTON See BURTON, BISHOP

BISHOPS CANNINGS See CANNINGS, BISHOP

BISHOPS CASTLE parish 1559 Shrops 19 miles nw Ludlow pop 2,007 sep juris archd Salop dioc Hereford

BISHOPS CAUNDLE Dorset See CAUNDLE BISHOP

BISHOP CROPWELL Notts See CROPWELL BISHOP

BISHOP MIDDLEHAM See MIDDLEHAM, BISHOPS

BISHOP NORTON Lincs See NORTON BISHOP

BISHOP'S CLEEVE See CLEEVE, BISHOPS

BISHOP'S DALE township parish Aysgarth N R York pop 108

BISHOP'S FEE Liberty parish St. Margaret Leics

BISHOP'S FONTHILL Wilts See FONTHILL, BISHOPS

BISHOP'S FROME Herefs See FROME, BISHOPS

BISHOP'S HULL See HULL, BISHOPS

BISHOP'S ITCHINGTON Warws See ITCHINGTON, BISHOPS

BISHOP'S LAVINGTON Wilts See LAVINGTON
BISHOP'S LYDEARD Somerset See LYDEARD
BISHOP'S NYMPTON Devon See NYMPTON, BISHOPS
BISHOP'S SIDE, HIGH and LOW township parish Ripon W R York
    pop 1,843
BISHOP'S STOKE Hamps See STOKE, BISHOPS
BISHOP'S STORTFORD Herefs See STORTFORD BISHOPS
BISHOP'S SUTTON Hamps See SUTTON, BISHOPS
BISHOP'S TACHBROOK parish Warws See TACKBROOK, BISHOPS
BISHOP'S TAWTON Devon See TAWTON, BISHOPS
BISHOP'S TEIGNTON Devon See TEIGNTON BISHOPS
BISHOP'S WEARMOUTH Durham See WEARMOUTH, BISHOP
BISHOP'S WICKHAM Essex See WICKHAM BISHOPS
BISHOP WILTON Yorks See WILTON, BISHOP
BISHOPSTON chapelry 1590 parish Old Stratford Warws
BISHOPTON parish 1636 Wilts 3-1/2 miles sw Wilton pop 663 archd
    and dioc Salisbury
BISHOPSTONE parish 1573 Wilts 5-3/4 miles e Swindon pop 688 pec
    juris of Prebendary of Bishopston in Cathedral of Salisbury
BISHOPSTONE parish 1727 Herefs 7 miles nw Hereford pop 278
    archd and dioc Hereford
BISHOPSTONE parish 1561 Sussex 1-3/4 miles nw Seaford pop 293
    archd Lewes dioc Chichester
BISHOPSTROW parish 1686 Wilts 1-1/2 miles se Warminster pop
    278 archd and dioc Salisbury
BISHOP'S WOOD township parish Brewood Staffs
BISHOP THORPE parish 1692 E R York 3-1/2 miles sw York pop 445
    originally called St Andrew's Thorpe archd and dioc York
BISHOPTON parish 1649 co Durham 6 miles nw Stockton comp town-
    ships Bishopton, East and West Newbiggins, Little Stainton pop
    513 archd and dioc Durham
BISHOPTON township Ripon W R York pop 118
BISHTON parish 4 miles se Caerleon co Monmouth pop 155 archd and
    dioc Llandaff
BISLEY parish 1547 Gloucs 3-1/2 miles ne Stroud pop 5,896 archd
    and dioc Gloucester Wesl Meth
BISLEY parish 1561 Surrey 4 miles se Bagshot pop 270 archd Surrey
    dioc Winchester
BISPHAM parish 1599 Lancs 3 miles nw Poulton comp townships
    Bispham with Norbreck, Layton with Warbrick pop 1,256 archd
    Richmond dioc Chester
BISPHAM chapelry parish Croston Lancs pop 256
BISTERN BARTLEY tything parish Eling 1561 incl regs of Ringswood
    Hamps
BITCHFIELD parish 1674 Lincs 3-1/4 miles nw Corby pop 135 archd
    and dioc Lincoln
BITCHFIELD township parish Stamfordham Northumberland pop 40
BITTADON parish 1712 Devon 6-1/4 miles nw Barnstaple pop 57

archd Barnstaple dioc Exeter

BITTERING, LITTLE parish 1733 Norfolk 5 miles nw East Dereham archd and dioc Norwich

BITTERLEY parish 1658 Shrops 4-1/2 miles ne Ludlow pop 1,194 archd Salop dioc Hereford

BITTERN tything parish South Stoneham Hamps pop 703 Wesl Meth

BITTESBY liberty parish Claybrooke Leics pop 11

BITTESWELL parish 1558 Leics 1 mile nw Lutterworth pop 439 archd Leicester dioc Lincoln

BITTISCOMBE hamlet parish Upton Somerset

BITTON parish 1571 Gloucs 6-1/4 miles se Bristol comp chapelries of Hanham, Oldland, hamlet of Bitton pop 8,703 archd and dioc Gloucester in Prebendary of Bitton in Cathedral Church of Salisbury

BIX BRAND parish 1577 co Oxford 4 miles nw Henley upon Thames pop 409 archd and dioc Oxford

BIX GIBWEN parish regs with Bix Brand co Oxford 2-1/2 miles nw Henley upon Thames archd and dioc Oxford

BIXLEY parish 1561 Norfolk 3 miles se Norwich pop 84 archd Norfolk dioc Norwich

BIXTON or BICKERSTON parish (regs incl with Barnham Broom) Norfolk nw Wymondham archd Norfolk dioc Norwich

BLABY parish 1560 Leics 4-1/2 miles sw Leicester pop 1,840 archd Leicester dioc Lincoln Wesl Meth, Bapt

BLACKAUTON parish 1538 Devon 5 miles nw Dartmouth pop 1,477 archd Totnes dioc Exeter Wesl Meth

BLACKBOROUGH parish 1695 incl with Kentisbury Devon 5 miles ne Cullompton archd and dioc Exeter

BLACKBROOK or BLAKEBROOK hamlet parish Kidderminster Worcs

BLACKBURN parish borough Lancs 31 miles se Lancaster comp Blackburn chapelries of Balderston, Billington, Great Harwood, Over Darwen, Mellor, Salesbury, Samlesbury, Tockholes and Walton le Dale, townships of Clayton le Dale, Cuerdale, Lower Darwen, Dinkley, Eccleshill, Little Harwood, Livesey, Osbaldeston, Pleasington, Ramsgrave, Rishton, Wilpshire and Witton, St Mary 1568, St John 1789 pop 59,791 archd and dioc Chester Bapt, Indep, Soc of Friends, Prim and Wesl Meth, Swedenborgians, Unit, Roman Cath

BLACK BOURTON co Oxford See BOURTON, BLACK

BLACK BURTON York See BURTON BLACK

BLACK CHAPEL chapelry parish Great Waltham Essex

BLACKDEN township parish Sandbach Ches pop 170

BLACKFORD chapelry 1824 parish Wedmore Somerset

BLACKFORD parish 1606 Somerset 4-1/4 miles sw Wincanton pop 192 archd Wells dioc Bath and Wells

BLACKFORDBY chapelry parish Ashby de la Zouch 1746 Leics pop 327 Wesl Meth

BLACKHEATH village parish Greenwich, Lewisham and Lee Kent

BLACKLAND parish 1757 Wilts 1-3/4 miles se Calne pop 65 Prebendary of Calne,Cathedral of Salisbury

BLACKLEY chapelry 1655 parish Manchester Lancs 3-1/2 miles ne Manchester pop 3,020 archd and dioc Chester Wesl Meth, Socinians

BLACKMANSTONE parish no regs Kent 3 miles ne New Romney pop 5 archd and dioc Canterbury

BLACKMORE parish 1602 Essex 3-1/2 miles nw Ingatestone pop 648 archd Essex dioc London

BLACKPOOL chapelry 1821 parish Bispham Lancs pop 800 archd Richmond dioc Chester

BLACKROD chapelry 1607 parish Bolton Lancs pop 2,591 archd and dioc Chester Wesl Meth

BLACKTHORN chapelry parish Ambrosden co Oxford pop 417 chapel in ruins

BLACKTOFT parish 1700 E R York 7-3/4 miles se Howden comp townships Blacktoft and Scalby pop 394 Pec court of Howdenshire

BLACK TORRINGTON Devon 1547 See TORRINGTON, BLACK

BLACKWALL hamlet parish Stepney Middlesex

BLACKWATER village parish Yately Hamps Bapt

BLACKWELL or BLACKHALL, HIGH township parish St Cuthbert Carlisle Cumberland pop 268

BLACKWELL or BLACKHALL, LOW township parish St Cuthbert Carlisle Cumberland pop 150

BLACKWELL chapelry parish Bakewell Derbys pop 69

BLACKWELL parish 1685 Derbs 3-1/4 miles ne Alfreton pop 432 archd Derby dioc Lichfield

BLACKWELL township parish Darlington Co Durham pop 271 Wesl Meth

BLACKWELL hamlet parish Tredington Worcs pop 176

BLACKWOOD joint township with Croborough parish Horton Staffs pop 527

BLACON joint township with Crabhall parish Holy Trinity Ches pop 72

BLADON parish 1545 co Oxford 2 miles s Woodstock pop 585 archd and dioc Oxford

BLAENAVON chapelry 1804 co Monmouth 5 miles sw Abergavenny pop 2,500 archd and dioc Llandaff Bapt

BLAGDON township parish Stannington Northumberland

BLAGDON tything parish Pitminster Somerset Wesl Meth

BLAGDON parish 1555 Somerset 6-1/4 miles ne Axbridge pop 1,109 archd Wells dioc Bath and Wells Meth

BLAGRAVE joint tything with Hadley parish Lambourn Berks pop 414

BLAISDON parish 1635 Gloucs 3-3/4 miles se Mitchel Dean pop 255 archd Hereford dioc Gloucester

BLAKEMERE parish 1662 Herefs 10-1/2 miles nw Hereford pop 190 Vicarage with Preston upon Wye in pec juris Dean of Hereford

BLAKENEY chapelry 1813 parish Awre Gloucs Bapt

BLAKENEY parish 1538 Norfolk 1-1/4 miles nw Clay pop 929 archd
Norfolk dioc Norwich Meth
BLACKENHALL township parish Wybunbury Ches pop 245
BLAKENHAM, GREAT parish 1549 Suffolk 3-1/2 miles se Needham
pop 192 archd Suffolk dioc Norwich
BLAKENHAM, LITTLE parish 1728 Suffolk 5 miles nw Ipswich pop
102 archd Suffolk dioc Norwich
BLAKESLEY parish 1538 co Northampton 4 miles nw Towcester pop
829 archd Northampton dioc Peterborough
BLANCHLAND, HIGH chapelry 1753 parish Shotley Northumberland
pop 454 archd Northumberland dioc Durham
BLANDFORD,ST MARY parish 1581 Dorset 3/4 mile s Blandford For-
um pop 363 archd Dorset dioc Bristol
BLANDFORD FORUM parish 1732 borough, earlier regs destroyed
Dorset 16 miles ne Dorchester pop 3,109 sep juris archd Dorset
dioc Bristol Indep, Wesl Meth
BLANKNEY parish 1558 Lincs 9-1/2 miles n Sleaford pop 543 archd
and dioc Lincoln
BLASTON, St Giles chapelry 1805 parish Medbourne, Leics earlier
records at Medbourne and Hallaton
BLASTON,ST MICHAEL chapelry 1634 parish Hallaton Leics
BLATCHINGTON, EAST parish 1563 Sussex 3 miles ne Brighton pop
170 archd Lewes dioc Chichester
BLATCHINGTON, WEST parish Sussex 2-1/4 miles nw Brighton pop
58 archd Lewes dioc Chichester
BLATCHINGWORTH chapelry parish Rochdale Lancs 3 miles ne Roch-
dale pop 4,221
BLATHERWYCKE parish 1621 co Northampton 8 miles ne Rockingham
pop 227 archd Northampton dioc Peterborough
BLAWITH chapelry 1728 parish Ulverstone Lancs pop 171 archd
Richmond dioc Chester
BLAXHALL parish 1673 Suffolk 3-3/4 miles ne Wickham Market pop
525 archd Suffolk dioc Norwich
BLAXTON township parish Finningley W R York pop 176
BLAZEY,ST parish 1608 Cornwall 4 miles ne St Austell pop 2,155
archd Cornwall dioc Exeter Wesl Meth
BLEADON parish 1713 Somerset 5-3/4 miles nw Axbridge pop 599
archd Wells dioc Bath and Wells
BLEANE Kent, See COSMUS, ST and DAMIAN
BLEASBY parish 1573 Notts 3-3/4 miles se Southwell pop 324 pec
juris of Chapter of Southwell
BLEASDALE chapelry parish Lancaster Lancs pop 236
BLEATARN hamlet parish Warcop Westm
BLECHINGDON parish 1559 co Oxford 5 miles ne Woodstock pop 641
archd and dioc Oxford
BLEDINGTON parish 1700 Gloucs 3-3/4 miles se Stow on the Wold
pop 335 archd and dioc Gloucester
BLEDLOW parish 1592 Bucks 5-1/2 miles se Thame pop 1,135 archd

Buckingham dioc Lincoln

BLENCARN township parish Kirkland Cumberland

BLENCOGO township parish Bromfield Cumberland pop 236

BLENCOW, GREAT township parish Dacre Cumberland

BLENCOW, LITTLE township parish Greystock Cumberland pop 60

BLENDWORTH parish 1586 Hamps 8 miles sw Petersfield pop 246
   archd and dioc Winchester

BLENHEIM PARK extra parochial near Woodstock co Oxford pop 83

BLENKINSOP township parish Haltwhistle Northumberland pop 344

BLENNERHASSET parish Torpenhow Cumberland pop 238 Indep

BLETCHINGLEY or BLECHINGLEY parish 1538 borough Surrey 24
   miles e Guildford pop 1,203 archd Surrey dioc Winchester

BLETCHLEY parish 1665 Bucks 1-1/2 miles sw Fenny Stratford pop
   1,254 archd Buckingham dioc Lincoln

BLETSOE parish 1582 Beds 6-1/2 miles nw Bedford pop 410 archd
   Bedford dioc Lincoln

BLEWBERRY parish 1588 Berks 4-1/2 miles ne East Ilsley comp
   chapelries of Aston Upthorp and Upton, liberty Nottingham Fee
   pop 1,056 pec juris Dean of Salisbury

BLICKLING parish 1559 Norfolk 1-1/4 miles nw Aylsham pop 365
   archd and dioc Norwich

BLIDESLOE tything parish Awre Gloucs

BLIDWORTH parith 1566 Notts 5 miles se Mansfield pop 901 pec
   juris of Southwell Bapt, Wesl Meth

BLINDBOTHEL township parish Brigham Cumberland pop 106

BLINDCRAKE township with Isall and Redmain parish Isall Cumberland

BLISLAND parish 1539 Cornwall 4-1/2 miles ne Bodmin pop 644
   archd Cornwall dioc Exeter Wesl Meth

BLISWORTH parish 1551 co Northampton 3-1/2 miles ne Towcester
   pop 769 archd Northampton dioc Peterborough

BLITHFIELD parish 1538 Staffs 4-1/4 miles n Rugeley pop 468 archd
   Stafford dioc Lichfield

BLOCKLEY parish 1538 in a detached portion of Worcs nw Moreton
   in the Marsh comp hamlets Aston Magna, Blockley, Ditchford,
   Dorne, Draycott, Horthwich and Paxford pop 2,015 pec juris of
   Bishop of Worcester

BLODWELL Shrops See LLAN Y BLODWELL

BLOFIELD parish 1545 Norfolk 4-1/2 miles sw Acle pop 1,092 archd
   and dioc Norwich

BLOOMSBURY, ST GEORGE Middlesex See LONDON

BLOORE IN TYRLEY township parish Drayton in Hales Staffs pop 397

BLORE RAY parish 1558 Staffs 4 miles nw Ashbourn comp township
   Blore with Swainscoe, part of chapelry Carlton pop 354 archd
   Stafford dioc Lichfield

BLOWNORTON parish 1562 Norfolk 6 miles se East Harling pop 411
   archd Norfolk dioc Norwich

BLOXHAM parish 1708 Lincs 5 miles nw Sleaford pop 76 archd and dioc Lincoln

BLOXHAM parish 1630 co Oxford 4 miles sw Banbury pop 1,573 archd and dioc Oxford Bapt

BLOXWICH chapelry 1733 parish Walsall Staffs Wesl Meth, Roman Cath

BLOXWORTH parish 1579 Dorset 5-1/4 miles nw Wareham, pop 251 pec juris Dean of Salisbury

BLUBBER HOUSES township parish Fewston W R York pop 118

BLUNDESTON parish 1558 Suffolk 3-1/2 miles nw Lowestoft pop 517 archd Suffolk dioc Norwich Wesl Meth

BLUNHAM parish 1571 Beds 5-1/4 miles nw Biggleswade pop 961 archd Bedford dioc Lincoln Bapt

BLUNSDON, St Andrew parish 1650 Wilts 4-1/4 miles sw Highworth pop 73 archd Wilts dioc Salisbury

BLUNSDON, BROAD chapelry 1679 parish Highworth Wilts pop 699

BLUNTISHAM parish 1538 Hunts 4-1/2 miles ne St Ives comp chapelry Earith pop 674 archd Huntingdon dioc Lincoln Bapt

BLURTON chapelry 1813 parish Trentham Staffs pop 849

BLYBOROUGH parish 1691 Lincs 9 miles ne Gainsborough pop 201 archd Stow dioc Lincoln

BLYFORD parish 1695 Suffolk

BLYMHILL parish 1561 Staffs 6 miles nw Brewood pop 566 archd Stafford dioc Lichfield

BLYTH parish 1556 Notts 31-1/4 miles ne Nottingham comp chapelry Austerfield, Bawtry township Ranskill, town of Blyth, townships Barnby Moor with Bilby, Styrrup and Torworth and Lordship of Hodsock pop 3,735 archd Nottingham dioc York Soc of Friends, Wesl Meth

BLYTH, NORTH joint township with Cambois parish Bedlington co Durham

BLYTH, SOUTH or BLYTH NOOK chapelry partly in parish Horton, chiefly in parish Earsdon Northumberland pop 1,769 Presb, Wesl Meth, New Connection Meth, Scotch Seceders

BLYTHBURGH parish 1690 Suffolk 4-1/4 miles sw Southwold pop 579 archd Suffolk dioc Norwich

BLYTHFORD parish 1695 Suffolk 2-3/4 miles se Halesworth pop 197 archd Suffolk dioc Norwich

BLYTON parish 1571 Lincs 4 miles ne Gainsborough pop 551 archd Stow dioc Lincoln Wesl Meth

BOARHUNT parish 1653 Hamps 1-3/4 miles ne Fareham pop 225 a donative

BOARSTALL parish 1640 Bucks 7-1/2 miles se Bicester pop 268 archd Buckingham dioc Lincoln

BOBBING parish 1738 Kent 1-1/4 miles nw Milton pop 364 archd and dioc Canterbury

BOBBINGTON parish 1571 Staffs 9 miles sw Wolverhampton pop 426 juris pec of Bridgenorth

BOBBINGWORTH or BOVINGER 1558 Essex 2-1/2 miles nw Chipping

Ongar pop 277 archd Essex dioc London

BOCKENFIELD township parish Felton Northumberland pop 144

BOCKHAMPTON tything parish Lambourn Berks

BOCKING parish 1558 Essex 1 mile n Braintree pop 3,128 pec juris Archbishop of Canterbury

BOCKLETON parish 1574 Worcs 5 miles s Tenbury pop 385 archd Salop dioc Hereford

BOCONNOC parish 1709 Cornwall 3-3/4 miles ne Lostwithiel pop 259 pec juris Dean and Chapter of Exeter

BODDINGTON parish 1656 Gloucs 3-3/4 miles nw Cheltenham pop 421 pec of Deerhurst

BODDINGTON, LOWER and UPPER parish 1558 co Northampton 9-3/4 miles sw Daventry pop 662 archd Northampton dioc Peterborough

BODENHAM parish 1584 Herefs 8-1/2 miles ne Hereford pop 998 archd and dioc Hereford Wesl Meth

BODENHAM tything parish Downton Wilts pop 309

BODHAM parish 1708 Norfolk 3-1/4 miles e Holt pop 308 archd and dioc Norwich

BODIAM parish 1557 Sussex 9 miles nw Winchelsea pop 349 archd Lewes dioc Chichester

BODICOTT chapelry 1563 parish East Adderbury co Oxford 1-3/4 miles se Banbury pop 779 Bapt

BODMIN parish 1558 Cornwall 20-1/2 miles sw Launceston pop 3,782 archd Cornwall dioc Exeter Bryanites, Countess of Huntington, Wesl Meth sep juris

BODNEY parish 1754 Norfolk 5-3/4 miles w Watton pop 110 archd Norfolk dioc Norwich

BOGNOR chapelry parish South Bersted Sussex Chapel built 1821 Indep, Wesl Meth

BOLAM township parish Gainford co Durham pop 115

BOLAM parish 1661 Northumberland 9-1/2 miles sw Morpeth comp townships Trewick, Bolam, Bolam Vicarage, Gallow Hill, Belsey, Bradford, Harnham and Shortflatt pop 608 archd Northumberland dioc Durham

BOLAS, GREAT parish 1582 Shrops 7-1/4 miles nw Newport pop 255 archd Salop dioc Lichfield

BOLD township parish Prescot Lancs pop 866

BOLD chapelry parish Aston Botterell Shrops

BOLDON parish 1571 co Durham 4-1/2 miles nw Sunderland comp East and West Boldon pop 855 archd and dioc Durham Wesl Meth

BOLDRE parish 1596 Hamps 2 miles n Lymington pop 2,111 archd and dioc Winchester Bapt

BOLDRON township parish Bowes N R York pop 148

BOLE parish 1755 Notts 3-1/2 miles sw Gainsborough pop 144 pec of Bole in Cathedral of York

BOLEHALL township parish Tamworth Warws

BOLINGBROKE parish 1538 Lincs 30 miles se Lincoln pop 725 archd

and dioc Lincoln Wesl Meth
BOLLEN FEE township parish Wilmslow Ches pop 1,784
BOLLINGTON township parishes of Bowdon and Rosthern Ches pop 268
BOLLINGTON township parish Prestbury Ches pop 2,685 Wesl Meth
BOLLINGHAM chapelry 1630 parish Eardisley Herefs
BOLNEY hamlet parish Harpsden co Oxford
BOLNEY parish 1541 Sussex 3-1/2 miles sw Cuckfield pop 635 archd Lewes dioc Chichester
BOLNHURST or BOLDENHURST parish 1685 Beds 7 miles ne Bedford pop 300 archd Bedford dioc Lincoln
BOLSOVER parish 1604 Derbys 28-1/2 miles ne Derby pop 1,429 archd Derby dioc Lichfield Indep, Wesl Meth
BOLTBY chapelry parish Felix Kirk N R York pop 342
BOLTERSTONE chapelry 1736 parish Ecclesfield W R York
BOLTON parish 1619 Cumberland 1-1/2 miles w Ireby pop 1,245 archd and dioc Carlisle Wesl Meth
BOLTON chapelry parish Edlingham Northumberland pop 117
BOLTON chapelry 1665 parish Morland Westm pop 391 Meth
BOLTON township parish Bishop Wilton E R York pop 103 Wesl Meth
BOLTON township parish Calverley W R York pop 671
BOLTON township parish Skipton W R York
BOLTON ABBEY chapelry 1689 parish Skipton W R York pop 112
BOLTON BY BOWLAND parish 1558 W R York 6-1/4 miles ne Clitheroe pop 1,774 archd and dioc York
BOLTON CASTLE chapelry 1684 parish Wensley N R York pop 269
BOLTON LE MOORS or GREAT BOLTON, ST PETER parish 1573 borough Lancs 43 miles se Lancaster comp town Bolton, chapelries Blackrod, Bradshaw, Darcy Lever, Rivington and Turton, townships Anglezarke, Breightmet, Edgworth, Entwisle, Harwood, Little Lever, Longworth, Quarlton, Sharples, Tonge with Haulgh, hamlet Lostock pop 63,034 archd and dioc Chester Indep, Unit, Soc of Friends, Swedenborgians, Meth, Roman Cath
BOLTON LE SANDS parish 1653 Lancs 4 miles n Lancaster comp chapelry Over Kellet and Slyne with Hest pop 1,781 Manor of Nether Kellet and Manor of Slyne with Hest exercised testamentary juris archd Richmond dioc Chester
BOLTON PERCY parish 1571 E R York 4 miles se Tadcaster comp township of Appleton Roebuck, Bolton Percy, Colton and Steeton pop 993 archd East Riding dioc York Wesl Meth
BOLTON UPON DEARNE parish 1560 W R York 7-1/4 miles ne Rotherham pop 556 archd and dioc York
BOLTON UPON SWALE chapelry 1653 parish Catterick N R York pop 85
BONBY parish 1649 Lincs 6-1/4 miles n Glandford Bridge pop 339 archd and dioc Lincoln
BONCHURCH parish 1734 Isle of Wight Hamps 10 miles se Newport pop 146 archd and dioc Winchester

BONDGATE township parish Ripon W R York
BONDLEIGH Devon See BUNDLEY
BONDS township parish Garstand Lancs
BONEHILL township parish Tamworth Staffs pop 283
BONGATE See APPLEBY
BONINGALE or BONINGHALL parish 1698 Shrops 5-1/4 miles se
  Shiffnall pop 168 archd Salop dioc Lichfield
BONNINGTON, St Rumwald parish 1679 Kent 6-1/2 miles se Ashford
  pop 127 archd and dioc Canterbury
BONNINGTON SUTTON Notts See SUTTON BONNINGTON
BONSALL parish 1634 Derbys 3-1/2 miles nw Wirksworth pop 1,315
  archd Derby dioc Lichfield Gen Bapt
BONWICK township parish Skipsea E R York pop 22
BOOKHAM, GREAT parish 1632 Surrey 2-1/2 miles sw Leatherhead
  pop 890 archd Surrey dioc Winchester
BOOKHAM, LITTLE parish 1642 Surrey 3 miles sw Leatherhead
  pop 191 archd Surrey dioc Winchester
BOOLEY township parish Stanton upon Hine Heath Shrops pop 138
BOOTH hamlet parish Howden E R York
BOOTH, NEW LAUND township parish Whalley Lancs
BOOTH, OLD LAUND township parish Mitton Lancs pop 476
BOOTHBY GRAFFOE parish 1720 Lancs 10 miles nw Sleaford pop
  173 archd and dioc Lincoln
BOOTHBY PAGNELL parish 1566 Lincs 5-1/4 miles nw Corby pop
  116 archd and dioc Lincoln
BOOTHEN township parish Stoke upon Trent Staffs pop 121
BOOTHS, HIGHER township parish Whalley Lancs pop 4,347
BOOTHS, LOWER township parish Whalley Lancs pop 2,178
BOOTLE parish 1655 Cumberland 5-3/4 miles se Ravenglass pop
  737 archd Richmond dioc Chester Indep
BOOTLE chapelry parish Walton on the Hill Lancs pop 1,133 chapel
  1827
BOOTON parish 1558 Norfolk 1-1/4 miles se Reepham pop 199
  archd and dioc Norwich
BORDEAN tything parish East Meon Hamps
BORDEN parish 1555 Kent 2-3/4 miles sw Sittingbourne pop 771
  archd and dioc Canterbury
BORDESLEY chapelry 1704 parish Aston Warws
BORDESLEY hamlet parish Tardebigg Worcs
BOREHAM parish 1559 Essex 3-1/2 miles ne Chelmsford pop 991
  archd Essex dioc London Roman Cath
BORESFORD township parish Brampton Bryan Herefs pop 109
BORLEY parish 1562 Essex 2-1/4 miles nw Sudbury pop 195 pec
  juris Archbishop of Canterbury
BORLEY township parish Ombersley Worcs
BOROUGHBRIDGE hamlet situated in parishes Ling, Othery, Middle-
  zoy and Weston Zoyland Somerset
BOROUGHBRIDGE chapelry parish Aldborough borough W R York

pop 950 Bapt, Wesl Meth

BOROUGH FEN extra parochial Peterborough co Northampton pop 200

BOROWBY township parish Leak N R York pop 350 Wesl Meth

BORROWBY township parish Lythe N R York pop 68

BORROWDALE chapelry 1775 parish Crosthwaite Cumberland pop 356 Dissenters at Grange and Rosthwaite

BORROWDON township parish Allenton Northumberland pop 174

BORWICK chapelry parish Warton Lancs pop 270

BOSBURY parish 1559 Herefs 4-1/2 miles nw Ledbury pop 1,061 archd and dioc Hereford

BOSCASTLE small sea port parishes Forrabury and Minster Cornwall Wesl Meth

BOSCOBEL extra parochial near Donington Shrops

BOSCOMBE parish 1695 Wilts 3-3/4 miles se Amesbury pop 148 archd and dioc Salisbury

BOSHAM parish 1557 Sussex 4 miles sw Chichester pop 1,181 archd and dioc Chichester

BOSLEY chapelry 1720 parish Prestbury Ches pop 597

BOSSALL parish 1613 N R York 10 miles ne York comp chapelry Sand Hutton, townships Bossall, Butter Crambe Claxton, Harton, Sand Hutton and part of Eaxton on the Moor in Wapentake of Bulmer pop 1,375 archd Cleveland dioc York

BOSSINEY with TREVENA borough, market town parish Tintagell Cornwall

BOSSINGTON chapelry 1763 parish Broughton Hamps pop 47

BOSTOCK township parish Davenham Ches pop 218

BOSTON parish 1557 Lincs 34 miles se Lincoln sep juris pop 11,240 archd and dioc Lincoln Gen and Part Bapt, Soc of Friends, Indep, Meth, Unit, Roman Cath, Jews

BOSTON township parish Bramham W R York chapel 1814 Wesl Meth

BOSWORTH, HUSBANDS parish 1557 Leics 6 miles sw Market Harborough pop 865 archd Leicester dioc Lincoln Part Bapt, Wesl Meth

BOSWORTH MARKET parish 1570 Leics 11-1/2 miles sw Leicester comp chapelries Barleston, Carlton, Shenton and Sutton Cheney, townships Barton in the Beans, part of township Osbaston pop 2,530 archd Leicester dioc Lincoln Bapt, Indep

BOTCHESTON township with Newton parish Ratby Leics pop 82

BOTESDALE chapelry parish Redgrave Suffolk pop 655 Extends into Rickinghall Superior and Inferior

BOTHAL parish 1678 Northumberland 3 miles e Morpeth comp townships Ashington with Sheepwash, Bothal Demesne, Longhurst, Old Moor and Pegsworth pop 755 archd Northumberland dioc Durham

BOTHAMSALL parish 1538 Notts 4-1/2 miles nw Tuxford pop 326 archd Nottingham dioc York

BOTHEL township parish Torpenhow Cumberland pop 405

BOTHENHAMPTON parish 1725 Dorset 1-1/4 miles se Bridport pop

424 archd Dorset dioc Bristol
BOTH HERGESTS township parish Kington Herefs pop 159
BOTLEY tything parish Cumner Berks pop 133
BOTLEY parish 1679 Hamps 6 miles s Southampton pop 722 archd
and dioc Winchester
BOTOLPH Sussex See BUTTOLPHS
BOTOLPH BRIDGE parish 1556 Hunts 2 miles sw Peterborough archd
Huntingdon dioc Lincoln
BOTTESFORD parish 1563 Leics 7 miles nw Grantham pop 1,320
archd Leicester dioc Lincoln Part Bapt
BOTTESFORD parish 1603 Lincs 8 miles w Glandford Bridge comp
townships Ashby and Burringham, hamlets Holm and Yaddles-
thorpe, township Crosby pop 1,229 archd Stow dioc Lincoln
BOTTESLAW township parish Stoke upon Trent Staffs pop 65
BOTTISHAM parish 1561 Cambs 6-1/2 miles sw Newmarket pop 1,302
archd and dioc Ely Part Bapt
BOTUSFLEMING parish 1548 Cornwall 3 miles nw Saltash pop 279
archd Cornwall dioc Exeter
BOUGHTON parish 1729 Norfolk 1-1/2 miles n Stoke Ferry pop 221
archd Norfolk dioc Norwich
BOUGHTON hamlet parish Weekley co Northampton
BOUGHTON parish 1549 co Northampton 3-3/4 miles n Northampton
pop 360 archd Northampton dioc Peterborough Wesl Meth
church desecrated
BOUGHTON parish 1686 Notts 1-3/4 miles ne Ollerton pop 295 archd
Nottingham dioc York
BOUGHTON ALUP parish 1558 Kent 4 miles ne Ashford pop 492
archd and dioc Canterbury
BOUGHTON, GREAT township parish Aldford Ches pop 900
BOUGHTON MALHERBE parish 1671 Kent 1-1/2 miles sw Lenham
pop 478 archd and dioc Canterbury
BOUGHTON MONCHELSEA parish 1560 Kent 4 miles se Maidstone
pop 1,025 archd and dioc Canterbury
BOUGHTON, SPITTLE extra parochial in Chester Ches pop 131
BOUGHTON UNDER BLEAN parish 1558 Kent 3 miles se Faversham
pop 1,300 pec of Archbishop of Canterbury Wesl Meth
BOULBY hamlet parish Easington N R York
BOULDON township parish Holdgate Shrops pop 49
BOULGE parish 1539 Suffolk 3 miles nw Woodbridge pop 55 archd
Suffolk dioc Norwich
BOULMER township parish Long Houghton Northumberland pop 140
BOULDSON tything parish Newent Gloucs pop 488
BOULSTONE parish 1562 Herefs 6 miles se Hereford pop 86 archd
and dioc Hereford
BOULTHAM parish 1716 Lincs 3 miles sw Lincoln pop 79 archd and
dioc Lincoln
BOULTON chapelry 1614 parish St Peter Derbys pop 175
BOURN parish 1564 Cambs 1-3/4 miles se Caxton pop 767 archd and

dioc Ely

BOURN tything parish Farnham Surrey

BOURN MOOR township Houghton le Spring co Durham pop 938 Wesl Meth

BOURNE parish 1562 Lincs 36 miles s Lincoln comp town Bourne, hamlets Cawthorpe and Dyke pop 2,569 archd and dioc Lincoln Bapt, Wesl Meth

BOURNE parish 1661 Hamps 3 miles nw Whitchurch pop 1,125 archd and dioc Winchester

BOURNE, EAST parish 1558 Sussex 7 miles s Hailsham pop 2,726 archd Lewes dioc Chichester Bapt, Indep, Wesl Meth

BOURNE, WEST parish 1550 Sussex 7-3/4 miles nw Chichester pop 2,031 archd and dioc Chichester

BOURTON tything parish Shrivenham Berks pop 302

BOURTON hamlet parish Buckingham Bucks

BOURTON chapelry 1810 parish Gillingham Dorset pop 810 Wesl Meth

BOURTON, BLACK parish 1542 co Oxford 5-1/2 miles se Burford pop 352 archd and dioc Oxford

BOURTON, FLAX parish 1701 Somerset 5-1/2 miles sw Bristol pop 219 archd Bath dioc Bath and Wells

BOURTON, GREAT and LITTLE chapelry parish Cropredy co Oxford pop 563

BOURTON ON THE HILL parish 1568 Gloucs 2 miles nw Moreton in the Marsh pop 553 archd and dioc Gloucester

BOURTON ON THE WATER parish 1654 Gloucs 4 miles sw Stow on the Wold pop 968 archd and dioc Gloucester Part Bapt

BOURTON UPON DUNSMOOR parish 1560 Warws 4 miles sw Dunchurch pop 367 archd Coventry dioc Lichfield

BOURTONHOLD hamlet parish Buckingham Bucks

BOUSTEAD HILL township parish Burgh upon the Sands Cumberland pop 63

BOVENY, Lower chapelry parish Burnham Bucks pop 207

BOVERIDGE or BEVERIDGE tything parish Cranborne Dorset

BOVEY, NORTH parish 1572 Devon 1-3/4 miles sw Moreton Hampstead pop 609 archd Totnes dioc Exeter

BOVEY TRACEY parish 1538 Devon 4 miles sw Chudleigh pop 1,697 archd Totnes dioc Exeter Bapt, Wesl Meth

BOVINGER Essex See BOBBINGWORTH

BOVINGDON chapelry 1674 parish Hemel Hempstead Herts pop 962

BOW or NYMETT TRACEY parish 1604 Devon 7-1/4 miles nw Crediton pop 962 archd Barnstaple dioc Exeter

BOW or STRATFORD LE BOW parish 1539 Middlesex 4-1/2 miles ne London pop 3,371 archd Middlesex dioc London Bapt, Wesl Meth

BOWBRIDGE hamlet parish Stroud Gloucs

BOWDEN, GREAT parish 1559 Leics 1-1/2 miles ne Market Harborough pop 3,346 archd Leicester dioc Lincoln

BOWDEN, LITTLE parish 1653 co Northampton 3/4 mile se Market

Harborough pop 346 archd Northampton dioc Peterborough

BOWDEN'S EDGE township parish Chapel en le Frith Derbys pop 1,067

BOWDON parish 1628 Ches 1 mile sw Altrincham comp town Althrincham, chapelry Carrington, townships Agden, Ashley, Baguley, Bollington, Bowdon, Dunham Massey, Hale, Partington, Timperley pop 8,200 archd and dioc Chester

BOWER CHALK parish 1653 Wilts 7-1/2 miles sw Wilton pop 370 archd and dioc Salisbury

BOWERS GIFFORD parish 1558 Essex 4-1/2 miles sw Rayleigh pop 231 archd Essex dioc London

BOWES parish 1670 N R York 6 miles nw Greta Bridge comp townships Boldron, Bowes, Gillmonby pop 1,145 archd Richmond dioc Chester Wesl Meth

BOWESDON hamlet parish Lowick Northumberland

BOWLAND township with Leagram parish Whalley Lancs pop 288

BOWLAND FOREST, HIGH township parish Slaidburn W R York pop 177

BOWLAND FOREST, LOW township parish Slaidburn W R York pop 344

BOWLING township parish Bradford W R York pop 5,958

BOWNESS parish 1642 Cumberland 12-1/4 miles nw Carlisle comp townships Anthorn, Bowness, Drumburgh and Fingland pop 1,196 archd and dioc Carlisle

BOWNESS village parish Windermere Westm

BOWOOD tything parish Netherbury Dorset

BOWOOD liberty parish Calne Wilts pop 81

BOWTHORP township with Menthorp parish Hemingbrough E R York

BOWTHORPE parish regs with Bowburgh Norfolk 3-1/2 miles nw Norwich

BOX parish 1587 Wilts 7 miles sw Chippenham pop 1,550 archd Wilts dioc Salisbury

BOXFORD parish 1558 Berks 4-1/2 miles nw Newbury pop 628 archd Berks dioc Salisbury Wesl Meth

BOXFORD parish 1557 Suffolk 16 miles sw Ipswich pop 1,088 archd Sudbury dioc Norwich

BOXGROVE parish 1561 Sussex 3-1/2 miles ne Chichester pop 778 archd and dioc Chichester

BOXLEY parish 1558 Kent 2-1/4 miles ne Maidstone pop 1,391 archd and dioc Canterbury

BOXTED parish 1559 Essex 5 miles n Colchester pop 832 archd Colchester dioc London

BOXTED parish 1538 Suffolk 5-3/4 miles ne Clare pop 239 archd Sudbury dioc Norwich

BOXWELL parish 1548 Gloucs 5 miles se Wootton under Edge pop 297 archd and dioc Gloucester

BOXWORTH parish 1588 Cambs 6-1/2 miles ne Caxton pop 283 archd and dioc Ely

BOYAT tything parish Otterbourne Hamps
BOYCUTT extra parochial near Stowe co Oxford
BOYLSTONE parish 1734 Derbys 7-1/2 miles s Ashbourn pop 330
  archd Derby dioc Lichfield Wesl Meth
BOYNTON parish 1563 E R York 2-1/2 miles nw Bridlington pop 114
  archd East Riding dioc York
BOYTON parish 1568 Cornwall 5 miles nw Launceston pop 557 archd
  Cornwall dioc Exeter
BOYTON parish 1539 Suffolk 3-3/4 miles Oxford pop 247 archd Suf-
  folk dioc Norwich
BOYTON parish 1560 Wilts 33 miles se Heytesbury pop 382 archd
  and dioc Salisbury
BOZEAT parish 1729 co Northampton 5-3/4 miles n Olney pop 812
  archd Northampton dioc Peterborough Wesl Meth
BRABOURNE   parish 1558 Kent 6-1/2 miles se Ashford pop 664
  archd and dioc Canterbury
BRACEBOROUGH parish 1593 Lincs 6 miles nw Market Deeping pop
  219 archd and dioc Lincoln
BRACEBRIDGE parish 1663 Lincs 2-1/4 miles sw Lincoln pop 158
  archd and dioc Lincoln
BRACEBY parish 1759 Lincs 4-1/2 miles nw Falkingham pop 123
  archd and dioc Lincoln
BRACE MEOLE parish 1681 Shrops 1-1/2 miles s Shrewsbury pop
  1,207 archd Salop dioc Hereford
BRACEWELL parish 1587 W R York 9 miles sw Skipton pop 160
  archd and dioc York
BRACKEN township chapelry Kilnwick E R York pop 28
BRACKENBOROUGH chapelry parish Little Grimsby Lincs pop 44
  incl in regs of Fotherby
BRACKENFIELD chapelry parish Morton Derbys pop 363
BRACKENHILL township parish Arthuret Cumberland pop 391
BRACKENHOLME township parish Hemingbrough E R York pop 69
BRACKENTHWAITE township parish Lorton Cumberland pop 130
BRACKLEY parish 1560 co Northampton 20 miles sw Northampton
  pop 2,107 archd Northampton dioc Peterborough Wesl Meth
BRACON ASH parish 1563 Norfolk 5-1/4 miles se Wymondham pop
  316 archd Norfolk dioc Norwich
BRADBORNE parish 1713 Derbys 5 miles ne Ashbourn comp chapel-
  ry Atlow, Ballidon, Brassington township Aldwark hamlet Lea
  Hill pop 1,297 archd Derby dioc Lichfield
BRADBURY township parish Sedgefield co Durham pop 147
BRADBY chapelry 1766 parish Repton Derbys 3 miles e Burton upon
  Trent pop 325
BRADDEN parish 1559 co Northampton 3-1/4 miles w Towcester pop
  165 archd Northampton dioc Peterborough
BRADDOCK Cornwall See BROADOAK
BRADENHAM parish 1627 Bucks 4-1/4 miles nw High Wycombe pop
  263 archd Buckingham dioc Lincoln

BRADENHAM, EAST parish 1695 Norfolk 5-3/4 miles sw East Dere-
ham pop 381 archd Norfolk dioc Norwich
BRADENHAM, WEST parish 1538 Norfolk 5-3/4 miles sw East Dere-
ham pop 370 archd Norfolk dioc Norwich
BRADESTON parish 1731 Norfolk 4-1/2 miles sw Acle pop 145 archd
and dioc Norwich
BRADFIELD parish 1539 Berks 8 miles w Reading pop 956 archd
Berks dioc Salisbury
BRADFIELD parish 1695 Essex 2-3/4 miles se Manningtree pop 964
archd Colchester dioc London Wesl Meth
BRADFIELD parish 1725 Norfolk 2-1/2 miles nw North Walsham pop
210 archd Norfolk dioc Norwich
BRADFIELD chapelry 1559 parish Ecclesfield W R York pop 5,504
Wesl Meth
BRADFIELD, ST CLARE parish 1538 Suffolk 6 miles se Bury St Ed-
munds pop 226 archd Sudbury dioc Norwich Wesl Meth
BRADFIELD, ST GEORGE 1555 Suffolk 5 miles se Bury St Edmunds
pop 489 archd Sudbury dioc Norwich
BRADFIELD COMBUST parish 1538 Suffolk 5-1/2 miles se Bury St
Edmunds pop 154 archd Sudbury dioc Norwich
BRADFORD parish 1538 Devon 6 miles ne Holsworthy pop 487 archd
Totnes dioc Exeter
BRADFORD township parish Manchester Lancs pop 166
BRADFORD township parish Bambrough Northumberland pop 36
BRADFORD township parish Bolam Northumberland pop 32
BRADFORD parish 1558 Somerset 4-1/4 miles sw Taunton pop 525
archd Taunton dioc Bath and Wells
BRADFORD parish 1596 W R York 10 miles se Leeds comp town
Bradford, chapelries North, Bierley, Hawarth, Heaton, Horton,
Shipley, Thornton and Wilsden, townships Allerton, Bowling, Clay-
ton, Eccleshill and Manningham pop 76,996 archd and dioc York
Bapt, Soc of Friends, Indep, Prim and Wesl Meth, Unit, Roman Cath
BRADFORD ABBAS parish 1579 Dorset 3-1/2 miles sw Sherborne
pop 595 archd Dorset dioc Bristol
BRADFORD, GREAT or BRADFORD ON AVON parish 1579 Wilts 8
miles se Bath pop 10,102 archd and dioc Salisbury
BRADFORD PEVERELL parish 1653 Dorset 3-1/4 miles nw Dorches-
ter pop 330 archd Dorset dioc Bristol
BRADFORD UPON AVON Wilts See BRADFORD, GREAT
BRADFORD, WEST township parish Mitton W R York pop 522
BRADING parish 1547 Isle of Wight Hamps 7 miles se Newport pop
2,227 archd and dioc Winchester Wesl Meth
BRADLE tything parish Church Knowles Dorset pop 97
BRADLEY tything parish Cumner Berks pop 6
BRADLEY township parish Malpas Ches pop 95
BRADLEY parish 1579 Derbys 3-1/4 miles se Ashbourn pop 323
archd Derby dioc Lichfield
BRADLEY tything parish Crediton Devon

BRADLEY tything parish Wooton under Edge Gloucs
BRADLEY hamlet chapelry of Holt parish Medbourne Leics
BRADLEY parish 1664 Lincs 3 miles sw Grimsby pop 98 archd and
dioc Lincoln
BRADLEY parish 1725 Hamps 6 miles nw Alton pop 103 archd and
dioc Winchester
BRADLEY chapelry 1562 parish Fladbury Worcs pop 236
BRADLEY FIELD hamlet chapelry Underbarrow parish Kendal Westm
BRADLEY, GREAT parish 1702 Suffolk 6-1/2 miles ne Haverhill pop
527 archd Sudbury dioc Norwich
BRADLEY parish 1538 Staffs 3-3/4 miles nw Penkridge pop 731
archd Stafford dioc Lichfield Wesl Meth
BRADLEY IN THE MOORS parish 1708 Staffs 4 miles se Cheadle pop
75 archd Stafford dioc Lichfield
BRADLEY, LITTLE parish 1561 Suffolk 6 miles ne Haverhill pop 22
archd Sudbury dioc Norwich
BRADLEY, LOWER and UPPER township parish Kildwick W R York
pop 614 Wesl Meth
BRADLEY, MAIDEN parish 1753 Somerset and Wilts 5-3/4 miles nw
Mere pop 659 archd and dioc Salisbury
BRADLEY, NORTH parish 1641 Wilts 2-1/2 miles s Strowbridge pop
2,477 archd Wilts dioc Salisbury Part Bapt
BRADLEY, WEST parish 1633 Somerset 4-3/4 miles se Glastonbury
pop 132 archd Wells dioc Bath and Wells
BRADMORE parish (no regs see Bunny) Notts 6-1/4 miles s Notting-
ham pop 369 archd Notthingham dioc York
BRADNINCH parish 1559 borough Devon 8 miles ne Exeter pop 1,524
sep juris archd and dioc Exeter Part Bapt
BRADNOP township parish Leek Staffs pop 467
BRADON, NORTH and SOUTH parish Somerset 3-3/4 miles ne Ilmin-
ster pop 34 archd Taunton dioc Bath and Wells
BRADPOLE parish 1695 Dorset 1-1/2 miles ne Bridport pop 1,018
archd Dorset dioc Bristol
BRADSHAW chapelry 1814 parish Bolton Lancs pop 773
BRADSHAW EDGE township parish Chapel en le Frith Derbys pop
1,768
BRADSTONE parish 1654 Devon 4-1/4 miles se Launceston pop 162
archd Totnes dioc Exeter
BRADSTONE hamlet parish Berkeley Gloucs pop 121
BRADWELL parish 1577 Bucks 3-1/2 miles se Stony Stratford pop
257 archd Buckingham dioc Lincoln
BRADWELL township parish Sandbach Ches pop 297
BRADWELL hamlet parish Hope Derbys pop 1,153 Wesl Meth, Unit
BRADWELL parish 1601 co Oxford
BRADWELL parish 1556 Suffolk 3 miles se Great Yarmouth pop 257
archd Suffolk dioc Norwich
BRADWELL ABBEY extra parochial Bucks 3-1/4 miles Stony Strat-
ford pop 17

BRADWELL JUXTA COGGESHALL parish 1704 Essex 2 miles sw
Great Coggeshall pop 318 archd Colchester dioc London
BRADWELL NEAR THE SEA parish 1558 Essex 12 miles e Maldon
pop 956 archd Essex dioc London
BRADWOOD WIDGER parish 1654 Devon 6 miles ne Launceston pop
879 archd Totnes dioc Exeter Wesl Meth
BRADWORTHY parish 1548 Devon 7 miles nw Holsworthy pop 1,027
archd Totnes dioc Exeter Wesl Meth
BRAFFERTON township parish Great Aycliffe co Durham pop 247
Meth
BRAFFERTON parish 1798 N R York 4 miles ne Boroughbridge, comp
township Thornton Bridge, Brafferton, Helperby pop 872 archd
Cleveland dioc York
BRAFIELD ON THE GREEN parish 1540 co Northampton 5 miles se
Northampton pop 460 archd Northampton dioc Peterborough
BRAILS parish 1570 Warws 4 miles se Shipston upon Stour pop 1,272
archd and dioc Worcester
BRAILSFORD parish 1647 Derbys 7-1/4 miles nw Derby pop 780
archd Derby dioc Lichfield Wesl Meth
BRAINTFIELD parish 1559 Herts 3-1/2 miles nw Hertford pop 204
archd Huntingdon dioc Lincoln
BRAINTREE parish 1660 Essex 11 miles ne Chelmsford pop 3,422
archd Middlesex dioc London Bapt, Soc of Friends, Indep, Meth
BRAISEWORTH parish 1709 Suffolk 1-3/4 miles sw Eye pop 156
archd Sudbury dioc Norwich
BRAITHWAITE township parish Crosthwaite Cumberland pop 245
BRAITHWAITE hamlet parish St Mary, Carlisle Cumberland
BRAITHWELL parish 1559 W R York 7 miles sw Doncaster comp
townships Braithwell, Bramley pop 745 archd and dioc York Wesl
Meth
BRAKES township parish Leintwardine Herefs pop 118
BRAMBER parish 1601 borough Sussex 1/2 mile se Steyning pop 97
archd and dioc Chichester
BRAMCOTE chapelry 1562 parish Attenborough Notts pop 562
BRAMCOTT hamlet parish Bulkington Warws
BRAMDEAN parish 1573 Hamps 4 miles se New Alresford pop 215
archd and dioc Winchester
BRAMERTON parish 1561 Norfolk 5-1/2 miles se Norwich pop 202
archd Norfolk dioc Norwich
BRAMFIELD parish 1539 Suffolk 2-1/4 miles se Halesworth pop 667
archd Suffolk dioc Norwich
BRAMFORD parish 1553 Suffolk 3-1/4 miles nw Ipswich pop 874
archd Norfolk dioc Norwich
BRAMHALL township parish Stockport Ches pop 1,401
BRAMHAM parish 1586 E R York 4-1/4 miles se Wetherby comp
townships Bramham, Clifford pop 2,403 pec juris Dean and Chapter of York Wesl Meth
BRAMHOPE township parish Otley W R York pop 359

BRAMLEY parish 1580 Hamps 4-1/2 miles ne Basingstoke pop 429 archd and dioc Winchester

BRAMLEY chapelry 1566 parish Shalford Surrey pop 842

BRAMLEY chapelry 1717 parish St Peter Leeds W R York pop 7,039 archd and dioc York Part Bapt, Wesl Meth

BRAMLEY township parish Braithwell W R York pop 290 Wesl Meth

BRAMPFORD SPEKE parish 1739 Devon 4-1/2 miles ne Exeter pop 374 archd and dioc Exeter

BRAMPTON parish 1663 Cumberland 9-1/2 miles ne Carlisle comp town Brampton, townships Easby and Naworth pop 3,345 archd and dioc Carlisle Indep, Prim and Wesl Meth, Presb

BRAMPTON parish 1658 Derbys 3-1/2 miles nw Chesterfield pop 3,594 archd Derby dioc Lichfield Prim and Wesl Meth

BRAMPTON parish 1653 Hunts 2-1/4 miles sw Huntingdon pop 1,064 archd Huntingdon dioc Lincoln

BRAMPTON chapelry parish Torksey Lincs pop 103

BRAMPTON parish 1600 Norfolk 2-3/4 miles se Aylsham pop 207 archd and dioc Norwich

BRAMPTON or BRAMPTON ASH parish 1580 co Northampton 3-3/4 miles ne Market Harborough pop 100 archd Northampton dioc Peterborough

BRAMPTON parish 1755 Suffolk 4-1/2 miles ne Halesworth pop 289 archd Suffolk dioc Norwich

BRAMPTON township parish Long Marton Westm

BRAMPSTON ABBOTS parish 1556 Herefs 1 mile n Ross pop 218 archd and dioc Hereford

BRAMPTON BIERLOW chapelry parish Wath upon Dearne W R York pop 1,462

BRAMPTON BRYAN parish 1598 Herefs 5-1/4 miles e Knighton comp Lordship of Stanage co Radnor South Wales, townships Brampton Bryan and Boresford with Pedwardine pop 249 archd Salop dioc Hereford

BRAMPTON CHAPEL parish with Church Brampton co Northampton 4-1/2 miles nw Northampton pop 206

BRAMPTON, CHURCH parish 1561 co Northampton 4-1/2 miles nw Northampton pop 176 archd Northampton dioc Peterborough

BRAMPTON EN LE MORTHEN township parish Treeton W R York pop 142

BRAMPTON, LITTLE township with Rod and Nash parish Presteigne Herefs

BRAMSHALL parish 1578 Staffs 2 miles sw Uttoxeter pop 170 archd Stafford dioc Lichfield

BRAMSHAW parish 1598 Wilts Hamps 6-1/4 miles nw Lyndhurst pop 799 pec juris Dean and Chapter of Salisbury

BRAMSHILL, GREAT tything parish Eversley Hamps pop 156

BRAMSHILL, LITTLE tything parish Eversley Hamps pop 10

BRAMSHOTT parish 1560 Hamps 4-1/2 miles nw Haslemere pop 1,210 archd and dioc Winchester

BRAMWITH, KIRK parish 1700 W R York 4-3/4 miles sw Thorne pop 211 archd and dioc York

BRANCASTER parish 1538 Norfolk 4-1/2 miles nw Burnham Westgate pop 851 archd Norfolk dioc Norwich

BRANCEPETH parish 1599 co Durham 4-1/4 miles sw Durham comp townships Brancepeth, Brandon with Byshottles, Crook with Billy Row, Hedley Hope, Hemlington Row, Stockley and Willington pop 1,449 archd and dioc Durham

BRANDESTON parish 1559 Suffolk 4 miles se Framlingham pop 569 archd Suffolk dioc Norwich

BRANDISTONE parish 1610 Norfolk 2-3/4 miles se Reepham pop 96 archd and dioc Norwich

BRANDON township with Byshottles parish Brancepeth co Durham pop 478

BRANDON township parish Eglingham Northumberland pop 160

BRANDON or BRANDON FERRY parish 1653 Suffolk 40 miles nw Ipswich pop 1,065 archd Sudbury dioc Norwich Wesl Meth

BRANDON hamlet with Bretsford parish Wolston Warws pop 379

BRANDON, LITTLE parish 1694 Norfolk 5 miles nw Wymondham pop 208 archd Norfolk dioc Norwich

BRANDSBURTON parish 1558 W R York 8-1/2 miles ne Beverley comp townships Brandsburton and Moor Town pop 611 archd East Riding dioc York Wesl Meth

BRANDS FEE liberty parish Hitchenden and Great and Little Missenden Bucks

BRANSBY township parish Stow Lincs pop 88

BRANSBY parish 1575 N R York 6-1/2 miles ne Easingwould pop 298 archd Cleveland dioc York

BRANSCOMBE parish 1539 Devon 4-3/4 miles e Sidmouth pop 829 pec juris of Dean and Chapter of Exeter

BRANSDALE, EAST SIDE township parish Kirby Moorside N R York

BRANSDALE, WEST SIDE township parish Kirkdale N R York

BRANSFORD chapelry 1767 parish Powick and Leigh Worcs pop 338

BRANSGORE chapelry parish Christchurch Hamps

BRANSON township parish Burton upon Trent Staffs pop 382

BRANSTONE parish 1591 Leics 8 miles ne Melton Mowbray pop 298 archd Leicester dioc Lincoln

BRANSTON parish 1626 Lincs 4-1/2 miles se Lincoln pop 859 archd and dioc Lincoln Wesl Meth

BRANTHAM parish 1634 Suffolk 2 miles ne Manningtree pop 367 archd Suffolk dioc Norwich

BRANTHWAITE township parish Dean Cumberland pop 317 Meth

BRANTINGHAM parish 1653 E R York 1-3/4 miles se South Cave comp township Thorpe Brantingham, chapelry Ellerker pop 468 pec court of Howdenshire

BRANTON township parish Eglingham Northumberland pop 110 Presb

BRANTON GREEN township with Upper Dunsforth parish Aldborough W R York

BRANXTON parish 1739 Northumberland 9-1/4 miles nw Wooler
pop 249 archd Northumberland dioc Durham
BRASHFIELD hamlet parish Mitchelmersh Hamps
BRASSINGTON chapelry 1716 parish Bradborne Derbys pop 714
archd Derby dioc Lichfield
BRASTED parish 1557 Kent 5 miles nw Seven Oaks pop 964 pec juris
Archbishop of Canterbury
BRATOFT parish 1685 Lincs 4-1/2 miles se Spilsby pop 201
BRATTLEBY parish 1686 Lincs 6-1/2 miles nw Lincoln pop 154
archd Stow dioc Lincoln
BRATTON chapelry 1542 parish Westbury Wilts pop 1,237 Part Bapt
BRATTON COVELLY parish 1555 Devon 8 miles sw Oakhampton
pop 787 archd Totnes dioc Exeter
BRATTON FLEMING parish 1673 Devon 5-3/4 miles ne Barnstaple
pop 534 archd Barnstaple dioc Exeter
BRATTON, ST MAUR also called BRATTON, BRATTON SEYMOUR
1754 Somerset 2-1/2 miles nw Wincanton pop 59 archd Wells
dioc Bath and Wells
BRAUGHING parish 1563 Herts 10 miles ne Hertford pop 1,266 archd
Middlesex dioc London Indep
BRAUNCEWELL parish 1760 Lincs 4-3/4 miles nw Sleaford pop 134
archd and dioc Lincoln
BRAUNSTON parish 1538 co Northampton 2-3/4 miles nw Daventry
pop 1,380 archd Northampton dioc Peterborough Calv Bapt,
Wesl Meth
BRAUNSTON or BRAUENSTONE parish 1553 co Rutland 2-1/2 miles
sw Oakham pop 424 archd Northampton dioc Peterborough
BRAUNSTONE chapelry 1561 parish Glenfield Leics pop 198
BRAUNSTONE FRITH extra parochial parish Glenfield Leics pop 8
BRAUNTON parish 1538 Devon 4-3/4 miles nw Barnstaple pop 2,947
juris Dean of Exeter Indep
BRAWBY township parish Salton E R York pop 199 Wesl Meth
BRAWITH township with Knayton parish Leak N R York
BRAXTED, GREAT parish 1558 Essex 2 miles ne Witham pop 471
archd Colchester dioc London
BRAXTED, LITTLE parish 1730 Essex 1 mile e Witham pop 92
archd Colchester dioc London
BRAY parish 1652 Berks comp Bray, Touchen, Water Oakley and part
of Maidenhead pop 3,880 archd Berks dioc Salisbury
BRAY EATON Beds See EATON, BRAY
BRAY, HIGH parish 1735 Devon 8 miles nw South Molton pop 280
archd Barnstaple dioc Exeter
BRAYBROOK parish 1653 co Northampton 2-1/2 miles se Market
Harborough pop 366 archd Northampton dioc Peterborough
Part Bapt
BRAYDON hamlet parish Purton Wilts pop 64
BRAYESWORTH parish 1709 Suffolk
BRAYFIELD, COLD parish 1693 Bucks 2-3/4 miles ne Olney pop 93

archd Buckingham dioc Lincoln

BRAYTOFT or BRATOFT parish 1685 Lincs 6 miles se Spilsby pop 201 archd and dioc Lincoln

BRAYTON township parish Aspatria Cumberland

BRAYTON, ST WILFRID parish 1615 W R York 1-3/4 miles sw Selby comp chapelry Barlow, townships Brayton, Burn, Gateforth, Hambleton and Thorpe Willoughby pop 1,612 pec Court of Selby

BREADSALL parish 1573 Derbys 3 miles ne Derby pop 565 archd Derby dioc Lichfield

BREAGE, ST parish 1559 Cornwall 3 miles nw Helston pop 5,149 archd Cornwall dioc Exeter Bryanites, Wesl Meth

BREAM, ST JAMES 1846 chapelry parish Newland Gloucs

BREAMORE parish 1675 Hamps 3 miles ne Fordingbridge pop 600 a donative dioc Winchester

BREANE parish 1730 Somerset 8-1/2 miles w Axbridge pop 134 archd Wells dioc Bath and Wells

BREARTON township parish Knaresborough W R York pop 248

BREASON or BREASTON chapelry 1719 parish Sawley Derbys pop 642 pec juris Prebendary of Sawley in Cathedral of Lichfield

BRECCLES, LITTLE hamlet parish Shropham Norfolk

BRECKENBROUGH township parish Kirby Wisk N R York

BRECCLES or BRECKLES parish 1540 Norfolk 5 miles se Watton pop 154 archd and dioc Norwich

BREDBURY township parish Stockport Ches pop 2,374

BREDE parish 1559 Sussex 6 miles ne Battle pop 1,046 archd Lewes dioc Chichester

BREDENBURY parish 1607 Herefs 3 miles nw Bromyard pop 54 archd and dioc Hereford

BREDFIELD parish 1711 Suffolk 3-1/4 miles sw Wickham Market pop 466 archd Suffolk dioc Norwich

BREDGAR parish 1559 Kent 3-1/4 miles sw Sittingburne pop 512 archd and dioc Canterbury Wesl Meth

BREDHURST parish 1545 Kent 4-1/2 miles se Chatham pop 147 pec juris of Archbishop of Canterbury

BREDICOT parish 1702 Worcs 3-3/4 miles e Worcester pop 52 archd and dioc Worcester

BREDON parish 1559 Worcs 3-3/4 miles ne Tewkesbury comp chapelries of Norton and Cutsdean, hamlets Bredon, Hardwick with Mittons, Kinsham and Westmancote pop 1,325 pec juris of rector

BREDON'S NORTON chapelry 1754 parish Bredon Worcs

BREDWARDINE parish 1723 Herefs 11-1/2 miles nw Hereford pop 436 archd and dioc Hereford

BREDY, LITTLE chapelry 1717 parish Long Bredy Dorset pop 165

BREDY, LONG parish 1627 Dorset 8 miles w Dorchester pop 333 archd Dorset dioc Bristol

BREEDON on HILL parish 1562 Leics 5-1/4 miles ne Ashby de la Zouch comp chapelries Worthington and Staunton Harrold, ham-

lets Tongue and Wilson and Liberty Newbold pop 2,656 archd
Leicester dioc Lincoln Wesl Meth
BREEM chapelry 1846 parish Newland Gloucs pop 393
BREIGHTMET township parish Bolton Lancs pop 1,026
BREIGHTON township parish Bubwith E R York pop 204
BREINTON parish 1662 Herefs 2-1/2 miles w Hereford pop 290 juris
of Consistory Court of Dean of Hereford
BREMHILL parish 1590 Wilts 4-1/4 miles e Chippenham pop 1,535
archd Wilts dioc Salisbury Moravian
BREMILHAM parish 1699 Wilts 2 miles sw Malmesbury pop 33 archd
Wilts dioc Salisbury
BRENCHLEY parish 1560 Kent 4-1/2 miles n Lamberhurst pop 2,602
archd and dioc Rochester Part Bapt
BRENDON parish 1620 Devon 15-1/2 miles e Ilfracombe pop 259
archd Barnstaple dioc Exeter
BRENKLEY township parish Ponteland Northumberland pop 42
BRENT, EAST parish 1556 Somerset 4-3/4 miles sw Axbridge pop
802 archd Wells dioc Bath and Wells Meth
BRENT ELEIGH or ELY parish 1580 Suffolk 1-3/4 miles se Laven-
ham pop 290 archd Sudbury dioc Norwich
BRENT, SOUTH parish 1677 Devon 7-3/4 miles sw Ashburton pop
1,248 archd Totnes dioc Exeter Wesl Meth
BRENT, SOUTH or BRENT KNOLL parish 1679 Somerset 6 miles sw
Axbridge pop 890 archd Wells dioc Bath and Wells Wesl Meth
BRENTFORD, NEW chapelry parish Hanwell, Middlesex pop 2,036
archd Middlesex dioc London
BRENTFORD, OLD chapelry 1828 parish Ealing Middlesex
BRENTWOOD market town Middlesex comp New Brentford and Old
Brentford pop 2,085 7 miles sw Hyde Park Corner, London
Part Bapt, Prim and Wesl Meth
BRENTINGBY chapelry in parish Thorpe Arnold and parish Wyfordby
Leics
BRENTOR parish 1720 Devon 4 miles n Tavistock pop 147 archd
Totnes dioc Exeter
BRENTWOOD chapelry 1695 parish South Weald Essex Indep
BRENZETT parish 1538 Kent 4-1/2 miles nw Romney pop 258 archd
and dioc Canterbury Wesl Meth
BREOCK, ST parish 1561 Cornwall 1 mile sw Wadebridge pop 1,450
pec juris of Bishop of Exeter
BREREHURST hamlet parish Wolstanton Staffs pop 900
BRERETON with SMETHWICK parish 1538 Ches 2-3/4 miles ne Sand-
bach pop 661 archd and dioc Chester Calvinistic Dissenters
BRESSINGHAM parish 1559 Norfolk 2-3/4 miles w Diss pop 655
archd Norfolk dioc Norwich
BRETBY See BRADBY parish 1766 Derbys
BRETFORTON parish 1538 Worcs 3-3/4 miles e Evesham pop 423
pec juris of Bishop of Worcester
BRETHERTON township parish Croston Lancs pop 828 Wesl Meth

BRETSFORD hamlet with Brandon parish Wolston Warws
BRETTENHAM parish 1777 Norfolk 4 miles se Thetford pop 65 archd
Norfolk dioc Norwich
BRETTENHAM parish 1584 Suffolk 3-3/4 miles nw Bildeston pop 366
archd Sudbury dioc Norwich
BRETTON, MONK chapelry 1750 parish Royston W R York pop 1,394
BRETTON, WEST chapelry 1750 parish Great Sandall and parish
Silkstone W R York
BREWARD ST or SIMONWARD parish 1558 Cornwall 6-3/4 miles ne
Bodmin pop 627 archd Cornwall dioc Exeter
BREWERS, ISLE Somerset See ISLE BREWERS
BREWHAM LODGE extra parochial Somerset
BREWHAM, NORTH and SOUTH parish 1660 Somerset 3-1/4 miles
ne Bruton pop 968 archd Wells dioc Bath and Wells
BREWHOUSE YARD extra parochial Notts pop 80
BREWOOD parish 1562 Staffs 10-1/2 miles sw Stafford comp town-
ships Brewood, Bishop's Wood, Hide and Wooley, Kiddermore
Green and Park Lanes, liberties of Chillington Coven and Somer-
ford pop 3,799 pec juris Dean of Lichfield Indep, Wesl Meth
BRIAVELL'S ST parish 1665 Gloucs 8 miles sw Blakeney pop 1,124
archd Hereford dioc Gloucester
BRICETT, GREAT parish 1680 Suffolk 3-3/4 miles ne Bildeston pop
284 archd Suffolk dioc Norwich
BRICETT, LITTLE parish Suffolk 4-1/2 miles sw Needham Market
archd Suffolk dioc Norwich
BRICKENDON liberty parish All Saints, Hertford, Herts pop 765
BRICKHILL, BOW parish 1687 Bucks 2 miles e Fenny Stratford pop
475 archd Buckingham dioc Lincoln
BRICKHILL, GREAT parish 1558 Bucks 2-3/4 miles se Fenny Strat-
ford pop 776 archd Buckingham dioc Lincoln Bapt, Wesl Meth
BRICKHILL, LITTLE parish 1559 Bucks 2 miles se Fenny Stratford
pop 514 pec juris Archbishop of Canterbury Wesl Meth
BRICKLEHAMPTON chapelry 1756 parish St Andrew, Pershore
Worcs pop 156
BRIDEKIRK parish 1584 Cumberland 2 miles nw Cockermouth comp
townships Bridekirk, Great Broughton, Little Broughton, Dovenby,
Popcastle with Goat, Ribton and Tallentire pop 1,902 archd and
dioc Carlisle
BRIDE, ST WENTLLOOG parish 1695 co Monmouth 5-1/4 miles s
Newport pop 200 archd and dioc Llandaff
BRIDE'S ST, NETHERWENT parish 1754 co Monmouth 7 miles se
Caerleon pop 163 archd and dioc Llandaff
BRIDDLESFORD hamlet parish Arreton Isle of Wight Hamps
BRIDESTOWE parish 1696 Devon 6 miles sw Oakhampton pop 907
archd Totnes dioc Exeter
BRIDFORD parish 1538 Devon 4 miles ne Moreton Hampstead pop
529 archd and dioc Exeter
BRIDGE parish 1579 Kent 3 miles se Canterbury pop 543 archd and

dioc Canterbury Wesl Meth

BRIDGEHAM parish 1558 Norfolk 2-1/2 miles sw East Harling pop 291 archd Norfolk dioc Norwich

BRIDGEMERE township parish Wybunbury Ches pop 236

BRIDGENORTH market town borough Shrops 20-1/2 miles se Shrewsbury pop 4,785 comp parishes St Mary Magdalene 1610, St Leonard 1556 sep juris pec of Bridgenorth Bapt, Indep

BRIDGE RULE parish 1561 Cornwall 4-1/2 miles w Holsworthy comp East Rule, Devon and West Rule pop 467 archd Totnes dioc Exeter

BRIDGE SOLLERS parish 1615 Herefs 5-3/4 miles nw Hereford pop 71 archd and dioc Hereford

BRIDGFORD, EAST parish 1557 Notts 8 miles ne Nottingham pop 938 archd Nottingham dioc York Wesl Meth

BRIDGFORD, WEST parish 1559 Notts 1-1/2 miles se Nottingham pop 388 archd Nottingham dioc York

BRIDGHAMPTON tything parish Yeovilton Somerset pop 103

BRIDGE WATER, ST MARY 1558, Holy Trin 1840, St John 1846 Somerset borough sep juris 35 miles se Bristol pop 7,807 archd Taunton dioc Bath and Wells Bapt, Soc of Friends, Indep, Wesl Meth, Unit

BRIDLINGTON parish 1564 E R York 38 miles ne York comp Bridlington, chapelries Grindall and Specton, townships Buckton, Hilderthorp and Sewerby with Marton, hamlet Easton pop 5,637 archd East Riding dioc York

BRIDPORT parish 1600 Dorset borough 14-3/4 miles w Dorchester pop 4,242 sep juris archd Dorset dioc Bristol Soc of Friends, Indep, Wesl Meth, Unit

BRIDSTOW parish 1560 Herefs 1-1/4 miles nw Ross pop 596 archd and dioc Hereford

BRIERDEAN township parish Earsdon Northumberland pop 67

BRIERLY township parish Felkirk W R York pop 483 Wesl Meth

BRIERLY HILL chapelry 1766 parish King's Swingford Staffs archd Stafford dioc Lichfield

BRIERS chapelry 1800 parish Halifax W R York See ANNE, ST

BRIERSCLIFFE township with Extwistle parish Whalley Lancs pop 1,755

BRIERTON township parish Stranton co Durham pop 22

BRIGG Lincs See GLANDFORD BRIDGE

BRIGHAM parish 1563 Cumberland 2 miles w Cockermouth comp Cockermouth, chapelries Buttermere, Embleto, Mosser and Setnurthey, townships Blindbothel, Brigham, Eaglesfield, Graysouthen and Whinfell pop 503 archd Richmond dioc Chester

BRIGHAM township parish Foston upon Wolds E R York pop 151 Wesl Meth

BRIGHOUSE township with Hipperholme parish Halifax W R York Wesl Meth

BRIGHTHAMPTON hamlet parish Bampton co Oxford

BRIGHTHELMSTONE or BRIGHTON parish 1558 borough Sussex 30 miles e London pop 40,634 archd Lewes dioc Chichester Indep, Soc of Friends, Countess of Huntingdon, Huntingtonians, Meth, Scotch Seceders, Roman Cath, Jews, Bethel chapel

BRIGHTLING parish 1560 Sussex 4 miles sw Battle pop 656 archd Lewes dioc Chichester

BRIGHTLINGSEA parish 1697 Essex 9 miles se Colchester pop 1,784 archd Colchester dioc London Wesl Meth

BRIGHTSIDE BIERLOW township parish Sheffield WR York pop 8,968

BRIGHTON See BRIGHTHELMSTONE

BRIGHTSTONE Hamps See BRIXTON

BRIGHT WALTHAM 1559 Berks See WALTHAM, BRIGHT

BRIGHTWELL parish 1564 Berks 2-1/2 miles nw Wallingford pop 573 archd Berks dioc Salisbury Dissenters

BRIGHTWELL parish 1653 Suffolk 5-1/2 miles se Ipswich pop 86 archd Suffolk dioc Norwich

BRIGHTWELL BALDWIN parish 1545 co Oxford 5-1/2 miles sw Tetsworth pop 332 archd and dioc Oxford

BRIGHTWELL PRIOR chapelry 1813 parish Newington co Oxford pop 52

BRIGHTWELL SALOME parish 1574 co Oxford 5-1/2 miles sw Tetsworth pop 216 archd and dioc Oxford

BRIGNALL parish 1588 N R York 1 mile sw Greta Bridge pop 232 archd Richmond dioc Chester

BRIGSLEY parish 1558 Lincs 5-1/4 miles sw Grimsby pop 108 archd and dioc Lincoln

BRIGSTOCK parish 1641 co Northampton 22 miles ne Northampton pop 1,167 archd Northampton dioc Peterborough

BRILL parish 1588 Bucks 7 miles nw Thame pop 1,283 archd Buckingham dioc Lincoln

BRILLEY chapelry 1581 parish Kington Herefs pop 539

BRIMFIELD parish 1566 Herefs 5 miles w Tenbury pop 581 archd and dioc Hereford

BRIMHAM hamlet chapelry Hartwith parish Kirby Malzeard W R York

BRIMINGTON chapelry 1759 parish Chesterfield Derbys pop 759

BRIMPSFIELD parish 1588 Gloucs 5-1/4 miles ne Painswick pop 382 archd and dioc Gloucester

BRIMPTON parish 1564 Berks 6 miles se Newbury pop 443 archd Berks dioc Salisbury

BRIMPTON or BRUMPTON parish 1699 Somerset 2-3/4 miles sw Yeovil pop 100 archd Wells dioc Bath and Wells

BRIMSCOMB PORT hamlet partly in Stroud and Minchinhampton Gloucs Wesl Meth

BRIMSLADE extra parochial liberty Wilts pop 186

BRIMSTAGE township parish Bromborrow Ches pop 136

BRIND township with Newsham parish Wressel E R York

BRINDLE parish 1558 Lancs 4-3/4 miles ne Chorley pop 1,558 archd
and dioc Chester
BRINDLEY township parish Acton Ches pop 153
BRINDLEYS extra parochial liberty E R York pop 2
BRINGHURST parish 1640 Leics 2-1/4 miles nw Rockingham comp
chapelry Great Easton, townships Bringhurst and Drayton pop
782 archd Leicester dioc Lincoln
BRINGTON parish 1685 Hunts 5-1/4 miles nw Kimbolton pop 150
archd Huntingdon dioc Lincoln
BRINGTON parish 1558 co Northampton 7 miles nw Northampton pop
887 archd Northampton dioc Peterborough Part Bapt
BRININGHAM parish 1709 Norfolk 3-3/4 miles sw Holt pop 277
archd Norfolk dioc Norwich
BRINKBURN, HIGH WARD township parish Long Framlington Northumberland pop 123
BRINKBURN, LOW WARD township parish Long Framlington North-
umberland pop 69
BRINKBURN, SOUTH SIDE township parish Felton Northumberland
pop 43
BRINKHILL parish 1562 Lincs 6-1/2 miles nw Spilsby pop 116 archd
and dioc Lincoln Wesl Meth
BRINKLEY parish 1684 Cambs 3-1/2 miles sw Newmarket pop 335
archd and dioc Ely
BRINKLOW parish 1558 Warws 6 miles nw Rugby pop 949 archd
Coventry dioc Lichfield Wesl Meth
BRINKWORTH parish 1653 Wilts 4-1/4 miles nw Wootton Bassett
pop 1,417 archd Wilts dioc Salisbury
BRINNINGTON township parish Stockport Ches pop 3,987
BRINSOP parish 1695 Herefs 5-1/2 miles nw Hereford pop 112 archd
and dioc Hereford
BRINSWORTH township parish Rotherham W R York pop 227
BRINTON parish 1547 Norfolk 3-1/2 miles sw Holt pop 199 archd
and dioc Norwich
BRISCO or BIRKSCEUGH township parish St Cuthbert, Carlisle Cum-
berland pop 305
BRISLEY parish 1698 Norfolk 6 miles nw East Dereham pop 362
archd and dioc Norwich
BRISLINGTON parish 1566 Somerset 3 miles se Bristol pop 1,294
a donative dioc Bristol
BRISTOL, a city, All Saints 1560; St Augustine 1577; Christ Church
1538; St John 1558; Cathedral Church 1669 (Holy Trinity); St
Leonard 1689; St Nicholas 1538; St Mary le Port 1560; St Mary
Redcliffe 1559; St Thomas 1552; St Michael 1658; St Peter 1653;
St Stephen 1559; Temple or Holy Cross 1588; St Werburgh 1559;
St James 1559; St Paul 1794; St Philip-St Jacob 1575;St George
1756 between counties of Gloucs and Somerset 34 miles sw
Gloucester dioc of Bristol except St Thomas and St Mary Red-
cliffe which are in archd Bath dioc Bath and Wells Bapt, Soc of

Friends, Connection of Countess of Huntingdon, Indep, Prim and
Wesl Meth, Moravians, Scotch Seceders, Swedenborgians, Unit,
Roman Cath, Jews, French Protestants
BRISTON parish 1689 Norfolk 4-1/2 miles sw Holt pop 1,037 archd
and dioc Norwich Wesl Meth
BRITFORD parish 1573 Wilts 1-1/2 miles se Salisbury pop 838 pec
juris Dean and Chapter of Salisbury
BRITWELL liberty parish Burnham Bucks
BRITWELL SALOME co Oxford See BRIGHTWELL SALOME
BRIXHAM parish 1556 Devon 27-3/4 miles s Exeter archd Totnes
dioc Exeter Wesl Meth
BRIXTON parish 1668 Devon 2-1/4 miles se Earl's Plympton pop
796 archd Totnes dioc Exeter
BRIXTON parish 1644 Isle of Wight Hamps 6-1/4 miles sw Newport
pop 641 pec juris of incumbent
BRIXTON parish 1824 Surrey 4-1/2 miles sw London archd Surrey
dioc Winchester Indep, Wesl Meth
BRIXTON DEVERILL parish 1653 Wilts 4-3/4 miles s Warminster
pop 197 archd and dioc Salisbury
BRIXWORTH parish 1546 co Northampton 6-1/2 miles n Northampton
pop 973 archd Northampton dioc Peterborough Wesl Meth
BROAD BLUNSDON Wilts See BLUNSDON, BROAD
BROADCAR hamlet parish Shropham Norfolk
BROAD CHALK parish 1538 Wilts 5-3/4 miles Wilton pop 796 archd
and dioc Salisbury
BROAD CLYST Devon See CLYST, BROAD
BROADFIELD parish incl regs of Cottered Herts 3 miles nw Bunting-
ford pop 10 archd Huntingdon dioc Lincoln
BROADFIELD tything parish Wrington Somerset
BROADGATE extra parochial liberty Leics pop 10 5 miles nw Lei-
cester
BROADHEMBURY parish 1538 Devon 5 miles nw Honiton pop 849
archd and dioc Exeter
BROADHEMPSTON Devon See HEMPSTON, BROAD
BROADHOLME hamlet parish Thorney Notts pop 67
BROADMAYNE parish 1693 Dorset 3-1/2 miles se Dorchester pop
362 archd Dorset dioc Bristol
BROADOAK parish 1555 Cornwall 6-3/4 miles sw Liskeard pop 301
pec juris Dean and Chapter of Exeter
BROADSTAIRS sea port 1828 parish St Peter Isle of Thanet Kent
Wesl Meth
BROADWARD township parish Leominster Herefs pop 347
BROADWAS parish 1676 Worcs 6-1/2 miles w Worcester pop 196
archd and dioc Worcester
BROADWATER parish 1558 Sussex 1 mile Worthing pop 4,576 archd
and dioc Chichester
BROADWAY parish 1673 Dorset 3 miles nw Melcombe Regis pop 385
archd Dorset dioc Bristol

BROADWAY parish 1678 Somerset 2-1/2 miles nw Ilminster pop 450
arohd Taunton dioc Bath and Wells
BROADWAY parish 1539 Worcs 5-3/4 miles se Evesham pop 1,517
pec juris of Bishop of Worcester Indep, Wesl Meth, Roman Cath
BROADWELL parish 1697 Gloucs 1-1/2 miles ne Stow on the Wold
pop 334 arohd and dioc Gloucester
BROADWELL parish 1601 co Oxford 5-1/4 miles s Burford pop 793
archd and dioc Oxford
BROADWINSOR parish 1562 Dorset 3 miles nw Beaminster comp tythings Childhay, Deberford Drimpton and Little Winsor pop 1,570
archd Dorset dioc Bristol
BROADWOOD KELLY parish 1654 Devon 5-1/2 miles ne Hatherleigh
pop 388 archd Totnes dioc Exeter
BROADWOOD WIDGER Devon See BRADWOOD WIDGER
BROBURY parish 1786 Herefs 8-3/4 miles e Hay pop 62 archd and
dioc Hereford
BROCKDISH parish 1558 Norfolk 3-1/4 miles sw Harleston pop 482
archd Norfolk dioc Norwich Wesl Meth
BROCKENHURST chapelry 1629 parish Boldre Hamps 4-1/4 miles
nw Lymington pop 841
BROCKFORD hamlet parish Wetheringsett Suffolk
BROCKHALL parish 1561 co Northampton 5 miles e Daventry pop 58
archd Northampton dioc Peterborough
BROCKHAMPTON tything parish Buckland Newton Dorset pop 162
BROCKHAMPTON hamlet parish Bishops' Cleeve Gloucs pop 223
BROCKHAMPTON chapelry township Norton parish Bromyard Herefs
BROCKHAMPTON parish 1578 Herefs 6-3/4 miles n Ross pop 153
pec juris of Dean of Hereford
BROCKHAMPTON tything parish Newington co Oxford
BROCKHOLES chapelry with Grimsargh parish Preston Lancs
BROCKLEBANK township parish Westward Cumberland pop 603
BROCKLESBY parish 1672 Lincs 7 miles ne Caistor pop 162 archd
and dioc Lincoln
BROCKLEY, ST NICHOLAS parish 1696 Somerset 9-3/4 miles ne Ax-
bridge pop 171 archd Bath dioc Bath and Wells
BROCKLEY, ST ANDREW parish 1560 Suffolk 6-3/4 miles sw Bury
St Edmunds pop 319 archd Sudbury dioc Norwich
BROCKMANTON township parish Puddlestone Herefs
BROCKSFIELD township parish Embleton Northumberland pop 29
BROCKTHORP or BROOKTHROP parish 1730 Gloucs 3 miles nw
Painswick pop 193 archd and dioc Gloucester
BROCKTON township parish Baswich Staffs pop 232
BROCKWORTH parish 1559 Gloucs 4 miles se Gloucester pop 390
archd and dioc Gloucester
BRODSWORTH parish 1538 W R York 5-1/2 miles nw Doncaster comp
townships Brodsworth with Pickburn and Scansby pop 447 pec
juris of Archbishop of York
BROGDEN township parish Barnoldwick W R York pop 229

BROKENBOROUGH parish incl in Westport Wilts 1-3/4 miles nw
Malmesbury pop 283 archd Wilts dioc Salisbury
BROKENHAUGH township parish Warden Northumberland pop 171
BROMBLOW a quarter parish Worthen Shrops
BROMBORROW parish 1621 Ches 5-1/4 miles ne Great Neston pop
449 archd and dioc Chester
BROMBY township parish Frodingham Lincs pop 115
BROME, SOUTH or SOUTHBROOM chapelry 1572 parish All Cannings
Wilts
BROMEHOLME hamlet parish Bacton Norfolk
BROMESWELL parish 1638 Suffolk 3 miles ne Woodbridge pop 178
archd Suffolk dioc Norwich
BROMFIELD parish 1654 Cumberland 6 miles sw Wigton comp town-
ships Blencogo and Dundraw, chapelry Allonby and townships
Bromfield with Crookdake and Scales, Langrigg with Mealrigg
with West Newton pop 2,342 archd and dioc Carlisle
BROMFIELD parish 1559 Shrops 3 miles nw Ludlow comp chapelry
Halford, townships Bromfield and Dinehope pop 630 archd Salop
dioc Hereford
BROMFLEET township parish South Cave E R York pop 190 Wesl
Meth
BROMHALL township parish Wrenbury Ches pop 181
BROMHAM parish 1570 Beds 3-3/4 miles ne Bedford pop 324 archd
Bedford dioc Lincoln
BROMHAM parish 1560 Wilts 4 miles nw Devizes pop 1,556 archd
and dioc Salisbury Bapt, Wesl Meth
BROMLEY parish 1558 Kent 10 miles se London archd and dioc Ro-
chester Indep, Meth
BROMLEY township parish Eccleshall Staffs pop 36
BROMLEY ABBOT'S parish 1558 Staffs 12-1/2 miles e Stafford comp
Bagot's Bromley, township Bromley Hurst pop 1,621 archd Staf-
ford dioc Lichfield Indep
BROMLEY BAGOT'S liberty parish Abbot's Bromley Staffs
BROMLEY, GREAT parish 1559 Essex 4-1/2 miles sw Manningtree
pop 697 archd Colchester dioc London
BROMLEY HURST township parish Abbot's Bromley Staffs
BROMLEY, KING'S parish 1673 Staffs 5-1/2 miles ne Lichfield pop
629 pec of Prebendary of Alrewas and Weeford
BROMLEY ST LEONARDS parish 1622 Middlesex 1/2 mile s Stratford
le Bow pop 4,846 archd Middlesex dioc London Wesl Meth
BROMLEY, LITTLE parish 1538 Essex 3-1/2 miles sw Manningtree
pop 383 archd Colchester dioc London
BROMPTON hamlet parish Gillingham Kent Wesl Meth
BROMPTON hamlet parish Kensington Middlesex Indep
BROMPTON township with Riston parish Church Stoke Shrops pop 206
BROMPTON chapelry 1594 parish Northallerton N R York pop 1,510
Prim and Wesl Meth
BROMPTON parish 1584 N R York 8-1/2 miles sw Scarborough comp

townships Brompton, Sawdon, Troutsdale, Snainton pop 1,337 archd Cleveland dioc York Wesl Meth

BROMPTON PATRICK parish 1558 N R York 3-3/4 miles nw Bedale comp townships Brompton Patrick, Newton le Willows, part of Arrowthorne, part of chapelry Hunton pop 1,051 archd Richmond dioc Chester

BROMPTON RALPH parish 1557 Somerset 3-1/2 miles n Wiveliscombe pop 424 archd Taunton dioc Bath and Wells

BROMPTON REGIS parish 1690 Somerset 4-1/4 miles ne Dulverton pop 802 archd Taunton dioc Bath and Wells

BROMPTON UPON SWALE township parish Easby N R York pop 455

BROMSBERROW parish 1558 Gloucs 3-1/2 miles se Ledbury pop 337 archd and dioc Gloucester

BROMSGROVE parish 1590 Worcs 13 miles ne Worcester borough pop 8,612 archd and dioc Worcester

BROMWICH, CASTLE chapelry 1619 parish Aston Warws

BROMWICH, WEST parish 1608 Staffs 3 miles se Wednesbury pop 15,327 archd Stafford dioc Lichfield Wesl Meth, Prim Meth, Bapt, Indep, Kilhamites

BROMYARD parish 1538 Herefs 14 miles ne Hereford pop 2,938 archd and dioc Hereford Indep

BRON Y GARTH township with Weston Rhyn parish St Martin Shrops pop 1,083

BROOK parish 1695 Kent 5 miles ne Ashford pop 175 archd and dioc Canterbury

BROOK or GASPER hamlet parish Stourton Somerset pop 303

BROOK parish Isle of Wight 1653 Hamps 8-1/4 miles sw Newport pop 125 archd and dioc Winchester

BROOKE parish 1558 Norfolk 7-1/4 miles se Norwich pop 736 archd Norfolk dioc Norwich

BROOKE parish 1576 co Rutland 3 miles sw Oakham pop 95 archd Northampton dioc Peterborough

BROOK END hamlet parish Northill Beds

BROOK END hamlet parish Shenley Bucks pop 240

BROOK STREET hamlet parish South Weald Essex

BROOKSBY parish 1767 Leics 6 miles sw Melton Mowbray pop 10 archd Leicester dioc Lincoln

BROOKHAMPTON township parish Holdgate Shrops pop 83

BROOKHAMPTON township parish Ombersley Worcs

BROOKLAND parish 1558 Kent 5 miles nw New Romney pop 434 archd and dioc Canterbury

BROOKTHORPE parish Gloucs See BROCKTHORP

BROOM hamlet parish Southill Beds pop 257

BROOM township parish St Oswald, city of Durham co Durham pop 93

BROOM parish 1666 Staffs 4 miles s Stourbridge pop 110 archd and dioc Worcester

BROOME parish 1538 Norfolk 2-1/2 miles ne Bungay pop 504 archd Norfolk dioc Norwich

BROOME parish 1559 Suffolk 2-1/4 miles n Rye pop 377 archd Sudbury dioc Norwich

BROOMFIELD parish 1546 Essex 2-1/2 miles n Chelmsford pop 747 archd Essex dioc London

BROOMFIELD parish 1579 Kent 6 miles se Maidstone pop 129 archd and dioc Canterbury

BROOMFIELD parish 1630 Somerset 4-3/4 miles n Taunton pop 503 pec juris of Dean of Wells

BROOMHAUGH township parish By Well St Andrew Northumberland pop 115

BROOMHILL Sussex and Kent pop 80 forms part of town of New Romney

BROOMHOPE township parish Birtley Northumberland

BROOMLEY township parish Bywell St Peter Northumberland pop 345

BROOM PARK township parish Edlingham Northumberland pop 53

BROOMRIDGE hamlet parish Ford Northumberland

BROOMSTHORPE hamlet parish East Rudham Norfolk pop 13

BROSELEY parish 1570 Shrops 4 miles e Wenlock pop 4,299 archd Salop dioc Hereford Wesl Meth, Bapt

BROTHERICK township parish Warkworth Northumberland pop 4

BROTHERTOFT chapelry 1708 parish Kirton Lincs 4 miles nw Boston pop 123

BROTHERTON parish 1562 W R York 3/4 mile nw Ferrybridge comp township Brotherton, Bryome with Poole and Sutton in W R York pop 1,623 pec juris Dean and Chapter of York Wesl Meth

BROTTON parish 1663 N R York 6 miles ne Guisbrough comp township Brotton, Kilton and Skinningrove pop 470 archd Cleveland dioc York Wesl Meth

BROUGH hamlet with Shatton parish Hope Derbys pop 78

BROUGH or BURG, UNDER STAINMOOR parish 1556 Westm 8 miles se Appleby comp chapelry Stainmore, township Brough Sowerby and Hilbeck, part of township of Kaber pop 1,882 archd and dioc Carlisle Indep, Prim and Wesl Meth

BROUGH township parish Catterick N R York pop 78

BROUGH FERRY township parish Elloughton E R Yorks

BROUGH SOWERBY township parish Brough Westm pop 155

BROUGHALL township parish Whitchurch Shrops

BROUGHAM parish 1681 Westm 1-3/4 miles se Penrith pop 171 archd and dioc Carlisle

BROUGHTON hamlet parish Bierton Bucks

BROUGHTON parish 1720 Bucks 3 miles se Newport Pagnell pop 172 archd Buckingham dioc Lincoln

BROUGHTON parish 1572 Hunts 5-3/4 miles ne Huntingdon pop 411 archd Huntingdon dioc Lincoln

BROUGHTON chapelry 1653 parish Preston Lancs pop 620

BROUGHTON township parish Manchester Lancs pop 1,589

BROUGHTON parish 1538 Lincs 3 miles nw Glandford Bridge pop 915

archd Stow dioc Lincoln
BROUGHTON parish 1560 co Northampton 2-3/4 miles sw Kettering
pop 533 archd Northampton dioc Peterborough
BROUGHTON parish 1683 co Oxford 3 miles sw Banbury pop 538
archd and dioc Oxford
BROUGHTON parish 1705 Shrops 7-1/2 miles n Shrewsbury pop 157
archd Salop dioc Lichfield
BROUGHTON parish 1639 Hamps 3 miles sw Stockbridge pop 897
archd and dioc Winchester Bapt, Indep, Wesl Meth
BROUGHTON chapelry 1907 parish Eccleshall Staffs pop 25 Prebend-
ary of Eccleshall
BROUGHTON township parish Appleton le Street N R York pop 111
Wesl Meth
BROUGHTON ASTLEY parish 1581 Leics 5-1/2 miles nw Lutterworth
comp townships Broughton Astley, Prime Thorp and Sutton in the
Elms pop 726 archd Leicester dioc Lincoln
BROUGHTON BRANT parish 1710 Lincs 8 miles e Newark pop 627
archd Stow dioc Lincoln Wesl Meth
BROUGHTON, CHURCH parish 1538 Derbys 8-1/2 miles e Uttoxeter
pop 521 archd Derby dioc Lichfield
BROUGHTON, EAST chapelry parish Cartmel Lancs pop 416
BROUGHTON, GIFFORD parish 1665 Wilts 2 miles w Melksham pop
735 archd and dioc Salisbury Part Bapt
BROUGHTON, GREAT township parish Bridekirk Cumberland pop 523
BROUGHTON, GREAT and LITTLE township parish Kirkby in Cleve-
land N R York pop 287
BROUGHTON HACKET parish 1761 Worcs 5-1/2 miles e Worcester
pop 153 archd and dioc Worcester
BROUGHTON IN AREDALE or BOLTON IN CRAVEN parish 1689 W
R York 3-1/2 miles sw Skipton pop 407 archd and dioc York
BROUGHTON IN FURNESS chapelry 1634 parish Kirkby Ireleth Lancs
BROUGHTON, LITTLE township parish Bridekirk Cumberland pop
297 Soc of Friends, Anabapt
BROUGHTON, NETHER parish 1572 Leics 5-3/4 miles nw Melton
Mowbray pop 415 archd Leicester dioc Lincoln
BROUGHTON POGGS or POGIS parish 1557 co Oxford 5-1/4 miles
sw Burford pop 158 archd and dioc Oxford
BROUGHTON SULNEY parish 1571 Notts 12-1/4 miles se Nottingham
pop 344 archd Nottingham dioc York
BROWN CANDOVER See CANDOVER BROWN
BROWNSHALL or BROWNSELL LANE hamlet parish Bishop's
Caundle Dorset
BROWNSOVER chapelry 1593 parish Clifton Warws pop 90
BROXA township parish Hackness N R York pop 74
BROXBURNE parish 1688 Herts 1-3/4 miles s Hodesdon pop 2,144
archd Middlesex dioc London
BROXHOLME parish 1643 Lincs 6-3/4 miles nw Lincoln pop 137
archd Stow dioc Lincoln

BROXTED parish 1654 Essex 3 miles sw Thaxted pop 694 archd Middlesex dioc London
BROXTON township parish Malpas Ches pop 454
BROXTOW chapelry parish Bilborough Notts
BRUEN STAPLEFORD Ches See STAPLEFORD, BRUEN
BRUERA See CHURTON HEATH
BRUERN extra parochial liberty co Oxford pop 41
BRUISYARD parish 1565 Suffolk 3-1/2 miles ne Framlingham pop 292 archd Suffolk dioc Norwich
BRUMHILL hamlet parish Weeting Norfolk
BRUMSTEAD parish 1560 Norfolk 6-3/4 miles se North Walsham pop 107 archd Norfolk dioc Norwich
BRUNDALL parish 1563 Norfolk 6 miles se Norwich pop 63 archd and dioc Norwich
BRUNDISH parish 1562 Suffolk 4-1/2 miles nw Framlingham pop 478 archd Suffolk dioc Norwich
BRUNDON Essex See BALLINGDON
BRUNSLOW township parish Edgton Shrops
BRUNSTOCK township parish Crosby upon Eden Cumberland pop 108
BRUNTINGTHORPE parish 1550 Leics 5-1/4 miles ne Lutterworth pop 382 archd Leicester dioc Lincoln
BRUNTON, EAST township parish Gosforth Northumberland pop 268
BRUNTON, WEST township parish Gosforth Northumberland pop 118
BRUSHFIELD township parish Bakewell Derbys pop 44
BRUSHFORD parish 1694 Devon 5-1/4 miles sw Chulmleigh pop 136 archd Barnstaple dioc Exeter
BRUSHFORD parish 1558 Somerset 1-3/4 miles se Dulverton pop 351 archd Taunton dioc Bath
BRUTON parish 1554 Somerset 12 miles se Wells pop 2,223 archd Wells dioc Bath and Wells Indep
BRUTON, HIGH and LOW township parish Embleton Northumberland pop 62
BRYANSTON parish 1598 Dorset 1-1/2 miles ne Blandford Forum pop 155 archd Dorset dioc Bristol
BRYANTS PIDDLE tything parish Aff Piddle Dorset
BRYMTON See BRIMPTON Somerset
BRYNGWYN parish 1643 co Monmouth 6-1/2 miles sw Monmouth pop 300 archd and dioc Llandaff
BRYNING township parish Kirkham Lancs pop 164
BUBBENHALL parish 1698 Warws 6 miles se Coventry pop 233 pec juris Bishop of Lichfield
BUBNELL township parish Bakewell Derbys
BUBWITH parish 1623 E R York 7 miles nw Howden comp townships Breighton, Bubwith, Foggathorpe, Gribthorpe with Willitoft, Harlthorpe and Spaldington pop 1,358 archd East Riding dioc York Wesl Meth
BUCKBY, LONG parish 1583 co Northampton 5 miles ne Daventry pop 2,978 archd Northampton dioc Peterborough Part Bapt

BUCKDEN parish 1559 Hunts 4-1/2 miles sw Huntingdon pop 1,095
pec juris of Bishop of Lincoln Wesl Meth

BUCKDEN township parish Arncliffe W R York pop 309

BUCKENHAM parish 1714 Norfolk 5 miles sw Acle pop 49 archd and
dioc Norwich

BUCKENHAM, NEW parish 1538 Norfolk 15-1/2 miles sw Norwich
pop 795 archd Norfolk dioc Norwich Meth

BUCKENHAM, OLD parish 1560 Norfolk 3 miles se Attleburgh pop
1,201 archd Norfolk dioc Norwich Sandemanians

BUCKENHAM, PARVA parish no regs Norfolk 6-1/2 miles sw Watton pop 51 archd Norfolk dioc Norwich

BUCKENHILL township parish Woolhope Herefs

BUCKERELL parish 1653 Devon 3 miles w Honiton pop 304 archd
and dioc Exeter

BUCKFASTLEIGH parish 1602 Devon 2-3/4 miles sw Ashburton pop
2,445 archd Totnes dioc Exeter Indep, Wesl Meth

BUCKHOLT FARM extra parochial liberty Hamps pop 8

BUCKHORN WESTON parish 1678 Dorset 8 miles nw Shaftesbury pop
403 archd Dorset dioc Bristol

BUCKHOW BANK township parish Dalston Cumberland pop 668

BUCKINGHAM parish 1559 Bucks borough sep juris 17 miles nw
Aylesbury comp chapelry Gawcott, hamlets Bourton, Bourtonhold
and Lenborough, precinct of Prebend End pop 3,610 pec juris of
Dean and Chapter of Lincoln Bapt, Soc of Friends, Indep, Wesl
Meth, Presb

BUCKLAND parish 1691 Berks 4-1/4 miles ne Great Farrington pop
946 archd Berks dioc Salisbury Bapt

BUCKLAND parish 1657 Bucks 3 miles nw Tring pop 510 pec of
Bierton Wesl Meth

BUCKLAND parish 1539 Gloucs 6 miles sw Chipping Campden pop
403 archd and dioc Gloucester

BUCKLAND parish 1659 Herts 2 miles sw Barkway pop 373 archd
Middlesex dioc London

BUCKLAND parish 1580 Kent 1-3/4 miles nw Dover pop 834 pec juris
of Bishop of Canterbury Wesl Meth

BUCKLAND parish Kent 3 miles nw Faversham pop 15 archd and
dioc Canterbury

BUCKLAND parish 1538 Somerset 6 miles sw Ilminster pop 646
archd Taunton dioc Bath and Wells

BUCKLAND parish 1560 Surrey 2-1/4 miles w Reigate pop 344 archd
Surrey dioc Winchester

BUCKLAND BREWER parish 1603 Devon 4-3/4 miles nw Great Torrington pop 1,096 archd Barnstaple dioc Exeter

BUCKLAND DINHAM parish 1569 Somerset 2-1/2 miles nw Frome
pop 532 pec juris of Prebendary of Buckland Denham Wesl Meth

BUCKLAND, EAST parish 1684 Devon 8 miles se Barnstaple pop 173
archd Barnstaple dioc Exeter Wesl Meth

BUCKLAND EGG parish 1653 Devon 3 miles ne Plymouth pop 1,117 archd Totnes dioc Exeter Wesl Meth

BUCKLAND FILLEIGH parish 1622 Devon 6-1/2 miles nw Hatherleigh pop 317 archd Barnstaple dioc Exeter

BUCKLAND IN THE MOOR parish 1693 Devon 3-1/2 miles nw Ashburton pop 139 pec juris Dean and Chapter of Exeter

BUCKLAND MONARCHORUM parish 1538 Devon 4 miles se Tavistock pop 1,274 archd Totnes dioc Exeter

BUCKLAND NEWTON parish 1568 Dorset 10-1/4 miles n Dorchester comp tythings Brockhampton with Knowle, Buckland Newton, Duntish, Mintern Parva and Plush pop 786 archd Dorset dioc Bristol

BUCKLAND RIPERS parish 1675 Dorset 3-1/2 miles nw Melcombe Regis pop 115 archd Dorset dioc Bristol

BUCKLAND TOUTSAINTS chapelry parish Loddiswell Devon pop 46

BUCKLAND, WEST parish 1625 Devon 7 miles se Barnstaple pop 273 archd Barnstaple dioc Exeter

BUCKLAND, WEST parish 1538 Somerset 2-3/4 miles e Wellington pop 793 archd Taunton dioc Bath and Wells Wesl Meth

BUCKLEBURY parish 1538 Berks 7-1/2 miles ne Newbury pop 1,300 archd Berks dioc Salisbury

BUCKLESHAM parish 1678 Suffolk 5 miles se Ipswich pop 274 archd Suffolk dioc Norwich

BUCKLEY or BULKELEY township parish Malpas Ches pop 185

BUCKMINSTER parish 1538 Leics 9-1/4 miles ne Melton Mowbray pop 842 archd Leicester dioc Lincoln

BUCKNALL parish 1708 Lincs 6-3/4 miles sw Horncastle pop 276 archd and dioc Lincoln

BUCKNALL parish 1758 Staffs 1-1/2 miles e Hanley pop 574 archd Stafford dioc Lichfield

BUCKNELL parish 1700 co Oxford 2-1/2 miles nw Bicester pop 274 archd and dioc Oxford

BUCKNELL parish 1598 Shrops 3-1/4 miles ne Knighton pop 465 archd Salop dioc Hereford

BUCKTHORPE See BUGTHORPE

BUCKTON township parish Bridlington E R York pop 171

BUCKWORTH parish 1664 Hunts 7 miles nw Huntingdon pop 136 archd Huntingdon dioc Lincoln

BUDBROOK parish 1539 Warws 1-1/2 miles nw Warwick pop 467 archd and dioc Worcester

BUDBY township parish Edwinstow Notts pop 139

BUDE seaport parish Stratton Cornwall Wesl Meth

BUDEAUX or BUDOCK, ST parish 1538 Devon 4-1/4 miles nw Plymouth pop 669 archd Totnes dioc Exeter

BUDLE township parish Bambrough Northumberland pop 103

BUDLEIGH, EAST parish 1555 Devon 4-1/2 miles sw Sidmouth pop 2,044 archd and dioc Exeter Wesl Meth

BUDOCK parish 1603 Cornwall 2 miles sw Falmouth pop 1,797 pec juris Bishop of Exeter Indep, Wesl Meth, Roman Cath

BUDVILLE, LANGFORD Somerset See LANGFORD, BUDVILLE

BUDWORTH, GREAT parish 1558 Ches 3 miles ne Northwich comp chapelry Hartford, townships Castle Northwich and Winnington, chapelries Northwich, Nether Peover and Witton with Twambrook, townships Allostock, Birches, Hulse, Lack Dennis, Lostock Graham, a portion of Rudheath, chapelries Aston by Budworth, Little Leigh and Stretton, townships Anderton, Antrobus, Barnton, Bartington, Great Budworth, Cogshall, Comberbach, Crowley, Dutton, Hull, with Appleton, Marbury, Marston, Little Peover, Pickmere, Plumley, Seven Oaks, Tabley, Inferior, Lower Whitley, Over Whitley, and Wincham pop 15,955 archd and dioc Chester

BUDWORTH, LITTLE parish 1561 Ches 3-3/4 miles ne Tarporley pop 621 archd and dioc Chester

BUERTON township parish Aldford Ches pop 59

BUERTON township parish Audlem Ches pop 464

BUGBROOKE parish 1657 co Northampton 5-3/4 miles sw Northampton pop 865 archd Northampton dioc Peterborough Part Bapt

BUGLAWTON township parish Astbury Ches pop 2,087 Wesl Meth

BUGLEY hamlet parish Gillingham Dorset

BUGTHORPE parish 1661 E R York 7-1/2 miles nw Pockington pop 300 pec juris of Prebendary of Bugthorpe

BUILDWAS parish 1659 Shrops 4 miles nw Much Wenlock pop 240 pec juris of Buildwas

BULBRIDGE parish incl regs of Wilton Wilts 3/4 mile s Wilton archd and dioc Salisbury

BULBY chapelry parish Irnham Lincs pop 176

BULCOTE chapelry parish Burton Joyce Notts pop 142

BULFORD parish 1608 Wilts 2 miles ne Amesbury pop 290 archd and dioc Salisbury

BULK township parish Lancaster Lancs pop 102

BULKINGTON parish 1606 Warws 4-1/2 miles se Nuneaton comp hamlets Barnacle, Bramcott, Marston Jabbett, Ryton and Weston pop 1,792 archd Coventry dioc Lichfield

BULKINGTON tything parish Keevil Wilts pop 249 Wesl Meth

BULKWORTHY chapelry parish Buckland Brewer 1714 Devon pop 198

BULLER'S GREEN township parish Morpeth Northumberland pop 203

BULLEY chapelry 1673 parish Churcham Gloucs pop 216

BULLINGHAM, LOWER hamlet parish Upper Bullingham Herefs pop 277

BULLINGHAM, UPPER and LOWER parish 1682 Herefs 2 miles s Hereford pop 397 prebend of Bullinghope in juris of Consistory Court of Dean of Hereford

BULLINGTON chapelry parish Goltho Lincs pop 50

BULLINGTON parish 1725 Hamps 5 miles sw Whitchurch pop 189 archd and dioc Winchester

BULLOCK'S HALL township parish Warkworth Northumberland pop 14

BULMER parish 1559 Essex 2 miles sw Sudbury pop 706 archd Middlesex dioc London

BULMER parish 1571 N R York 7 miles sw New Malton comp chapelry Henderskelf, townships Bulmer and Welburn pop 901 archd Cleveland dioc York

BULPHAN parish 1722 Essex 3 miles nw Horndon on the Hill pop 236 archd Essex dioc London

BULVERHITHE parish Bexhill Sussex pop 51

BULWELL parish 1621 Notts 3-3/4 miles nw Hottingham pop 2,611 archd Nottingham dioc York Wesl Meth

BULWICK parish 1563 co Northampton 6-1/2 miles ne Rockingham pop 482 archd Northampton dioc Peterborough

BUMPSTEAD HELION parish 1558 Essex 8-3/4 miles ne Thaxted pop 847 archd Colchester dioc London

BUMPSTEAD, STEEPLE parish 1676 Essex 8-3/4 miles nw Castle Hedingham pop 1,080 archd Middlesex dioc London

BUNBURY parish 1559 Ches 3-1/2 miles se Tarporley comp chapelry Burwardsley, townships Alpraham, Beeston, Bunbury, Calveley, Haughton, Peckforton, Ridley, Spurstow, Tilston Fernall, Tiverton and Wardley pop 4,373 archd and dioc Chester Wesl Meth

BUNCTON chapelry parish Ashington Sussex

BUNDLEY parish 1734 Devon 6-3/4 miles sw Chulmeigh pop 339 archd Barnstaple dioc Exeter

BUNGAY market town 1538 Suffolk 40 miles ne Ipswich, Bungay comp parishes St Mary 1538, Holy Trinity 1557 archd Suffolk dioc Norwich Wesl Meth, Presb, Roman Cath

BUNNY parish 1556 Notts 7-1/4 miles s Nottingham pop 371 archd Nottingham dioc York

BUNTINGFORD chapelry parishes Aspenden, Layston, Throcking and Wyddiall Herts Soc of Friends, Indep

BUNWELL parish 1551 Norfolk 3 miles ne New Buckenham pop 947 archd Norfolk dioc Norwich

BURASTON chapelry with Whetmore parish Burford Shrops

BURBAGE chapelry 1562 parish Aston Flamville Leics pop 1,618 Wesl Meth

BURBAGE parish 1561 Wilts 4-3/4 miles ne Pewsey pop 1,448 pec juris of Dean of Salisbury, the Prebendary of Hurtborne and Burbage

BURCOMBE, SOUTH parish 1682 Wilts 1-3/4 miles sw Wilton pop 419 archd and dioc Salisbury

BURCOTT hamlet parish Dorchester co Oxford pop 163

BURDON hamlet parish High Hampton Devon

BURDON township parish Bishop Wearmouth co Durham pop 162

BURDON, GREAT township parish Haughton le Skerne co Durham pop 102

BURE tything parish Christchurch Hamps

BURES parish 1538 partly in Essex chiefly in Suffolk 5 miles se Sudbury pop 1,559 archd Sudbury dioc Norwich

BURES, MOUNT parish 1540 Essex 6 miles ne Halstead pop 262 archd Colchester dioc London

BURFORD, parish 1612 co Oxford 18-1/2 miles nw Oxford pop 1,866
    archd and dioc Oxford Bapt, Soc of Friends, Wesl Meth
BURFORD parish 1558 Shrops 1-1/2 miles sw Tenbury comp chapel-
    ries Buraston with Whetmore, Nash with Tilsop and Weston and
    Whitton, township Burford pop 1,086 archd Salop dioc Hereford
BURGATE parish 1560 Suffolk 4-1/2 miles nw Eye pop 243 archd
    Sudbury dioc Norwich
BURGH NEXT AYLSHAM parish 1563 Norfolk 2 miles se Aylsham
    pop 247 archd and dioc Norwich
BURGH parish 1739 Norfolk 3-3/4 miles ne Acle pop 491 archd and
    dioc Norwich
BURGH Norfolk See WHEATACRE BURGH
BURGH parish 1547 Suffolk 3-3/4 miles nw Woodbridge pop 252 archd
    Suffolk dioc Norwich
BURGH APTON parish 1556 Norfolk 8-1/2 miles se Norwich pop 509
    archd and dioc Norwich
BURGH, CASTLE parish 1694 Suffolk 4 miles sw Great Yarmouth
    pop 270 archd Suffolk dioc Norwich
BURGH IN THE MARSH parish 1538 Lincs 7-1/2 miles se Spilsby
    pop 906 archd and dioc Lincoln
BURGH, LITTLE parish 1594 Norfolk 4-1/2 miles sw Holt archd and
    dioc Norwich
BURGH MATTISHALL parish 1653 Norfolk 5-1/2 miles se East Dere-
    ham pop 210 archd Suffolk dioc Norwich Wesl Meth
BURGH, SOUTH parish 1558 Norfolk 2-1/2 miles nw Hingham pop
    261 archd Norfolk dioc Norwich
BURGH UPON BAINE parish 1735 Lincs 7 miles w Louth pop 131
    archd and dioc Lincoln
BURGH UPON THE SANDS parish 1695 Cumberland comp townships
    Boustead Hill, Burgh upon the Sands or Burgh Head, Longburgh,
    Moorhouse and Westend pop 1,372 5-1/2 miles nw Carlisle
    archd and dioc Carlisle
BURGH WALLIS parish 1597 W R York 7-1/4 miles nw Doncaster
    pop 223 archd and dioc York
BURGHAM tything parish Worplesdon Surrey
BURGHCLERE parish 1559 Hamps 7-1/2 miles n Whitchurch pop 802
BURGHFIELD parish 1559 Berks 4-1/2 miles sw Reading pop 965
    archd Berks dioc Salisbury
BURGHILL parish 1655 Herefs 4 miles nw Hereford pop 856 archd
    and dioc Hereford
BURHAM parish 1626 Kent 1-3/4 miles nw Aylesford pop 287 archd
    and dioc Rochester
BURIAN, ST or BURYAN ST parish 1653 Cornwall 6 miles sw Pen-
    zance pop 1,707 a peculiar
BURITON parish 1678 Hamps 2-1/4 miles sw Petersfield pop 822
    archd and dioc Winchester
BURLAND township parish Acton Ches pop 515
BURLATON chapelry parish Sheriff Hales Staffs

BURLESCOMBE parish 1579 Devon 4-1/2 miles sw Wellington comp tythings Burlescombe, Westleigh, South Appledore and Ayshford pop 999 archd and dioc Exeter

BURLESTONE parish 1692 Dorset 6 miles ne Dorchester pop 67 archd Dorset dioc Bristol

BURLEY on the HILL parish 1577 co Rutland 2 miles ne Oakham pop 232 archd Northampton dioc Peterborough

BURLEY tything parish Ringwood Hamps pop 341

BURLEY chapelry parish St Peter Leeds W R York

BURLEY chapelry 1774 parish Otley W R York pop 1,448 archd and dioc York Wesl Meth

BURLEY DAM chapelry 1770 parish Acton Ches

BURLEY LODGE extra parochial liberty Hamps pop 33

BURLINGHAM, ST ANDREW parish 1538 Norfolk 2-1/2 miles sw Acle pop 225 archd Norfolk dioc Norwich

BURLINGHAM, ST EDMUND parish 1554 Norfolk 3 miles sw Acle archd Norfolk dioc Norwich

BURLINGHAM, ST PETER parish 1560 Norfolk 2-1/2 miles sw Acle pop 102 archd Norfolk dioc Norwich

BURMARSH parish 1572 Kent 4-1/2 miles sw Hythe pop 105 archd and dioc Canterbury

BURMINGTON chapelry 1582 parish Wolford Warws pop 205

BURN township parish Brayton W R York pop 244

BURNAGE township parish Manchester Lancs pop 507

BURNASTON hamlet parish Etwall Derbys pop 134

BURNBY parish 1584 E R York 2-3/4 miles se Pocklington pop 93 archd East Riding dioc York

BURNESIDE chapelry 1717 parish Kendall Westm comp townships Strickland Ketle and Strickland Roger pop 712

BURNESTON parish 1566 N R York 4 miles se Bedale comp chapelry Leeming with Exelby and Newton, townships Burneston, Carthorp Gatenby and Theakstone pop 1,430 archd Richmond dioc Chester Wesl Meth

BURNETT parish 1749 Somerset 2 miles se Keynsham pop 82 archd Bath dioc Bath and Wells

BURNHAM parish 1561 Bucks 3-3/4 miles nw Eton comp chapelry Lower Boveny, liberties Upper Boveny, Britwell, East Burnham, Cippenham, Toun and Wood pop 2,137 archd Buckingham dioc Lincoln Dissenters

BURNHAM parish 1559 Essex 19-1/2 miles se Chelmsford pop 1,393 archd Essex dioc London Wesl Meth

BURNHAM or BURNHAM on the SEA parish 1630 Somerset 9-1/4 miles sw Axbridge pop 1,113 archd Wells dioc Bath and Wells

BURNHAM DEEPDALE parish 1539 Norfolk 2-1/4 miles nw Burnham Westgate pop 95 archd Norfolk dioc Norwich

BURNHAM, EAST liberty parish Burnham Bucks

BURNHAM MARKET or BURNHAM, WEST GATE parish 1538 Norfolk 36-1/2 miles nw Norwich pop 1,022 archd Norfolk dioc Norwich

Indep
BURNHAM NORTON parish 1559 Norfolk 1-1/4 miles n Burnham
Westgate pop 183 archd Norfolk dioc Norwich
BURNHAM OVERY parish 1653 Norfolk 1-1/2 miles ne Burnham
Westgate pop 610 archd Norfolk dioc Norwich
BURNHAM SUTTON parish 1563 Norfolk 3/4 mile se Burnham West-
gate archd Norfolk dioc Norwich
BURNHAM THORPE parish 1559 Norfolk 1-1/2 miles se Burnham
Westgate pop 363 archd Norfolk dioc Norwich
BURNHAM ULPH parish incl with Burnham Sutton Norfolk 3/4 mile
ne Burnham Westgate pop 364 archd Norfolk dioc Norwich
BURNISTON township parish Scalby N R York pop 317 Wesl Meth
BURNLEY chapelry 1562 parish Whalley Lancs pop 7,551 archd and
dioc Chester Bapt, Indep, Wesl Meth, Roman Cath
BURNOP township parish Lanchester co Durham pop 133 Wesl Meth
BURNSALL parish 1559 N R York 9-1/2 miles ne Skipton comp chap-
elries Coniston with Kilnsay and Rilsdon, townships Appletree-
wick, Burnsall with Thorn sub Montem, Graco, Hartlington and
Hetton with Bordley pop 1,385 archd and dioc York
BURNTWOOD chapelry 1820 parish St Michael, Lichfield Staffs pop
432 pec juris Dean and Chapter of Lichfield
BURPHAM parish 1653 Sussex 2-1/2 miles ne Arundel pop 273 archd
and dioc Chichester
BURRALS township parish Appleby St Lawrence Westm pop 90
BURREL township with Cowling parish Bedale N R York pop 139
BURRINGHAM, EAST chapelry parish Bottesford Lincs pop 410
Wesl Meth
BURRINGTON parish 1592 Devon 4 miles nw Chulmleigh pop 987
archd Barnstaple dioc Exeter
BURRINGTON parish 1541 Herefs 4-1/2 miles sw Ludlow pop 230
archd Salop dioc Hereford
BURRINGTON parish 1687 Somerset 5-1/2 miles nw Axbridge pop
579 archd Bath dioc Bath and Wells
BURROUGH parish 1612 Leics 5-1/2 miles s Melton Mowbray pop
173 archd Leicester dioc Lincoln
BURROUGH GREEN parish 1571 Cambs 5 miles s Newmarket pop
421 archd and dioc Ely
BURROW township parish Tunstall Lancs pop 306
BURROW ASH hamlet parish Ockbrook Derbys
BURSCOUGH township parish Ormskirk Lancs pop 2,244
BURSLEDON chapelry 1660 parish Hound Hamps pop 503
BURSLEM parish 1639 Staffs 3 miles nw Newcastle pop 12,714 archd
Stafford dioc Lichfield Bapt, Indep, Prim and Wesl Meth, New
Connection, Roman Cath
BURSTALL parish 1542 Suffolk 4-1/2 miles w Ipswich pop 199 archd
Suffolk dioc Norwich
BURSTEAD, GREAT parish 1558 Essex 2 miles se Billericay pop
1,977 archd Essex dioc London

BURSTEAD, LITTLE parish 1681 Essex 2-1/4 miles sw Billericay pop 204 archd Essex dioc London

BURSTOCK parish 1658 Dorset 4-1/4 miles nw Beaminster pop 261 archd Dorset dioc Bristol

BURSTON parish 1653 Norfolk 2-3/4 miles ne Diss pop 377 archd Norfolk dioc Norwich

BURSTOW parish 1547 Surrey 8 miles se Reigate pop 736 deanery of Croydon pec juris of Archbishop of Canterbury

BURSTWICK parish 1747 E R York 3 miles se Hedon comp townships Burstwick and Ryhill with Camerton pop 669 archd East Riding dioc York

BURTHOLME township parish Lanercost Abbey Cumberland pop 239

BURTLE chapelry 1839 parishes of Edington and Moorlinch

BURTHOPE Gloucs See EAST LEACH MARTIN

BURTON township parish Tarvin Ches pop 84

BURTON parish 1538 Ches 2-1/2 miles se Great Neston comp townships Burton and Puddington pop 458 archd and dioc Chester

BURTON township parish Bambrough Northumberland pop 76

BURTON chapelry parish Much Wenlock Shrops

BURTON tything parish Christchurch Hamps

BURTON or BODEKTON parish 1559 Sussex 3-1/2 miles sw Petworth pop 7 archd and dioc Chichester Roman Cath

BURTON hamlet parish Warcop Westm

BURTON township with Walden parish Aysgarth N R York pop 545 Wesl Meth

BURTON AGNES parish 1700 E R York 6-1/2 miles ne Great Driffield comp townships Burton Agnes, Gransmoor, Haisthorp and Thornholm pop 653 archd East Riding dioc York

BURTON BISHOP parish 1562 E R York 2-1/2 miles w Beverley pop 556 archd East Riding dioc York Part Bapt

BURTON BLACK chapelry parish Thornton in Lonsdale W R York pop 711

BURTON BRADSTOCK parish 1614 Dorset 2-3/4 miles se Bridport pop 1,068 archd Dorset dioc Bristol

BURTON BY LINCOLN parish 1558 Lincs 2-1/4 miles nw Lincoln pop 177 archd Stow dioc Lincoln

BURTON, CHERRY parish 1561 E R York 3 miles nw Beverly pop 447 archd East Riding dioc York

BURTON COGGLES parish 1564 Lincs 1-3/4 miles nw Corby pop 246 archd and dioc Lincoln

BURTON CONSTABLE township parish Fingall N R York pop 257

BURTON DASSETT parish 1660 Warws 5-1/4 miles e Kington pop 673 archd Coventry dioc Lichfield

BURTON EXTRA township parish Burton upon Trent Staffs pop 910

BURTON FLEMING or NORTH parish 1538 E R York 3-1/4 miles sw Hunmanby pop 414 archd East Riding dioc York Wesl Meth

BURTON GATE parish 1575 Lincs 5 miles se Gainsborough pop 110 archd Stow dioc Lincoln

BURTON HASTINGS parish 1574 Warws 4-1/4 miles se Nuneaton pop
253 archd Coventry dioc Lichfield

BURTON HILL tything parish Malmesbury Wilts pop 165

BURTON IN KENDAL parish 1653 Lancs 34-1/2 miles sw Appleby
comp Burton in Kendal, township Holme in Westm, township
Dalton pop 1,931 archd Richmond dioc Chester Indep

BURTON JOYCE parish 1559 Notts 5 miles ne Nottingham pop 676
archd Notthingham dioc York

BURTON KIRK parish 1543 W R York 5-1/2 miles se Huddersfield
comp chapelry Cumberworth Half, townships Cartworth, Foulston,
Hepworth, Kirk Burton, Shelley, Shepley, Thurstonland and Wooldale pop 15,731 archd East Riding dioc York Wesl Meth

BURTON LATIMER parish 1538 co Northampton 3 miles se Kettering
pop 995 archd Northampton dioc Peterborough

BURTON LAZARS chapelry 1718 parish Melton Mowbray Leics pop
258

BURTON LEONARD parish 1672 E R and W R York 5 miles nw Knaresborough pop 553 pec juris Dean and Chapter of York Wesl Meth

BURTON, LONG parish 1590 Dorset 3 miles se Sherborne pop 361
pec juris Dean of Salisbury

BURTON ON THE WOLDS township parish Prestwould Leics pop 411
Wesl Meth

BURTON OVERY parish 1575 Leics 7-1/2 miles se Leicester pop
418 archd Leicester dioc Lincoln

BURTON PEDWARDINE parish 1736 Lincs 4-1/2 miles se Sleaford
pop 106 archd and dioc Lincoln

BURTON PIDSEA parish 1708 E R York 11-1/2 miles ne Kingston
upon Hull pop 387 pec juris Dean and Chapter of York Wesl Meth

BURTON SALMON township parish Monk Fryston W R York pop 142

BURTON UPON STATHER parish 1567 Lincs 35-1/2 miles nw Lincoln pop 760 archd Stow dioc Lincoln

BURTON UPON TRENT parish 1539 Staffs 24 miles e Stafford comp
townships Branson, Burton Extra Horninglow and Stretton, chapelry of Chilcote and township of Winshill Derbys pop 6,988 pec
juris of Lord of Manor Gen and Part Bapt, Indep, Prim and Wesl
Meth

BURTON UPON URE township parish Masham N R York pop 254

BURTON, WEST parish 1602 Notts 3-1/4 miles sw Gainsborough pop
40 archd Nottingham dioc York

BURTONWOOD chapelry 1688 parish Warrington Lancs pop 944 archd
and dioc Chester

BURWARDSLEY chapelry 1813 parish Bunbury Ches pop 394

BURWARTON parish 1575 Shrops 9-3/4 miles ne Ludlow pop 112
archd Salop dioc Hereford

BURWASH parish 1558 Sussex 6 miles se Wadhurst pop 1,966 archd
Lewes dioc Chichester

BURWELL parish 1562 Cambs 4 miles nw Newmarket pop 1,668
archd Sudbury dioc Norwich

BURWELL parish 1586 Lincs 5-1/2 miles se Louth pop 181 archd
and dioc Lincoln
BURWELL tything parish Hambledon Hamps
BURY parish 1561 Hunts 1 miles s Ramsey pop 358 archd Huntingdon
dioc Lincoln
BURY parish 1590 Lancs borough 9 miles nw Manchester comp chap-
elry Heap, Higher Tottington and Lower Tottington, township El-
ton and Walmersley, Coupe Lench with Newhallhey and Hall Carr,
Henheads and Musbury pop 47,829 archd and dioc Chester Indep,
Prim and Wesl Meth, New Connection Meth, Presb, Unit, Roman
Cath
BURY hamlet parish Brompton Regis Somerset
BURY parish 1560 Sussex 4 miles n Arundel pop 547 archd and dioc
Chichester
BURY ST EDMUNDS market town 1538 Suffolk 26-1/2 miles nw Ips-
wich pop 11,436 Excl juris St Mary 1548, St James 1538 Indep,
Bapt, Soc of Friends, Meth, Unit, Roman Cath
BURYAN, ST Cornwall See BURIAN
BURYTHORP parish 1720 E R York 4-3/4 miles s New Malton pop
211 archd East Riding dioc York Wesl Meth
BUSBY, GREAT township parish Stokesley N R York pop 106
BUSCOT or BURWASCOT parish 1676 Berks 1 mile se Lechlande
pop 416 archd Berks dioc Salisbury
BUSHBURY parish 1747 Staffs 2-3/4 miles ne Wolverhampton comp
township Essington, hamlet Moseley pop 1,275 archd Stafford
dioc Lichfield
BUSHBY hamlet parish Thurnby Leics pop 86
BUSHEY parish 1684 Herts 1-1/4 miles se Watford pop 1,586 archd
St Albans dioc London
BUSHLEY parish 1538 Worcs 2-1/4 miles nw Tewkesbury pop 313
archd and dioc Worcester
BUSLINGTHORPE parish 1762 Lincs 4 miles sw Market Rasen pop
55 archd Stow dioc Lincoln
BUSTABECK township parish Castle Sowerby Cumberland pop 237
BUSTON, HIGH township parish Warkworth Northumberland pop 92
BUSTON, LOW township parish Warkworth Northumberland pop 102
BUTCOMBE parish 1692 Somerset 8-1/2 miles ne Axbridge pop 242
archd Bath dioc Bath and Wells
BUTELAND township with Broomhope parish Birtley Northumberland
BUTLEIGH parish 1578 Somerset 4-1/2 miles se Glastonbury pop
952 Bishop of Bath and Wells
BUTLEY township parish Prestbury Ches pop 808 Wesl Meth
BUTLEY parish 1785 Suffolk 7-1/4 miles ne Woodbridge pop 356
archd Suffolk dioc Norwich
BUTSFIELD township parish Lanchester co Durham pop 285
BUTTER CRAMBE chapelry 1635 parish Bossall N R York pop 176
BUTTERLAW township parish Newburn Northumberland pop 30
BUTTERLEIGH parish 1698 Devon 3-1/4 miles se Tiverton pop 142

archd and dioc Exeter

BUTTERLEY hamlet township Ripley parish Pentrich Derbys

BUTTERLEY township parish Edwin Ralph Herefs

BUTTERMERE chapelry 1801 parish Brigham Cumberland pop 137 archd Richmond dioc Chester

BUTTERMERE parish 1727 Wilts 5-1/4 miles s Hungerford pop 89 archd Wilts dioc Salisbury

BUTTERTON township parish Trentham Staffs pop 35

BUTTERTON chapelry 1686 parish Mayfield Staffs pop 346

BUTTERWICK tything parish Folke Dorset

BUTTERWICK township parish Sedgefield co Durham pop 38

BUTTERWICK parish 1658 Lincs 4-1/4 miles ne Boston pop 504 archd and dioc Lincoln Wesl Meth

BUTTERWICK chapelry 1796 parish Fox Holes E R York pop 100

BUTTERWICK township parish Barton le Street N R York pop 56

BUTTERWICK, EAST township parish Messingham Lincs pop 326 Wesl Meth

BUTTERWICK, WEST chapelry parish Owston Lincs pop 798 Wesl Meth

BUTTERWORTH township parish Rochdale Lancs pop 5,648

BUTTOLPHS parish 1607 Sussex 1-1/2 miles se Steyning pop 81 archd and dioc Chichester

BUTTSBURY parish 1657 Essex 7 miles sw Chelmsford pop 515 archd Essex dioc London

BUXHALL parish 1558 Suffolk 3-1/4 miles sw Stow Market pop 466 archd Sudbury dioc Norwich

BUXLOW chapelry, hamlet parish Knodishall Suffolk

BUXTED parish 1567 Sussex 1-3/4 miles ne Uckfield pop 1,642 deanery of South Malling within pec juris of Archbishop of Canterbury

BUXTON chapelry 1718 parish Bakewell Derbys pop 1,211 Indep, Wesl Meth, Unit

BUXTON township with Coxhall parish Bucknill Herefs pop 120

BUXTON parish 1665 Norfolk 3-1/4 miles nw Coltishall pop 610 archd and dioc Norwich Part Bapt

BWLCH township parish Cwmyoy Herefs pop 87

BYAL FEN extra parochial liberty Isle of Ely Cambs

BYERS GREEN township parish St Andrew Auckland co Durham pop 206

BYFIELD parish 1636 co Northampton 7-1/4 miles se Daventry pop 952 archd Northampton dioc Peterborough

BYFLEET parish 1698 Surrey 2-1/2 miles nw Cobham pop 510 archd Surrey dioc Winchester Part Bapt

BYFORD parish 1660 Herefs 7-1/2 miles nw Hereford pop 187 archd and dioc Hereford

BYGRAVE parish 1765 Herts 2 miles ne Baldock pop 145 archd Huntingdon dioc Lincoln

BYKER township parish All Saints, Newcastle Northumberland pop

5,176 Wesl Meth
BYLAND CUM MEMBRIS township parish Coxwold N R York pop 365
BYLAND, OLD parish 1653 N R York 4-3/4 miles nw Helmsley pop
163 archd Cleveland dioc York
BYLAUGH parish 1557 Norfolk 5-1/4 miles ne East Dereham pop 62
archd and dioc Norwich
BYLEY township parish Middlewich Ches pop 123
BYRNESS chapelry 1797 parish Elsdon Northumberland
BYROME township with Pool parish Brotherton E R York and W R York
BYSHOTTLES township with Brandon parish Brancepeth co Durham
BYTHAM, CASTLE parish 1597 Lincs 5 miles sw Corby comp chapel-
ry Holywell with Awnby and hamlet Counthorpe pop 781 archd
and dioc Lincoln Wesl Meth
BYTHAM, LITTLE parish 1681 Lincs 5 miles s Corby pop 237 archd
and dioc Lincoln
BYTHORN parish 1571 Hunts 6-1/2 miles nw Kimbolton pop 313
archd Huntingdon dioc Lincoln Part Bapt
BYTON parish 1763 Herefs 4-1/2 miles se Presteign pop 155 archd
and dioc Hereford
BYWELL St Andrew parish 1668 Northumberland comp townships
Bearl, Broomhaugh, Riding, Stocksfield Hall, Styford pop 436
archd Northumberland dioc Durham
BYWELL St Peter parish 1663 Northumberland comp chapelry Whit-
tonstall, townships East Acomb, Broomley, Espershields with
Millshields, High Fotherly, Heally, Newlands, Newton, Newton Hall
and Stelling, part township of Bywell St Andrew and St Peter
pop 1,478 8 miles se Hexham archd Northumberland dioc Durham Bapt, Soc of Friends, Wesl Meth
CABOURN parish 1559 Lincs 1-3/4 miles ne Caistor pop 173 archd
and dioc Lincoln
CABUS township parish Garstang Lancs pop 267
CADBURY parish 1756 Devon 6-1/4 miles sw Tiverton pop 256 archd
and dioc Exeter
CADBURY, NORTH parish 1558 Somerset 3-1/4 miles s Castle Cary
pop 1,109 archd Wells dioc Bath and Wells
CADBURY, SOUTH parish 1559 Somerset 4-1/2 miles s Castle Cary
pop 231 archd Wells dioc Bath and Wells
CADDINGTON parish 1558 Beds 1-3/4 miles sw Luton pop 1,563
archd Bedford dioc Lincoln
CADEBY parish 1574 Leics 1-1/4 miles se Market Bosworth pop 361
archd Leicester dioc Lincoln
CADEBY hamlet parish Wyham Lincs
CADEBY or CATEBY township parish Sprotbrough W R York pop 178
CADELEIGH parish 1665 Devon 4-1/4 miles sw Tiverton pop 236
archd and dioc Exeter
CADLEY extra parochial liberty Wilts
CADNAM hamlet in parishes Eling and Minstead Hamps Wesl Meth
CADNEY parish 1564 Lincs 2-3/4 miles se Glandford Bridge pop

334 arch and dioc Lincoln

CADWELL tything parish Brightwell Baldwin co Oxford

CAENBY parish 1713 Lincs 7-1/4 miles w Market Rasen pop 176
    archd Stow dioc Lincoln

CAERLEON market town parish Llangattock co Monmouth 20-1/2
    miles sw Monmouth pop 1,071 Bapt, Indep, Wesl Meth

CAERTON ULTRA PONTEM hamlet parish Christchurch co Monmouth

CAER WENT parish 1752 co Monmouth 5-1/2 miles sw Chepstow
    pop 444 archd and dioc Llandaff Part Bapt

CAINHAM parish 1558 Shrops 3-1/2 miles se Ludlow pop 1,005 archd
    Salop dioc Hereford

CAIN'S CROSS hamlet in parishes Stroud and Stonehouse Gloucs

CAISTOR or CASTOR parish 1583 Lincs 23 miles ne Lincoln pop
    1,525 pec juris of Prebendary of Caistor in Cathedral Church of
    Lincoln Indep, Meth

CAISTOR parish 1557 Norfolk 3-3/4 miles s Norwich pop 193 archd
    and dioc Norwich

CAISTOR, NEAR YARMOUTH parish 1563 Norfolk 19-1/2 miles e
    Norwich pop 864 archd and dioc Norwich

CAISTRON township parish Rothbury Northumberland pop 43

CALBOURN parish 1562 Isle of Wight Hemps 5-1/4 miles sw Newport
    pop 844 pec juris of incumbent

CALCEBY parish 1622 Lincs 4-3/4 miles w Alford pop 54 archd and
    dioc Lincoln

CALCETHORPE parish 1651 Lincs 6 miles nw Louth pop 72 archd
    and dioc Lincoln

CALDBECK parish 1640 Cumberland 8 miles se Wigton comp town-
    ships High Caldbeck, Low Caldbeck and Haltcliffe Caldbeck pop
    1,578 archd and dioc Carlisle

CAMBRIDGE township parish Coverham N R York pop 107

CALDECOT parish Norfolk 4 miles ne Stoke Ferry pop 63 archd
    Norfolk dioc Norwich

CALDECOTE parish 1662 Cambs 4 miles se Caxton pop 112 archd
    and dioc Ely

CALDECOTE parish 1725 Warws 3-3/4 miles se Atherstone pop 106
    archd Coventry dioc Lichfield

CALDECOTT township parish Shocklach Ches pop 75

CALDECOTT parish 1726 Herts 3 miles nw Baldock pop 39 archd
    Huntingdon dioc Lincoln

CALDECOTT chapel 1605 parish Liddington co Rutland pop 226

CALDER BRIDGE hamlet parish Beckermet St Bridget's Cumberland

CALDEY, GREAT and LITTLE township parish West Kirby Ches
    pop 102

CALDICOT parish 1716 co Monmouth 6 miles sw Chepstow pop 583
    archd and dioc Llandaff Wesl Meth

CALDICOTE parish 1739 Hunts 1-1/2 miles sw Stilton pop 48 archd
    Huntingdon dioc Lincoln

CALDICOTTS, LOWER and UPPER hamlet parish Northill Beds

pop 415

CALDWELL township parish Stanwick St John's N R York pop 204

CALLALEY township parish Whittingham Northumberland pop 303

CALLERTON, BLACK township parish Newburn Northumberland pop 438

CALLERTON, HIGH township parish Ponteland Northumberland pop 136

CALLERTON, LITTLE township parish Ponteland Northumberland pop 36

CALLINGTON or KELLINGTON parish 1558 Cornwall 11 miles se Launceston pop 1,388 archd Cornwall dioc Exeter Indep, Wesl Meth

CALLOW hamlet parish Wirksworth Derbys pop 101

CALLOW parish 1576 Herefs 3-3/4 miles sw Hereford pop 148 pec juris Dean of Hereford

CALMSDEN tything parish North Cerney Gloucs

CALNE parish 1538 borough Wilts 30 miles nw Salisbury pop 4,876 pec juris Prebendal of Calne Bapt, Soc of Friends, Meth, Unit

CALOW hamlet parish Chesterfield Derbys pop 569

CALSTOCK parish 1654 Cornwall 5-1/4 miles e Callington pop 2,328 archd Cornwall dioc Exeter

CALSTONE WILLINGTON parish 1716 Wilts 3 miles se Calne pop 32 archd Wilts dioc Salisbury

CALTHORPE parish 1539 Norfolk 3-1/4 miles nw Aylsham pop 206 archd and dioc Norwich

CALTHWAITE township parish Hesket in the Forest Cumberland pop 210

CALTON chapelry 1762 in parishes Blore and Croxden, Mayfield and Waterfall Staffs pop 215 archd Stafford dioc Lichfield

CALTON township parish Kirkby in Malham Dale W R York pop 79

CALVELEY township parish Bunbury Ches pop 170

CALVER township parish Bakewell Derbys pop 616

CALVERHALL chapelry 1668 parish Prees Shrops pop 322 pec juris Prebendary of Press in Cathedral Church of Lichfield

CALVERLEIGH parish 1679 Devon 2-1/4 miles nw Tiverton pop 91 archd and dioc Exeter

CALVERLEY parish 1574 W R York 4-1/2 miles ne Bradford comp chapelries Idle and Pudsey, townships Bolton, Calverley with Farsley pop 16,184 archd and dioc York

CALVERTON parish 1559 Bucks 1 mile s Stony Stratford pop 425 archd Buckingham dioc Lincoln

CALVERTON parish 1568 Notts 7 miles ne Nottingham pop 1,196 pec juris of Chapter of the Collegiate Church of Southwell Wesl Meth

CALWICK township parish Ellastone Staffs pop 136

CAM parish 1569 Gloucs 1 mile n Dursley pop 2,071 archd and dioc Gloucester Indep, Wesl Meth

CAMBERWELL parish 1558 Surrey 3-1/4 miles s London pop 28,231 archd Surrey dioc Winchester Bapt, Indep, Meth

CAMBLESFORTH township parish Drax W R York pop 260

CAMBO township parish Hartburn Northumberland pop 108

CAMBOIS joint township with North Blyth parish Bedlington co Durham

CAMBORNE parish 1538 Cornwall 4 miles sw Redruth pop 7,699 arch Cornwall dioc Exeter Wesl Meth, Bryanites

CAMBRIDGE University town Borough Cambs 51 miles ne London pop 20,917 sep juris All Saints 1548, St Andrew the Great 1635, St Andrew the Less or Barnwell 1753, St Benedict 1539, St Botolph 1564, St Clement 1567, St Edward 1558, St Giles 1596, St Peter 1586, St Mary the Great 1559, St Mary the Less 1557, St Michael 1538, St Sepulchre 1567, Holy Trinity 1566 Bapt, Soc of Friends, Indep, Prim and Wesl Meth

CAMBRIDGE hamlet parish Slimbridge Gloucs

CAMDEN TOWN chapelry 1828 parish Pancras Middlesex Indep, Wesl Meth

CAMEL, QUEEN parish 1639 Somerset 5-1/2 miles ne Ilchester pop 664 archd Wells dioc Bath and Wells Wesl Meth

CAMEL, WEST parish 1678 Somerset 3-1/2 miles ne Ilchester pop 322 archd Wells dioc Bath and Wells

CAMELEY parish 1561 Somerset 4-3/4 miles s Pensford pop 658 archd Wells dioc Bath and Wells

CAMELFORD town parish Lanteglos borough Cornwall 16 miles sw Launceston sep juris Wesl Meth

CAMERTON parish 1684 Somerset 6-3/4 miles sw Bath pop 1,326 archd Wells dioc Bath and Wells Bapt, Wesl Meth

CAMERTON joint township with Ryhill parish Burstwick E R York

CAMMERINGHAM parish 1662 Lincs 7-1/4 miles nw Lincoln pop 134 archd Stow dioc Lincoln

CAMMERTON parish 1599 Cumberland 3 miles ne Workington comp townships Cammerton and Seaton pop 846 archd and dioc Carlisle

CAMPDEN, BROAD hamlet parish Chipping Campden Gloucs pop 262

CAMPDEN, CHIPPING parish 1616 Gloucs 29 miles ne Gloucester comp market town Chipping Campden, hamlets Berrington, Broad Campden and Wessington with Combe pop 2,038 archd and dioc Gloucester Bapt, Wesl Meth

CAMPSALL parish 1563 W R York 8 miles nw Doncaster comp townships Askern, Campsall, Finwick, Moss, Norton and Sutton pop 1,974 archd and dioc York

CAMPSEA ASH parish 1559 Suffolk 2 miles e Wickham Market pop 392 archd Suffolk dioc Norwich

CAMPTON parish 1568 Beds 3-3/4 miles ne Silsoe pop 1,212 archd Bedford dioc Lincoln

CANDLESBY parish 1753 Lincs 3-1/4 miles ne Spilsby pop 216 archd and dioc Lincoln

CANDOVER, BROWN parish 1611 Hamps 4-3/4 miles ne New Alresford pop 284 archd and dioc Winchester

CANDOVER, CHILTON parish 1612 Hamps 5 miles n New Alresford pop 130 archd and dioc Winchester

CANDOVER, PRESTON parish 1688 Hamps 6 miles ne New Alresford pop 442 archd and dioc Winchester
CANEWDON parish 1636 Essex 3-1/2 miles ne Rochford pop 675 archd Essex dioc London
CANFIELD, GREAT parish 1538 Essex 3-1/2 miles se Great Dunmow pop 511 archd Middlesex dioc London
CANFIELD, LITTLE parish 1560 Essex 2-3/4 miles sw Great Dunmow pop 277 archd Middlesex dioc London
CANFORD, GREAT parish 1656 Dorset 2-1/4 miles se Wimborne Minster comp chapelry Kingston, tythings Longfleet and Parkston pop 3,100 royal pec
CANN parish 1563 Dorset 1-1/2 miles se Shaftesbury pop 435 archd Dorset dioc Bristol
CANNINGS, BISHOPS parish 1591 Wilts 3 miles ne Devizes pop 3,350 pec juris Dean and Chapter of Salisbury
CANNINGTON parish 1559 Somerset 3-1/2 miles nw Bridgewater pop 1,437 archd Taunton dioc Bath and Wells
CANNOCK parish 1744 Staffs 4-1/2 miles se Penkridge comp townships Cannock, Cannock Wood, Cheslyn Hay, Hednesford with Leacroft, Huntington and Great Wyrley pop 3,116 pec juris of Dean and Chapter of Lichfield Indep, Wesl Meth
CANNOCK WOOD township parish Cannock Staffs
CANNONBY, CROSS parish 1663 Cumberland 2-3/4 miles ne Maryport comp chapelry Maryport, townships Birkby, Cross Cannonby, Crosby pop 4,243 archd and dioc Carlisle
CANNON FROME Herefs See FROOME, CANNON
CANON PION or PYON parish 1707 Herefs 4-1/2 miles se Weobley pop 663 Cons Court of Dean of Hereford
CANON TEIGN hamlet parish Christow Devon
CANTELOSE or CANTELOFF parish regs in Hetherset Norfolk 4 miles se Norwich archd and dioc Norwich
CANTERBURY Kent 26 miles se Rochester pop 13, 924 sep juris All Saints 1559, St Mary in the Castle 1558, St Mildred 1558, St Alphege 1558, St Mary 1640, St Andrew 1563, St Mary Bredman 1558, Cathedral Christ Church 1564, St Dunston 1559, St George the Martyr 1538, St Mary Magdalen 1634, St Margaret 1653, St Martin 1662, St Paul 1562, St Mary Bredin 1633, St Peter 1560, Holy Cross 1568   Bapt, Soc of Friends, Indep, Wesl Meth, Jews
CANTELEY parish 1559 Norfolk 5 miles sw Acle pop 265 archd and dioc Norwich
CANTLEY parish 1538 W R York 4-1/2 miles se Doncaster pop 634 archd and dioc York
CANTSFIELD township parish Tunstall Lancs pop 88
CANVERY ISLAND chapelry parishes of North and South Benfleet, Bowers Gifford, Laindon, Pitsea, Vance, Leigh, Prettlewell and Southchurch Essex
CANWELL extra parochial liberty 5-1/4 miles sw Tamworth Staffs pop 24

CANWICK parish 1681 Lincs 2-1/4 miles se Lincoln pop 201 archd
and dioc Lincoln
CAPEL hamlet 1785 parish Butley Suffolk pop 190
CAPEL parish 1538 Suffolk 6 miles se Hadleigh pop 628 archd Suf-
folk dioc Norwich
CAPEL parish 1653 Surrey 6 miles se Dorking pop 915 Donative in
patronage of Duke of Norfolk
CAPEL LE FERNE parish 1592 Kent 3-1/4 miles ne Folkestone pop
203 archd and dioc Canterbury
CAPESTHORNE chapelry 1722 parish Prestbury Ches pop 72
CAPHEATON township parish Kirk Whelpington Northumberland pop
232
CAPLAND tything parishes of Beer Crocombe and Broadway Somerset
CAPLE or CAPEL chapelry 1754 parish Tudeley Kent pop 399
CAPPENHURST township parish Shotwick Ches pop 159
CARBROOKE parish 1539 Norfolk 2-3/4 miles ne Watton pop 789
archd and dioc Norwich
CARBURTON chapelry 1538 parish Edwinstow Notts pop 143
CAR COLSTON parish 1570 Notts 9 miles sw Newark pop 213 archd
Nottingham dioc York Wesl Meth
CARDEN township parish Tilston Ches pop 249
CARDESTON parish 1706 Shrops 6 miles w Shrewsbury pop 314 archd
Salop dioc Hereford
CARDINGTON parish 1574 Beds 3 miles se Bedford pop 1,304 archd
Bedford dioc Lincoln Wesl Meth, Part Bapt
CARDINGTON parish 1598 Shrops 4 miles ne Church Stretton pop 718
archd Salop dioc Hereford
CARDINHAM parish 1701 Cornwall 3-3/4 miles ne Bodwin pop 728
archd Cornwall dioc Exeter
CAREBY parish 1562 Lincs 6-1/2 miles n Stanford pop 75 archd and
dioc Lincoln
CARGO or CRAGHOW township parish Stanwick Cumberland pop 242
CARHAISE ST MICHAEL Cornwall See MICHAEL, ST CARHAISE
CARHAM parish 1684 Northumberland 3-1/2 miles sw Coldstream
comp townships Carham with Shidlaw, Downham, Hagg, New Lear-
mouth, West Learmouth, East Mindrim, West Mindrim, Moneylaws,
Preston, Tythehill, Wark, Wark Common pop 1,174 archd North-
umberland dioc Durham
CARHAMPTON parish 1634 Somerset 1-1/2 miles se Dunster pop
658 pec juris Dean of Wells
CARISBROOKE parish 1695 Isle of Wight Hamps 1 mile sw Newport
comp hamlets Billingham, Bowcomb and Carisbrooke, part of
Newport pop 4,713 archd and dioc Winchester
CARKIN township parish Forcett N R York pop 46
CARLATTON extra parochial liberty 9-1/2 miles se Carlisle Cum-
berland pop 70
CARLBY parish 1660 Lincs 5-1/4 miles ne Stamford pop 206 archd
and dioc Lincoln

CARLEBURY hamlet parish Coniscliffe co Durham
CARLETON township parish Dregg Cumberland
CARLETON township parish St Cuthbert, Carlisle Cumberland pop 189
CARLETON chapelry parish Red Marshall Durham pop 183
CARLETON township parish Poulton Lancs pop 319
CARLETON parish 1544 Norfolk 8-1/2 miles se Norwich pop 96 archd Norfolk dioc Norwich
CARLETON in CLEVELAND parish 1700 N R York 3-1/4 miles sw Stokesley pop 256 archd Cleveland dioc York Wesl Meth
CARLETON by SNAITH parish 1618 W R York 1-1/2 miles ne Snaith pop 808 pec Snaith
CARLETON township parish Pontefract W R York pop 155
CARLETON in CRAVEN parish 1538 W R York 2 miles se Otley pop 1,265 archd and dioc York
CARLETON FOREHOE parish 1699 Norfolk 3-1/4 miles nw Wymondham pop 132 archd Norfolk dioc Norwich
CARLISLE Cumberland 302 miles nw London pop 20,006 St Mary 1648, St Cuthbert 1693, St Mary's includes townships Abbey Street, Castle Street, Fisher Street, Scotch Street, Caldergate, Rickergate and Cummersdale, chapelry Wreay; St Cuthbert includes townships Botchergate, Botcherby, Brisco and English street, High Blackwell, Low Blackwell, Carleton, Harraby, Upperby sep juris Bapt, Soc of Friends, Indep, Wesl Meth, Presb, Roman Cath
CARLTON parish 1554 Beds 1-1/2 miles s Harrold pop 424 archd Bedford dioc Lincoln Part Bapt
CARLTON parish 1725 Cambs 5-1/2 miles s Newmarket pop 363 archd and dioc Ely
CARLTON chapelry 1714 parish Market Bosworth Leics pop 201
CARLTON hamlet parish Gedling Notts pop 1,704 Wesl Meth
CARLTON parish 1538 Suffolk 1/4 miles nw Saxmundham pop 130 archd Suffolk dioc Norwich
CARLTON chapelry Parish Husthwaite N R York pop 163
CARLTON township parish Coverham N R York pop 301
CARLTON township parish Rothwell W R York pop 1,463
CARLTON township parish Guiseley W R York pop 181
CARLTON township parish Royston W R York pop 340
CARLTON, CASTLE parish 1570 Lincs 6-3/4 miles se Louth pop 54 archd and dioc Lincoln
CARLTON COLVILLE parish 1710 Suffolk 3-3/4 miles sw Lowestoft pop 745 archd Suffolk dioc Norwich Wesl Meth
CARLTON CURLIEU parish 1749 Leics 7-1/2 miles nw Market Harborough pop 182 archd Leicester dioc Lincoln
CARLTON, EAST parish 1544 Norfolk 4-3/4 miles e Wymondham pop 314 archd Norfolk dioc Norwich
CARLTON, EAST parish 1625 co Northampton 3 miles sw Rockingham pop 95 archd Northampton dioc Peterborough
CARLTON, GREAT parish 1561 Lincs 6-1/2 miles se Louth pop 280

archd and dioc Lincoln Wesl Meth
CARLTON HIGHDALE township parish Coverdale N R York pop 365
CARLTON IN LINDRICK parish 1559 Notts 3-3/4 miles ne Workshop
pop 974 archd Nottingham dioc York
CARLTON ISLEBECK or MINIOT chapelry 1706 parish Thirsk N R.
York pop 238
CARLTON, LITTLE parish 1726 Lincs 6 miles se Louth pop 131
archd and dioc Lincoln
CARLTON LE MOORLANDS parish 1562 Lincs 10 miles sw Lincoln
pop 328 archd and dioc Lincoln Part Bapt
CARLTON, NORTH parish 1653 Lincs 4-1/2 miles nw Lincoln pop
180 pec juris Dean and Chapter of Lincoln
CARLTON RODE parish 1560 Norfolk 2-1/2 miles ne New Buckenham
pop 916 archd Norfolk dioc Norwich Part Bapt
CARLTON SCROOP parish 1558 Lincs 6-1/4 miles ne Grantham pop
199 archd and dioc Lincoln
CARLTON, SOUTH parish 1653 Lincs 3-1/2 miles nw Lincoln pop
204 pec juris Dean and Chapter of Lincoln
CARLTON UPON TRENT chapelry parish Norwell Notts pop 265
CARNABY parish 1596 E R York 3 miles sw Bridlington pop 155
archd East Riding dioc York
CARNFORTH township parish Warton Lancs pop 299
CARPERBY township parish Aysgarth N R York pop 320
CARRINGTON chapelry 1759 parish Bowdon Ches
CARRINGTON chapelry 1812 parish Helpringham Lincs pop 149
CARROCK or CANNOCK, PASSAGE chapelry parish St Veep Cornwall
CARROW hamlet parish Warden Northumberland
CARSHALTON parish 1538 Surrey 11 miles sw London pop 1,919
archd Surrey dioc Winchester Roman Cath
CARSINGTON parish 1592 Derbys 2-1/4 miles sw Wirksworth pop
286 archd Derby dioc Lichfield
CARSWELL, ABBOT'S Devon See KERSWELL, ABBOT'S
CARTER MOOR hamlet parish Ponteland Northumberland
CARTHORP township parish Burneston N R York pop 304 Wesl Meth
CARTMEL parish 1559 Lancs 14 miles nw Lancaster comp market
town Cartmel, chapelries Broughton, Cartmel Fell and Staveley,
townships Lower Allithwaite, Upper Allithwaite, Lower Holker and
Upper Holker pop 4,802 archd Richmond dioc Chester
CARTMEL FELL chapelry 1754 parish Cartmel Lancs pop 347
CARTWORTH township parish Kirk Burton W R York pop 1,796
CARWOOD Shrops See SIBDON CARWOOD
CARY COATS township parish Throckrington Northumberland pop 42
CASHIO or CASHIOBURY hamlet parish Watford Herts
CASSINGTON parish 1653 co Oxford 6-3/4 miles nw Oxford pop 428
archd and dioc Oxford
CASSOP township parish Kelloe co Durham pop 69
CASTERTON township parish Kirkby Lonsdale Westm pop 302
CASTERTON hamlet parish Ilam Staffs

CASTERTON, GREAT parish 1665 co Rutland 2-1/4 miles nw Stamford pop 353 archd Northampton dioc Peterborough
CASTERTON, LITTLE parish 1559 co Rutland 2-1/4 miles nw Stamford pop 135 archd Northampton dioc Peterborough
CASTLE ACRE parish 1695 Norfolk 4 miles n Swaffham pop 1,333 archd and dioc Norwich Bapt, Wesl Meth
CASTLE ASHBY co Northampton See ASHBY CASTLE
CASTLE CAMPS parish 1565 Cambs 5-3/4 miles se Linton pop 734 archd and dioc Ely
CASTLE CARROCK parish 1679 Cumberland 4-1/2 miles se Brampton pop 383 archd and dioc Carlisle
CASTLE CARY parish 1564 Somerset 11 miles ne Somerton pop 1,794 archd Wells dioc Bath and Wells Indep, Wesl Meth
CASTLE CHURCH parish 1567 Staffs 1 mile sw Stafford pop 1,374 archd Stafford dioc Lichfield
CASTLE COMBE parish 1653 Wilts 6-1/2 miles nw Chippenham pop 655 archd Wilts dioc Salisbury
CASTLE EATON parish 1549 Wilts 5 miles nw Highworth pop 302 archd Wilts dioc Salisbury
CASTLE MORTON parish 1558 Worcs 5 miles sw Upton upon Severn pop 879 archd and dioc Worcester
CASTLE NORTHWICH township parish Great Budworth Ches pop 692
CASTLE RISING parish 1573 borough Norfolk 43 miles nw Norwich pop 358 pec juris of Rector
CASTLE THORPE parish 1562 Bucks 3 miles ne Stony Stratford pop 366 archd Buckingham dioc Lincoln
CASTLEFORD parish 1653 W R York 3-1/2 miles nw Pontefract comp townships Castleford and Glass Houghton pop 1,587 archd and dioc York Wesl Meth
CASTLETON parish 1645 Derbys 4-1/2 miles n Tideswell pop 1,329 archd Derby dioc Lichfield Wesl Meth
CASTLETON parish 1715 Dorset 1 miles ne Sherborne pop 186 pec juris of Dean of Salisbury
CASTLETON township parish Rochdale Lancs pop 11,079
CASTLETON hamlet parish Marshfield co Monmouth
CASTLE VIEW extra parochial liberty adjoining Leicester Leics pop 127
CASTLEY township parish Leathley W R York pop 118
CASTON parish 1539 Norfolk 3-1/2 miles se Watton pop 541 archd and dioc Norwich Wesl Meth
CASTOR Lincs See CAISTOR
CASTOR parish 1538 co Northampton 4-1/2 miles w Peterborough comp chapelries of Sutton and Upton hamlet of Ailesworth pop 1,198 archd Northampton dioc Peterborough
CATCHBURN township parish Morpeth Northumberland pop 189
CATCHERSIDE township parish Kirkwhelpington Northumberland pop 14
CATCLIFFE township parish Rotherham W R York pop 196

CATERHAM parish 1543 Surrey 3-1/4 miles nw Godstone pop 449 archd Surrey dioc Winchester

CATCOTT chapelry 1733 parish Moorlinch Somerset pop 651

CATEBY Yorks See CADEBY

CATESBY parish 1705 co Northampton 3-3/4 miles sw Daventry comp Upper and Nether Catesby hamlet Newbold Ground pop 103 archd Northampton dioc Peterborough

CATFIELD parish 1723 Norfolk 7-1/2 miles ne Coltishall pop 602 archd Norfolk dioc Norwich

CATFOSS township parish Sigglesthorne E R York pop 54

CATHERINE, ST parish 1752 Somerset 4 miles ne Bath pop 154 archd Bath dioc Bath and Wells

CATHERINGTON parish 1602 Hamps 6-3/4 miles sw Petersfield pop 944 archd and dioc Winchester

CATHERSTON LEWSTON parish incl in Charmouth regs Dorset 2-3/4 miles ne Lyme Regis pop 27 archd Dorset dioc Bristol

CATMERE parish 1724 Berks 3-1/2 miles sw East Ilsley pop 88 archd Berks dioc Salisbury

CATON chapelry 1585 parish Lancaster Lancs pop 1,166

CATSFIELD parish 1611 Sussex 3 miles sw Battle pop 619 archd Lewes dioc Chichester

CATTAL township parish Hunsingore W R York pop 208

CATTERAL township parish Garstand Lancs pop 457

CATTERICK parish 1653 N R York 5 miles se Richmond comp townships of Ellerton upon Swale, Kiplin, Scorton, Uckerby and Whitwell, chapelry Hudswell, Hipswell, townships Appleton, Brough, Catterick, Colbourne, St Martin's, Killerby, Scotton and Tunstall pop 2,921 archd Richmond dioc Chester

CATTERLEN township parish Newton Rigny Cumberland pop 125

CATTERTON township parish Tadcaster E R York pop 62

CATTHORPE parish 1573 Leics 4-1/2 miles se Lutterworth pop 199 archd Leicester dioc Lincoln

CATTISTOCKE parish 1558 Dorset 9-1/4 miles nw Dorchester pop 427 archd Dorset dioc Bristol

CATTO joint township with Landmoth N R York

CATTON chapelry parish Croxall Derbys pop 75

CATTON parish 1688 Norfolk 2-1/2 miles n Norwich pop 592 pec juris Dean and Chapter of Norwich

CATTON parish 1592 E R York 9 miles ne York comp townships Kexby and West Stamford Bridge with Scoreby, townships High Catton, Low Catton, East Stamford Bridge pop 1,095 archd East Riding dioc York Wesl Meth

CATTON township parish Topcliffe N R York pop 102

CATWICK parish 1583 E R York 8 miles ne Beverley pop 213 archd East Riding dioc York

CATWORTH, GREAT parish 1561 Hunts 4 miles nw Kimbolton pop 564 archd Huntingdon dioc Lincoln

CATWORTH, LITTLE chapelry parish Long Stow Hunts

CAUDERY joint township with Rudyard parish Leek Staffs
CAULDON parish 1580 Staffs 6-3/4 miles nw Ashbourn pop 347 archd
  Stafford dioc Lichfield
CAULDWELL chapelry 1679 parish Stapenhill Derbys pop 172
CAULK parish 1699 Derbys 4-1/4 miles ne Ashby de la Zouch pop 58
  archd Derby dioc Lichfield
CAUNDLE, BISHOP parish 1570 Dorset 5 miles se Sherborne pop
  376 archd Dorset dioc Bristol
CAUNDLE MARSH parish 1704 Dorset 3-3/4 miles se Sherborne pop
  70 pec juris Dean of Salisbury
CAUNDLE PURSE parish 1730 Dorset 1-1/2 miles se Milborne Port
  pop 180 archd Dorset dioc Bristol
CAUNDLE STOURTON parish 1670 Dorset 3-1/2 miles se Milborne
  Port pop 349 archd Dorset dioc Bristol
CAUNDLE WAKE tything parish Bishop Caundle Dorset pop 36
CAUNTON parish 1709 co Notts 5-1/2 miles nw Newark pop 542 pec
  juris Chapter of Collegiate Church of Southwell
CAUSEY PARK township parish Hebburn Northumberland pop 98
CAVE, NORTH parish 1678 E R York 6-3/4 miles se Market Weighton
  comp townships North Cave, South Cliff, Drewton with Everthorp
  pop 1,000 archd East Riding dioc York Soc of Friends, Prim and
  Wesl Meth
CAVE, SOUTH 1558 E R York 27 miles se York comp market town
  South Cave, townships Bromfleet and Flaxfleet pop 1,200 pec of
  South Cave Meth
CAVENDISH parish 1594 Suffolk 2-1/4 miles ne Clare pop 1,214
  archd Sudbury dioc Norwich
CAVENHAM parish 1539 Suffolk 4-1/2 miles se Mildenhall pop 261
  archd Sudbury dioc Norwich
CAVERSFIELD parish 1640 Bucks 2 miles n Bicester pop 123 archd
  Buckingham dioc Lincoln
CAVERSHAM parish 1597 co Oxford 1 mile n Reading pop 1,369 archd
  and dioc Oxford
CAVERSWALL parish 1559 Staffs 3-3/4 miles w Cheadle pop 1,207
  archd Stafford dioc Lichfield Wesl Meth
CAVIL joint township with Portington parish Eastrington E R York
CAWKWELL parish 1683 Lincs 7-1/2 miles ne Horncastle pop 44
  archd and dioc Lincoln
CAWOOD hamlet chapelry Arkolme parish Melling Lancs
CAWOOD parish 1591 W R York 9-1/2 miles sw York pop 1,173 pec
  juris Prebendary of Wistow in Cathedral Church of York Wesl
  Meth
CAWSTON parish 1538 Norfolk 3-1/4 miles ne Reepham pop 1,110
  archd and dioc Norwich
CAWTHORNE parish 1653 W R York 4-1/2 miles nw Barnsley pop
  1,491 archd and dioc York Wesl Meth
CAWTHORPE hamlet parish Bourne Lincs pop 71
CAWTHORPE, LITTLE parish 1679 Lincs 3 miles se Louth pop 137

archd and dioc Lincoln

CAWTON township parish Gilling N R York pop 89

CAXTON parish 1741 Cambs 10-1/2 miles sw Cambridge pop 417 archd and dioc Ely

CAYTHORPE parish 1663 Lincs 9 miles ne Grantham pop 720 archd and dioc Lincoln Wesl Meth

CAYTHORPE township parish Lowdham Notts pop 289

CAYTON parish 1684 N R York 4 miles se Scarborough comp townships Cayton Deepdale with Killerby and Osgodby pop 514 archd East Riding dioc York Prim and Wesl Meth

CERNE or CERNE ABBAS parish 1653 Dorset 8 miles nw Dorchester pop 1,209 archd Dorset dioc Bristol Indep

CERNE, NETHER parish 1694 Dorset 5-3/4 miles nw Dorchester pop 83 archd Dorset dioc Bristol

CERNE, UPPER parish 1650 Dorset 9 miles nw Dorchester pop 88 archd Dorset dioc Bristol

CERNEY, NORTH parish 1568 Gloucs 4 miles n Cirencester pop 622 archd and dioc Gloucester

CERNEY, SOUTH parish 1583 Gloucs 3-3/4 miles se Cirencester pop 980 archd and dioc Gloucester

CHACELEY See CHASELEY

CHACEWATER chapelry 1828 parishes Kenwyn and St Kea Cornwall Bapt, Bryanites, Prim and Wesl Meth

CHACKMORE hamlet parish Radclive Bucks

CHAD KIRK chapelry 1747 parish Stockport Ches archd and dioc Chester

CHADD, ST chapelry Ches

CHADDENWICKE joint tything with Woodlands parish Mere Wilts

CHADDERTON chapelry parish Oldham Lancs pop 5,476

CHADDESDEN parish 1718 Derbys 2-1/2 miles e Derby pop 469 archd Derby dioc Lichfield

CHADDESLEY CORBETT parish 1538 Worcs 5 miles nw Bromsgrove pop 1,404 archd and dioc Worcester

CHADDLEWORTH parish 1538 Berks 6-1/2 miles sw East Ilsley pop 494 archd Berks dioc Salisbury

CHADKIRK chapelry 1747 parish Stockport Ches

CHADLINGTON, EAST chapelry 1561 parish Charlbury co Oxford pop 681

CHADLINGTON, WEST tything parish Charlbury co Oxford

CHADSHUNT chapelry 1701 parish Bishop's Itchington Warws pop 45 pec juris Prebendary of Colwich and Bishop's Itchington in Cathedral Church Lichfield

CHADWELL parish 1539 Essex 3 miles s Orsett pop 180 archd Essex dioc London

CHADWELL a ward parish Barking Essex pop 733

CHADWELL chapelry parish Rothley Leics pop 103

CHADWICK hamlet parish Bromsgrove Worcs

CHAFFCOMBE parish 1678 Somerset 3-1/4 miles sw Ilminster pop

243 archd Taunton dioc Bath and Wells

CHAGFORD parish 1598 Devon 15 miles sw Exeter pop 1,868 archd and dioc Exeter

CHAIGLEY township parish Mitton Lancs

CHAILEY parish 1538 Sussex 6-1/2 miles nw Lewes pop 1,030 archd Lewes dioc Chichester

CHALBURY parish 1629 Dorset 5 miles ne Wimborne Minster pop 157 archd Dorset dioc Bristol

CHALCOMBE parish 1566 co Northampton 3-3/4 miles ne Banbury pop 493 archd Northampton dioc Peterborough

CHALDON parish 1564 Surrey 3 miles ne Gatton pop 173 archd Surrey dioc Winchester

CHALDON HERRING parish 1622 Dorset 10-1/2 miles sw Wareham pop 270 archd and dioc Bristol

CHALE Isle of Wight parish 1679 Hamps 7 miles sw Newport pop 544 archd and dioc Winchester

CHALFIELD, GREAT parish 1545 Wilts 3-1/2 miles w Melksham pop 83 archd and dioc Salisbury

CHALFIELD, LITTLE extra parochial parish Great Chalfield Wilts

CHALFONT St Giles parish 1584 Bucks 3-3/4 miles se Amersham pop 1,297 archd Buckingham dioc Lincoln Soc of Friends, Indep

CHALFONT St Peters parish 1539 Bucks 4 miles ne Beaconfield pop 1,416 archd Buckingham dioc Lincoln

CHALFORD hamlet parish Bisley Gloucs

CHALFORD liberty parish Aston Rowant co Oxford

CHALGRAVE parish 1539 Beds 3-3/4 miles nw Dunstable pop 746 archd Bedford dioc Lincoln Wesl Meth at Tebworth

CHALGROVE parish 1538 co Oxford 5-3/4 miles sw Tetsworth pop 549 archd and dioc Oxford Bapt

CHALK parish 1661 Kent 1-3/4 miles se Gravesend pop 333 archd and dioc Rochester

CHALLACOMBE parish 1676 Devon 10 miles ne Barnstaple pop 240 archd Barnstaple dioc Exeter

CHALLOCK parish 1558 Kent 4-1/4 miles e Charing pop 363 pec juris of Archbishop of Canterbury

CHALLOW, EAST chapelry 1711 parish Letcombe Regis Berks pop 328

CHALLOW, WEST chapelry 1653 parish Letcombe Regis Berks pop 148

CHALTON or CHALKTON parish 1538 Hamps 5-1/2 miles sw Petersfield pop 550 archd and dioc Winchester

CHALVEY hamlet parish of Upton Bucks Indep

CHALVINGTON parish 1538 Sussex 5 miles w Hailsham pop 188 archd Lewes dioc Chichester

CHAPEL or PONTISBRIGHT, Essex See PONTISBRIGHT

CHAPEL ALLERTON York See ALLERTON, CHAPEL

CHAPEL EN LE FRITH parith 1620 Derbys 41 miles nw Derby comp townships Bradshaw Edge, Bowden's Edge, Coomb's Edge pop

3,320 pec juris Dean and Chapter of Lichfield Wesl Meth
CHAPEL HILL parish 1695 co Monmouth 4-1/4 miles n Chepstow
pop 590 archd and dioc Llandaff
CHAPEL LE DALE Ingleton Fells chapelry 1754 parish Ingleton WR
York
CHAPEL POINT or PORT EAST sea port and chapelry, parish Gorran
Cornwall
CHAPEL SUCKEN township parish Millom Cumberland pop 291
CHAPEL THORPE chapelry parish Great Sandall W R York
CHAPELWICK chapelry parish Ashbury Berks
CHARBOROUGH parish See MORDEN Dorset 6-1/4 miles se Bland-
ford Forum archd Dorset dioc Bristol
CHARCOMBE extra parochial liberty Somerset
CHARD parish 1649 Somerset 13 miles se Taunton comp Chard,
tythings of Crim Chard, Old Chard, South Chard, Tatworth with
Forton pop 5,141 archd Taunton dioc Bath and Wells Part Bapt
CHARDSTOCK parish 1597 Dorset 4-1/2 miles sw Chard pop 1,357
pec juris Prebendary of Chadstock in Cathedral Church of Salis-
bury
CHARFIELD parish 1587 Gloucs 2-1/4 miles nw Wickwar pop 487
archd and dioc Gloucester
CHARFORD, NORTH parish no regs Hamps 3-1/2 miles ne Fording-
bridge archd and dioc Winchester pop 138
CHARFORD, SOUTH tything parish North Charford Hamps pop 67
CHARING parish 1590 Kent 13-1/2 miles se Maidstone pop 1,237
dioc Canterbury Epis Cons of Canterbury Wesl Meth
CHARINGWORTH hamlet parish Ebrington Gloucs
CHARLBURY parish 1559 co Oxford 6-3/4 miles nw Woodstock comp
chapelries of East Chadlington and Chilson, tything West Chad-
lington, hamlets Fawler, Finstock and Wallcott pop 3,027 archd
and dioc Oxford Wesl Meth
CHARLCOMBE parish 1709 Somerset 1-1/2 miles n Bath pop 107
archd Bath dioc Bath and Wells
CHARLCOTE parish 1539 Warws 6 miles nw Kington pop 297 archd
and dioc Worcester
CHARLCOTT tything parish Whitchurch Hamps
CHARLES parish 1538 Devon 9 miles e Barnstaple pop 343 archd
Barnstaple dioc Exeter Bapt, Wesl Meth
CHARLESTOWN sea port parish St Austell Cornwall
CHARLESWORTH chapelry parish Glossop Derbys pop 1,206
CHARLETON parish 1562 Devon 2-1/2 miles se Kingsbridge pop 644
archd Totnes dioc Exeter
CHARLETON hamlet parish Newbottle and King's Sutton co North-
ampton
CHARLETON, QUEEN parish 1562 Somerset 2-3/4 miles ne Pens-
ford pop 168 archd Bath dioc Bath and Wells
CHARLEY extra parochial liberty 4-3/4 miles sw Loughboro Leics
pop 41

CHARLEY township parish Farewell Staffs
CHARLINCH parish 1744 Somerset 4-1/2 miles nw Bridgewater pop
199 archd Taunton dioc Bath and Wells
CHARLTON hamlet parish Wantage Berks pop 255
CHARLTON tything parish Henbury Gloucs pop 310
CHARLTON parish 1564 Kent 1 mile ne Dover pop 1,637 archd and
dioc Canterbury
CHARLTON parish 1562 Kent 6-1/2 miles e London pop 2,327 archd
and dioc Rochester
CHARLTON hamlet parish Kilmersdon Somerset
CHARLTON tything parish Shepton Mallet Somerset
CHARLTON tything parish Singleton Sussex
CHARLTON tything parish Donhead St Mary Wilts
CHARLTON parish 1661 Wilts 2-1/4 miles ne Malmesbury pop 645
archd Wilts dioc Salisbury
CHARLTON parish 1695 Wilts 4 miles sw Pewsey pop 183 archd and
dioc Salisbury
CHARLTON hamlet parish Cropthorn Worcs pop 276
CHARLTON, ABBOT'S parish 1727 Gloucs 2-3/4 miles se Winch-
combe pop 11 archd and dioc Gloucester
CHARLTON ADAM parish 1704 Somerset 3 miles e Somerton pop
480 archd Wells dioc Bath and Wells
CHARLTON, CROSS extra parochial liberty 5 miles n Frome Somer-
set
CHARLTON, EAST township parish Bellingham Northumberland pop
151
CHARLTON HORETHORNE parish 1739 Somerset 5-1/2 miles se
Wincanton pop 485 archd Wells dioc Bath and Wells
CHARLTON KING'S parish 1538 Gloucs 2 miles se Cheltenham pop
2,478 archd and dioc Gloucester Bapt
CHARLTON MACKREL parish 1575 Somerset 3 miles e Somerton
pop 366 archd Wells dioc Bath and Wells
CHARLTON MARSHALL parish 1575 Dorset 1-3/4 miles se Bland-
ford Forum pop 324 archd Dorset dioc Bristol
CHARLTON MUSGRAVE parish 1538 Somerset 1 mile ne Wincanton
pop 415 archd Wells dioc Bath and Wells
CHARLTON, NORTH township parish Ellingham Northumberland
pop 244
CHARLTON, SOUTH township parish Ellingham Northumberland
pop 187
CHARLTON UPON OTMORE parish 1577 co Oxford 5-3/4 miles sw
Bicester pop 658 archd and dioc Oxford
CHARLTON, WEST township parish Bellingham Northumberland
pop 188
CHARLWOOD parish 1585 Surrey 7 miles sw Reigate pop 1,176 pec
juris Archbishop of Canterbury
CHARMINSTER parish 1561 Dorset 2 miles nw Dorchester pop 596
pec juris Dean of Salisbury

CHARMOUTH parish 1653 Dorset 2 miles ne Lyme Regis pop 724 archd Dorset dioc Bristol

CHARNDON hamlet parish Twyford Bucks pop 160

CHARNES township parish Eccleshall Staffs pop 79

CHARNEY chapelry 1700 parish Longworth Berks pop 270

CHARNHAM STREET tything parish Hungerford Wilts pop 432

CHARNOCK HEATH township parish Standish Lancs pop 841

CHARNOCK RICHARD township parish Standish Lancs pop 755

CHARSFIELD parish 1727 Suffolk 3-1/2 miles nw Wickham Market pop 558 archd Suffolk dioc Norwich Part Bapt

CHART joint tything with Pitfolf parish Frensham Surrey pop 618

CHART, GREAT parish 1558 Kent 2 miles sw Ashford pop 771 archd and dioc Canterbury Wesl Meth

CHART, LITTLE parish 1562 Kent 2 miles sw Charing pop 315 archd and dioc Canterbury

CHART, SUTTON parish 1558 Kent 5 miles se Maidstone pop 610 archd and dioc Canterbury

CHARTERHOUSE HINTON Somerset See HINTON CHARTERHOUSE

CHARTERHOUSE ON MENDIP district Somerset pop 105

CHARTHAM parish 1558 Kent 3-1/2 miles sw Canterbury pop 895 archd and dioc Canterbury Wesl Meth

CHARTINGTON township parish Rothbury Northumberland pop 93

CHARTLEY LODGE extra parochial liberty 7-1/2 miles ne Stafford Staffs pop 9

CHARWELTON parish 1697 co Northampton 6 miles sw Daventry pop 266 archd Northampton dioc Peterborough

CHASELEY parish 1538 Worcs 3 miles sw Tewkesbury pop 354 archd and dioc Worcester

CHASEWATER Cornwall See CHACEWATER

CHASTLETON parish 1586 co Oxford 5 miles nw Chipping Norton pop 238 archd and dioc Oxford

CHATBURN township parish Whalley Lancs pop 591

CHATCULL township parish Eccleshall Staffs pop 66

CHATHAM parish 1568 borough Kent 8 miles ne Maidstone pop 16,485 archd and dioc Rochester Bapt, Indep, Wesl Meth, Unit

CHATHILL township parish Ellingham Northumberland pop 30

CHATLEY hamlet parish Great Leighs Essex pop 539

CHATSWORTH extra parochial liberty 3-1/4 miles ne Bakewell Derbys

CHATTERIS parish 1613 Cambs 8-3/4 miles ne Ramsey pop 4,177 pec juris Bishop of Ely Part Bapt, Wesl Meth

CHATTERLEY township parish Wolstanton Staffs pop 308

CHATTISHAM parish 1559 Suffolk 4-1/2 miles se Hadleigh pop 241 archd Suffolk dioc Norwich

CHATTON parish 1715 Northumberland 4 miles e Wooler pop 1,632 archd Northumberland dioc Durham

CHAWLEY tything parish Cumner Berks pop 69

CHAWLEY parish 1544 Devon 2 miles se Chulmleigh pop 865 archd

Barnstaple dioc Exeter
CHAWTON parish 1596 Hamps 1-1/4 miles sw Alton pop 446 archd
and dioc Winchester
CHEADLE parish 1558 Ches 3 miles sw Stockport comp townships
Cheadle Bulkeley, Cheadle Moseley, Handforth with Boxden
pop 8,154 archd and dioc Chester Meth, Roman Cath
CHEADLE parish 1569 Staffs 14 miles ne Stafford pop 4,119 archd
Stafford dioc Lichfield Indep, Wesl Meth, New Connection Meth,
or Kilhamites, Roman Cath
CHEAM parish 1538 Surrey 1-1/2 miles ne Ewell pop 997 in exempt
deanery of Croydon, pec juris of Archbishop of Canterbury
CHEAPSIDES extra parochial liberty E R York pop 57
CHEARSLEY parish 1570 Bucks 3-1/4 miles ne Thame pop 337
archd Buckingham dioc Lincoln
CHEBSEY parish 1713 Staffs 2 miles se Eccleshall pop 414 archd
Stafford dioc Lichfield
CHECKENDON parish 1719 co Oxford 6-3/4 miles se Wallingford
pop 346 archd and dioc Oxford
CHECKLEY joint township with Wrinchill parish Wybunbury Ches
pop 235
CHECKLEY parish 1625 Staffs 5-1/2 miles nw Uttoxeter pop 2,247
archd Stafford dioc Lichfield Indep, Wesl Meth
CHEDBURGH parish 1538 Suffolk 6-1/4 miles sw Bury St Edmund's
pop 295 archd Sudbury dioc Norwich
CHEDDER parish 1678 Somerset 2-1/2 miles se Axbridge pop 1,980
pec juris of Dean and Chapter of Wells Wesl Meth
CHEDDINGTON parish 1558 Bucks 2 miles nw Ivinghoe pop 375
archd Buckingham dioc Lincoln
CHEDDLETON parish 1696 Staffs 3 miles sw Leek pop 1,664 archd
Stafford dioc Lichfield Wesl Meth
CHEDDON FITZPAINE parish 1558 Somerset 2-3/4 miles ne Taunton
pop 325 archd Taunton dioc Bath and Wells
CHEDGRAVE parish 1550 Norfolk 7 miles nw Beccles pop 353 archd
Norfolk dioc Norwich
CHEDINGTON parish 1756 Dorset 4 miles ne Beaminster pop 178
archd Dorset dioc Bristol
CHEDISTON parish 1653 Suffolk 2 miles nw Halesworth pop 409
archd Suffolk dioc Norwich
CHEDWORTH parish 1653 Gloucs 5-1/2 miles sw Northleach pop
1,026 archd and dioc Gloucester
CHEDZOY parish 1558 Somerset 2-3/4 miles ne Bridgewater pop
549 archd Taunton dioc Bath and Wells
CHEESEBURN GRANGE township parish Stamfordham Northumber-
land pop 71
CHEETHAM chapelry 1794 parish Manchester Lancs pop 4,025 Wesl
Meth
CHELBOROUGH, EAST parish 1682 Dorset 5-3/4 miles ne Beamin-
ster pop 83 archd Dorset dioc Bristol

119

CHELBOROUGH, WEST parish 1660 Dorset 5-1/2 miles ne Beamin-
ster pop 62 archd Dorset dioc Bristol
CHELDON parish 1708 Devon 3 miles se Chulmleigh pop 90 archd
Barnstaple dioc Exeter
CHELFORD chapelry 1674 parish Prestbury Ches pop 191
CHELL township parish Wolstanton Staffs pop 535
CHELLASTON parish 1570 Derbys 4-1/2 miles se Derby pop 352
archd Derby dioc Lichfield Wesl Meth
CHELLESWORTH or CHELSWORTH parish 1559 Suffolk 1-1/4 miles
se Bildeston pop 346 archd Sudbury dioc Norwich
CHELLINGTON parish 1567 Beds 7 miles ne Olney pop 119 archd
Bedford dioc Lincoln
CHELMARSH parish 1556 Shrops 4 miles se Bridgenorth pop 439
archd Salop dioc Hereford
CHELMERTON chapelry 1580 parish Bakewell Derbys 4-1/4 miles
sw Tideswell pop 268 pec juris Dean and Chapter of Lichfield
Wesl Meth, Presb
CHELMONDISTON parish 1727 Suffolk 6-1/4 miles se Ipswich pop
480 archd Suffolk dioc Norwich
CHELMSFORD parish 1538 Essex 29 miles ne London pop 5,435
Commissary of Essex and Herts Indep, Soc of Friends, Wesl Meth
CHELSEA parish 1559 Middlesex pop 32,371 archd and dioc Middle-
sex Bapt, Indep, Wesl Meth
CHELSFIELD parish 1538 Kent 6-1/4 miles se Bromley pop 796
archd and dioc Rochester
CHELSHAM chapelry 1669 parish Warlingham Surrey 7 miles se
Croydon pop 279
CHELSWORTH Suffolk See CHELLESWORTH
CHELTENHAM parish 1558 Gloucs borough 8 miles ne Gloucester
archd and dioc Gloucester Bapt, Soc of Friends, Countess of
Huntingdon, Indep, Wesl Meth, Roman Cath
CHELVESTON parish 1579 co Northampton 2 miles ne Higham Fer-
rers pop 332 archd Northampton dioc Peterborough
CHELVEY parish 1735 Somerset 8 miles sw Bristol pop 70 archd
Bath dioc Bath and Wells
CHELWOOD parish 1783 Somerset 2 miles se Pensford pop 246 archd
Bath dioc Bath and Wells Indep
CHELWORTH tything parish St Sampson Wilts
CHENIES parish 1592 Bucks 5 miles ne Amersham pop 649 archd
Buckingham dioc Lincoln Part Bapt
CHEPSTOW parish 1596 co Monmouth 15 miles se Monmouth pop
3,524 archd and dioc Llandaff Bapt, Indep, Wesl Meth, Roman Cath
CHERHILL parish 1690 Wilts 3 miles e Calne pop 404 pec juris
Treasurer of the Cathedral Church of Salisbury
CHERINGTON parish 1568 Gloucs 4 miles ne Tetbury pop 251 archd
and dioc Gloucester
CHERINGTON parish 1538 Warws 3-3/4 miles se Shipston upon Stour
pop 328 archd and dioc Worcester

CHERITON parish 1562 Kent 2-1/4 miles nw Folkestone pop 1,143
   archd and dioc Canterbury
CHERITON parish 1557 Hamps 2-1/2 miles sw New Alresford pop
   722 pec juris of incumbent
CHERITON, BISHOP parish 1538 Devon 10 miles nw Exeter pop 799
   archd and dioc Exeter
CHERITON FITZPAINE parish 1660 Devon 4-3/4 miles ne Crediton
   pop 1,085 archd and dioc Exeter
CHERITON, NORTH parish 1558 Somerset 3 miles sw Wincanton
   pop 246 archd Wells dioc Bath and Wells
CHERITON, SOUTH hamlet parish Horsington Somerset
CHERRINGTON township parish Edgmond Shrops pop 192
CHERRY BURTON Yorks See BURTON CHERRY
CHERTSEY parish 1606 Surrey 13 miles ne Guildford pop 4,795 archd
   Surrey dioc Winchester Bapt, Meth, Presb
CHESEL hamlet parish West Winteslow Wilts
CHESELBORNE parish 1644 regs to 1630 damaged by fire Dorset
   10-1/2 miles sw Blandford Forum pop 351 archd Dorset dioc
   Bristol
CHESHAM parish 1538 Bucks 30 miles se Buckingham comp chapelry
   Lattimers with hamlets Waterside, Botley, Ashley Green, Billing-
   ton, Chartridge, Hundridge with Ashridge pop 5,388 archd Buck-
   ingham dioc Lincoln
CHESHAM BOIS parish 1562 Bucks 1-1/4 miles se Chesham pop 157
   archd Buckingham dioc Lincoln
CHESHUNT parish 1559 Herts 8 miles se Hertford comp three wards
   of Cheshunt Street, Waltham Cross and Woodside pop 5,021
   archd Middlesex dioc London
CHESLYN HAY township parish Cannock Staffs pop 648
CHESSINGTON parish 1656 Surrey 2-3/4 miles nw Ewell pop 189
   archd Surrey dioc Winchester
CHESTER CITY Ches 17 miles s Liverpool pop 21,363 comp Cathedral 1687, St Bridget 1649, St John the Baptist 1559, St Martin 1680,
   St Michael 1581, St Olave 1612, St Peter 1559, St Mary 1628, St
   Oswald 1580, Holy Trinity 1654 archd and dioc Chester Bapt, Soc
   of Friends, Countess of Huntingdon, Indep, Welsh and Wesl Meth,
   New Connection Meth, Sandemanians, Unit, Roman Cath
CHESTER LE STREET parish 1582 co Durham 6-1/4 miles n Durham
   comp chapelry Great Lumley, townships Lambton, Little Lumley,
   chapelries Lamesley, Tanfield, townships Beamish, Birtley, Ches-
   ter le Street, Edmondsley, Harraton, Hedley, Kibblesworth, Lintz
   Green, Pelton, Plawsworth, Ravensworth, Urpeth, Ouston, Wald-
   ridge pop 15,378 archd and dioc Durham Indep, Prim and Wesl
   Meth
CHESTER, LITTLE township parish St Alkmund Derbys pop 181
CHESTERBLADE chapelry parish Evercreech Somerset
CHESTERFIELD parish 1558 Derbys 25 miles ne Derby comp chap-
   elries Brimington, Temple Normanton, townships Hasland, Tapton,

Walton, hamlets Calow, Newbold with Dunstan, Pilsley pop 10,683
sep juris archd Derby dioc Lichfield Bapt, Soc of Friends, Indep,
Prim and Wesl Meth, Sandemanians, Unit

CHESTERFORD, GREAT parish 1586 Essex 4 miles nw Saffron Walden pop 873 archd Colchester dioc London

CHESTERFORD, LITTLE parish 1559 Essex 3 miles nw Saffron Walden pop 211 archd Colchester dioc London

CHESTERHOPE hamlet parish Corsenside Northumberland

CHESTERTON parish 1564 Cambs 1-1/4 miles ne Cambridge pop
1,174 archd and dioc Ely

CHESTERTON parish 1561 Hunts 4-1/2 miles nw Stilton pop 105
archd Huntingdon dioc Lincoln

CHESTERTON parish 1540 co Oxford 2 miles sw Bicester pop 382
archd and dioc Oxford

CHESTERTON township parish Wolstanton Staffs pop 960 Wesl Meth

CHESTERTON parish 1538 Warws 5-1/2 miles ne Kington pop 188
archd Coventry dioc Lichfield

CHESTERTON, LITTLE Warws See KINGTON

CHESWARDINE parish 1558 Shrops 4-1/2 miles se Drayton pop 1,051
archd Stafford dioc Lichfield

CHETNOLE chapelry parish Yetminster Dorset pop 236

CHETTISCOMBE chapelry parish Tiverton Devon

CHETTISHAM chapelry 1701 parish St Mary Ely Cambs

CHETTLE parish 1538 Dorset 7 miles ne Blandford Forum pop 129
archd Dorset dioc Bristol

CHETTON parish 1538 Shrops 4 miles sw Bridgenorth pop 627 archd
Salop dioc Hereford

CHETWOOD parish 1756 Bucks 5 miles sw Buckingham pop 149
archd Buckingham dioc Lincoln

CHETWYND parish 1585 Shrops 1-3/4 miles nw Newport pop 766
archd Salop dioc Lichfield

CHEVELEY parish 1559 Cambs 3-1/4 miles se Newmarket pop 541
archd Sudbury dioc Norwich

CHEVENING parish 1561 Kent 3-1/4 miles nw Seven Oaks pop 901
pec deanery of Shoreham

CHEVERELL, GREAT parish 1653 Wilts 2-1/2 miles w East Lavington pop 576 archd and dioc Salisbury

CHEVERELL, LITTLE parish 1653 Wilts 1-3/4 miles sw East Lavington pop 259 archd and dioc Salisbury

CHEVETT township parish Royston W R York pop 38

CHEVINGTON parish 1559 Suffolk 5-1/2 miles sw Bury St Edmunds
pop 573 archd Sudbury dioc Norwich

CHEW, MAGNA parish 1558 Somerset 3 miles w Pensford pop 2,048
archd Bath dioc Bath and Wells Wesl Meth

CHEW STOKE parish 1663 Somerset 4-1/4 miles sw Pensford pop
693 archd Bath dioc Bath and Wells Wesl Meth

CHEWTON tything parish Milton Hamps

CHEWTON MINDIP parish 1561 Somerset 5-3/4 miles ne Wells pop

1,315 archd Wells dioc Bath and Wells Wesl Meth

CHICH Essex See OSYTH, ST

CHICHELEY parish 1539 Bucks 2-1/4 miles ne Newport Pagnell pop 218 archd Buckingham dioc Lincoln

CHICHESTER City Sussex 62 miles sw London pop 8,270 comp All Saints 1557, St Andrew 1568, St Martin 1684, St Olave 1569, St Pancras 1559, St Peter the Great 1558, St Peter the Less 1679, St Bartholomew 1571 pec of deanery of South Malling and pec of Dean of Chichester Soc of Friends, Indep, Huntingtonians, Wesl Meth, Unit

CHICKERELL, WEST parish 1723 Dorset 3 miles nw Weymouth pop 476 archd Dorset dioc Bristol

CHICKLADE parish 1721 Wilts 1 mile n Hindon pop 127 archd and dioc Salisbury

CHICKNEY parish 1554 Essex 3-1/2 miles sw Thaxted pop 72 archd Middlesex dioc London

CHICKSANDS extra parochial liberty 1-1/2 miles nw Shefford Beds pop 66

CHICKSGROVE tything parish Tisbury Wilts

CHICKSTON hamlet parish Littleham Devon

CHICKWARD township with Pembers Oak and Lilwall parish Kington Herefs pop 381

CHIDDEN tything parish Hambledon Hamps

CHIDDINGFORD parish 1563 Surrey 4-1/2 miles ne Haslemere pop 1,095 archd Surrey dioc Winchester

CHIDDINGLY parish 1621 Sussex 5-1/2 miles nw Hailsham pop 902 archd Lewes dioc Chichester

CHIDDINGSTONE parish 1558 Kent 7-1/2 miles sw Tonbridge pop 1,223 pec deanery of Shoreham

CHIDEOCK parish 1654 Dorset 2-3/4 miles w Bridgeport pop 838 archd Dorset dioc Bristol

CHIDHAM parish 1652 Sussex 6 miles sw Chichester pop 320 archd and dioc Chichester

CHIDLOW township parish Malpas Ches pop 15

CHIEVELEY parish 1560 Berks 5-1/4 miles ne Newbury pop 1,837 archd Berks dioc Salisbury Wesl Meth

CHIGNAL parish 1723 Essex 3-1/2 miles nw Chelmsford pop 222 archd Essex dioc London

CHIGNAL SMEALY parish 1600 Essex 4-3/4 miles nw Chelmsford pop 75 archd Essex dioc London

CHIGWELL parish 1555 Essex 6 miles s Epping pop 1,815 archd Essex dioc London Part Bapt

CHILBOLTON parish 1699 Hamps 4 miles se Andover pop 375 pec of the incumbent

CHILCOMB parish 1556 Hamps 2 miles se Winchester pop 192 pec juris of incumbent

CHILCOMBE parish 1748 Dorset 4-3/4 miles se Bridport pop 35 archd Dorset dioc Bristol

CHILCOMPTON parish 1649 Somerset 6-3/4 miles ne Shepton Mallet pop 487 pec of Dean of Wells Wesl Meth

CHILCOTE chapelry 1595 parish Burton upon Trent Derbys pop 191 archd Stafford dioc Lichfield

CHILDERDITCH parish 1538 Essex 3 miles se Brentwood pop 251 archd Essex dioc London

CHILDERLEY parish no regs Cambs 7-1/2 miles nw Cambridge pop 96 archd and dioc Ely

CHILDREY parish 1558 Berks 2-1/2 miles w Wantage pop 562 archd Berks dioc Salisbury Wesl Meth

CHILD'S ERCALL Shrops See ERCALL, CHILD'S

CHILDWALL parish 1556 Lancs 4-1/4 miles se Liverpool comp chapelries Garston, Hale, Wavertree, Much Woolton, townships Allerton, Childwall, Halewood, Speke, Little Woolton pop 7,706 archd and dioc Chester

CHILFROOM parish 1709 Dorset 9 miles nw Dorchester pop 111 archd Dorset dioc Bristol

CHILHAM parish 1558 Kent 6-1/2 miles sw Canterbury pop 1,140 archd and dioc Canterbury

CHILHAMPTON chapelry parish South Newton Wilts

CHILLENDEN parish 1559 Kent 3-3/4 miles se Wingham pop 1,541 archd and dioc Canterbury

CHILLESFORD parish 1740 Suffolk 3-1/4 miles nw Oxford pop 179 archd Suffolk dioc Norwich

CHILLINGHAM parish 1696 Northumberland 5 miles se Wooler comp townships Chillingham, Hebburn, Newton pop 477 archd Northumberland dioc Durham

CHILLINGTON parish 1750 prev incl with Cudworth Somerset 4 miles nw Crewkerne pop 311 archd Taunton dioc Bath and Wells

CHILLINGTON liberty parish Brewood Staffs

CHILMARK parish 1653 Wilts 4 miles e Hindon pop 507 archd and dioc Salisbury

CHILSON tything parish Charlbury co Oxford pop 251

CHILSWELL liberty parish Cumner Berks pop 12

CHILTHORNE DOMER parish 1678 Somerset 2 miles s Ilchester pop 236 archd Wells dioc Bath and Wells

CHILTINGTON, EAST chapelry 1651 parish Westmeston Sussex pop 258

CHILTINGTON, WEST parish 1558 Sussex 8-1/2 miles nw Steyning pop 718 archd and dioc Chichester

CHILTON parish 1584 Berks 3-1/4 miles n East Ilsley pop 274 archd Berks dioc Salisbury

CHILTON parish 1730 Bucks 3-1/2 miles nw Thame pop 314 archd Buckingham dioc Lincoln

CHILTON township parish Merrington co Durham pop 168

CHILTON parish 1623 Suffolk 1-3/4 miles ne Sudbury pop 108 archd Sudbury dioc Norwich

CHILTON hamlet parish Clare Suffolk

CHILTON CANDOVER Hamps See CANDOVER CHILTON
CHILTON CANTILO parish 1714 Somerset 3-3/4 miles e Ilchester
pop 127 archd Wells dioc Bath and Wells
CHILTON FOLIATT parish 1569 Wilts 2-1/4 miles nw Hungerford
pop 761 archd Wilts dioc Salisbury Wesl Meth
CHILTON TRINITY parish 1735 Somerset 1-1/2 miles nw Bridge-
water pop 49 archd Taunton dioc Bath and Wells
CHILTON UPON POLDON chapelry 1654 parish Moorlinch Somerset
pop 423
CHILVERS COTON parish 1654 Warws 3/4 miles sw Nuneaton pop
2,494 archd Coventry dioc Lichfield Wesl Meth
CHILWELL hamlet parish Attenborough Notts pop 892
CHILWORTH hamlet parish Great Milton co Oxford pop 85
CHILWORTH parish 1721 Hamps 4 miles se Romsey pop 150 archd
and dioc Winchester
CHILWORTH or ST MARTHA parish 1779 Surrey 2-3/4 miles se
Guildford pop 195 Donative of Proprietor of the Chilworth Estate
CHIMNELL township parish Whitchurch Shrops
CHIMNEY hamlet parish Bampton co Oxford pop 42
CHINEHAM tything parish Monk's Sherborne Hamps
CHINGFORD parish 1715 Essex 9-1/2 miles ne London pop 963 archd
Essex dioc London
CHINLEY chapelry 1729 parish Glossop Derbys 2-1/2 miles nw
Chapel en le Frith pop 993   Wesl Meth
CHINNOCK, EAST parish 1647 Somerset 5 miles sw Yeovil pop 673
archd Wells dioc Bath and Wells
CHINNOCK, MIDDLE parish 1695 Somerset 3-1/2 miles ne Crew-
kerne pop 173 archd Wells dioc Bath and Wells
CHINNOCK, WEST parish 1678 Somerset 3 miles ne Crewkerne pop
523 archd Wells dioc Bath and Wells Wesl Meth
CHINNOR parish 1581 co Oxford 3-1/2 miles ne Watlington pop
1,225 archd and dioc Oxford
CHIPCASE chapelry parish Chollerton Northumberland pop 422
CHIPLEY hamlet parish Clare Suffolk
CHIPPENHAM parish 1559 Cambs 4-1/2 miles ne Newmarket pop
665 archd Sudbury dioc Norwich
CHIPPENHAM parish 1578 borough Wilts 33 miles nw Salisbury
comp Chippenham, tythings Allington, Tytherton Stanley with
Nethermore pop 4,333 archd Wilts dioc Salisbury Bapt, Indep,
Wesl Meth
CHIPPING parish 1559 Lancs 9-1/4 miles nw Clitheroe comp town-
ships Chipping, Thornley with Wheatley pop 1,850 archd Rich-
mond dioc Chester
CHIPPING CAMPDEN Gloucs See CAMPDEN, CHIPPING
CHIPPINGHURST hamlet parish Cuddesden co Oxford pop 30
CHIPSTABLE parish 1694 Somerset 2-3/4 miles sw Wiveliscombe
pop 343 archd Taunton dioc Bath and Wells
CHIPSTEAD parish 1656 Surry 2-3/4 miles ne Gatton pop 522 archd

Surrey dioc Winchester

CHIRBURY parish 1629 Shrops 3-1/4 miles ne Montgomery pop 1,575 archd Salop dioc Hereford

CHIRDON township parish Greystead Northumberland pop 77

CHIRTON township parish Tynemouth Northumberland pop 4,973

CHIRTON parish 1585 Wilts

CHISELHAMPTON parish 1556 co Oxford 8 miles n Wallingford pop 126 pec court of Corchester

CHISELHURST parish 1558 Kent 11 miles se London archd and dioc Rochester Wesl Meth

CHISENBURY tything parish Nether Avon Wilts

CHISHALL, GREAT parish 1583 Essex 8-1/4 miles nw Saffron Walden pop 271 archd Colchester dioc London

CHISHALL, LITTLE parish 1577 Essex 8-1/4 miles sw Saffron Walden pop 106 archd Colchester dioc London

CHISLEBOROUGH parish 1558 Somerset 4 miles ne Crewkerne pop 483 archd Wells dioc Bath and Wells

CHISLEDON parish 1641 Wilts 3-1/2 miles se Swindon pop 1,148 archd Wilts dioc Salisbury

CHISLETT parish 1538 Kent 7 miles ne Canterbury archd and dioc Canterbury

CHISWICK parish 1678 Middlesex 4-1/2 miles sw London pop 4,994 pec juris of Dean and Chapter of St Paul's London

CHISWORTH township parish Glossop Derbys

CHITHURST chapelry 1739 parish Iping Sussex pop 172

CHITTERN All Saints parish 1653 Wilts 4 miles ne Heytesbury pop 382 archd and dioc Salisbury

CHITTERN St Mary parish 1653 Wilts 3-3/4 miles ne Heytesbury pop 183 archd and dioc Salisbury

CHITTLEHAMPTON parish 1575 Devon 5-1/4 miles w South Molton pop 1,897 archd Barnstaple dioc Exeter

CHITTOE tything parish Bishop's Cannings Wilts pop 220

CHIVELSTONE parish 1684 Devon 6 miles Kingsbridge pop 601 archd Totnes dioc Exeter

CHIVESFIELD Herts See GRAVELEY

CHIVINGTON, EAST township parish Warkworth Northumberland pop 234

CHIVINGTON, WEST township parish Warkworth Northumberland pop 117

CHOBHAM parish 1654 Surrey 4-1/2 miles se Bagshot pop 1,937 archd Surrey dioc Winchester Wesl Meth

CHOCKNELL hamlet parish Leigh Worcs

CHOLDERTON, EAST chapelry parish Amport Hamps

CHOLDERTON, WEST parish 1616 Wilts 5 miles ne Amesbury pop 161 archd and dioc Salisbury

CHOLESBURY Bucks See CHOULSBURY

CHOLLERTON parish 1647 Northumberland 6 miles n Hexham comp chapelry Chipchase with Gunnerton, townships Barrasford, Chol-

lerton, Colwell with Swinburn, part of township Broomhope with
Buteland pop 1,252 archd Northumberland dioc Durham
CHOLMONDELEY township parish Malpas Ches pop 272
CHOLMONDSTONE township parish Acton Ches pop 180
CHOLSEY parish 1540 Berks 2-1/2 miles se Wallingford pop 983
archd Berks dioc Salisbury
CHOPPINGTON township parish Bedlington co Durham and co North-
umberland
CHOPWELL township parish Ryton co Durham pop 254
CHORLEY township parish Wilmslow Ches pop 474
CHORLEY township parish Wrenbury Ches pop 168
CHORLEY parish 1550 Lancs 32 miles se Lancaster pop 9,282 archd
and dioc Chester Indep, Wesl Meth, Unit, Roman Cath
CHORLTON township parish Malpas Ches pop 155
CHORLTON township parish Wybunbury Ches pop 109
CHORLTON township parish Backford Ches pop 86
CHORLTON chapelry 1737 parish Manchester Lancs pop 666
CHORLTON chapelry 1564 parish Eccleshall Staffs pop 251
CHORLTON HILL township parish Eccleshall Staffs pop 135
CHORLTON ROW chapelry parish Manchester Lancs pop 20,569
Indep, Wesl Meth
CHOULESBURY parish 1583 Bucks 4 miles nw Chesham pop 127
archd Buckingham dioc Lincoln
CHOWBENT village, chapelry Atherton parish Leigh Lancs Unit
CHOWLEY township parish Coddington Ches pop 70
CHRISHALL parish 1662 Essex 6-1/2 miles nw Saffron Walden pop
487 archd Essex dioc London
CHRIST CHURCH Middlesex See SPITALFIELDS
CHRISTCHURCH parish 1698 co Monmouth 2-1/4 miles ne Newport
pop 862 archd and dioc Llandaff
CHRISTCHURCH parish 1576 Hamps 21-1/2 miles sw Southampton
comp tythings of Town and Street, Winkton with Burton, Bure
with Hinton, Hurn with Parley, Ilford with Tuckton pop 5,344
archd and dioc Winchester Indep, Roman Cath
CHRIST CHURCH parish 1671 Surrey pop 13,705 archd Surrey dioc
Winchester
CHRISTIAN MALFORD parish 1653 Wilts 5-1/2 miles ne Chippen -
ham comp chapelry Avon pop 1,006 archd Wilts dioc Salisbury
Indep
CHRISTLETON parish 1678 Ches 2-1/4 miles se Chester comp town-
ships Christledon, Cotton Abbots, Cotton Edmund's, Littleton,
Rowton pop 893 archd and dioc Chester Wesl Meth
CHRISTON parish 1668 Somerset 5 miles nw Axbridge pop 83 archd
Wells dioc Bath and Wells
CHRISTOW parish 1557 Devon 5-1/2 miles nw Chudleigh pop 601
archd and dioc Exeter
CHUDLEIGH parish 1558 Devon 9 miles sw Exeter pop 2,278 pec
juris of Bishop of Exeter

CHULMLEIGH parish 1653 Devon 21-1/2 miles nw Exeter pop 1,573
  archd Barnstaple dioc Exeter Indep, Wesl Meth
CHUNAT township parish Glossop Derbys pop 119
CHURCHAM parish 1541 Gloucs 4-1/2 miles nw Gloucester pop 908
  archd Hereford dioc Gloucester
CHURCH BRAMPTON co Northampton See BRAMPTON, CHURCH
CHURCHDOWN parish 1653 Gloucs 3 miles ne Gloucester comp town-
  ships Churchdown and Hucklecote pop 982 archd and dioc Glou-
  cester
CHURCH END township parish Shenley Bucks pop 240
CHURCHENFORD hamlet parish Church Stanton Devon
CHURCHFIELD hamlet parish Oundle co Northampton
CHURCHILL parish 1630 co Oxford 3 miles sw Chipping Norton pop
  633 archd and dioc Oxford
CHURCHILL parish 1653 Somerset 4-3/4 miles ne Axbridge pop 985
  pec of Banwell
CHURCHILL parish 1564 Worcs 3-1/2 miles ne Kidderminster pop
  114 archd and dioc Worcester
CHURCHILL parish 1540 Worcs 5-1/2 miles se Worcester pop 161
  archd and dioc Worcester
CHURCHOVER parish 1658 Warws 4-1/4 miles ne Rugby pop 295
  archd Coventry dioc Lichfield
CHURCH STANTON parish 1662 Devon 11 miles ne Honiton pop 977
  archd and dioc Exeter
CHURCHSTOW parish 1538 Devon 2-3/4 miles nw Kingsbridge pop
  326 archd Totnes dioc Exeter
CHURCH TOWN chapelry 1633 parish Whalley Lancs pop 979 archd
  and dioc Chester Wesl Meth
CHURSTON FERRERS parish 1590 Devon 1-1/2 miles nw Brixham
  pop 763 archd Totnes dioc Exeter
CHURTON township parish Aldford Ches pop 238
CHURTON township parish Farndon Ches pop 122
CHURTON or CHIRKTON parish 1585 Wilts 4-1/4 miles ne East
  Lavington pop 409 archd and dioc Salisbury
CHURTON HEATH or BRUERA chapelry 1657 parish Aldford Ches
  pop 14
CHURWELL township parish Batley W R York pop 1,023 Wesl Meth
CHUTE parish 1580 Wilts 3-3/4 miles ne Ludgershall pop 501 pec
  juris of Prebendary of Chute and Chisenbury in Cathedral Church
  of Salisbury
CHUTE FOREST extra parochial district 4-3/4 miles ne Ludgershall
  Wilts pop 110
CIPPENHAM liberty parish Burnham Bucks
CIRCOURT joint chapelry with Goosey parish Stanford in the Vale
  Berks
CIRENCESTER 1560 borough Gloucs 17 miles se Gloucester comp
  tythings of Barton Chesterton, Oakley, Spirringate and Wiggott
  pop 5,420 archd and dioc Gloucester Bapt, Soc of Friends, Indep,

Wesl Meth, Unit
CLACK hamlet parish Lineham Wilts
CLACKHEATON chapelry 1761 parish Birstall W R York pop 3,317
   Indep, Moravians
CLACTON, GREAT parish 1542 Essex 14-1/2 miles se Colchester
   pop 1,149 archd Colchester dioc London Wesl Meth
CLACTON, LITTLE parish 1538 Essex 12-1/2 miles se Colchester
   pop 546 archd Colchester dioc London
CLAIFE township parish Hawkeshead Lancs pop 463
CLAINES parish 1538 Worcs 2-1/2 miles n Worcester pop 5,568 pec
   juris Bishop of Worcester
CLANNABOROUGH parish 1696 Devon 1-1/2 miles ne Bow pop 58
   archd Barnstaple dioc Exeter
CLANDON, EAST parish 1558 Surrey 4 miles ne Guildford pop 281
   archd Surrey dioc Winchester
CLANDON, WEST parish 1536 Surrey 3 miles ne Guildford pop 389
   archd Surrey dioc Winchester
CLANFIELD parish 1615 co Oxford 5 miles ne Lechlade pop 529
   archd and dioc Oxford
CLANFIELD parish 1547 Hamps 5-3/4 miles sw Petersfield pop 210
   archd and dioc Winchester
CLAPCOT liberty parish Allhallows, Wallingford Berks pop 130
CLAPHAM parish 1696 Beds 2-1/2 miles nw Bedford pop 298 archd
   Bedford dioc Lincoln
CLAPHAM parish 1552 Surrey 4 miles s London pop 9,958 archd
   Surrey dioc Winchester Indep, Bapt
CLAPHAM parish 1685 Sussex 5 miles se Arundel pop 229 archd
   and dioc Chichester
CLAPHAM parish 1596 W R York 6 miles nw Settle comp townships
   Austwick, Clapham, with Newby, Lawkland pop 1,909 archd Rich-
   mond dioc Chester
CLAPTON Cambs See CROYDON
CLAPTON chapelry parish Bourton on the Water Gloucs pop 109
CLAPTON hamlet parish St John Hackney Middlesex Indep, Wesl Meth
CLAPTON parish 1558 co Northampton 5-1/4 miles ne Thrapston pop
   99 archd Northampton dioc Peterborough
CLAPTON tything parish Midsummer Norton Somerset
CLAPTON parish 1558 Somerset 9-1/4 miles w Bristol pop 167
   archd Bath dioc Bath and Wells
CLARE parish 1558 Suffolk 18 miles sw Bury St Edmund's pop 1,619
   archd Sudbury dioc Norwich
CLAREBOROUGH parish 1563 Notts 2-1/2 miles ne East Retford
   pop 2,106 archd Nottingham dioc York
CLARENDON PARK extra parochial liberty 3-1/2 miles se Salisbury
   Wilts pop 177
CLARETON township parish Allerton Mauleverer W R York pop 20
CLAREWOOD township parish Corbridge Northumberland pop 71
CLATFORD tything parish Preshute Wilts

CLATFORD, GOODWORTH parish 1538 Hamps 2 miles s Andover
pop 414 archd and dioc Winchester

CLATFORD, UPPER parish 1570 Hamps 1 mile s Andover pop 487
archd and dioc Winchester

CLATTERCOTT extra parochial liberty 6 miles n Banbury co Oxford
pop 9

CLATWORTHY parish 1558 Somerset 4 miles nw Wiveliscombe pop
246 archd Taunton dioc Bath and Wells

CLAUGHTON joint township with Grange parish Bidstone Ches pop 224

CLAUGHTON township parish Garstang Lancs pop 842

CLAUGHTON parish 1701 Lancs 7-1/2 miles ne Lancaster pop 116
archd Richmond dioc Chester

CLAVERDON parish 1593 Warws 3-1/2 miles se Henley in Arden
pop 666 archd and dioc Worcester

CLAVERING parish 1555 Essex 7-1/2 miles nw Stanstead Mountfitchet pop 1,134 archd Colchester dioc London

CLAVERLEY parish 1568 Shrops 5-1/2 miles e Bridgenorth pop
1,521 pec of Bridgenorth

CLAVERTON parish 1582 Somerset 2-1/2 miles se Bath pop 156
archd Bath dioc Bath and Wells

CLAWRPLWYF hamlet parish Wynyddyslwyn co Monmouth pop 1,918

CLAWTON parish 1694 Devon 3-1/2 miles s Holsworthy pop 570
archd Totnes dioc Exeter

CLAXBY parish 1699 lincs 3 miles s Alford pop 101 archd and dioc
Lincoln

CLAXBY parish 1556 Lincs 4 miles n Market Rasen pop 205 archd
and dioc Lincoln

CLAXBY PLUCKACRE See MOORBY

CLAXTON township parish Greatham co Durham pop 32

CLAXTON or LONG CLAWSON parish 1558 Leics 6 miles nw Melton
Mowbray pop 776 archd Leicester dioc Lincoln Wesl Meth

CLAXTON parish 1747 Norfolk 7-1/2 miles se Norwich pop 192
archd Norfolk dioc Norwich Bapt

CLAXTON township parish Bossall N R York pop 163

CLAYBROOKE parish 1705 Leics 4-3/4 miles nw Lutterworth comp
chapelry Little Wigston, townships Great Claybrooke, Little Claybrooke, liberty of Bittesby, hamlet Ullesthorpe pop 1,242 archd
Leicester dioc Lincoln

CLAYBROOKE, LITTLE township parish Claybrooke Leics pop 82

CLAY COTON co Northampton See COTTON, CLAY

CLAYDON chapelry 1569 parish Cropredy co Oxford pop 291

CLAYDON parish 1559 Suffolk 3-1/2 miles nw Ipswich pop 402 archd
Suffolk dioc Norwich

CLAYDON, EAST parish 1584 Bucks 2-3/4 miles sw Winslow pop
336 archd Buckingham dioc Lincoln

CLAYDON, MIDDLE parish 1630 Bucks 4 miles sw Winslow pop 136
archd Buckingham dioc Lincoln

CLAYDON, STEEPLE parish 1575 Bucks 5-1/2 miles w Winslow

pop 881 archd Buckingham dioc Lincoln

CLAYHANGER parish 1538 Devon 4-3/4 miles ne Bampton pop 272 archd and dioc Exeter

CLAYHIDON parish 1637 Devon 4 miles se Wellington pop 767 archd and dioc Exeter

CLAY LANE township parish North Wingfield Derbys pop 564

CLAYPOLE parish 1538 Lincs 5 miles se Newark pop 586 archd and dioc Lincoln Wesl Meth

CLAYTHORPE chapelry parish Belleau Lincs pop 61

CLAYTHORPE hamlet parish Burton in Kendal Westm

CLAYTON liberty parish Stoke upon Trent Staffs pop 171

CLAYTON parish 1601 Sussex 2-1/4 miles se Hurst Pierrepoint pop 489 archd Lewes dioc Chichester

CLAYTON township parish South Stainley W R York

CLAYTON township parish Bardford W R York pop 4,469 Wesl Meth

CLAYTON joint parish 1577 W R York 9 miles ne Barnsley archd and dioc York

CLAYTON GRIFFITH township parish Trentham Staffs pop 53

CLAYTON LE DALE township parish Blackburn Lancs pop 551

CLAYTON le MOORS township parish Whalley Lancs pop 2,171

CLAYTON le WOODS township parish Leyland Lancs pop 926

CLAYTON, WEST township parish High Hoyland W R York pop 887

CLAYWORTH parish 1545 Notts 6 miles ne East Retford pop 577 archd Nottingham dioc York Wesl Meth

CLEADON township parish Whitburn co Durham

CLEARWELL chapelry parish Newland Gloucs pop 678

CLEASBY parish 1712 N R York 3 miles sw Darlington pop 162 archd Richmond dioc Chester

CLEATHAM township parish Manton Lincs pop 76

CLEATLAM township parish Staindrop and Fainford co Durham pop 94

CLEATOR parish 1572 Cumberland 2-1/4 miles n Egremont pop 487 archd Richmond dioc Chester

CLECKHEATON Yorks See CLACKHEATON

CLEE parish 1562 Lincs 2-1/4 miles se Grimsby pop 674 archd and dioc Lincoln

CLEE parish 1634 Shrops 8-1/4 miles ne Ludlow pop 294 archd Salop dioc Hereford

CLEER, ST parish 1678 Cornwall 2-3/4 miles nw Liskeard pop 982 archd Cornwall dioc Exeter

CLEETHORPE township parish Clee Lincs pop 497 Wesl Meth

CLEEVE, BISHOP'S parish 1563 Gloucs 3-1/4 miles ne Cheltenham comp chapelry Stoke Orchard, township Bishop's Cleve, hamlets Gotherington, Southam with Brockampton and Woodmancott pop 1,642 pec juris of rector

CLEEVE, CHAPEL hamlet parish Old Cleeve Somerset

CLEEVE, OLD parish 1661 Somerset 3-3/4 miles se Dunster pop 1,347 archd Taunton dioc Bath and Wells Wesl Meth

CLEEVE, PRIOR'S parish 1598 Worcs 5-1/2 miles ne Evesham pop 368 archd and dioc Worcester

CLEHONGER parish 1671 Herefs 3-1/2 miles sw Hereford pop 365 Cons court of Dean of Hereford

CLEMENT'S,ST parish 1543 Cornwall 2 miles e Truro pop 2,885 archd Cornwall dioc Exeter

CLEMENT'S, ST parish 1666 co Oxford 3 miles nw Oxford pop 1,836 archd and dioc Oxford

CLENCHWHARTON parish 1720 Norfolk 2-3/4 miles w King's Lynn pop 478 archd and dioc Norwich

CLENNELL township parish Allenton Northumberland pop 15

CLENT parish 1562 Staffs and Worcs 3-1/4 miles se Stourbridge pop 922 archd and dioc Worcester Wesl Meth

CLEOBURY MORTIMER parish 1603 Shrops 32 miles se Shrewsbury pop 1,716 archd Salop dioc Hereford Wesl Meth, Roman Cath

CLERBURY, NORTH parish 1680 Shrops 8 miles sw Bridgenorth pop 187 archd Salop dioc Hereford

CLERKENWELL parish Middlesex adj city of London pop 47,634 comp St James 1560, St John's 1723, St Marks 1791 archd and dioc London Countess of Huntingdon, Bapt, Soc of Friends, Indep, Wesl and other Meth, Scotch Church, Welsh Chapel

CLETHER, ST parish 1640 Cornwall 7 miles e Camelford pop 171 archd Cornwall dioc Exeter

CLEVEDON parish 1727 Somerset 14 miles sw Bristol pop 1,147 archd Bath dioc Bath and Wells

CLEVEDON, MILTON parish 1595 Somerset 2-1/4 miles nw Bruton pop 242 archd Wells dioc Bath and Wells

CLEVELAND PORT hamlet parish Ormesby N R York

CLEVELEY hamlet parish Church Enstone co Oxford

CLEVELY township chiefly in parish Garstang Lancs pop 140

CLEVERTON township parish Lea Wilts

CLEWER parish 1653 Berks 1 mile w New Windsor pop 3,011 archd Berks dioc Salisbury Wesl Meth, Roman Cath

CLEY parish 1538 Norfolk 26 miles nw Norwich pop 827 archd and dioc Norwich Wesl Meth

CLEYGATE manor parish Thames Ditton Surrey pop 708

CLIBURN parish 1565 Westm 7-1/4 miles nw Appleby pop 229 archd and dioc Carlisle

CLIDDESDEN parish 1636 Hamps 1-3/4 miles sw Basingstoke pop 329 archd and dioc Winchester

CLIEVELOAD chapelry parish Powick Worcs pop 29

CLIFF joint township with Lund parish Hemingbrough E R York pop 490 Wesl Meth

CLIFFE AT HOO parish 1558 Kent 5 miles nw Rochester pop 832 pec juris of incumbent

CLIFFE Sussex See LEWES

CLIFFE township parish Manfield N R York pop 68 Roman Cath

CLIFFE, KING'S parish 1590 co Northampton 31 miles ne Northamp-

ton pop 1,173 archd Northampton dioc Peterborough
CLIFFE, NORTH township parish Sancton E R York pop 85
CLIFFE PYPARD parish 1576 Wilts 4 miles s Wootton Bassett comp
tythings Broadtown, Cliffe, Thornhill pop 885 archd Wilts dioc
Salisbury
CLIFFE, SOUTH township parish North Cave E R York pop 104
CLIFFE, WEST parish 1576 Kent 2-3/4 miles ne Dover pop 82 archd
and dioc Canterbury
CLIFFORD parish 1690 Herefs 9-1/2 miles sw Kington pop 807 archd
and dioc Hereford
CLIFFORD township parish Bramham W R York pop 1,166 Wesl Meth
CLIFFORD CHAMBERS parish 1538 Gloucs 2-3/4 miles sw Stratford
upon Avon pop 336 archd and dioc Gloucester
CLIFTON parish 1538 Beds 1-1/2 miles ne Shefford pop 664 archd
Bedford dioc Lincoln
CLIFTON or ROCK SAVAGE township parish Runcorn Ches pop 36
CLIFTON chapelry parish Ashbourn Derbys pop 839
CLIFTON parish 1538 Gloucs 1-1/4 miles w Bristol pop 12,032 archd
Gloucester dioc Bristol Countess of Huntingdon's Connection,
Wesl Meth
CLIFTON township parish Kirkham Lancs pop 508
CLIFTON township parish Eccles Lancs pop 1,277
CLIFTON township parish Stannington Northumberland
CLIFTON parish 1573 Notts 4-1/4 miles sw Nottingham pop 405
archd Nottingham dioc York
CLIFTON township parish Deddington co Oxford pop 268 Wesl Meth
CLIFTON parish 1676 Westm 2-3/4 miles se Penrith pop 288 archd
and dioc Carlisle
CLIFTON township parish St Michael le Belfrey and St Olave, Mary-
gate N R York pop 715
CLIFTON township parish Fewston W R York pop 415
CLIFTON township parish Otley W R York
CLIFTON chapelry parish Dewsbury W R York pop 2,408
CLIFTON CAMPVILLE parish 1662 Staffs 5-3/4 miles ne Tamworth
comp chapelry Harleston, township Haunton pop 801 archd Staf-
ford dioc Lichfield
CLIFTON, GREAT chapelry parish Workington Cumberland pop 286
CLIFTON HAMPDEN parish 1578 co Oxford 3-1/4 miles se Abingdon
pop 288 pec of Dorchester
CLIFTON, LITTLE township parish Workington Cumberland pop 221
CLIFTON MABANK parish See BRADFORD ABBAS Dorset 5-1/2
miles sw Sherborne pop 60 formerly pec juris Dean of Salisbury
united 1824 to Bradford Abbas archd Dorset dioc Bristol
CLIFTON, NORTH parish 1539 Notts 6 miles ne Tuxford comp township South Clifton, hamlets Harby, Spalford pop 949 archd Nottingham dioc York
CLIFTON REYNES parish 1653 Bucks 2-1/2 miles e Olney pop 246
archd Buckingham dioc Lincoln

CLIFTON, SOUTH township parish North Clifton Notts pop 340
CLIFTON UPON DUNSMOOR parish 1594 Warws 2-1/4 miles ne
    Rugby pop 597 archd Coventry dioc Lichfield
CLIFTON UPON TEME parish 1598 borough Worcs 10-1/4 miles ne
    Worcester pop 488 archd Salop dioc Hereford Wesl Meth
CLIFTON UPON URE township parish Thornton Watlass N R York
    pop 43
CLIMPING parish 1678 Sussex 7 miles sw Arundel pop 269 archd
    and dioc Chichester
CLINCH township parish Ingram Northumberland
CLINT township parish Ripley W R York pop 404
CLIPPESBY parish 1732 Norfolk 3 miles ne Acle pop 79 archd and
    dioc Norwich
CLIPSHAM parish 1726 co Rutland 9-3/4 miles ne Oakham archd
    Northampton dioc Peterborough
CLIPSTON parish 1667 co Northampton 4 miles sw Market Harbor-
    ough pop 807 archd Northampton dioc Peterborough
CLIPSTON township parish Plumtree Notts pop 82
CLIPSTONE township parish Edwinstow Notts pop 228
CLIST St George parish 1565 Devon 1-1/2 miles ne Topsham pop 359
    archd and dioc Exeter
CLIST St Lawrence parish 1539 Devon 5 miles se Cullompton pop
    185 archd and dioc Exeter
CLIST St Mary parish 1662 Devon 2-1/4 miles ne Topsham pop 137
    archd and dioc Exeter
CLIST, BROAD parish 1653 Devon 5-3/4 miles ne Exeter pop 2,085
    archd and dioc Exeter
CLIST HONITON parish 1683 Devon 4-1/2 miles ne Exeter pop 426
    pec Dean and Chapter of Exeter
CLIST HYDON parish 1548 Devon 3-3/4 miles se Cullompton pop
    297 archd and dioc Exeter
CLIST SACKVILLE chapelry parishes Clist St Mary, Farringdon and
    Sowton Devon
CLITHEROE town and chapelry 1570 parish Whalley borough Lancs
    pop 5,213 archd and dioc Chester Indep, Meth, Roman Cath
CLIVE township parish Middlewich Ches pop 123
CLIVE chapelry 1667 parish St Mary, Shrewsbury Shrops pop 333
CLIVIGER chapelry 1742 parish Whalley Lancs pop 1,598
CLIXBY chapelry parish Caistor Lincs pop 46
CLOATLY tything parish Hankerton Wilts pop 88
CLODOCK parish 1714 Herefs 16 miles sw Hereford comp chapelries
    Crasswell, Llaveynoe and Longton, township Newton pop 1,863
    archd Brecon dioc St David's
CLOFFOCK extra parochial liberty adjoining parish Workington Cum-
    berland
CLOFORD parish 1561 Somerset 4-1/2 miles sw Frome pop 302
    archd Wells dioc Bath and Wells Wesl Meth
CLOPHILL parish 1568 Beds 1-3/4 miles ne Silsoe pop 972 archd

Bedford dioc Lincoln Wesl Meth

CLOPTON parish 1735 Suffolk 4 miles nw Woodbridge pop 468 archd
Suffolk dioc Norwich

CLOSWORTH parish 1685 Somerset 4-1/2 miles se Yeovil pop 195
archd Wells dioc Bath and Wells

CLOTHALL parish 1717 Herts 2-1/4 miles se Baldock pop 444 archd
Huntingdon dioc Lincoln

CLOTHERHOLME township parish Ripon W R York pop 14

CLOTTON HOOFIELD township parish Tarvin Ches pop 401

CLOUGHTON chapelry 1754 parish Scalby N R York pop 415

CLOVELLY parish 1686 Devon 11 miles sw Bideford pop 907 archd
Barnstaple dioc Exeter Wesl Meth

CLOWHOUSE township parish Heddon on the Wall Northumberland

CLOWNE parish 1570 Derbys 8 miles ne Chesterfield pop 637 archd
Derby dioc Lichfield

CLUN parish 1653 borough Shrops 26 miles sw Shrewsbury comp
market town Clun,townships Edeclift, Hobendrid, Newcastle pop
1,996 archd Salop dioc Hereford Wesl Meth

CLUNBURY parish 1574 Shrops 6-1/2 miles se Bishop's Castle comp
townships Clunbury with Obley, Clunton with Rempton pop 959
archd Salop dioc Hereford

CLUNGUNFORD parish 1559 Shrops 9 miles se Bishop's Castle pop
488 archd Salop dioc Hereford

CLUNTON township parish Clunbury Shrops pop 529

CLUTTON township parish Farndon Ches pop 100

CLUTTON parish 1693 Somerset 3-1/4 miles se Pensford pop 1,287
archd Bath dioc Bath and Wells Meth, Indep

CLYTHA chapelry parish Llanarth co Monmouth pop 331

COAL ASTON township parish Dronfield Derbys pop 300

COALEY parish 1582 Glouce 3-3/4 miles ne Dursley pop 1,124 archd
and dioc Gloucester Wesl Meth

COANWOOD, EAST township parish Haltwhistle Northumberland
pop 156

COASTAMOOR township parish Heighington co Durham pop 13

COATES parish 1566 Gloucs 3-3/4 miles sw Cirencester pop 343
archd and dioc Gloucester

COATES township parish Prestwould Leics pop 68

COATES parish 1661 Lincs 9-1/2 miles nw Lincoln pop 55 archd
Stow dioc Lincoln

COATES parish incl regs Burton Sussex 4 miles se Petworth pop
75 archd and dioc Chichester

COATES township parish Barnoldwick W R York pop 88

COATES, GREAT parish 1653 Lincs 4 miles w Grimsby pop 235
archd and dioc Lincoln

COATES, LITTLE parish 1726 Lincs 3-1/4 miles sw Grimsby pop
49 archd and dioc Lincoln

COATES, NORTH parish 1659 Lincs 10 miles ne Louth pop 215
archd and dioc Lincoln

COATHAM, EAST hamlet parish Kirkleatham N R York
COATHAM MUNDEVILLE township parish Haughton le Skerne co
Durham pop 175
COATHILL township parish Wetheral Cumberland
COATON hamlet parish Ravensthorpe co Northampton pop 116
COATON CLAY parish 1541 co Northampton 6-1/4 miles ne Rugby
pop 83 archd Northampton dioc Peterborough
COAT YARDS or COAL YARDS township parish Nether Witton North-
umberland pop 20
COBERLEY Gloucs See CUBBERLEY
COBHAM parish 1653 Kent 5 miles w Rochester pop 732 archd and
dioc Rochester
COBHAM parish 1562 Surrey 10 miles ne Guildford pop 1,422 archd
Surrey dioc Winchester
COBLEY joint hamlet with Tutnal parish Tardebig Warws
COBRIDGE hamlet parishes Burslem and Stoke upon Trent Staffs
Roman Cath, New Connection of Meth
COCKEN township parish Houghton le Spring co Durham pop 71
COCKERHAM parish 1592 Lancs 5-1/2 miles nw Garstang comp
chapelry Elle, township Cockerham pop 2,794 archd Richmond
dioc Chester
COCKERINGTON, SOUTH parish 1670 Lincs 4-1/4 miles ne Louth
pop 214 archd and dioc Lincoln
COCKERINGTON, NORTH parish 1646 Lincs 4-3/4 miles ne Louth
pop 202 archd and dioc Lincoln
COCKERMOUTH town borough parochial chapelry parish Brigham
1632 borough Cumberland 25 miles sw Carlisle pop 4,536 archd
Richmond dioc Chester Soc of Friends, Indep, Wesl Meth
COCKERSAND ABBEY extra parochial liberty Lancs
COCKERSTON township parish Darlington co Durham pop 522 Wesl
Meth
COCKEY chapelry parish Middleton Lancs Unit
COCKFIELD parish 1578 co Durham 8-1/2 miles ne Barnard Castle
pop 790 archd and dioc Durham
COCKFIELD parish 1561 Suffolk 4-1/4 miles nw Lavenham pop 1,023
archd Sudbury dioc Norwich
COCKING parish 1558 Sussex 2-1/2 miles s Midhurst pop 453 archd
and dioc Chichester
COCKINGTON parish 1628 Devon 2-1/2 miles w Torbay pop 223
archd Totnes dioc Exeter
COCKLAW township parish St John Lee Northumberland pop 188
COCKLE PARK township parish Hebburn Northumberland pop 78
COCKLEY CLEY parish 1731 Norfolk 4 miles sw Swaffham pop 218
archd Norfolk dioc Norwich
COCKSHUT chapelry 1772 parish Ellesmere Shrops
COCKTHORPE parish 1560 Norfolk 5-1/2 miles sw Clay pop 41
archd and dioc Norwich
COCKTHORPE chapelry parish Ducklington co Oxford

CODDENHAM parish 1539 Suffolk 3-3/4 miles se Needham Market
pop 913 archd Suffolk dioc Norwich Wesl Meth
CODDINGTON parish 1681 Ches 6 miles nw Malpas comp townships
Aldersey, Chowley and Coddington pop 345 archd and dioc Chester
CODDINGTON parish 1675 Herefs 7 miles nw Ledbury pop 164 archd
and dioc Hereford
CODDINGTON parish 1676 Notts 2-1/2 miles ne Newark pop 435
archd Nottingham dioc York
CODFORD St Mary parish 1653 Wilts 4 miles se Heytesbury pop 287
archd and dioc Salisbury
CODFORD St Peter parish 1680 Wilts 3-1/2 miles se Heytesbury
pop 387 archd and dioc Salisbury
CODICOTE parish 1559 Herts 2 miles nw Welwyn pop 805 archd St
Albans dioc London Bapt
CODNOR township with Loscoe parish Heanor Derbys pop 1,439
CONDOR CASTLE extra parochial Derbys pop 637
CODRINGTON tything parish Wapley Gloucs
CODSALL parish 1587 Staffs 5 miles nw Wolverhampton
Tettenhall
COEDKERNEW parish 1733 co Monmouth 4-1/4 miles sw Newport
pop 149 archd and dioc Llandaff
COFFINSWELL parish 1560 Devon 3 miles se Newton Bushell pop
265 pec Dean and Chapter of Exeter
COFTON HACKETT parish 1550 Worcs 5 miles ne Bromsgrove archd
and dioc Worcester
COGDEAN hamlet parish Sturminster Marshall Dorset
COGENHOE parish 1558 co Northampton 5-1/4 miles e Northampton
pop 276 archd Northampton dioc Peterborough
COGGES parish 1653 co Oxford 1-1/2 miles se Witney pop 673 archd
and dioc Oxford
COGGESHALL, GREAT parish 1584 Essex 16 miles ne Chelmsford
pop 3,227 archd Colchester dioc London Bapt, Soc of Friends,
Indep, Wesl Meth
COGGESHALL, LITTLE hamlet parish Great Coggeshall Essex pop
455
COGSHALL township parish Great Budworth Ches pop 77
COKER, EAST parish 1560 Somerset 2-1/2 miles sw Yeovil pop 1,330
archd Wells dioc Bath and Wells
COKER, NORTH hamlet parish East Coker Somerset
COKER, WEST parish 1697 Somerset 3-1/2 miles sw Yeovil pop
1,013 archd Wells dioc Bath and Wells
COLAN parish 1665 Cornwall 3-1/2 miles sw St Columb Major pop
261 archd Cornwall dioc Exeter Wesl Meth
COLBOURNE township parish Catterick N R York pop 103
COLBY parish 1552 Norfolk 3-1/4 miles ne Aylsham archd and dioc
Norwich
COLBY township parish St Lawrence Westm pop 148

COLCHESTER town borough Essex 22 miles ne Chelmsford pop
13,766 sep juris comp All Saints 1610, Holy Trinity 1696, St
Botolph 1560, St Giles 1692, St James 1560, St Leonard 1542, St
Martin 1622, St Mary Magdalen 1721, St Mary the Virgin 1561, St
Nicholas 1541, St Peter 1611, St Runwald 1576 archd Colchester
dioc London Bapt, Indep, Soc of Friends, Wesl Meth, Unit
COLD ASHBY co Northampton See ASHBY, COLD
COLDCOATS township parish Ponteland Northumberland pop 36
COLD DUNGHILLS extra parochial district parish St Clement Ipswich
Suffolk
COLD MARTIN township parish Chatton Northumberland
COLDMEECE township parish Eccleshall Staffs pop 60
COLDRED parish 1560 Kent 5 miles nw Dover pop 139 archd and
dioc Canterbury
COLDREY extra parochial liberty parish Froyle Hamps pop 22
COLDWELL township parish Kirkwhelpington Northumberland pop 6
COLE tything parish Pitcomb Somerset
COLE tything parish Malmesbury Wilts pop 43
COLEBROKE parish 1558 Devon 4-1/2 miles w Crediton pop 880
pec Dean and Chapter of Exeter
COLEBY parish 1561 Lincs 6-3/4 miles s Lincoln pop 415 archd and
dioc Lincoln
COLEDALE township parish Crosthwaite Cumberland pop 253
COLEFORD chapelry parish Newland Gloucs pop 2,193 Part Bapt
COLEFORD hamlet parish Kilmersdon Somerset
COLEMORE parish 1563 Hamps 5-3/4 miles sw Alton pop 164 archd
and dioc Winchester
COLE ORTON parish 1612 Leics 2 miles e Ashby de la Zouch pop 848
archd Leicester dioc Lincoln
COLERIDGE parish 1556 Devon 5 miles se Chulmleigh pop 644 archd
Barnstaple dioc Exeter
COLERNE parish 1661 Wilts 7 miles sw Chippenham pop 931 archd
Wilts dioc Salisbury Indep
COLESBORNE parish 1632 Gloucs 7-1/2 miles nw Cirencester pop
252 archd and dioc Gloucester
COLESHILL chapelry parish Amersham Herts and Beaconsfield Bucks
pop 497
COLESHILL parish 1559 Berks 3-3/4 miles sw Great Farringdon
pop 351 archd Berks dioc Salisbury
COLESHILL parish 1538 Warws 103-1/2 miles nw London pop 1,853
archd Coventry dioc Lichfield Wesl Meth
COLEY chapelry parish Halifax W R York
COLKERK parish 1538 Norfolk 2 miles s Fakenham pop 316 archd
and dioc Norwich
COLLIERLY township parish Lanchester co Durham pop 526 Wesl
Meth
COLLINGBOURN DUCIS parish 1653 Wilts 2-3/4 miles nw Ludger-
shall pop 458 pec Lord Warden of Savernake Forest

COLLINGBOURN KINGSTONE parish 1653 Wilts 4 miles nw Ludgershall pop 913 archd Wilts dioc Salisbury Wesl Meth
COLLINGHAM parish 1579 W R York 2 miles sw Wetherby pop 414 archd and dioc York
COLLINGHAM, NORTH parish 1558 Notts 5-3/4 miles ne Newark pop 881 archd Nottingham dioc York Part Bapt
COLLINGHAM, SOUTH parish 1558 Notts 5-1/2 miles ne Newark pop 727 archd Nottingham dioc York Wesl Meth
COLLINGTON parish 1566 Herefs 4-1/2 miles n Bromyard pop 160 archd and dioc Hereford
COLLINGTREE parish 1677 co Northampton 3-1/4 miles s Northampton pop 194 archd Northampton dioc Peterborough Wesl Meth
COLLITON ROW tything parish Holy Trinity Dorchester Dorset
COLLUMPTON Devon See CULLOMPTON
COLLY WESTON parish 1541 co Northampton 3-3/4 miles sw Stamford pop 394 archd Northampton dioc Peterborough
COLMER Hamps See COLEMER
COLMWORTH parish 1735 Beds 5-1/2 miles sw St Neots pop 468 archd Bedford dioc Lincoln
COLN parish 1561 Gloucs 3 miles sw Northleach pop 176 archd and dioc Gloucester
COLN, ST ALDWIN'S parish 1650 Gloucs 3 miles n Dairford pop 441 archd and dioc Gloucester
COLN ROGERS parish 1754 Gloucs 4 miles sw Northleach pop 135 archd and dioc Gloucester
COLNBROOK chapelry 1760 parishes of Horton, Iver and Langley Marsh Bucks Bapt
COLNE parish 1668 Hunts 2-1/4 miles se Somersham pop 476 archd Huntingdon dioc Lincoln
COLNE chapelry 1599 parish Whalley Lancs pop 8,080 Bapt, Indep, Wesl Meth
COLNE EARL'S parish 1559 Essex 3-1/2 miles se Halstead archd Colchester dioc London Part Bapt
COLNE, ENGAIN parish 1629 Essex 2-3/4 miles e Halstead pop 618 archd Colchester dioc London
COLNE, WAKES parish 1690 Essex 5-1/2 miles se Halstead pop 442 archd Colchester dioc London
COLNE, WHITE parish 1558 Essex 4-1/2 miles e Halstead pop 384 archd Colchester dioc London
COLNEY parish 1750 Norfolk 2-3/4 miles sw Norwich pop 90 archd Norfolk dioc Norwich
COLSTERWORTH parish 1572 Lincs 32-1/2 miles sw Lincoln comp township Twyford pop 889 archd and dioc Lincoln Wesl Meth
COLSTON BASSET parish 1591 Notts 10 miles se Nottingham pop 387 archd Nottingham dioc York
COLTISHALL parish 1558 Norfolk 8-1/2 miles ne Norwich pop 868 archd and dioc Norfolk Wesl Meth
COLTON parish 1542 Norfolk 5-3/4 miles n Wymondham pop 280

archd Norfolk dioc Norwich

COLTON parish 1647 Staffs 2 miles ne Rugeley pop 675 archd Stafford dioc Lichfield

COLTON or COULTON parish 1632 Lancs 5-1/2 miles ne West Coulton comp chapelries Finthwaite, Waverthwaite and Rusland, townships East Coulton, West Coulton, Nibthwaite pop 1,786 archd Richmond dioc Chester

COLTON township parish Bolton Percy in the Ainsty city York E R York pop 150

COLUMB DAVID tything parish Hemyock Devon

COLUMB ST MAJOR parish 1539 Cornwall 32 miles sw Launceston pop 2,790 archd Cornwall dioc Exeter Bryanites, Indep, Prim and Wesl Meth

COLUMB ST MINOR parish 1560 Cornwall 5-1/4 miles sw St Columb Major pop 1,406 archd Cornwall dioc Exeter

COLVESTON parish (incl in regs of Didlington) Norfolk 6-1/2 miles ne Brandon pop 34 archd Norfolk dioc Norwich

COLWALL parish 1651 Herefs 3-3/4 miles ne Ledbury pop 909 archd and dioc Hereford

COLWELL joint township with Swinburn parish Chollerton Northumberland pop 411

COLWICH parish 1590 Staffs 3 miles ne Rugeley comp chapelry Fradswell township Colwich pop 1,918 pec prebendary of Colwich and Bishop's Itchington in the Cathedral Church of Lichfield

COLWICK parish 1569 Notts 2-1/2 miles e Nottingham pop 145 archd Nottingham dioc York

COLYFORD hamlet parish Colyton Devon

COLYTON or CULLITON parish 1538 Devon 22 miles e Exeter pop 2,182 pec Dean and Chapter of Exeter Indep, Unit

COLYTON RAWLEIGH parish 1673 Devon 3-1/4 miles w Sidmouth pop 857 archd and dioc Exeter

COMBE joint hamlet Wessington parish Chipping Campden Gloucs

COMBE tything parish Wotton under Edge Gloucs

COMBE tything parish Crewkerne Somerset

COMBE parish 1678 Somerset 2-1/2 miles nw Chard pop 1,202 pec Dean and Chapter of Wells

COMBE parish 1560 Hamps 6-3/4 miles se Great Bedwin pop 193 archd and dioc Winchester

COMBE tything parish Endford Wilts

COMBE ABBAS Somerset See ABBAS COMBE

COMBE, ENGLISH parish 1728 Somerset 2-3/4 miles se Bath pop 388 archd Bath dioc Bath and Wells

COMBE FIELDS or COMBE ABBEY extra parochial liberty 5-1/4 miles e Coventry Warws pop 170

COMBE FLOREY parish 1566 Somerset 6 miles ne Wiveliscombe pop 316 archd Bath dioc Bath and Wells

COMBE HAY parish 1538 Somerset 3-1/2 miles sw Bath pop 260 archd Wells dioc Bath and Wells

COMBE HILL township parish Netherwitton Northumberland
COMBE, LONG parish 1646 co Oxford 5 miles sw Woodstock pop
619 pec Rector and Fellows of Lincoln College Oxford
COMBE MARTIN parish 1736 Devon 4-1/2 miles e Ilfracombe pop
1,031 archd Barnstaple dioc Exeter Wesl Meth
COMBE, MONCTON parish 1561 Somerset 3-1/2 miles se Bath pop
1,031 archd Wells dioc Bath and Wells
COMBEINTEIGNHEAD parish 1653 Devon 3 miles e Newton Bushell
pop 460 archd and dioc Exeter
COMBERBACH township parish Great Budworth Ches pop 295 Wesl
Meth
COMBERTON parish 1560 Cambs 5-3/4 miles sw Cambridge archd
and dioc Ely
COMBERTON, GREAT parish 1540 Worcs 2-3/4 miles se Pershore
pop 229 archd and dioc Worcester
COMBERTON, LITTLE parish 1540 Worcs 2-1/2 miles se Pershore
pop 219 archd and dioc Worcester
COMB PYNE parish 1681 Devon 3-3/4 miles se Colyton pop 142
archd and dioc Exeter
COMB RAWLEIGH parish 1653 Devon 1-1/2 miles nw Honiton pop
296 archd and dioc Exeter
COMBROOK chapelry 1701 parish Kington Warws pop 282 Wesl Meth
COMBS parish 1568 Suffolk 2 miles se Stow Market pop 950 archd
Sudbury dioc Norwich
COMMON DALE township parish Guilsbrough N R York pop 78
COMP, GREAT hamlet parish Wrotham Kent
COMPSTALL village parish Stockport Ches pop 1,600 Wesl Meth
COMPTON parish 1553 Berks 2-1/4 miles se East Ilsley pop 554
archd Berks dioc Salisbury
COMPTON hamlet parish Ashburn Derbys
COMPTON tything parish Newent Gloucs pop 428
COMPTON tything parish Henbury Gloucs pop 159
COMPTON parish 1678 Hamps 2-1/2 miles sw Winchester pop 255
pec of the incumbent
COMPTON parish 1639 Surrey 3-1/4 miles sw Guildford pop 455
archd Surrey dioc Winchester
COMPTON parish 1558 Sussex 9 miles sw Midhurst pop 241 archd
and dioc Chichester
COMPTON ABBAS or WEST COMPTON parish 1538 Dorset 9 miles
nw Dorchester pop 69 archd Dorset dioc Bristol
COMPTON ABBAS parish 1650 Dorset 3-1/2 miles se Shaftesbury
pop 401 archd Dorset dioc Bristol
COMPTON ABDALE parish 1720 Gloucs 4-1/4 miles nw Northleach
pop 188 archd and dioc Gloucester
COMPTON BASSETT parish 1558 Wilts 2-1/4 miles ne Calne pop 538
pec Prebendary of Combe and Harnham in the Cathedral Church
of Salisbury
COMPTON BEAUCHAMP parish 1552 Berks 6-1/2 miles sw Great
Farringdon pop 156 archd Berks dioc Salisbury

COMPTON BISHOP parish 1641 Somerset 2-1/4 miles nw Axbridge
pop 554 pec Prebendary of Compton Bishop in the Cathedral
Church of Wells
COMPTON CHAMBERLAIN parish 1538 Wilts 4-1/2 miles sw Wilton
pop 309 archd and dioc Salisbury
COMPTON DANDO parish 1652 Somerset 2 miles ne Pensford pop
382 archd Bath dioc Bath and Wells Wesl Meth
COMPTON DUNDON parish 1682 Somerset 2-3/4 miles n Somerton
pop 623 pec of Prebendary of Compton Dundon in Cathedral
Church of Wells
COMPTON DURVILLE tything parish South Petherton Somerset
COMPTON, EAST tything parish Pilton Somerset
COMPTON, FENNY parish 1626 Warws 5-3/4 miles ne Kington pop
565 archd Coventry dioc Lichfield
COMPTON GIFFORD tything parish Charles the Martyr, Plymouth
Devon pop 229
COMPTON GREENFIELD parish 1583 Gloucs 6-1/4 miles nw Bristol
pop 40 pec of Bishop of Bristol
COMPTON, LITTLE parish 1588 Gloucs 4-1/2 miles nw Chipping
Norton pop 314 archd and dioc Gloucester
COMPTON, LONG parish 1670 Warws 4-1/4 miles nw Chipping Nor-
ton pop 891 archd and dioc Worcester Wesl Meth
COMPTON MARTIN parish 1559 Somerset 8 miles n Wells pop 572
archd Bath dioc Bath and Wells
COMPTON, NETHER parish 1538 Dorset 2-3/4 miles nw Sherborne
pop 415 pec Dean of Salisbury
COMPTON, OVER parish 1726 Dorset 3-1/2 miles nw Sherborne pop
139 pec Dean of Salisbury
COMPTON PAUNCEFOOT parish 1559 Somerset 5 miles sw Wincan-
ton pop 228 archd Wells dioc Bath and Wells
COMPTON SCORPION hamlet parish Ilmington Warws
COMPTON VALLENCE parish 1655 Dorset 7-1/4 miles nw Dorches-
ter pop 104 archd Dorset dioc Bristol
COMPTON VERNEY extra parochial liberty Warws pop 56
COMPTON, WEST tything parish Pilton Somerset
COMPTON, WEST Dorset See COMPTON ABBAS
COMPTON WYNIATES parish 1683 Warws 5-1/4 miles ne Shipston
upon Stour pop 23 archd and dioc Worcester
CONDERTON hamlet parish Overbury Worcs pop 112
CONDICOTE parish 1663 Gloucs 3-1/2 miles nw Stow on the Wold
pop 142 archd and dioc Gloucester
CONDOVER parish 1570 Shrops 4-1/2 miles s Shrewsbury pop 1,455
archd Salop dioc Lichfield
CONEYSTHORPE township parish Barton in the Street N R York pop
190
CONEYTHORPE township parish Goldsborough W R York pop 96
CONEY WESTON Suffolk See WESTON, CONEY
CONGERSTON parish 1593 Leics 3-3/4 miles nw Market Bosworth

pop 170 archd Leicester dioc Lincoln
CONGHALL or COUGHALL township parish Backford Ches pop 26
CONGHAM parish 1581 Norfolk 3-1/2 miles se Castle Rising pop 290
archd and dioc Norwich
CONGLETON chapelry parish Astbury Ches pop 1,352 sep juris
Indep, Prim and Wesl Meth, Unit, Roman Cath
CONGRESBURY parish 1543 Somerset 7-1/2 miles nw Axbridge pop
1,327 archd Wells dioc Bath and Wells
CONHOPE township parish Aymestrey Herefs pop 193
CONINGSBY parish 1561 Lincs 1 mile ne Tattershall pop 1,773 archd
and dioc Lincoln Gen Bapt, Prim and Wesl Meth
CONINGTON parish 1538 Cambs 3-1/4 miles se St Ives pop 203 archd
and dioc Ely
CONINGTON parish 1583 Hunts 3 miles se Stilton pop 204 archd
Huntingdon dioc Lincoln
CONISBROUGH parish 1555 W R York 6-1/2 miles ne Rotherham pop
1,347 archd and dioc York Wesl Meth
CONISCLIFFE parish 1590 co Durham 4 miles nw Darlington comp
townships High Coniscliffe, Low Coniscliffe pop 234 archd and
dioc Durham
CONISCLIFFE, LOW township parish Coniscliffe co Durham pop 140
CONISHOLM parish 1559 Lincs 8-1/4 miles ne Louth pop 170 archd
and dioc Lincoln Wesl Meth
CONISTON township parish Swine E R York pop 162
CONISTON chapelry 1567 parish Burnsall W R York pop 116
CONISTON, COLD township parish Gargrave W R York pop 336
CONISTON, MONK joint township with Skelwith parish Hawkeshead
Lancs pop 397
CONISTONE, CHURCH chapelry 1673 parish Ulverstone Lancs pop
587 archd Richmond dioc Chester
CONOCK tything parish Churton Wilts pop 143
CONONLEY joint township with Farnhill parish Kildwick W R York
CONSIDE joint township with Knitsley parish Lanchester co Durham
pop 146
CONSTANTINE parish 1581 Cornwall 7-1/2 miles sw Falmouth pop
2,004 archd Cornwall dioc Exeter Wesl Meth
COOKBURY parish 1749 Devon 4-3/4 miles ne Holsworthy pop 290
archd Totnes dioc Exeter
COOKHAM parish 1656 Berks 2-1/2 miles ne Maidenhead pop 3,337
archd Berks dioc Salisbury Indep
COOKLEY parish 1538 Suffolk 2-1/2 miles sw Halesworth pop 287
archd Suffolk dioc Norwich
COOLING parish 1707 Kent 2 miles ne Rochester pop 131 archd and
dioc Rochester
COOL PILATE township parish Acton Ches pop 48
COOMBE township parish Presteign Herefs pop 101
COOMBE BISSET parish 1636 Wilts 3-1/2 miles sw Salisbury pop
358 archd and dioc Salisbury

COOMBE KEYNES parish 1538 Dorset 6 miles sw Wareham pop 113 archd Dorset dioc Bristol

COOMBS parish 1538 Sussex 2 miles se Steyning pop 71 archd and dioc Chichester

COOMBS EDGE township parish Chapel en le Frith Derbys pop 367

COPDOCK parish 1701 Suffolk 3-3/4 miles sw Ipswich pop 310 archd Suffolk dioc Norwich

COPFORD parish 1558 Essex 4 miles sw Colchester pop 611 archd Colchester dioc London

COPGROVE parish 1586 W R York 4-3/4 miles sw Boroughbridge pop 120 archd Richmond dioc Chester

COPLE parish 1563 Beds 4 miles se Bedford pop 643 archd Bedford dioc Lincoln

COPLESTONE hamlet parish Colebroke Devon

COPMANFORD See UPTON Hunts

COPMANTHORPE chapelry 1759 parish St Mary Bishopshill Junior, York E R York pop 293 Wesl Meth

COPP chapelry parish St Michael upon Wyre Lancs

COPPENHALL parish 1653 Ches 5 miles ne Nantwich comp townships Church Coppenhall and Monks Coppenhall pop 498 archd and dioc Chester

COPPENHALL chapelry 1678 parish Penkridge Staffs pop 100

COPPINGFORD parish See UPTON Hunts 6-1/2 miles s Stilton pop 44 archd Huntingdon dioc Lincoln

COPPIN SIKE extra parochial liberty near Kirton Lincs pop 67

COPPULL chapelry 1765 parish Standish Lancs pop 908

COPSTON, MAGNA chapelry parish Monks Kirby Warws

COPSTON, PARVA hamlet parish Wolvey Warws

CORBRIDGE parish 1657 Northumberland 4-1/2 miles e Hexham comp chapelry Halton, townships Aydon, Aydon Castle, Clarewood, Corbridge, Dilston, Halton Shields, Thornborough, Great Whittington, Little Whittington pop 2,101 archd Northumberland dioc Durham Indep, Wesl Meth, Roman Cath

CORBY parish 1561 Lincs 33 miles se Lincoln pop 654 archd and dioc Lincoln

CORBY parish 1684 co Northampton 2-1/2 miles se Rockingham pop 684 archd Northampton dioc Peterborough

CORBY, GREAT township parish Wetheral Cumberland pop 1,285

CORBY, LITTLE township parish Warwick Cumberland pop 313

CORELY parish 1543 Shrops 4 miles sw Cleobury Mortimer pop 553 archd Salop dioc Hereford

CORFE parish 1673 Somerset 3-1/2 miles s Taunton pop 271 archd Taunton dioc Bath and Wells

CORFE CASTLE parish 1653 borough Dorset 23 miles se Dorchester pop 1,712 sep juris pec Corfe Castle

CORFE MULLEN chapelry 1652 parish Sturminster Marshall Dorset pop 603

CORHAMPTON parish 1677 Hamps 4 miles ne Bishop's Waltham pop

125 archd and dioc Winchester

CORLEY parish 1540 Warws 4-3/4 miles nw Coventry pop 307 archd Coventry dioc Lichfield

CORNARD, GREAT parish 1540 Suffolk 1-1/4 miles se Sudbury pop 819 archd Sudbury dioc Norwich

CONARD, LITTLE parish 1565 Suffolk 2-1/2 miles se Sudbury pop 345 archd Sudbury dioc Norwich

CORNBROUGH township parish Sheriff Hutton N R York pop 59

CORNELLY parish 1559 Cornwall 3/4 mile w Tregoney pop 170 archd Cornwall dioc Exeter

CORNEY parish 1754 Cumberland 4 miles se Ravenglass pop 292 archd Richmond dioc Chester

CORNFORTH township parish Bishop Middleham co Durham pop 353

CORNHILL chapelry 1695 parish Norham co Durham pop 765

CORNSAY township parish Lanchester co Durham pop 230

CORNWELL parish 1662 co Oxford 4 miles w Chipping Norton pop 110 archd and dioc Oxford

CORNWOOD parish 1685 Devon 5 miles ne Earl's Plympton pop 1,056 archd Totnes dioc Exeter

CORNWORTHY parish 1563 Devon 4-1/4 miles se Totnes pop 567 archd Totnes dioc Exeter

CORPUSTY parish 1726 Norfolk 6 miles nw Aylshamp pop 468 archd and dioc Norwich

CORRIDGE township parish Hartburn Northumberland pop 23

CORRINGHAM parish 1557 Essex 3 miles e Horndon on the Hill pop 234 archd Essex dioc London

CORRINGHAM parish 1647 Lincs 4 miles ne Gainsborough comp villages Great and Little Corringham pop 559 pec Prebendary of Corringham in Cathedral Church of Lincoln Wesl Meth

CORSCOMBE parish 1595 Dorset 3-1/2 miles ne Beaminster pop 714 archd Dorset dioc Bristol

CORSE parish 1661 Gloucs 5-1/2 miles ne Newent pop 476 archd and dioc Gloucester

CORSENSIDE parish 1726 Northumberland 5-3/4 miles ne Bellingham pop 524 archd Northumberland dioc Durham

CORSHAM parish 1553 Wilts 4 miles sw Chippenham pop 2,952 sep juris pec of incumbent Indep, Bapt

CORSLEY parish 1686 Wilts 3-1/4 miles nw Warminster comp Great and Little Corsley pop 1,729 archd and dioc Salisbury

CORSTON parish 1568 Somerset 3-3/4 miles w Bath pop 433 archd Bath dioc Bath and Wells

CORSTON chapelry parish Malmesbury Wilts pop 219

CORTON hamlet parish Portisham Dorset

CORTON parish 1579 Suffolk 3 miles n Lowestoft pop 410 archd Suffolk dioc Norwich

CORTON township parish Boyton Wilts

CORTON hamlet parish Cliffe Pypard Wilts

CORTON DENHAM parish 1538 Somerset 4 miles n Sherborne pop

494 archd Wells dioc Bath and Wells

CORTON HACKETT Worcs See COFTON HACKETT

CORYTON parish 1654 Devon 6-1/4 miles nw Tavistock pop 314 archd Totnes dioc Exeter

COSBY parish 1557 Leics 6-3/4 miles sw Leicester pop 1,009 archd Leicester dioc Lincoln

COSFORD hamlet parish Newbold upon Avon Warws pop 63

COSGROVE parish 1691 co Northampton 1-1/2 miles ne Stony Stratford pop 624 archd Northampton dioc Peterborough

COSMUS ST DAMIAN IN THE BLEAN parish 1558 Kent 2-1/4 miles nw Canterbury pop 554 archd and dioc Canterbury

COSSAL parish 1654 Notts 6-1/2 miles nw Nottingham pop 341 archd Nottingham dioc York

COSSINGTON parish 1544 Leics 2-3/4 miles se Mountsorrel pop 283 archd Leicester dioc Lincoln

COSSINGTON parish 1675 Somerset 4-1/4 miles ne Bridgwater pop 280 archd Wells dioc Bath and Wells

COSTESSY or COSSEY parish 1538 Norfolk 4-1/2 miles ne Norwich pop 1,098 archd Norfolk dioc Norwich

COSTOCK or CORTLINGSTOCK parish 1558 Notts 9-1/2 miles s Nottingham pop 412 archd Nottingham dioc York

COSTON parish 1561 Leics 7 miles ne Melton Mowbray pop 170 archd Leicester dioc Lincoln

COSTON parish 1704 Norfolk 4-1/2 miles nw Wymondham pop 64 archd Norfolk dioc Norwich

COTE joint hamlet with Aston parish Bampton co Oxford

COTES township parish Eccleshall Staffs pop 261

COTES DE VAL hamlet parish Kimcote Leics pop 6

COTGRAVE parish 1559 Notts 6 miles se Nottingham pop 842 archd Nottingham dioc York Wesl Meth

COTHAM hamlet parish Keelby Lincs

COTHAM parish 1587 Notts 4-1/2 miles s Newark pop 74 archd Nottingham dioc York

COTHELSTON parish 1664 Somerset 7 miles nw Taunton pop 120 archd Taunton dioc Bath and Wells

COTHERIDGE parish 1653 Worce 3-3/4 miles w Worcester pop 276 archd and dioc Worcester

COTHERSTON township parish Romaldkirk N R York pop 631 Soc of Friends, Indep, Wesl Meth

COTLEIGH parish 1653 Devon 3 miles ne Honiton pop 240 archd and dioc Exeter

COTNESS township parish Howden E R York pop 29

COTON parish 1538 Cambs 3 miles nw Cambridge pop 225 archd and dioc Ely

COTON township parish Hanbury Staffs pop 56

COTON joint liberty with Hopton parish St Mary, Stafford Staffs

COTON IN THE ELMS township parish Lullington Derbys pop 264

COTTAM township parish Preston Lancs

COTTAM chapelry 1695 parish South Leverton Notts pop 77
COTTENHAM parish 1572 Cambs 6-3/4 miles n Cambridge pop 1,635
    archd and dioc Ely Part Bapt
COTTERED parish 1558 Herts 3-1/4 miles w Buntingford pop 436
    archd Huntingdon dioc Lincoln
COTTERSTOCK parish 1632 co Northampton 2 miles ne Oundle pop
    161 archd Northampton dioc Peterborough
COTTESBACH parish 1558 Leics 1-1/2 miles sw Lutterworth pop
    108 archd Leicester dioc Lincoln
COTTESBROOK parish 1630 co Northampton 8-3/4 miles nw North-
    ampton pop 226 archd Northampton dioc Peterborough
COTTESFORD parish 1651 co Oxford 6 miles n Bicester pop 163
    archd and dioc Oxford
COTTESMORE parish 1655 co Rutland 4-1/4 miles ne Oakham pop
    631 archd Northampton dioc Peterborough
COTTINGHAM parish 1574 co Northampton 2 miles sw Rockingham
    pop 903 archd Northampton dioc Peterborough Wesl Meth
COTTINGHAM parish 1563 E R York 4-1/2 miles nw Kingston upon
    Hull pop 2,575 archd East Riding dioc York
COTTINGWITH, EAST chapelry parish Aughton E R York pop 310
    Wesl Meth
COTTINGWITH, WEST township parish Thorganby E R York
COTTLES extra parochial liberty Little Chalfield Wilts
COTTON township parish Sandbach Ches pop 86
COTTON township parish Wem Shrops pop 438
COTTON chapelry parish Alveson Staffs pop 471
COTTON parish 1538 Suffolk 2 miles nw Mendlesham pop 585 archd
    Sudbury dioc Norwich Wesl Meth
COTTON or COTTAM chapelry parish Langtoft E R York pop 25
COTTON township parish Hovingham N R York pop 131
COTTON, ABBOT'S township parish Christleton Ches pop 11
COTTON, EDMUND'S township parish Christleton Ches pop 79
COTTON FAR hamlet parish Hardingstone co Northampton
COUGHTON hamlet parish Walford Herefs
COUGHTON parish 1673 Warws 2 miles nw Alcester pop 1,010 archd
    and dioc Worcester
COULDSNOUTH joint township with Thompson's Walls parish Kirk-
    newton Northumberland pop 41
COULSDON parish 1653 Surrey 5 miles sw Croydon pop 516 archd
    Surrey dioc Winchester
COULSTON, EAST parish 1714 Wilts 5 miles ne Westbury pop 103
    archd Wilts dioc Salisbury
COULSTON, WEST joint tything with Baynton parish Edington Wilts
COUND parish 1608 Shrops 6-1/2 miles nw Much Wenlock pop 680
    archd Salop dioc Lichfield
COUNDEN GRANGE township parish St Andrew Auckland co Durham
    pop 44
COUNDON township parish St Andrew Auckland co Durham pop 475
COUNDON hamlet parish Holy Trinity, Coventry Warws pop 192

COUNTESS THORPE chapelry 1577 parish Blaby Leics pop 839
COUNTHORPE hamlet parish Bytham Castle Lincs pop 65
COUNTISBURY parish 1676 Devon 15-1/2 miles ne Ilfracombe pop
187 archd Barnstaple dioc Exeter
COUPE LENCH joint township with Newhallhey and Hall Carr parish
Bury Lancs pop 1,519
COUPLAND township parish Kirknewton Northumberland pop 100
COURAGE tything parish Chieveley Berks
COURLAND Somerset See CURLAND
COURTEENHALL parish 1538 co Northampton 5-1/4 miles s North-
ampton pop 120 archd Northampton dioc Peterborough
COVE tything parish Yately Hamps pop 443
COVE, CHAPEL chapelry parish Tiverton Devon
COVE, NORTH parish 1696 Suffolk 2-3/4 miles se Beccles pop 218
archd Suffolk dioc Norwich Wesl Meth
COVE, SOUTH parish 1555 Suffolk 3 miles n Southwold pop 183
archd Suffolk dioc Norwich
COVEHITHE Suffolk See NORTH HALES
COVEN liberty parish Brewood Staffs Wesl Meth
COVENEY parish 1676 Cambs 6 miles nw Ely pop 1,170 archd and
dioc Ely
COVENHAM parish 1566 Lincs 5-1/2 miles ne Louth pop 222 archd
and dioc Lincoln Wesl Meth
COVENHAM parish 1597 Lincs 5-1/2 miles ne Louth pop 163 archd
and dioc Lincoln
COVENTRY city Warws 10 miles ne Warwick pop 27,070 comp St
Michael 1698, Holy Trinity 1561, St John 1734 archd Coventry
dioc Lichfield Bapt, Soc of Friends, Indep, Wesl Meth, Unit,
Roman Cath
COVERHAM parish 1707 N R York 1-3/4 miles sw Middleham comp
townships Agelthorpe, Caldbridge, Carlton, Carlton Highdale,
Melmerby, West Scrafton pop 1,233 archd Richmond dioc Chester
COVINGTON parish 1539 Hunts 3-1/4 miles nw Kimbolton pop 146
archd Huntingdon dioc Lincoln
COWARNE, LITTLE parish 1563 Herefs 4-1/4 miles sw Bromyard
pop 180 archd and dioc Hereford
COWARNE, MUCH parish 1559 Herefs 5-3/4 miles sw Bromyard
pop 573 archd and dioc Hereford
COWBIT parish 1700 Lincs 5-1/2 miles ne Crowland pop 556 archd
and dioc Lincoln Wesl Meth
COWDEN parish 1566 Kent 9 miles w Tonbridge Wells pop 689 archd
and dioc Rochester
COWDON, GREAT and LITTLE parish incl in regs Mappleton E R
York Great Cowdon 14-1/4 miles and Little Cowdon 12-3/4 miles
ne Kingston upon Hull pop 146 archd East Riding, dioc York
COWES, EAST hamlet parish Whippingham Isle of Wight Hamps Indep
COWES, WEST chapelry 1679 parish Northwood Isle of Wight Hamps
Bapt, Wesl Meth, Roman Cath
COWFOLD parish 1558 Sussex 7 miles se Horsham pop 809 archd

Lewes dioc Chichester

COWGROVE or KINSON tything parish Wimborne Winster Dorset pop 728

COWICK chapelry parish St Thomas the Apostle Exeter Devon

COWICK township parish Snaith W R York pop 928

COWLAM parish no regs E R York 6-1/2 miles nw Great Driffield pop 49 archd East Riding dioc York

COWLEY hamlet parish Dronfield Derbys

COWLEY parish 1676 Gloucs 6-1/2 miles se Cheltenham pop 323 archd and dioc Gloucester

COWLEY parish 1562 Middlesex 1-1/2 miles se Uxbridge pop 315 archd Middlesex dioc London

COWLEY parish 1678 co Oxford 2-1/2 miles se Oxford pop 558 archd and dioc Oxford

COWLEY township parish Gnosall Staffs

COWLING parish 1559 Suffolk 8-1/4 miles nw Clare pop 845 archd Sudbury dioc Norwich

COWLING township parish Bedale N R York

COWLING township parish Kildwick W R York pop 2,249

COWPEN township parish Horton Northumberland pop 2,081

COWPEN BEWLEY township parish Billingham co Durham pop 137

COWSBY parish 1679 N R York 6-1/4 miles ne Thirsk pop 89 pec of Allerton and Allertonshire

COWSHUISH tything hamlet Toulton parish Kingston Somerset

COWTHORN township parish Middleton N R York pop 18

COWTHORP parish 1568 W R York 3-3/4 miles ne Wetherby pop 146 archd and dioc York

COWTON, EAST parish 1754 N R York 7 miles ne Catterick pop 374 archd Richmond dioc Chester

COWTON, NORTH township parish Gilling N R York pop 264

COWTON, SOUTH chapelry 1568 parish Gilling N R York pop 163

COXFORD hamlet parish East Rudham Norfolk

COXHALL joint township with Buxton parish Bucknill Herefs

COXHOE township parish Kelloe co Durham pop 154

COXLODGE township parish Gosforth Northumberland pop 965 Wesl Meth

COXWELL, GREAT parish 1557 Berks 1-3/4 miles se Great Farringdon pop 337 archd Berks dioc Salisbury

COXWELL, LITTLE chapelry parish Farringdon Berks pop 304

COXWOLD parish 1583 N R York 5 miles n Easingwould comp chapelry Birdforth, townships Angram Grange, Byland cum Membris, Coxwold, Newborough, Oulston, Thornton with Baxly, Wildon Grange, Yearsley pop 1,380 archd Cleveland dioc York

COZENLEY township parish Kirby Malzeard W R York pop 701

CRABHALL township parish Holy Trinity, Chester Ches

CRACKENTHORPE township parish Bongate or St Michael Appleby Westm pop 115

CRACO township parish Burnsall W R York pop 150 Wesl Meth

CRADLEY parish 1560 Herefs 7 miles ne Ledbury comp townships East and West Cradley pop 1,509 archd and dioc Hereford

CRADLEY chapelry 1798 parish Hales Owen Worcs pop 2,022 Wesl Meth, Bapt, Unit

CRADLEY, WEST township parish Cradley Herefs pop 733

CRAIKE parish 1538 co Durham and N R York 3-1/4 miles ne Easingwould pop 607 pec of Dean and Chapter of Durham Wesl Meth

CRAKEHALL township parish Topcliffe N R York

CRAKEHALL township parish Bedale N R York pop 580 Bapt, Wesl Meth

CRAKEMARSH township parish Uttoxeter Staffs

CRAMBE parish 1710 N R York 6-1/4 miles sw New Malton comp townships Barton le Willows, Crambe, Whitwell on the Hill pop 573 archd Cleveland dioc York

CRAMLINGTON chapelry 1665 parish St Andrew, Newcastle Northumberland pop 931

CRANAGE township parish Sandbach Ches pop 438

CRANBORNE parish 1602 Dorset 30 miles ne Dorchester comp tythings Alderholt, Beveridge, Farewood, hamlet Crendall, tything Blagdon, Monckton up Wimborne pop 2,158 archd Dorset dioc Bristol

CRANBROOKE parish 1553 Kent 14 miles se Maidstone pop 3,844 archd and dioc Canterbury Part Bapt, Huntingtonians, Indep, Wesl Meth, Unit

CRANFIELD parish 1653 Beds 7 miles nw Ampthill pop 1,250 archd Bedford dioc Lincoln

CRANFORD parish 1564 Middlesex 2-1/2 miles nw Hounslow pop 377 archd Middlesex dioc London

CRANFORD parish 1695 co Northampton 4-1/4 miles se Kettering pop 564 archd Northampton dioc Peterborough

CRANFORD parish 1627 co Northampton 4 miles se Kettering archd Northampton dioc Peterborough

CRANHAM parish 1559 Essex 2-3/4 miles se Hornchurch pop 300 archd Essex dioc London

CRANHAM parish 1666 Gloucs 2-1/2 miles ne Painswick pop 394 archd and dioc Gloucester

CRANLEY parish 1608 Surrey 7-1/4 miles se Godalming pop 1,320 archd Surrey dioc Winchester

CRANMORE, EAST parish 1716 Somerset 4-1/4 miles e Shepton Mallet pop 64 archd Wells dioc Bath and Wells

CRANMORE, WEST parish 1563 Somerset 3-1/2 miles e Shepton Mallet pop 298 archd Wells dioc Bath and Wells

CRANOE parish 1653 Leics 6 miles ne Market Harborough pop 100 archd Leicester dioc Lincoln

CRANSFORD parish 1653 Suffolk 2-1/4 miles ne Framlingham pop 323 archd Suffolk dioc Norwith

CRANSLEY parish 1561 co Northampton 3 miles sw Kettering pop 308 archd Northampton dioc Peterborough

CRANTOCK parish 1559 Cornwall 7 miles nw St Michael pop 458

archd Cornwall dioc Exeter

CRANWELL parish 1564 Lincs 4 miles nw Sleaford pop 229 archd and dioc Lincoln

CRANWICK parish 1732 Norfolk 6 miles se Stoke Ferry pop 88 archd Norfolk dioc Norwich

CRANWORTH parish 1653 Norfolk 6 miles ne Watton pop 323 archd Norfolk dioc Norwich

CRASSWALL chapelry parish Clodock Herefs pop 374

CRASTER township parish Embleton Northumberland pop 212

CRATFIELD parish 1538 Suffolk 5-1/2 miles sw Halesworth pop 692 archd Suffolk dioc Norwich

CRATHORNE parish 1723 N R York 3-1/4 miles se Yarm pop 304 archd Cleveland dioc York Prim Meth, Roman Cath

CRAWCROOK township parish Ryton co Durham pop 340

CRAWFORD TARRANT parish 1597 Dorset 3-1/2 miles se Blandford Forum pop 78 archd Dorset dioc Bristol

CRAWLEY township parish Eglingham Northumberland pop 32

CRAWLEY hamlet parish Witney co Oxford pop 275

CRAWLEY parish 1649 Hamps 5 miles nw Winchester pop 484 pec of incumbent

CRAWLEY parish 1653 Sussex 9-1/2 miles nw Cuckfield pop 394 archd Lewes dioc Chichester

CRAWLEY HUSBORN Beds See HUSBORN CRAWLEY

CRAWLEY, NORTH Bucks See CROWLEY

CRAY parish 1579 Kent 2 miles sw Foot's Cray pop 905 pec of Archbishop of Canterbury

CRAY FOOTS parish 1559 Kent 12-1/2 miles se London pop 308 archd and dioc Rochester

CRAY, NORTH parish 1538 Kent 1 mile ne Foot's Cray pop 342 archd and dioc Rochester

CRAY, ST PAUL'S parish 1579 Kent 1-1/2 miles s Foot's Cray pop 411 archd and dioc Rochester

CRAYFORD parish 1558 Kent 13 miles se London pop 2,022 pec of Archbishop of Canterbury Part Bapt

CREACOMBE parish 1695 Devon 8-1/4 miles se South Molton pop 43 archd Barnstaple dioc Exeter

CREAKE, NORTH parish 1538 Norfolk 3 miles se Burnham Westgate pop 651 archd Norfolk dioc Norwich

CREAKE, SOUTH parish 1538 Norfolk 4 miles se Burnham Westgate pop 831 archd Norfolk dioc Norwich

CREATON, GREAT parish 1688 co Northampton 7-1/4 miles nw Northampton pop 543 archd Northampton dioc Peterborough

CREATON, LITTLE hamlet parish Spratton co Northampton pop 100

CREDENHILL parish 1671 Herefs 4-1/2 miles nw Hereford pop 235 archd and dioc Hereford

CREDITON parish 1564 Devon 8 miles nw Exeter comp tythings Borough, Canon fee, Knowle, Rudge, Town, Uford, Uton, Woodland pop 5,922 pec of Bishop of Exeter Bapt, Indep, Wesl Meth, Unit

CREECH parish 1668 Somerset 3-1/2 miles ne Taunton pop 1,116 archd Taunton dioc Bath and Wells

CREECH, EAST tything parish Church Knowle Dorset pop 204

CREED parish 1653 Cornwall 3/4 mile s Grampound pop 973 archd Cornwall dioc Exeter

CREEKSEA parish 1749 Essex 2 miles nw Burnham pop 154 archd Essex dioc London

CREETING, ALL SAINTS parish 1705 Suffolk 1-3/4 miles n Needham Market pop 294 archd Sudbury dioc Norwich

CREETING, ST MARY parish 1681 Suffolk 1-1/2 miles ne Needham Market pop 129 archd Suffolk dioc Norwich

CREETING, ST OLAVE parish no regs Suffolk 2-1/2 miles ne Needham Market pop 44 archd Suffolk dioc Norwich

CREETING, ST PETER or WEST, CREETING parish 1558 Suffolk 2-1/2 miles nw Needham Market pop 166 archd Sudbury dioc Norwich

CREETON parish 1692 Lincs 3-3/4 miles se Corby pop 66 archd and dioc Lincoln

CREIGHTON township parish Uttoxeter Staffs

CRENDAL hamlet parish Cranborne Dorset

CRENDON, LONG parish 1559 Bucks 2-1/4 miles nw Thame pop 1,381 archd Buckingham dioc Lincoln Part Bapt

CRESLOW Bucks See WHITCHURCH

CRESSAGE chapelry 1605 parish Cound Shrops pop 276

CRESSING parish 1733 Essex 3-1/4 miles se Braintree pop 551 archd Colchester dioc London

CRESSINGHAM, GREAT parish 1557 Norfolk 4-1/2 miles nw Watton pop 449 pec in which rector exercises jurisdiction.

CRESSINGHAM, LITTLE parish 1681 Norfolk 3 miles w Watton pop 276 archd Norfolk dioc Norwich

CRESSWELL township parish Woodhorn Northumberland pop 251

CRESSY HALL chapelry parish Surfleet Lincs

CRESWELL extra parochial Staffs 3 miles sw Cheadle pop 11

CRETINGHAM parish 1558 Suffolk 4-1/2 miles sw Framlingham pop 387 archd Suffolk dioc Norwich

CREWE township parish Farndon Ches pop 51

CREWE township parish Barthomley Ches pop 295

CREWKERNE parish 1551 Somerset 10 miles sw Ilchester pop 3,789 archd Taunton dioc Bath and Wells Part Bapt, Unit

CRICH parish 1600 Derbys 4-3/4 miles sw Alfreton comp townships Crich, Wessington, hamlet Tansley pop 3,087 archd Derby dioc Lichfield Wesl Meth

CRICK hamlet parish Caerwent co Monmouth pop 131

CRICK parish 1559 co Northampton 6-1/2 miles ne Daventry pop 945 archd Northampton dioc Peterborough

CRICKET parish 1564 Somerset 5 miles s Crewkerne pop 86 archd Taunton dioc Bath and Wells

CRICKET MALHERBIE parish 1723 Somerset 2-1/4 mi les s Ilminster pop 28 archd Taunton dioc Bath and Wells

CRICKLADE town borough Wilts 44-1/2 miles nw Salisbury pop 1,642 comp St Sampson 1673, St Mary 1683 archd Wilts dioc Salisbury Indep, Wesl Meth

CRICKSEA Essex See CREEKSEA

CRIDLING STUBBS township parish Womersley W R York pop 118

CRIGGLESTONE township parish Great Sandall W R York pop 1,266 Part Bapt

CRIMPLESHAM parish 1561 Norfolk 2-1/2 miles e Downham Market pop 320 archd Norfolk dioc Norwich

CRINGLEFORD parish 1560 Norfolk 2-1/2 miles sw Norwich pop 177 archd Norfolk dioc Norwich

CRIPTON tything parish Winterbourn Came Dorset pop 18

CRITCHELL or CRICHEL, LONG parish 1663 Dorset 6-1/2 miles sw Cranborne pop 138 archd Dorset dioc Bristol

CRITCHELL or CRICHEL, MORE parish 1664 Dorset 6 miles sw Cranborne pop 304 archd Dorset dioc Bristol

CROBOROUGH joint township with Blackwood parish Horton Staffs

CROCK STREET hamlet parishes Combe St Nicholas and Donyatt Somerset

CROCKERN WELL hamlet parishes Bishop Cheriton and Drewsteignton Devon

CROCKERNE PILL hamlet parish Easton in Gordano Somerset

CROFT parish 1565 Herefs 5-1/2 miles nw Leominster pop 128 archd and dioc Hereford

CROFT joint township with Southworth parish Winwick Lancs

CROFT parish 1583 Leics 6-1/4 miles ne Hinckley pop 284 archd Leicester dioc Lincoln

CROFT parish 1559 Lincs 1-3/4 miles ne Wainfleet pop 546 archd and dioc Lincoln

CROFT parish 1617 N R York 3-1/2 miles s Darlington comp townships Croft, Dalton upon Tees, part of Stapleton pop 692 archd Richmond dioc Chester

CROFTON township parish Thursby Cumberland pop 106

CROFTON village parish Orpington Kent

CROFTON township parish Diddlebury Shrops

CROFTON chapelry parish Titchfield Hamps

CROFTON parish 1615 W R York 3-3/4 miles se Wakefield pop 361 archd and dioc York

CROGDEAN township parish Kirk Whelpington Northumberland pop 9

CROGLIN parish 1644 Cumberland 5 miles ne Kirk Oswald pop 362 archd and dioc Carlisle

CROKEHAM hamlet parish Thatcham Berks

CROMER parish 1689 Norfolk 21 miles n Norwich pop 1,232 archd Norfolk dioc Norwich Wesl Meth

CROMFORD chapelry parish Wirksworth Derbys pop 1,291 Wesl Meth

CROMHALL, ABBOT'S parish 1653 Gloucs 2-1/2 miles nw Wickwar pop 761 archd and dioc Gloucester

CROMHALL, LYGON tything parish Abbot's Cromhall Gloucs
CROMPTON township parish Oldham cum Prestwich Lancs pop 7,004
CROMWELL parish 1650 Notts 5-1/4 miles n Newark pop 184 archd
  Nottingham dioc York
CRONDALL parish 1567 Hamps 3 miles nw Farnham comp tythings
  Ewshott, Dippenhall, Crondall with Swanthorpe and Crookham
  pop 2,010 archd and dioc Winchester
CRONTON township parish Prescot Lancs pop 293
CROOK joint township with Billy Row parish Brancepeth co Durham
CROOK chapelry 1742 parish Kendal Westm pop 246
CROOKDAKE joint township with Bromfield and Scales parish Brom-
  field Cumberland
CROOKHAM tything parish Crondall Hamps pop 650
CROOKHOUSE township parish Kirk Newton Northumberland pop 20
CROOM hamlet parish Sledmere E R York
CROOME D'ABITOT parish 1560 Worcs 4 miles sw Pershore pop
  144 archd and dioc Worcester
CROOME, EARL'S parish 1647 Worcs 2 miles ne Upton upon Severn
  pop 192 archd and dioc Worcester
CROOME HILL parish 1721 Worcs 3-1/4 miles e Upton upon Severn
  pop 215 archd and dioc Worcester
CROPREDY parish 1538 co Oxford 4 miles ne Banbury comp chapel-
  ry Mollington, Bourton, Claydon, Wardington, hamlet Prescott
  pop 2,601 pec of Dean and Chapter of Lincoln Wesl Meth
CROPSTON township parish Thurcaston Leics pop 115
CROPTHORN parish 1557 Worcs 4-1/4 miles se Pershore pop 690
  archd and dioc Worcester
CROPTON township parish Middleton N R York pop 330 Wesl Meth
CROPTON parish 1754 Yorks 4-1/2 miles nw Pickering archd Cleve-
  land dioc York
CROPWELL, BISHOP parish 1539 Notts 8 miles se Nottingham pop
  473 pec of Collegiate Church of Southwell Wesl Meth
CROPWELL BUTLER chapelry parish Tythby Notts pop 551 Wesl
  Meth
CROSBY township parish Cross Cannonby Cumberland pop 197
CROSBY township parish Bottesford Lincs pop 174
CROSBY township parish Leak N R York pop 37
CROSBY GARRETT parish 1559 Westm 3 miles nw Kirby Stephen
  comp townships Crosby Garrett, Little Musgrave pop 286 archd
  and dioc Carlisle
CROSBY, GREAT chapelry 1749 parish Sephton Lancs pop 1,201
  archd and dioc Chester
CROSBY, HIGH township parish Crosby upon Eden Cumberland pop
  133
CROSBY, LITTLE township parish Sephton Lancs pop 414
CROSBY, LOW township parish Crosby upon Eden Cumberland pop
  184
CROSBY RAVENSWORTH parish 1570 Westm 4 miles ne Orton pop

928 archd and dioc Carlisle

CROSBY UPON EDEN parish 1649 Cumberland 3-3/4 miles ne Carlisle comp townships Brunstock, High Crosby, Low Crosby, Walby pop 497 archd and dioc Carlisle

CROSCOMBE parish 1558 Somerset 1-3/4 miles nw Shepton Mallet pop 803 archd Wells dioc Bath and Wells

CROSCRAKE chapelry 1796 parish Heversham Westm

CROSS ST Hamps See WINCHESTER

CROSS HANDS hamlet parish Old Sodbury Gloucs

CROSSLAND, NORTH and SOUTH chapelry parish Almondbury W R York pop 2,258

CROSSTONE chapelry 1640 parish Halifax W R York

CROSS WAY HAND hamlet parish Southwick co Northampton pop 12

CROSTHWAITE parish 1566 Cumberland 1/2 mile nw Keswick comp chapelries Borrowdale, Newlands, Thornthwaite, townships Braithwaite, Coledale or Portingscale, chapelry St John Castlerigg with Wythburn, town Keswick and township Under Skiddaw pop 4,344 archd and dioc Carlisle

CROSTHWAITE chapelry 1570 parish Heversham Westm pop 721

CROSTON parish 1543 Lancs 6-1/2 miles w Chorley comp chapelries Becconsall with Hesketh and Tarleton, townships Bispham, Bretherton, Croston, Mawdesley, Ulnes Walton pop 6,278 archd and dioc Chester

CROSTWICK parish 1562 Norfolk 3 miles sw Coltishall pop 143 archd Norfolk dioc Norwich

CROSTWIGHT parish 1698 Norfolk 3-1/2 miles se North Walsham pop 79 archd and dioc Norwich

CROUCH END hamlet parish Hornsey Middlesex

CROUGHTON township parish St Oswald Chester Ches pop 39

CROUGHTON parish 1663 co Northampton 3-1/2 miles sw Brackley pop 450 archd Northampton dioc Peterborough

CROWAN parish 1692 Cornwall 6 miles nw Helston pop 4,332 archd Cornwall dioc Exeter Wesl Meth, Bryanites

CROWBOROUGH Staffs See CROBOROUGH

CROWCOMBE parish 1641 Somerset 7 miles ne Wiveliscombe pop 691 archd Taunton dioc Bath and Wells

CROWELL parish 1594 co Oxford 5 miles se Tetsworth pop 159 archd and dioc Oxford

CROWFIELD chapelry parish Coddenham Suffolk pop 360

CROWHURST parish 1567 Surrey 4-1/2 miles se Godstone pop 212 archd Surrey dioc Winchester

CROWHURST parish 1558 Sussex 2-3/4 miles s Battle pop 370 archd Lewes dioc Chichester

CROWLAND or CROYLAND parish 1639 Lincs 51 miles se Lincoln pop 2,278 archd and dioc Lincoln Wesl Meth

CROWLE parish 1561 Lincs 35 miles nw Lincoln pop 1,889 archd Stowe dioc Lincoln Indep, Wesl Meth

CROWLE parish 1539 Worcs 5-1/2 miles se Droitwich pop 526 archd and dioc Worcester

CROWLEY township parish Great Budworth Ches pop 133

CROWLEY, NORTH parish 1558 Bucks 3-1/2 miles ne Newport Pagnell pop 791 archd Buckingham dioc Lincoln

CROWMARSH GIFFORD parish 1575 co Oxford 1/2 mile e Wallingford pop 325 archd and dioc Oxford

CROWNTHORPE parish 1700 Norfolk 2-1/4 miles nw Wymondham pop 106 archd Norfolk dioc Norwich

CROWTON township parish Weaverham Ches pop 361

CROXALL parish 1586 Derbys 7-1/2 miles n Tamworth comp township Oakley, chapelry Catton pop 292 archd Derby dioc Lichfield

CROXBYparish no regs Lincs 5-1/4 miles se Caistor pop 73 archd and dioc Lincoln

CROXDALE chapelry 1696 parish St Oswald Durham co Durham Roman Cath

CROXDEN parish 1648 Staffs 5-1/2 miles nw Uttoxeter pop 272 archd Stafford dioc Lichfield

CROXTETH PARK extra parochial liberty Lancs 4 miles nw Prescot pop 42

CROXTON parish 1538 Cambs 4-1/2 miles nw Caxton pop 245 archd and dioc Ely

CROXTON township parish Middlewich Ches pop 43

CROXTON parish 1562 Lincs 7-1/2 miles ne Glandford Bridge pop 103 archd and dioc Lincoln

CROXTON chapelry parish Fulmondeston Norfolk

CROXTON parish 1558 Norfolk 2 miles n Thetford pop 278 archd Norfolk dioc Norwich

CROXTON township parish Eccleshall Staffs pop 836

CROXTON KERRIAL parish 1559 Leics 7 miles se Grantham pop 594 archd Leicester dioc Lincoln

CROXTON, SOUTH parish 1662 Leics 8-1/4 miles ne Leicester pop 315 archd Leicester dioc Lincoln

CROYDON parish 1672 Cambs 6 miles se Caxton pop 434 archd and dioc Ely

CROYDON parish 1538 Surrey 9-1/2 miles s London pop 12,447 pec of Archbishop of Canterbury Bapt, Soc of Friends, Indep, Wesl Meth

CROYLAND Lincs See CROWLAND

CRUCKTON township parish Pontesbury Shrops

CRUDWELL parish 1659 Wilts 4 miles ne Malmesbury pop 604 archd Wilts dioc Salisbury

CRUMPSALL township parish Manchester Lancs pop 1,878

CRUNDALE parish 1554 Kent 8 miles sw Canterbury pop 263 archd and dioc Canterbury

CRUTCH extra parochial district Worcs 2 miles w Droitwich

CRUWYS MORCHARD parish 1572 Devon 5-1/4 miles w Tiverton pop 634 archd Barnstaple dioc Exeter

CRUX EASTON parish 1702 Hamps 6-1/4 miles nw Whitchurch pop 97 archd and dioc Winchester

CUBBERLY parish 1546 Gloucs 5-1/2 miles se Cheltenham pop 181 archd and dioc Gloucester Bapt

CUBBINGTON parish 1559 Warws 5 miles ne Warwick pop 677 archd Coventry dioc Lichfield

CUBERT parish 1653 Cornwall 10 miles ne Truro pop 487 archd Cornwall dioc Exeter

CUBLEY parish 1566 Derbys 6 miles sw Ashbourn pop 471 archd Derby dioc Lichfield

CUBLINGTON parish 1566 Bucks 6-3/4 miles ne Aylesbury pop 284 archd Buckingham dioc Lincoln

CUBY Cornwall See TREGONEY

CUCKFIELD parish 1598 Sussex 25 miles ne Chichester pop 2,586 archd Lewes dioc Chichester Unit

CUCKLINGTON parish 1558 Somerset 2-3/4 miles se Wincanton pop 280 archd Wells dioc Bath and Wells

CUCKNEY or NORTON CUCKNEY parish 1632 Notts 5-1/2 miles sw Worksop comp township Holbeck, Langwith, Norton pop 1,638 archd Nottingham dioc York

CUDDESDEN parish 1541 co Oxford 6-1/2 miles se Oxford comp chapelries Denton, Wheatley, hamlet Chippinghurst pop 1,460 archd and dioc Oxford

CUDDINGTON parish 1653 Bucks 5-1/4 miles sw Aylesbury pop 620 archd Buckingham dioc Lincoln Part Bapt

CUDDINGTON township parish Malpas Ches pop 260

CUDDINGTON township parish Weaverham Ches pop 277

CUDDINGTON parish no regs Surrey 3/4 miles ne Ewell pop 138 archd Surrey dioc Winchester

CUDHAM parish 1653 Kent 7-1/4 miles se Bromley pop 660 archd and dioc Rochester

CUDWORTH parish 1699 Somerset 3 miles se Ilminster pop 146 pec Prebendary of Cudworth in Cathedral Church of Wells

CUDWORTH township parish Royston W R York pop 451 Wesl Meth

CUERDALE township parish Blackburn Lancs pop 118

CUERDEN township parish Leyland Lancs pop 592

CUERDLEY township parish Prescot Lancs pop 319

CUGLEY tything parish Newent Gloucs pop 372

CULBONE or KILNER parish 1625 Somerset 9 miles nw Minehead pop 62 archd Taunton dioc Bath and Wells

CULCHETH township parish Winwick Lancs pop 2,503

CULFORD parish 1560 Suffolk 4-3/4 miles nw Bury St Edmund's pop 327 archd Sudbury dioc Norwich

CULGAITH chapelry 1758 parish Kirkland Cumberland pop 257

CULHAM parish 1650 co Oxford 1 mile se Abingdon pop 404 archd and dioc Oxford

CULLERCOATS township parish Tynemouth Northumberland pop 542

CULLINGWORTH hamlet parish Bingley W R York Wesl Meth

CULLOMPTON parish 1601 Devon 12 miles ne Exeter pop 3,813

archd and dioc Exeter Bapt, Bryanites, Soc of Friends, Indep, Wesl Meth, Unit

CULMINGTON parish 1575 Shrops 5-1/2 miles nw Ludlow pop 515 archd Salop dioc Hereford

CULMSTOCK parish 1645 Devon 7 miles ne Cullompton pop 1,519 pec Dean and Chapter of Exeter Bapt, Soc of Friends, Wesl Meth

CULPHO parish 1700 Suffolk 3-1/2 miles nw Woodbridge pop 64 archd Suffolk dioc Norwich

CULVERLANDS tything parish Farnham Surrey pop 443

CULVERTHORPE chapelry 1559 parish Haydor Lincs pop 109

CULWORTH parish 1563 co Northampton 7-3/4 miles ne Banbury pop 606 archd Northampton dioc Peterborough

CUMBERWORTH parish 1562 Lincs 4-1/4 miles se Alford pop 188 archd and dioc Lincoln

CUMBERWORTH chapelry 1653 parish Silkstone W R York pop 2,554

CUMDEVOCK township parish Dalston Cumberland pop 348

CUMMERSDALE township parish St Mary Carlisle Cumberland pop 488

CUMNER parish 1559 Berks 5-1/4 miles nw Abingdon comp township Cumner, tything Botley, Bradley, Chawley, Henwood, Hill end, Straud, Swinford, Whitely, liberty Chilswell pop 1,364 archd Berks dioc Salisbury

CUMREW parish 1731 Cumberland 6 miles n Kirk Oswald comp townships Cumrew Inside, Cumrew Outside pop 212 archd and dioc Carlisle

CUMWHINTON joint township with Coathill parish Wetheral Cumberland pop 575 Wesl Meth

CUMWHITTON parish 1694 Cumberland 9-1/4 miles se Carlisle comp townships Cumwhitton, Moorthwaite with Northscaugh pop 579 archd and dioc Carlisle

CUNDALL parish 1582 W R York 5 miles ne Boroughbridge comp townships Cundall with Leckby, Norton le Clay pop 394 archd Richmond dioc Chester

CUNSALL township parish Cheddleton Staffs pop 197

CUNSCOUGH district parish Halsall Lancs

CUPERNHAM tything parish Romsey Hamps

CURBAR hamlet parish Bakewell Derbys pop 227

CURBOROUGH joint township with Elmhurst parish St Chad, Lichfield Staffs pop 212

CURBRIDGE hamlet parish Witney co Oxford pop 398

CURDWORTH parish 1653 Warws 3 miles nw Coleshill pop 617 archd Coventry dioc Lichfield

CURLAND parish 1634 Somerset 5-3/4 miles se Taunton pop 167 archd Taunton dioc Bath and Wells Wesl Meth

CURRY MALLET parish 1682 Somerset 5-3/4 miles ne Ilminster pop 496 archd Taunton dioc Bath and Wells

CURRY, NORTH parish 1539 Somerset 6-1/2 miles ne Taunton pop 1,833 pec Dean and Chapter of Wells Bapt, Wesl Meth

CURRY, RIVELL parish 1642 Somerset 2-1/2 miles sw Langport
pop 1,444 archd Taunton dioc Bath and Wells
CURY parish 1690 Cornwall 4-3/4 miles se Helston pop 523 archd
Cornwall dioc Exeter Wesl Meth
CUSOP parish 1754 Herefs 2 miles se Hay pop 252 archd and dioc
Hereford
CUSTHORPE hamlet parish West Acre Norfolk
CUTCOMBE parish 1624 Somerset 5-1/4 miles sw Dunster pop 709
archd Taunton dioc Bath and Wells
CUTSDEAN chapelry 1696 parish Bredon Worcs pop 166
CUTTHORPE hamlet parish Brampton Derbys
CUXHAM parish 1577 co Oxford 5 miles sw Tetsworth pop 207 archd
and dioc Oxford
CUXTON parish 1560 Kent 2-3/4 miles sw Rochester pop 298 archd
and dioc Rochester
CUXWOLD parish 1683 Lincs 4 miles e Caistor pop 79 archd and
dioc Lincoln
CWMCARVAN parish 1660 co Monmouth 3-1/2 miles sw Monmouth
pop 301 archd and dioc Llandaff
CWMYOY parish 1708 Herefs 8-1/2 miles nw Abergavenny pop 658
archd Brecon dioc St David
DACRE parish 1559 Cumberland 5 miles sw Penrith comp townships
Dacre, Great Blencow, Newbiggin, Soulby, Stainton pop 995 archd
and dioc Carlisle
DACRE township parish Ripon W R York pop 698
DADLINGTON chapelry 1734 parish Hinckley Leics 3 miles nw Hin-
ckley pop 169
DAGENHAM parish 1598 Essex 3-1/2 miles sw Romford pop 2,118
archd Essex dioc London
DAGLINGWORTH parish 1561 Gloucs 2-3/4 miles nw Cirencester
pop 239 archd and dioc Gloucester
DAGNELL chapelry parish Eddlesborough Bucks pop 304
DAGWORTH hamlet parish Old Newton Suffolk
DALBURY parish 1545 Derbys 6-1/2 miles sw Derby pop 256 archd
Derby dioc Lichfield
DALBY parish 1721 Lincs 2-3/4 miles n Spilsby pop 99 pec Dean and
Chapter of Lincoln
DALBY parish 1657 N R York 9-1/2 miles sw New Malton pop 155
archd Cleveland dioc York
DALBY, MAGNA parish 1591 Leics 3-3/4 miles sw Melton Mowbray
pop 511 archd Leicester dioc Lincoln
DALBY ON THE WOLDS, or DALBY, OLD parish 1725 Leics 6-1/2
miles nw Melton Mowbray pop 393 pec Old Dalby Wesl Meth
DALBY, PARVA parish 1559 Leics 4-1/2 miles se Melton Mowbray
pop 194 archd Leicester dioc Lincoln
DALDERBY parish 1690 Lincs 3 miles sw Horncastle pop 42 archd
and dioc Lincoln
DALE ABBEY extra parochial liberty 1667 Derbys pec of Dale Abbey

DALE TOWN township parish Hawnby N R York pop 53

DALHAM parish 1558 Suffolk 5 miles se Newmarket pop 538 archd Sudbury dioc Norwich

DALLINGHOO parish 1559 Suffolk 2-3/4 miles sw Wickham Market pop 354 archd Suffolk dioc Norwich

DALLINGTON parish 1577 co Northampton 1-3/4 miles nw Northampton pop 479 archd Northampton dioc Peterborough

DALLINGTON parish 1643 Sussex 6 miles nw Battle pop 577 archd Lewes dioc Chichester

DALPOOL hamlet parish Thurstaston Ches

DALSCOTE hamlet parish Pattishall co Northampton

DALSTON parish 1570 Cumberland 4-1/2 miles sw Carlisle comp chapelry Ivegill, townships Buckhowbank, Cumdevock, Dalston, Hawkesdale, Raughton with Gatesgill pop 3,023 archd and dioc Carlisle

DALSTON hamlet parish Hackney Middlesex

DALTON township parish Burton in Kendal Lancs pop 131

DALTON township parish Wigan Lancs pop 468

DALTON hamlet parish Hexham Northumberland

DALTON township parish Newburn Northumberland pop 106

DALTON township parish Topcliffe N R York pop 252

DALTON township partly in parish Croft chiefly in parish Kirkby Ravensworth N R York pop 308 Wesl Meth

DALTON township parish Kirk Heaton W R York pop 3,060

DALTON township parish Rotherham W R York pop 187

DALTON LE DALE parish 1653 co Durham 6 miles s Sunderland comp townships Dalton le Dale, Dawdon, Cold Hesleton, East Morton pop 1,305 archd and dioc Durham

DALTON IN FURNESS parish 1565 Lancs 25 miles nw Lancaster comp market town Dalton, chapelry Ireleth, townships Hawcoat above town, Yarleside pop 2,697 archd Richmond dioc Chester Wesl Meth

DALTON HOLME York See DALTON, SOUTH

DALTON, NORTH parish 1653 E R York 7-1/2 miles sw Great Driffield comp townships North Dalton, Neswick pop 525 archd East Riding dioc York

DALTON PIERCY township parish Hart co Durham pop 79

DALTON, SOUTH parish 1653 E R York 6 miles nw Beverley pop 273 archd East Riding dioc York

DALTON UPON TEES township parish Croft N R York pop 196

DALWOOD chapelry 1568 parish Stockland Dorset 3-3/4 miles nw Axminster pop 434

DAMERHAM, SOUTH parish 1678 Wilts 4 miles ne Cranbourn pop 716 archd and dioc Salisbury

DANBURY parish 1673 Essex 5-1/2 miles se Chelmsford pop 1060 archd Essex dioc London

DANBY parish 1585 N R York 9-1/2 miles se Guilsbrough pop 1,392 archd Cleveland dioc York

DANBY WISK parish 1621 N R York 3-1/2 miles nw North Allerton
comp chapelry Yafforth, township Danby Wisk pop 508 archd
Richmond dioc Chester
DANTHORPE township parish Humbleton E R York pop 52
DARENTH parish 1631 Kent 2-1/2 miles se Dartford pop 588 pec
archbishop of Canterbury
DARESBURY chapelry 1617 parish Runcorn Ches 5-1/2 miles ne
Frodsham pop 143 archd and dioc Chester
DARFIELD parish 1628 W R York 5-1/4 miles se Barnsley comp
chapelry Worsbrough, townships Ardsley, Billingley, Darfield,
Great Houghton, Little Houghton, Wombwell pop 5,703 archd and
dioc York
DARLASTON parish 1539 Staffs 1-1/2 miles nw Wednesbury pop 6,647
archd Stafford dioc Lichfield Indep, Wesl Meth
DARLASTON liberty parish Stone co Staffs
DARLESTON hamlet parish Prees Shrops
DARLEY (DARLEY DALE) parish 1541 Derbys 3 miles nw Matlock
pop 1,937 archd Derby dioc Lichfield
DARLEY joint township with Menwith parish Hampsthwaite W R York
DARLEY ABBEY chapelry parish St Alkmund Derbys pop 1,170 archd
Derby dioc Lichfield
DARLINGSCOTT hamlet parish Tredington Worcs pop 166
DARLINGTON chapelry borough 1590 co Durham 18-1/2 miles s
Durham comp town Darlington, townships Archdeacon Newton,
Blackwell, Cockerton pop 9,417 archd and dioc Durham Part
Bapt, Soc of Friends, Indep, Prim and Wesl Meth, Roman Cath
DARLTON chapelry 1568 parish Dunham co Notts pop 162
DARMSDEN hamlet parish Barking
DARNALL hamlet 1719 parish Sheffield W R York Wesl Meth
DARNHALL township parish Whitegate or New Church Ches pop 198
DARRAS HALL township parish Ponteland Northumberland pop 15
DARRINGTON parish 1568 W R York 2-3/4 miles se Pontefract comp
townships Darrington, Stapleton pop 619 archd and dioc York
Wesl Meth
DARSHAM parish 1539 Suffolk 5-1/4 miles ne Saxmundham pop 513
archd Suffolk dioc Norwich
DARTFORD parish 1561 Kent 15 miles se London pop 4,715 archd
and dioc Rochester various denominations of dissenters
DARTINGTON parish 1538 Devon 2 miles nw Totnes pop 618 archd
Totnes dioc Exeter
DARTMOOR FOREST township parish Lydford Devon pop 353
DARTMOUTH seaport market town borough sep juris Devon 30-3/4
miles sw Exeter pop 4,597 comp parishes St Petrox 1652, St
Savior and Townstall (St Clement) archd Totnes dioc Exeter
Bapt, Indep, Wesl Meth
DARTON parish 1558 W R York 3-1/4 miles nw Barnsley comp town-
ships Barugh, Darton, Kexborough pop 2,960 archd and dioc York
DARWEN, LOWER township parish Blackburn Lancs pop 2,667

DARWEN, OVER chapelry parish Blackburn Lancs pop 6,972 archd
and dioc Chester Wesl Meth and others
DASSET, AVON parish 1559 Warws 5-1/4 miles se Kington pop 226
pec Bishop of Lichfield
DASSET BURTON See BURTON DASSET
DATCHETT parish 1559 Bucks 2 miles se Eton pop 802 archd Buckingham dioc Lincoln Part Bapt
DATCHWORTH parish 1570 Herts 3-1/4 miles ne Welwyn pop 593
archd Huntingdon dioc Lincoln
DAUNTSEY parish 1653 Wilts 4-3/4 miles se Malmesbury pop 561
archd and dioc Salisbury
DAVENHAM parish 1560 Ches 2-1/4 miles s Northwich comp townships Bostock, Davenham, Eaton, Leftwich, Moulton, Newhall, Rudheath, Shipbrook, Shurlach, Stanthorne, Wharton, Whatcroft pop
4,515 archd and dioc Chester
DAVENPORT township parish Astbury Ches pop 103
DAVENTRY parish borough 1560 sep juris co Northampton 12-1/4
miles nw Northampton pop 3,646 archd Northampton dioc Peterborough
DAVIDSTOW parish 1710 Cornwall 3-1/2 miles ne Camelford pop
389 archd Cornwall dioc Exeter
DAVINGTON parish 1549 Kent 1/2 mile nw Faversham pop 157 archd
and dioc Canterbury
DAWDON township parish Dalton le Dale co Durham pop 1,022
DAWLEY, MAGNA parish 1666 Shrops 4 miles sw Shiffnall pop 6,877
archd Salop dioc Lichfield Wesl Meth
DAWLISH parish 1627 Devon 2-3/4 miles ne Teignmouth pop 3,151
pec Dean and Chapter of Exeter Indep, Wesl Meth
DAY, ST chapelry parish Gwennap Cornwall archd Cornwall dioc
Exeter Bapt, Bryanites, Wesl Meth
DAYLESFORD parish 1674 Worcs 3-1/2 miles e Stow on the Wold
pop 88 pec Bishop of Worcester
DEAL parish, borough 1559 Kent 18 miles se Canterbury pop 7,268
exempt from jurisdiction of archdeacon dioc Canterbury Part
Bapt, Indep, Calv and Wesl Meth
DEAN parish 1542 Cumberland 5 miles sw Cockermouth comp town-
ships Branthwaite, Dean, Ullock with Pardsey, Dean Scales pop
866 archd Richmond dioc Chester
DEAN parish 1637 Lancs 1-3/4 miles sw Great Bolton comp chapelries Farnworth, Little Hulton, Horwich, West Houghton, townships
Heaton, Middle Hulton, Over Hulton, Halliwell, Kearsley, Rumworth
pop 22,994 archd and dioc Chester some dissenting places of
worship
DEAN hamlet parish Spelsbury co Oxford
DEAN parish 1659 Hamps 5-1/2 miles sw Basingstoke pop 163 archd
and dioc Winchester
DEAN, EAST chapelry 1682 parish Mottisfont Hamps pop 173 archd
and dioc Winchester

DEAN, EAST parish 1653 Sussex 7 miles se Midhurst pop 391 archd Lewes dioc Chichester

DEAN, FOREST extra parochial liberty Gloucs 5 miles sw Newnham comp divisions Denby walk, Herbert's walk, Little Dean walk, Speech House walk, Worcester walk, York walk pop 7,014 archd and dioc Gloucester chapelries Christ Church, Holy Trinity, St Paul's

DEAN, HILL hamlet parish Sandbach Ches

DEAN, LITTLE parish 1684 Gloucs 1-3/4 miles nw Newnham pop 617 archd and dioc Gloucester

DEAN, MITCHELL parish 1680 Gloucs 11 miles w Gloucester pop 601 archd Hereford dioc Gloucester

DEAN, NETHER parish 1566 Beds 3-1/2 miles sw Kimbolton pop 513 archd Bedford dioc Lincoln Wesl Meth

DEAN PRIOR parish 1561 Devon 4 miles sw Ashburton pop 561 archd Totnes dioc Exeter

DEAN PRIOR'S chapelry 1538 parish Colemore Hamps pop 166

DEAN RAW township parish Warden Northumberland pop 654

DEAN ROW hamlet parish Wilmslow Ches Unit

DEAN SCALES joint township with Ullock and Pardsey parish Dean Cumberland pop 356

DEAN, UPPER hamlet parish Nether Dean Beds

DEAN, WEST parish 1631 Sussex 6-1/2 miles sw Midhurst pop 641 archd and dioc Chichester

DEAN, WEST parish 1554 Sussex 3 miles e Seaford pop 150 archd Lewes dioc Chichester

DEAN, WEST parish 1538 Wilts 7 miles se Salisbury pop 360 archd and dioc Salisbury

DEANHAM township parish Hartburn Northumberland pop 46

DEARHAM parish 1662 Cumberland 6-1/4 miles nw Cockermouth comp townships Dearham, Ellenborough with Unerigg pop 1,449 archd and dioc Carlisle

DEARNBROOK hamlet parish Arncliffe W R York

DEBACH parish 1539 Suffolk 4-1/4 miles nw Woodbridge pop 133 archd Suffolk dioc Norwich

DEBDEN parish 1557 Essex 4-1/4 miles nw Thaxted pop 985 archd Colchester dioc London

DEBENHAM parish 1559 Suffolk 13 miles n Ipswich pop 1,629 archd Suffolk dioc Norwich

DEBTLING parish 1558 Kent 2-3/4 miles ne Maidstone pop 372 archd and dioc Canterbury

DECUMANS, ST parish 1600 Somerset 5-1/4 miles se Dunster comp market town Watchett pop 2,120 pec Prebendary of St Decuman's, Cathedral Church of Wells Wesl Meth, Bapt

DEDDINGTON parish 1631 co Oxford 16 miles nw Oxford pop 2,078 archd and dioc Oxford Wesl Meth

DEDHAM parish 1560 Essex 4 miles nw Manningtree pop 1,770 archd Colchester dioc London

DEDWORTH hamlet parish New Windsor Berks pop 137

DEENE parish 1558 co Northampton 5-1/2 miles ne Rockingham pop 453 archd Northampton dioc Peterborough

DEENTHORPE hamlet parish Deene co Northampton pop 225

DEEP DALE hamlet parish Arncliffe W R York

DEEPING parish 1674 Lincs 3/4 mile e Market Deeping pop 1,587 archd and dioc Lincoln Wesl Meth

DEEPING FEN extra parochial liberty Lincs 6 miles sw Spalding pop 790

DEEPING GATE hamlet parish Maxey co Northampton pop 155

DEEPING, MARKET parish 1709 Lincs 43 miles se Lincoln pop 1,091 archd and dioc Lincoln

DEEPING, WEST parish 1657 Lincs 1-1/2 miles sw Market Deeping pop 301 archd and dioc Lincoln

DEERHURST parish 1559 Gloucs 2 miles sw Tewkesbury pop 869 pec Deerhurst

DEFFORD chapelry 1540 parish St Andrew, Pershore Worcs pop 383 archd and dioc Worcester

DEIGHTON chapelry 1686 parish Northallerton N R York pop 146

DEIGHTON township parish Escrick E R York pop 179

DEIGHTON, KIRK parish 1600 W R York 1-3/4 miles nw Wetherby comp townships Kirk Deighton, North Deighton pop 506 archd and dioc York Wesl Meth

DELAMERE parish 1817 Ches 5-3/4 miles w Northwich comp townships Delamere, Eddisbury, Oakmere pop 828 archd and dioc Chester

DELAPREE hamlet parish Hardingstone co Northampton

DEMBLEBY parish 1573 Lincs 6 miles nw Folkingham pop 66 archd and dioc Lincoln

DENBURY parish 1559 borough Devon 2-1/2 miles sw Newton Abbots pop 464 archd Totnes dioc Exeter

DENBY parish 1577 Derbys 8 miles ne Derby pop 1,272 archd Derby dioc Lichfield

DENBY chapelry parish Penistone W R York pop 1,295 Wesl Meth

DENCHWORTH parish 1570 Berks 2-1/2 miles nw Wantage pop 213 archd Berks dioc Salisbury

DENDRON chapelry 1788 parish Aldingham Lancs archd Richmond dioc Chester

DENERDISTAN, otherwise DENSTON parish 1561 Suffolk 5-3/4 miles n Clare pop 341 archd Sudbury dioc Norwich

DENFORD parish 1597 co Northampton 1-1/2 miles s Thrapston pop 319 archd Northampton dioc Peterborough

DENGE MARSH locally in parish of Lydd Kent

DENGIE parish 1559 Essex 4 miles sw Bradwell pop 249 archd Essex dioc London

DENHAM parish 1653 Bucks 2-1/2 miles nw Uxbridge pop 1,169 archd Buckingham dioc Lincoln Wesl Meth

DENHAM parish 1708 Suffolk 2 miles e Eye pop 276 archd Suffolk dioc Norwich

DENHAM parish 1539 Suffolk 7-1/2 miles sw Bury St Edmunds pop 191 archd Sudbury dioc Norwich

DENMEAD tything parish Hambledon Hamps

DENNABY township parish Mexborough W R York pop 130

DENNEY hamlet parish Waterbeach Cambs

DENNINGTON parish 1570 Suffolk 2-3/4 miles n Framlingham pop 1,000 archd Suffolk dioc Norwich

DENNIS, ST parish 1687 Cornwall 5-1/2 miles se St Columb Major pop 721 archd Cornwall dioc Exeter Wesl Meth

DENSHANGER or Deanshanger hamlet parish Passenham co Northampton

DENSTON township parish Alveton Staffs pop 250

DENSTON Suffolk See DENERDISTAN

DENT chapelry 1611 Parish Sedbergh W R York pop 1,840 archd Richmond dioc Chester Indep

DENTON chapelry 1586 parish Gainford co Durham pop 144

DENTON parish 1546 Hunts 1-3/4 miles sw Stilton pop 85 archd Huntingdon dioc Lincoln

DENTON parish 1560 Kent 9 miles se Canterbury pop 314 archd and dioc Canterbury

DENTON parish incl in regs of Chalk Kent

DENTON chapelry 1694 parish Manchester Lancs pop 2,792 archd and dioc Chester Wesl Meth

DENTON parish 1558 Lincs 4 miles sw Grantham pop 553 archd and dioc Lincoln

DENTON parish 1559 Norfolk 4-1/4 miles ne Harleston pop 580 archd Norfolk dioc Norwich

DENTON parish 1540 co Northampton 6-1/4 miles se Northampton pop 527 archd Northampton dioc Peterborough

DENTON chapelry parish Cuddesden co Oxford pop 137

DENTON parish 1600 Sussex 1-1/2 miles ne Newhaven pop 117 archd Lewes dioc Chichester

DENTON chapelry 1754 parish Otley W R York pop 179

DENTON, EAST township parish Newburn Northumberland pop 524

DENTON, NETHER parish 1703 Cumberland 5-1/2 miles ne Brampton pop 290 archd and dioc Carlisle

DENTON, UPPER parish see regs of Lanercost and Nether Denton Cumberland 6-1/2 miles ne Brampton pop 106 archd and dioc Carlisle

DENTON, WEST township parish Newburn Northumberland pop 455

DENVER parish 1653 Norfolk 1-1/4 miles s Downham Market pop 850 archd Norfolk dioc Norwich

DENWICK hamlet parish Alnwick Northumberland

DEOPHAM parish 1560 Norfolk 3-3/4 miles sw Wymondham pop 506 archd Norfolk dioc Norwich Wesl Meth

DEPDEN parish 1538 Suffolk 7-1/4 miles sw Bury St Edmund's pop 329 archd Sudbury dioc Norwich

DEPTFORD town Kent 4 miles e London pop 21,350 St Nicholas 1730,

St Paul 1563 archd and dioc Rochester Bapt, Soc of Friends, Indep, Wesl Meth, Unit

DEPTFORD tything parish Wily Wilts

DERBY market town, borough sep juris Derbys 15 miles w Nottingham pop 23,607 All Saints 1558, St Werburgh 1562, St Alkmund 1538, St Peter 1558, St Michael 1559 archd Derby dioc Lichfield Gen and Part Bapt, Soc of Friends, Indep, Wesl Meth, New and Old Connexion, Swedenborgians, Unit, Roman Cath

DERBY HILLS extra parochial liberty Derbys 9 miles s Derby pop 76

DERBY, WEST chapelry parish Walton on the Hill Lancs pop 6,304

DEREHAM, EAST parish 1538 Norfolk 16 miles nw Norwich pop 3,913 archd Norfolk dioc Norwich Part Bapt, Indep, Wesl Meth

DEREHAM, WEST parish 1558 Norfolk 3-1/4 miles nw Stoke Ferry pop 496 archd Norfolk dioc Norwich

DERITEND chapelry 1699 parish Aston Warws archd Coventry dioc Lichfield

DERSINGHAM parish 1710 Norfolk 4-1/2 miles ne Castle Rising pop 534 archd and dioc Norwich

DERTHORPE chapelry parish Well Lincs

DERWENT chapelry parish Hathersage Derbys pop 153

DESBOROUGH parish 1571 co Northampton 1-3/4 miles nw Rothwell pop 988 archd Northampton dioc Peterborough Wesl Meth, Unit

DESFORD parish 1559 Leics 5 miles e Market Bosworth pop 971 archd Leicester dioc Lincoln

DETCHANT township parish Belford Northumberland pop 180

DETHWICK LEA chapelry parish Ashover Derbys pop 675

DEUXHILL parish 1655 Shrops 4 miles s Bridgenorth pop 55 archd Salop dioc Hereford

DEVEREUX parish 1669 Herefs 7-3/4 miles sw Hereford pop 201 archd and dioc Hereford

DEVERHILL (LONGBRIDGE) parish 1682 Wilts 2-1/2 miles s Warminster pop 1,307 archd and dioc Salisbury

DEVERHILL (MONCKTON) parish 1695 Wilts 4-1/4 miles ne Mere pop 204 archd and dioc Salisbury

DEVIL'S HOUSE parish Woolwich Kent

DEVIZES market town borough sep juris Wilts 22 miles nw Salisbury pop 4,562 pec Bishop of Salisbury comp St John 1559, St Mary 1569 Part Bapt, Soc of Friends, Indep, Presb, Wesl Meth

DEVONPORT Naval Arsenal borough parish Stoke Damarel Devon 1-1/2 miles w Plymouth pop 34,883 St Aubyn's 1771, St John's 1709 Part Bapt, Indep, Wesl Meth, Moravians, Unit

DEWCHURCH, LITTLE parish 1730 Herefs 6 miles se Hereford pop 369 archd and dioc Hereford

DEWCHURCH, MUCH parish 1559 Herefs 6-1/2 miles sw Hereford pop 573 archd and dioc Hereford

DEWLISH parish 1627 Dorset 9-1/2 miles sw Blandford Forum pop 361 archd Dorset dioc Bristol

DEWSALL parish 1582 Herefs 5-1/2 miles sw Hereford pop 44 juris
Cons Court of Dean of Hereford
DEWSBURY parish 1538 W R York 34 miles sw York comp Dewsbury,
chapelry Ossett, township Soothill, chapelry Clifton, township
Hartshead pop 19,854 archd and dioc York Soc of Friends, Indep,
Wesl Meth
DIBDEN parish 1664 Hamps 3 miles sw Southampton pop 418 archd
and dioc Winchester
DICKLEBURGH parish 1540 Norfolk 2 miles ne Scole pop 815 archd
Norfolk dioc Norwich
DIDBROOK parish 1558 Gloucs 2-3/4 miles ne Winchcombe pop 240
archd and dioc Gloucester
DIDCOT Berks See DUDCOTE
DIDDINGTON parish 1688 Hunts 3-3/4 miles n St Neots pop 208 archd
Huntingdon dioc Lincoln
DIDDLEBURY parish 1583 Shrops 8-1/2 miles n Ludlow comp town-
ships Diddlebury, Middlehope, Peaton, Sutton pop 920 archd Salop
dioc Hereford
DIDLING parish see regs of Trayford Sussex 4 miles sw Midhurst
pop 82 archd and dioc Chichester
DIDLINGTON tything parish Chalbury Dorset
DIDLINGTON parish 1717 Norfolk 6 miles se Stoke Ferry pop 86
archd Norfolk dioc Norwich
DIDMARTON parish 1567 Gloucs 4-3/4 miles sw Tetbury pop 103
archd and dioc Gloucester
DIDSBURY chapelry 1561 parish Manchester Lancs pop 1,067 archd
and dioc Chester
DIGBY parish 1679 Lincs 6 miles ne Sleaford pop 319 archd and dioc
Lincoln
DIGSWELL parish 1538 Herefs 1-1/4 miles se Welwyn pop 196
archd Huntingdon dioc Lincoln
DILHAM parish 1563 Norfolk 4-3/4 miles se North Walsham pop 450
archd Norfolk dioc Norwich
DILHORNE parish 1558 Staffs 2-1/4 miles w Cheadle pop 1,510 archd
Stafford dioc Lichfield Wesl Meth
DILLIKER township parish Kendal Westm pop 109
DILLINGTON hamlet parish East Dereham Norfolk pop 33
DILSTON township parish Corbridge Northumberland pop 175
DILTON chapelry 1585 parish Westbury Wilts pop 2,172
DILWORTH township parish Ribchester Lancs pop 874
DILWYN parish 1558 Herefs 2-1/2 miles ne Weobley pop 1,035 archd
and dioc Hereford
DINCHOPE township parish Bromfield Shrops pop 83
DINDER parish 1696 Somerset 2 miles se Wells pop 210 pec Dean of
Wells
DINEDOR parish 1750 Herefs 4-1/2 miles se Hereford pop 314 juris
Cons Court of Dean of Hereford
DINGESTOW parish 1755 co Monmouth 4 miles sw Monmouth pop 198

archd and dioc Llandaff

DINGLEY parish 1583 co Northampton 2-1/2 miles ne Market Harborough pop 160 archd Northampton dioc Peterborough

DINHAM hamlet parish Llanvair Discord co Monmouth pop 24

DINKLEY township parish Blackburn Lancs pop 223

DINMORE extra parochial liberty Herefs 9 miles nw Hereford pop 21

DINMORE extra parochial liberty parish Clungunford Shrops pop 12

DINNINGTON township parish Ponteland Northumberland pop 354

DINNINGTON chapelry 1592 parish Seavington, St Michael Somerset pop 187

DINNINGTON parish 1730 W R York 7 miles nw Worksop pop 233 archd and dioc York

DINSDALE, LOW parish 1556 co Durham 6 miles se Darlington pop 169 archd and dioc Durham

DINSDALE, OVER township parish Sockburn N R York pop 58

DINTING township parish Glossop Derbys

DINTON parish 1562 Bucks 4 miles sw Aylesbury comp hamlet Aston Mollins, liberty Moreton pop 893 archd Buckingham dioc Lincoln

DINTON parish 1558 Wilts 5 miles w Wilton pop 536 archd and dioc Salisbury dissenters

DIPPENHALL tything parish Crondall Hamps pop 324

DIPTFORD parish 1653 Devon 5-3/4 miles sw Totnes pop 735 archd Totnes dioc Exeter

DIRHAM or DYRHAM parish 1568 Gloucs 4 miles nw Marshfield pop 516 archd and dioc Gloucester

DISCOVE tything parish Bruton Somerset pop 35

DISEWORTH parish 1656 Leics 6 miles nw Loughborough pop 764 archd Leicester dioc Lincoln Wesl Meth

DISHFORTH chapelry parish Topcliffe N R York pop 332 Part Bapt

DISHLEY chapelry 1681 parish Thorpacre Leics pop 366

DISS parish 1551 Norfolk 22 miles sw Norwich pop 2,934 archd Norfolk dioc Norwich Soc of Friends, Part Bapt, Indep, Wesl Meth, Unit

DISSINGTON, NORTH township parish Newburn Northumberland pop 76

DISSINGTON, SOUTH township parish Newburn Northumberland pop 77

DISTINGTON parish 1653 Cumberland 4-1/4 miles ne Whitehaven pop 960 archd Richmond dioc Chester

DISTLEY chapelry 1591 parish Stockport Ches pop 2,037 archd and dioc Chester

DITCHAMPTON parish (no regs) Wilts 1/4 mile n Wilton archd and dioc Salisbury

DITCHBURN, EAST and WEST township parish Ellingham Northumberland pop 77

DITCHEAT parish 1562 Somerset 3-1/4 miles nw Castle Cary pop 1,238 archd Wells dioc Bath and Wells Wesl Meth

DITCHELLING or DITCHLING parish 1556 Sussex 3 miles se Hurst

Pierrepoint pop 917 archd Lewes dioc Chichester Indep, Unit
DITCHES joint township with Lowe parish Wem Shrops
DITCHFORD parish (See STRETTON ON THE FOSS) Warws 3 miles
    sw Shipston upon Stour archd Gloucester dioc Worcester
DITCHFORD hamlet parish Blockley Worcs
DITCHINGHAM parish 1559 Norfolk 13-1/2 miles ne Norwich pop 962
    archd Norfolk dioc Norwich
DITTERIDGE parish 1584 Wilts 7-3/4 miles sw Chippenham pop 83
    archd Wilts dioc Salisbury
DITTISHAM parish 1650 Devon 5-1/2 miles nw Dartmouth pop 816
    archd Totnes dioc Exeter
DITTON chapelry parish Stoke Poges Bucks
DITTON parish 1663 Kent 3-1/2 miles nw Maidstone pop 218 archd
    and dioc Rochester
DITTON township parish Prescot Lancs pop 466
DITTON, FEN parish 1538 Cambs 2-3/4 miles ne Cambridge pop 528
    pec Bishop of Ely
DITTON, LONG parish 1564 Surrey 2-1/4 miles sw Kingston upon
    Thames pop 627 archd Surrey dioc Winchester
DITTON, PRIORS parish 1673 Shrops 7-3/4 miles sw Bridgenorth
    pop 584 archd Salop dioc Hereford
DITTON, THAMES parish 1661 Surrey 2-1/4 miles sw Kingston upon
    Thames pop 1878 archd Surrey dioc Winchester Indep
DITTON, WOOD parish 1567 Cambs 2-3/4 miles se Newmarket pop
    888 archd Sudbury dioc Norwich
DIXON or DICKLESTON hamlet parish Alderton Gloucs
DIXTON, HADNOCK hamlet parish Newton Dixton co Monmouth pop
    447
DIXTON, NEWTON parish 1661 co Monmouth 1-1/2 miles ne Mon-
    mouth comp hamlets Hadnock Dixton, Newton Dixton pop 672
    archd and dioc Hereford
DOBCROSS chapelry 1787 parish Rochdale W R York archd and dioc
    Chester
DOCKER township parish Kendal Westm pop 95
DOCKING parish 1558 Norfolk 5-1/4 miles sw Burnham Westgate
    pop 1,406 archd Norfolk dioc Norwich
DOCKINGFIELD tything parish Frensham Hamps pop 169
DOCKLOW parish 1584 Herefs 5-1/2 miles se Leominster pop 199
    archd and dioc Hereford
DODBROOKE parish 1725 Devon 1/2 mile e Kingsbridge pop 1,038
    archd Totnes dioc Exeter
DODCOT township partly in parish Wrenbury chiefly in Audlem Ches
    pop 637
DODDENHAM parish 1538 Worcs 7-1/4 miles nw Worcester pop 283
    archd and dioc Worcester
DODDERHILL parish 1651 Worcs 1/2 mile n Droitwich pop 1,799
    archd and dioc Worcester
DODDERSHALL hamlet parish Quainton Bucks

DODDINGHURST parish 1560 Essex 3-1/2 miles n Brentwood pop
372 archd and dioc Exeter
DODDINGTON parish 1681 Cambs 4-1/2 miles sw March comp chapelries Benwick, Marsh, hamlet Wimblington pop 7,527 pec Bishop
of Ely
DODDINGTON township parish Wybunbury Ches pop 37
DODDINGTON parish 1589 Kent 4-3/4 miles se Sittingbourne pop 466
archd and dioc Canterbury Wesl Meth
DODDINGTON parish 1690 Lincs 6-1/2 miles sw Lincoln pop 223
archd and dioc Lincoln
DODDINGTON parish 1688 Northumberland 3 miles ne Wooler comp
townships Doddington, Earl (otherwise Yeard) Hill, Ewart, Hum-
bleton, Nesbitt pop 903 archd Northumberland dioc Durham
DODDINGTON, DRY parish See WESTBOROUGH Lincs 8 miles nw
Grantham pop 230 archd and dioc Lincoln
DODDINGTON, GREAT parish 1560 co Northampton 2-1/2 miles sw
Wellingborough pop 442 archd Northampton dioc Peterborough
DODDISCOMBSLEIGH parish 1678 Devon 6 miles sw Exeter pop 392
archd and dioc Exeter
DODDLESTON parish 1570 Ches 5 miles sw Chester comp townships
Doddleston, Lower Kinnerton pop 356 archd and dioc Chester
DODFORD parish 1581 co Northampton 3 miles se Daventry pop 279
archd Northampton dioc Peterborough
DODINGTON parish 1575 Gloucs 2-1/2 miles se Chipping Sodbury
pop 113 archd and dioc Gloucester
DODINGTON township parish Whitchurch Shrops
DODINGTON parish 1538 Somerset 9-1/2 miles nw Bridgewater pop
93 archd Taunton dioc Bath and Wells
DODNASH parish Bentley Suffolk Wesl Meth
DODWORTH township parish Silkstone W R York pop 1,779
DOGDYKE township parish Billinghay Lincs pop 215
DOGMERSFIELD parish 1695 Hamps 2 miles ne Odiham pop 272
archd and dioc Winchester
DOGS, ISLE OF or STEPNEY MARSH parish Stepney Middlesex Indep
DOGSTHORPE chapelry parish St John the Baptist Peterborough co
Northampton pop 443
DOLTON parish 1608 Devon 7 miles ne Hatherleigh pop 870 archd
Barnstaple dioc Exeter
DOMINICK (ST) parish 1539 Cornwall 2-3/4 miles se Callington pop
726 archd Cornwall dioc Exeter
DONCASTER parish 1557 sep juris W R York 37 miles sw York comp
townships Balby with Hexthorp, Long Sandal with Wheatley, Lang-
thwaite with Tilts pop 11,572 archd and dioc York Soc of
Friends, Indep, Wesl Meth, Unit
DONHEAD parish 1645 Wilts 5-1/2 miles se Hindon pop 804 archd
and dioc Salisbury
DONHEAD parish 1678 Wilts 5-1/2 miles s Hindon pop 1,520 archd
and dioc Salisbury

DONINGTON parish 1642 Lincs 32 miles se Lincoln pop 1,759 archd and dioc Lincoln Part Bapt, Wesl Meth

DONINGTON parish 1556 Shrops 5-1/4 miles se Shiffnall pop 313 archd Salop dioc Lichfield

DONINGTON, CASTLE parish 1539 Leics 9-1/2 miles ne Ashby de la Zouch pop 3,182 archd Leicester dioc Lincoln Indep, Wesl Meth

DONINGTON UPON BAIN parish 1653 Lincs 6-3/4 miles sw Louth pop 300 archd and dioc Lincoln

DONISTHORPE hamlet partly in parish Nether Seal, Leics partly in parish Church Gresley, Derbys

DONNINGTON tything parish Shaw Berks

DONNINGTON hamlet parish Stow on the Wold Gloucs pop 200

DONNINGTON parish 1690 Herefs 2-1/2 miles sw Ledbury pop 124 archd and dioc Hereford

DONNINGTON joint chapelry with Hugglescote parish Ibstock Leics pop 786

DONNINGTON parish 1559 Sussex 2 miles sw Chichester pop 228 archd and dioc Chichester

DONNINGTON WOOD chapelry parish Lilleshall Shrops Part Bapt

DONYATT parish 1719 Somerset 2-1/4 miles sw Ilminster pop 557 archd Taunton dioc Bath and Wells

DONYLAND, EAST parish 1731 Essex 3-1/4 miles se Colchester pop 692 archd Colchester dioc London

DONYLAND, WEST Essex See BERECHURCH

DORCHESTER market town, borough sep juris Dorset 120 miles sw London pop 3,033 All Saints, commonly called All Hallows 1654, Holy Trinity 1653, St Peter's 1653 archd Dorset dioc Bristol Bapt, Indep, Wesl Meth, Unit

DORCHESTER parish 1638 co Oxford 8-1/2 miles se Oxford pop 866 pec Dorchester

DORE chapelry 1813 Derbys pop 527 parish Dronfield archd Derby dioc Lichfield

DORE ABBEY parish 1634 Herefs 12 miles sw Hereford pop 533 archd and dioc Hereford

DORKING parish 1538 Surrey 12 miles s Guildford pop 4,711 archd Surrey dioc Winchester Soc of Friends, Indep

DORMINGTON parish Herefs 5-1/2 miles se Hereford pop 148 archd and dioc Hereford

DORMSDEN chapelry parish Barking Suffolk pop 73

DORMSTON parish 1716 Worcs 7 miles nw Alcester pop 157 archd and dioc Worcester

DORNE hamlet parish Blockley Worcs

DORNEY parish 1538 Bucks 2-1/4 miles nw Eton pop 268 archd Bucking dioc Lincoln

DORNFORD hamlet parish Chesterton Hunts

DORRINGTON parish 1655 Lincs 4-3/4 miles n Sleaford pop 371 archd and dioc Lincoln

DORRINGTON township parish Muckleston Shrops pop 197

DORSINGTON parish 1593 Gloucs 8 miles nw Chipping Campden pop
122 archd and dioc Gloucester

DORSINGTON, LITTLE hamlet parish Welford Warws

DORSTONE parish 1733 Herefs 8 miles se Hay comp townships Lower
Dorstone, Upper Dorstone pop 571 archd and dioc Hereford

DORTON parish 1694 Bucks 5-1/2 miles nw Thame pop 158 archd
Buckingham dioc Lincoln

DOSTHILL hamlet parish Tamworth Warws

DOTTON extra parochial liberty Devon 6-1/2 miles e Topsham pop 20

DOUGHTON joint parish with Dunton Norfolk

DOUGLAS chapelry parish Eccleston Lancs

DOULTING parish 1563 Somerset 2 miles e Shepton Mallet pop 630
archd Wells dioc Bath and Wells

DOVENBY township parish Bridekirk Cumberland pop 247

DOVER COURT Essex See HARWICH

DOVERDALE parish 1755 Worcs 3-1/4 miles nw Droitwich pop 72
archd and dioc Worcester

DOVERIDGE parish 1574 Derbys 1-3/4 miles ne Uttoxeter pop 792
archd Derby dioc Lichfield

DOVOR or DOVER parish borough sep juris Kent 16 miles se Canterbury pop 11,922 St James 1594, St Mary 1557 pec Archbishop
of Canterbury Gen and Part Bapt, Soc of Friends, Indep, Wesl
Meth, Unit, Roman Cath

DOWDESWELL parish 1575 Gloucs 4-1/4 miles se Cheltenham pop
232 pec Withington

DOWLAND parish 1742 Devon 5 miles ne Hatherleigh archd Barnstaple dioc Exeter

DOWLES parish 1572 Shrops 1-1/4 miles nw Bewdley pop 62 archd
Salop dioc Hereford

DOWLISH WAKE parish 1636 Somerset 1-3/4 miles se Ilminster pop
380 archd Taunton dioc Bath and Wells

DOWLISH, WEST parish Somerset 1 mile se Ilminster pop 38 archd
Taunton dioc Bath and Wells

DOWN parish 1538 Kent 2 miles sw Farnborough pop 421 pec Archbishop of Canterbury Bapt

DOWN parish 1688 Devon 2-3/4 miles ne Bow pop 407 archd and dioc
Exeter

DOWN, EAST parish 1538 Devon 6-3/4 miles ne Barnstaple pop 446
archd Barnstaple dioc Exeter

DOWN, WEST parish 1583 Devon 7 miles nw Barnstaple pop 628
archd Barnstaple dioc Exeter

DOWNHAM parish 1558 Cambs 3 miles nw Ely pop 1,722 pec Bishop
of Ely Part Bapt

DOWNHAM parish 1558 Essex 4-1/4 miles ne Billericay pop 271
archd Essex dioc London

DOWNHAM chapelry 1653 parish Whalley Lancs pop 552 archd and
dioc Chester Wesl Meth

DOWNHAM township parish Wymondham Norfolk pop 1,165

DOWNHAM MARKET parish 1554 Norfolk 42-1/2 miles w Norwich
pop 2,198 archd Norfolk dioc Norwich Part Bapt, Soc of Friends,
Indep, Wesl Meth
DOWNHAM SANTON parish 1576 Suffolk 2-3/4 miles ne Brandon Fer-
ry pop 66 archd Sudbury dioc Norwich
DOWNHEAD chapelry 1695 parish Doulting Somerset pop 221 archd
Wells dioc Bath and Wells
DOWNHEAD hamlet parish West Camel Somerset
DOWNHOLME parish 1736 N R York 4-3/4 miles sw Richmond comp
townships Downholme, Ellerton Abbey, Stainton, Walburn pop 235
archd Richmond dioc Chester
DOWNSIDE tything parish Midsummer Norton Somerset
DOWNTON parish 1728 Herefs 5-1/2 miles sw Ludlow pop 111 archd
Salop dioc Hereford
DOWNTON parish borough 1602 Wilts 6-3/4 miles se Salisbury pop
3,519 archd and dioc Salisbury Gen and Part Bapt, Wesl Meth
DOWSBY parish 1670 Lincs 6 miles ne Bourne pop 230 archd and
dioc Lincoln
DOXFORD township parish Ellingham Northumberland pop 79
DOYNTON parish 1566 Gloucs 7 miles sw Chipping Sodbury pop 448
archd and dioc Gloucester
DRAKELOW township parish Church Gresley Derbys pop 77
DRAUGHTON parish 1559 co Northampton 7-1/2 miles sw Kettering
pop 176 archd Northampton dioc Peterborough
DRAUGHTON township parish Skipton W R York pop 223
DRAX parish 1597 W R York 4 miles ne Snaith comp townships Cam-
blesforth, Drax, Long Drax, Newland pop 1,032 archd and dioc
York Wesl Meth
DRAX, LONG township parish Drax W R York pop 140
DRAYCOT tything parish Bourton upon Dunsmoor Warws
DRAYCOT CERNE parish 1691 Wilts 4 miles ne Chippenham pop 180
archd Wilts dioc Salisbury
DRAYCOT FOLIATT parish no regs Wilts 4-1/2 miles se Swindon
pop 19 archd Wilts dioc Salisbury
DRAYCOT FOLIATT chapelry parish Wilcot Wilts
DRAYCOTT liberty parish Sawley Derbys pop 1,074 Wesl Meth
DRAYCOTT tything parish Limington Somerset pop 31
DRAYCOTT hamlet partly in parish Chedder partly in Rodney Stoke
Somerset
DRAYCOTT township parish Hanbury Staffs pop 288
DRAYCOTT hamlet parish Blockley Worcs pop 197
DRAYCOTT IN THE MOORS parish 1669 Staffs 2-1/4 miles sw
Cheadle pop 539 archd Stafford dioc Lichfield Roman Cath
DRAYCOTT MOORE hamlet parish Longworth Berks pop 224
DRAYTON chapelry 1754 parish St Helen Abingdon Berks pop 506
archd Berks dioc Salisbury
DRAYTON township parish Bringhurst Leics pop 156
DRAYTON parish 1558 Norfolk 4-1/2 miles nw Norwich pop 349

archd and dioc Norwich

DRAYTON hamlet parish Daventry co Northampton

DRAYTON parish 1577 co Oxford 2 miles nw Banbury pop 184 archd and dioc Oxford

DRAYTON parish 1568 co Oxford 5 miles n Wallingford pop 333 pec Dorchester

DRAYTON parish 1558 Somerset 2 miles sw Langport pop 519 archd Taunton dioc Bath and Wells

DRAYTON township parish Penkridge Staffs

DRAYTON township parish Old Stratford Warws

DRAYTON BASSETT parish 1560 Staffs 2-3/4 miles sw Tamworth pop 459 archd Stafford dioc Lichfield

DRAYTON BEAUCHAMP parish 1538 Bucks 2 miles nw Tring pop 275 archd Buckingham dioc Lincoln

DRAYTON, DRY parish 1564 Cambs 5 miles nw Cambridge pop 432 archd and dioc Ely

DRAYTON, EAST parish 1737 Notts 4 miles ne Tuxford pop 256 pec Dean and Chapter of York

DRAYTON, FEN parish 1573 Cambs 3-3/4 miles se St Ives pop 319 archd and dioc Ely

DRAYTON, FENNY parish 1712 Leics 6 miles nw Hinckley pop 127 archd Leicester dioc Lincoln

DRAYTON IN HALES or MARKET DRAYTON parish 1558 Shrops 19-1/4 miles ne Shrewsbury comp Drayton in Hales, Drayton Division, townships Almington, Bloore in Tyrley and Hales pop 4,619 archd Salop dioc Lichfield except that portion of the parish lying in co Stafford which is within pec manor of Tyrley dioc Lichfield Part Bapt, Indep, Wesl Meth

DRAYTON PARSLOW parish 1559 Bucks 5-1/4 miles ne Winslow pop 416 archd Buckingham dioc Lincoln

DRAYTON, WEST parish 1568 Middlesex 3-1/4 miles ne Colnbrook pop 662 pec Dean and Chapter of St Paul's London

DRAYTON, WEST chapelry 1632 parish East Markham Notts pop 108

DREGG (GRIGG) parish 1631 Cumberland 3 miles nw Ravenglass comp townships Carleton and Dregg pop 432 archd Richmond dioc Chester

DREWSTEIGNTON Devon See TEIGNTON, DREWS

DREWTON township parish North Cave E R York pop 149

DRIBY parish 1622 Lincs 4-3/4 miles sw Alford pop 89 archd and dioc Lincoln

DRIFFIELD parish 1561 Gloucs 4-1/2 miles se Cirencester pop 146 archd and dioc Gloucester

DRIFFIELD, GREAT parish 1556 E R York 29 miles ne York comp Great Driffield, chapelry Little Driffield, township Emswell with Kelley thorpe pop 2,854 pec Precentor in Cathedral Church of York Bapt, Indep, Prim and Wesl Meth

DRIFFIELD, LITTLE chapelry 1578 parish Great Driffield E R York pop 92 pec Precentor in Cathedral Church of York Wesl Meth

DRIGG 1631 Cumberland

DRIGHLINGTON chapelry parish Birstall W R York pop 1,676

DRINGHOE township parish Skipsea E R York pop 152

DRINGHOUSES township partly in parish Holy Trinity, Micklegate, York and partly in parish Acomb, Ainsty of city of York chiefly in parish St Mary Bishopshill Senior E R York pop 194

DRINKSTONE parish 1666 Suffolk 6-1/2 miles nw Stow Market pop 469 archd Sudbury dioc Norwich

DROITWICH market town borough Worcs 6-3/4 miles ne Worcester pop 2,487 St Andrew 1571, St Peter 1544 archd and dioc Worcester Indep, Wesl Meth

DRONFIELD parish 1560 Derbys 6 miles nw Chesterfield comp chapelries Dore, Holmesfield, townships Coal Aston, Unstone, hamlet Totley pop 3,974 archd Derby dioc Lichfield Soc of Friends, Indep, Wesl Meth

DROXFORD parish 1633 Hamps 3-1/4 miles ne Bishop's Waltham pop 1,620 pec the Incumbent

DROYLSDEN township parish Manchester Lancs pop 2,996

DRUMBURGH township parish Bowness Cumberland pop 384

DRURIDGE hamlet parish Woodhorn Northumberland

DRYBECK township parish St Lawrence, Appleby Westm pop 92

DRY DRAYTON Cambs See DRAYTON, DRY

DRYPOOL parish 1587 E R York 1/2 mile e Kingston upon Hull comp townships Drypool, Southcastle pop 2,935 archd East Riding dioc York Wesl Meth

DUCKINGTON township parish Malpas Ches pop 66

DUCKLINGTON parish 1550 co Oxford 1-3/4 miles s Witney pop 509 archd and dioc Oxford

DUCKMANTON See SUTTON CUM DUCKMANTON

DUDCOTE parish 1562 Berks 6 miles nw Wallingford pop 181 archd Berks dioc Salisbury

DUDDEN township parish Tarvin Ches pop 203

DUDDINGTON parish 1733 co Northampton 6 miles nw Wansford pop 364 pec Prebendary of Gretton Indep

DUDDO township parish Norham co Durham situated in Northumberland pop 356

DUDDO township parish Stannington Northumberland

DUDLESTON chapelry 1693 parish Ellsmere Shrops archd Salop dioc Lichfield

DUDLEY parish borough 1540 Worcs 26 miles ne Worcester pop 23,043 archd and dioc Worcester Prim Meth, Kilhamites, Wesl Meth, Bapt, Soc of Friends, Indep, Unit

DUESHILL township chapelry Hallystone Northumberland pop 45

DUFFIELD parish 1598 Derbys 4-1/4 miles n Derby comp chapelries Belper, Heage Holbrook, Turnditch, townships Hazlewood, Shottle with Postern, Windley pop 14,683 archd Derby dioc Lichfield Gen Bapt, Wesl Meth, Unit

DUFFIELD, NORTH township parish Skipwith E R York pop 344

DUFFIELD, SOUTH township parish Hemingbrough E R York pop 202 Wesl Meth

DUFFRIN hamlet parish Bassaleg co Monmouth pop 213

DUFTON parish 1570 Westm 3-1/4 miles n Appleby pop 554 archd and dioc Carlisle Wesl Meth

DUGGLEBY township parish Kerby Grindalyth E R York pop 186

DUKESHAGG township parish Ovingham Northumberland pop 9

DUKINFIELD township parish Stockport Ches pop 14,681 Indep, Wesl Meth, Moravian, Unit, Roman Cath

DULAS parish 1770 Herefs 13-1/2 miles sw Hereford pop 58 archd Brecon dioc St David's

DULLINGHAM parish 1558 Cambs 3-3/4 miles sw Newmarket pop 684 archd and dioc Ely

DULOE parish 1668 Cornwall 3-3/4 miles nw West Looe pop 928 archd Cornwall dioc Exeter

DULVERTON parish 1558 Somerset 13 miles w Wiveliscombe pop 1,285 archd Taunton dioc Bath and Wells

DULWICH hamlet parish Camberwell Surrey Chapel college 1616

DUMBLETON parish 1738 Gloucs 6 miles nw Winchcombe pop 420 archd and dioc Gloucester

DUMMER parish 1540 Hamps 5 miles sw Basingstoke pop 383 archd and dioc Winchester

SUMMER ANDREWS SWATHLING extra parochial liberty Hamps

DUNCHIDEOCK parish 1538 Devon 4-1/2 miles sw Exeter pop 182 archd and dioc Exeter

DUNCHURCH parish 1538 Warws 15 miles ne Warwick pop 1,310 archd Coventry dioc Lichfield

DUNCTON parish 1545 Sussex 3-1/2 miles sw Petworth pop 272 archd and dioc Chichester

DUNDRAW township parish Broomfield Cumberland pop 269

DUNDRY parish 1654 Somerset 5-1/2 miles nw Pensford pop 583 archd Bath dioc Bath and Wells

DUNHAM township parish Thornton Ches pop 322

DUNHAM parish 1654 Notts 5-3/4 miles ne Tuxford pop 557 pec Prebendary of Dunham, Collegiate Church of Southwell

DUNHAM, GREAT parish 1539 Norfolk 5-1/4 miles ne Swaffham pop 511 archd and dioc Norwich

DUNHAM, LITTLE parish 1562 Norfolk 4 miles ne Swaffham pop 290 archd and dioc Norwich

DUNHAM MASSEY township parish Bowdon Ches pop 1,105

DUNHOLM parish 1564 Lincs 6 miles ne Lincoln pop 237 pec Dean and Chapter of Lincoln

DUNKERTON parish 1748 Somerset 5 miles sw Bath pop 718 archd Wells dioc Bath and Wells

DUNKESWELL parish 1749 Devon 5-1/2 miles nw Honiton pop 414 donative

DUNKESWITH township parish Harewood W R York pop 261

DUNKIRK VILLE extra parochial liberty Kent 5 miles nw Canterbury

pop 613

DUNMOW, GREAT parish 1538 Essex 12-1/2 miles nw Chelmsford pop 2,462 archd Middlesex dioc London Bapt, Soc of Friends, Indep

DUNMOW, LITTLE parish 1555 Essex 2-1/4 miles se Great Dunmow pop 378 archd Middlesex dioc London

DUNNEDALE chapelry parish Kirby Ireleth Lancs pop 148

DUNNINGTON township parish Beeford E R York pop 61

DUNNINGTON parish 1583 E R York 4-1/2 miles ne York pop 713 archd Cleveland dioc York

DUNNINGWORTH hamlet parish Tunstall Suffolk

DUNNOCKSHAW township parish Whalley Lancs pop 46

DUNSBY parish 1538 Lincs 4 miles ne Bourne pop 172 archd and dioc Lincoln

DUNSBY parish no regs Lincs 4 miles nw Sleaford archd and dioc Lincoln

DUNSCROFT hamlet parish Hatfield W R York

DUNSDEN joint liberty with Eye parish Sonning co Oxford pop 887

DUNSFORD parish 1628 Surrey 5-3/4 miles se Godalming pop 567 archd Surrey dioc Winchester

DUNSFORD parish 1599 Devon 7 miles sw Exeter pop 903 archd and dioc Exeter

DUNSFORTH, LOW chapelry parish Aldborough W R York pop 133 pec Dean and Chapter of York

DUNSFORTH, UPPER township parish Aldborough W R York pop 163

DUNSLEY township parish Whitby N R York

DUNSTABLE parish 1558 Beds 18 miles sw Bedford pop 2,117 archd Bedford dioc Lincoln Bapt, Wesl Meth

DUNSTALL township parish Tatenhill Staffs pop 204

DUNSTALL township parish Tamworth Staffs

DUNSTAN joint hamlet with Newbold parish Chesterfield Derbys

DUNSTAN (ST) parish Kent 1/4 mile nw Canterbury pop 809 archd and dioc Canterbury

DUNSTER parish 1559 Somerset 38 miles nw Somerton pop 983 archd Taunton dioc Bath and Wells

DUNSTEW parish 1654 co Oxford 2-1/2 miles se Deddington pop 450 archd and dioc Oxford

DUNSTON parish 1691 Lincs 8-1/4 miles se Lincoln pop 423 archd and dioc Lincoln

DUNSTON parish 1555 Norfolk 4 miles s Norwich pop 102 archd Norfolk dioc Norwich

DUNSTON township parish Embleton Northumberland

DUNSTON chapelry parish Penkridge Staffs pop 272

DUNTERTON parish 1583 Devon 5 miles se Launceston pop 207 archd Totnes dioc Exeter

DUNTHORPE hamlet parish Heythorpe co Oxford

DUNTISH tything parish Buckland Newton Dorset

DUNTON parish 1553 Beds 3-1/2 miles se Biggleswade pop 413 archd

Bedford dioc Lincoln

DUNTON parish 1576 Bucks 5 miles se Winslow pop 116 archd Buckingham dioc Lincoln

DUNTON parish 1538 Essex 3-1/2 miles nw Horndon on the Hill pop 133 archd Essex dioc Lincoln

DUNTON joint parish with Doughton 1785 Norfolk 3 miles nw Fakenham pop 126 archd Norfolk dioc Norwich

DUNTON BASSETT parish 1653 Leics 3-3/4 miles n Lutterworth archd Leicester dioc Lincoln

DUNTSBOURN ABBOTS parish 1607 Gloucs 5 miles nw Cirencester pop 282 archd and dioc Gloucester

DUNTSBOURN LEER township parish Abbot's Duntsbourn Gloucs pop 111

DUNTSBOURNE ROUSE parish 1545 Gloucs 3-3/4 miles nw Cirencester pop 126 archd and dioc Gloucester

DUNWICH parish 1672 borough sep juris Suffolk 29 miles ne Ipswich pop 232 archd Suffolk dioc Norwich

DUNWOOD extra parochial liberty 3 miles nw Romsey Hamps

DURHAM city co Durham 67 miles se Carlisle St Giles 1584, St Margaret 1558, St Mary 1571, St Mary the Less 1559, St Nicholas 1540, Cathedral 1609, St Oswald 1538 archd and dioc Durham Soc of Friends, Indep, Prim and Wesl Meth, Roman Cath

DURLEIGH parish 1683 Somerset 1-1/2 miles sw Bridgewater pop 139 archd Taunton dioc Bath and Wells

DURLEY chapelry 1562 parish Upham Hamps pop 361

DURLEY tything parish Eling Hamps

DURNFORD parish 1574 Wilts 2-1/4 miles sw Amesbury pop 481 pec Prebendary of Durnford

DURRINGTON chapelry parish Tarring Sussex pop 162

DURRINGTON parish 1591 Wilts 3 miles n Amesbury pop 467 archd and dioc Salisbury

DURSLEY parish 1639 Gloucs 15 miles sw Gloucester pop 3,226 archd and dioc Gloucester Indep, Wesl Meth

DURSTON parish 1696 Somerset 4-3/4 miles ne Taunton pop 226 archd Taunton dioc Bath and Wells

DURWESTON parish 1793 Dorset 3 miles nw Blandford Forum pop 418 archd Dorset dioc Bristol

DUSTON parish 1692 co Northampton 1-3/4 miles nw Northampton pop 603 archd Northampton dioc Peterborough

DUTTON township parish Great Budworth Ches pop 329

DUTTON township parish Ribchester Lancs pop 490

DUXBURY township parish Standish Lancs pop 213

DUXFORD comp parishes St Peter, St John 1685 Cambs 6-1/4 miles w Linton pop 670 archd and dioc Ely

DYKE hamlet parish Bourne Lincs pop 143

DYMCHURCH parish 1624 Kent 4 miles ne New Romney pop 521 archd and dioc Canterbury Wesl Meth

DYMOCK parish 1538 Gloucs 3-3/4 miles nw Newent pop 1656 archd

Hereford dioc Gloucester

DYRHAM Gloucs See DIRHAM

EACHWICK township parish Heddon on the Wall Northumberland pop 113

EAGLE parish 1588 Lincs 7-1/2 miles sw Lincoln pop 477 archd and dioc Lincoln Wesl Meth

EAGLE HALL hamlet parish Eagle Lincs

EAGLE WOODHOUSE extra parochial liberty parish Eagle Lincs

EAGLESCLIFFE parish 1539 co Durham 3 miles sw Stockton comp townships Aislaby, Eaglescliffe, Newsham pop 625 archd and dioc Durham

EAGLESFIELD township parish Brigham Cumberland pop 411

EAKLEY hamlet parish Stoke Goldington Bucks

EAKRING parish 1563 Notts 3-3/4 miles se Ollerton pop 598 archd Nottingham dioc York

EALING parish 1582 Middlesex 6-1/2 miles w London pop 7,783 archd Middlesex dioc London Indep

EAMONT BRIDGE township parish Barton Westm pop 327

EARDINGTON township parish Quatford Shrops pop 325

EARDISLAND parish 1614 Herefs 5 miles w Leominster pop 813 archd and dioc Hereford

EARDISLEY parish 1630 Herefs 6-1/4 miles sw Kington pop 825 archd and dioc Hereford

EARDLEY END township parish Audley Staffs pop 165

EARESBY chapelry parish Spilsby Lincs

EARITH chapelry parish Bluntisham Hunts pop 707

EARL (otherwise YEARD) HILL township parish Doddington Northumberland pop 86

EARL FRAMINGHAM Norfolk See FRAMINGHAM, EARL

EARL SHILTON chapelry parish Kirby Mallory Leics pop 2,017 Indep, Wesl Meth

EARL STOKE chapelry parish Melksham Wilts pop 420

EARLDOMS extra parochial liberty Wilts 4 miles se Downton

EARLHAM See NORWICH

EARLY liberty parish Sonning Berks pop 441

EARNLEY parish 1562 Sussex 6-1/2 miles sw Chichester archd and dioc Chichester

EARNSFORD liberty parish Binley Warws

EARNSHILL parish incl in regs Hambridge Somerset 5 miles sw Langport pop 12 archd Taunton dioc Bath and Wells

EARSDON parish 1589 Northumberland 4 miles nw North Shields comp townships Blackworth, South Blyth with Newsham, Brierdean, Earsdon, Hartley, Holywell, Seaton Delaval, Sighill pop 6,640 archd Northumberland dioc Durham

EARSDON township parish Hebburn Northumberland pop 100

EARSDON FOREST township parish Hebburn Northumberland pop 32

EARSHAM parish 1559 Norfolk 1 mile sw Bungay pop 759 archd Norfolk dioc Norwich

EARSWICK township partly in parish Strensall chiefly in Huntington N R York pop 66

EARTHAM parish Sussex 5-3/4 miles ne Chichester pop 113 archd and dioc Chichester

EARTHCOTT GAUNTS tything parish Almondsbury Gloucs pop 125

EASBY township parish Brampton Cumberland pop 98

EASBY parish 1670 N R York 1-1/2 miles se Richmond comp townships Aske, Easby, Skeeby, Brompton on Swale pop 822 archd Richmond dioc Chester

EASBY township parish Stokesley N R York pop 151

EASEBOURNE parish 1538 Sussex 1 mile ne Midhurst pop 1,503 archd and dioc Chichester

EASENHALL hamlet parish Monks Kirby Warws pop 202

EASHING tything parish Godalming Surrey

EASINGTON hamlet parish Chilton Bucks

EASINGTON parish 1571 co Durham 9-1/2 miles e Durham comp townships Easington, Haswell, Hawthorn, Shotton pop 1,390 archd and dioc Durham Wesl Meth

EASINGTON Gloucs See AMPNEY

EASINGTON township parish Belford Northumberland pop 203

EASINGTON parish 1583 co Oxford 4 miles sw Tetsworth pop 13 archd and dioc Oxford

EASINGTON parish 1585 E R York 6-1/2 miles se Patrington comp townships Easington, Out Newton pop 542 archd East Riding dioc York

EASINGTON parish 1606 N R York 9-1/2 miles ne Guilsborough pop 477 archd Cleveland dioc York Wesl Meth

EASINGTON township parish Slaidburn W R York pop 424

EASINGTON GRANGE township parish Belford Northumberland pop 63

EASINGWOULD parish 1599 N R York 13 miles nw York comp Easingwould, chapelry Raskelf pop 2,381 archd Cleveland dioc York Indep, Prim and Wesl Meth

EAST BOURNE Sussex See BOURNE, EAST

EASTBRIDGE extra parochial liberty near Canterbury Kent pop 30

EASTBRIDGE parish incl in regs Dymchurch Kent 5 miles ne New Romney pop 16 archd and dioc Canterbury

EASTBURN township parish Kirk Burn E R York pop 14

EASTBURN township parish Kildwick W R York

EASTBURY parish Lambourn Berks pop 419 Wesl Meth

EASTBY township parish Skipton W R York pop 891 Wesl Meth

EAST CHURCH parish 1677 Kent 5 miles se Queenborough pop 857 archd and dioc Canterbury Wesl Meth

EASTCOTT tything parish Urchfont Wilts pop 110

EASTCOTTS chapelry parish Cardington Beds pop 710

EASTCOURT tything parish Crudwell Wilts

EASTER, GOOD parish 1538 Essex 7 miles nw Chelmsford pop 487 pec Bishop of London

EASTER, HIGH parish 1654 Essex 5 miles sw Great Dunmow pop 862 archd Middlesex dioc London

EASTERGATE parish 1563 Sussex 5-1/4 miles sw Arundel pop 208 archd and dioc Chichester

EASTERTON tything parish East Lavington Wilts pop 417

EASTFIELD hamlet parish St John Peterborough co Northampton pop 250

EASTGATE hamlet parish Stanhope co Durham Wesl Meth

EASTHAM parish 1598 Ches 5 miles ne Great Neston comp townships Eastham, Hooton, Nether Pool, Over Pool, Great Sutton, Little Sutton, Thornton Childer pop 1,644 archd and dioc Chester

EASTHAM parish 1571 Worcs 4-1/4 miles e Tenbury comp chapelries Child Hanley, Orleton pop 677 archd Salop dioc Hereford

EASTHAMSTEAD Berks See HAMPSTEAD, EAST

EASTHOPE parish 1624 Shrops 4-3/4 miles sw Much Wenlock pop 103 archd Salop dioc Hereford

EASTHORPE parish 1572 Essex 4-1/4 miles se Great Coggeshall pop 167 archd Colchester dioc London

EASTHORPE hamlet parish Southwell Notts

EASTINGTON chapelry parish Naunton Gloucs pop 266

EASTINGTON parish 1558 Gloucs 5 miles nw Stroud comp hamlets Alkerton, Church End, Eastington, Mill End, Muddleshole, Nastend, Nuppend, Westend pop 1,770 archd and dioc Gloucester Bapt, Wesl Meth

EASTLEACH MARTIN otherwise BURTHORPE parish 1538 Glouc 4 miles n Lechdale pop 159 archd and dioc Gloucester

EAST LEACH TURVILLE parish 1654 Gloucs 4 miles ne Lechdale pop 370 archd and dioc Gloucester

EASTLEY tything parish South Stoneham Hamps

EASTLING parish 1558 Kent 5 miles sw Faversham pop 420 archd and dioc Canterbury

EASTMOORE hamlet parish Barton Bendish Norfolk

EASTNOR parish 1561 Herefs 2-1/4 miles se Ledbury pop 493 archd and dioc Hereford

EASTOFT chapelry parish Crowle Lincs pop 224

EASTOFT township parish Adlingfleet W R York pop 157

EASTON parish 1708 Hunts 3-1/2 miles ne Kimbolton pop 151 pec Prebendary of Longstow

EASTON hamlet parish South Stoke Lincs pop 221

EASTON parish 1678 Norfolk 6-3/4 miles nw Norwich pop 239 archd Norfolk dioc Norwich Bapt

EASTON or EASTON ON THE HILL parish 1579 co Northampton 2-1/2 miles sw Stamford pop 769 archd Northampton dioc Peterborough

EASTON parish 1692 Hamps 2-3/4 miles ne Winchester pop 494 pec the incumbent

EASTON parish 1561 Suffolk 2-1/2 miles nw Wickham Market pop 362 archd Suffolk dioc Norwich

EASTON parish 1580 Wilts 3-1/4 miles ne Pewsey pop 488 donative

EASTON hamlet parish Bridlington E R York pop 17

EASTON BAVENTS parish incl in regs of Benacre Suffolk 2 miles ne Southwold pop 16 archd Suffolk dioc Norwich

EASTON, GREAT parish 1561 Essex 2-1/2 miles nw Great Dunmow pop 840 archd Middlesex dioc London

EASTON, GREY parish 1654 Wilts 3-1/2 miles w Malmesbury pop 151 archd Wilts dioc Salisbury

EASTON IN GORDANO parish 1559 Somerset 7-1/4 miles nw Bristol pop 2,255 pec Prebendary of Easton, Cathedral Church of Wells Wesl Meth

EASTON, LITTLE parish 1559 Essex 2-1/4 miles nw Great Dunmow pop 350 archd Middlesex dioc London

EASTON, MAGNA chapelry 1722 parish Bringhurst Leics pop 541

EASTON MAUDIT parish 1539 co Northampton 6-1/2 miles s Wellingborough pop 210 archd Northampton dioc Peterborough

EASTON NESTON parish 1559 co Northampton 1-1/4 miles e Towcester pop 144 archd Northampton dioc Peterborough

EASTON PERCEY tything parish Kington St Michael Wilts

EASTRIDGE tything parish Ramsbury Wilts pop 302

EASTRINGTON parish 1563 E R York 3-1/4 miles ne Howden comp townships Bellasize, Eastrington, Gilberdike, Newport Wallingfen, Portingten with Cavil pop 1,676 pec Howdenshire Wesl Meth

EASTRIP extra parochial liberty Somerset near Bruton pop 12

EASTROP parish 1750 Hamps 1/2 mile n Basingstoke pop 69 archd and dioc Winchester

EASTRY parish 1559 Kent 2-3/4 miles sw Sandwich pop 1,245 pec Archbishop of Canterbury Wesl Meth

EAST VILLE township not dependent on any parish Lincs 3/4 mile ne Boston pop 136

EASTWELL parish 1538 Kent 3-1/4 miles n Ashford pop 97 archd and dioc Canterbury

EASTWELL parish 1719 Leics 7 miles ne Melton Mowbray pop 125 archd Leicester dioc Lincoln

EASTWICK parish 1555 Herts 4 miles sw Sawbridgeworth pop 169 archd Middlesex dioc London

EASTWOOD parish 1685 Essex 1-1/2 miles sw Rochford pop 531 archd Essex dioc London

EASTWOOD parish 1711 Notts 9 miles nw Nottingham pop 1,395 archd Nottingham dioc York Wesl Meth

EATHORPE hamlet parish Wappenbury Warws pop 145

EATINGTON parish 1661 Warws pop 728 archd and dioc Worcester Bapt

EATON township parish Appleton Berks pop 109

EATON township parish Eccleston Ches pop 73

EATON township parish Tarporley Ches pop 502

EATON township parish Prestbury Ches pop 525

EATON township parish Davenham Ches pop 13

EATON township parish Ashbourn Derbys pop 60

EATON 1568 Norfolk See NORWICH

EATON parish 1751 Leics 8 miles ne Melton Mowbray pop 350 archd Leicester dioc Lincoln Wesl Meth

EATON parish 1660 Notts 2-1/4 miles s East Retford pop 234 pec Chapter of Collegiate Church of Southwell

EATON township parish Stoke upon Tern Shrops pop 148

EATON or EATON UNDER HEYWOOD parish 1688 Shrops 4-1/4 miles se Church Stretton pop 539 archd Salop dioc Hereford

EATON, BISHOP parish 1588 Herefs 5 miles w Hereford pop 489 Cons Court of Dean of Hereford

EATON, BRAY parish 1559 Beds 3-1/2 miles sw Dunstable pop 957 archd Bedford dioc Lincoln Wesl Meth

EATON, CHURCH parish 1538 Staffs 5-1/2 miles nw Penkridge pop 922 archd Stafford dioc Lichfield

EATON CONSTANTINE parish 1684 Shrops 5-1/4 miles nw Much Wenlock pop 244 archd Salop dioc Lichfield

EATON HASTINGS parish 1574 Berks 3-1/4 miles nw Great Farringdon pop 167 archd Berks dioc Salisbury

EATON, LITTLE chapelry 1791 parish St Alkmund Derby Derbys pop 610 pec Dean and Chapter of Lichfield

EATON, LONG chapelry parish Sawley Derbys pop 750 pec Prebendary of Sawley Wesl Meth

EATON SOCON parish 1577 Beds 1-1/2 miles sw St Neot's pop 2,490 archd Bedford dioc Lincoln

EATON TREGOES township parish Foy Herefs

EAVES township parish Stoke upon Trent Staffs pop 281

EAVESTONE township parish Ripon W R York pop 82

EBBERSTON parish 1678 N R York 5-3/4 miles e Pickering pop 509 pec Dean of York Wesl Meth

EBBESBORNE WAKE parish 1653 Wilts 8-1/2 miles sw Wilton pop 278 archd and dioc Salisbury Indep

EBBS FLEET hamlet parish Minster Kent

EBCHESTER chapelry 1610 parish Lanchester co Durham pop 255 archd and dioc Durham

EBONY parish 1708 Kent 4-1/4 miles se Tenterden pop 165 archd and dioc Canterbury

EBRINGTON parish 1653 Gloucs 1-3/4 miles ne Chipping Campden pop 573 archd and dioc Gloucester

ECCHINSWELL chapelry parish Kingsclere Hamps pop 449

ECCLES parish 1564 Lancs 4 miles w Manchester comp chapelries Pendleton, Worsley, Ellenbrook, townships Barton, Clifton, Pendlebury pop 28,083 archd and dioc Chester Indep, Wesl Meth, Roman Cath

ECCLES parish 1678 Norfolk 9-1/2 miles se North Walsham pop 212 archd Norfolk dioc Norwich

ECCLES parish 1678 Norfolk 2-1/2 miles ne East Harling pop 122 archd Norfolk dioc Norwich

ECCLESALL BIERLOW chapelry 1784 parish Sheffield W R York pop 14,279 archd and dioc York

ECCLESFIELD parish 1558 W R York 5-1/2 miles n Sheffield comp chapelry Bradfield, townships Aldward, Ecclesfield pop 13,415 archd and dioc York Wesl Meth

ECCLESHALL parish 1573 Staffs 7-1/4 miles nw Stafford comp Eccleshall, chapelries Broughton, Chorlton, townships Aspley, Bromley, Charnes, Chatfull, Chorlton Hill, Coldmeece, Cotes, Croston, Horseley, Mitmeece, Pershall, Podmore, Slindon, Great Sugnall, Little Sugnall, Three Farms, Walton, Wootton pop 4,471 pec Prebendary of Eccleshall Indep

ECCLESHILL township parish Blackburn Lancs pop 715

ECCLESHILL township parish Bradford W R York pop 2,570 Wesl Meth, Indep

ECCLESTON parish 1593 Ches 2-3/4 miles s Chester comp townships Eaton, Eccleston pop 361 archd and dioc Chester

EDGBOLTON township parish Shawbury Shrops pop 421

EDGCOTE parish 1690 co Northampton 6-1/4 miles ne Banbury pop 96 archd Northampton dioc Peterborough

EDGE township parish Malpas Ches pop 310

EDGE tything parish Painswick Gloucs pop 1,529

EDGE township parish Pontesbury Shrops

EDGECOTT parish 1539 Bucks 8 miles sw Winslow pop 180 archd Buckingham dioc Lincoln

EDGEFIELD parish 1653 Norfolk 2-3/4 miles s Holt pop 774 archd and dioc Norwich

EDGE HILL chapelry parish Walton on the Hill Lancs Bapt

EDGE HILL township parish St Michael Lichfield Staffs pop 93

EDGERLEY township parish Alford Ches pop 11

EDGEWORTH parish 1554 Gloucs 6-1/2 miles nw Cirencester pop 116 archd and dioc Gloucester

EDGMOND parish 1680 Shrops 1-3/4 miles w Newport comp chapelries Church Aston, Tibberton, townships Cherrington, Chetwynd Aston pop 2,300 archd Salop dioc Lichfield

EDGTON parish 1722 Shrops 4-1/2 miles se Bishop's Castle pop 232 archd Salop dioc Hereford

EDGWARE parish 1717 Middlesex 8 miles nw London pop 591 archd Middlesex dioc London

EDGWORTH township parish Bolton Lancs pop 2,168 Indep

EDINGHALL otherwise EDINGALE parish 1573 partly in Staffs partly in Derbys 6 miles nw Tamworth pec Prebendary Alrewas and Weeford

EDINGLEY parish 1538 Notts 3 miles nw Southwell pop 398 pec Chapter of Collegiate Church of Southwell

EDINGTHORPE parish 1560 Norfolk 3 miles ne North Walsham pop 188 archd Norfolk dioc Norwich

EDINGTON township parish Mitford Northumberland pop 41

EDINGTON chapelry parish Moorlinch Somerset pop 401

missing entries (see the leaf before page 1)

184

EDINGTON parish 1695 Wilts 3-3/4 miles ne Westbury comp tythings Baynton with West Coulston, Edington, Tinhead pop 1,112 archd and dioc Salisbury

EDINGWORTH hamlet partly in parish East Brent partly in parish Lympsham Somerset

EDITH WESTON parish 1585 co Rutland 5-3/4 miles se Oakham pop 337 archd Northampton dioc Peterborough

EDLASTON parish 1573 Derbys 2-1/2 miles s Ashbourn pop 225 archd Derby dioc Lichfield

EDLINGHAM parish 1659 Northumberland 6 miles sw Alnwick comp chapelry Bolton, townships Abberwick, Broom Park, Edlingham, Learchild, Lemmington pop 568 archd Northumberland dioc Durham

EDLESBOROUGH Bucks See EDDLESBOROUGH

EDLINGTON parish 1562 Lincs 2 miles nw Horncastle pop 216 archd and dioc Lincoln

EDLINGTON parish 1731 W R York 5-1/4 miles sw Doncaster pop 129 archd and dioc York

EDMONDBYERS parish 1700 co Durham 12 miles nw Wolsingham comp chapelry Hunstonworth, township Edmondbyers pop 995 archd and dioc Durham

EDMONDSLEY township parish Chester le Street co Durham pop 150

EDMONDSTRIP BENHAM tything parish Kingsclere Hamps

EDMONDSTRIP LANCES tything parish Kingsclere Hamps

EDMONDTHORPE parish 1560 Leics 7 miles se Melton Mowbray pop 211 archd Leicester dioc Lincoln

EDMONSHAM parish 1573 Dorset 1-1/2 miles se Cranborne pop 271 archd Dorset dioc Bristol

EDMONTON parish 1558 Middlesex 7 miles n London pop 8,192 archd Middlesex dioc London Bapt, Soc of Friends, Indep, Wesl Meth

EDSTASTON chapelry 1712 parish Wem Shrops pop 397

EDSTOCK hamlet parish Cannington Somerset pop 13

EDSTON hamlet parish Wooton Waven Warws

EDSTON, GREAT parish 1557 N R York 6-1/2 miles sw Pickering pop 156 archd Cleveland dioc York

EDSTON, LITTLE township parish Sinnington N R York pop 13

EDWALTON parish 1538 Notts 3-1/2 miles se Nottingham pop 130 archd Nottingham dioc York

EDWARDSTONE parish 1645 Suffolk 1-3/4 miles nw Boxford pop 503 archd Sudbury dioc Norwich

EDWIN LOACH parish 1570 Herefs 3 miles ne Bromyard pop 62 archd Salop dioc Hereford

EDWIN RALPH parish 1748 Herefs 2 miles n Bromyard pop 170 archd and dioc Hereford

EDWINSTOWE parish 1634 Notts 1-1/2 miles sw Ollerton comp chapelries Carburton, Ollerton, Perlethorpe, townships Budby, Clipstone pop 1,992 archd Nottingham dioc York Wesl Meth

EDWORTH parish 1552 Beds 3-3/4 miles se Biggleswade pop 95

archd Bedford dioc Lincoln

EFFINGHAM parish 1565 Surrey 3-3/4 miles sw Leatherhead pop
565 archd Surrey dioc Winchester

EFFORD tything chapelry Harbridge Hamps

EGBROUGH township parish Kellington W R York pop 220

EGDEAN parish 1646 Sussex 2 miles se Tetworth pop 88 archd and
dioc Chichester

EGERTON township parish Malpas Ches pop 114

EGERTON parish 1684 Kent 3-1/4 miles sw Charing pop 866 archd
and dioc Canterbury

EGG BUCKLAND Devon See BUCKLAND, EGG

EGGESFORD parish 1586 Devon 2-1/2 miles s Chulmleigh pop 168
archd Barnstaple dioc Exeter

EGGINGTON chapelry 1553 parish Leighton Buzzard Beds pop 348
pec Prebendary of Leighton Buzzard, Cathedral Church of Lincoln

EGGINTON parish 1561 Derbys 4-1/4 miles ne Burton upon Trent
pop 361 archd Derby dioc Lichfield

EGGLESTON ABBEY township parish Rokeby N R York

EGGLESTONE chapelry 1795 parish Middleton in Tresdale co Durham pop 623 archd and dioc Durham

EGGLETON township parish Bishop's Froome Herts pop 153

EGHAM parish 1560 Surrey 20 miles sw London pop 4,203 archd
Surrey dioc Winchester Wesl Meth

EGLETON chapelry 1538 parish Oakham co Rutland pop 137

EGLINGHAM parish 1662 Northumberland 7-1/2 miles nw Alnwick
comp townships Bassington, Beanly, New Bewick, Old Bewick,
Brandon, Branton, Crawley, East Ditchburn, West Ditchburn, Eg-
lingham, Hareup, Hedgeley, East Lilburn, West Lilburn, Shipley,
Titlington, Wooperton pop 1,633 archd Northumberland dioc
Durham

EGLOSHAYLE parish 1600 Cornwall pop 1,335 pec Bishop of Exeter

EGLOSKERRY parish 1574 Cornwall 3-3/4 miles nw Launceston pop
535 archd Cornwall dioc Exeter Wesl Meth

EGMANTON parish 1653 Notts 1-1/4 miles s Tuxford pop 341 archd
Nottingham dioc York Wesl Meth

EGMERE parish Norfolk 2-1/2 miles nw Little Walsingham pop 46
archd and dioc Norwich

EGREMONT parish borough 1630 Cumberland 42-1/2 miles sw Carlisle pop 1,741 archd Richmond dioc Chester Wesl Meth

EGTON chapelry 1791 parish Ulverstone Lancs pop 496 archd Richmond dioc Chester

EGTON parish 1622 N R York 6-1/4 miles sw Whitby pop 1,071
archd Cleveland Dioc York Roman Cath

EISEY parish 1571 Wilts 1 mile ne Cricklade pop 167 archd Wilts
dioc Salisbury

ELBERTON parish 1653 Gloucs 2-1/2 miles sw Thornbury pop 199
pec Bishop of Bristol

ELDEN parish 1651 Hamps 4-1/2 miles se Stockbridge archd and dioc Winchester

ELDEN Suffolk See ELVEDON

ELDERSFIELD parish 1718 Worcs 7 miles sw Tewkesbury pop 787 archd and dioc Worcester Dissenters

ELDON township parish St Andrew, Auckland co Durham pop 129

ELDROTH hamlet parish Clapham W R York

ELFORD township parish Bambrough Northumberland pop 149

ELFORD parish 1552 Staffs 4-1/2 miles nw Tamworth pop 483 archd Stafford dioc Lichfield

ELHAM parish 1566 Kent 7 miles nw Folkstone pop 1,302 archd and dioc Canterbury Wesl Meth

ELING parish 1537 Hamps 5 miles nw Southampton pop 4,624 archd and dioc Winchester Indep

ELISHAW hamlet parish Elsdon Northumberland

ELKINGTON parish no regs co Northampton 11 miles ne Daventry pop 43

ELKINGTON, NORTH parish 1757 Lincs 4-1/4 miles nw Louth pop 100 archd and dioc Lincoln

ELKINGTON, SOUTH parish 1701 Lincs 2-1/4 miles nw Louth pop 271 archd and dioc Lincoln

ELKSLEY parish 1620 Notts 4 miles nw Tuxford pop 377 archd Nottingham dioc York

ELKSTONE parish 1592 Gloucs 7-1/4 miles nw Cirencester pop 299 archd and dioc Gloucester

ELKSTONE chapelry 1791 parish Allstonefield Staffs pop 626 archd Stafford dioc Lichfield

ELLA, KIRK parish 1558 E R York 5 miles nw Kingston upon Hull comp townships Kirk Ella, West Ella, portion of townships Anlaby, Willerby pop 974 archd and dioc York

ELLAND chapelry 1559 W R York pop 5,500 archd and dioc York four places of worship for dissenters

ELLASTONE parish 1540 Staffs 4-1/2 miles sw Ashbourn comp townships Calwick, Prestwood, Ramshorn, Stanton, Wooton pop 1,344 archd Stafford dioc Lichfield

ELLEL chapelry parish Cockerham Lancs pop 2,217

ELLENBOROUGH joint township with Unerigg parish Dearham Cumberland pop 713

ELLENBROOK chapelry 1765 parish Eccles Lancs

ELLENHALL parish 1539 Staffs 2-1/4 miles se Eccleshall pop 286 archd Stafford dioc Lichfield

ELLENBECK township parish Osmotherley N R York pop 79

ELLERBURN parish 1691 N R York 3-1/4 miles Pickering comp chapelry Wilton pop 192 pec Dean of York

ELLERBY township parish Swine E R York pop 251

ELLERBY township parish Lythe N R York pop 64

ELLERKER chapelry parish Brantingham E R York pop 278 Wesl Meth

ELLERTON ABBEY township parish Downholme N R Yock pop 61

ELLERTON PRIORY parish 1680 E R York 9 miles nw Howden pop 305 archd East Riding dioc York Wesl Meth

ELLERTON UPON SWALE township parish Catterick N R York pop 147

ELLESBOROUGH parish 1603 Bucks 2-1/2 miles sw Wendover pop 665 archd Buckingham dioc Lincoln

ELLESMERE parish 1653 Shrops 16-1/2 miles nw Shrewsbury comp chapelries Cockshut, Dudlaston, Penley pop 6,540 archd Salop dioc Lichfield

ELLINGHAM parish 1538 Norfolk 2-3/4 miles ne Bungay pop 333 archd Norfolk dioc Norwich

ELLINGHAM parish 1695 Northumberland 8-1/2 miles n Alnwick comp townships North Charlton, South Charlton, Chathill, Doxford, Ellingham and Preston pop 1,125 archd Northumberland dioc Durham

ELLINGHAM parish 1596 Hamps 2-1/2 miles nw Ringwood pop 420 archd and dioc Winchester

ELLINGHAM, GREAT parish 1630 Norfolk 2 miles nw Attleburgh pop 882 archd and dioc Norwich Bapt

ELLINGHAM, LITTLE parish 1649 Norfolk 3-3/4 miles nw Attleburgh pop 240 archd and dioc Norwich

ELLINGSTRING township parish Masham N R York pop 228 Wesl Meth

ELLINGTON parish 1608 Hunts 5-1/2 miles nw Huntingdon pop 376 archd Huntingdon dioc Lincoln

ELLINGTON township parish Woodhorn Northumberland pop 270

ELLINGTON, NETHER and OVER township parish Masham N R York pop 148

ELLISFIELD parish 1540 Hamps 4 miles s Basingstoke pop 245 archd and dioc Winchester

ELLOUGH parish 1540 Suffolk 3 miles se Beccles pop 146 archd Suffolk dioc Norwich

ELLOUGHTON parish 1657 E R York 2-1/2 miles se South Cave pop 355 Prebendary of Wetwant Calv and Wesl Meth

ELLSTHORP hamlet parish Edenham Lincs

ELM parish 1539 Cambs 2 miles se Wisbech   pop 1,410 pec Bishop of Ely

ELM parish 1697 Somerset 2-1/4 miles nw Frome comp hamlets Great Elm and Little Elm pop 427 archd Wells dioc Bath and Wells

ELMBRIDGE chapelry 1570 parish Dodderhill Worcs pop 334

ELMDON parish 1618 Essex 5-1/2 miles nw Saffron Walden pop 697 archd Colchester dioc London

ELMDON parish 1538 Warws 4-3/4 miles sw Coleshill pop 157 archd Coventry dioc Lichfield

ELMER township parish Topcliffe N R York pop 77

ELMHAM, NORTH parish 1538 Norfolk 5-1/4 miles nw East Dereham pop 1,153 archd Norfolk dioc Norwich

ELMHAM, SOUTH (ALL SAINTS) parish 1708 Suffolk 5 miles nw
Halesworth pop 239 archd Suffolk dioc Norwich
ELMHAM, SOUTH ST CROSS or SANDCROFT parish Suffolk 4 miles
ne Harleston pop 234 archd Suffolk dioc Norwich
ELMHAM, SOUTH ST JAMES parish 1705 Suffolk 5-1/2 miles nw
Halesworth pop 263 archd Suffolk dioc Norwich
ELMHAM, SOUTH ST MARGARET parish 1679 Suffolk 6-1/4 miles
nw Halesworth pop 169 archd Suffolk dioc Norwich
ELMHAM, SOUTH ST MICHAEL parish 1559 Suffolk 6 miles nw
Halesworth pop 147 archd Suffolk dioc Norwich
ELMHAM, SOUTH ST NICHOLAS parish no regs Suffolk 6-1/4 miles
nw Halesworth pop 101 archd Suffolk dioc Norwich
ELMHAM, SOUTH ST PETER parish 1695 Suffolk 3-3/4 miles s
Bungay pop 122 archd Suffolk dioc Norwich
ELMHURST joint township with Curborough parish St Chad Lichfield
Staffs pop 37
ELMINGTON hamlet parish Oundle co Northampton
ELMLEY CASTLE parish 1665 Worcs 4-3/4 miles sw Evesham pop
333 archd and dioc Worcester
ELMLEY, ISLE OF parish Kent 3-1/2 miles se Queenborough pop
29 archd and dioc Canterbury
ELMLEY LOVETT parish 1539 Worcs 4 miles se Stourport pop 432
archd and dioc Worcester
ELMORE hamlet parish Motcomb Dorset
ELMORE parish 1560 Gloucs 6-1/2 miles sw Gloucester pop 401
archd and dioc Gloucester
ELMSALL, NORTH township parish South Kirkby W R York pop 256
ELMSALL, SOUTH township parish South Kirkby W R York pop 494
ELMSETT parish 1684 Suffolk 4 miles ne Hadleigh pop 437 archd
Sudbury dioc Norwich
ELMSTEAD parish 1557 Essex 4-1/2 miles ne Colchester pop 732
archd Colchester dioc London Wesl Meth
ELMSTED parish 1538 Kent 8 miles ne Ashford pop 502 archd and
dioc Canterbury
ELMSTHORPE parish no regs Leics 3 miles ne Hinckley pop 34
archd Leicester dioc Lincoln
ELMSTONE parish 1552 Kent 2-1/4 miles ne Wingham pop 97 archd
and dioc Canterbury
ELMSTONE HARDWICKE parish 1564 Gloucs 3-3/4 miles nw Chel-
tenham pop 372 archd and dioc Gloucester
ELMSWELL parish 1659 Suffolk 5-3/4 miles nw Stow Market pop 694
archd Sudbury dioc Norwich Wesl Meth
ELMTON parish 1599 Derbys 9 miles ne Chesterfield pop 340 archd
Derby dioc Lichfield
ELSDON parish 1672 Northumberland 18-1/2 miles nw Morpeth comp
townships Elsdon ward, Monkridge ward, Otterburn ward, Roches-
ter ward, Troughend ward, Woodside ward pop 1,724 archd
Northumberland dioc Durham

ELSENHAM parish 1730 Essex 2 miles ne Stansted Mountfitchet pop 483 archd Colchester dioc London

ELSFIELD parish 1686 co Oxford 3-1/4 miles ne Oxford pop 185 archd and dioc Oxford

ELSHAM parish 1566 Lincs 5 miles ne Glandford Bridge pop 471 archd and dioc Lincoln

ELSING parish 1558 Norfolk 5 miles ne East Dereham pop 437 archd Norfolk dioc Norwich

ELSLACK township parish Broughton in Aredale W R York pop 407

ELSTEAD parish 1540 Surrey 4-3/4 miles w Godalming pop 711 archd Surrey dioc Winchester

ELSTEAD parish 1571 Sussex 4-1/2 miles sw Midhurst pop 174 archd and dioc Chichester

ELSTOB township parish Stainton co Durham pop 94

ELSTON township parish Preston Lancs pop 64

ELSTON parish 1572 Notts 5-1/2 miles sw Newark pop 552 archd Nottingham dioc York

ELSTON chapelry 1584 parish East Stoke Notts Wesl Meth

ELSTON tything parish Orcheston St George Wilts

ELSTONE COMBE hamlet parish Yeovil Somerset

ELSTOW parish 1641 Beds 1-1/4 miles sw Bedford pop 561 archd Bedford dioc Lincoln

ELSTREE or IDLESTREE parish 1656 Herts 3 miles nw Edgware pop 341 archd St Albans dioc London

ELSTRONWICK chapelry parish Humbleton E R York pop 153

ELSWICK township parish St Michael Lancs pop 327

ELSWICKE township parish St John Newcastle Northumberland pop 787

ELSWORTH parish 1538 Cambs 4-1/2 miles ne Caxton pop 689 archd and dioc Ely

ELTHAM parish 1583 Kent 8-1/2 miles se London pop 2,129 archd and dioc Rochester Indep

ELTISLEY parish 1653 Cambs 3 miles nw Caxton pop 340 archd and dioc Ely

ELTON township parish Thornton Ches pop 210

ELTON township parish Warmingham Ches pop 430

ELTON chapelry 1691 parish Youlgrave Derbys pop 595 archd Derby dioc Lichfield

ELTON parish 1573 co Durham 3-1/2 miles sw Stockton upon Tees pop 103 archd and dioc Durham

ELTON parish 1657 Herefs 4-3/4 miles sw Ludlow pop 85 archd and dioc Hereford

ELTON parish 1560 Hunts 4-3/4 miles ne Oundle pop 780 archd Huntingdon dioc Lincoln Wesl Meth

ELTON township parish Bury Lancs pop 4054

ELTON or ELTON ON THE HILL parish 1592 Notts 4-1/4 miles se Bingham pop 91 archd Nottingham dioc York

ELTRINGHAM township parish Ovingham Northumberland pop 50

ELVASTON parish 1652 Derbys 5 miles se Derby pop 522 archd
Derby dioc Lichfield

ELVEDON otherwise ELDEN parish 1651 Suffolk 32 miles sw Thetford pop 248 archd Sudbury dioc Norwich

ELVETHAM parish 1638 Hamps 1-1/4 miles se Hartford Bridge pop 481 archd and dioc Winchester

ELVINGTON parish 1600 E R York 7 miles se York pop 391 archd Cleveland dioc York Wesl Meth

ELWICK township parish Hart co Durham pop 232

ELWICK township parish Belford Northumberland pop 79

ELWICK HALL parish 1592 co Durham 9 miles ne Stockton upon Tees pop 169 archd and dioc Durham

ELWORTHY parish 1685 Somerset 5-1/4 miles n Wiveliscombe pop 210 archd Taunton dioc Bath and Wells

ELY city Cambs 16 miles ne Cambridge pop 6,189 St Mary 1670, Cathedral 1691, Holy Trinity 1559 pec Dean and Chapter Bapt, Countess of Huntingdon's connexion, Indep, Wesl Meth

ELYAUGH township parish Felton Northumberland pop 13

EMBER hamlet parish Thames Ditton Surrey pop 1,170

EMBERTON parish 1659 Bucks 1-1/2 miles s Olney pop 598 archd Buckingham dioc Lincoln

EMBLETON chapelry 1625 parish Brigham Cumberland pop 442 archd Richmond dioc Chester

EMBLETON chapelry parish Sedgefield co Durham pop 105

EMBLETON parish 1682 Northumberland 7-1/4 miles ne Alnwick comp chapelries Rennington, Rock, townships Brocksfield, High Bruton, Low Bruton, Craster, Dunston, Embleton, Fallowdon, Newton, Stamford pop 1,923 archd Northumberland dioc Durham

EMBLEY tything parish East Wellow Hamps

EMBORROW, IN and OUT parish 1569 Somerset 5-1/2 miles ne Wells pop 207 archd Wells dioc Bath and Wells

EMBSAY township parish Skipton W R York pop 891

EMLEY parish 1600 W R York 7-1/2 miles se Huddersfield pop 1,445 archd and dioc York

EMMINGTON parish 1539 co Oxford 3-1/4 miles se Thame pop 80 archd and dioc Oxford

EMNETH parish 1681 Norfolk 2-1/2 miles se Wisbech pop 995 pec Bishop of Ely

EMPINGHAM parish 1559 co Rutland 6-1/4 miles se Oakham pop 913 pec Prebendary of Empingham

EMPSHOTT parish 1718 Hamps 5 miles n Petersfield pop 149 archd and dioc Winchester

EMSWELL township parish Driffield E R York pop 102

EMSWORTH tything parish Warblington Hamps

ENBORNE parish 1666 Berks 2-1/4 miles sw Newbury pop 420 archd Berks dioc Salisbury

ENDELLION parish 1684 Cornwall 5-1/4 miles n Wade Bridge pop

1,218 archd Cornwall dioc Exeter

ENDERBY parish 1559 Leics 4-1/2 miles se Leicester pop 1,141 archd Leicester dioc Lincoln

ENDERBY, BAG parish 1561 Lincs 5-1/2 miles nw Spilsby pop 114 archd and dioc Lincoln

ENDERBY, MAVIS parish 1579 Lincs 1-3/4 miles nw Spilsby pop 203 archd and dioc Lincoln

ENDERBY, WOOD parish 1561 Lincs 4 miles se Horncastle pop 210 archd and dioc Lincoln

ENDON chapelry 1730 parish Leek Staffs pop 487 archd Stafford dioc Lichfield

ENFIELD parish 1550 Middlesex 10 miles ne London pop 8,812 archd Middlesex dioc London Indep, Wesl Meth, Presb

ENFORD parish 1631 Wilts 8-1/4 miles nw Ludgershall pop 961 archd and dioc Salisbury

ENGLEFIELD parish 1559 Berks 6 miles w Reading pop 411 archd Berks dioc Salisbury

ENGLISH COMBE 1728 Somerset See COMBE, ENGLISH

ENHAM, KING'S hamlet parish Andover Hamps

ENHAM, KNIGHT'S parish 1683 Hamps 1-3/4 miles n Andover pop 123 archd and dioc Winchester

ENMORE parish 1653 Somerset 4 miles sw Bridgewater pop 294 archd Taunton dioc Bath and Wells

ENNERDALE chapelry 1643 parish St Bees Cumberland pop 611 archd Richmond dioc Chester

ENODER, ST parish 1571 Cornwall 2-3/4 miles ne St Michael's pop 1,124 archd Cornwall dioc Exeter Bryanites, Wesl Meth

ENODOCK, ST chapelry parish St Minver Cornwall

ENSHAM parish 1653 co Oxford 5-1/2 miles se Witney pop 1,858 archd and dioc Oxford Indep

ENSON township parish St Mary Lichfield Staffs

ENSTONE, CHURCH parish 1558 co Oxford 15-3/4 miles nw Oxford comp hamlets Cleveley, Church Enstone, Neat Enstone, Gagingwell, Lidstone, Radford pop 742 archd and dioc Oxford Wesl Meth

ENTWISLE township parish Bolton Lancs pop 701

ENVILLE parish 1627 Staffs 5 miles nw Stourbridge pop 766 archd Stafford dioc Lichfield

EPPERSTONE parish 1582 Notts 6 miles se Southwell pop 518 archd Nottingham dioc York Wesl Meth

EPPING parish 1539 Essex 17-1/2 miles sw Chelmsford comp Epping Upland, hamlet Ryhill pop 2,313 pec court of Commissary London Indep, Soc of Friends

EPPLEBY township parish Gilling N R York pop 206

EPPLETON, GREAT township parish Houghton le Spring co Durham pop 47

EPPLETON, LITTLE township parish Houghton le Spring co Durham

pop 17

EPSOM parish 1695 Surrey 16 miles se Guildford pop 3,231 archd Surrey dioc Winchester Indep

EPWELL chapelry 1577 parish Swalcliffe co Oxford pop 367

EPWORTH parish 1540 Lincs 23-3/4 miles nw Lincoln pop 1,825 archd Stow dioc Lincoln Bapt, Soc of Friends, Old and New Connection Meth, Prim Meth

ERCALL, CHILD'S parish 1570 Shrops 7 miles nw Newport pop 416 archd Salop dioc Lichfield

ERCALL, MAGNA parish 1585 Shrops 6 miles nw Wellington pop 2,048 archd Salop dioc Lichfield

ERDINGTON chapelry parish Aston Warws

ERISWELL parish 1669 Suffolk 3 miles ne Mildenhall pop 403 archd Sudbury dioc Norwich

ERITH parish 1560 Kent 2-1/4 miles n Crayford pop 1,533 archd and dioc Rochester

ERLESTOKE See STOKE ERLE

ERME, ST parish 1671 Cornwall 3-1/4 miles ne Truro pop 586 archd Cornwall dioc Exeter

ERMINGTON parish 1603 Devon 2 miles nw Modbury pop 1,471 archd Totnes dioc Exeter

ERNEY, ST chapelry parish Landrake Cornwall

ERPINGHAM parish 1559 Norfolk 3 miles ne Aylsham pop 434 archd and dioc Norwich

ERPINGDEN chapelry parish Halifax W R York pop 1,933

ERTH, ST parish 1563 Cornwall 4 miles ne Marazion pop 1,922 archd Cornwall dioc Exeter Calv, Wesl Meth

ERVAN parish 1674 Cornwall 4 miles sw Padstow pop 453 pec Bishop of Exeter Wesl Meth

ERWARTON parish 1558 Suffolk 8-1/4 miles se Ipswich pop 179 archd Suffolk dioc Norwich

ERYHOLME chapelry 1568 parish Gilling N R York pop 172 archd Richmond dioc Chester

ESCOMBE chapelry 1545 co Durham pop 282 archd and dioc Durham

ESCRICK parish 1617 E R York 6 miles se York comp townships Deighton, Escrick pop 896 archd Cleveland dioc York

ESH or ASH chapelry 1567 parish Lanchester co Durham pop 486 archd and dioc Durham

ESHAM hamlet parish Syleham Suffolk

ESHER parish 1678 Surrey 13-1/2 miles ne Guildford pop 1,215 archd Surrey dioc Winchester

ESHOLT township parish Otley W R York pop 404

ESHOTT township parish Felton Northumberland pop 132

ESHTON township parish Gargrave W R York pop 82

ESKDALE chapelry 1626 parish St Bees Cumberland pop 354 archd Richmond dioc Chester

ESKDALE SIDE chapelry 1676 parish Whitby N R York pop 277 archd Cleveland dioc York

ESKE township parish St John Beverley E R York pop 17
ESP GREEN hamlet parish Lanchester co Durham
ESPERSHIELDS township parish Bywell St Peter Northumberland pop 195
ESSENDINE chapelry 1600 parish Ryall co Rutland pop 156
ESSENDON parish 1653 Herts 3-1/2 miles e Bishop's Hatfield pop 672 archd Huntingdon dioc Lincoln
ESSINGTON township parish Bushbury Staffs pop 598
ESTON hamlet parish Arthuret Cumberland
ESTON chapelry 1590 parish Ormsby N R York pop 334 archd Cleveland dioc York
ETALL township parish Ford Northumberland
ETCHELLS township parish partly in parish Northern or Northende partly in Stockport Ches pop 1, 443
ETCHILHAMPTON chapelry 1630 parish Allcannings Wilts pop 270
ETCHINGHAM parish 1564 Sussex 6-3/4 miles se Wadhurst pop 631 archd Lewes dioc Chichester
ETLOE tything parish Awre Gloucs
ETON parish 1594 Bucks 1 mile n Windsor pop 3,232 pec Provost of Eton College
ETRURIA hamlet formerly in parish Stoke upon Trent now in Shelton Staffs Wesl Meth
ETTERBY township parish Stanwix Cumberland pop 110
ETTINGTON See EATINGTON
ETTON parish 1587 co Northampton 7 miles nw Peterborough pop 118 archd Northampton dioc Peterborough
ETTON parish 1557 E R York 4-1/4 miles nw Beverley pop 407 archd East Riding dioc York
ETWALL parish 1558 Derbys 6 miles sw Derby comp townships Etwall, Bearward Cote, hamlet Burnaston pop 605 archd Derby dioc Lichfield
EUSTON parish 1708 Suffolk 3-1/2 miles se Thetford pop 202 archd Sudbury dioc Norwich
EUXTON chapelry 1774 parish Leyland Lancs pop 1,501 archd and dioc Chester
EVAL, ST parish 1695 Cornwall 4-1/2 miles nw St Columb Major pop 354 pec Bishop of Exeter Bryanites, Wesl Meth
EVEDON parish 1560 Lincs 2-3/4 miles ne Sleaford pop 86 archd and dioc Lincoln
EVENLEY parish 1694 co Northampton 1 mile sw Brackley pop 506 archd Northampton dioc Peterborough
EVENLOAD parish 1561 Worcs 3 miles se Moreton in the Marsh pop 312 pec Bishop of Worcester
EVENWOOD township parish St Andrew Auckland co Durham pop 1,019 Wesl Meth
EVERCREECH parish 1541 Somerset 3-3/4 miles se Shepton Mallet pop 1,490 pec Dean of Wells Wesl Meth
EVERDON parish 1558 co Northampton 4-1/4 miles se Daventry pop

745 archd Northampton dioc Peterborough Indep

EVERINGHAM parish 1653 E R York 5 miles nw Market Weighton pop 276 archd East Riding dioc York Roman Cath

EVERLEY parish 1598 Wilts 4-3/4 miles nw Ludgershall pop 352 archd Wilts dioc Salisbury

EVERLEY township parish Hackness N R York

EVERSAW hamlet parish Biddlesdon Bucks

EVERSDEN, GREAT parish 1541 Cambs 7 miles se Caxton pop 316 archd and dioc Ely

EVERSDEN, LITTLE parish 1703 Cambs 7-3/4 miles se Caxton pop 196 archd and dioc Ely

EVERSHOLT parish 1628 Beds 2-1/2 miles se Woburn pop 901 archd Bedford dioc Lincoln

EVERSHOT chapelry 1694 parish Frome St Quintin Dorset pop 569

EVERSLEY parish 1559 Hamps 2 miles n Hartford Bridge pop 755 archd and dioc Winchester

EVERTHORP joint township with Drewton parish North Cave E R York pop 149

EVERTON parish 1653 Beds 4-3/4 miles ne Biggleswade pop 396 archd Bedford dioc Lincoln

EVERTON chapelry parish Walton on the Hill Lancs pop 4,518

EVERTON parish 1567 Notts 2-3/4 miles se Bawtry pop 786 archd Nottingham dioc York

EVESBATCH parish 1700 Herefs 5-1/2 miles se Bromyard pop 84 archd and dioc Hereford

EVESHAM market town borough Worcs 15 miles se Worcester pop 3,026 sep juris All Saints 1538, St Lawrence 1556, St Peter Bengworth formerly pec Evesham archd and dioc Worcester Bapt, Soc of Friends, Wesl Meth, Unit

EVINGTON hamlet parish Leigh Gloucs

EVINGTON parish 1601 Leics 3-1/4 miles se Leicester pop 260 pec Lord of Manor of Evington

EWART township parish Doddington Northumberland pop 173

EWE, ST parish 1559 Cornwall 4 miles ne Tregoney pop 1,699 archd Cornwall dioc Exeter

EWELL parish 1581 Kent 2-1/2 miles nw Dover pop 425 archd and dioc Canterbury

EWELL parish 1603 Surrey 5-1/2 miles nw Kingston pop 1,851 archd Surrey dioc Winchester Indep

EWELME parish 1599 co Oxford 3-1/4 miles ne Wallingford pop 619 archd and dioc Oxford

EWEN tything parish Kemble Wilts

EWERBY parish 1694 Lincs 3-3/4 miles ne Sleaford pop 345 archd and dioc Lincoln

EWESLEY township parish Nether Witton Northumberland pop 22

EWHURST parish 1682 Hamps 6 miles nw Basingstoke pop 28 archd and dioc Winchester

EWHURST parish 1614 Surrey 9-1/4 miles nw Godalming pop 828

archd Surrey dioc Winchester

EWHURST parish 1558 Sussex 4 miles ne Roberts Bridge pop 1,200 archd Lewes dioc Chichester

EWSHOTT tything parish Crondall Hamps pop 526

EWYAS HARROLD parish 1734 Herefs 12-1/2 miles sw Hereford pop 344 archd Brecon dioc St David's

EXBOURNE parish 1540 Devon 4-3/4 miles se Hatherleigh pop 509 archd Totnes dioc Exeter

EXBURY chapelry parish Fawley Hamps pop 325

EXELBY township parish Burneston N R York pop 633

EXETER city Devon 10 miles nw Exmouth pop 28,201 comp parishes Allhallows 1561, Goldsmith Street, Allhallows on the Walls 1694, St Edmund 1571, St George 1681, St John 1682, St Kerrian 1558, St Petrock 1538, St Lawrence 1604, St Martin 1572, St Pancras 1664, St Mary Arches 1538, St Mary Major's 1561, St Mary Steps 1654, St Olave 1601, St Paul 1562, St Stephen 1668, Holy Trinity 1605, St David 1559, St Sidwell 1569, St Leonard 1758, St Thomas 1554, The Cathedral 1594 Bapt, Soc of Friends, Indep, Wesl and other Meth, Unit, Roman Cath

EXFORD parish 1609 Somerset 8-1/2 miles nw Dulverton pop 447 archd Taunton dioc Bath and Wells

EXHALL parish 1540 Warws 4-3/4 miles ne Coventry pop 840 archd Coventry dioc Lichfield

EXHALL parish 1539 Warws 2-1/4 miles se Alcester pop 241 archd and dioc Worcester

EXMINSTER parish 1562 Devon 4 miles se Exeter pop 1,113 archd and dioc Exeter

EXMOOR extra parochial liberty moorland Somerset pop 52

EXMOUTH chapelry parish Withycombe Rawleigh chiefly in Littleham Devon Indep, Wesl Meth

EXNING parish 1558 Suffolk 2 miles nw Newmarket pop 917 archd Sudbury dioc Norwich Wesl Meth

EXTON parish 1597 co Rutland 5-1/4 miles ne Oakham pop 751 archd Northampton dioc Peterborough

EXTON parish 1559 Somerset 4 miles ne Dulverton pop 347 archd Taunton dioc Bath and Wells

EXTON parish 1579 Hamps 4-3/4 miles ne Bishop's Waltham pop 283 pec the incumbent

EXTWISTLE township parish Whalley Lancs

EYAM parish 1630 Derbys 1-1/2 miles nw Stony Middleton comp townships Eyam, Woodland Eyam, hamlet Foolow pop 1,372 archd Derby dioc Lichfield Wesl Meth

EYDON parish 1538 co Northampton 9-1/2 miles sw Daventry pop 630 archd Northampton dioc Peterborough

EYE parish 1573 Herefs 3-1/2 miles n Leominster comp townships Ashton, Eye Moreton, Luston pop 720 archd and dioc Hereford

EYE parish 1543 co Northampton 3-1/4 miles ne Peterborough pop 1,122 archd Northampton dioc Peterborough Wesl Meth

EYE parish 1538 borough Suffolk 20-1/2 miles n Ipswich pop 2,313 sep juris archd Sudbury dioc Norwich Bapt, Wesl Meth

EYE MORETON township parish Eye Herefs

EYFORD extra parochial liberty 2-1/2 miles sw Stow on the Wold Gloucs pop 55

EYKE parish 153 8 Suffolk 3-3/4 miles ne Woodbridge pop 485 archd Suffolk dioc Norwich

EYNESBURY parish 1539 Hunts 1/2 mile s St Neots pop 957 archd Huntingdon dioc Lincoln

EYNESFORD parish 1538 Kent 6 miles se Foot's Cray pop 1,277 pec Archbishop of Canterbury Bapt

EYTHORN parish 1558 Kent 6-1/2 miles nw Dover pop 422 archd and dioc Canterbury Bapt

EYTHORPE hamlet parish Waddesdon Bucks

EYTON parish 1682 Herefs 2-1/4 miles nw Leominster pop 177 archd and dioc Hereford

EYTON township parish Abberbury Shrops

EYTON UPON SEVERN chapelry parish Wroxeter Shrops

EYTON UPON THE WILD MOORS parish 1698 Shrops 2-1/2 miles n Wellington pop 350 archd Salop dioc Lichfield

EYWORTH parish 1538 Beds 4-1/2 miles n Biggleswade pop 129 archd Bedford dioc Lincoln

FACCOMBE parish 1585 Hamps 5-1/2 miles ne Andover pop 290 archd and dioc Winchester Wesl Meth

FACEBY chapelry 1707 parish Whorlton N R York pop 143

FADDILEY township parish Acton Ches pop 316 Wesl Meth

FADMORE township parish Kirby Moorside N R York pop 158

FAILSWORTH township parish Manchester Lancs pop 3,667

FAIRBURN township parish Ledsham W R York pop 465

FAIRFIELD chapelry 1738 parish Hope Derbys pop 482 pec of Dean and Chapter of Lichfield

FAIRFIELD parish 1558 Kent 6-3/4 miles nw New Romney pop 89 archd and dioc Canterbury

FAIRFIELD hamlet parish Manchester Lancs Moravians

FAIRFIELD hamlet parish Stogursey Somerset

FAIRFIELD HEAD township parish Allstonefield Staffs pop 1,017

FAIRFORD parish 1617 borough Gloucs 24 miles se Gloucester pop 1,574 archd and dioc Gloucester Bapt, Indep

FAIRHAUGH township parish Allenton Northumberland pop 4

FAIRLIGHT parish 1651 Sussex 2-1/2 miles ne Hastings pop 533 archd Lewes dioc Chichester

FAIRSTED parish 1537 Essex 4 miles nw Witham pop 258 archd Colchester dioc London

FAITH, ST parish Hamps pop 394 pec Bishop of Winchester (Same as St Cross Winchester)

FAKENHAM parish 1719 Norfolk 25-1/2 miles nw Norwich pop 2,085 archd Norfolk dioc Norwich Bapt, Indep, Prim and Wesl Meth

FAKENHAM, MAGNA parish 1559 Suffolk 5 miles se Thetford pop

204 archd Sudbury dioc Norwich

FAKENHAM, PARVA hamlet parish Euston Suffolk

FALDINGWORTH parish 1560 Lincs 5 miles sw Market Rasen pop 296 archd Stow dioc Lincoln

FALFIELD chapelry parish Thornbury Gloucs

FALKENHAM parish 1538 Suffolk 8-1/2 miles se Ipswich pop 297 archd Suffolk dioc Norwich

FALKINGHAM or FOLKINGHAM parish 1583 Lincs 26-1/2 miles se Lincoln pop 744 archd and dioc Lincoln

FALLOWDON township parish Embleton Northumberland pop 105

FALLOWFIELD township parish St John Lee Northumberland pop 70

FALLOWLEES township parish Rothbury Northumberland pop 8

FALLYBROOM township parish Prestbury Ches pop 25

FALMER parish 1642 Sussex 4 miles ne Brighton pop 432 archd Lewes dioc Chichester

FALMOUTH parish 1663 Cornwall 54 miles se Launceston pop 7,284 pec Bishop of Exeter Bapt, Bryanites, Soc of Friends, Indep, Prim and Wesl Meth, Unit

FALSGRAVE township borough Scarborough N R York pop 391

FALSTONE parish 1742 Northumberland 8 miles nw Bellingham comp township Falstone Plashets, Wellhaugh pop 1,421 archd Northumberland dioc Durham

FAMBRIDGE, NORTH parish 1556 Essex 5 miles nw Rochford pop 148 archd Essex dioc London

FAMBRIDGE, SOUTH parish 1754 Essex 3-1/2 miles nw Rochford pop 91 archd Essex dioc London

FANGFOSS parish 1715 E R York 4 miles nw Pocklington pop 155 pec of Dean of York

FARCETT chapelry 1650 parish Standground Hunts pop 536

FAREHAM parish 1559 Hamps 12 miles se Southampton pop 4,402 pec of incumbent Indep, Wesl Meth

FAREWELL parish 1693 Staffs 2 miles nw Lichfield pop 200 pec Dean and Chapter of Lichfield

FARFORTH parish 1784 Lincs 6-1/4 miles sw Louth pop 91 archd and dioc Lincoln

FARINGDON parish 1558 Hamps 3 miles sw Alton pop 504 archd and dioc Winchester

FARLAM parish 1700 Cumberland 3 miles se Brampton comp townships East Farlam, West Farlam pop 816 archd and dioc Carlisle

FARLEIGH, EAST parish 1580 Kent 2-1/2 miles sw Maidstone pop 1,461 pec Archbishop of Canterbury

FARLEIGH HUNGERFORD parish 1673 Somerset 7 miles se Bath pop 168 archd Wells dioc Bath and Wells

FARLEIGH WALLOP parish (united with Cliddesdon) Hamps 3-3/4 miles sw Basingstoke pop 108 archd and dioc Winchester

FARLEIGH, WEST parish 1558 Kent 3-1/4 miles sw Maidstone pop 392 archd and dioc Rochester

FARLETON township parish Melling Lancs pop 90

FARLETON township parish Beetham Westm pop 90

FARLEY township parish Alveton Staffs pop 450

FARLEY parish 1672 Surrey 5 miles se Croydon pop 83 archd Surrey dioc Winchester

FARLEY chapelry 1570 parish Alderbury Wilts pop 254 pec Treasurer in Cathedral Church of Salisbury

FARLEY CHAMBERLAYNE parish 1593 Hamps 5-3/4 miles sw Winchester pop 165 archd and dioc Winchester

FARLINGTON parish 1538 Hamps 2-1/4 miles sw Havant pop 778 archd and dioc Winchester

FARLINGTON chapelry 1614 parish Sheriff Hutton N R York pop 152

FARLOW chapelry parish Sparsholt Berks pop 376

FARLOW chapelry parish Stottesdon Herefs pop 345

FARLSTHORP parish 1655 Lincs 1-3/4 miles se Alford pop 94 archd and dioc Lincoln

FARMSNBY township in parishes Ellerburn and Thornton Dale N R York pop 431

FARMBOROUGH parish 1559 Somerset 3-3/4 miles se Pensford pop 924 archd Bath dioc Bath and Wells Wesl Meth

FARMCOT chapelry parish Lower Guyting Gloucs

FARMINGTON parish 1613 Gloucs 2 miles ne Northleach pop 311 archd and dioc Gloucester

FARNBOROUGH parish 1739 Berks 5 miles nw East Ilsley pop 229 archd Berks dioc Salisbury

FARNBOROUGH chapelry 1558 parish Chelsfield Kent pop 638

FARNBOROUGH parish 1584 Hamps 5-1/2 miles ne Farnham pop 334 archd and dioc Winchester

FARNBOROUGH parish 1558 Warws 6-1/2 miles se Kington pop 365 archd Coventry dioc Lichfield

FARNDALE chapelry parish Lastingham N R York pop 474

FARNDALE EASTSIDE township parish Lastingham N R York pop 405

FARNDISH parish 1587 Beds 4-1/2 miles sw Higham Ferrers pop 81 archd Bedford dioc Lincoln

FARNDON parish 1603 Ches 8-3/4 miles s Chester comp townships Barton, Churton by Farndon, Clutton, Crewe, Farndon pop 864 archd and dioc Chester Calv Meth

FARNDON hamlet parish Woodford co Northampton

FARNDON parish 1559 Notts 2-1/4 miles sw Newark pop 570 archd Nottingham dioc York

FARNDON, EAST parish 1562 co Northampton 2 miles sw Market Harborough pop 250 archd Northampton dioc Peterborough

FARNHAM parish 1647 Wilts and Dorset 8 miles nw Cranborne pop 314 archd Dorset dioc Bristol

FARNHAM parish 1558 Essex 3-1/4 miles nw Stansted Mountftchet pop 524 archd Colchester dioc London

FARNHAM township parish Allenton Northumberland pop 47

FARNHAM parish 1707 Suffolk 2-3/4 miles sw Saxmundham pop 216 archd Suffolk dioc Norwich

FARNHAM parish 1539 Surrey 10 miles sw Guildford comp market town Farnham tythings Badshot, with Runfold, Culverlands with Tilford, Runwick and Wrecklesham with Bourn pop 5,858 archd Surry dioc Winchester Indep

FARNHAM parish 1569 W R York 2-1/4 miles n Knaresborough comp townships Farnham, Ferensby, Scotton pop 614 pec of honour of Knaresborough

FARNHAM ROYAL parish 1635 Bucks 3-1/2 miles n Eton pop 1,193 archd Buckingham dioc Lincoln Dissenters

FARNHAM TOLLARD tything parish Farnham Dorset pop 220

FARNHILL township parish Kildwick W R York pop 1, 567

FARNHURST parish 1547 Sussex 5 miles ne Midhurst pop 769 archd and dioc Chichester

FARNINGHAM parish 1589 Kent 5-1/2 miles se Foot's Cray pop 701 pec of Archbishop of Canterbury

FARN ISLANDS seventeen small islands parish Holy Island co Durham

FARNLEY chapelry parish Otley W R York pop 196 archd and dioc York

FARNLEY chapelry 1772 parish St Peter Leeds W R York pop 1,591

FARNLEY TYAS chapelry parish Almondbury W R York pop 849

FARNSFIELD parish 1572 Notts 4 miles nw Southwell pop 1,010 pec of Chapter of the Collegiate Church of Southwell Part Bapt, Wesl Meth

FARNWORTH chapelry 1538 parish Dean Lancs pop 2,928 Indep

FARNWORTH chapelry parish Prescot Lancs

FARRINGDON parish 1678 Devon 4-3/4 miles ne Topsham pop 377 archd and dioc Exeter

FARRINGDON chapelry parish Twerne Courtnay Dorset

FARRINGDON, GREAT parish 1582 Berks 35 miles nw Reading comp market town Farringdon, chapelry Little Coxwell, tything Hospital, Wadley or Littleworth with Thrupp pop 3,033 formerly prebend in Salisbury Cathedral now pec Lord of Manor Bapt

FARRINGDON, LITTLE chapelry parish Langford Berks pop 156

FARRINGTON township parish Penwortham Lancs pop 672

FARRINGTON OURNEY chapelry 1680 parish Chewton Mendip Somerset pop 568 Wesl Meth

FARSLEY township parish Calverley W R York pop 2, 637 Bapt

FARTHINGHOE parish 1560 co Northampton 4-3/4 miles nw Brackley pop 356 archd Northampton dioc Peterborough

FARTHINGSTONE parish 1538 co Northampton 5 miles se Daventry pop 293 archd Northampton dioc Peterborough

FARWAY parish 1567 Devon 3 miles se Honiton pop 360 archd and dioc Exeter

FAUGH township parish Hayton Cumberland pop 333

FAULD township parish Hanbury Staffs pop 45

FAULKBOURN parish 1574 Essex 2 miles nw Witham pop 161 archd

Colchester dioc London

FAVERSHAM parish 1620 Kent 8 miles w Canterbury pop 4,429 sep juris archd and dioc Canterbury Bapt, Indep, Wesl Meth

FAVINLEY or FARNLAWS township parish Hartburn Northumberland pop 15

FAWCET FOREST township parish Orton Westm pop 61

FAWDINGTON township parish Cundall N R York pop 48

FAWDON township parish Gosforth Northumberland pop 707

FAWDON township parish Ingram Northumberland pop 67

FAWKHAM parish 1568 Kent 5-3/4 miles se Dartford pop 204 archd and dioc Rochester

FAWLER hamlet parish Charlbury co Oxford pop 134

FAWLEY parish 1540 Berks 5-1/2 miles s Wantage pop 194 archd Berks dioc Salisbury

FAWLEY parish 1573 Bucks 3 miles nw Henley upon Thames pop 254 archd Buckingham dioc Lincoln

FAWLEY chapelry parish Fownhope Herefs

FAWLEY parish 1673 Hamps 6 miles se Southampton pop 1,839 pec of incumbent Wesl Meth

FAWNS township parish Kirkwhelpington Northumberland pop 7

FAWSLEY parish 1585 co Northampton 4 miles sw Daventry pop 22 archd Northampton dioc Peterborough

FAXFLEET township parish South Cave E R York pop 177

FAXTON chapelry 1653 parish Lamport co Northampton pop 103

FAZAKERLEY township parish Walton on the Hill Lancs pop 407

FAZELY chapelry parish Tamworth Staffs pop 1,139

FEARBY township parish Masham N R York pop 249

FEARNHEAD township parish Warrington Lancs

FEATHERSTON township parish Haltwhistle Northumberland pop 274

FEATHERSTONE chapelry parish Wolverhampton Staffs pop 34

FEATHERSTONE parish 1558 W R York 3-1/2 miles w Pontefract comp townships Ackton, Whitwood, Featherstone, Peerston Jaglin pop 945 archd and dioc York

FECKENHAM parish 1538 Worcs 7 miles se Droitwich pop 2,762 archd and dioc Worcester Indep

FEERING parish 1563 Essex 1-1/4 miles ne Kelvedon pop 735 archd Colchester dioc London

FELBRIGGE parish 1700 Norfolk 3 miles sw Cromer pop 155 archd Norfolk dioc Norwich

FELIX KIRK parish 1598 N R York 4 miles ne Thirsk comp township Felix Kirk West Riding, chapelry Boltby, townships Sutton under Whitestone Cliff and Thirlby pop 911 archd Cleveland dioc York

FELIXSTOWE parish 1653 Suffolk 11-1/2 miles se Ipswich pop 363 archd Suffolk dioc Norwich

FELKINGTON township parish Norham co Durham and Northumberland pop 141

FELKIRK parish 1701 W R York 6-1/4 miles ne Barnsley comp townships Brierly, Havercroft with Cold Hiendley, South Hiendley and

Shafton pop 1,156 archd and dioc York

FELLISCLIFFE township parish Hampsthwaite W R York pop 351

FELLSIDE township parish Whickham co Durham pop 419

FELLY hamlet parish Annesley Notts pop 67

FELMERSHAM parish 1660 Beds 7 miles nw Bedford pop 448 archd Bedford dioc Lincoln

FELMINGHAM parish 1754 Norfolk 2-1/2 miles sw North Walsham pop 394 archd Norfolk dioc Norwich

FELPHAM parish 1557 Sussex 8 miles sw Arundel pop 588 archd and dioc Chichester

FELSHAM parish 1656 Suffolk 6-3/4 miles sw Stow Market pop 401 archd Sudbury dioc Norwich

FELSTEAD parish 1558 Essex 4 miles se Great Dunmow pop 1,788 archd Middlesex dioc London

FELTHAM parish 1634 Middlesex 4 miles sw Hounslow pop 924 archd Middlesex dioc London

FELTHORPE parish 1712 Norfolk 7 miles nw Norwich pop 502 archd and dioc Norwich

FELTON parish 1637 Herefs 8 miles ne Hereford pop 122 archd and dioc Hereford

FELTON parish 1653 Northumberland 9 miles s Alnwick comp township Acton with Old Felton, Elyaugh, Felton Greens with Glantless, Swarland, Bockenfield, Eshott, East and West Thriston with Shothaugh, Brickburn South side pop 1,619 archd Northumberland dioc Durham Presb

FELTON Somerset See WHITCHURCH

FELTON, OLD township parish Felton Northumberland

FELTON, WEST parish 1628 Shrops 5 miles se Oswestry pop 1,093 archd Salop dioc Lichfield

FELTWELL parish 1562 Norfolk 6-1/2 miles s Stoke Ferry pop 1,231 archd Norfolk dioc Norwich Wesl Meth

FEN DRAYTON See DRAYTON FEN Cambs

FENBY hamlet parish Ashby Lincs

FENCOT hamlet parish Charlton upon Otmore co Oxford pop 300

FENCOTT township parish Docklow Herefs

FENHAM township parish St Andrew, Newcastle Northumberland pop 100

FENITON parish 1549 Devon 4 miles sw Honiton pop 343 archd and dioc Exeter

FENNY COMPTON Warws See COMPTON, FENNY

FENNY DRAYTON See DRAYTON FENNY Leics

FENROTHER township parish Hebburn Northumberland pop 90

FEN STANTON parish 1612 Hunts 2-1/2 miles sw St Ives pop 968 archd Huntingdon dioc Lincoln

FENTON township parish Hayton Cumberland pop 333

FENTON chapelry 1539 parish Beckingham Lincs pop 102

FENTON hamlet parish Kettlethorpe Lincs pop 226

FENTON hamlet parish Wooler Northumberland

FENTON CALVERT township parish Stoke upon Trent Staffs pop 2,708
FENTON, KIRK parish 1630 W R York 5 miles se Tadcaster comp
 townships Biggin, Little Fenton, Kirk Fenton pop 649 pec of Pre-
 bendary of Kirk Fenton
FENTON, LITTLE township parish Kirk Fenton W R York pop 102
FENTON VIVIAN township parish Stoke upon Trent Staffs pop 1,002
FENWICK township parish Stamfordham Northumberland pop 80
FENWICK township parish Campsall W R York pop 286 Wesl Meth
FEOCK, ST parish 1671 Cornwall 5 miles s Truro pop 1,210 archd
 Cornwall dioc Exeter Bapt, Calvinists, Wesl Meth
FERENSBY township parish Farnham W R York pop 133
FERNHAM hamlet parish Shrivenham Berks pop 239
FERNILEE township parish Hope Derbys pop 418
FERRIBY, NORTH parish 1730 E R York 5-1/4 miles se South Cave
 comp townships North Ferriby and Swanland pop 823 archd East
 Riding dioc York
FERRIBY, SOUTH parish 1538 Lincs 3-1/4 miles sw Barton upon
 Humber pop 500 archd and dioc Lincoln Wesl Meth
FERRING parish 1558 Sussex 3-3/4 miles w Worthing pop 258 archd
 and dioc Chichester
FERRY BRIDGE hamlet parish Ferry Frystone W R York Wesl Meth
FERRY EAST chapelry parish Scotton Lincs pop 141 Wesl Meth
FERRY HILL chapelry parish Merrington co Durham pop 591
FERSFIELD parish 1565 Norfolk 4-1/4 miles nw Diss pop 292 archd
 Norfolk dioc Norwich
FETCHAM parish 1559 Surrey 1-1/4 miles w Leatherhead pop 384
 archd Surrey dioc Winchester
FEWCOT hamlet parish Stoke Lyne co Oxford pop 198
FEWSTON parish 1593 W R York 7 miles n Otley comp townships
 Blubberhouses, Clifton with Norwood, Fewston, Thurcross, Great
 Timble pop 2,035 pec of honor of Knaresborough
FIDDINGTON tything parish Ashchurch Gloucs pop 172
FIDDINGTON parish 1706 Somerset 7-1/4 miles nw Bridgewater pop
 210 archd Taunton dioc Bath and Wells
FIELD township parish Leigh Staffs pop 82
FIELD DALLING parish 1538 Norfolk 5 miles ne Little Walsingham
 pop 400 archd and dioc Norwich
FIFEHEAD MAGDALENE parish 1564 Dorset 6 miles sw Shaftesbury
 pop 241 archd Dorset dioc Bristol
FIFEHEAD NEVILLE parish 1573 Dorset 10-1/2 miles nw Blandford
 Forum pop 101 archd Dorset dioc Bristol
FIFIELD parish 1712 co Oxford 4-1/2 miles nw Burford pop 163
 pec Chancellor of Cathedral Church of Salisbury
FIFIELD hamlet parish Bensington co Oxford pop 13
FIFIELD BAVANT parish 1695 Wilts 6-3/4 miles sw Wilton pop 49
 archd and dioc Salisbury
FIGHELDEAN parish 1653 Wilts 4-1/4 miles n Amesbury pop 531
 pec Treasurer in Cathedral Church of Salisbury

FILBY parish 1599 Norfolk 3 miles nw Caistor pop 464 archd Norfolk
dioc Norwich Wesl Meth, Unit
FILEY parish 1573 E R York 2-1/2 miles ne Hunmanby pop 1,192
archd East Riding dioc York
FILGROVE parish 1629 Bucks 3-3/4 miles n Newport Pagnell archd
Buckingham dioc Lincoln
FILKINS hamlet parish Broadwell co Oxford pop 473
FILLEIGH parish 1726 Devon 3-3/4 miles nw South Molton pop 329
archd Barnstaple dioc Exeter
FILLINGHAM parish 1661 Lincs 10 miles nw Lincoln pop 308 archd
Stow dioc Lincoln
FILLONGLEY parish 1538 Warws 6-1/4 miles nw Coventry pop 981
archd Coventry dioc Lichfield
FILTON parish 1654 Gloucs 3-3/4 miles ne Bristol pop 217 pec of
Bishop of Bristol
FIMBER chapelry parish Wetwang E R York pop 139
FINBOROUGH, GREAT parish 1558 Suffolk 2-3/4 miles sw Stow
Market pop 421 archd and dioc Norwich
FINBOROUGH, LITTLE parish 1558 Suffolk 3-3/4 miles sw Stow
Market pop 73 archd Sudbury dioc Norwich
FINCHAM parish 1541 Norfolk 5 miles ne Downham Market pop 756
archd Norfolk dioc Norwich Wesl Meth
FINCHAMPSTEAD parish 1653 Berks 3-3/4 miles sw Wokingham pop
575 archd Berks dioc Salisbury
FINCHINGFIELD parish 1617 Essex 5-1/2 miles ne Thaxted pop
2,101 archd Middlesex dioc London Indep
FINCHLEY parish 1560 Middlesex 7 miles nw London pop 3,210
archd Middlesex dioc London Indep, Wesl Meth
FINDERN chapelry 1558 parish Mickleover Derbys pop 410 Unit
FINDON parish 1566 Sussex 4 miles sw Steyning pop 544 archd and
dioc Chichester
FINEDON or THINGDON parish 1539 co Northampton 3-1/2 miles ne
Wellingborough pop 1,292 archd Northampton dioc Peterborough
Wesl Meth
FINESHADE parish no regs co Northampton 8 miles nw Oundle pop
68 a donative
FINGALL parish 1593 N R York 5 miles ne Middleham comp town-
ships Akebar, Burton, Constable, Fingall, Hang Hutton pop 460
archd Richmond dioc Chester
FINGEST parish 1607 Bucks 5-1/2 miles nw Great Marlow pop 340
archd Buckingham dioc Lincoln
FINGLAND township parish Bowness Cumberland pop 194
FINGRINGHOE parish 1653 Essex 4-1/4 miles se Colchester pop 542
archd Colchester dioc London
FINMERE parish 1566 co Oxford 8 miles ne Bicester pop 373 archd
and dioc Oxford
FINNINGHAM parish 1560 Suffolk 6-1/4 miles sw Eye pop 497 archd
Sudbury dioc Norwich

FINNINGLEY parish 1557 W R York 4 miles ne Bawtry comp township Aukley Notts and Blaxton pop 962 archd Nottingham dioc York

FINSTHWAITE chapelry 1725 parish Coulton Lancs archd Richmond dioc Chester

FINSTOCK hamlet parish Charlbury co Oxford pop 519

FIRBANK chapelry 1746 parish Kirby Lonsdale Westm pop 190

FIRBECK parish 1721 W R York 4-1/2 miles sw Tickhill pop 178 archd and dioc York pec of Chancellor in Cathedral Church of York

FIRBY township parish Westow E R York pop 38

FIRBY township parish Bedale N R York

FIRLE, WEST parish 1668 Sussex 4-3/4 miles se Lewes pop 618 archd Lewes dioc Chichester

FIRSBY parish 1717 Lincs 5 miles se Spilsby pop 142 archd and dioc Lincoln

FIRSBY, EAST parish 1717 Lincs 6-1/2 miles sw Market Rasen pop 29 archd Stow dioc Lincoln

FIRSBY, WEST township parish East Firsby Lincs pop 30

FISHBOURN, NEW parish 1589 Sussex 1-1/4 miles w Chichester pop 291 pec Dean of Chichester

FISHBOURN, OLD hamlet parish New Fishbourn Sussex

FISHBURN township parish Sedgefield co Durham pop 212 Wesl Meth

FISHERTON ANGER parish 1653 Wilts near Salisbury pop 1,496 archd and dioc Salisbury Bapt, Wesl Meth

FISHERTON DE LA MERE parish 1561 Wilts 10 miles sw Amesbury pop 309 archd and dioc Salisbury

FISHERWICK township parish St Michael Lichfield Staffs pop 96

FISHLAKE parish 1561 W R York 4-1/2 miles w Thorne comp chapelry Sykehouse pop 1,334 archd and dioc York

FISHLEY parish Norfolk 3/4 mile n Acle archd and dioc Norwich

FISHTOFT parish 1696 Lincs 3 miles se Boston pop 463 archd and dioc Lincoln

FISHWICK township parish Preston Lancs pop 759

FISHERTON parish 1539 Lincs 4-1/2 miles e Lincoln pop 330 archd Stow dioc Lincoln

FISHERTON chapelry parish Rolleston Notts pop 314 Wesl Meth

FITLING township parish Humbleton E R York pop 103

FITTLETON parish 1623 Wilts 8-1/4 miles sw Ludgershall pop 331 archd and dioc Salisbury

FITTLEWORTH parish 1559 Sussex 3-1/4 miles se Petworth pop 668 archd and dioc Chichester

FITZ parish 1559 Shrops 5-1/2 miles nw Shrewsbury pop 211 archd Salop dioc Lichfield

FITZHEAD parish 1558 Somerset 2-3/4 miles ne Wiveliscombe pop 311 pec Prebendary of Wiveliscombe in Cathedral Church of Wells

FIVEHEAD parish 1654 Somerset 5 miles sw Langport pop 387 archd

Taunton dioc Bath and Wells

FIXBY township parish Halifax W R York pop 348

FLADBURY parish 1560 Worcs 4 miles e Pershore comp chapelries
Stock with Bradley, Throckmorton and Wyre Piddle, township Hill
with Moor, hamlet Hob Lench pop 1,407 pec of the rector

FLAGG township parish Bakewell Derbys pop 232

FLAMBOROUGH parish 1564 E R York 4 miles ne Bridlington pop
975 archd East Riding dioc York Prim and Wesl Meth

FLAMSTEAD parish 1548 Herts 2-3/4 miles nw Redbourn pop 1,462
archd Huntingdon dioc Lincoln

FLASBY township parish Gargrave W R York pop 143

FLASHBROOK township parish Abdaston Staffs pop 99

FLAT HOLMES island parish Uphill Somerset

FLAUNDEN chapelry 1729 parish Hemel Hempstead Herts pop 316

FLAVEL FLYFORD Worcs See FLYFORD FLAVEL

FLAWBOROUGH chapelry 1680 parishes Orston and Staunton Notts
pop 80

FLAWITH township parish Alne N R York pop 94

FLAX BOURTON Somerset See BOURTON FLAX

FLAXBY township parish Goldsborough W R York pop 96

FLAXLEY parish 1648 Gloucs 3 miles ne Newnham pop 186 archd
Hereford dioc Gloucester

FLAXTON ON THE MOOR township parish Bossall N R York pop
355 Wesl Meth

FLECKNEY parish 1637 Leics 7-1/4 miles nw Market Harborough
pop 514 archd Leicester dioc Lincoln

FLEDBOROUGH parish 1562 Notts 5-1/4 miles ne Tuxford pop 86
archd Nottingham dioc York

FLEET parish 1663 Dorset 4 miles nw Weymouth pop 122 archd
Dorset dioc Bristol

FLEET parish 1652 Lincs 2 miles se Holbeach pop 794 archd and
dioc Lincoln

FLEETHAM township parish Bambrough Northumberland pop 93

FLEMPTON parish 1561 Suffolk 4-3/4 miles nw Bury St Edmund's
pop 188 archd Sudbury dioc Norwich

FLETCHING parish 1554 Sussex 3-3/4 miles nw Uckfield pop 1,870
archd Lewes dioc Chichester

FLETTON parish 1616 Hunts 1 mile se Peterborough pop 189 archd
Huntingdon dioc Lincoln

FLIMBY parish 1696 Cumberland 2-1/2 miles sw Maryport pop 404
archd and dioc Carlisle

FLINTHAM parish 1576 Notts 6-1/2 miles sw Newark pop 545 archd
Nottingham dioc York Wesl Meth

FLINTON township parish Humbleton E R York pop 126

FLITCHAM parish 1754 Norfolk 4-3/4 miles ne Castle Rising pop
323 archd and dioc Norwich

FLITTON parish 1581 Beds 1-1/2 miles w Silsoe pop 1,184 archd
Bedford dioc Lincoln

FLITWICK parish 1661 Beds 2-3/4 miles sw Ampthill pop 636 archd
Bedford dioc Lincoln
FLIXBOROUGH parish 1660 Lincs 11 miles nw Glandford Bridge pop
210 archd Stow dioc Lincoln
FLIXTON parish 1570 Lancs 7 miles nw Manchester comp townships
Flixton, Urmston pop 2,099 archd and dioc Chester pec Prebend-
ary of Flixton Wesl Meth
FLIXTON parish 1544 Suffolk 3 miles nw Lowestoft pop 39 archd
Suffolk dioc Norwich
FLIXTON parish Suffolk 3 miles sw Bungay pop 206 archd Suffolk
dioc Norwich
FLIXTON township parish Folkton E R York pop 251
FLOCKTON chapelry 1716 parish Thornhill W R York pop 995 archd
and dioc York Indep
FLOOKBOROUGH chapelry parish Cartmell Lancs
FLOORE parish 1652 co Northampton 7-1/4 miles w Northampton
pop 955 archd Northampton dioc Peterborough
FLORDON parish 1558 Norfolk 3-1/4 miles nw St Mary Stratton pop
164 archd Norfolk dioc Norwich
FLOTTERTON township parish Rothbury Northumberland pop 95
FLOWTON parish 1572 Suffolk 5-3/4 miles nw Ipswich pop 185 archd
Suffolk dioc Norwich
FLUSHING sea port parish Mylor Cornwall Bapt, Bryanites, Wesl
Meth, Unit
FLYFORD FLAVEL parish 1679 Worcs 8-3/4 miles se Worcester
pop 154 archd and dioc Worcester
FLYFORD GRAFTON parish 1676 Worcs 8 miles e Worcester pop
242 archd and dioc Worcester
FOBBING parish 1539 Essex 3-1/2 miles e Horndon on the Hill pop
391 archd Essex dioc London
FOCKERBY township parish Adlingfleet W R York pop 103
FOGGATHORPE township parish Bubwith E R York pop 128 Wesl
Meth
FOLESHILL parish 1564 Warws 2-1/2 miles ne Coventry pop 6,969
archd Coventry dioc Lichfield Indep, Wesl Meth
FOLKE parish 1538 Dorset 3-1/4 miles se Sherborne pop 281 pec of
Dean of Salisbury
FOLKESTONE parish 1635 Kent 37-1/4 miles se Maidstone pop 4,296
sep juris archd and dioc Canterbury Bapt, Soc of Friends, Wesl
Meth
FOLKINGHAM parish 1583 Lincs See FALKINGHAM
FOLKINGTON parish 1560 Sussex 4-1/2 miles sw Hailsham pop 168
archd Lewes dioc Chichester
FOLKSWORTH parish 1563 Hunts 1-1/2 miles nw Stilton pop 185
archd Huntingdon dioc Lincoln
FOLKTON parish 1665 E R York 6 miles se Scarborough comp town-
ships Flixton and Folkton pop 455 archd East Riding dioc York
FOLLYFOOT township parish Spofforth W R York pop 327 Wesl Meth

FONTHILL, BISHOP'S parish 1754 Wilts 1-1/2 miles ne Hindon pop
211 archd and dioc Salisbury
FONTHILL, GIFFORD parish 1664 Wilts 1-3/4 miles se Hindon pop
442 archd and dioc Salisbury
FONTMELL, MAGNA parish 1653 Dorset 4-1/4 miles s Shaftesbury
pop 743 archd Dorset dioc Bristol Wesl Meth
FOOLOW township parish Eyam Derbys pop 248 Wesl Meth
FOOTHOG township parish Cwmyoy Herefs pop 127
FOOT'S CRAY Kent See CRAY, FOOTS
FORCETT parish 1596 N R York 7 miles ne Richmond comp town-
ships Barforth, Carkin, Forcett, Ovington pop 430 archd Richmond
dioc Chester
FORD hamlet parish Dinton Bucks
FORD township parish Bidstone Ches
FORD hamlet parish North Wingfield Derbys
FORD Hamps See FORDINGBRIDGE
FORD chapelry parish Bishop Wearmouth co Durham pop 911
FORD township parish Sephton Lancs
FORD parish 1683 Northumberland 9 miles sw Wooler pop 2,110
archd Northumberland dioc Durham Bapt, Presb
FORD parish 1589 Shrops 4-3/4 miles nw Shrewsbury pop 263 archd
Salop dioc Hereford
FORD parish 1627 Sussex 5-1/2 miles sw Arundel pop 81 archd and
dioc Chichester
FORD tything parish Idmiston Wilts pop 48
FORDHALL hamlet parish Wootton Waven Warws
FORDHAM parish 1567 Cambs 5-1/2 miles n Newmarket pop 1,326
archd Sudbury dioc Norwich Indep
FORDHAM parish 1561 Essex 6 miles nw Colchester pop 727 archd
Colchester dioc London
FORDHAM parish 1576 Norfolk 2-1/2 miles s Downham Market pop
133 archd Norfolk dioc Norwich
FORDINGBRIDGE parish 1642 Hamps 20 miles nw Southampton pop
2,611 archd and dioc Winchester Indep, Soc of Friends
FORDINGTON parish 1705 Dorset pop 2,030 pec Dean of Salisbury
FORDINGTON incl regs of Ulceby Lincs
FORDLEY formerly parish now with Middleton 1653 Suffolk 3-3/4
miles ne Saxmundham archd Suffolk dioc Norwich
FORDON chapelry parish Hunmanby E R York
FORDSBRIDGE indep chapelry 1742 Herefs pop 33 archd and dioc
Hereford
FORDWICH parish 1683 Kent 2 miles ne Canterbury pop 287 archd
and dioc Canterbury
FOREBRIDGE township parish Castle Church Staffs
FOREMARK parish 1662 Derbys 6-1/2 miles sw Derby pop 221 archd
Derby dioc Lichfield
FOREST Ches See MACCLESFIELD FOREST
FOREST township parish Middleton in Teesdale co Durhăm comp

Ettersgill, Middle Forest, Harwood pop 760

FOREST HILL parish 1564 co Oxford 5 miles ne Oxford pop 142 archd and dioc Oxford

FOREST QUARTER township parish Stanhope co Durham pop 4,741

FORMBY chapelry 1711 parish Walton on the Hill Lancs pop 1,312

FORNCETT St Mary parish 1561 Norfolk 3 miles nw St Mary Stratton pop 288 archd Norfolk dioc Norwich

FORNCETT St Peter parish Norfolk 2-3/4 miles nw St Mary Stratton pop 727 archd Norfolk dioc Norwich

FORNHAM parish 1558 Suffolk 2-1/4 miles nw Bury St Edmund's pop 310 archd Sudbury dioc Norwich

FORNHAM St Geneveve parish Suffolk 4-1/4 miles nw Bury St Edmund's pop 73 archd Sudbury dioc Norwich

FORNHAM St Martin parish 1539 Suffolk 2 miles n Bury St Edmund's pop 276 archd Sudbury dioc Norwich

FORRABURY parish 1710 Cornwall 5 miles nw Camelford pop 358 archd Cornwall dioc Exeter

FORSBROOK township parish Dilhorne Staffs pop 754

FORSCOTE parish 1691 Somerset 7-1/2 miles sw Bath pop 102 archd Wells dioc Bath and Wells

FORSTER'S BOOTH hamlet in parishes Cold Higham and Pattishall co Northampton

FORTHAMPTON parish 1678 Gloucs 2-1/2 miles w Tewkesbury pop 459

FORTON township parish Garstang Lancs pop 662 Indep

FORTON tything parish Chard Somerset

FORTON parish 1558 Staffs 1-1/2 miles ne Newport pop 904 archd Stafford dioc Lichfield

FOSDYKE parish 1558 Lincs 6 miles nw Holbeach pop 401 archd and dioc Lincoln

FOSTON township parish Scropton Derbys

FOSTON parish 1653 Leics 6-3/4 miles se Leicester pop 32 archd Leicester dioc Lincoln

FOSTON parish 1560 Lincs 5-3/4 miles nw Grantham pop 441 archd and dioc Lincoln

FOSTON parish 1587 N R York 11-1/4 miles ne York comp townships Foston, Thornton upon Clay pop 283 archd Cleveland dioc York

FOSTON UPON THE WOLDS parish 1653 E R York 6-1/2 miles se Great Driffield comp townships Brigham, Foston upon the Wolds, Gembling, Great Kelk pop 715 archd East Riding dioc York Wesl Meth, Calvinistic dissenters

FOTHERBY parish 1568 Lincs 3-1/4 miles nw Louth pop 207 archd and dioc Lincoln

FOTHERINGAY parish 1557 co Northampton 3-1/2 miles ne Oundle pop 280 archd Northampton dioc Peterborough

FOTHERLEY, HIGH township parish Bywell St Peter Northumberland pop 105

FOULBY hamlet parish Wragby W R York

FOULDEN parish 1538 Norfolk 5 miles se Stoke Ferry pop 500 archd
   Norfolk dioc Norwich
FOULK STAPLEFORD Ches See STAPLEFORD, FOULK
FOULMIRE parish 1561 Cambs 5-1/2 miles ne Royston pop 547
   archd and dioc Ely
FOULNESS parish 1695 Essex 9 miles ne Rochford pop 630 court of
   Commissary of Essex and Herts, concurrently with Consistorial
   Court of the Bishop of London
FOULNEY island parish Dalton in Furness Lancs
FOULRIDGE township parish Whalley Lancs pop 1,418
FOULSHAM parish 1746 Norfolk 18 miles nw Norwich pop 958 archd
   Norfolk dioc Norwich Bapt
FOULSTON township parish Kirk Burton W R York pop 1,573
FOULTON hamlet parish Ramsey Essex
FOUNTAIN'S EARTH township parish Kirkby Malzeard W R York
   pop 413
FOVANT parish 1541 Wilts 7 miles sw Wilton pop 553 archd and
   dioc Salisbury
FOWBERRY township parish Chatton Northumberland
FOWEY parish 1543 borough Cornwall 29 miles sw Launceston pop
   1,767 archd Cornwall dioc Exeter Wesl Meth, Indep
FOWNHOPE parish 1538 Herefs 7 miles se Hereford pop 1,006
   archd and dioc Hereford
FOXCOTE chapelry parish Andover Hamps pop 95
FOXCOTT parish 1664 Bucks 2 miles ne Buckingham pop 107 archd
   Buckingham dioc Lincoln
FOXEARTH parish 1551 Essex 3-1/2 miles nw Sudbury pop 466
   archd Middlesex dioc London
FOXHALL parish no regs Suffolk 4-1/4 miles se Ipswich pop 190
   archd Suffolk dioc Norwich
FOXHAM chapelry parish Bremhill Wilts
FOXHOLES parish 1654 E R York 10-1/2 miles nw Great Driffield
   comp chapelry Butterwick, township Foxholes with Bouthorp pop
   277 archd East Riding dioc York Wesl Meth
FOXLEY parish 1700 Norfolk 2 miles se Foulsham pop 274 archd
   Norfolk dioc Norwich
FOXLEY parish 1713 Wilts 2-1/2 miles sw Malmesbury pop 67
   archd Wilts dioc Salisbury
FOXT township parish Ipstones Staffs
FOXTON parish 1678 Cambs 6 miles sw Cambridge pop 408 archd
   and dioc Ely
FOXTON township parish Sedgefield co Durham pop 73
FOXTON parish 1690 Leics 3 miles nw Market Harborough pop 346
   archd Leicester dioc Lincoln Part Bapt
FOY parish 1570 Herefs 3-3/4 miles n Ross pop 290 archd and dioc
   Hereford
FRADLEY hamlet parish Alrewas Staffs pop 382
FRADSWELL chapelry 1578 parish Colwich Staffs pop 199 pec Pre-

bendary of Colwich

FRAISTHORP parish E R York 4-3/4 miles sw Bridlington pop 103 archd East Riding dioc York

FRAMCOTE chapelry parish Lower or Power Guiting Gloucs

FRAMFIELD parish 1538 Sussex 1-1/2 miles se Uckfield pop 1,468 pec of Archbishop of Canterbury

FRAMINGHAM, EARL parish 1721 Norfolk 5 miles se Norwich pop 74 archd Norfolk dioc Norwich

FRAMINGHAM, PIGOT parish 1555 Norfolk 5-1/2 miles se Norwich pop 302 archd Norfolk dioc Norwich

FRAMLINGHAM parish 1560 Suffolk 18 miles ne Ipswich pop 2,445 archd Suffolk dioc Norwich Indep, Wesl Meth, Unit

FRAMLINGTON, LONG parish 1653 Northumberland 11 miles nw Morpeth comp townships Brinkburn High, Brinkburn Low, Long Framlington pop 735 archd Northumberland dioc Durham Presb

FRAMPTON parish 1654 Dorset 5-3/4 miles nw Dorchester pop 376 archd Dorset dioc Bristol

FRAMPTON tything parish Sapperton Gloucs pop 178

FRAMPTON parish 1538 Lincs 3-1/4 miles s Boston pop 706 archd and dioc Lincoln

FRAMPTON COTTERELL parish 1561 Gloucs 8 miles ne Bristol pop 1,816 archd and dioc Gloucester Indep, Wesl Meth

FRAMPTON UPON SEVERN parish 1625 Gloucs 8 miles nw Stroud pop 1,055 archd and dioc Gloucester Indep

FRAMSDEN parish 1575 Suffolk 4 miles se Debenham pop 642 archd Suffolk dioc Norwich

FRANKBY township parish West Kirby Ches pop 114

FRANKLEY chapelry 1598 parish Hagley Worcs 3-3/4 miles se Hales Owen pop 176

FRANKTON parish 1559 Warws 4-1/2 miles sw Dunchurch pop 261 archd Coventry dioc Lichfield

FRANSHAM, GREAT parish 1560 Norfolk 6-1/4 miles ne Swaffham pop 323 archd and dioc Norwich

FRANSHAM, LITTLE parish 1538 Norfolk 5-3/4 miles ne Swaffham pop 234 archd and dioc Norwich

FRANT parish 1544 Sussex 2 miles se Tonbridge Wells pop 2,071 archd Lewes dioc Chichester

FRATING parish 1560 Essex 6 miles se Colchester pop 269 archd Colchester dioc London

FRECKENHAM parish 1550 Suffolk 3-1/4 miles sw Mildenhall pop 427 pec of Bishop of Rochester

FRECKLETON township parish Kirkham Lancs pop 909 Indep

FREEBY chapelry 1604 parish Melton Mowbray Leics pop 120 Indep

FREEFOLK chapelry parish Whitchurch Hamps pop 73

FREEFORD hamlet parish St Michael, Lichfield Staffs pop 17

FREEHOLDERS' QUARTER township parish Longhorsley Northumberland pop 127

FREETHORPE parish 1755 Norfolk 4 miles s Acle pop 289 archd and dioc Norwich

FREMINGTON parish 1602 Devon 3 miles sw Barnstaple pop 1,180 archd Barnstaple dioc Exeter

FRENCH MOOR tything parish Broughton Hamps

FRENSHAM parish 1649 Surrey 4 miles s Farnham comp tything Dockingfield Hamps pop 1,388 archd Surrey dioc Winchester

FRENZE or THORPE, PARVA parish 1651 Norfolk 1-1/4 miles ne Diss pop 50 archd Norfolk dioc Norwich

FRESDON tything parish Highworth Wilts pop 21

FRESHFORD parish 1705 Somerset 4-3/4 miles se Bath pop 666 archd Bath dioc Bath and Wells Wesl Meth

FRESHWATER parish 1576 Hamps 1-3/4 miles sw Yarmouth pop 1,184 archd and dioc Winchester Wesl Meth

FRESSINGFIELD parish 1554 Suffolk 7-1/4 miles ne Eye pop 1,352 archd Suffolk dioc Norwich

FRESTON parish 1538 Suffolk 3-1/2 miles s Ipswich pop 183 archd Suffolk dioc Norwich

FRETHERNE parish 1631 Gloucs 9-1/2 miles nw Stroud pop 224 archd and dioc Gloucester

FRETTENHAM parish 1558 Norfolk 2-1/4 miles sw Coltishall pop 269 archd and dioc Norwich

FRICKLEY parish 1577 W R York 10-1/2 miles ne Barnsley pop 321 archd and dioc York

FRIDAYTHORPE parish 1687 E R York 9 miles ne Pocklington pop 283 pec Prebendary of Wetwang Wesl Meth

FRIERMERE chapelry 1769 parish Rochdale Lancs

FRIERING Essex See FRYERNING

FRIESDEN hamlet parish Piglesthorne Bucks

FRIESTHORPE parish 1620 Lincs 5-3/4 miles sw Market Rasen pop 46 pec Dean and Chapter of Lincoln

FRIESTON parish 1657 Lincs 3-1/4 miles e Boston pop 1,089 archd and dioc Lincoln Wesl Meth

FRILFORD chapelry parish Marcham Berks pop 129

FRILSHAM parish 1711 Berks 6-1/4 miles se East Ilsley pop 192 archd Berks dioc Salisbury

FRIMLEY chapelry 1590 parish Ash Surrey pop 1,351

FRINDSBURY parish 1669 Kent 2 miles nw Rochester pop 1,826 archd and dioc Rochester Wesl Meth

FRING parish 1671 Norfolk 8 miles sw Burnham Westgate pop 127 archd Norfolk dioc Norwich

FRINGFORD parish 1586 co Oxford 3-1/4 miles ne Bicester pop 358 archd and dioc Oxford

FRINSTED parish 1714 Kent 4-1/2 miles sw Sittingbourne pop 183 archd and dioc Canterbury

FRINTON parish 1754 Essex 13 miles se Manningtree pop 35 archd Colchester dioc London

FRISBY chapelry parish Gaulby Leics pop 21

FRISBY ON THE WREAK parish 1659 Leics 4-1/2 miles sw Melton

Mowbray pop 442 archd Leicester dioc Lincoln Wesl Meth

FRISKNEY parish 1558 Lincs 4 miles sw Wainfleet pop 1,457 archd and dioc Lincoln Wesl Meth

FRISTON parish 1543 Suffolk 3 miles se Saxmundham pop 466 archd Suffolk dioc Norwich

FRISTON parish 1546 Sussex 3 miles sw East Bourne pop 89 archd Lewes dioc Chichester

FRITH township parish Wrenbury Ches

FRITHAM tything parish Bramshaw Hamps

FRITHELSTOCK parish 1556 Devon 2 miles w Great Torrington pop 696 archd Barnstaple dioc Exeter

FRITH VILLE extra parochial liberty Lincs pop 261 attend Carrington

FRITTENDEN parish 1558 Kent 4-1/4 miles ne Cranbrooke pop 816 archd and dioc Canterbury

FRITTON parish 1558 Norfolk 2-1/2 miles ne St Mary Stratton pop 243 archd Norfolk dioc Norwich

FRITTON parish 1706 Suffolk 7-1/4 miles nw Lowestoft pop 170 archd Suffolk dioc Norwich

FRITWELL parish 1558 co Oxford 5 miles nw Bicester pop 494 archd and dioc Oxford

FRIZINGTON, HIGH and LOW township parish Arlecdon Cumberland

FROBURY tything parish Kingsclere Hamps

FROCESTER parish 1559 Gloucs 5-1/2 miles sw Stroud pop 414 archd and dioc Gloucester

FRODESLEY parish 1547 Shrops 8-3/4 miles nw Much Wenlock pop 186 archd Salop dioc Lichfield

FRODINGHAM parish 1638 Lincs 8-1/2 miles nw Glandford Bridge comp townships Bromby and Scunthorpe pop 425 archd Stow dioc Lincoln

FRODINGHAM, NORTH parish 1559 E R York 5-1/2 miles se Great Driffield pop 711 archd East Riding dioc York Indep, Prim and Wesl Meth

FRODINGHAM, SOUTH township parish Owthorne E R York pop 60

FRODSHAM parish 1558 Ches 10 miles ne Chester comp market town Frodsham, chapelry Alvanley, lordship Frodsham, townships Helsby, Kingsley, Manley, Newton, Norley pop 5,547 archd and dioc Chester Wesl Meth

FROGGATT township parish Bakewell Derbys pop 167

FROG STREET township parish Presteign Herefs

FROME SELWOOD or FROME parish 1558 Somerset 25 miles ne Ilchester pop 12,240 archd Wells dioc Bath and Wells Bapt, Soc of Friends, Indep, Wesl Meth, Presb

FROMEHAMPTON township parish Marden Herefs

FROME, BISHOP'S parish 1564 Herefs 4-1/2 miles se Bromyard comp townships Bishop's Frome, Eggleston, Halmonds Froome, Leadon, Walton pop 948 archd and dioc Hereford

FROOME, CANON parish 1680 Herefs 6 miles nw Ledbury pop 98

archd and dioc Hereford

FROOME, CASTLE parish 1678 Herefs 7 miles nw Ledbury pop 223 archd and dioc Hereford

FROOME, HALMONDS township parish Bishop's Froome Herefs pop 368

FROOME, ST QUINTIN parish 1653 Dorset 9-1/2 miles ne Beaminster pop 143 archd Dorset dioc Bristol

FROOME VAUCHURCH parish 1642 Dorset 7-1/2 miles nw Dorchester pop 135 archd Dorset dioc Bristol

FROSTENDEN parish 1538 Suffolk 4-3/4 miles nw Southwold pop 273 archd Suffolk dioc Norwich

FROSTERLEY hamlet parish Stanhope co Durham Wesl Meth

FROWLESWORTH parish 1538 Leics 4-3/4 miles nw Lutterworth pop 278 archd Leicester dioc Lincoln

FROXFIELD chapelry 1545 parish East Meon Hamps pop 618

FROXFIELD parish 1561 Wilts 3-1/4 miles sw Hungerford pop 581 archd Wilts dioc Salisbury

FROYLE parish 1697 Hamps 3-3/4 miles ne Alton pop 777 archd and dioc Winchester

FRYERN BARNET Middlesex See BARNET, FRYERN

FRYERNING parish 1595 Essex 1 mile nw Ingatestone pop 670 archd Essex dioc London

FRYSTONE, FERRY parish 1674 W R York 3/4 mile nw Ferry Bridge pop 833 pec of Dean and Chapter of York

FRYSTONE, MONK parish 1538 W R York 4 miles ne Ferry Bridge comp townships Burton Salmon, Hillam, Monk Frystone pop 863 archd and dioc York

FRYTON township parish Hovingham N R York pop 60

FUGGLESTONE parish 1568 Wilts 3/4 mile e Wilton pop 515 archd Wilts dioc Salisbury

FULBECK parish 1563 Lincs 10-1/4 miles ne Grantham pop 650 archd and dioc Lincoln

FULBOURN parish 1538 Cambs 5 miles se Cambridge pop 1,207 archd and dioc Ely Indep

FULBROOK hamlet parish Hogshaw Bucks

FULBROOK parish 1615 co Oxford 3/4 mile ne Burford pop 361 archd and dioc Oxford

FULBROOK parish no regs Warws 4 miles ne Stratford upon Avon pop 77 archd and dioc Worcester

FULFORD tything in parishes Cheriton Fitzpaine and Shoebrook and Crediton Devon

FULFORD chapelry 1800 parish Stone Staffs

FULFORD AMBO parish 1653 W R York 1-1/2 miles s York comp townships Fulford Gate, Fulford Water pop 934 archd and dioc York Wesl Meth

FULFORD WATER township parish Fulford Ambo E R York pop 29

FULHAM parish 1674 Middlesex 4 miles sw London pop 17,537 archd Middlesex dioc London Indep

FULKING hamlet parish Edburton Essex pop 166

FULLAWAY tything parish Allcannings Wilts pop 6

FULLETBY parish 1750 Lincs 3-1/2 miles ne Horncastle pop 250 archd and dioc Lincoln

FULMER parish 1688 Bucks 4-1/2 miles se Beaconfield pop 391 archd Buckingham dioc Lincoln

FULMODESTON parish 1555 Norfolk 5 miles e Fakenham pop 391 archd Norfolk dioc Norwich

FULNECK hamlet parish Calverley W R York Moravians

FULNETBY chapelry parish Rand Lincs pop 53

FULSHAW township parish Wilmslow Ches pop 291

FULSTOW parish 1589 Lincs 7-1/4 miles n Louth pop 448 archd and dioc Lincoln Wesl Meth

FULWELL township parish Monk Wearmouth co Durham pop 158

FULWOOD township parish Lancaster Lancs pop 500

FULWOOD extra parochial liberty Notts 4-1/2 miles sw Mansfield pop 12

FUNDENHALL parish 1559 Norfolk 5 miles nw St Mary Stratton pop 394 archd Norfolk dioc Norwich

FUNTINGTON parish 1564 Sussex 5 miles nw Chichester pop 969 archd and dioc Chichester

FURLAND tything parish Crewkerne Somerset

FURNESS ABBEY Lancs See DALTON IN FURNESS

FURTHO parish 1696 co Northampton 2 miles nw Stony Stratford pop 16 archd Northampton dioc Peterborough

FYFIELD parish 1587 Berks 4-1/2 miles nw Abingdon pop 403 archd Berks dioc Salisbury

FYFIELD parish 1538 Essex 2-3/4 miles ne Chipping Ongar pop 572 archd Essex dioc London

FYFIELD parish 1628 Hamps 4-3/4 miles nw Andover pop 211 archd and dioc Winchester

FYFIELD tything parish Endford Wilts pop 157

FYFIELD chapelry 1732 parish Overton Wilts

FYLINGDALES parish 1653 N R York 4-1/2 miles se Whitby pop 5,135 archd Cleveland dioc York

FYLTON, Gloucs See FILTON

GADDESBY chapelry 1698 parish Rothley Leics pop 276

GADDESDEN, GREAT parish 1558 Herts 2-1/2 miles nw Hemel Hemstead pop 988 archd Huntingdon dioc Lincoln

GADDESDEN, LITTLE parish 1681 Herts 5-3/4 miles ne Berkhamstead pop 492 archd Huntingdon dioc Lincoln

GAGINWELL hamlet parish Church Enstone co Oxford

GAINFORD parish 1560 co Durham 7-3/4 miles nw Darlington comp chapelry Denton, townships Houghton Lee Side, chapelries Barnard Castle and Whorlton, townships Bolam, Gainford, Headlam, Langton, Marwood, Morton, Tynemouth, Pierse Bridge, Staunton with Steatlam Summerhouse, Westwick and part of Cleatlam pop 7,430 archd and dioc Durham Wesl Meth

GAINSBOROUGH parish 1564 Lincs 18-1/4 miles nw Lincoln comp town Gainsborough, hamlets Morton, East Stockwith, Thorrock and Walkerith pop 7,535 archd Stowe dioc Lincoln Bapt, Soc of Friends, Indep, Prim and Wesl Meth, Presb

GALBY Leics See GAULBY

GALHAMPTON hamlet parish North Cadbury Somerset

GALLOW HILL township parish Bolam Northumberland pop 33

GALTON tything parish Owermoigne Dorset

GAMBLESBY township parish Addingham Cumberland pop 301 Wesl Meth, Indep

GAMELSBY township parish Aikton Cumberland Wesl Meth

GAMLINGAY parish 1698 Cambs 2-1/4 miles ne Potton pop 1,319 archd and dioc Ely Bapt

GAMPSTON hamlet parish West Bridgford Notts pop 107

GAMSTON parish 1544 Notts 3-1/2 miles s East Retford pop 306 archd Nottingham dioc York

GANAREW parish 1635 Herefs 3 miles ne Monmouth pop 148 archd and dioc Hereford Wesl Meth

GANSTEAD township parish Swine E R York pop 79

GANTHORPE township parish Terrington N R York pop 110

GANTON parish 1553 E R York 9-1/4 miles sw Scarborough pop 275 archd East Riding dioc York

GARBOLDISHAM parish 1609 Norfolk 4-1/4 miles se East Harling pop 718 archd Norfolk dioc Norwich

GARENDON extra parochial liberty 2 miles sw Loughboro Leics pop 51

GARFORD chapelry parish Marcham Berks pop 209

GARFORTH, WEST parish 1663 W R York 7 miles e Leeds pop 782 archd and dioc York Indep, Wesl Meth

GARGRAVE parish 1558 W R York 4-1/2 miles nw Skipton comp townships Bank Newton, Cold Coniston, Eshton, Flasby with Winterburn and Gargrave pop 1,748 archd and dioc York Wesl Meth

GARMONDSWAY MOOR township parish Bishop's Middleham co Durham pop 43

GARRETT hamlet parish Wandsworth Surrey

GARRIGILL chapelry 1699 parish Alston Cumberland pop 1,614 Indep, Prim and Wesl Meth

GARRISON SIDE extra parochial Kinston upon Hill E R York pop 366

GARRISON township parish Haukeswell N R York pop 60

GARSDALE chapelry 1608 parish Sedbergh W R York pop 657 archd Richmond dioc Chester

GARSDON parish 1737 Wilts 2 miles ne Malmesbury pop 234 archd Wilts dioc Salisbury

GARSINGTON parish 1562 co Oxford 5 miles se Oxford pop 597 archd and dioc Oxford

GARSTANG parish 1567 Lancs 11 miles se Lancaster comp town Garstang, townships Barnacre with Bonds, Billisborrow, Cabus, Catteral, Claughton, Forton, Kirkland, Nateby, Winmarleighm

Nether Wyersdale, part of Cleverly, hamlet Holleth pop 6,927 archd Richmond dioc Chester Indep, Wesl Meth, Roman Cath

GARSTON chapelry 1777 parish Childwall Lancs pop 1,147 archd and dioc Chester

GARSTON, EAST parish 1554 Berks 2-3/4 miles se Lambourn pop 699 archd Berks dioc Salisbury Wesl Meth

GARTHORP township parish Luddington Lincs pop 454

GARTHORPE parish 1568 Leics 5-3/4 miles ne Melton Mowbray pop 117 archd Leicester dioc Lincoln

GARTON IN HOLDERNESS parish 1593 E R York 12 miles ne Kingston upon Hull pop 297 archd East Riding dioc York Wesl Meth

GARTON UPON THE WOLDS parish 1653 E R York 3 miles nw Great Driffield pop 428 archd East Riding dioc York Wesl Meth

GARVESTONE parish 1538 Norfolk 5 miles se East Dereham pop 333 archd and dioc Norwich

GARWAY parish 1664 Herefs 7 miles nw Monmouth pop 513 archd and dioc Hereford Bapt

GASPER Somerset See BROOK

GASTHORPE parish Incl regs of Riddlesworth Norfolk 4-1/2 miles s East Harling pop 112 archd Norfolk dioc Norwich

GATCOMB parish 1560 Isle of Wight Hamps 3-3/4 miles sw Newport pop 263 archd and dioc Winchester

GATCOMBE hamlet parish Colyton Devon

GATEFORTH township parish Brayton W R York pop 223

GATELEY parish 1682 Norfolk 5-1/2 miles se Fakenham pop 120 archd and dioc Norwich

GATENBY township parish Burneston N R York pop 69

GATESGILL township parish Dalston Cumberland

GATESHEAD parish 1559 co Durham 1 mile se Newcastle borough pop 15,177 archd and dioc Durham Wesl Meth, Meth of New Connection, Presb

GATESHEAD FELL parish 1824 co Durham 3 miles s Newcastle archd and dioc Durham Bapt, Wesl Meth

GATTON parish 1599 borough Surrey 22 miles ne Guildford pop 145 archd Surrey dioc Winchester

GAULBY parish 1583 Leics 8 miles se Leicester pop 118 archd Leicester dioc Lincoln

GAUTBY parish 1571 Lincs 6-1/2 miles nw Horncastle pop 109 archd and dioc Lincoln

GAWCOTT chapelry 1806 parish Buckingham Bucks

GAWSWORTH parish 1557 Ches 3-1/2 miles sw Macclesfield pop 847 archd and dioc Chester

GAYDON chapelry 1701 parish Bishop's Itchington Warws pop 213

GAYHURST parish 1728 Bucks 2-3/4 miles nw Newport Pagnell pop 118 archd Buckingham dioc Lincoln

GAYLES township parish Kirkby Ravensworth N R York pop 223

GAYTON township parish Heswall Ches pop 110

GAYTON parish 1702 Norfolk 7-1/4 miles e Lynn Regis pop 711

archd and dioc Norwich Wesl Meth

GAYTON parish 1558 co Northampton 4-1/4 miles ne Towcester pop 461 archd Northampton dioc Peterborough

GAYTON parish 1594 Staffs 6 miles ne Stafford pop 296 archd Stafford dioc Lichfield

GAYTON LE MARSH parish 1687 Lincs 5-3/4 miles nw Alford pop 306 archd and dioc Lincoln

GAYTON LE WOLD parish 1773 Lincs 6-1/4 miles sw Louth pop 127 archd and dioc Lincoln

GAYTON THORPE parish 1575 Norfolk 8 miles nw Swaffham pop 169 archd and dioc Norwich

GAYWOOD parish 1562 Norfolk 3/4 mile ne Lynn Regis pop 924 archd and dioc Norwich

GAZELEY parish 1539 Suffolk 5-1/4 miles ne Newmarket pop 737 archd Sudbury dioc Norwich

GEDDING parish 1543 Suffolk 6-3/4 miles w Stow Market pop 147 archd Sudbury dioc Norwich

GEDDINGTON parish 1680 co Northampton 3-1/2 miles ne Kettering pop 795 archd Northampton dioc Peterborough

GEDLING parish 1558 Notts 3-1/2 miles ne Nottingham pop 2,343 archd Nottingham dioc York

GEDNEY parish 1558 Lincs 3 miles e Holbeach pop 1,862 archd and dioc Lincoln

GEDNEY HILL chapelry 1693 parish Gedney Lincs pop 371 archd and dioc Lincoln

GELDESTONE parish 1657 Norfolk 2-1/4 miles nw Beccles pop 340 archd and dioc Norwich

GEMBLING township parish Foston upon Wolds E R York pop 78

GENNYS, ST parish 1702 Cornwall 10 miles ne Camelford pop 761 archd Cornwall dioc Exeter

GEORGEHAM parish 1538 Devon 8 miles nw Barnstaple pop 925 archd Barnstaple dioc Exeter

GERMANS, ST parish 1590 borough Cornwall 19 miles se Launceston pop 2,586 pec of Bishop of Exeter

GERMANS WEEK parish 1652 Devon 11 miles sw Oakhampton pop 370 archd Totnes dioc Exeter

GERMOE parish 1668 Cornwall 5-3/4 miles nw Helston pop 1,175 archd Cornwall dioc Exeter Wesl Meth

GERRANS parish 1538 Cornwall 7 miles sw Tregony pop 766 pec of Bishop of Exeter Indep, Wesl Meth

GESTINGTHORPE parish 1609 Essex 3 miles ne Castle Hedingham pop 801 Commissary of Essex and Herts, concurrently with Bishop of London

GIDDING, GREAT parish 1564 Hunts 5 miles sw Stilton pop 452 archd Huntingdon dioc Lincoln

GIDDING, LITTLE parish 1657 Hunts 5-3/4 miles sw Stilton pop 48 archd Huntingdon dioc Lincoln

GIDDING, STEEPLE parish 1571 Hunts 6 miles sw Stilton pop 86 archd Huntingdon dioc Lincoln

GIDLEY parish 1599 Devon 8-1/4 miles se Oakhampton pop 155 archd and dioc Exeter

GIFFORD FONTHILL Wilts See FONTHILL, GIFFORD

GIGGLESWICK parish 1558 W R York 3/4 mile nw Settle comp townships Giggleswick, Ratmill, Settle, Stainforth pop 3,017 archd and dioc York

GILBERDIKE township parish Eastrington E R York pop 632

GILBY hamlet parish Pilham Lincs

GILCRUX parish 1589 Cumberland 5-1/2 miles Cockermouth pop 382 archd and dioc Carlisle

GILDEN WELLS township parish Laughton en le Morthen W R York pop 81

GILDERSOME chapelry parish Batley W R York pop 1,652 Bapt, Wesl Meth

GILES, ST IN THE WOOD parish 1556 Devon 3 miles se Great Torrington pop 894 archd and dioc Exeter

GILES, ST ON THE HEATH parish 1653 Devon 4-1/2 miles ne Launceston pop 357 archd Cornwall dioc Exeter

GILL township parish Greystock Cumberland

GILLIMOOR township parish Kirby Moorside N R York pop 179 Wesl Meth

GILLING parish 1570 N R York 3 miles ne Richmond comp chapelries South Cowton and Eryholme, townships North Cowton, Eppleby and Gilling pop 1,704 archd Richmond dioc Chester Wesl Meth

GILLING, EAST parish 1639 N R York 5-1/4 miles s Helmsley comp townships Cawton, Gilling and Grimston pop 371 archd Cleveland dioc York

GILLINGHAM parish 1559 Dorset 4 miles nw Shaftesbury pop 3,330 pec of the Lord of the Manor Wesl Meth

GILLINGHAM parish 1558 Kent 1-1/2 miles ne Chatham pop 6,734 pec Archbishop of Canterbury Wesl Meth

GILLINGHAM parish 1541 Norfolk 1-1/4 miles nw Beccles pop 369 archd Norfolk dioc Norwich

GILLMONDBY township parish Bowes N R York pop 98

GILMORTON parish 1618 Leics 3 miles ne Lutterworth pop 830 archd Leicester dioc Lincoln

GILROE extra parochial liberty Leics 1-1/2 miles nw Leicester pop 11

GILSTONE parish 1558 Herts 3-1/2 miles sw Sawbridgeworth pop 233 archd Middlesex dioc London

GIMINGHAM parish 1558 Norfolk 4 miles n North Walsham pop 353 archd Norfolk dioc Norwich

GINGE, WEST tything parish Lockinge Berks

GIPPING chapelry parish Stowmarket Suffolk pop 87

GIRSBY township parish Sockburn N R York pop 83

GIRTON parish 1629 Cambs 3 miles nw Cambridge pop 338 archd and dioc Ely

GIRTON parish 1680 Notts 8 miles se Tuxford pop 187 archd Nottingham dioc York

GISBURN parish 1558 W R York 10-1/2 miles sw Skipton comp townships Gisburn, Gisburn Forest, Horton, Middop, Nappa, Newsholme, Paythorne, Rimmington, Swinden pop 2,306 archd and dioc York

GISBURN FOREST township parish Gisburn W R York pop 400

GISLEHAM parish 1559 Suffolk 4-1/2 miles sw Lowestoft pop 262 archd Suffolk dioc Norwich

GISLINGHAM parish 1558 Suffolk 5 miles sw Eye pop 660 archd Sudbury dioc Norwich Wesl Meth

GISSING parish 1702 (earlier destroyed) Norfolk 4-1/4 miles ne Diss pop 598 archd Norfolk dioc Norwich Wesl Meth

GITTISHAM parish 1559 Devon 2-3/4 miles sw Honiton pop 370 archd and dioc Exeter

GIVENDALE township parish Ripon W R York pop 35

GIVENDALE or GWENDALE, GREAT parish 1658 E R York 3-1/2 miles ne Pocklington comp townships of Great Givendale and Grimthorpe pop 78 pec of Dean of York

GLAISDALE parish 1758 N R York 10 miles sw Whitby pop 1,004 archd Cleveland dioc York Wesl Meth

GLANDFORD parish 1654 Norfolk 1-1/2 miles sw Clay pop 102 archd and dioc Norwich

GLANDFORD BRIGG or BRIDGE chapelry parish Wrawby Lincs pop 1,780 Indep, Prim and Wesl Meth, Roman Cath

GLANTLEES township parish Felton Northumberland pop 56

GLANTON township parish Whittingham Northumberland pop 534 Presb

GLAPTHORN parish 1614 co Northampton 1-1/2 miles nw Oundle pop 353 archd Northampton dioc Peterborough

GLAPTON township parish Clifton Notts

GLAPWELL township in parishes Ault Hucknall and Bolsover Derbys pop 99

GLASCOED hamlet parish Usk co Monmouth pop 198 Bapt

GLASCOTE township parish Tamworth Warws

GLASS HOUSE YARD liberty Finsbury Middlesex pop 1,312

GLASSONBY township parish Addingham Cumberland pop 167

GLASTON township parish Aldingham Lancs

GLASTON parish 1555 co Rutland 2 miles ne Uppingham pop 229 archd Northampton dioc Peterborough

GLASTONBURY market town Somerset 7-1/2 miles ne Somerton pop 2,984 pec of Glastonbury comp St Benedict 1740, St John the Baptist 1603 Bapt, Soc of Friends, Wesl Meth, Indep

GLATTON parish 1578 Hunts 2-1/4 miles sw Stilton pop 348 archd Huntingdon dioc Lincoln

GLAZELEY parish (regs with Deuxhill) Shrops 3-1/2 miles sw Bridgenorth pop 47 archd Salop dioc Hereford

GLEMHAM, GREAT parish 1569 Suffolk 4-1/2 miles sw Saxmundham pop 399 archd Suffolk dioc Norwich

GLEMHAM, LITTLE parish 1551 Suffolk 3 miles ne Wickham Market pop 361 archd Suffolk dioc Norwich

GLEMSFORD parish 1550 Suffolk 4-1/4 miles ne Clare pop 1,470 archd Sudbury dioc Norwich

GLEN, MAGNA parish 1687 Leics 6 miles se Leicester pop 770 archd and dioc Lincoln

GLEN, PARVA chapelry parish Aylestone Leics pop 160

GLENDON parish no regs co Northampton 3 miles nw Kettering pop 44 archd Northampton dioc Peterborough

GLENFIELD parish 1604 Leics 3-1/2 miles nw Leicester comp chapelries Braunstone, Kirby Muxloe, liberties Braunstone Frith, Glenfield Frith, Kirby Frith pop 1,166 pec of Lord of manor of Grosby Wesl Meth

GLENFIELD FRITH liberty parish Glenfield Leics

GLENTHAM parish 1690 Lincs 8 miles nw Market Rasen pop 399 pec of Dean of Lincoln Wesl Meth

GLENTWORTH parish 1586 Lincs 11-1/2 miles nw Lincoln pop 298 archd Stow dioc Lincoln

GLEWSTON township parish Goodrich Herefs pop 154

GLIDDEN tything parish Hambledon Hamps

GLINTON parish 1567 co Northampton 3 miles se Market Deeping pop 414 archd Northampton dioc Peterborough

GLOOSTON parish 1685 Leics 5-3/4 miles ne Market Harborough pop 177 archd Leicester dioc Lincoln

GLORORUM township parish Bambrough Northumberland pop 47

GLOSSOP parish 1620 Derbys 10 miles n Chapel en le Frith comp chapelries Charlesworth, Chinley Bugsworth with Brownside, Hayfield and Mellor, townships Chunat, Dinting, Glossop, Great Hamlet, Hadfield, Ludworth with Chisworth, Padfield, Simondsley and Whitfield, hamlets Beard, Kinder, Olerset, Thornsett and Whittle, liberty Phoside pop 18,080 archd Derby dioc Lichfield Indep, Wesl Meth

GLOSTERHILL township parish Warkworth Northumberland pop 28

GLOUCESTER city Gloucs 34 miles ne Bristol pop 11,933 comp St Aldate 1572, St Catherine 1687, St John 1558, St Mary de Crypt 1653, St Mary de Lode 1675, Holy Trinity 1557, St Michael 1553, St Nicholas 1558, Cathedral Church 1661 archd and dioc Gloucester Bapt, Soc of Friends, Countess of Huntingdon's Connection, Indep, Wesl Meth, Unit, Roman Cath

GLOVERSTONE township parish St Mary, Chester Ches

GLUSBURN township parish Kildwick W R York pop 987

GLUVIAS, ST parish 1645 Cornwall comp Penryn pop 4,490 pec Bishop of Exeter Wesl Meth

GLYMPTON parish 1667 co Oxford 4 miles nw Woodstock pop 125 archd and dioc Oxford

GLYND parish 1558 Sussex 3-1/4 miles se Lewes pop 276 pec Archbishop of Canterbury

GNOSALL parish 1572 Staffs 6-1/2 miles sw Stafford comp townships

Cowley, Gnosall, Knightly, part of Apeton, Alstone, Brough and Rule, hamlet Moreton   pop 3,358 pec of Lord of manor of Gnosall

GOADBY chapelry 1745 parish Billesden Leics pop 98

GOADBY MARWOOD parish 1656 Leics 5-1/2 miles ne Melton Mowbray pop 161 archd Leicester dioc Lincoln

GOADLAND or GOATHLAND chapelry 1669 parish Pickering N R York pop 326 pec Dean of York

GOAT township parish Bridekirk Cumberland pop 461

GOATHILL parish 1699 Somerset 2-1/4 miles e Sherborne pop 35 archd Wells dioc Bath and Wells

GOATHURST parish 1559 Somerset 3-1/2 miles sw Bridgewater pop 349 archd Taunton dioc Bath and Wells

GODALMING parish 1582 Surrey 4 miles sw Guildford pop 4,529 archd Surrey dioc Winchester Gen Bapt, Soc of Friends, Indep, Wesl Meth

GODINGTON parish 1672 co Oxford 5-1/2 miles ne Bicester pop 118 archd and dioc Oxford

GODLEY township parish Mottram in Longden Dale Ches pop 636

GODMANCHESTER parish 1604 Hunts 3/4 mile se Huntingdon pop 2,146 archd Huntingdon dioc Lincoln

GODMANSTONE parish 1654 Dorset 5 miles nw Dorchester pop 152 archd Dorset dioc Bristol

GODMERSHAM parish 1600 Kent 6-1/4 miles ne Ashford pop 444 pec Archbishop of Canterbury

GODNEY chapelry 1741 parish Meare Somerset

GODOLPHIN hamlet parish Breage Cornwall

GODSFIELD extra parochial liberty Hamps 3 miles ne New Alresford pop 4

GODSHILL tything parish Fordingbridge Hamps pop 211

GODSHILL parish 1678 Isle of Wight Hamps 5-1/2 miles se Newport pop 1,305 archd and dioc Winchester Wesl Meth

GODSTONE parish 1662 Surrey 19 miles se London pop 1,397 archd Surrey dioc Winchester

GODWICK parish incl in regs Titteshall Norfolk 5-3/4 miles sw Fakenham

GOLBORN BELLOW township parish Tattenhall Ches pop 96

GOLBORN DAVID township parish Handley Ches pop 80

GOLBORNE township parish Winwick Lancs pop 1,532

GOLCAR chapelry parish Huddersfield W R York pop 3,134

GOLDCLIFF parish 1728 co Monmouth 4-1/2 miles se Newport pop 270 archd and dioc Llandaff

GOLDHANGER parish 1558 Essex 4-1/4 miles ne Maldon pop 496 archd Colchester dioc London

GOLDINGTON parish 1559 Beds 1-3/4 miles ne Bedford pop 494 archd and dioc Lincoln

GOLDSBOROUGH parish 1707 W R York 2-3/4 miles se Knaresborough comp townships Coneythorpe, Flaxby and Goldsborough pop 359 archd Richmond dioc Chester

GOLDSHAW BOOTH chapelry 1732 parish Whalley Lancs pop 763

GOLTHO parish 1672 Lincs 1-1/2 miles sw Wragby pop 93 pec Bishop of Lincoln

GOMELDON tything parish Idmiston Wilts

GOMERSALL township parish Birstall W R York pop 6,189 Indep, Moravians, Wesl Meth

GOMERSHAY tything parish Stalbridge Dorset pop 90

GONALDSTON parish 1598 Notts 4-3/4 miles sw Southwell pop 107 archd Nottingham dioc York

GONERBY, GREAT parish 1560 Lincs 1-1/2 miles nw Grantham pop 916 archd and dioc Lincoln

GONERBY, LITTLE township parish Grantham Lincs pop 1,720

GOOD EASTER Essex See EASTER GOOD

GOODERSTONE parish 1702 Norfolk 4-1/4 miles ne Stoke Ferry pop 476 archd Norfolk dioc Norwich

GOODLEIGH parish 1538 Devon 2-3/4 miles ne Barnstaple pop 442 archd Barnstaple dioc Exeter Indep

GOODMANHAM parish 1678 E R York 1-1/4 miles ne Market Weighton pop 268 archd East Riding dioc York

GOODNESTONE parish 1569 Kent 2 miles e Faversham pop 74 archd and dioc Canterbury

GOODNESTONE parish 1569 2-1/2 miles se Wingham pop 486 archd and dioc Canterbury

GOODRICH or GODERICH parish 1558 Herefs 5-1/4 miles sw Ross comp townships Glewston, Goodrich and Huntisham pop 792 archd and dioc Hereford

GOODSHAW BOOTH See GOLDSHAW BOOTH

GOOLE township parish Snaith W R York pop 1,671 Indep

GOOSEY chapelry parish Stamford in the Vale Berks pop 203

GOOSNARGH chapelry 1635 parish Kirkham Lancs pop 1,844

GOOSTREY chapelry 1561 parish Sandbach Ches pop 292

GOPSALL extra parochial liberty Leics 4-1/2 miles nw Market Bosworth pop 7

GORAN ST Cornwall See GORRAN

GORE END parish Birchington Kent

GOREFIELDS extra parochial liberty Bucks 3 miles nw Newport Pagnell

GORING parish 1670 co Oxford 6-1/4 miles sw Wallingford pop 933 archd and dioc Oxford Indep

GORING parish 1560 Sussex 2-1/2 miles w Worthing pop 527 archd and dioc Chichester

GORLESTON parish 1674 near Gt Yarmouth Suffolk pop 2,116 archd Suffolk dioc Norwich Indep, Wesl Meth

GORNALL, LOWER hamlet parish Sedgley Staffs

GORRAN parish 1661 Cornwall 5-3/4 miles se Tregoney pop 1,205 archd Cornwall dioc Exeter Wesl Meth

GORTON chapelry 1570 parish Manchester Lancs pop 2,623

GOSBECK parish 1561 Suffolk 4-3/4 miles ne Needham Market pop

319 archd Suffolk dioc Norwich

GOSBERTON parish 1659 Lincs 6 miles nw Spalding pop 1,951 archd and dioc Lincoln

GOSEBRADON parish no regs Somerset 5 miles n Ilminster archd Taunton dioc Bath and Wells

GOSFIELD parish 1538 Essex 2-3/4 miles sw Halstead pop 512 archd Middlesex dioc London

GOSFORD township parish Kidlington co Oxford pop 45

GOSFORTH parish 1571 Cumberland 6-3/4 miles se Egremont comp townships High Bolton, Low Bolton, Bornwood pop 935 archd Richmond dioc Chester

GOSFORTH parish 1699 Northumberland 4-1/4 miles n Newcastle comp townships East Brunton, West Brunton, Coxlodge, Fawdon, East Kenton, West Kenton pop 3,546 archd Northumberland dioc Durham

GOSPORT sea port 1696 parish Alverstoke borough Hamps 17-1/2 miles se Southampton pop 6,798 pec of Bishop of Winchester Indep, Wesl Meth, Roman Cath

GOSWICK hamlet parish Holy Island co Durham

GOTHAM parish 1560 Notts 7-1/2 miles sw Nottingham pop 748 archd Nottingham dioc York Wesl Meth

GOTHERINGTON hamlet parish Bishop's Cleeve Gloucs pop 373

GOUDHURST parish 1558 Kent 13 miles sw Maidstone pop 2,758 archd and dioc Rochester Wesl Meth

GOULSBY or GOULCEBY parish 1686 Lincs 6-3/4 miles sw Louth pop 252 archd and dioc Lincoln Wesl Meth

GOURNAL chapelry parish Sedgley Staffs

GOWDALL township parish Snaith W R York pop 260

GOWTHORPE chapelry parish Swardeston Norfolk

GOWTHORPE township parish Bishop Wilton E R York pop 106

GOXHILL parish 1590 Lincs 5-1/2 miles se Barton upon Humber pop 801 archd and dioc Lincoln Wesl Meth

GOXHILL parish 1561 E R York 11-1/2 miles ne Beverley pop 65 archd East Riding dioc York

GOYTREY parish 1695 co Monmouth 5 miles nw Usk pop 521 archd and dioc Llandaff

GRABY hamlet parish Aslackby Lincs

GRACE DIEU extra parochial liberty 5 miles ne Ashby de la Zouch Leics

GRACE DIEU PARK extra parochial liberty 4-1/2 miles sw Monmouth co Monmouth

GRADE parish 1707 Cornwall 10 miles se Helston pop 306 archd Cornwall dioc Exeter

GRAFFHAM parish 1581 Hunts 4-3/4 miles ne Kimbolton pop 281 archd Huntingdon dioc Lincoln

GRAFFHAM parish 1665 Sussex 4-3/4 miles se Midhurst pop 372 archd and dioc Chichester

GRAFTON township parish Tilston Ches pop 18

GRAFTON township parish Beckford Gloucs
GRAFTON township parish All Saints, Hereford Herefs pop 56
GRAFTON township parish Langford co Oxford pop 71
GRAFTON parish (regs with Marton) W R York 2-1/2 miles se
Aldborough
GRAFTON ARDEN township parish Temple Grafton Warws
GRAFTON, EAST tything parish Graft Bedwin Wilts
GRAFTON, FLYFORD Worcs See FLYFORD GRAFTON
GRAFTON MANOR extra parochial liberty 1-3/4 miles sw Broms-
grove Worcs pop 45
GRAFTON REGIS parish 1584 co Northampton 4-3/4 miles se Tow-
cester pop 241 archd Northampton dioc Peterborough
GRAFTON, TEMPLE parish 1695 Warws 3-1/4 miles se Alcester
pop 374 archd and dioc Worcester
GRAFTON UNDERWOOD parish 1678 co Northampton 4-3/4 miles
ne Kettering pop 290 archd Northampton dioc Peterborough
GRAIG hamlet parish Bassaleg co Monmouth pop 581
GRAIN, ISLE parish 1653 Kent 1-3/4 miles nw Sheerness pop 240
pec of Archbishop of Canterbury Indep
GRAINSBY parish 1561 Lincs 7 miles s Great Grimsby pop 116 archd
and dioc Lincoln
GRAINTHORPE parish 1653 Lincs 8-1/4 miles ne Louth pop 517
archd and dioc Lincoln
GRAISLEY tything parish Sulhampstead Abbots' Berks pop 66
GRAMPOUND or GRAND PONT tything parish St Aldate's Oxford
Berks pop 337
GRAMPOUND town borough in parishes Probus and Creed Cornwall
40 miles sw Launceston pop 715
GRANBY parish 1567 Notts 4 miles se Bingham pop 342 archd Not-
tingham dioc York Wesl Meth
GRANDBOROUGH parish 1538 Bucks 1-3/4 miles s Winslow pop 341
archd St Albans dioc London
GRANDBOROUGH parish 1581 Worws 3-1/4 miles s Dunchurch pop
528 archd Coventry dioc Lichfield
GRANGE township parish Bidstone Ches
GRANGE township parish West Kirby Ches pop 124
GRANGE township parish Leintwardine Herefs pop 218
GRANGE or GRENCH hamlet parish Gillingham Kent pop 134
GRANGE township parish Swine E R York
GRANGE, CHAPEL hamlet parish Oswald Kirk N R York
GRANSDEN, GREAT parish 1538 Hunts 7-1/4 miles se St Neot's pop
527 archd Huntingdon dioc Lincoln Bapt
GRANSDEN, LITTLE parish 1730 Cambs 3 miles sw Caxton pop 251
pec of Bishop of Ely
GRANSMOOR township parish Burton Agnes E R York pop 93
GRANTCHESTER parish 1539 Cambs 2-1/4 miles sw Cambridge pop
468 archd and dioc Ely
GRANTHAM parish 1563 borough Lincs 24 miles sw Lincoln comp

town Grantham, township Manthorp with Little Gonerby, Harrowby and Spittlegate pop 7,427 archd and dioc Lincoln Huntingtonians, Indep, Wesl Meth

GRANTLEY township parish Ripon W R York pop 243

GRAPPENHALL parish 1574 Ches 2-3/4 miles se Warrington comp chapelry Latchford, township Grappenhall pop 2,607 archd and dioc Chester

GRASMERE parish 1571 Westm 4 miles nw Ambleside comp chapelries Ambleside and Langdales, townships Grasmere and Rydal with Loughrigg pop 2,083 archd Richmond dioc Chester

GRASBY parish 1653 Lincs 3-1/4 miles nw Caistor pop 283 archd and dioc Lincoln

GRASSGARTH hamlet parish Kendal Westm

GRASSINGTON township parish Linton W R York pop 1,067 Wesl Meth

GRASSTHORPE township parish Marnham Notts pop 118

GRATELY parish 1624 Hamps 6-1/2 miles sw Andover pop 130 archd and dioc Winchester

GRATTON hamlet parish Youlgrave Derbys pop 26

GRATWICH parish 1598 Staffs 4-3/4 miles sw Uttoxeter pop 116 archd Stafford dioc Lichfield

GRAVELEY parish 1642 Cambs 6-1/2 miles nw Caxton pop 255 archd and dioc Ely

GRAVELEY parish 1551 Herts 2 miles n Stevenage pop 331 archd Huntingdon dioc Lincoln

GRAVELTHORPE Yorks See GREWELTHORPE

GRAVENEY parish 1653 Kent 3 miles ne Faversham pop 197 archd and dioc Canterbury

GRAVENHANGER township parish Muckleston Shrops pop 198

GRAVENHURST, LOWER parish 1705 Beds 3 miles e Silsoe pop 77 archd Bedford dioc Lincoln

GRAVENHURST, UPPER parish 1567 Beds 3 miles ne Silsoe pop 318 archd Bedford dioc Lincoln

GRAVESEND parish 1547 Kent 15-1/2 miles nw Maidstone pop 5,097 archd and dioc Rochester Indep, Wesl Meth Sep juris

GRAVESHIP, NETHER township parish Kendal Westm pop 312

GRAYS See THURROCK GRAYS Essex

GRAYINGHAM parish 1576 Lincs 1-1/2 miles s Kirton pop 137 archd Stow dioc Lincoln

GRAYRIGG chapelry 1724 parish Kendal Westm pop 242 Soc of Friends

GRAYSOUTHEN township parish Brigham Cumberland pop 555

GREASBROUGH chapelry 1747 parish Rotherham W R York pop 1,290 Wesl Meth

GREASBY township parish West Kirby Ches pop 141

GREASLEY parish 1600 Notts 7 miles nw Nottingham pop 4,583 archd Nottingham dioc York

GREAT ABINGTON Cambs See ABINGTON, GREAT

GREATFORD parish 1754 Lincs 4-3/4 miles nw Market Deeping pop
296 archd and dioc Lincoln

GREATHAM parish 1566 co Durham 7 miles ne Stockton upon Tees
comp townships Claxton and Greatham pop 551 archd and dioc
Durham

GREATHAM parish 1571 Hamps 5 miles ne Peterfield pop 238 archd
and dioc Winchester

GREATHAM parish inc regs of Wiggonholt Sussex 7-1/4 miles ne
Arundel pop 79 archd and dioc Chichester

GREAT HAMLET township parish Glossop Derbys pop 1,092

GREATWORTH parish 1757 co Northampton 6 miles nw Brackley pop
214 archd Northampton dioc Peterborough

GREAT YATE township parish Croxden Staffs

GREENCROFT township parish Lanchester co Durham pop 235

GREENFIELD hamlet parish Aby Lincs

GREENFIELD liberty parish Watlington co Oxford

GREENFORD parish 1539 Middlesex 4-1/2 miles ne Hounslow pop
477 juris of Commissary of London Bapt

GREENHALGH township parish Kirkham Lancs pop 408

GREENHAM chapelry 1607 parish Thatcham Berks pop 1,061

GREEN HAMMERTON Yorks See HAMMERTON, GREEN

GREENHILL extra parochial liberty Lincs pop 7

GREENHILL hamlet parish Harrow on the Hill Middlesex

GREENHILL LANE township parish Alfreton Derbys

GREENHOW township parish Ingle by Greenhow N R York pop 94

GREENHYTHE hamlet parish Swanscombe Kent

GREENLEIGHTON township parish Hartburn Northumberland pop 20

GREENS township parish Felton Northumberland pop 56

GREENSIDE HILL township parish Ingram Northumberland pop 71

GREENS NORTON parish 1565 co Northampton 1-3/4 miles nw Towcester pop 771 archd Northampton dioc Peterborough

GREENSTEAD parish 1676 Essex 1 mile e Colchester pop 598 archd
Essex dioc London

GREENSTEAD parish 1561 Essex 1-1/4 miles sw Chipping Ongar
pop 134 archd Colchester dioc London

GREENWICH parish 1615 borough Kent 6 miles se London pop 24,553
archd and dioc Rochester Bapt, Indep, Wesl Meth, Roman Cath

GREET chapelry parish Winchcombe Gloucs

GREET parish 1728 Shrops 2-1/2 miles nw Tenbury pop 93 archd
Salop dioc Hereford

GREETHAM parish 1653 Lincs 3-1/4 miles ne Horncastle pop 152
archd and dioc Lincoln

GREETHAM parish 1576 co Rutland 6 miles ne Oakham pop 505 archd
Northampton dioc Peterborough

GREETLAND chapelry parish Halifax W R York pop 5,500 Wesl Meth

GREETWELL parish 1723 Lincs 2-1/4 miles e Lincoln pop 42 archd
Stow dioc Lincoln

GREGORY ST extra parochial liberty near Canterbury Kent pop 833

GREINTON parish 1728 Somerset 6-1/2 miles sw Glastonbury pop 219 archd Wells dioc Bath and Wells

GRENDON parish 1559 co Northampton 5-1/2 miles sw Wellingborough pop 622 archd Northampton dioc Peterborough

GRENDON parish 1570 Warws 3-1/4 miles nw Atherstone pop 577 archd Coventry dioc Lichfield

GRENDON BISHOP'S parish 1662 Herefs 4-1/4 miles nw Bromyard pop 229 archd and dioc Hereford

GRENDON UNDERWOOD parish 1653 Bucks 6-3/4 miles se Bicester pop 379 archd Buckingham dioc Lincoln

GRENDON WARREN chapelry parish Pencombe Herefs

GRESHAM parish 1560 Norfolk 4-1/4 miles sw Cromer pop 362 archd Norfolk dioc Norwich

GRESLEY, CASTLE hamlet parish Church Gresley Derbys pop 126

GRESLEY, CHURCH parish 1584 Derbys 5 miles se Burton upon Trent comp chapelry Swadlincote, townships Drakelow and Linton, hamlet Castle Gresley and Oakthorpe and Donisthorpe pop 1,543 archd Derby dioc Lichfield

GRESSENHALL parish 1538 Norfolk 2-3/4 miles nw East Dereham pop 924 archd and dioc Norwich

GRESSINGHAM chapelry 1710 parish Lancaster Lancs pop 177 archd Richmond dioc Chester

GRESTLY township parish Wybunbury Ches

GRETA BRIDGE hamlet parish Brignall N R York

GRETFORD Lincs See GREATFORD

GRETTON chapelry parish Winchcombe Gloucs Wesl Meth

GRETTON parish 1556 co Northampton 2-3/4 miles ne Rockingham pop 762 pec of Prebendary of Gretton Bapt

GREWELL parish 1604 Hamps 1-3/4 miles w Odiham pop 287 archd and dioc Winchester

GREWELTHORPE or GRAVELTHORPE township parish Kirby Malzeard W R York pop 571

GREY EASTON Wilts See EASTON GREY

GREY'S FOREST township parish Kirknewton Northumberland pop 44

GREYSTEAD or GAYSTEAD parish 1818 Northumberland 5 miles nw Bellingham comp townships Chirdon and Smalesmouth pop 250 archd Northumberland dioc Durham

GREYSTOCK or GREYSTOKE parish 1559 Cumberland 5 miles nw Penrith comp chapelries Matterdale, Mungrisdale, Threlkeld and Water Millock, townships Berrier with Murrah, Little Blencow, Greystock, Hutton John, Hutton Roof, Hutton Soil, Johnby and Motherby with Gill pop 2,565 archd and dioc Carlisle

GREYWELL Hamps See GREWELL

GRIBTHORPE township parish Bubwith E R York pop 108

GRIMLEY parish 1573 Worcs 4-1/2 miles nw Worcester pop 711 archd and dioc Worcester

GRIMOLDBY parish 1563 Lincs 5 miles e Louth pop 311 archd and dioc Lincoln

GRIMSARGH chapelry parish Preston Lancs pop 310

GRIMSBY, GREAT or GRIMSBY parish 1538 borough Lincs 35 miles ne Lincoln pop 4,225 sep juris archd and dioc Lincoln Bapt, Indep, Prim and Wesl Meth

GRIMSBY, LITTLE parish 1593 Lincs 3-1/4 miles n Louth pop 52 archd and dioc Lincoln

GRIMSTEAD, EAST chapelry parish West Dean Wilts pop 122

GRIMSTEAD, WEST parish 1717 Wilts 5 miles se Salisbury pop 186 archd and dioc Salisbury

GRIMSTON parish 1635 Leics 5 miles nw Melton Mowbray pop 185 pec Lord of manor of Rothley

GRIMSTON township parish Dunnington E R York pop 70

GRIMSTON township parish Gilling N R York pop 68

GRIMSTON township parish Kirby Wharfe W R York pop 63

GRIMSTON, NORTH parish 1686 E R York 4-1/2 miles se New Malton pop 158 pec Prebendary of Langtoft

GRIMSTONE tything parish Stratton Dorset

GRIMSTONE parish 1552 Norfolk 4-1/4 miles se Castle Rising pop 1,060 archd and dioc Norwich

GRIMTHORPE township parish Givendale E R York pop 19

GRINDALL chapelry 1592 parish Bridlington E R York pop 121

GRINDLETON chapelry 1744 parish Mitton W R York pop 1,103

GRINDLEY township parish Malpas Ches pop 328

GRINDLOW township parish Hope Derbys pop 87

GRINDON township parish Norham co Durham and Northumberland pop 162

GRINDON parish 1565 co Durham 5-1/2 miles nw Stockton upon Tees comp townships Grindon and Whitton pop 384 archd and dioc Durham

GRINDON parish 1697 Staffs 7-1/4 miles se Leek pop 431 archd Stafford dioc Lichfield

GRINGLEY ON THE HILL parish 1678 Notts 6 miles se Bawtry pop 737 pec of Lord of the manor

GRINSDALE parish 1739 Cumberland 2-3/4 miles nw Carlisle pop 135 archd and dioc Carlisle

GRINSHILL parish 1592 Shrops 7-1/2 miles ne Shrewsbury pop 203 archd Salop dioc Lichfield

GRINSTEAD, EAST parish 1558 borough Sussex 19-3/4 miles n Lewes pop 3,364 archd Lewes dioc Chichester Countess of Huntingdon's

GRINSTEAD, WEST parish 1558 Sussex 7-1/2 miles s Horsham pop 1,292 archd and dioc Chichester

GRINSTHORPE hamlet parish Edenham Lincs

GRINTON parish 1640 N R York 9-1/2 miles sw Richmond pop 4,854 archd and dioc Chester

GRISTHORPE township parish Filey N R York pop 217

GRISTON parish 1652 Norfolk 2 miles se Watton pop 208 archd and dioc Norwich

GRITFORD hamlet parish Sandy Beds
GRITTENHAM tything parish Brinkworth Wilts pop 148
GRITTLETON parish 1577 Wilts 7 miles nw Chippenham pop 438 archd
    Wilts dioc Salisbury Bapt
GROOBY hamlet parish Ratby Leics pop 335
GROOMBRIDGE chapelry parish Speldhurst Kent
GROSMONT parish 1589 co Monmouth 12 miles n Monmouth pop 690
    archd and dioc Llandaff
GROTTON parish 1562 Suffolk 1 mile nw Boxford pop 577 archd Sud-
    bury dioc Norwich
GROVE hamlet parish Wantage Berks pop 520
GROVE parish 1689 Bucks 2-1/2 miles s Leighton Buzzard pop 21
    archd Buckingham dioc Lincoln
GROVE parish 1726 Notts 2-3/4 miles se East Retford pop 121 archd
    Nottingham dioc York
GROVELEY extra parochial liberty Wilts 4 miles nw Wilton pop 33
GRUNDISBURGH parish 1540 Suffolk 3 miles nw Woodbridge pop 835
    archd Suffolk dioc Norwich Bapt
GRUNTY FEN HOUSE extra parochial liberty Cambs 4 miles sw Ely
GUELDABLE township parish Leak N R York pop 126
GUESTLING parish 1686 Sussex 3-3/4 miles sw Winchelsea pop 768
    archd Lewes dioc Chichester
GUESTWICK parish 1558 Norfolk 2-1/2 miles ne Foulsham pop 188
    archd Norfolk dioc Norwich Indep
GUILDEN MORDEN Cambs See MORDEN, GUILDEN
GUILDON SUTTON Ches See SUTTON, GUILDEN
GUILDFORD town borough Surrey 30 miles sw London pop 3,813
    comp Holy Trinity 1558, St May the Virgin 1540, St Nicholas 1561,
    sep juris archd Surrey dioc Winchester Bapt, Soc of Friends,
    Indep, Wesl Meth
GUILDFORD or GUILDEFORD, EAST parish 1705 Sussex 1-3/4 miles
    ne Rye pop 126 archd Lewes dioc Chichester
GUILSBOROUGH parish 1560 co Northampton 9-1/4 miles nw North-
    ampton pop 1,069 archd Northampton dioc Peterborough Bapt
GUISBOROUGH or GUILSBROUGH parish 1661 N R York 49 miles n
    York comp town Guisborough, townships Dale Common, Hutton
    Locras, Pinchingthorpe and Tocketts pop 2,210 archd Cleveland
    dioc York Soc of Friends, Indep, Wesl Meth
GUISLEY parish 1586 W R York 3 miles sw Otley comp chapelries
    Horsforth and Rawden, townships Carlton, Guisley and Yeaden
    pop 10,028 archd and dioc York Wesl Meth
GUIST parish 1557 Norfolk 2 miles nw Foulsham pop 363 archd Nor-
    folk dioc Norwich
GUITING See GUYTING
GULVAL parish 1598 Cornwall 1-1/2 miles ne Penzance pop 1,467
    archd Cornwall dioc Exeter Wesl Meth
GUMLEY parish 1694 Leics 4-1/2 miles nw Market Harborough pop
    272 archd Leicester dioc Lincoln

GUNBY parish 1715 Lincs 2-3/4 miles sw Colsterworth pop 152 archd and dioc Lincoln

GUNBY parish 1724 Lincs 5-1/4 miles e Spilsby pop 75 archd and dioc Lincoln

GUNHOUSE hamlet parish West Halton Lincs

GUNNERSBURY hamlet parish Acton Middlesex

GUNNERTON chapelry parish Chollerton Northumberland pop 422

GUNTHORPE parish 1558 Norfolk 5-1/4 miles sw Holt pop 316 archd and dioc Norwich

GUNTHORPE hamlet parish Paston co Northampton pop 48

GUNTHORPE township parish Lowdham Notts pop 383 Wesl Meth

GUNTHORPE hamlet parish Belton co Rutland pop 4

GUNTHWAITE township parish Penistone W R York pop 99

GUNTON parish 1723 Norfolk 4-1/4 miles nw North Walsham pop 84 archd Norfolk dioc Norwich

GUNTON parish 1759 Suffolk 1-1/2 miles nw Lowestoft pop 63 archd Suffolk dioc Norwich

GUNVILLE TARRANT Dorset See TARRANT GUNVILLE

GUNWALLOE parish 1716 Cornwall 5 miles s Helston pop 284 archd Cornwall dioc Exeter Wesl Meth

GUSSAGE parish 1560 Dorset 5 miles sw Cranborne pop 373 archd Dorset dioc Bristol

GUSSAGE chapelry parish Handley Dorset

GUSSAGE parish 1653 Dorset 6 miles sw Granborne pop 233 archd Dorset dioc Bristol

GUSTON parish 1664 Kent 2 miles ne Dovor pop 197 pec of Archbishop of Canterbury

GUTON hamlet parish Brandistone Norfolk

GUY'S CLIFF hamlet parish Leek Wootton Warws

GUYSON township parish Shilbottle Northumberland pop 197

GUYTING, LOWER or GUYTING POWER parish 1560 Gloucs 6 miles se Winchcombe pop 792 archd and dioc Gloucester

GUYTING, TEMPLE parish 1647 Gloucs 4-3/4 miles se Winchcombe pop 520 archd and dioc Gloucester

GWEEK small port in English channel extending into parishes Constantine, St Keverne, Landewednack, Manaccan, Mawgan, Mawnan, Ruan Minor and Wendron Cornwall 3-1/2 miles se Helston

GWEHELLOG hamlet parish Usk co Monmouth pop 418

GWENNAP parish 1658 Cornwall 3-1/2 miles se Rudruth pop 8,539 archd Cornwall dioc Exeter Bapt, Bryanites, Wesl Meth

GWERNESNEY parish 1757 co Monmouth 2-1/2 miles ne Usk pop 62 archd and dioc Llandaff

GWINEAR parish 1560 Cornwall 3-1/4 miles sw Camborne pop 2,728 archd Cornwall dioc Exeter Wesl Meth

GWITHIAN parish 1717 Cornwall 7-1/2 miles w Redruth pop 539 archd Cornwall dioc Exeter Wesl Meth

GYHIRN chapelry parish St Mary Wisbeach Cambs

HABBERLEY parish 1670 Shrops 9 miles sw Shrewsbury pop 128 archd Salop dioc Hereford

HABROUGH parish 1540 Lincs 10 miles nw Great Grimsby pop 313 archd and dioc Lincoln Wesl Meth

HABTON, GREAT township parish Kirby Misperton N R York pop 122

HABTON, LITTLE township parish Kirby Misperton N R York pop 56

HACCOMBE parish no regs Devon 3 miles se Newton Abbot's pop 13 pec Bishop of Exeter

HACCONBY parish 1653 Lincs 3-1/2 miles ne Bourne pop 381 archd and dioc Lincoln

HACEBY parish 1703 Lincs 8-1/4 miles e Grantham pop 66 archd and dioc Lincoln

HACHESTON parish 1560 Suffolk 2 miles ne Wickham Market pop 549 archd Suffolk dioc Norwich

HACKERSALL township parish Lancaster Lancs

HACKFORD parish 1559 Norfolk 1-3/4 miles sw Reepham pop 698 archd Norfolk dioc Norwich

HACKFORD parish 1689 Norfolk 4 miles nw Wymondham pop 229 archd Norfolk dioc Norwich

HACKFORTH township parish Hornby N R York pop 142

HACKINGTON parish 1567 Kent 1-1/4 miles n Canterbury pop 436 archd and dioc Canterbury

HACKLESTON hamlet parish Piddington co Northampton pop 425 Part Bapt

HACKLESTONE tything parish Fittleton Wilts Gen and Part Bapt

HACKNESS parish 1567 N R York 6-1/2 miles nw Scarborough comp chapelry Harwood Dale with Silpho, townships Broxa, Hackness, Suffield with Everley pop 749 archd East Riding dioc York

HACKNEY parish 1555 Middlesex 2 miles ne London comp districts Hackney St John, South Hackney, West Hackney pop 31,047 Commissary of London Bapt, Indep, Wesl Meth, Unit

HACKTHORN parish 1653 Lincs 8 miles ne Lincoln pop 244 archd Stow dioc Lincoln

HADDENHAM parish 1653 Bucks 3 miles ne Thame pop 1,477 archd Buckingham dioc Lincoln Bapt

HADDENHAM parish 1574 Cambs 6-1/2 miles sw Ely pop 1,929 pec Bishop of Ely Bapt, Wesl Meth

HADDESLEY, CHAPEL chapelry parish Birkin W R York pop 196

HADDESLEY, WEST township parish Birkin W R York pop 296

HADDINGTON township partly in parish Auburn partly in South Hyckham Lincs pop 123

HADDISCOE parish 1558 Norfolk 4-3/4 miles ne Beccles pop 383 archd Norfolk dioc Norwich

HADDON parish 1540 Hunts 3 miles nw Stilton pop 130 archd Huntingdon dioc Lincoln

HADDON, EAST parish 1552 co Northampton 7-1/2 miles nw Northampton pop 644 archd Northampton dioc Peterborough

HADDON, OVER township parish Bakewell Derbys pop 242

HADDON, WEST parish 1653 co Northampton 7-1/4 miles ne Daventry pop 909 archd Northampton dioc Peterborough Bapt, Wesl Meth

HADFIELD township parish Glossop Derbys pop 1,270 Wesl Meth

HADHAM, LITTLE parish 1559 Herts 3 miles ne Bishop's Stortford pop 878 Commissary of Essex and Herts, Consistorial Court of Bishop of London

HADHAM, MUCH parish 1559 Herts 4-1/4 miles sw Bishop's Stortford pop 1,268 pec Commissary of Essex and Herts, Consistorial Court of Bishop of London Indep

HADLEIGH parish 1568 Essex 2-1/4 miles nw Leigh pop 365 archd Essex dioc London

HADLEIGH parish 1557 Suffolk 10-1/2 miles sw Ipswich pop 3,425 pec Bocking Bapt, Indep, Wesl Meth

HADLEIGH, HAMLET chapelry parish Boxford Suffolk pop 214

HADLEY tything parish Lambourne Berks

HADLEY, MONKEN parish 1619 Middlesex 3/4 mile ne Chipping Barnet pop 979 Commissary of London

HADLOW parish 1558 Kent 3-1/2 miles ne Tombridge pop 1,853 archd and dioc Rochester Bapt, Wesl Meth

HADNALL EASE chapelry parish Middle Shrops pop 398

HADSOR or HADZOR parish 1554 Worcs 1-1/4 miles se Droitwich pop 100 archd and dioc Worcester

HADSPEN tything parish Pitcomb Somerset

HADSTOCK parish 1559 Essex 1-1/2 miles sLinton pop 424 Commissary of Essex and Herts, Consistorial Court of Bishop of London

HADSTON township parish Warkworth Northumberland pop 11

HAGBORNE parish 1662 Berks 5-1/2 miles sw Wallingford comp liberties East Hagborne, West Hagborne pop 782 archd Berks dioc Salisbury

HAGBORNE, WEST liberty parish Hagborne Berks pop 220

HAGGERSTON parish 1830 Middlesex 1-1/2 miles ne London archd and dioc London Indep, Wesl Meth

HAGHMON or HAUGHMOND, ABBEY extra parochial liberty Shrops 4-1/4 miles ne Shrewsbury

HAGLEY parish 1538 Worcs 2 miles s Stourbridge pop 691 archd and dioc Worcester

HAGLOE tything parish Awre Gloucs

HAGNABY parish 1684 Lincs 5 miles sw Spilsby pop 71 archd and dioc Lincoln

HAGNABY hamlet parish Hannay Lincs pop 97

HAGWORTHINGHAM parish 1562 Lincs 4-1/2 miles nw Spilsby pop 593 archd and dioc Lincoln

HAIGH township parish Wigan Lancs pop 1,271

HAIGHTON township parish Preston Lancs pop 192

HAILES chapelry parish Didbrook Gloucs pop 123

HAILEY chapelry parish Witney co Oxford pop 1,236

HAILSHAM parish 1558 Sussex 52 miles e Chichester pop 1,445

archd Lewes dioc Chichester Bapt

HAIL WESTON parish 1563 Hunts 2-1/4 miles nw St Neots pop 346
    archd Huntingdon dioc Lincoln Part Bapt

HAINFORD parish 1556 Norfolk 2-1/2 miles w Coltishall pop 605
    archd and dioc Norwich

HAINTON parish 1632 Lincs 6-1/4 miles ne Wragby pop 268 pec
    Dean and Chapter of Lincoln

HAISTHORP township parish Agnes Burton E R York pop 117

HALAM parish 1560 Notts 1-1/2 miles nw Southwell pop 371 pec
    Collegiate Church of Southwell

HALBERTON parish 1606 Devon 3-1/2 miles e Tiverton pop 1,598
    archd and dioc Exeter

HALDEN, HIGH parish 1558 Kent 3-1/2 miles ne Tenterden pop 649
    archd and dioc Canterbury

HALDENBY township parish Adlingfleet W R York pop 157

HALE township parish Bowdon Ches pop 945

HALE parish 1545 Cumberland 2-1/2 miles se Egremont pop 279
    archd Richmond dioc Chester

HALE township parish Wrotham Kent

HALE chapelry 1572 parish Childwall Lancs pop 572 archd and dioc
    Chester

HALE parish 1618 Hamps 4 miles ne Fordingbridge pop 203 archd
    and dioc Winchester

HALE, GREAT parish 1538 Lincs 5-3/4 miles se Sleaford pop 966
    archd and dioc Lincoln

HALE, LITTLE township parish Great Hale Lincs pop 299

HALE WESTON Hunts See HAIL WESTON

HALES NORTH See COVEHITHE Suffolk

HALES parish 1674 Norfolk 4-1/2 miles nw Beccles pop 314 archd
    Norfolk dioc Norwich

HALES township parish Drayton in Hales Staffs

HALES OWEN parish 1559 Worcs 35 miles se Shrewsbury comp
    town Halesowen, chapelry Cradley, hamlets Luttley, Warley Wig-
    orn pop 12,839 archd and dioc Worcester Indep, Wesl Meth

HALESWORTH parish 1653 Suffolk 30-1/2 miles ne Ipswich pop
    2,473 archd Suffolk dioc Norwich Bapt, Indep, Unit

HALEWOOD township parish Childwall Lancs pop 930

HALFORD chapelry parish Bromfield Shrops pop 113

HALFORD or HALFORD BRIDGE parish 1545 Warws 4 miles n Ship-
    ston upon Stour pop 315 archd and dioc Worcester

HALIFAX parish 1538 borough W R York 42 miles se York comp
    town Halifax, chapelries Coley, Elland with Greetland, Heptonstall,
    Rastrick, Sowerby, townships Barkisland, Erringden, Fixby, Hip-
    perholme with Brighouse, Langfield, Midgley, Norland, Overdon,
    North Owram, South Owram, Rishworth, Self, Skircoat, Soyland,
    Stainland, Stansfield, Wadsworth, Warley pop 109,899 archd and
    dioc York Bapt, Soc of Friends, Indep, Wesl Meth, Unit

HALLABROW hamlet parish High Littleton Somerset

HALLAM, KIRK parish 1700 Derbys 8-3/4 miles ne Derby pop 486 archd Derby dioc Lichfield

HALLAM, NETHER township parish Sheffield W R York pop 4,658

HALLAM, UPPER township parish Sheffield W R York pop 1,035

HALLAM, WEST parish 1545 Derbys 8 miles ne Derby pop 710 archd Derby dioc Lichfield

HALLATON parish 1563 Leics 7 miles ne Market Harborough pop 653 archd Leicester dioc Lincoln Bapt

HALL CARR township parish Bury Lancs

HALLEN incl in regs Henbury Gloucs

HALL GARTH township parish Pittington co Durham pop 1,632

HALLING parish 1705 Kent 4-3/4 miles sw Rochester pop 431 archd and dioc Rochester

HALLINGBURY, GREAT parish 1538 Essex 2 miles se Bishop's Stortford pop 695 archd Middlesex dioc London

HALLINGBURY, LITTLE parish 1690 Essex 4-1/4 miles ne Harlow pop 483 Commissary of Essex and Herts

HALLINGTON parish incl regs Raithby Lincs 2 miles sw Louth pop 67 archd and dioc Lincoln

HALLINGTON township parish St John Lee Northumberland pop 120

HALLIWELL township parish Dean Lancs pop 2,963

HALLOUGHTON parish 1625 Notts 1-3/4 miles sw Southwell pop 103 pec Prebendary of Halloughton

HALLOW chapelry 1538 parish Grimley Worcs pop 1,227

HALLOWICKS hamlet parish Medenham Bucks

HALLYSTONE parish incl Alwinton regs Northumberland 7 miles nw Rothbury comp townships Barrow, Dueshill, Hallystone, Harbottle, Linsheeles pop 462 archd Northumberland dioc Durham

HALMER END liberty parish Audley Staffs pop 681

HALSALL parish 1606 Lancs 3 miles nw Ormskirk comp chapelries Lydiate, Maghull, Melling, townships Down Holland, Halsall pop 4,159 archd and dioc Chester

HALSE hamlet parish St Peter Brackley co Northampton

HALSE parish 1558 Somerset 4 miles e Wiveliscombe pop 444 archd Taunton dioc Bath and Wells

HALSHAM parish 1563 E R York 6 miles se Hedon pop 302 archd East Riding dioc York

HALSTEAD parish 1564 Essex 17-1/2 miles ne Chelmsford pop 4,637 pec Commissary of Essex and Herts, Consistorial Court of Bishop of London Bapt, Soc of Friends, Indep

HALSTEAD parish 1561 Kent 5-1/4 miles nw Seven Oaks pop 242 pec Archbishop of Canterbury Bapt, Indep

HALSTEAD township parish Tilton Leics pop 162 Wesl Meth

HALSTOCK parish 1698 Dorset 6-1/2 miles ne Beaminster pop 554 pec Prebendary of Lyme and Halstock

HALSTON extra parochial liberty 1686 Shrops 3-1/2 miles ne Oswestry pop 17

HALSTOW, HIGH parish 1662 Kent 5-3/4 miles ne Rochester pop 351 archd and dioc Rochester

HALSTOW, LOWER parish 1691 Kent 4 miles nw Milton pop 221 archd and dioc Canterbury

HALTHAM UPON BAIN parish 1561 Lincs 5-1/4 miles sw Horncastle pop 143 archd and dioc Lincoln

HALTON parish 1606 Bucks 2 miles ne Wendover pop 209 pec Archbishop of Canterbury

HALTON chapelry 1732 parish Runcorn Ches pop 1,322 archd and dioc Chester

HALTON parish 1592 Lancs 2-1/2 miles ne Lancaster pop 834 pec Lord of the manor

HALTON chapelry 1654 parish Corbridge Northumberland pop 78

HALTON, EAST parish 1574 Lincs 7-1/2 miles se Barton upon Humber pop 515 archd and dioc Lincoln Wesl Meth

HALTON, EAST township parish Skipton W R York pop 144

HALTON GILL chapelry parish Arncliffe W R York pop 88

HALTON HOLEGATE parish 1567 Lincs 1-1/2 miles se Spilsby pop 520 archd and dioc Lincoln

HALTON SHIELDS township parish Corbridge Northumberland pop 56

HALTON, WEST parish 1538 Lincs 8-1/2 miles w Barton upon Humber pop 359 archd Stow dioc Lincoln

HALTON, WEST township parish Arncliffe W R York pop 171

HALTWHISTLE parish 1656 Northumberland 36 miles w Newcastle comp town Haltwhistle, townships Bellester, Blenkinsop, East Coanwood, Featherston, Hartley Burn, Henshaw, Melkridge, Plainmellor, Ridley, Thirlwall, Thorngrafton, Wall Town pop 4,119 archd Northumberland dioc Durham Prim Meth, Presb

HALVERGATE parish 1550 Norfolk 3-3/4 miles se Acle pop 465 archd and dioc Norwich

HALWELL parish 1695 Devon 6-1/2 miles se Holsworthy pop 230 archd Totnes dioc Exeter

HALWELL parish 1559 Devon 5-1/4 miles sw Totnes pop 474 archd Totnes dioc Devon

HAM tything parish Berkeley Gloucs pop 903

HAM parish 1552 Kent 2-3/4 miles s Sandwich pop 38 archd and dioc Canterbury

HAM tything parish Baughurst Hamps

HAM hamlet parish Kingston upon Thames Surrey pop 1,079 Indep

HAM parish 1720 Wilts 3-3/4 miles s Hungerford pop 205 archd Wilts dioc Salisbury

HAM, EAST parish 1695 Essex 6 miles e London pop 1,543 archd Essex dioc London Wesl Meth

HAM, HIGH parish 1569 Somerset 3 miles n Langport pop 1,027 archd Wells dioc Bath and Wells Wesl Meth

HAM, LONG Dorset See HAM PRESTON

HAM, LOW chapelry parish High Ham Somerset

HAM, WEST parish 1653 Essex 4 miles ne London comp wards All Saints, Church Street, Plaistow, Stratford Langthorne pop 11,580 archd Essex dioc London Indep, Unit

HAMBLE EN LE RICE parish 1673 Hamps 4-3/4 miles se Southampton pop 318 archd and dioc Winchester

HAMBLEDEN parish 1566 Bucks 4 miles w Great Marlow pop 1,357 archd Buckingham dioc Lincoln Indep

HAMBLEDON parish 1601 Hamps 6 miles se Bishop's Waltham comp tythings Hambledon, Chidden, Denmead, Farvisl, Glidden pop 2,026 pec Vicar

HAMBLEDON parish 1617 Surrey 3-1/2 miles sw Godalming pop 437 archd Surrey dioc Winchester

HAMBLETON chapelry parish Kirkham Lancs pop 334

HAMBLETON parish 1558 co Rutland 3 miles se Oakham pop 297 archd Northampton dioc Peterborough

HAMBLETON township parish Brayton W R York pop 494

HAMBROOK chapelry parish Winterbourne Gloucs pop 950

HAMERINGHAM parish 1744 Lincs 3-3/4 miles se Horncastle pop 158 archd and dioc Lincoln

HAMERTON parish 1752 Hunts 7 miles sw Stilton pop 129 archd Huntingdon dioc Lincoln

HAMFOLLOW hamlet parish Berkeley Gloucs pop 645

HAMMERSMITH chapelry 1751 parish Fulham Middlesex pop 10,222 archd Middlesex dioc London Bapt, Soc of Friends, Indep, Wesl Meth, Roman Cath

HAMMERTON, GREEN township parish Whixley W R York pop 330 Wesl Meth

HAMMERTON, KIRK parish 1714 W R York 8 miles se Aldborough comp township Wilstrop with Ainsty of city of York pop 382 archd Richmond dioc Chester Wesl Meth

HAMMERWICH parish 1720 Staffs 3-3/4 miles sw Lichfield pop 218 pec Dean of Lichfield

HAMMOON parish 1656 Dorset 7 miles sw Shaftesbury pop 54 archd Dorset dioc Bristol

HAMPDEN, GREAT parish 1557 Bucks 3-1/4 miles nw Great Missenden pop 286 archd Buckingham dioc Lincoln

HAMPDEN, LITTLE parish 1672 Bucks 3-1/4 miles nw Great Missenden pop 105 archd Buckingham dioc Lincoln

HAMPHALL township parish Adwick le Street W R York pop 128

HAMPNETT parish 1590 Gloucs 1-1/2 miles nw Northleach pop 187 archd and dioc Gloucester

HAMPNETT, WEST parish 1734 Sussex 1-1/2 miles ne Chichester pop 449 archd and dioc Chichester

HAMPRESTON parish 1617 Dorset 3-1/2 miles se Wimborne Minster comp hamlet Long Ham, Hamps pop 883 archd Dorset dioc Bristol

HAMPSTEAD parish 1560 Middlesex 4 miles nw London pop 7,263 archd Middlesex dioc London Bapt, Wesl Meth, Unit, Roman Cath

HAMPSTEAD, EAST parish 1558 Berks 4 miles se Wokingham pop 647 archd Berks dioc Salisbury

HAMPSTEAD MARSHALL parish 1675 Berks 4 miles sw Newbury
pop 313 archd Berks dioc Salisbury
HAMPSTEAD MORETON Devon See MORETON HAMPSTEAD
HAMPSTEAD NORRIS parish 1538 Berks 3-3/4 miles se East Ilsley
pop 1,179 archd Berks dioc Salisbury Indep, Wesl Meth
HAMPSTHWAITE parish 1603 W R York 1-1/2 miles sw Ripley comp
chapelry Thornthwaite with Padside, townships Eirstwith, Fellis-
cliffe, Hampsthwaite, Menwith with Darley pop 2,589 pec honor
of Knaresborough
HAMPTON township parish Malpas Ches pop 273
HAMPTON parish 1554 Middlesex 13-1/2 miles sw London pop 3,992
archd Middlesex dioc London Indep
HAMPTON, BISHOP'S parish 1669 Herefs 4 miles se Hereford pop
753 juris Consistory Court of Dean of Hereford
HAMPTON CHARLES hamlet parish Bockleton Herefs pop 91
HAMPTON COURT extra parochial liberty parish Hope under Din-
more Herefs
HAMPTON GAY parish 1621 co Oxford 2-3/4 miles se Woodstock
pop 36 archd and dioc Oxford
HAMPTON, GREAT parish 1539 Worcs 1 mile sw Evesham pop 290
pec Bishop of Worcester
HAMPTON, HIGH parish 1653 Devon 3-1/2 miles w Hatherleigh
archd Totnes dioc Exeter
HAMPTON, HILL hamlet parish Martley Worcs pop 165
HAMPTON IN ARDEN parish 1599 Warws 4 miles ne Solihull comp
chapelries Balsall, Knowle, hamlets Kinwalsey, Nuthurst pop
1,894 archd Coventry dioc Lichfield
HAMPTON, LITTLE parish 1539 Sussex 4 miles s Arundel pop 1,625
archd and dioc Chichester
HAMPTON, LITTLE township parish Great Hampton Worcs
HAMPTON LOVETT parish 1666 Worcs 1-1/2 miles nw Droitwich
pop 143 archd and dioc Worcester
HAMPTON LUCY otherwise HISHOP'S HAMPTON parish 1556 Warws
4-1/4 miles ne Stratford upon Avon pop 540 pec Rector
HAMPTON, MAISEY parish 1570 Gloucs 2-1/4 miles sw Fairford
pop 364 archd and dioc Gloucester
HAMPTON, MINCHIN parish 1558 Gloucs 14 miles s Gloucester
comp chapelry Rodborough, part of Nailsworth, town Minchin
Hampton pop 7,255 archd and dioc Gloucester Bapt, Wesl Meth
HAMPTON, NETHER chapelry 1755 parish Wilton Wilts pop 143
HAMPTON POYLE parish 1540 co Oxford 3-3/4 miles se Woodstock
pop 156 archd and dioc Oxford
HAMPTON, WELSH parish 1725 Shrops 2-3/4 miles ne Ellesmere
pop 532 pec Lord of the manor
HAMPTON WICK chapelry parish Hampton Middlesex pop 1,463
HAMSEY parish 1583 Sussex 2 miles n Lewes pop 608 archd Lewes
dioc Chichester
HAMSTALL RIDWARE parish 1598 Staffs 5-1/2 miles ne Rugeley

pop 443 archd Stafford dioc Lichfield

HAMSTEELS township parish Lanchester co Durham

HAMSTERLEY chapelry 1588 parish St Andrew Auckland co Durham pop 503 archd and dioc Durham Bapt

HAMWORTHY chapelry parish Sturminster Marshall Dorset pop 308

HANBURY parish 1574 Staffs 6-3/4 miles nw Burton upon Trent comp chapelries Marchington, Newborough, townships Coton, Fauld, Hanbury-Woodene, Marchington, Woodlands, hamlet Subby Lane pop 2,160 archd Stafford dioc Lichfield

HANBURY parish 1577 Worcs 4 miles ne Droitwich pop 1,073 pec the Rector

HANBURY WOODEND township parish Hanbury Staffs pop 291

HANBY hamlet parish Lavington Lincs

HANDBOROUGH parish 1560 co Oxford 5-1/4 miles ne Witney pop 883 archd and dioc Oxford

HANDCHURCH township parish Trentham Staffs pop 169

HANDFORD township parish Trentham Staffs pop 607

HANDFORTH township parish Cheadle Ches pop 1,980

HANDLEY parish 1570 Ches 7-3/4 miles se Chester pop 389 archd and dioc Chester

HANDLEY parish 1754 Dorset 5-1/2 miles nw Cranborne pop 889 archd Dorset dioc Bristol

HANDSACRE joint parish with Armitage Staffs 3-1/2 miles se Rugeley pop 977 pec Prebendary of Handsacre and Armitage

HANDSWORTH parish 1558 Staffs 2-1/4 miles nw Birmingham pop 4,944 archd Stafford dioc Lichfield

HANDSWORTH parish 1558 W R York 4-1/2 miles se Sheffield pop 2,338 pec Chancellor, Cathedral Church of York

HANFORD extra parochial liberty 1669 Dorset 5-1/4 miles nw Blandford pop 10

HANGLETON parish 1727 Sussex 4-1/2 miles nw Brighton pop 64 archd Lewes dioc Chichester

HANHAM, ABBOTS chapelry 1586 parish Bitton Gloucs pop 1212

HANKELOW township parish Audlem Ches pop 289

HANKERTON parish 1699 Wilts 3-1/2 miles ne Malmesbury pop 413 archd Wilts dioc Salisbury

HANLEY chapelry 1754 parish Stoke upon Trent Staffs pop 7,121 archd Stafford dioc Lichfield Bapt, Indep, Wesl and other Meth, Unit, Roman Cath

HANLEY CASTLE parish 1538 Worcs 1-1/4 miles nw Upton upon Severn pop 1,653 archd and dioc Worcester Roman Cath

HANLEY CHILD chapelry parish Eastham Worcs pop 210

HANLEY WILLIAM parish 1586 Worcs 6 miles se Tenbury pop 141 archd Salop dioc Hereford

HANLITH township parish Kirby in Malham Dale W R York pop 42

HANNAY or HANNAH parish 1559 Lincs 3-3/4 miles ne Alford pop 97 a donative

HANNEY, EAST township parish West Hanney Berks pop 631

HANNEY, WEST parish 1565 Berks 3-3/4 miles ne Wantage pop 1,161 archd Berks dioc Salisbury

HANNINGFIELD, EAST parish 1612 Essex 4-1/4 miles sw Danbury pop 447 archd Essex dioc London

HANNINGFIELD, SOUTH parish 1558 Essex 6 miles sw Danbury pop 214 archd Essex dioc London

HANNINGFIELD, WEST parish 1558 Essex 6 miles sw Danbury pop 480 archd Essex dioc London

HANNINGTON parish 1538 co Northampton 6-3/4 miles nw Wellingborough pop 196 archd Northampton dioc Peterborough

HANNINGTON parish 1771 Hamps 7-1/2 miles nw Basingstoke pop 287 pec Rector

HANNINGTON parish 1571 Wilts 1-3/4 miles nw Highworth pop 415 archd Wilts dioc Salisbury

HANSLOPE parish 1570 Bucks 4-1/2 miles ne Stony Stratford pop 1,623 archd Buckingham dioc Lincoln Bapt

HANTHORPE or HARMTHORPE chapelry parish Morton Lincs pop 166

HANWELL parish 1571 Middlesex 8 miles w London pop 1,213 archd Middlesex dioc London Indep

HANWELL parish 1586 co Oxford 3 miles nw Banbury pop 288 archd and dioc Oxford

HANWOOD, GREAT parish 1559 Shrops 3-3/4 miles sw Shrewsbury pop 156 archd Salop dioc Hereford

HANWOOD, LITTLE township parish Pontesbury Shrops

HANWORTH parish 1731 Middlesex 3-1/4 miles sw Hounslow pop 671 juris Commissary of London concurrently with Bishop of London

HANWORTH parish 1721 Norfolk 5-1/2 miles ne Aylsham pop 276 archd Norfolk dioc Norwich

HANWORTH, COLD parish 1725 Lincs 8-3/4 miles ne Lincoln pop 63 archd Stow dioc Lincoln

HANWORTH, POTTER Lincs See POTTER HANWORTH

HAPPISBURGH parish 1558 Norfolk 6-1/4 miles e North Walsham pop 582 archd Norfolk dioc Norwich

HAPSFORD township parish Thornton Ches pop 83

HAPTON township parish Whalley Lancs pop 583

HAPTON parish 1653 Norfolk 3-1/2 miles nw St Mary Stratton pop 200 archd Norfolk dioc Norwich Unit

HARAM township parish Helmsley N R York pop 445

HARBERTON parish 1621 Devon 2 miles sw Totnes pop 1,584 archd Totnes dioc Exeter Bapt

HARBLEDOWN parish 1557 Kent 1-1/4 miles sw Canterbury pop 819 archd and dioc Canterbury

HARBONE or HARBORNE parish 1538 Staffs 3-3/4 miles sw Birmingham pop 4,227 pec Dean and Chapter of Lichfield

HARBOROUGH, MAGNA parish 1540 Warws 3-3/4 miles nw Rugby pop 365 archd Coventry dioc Lichfield

HARBOROUGH, MARKET market town 1588 parish Bowden Magna Leics 17 miles n Northampton pop 2,272 archd Leicester dioc Lincoln Indep, Wesl Meth

HARBOTTLE township parish Hallystone Northumberland pop 165 Presb

HABROUGHAM EAVES township parish Whalley Lancs pop 5,817

HARBRIDGE chapelry 1563 Hamps pop 322 pec vicar of Ringwood

HARBURY otherwise HARBERSBURY parish 1564 Warws 3-3/4 miles sw Southam pop 997 archd Coventry dioc Lichfield Wesl Meth

HARBY parish 1700 Leics 8-3/4 miles n Melton Mowbray pop 488 archd Leicester dioc Lincoln

HARBY chapelry parish North Clifton Notts pop 304 Wesl Meth

HARCOURT township parish Stanton upon Hine Heath Shrops pop 35

HARDENHUISH parish 1730 Wilts 1-1/4 miles nw Chippenham pop 116 archd Wilts dioc Salisbury

HARDHAM parish 1642 Sussex 6 miles se Petworth pop 134 archd and dioc Chichester

HARDHORN township parish Poulton Lancs pop 409

HARDINGHAM parish 1557 Norfolk 5-3/4 miles nw Wymondham pop 560 archd Norfolk dioc Norwich

HARDINGSTONE parish 1562 co Northampton 2 miles se Northampton pop 1,036 archd Northampton dioc Peterborough

HARDINGTON parish incl in regs of Hemington Somerset 4-1/4 miles nw Frome pop 28 archd Wells dioc Bath and Wells

HARDINGTON MANDEVILLE parish 1687 Somerset 4-1/2 miles sw Yeovil pop 603 archd Wells dioc Bath and Wells

HARDLEY parish 1715 Norfolk 7 miles sw Acle pop 211 archd Norfolk dioc Norwich

HARDMEAD parish 1556 Bucks 5 miles ne Newport Pagnell pop 83 archd Buckingham dioc Lincoln

HARDRES, LOWER parish 1558 Kent 3 miles s Canterbury pop 259 archd and dioc Canterbury

HARDRES, UPPER parish 1565 Kent 4-3/4 miles s Canterbury pop 311 archd and dioc Canterbury

HARDROW chapelry 1755 parish Aysgarth N R York archd Richmond dioc Chester

HARDWICK hamlet parish Monk Hesleton co Durham

HARDWICK chapelry 1566 parish Standish Gloucs pop 459

HARDWICK parish 1561 Norfolk 3 miles se St Mary Stratton pop 224 archd Norfolk dioc Norwich Wesl Meth

HARDWICK hamlet Norfolk

HARDWICK parish 1559 co Northampton 3-1/4 miles nw Wellingborough pop 86 archd Northampton dioc Peterborough

HARDWICK extra parochial liberty parish Hawstead Suffolk

HARDWICK, EAST township parish Pontefract W R York pop 139

HARDWICK PRIORS parish 1660 Warws 5-3/4 miles se Southam pop 296 archd Coventry dioc Lichfield

HARDWICK, WEST township parish Wragby W R York pop 85

HARDWICKE parish 1558 Bucks 3-1/2 miles nw Aylesbury pop 640 archd Buckingham dioc Lincoln

HARDWICKE parish 1564 Cambs 5-1/2 miles ne Caxton pop 90 pec Bishop of Ely

HARDWICKE hamlet parish Abergavenny co Monmouth pop 127

HARDWICKE hamlet parish Ducklington co Oxford pop 103

HARDWICKE parish 1758 co Oxford 5 miles n Bicester pop 80 archd and dioc Oxford

HARDY chapelry parish Manchester Lancs

HAREBY parish 1587 Lincs 4-1/4 miles w Spilsby pop 81 archd and dioc Lincoln

HAREFIELD parish 1538 Middlesex 4-1/4 miles n Uxbridge pop 1,285 juris Commissary of London, Consistorial Court of Bishop

HARESCOMB parish 1741 Gloucs 2-1/2 miles nw Painswick pop 121 archd and dioc Gloucester

HARESFIELD parish 1558 Gloucs 6 miles sw Gloucester pop 611 archd and dioc Gloucester

HAREUP or HAREHOPE township parish Eglingham Northumberland pop 50

HAREWOOD parish 1671 Herefs 5-1/2 miles nw Ross pop 85 pec Bishop of Hereford

HAREWOOD parish 1614 W R York 6-1/2 miles sw Wetherby comp townships Dunkeswith, Weston, East Keswick, Alwoodley, Harewood, Weardley, Wigton, Wike pop 2,463 archd and dioc York Wesl Meth

HARFORD parish 1724 Devon 2-1/2 miles n Ivy Bridge pop 210 archd Totnes dioc Exeter

HARGHAM parish 1561 Norfolk 3-1/2 miles sw Attleburgh pop 77 archd Norfolk dioc Norwich

HARGRAVE chapelry 1631 parish Tarvin Ches archd and dioc Chester

HARGRAVE parish 1572 co Northampton 3-1/2 miles nw Kimbolton pop 203 archd Northampton dioc Peterborough

HARGRAVE parish 1710 Suffolk 6-1/2 miles sw Bury St Edmund's pop 394 archd Sudbury dioc Norwich

HARKSTEAD parish 1654 Suffolk 6-1/2 miles se Ipswich pop 329 archd Suffolk dioc Norwich

HARLAXTON parish 1558 Lincs 3 miles sw Grantham pop 390 archd and dioc Lincoln

HARLE, KIRK parish 1692 Northumberland 13-1/2 miles sw Morpeth comp chapelry Kirkheaton, townships Hawick, Kirk Harle pop 367 incl Beldridge, Greatlaw, Kidlaw, Mirlow House, Shield Hill, Thrivewell archd Northumberland dioc Durham

HARLE, LITTLE township parish Kirkwhelpington Northumberland pop 64

HARLE, WEST township parish Kirkwhelpington Northumberland pop 55

HARLESTON 1558 parish Reddenhall Norfolk Indep, Wesl Meth

HARLESTON chapelry 1693 parish Clifton Campville Staffs pop 218
HARLESTON parish 1561 Suffolk 3 miles nw Stow Market pop 89
    archd Sudbury dioc Norwich
HARLESTONE parish 1570 co Northampton 4 miles nw Northampton
    pop 645 archd Northampton dioc Peterborough
HARLEY parish 1745 Shrops 2-1/4 miles nw Much Wenlock pop 257
    archd Salop dioc Lichfield
HARLING, EAST parish 1544 Norfolk 22 miles sw Norwich pop 1,031
    archd Norfolk dioc Norwich Soc of Friends, Wesl Meth
HARLING, MIDDLE hamlet, formerly parish Norfolk
HARLING, WEST parish 1583 Norfolk 2-1/4 miles sw East Harling
    pop 107 archd Norfolk dioc Norwich
HARLINGTON parish 1647 Beds 5-1/4 miles s Ampthill pop 481
    archd Bedford dioc Lincoln
HARLINGTON parish 1540 Middlesex 4 miles nw Hounslow pop 648
    archd Middlesex dioc London Bapt
HARLOW parish 1629 Essex 17 miles nw Chelmsford pop 2,101 archd
    Middlesex dioc London Bapt
HARLOWHILL township parish Ovingham Northumberland pop 149
HARLTHORPE township parish Bubwith W R York pop 105
HARLTON parish 1636 Cambs 6-1/2 miles sw Cambridge pop 223
    archd and dioc Ely
HARMBY township parish Spennithorn N R York pop 233
HARMONDSWORTH parish 1670 Middlesex 2-1/2 miles ne Colnbrook
    pop 1,276 archd Middlesex dioc London
HARMSTON parish 1563 Lincs 6 miles s Lincoln pop 405 archd and
    dioc Lincoln
HARNHAM township parish Bolam Northumberland pop 73
HARNHAM, WEST parish 1568 Wilts 1-1/2 miles sw Salisbury pop
    256 pec Prebendal Court of Coombe and Harnham
HARNHILL parish 1730 Gloucs 4 miles se Cirencester pop 71 archd
    and dioc Gloucester
HARPENDEN parish 1562 Herts 3 miles ne Redburn pop 1,972 archd
    Huntingdon dioc Lincoln Indep, Wesl Meth
HARPFORD parish 1569 Devon 3-1/2 miles nw Sidmouth pop 307
    archd and dioc Exeter
HARPHAM parish 1720 E R York 5-1/2 miles ne Great Driffield pop
    240 archd East Riding dioc York Wesl Meth
HARPLEY parish 1722 Norfolk 8 miles ne Castle Rising pop 370
    archd and dioc Norwich
HARPOLE parish 1538 co Northampton 4 miles w Northampton pop
    711 archd Northampton dioc Peterborough Bapt
HARPSDEN parish 1558 co Oxford 1-3/4 miles s Henley upon Thames
    pop 238 archd and dioc Oxford
HARPSWELL parish 1559 Lincs 7-3/4 miles se Gainsborough pop 73
    archd Stow dioc Lincoln
HARPTON, LOWER township parish Old Radnor Herefs pop 68
HARPTREE, EAST parish 1663 Somerset 7 miles ne Wells pop 695

pec Prebendary of East Harptree Wesl Meth

HARPTREE, WEST parish 1655 Somerset 8 miles ne Wells pop 536 archd Bath dioc Bath and Wells

HARPURHEY township parish Manchester Lancs pop 463

HARRABY township parish St Cuthbert, Carlisle Cumberland pop 66

HARRATON township parish Chester le Street co Durham pop 2,171

HARRIETSHAM parish 1538 Kent 7-1/2 miles se Maidstone pop 704 archd and dioc Canterbury

HARRINGTON parish 1653 Cumberland 2-1/2 miles s Workington pop 1,758 archd Richmond dioc Chester Prim and Wesl Meth

HARRINGTON parish 1697 Lincs 5-1/4 miles nw Spilsby pop 70 archd and dioc Lincoln

HARRINGTON parish 1673 co Northampton 3 miles sw Rothwell pop 191 archd Northampton dioc Peterborough

HARRINGWORTH parish 1695 co Northampton 3-3/4 miles se Uppingham pop 358 archd Northampton dioc Peterborough

HARROGATE township 1758 parish Knaresboro W R York pop 2,812 archd Richmond dioc Chester Low Harrogate church erected 1824 Indep, Wesl Meth

HARROLD parish 1598 Beds 8 miles nw Bedford pop 995 archd Bedford dioc Lincoln Indep

HARROW ON THE HILL parish 1558 Middlesex 9 miles nw London pop 3,861 pec Archbishop of Canterbury Bapt, Wesl Meth

HARROWBY township parish Grantham Lincs pop 54

HARROWDEN, GREAT parish 1672 co Northampton 2-1/4 miles nw Wellingborough pop 148 archd Northampton dioc Peterborough

HARROWDEN, LITTLE parish 1653 co Northampton 3 miles nw Wellingborough pop 465 archd Northampton dioc Peterborough

HARSLEY, EAST parish 1693 N R York 6-3/4 miles ne North Allerton pop 436 archd Cleveland dioc York

HARSLEY, WEST township parish Osmotherley N R York pop 66

HARSTON parish 1686 Cambs 5-1/2 miles sw Cambridge pop 562 archd and dioc Ely

HARSTON parish 1707 Leics 6 miles sw Grantham pop 182 archd Leicester dioc Lincoln

HARSWELL parish 1653 E R York 3-1/2 miles sw Market Weighton pop 70 archd East Riding dioc York

HART parish 1577 co Durham 4-1/2 miles nw Hartlepool comp townships Dalton, Piercy, Elwick, Hart, Throston pop 624 archd Northumberland dioc Durham

HARTBURN township parish Stockton upon Tees co Durham pop 152

HARTBURN parish 1678 Northumberland 7 miles w Morpeth comp townships High Angerton, Low Angerton, Corridge, Hartburn, Hartburn Grange, Highlaws, Longwitton, North Middleton, South Middleton, Rothley, East Thornton, West Thornton, Todridge, Whitridge, Cambo, Deanham, Favinley, otherwise Farnlaws, Greenleighton, Hartington, Hartington Hall, Harwood, East Shafto, West Shafto, Wallington Demesne pop 1,440 archd Northumberland dioc Durham

HARTBURN GRANGE township parish Hartburn Northumberland pop 66

HARTEST parish 1556 Suffolk 7 miles ne Clare pop 761 archd Sudbury dioc Norwich

HARTFIELD parish 1648 Sussex 6 miles se East Grinsted comp North and South Hartfield pop 1,455 archd Lewes dioc Chichester Wesl Meth

HARTFORD chapelry parish Great Budworth Ches pop 863

HARTFORD parish 1538 Hunts 1-1/2 miles ne Huntingdon pop 452 archd Huntingdon dioc Lincoln

HARTFORD BRIDGE hamlet partly in parish Elvetham partly in Hartley Wintney Hamps

HARTFORD, EAST township parish Horton Northumberland pop 12

HARTFORD, WEST township parish Horton Northumberland pop 55

HARTGROVE chapelry parish Fontmell Magna Dorset pop 187

HARTHILL parish 1730 Ches 7 miles sw Tarporley pop 166 archd and dioc Chester

HARTHILL or HARTLE township parish Bakewell Derbys pop 65

HARTHILL parish 1586 W R York 9-3/4 miles se Rotherham pop 632 archd and dioc York

HARTING parish 1567 Sussex 7 miles sw Midhurst pop 1,290 archd and dioc Chichester Indep

HARTINGTON parish 1610 Derbys 9-1/2 miles sw Bakewell, comp townships Town Quarter, Middle Quarter with Earl Sterndale, Nether Quarter, Upper Quarter pop 2,103 pec Dean's Court for manor of Hartington Wesl Meth

HARTINGTON township parish Hartburn Northumberland pop 66

HARTINGTON HALL township parish Hartburn Northumberland pop 44

HARTLAND parish 1578 Devon 13-1/4 miles sw Bideford pop 2,143 archd Barnstaple dioc Exeter Indep

HARTLEBURY parish 1540 Worcs 2 miles se Stourport pop 1,948 pec Rector

HARTLEPOOL parish 1566 co Durham 19 miles se Durham pop 1,330 archd and dioc Durham Wesl Meth

HARTLEY parish 1712 Kent 6-3/4 miles se Dartford pop 182 archd and dioc Rochester

HARTLEY township parish Earsdon Northumberland pop 1,850 Prim and Wesl Meth

HARTLEY township parish Kirkby Stephen Westm pop 125

HARTLEY BURN township parish Haltwhistle Northumberland pop 161

HARTLEY DAMMER liberty parish Shinfield Berks pop 381

HARTLEY MAUDIT parish 1672 Hamps 2-3/4 miles se Alton pop 69 archd and dioc Winchester

HARTLEY ROW hamlet parish Hartley Wintney Hamps

HARTLEY WESTPALL parish 1558 Hamps 5 miles w Hartford Bridge pop 283 archd and dioc Winchester

HARTLEY WINTNEY parish 1658 Hamps 1-3/4 miles sw Hartford Bridge pop 1,139 archd and dioc Winchester

HARTLINGTON township parish Burnsall W R York pop 115

HARTLIP parish 1538 Kent 6 miles se Chatham pop 363 archd and dioc Canterbury

HARTLEY tything parish Mintern Magna Dorset

HARTOFT township parish Middleton N R York pop 142

HARTON township parish Jarrow co Durham pop 217

HARTON township parish Bossall N R York pop 169

HARTPURY parish 1571 Gloucs 4-1/4 miles se Newent pop 880 archd and dioc Gloucester

HARTS GROUNDS otherwise GIBBET HILLA extra parochial district parish Gosberton Lincs pop 43

HARTSHEAD township parish Ashton under Line Lancs

HARTSHEAD chapelry 1612 parish Dewsbury W R York pop 2,408 archd and dioc York

HARTSHILL hamlet parish Mancetter Warwick pop 909

HARTSHORN parish 1594 Derbys 3 miles nw Ashby de la Zouch pop 1,204 archd Derby dioc Lichfield Wesl Meth

HARTSIDE township parish Ingram Northumberland

HARTSOP chapelry parish Barton Westm pop 400

HARTWELL parish 1550 Bucks 2 miles sw Aylesbury pop 137 archd Buckingham dioc Lincoln

HARTWELL parish 1684 co Northampton 7-1/4 miles se Northampton pop 531 archd Northampton dioc Peterborough

HARTWITH chapelry 1751 parish Kirby Malzeard W R York pop 943 pec Prebendal of Masham

HARTY, ISLE OF parish 1679 Kent 9 miles se Queenborough pop 67 archd and dioc Canterbury

HARVINGTON parish 1573 Worcs 4 miles ne Evesham pop 318 archd and dioc Worcester

HARWELL parish 1558 Berks 6-1/2 miles ne Wantage pop 780 archd Berks dioc Salisbury

HARWICH market town, borough 1539 Essex 42 miles ne Chelmsford pop 4,297 sep juris comp parishes Dover Court All Saints 1706, St Nicholas archd Colchester dioc London

HARWOOD chapelry 1780 parish Middleton in Teasdale co Durham

HARWOOD township parish Bolton Lancs pop 2,011

HARWOOD township parish Hartburn Northumberland pop 47

HARWOOD DALE chapelry parish Hackness N R York pop 336

HARWOOD, GREAT chapelry 1560 parish Blackburn Lancs pop 2,436 archd and dioc Chester

HARWOOD, LITTLE township parish Blackburn Lancs pop 341

HARWORTH parish 1538 Notts 2-3/4 miles sw Bawtry pop 526 archd Nottingham dioc York

HASCOMB parish 1646 Surrey 3-3/4 miles se Godalming pop 317 archd Surrey dioc Winchester

HASELBEECH parish 1653 co Northampton 11-1/4 miles nw Northampton pop 140 archd Northampton dioc Peterborough

HASELBURY BRYAN parish 1562 Dorset 10 miles nw Blandford Forum pop 611 archd Dorset dioc Bristol

HASELEY parish 1588 Warws 3-1/2 miles nw Warwick pop 194 archd and dioc Worcester

HASELEY, GREAT parish 1538 co Oxford 3-1/4 miles w Tetsworth pop 749 archd and dioc Oxford

HASELEY, LITTLE township parish Great Haseley co Oxford pop 114

HASELOR township parish St Michael Lichfield Staffs pop 36

HASELOR parish 1594 Warws 2-1/2 miles e Alcester pop 349 archd and dioc Worcester

HASELWOOD or HASLEWOOD chapelry no regs Suffolk pop 90

HASFIELD parish 1559 Gloucs 6 miles n Gloucester pop 245 pec Deerhurst

HASKETON parish 1545 Suffolk 1-3/4 miles nw Woodbridge pop 517 archd Suffolk dioc Norwich

HASLAND township parish Chesterfield Derbys pop 889

HASLE township parish Wragby W R York pop 134

HASLEBURY parish (incl in regs of Box) Wilts 6-1/2 miles sw Chippenham archd Wilts dioc Salisbury

HASLEBURY PLUCKNETT parish 1672 Somerset 2-1/4 miles ne Crewkerne pop 826 pec Prebendary of Haslebury

HASLEMERE parish 1594 borough Surrey 12-1/2 miles SW Guildford pop 849 archd Surrey dioc Winchester Indep

HASLINGDEN chapelry 1620 parish Whalley Lancs pop 7,776 archd and dioc Chester Bapt, Indep, Wesl Meth, Sandemanians, Swedenborgians

HASLINGFIELD parish 1709 Cambs 5-1/2 miles sw Cambridge pop 559 archd and dioc Ely

HASLINGTON chapelry 1648 parish Barthomley Ches pop 1,028 archd and dioc Chester Indep

HASSALL township parish Sandbach Ches pop 200

HASSINGHAM parish 1563 Norfolk 4 miles sw Acle pop 140 archd and dioc Norwich

HASSOP hamlet parish Bakewell Derbys pop 121

HASTINGLEIGH parish 1730 Kent 6-1/2 miles ne Ashford pop 216 archd and dioc Canterbury

HASTINGS parish borough sep juris Sussex 69 miles e Chichester pop 10,097 All Saints 1559, St Clement 1558 archd and dioc Chichester Bapt, Bryanites, Huntingtonians, Indep, Wesl Meth

HASTINGWOOD hamlet parish North Weald Essex

HASWELL township parish Easington co Durham pop 263

HATCH hamlet parish Northill Beds pop 241

HATCH hamlet parish Kingston upon Thames Surrey pop 1,079

HATCH BEAUCHAMP parish 1760 Somerset 6-3/4 miles nw Ilminster pop 324 archd Taunton dioc Bath and Wells Bapt

HATCH, EAST chapelry parish Tisbury Wilts

HATCH, WEST parish 1606 Somerset 4-3/4 miles se Taunton pop

396 pec Dean and Chapter of Wells

HATCLIFFE parish 1696 Lincs 6-3/4 miles se Caistor pop 96 pec Collegiate Church of Southwell

HATFIELD parish 1615 Hereford 7 miles nw Bromyard pop 155 archd and dioc Hereford

HATFIELD parish 1566 W R York 3 miles sw Thorne comp townships Hatfield, Stainforth pop 3,000 archd and dioc York Indep

HATFIELD, BISHOP'S parish 1653 Herts 7 miles sw Hereford pop 3,598 archd Huntingdon dioc Lincoln Indep

HATFIELD BROAD OAK parish 1558 Essex 6 miles ne Harlow comp townships Brumsend quarter, Heath quarter, Town quarter, Woodrow quarter pop 1,825 juris Commissary Essex and Herts, Consistorial Court of Bishop of London Wesl Meth

HATFIELD, GREAT township parish Sigglesthorne E R York pop 146

HATFIELD PEVERELL parish 1626 Essex 3-1/4 miles sw Witham pop 1,313 archd Colchester dioc London

HATFORD parish 1538 Berks 3-1/2 miles se Great Farringdon pop 123 archd Berks dioc Salisbury

HATHERALL Lancs See HOTHERSALL

HATHERLEIGH parish 1558 borough sep juris Devon 29 miles nw Exeter pop 1,606 archd Totnes dioc Exeter Indep

HATHERLEY, DOWN parish 1563 Gloucs 3-1/4 miles ne Gloucester pop 150 archd and dioc Gloucester

HATHERLEY, UP joint chapelry with Great Shurdington Gloucs 2-1/2 miles sw Cheltenham pop 21 archd and dioc Gloucester

HATHERN parish 1563 Leics 2-3/4 miles nw Loughborough pop 1,289 archd Leicester dioc Lincoln Wesl Meth

HATHEROP parish 1670 Gloucs 3 miles n Fairford pop 326 archd and dioc Gloucester

HATHERSAGE parish 1627 Derbys 5-1/4 miles ne Stonet Middleton comp chapelries Darwent, Middleston Stoney, hamlets Bamford, Hathersage, Outseats pop 1,794 archd Derby dioc Lichfield Wesl Meth, Roman Cath

HATHERTON township parish Wybunbury Ches pop 447

HATHERTON township parish Wolverhampton Staffs pop 320

HATLEY parish 1589 Cambs 4 miles ne Potton pop 119 archd and dioc Ely

HATLEY, COCKAYNE parish 1701 Beds 6 miles ne Biggleswade pop 125 archd Bedford dioc Lincoln

HATLEY, EAST parish 1585 Cambs 4-1/2 miles ne Potton pop 104 archd and dioc Ely

HATTERSLEY township parish Mottram in Longden Dale Ches pop 477

HATTON township parish Waverton Ches pop 150

HATTON township parish Runcorn Ches pop 391

HATTON hamlet parish Marston upon Dover Derbys pop 211

HATTON parish 1552 Lincs 3-1/4 miles se Wragby pop 165 archd and dioc Lincoln

HATTON hamlet parish East Bedfont Middlesex

HATTON township parish Shiffnall Shrops pop 571

HATTON parish 1538 Warws 3-1/4 miles nw Warwick comp chapelries Beausall, Shrewley pop 815 archd and dioc Worcester

HATTON, HIGH township parish Stanton upon Hine Heath Shrops pop 208

HAUGH extra parochial liberty 1762 Lincs 2-3/4 miles w Alford pop 8

HAUGHAM parish 1756 Lincs 3-3/4 miles s Louth pop 92 archd and dioc Lincoln

HAUGHLEY parish 1558 Suffolk 2-3/4 miles nw Stow Market pop 908 archd Sudbury dioc Norwich

HAUGHMOND, ABBERY Shrops See HAGHMON ABBEY

HAUGHTON township parish Bunbury Ches pop 172

HAUGHTON township parish Simonbourn Northumberland pop 154

HAUGHTON parish 1570 Staffs 4 miles sw Stafford pop 490 archd Stafford dioc Lichfield

HAUGHTON LE SKERNE parish 1569 co Durham 1-3/4 miles ne Darlington comp townships Brampton, Great Burdon, Haughton, Whessoe, chapelry Sadberge, township Coatham Mundeville pop 1,603 archd and dioc Durham Wesl Meth

HAUKSWELL parish 1592 N R York 5-1/4 miles s Richmond comp townships Barton, Garriston, East Haukswell, West Haukswell pop 361 archd Richmond dioc Chester

HAULGH township parish Bolton Lancs

HAULT HUCKNALL Derbys See AULT HUCKNALL

HAUNTON township parish Clifton Campbille Staffs pop 214

HAUTBOYS, GREAT parish 1563 Norfolk 3/4 mile nw Coltishall pop 141 archd and dioc Norwich

HAUTBOYS, LITTLE parish incl in regs of Lammas Norfolk 2 miles nw Coltishall pop 303 archd and dioc Norwich

HAUXLEY township parish Warkworth Northumberland pop 143

HAUXTON parish 1560 Cambs 4-1/2 miles sw Cambridge pop 235 archd and dioc Ely

HAVANT parish 1653 Hamps 21-1/4 miles se Southampton pop 2,063 pec Incumbent Indep, Roman Cath

HAVENGORE MARSH extra parochial liberty Essex 7 miles se Rochford pop 21

HAVENINGHAM parish 1539 Suffolk 5-1/2 miles sw Halesworth pop 423 archd Suffolk dioc Norwich

HAVERAH PARK extra parochial liberty W R York 8 miles sw Knaresboro pop 96

HAVERBRACK township parish Beetham Westm pop 120

HAVERCROFT township parish Felkirk W R York pop 153

HAVERHILL parish 1670 Suffolk 28 miles sw Bury St Edmund's pop 2,025 archd Sudbury dioc Norwich Bapt, Indep

HAVERHOLM PRIORY extra parochial liberty Lincs 4 miles ne Sleaford

HAVERING ATTE BOWER parish 1671 Essex 3 miles n Romford pop

332 pec Hornchurch and Havering atte Bower

HAVERINGLAND parish 1694 Norfolk 4-1/4 miles se Reepham pop 181 archd Norfolk dioc Norwich

HAVERSHAM parish 1665 Bucks 3-1/2 miles sw Newport Pagnell pop 313 archd Buckingham dioc Lincoln

HAVERTHWAITE chapelry parish Coulton Lancs

HAW hamlet parish Tirley Gloucs

HAWCOAT, ABOVE TOWN township parish Dalton in Furness Lancs pop 848

HAWERBY parish 1598 Lincs 10-1/2 miles nw Louth pop 66 pec Chapter of Collegiate Church of Southwell

HAWES chapelry 1695 parish Bassenthwaite Cumberland

HAWES chapelry parish Aysgarth N R York pop 1,559 Soc of Friends, Sandemanians

HAWICK township parish Kirkharle Northumberland pop 18

HAWKCHURCH parish 1663 Dorset 3-1/4 miles ne Axminster comp tything Wyldecourt, Phillyholme pop 886 archd Dorset dioc Bristol

HAWKEDON parish 1709 Suffolk 6 miles ne Clare pop 328 archd Sudbury dioc Norwich

HAWKESBURY parish 1603 Gloucs 3-3/4 miles se Wickwar comp tythings Little Badminton, Hawkesbury, Killcot, Hillesley, Saddlewood, Tresham, Upton pop 2,182 archd and dioc Gloucester

HAWKESDALE township parish Dalston Cumberland pop 427

HAWKESHEAD parish 1568 Lancs 28 miles nw Lancaster comp town of Hawkeshead, chapelry Satterthwaite, townships Claife, Monk Coniston with Skellwith pop 2,060 archd Richmond dioc Chester

HAWKHILL township parish Lesbury Northumberland

HAWKHURST parish 1550 Kent 5 miles sw Cranbrooke pop 2,428 archd and dioc Canterbury

HAWKINGE parish 1691 Kent 2-1/2 miles n Folkestone pop 131 archd and dioc Canterbury

HAWKLEY parish 1797 earlier entries in regs of Newton Valence Hamps 3-3/4 miles n Petersfield pop 277 archd and dioc Winchester Indep

HAWKRIDGE parish 1655 Somerset 4-1/4 miles nw Dulverton pop 67 archd Taunton dioc Bath and Wells

HAWKSWITH township parish Arncliffe W R York pop 81

HAWKSWORTH parish 1569 Notts 8 miles sw Newark pop 212 archd Nottingham dioc York

HAWKSWORTH township parish Otley W R York pop 327

HAWKWELL parish 1692 Essex 1-3/4 miles nw Rochford pop 329 archd Essex dioc London

HAWKWELL township parish Stamfordham Northumberland pop 150

HAWLEY tything parish Yately Hamps pop 747

HAWLING parish 1677 Gloucs 4-1/2 miles se Winchcombe pop 240 archd and dioc Gloucester

HAWNBY parish 1653 N R York 6-1/4 miles nw Helmsley comp townships Arden with Ardenside, Bilsdale Westside, Dale Town, Hawnby, Snilesby pop 754 archd Cleveland dioc York Wesl Meth

HAWNES Beds See HAYNES

HAWORTH chapelry 1645 parish Bradford W R York pop 5,835 Bapt, Wesl Meth

HAWRIDGE parish 1725 Bucks 3 miles nw Chesham pop 217 archd Buckingham dioc Lincoln

HAWSKER township parish Whitby N R York pop 654

HAWSTEAD parish 1558 Suffolk 4 miles s Bury St Edmund's pop 414 archd Sudbury dioc Norwich

HAWTHORN township parish Easington co Durham pop 162

HAWTHORP chapelry parish Irnham Lincs pop 176

HAWTON parish 1564 Notts 2 miles sw Newark pop 258 archd Nottingham dioc York

HAXBY parish 1667 N R York 4-3/4 miles n York pop 412 pec Prebendary of Strensall Wesl Meth

HAXEY parish 1559 Lincs 8 miles nw Gainsborough pop 1,868 archd Stow dioc Lincoln Wesl Meth

HAYDOCK township parish Winwick Lancs pop 934

HAYDON parish 1711 Dorset 3 miles se Sherborne pop 123 pec Dean of Sarum

HAYDON parish 1538 Essex 7-1/2 miles nw Saffron Walden pop 259 Commissary Essex and Herts, Consistorial Court of Bishop of London

HAYDON BRIDGE chapelry 1654 parish Warden Northumberland pop 338 Indep, Wesl Meth

HAYDOR parish 1559 Lincs 6-1/2 miles ne Grantham pop 575 pec Prebendary of Haydor

HAYES parish 1539 Kent 2 miles s Bromley pop 504 pec Archbishop of Canterbury

HAYES parish 1638 Middlesex 3-1/2 miles se Uxbridge pop 1,575 pec Archbishop Indep

HAYFIELD chapelry 1622 parish Glossop Derbys archd Derby dioc Lichfield Indep, Meth

HAYLE and COPPER HOUSE sea port partly in parishes St Erth, Phillack and Uny Lelant Cornwall Wesl Meth

HAYLING, NORTH parish 1571 Hamps 2 miles se Havant pop 294 archd and dioc Winchester

HAYLING, SOUTH parish 1672 Hamps 4-1/2 miles s Havant pop 588 archd and dioc Winchester

HAYNES parish 1596 Beds 4 miles ne Ampthill pop 847 archd Bedford dioc Lincoln

HAYNFORD See HAINFORD

HAYTON township parish Aspatria Cumberland pop 253

HAYTON parish 1620 Cumberland 8 miles ne Carlisle comp townships Faugh with Fenton, Hayton, Talkin pop 1,291 archd and dioc Carlisle

HAYTON parish 1655 Notts 3 miles ne East Retford pop 256 archd

Nottingham dioc York

HAYTON parish 1610 E R York 2 miles se Pocklington comp chapelry Beilby, township Hayton pop 434 pec Dean of York

HAYWOOD FOREST extra parochial liberty Herefs 2-1/2 miles sw Hereford pop 126

HAZELEIGH parish 1575 Essex 2-3/4 miles sw Maldon pop 119 archd Essex dioc London

HAZELY HEATH tything parish Heckfield Hamps pop 313

HAZLEBADGE liberty parish Hope Derbys pop 63

HAZLETON parish 1597 Gloucs 4 miles nw Northleach pop 287 archd and dioc Gloucester

HAZLEWOOD township parish Duffield Derbys pop 390 Wesl Meth

HAZLEWOOD extra parochial parish Tadcaster W R York pop 330

HAZLEWOOD township parish Skipton W R York pop 221

HAZON township parish Shilbottle Northumberland pop 92

HEACHAM parish 1558 Norfolk 9 miles ne Castle Rising pop 733 archd Norfolk dioc Norwich

HEADBOURN WORTHY Hamps See WORTHY, HEADBOURN

HEADCORN parish 1560 Kent 8-1/2 miles se Maidstone pop 1,193 archd and dioc Canterbury Wesl Meth

HEADINGLEY chapelry 1723 parish St Peter Leeds W R York pop 3,849 archd and dioc York

HEADINGTON parish 1683 co Oxford 1-1/2 miles ne Oxford pop 1,388 archd and dioc Oxford

HEADLAM township parish Gainford co Durham pop 109

HEADLEY parish 1539 Hamps 6-1/2 miles sw Farnham pop 1,228 archd and dioc Winchester

HEADLEY parish 1663 Surrey 2-3/4 miles se Leatherhead pop 253 archd Surrey dioc Winchester

HEADON parish 1566 Notts 4 miles se East Retford pop 248 archd Nottingham dioc York

HEADWORTH township parish Jarrow co Durham

HEAGE chapelry parish Duffield Derbys pop 1,845 Bapt, Indep, Prim and Wesl Meth

HEALAUGH parish 1687 E R York 3-1/4 miles ne Tadcaster pop 212 archd and dioc York

HEALEY township parish Masham N R York pop 400

HEALING parish 1571 Lincs 5-1/2 miles w Great Grimsby pop 102 archd and dioc Lincoln

HEALY township parish Bywell St Peter Northumberland pop 54

HEALY township parish Netherwitton Northumberland pop 44

HEANOR parish 1559 Derbys 9 miles ne Derby comp town Heanor, townships Codnor with Lascow, Shipley pop 5,380 archd Derby dioc Lichfield Indep, Wesl Meth

HEANTON PUNCHARDEN parish 1657 Devon 4-1/2 miles nw Barnstaple pop 586 archd Barnstaple dioc Exeter

HEAP chapelry parish Bury Lancs pop 10,429 Indep, Wesl Meth

HEAPEY chapelry parish Leyland Lancs pop 465

HEAPHAM parish 1558 Lincs 5 miles se Gainsborough pop 143 archd Stow dioc Lincoln

HEATH chapelry parish Leighton Buzzard Beds pop 784 Wesl Meth

HEATH parish 1682 Derbys 5-1/4 miles se Chesterfield pop 382 archd Derby dioc Lichfield

HEATH township parish Leintwardine Herefs pop 51

HEATH or HETHE parish 1679 co Oxford 4 miles ne Bicester pop 414 archd and dioc Oxford Wesl Meth

HEATH chapelry parish Stoke St Milborough Shrops pop 42

HEATH township parish Warmfield W R York

HEATH, UPPER township parish Worthen Shrops

HEATHENCOTE hamlet parish Paulers Pury co Northampton

HEATHER parish 1619 Leics 5-1/2 miles nw Market Bosworth pop 449 archd Leicester dioc Lincoln

HEATHERCLEUGH chapelry parish Stanhope co Durham

HEATHFIELD parish 1703 Somerset 5-1/4 miles nw Taunton pop 136 archd Taunton dioc Bath and Wells

HEATHFIELD parish 1582 Sussex 8-1/2 miles ne Haylsham pop 1,801 archd Lewes dioc Chichester

HEATHPOOL township parish Kirk Newton Northumberland pop 43

HEATHWAITE township parish Kirkby Ireleth Lancs

HEATHY LEE township parish Allstonefield Staffs pop 689

HEATON township parish Lancaster Lancs pop 170

HEATON township parish Dean Lancs pop 719

HEATON township parish All Saints, Newcastle Northumberland pop 501

HEATON township parish Leek Staffs pop 402

HEATON chapelry parish Bradford W R York pop 1,452 Wesl Meth

HEATON, GREAT township parish Oldham Lancs pop 181

HEATON, KIRK parish 1653 W R York 2 miles ne Huddersfield comp townships Dalton, Kirk Heaton, Lepton, Upper Whitley pop 10,020 archd and dioc York

HEATON, LITTLE township parish Oldham Lancs pop 771

HEATON NORRIS chapelry 1767 parish Manchester Lancs pop 11,238 archd and dioc Chester Indep

HEAVITREE parish 1653 Devon 1 mile e Exeter pop 1,932 pec Dean and Chapter of Exeter

HEBBURN township parish Chillingham Northumberland pop 137

HEBBURN parish 1680 Northumberland 3 miles nw Morpeth comp townships Causey Park, Cockle Park, Earsdon, Earsdon Forest, Fenrother, Hebburn, Tritlington pop 564 archd Northumberland dioc Durham

HEBDEN township parish Linton W R York pop 491 Bapt, Wesl Meth

HECK or HICK township parish Snaith W R York pop 236

HECKFIELD parish 1538 Hamps 3-3/4 miles nw Hartford Bridge comp chapelry Mattingley, tythings Heckfield, Holdshott, greater portion of Hazely Heath pop 1,202 archd and dioc Winchester

HECKINGHAM parish 1560 Norfolk 6 miles nw Beccles pop 183

archd Norfolk dioc Norwich

HECKINGTON parish 1559 Lincs 5 miles se Sleaford pop 1,480 archd and dioc Lincoln Bapt

HECKMONDWIKE chapelry parish Birstall W R York pop 2,793 Indep, Wesl Meth

HEDDINGTON parish 1538 Wilts 3 miles s Calne pop 310 archd Wilts dioc Salisbury

HEDDON, BLACK township parish Stamfordham Northumberland pop 64

HEDDON, EAST township parish Heddon on the Wall Northumberland pop 57

HEDDON ON THE WALL parish 1656 Northumberland 7 miles nw Newcastle upon Tyne comp townships East Heddon, Heddon on the Wall, West Heddon, Houghton with Clowhouse, Whitchester pop 774 archd Northumberland dioc Durham

HEDDON, WEST township parish Heddon on the Wall Northumberland pop 42

HEDENHAM parish 1559 Norfolk 3-1/4 miles nw Bungay pop 356 archd Norfolk dioc Norwich

HEDGELEY township parish Eglingham Northumberland pop 43

HEDGERLEY parish 1539 Bucks 3 miles se Beaconfield pop 187 archd Buckingham dioc Lincoln

HEDGERLEY DEAN hamlet parish Farnham Royal Bucks pop 171

HEDINGHAM, CASTLE parish 1558 Essex 19 miles ne Chelmsford pop 1,220 archd Middlesex dioc London Indep

HEDINGHAM SIBLE parish 1680 Essex 3/4 mile sw Castle Heding-ham pop 2,194 Commissary Essex and Herts, Consistorial Court of Bishop of London Bapt

HEDLEY township parish Chester le Street co Durham pop 44

HEDLEY township parish Ovingham Northumberland pop 193

HEDLEY HOPE township parish Brancepeth co Durham pop 72

HEDLEY WOODSIDE township parish Ovingham Northumberland pop 60

HEDNESFORD township parish Cannock Staffs

HEDON or HEYDON parish 1549 borough E R York 44 miles se York pop 1,080 sep juris pec Archbishop of York Bapt, Indep, Wesl Meth, Roman Cath

HEDSOR parish 1678 Bucks 4-1/4 miles se Great Marlow pop 207 archd Buckingham dioc Lincoln

HEELYFIELD township parish Muggleswick co Durham pop 159

HEENE hamlet parish West Tarring Sussex pop 153

HEIGHAM See NORWICH

HEIGHAM, POTTER parish 1538 Norfolk 7 miles ne Acle pop 367 archd Norfolk dioc Norwich

HEIGHINGTON parish 1559 co Durham 6-1/2 miles nw Darlington comp townships Coastamoor, Heighington, Killerby, Midridge, Redworth, School Aycliffe, Walworth pop 1,739 archd and dioc Durham Wesl Meth

HEIGHINGTON chapelry parish Washingborough Lincs pop 552 Wesl
Meth
HEIGHLEY township parish Mitford Northumberland pop 117
HEIGHTINGTON chapelry parish Rock Worcs
HEIGHTON, SOUTH parish 1700 Sussex 1-3/4 miles ne Newhaven
pop 91 archd Lewes dioc Chichester
HELBECK LANDS chapelry parish Aysgarth N R York
HELEN'S ST parish 1653 Isle of Wight Hamps 9 miles e Newport
pop 953 archd and dioc Winchester Wesl Meth
HELFORD sea port parish Manaccan Cornwall Indep
HELHOUGHTON parish 1540 Norfolk 4-1/4 miles sw Fakenham pop
318 archd and dioc Norwich
HELLABY township parish Stainton W R York
HELLAND parish 1722 Cornwall 2-1/2 miles ne Bodmin pop 285
archd Cornwall dioc Exeter Wesl Meth
HELLESDON parish 1562 Norfolk 2-3/4 miles nw Norwich pop 443
archd and dioc Norwich
HELLIDON parish 1571 co Northampton 5 miles se Daventry pop 426
archd Northampton dioc Peterborough Wesl Meth
HELLIFIELD township parish Long Preston W R York pop 250
HELLINGHILL township parish Rothbury Northumberland pop 109
HELLINGLY parish 1618 Sussex 2-1/4 miles nw Haylsham pop 1,504
archd Lewes dioc Chichester Wesl Meth
HELLINGTON Norfolk See HILLINGTON
HELMDON parish 1572 co Northampton 6 miles n Brackley pop 515
archd Northampton dioc Peterborough
HELMINGHAM parish 1559 Suffolk 5 miles se Debenham pop 286
archd Suffolk dioc Norwich
HELMINGTON township parish St Andrew Auckland co Durham
HELMSLEY parish 1575 N R York 23 miles n York comp town Helms-
ley, joint chapelry Bilsdale Midcable with Bilsdale Birkham, town-
ships Haram, Laskill Pasture, Pockley, Rivaulx, Sproxton pop
3,411 archd Cleveland dioc York Soc of Friends, Wesl Meth
HELMSLEY, GATE parish 1689 N R York 6-1/4 miles ne York pop
243 pec Prebendary of Osbaldwick
HELMSLEY, UPPER parish 1642 N R York 7-1/2 miles ne York
pop 66 archd Cleveland dioc York
HELPERBY township parish Brafferton N R York pop 673
HELPERTHORP parish 1733 E R York 12 miles e New Malton pop
131 pec Dean and Chapter of York
HELPRINGHAM parish 1560 Lincs 7-1/2 miles ne Falkingham pop
750 archd and dioc Lincoln Indep
HELPSTONE parish 1685 co Northampton 3-3/4 miles sw Market
Deeping pop 485 archd Northampton dioc Peterborough
HELSBY township parish Frodsham Ches pop 534
HELSINGTON chapelry 1728 parish Kendal Westm pop 296 archd
Richmond dioc Chester
HELSTON chapelry 1598 parish Wendron borough Cornwall pop 3,293

sep juris archd Cornwall dioc Exeter Bapt, Wesl Meth

HELTON township parish Askham Westm pop 192

HELTON or HILTON township parish Bongate of St Michael Appleby Westm pop 311

HEMBLINGTON parish 1562 Norfolk 4 miles nw Acle pop 238 archd and dioc Norwich

HEMBURY, BROAD Devon See BROADHEMBURY

HEMINGBROUGH parish 1605 E R York 4-1/4 miles se Selby comp chapelry Barlby, townships Brackenholme with Woodall, Cliff with Lund, South Duffield, Hemingbrough, Menthorpe with Bowthorn, Osgodby pop 1,806 pec Howdenshire

HEMINGBY parish 1597 Lincs 3-3/4 miles nw Horncastle pop 366 archd and dioc Lincoln Wesl Meth

HEMINGFORD, ABBOTS parish 1693 Hunts 2-1/2 miles w St Ives pop 484 archd Huntingdon dioc Lincoln

HEMINGFORD, GREY parish 1673 Hunts 1-3/4 miles sw St Ives pop 556 archd Huntingdon dioc Lincoln

HEMINGSTONE or HELMINGSTONE parish 1553 Suffolk 4-3/4 miles se Needham Market pop 342 archd Suffolk dioc Norwich

HEMINGTON township parish Lockington Leics pop 389

HEMINGTON parish 1563 co Northampton 5-1/2 miles se Oundle pop 133 archd Northampton dioc Peterborough

HEMINGTON parish 1539 Somerset 5-1/4 miles nw Frome pop 384 archd Wells dioc Bath and Wells

HEMLEY parish 1698 Suffolk 5 miles se Woodbridge pop 69 archd Suffolk dioc Norwich

HEMLINGTON township parish Stainton N R York pop 83

HEMLINGTON ROW township parish Brancepeth co Durham pop 97

HEMPHOLME township parish Leven E R York pop 102

HEMPNALL parish 1560 Norfolk 3-3/4 miles ne St Mary Stratton pop 1,225 archd Norfolk dioc Norwich

HEMPSTEAD parish 1664 Essex 5-1/2 miles ne Thaxted pop 708 archd Essex dioc London

HEMPSTEAD parish 1558 Gloucs 1-3/4 miles sw Gloucester pop 999 archd and dioc Gloucester

HEMPSTEAD parish 1558 Norfolk 8-3/4 miles se North Walsham pop 209 archd Norfolk dioc Norwich

HEMPSTEAD parish 1707 Norfolk 2 miles se Holt pop 286 archd and dioc Norwich

HEMPSTEAD, HEMEL parish 1558 Herts 19-1/2 miles sw Hertford comp town Hemel Hempstead, chapelries Bovingdon, Flaunden pop 6,037 archd Huntingdon dioc Lincoln Bapt, Soc of Friends, Huntingtonians

HEMPSTON, BROAD parish 1678 Devon 4 miles se Ashburton pop 748 archd Totnes dioc Exeter Wesl Meth

HEMPSTON, LITTLE parish 1539 Devon 1-3/4 miles ne Totnes pop 321 archd Totnes dioc Exeter

HEMPTON tything parish Almondsbury Gloucs pop 424

HEMPTON parish no regs Norfolk 1 mile sw Fakenham pop 411 archd and dioc Norwich

HEMPTON township parish Deddington co Oxford pop 220

HEMSBY parish 1566 Norfolk 4-1/2 miles nw Caistor pop 560 archd and dioc Norwich

HEMSWELL parish 1676 Lincs 7-1/2 miles e Gainsborough pop 347 archd Stow dioc Lincoln Wesl Meth

HEMSWORTH parish 1685 W R York 6-1/2 miles sw Pontefract pop 937 archd and dioc York Wesl Meth

HEMYOCK parish 1635 Devon 5-1/4 miles s Wellington pop 1,228 archd and dioc Exeter

HENBURY township parish Prestbury Ches pop 421

HENBURY parish 1538 Gloucs 4-1/2 miles nw Bristol comp tythings King's Weston, Lawrence Weston, joint chapelries Redwick with Northwick, township Henbury, chapelry Aust, tythings Charlton, Compton pop 2,351 pec Consistory Court of Bishop of Bristol

HENDERSKELF chapelry parish Bulmer N R York pop 150

HENDON parish 1653 Middlesex 7 miles nw London pop 3,110 Commissary of London, Consistorial Court of Bishop Indep, Wesl Meth

HENDRED, EAST parish 1538 Berks 4-1/2 miles ne Wantage pop 865 archd Berks dioc Salisbury Roman Cath

HENDRED, WEST parish 1559 Berks 3-3/4 miles e Wantage pop 335 archd Berks dioc Salisbury

HENFIELD parish 1596 Sussex 5-3/4 miles ne Steyning pop 1,516 archd Lewes dioc Chichester

HENGRAVE parish incl in regs of Flempton Suffolk 3-3/4 miles nw Bury St Edmund's pop 238 archd Sudbury dioc Norwich

HENHAM parish 1539 Essex 4 miles ne Stansted Mountfitchet pop 863 Commissary of Essex and Herts, Consistorial Court of Bishop of London Indep

HENHAM hamlet parish Wangford Suffolk pop 156

HENHEADS township parish Bury Lancs pop 202

HENHULL township parish Acton Ches pop 62

HENLEY parish 1559 Suffolk 5 miles n Ipswich pop 305 archd Suffolk dioc Norwich

HENLEY, COLD chapelry parish Whitchurch Hamps

HENLEY ARDEN chapelry 1672 parish Wootton Wawen Warws pop 1,214 archd and dioc Worcester Bapt

HENLEY UPON THAMES 1558 co Oxford 23 miles se Oxford pop 3,618 sep juris archd and dioc Oxford Bapt, Soc of Friends, Indep

HENLLIS parish 1754 co Monmouth 3-3/4 miles nw Newport pop 204 archd and dioc Llandaff

HENLOW parish 1558 Beds 4-1/4 miles sw Biggleswade pop 724 archd Bedford dioc Lincoln

HENNOCK parish 1544 Devon 3 miles nw Chudleigh pop 747 archd Totnes dioc Exeter Wesl Meth

HENNOR hamlet parish Leominster Herefs

HENNEY, GREAT parish 1695 Essex 2-3/4 miles sw Sudbury pop

414 archd Middlesex dioc London

HENNY, LITTLE parish no regs Essex 2-1/4 miles s Sudbury pop 53 archd Middlesex dioc London

HENSALL township parish Snaith W R York pop 250

HENSHAW township parish Halt Whistle Northumberland pop 619

HENSINGHAM chapelry 1811 parish St Bees, Allerdale Cumberland pop 936 archd Richmond dioc Chester

HENSINGTON hamlet parish Bladon co Oxford pop 143

HENSTEAD parish 1539 Suffolk 5-3/4 miles se Beccles pop 566 archd Suffolk dioc Norwich

HENSTRIDGE parish 1653 Somerset 6-1/2 miles se Wincanton pop 1,074 pec Prebendary of Henstridge

HENTLAND parish 1558 Herefs 4-1/2 miles nw Ross pop 618 archd and dioc Hereford

HENTON liberty parish Chinnor co Oxford pop 216

HEPPLE township parish Rothbury Northumberland pop 101

HEPPLE DEMESNE township parish Rothbury Northumberland pop 59

HEPSCOT township parish Morpeth Northumberland pop 174

HEPSTONSTALL chapelry 1593 parish Halifax W R York pop 4,661 archd and dioc York

HEPWORTH parish 1688 Suffolk 4-1/2 miles sw Botesdale pop 542 archd Sudbury dioc Norwich

HEPWORTH township parish Kirk Burton W R York pop 1,229 Wesl Meth

HEREFORD city Herefs 135 miles nw London pop 10,282 sep juris All Saints 1669, St John the Baptist 1687, St Martin 1559, St Nicholas 1556, St Owen 1626, St Peter 1556 Consistory Court of Dean of Hereford Soc of Friends, Indep, Huntingdon's Connection, Wesl Meth, Roman Cath

HEREFORD, LITTLE parish 1725 Herefs 3 miles w Tenbury pop 477 pec Chancellor of Choir, Cathedral Church of Hereford

HERGESTS, BOTH township parish Kinton Herefs pop 159

HERMITAGE parish 1712 Dorset 7 miles se Sherborne pop 124 pec Dean of Sarum

HERNE parish 1558 Kent 5-3/4 miles ne Canterbury pop 1,876 pec Archbishop of Canterbury Indep, Wesl Meth

HERNHILL parish 1557 Kent 3-1/2 miles se Faversham pop 507 pec Archbishop of Canterbury

HERRIARD parish 1666 Hamps 4-3/4 miles se Basingstoke pop 426 archd and dioc Winchester

HERRINGBY parish incl in regs of Stokesby Norfolk 3-1/4 miles se Acle pop 324 archd and dioc Norwich

HERRINGFLEET parish 1706 Suffolk 6 miles nw Lowestoft pop 183 archd Suffolk dioc Norwich

HERRINGSTONE or WINTERBOURNE HERRINGSTONE chapelry parish West Chickerell Dorset pop 46

HERRINGSWELL parish 1748 Suffolk 3-1/4 miles se Mildenhall pop 239 archd Sudbury dioc Norwich

HERRINGTON, EAST and MIDDLE township parish Houghton le Spring co Durham pop 229

HERRINGTON, WEST township parish Houghton le Spring co Durham pop 381

HERTFORD market town, borough Herts 21 miles n London pop 5,247 sep juris parishes All Saints 1559, liberties Little Amwell, Brickendon parish All Saints, St Andrew 1560 archd Huntingdon dioc Lincoln Bapt, Soc of Friends, Countess of Huntingdon's Connection, Wesl Meth

HERTINGFORDBURY parish 1679 Herts 11-3/4 miles sw Hertford pop 753 archd Huntingdon dioc Lincoln

HESKET IN THE FOREST parish 1662 Cumberland 9 miles nw Penrith comp townships Calthwaite, Nether and Upper Hesket, Itonfield, Petterell Crooks, Plumpton Street pop 2,107 archd and dioc Carlisle

HESKET NEWMARKET market town, township Caldbeck Haltcliffe parish Caldbeck Cumberland Soc of Friends

HESKETH chapelry 1745 parish Croston Lancs

HESKIN township parish Eccleston Lancs pop 324

HESLERTON, EAST chapelry parish West Heslerton E R York pop 215 Wesl Meth

HESLERTON, WEST parish 1561 E R York 8 miles ne New Malton comp chapelry East Heslerton, township West Heslerton pop 514 archd East Riding dioc York

HESLETON, COLD township parish Dalton le Dale co Durham pop 112

HESLETON, MONK parish 1578 co Durham 10 miles se Durham comp townships Hulam or Holom, Hutton Henry, Monk Hesleton, Nesbit, Sheraton, Thorpe Bulmer pop 501 archd and dioc Durham

HESLEY HURST township parish Rothbury Northumberland pop 40

HESLINGTON parish 1653 E R York 1-1/2 miles se York pop 536 pec Prebendary of Ampleforth

HESSETT parish 1538 Suffolk 6 miles se Bury St Edmund's pop 428 archd Sudbury dioc Norwich

HESSEY township parish Moor Monkton, Ainsty of city E R York pop 170

HESSLE parish 1561 E R York 5-1/4 miles sw Longston upon Hull pop 1,172 archd East Riding dioc York Wesl Meth

HEST township parish Bolton le Sands Lancs pop 286

HESTERCOMBE hamlet parish Kingston Somerset

HESTON parish 1560 Middlesex pop 3,407 archd Middlesex dioc London

HESWALL parish 1559 Ches 3-3/4 miles nw Great Neston comp townships Gayton, Heswall with Oldfield pop 406

HETHE co Oxford See HEATH

HETHEL parish 1710 Norfolk 4-1/2 miles se Wymondham pop 184 archd Norfolk dioc Norwich

HETHERSETT parish 1616 Norfolk 3-3/4 miles ne Wymondham pop

1,080 archd Norfolk dioc Norwich

HETHERSGILL township parish Kirk Linton Cumberland pop 743

HETT township parish Merrington co Durham pop 227

HETTON township parish Burnsall W R York pop 176

HETTON LE HOLE township parish Houghton le Spring co Durham pop 5,887 Bapt, Kilhamites, Prim and Wesl Meth

HEUGH township parish Stamfordham Northumberland pop 472

HEVER parish 1632 Kent 8-1/2 miles sw Tonbridge pop 559 pec Archbishop of Canterbury

HEVERSHAM parish 1601 Westm 1-1/2 miles n Milnthorpe comp chapelries Crosthwaite with Lyth, Stainton, townships Hincaster, Levens, Milnthorpe with Heversham, Preston Richard, Sedgwick, incl Levens, small portion of Kendal pop 4,162 archd Richmond dioc Chester Wesl Meth

HEVINGHAM or HEVENINGHAM parish 1654 Norfolk 3 miles se Aylsham pop 931 archd and dioc Norwich

HEWELSFIELD parish 1664 Gloucs 5-1/2 miles ne Chepstow pop 535 archd Hereford dioc Gloucester

HEWICK BRIDGE township parish Ripon W R York pop 95

HEWICK COPT township parish Ripon W R York pop 160

HEWISH parish 1603 Wilts 3 miles nw Pewsey pop 128 archd Wilts dioc Salisbury

HEWORTH township parish St Cuthbert, St Giles N R York pop 268

HEWORTH, NETHER chapelry 1808 earlier incl regs Jarrow parish Jarrow co Durham pop 5,424

HEXGRAVE PARK township parish Southwell Notts

HEXHAM parish 1655 Northumberland 20 miles w Newcastle upon Tyne comp town Hexham, wards Gilligate, Hencoats, Market, Priestpople, district Hexhamshire, townships High Quarter, Low Quarter, Middle Quarter (North), Middles Quarter (South), West Quarter pop 6,042 pec Archbishop of York Indep

HEXTHORPE township parish Doncaster W R York pop 420

HEXTON parish 1538 Herts 5-1/4 miles nw Hitchin pop 294 archd St Albans dioc London

HEXWOOD tything parish Cumner Berks pop 39

HEY chapelry 1743 parish Ashton under Line Lancs

HEYBRIDGE parish 1558 Essex 1 mile ne Maldon pop 1,064 pec Dean and Chapter of St Paul's London

HEYDON parish 1538 Norfolk 3-1/2 miles ne Reepham pop 350 archd and dioc Norwich

HEYFORD, LOWER parish 1539 co Oxford 6 miles nw Bicester pop 541 archd and dioc Oxford

HEYFORD, NETHER parish 1558 co Northampton 7 miles sw Northampton pop 507 archd Northampton dioc Peterborough

HEYFORD, UPPER parish co Northampton 6-1/4 miles w Northampton pop 112

HEYFORD, WARREN or UPPER parish 1558 co Oxford 6 miles nw Bicester pop 326 archd and dioc Oxford

HEYHOUSES township parish Whalley Lancs pop 155

HEYSHAM parish 1650 Lancs 5 miles w Lancaster pop 582 archd Richmond dioc Chester

HEYSHOT parish 1690 Sussex 2-1/2 miles se Midhurst pop 358 archd and dioc Chichester

HEYTESBURY parish 1653 borough Wilts 3-1/2 miles se Warminster pop 1,412 pec Dean of Sarum Indep

HEYTHORP parish 1607 co Oxford 3-1/4 miles ne Chipping Norton pop 123 archd and dioc Oxford

HEYWOOD chapelry 1733 parish Bury Lancs archd and dioc Oxford

HIBALSTOW parish 1632 Lincs 3-3/4 miles sw Glandford Bridge pop 632 archd Stow dioc Lincoln Wesl Meth

HIBBURN Northumberland See HEBBURN

HICKLETON parish 1694 W R York 6 miles nw Doncaster pop 154 archd and dioc York

HICKLING parish 1654 Norfolk 10-1/2 miles ne Coltishall pop 762 archd Norfolk dioc Norwich

HICKLING parish 1646 Notts 8-1/4 miles nw Melton Mowbray pop 529 archd Nottingham dioc York Wesl Meth

HIDCOTE BATRIM hamlet parish Mickleton Gloucs

HIDDON tything parish Hungerford Berks pop 479

HIDE, WEST chapelry 1660 parish Stoke Edith Herefs pop 196

HIENDLEY, COLD township parish Felkirk W R York pop 153

HIENDLEY, SOUTH township parish Felkirk W R York pop 272

HIGHAM hamlet parish Shirland Derbys pop 595

HIGHAM parish 1653 Kent 4-1/2 miles nw Derby pop 703 archd and dioc Rochester

HIGHAM parish 1538 Suffolk 4-3/4 miles s Hadleigh pop 260 archd Suffolk dioc Norwich

HIGHAM BOOTH township parish Whalley Lancs pop 1,038 Wesl Meth

HIGHAM, COLD parish 1556 co Northampton 3-1/2 miles nw Towcester pop 391 archd Northampton dioc Peterborough

HIGHAM DYKES townships parish Ponteland Northumberland pop 15

HIGHAM FERRERS parish 1573 borough co Northampton 15-1/2 miles ne Northampton pop 965 sep juris archd Northampton dioc Peterborough Wesl Meth

HIGHAM GOBION parish 1558 Beds 2-3/4 miles se Silsoe pop 108 archd Beds dioc Lincoln

HIGHAM GREEN hamlet parish Gazeley Suffolk pop 311

HIGHAM ON THE HILL parish 1707 Leics 3-1/4 miles nw Hinckley pop 560 archd Leicester dioc Lincoln

HIGHAM PARK extra parochial liberty co Northampton 3-1/2 miles se Highham Ferrers pop 15

HIGHAMPTON Devon See HAMPTON, HIGH

HIGH BRAY parish 1735 Devon

HIGHCLERE parish 1656 Hamps 8-1/2 miles nw Whitchurch pop 444 pec Incumbent

HIGHEAD or IVEGILL chapelry 1709 parish Dalston Cumberland pop

141 archd and dioc Carlisle

HIGHGATE chapelry 1633 parish St Pancras chiefly in parish Hornsey Middlesex Bapt, Indep, Wesl Meth

HIGHLAWS township parish Hartburn Northumberland pop 18

HIGHLEY parish 1551 Shrops 7-1/2 miles se Bridgenorth pop 404 archd Salop dioc Hereford

HIGHLOW township parish Hope Derbys pop 62

HIGHNAM hamlet parish Churcham Gloucs pop 327

HIGHWAY parish 1742 Wilts 4-1/2 miles ne Calne pop 148 archd Wilts dioc Salisbury

HIGHWEEK parish 1653 Devon 1 mile nw Newton Abbots pop 1,109 archd Totnes dioc Exeter

HIGHWORTH parish 1538 borough Wilts 48 miles ne Salisbury comp Highworth, chapelries Broad Blunsdon, South Marston, Sevenhampton, tythings Fresdon, Eastrop with Westrop pop 3,127 pec Prebendary of Highworth Indep

HILARY, ST parish 1692 Cornwall comp market town Marazion pop 3,121 archd Cornwall dioc Exeter

HILBECK township parish Brough Westm pop 54

HILBOROUGH parish 1561 Norfolk 6 miles s Swaffham pop 310 archd Norfolk dioc Norwich

HILCOTT tything parish North Newton Wilts

HILDENLEY township parish Appleton le Street N R York pop 12

HILDERSHAM parish 1560 Cambs 1-3/4 miles nw Linton pop 214 archd and dioc Ely

HILDERSTONE liberty parish Stone Staffs

HILDERTHORP township parish Bridlington E R York pop 73

HILFIELD chapelry 1565 parish Sydling St Nicholas Dorset pop 150

HILGAY parish 1583 Norfolk 3-1/2 miles se Downham Market pop 1,176 archd Norfolk dioc Norwich

HILL parish 1653 Gloucs 3-1/2 miles ne Thornbury pop 257 archd and dioc Gloucester

HILL township parish Fladbury Worcs pop 304

HILL, CROOM Worcs See CROOM HILL

HILL DEVERILL parish 1648 Wilts 3 miles s Warminster pop 129 pec Dean of Salisbury

HILL END tything parish Cumner Berks pop 102

HILL FARRANCE parish 1702 Somerset 4-1/4 miles w Taunton pop 579 archd Taunton dioc Bath and Wells

HILL TOP township parish Wragby W R York pop 86

HILLAM township parish Monk Fryston W R York pop 291

HILLESDON parish 1595 Bucks 3-3/4 miles sw Buckingham pop 251 archd Buckingham dioc Lincoln

HILLESLEY tything parish Hawkesbury Gloucs pop 630

HILLINGDON parish 1549 Middlesex 13-1/2 miles nw London pop 6,885 archd Middlesex dioc London

HILLINGTON parish 1694 Norfolk 4 miles e Castle Rising pop 289 archd and dioc Norwich

HILLINGTON parish 1562 Norfolk 6-3/4 miles se Norwich pop 52
archd and dioc Norwich

HILLMARTON parish 1645 Wilts 3-1/4 miles ne Calne pop 791 archd
and dioc Salisbury

HILLMORTON parish 1564 Warws 3 miles se Rugby pop 873 archd
Coventry dioc Lichfield Wesl Meth

HILPERTON parish 1694 Wilts 1-1/4 miles nw Trowbridge pop 1,067
archd and dioc Salisbury Bapt, Wesl Meth

HILSTON parish 1654 E R York 14 miles ne Kingston upon Hull pop
43 archd East Riding dioc York

HILTON township parish Marston upon Dove Derbys pop 651

HILTON parish 1603 Dorset 7-1/2 miles sw Blandford Forum pop
685 archd Dorset dioc Bristol

HILTON township parish Staindrop co Durham pop 118

HILTON parish 1558 Hunts 3-1/2 miles sw St Ives pop 329 archd
Huntingdon dioc Lincoln

HILTON township parish Wolverhampton Staffs pop 45

HILTON Westm See HELTON

HILTON IN CLEVELAND parish 1698 N R York 3-1/4 miles se
Yarm pop 113 archd Cleveland dioc York

HIMBLETON parish 1713 Worcs 4-1/2 miles se Droitwich pop 478
archd and dioc Worcester

HIMLEY parish 1660 Staffs 3-3/4 miles w Dudley pop 421 Stafford
dioc Lichfield

HINCASTER township parish Heversham Westm pop 156

HINCHINBROOK parish Hunts 1 mile w Huntingdon

HINCKLEY parish 1554 Leics 13 miles sw Leicester comp town
Hinckley, chapelries Dadlington, Stoke Golding, hamlet Wykin
pop 7,180 archd Leicester dioc Lincoln Gen Bapt, Soc of Friends,
Indep, Wesl Meth, Unit, Roman Cath

HINDERCLAY parish 1567 Suffolk 2 miles nw Botesdale pop 405
archd Sudbury dioc Norwich

HINDERWELL parish 1601 N R York 9 miles nw Whitby comp townships Hinderwell, Roxby pop 1,881 archd Cleveland dioc York

HINDLEY chapelry 1698 parish Wigan Lancs pop 4,575 archd and
dioc Chester Indep, Unit

HINDLIP Worcs See HINLIP

HINDOLVESTON parish 1693 Norfolk 3-1/4 miles nw Foulsham pop
797 archd Norfolk dioc Norwich

HINDON chapelry parish East Knoyle borough 1599 Wilts pop 921
archd Wilts dioc Salisbury Indep

HINDRINGHAM parish 1660 Norfolk 3-3/4 miles se Little Walsingham pop 784 archd and dioc Norwich

HINGHAM parish 1601 Norfolk 14 miles sw Norwich pop 1,539 archd
Norfolk dioc Norwich

HINKSEY, NORTH parish 1703 Berks 1-1/2 miles w Oxford pop 187
archd Berks dioc Salisbury

HINKSEY, SOUTH parish 1670 Berks 1-1/2 miles s Oxford pop 157 archd Berks dioc Salisbury

HINLIP parish 1612 Worcs 3-1/2 miles ne Worcester pop 134 archd and dioc Worcester

HINSTOCK parish 1695 Shrops 5-3/4 miles nw Newport pop 805 archd Salop dioc Lichfield

HINTLESHAM parish 1652 Suffolk 4-1/2 miles ne Hadleigh pop 578 archd Suffolk dioc Norwich

HINTON tything parish Berkeley Gloucs pop 162   Wesl Meth

HINTON tything parish Dirham Gloucs

HINTON hamlet parish Woodford co Northampton

HINTON township parish Whitchurch Shrops

HINTON parish 1632 Somerset 2-1/4 miles nw Crewkerne pop 850 archd Taunton dioc Bath and Wells

HINTON chapelry parish Christchurch Hamps

HINTON AMPNER parish 1561 Hamps 4 miles se New Alresford archd and dioc Winchester

HINTON BLEWETT parish 1563 Somerset 8 miles ne Wells pop 325 archd Bath dioc Bath and Wells

HINTON, BROAD parish 1682 Wilts 8 miles nw Marlborough pop 700 archd Wilts dioc Salisbury

HINTON, BROAD liberty parish Hurst Wilts pop 519

HINTON, CHARTERHOUSE parish 1546 Somerset 5 miles se Bath pop 735 archd Wells dioc Bath and Wells

HINTON, CHERRY parish 1538 Cambs 2-3/4 miles se Cambridge pop 574 archd and dioc Ely

HINTON, GREAT tything parish Steeple Ashton Wilts pop 234

HINTON IN THE HEDGES parish 1558 co Northampton 1-1/2 miles w Brackley pop 173 archd Northampton dioc Peterborough

HINTON, LITTLE parish 1649 Wilts 5-1/4 miles e Swindon pop 310 archd and dioc Salisbury

HINTON MARTELL parish 1661 Dorset 4-1/4 miles ne Wimborne Minster pop 267 archd Dorset dioc Bristol

HINTON, ST MARY parish 1581 Dorset 8 miles sw Shaftesbury pop 303 archd Dorset dioc Bristol

HINTON ON THE GREEN parish 1735 Gloucs 2-3/4 miles sw Evesham pop 209 archd and dioc Gloucester

HINTON, PARVA or STANDBRIDGE parish 1621 Dorset 2-1/2 miles nw Wimborne Minster pop 36 archd Dorset dioc Bristol

HINTON, TARRANT parish 1545 Dorset 4-3/4 miles ne Blandford Forum pop 241 archd Dorset dioc Bristol

HINTON WALDRIST parish 1551 Berks 6-1/4 miles ne Great Farrington pop 348 archd Berks dioc Salisbury

HINTS parish 1558 Staffs 4 miles sw Tamworth pop 225 pec Prebendal court of Handsacre and Armitage

HINXHILL parish 1577 Kent 2-1/2 miles se Ashford pop 163 archd and dioc Canterbury

HINXTON parish 1538 Cambs 5-1/2 miles sw Linton pop 333 archd and dioc Ely

HINXWORTH parish 1739 Herts 5-1/2 miles n Baldock pop 295 archd
Huntingdon dioc Lincoln
HIPPENSCOMBE extra parochial liberty Wilts 4 miles ne Ludgershall
pop 58
HIPPERHOLME township parish Halifax W R York pop 4,977 Indep
HIPSWELL chapelry 1665 parish Catterwick N R York pop 293 archd
Richmond dioc Chester
HISTON parish 1655 Cambs 3-1/2 miles nw Cambridge pop 784
archd and dioc Ely
HITCHAM parish 1559 Bucks 2-1/4 miles ne Maidenhead pop 232
archd Buckingham dioc Lincoln
HITCHAM parish 1575 Suffolk 1-3/4 miles nw Bildeston pop 1,022
archd Sudbury dioc Norwich
HITCHENDEN or HUGHENDEN parish 1559 Bucks 1-3/4 miles n
High Wycombe pop 1,457 archd Buckingham dioc Lincoln
HITCHIN parish 1562 Herts 15-1/2 miles nw Hertford pop 5,211
archd Huntingdon dioc Lincoln Bapt, Soc of Friends, Countess of
Huntingdon's, Indep
HITTISLEIGH parish 1676 Devon 7-1/2 miles sw Crediton pop 168
archd and dioc Exeter
HOARCROSS township parish Yoxhall Staffs
HOATH parish 1554 Kent 5-1/4 miles ne Canterbury pop 360 pec
Archbishop of Canterbury
HOATHLY, EAST parish 1560 Sussex 5 miles se Uckfield pop 505
archd Lewes dioc Chichester
HOATHLY, WEST parish 1645 Sussex 4-1/4 miles sw East Grinstead
pop 980 archd Lewes dioc Chichester Wesl Meth
HOBENDRID township parish Clun Shrops pop 285
HOB LENCH or ABBOTS LENCH hamlet parish Fladbury Worcs pop
116
HOBY parish 1562 Leics 5-3/4 miles sw Melton Mowbray pop 357
archd Leicester dioc Lincoln
HOCKENHULL township parish Tarvin Ches pop 35
HOCKERING parish 1561 Norfolk 5-1/2 miles e East Dereham pop
438 archd Norfolk dioc Norwich
HOCKERTON parish 1582 Notts 2 miles ne Southwell pop 108 archd
Nottingham dioc York
HOCKHAM parish 1563 Norfolk 4-1/2 miles nw East Harling comp
Great and Little Hockham pop 565 archd Norfolk dioc Norwich
HOCKLEY parish 1732 Essex 2-1/4 miles ne Rayleigh pop 777
archd Essex dioc London
HOCKLIFFE parish 1620 Beds 3-1/2 miles ne Leighton Buzzard pop
460 archd Bedford dioc Lincoln Indep
HOCKMOOR hamlet parish Iffley co Oxford
HOCKWOOD parish 1664 Norfolk 4-1/2 miles nw Brandon Ferry pop
878 archd Norfolk dioc Norwich
HOCKWORTHY parish 1577 Devon 6 miles se Bampton pop 335
archd and dioc Exeter

HODDESDON chapelry parish Broxburn Herts pop 1,615 Soc of Friends, Indep

HODDINGTON tything parish Upton Gray Hamps

HODNEL extra parochial liberty Warws 3 miles se Southam pop 9

HODNET parish 1657 Shrops 6 miles se Drayton in Hales pop 2,097 archd Salop dioc Lichfield

HODSOCK lordship parish Blyth Notts pop 228

HOE Norfolk See HOO

HOFFE township parish St Lawrence Appleby Westm pop 99

HOGHTON chapelry parish Leyland Lancs pop 2,198

HOGNASTON parish 1661 Derbys 5 miles sw Wirksworth pop 271 archd Derby dioc Lichfield

HOGSHAW parish incl in regs Quainton Bucks 4 miles sw Winslow pop 48

HOGSTHORPE parish 1574 Lincs 6-1/4 miles se Alford pop 698 archd and dioc Lincoln Wesl Meth

HOGSTON parish 1547 Bucks 3-3/4 miles se Winslow pop 173 archd Buckingham dioc Lincoln

HOLBEACH parish 1560 Lincs 12 miles s Boston pop 3,890 archd and dioc Lincoln

HOLBECK extra parochial liberty Lincs 4 miles ne Horncastle

HOLBECK township parish Cuckney Notts pop 244

HOLBECK chapelry 1717 parish St Peter, Leeds W R York pop 14,210 archd and dioc York Wesl Meth

HOLBETON parish 1620 Devon 7 miles sw Ermbridge pop 1,107 archd Totnes dioc Exeter

HOLBROOK chapelry parish Duffield Derbys pop 703

HOLBROOK parish 1559 Suffolk 5 miles se Ipswich pop 762 archd Stafford dioc Norwich Wesl Meth

HOLCOM tything parish Newington co Oxford

HOLCOMBE chapelry 1726 parish Bury Lancs archd and dioc Chester

HOLCOMBE parish 1698 Somerset 6-1/2 miles ne Shepton Mallet pop 538 archd Wells dioc Bath and Wells Wesl Meth

HOLCOMBE BURNELL parish 1657 Devon 4-1/2 miles sw Exeter pop 264 archd and dioc Exeter

HOLCOMBE ROGUS parish 1540 Devon 6 miles sw Wellington pop 915 archd and dioc Exeter

HOLCOT parish 1559 co Northampton 7-1/2 miles nw Wellingborough pop 433 archd Northampton dioc Peterborough

HOLCUTT parish 1658 Beds 4-1/2 miles n Woburn pop 49 archd Bedford dioc Lincoln

HOLDENBY parish 1754 co Northampton 6-1/2 miles nw Northampton pop 181 archd Northampton dioc Peterborough

HOLDENHURST chapelry 1679 parish Christchurch Hamps pop 733 archd and dioc Winchester

HOLDFAST hamlet parish Ripple Worcs

HOLDGATE parish 1662 Shrops 8-3/4 miles sw Much Wenlock comp townships Bouldon, Brookhampton, Holdgate pop 188 archd Salop dioc Hereford

HOLDINGHAM hamlet parish New Sleaford Lincs pop 137

HOLDSHOTT tything parish Heckfield Hamps

HOLDFORD parish 1558 Somerset 10-1/2 miles nw Bridgwater pop 188 archd Taunton dioc Bath and Wells

HOLGATE township parish St Mary Bishopshill Junior, Ainsty of city E R York pop 97

HOLKER, LOWER township parish Cartmel Lancs pop 1,021

HOLKER, UPPER township parish Cartmel Lancs pop 1,095

HOLKHAM parish 1542 Norfolk 3 miles w Wells pop 792 archd and dioc Norfolk

HOLLACOMBE parish 1638 Devon 2-1/2 miles se Holsworthy pop 100 archd Totnes dioc Exeter

HOLLAND, DOWN township parish Halsall Lancs pop 704

HOLLAND, FEN district Lincs 8-1/4 miles nw Boston

HOLLAND, GREAT parish 1539 Essex 12-1/2 miles se Manningtree pop 425 archd Colchester dioc London

HOLLAND, LITTLE parish 1561 incl regs Great Clacton Essex 16 miles se Colchester pop 76 Commissary of Essex and Herts, Consistorial Court of Bishop of London

HOLLAND, UP chapelry parish Wigan Lancs pop 3,040

HOLLESLEY parish 1623 Suffolk 7-1/4 miles se Woodbridge pop 604 archd Suffolk dioc Norwich

HOLLETH hamlet parish Garstang Lancs pop 50

HOLLINGBOURN parish 1556 Kent 6 miles e Maidstone pop 943 pec Archbishop of Canterbury Wesl Meth

HOLLINGFARE chapelry 1654 parish Warrington Lancs archd and dioc Chester

HOLLINGTON township parish Longford Derbys pop 343

HOLLINGTON parish 1636 Sussex 2-3/4 miles nw Hastings pop 338 archd Lewes dioc Chichester

HOLLINGWORTH township parish Mottram in Longden Dale Ches pop 1,760

HOLLINSCLOUGH township parish Allstonefield Staffs pop 564

HOLLINWOOD chapelry 1769 parish Oldham Lancs

HOLLOWAY hamlet parish Ashover Derbys

HOLLOWAY district parish Islington Middlesex 3 miles n London Commissary of London, concurrently with Bishop Indep

HOLLOWELL hamlet parish co Northampton pop 318

HOLLYN parish 1564 E R York 3 miles ne Patrington comp chapelry Withernsea, township Hollyn pop 351 archd East Riding dioc York

HOLM hamlet parish Bottesford Lincs pop 49

HOLM township parish Pickhill N R York pop 110

HOLME hamlet parish Biggleswade Beds

HOLME township parish Bakewell Derbys

HOLME chapelry 1683 parish Blatton Hunts pop 359 archd Huntingdon dioc Lincoln

HOLME in CLIVIGER chapelry 1742 parish Whalley Lancs archd and dioc Chester

HOLME chapelry 1711 parish North Muskham Notts pop 121

HOLME township parish Burton Kendal Westm pop 649 Indep

HOLME township parish Almondbury W R York pop 630

HOLME, BALDWIN township parish Orton Cumberland pop 235

HOLME, ST BENET hamlet parish Horning Norfolk

HOLME CULTRAM parish 1581 Cumberland 6-1/2 miles nw Wigton comp Abbey Quarter, East Waver Quarter, Low Quarter, St Cuthbert's Quarter pop 3,056 archd and dioc Carlisle Soc of Friends

HOLME, EAST extra parochial liberty Dorset 2-1/2 miles sw Wareham pop 55

HOLME HALE parish 1538 Norfolk 5 miles nw Watton pop 447 archd Norfolk dioc Norwich

HOLME NEXT RUNCTON parish 1562 Norfolk 4-1/4 miles n Downham Market pop 225 archd Norfolk dioc Norwich

HOLME LACY parish 1562 Herefs 6 miles se Hereford pop 430 archd and dioc Hereford

HOLME NEXT THE SEA parish 1704 Norfolk 8-1/2 miles nw Burnham Westgate pop 268 archd Norfolk dioc Norwich

HOLME, NORTH township parish Kirkdale N R York pop 21

HOLME ON THE WOLDS parish 1654 E R York 6-1/4 miles nw Beverly pop 136 archd East Riding dioc York

HOLME PIERREPOINT parish 1564 Notts 5 miles se Nottingham pop 205 archd Nottingham dioc York

HOLME, SOUTH township parish Hovingham N R York pop 65

HOLME UPON SPALDING MOOR parish 1559 E R York 5 miles sw Market Weighton pop 1,438 archd East Riding dioc York Wesl Meth, Roman Cath

HOLMFIRTH chapelry 1797 parish Kirkburton W R York archd and dioc York Indep, Wesl Meth

HOLMER parish 1712 Herefs 2 miles n Hereford pop 556 Consistory Court of Dean of Hereford

HOLMESCALES hamlet parish Kendal Westm

HOLMESFIELD chapelry 1730 parish Dronfield Derbys pop 499 archd Derby dioc Lichfield

HOLMPTON parish 1739 E R York 3-1/2 miles ne Patrington pop 239 archd East Riding dioc York Wesl Meth

HOLMSIDE township parish Lanchester co Durham pop 218

HOLNE parish 1603 Devon 4 miles w Ashburton pop 369 archd Totnes dioc Exeter

HOLNEST parish 1589 Dorset 4-3/4 miles se Sherborne pop 159 pec Dean of Sarum

HOLSWORTHY parish 1563 Devon 42 miles nw Exeter pop 1,628 archd Totnes dioc Exeter Indep, Wesl Meth

HOLT tything parish Wimborne Minster Dorset pop 1,265

HOLT chapelry parish Medbourne Leics pop 42

HOLT parish 1557 Norfolk 23 miles nw Norwich pop 1,622 archd and dioc Norwich Soc of Friends, Wesl Meth

HOLT chapelry 1580 parish Great Bradford Wilts pop 839 Indep
HOLT parish 1538 Worcs 6 miles nw Worcester pop 635 archd and
dioc Worcester
HOLTBY parish 1679 N R York 5-1/2 miles ne York pop 157 pec
Howdenshire
HOLTON BICKERING parish 1560 Lincs 2-1/2 miles nw Wragby pop
168 archd and dioc Lincoln
HOLTON parish 1633 co Oxford 6 miles e Oxford pop 277 archd and
dioc Oxford
HOLTON parish 1558 Somerset 2-1/2 miles sw Wincanton pop 209
archd Wells dioc Bath and Wells
HOLTON ST MARY 1568 Suffolk 4-3/4 miles se Hadleigh pop 194
archd Suffolk dioc Norwich
HOLTON ST PETER parish 1538 Suffolk 1-1/4 miles ne Halesworth
pop 435 archd Suffolk dioc Norwich
HOLTON LE CLAY parish 1750 Lincs 5 miles se Great Grimsby pop
207 archd and dioc Lincoln
HOLTON LE MOOR chapelry parish Caistor Lincs pop 150 Wesl Meth
HOLVERSTONE parish incl in regs Burgh Apton Norfolk 6 miles se
Norwich pop 33 archd Norfolk dioc Norwich
HOLWELL parish 1560 Beds 3 miles nw Hitchin pop 167 archd Bed-
ford dioc Lincoln
HOLWELL chapelry parish Ab Kettleby Leics pop 131
HOLWELL chapelry parish Broadwell co Oxford pop 96
HOLWELL parish 1653 Dorset 5-3/4 miles se Sherborne pop 405
archd Dorset dioc Bristol
HOLWICK township parish Romaldkirk N R York pop 208
HOLYBOURNE parish 1690 Hamps 1-1/2 miles ne Alton pop 487
archd and dioc Winchester
HOLY CROSS hamlet parish Clent Worcs Bapt
HOLYFIELD hamlet parish Waltham Abbey Essex pop 332
HOLY ISLAND or LINDISFARN parish 1578 locally north of North-
umberland co Durham 5-1/2 miles ne Belford pop 836 archd
Northumberland dioc Durham
HOLY OAKES liberty parish Dry Stoke Leics pop 3
HOLYWELL hamlet parish Shitlington Beds
HOLYWELL parish 1667 Hunts 2 miles se St Ives pop 951 archd
Huntingdon dioc Lincoln
HOLYWELL chapelry 1558 parish Castle Bytham Lincs pop 119
HOLYWELL township parish Earsdon Northumberland pop 478
HOMERSFIELD parish 1558 Suffolk 4-1/4 miles sw Bungay pop 233
archd Suffolk dioc Norwich
HOMINGTON parish 1675 Wilts 3-1/2 miles sw Salisbury pop 200
pec Dean and Chapter of Salisbury
HONEYBOURNE,CHURCH parish 1673 Worcs 4 miles nw Chipping
Campden pop 108 pec Bishop of Worcester Wesl Meth
HONEYBOURNE, COW parish incl in regs Church Honeybourne
Gloucs 4 miles nw Chipping Campden pop 329

HONEYCHURCH parish 1728 Devon 6-3/4 miles se Hatherleigh pop
72 archd Totnes dioc Exeter

HONILY parish 1745 Warws 6-3/4 miles nw Warwick pop 60 archd
Coventry dioc Lichfield

HONING parish 1630 Norfolk 3-3/4 miles se North Walsham pop 307
archd Norfolk dioc Norwich

HONINGHAM parish 1561 Norfolk 7-1/2 miles nw Norwich pop 365
archd Norfolk dioc Norwich

HONINGHAM Warws See HUNNINGHAM

HONINGTON parish 1561 Lincs 5 miles ne Grantham pop 177 archd
and dioc Lincoln

HONINGTON parish 1559 Suffolk 2-3/4 miles nw Ixworth pop 248
archd Sudbury dioc Norwich

HONINGTON parish 1571 Warws 1-1/2 miles ne Shipston upon Stour
pop 341 archd and dioc Worcester

HONITON parish 1598 borough Devon 16 miles ne Exeter pop 3,509
archd and dioc Exeter Bapt, Indep, Wesl Meth, Unit

HONLEY chapelry parish Almondbury W R York pop 4,523 Indep,
Wesl Meth

HOO parish 1733 Norfolk 2-1/2 miles ne East Dereham pop 235
archd Norfolk dioc Norwich

HOO parish 1653 Suffolk 4-1/4 miles nw Wickham Market pop 186
archd Suffolk dioc Norwich

HOO otherwise St WERBURGH parish 1587 Kent 4-1/2 miles ne
Rochester pop 910 archd and dioc Rochester

HOO ST MARY parish 1695 Kent 6-3/4 miles ne Rochester pop 296
archd and dioc Rochester

HOO ALLHALLOWS See ALLHALLOWS HOO

HOOD township parish Kilburn N R York pop 21

HOOE parish 1609 Sussex 8 miles sw Battle pop 525 archd Lewes
dioc Chichester

HOOK hamlet parish Kingston upon Thames Surrey pop 189

HOOKE parish Dorset 4-1/4 miles se Beaminster pop 269 archd
Dorset dioc Bristol

HOOKE chapelry 1683 parish Snaith W R York pop 650 pec Snaith
Wesl Meth

HOOLE township parish Plemonstall Ches pop 249

HOOLE parish 1673 Lancs 8 miles sw Preston comp townships Much
Hoole, Little Hoole pop 934 archd and dioc Chester

HOON township parish Marston upon Dove Derbys pop 31

HOOSE township parish West Kirby Ches pop 196

HOOTON township parish Eastham Ches pop 103

HOOTON LEVETT township parish Maltby W R York pop 92

HOOTON PAGNELL parish 1538 W R York 7-1/2 miles nw Doncaster
comp townships Bilham, Hooton Pagnell, Stotford pop 425 archd
and dioc York

HOOTON ROBERTS parish 1702 W R York 4-1/2 miles ne Rotherham pop 178 archd and dioc York

HOPE parish 1599 Derbys 6 miles ne Tideswell comp chapelry Fairfield, townships Fernilee, Grindlow, Highlow, Hope, Stoke, hamlets Abney, Aston with Thornton, Bradwell, Brough with Shatton, Great Hucklow, Nether Padley, Offerton, Thornhill, Woodland Hope, liberties Hazelbadge, Little Hucklow pop 3,927 pec Dean and Chapter of Lichfield

HOPE parish incl in regs New Romsey Kent 1 mile nw New Romney pop 24 archd and dioc Canterbury

HOPE township parish Barningham N R York pop 35

HOPE BAGGOT parish 1754 Shrops 6-1/4 miles se Ludlow pop 62 archd Salop dioc Hereford

HOPE BOWDLER parish 1564 Shrops 2 miles se Church Stretton pop 202 archd Salop dioc Hereford

HOPE MANSELL parish 1556 Herefs 5 miles se Ross pop 141 archd and dioc Hereford

HOPE, SOLLERS See SOLLERS HOPE

HOPE UNDER DINMORE parish 1701 Herefs 4-3/4 miles se Leominster pop 555 archd and dioc Hereford

HOPESAY parish 1678 Shrops 6 miles se Bishop's Castle pop 571 archd Salop dioc Hereford

HOPLEY'S GREEN township parish Almeley Herefs

HOPPEN township parish Bambrough Northumberland pop 43

HOPPERTON township parish Allerton Mauleverer W R York

HOPSFORD hamlet parish Withy Brook Warws

HOPTON township parish Wirksworth Derbys pop 118

HOPTON joint liberty with Coton parish St Mary, Stafford Staffs pop 642

HOPTON parish 1691 Suffolk 7-1/2 miles ne Ixworth pop 581 archd Suffolk dioc Norwich

HOPTON parish 1673 Suffolk 4-3/4 miles nw Lowestoft pop 260 archd Suffolk dioc Norwich

HOPTON, CASTLE parish 1538 Shrops 9 miles se Bishop's Castle pop 145 archd Salop dioc Hereford

HOPTON IN THE HOLE or HOPTON CANGFORD parish no regs Shrops 5 miles ne Ludlow pop 30 archd Salop dioc Hereford

HOPTON, MONK parish 1698 Shrops 4-1/2 miles s Much Wenlock pop 208 archd Salop dioc Hereford

HOPTON WAFERS parish 1729 Shrops 2-3/4 miles nw Cleobury Mortimer pop 473 archd Salop dioc Hereford

HOPWAS HAYES extra parochial liberty parish Tamworth Staffs pop 2

HOPWELL liberty parish Sawley Derbys pop 23

HOPWOOD township parish Middleton Lancs pop 1,413

HORBLING parish 1653 Lincs 3-3/4 miles ne Falkingham pop 559 archd and dioc Lincoln

HORBURY chapelry 1598 parish Wakefield W R York pop 2,400 archd and dioc York

HORDERLEY extra parochial liberty Shrops 6 miles se Bishop's Castle pop 150

HORDLE parish 1754 Hamps 4-1/2 miles sw Lymington pop 699 archd and dioc Winchester

HORDLEY parish 1686 Shrops 3 miles sw Ellesmere pop 325 archd Salop dioc Lichfield

HORFIELD parish 1543 Gloucs 2-1/2 miles n Bristol pop 328 pec Bishop of Bristol

HORHAM parish 1594 Suffolk 4-1/4 miles se Eye pop 464 archd Suffolk dioc Norwich Bapt

HORKSLEY, GREAT parish 1558 Essex 1-3/4 miles sw Nayland pop 697 archd Colchester dioc London

HORKSLEY, LITTLE parish 1568 Essex 2-1/2 miles sw Nayland pop 223 archd Colchester dioc London

HORKSTOW parish 1562 Lincs 4-1/2 miles sw Barton upon Humber pop 240 archd and dioc Lincoln

HORLEY parish 1538 co Oxford 3-3/4 miles nw Banbury pop 881 pec Banbury Wesl Meth

HORLEY parish 1578 Surrey 5-3/4 miles se Reigate pop 1,164 archd Surrey dioc Winchester

HORMEAD, GREAT parish 1538 Herts 2-1/2 miles e Buntingford pop 576 archd Middlesex dioc London

HORMEAD, LITTLE parish 1588 Herts 2-3/4 miles se Buntingford pop 107 Commissary of Essex and Herts, with Consistorial Court of Bishop of London

HORN parish incl in regs of Exton co Rutland 6 miles nw Stamford pop 18 archd Northampton dioc Peterborough

HORNBLOTTON parish 1763 Somerset 4-1/2 miles nw Castle Cary pop 118 archd Wells dioc Bath and Wells

HORNBY chapelry 1742 parish Melling Lancs pop 383 archd Richmond dioc Chester

HORNBY township parish Great Smeaton N R York pop 262 Wesl Meth

HORNBY parish 1582 N R York 4 miles sw Catterick comp townships Ainderby Myers with Holtby, Hackforth, Hornby, Arrowthorne, Hunton pop 364 pec Dean and Chapter of York

HORNCASTLE parish 1559 Lincs 21 miles e Lincoln pop 3,988 archd and dioc Lincoln Bapt, Indep, Prim and Wesl Meth

HORNCHURCH parish 1576 Essex 14-1/4 miles se London pop 2,186 pec Hornchurch and Havering atte Bower

HORNCLIFFE township parish Norham co Durham but locally in Northumberland pop 369

HORNDON, EAST parish 1558 Essex 4 miles se Brentwood pop 438 archd Essex dioc London

HORNDON ON THE HILL parish 1672 Essex 16-1/2 miles sw Chelmsford pop 511 archd Essex dioc London

HORNDON, WEST incl regs Ingrave Essex 3-1/2 miles se Brentwood pop 63 archd Essex dioc London

HORNE parish 1614 Surrey 5-1/2 miles sw Godstone pop 595 archd Surrey dioc Winchester

HORNING parish 1558 Norfolk 6 miles nw Acle pop 468 archd Norfolk dioc Norwich

HORNINGHOLD parish 1661 Leics 4-1/2 miles sw Uppingham pop 97 archd Leicester dioc Lincoln

HORNINGLOW township parish Burton upon Trent Staffs pop 391

HORNINGSEA parish 1628 Cambs 4-1/4 miles ne Cambridge pop 272 pec Bishop of Ely

HORNINGSHAM parish 1561 Wilts 4-1/2 miles sw Warminster pop 1,323 pec Dean of Salisbury Indep

HORNINGSHEATH parish 1558 Suffolk 2 miles sw Bury St Edmund's comp Great and Little Horningsheath pop 586 archd Sudbury dioc Norwich

HORNINGTOFT parish 1541 Norfolk 5 miles se Fakenham pop 293 archd and dioc Norwich

HORNSEA parish 1654 E R York 42 miles se York pop 780 archd East Riding dioc York Indep, Wesl Meth

HORNSEY parish 1653 Middlesex 5-1/2 miles nw London comp part Highgate, hamlets Crouch End, Muswell Hill, Stroud Green pop 4,856 juris Commissary of London, with Consistorial Episcopal Court Bapt

HORNTON parish 1703 co Oxford 6-1/2 miles nw Banbury pop 551 Dean and Chapter of Lincoln

HORSEDOWN extra parochial liberty Devon See AXMOUTH

HORRINGER Suffolk See HORNINGSHEATH

HORSEHEATH parish 1558 Cambs 3-1/2 miles ne Linton pop 430 archd and dioc Ely

HORSEHOUSE chapelry parish Coverham N R York

HORSELEY township parish Eccleshall Staffs pop 491

HORSELL parish 1653 Surrey 4-1/2 miles nw Ripley pop 673 archd Surrey dioc Winchester

HORSEMONDEN parish 1561 Kent 2-3/4 miles ne Lamberhurst pop 1,197 archd and dioc Rochester

HORSENDON parish 1637 Bucks 7 miles nw Great Missenden pop 37 archd Buckingham dioc Lincoln

HORSEPATH parish 1561 co Oxford 4 miles se Oxford pop 275 archd and dioc Oxford

HORSEPOOL township parish Thornton Leics

HORSEY NEXT THE SEA parish 1559 Norfolk 8-3/4 miles nw Caistor pop 111 archd Norfolk dioc Norwich

HORSFORD parish 1597 Norfolk 5 miles nw Norwich pop 543 archd and dioc Norwich

HORSFORTH chapelry 1693 parish Guisley W R York pop 3,425 archd and dioc York Bapt, Wesl Meth

HORSHAM parish 1695 Norfolk 4-3/4 miles nw Norwich pop 1,279 archd and dioc Norwich

HORSHAM parish 1540 borough Sussex 29 miles ne Chichester pop 5,105 archd and dioc Chichester Bapt, Soc of Friends, Indep, Wesl Meth, Roman Cath

HORSINGTON parish 1558 Lincs 4-3/4 miles w Horncastle pop 323

archd and dioc Lincoln

HORSINGTON parish 1559 Somerset 4 miles sw Wincanton pop 968
archd Wells dioc Bath and Wells Bapt

HORSLEY parish 1558 Derbys 6-1/4 miles ne Derby comp townships
Horsley, Horsley Woodhouse, Kilbourne pop 1,948 archd Derby
dioc Lichfield

HORSLEY parish 1587 Gloucs 3 miles sw Minchin Hampton pop 3,690
archd and dioc Gloucester Bapt, Wesl Meth

HORSLEY township parish Ovingham Northumberland pop 293 Presb

HORSLEY, EAST parish 1666 Surrey 5-1/2 miles sw Leatherhead
pop 291 pec Archbishop of Canterbury

HORSLEY, LONG parish 1668 Northumberland 6-3/4 miles nw Morpeth comp townships Bigge's Quarter, Freeholders Quarter, Longshaws, Riddle's Quarter, Stanton, Todburn, Wingates, Witton Shels
pop 952 archd Northumberland dioc Durham Roman Cath

HORSLEY, WEST parish 1600 Surrey 6-1/2 miles sw Leatherhead
pop 702 archd Surrey dioc Winchester

HORSLEY WOODHOUSE township parish Horsley Derbys pop 709

HORSTEAD parish 1558 Norfolk 1/2 mile w Coltishall pop 593 archd
and dioc Norwich

HORSTED KEYNES parish 1638 Sussex 6 miles ne Cuckfield pop 782
archd Lewes dioc Chichester

HORSTED, LITTLE parish 1540 Sussex 2 miles s Uckfield pop 300
archd Lewes dioc Chichester

HORTON hamlet parish Ivinghoe Bucks pop 223

HORTON parish 1571 Bucks 1-1/4 miles sw Colnbrook pop 804 archd
Buckingham dioc Lincoln

HORTON township parish Tilston Ches pop 148

HORTON township parish Tarvin Ches pop 36

HORTON parish 1653 Dorset 5 miles sw Cranborne pop 421 archd
Dorset dioc Bristol

HORTON parish 1567 Gloucs 3-3/4 miles ne Chipping Sudbury pop
477 archd and dioc Gloucester

HORTON chapelry parish Chartham Kent

HORTON parish 1605 co Northampton 6-1/2 miles se Northampton
pop 115 archd Northampton dioc Peterborough

HORTON parish 1648 Northumberland 7-1/4 miles se Morpeth comp
townships Bedside, Cowpen, East Hartford, West Hartford, Horton
pop 2,423 archd Northumberland dioc Durham

HORTON hamlet parish Beckley co Oxford

HORTON parish incl in regs Ilminster Somerset

HORTON township parish Wem Shrops pop 97

HORTON parish 1653 Staffs 2-3/4 miles nw Leek pop 970 archd Stafford dioc Lichfield

HORTON chapelry 1808 parish Bradford W R York pop 10,782 archd
and dioc York Wesl Meth

HORTON township parish Gisburn W R York pop 200

HORTON GRANGE township parish Ponteland Northumberland pop 64

HORTON HAY township parish Horton Staffs

HORTON IN RIBBLESDALE parish 1556 W R York 5-1/2 miles n Settle pop 567 archd and dioc York

HORTON, KIRBY parish 1678 Kent 4 miles se Dartford pop 666 archd and dioc Rochester

HORTON, MONKS parish 1558 Kent 5 miles nw Hythe pop 156 archd and dioc Canterbury

HORWICH chapelry 1695 parish Dean Lancs pop 3,502 archd and dioc Chester Indep, Presb, Wesl Meth

HORWOOD parish 1653 Devon 5-1/2 miles sw Barnstaple pop 130 archd Barnstaple dioc Exeter

HORWOOD, GREAT parish 1600 Bucks 2-1/4 miles n Winslow pop 720 archd Buckingham dioc Lincoln Indep

HORWOOD, LITTLE parish 1568 Bucks 2-1/2 miles ne Winslow pop 431 archd St Albans dioc London

HOSE parish 1625 Leics 6-3/4 miles nw Melton Mowbray pop 385 archd Leicester dioc Lincoln

HOSPITAL tything parish Farringdon Berks

HOTHAM parish 1706 E R York 1-1/2 miles ne North Cave pop 286 archd East Riding dioc York

HOTHERSALL township parish Ribchester Lancs

HOTHFIELD parish 1570 Kent 3-1/4 miles nw Ashford pop 410 archd and dioc Canterbury

HOTHORPE hamlet parish Theddingworth co Northampton pop 26

HOTON chapelry 1653 parish Prestwould Leics pop 401 Wesl Meth

HOUGH township parish Wybunbury Ches pop 252

HOUGH ON THE HILL parish 1646 Lincs 7 miles n Grantham pop 565 archd and dioc Lincoln

HOUGHAM parish 1659 Kent 2-1/2 miles sw Dover pop 1,151 archd and dioc Canterbury

HOUGHAM parish 1562 Lincs 6-1/4 miles nw Grantham pop 304 archd and dioc Lincoln

HOUGHTON township parish Stanwix Cumberland pop 384

HOUGHTON parish 1633 Hunts 2 miles nw St Ives pop 372 archd Huntingdon dioc Lincoln

HOUGHTON township parish Manchester Lancs pop 2,914 Wesl Meth

HOUGHTON township parish Winwick Lancs pop 286

HOUGHTON township parish Heddon on the Wall Northumberland pop 122

HOUGHTON parish no regs Notts 3-3/4 miles nw Tuxford pop 55

HOUGHTON parish 1669 Hamps 2-1/2 miles sw Stockbridge pop 435 pec incumbent

HOUGHTON parish 1560 Sussex 3-1/2 miles n Arundel pop 174 archd and dioc Chichester

HOUGHTON E R York See SANCTON

HOUGHTON CONQUEST parish 1595 Beds 2-1/4 miles ne Ampthill pop 796 archd Bedford dioc Lincoln Wesl Meth

HOUGHTON, GLASS township parish Castleford W R York pop 446

HOUGHTON, GREAT parish 1558 co Northampton 2-3/4 miles se
Northampton pop 305 archd Northampton dioc Peterborough
HOUGHTON, GREAT township parish Darfield W R York pop 292
HOUGHTON, HANGING hamlet parish Lamport co Northampton pop
114
HOUGHTON IN THE HOLE parish 1558 Norfolk 3/4 mile sw Little
Walsingham pop 215 archd Norfolk dioc Norwich
HOUGHTON LEE SIDE township parish Gainford co Durham pop 130
HOUGHTON LE SPRING parish 1563 co Durham 6-3/4 miles ne Dur-
ham comp town Houghton le Spring, chapelries Painshaw, West
Rainton, townships South Bidick, Bourn Moor, Cocken, Great Ep-
pleton, Little Eppleton, East and Middle Herrington, West Herring-
ton, Hetton le Hole, Moorhouse, Moorsley, Morton Grange, New-
bottle, Offerton, East Rainton, Warden Law pop 20,524 archd
and dioc Durham Bapt, Indep, Wesl Meth
HOUGHTON, LITTLE parish 1540 co Northampton 3-1/2 miles se
Northampton pop 539 archd Northampton dioc Peterborough
HOUGHTON, LITTLE township parish Long Houghton Northumber-
land pop 80
HOUGHTON, LITTLE township parish Darfield W R York pop 132
HOUGHTON, LONG parish 1646 Northumberland 3-3/4 miles ne
Alnwick comp townships Boulmer with Seaton House, Little
Houghton, Long Houghton, Little Mill pop 690 archd Northumber-
land dioc Durham
HOUGHTON, NEW parish 1654 Norfolk 9-1/4 miles sw Fakenham
pop 277 archd Norfolk dioc Norwich
HOUGHTON ON THE HILL parish 1653 Leics 6-1/2 miles se Lei-
cester pop 395 archd Leicester dioc Lincoln
HOUGHTON ON THE HILL parish 1695 Norfolk 4-1/4 miles nw Wat-
ton pop 52 archd Norfolk dioc Norwich
HOUGHTON REGIS parish 1538 Beds 1-3/4 miles n Dunstable pop
1,424 archd Bedford dioc Lincoln
HOUGHTON, WEST chapelry 1732 parish Dean Lancs pop 4,500
Wesl Meth
HOUND parish 1660 Hamps 3-3/4 miles se Southampton pop 417
archd and dioc Winchester
HOUNDSTREET tything parish Marksbury Somerset
HOUNSLOW chapelry 1708 parish Isleworth Middlesex archd Middle-
sex dioc London Indep, Wesl Meth
HOUSHAM township parish Cadney Lincs
HOVE parish 1538 Sussex 2 miles nw Brighton pop 1,360 archd
Lewes dioc Chichester
HOVERINGHAM parish 1655 Notts 5 miles s Southwell pop 347 archd
Nottingham dioc York
HOVETON ST JOHN parish 1673 Norfolk 2-1/2 miles se Coltishall
pop 293 archd and dioc Norwich
HOVETON ST PETER parish 1624 Norfolk 2-1/2 miles se Coltishall
pop 129 archd and dioc Norwich

HOVINGHAM parish 1642 N R York 8 miles nw New Malton comp
township Scackleton, Aryholme with Hawthorpe, Wath pop 1,155
archd Cleveland dioc York Wesl Meth
HOW BOUND township parish Castle Sowerby Cumberland pop 197
HOW CAPLE parish 1677 Herefs 6 miles ne Ross pop 137 archd and
dioc Hereford
HOWDEN parish 1543 E R York 21 miles se York comp town Howden,
chapelries Barmby on the Marsh, Laxton, townships Asselby,
Balkholme, Belby, Cotness, Kilpin, Knedlington, Metham, Saltmarsh,
Skelton, Thorpe, Yorkfleet pop 4,531 pec Howdenshire dioc York
Indep, Wesl Meth, Sandemanians
HOWDEN PANS township parish Wallsend Northumberland Wesl Meth
HOWE parish 1734 Norfolk 6-1/2 miles se Norwich pop 119 archd
Norfolk dioc Norwich
HOWE township parish Pickhill N R York pop 33
HOWELL parish 1710 Lincs 5 miles ne Sleaford pop 71 archd and
dioc Lincoln
HOWGILL chapelry parish Sedbergh W R York
HOWGRAVE township parish Kirklington N R York pop 25
HOWGRAVE township parish Pickhill N R York
HOWGRAVE township parish Ripon W R York pop 38
HOWICK township parish Penwortham Lancs pop 132
HOWICK extra parochial liberty co Monmouth pop 47
HOWICK parish 1678 Northumberland 5-1/2 miles ne Alnwick pop
208 archd Northumberland dioc Durham
HOWSHAM township parish Scrayingham E R York pop 240
HOWTELL township parish Kirk Newton Northumberland pop 195
HOXNE parish 1572 Suffolk 3-1/4 miles ne Eye pop 1,243 archd Suf-
folk dioc Norwich
HOXTON district parish St Leonard, Shoreditch Middlesex 1/2 mile
ne London constituted parish 1830 archd Middlesex dioc London
Indep, Wesl Meth, Meth of New Connection
HOYLAND, HIGH parish 1720 W R York 5-1/2 miles nw Barnsley
comp townships West Clayton, High Hoyland, township Skelman-
thorpe pop 1,118 archd and dioc York
HOYLAND, NETHER chapelry 1740 parish Wath upon Dearn W R
York pop 1,670 archd and dioc York
HOYLAND SWAINE township parish Silkstone W R York pop 790
HUBBERHOLME chapelry 1663 parish Arncliffe W R York archd and
dioc York
HUBY township parish Sutton on the Forest N R York pop 526 Soc of
Friends, Prim and Wesl Meth
HUCKING parish 1556 Kent 7 miles ne Maidstone pop 139 archd and
dioc Canterbury
HUCKLE COT hamlet parish Church Down Gloucs pop 465
HUCKLOW, GREAT hamlet parish Hope Derbys pop 253 Presb, Wesl
Meth, Unit
HUCKLOW, LITTLE liberty parish Hope Derbys pop 168

HUCKNALL UNDER HUTHWAITE hamlet parish Sutton in Ashfield Notts pop 929 Wesl Meth

HUCKNALL TORKARD parish 1559 Notts 6-1/2 miles nw Nottingham pop 2,200 archd Nottingham dioc York Gen Bapt, Prim and Wesl Meth'

HUDDERSFIELD parish 1606 borough W R York 40 miles sw York comp town Huddersfield, chapelries Lindley, Longwood, Seammonden, Slaithwaite, portion Marsden, township Golcar pop 31,041 pec Manorial Court of Marsden Bapt, Soc of Friends, Indep, Prim and Wesl Meth, Meth of New Connection, Southcotians, Roman Cath

HUDDINGTON parish 1695 Worcs 4-3/4 miles se Droitwich pop 111 archd and dioc Worcester

HUDDLESTON township parish Sherburn W R York pop 212

HUDNALL hamlet parish Eddlesborough Bucks pop 96

HUDSWELL chapelry 1602 parish Catterick N R York pop 291 archd Richmond dioc Chester

HUELSFIELD Gloucs See HEWELSFIELD

HUGGATE parish 1539 E R York 7-1/2 miles ne Pocklington pop 439 archd East Riding dioc York Wesl Meth

HUGGLESCOTE joint chapelry with Donnington 1583 parish Ibstock Leics pop 786

HUGHENDEN Bucks See HITCHENDON

HUGHLEY parish 1576 Shrops 4-1/4 miles sw Much Wenlock pop 115 archd Salop dioc Hereford

HUGIL chapelry 1732 parish Kendal Westm pop 367 archd Richmond dioc Chester

HUISH Wilts See HEWISH

HUISH parish 1595 Devon 5-1/2 miles n Hatherleigh pop 131 archd Barnstaple dioc Exeter

HUISH CHAMPFLOWER parish 1677 Somerset 2-3/4 miles nw Wiveliscombe pop 345 archd Taunton dioc Bath and Wells

HUISH EPISCOPI parish 1678 Somerset 1/2 mile e Langport pop 574 pec Archdeacon of Wells

HUISH, NORTH parish 1655 Devon 4-3/4 miles ne Modbury pop 457 archd Totnes dioc Exeter

HUISH, SOUTH parish 1576 Devon 3-3/4 miles sw Kingsbridge pop 357 archd Totnes dioc Exeter

HUISH ROAD chapelry parish Carhampton Somerset

HULAM or HOLOM township parish Monk Hesleton co Durham pop 15

HULCOTE hamlet parish Easton Neston co Northampton

HULCOTT parish 1539 Bucks 3 miles ne Aylesbury pop 145 archd Buckingham dioc Lincoln

HULL township parish Great Budworth Ches pop 1,699

HULL See KINSTON UPON HULL

HULL, BISHOPS parish 1562 Somerset 1-1/2 miles w Taunton pop 1,155 archd Taunton dioc Bath and Wells

HULLAND township parish Ashbourn Derbys pop 234

HULLAND WARD hamlet parish Ashbourn Derbys pop 286
HULLAND WARD INTACKS township parish Ashbourn Derbys pop 46
HULLAVINGTON parish 1694 Wilts 4-3/4 miles sw Malmesbury pop 563 archd Wilts dioc Salisbury
HULME township parish Middlewich Ches
HULME chapelry parish Manchester Lancs pop 9,624
HULME township parish Caverswall Staffs
HULME, CHURCH chapelry 1613 parish Sandbach Ches pop 406 archd and dioc Chester
HULME, LEVENS township parish Manchester Lancs pop 1,086
HULME WALFIELD township parish Astbury Ches pop 109
HULSE township parish Great Budworth Ches pop 55
HULTON ABBEY township parish Burslem Staffs pop 501 Wesl Meth
HULTON, LITTLE chapelry 1768 parish Dean Lancs pop 2,981 archd and dioc Chester
HULTON, MIDDLE township parish Dean Lancs pop 934
HULTON, OVER township parish Dean Lancs pop 538
HULVERSTREET hamlet parish Henstead Suffolk pop 297
HUMBER parish 1588 Herefs 4 miles se Leominster pop 219 archd and dioc Hereford
HUMBERSHOE hamlet parish Studham Beds
HUMBERSTON parish 1748 Lincs 4-1/2 miles se Great Grimsby pop 258 archd and dioc Lincoln Wesl Meth
HUMBERSTONE parish 1683 Leics 2-3/4 miles ne Leicester pop 470 archd Leicester dioc Lincoln Wesl Meth
HUMBERTON township parishes Kirby on the Moor and Aldborough W R York pop 188
HUMBLETON township parish Doddington Northumberland pop 171
HUMBLETON parish 1577 E R York 9-1/4 miles ne Kingston upon Hull comp chapelry Elstronwick, townships Danthorpe, Fitling, Flinton, Humbleton pop 579 archd East Riding dioc York
HUMBY, GREAT hamlet parish Somerby Lincs
HUMBY, LITTLE hamlet parish Ropsley Lincs pop 76
HUMSHAUGH chapelry parish Simonburn Northumberland pop 381
HUNCOAT township parish Whalley Lancs pop 502 Bapt
HUNCOTE hamlet parish Narborough Leics pop 355
HUNDERSFIELD chapelry parish Rochdale Lancs
HUNDERTHWAITE township parish Romald Kirk N R York pop 297
HUNDLEBY parish 1707 Lincs 1 mile nw Spilsby pop 420 archd and dioc Lincoln
HUNDON parish 1538 Suffolk 3-1/4 miles nw Clare pop 1,121 archd Sudbury dioc Norwich
HUNGERFORD parish 1559 Berks 26 miles sw Reading comp town Hungerford, tythings Eddington with Hiddon, Sandon Fee, Charnham Street pop 2,715 pec Dean and Canons of Windsor Indep, Wesl Meth
HUNGERTON parish 1614 incl in regs Harlaxton Leics 7 miles ne Leicester comp chapelry Ingarsby, liberty Baggrave, hamlet

Quenby pop 260 archd Leichester dioc Lincoln

HUNGERTON parish 1558 Lincs 4-3/4 miles sw Grantham pop 128 archd and dioc Lincoln

HUNMANBY parish 1584 E R York 8-1/4 miles se Scarborough pop 1,079 archd East Riding dioc York Bapt, Wesl Meth

HUNNINGHAM parish 1718 Warws 5-1/2 miles nw Southam pop 212 archd Coventry dioc Lichfield

HUNSDON parish 1546 Herts 5 miles sw Sawbridgeworth pop 592 archd Middlesex dioc London

HUNSHELF township parish Penistone W R York pop 531

HUNSINGORE parish 1656 W R York 4 miles ne Wetherby comp townships Cattal, Hunsingore, Great Ribston with Walshford pop 595 pec lord of the Manor

HUNSLET or HUNFLEET chapelry 1686 parish Leeds W R York pop 12,074 archd and dioc York Wesl Meth, New Connection Meth

HUNSONBY township parish Addingham Cumberland pop 146 Wesl Meth

HUNSTANTON parish 1538 Norfolk 10 miles w Burnham Westgate pop 432 archd Norfolk dioc Norwich

HUNSTERTON township parish Wybunbury Ches pop 226

HUNSTON parish 1559 Suffolk 8-1/2 miles nw Stow Market pop 185 archd Sudbury dioc Norwich

HUNSTON parish 1678 Sussex 2-1/2 miles s Chichester pop 173 archd and dioc Chichester

HUNSTONWORTH chapelry 1724 parish Edmondbyers co Durham pop 511 archd and dioc Durham

HUNSWORTH township parish Birstall W R York pop 878

HUNTINGDON town, borough Hunts 59 miles nw London pop 3,267 sep juris comp All Saints 1558, St Benedict 1574, St John the Baptist 1585, St Mary 1593 archd Huntingdon dioc Lincoln Bapt, Soc of Friends, Indep, Wesl Meth

HUNTINGFIELD parish 1539 Suffolk 4 miles sw Halesworth pop 400 archd Suffolk dioc Norwich

HUNTINGFORD tything parish Wooton under Edge Gloucs

HUNTINGTON township parish St Oswald, Chester Ches pop 112

HUNTINGTON chapelry 1754 parish Holmer Herefs pop 69 pec Dean of Hereford

HUNTINGTON chapelry 1718 parish Kington Herefs pop 264 Indep

HUNTINGTON township parish Cannock Staffs pop 106

HUNTINGTON parish 1592 N R York 3 miles ne York comp townships Huntington, portion Earswick, Towthorpe pop 626 archd Cleveland dioc York

HUNTISHAM township parish Goodrich Herefs pop 119

HUNTLEY parish 1660 Gloucs 4-1/2 miles sw Newent pop 464 archd Hereford dioc Gloucester

HUNTON parish 1585 Kent 6 miles sw Maidstone pop 765 pec Archbishop of Canterbury

HUNTON chapelry 1564 parish Crawley Hamps pop 112 pec Rector of Crawley

HUNTON chapelry incl in regs of Brompton Patrick N R York pop 535

HUNTSHAM parish 1558 Devon 3 miles se Bampton pop 170 archd and dioc Exeter

HUNTSHAW parish 1746 Devon 3 miles ne Great Torrington pop 312 archd Barnstaple dioc Exeter

HUNTSPILL parish 1654 Somerset 7-1/2 miles ne Bridgewater pop 1,503 archd Wells dioc Bath and Wells Bapt

HUNWICK township parish St Andrew Auckland co Durham pop 164

HUNWORTH parish 1653 Norfolk 2-1/2 miles sw Holt pop 285 archd and dioc Norwich

HURDSFIELD township parish Prestbury Ches pop 3,083

HURLESTON township parish Acton Ches pop 198

HURLEY parish 1563 Berks 4-3/4 miles nw Maidenhead pop 1,150 archd Berks dioc Salisbury

HURN tything parish Christchurch Hamps

HURSLEY parish 1600 Hamps 4-1/2 miles sw Winchester pop 1,418 pec Incumbent

HURST parish 1583 Wilts 3-1/2 miles nw Wokingham comp liberties Whistley Hurst, Newland, Winnersh, Broad Hinton pop 2,334 pec Dean of Salisbury

HURST parish no regs Kent 5-1/2 miles w Hythe pop 40 archd and dioc Canterbury

HURST township parish Woodhorn Northumberland pop 39

HURST, COURTNEY township parish Birkin W R York pop 117

HURST, LONG township parish Bothall Northumberland pop 216

HURSTMONCEAUX parish 1538 Sussex 4 miles e Hailsham pop 1,338 archd Lewes dioc Chichester Indep

HURST, OLD parish 1653 Hunts 4-1/4 miles nw St Ives pop 150 archd Huntingdon dioc Lincoln

HURSTPIERREPOINT parish 1558 Sussex 11 miles nw Lewes pop 1,484 archd Lewes dioc Chichester

HURST, TEMPLE township parish Birkin W R York pop 135

HURSTBOURN parish 1604 Hamps 2 miles sw Whitchurch pop 490 pec incumbent

HURSTBOURN TARRANT parish 1546 Hamps 5-1/2 miles ne Andover pop 786 archd and dioc Winchester

HURSTLEY township parish Letton Herefs pop 66

HURSTWICK township parish Wragby W R York pop 142

HURWORTH parish 1559 co Durham 3-3/4 miles se Darlington comp townships Hurworth, Neasham or Nysam pop 1,348 archd and dioc Durham Wesl Meth

HUSBORN CRAWLEY parish 1558 Beds 2-1/2 miles ne Woburn pop 680 archd Bedford dioc Lincoln

HUSTHWAITE parish 1674 N R York 4 miles nw Easingwould comp chapelry Carlton, township Husthwaite pop 539 pec Dean and Chapter of York

HUTTOFT parish 1562 Lincs 4 miles e Alford pop 470 archd and dioc Lincoln Wesl Meth

HUTTON parish 1654 Essex 2-1/2 miles w Billericay pop 381 archd Essex dioc London

HUTTON township parish Penwortham Lancs pop 715

HUTTON township parish Warton Lancs pop 263

HUTTON parish 1715 Somerset 7 miles nw Axbridge pop 381 archd Wells dioc Bath and Wells

HUTTON township parish Long Marston E R York pop 116

HUTTON township parish Rudby in Cleveland N R York pop 1,027

HUTTON BONVILLE chapelry 1727 parish Birkby N R York pop 112 pec Bishop of Durham for Allerton and Allertonshire

HUTTON BUSHELL parish 1572 N R York 6 miles sw Scarborough comp townships West Ayton, Hutton Bushell pop 671 archd Cleveland dioc York

HUTTON CONYERS extra parochial liberty N R York 1-3/4 miles ne Ripon pop 159

HUTTON CRANSWICK parish 1653 E R York 3-1/2 miles s Great Driffield comp townships Hutton Cranswick, Botsea, Sunderland-wick pop 1,118 archd East Riding dioc York

HUTTON, HANG township parish Fingall N R York pop 23

HUTTON, HENRY township parish Monk Hesleton co Durham pop 162 Roman Cath

HUTTON IN THE FOREST parish 1729 Cumberland 5-1/2 miles nw Penrith comp townships Hutton in the Forest, Thomas Close pop 273 archd and dioc Carlisle

HUTTON I' TH' HAY township parish Kendal Westm

HUTTON JOHN township parish Greystock Cumberland pop 27

HUTTON LE HOLE township parish Lastingham N R York pop 276

HUTTON LOCRAS township parish Guisbrough N R York pop 52

HUTTON MAGNA parish 1670 N R York 3-1/4 miles se Greta Bridge comp townships Hutton Magna with Lane Head, Wesl Layton pop 319 archd Richmond dioc Chester

HUTTON MULGRAVE township parish Lythe N R York pop 85

HUTTON, NEW chapelry 1741 parish Kendal Westm pop 172 archd Richmond dioc Chester

HUTTON, OLD chapelry 1754 parish Kendal Westm pop 429 archd Richmond dioc Chester

HUTTON, ROOF township parish Greystock Cumberland pop 189

HUTTON ROOF chapelry parish Kirby Lonsdale Westm pop 351

HUTTON, SAND chapelry 1706 parish Thirsk N R York pop 275 archd Cleveland dioc York Wesl Meth

HUTTON, SAND township parish Bossall N R York pop 161

HUTTON SESSAY township parish Sessay N R York

HUTTON, SHERIFF parish 1628 N R York 11 miles ne York comp chapelry Farlington, townships Cornbrough, Lillings Ambo, Sheriff Hutton, Stittenham pop 1,371 archd Cleveland dioc York Prim and Wesl Meth

HUTTON, SOIL township parish Greystock Cumberland pop 338

HUTTONS AMBO parish 1714 N R York 3 miles sw New Malton pop 412 archd Cleveland dioc York Wesl Meth

HUXHAM parish 1667 Devon 3-3/4 miles ne Exeter pop 172 archd and dioc Exeter

HUXLEY township parish Waverton Ches pop 246

HUYTON parish 1578 Lancs 1-1/2 miles sw Prescot comp townships Huyton, Knowsley, Robby, Tarbock pop 3,412 archd and dioc Chester

HYCKHAM, NORTH parish 1695 Lincs 4-3/4 miles sw Lincoln pop 317 archd and dioc Lincoln

HYCKHAM, SOUTH parish (incl in regs of North Hyckham) Lincs 6 miles sw Lincoln pop 116 archd and dioc Lincoln

HYDE hamlet parish Luton Beds pop 537

HYDE chapelry parish Stockport Ches pop 7,144 Indep, Wesl Meth, Unit

HYDE ASH hamlet parish Leominster Herefs

HYDE PASTURES extra parochial liberty Warws 2-1/4 miles e Nuneaton

HYLTON township parish Monkwearmouth co Durham pop 420

HYTHE parish 1556 borough Kent 33 miles se Maidstone pop 2,287 sep juris pec Archbishop of Canterbury Indep, Wesl Meth

HYTHE chapelry parish Fawley Hamps

HYTHE, WEST parish 1730 Kent 2 miles sw Hythe pop 168 archd and dioc Canterbury

IBBERTON parish 1761 Dorset 7 miles nw Blandford Forum pop 225 archd Dorset dioc Bristol

IBLE township parish Wirksworth Derbys pop 113

IBSLEY chapelry 1654 parish Fordingbridge Hamps pop 316

IBSTOCK parish 1568 Leics 4-3/4 miles n Market Bosworth pop 1,830 archd Leicester dioc Lincoln Wesl Meth

ICCOMB parish 1545 Gloucs 3 miles se Stow on the Wold pop 148 pec Bishop of Worcester

ICKBOROUGH parish 1755 Norfolk 6 miles ne Brandon Ferry pop 197 archd Norfolk dioc Norwich

ICKENHAM parish 1538 Middlesex 2-3/4 miles ne Uxbridge pop 297 Commissary of London, concurrently with Consistorial Court of the Bishop

ICKFORD parish 1561 co Oxford and Bucks 4-1/4 miles nw Thame pop 368 archd Buckingham dioc Lincoln Bapt

ICKHAM parish 1557 Kent 1-3/4 miles nw Wingham pop 567 in exempt deanery of Shoreham pec of Archbishop of Canterbury

ICKLEFORD parish 1749 Herts 1-3/4 miles n Hitchin pop 502 archd Huntingdon dioc Lincoln

ICKLESHAM parish 1669 Sussex 2 miles sw Winchelsea pop 604 archd Lewes dioc Chichester

ICKLETON parish 1558 Cambs 4-3/4 miles sw Linton pop 682 archd and dioc Ely

ICKLINGHAM parish 1560 Suffolk 3-1/2 miles se Mildenhall pop 473 archd Sudbury dioc Norwich

ICKWELL hamlet parish Northill Beds

ICKWORTH parish 1566 Suffolk 2-1/2 miles sw Bury St Edmund's pop 43 archd Sudbury dioc Norwich

IDBURY parish 1754 co Oxford 5-1/2 miles nw Burford pop 185 archd and dioc Oxford

IDDESLEIGH parish 1540 Devon 3 miles ne Hatherleigh pop 574 archd Barnstaple dioc Exeter

IDE parish 1653 Devon 2-1/4 miles sw Exeter pop 757 pec Dean and Chapter of Exeter

IDEFORD parish 1598 Devon 2-1/2 miles se Chudleigh pop 381 archd Totnes dioc Exeter

IDE HILL chapelry parish Sundridge Kent

IDEN parish 1559 Sussex 2-1/4 miles n Rye pop 517 archd Lewes dioc Chichester Wesl Meth

IDLE chapelry parish Calverley W R York pop 5,416 Bapt, Indep, Wesl Meth

IDLESTREE Herts See ELSTREE

IDLICOTE parish 1556 Warws 3-1/4 miles ne Shipton upon Stour pop 82 archd and dioc Worcester

IDMISTON parish 1577 Wilts 5-1/4 miles ne Salisbury comp chapelry Porton, tythings Ford Gomeldon, Idmiston and Shripple pop 520 archd and dioc Salisbury

IDRIDGEHAY township parish Wirksworth Derbys pop 182

IDSTONE tything parish Ashbury Berks pop 192

IDSWORTH chapelry parish Chalton Hamps pop 315

IFIELD parish 1751 Kent 2-1/2 miles se Gravesend pop 72 pec deanery Shoreham

IFIELD parish 1568 Sussex 7 miles ne Horsham pop 916 archd Lewes dioc Chichester

IFLEY parish 1572 co Oxford 1-3/4 miles se Oxford pop 656 archd and dioc Oxford

IFORD tything parish Christchurch Hamps

IFORD parish 1654 Sussex 2-1/4 miles sw Lewes pop 187 archd Lewes dioc Chichester

IFORD hamlet parish Westwood Wilts

IFTON parish no regs co Monmouth 6 miles sw Chepstow pop 42 archd and dioc Llandaff

IFTON RHYN township parish St Martin Shrops pop 1,016

IGHTENHILL PARK township parish Whalley Lancs pop 164

IGHTFIELD parish 1557 Shrops 4-1/4 miles se Whitchurch pop 301 archd Salop dioc Lichfield

IGHTHAM parish 1559 Kent 1-3/4 miles sw Wrotham pop 1,017 pec deanery of Shoreham

IGBOROUGH Norfolk See ICKBOROUGH

IKEN parish 1669 Suffolk 5 miles nw Orford pop 382 archd Suffolk dioc Norwich

ILAM parish 1656 Staffs 4-1/4 miles nw Ashbourn pop 210 archd

Stafford dioc Lichfield

ILCHESTER parish 1690 borough Somerset 4 miles se Somerton pop 1,095 archd Wells dioc Bath and Wells Indep

ILDERTON parish 1724 Northumberland 4-1/4 miles se Wooler comp townships Ilderton, Middleton Hall, North Middleton, South Middleton, Roddam and Rosedon pop 602 archd Northumberland dioc Durham

ILFORD, GREAT chapelry parish Barking Essex pop 3,512 Bapt, Wesl Meth

ILFORD, LITTLE parish 1539 Essex 7 miles ne London pop 115 archd Essex dioc London

ILFRACOMBE or ILFORDCOMBE parish 1567 Devon 11 miles nw Barnstaple pop 4,000 archd Barnstaple dioc Exeter Indep, Wesl Meth

ILKESTON parish 1586 Derbys 9-1/2 miles ne Derby pop 4,446 archd Derby dioc Lichfield Gen and Part Bapt, Indep, Wesl Meth, Unit

ILKETSHALL ST ANDREW parish 1542 Suffolk 3-3/4 miles se Bungay pop 512 archd Suffolk dioc Norwich

ILKETSHALL ST JOHN parish 1538 Suffolk 2 miles se Bungay pop 72 archd Suffolk dioc Norwich

ILKETSHALL ST LAWRENCE parish 1559 Suffolk 3-1/4 miles se Bungay pop 242 archd Suffolk dioc Norwich

ILKETSHALL ST MARGARET parish 1538 Suffolk 2-3/4 miles se Bungay pop 309 archd Suffolk dioc Norwich

ILKLEY parish 1597 W R York 5-3/4 miles nw Otley comp townships Middleton with Stockhill, Nesfield with Langbar, Ilkley pop 1,063 archd and dioc York

ILLINGTON parish 1672 Norfolk 3-1/2 miles nw East Harling pop 91 archd Norfolk dioc Norwich

ILLINGWORTH chapelry 1695 parish Halifax W R York Wesl Meth

ILLMIRE parish 1660 Bucks 4-1/2 miles se Thame pop 78 archd Buckingham dioc Lincoln

ILLOGAN parish 1539 Cornwall 2-3/4 miles nw Rudruth pop 6,072 archd Cornwall dioc Exeter Wesl Meth, Bryanites

ILMINGTON parish 1588 Gloucs and Warws 4 miles nw Shipston upon Stour pop 859 archd and dioc Worcester

ILMINSTER parish 1652 Somerset 13 miles sw London pop 2,957 pec of Manor of Ilminster Indep, Wesl Meth, Unit

ILSINGTON parish 1558 Devon 4-3/4 miles ne Ashburton pop 1,298 archd Totnes dioc Exeter

ILSLEY, EAST parish 1653 Berks 16 miles se Reading pop 738 archd Berks dioc Salisbury Wesl Meth

ILSLEY, WEST parish 1558 Berks 2 miles nw East Ilsley pop 425 archd Berks dioc Salisbury

ILSTON ON THE HILL chapelry 1654 parish Carlton Curlieu and King's Norton Leics pop 131

ILTON parish 1642 Somerset 2-1/4 miles nw Ilminster pop 530 no juris

ILTON township parish Masham N R York pop 233

IMBER parish 1709 Wilts 4-3/4 miles sw East Lavington pop 604 archd and dioc Salisbury

IMMINGHAM parish 1562 Lincs 10 miles nw Grimsby pop 199 archd and dioc Lincoln

IMPINGTON parish 1562 Cambs 3-1/4 miles n Cambridge pop 211 archd and dioc Ely

INCE parish 1687 Ches 6 miles sw Frodsham pop 487 archd and dioc Chester

INCE township parish Wigan Lancs pop 1,903

INCE BLUNDELL township parish Sephton Lancs pop 505

INGARSBY chapelry parish Hungerton Leics pop 29

INGATESTONE parish 1558 Essex 6 miles sw Chelmsford pop 789 archd Essex dioc London Indep

INGBIRCHWORTH township parish Penistone W R York pop 371

INGERTHORPE township parish Ripon W R York pop 48

INGESTRIE parish 1691 Staffs 3-3/4 miles ne Stafford pop 116 archd Stafford dioc Lichfield

INGHAM parish 1567 Lincs 8-1/4 miles nw Lincoln pop 361 archd Stow dioc Lincoln

INGHAM parish 1801 Norfolk 8-1/2 miles se North Walsham pop 419 archd Norfolk dioc Norwich Bapt

INGHAM parish 1538 Suffolk 4-3/4 miles n Bury St Edmund's pop 226 archd Suffolk dioc Norwich

INGLEBY township parish Foremark Derbys pop 163

INGLEBY township parish Saxelby Lincs

INGLEBY ARNCLIFFE Yorks See ARNCLIFFE, INGLEBY

INGLEBY BERWICK township parish Stainton N R York pop 177

INGLEBY GREENHOW parish 1539 N R York 4-1/2 miles se Stokesley comp townships Battersby, Greenhow, Ingleby Greenhow pop 368 archd Cleveland dioc York

INGLESHAM parish 1589 in Berks and Wilts 3-1/4 miles n Highworth pop 133 archd Wilts dioc Salisbury

INGLETON township parish Gainford co Durham pop 355 Prim Meth

INGLETON chapelry 1607 parish Bentham W R York pop 1,228

INGLISH COMBE Somerset See COMBE, ENGLISH

INGOE township parish Stamfordham Northumberland pop 242

INGOL township parish Preston Lancs pop 687

INGOLDESTHORPE parish 1754 Norfolk 5-3/4 miles ne Castle Rising pop 286 archd Norfolk dioc Norwich

INGOLDMELLS parish 1723 Lincs 9-3/4 miles se Alford pop 206 archd and dioc Lincoln

INGOLDSBY parish 1566 Lincs 5-1/4 miles ne Corby pop 345 archd and dioc Lincoln

INGRAM parish 1682 Northumberland 7-1/2 miles se Wooler comp townships Fawdon, Clinch with Hartside, Ingram, Linop with Greenside Hill, Reaveley pop 205 archd Northumberland dioc Durham

INGRAVE parish 1560 Essex 2 miles se Brentwood pop 402 archd

Essex dioc London

INGTHORP hamlet parish Tinwell co Rutland

INGWORTH parish 1558 Norfolk 2 miles n Aylsham pop 191 archd
and dioc Norwich

INHURST tything parish Baughurst Hamps

INKBERROW parish 1675 Worcs 5-1/4 miles w Alcester pop 1,734
archd and dioc Worcester

INKPEN parish 1633 Berks 4 miles se Hungerford pop 729 archd
Berks dioc Salisbury Wesl Meth

INSKIP township parish St Michael on Wyre Lancs pop 793 Bapt

INSTOW parish 1717 Devon 3 miles ne Bideford pop 369 archd
Barnstaple dioc Exeter

INTWOOD parish 1557 Norfolk 4 miles sw Norwich pop 52 archd
Norfolk dioc Norwich

INWARDLEIGH parish 1699 Devon 3-3/4 miles nw Oakhampton pop
638 archd Totnes dioc Exeter

INWORTH parish 1731 Essex 1-1/2 miles se Kelvedon pop 443 archd
Colchester dioc London

IPING parish 1664 Sussex 2-3/4 miles nw Midhurst pop 338 archd
and dioc Colchester

IPPLEPEN parish 1558 Devon 3-3/4 miles sw Newton Abbots pop
1,164 archd Totnes dioc Exeter Wesl Meth

IPPOLITTS parish 1710 Herts 1-1/2 miles se Hitchin pop 874 archd
Huntingdon dioc Lincoln

IPSDEN chapelry 1569 parish North Stoke co Oxford pop 582

IPSLEY parish 1615 Warws 6-1/4 miles nw Alcester pop 830 archd
and dioc Worcester

IPSTONE parish 1665 Bucks 7 miles nw Great Marlow pop 313
archd and dioc Oxford

IPSTONES parish 1561 Staffs 5 miles ne Cheadle pop 1,325 archd
Stafford dioc Lichfield

IPSWICH town borough Suffolk 25 miles se Bury St Edmund's pop
20,454 comp parishes St Clement 1563, St Helen 1677, St Lawrence
1539, St Margaret 1538, St Mary at Elms 1557, St Mary at the
Quay 1559, St Mary Stoke 1565, St Mary le Tower 1538, St Matthew 1559, St Nicholas 1539, St Peter 1657, St Stephen 1585
archd Suffolk dioc Norwich Gen and Part Bapt, Soc of Friends,
Indep, Wesl Meth, Unit, Roman Cath

IRBY township parish Woodchurch Ches pop 123

IRBY IN THE MARSH parish 1566 Lincs 5 miles se Spilsby pop 96
archd and dioc Lincoln

IRBY UPON HUMBER parish 1558 Lincs 6 miles sw Great Grimsby
pop 263 archd and dioc Lincoln

IRCHESTER parish 1622 co Northampton 3 miles se Wellingborough
pop 797 archd Northampton dioc Peterborough Wesl Meth

IREBY parish 1705 Cumberland 6-1/2 miles sw Wigton comp townships High Ireby, Low Ireby pop 499 archd and dioc Carlisle

IREBY township parish Tatham Lancs pop 109

IRELETH chapelry parish Dalton in Furness Lancs pop 591

IRETON, KIRK parish 1572 Derbys 2-1/2 miles sw Wirksworth pop 744 archd Derby dioc Lichfield Indep

IRETON, WOOD township parish Kirk Ireton Derbys pop 138

IRMINGLAND parish Norfolk 5-1/4 miles nw Aylsham pop 16 archd and dioc Norwich

IRNHAM parish 1559 Lincs 2-1/2 miles ne Corby pop 394 archd and dioc Lincoln

IRON ACTON Gloucs See ACTON, IRON

IRON BROCK GRANGE hamlet parish Wirksworth Derbys pop 27

IRSTEAD parish 1538 Norfolk 6-1/2 miles e Coltishall pop 169 archd Norfolk dioc Norwich

IRTHINGTON parish 1704 Cumberland 3 miles nw Brampton comp townships Irthington, Leversdale, Newby, Newtown pop 1,023 archd and dioc Carlisle

IRTHLINGBOROUGH parish 1562 co Northampton 2 miles nw Higham Ferrers pop 1,262 archd Northampton dioc Peterborough Bapt, Wesl Meth

IRTON parish 1697 Cumberland 4-1/2 miles ne Ravenglass pop 531 archd Richmond dioc Chester

IRTON township parish Seamer N R York pop 107

ISALL parish 1669 Cumberland 3-3/4 miles ne Cockermouth comp townships Blinderake with Isall, Redmain, Isall Old Park, Sunderland pop 508 archd and dioc Carlisle

ISALL OLD PARK township parish Isall Cumberland pop 108

ISFIELD parish 1570 Sussex 3-1/4 miles sw Uckfield pop 581 pec of Archbishop of Canterbury

ISHAM parish 1701 co Northampton 3-1/2 miles se Kettering pop 318 archd Northampton dioc Peterborough

ISHLAWREOED hamlet parish Bedwelty co Monmouth pop 2,070

ISLE ABBOTTS parish 1558 Somerset 4-3/4 miles nw Ilminster pop 380 archd Taunton dioc Bath and Wells Bapt

ISLE BREWERS parish 1705 Somerset 5-1/4 miles sw Langport pop 254 archd Taunton dioc Bath and Wells

ISLEHAM parish 1566 Cambs 4-1/4 miles w Mildenhall pop 1,942 pec Bishop of Rochester Bapt, Indep

ISLEWORTH parish 1566 Middlesex 9 miles sw London pop 5,590 archd Middlesex dioc London Soc of Friends, Indep, Wesl Meth, Roman Cath

ISLEY WALTON chapelry 1710 parish Kegworth Leics pop 72

ISLINGTON parish 1557 Middlesex 2 miles nw London pop 37,316 commissary of London, concurrently with Consistorial Court of the Bishop Indep, Wesl Meth

ISLINGTON parish 1588 Norfolk 3-3/4 miles sw Lynn Regis pop 238 archd and dioc Norwich

ISLIP parish 1695 co Northampton 1 mile nw Thrapston pop 562 archd Northampton dioc Peterborough Bapt

ISLIP parish 1590 co Oxford 5 miles ne Oxford pop 645 archd and dioc Oxford

ISSEY, ST parish 1596 Cornwall 3-1/2 miles se Padstor pop 720 pec Bishop of Exeter Indep, Wesl Meth

ITCHENOR, WEST parish 1561 Sussex 6-1/2 miles sw Chichester pop 237 archd and dioc Chichester

ITCHIN ABBAS parish 1586 Hamps 3-1/2 miles nw New Alresford pop 243 archd and dioc Winchester

ITCHIN STOKE parish 1719 Hamps 2 miles nw New Alresford pop 267 archd and dioc Winchester

ITCHINGFIELD parish 1700 Sussex 3-1/4 miles sw Horsham pop 356 archd and dioc Chichester

ITCHINGSWELL Hamps See ECCHINSWELL

ITCHINGTON tything parish Tytherington Gloucs pop 126

ITCHINGTON, BISHOP'S parish 1559 Warws 3-3/4 miles sw Southam comp hamlets Upper and Lower Itchington, chapelries Chadshunt, Gaydon pop 421 pec Prebendary of Colwich and Bishop's Itchington in Cathedral Church of Litchfield

ITCHINGTON, LONG parish 1653 Warws 2 miles nw Southam pop 911 archd Coventry dioc Lichfield

ITONFIELD township parish Hesket in the Forest Cumberland pop 234

ITTERINGHAM parish 1560 Norfolk 4-1/4 miles nw Aylesham pop 343 archd and dioc Norwich

ITTON parish 1773 co Monmouth 3-1/4 miles nw Chepstow pop 141 archd and dioc Llandaff

IVE, ST parish 1651 Cornwall 4-1/4 miles sw Callington pop 656 archd Cornwall dioc Exeter

IVEGILL Cumberland See HIGHEAD

IVER parish 1605 Bucks 2-1/2 miles ne Colnbrook pop 1,870 archd Buckingham dioc Lincoln

IVES, ST parish 1686 borough Cornwall 9 miles ne Penzance sep juris pop 4,776 archd Cornwall dioc Exeter Countess of Huntingdon's, Prim and Wesl Meth

IVES, ST parish 1566 Hunts 6 miles e Huntingdon pop 3,314 archd Huntingdon dioc Lincoln Bapt, Wesl Meth

IVESTONE township parish Lanchester Co Durham pop 212

IVINGHOW parish 1559 Bucks 9 miles ne Aylesbury comp town Ivinghoe, hamlets Aston, Norton with Seabrook, St Margaret pop 1,654 archd Buckingham dioc Lincoln Bapt, Wesl Meth

IVINGTON chapelry parish Leominster Herefs pop 602

IVY BRIDGE village in parishes Cornwood, Ermington, Harford, Ugborough Devon Wesl Meth

IVY CHURCH parish 1564 Kent 3 miles nw New Romney pop 198 archd and dioc Canterbury

IVY CHURCH chapelry parish Alderbury Wilts

IWADE parish 1560 Kent 2 miles nw Milton pop 134 archd and dioc Canterbury

IWERNE COURTNAY or SHROTON parish 1562 Dorset 7 miles e

Shaftesbury pop 557 archd Dorset dioc Bristol

IWERNE MINSTER parish 1742 Dorset 5 miles s Shaftesbury pop 634 archd Dorset dioc Bristol

IWERNE STAPLETON parish 1755 Dorset 3-1/2 miles n Blandford archd Dorset dioc Bristol

IXWORTH parish 1559 Suffolk 7 miles ne Bury St Edmund's pop 1,061 archd Sudbury dioc Norwich

IXWORTH THORPE Suffolk See THORPE BY IXWORTH

JACKFIELD parish 1759 Shrops 1 mile ne Broseley archd Salop dioc Hereford

JACOBSTOW parish 1653 Cornwall 8-1/2 miles sw Stratton pop 638 archd Cornwall dioc Exeter

JACOBSTOWE parish 1586 Devon 3-1/2 miles se Hatherleigh pop 293 archd Totnes dioc Exeter

JAMES, ST chapelry parish Bishop's Cannings Wilts pop 1,765

JARROW parish 1572 co Durham 2-3/4 miles sw South Sheilds comp chapelries Heworth, South Sheilds, townships Harton, Monkton with Jarrow and Westoe pop 3,598 archd and dioc Durham Wesl Meth

JAY township parish Leintwardine Herefs

JESMOND township parish St Andrew, Newcastle Northumberland pop 1,393

JEVINGTON parish 1661 Sussex 3 miles nw East Bourne pop 350 archd Lewes dioc Chichester

JOHN, ST parish 1616 Cornwall 6 miles se St Germans pop 150 archd Cornwall dioc Exeter

JOHN, ST York See LETWELL

JOHN, ST CASTERIGG chapelry 1776 parish Crosthwaite Cumberland pop 567 archd and dioc Carlisle

JOHN'S ST, CHAPEL co Durham See WEARDALE, ST JOHN

JOHNBY township parish Greystock Cumberland pop 86

JULIOT, ST parish 1656 Cornwall 6 miles ne Camelford pop 271 archd Cornwall dioc Exeter Bryanites

JUST, ST parish 1599 Cornwall 7 miles nw Penzance pop 4,667 archd Cornwall dioc Exeter Soc of Friends, Bapt, Wesl Meth

JUST, ST in ROSELAND parish 1538 Cornwall 2 miles n St Mawes comp town St Mawes pop 1,558 archd Cornwall dioc Exeter

KABER township parishes Brough and Kirby Stephen Westm pop 180

KEA parish 1701 Cornwall 3-1/2 miles se Truro pop 3,896 archd Cornwall dioc Exeter Soc of Friends, Wesl Meth

KEADBY township parish Althorp Lincs pop 309

KEAL, EAST parish 1708 Lincs 1-3/4 miles sw Spilsby pop 357 archd and dioc Lincoln Wesl Meth

KEAL, WEST parish 1623 Lincs 3 miles sw Spilsby pop 484 archd and dioc Lincoln Wesl Meth

KEARSLEY township parish Dean Lancs pop 2,705

KEARSLEY township parish Stamfordham Northumberland pop 16

KECKWICK township parish Runcorn Ches pop 74

KEDDINGTON parish 1563 Lincs 1-1/2 miles ne Louth pop 172 archd

and dioc Lincoln

KEDINGTON or KETTON parish 1651 Suffolk 4-1/2 miles nw Clare pop 626 archd Sudbury dioc Norwich

KEDLESTON parish 1600 Derbys 4-1/2 miles nw Derby pop 134 archd Derby dioc Lichfield

KEELBY parish 1565 Lincs 7 miles ne Caistor pop 638 archd and dioc Lincoln Wesl Meth

KEELE parish 1540 Staffs 2-1/2 miles sw Newcastle under Lyne pop 1,130 archd Stafford dioc Lichfield Wesl Meth

KEEVIL parish 1559 Wilts 4 miles e Trowbridge pop 692 archd Wilts dioc Salisbury

KEGWORTH parish 1556 Leics 6 miles nw Loughborough pop 1,821 archd Leicester dioc Lincoln Bapt, Wesl Meth

KEIGHLEY parish 1562 W R York 4 miles w Bingley pop 11,176 archd and dioc York Bapt, Indep, Wesl Meth, Swedenborgians

KEINTON MANSFIELD parish 1731 Somerset 4-1/4 miles ne Somerton pop 459 archd Wells dioc Bath and Wells

KEISBY hamlet parish Lavington Lincs pop 65

KELBY chapelry parish Haydor Lincs pop 104

KELDHOLME hamlet parish Kirby Moorside N R York

KELFIELD hamlet parish Owston Lincs

KELFIELD township parish Stillingfleet E R York pop 302 Wesl Meth

KELHAM parish 1663 Notts 2 miles nw Newark pop 189 archd Nottingham dioc York

KELK, GREAT township parish Foston upon Wolds E R York pop 178

KELK, LITTLE extra parochial liberty E R York 5-3/4 miles ne Great Driffield pop 50

KELLASNERGH township parish Kirkham Lancs

KELLAWAYS parish 1800 Wilts 3 miles ne Chippenham pop 20 archd Wilts dioc Salisbury

KELLET, NETHER township parish Bolton le Sands Lancs pop 354

KELLET, OVER chapelry 1653 parish Bolton le Sands Lancs pop 446

KELLEYTHORPE township parish Driffield E R York pop 102

KELLING parish 1558 Norfolk 2 miles ne Holt pop 213 archd and dioc Norwich

KELLINGTON Cornwall See CALLINGTON

KELLINGTON parish 1637 W R York 7 miles ne Pontefract comp townships Beaghall, Egbrough, Kellington and Whitley pop 1,388 archd and dioc York

KELLOE parish 1693 co Durham 6-1/2 miles se Durham comp townships Cassop, Coxhoe, Church Kelloe, Quarrington, Thornley and Wingate pop 663 archd and dioc Durham

KELLY parish 1653 Devon 6 miles se Launceston pop 250 archd Totnes dioc Exeter

KELMARSH parish 1599 co Northampton 5-1/2 miles sw Rothwell pop 159 archd Northampton dioc Peterborough

KELMSCOTT parish 1601 co Oxford 2 miles e Lechlade pop 140 archd and dioc Oxford

KELSALE parish 1538 Suffolk 1 mile n Saxmundham pop 1,103 archd Suffolk dioc Norwich

KELSALL township parish Tarvin Ches pop 648 Wesl Meth

KELSEY, NORTH parish 1621 Lincs 5 miles w Caistor pop 648 pec Dean and Chapter of Lincoln Wesl Meth

KELSEY, SOUTH parish 1559 Lincs 5-3/4 miles sw Caistor pop 632 archd and dioc Lincoln

KELSHALL parish 1538 Herts 3-1/2 miles sw Royston pop 251 archd Huntingdon dioc Lincoln

KELSTERN parish 1651 Lincs 5-1/2 miles nw Louth pop 200 archd and dioc Lincoln Wesl Meth

KELSTON parish 1538 Somerset 3-3/4 miles nw Bath pop 274 archd Bath dioc Bath and Wells

KELVEDON parish 1558 Essex 12-3/4 miles ne Chelmsford pop 1,463 archd Colchester dioc London Indep

KELVEDON HATCH parish 1561 Essex 2-3/4 miles se Chipping Ongar pop 361 archd Essex dioc London

KEMBERTON parish 1659 Shrops 3 miles sw Shiffnall pop 282 archd Salop dioc Lichfield

KEMBLE parish 1679 Wilts 4 miles w Cirencester pop 482 archd Wilts dioc Salisbury

KEMERTON parish 1572 Gloucs 4-1/2 miles ne Tewkesbury pop 599 archd and dioc Gloucester Wesl Meth

KEMEYS COMMANDER parish 1696 co Monmouth 4 miles nw Usk pop 75 archd and dioc Llandaff

KEMEYS INFERIOR parish 1701 co Monmouth 3 miles ne Caerleon pop 133 archd and dioc Llandaff

KEMPLEY parish 1677 Gloucs 5-1/2 miles nw Newent pop 302 archd Hereford dioc Gloucester

KEMPSEY parish 1688 Worcs 4-1/4 miles s Worcester pop 1,314 archd and dioc Worcester

KEMPSFORD parish 1653 Gloucs 3 miles s Fairford pop 885 archd and dioc Gloucester

KEMPSHOT tything parish Winslade Hamps

KEMPSTON parish 1570 Beds 2-3/4 miles sw Bedford pop 1,571 archd Bedford dioc Lincoln Wesl Meth

KEMPSTON parish 1721 Norfolk 6-3/4 miles ne Swaffham pop 59 archd and dioc Norwich

KEMSING parish 1561 Kent 4 miles ne Seven Oaks pop 399 archd and dioc Rochester

KENARDINGTON parish 1544 Kent 7 miles se Tenterden pop 186 archd and dioc Canterbury

KENCHESTER parish 1757 Herefs 5 miles nw Hereford pop 118 archd and dioc Hereford

KENCOTT parish 1584 co Oxford 5 miles s Burford pop 199 archd and dioc Oxford

KENDAL parish 1558 borough Westm 23 miles sw Appleby comp town Kirkby Kendal, chapelries Crook, Grayrigg, Helsington, Hugil,

Kentmere, Long Sleddale, Natland, New Hutton, Over Stayeley, Old Hutton with Holmescales, Selside with Whitwell, Underbarrow with Bradleyfield and Winster, townships Docker, Kirkland, Lambrigg, Nether Graveship, Nether Staveley, Patton, Scathwaiterigg, Hay with Hutton in the Hay, Skelsmergh, Kettle Strickland, Strickland Roger, Whinfell, portion of Fawcet Forest pop 17,427 archd Richmond dioc Chester Bapt, Soc of Friends, Glassites, Indep, Inghamites, Prim and Wesl Meth, Scotch Seceders, Unit Roman Cath

KENDER CHURCH parish 1757 Herefs 11-1/4 miles sw Hereford pop 75 archd and dioc Hereford

KENELM, ST chapelry 1736 parish Hales Owen Worcs

KENILWORTH parish 1630 Warws 5 miles n Warwick pop 3,097 archd Coventry dioc Lichfield Bapt, Indep, Presb

KENLEY parish 1682 Shrops 4-1/2 miles nw Much Wenlock pop 281 archd Salop dioc Lichfield

KENN parish 1538 Devon 4-1/4 miles s Exeter pop 982 archd and dioc Exeter

KENN parish 1540 Somerset 10 miles n Axbridge pop 273 pec Prebendary of Yatton

KENNERLEY or KENNERLEIGH parish 1645 Devon 5 miles nw Crediton pop 110 Consistory Court of Bishop of Exeter

KENNETT parish 1735 Cambs 5 miles ne Newmarket pop 195 archd Sudbury dioc Norwich

KENNETT, EAST parish 1655 Wilts 4-1/2 miles sw Marlborough pop 103 archd Wilts dioc Salisbury

KENNETT, WEST hamlet tything East and West Kennett parish Avebury Wilts pop 118

KENNINGHALL parish 1558 Norfolk 3 miles se East Harling pop 1,251 archd Norfolk dioc Norwich Bapt

KENNINGTON chapelry parish Radley Berks pop 141

KENNINGTON parish 1671 Kent 2 miles ne Ashford pop 461 archd and dioc Canterbury

KENNINGTON district in parish Lambeth Surrey Indep, Bapt, Wesl Meth

KENNYTHORPE township parish Langton E R York pop 75

KENSINGTON parish 1539 Middlesex 2 miles sw London pop 20,902 archd Middlesex dioc London Bapt, Indep, Roman Cath

KENSWICK chapelry parish Knightwick Worcs pop 15

KENSWORTH parish 1615 Herts 2-1/2 miles nw Market Street pop 732 archd Huntingdon dioc Lincoln

KENT CHURCH parish 1686 Herefs 13 miles sw Hereford pop 320 archd and dioc Hereford

KENTFORD parish 1709 Suffolk 4-1/2 miles ne Newmarket pop 173 archd Sudbury dioc Norwich

KENTISBERE parish 1695 Devon 3-3/4 miles ne Cullompton pop 1,336 archd and dioc Exeter

KENTISBURY parish 1675 Devon 8 miles se Ilfracombe pop 340

archd Barnstaple dioc Exeter Bapt

KENTISH TOWN chapelry parish St Pancras Middlesex Indep, Wesl Meth

KENTMERE chapelry 1701 parish Kendal Westm pop 191

KENTON parish 1694 borough Devon 8-3/4 miles se Exeter pop 2,050 archd and dioc Exeter

KENTON township parish Gosforth Northumberland pop 1,106

KENTON parish 1538 Suffolk 2-1/4 miles ne Debenham pop 261 archd Suffolk dioc Norwich

KENWYN parish 1559 Cornwall 1 mile nw Truro pop 8,492 archd Cornwall dioc Exeter

KENYON township parish Winwick Lancs pop 349

KEPWICK township parish Over Silton N R York pop 152

KERDISTON parish incl in regs of Reepham Norfolk 1-1/2 miles nw Reepham pop 211 archd Norfolk dioc Norwich

KERESLEY hamlet parish St Michael Coventry Warws pop 412

KERMINGHAM township parish Swettenham Ches pop 174

KERSALL hamlet parish Kneesall Notts pop 94

KERSEY parish 1542 Suffolk 1-3/4 miles nw Hadleigh pop 700 archd Sudbury dioc Norwich

KERSWELL, ABBOTS parish 1607 Devon 1-3/4 miles s Newton Bushell pop 442 archd Totnes dioc Exeter

KERSWELL, KING'S parish 1702 Devon 2-3/4 miles se Newton Bushell pop 771 archd Totnes dioc Exeter Indep, Wesl Meth

KESGRAVE parish 1658 Suffolk 3-3/4 miles ne Ipswich pop 101 archd Suffolk dioc Norwich

KESSINGLAND parish 1561 Suffolk 5-1/4 miles sw Lowestoft pop 666 archd Suffolk dioc Norwich Wesl Meth

KESTON parish 1541 Kent 5 miles se Bromley pop 391 pec deanery Shoreham

KESWICK market town parish Crosthwaite Cumberland pop 2,159 Indep, Wesl Meth

KESWICK parish 1538 Norfolk 3 miles sw Norwich pop 120 archd Norfolk dioc Norwich

KESWICK EAST township parish Harewood W R York pop 365 Wesl Meth

KETBY parish Lincs 8-1/2 miles nw Spilsby pop 237 archd and dioc Lincoln

KETTERING parish 1637 co Northampton 15 miles ne Northampton pop 4,099 archd Northampton dioc Peterborough Bapt, Soc of Friends, Indep, Wesl Meth

KETTERINGHAM parish 1558 Norfolk 3-3/4 miles ne Wymondham pop 215 archd Norfolk dioc Norwich

KETTLEBASTON parish 1578 Suffolk 2-1/4 miles nw Bildeston pop 202 archd Sudbury dioc Norwich

KETTLEBURGH parish Suffolk 2-1/4 miles sw Framlingham pop 388 archd Suffolk dioc Norwich

KETTLEBY hamlet parish Wrawby Lincs

KETTLESHULME township parish Prestbury Ches pop 232 Wesl Meth

KETTLESTONE parish 1540 Norfolk 3-1/4 miles ne Fakenham pop 221 archd Norfolk dioc Norwich

KETTLETHORPE parish 1653 Lincs 9-1/2 miles nw Lincoln pop 463 archd Stow dioc Lincoln

KETTLEWELL parish 1698 W R York 16 miles ne Settle pop 673 archd and dioc York

KETTON township parish Lamplugh Cumberland

KETTON parish 1561 co Rutland 4 miles sw Stamford pop 810 pec Prebendary of Ketton Indep

KEVERNE, ST parish 1580 Cornwall 11 miles se Helston pop 2,437 archd Cornwall dioc Exeter Bapt, Bryanites, Wesl Meth

KEVERSTONE township parish Staindrop co Durham

KEW parish 1714 Surrey 6-1/2 miles sw London pop 837 archd Surrey dioc Winchester

KEW, ST parish 1564 Cornwall 4-1/4 miles ne Wadebridge pop 1,316 archd Cornwall dioc Exeter Wesl Meth

KEWSTOKE parish 1667 Somerset 9-1/2 miles nw Axbridge pop 467 archd Wells dioc Bath and Wells

KEXBOROUGH township parish Darton W R York pop 548

KEXBY township parish Upton Lincs pop 227

KEXBY township parish Catton E R York pop 160

KEYHAM chapelry 1563 parish Rothley Leics pop 172

KEYHAVEN tything parish Milford Hamps

KEYINGHAM parish 1618 E R York 5 miles se Hedon pop 636 archd East Riding dioc York Wesl Meth

KEYMER parish 1601 Sussex 2-1/4 miles se Hurstpierrepoint pop 681 archd Lewes dioc Chichester

KEYNE, ST parish 1539 Cornwall 2-1/2 miles s Liskeard pop 201 archd Cornwall dioc Exeter

KEYNSHAM parish 1629 Somerset 7-1/4 miles nw Bath pop 2,142 archd Bath dioc Bath and Wells Bapt, Wesl Meth

KEYSOE parish 1735 Beds 4-1/2 miles sw Kimbolton pop 718 archd Bedford dioc Lincoln Bapt

KEYSTON parish 1637 Hunts 3-1/4 miles se Thrapston pop 198 archd Huntingdon dioc Lincoln

KEYTHORPE liberty parish Tugby Leics pop 16

KEYWORTH parish 1653 Notts 6-3/4 miles se Nottingham pop 552 archd Nottingham dioc York Indep

KIBBLESTONE liberty parish Stone Staffs

KIBBLESWORTH township parish Chester le Street co Durham pop 246

KIBWORTH BEAUCHAMP parish 1574 Leics 5-1/4 miles nw Market Harborough comp chapelry Kidworth, township Smeeton Westerby pop 1,500 archd Leicester dioc Lincoln Indep, Wesl Meth

KIBWORTH HARCOURT chapelry parish Kibworth Beauchamp Leics pop 421

KIDBROOKE liberty anciently a parish Kent 2 miles sw Woolwich

pop 458

KIDDAL township parish Barwick in Elmett W R York

KIDDERMINSTER parish 1539 Worcs 14 miles n Worcester comp town and borough of Kidderminster, chapelry Lower Mitton, hamlet Wribbenhall pop 20,865 sep juris archd and dioc Worcester Bapt, Indep, Wesl Meth, Unit

KIDDINGTON parish 1570 co Oxford 3-1/4 miles se Neat Enstone pop 292 archd and dioc Oxford

KIDLAND extra parochial liberty Northumberland 12 miles nw Rothbury pop 69

KIDLINGTON parish 1574 co Oxford 4 miles se Woodstock comp townships Gosford, Water Easton, hamlet Thrup pop 1,217 archd and dioc Oxford

KIGBEAR hamlet parish Oakhampton Devon

KILBOURNE township parish Horsley Derbys pop 590

KILBURN hamlet parish St John Middlesex

KILBURN parish 1600 W R York 7 miles nw Easingwould comp townships Hood with Osgoodby Grange, Kilburn pop 529 archd Cleveland dioc York

KILBY parish 1653 Leics 6-1/2 miles se Leicester pop 434 archd Leicester dioc Lincoln

KILDALE parish 1719 prior incl in Ingleby Greenhow N R York 5-3/4 miles ne Stokesley pop 188 archd Cleveland dioc York

KILDWICK parish 1572 W R York 4 miles se Skipton comp chapelry Silsden, townships Bradley's Both, Cowling, Farnhill with Cononley, Glusburn, Kildwick, Steeton with Eastburn, Stirton with Thorlby and Sutton pop 9,926 pec of Dean of York

KILGWRRWG or KILGARROCK parish 1813 co Monmouth 5-3/4 miles se Usk pop 129 archd and dioc Llandaff

KILHAM township parish Kirk Newton Northumberland pop 217

KILHAM parish 1653 E R York 5-1/2 miles ne Great Driffield pop 1,042 pec Dean of York Bapt, Wesl Meth

KILKHAMPTON parish 1539 Cornwall 3-1/2 miles ne Stratton pop 1,126 archd Cornwall dioc Exeter Wesl Meth

KILLAMARSH parish 1638 Derbys 9 miles ne Chesterfield pop 774 archd Derby dioc Lichfield

KILLCOT tything parish Newent Gloucs

KILLCOTT tything parish Hawkesbury Gloucs pop 306

KILLERBY township parish Heighington co Durham pop 95

KILLERBY township parish Catterick N R York pop 62

KILLINGHALL township parish Ripley W R York pop 545 Wesl Meth

KILLINGHOLME parish 1564 Lincs 12 miles nw Grimsby pop 480 archd and dioc Lincoln Bapt, Wesl Meth

KILLINGTON chapelry 1619 parish Kirby Lonsdale Westm pop 302

KILLINGWORTH township parish Long Benton Northumberland Wesl Meth

KILLPECK parish 1673 Herefs 8-3/4 miles sw Hereford pop 285 archd and dioc Hereford

KILMERSDON parish 1653 Somerset 6 miles nw Frome comp hamlets Charlton, Coleford, Kilmersdon, Kilmersdon Common, Luckington, Lypeat pop 2,129 archd Wells dioc Bath and Wells Presb, Meth

KILMESTON parish 1661 Hamps 4-1/2 miles s New Alresford pop 255 pec of incumbent

KILMINGTON parish 1723 Devon 1-1/2 miles sw Axminster pop 540 archd and dioc Exeter

KILMINGTON parish 1582 Somerset 6-1/2 miles ne Bruton pop 580 archd Wells dioc Bath and Wells

KILNER Somerset See CULBONE

KILNSAY hamlet parish Burnsall W R York

KILNSEA parish 1711 E R York 8-1/2 miles se Patrington pop 158 archd East Riding dioc York

KILNWICK parish 1575 E R York 7 miles sw Great Driffield comp chapelry Beswick, townships Bracken, Kilnwick and portion of Lockington pop 581 archd East Riding dioc York

KILNWICK PERCY parish 1688 E R York 2 miles ne Pocklington pop 49 pec of Dean of York

KILPIN township parish Howden E R York pop 349

KILSBY parish 1754 co Northampton 5-1/2 miles nw Daventry pop 687 archd Northampton dioc Peterborough Indep

KILTON parish 1683 Somerset 10-1/2 miles nw Bridgewater pop 141 archd Taunton dioc Bath and Wells

KILTON township parish Brotton N R York pop 80

KILVE parish 1538 Somerset 11-1/2 miles nw Bridgewater pop 233 archd Taunton dioc Bath and Wells

KILVERSTONE parish 1558 Norfolk 1-3/4 miles ne Thetford pop 36 archd Norfolk dioc Norwich

KILVINGTON parish 1538 Notts 7 miles s Newark pop 45 archd Nottingham dioc York

KILVINGTON, NORTH township parish Thornton le Street N R York pop 64 Roman Cath

KILVINGTON, SOUTH parish 1572 N R York 1-1/2 miles n Thirsk comp townships South Kilvington, Thornbrough, Upsal pop 414 archd Cleveland dioc York

KILWORTH, NORTH parish 1553 Leics 5 miles se Lutterworth pop 390 archd Leicester dioc Lincoln

KILWORTH, SOUTH parish 1559 Leics 5 miles ese Lutterworth pop 437 archd Leicester dioc Lincoln Wesl Meth

KIMBERLEY parish 1753 Norfolk 3-1/2 miles nw Wymondham pop 138 archd Norfolk dioc Norwich Wesl Meth

KIMBERLEY hamlet parish Greasley Notts

KIMBERWORTH township parish Rotherham W R York pop 4,031 Indep, Wesl Meth

KIMBLE, GREAT parish 1701 Bucks 3-1/4 miles sw Wendover pop 436 archd Buckingham dioc Lincoln

KIMBLE, LITTLE parish 1657 Bucks 3 miles sw Wendover pop 176 archd Buckingham dioc Lincoln

KIMBLEWORTH parish no regs co Durham 3 miles nw Durham pop 36 Dean and Chapter of Durham now extra parochial liberty

KIMNOLTON parish 1565 Herefs 3 miles ne Leominster pop 719 archd and dioc Hereford

KIMBOLTON parish 1647 Hunts 10-1/2 miles sw Huntingdon pop 1,584 archd Huntingdon dioc Lincoln Bapt, Indep, Moravians, Wesl Meth

KIMCOTE parish 1653 Leics 3-1/2 miles ne Lutterworth pop 490 archd Leicester dioc Lincoln

KIMMERIDGE parish 1700 Dorset 4-1/4 miles sw Corfe Castle pop 124 a donative

KIMPTON parish 1559 Herts 4-1/2 miles nw Welwyn pop 944 archd Huntingdon dioc Lincoln

KIMPTON parish 1589 Hamps 3 miles se Ludgershall pop 383 archd and dioc Winchester

KINDER hamlet parish Glossop Derbys pop 104

KINDERTON township parish Middlewich Ches pop 493

KINETON Warws See KINGTON

KINFARE or KINVER parish 1560 Staffs 4 miles sw Stourbridge pop 1,831 archd Stafford dioc Lichfield

KINGCOMBE tything parish Tollerporcorum Dorset pop 189

KINGERBY parish 1765 Lincs 5 miles nw Market Rasen pop 95 archd and dioc Lincoln

KINGHAM parish 1646 co Oxford 4-1/4 miles se Chipping Norton pop 504 archd and dioc Oxford

KINGMOOR extra parochial liberty Cumberland 2 miles nw Carlisle pop 426

KINGSBRIDGE parish 1612 Devon 36 miles sw Exeter pop 1,586 archd Totnes dioc Exeter Bapt, Soc of Friends, Indep, Wesl Meth

KING'S BROMLEY Staffs See BROMLEY, KING'S

KINGSBURY parish 1732 Middlesex 7-1/2 miles nw London pop 463 pec Dean and Chapter of St Paul's London

KINGSBURY parish 1537 Warws 5-1/4 miles ne Coleshill pop 1,314 archd Coventry dioc Lichfield

KINGSBURY EPISCOPI parish 1557 Somerset 4-3/4 miles se Langport comp tythings Barrow, Kingsbury Episcopi, East Lambrook, West Lambrook with Lake, Stembridge pop 1,695 archd Taunton dioc Bath and Wells Wesl Meth

KING'S CAPLE parish 1683 Herefs 5-1/4 miles nw Ross pop 280 archd and dioc Hereford

KINGSCLERE parish 1538 Hamps 9 miles ne Whitchurch pop 3,151 archd and dioc Winchester Wesl Meth, Indep

KINGSCOTE parish 1651 Gloucs 4-3/4 miles nw Tetbury pop 276 archd and dioc Gloucester

KING'S CLIFFE co Northampton See CLIFFE, KINGS

KINGSDON parish 1559 Somerset 2-1/4 miles se Somerton pop 610 archd Wells dioc Bath and Wells Indep

KINGSDOWN parish 1725 Kent 2-3/4 miles nw Wrotham pop 431

archd and dioc Rochester

KINGSDOWN parish 1560 Kent 3-1/2 miles s Sittingbourne pop 94 archd and dioc Canterbury

KINGSEY parish 1538 Bucks 3 miles ne Thame pop 222 archd Buckingham dioc Lincoln

KINGSFORD hamlet parish Wolverley Worcs

KINGSHOLME hamlet in parishes St Catherine and St Mary de Lode city of Gloucester

KINGSLAND parish 1538 Herefs 4-1/2 miles nw Leominster pop 1,074 archd and dioc Hereford

KINGSLAND chapelry parish Islington Middlesex Indep

KINGSLEY township parish Frodsham Ches pop 934 Wesl Meth

KINGSLEY parish 1568 Hamps 4-1/2 miles se Alton pop 345 archd and dioc Winchester

KINGSLEY parish 1561 Staffs 2-3/4 miles ne Cheadle pop 1,416 archd Stafford dioc Lichfield Wesl Meth

KINGS LYNN Norfolk See LYNN, KINGS

KINGSMARSH extra parochial liberty Ches 5-1/2 miles nw Malpas pop 70

KINGSBORTH parish 1538 Kent 2-3/4 miles s Ashford pop 386 archd and dioc Canterbury

KING'S NORTON Worcs See NORTON, KINGS

KINGSTHORPE parish 1540 co Northampton 2 miles nw Northampton pop 1,344 archd Northampton dioc Peterborough

KINGSTON parish 1654 Cambs 3-3/4 miles se Caxton pop 293 archd and dioc Ely

KINGSTON parish 1630 Devon 3-1/2 miles sw Modbury pop 504 archd Totnes dioc Exeter Wesl Meth

KINGSTON or KINSON chapelry 1728 parish Canford Magna Dorset pop 775

KINGSTON parish 1677 Somerset 3-3/4 miles n Taunton pop 892 archd Taunton dioc Bath and Wells Indep

KINGSTON parish 1714 Somerset 1-1/2 miles se Ilminster pop 292 archd Wells dioc Bath and Wells

KINGSTON parish 1647 Hamps 6-1/2 miles sw Newport pop 83 archd and dioc Winchester

KINGSTON parish 1571 Staffs 3-1/2 miles sw Uttoxeter pop 368 archd Stafford dioc Lichfield

KINGSTON parish 1570 Sussex 4-1/4 miles se Little Hampton pop 61 archd Lewes dioc Chichester

KINGSTON BAGPUZE parish 1539 Berks 6-1/4 miles w Abingdon pop 306 archd Berks dioc Salisbury

KINGSTON BLOUNT liberty parish Aston Rowant co Oxford

KINGSTON BY SEA or KINGSTON BOWSEY parish 1591 Sussex 1-1/2 miles e New Shoreham pop 60 archd Lewes dioc Chichester

KINGSTON DEVERILL parish 1706 Wilts 3-1/2 miles ne Mere pop 380 archd and dioc Salisbury

KINGSTON LISLE chapelry parish Sparsholt Berks pop 376 Bapt

KINGSTON NEAR LEWES parish 1654 Sussex 2 miles sw Lewes pop 160 archd Lewes dioc Chichester

KINGSTON RUSSELL extra parochial liberty Dorset pop 76

KINGSTON SEYMOUR parish 1727 Somerset 8-1/2 miles nw Axbridge pop 368 archd Bath dioc Bath and Wells

KINGSTON UPON HULL sea port E R York 39 miles se York comp Holy Trinity 1558, St Mary 1564, Kirk Ella, North Ferriby, Hessle extra parochial district Garrison Side pop 36,293 archd East Riding dioc York Gen and Part Bapt, Soc of Friends, Countess of Huntingdon's, Indep, Prim, Wesl and New Connection Meth, Swedenborgians, Unit, Roman Cath, Jews

KINGSTON UPON SOAR parish 1657 Notts 1-1/4 miles sw Kegworth pop 175 archd and dioc York

KINGSTON UPON THAMES parish 1542 Surry 17-1/2 miles ne Guildford comp market town Kingston sep juris, hamlets Ham with Hatch and Hook pop 7,257 archd Surrey dioc Winchester Bapt, Soc of Friends, Indep

KINGSTON WINTERBOURNE Dorset See WINTERBOURNE, KINGSTON

KINGSTONE parish 1659 Herefs 7 miles sw Hereford pop 492 Consistory Court Dean of Hereford

KINGSTONE parish 1558 Kent 5-1/4 miles se Canterbury pop 282 archd and dioc Canterbury

KINGSWEAR parish 1601 Devon 3-1/4 miles sw Brixham pop 275 archd Totnes dioc Exeter

KINGSWINFORD Staffs See SWINFORD, KING'S

KINGSWOOD hamlet parish Ludgershall Bucks

KINGSWOOD township parish Delamere Ches pop 86

KINGSWOOD liberty parish Shotwick Ches

KINGSWOOD parish 1598 Gloucs 4 miles ne Bristol archd Dorset dioc Bristol

KINGSWOOD liberty parish Ewell Surrey pop 221

KINGSWOOD hamlet parish Lapworth Warws Unit

KINGSWOOD parish 1598 Gloucs 5-1/4 miles sw Dursley pop 1,446 archd and dioc Gloucester Indep, Wesl Meth

KINGTHORP township parish N R York pop 42

KINGTON tything parish Thornbury Gloucs

KINGTON parish 1667 Herefs 19 miles nw Hereford comp town Kington, townships Barton and Bradnor with Rustrock, Chickward and Pembers Oak with Lilwall and Both Hergists pop 3,111 archd and dioc Hereford Bapt, Wesl Meth

KINGTON or KINETON parish 1538 Warws 10-1/2 miles se Warwick comp town Kington, chapelry Combrook pop 1,102 archd and dioc Worcester

KINGTON or LITTLE CHESTERTON hamlet parish Chesterton Warws

KINGTON parish 1563 Wilts 3 miles nw Chippenham comp tytings Easton Percy, Kington St Michael, Langley pop 1,091 archd Wilts dioc Salisbury

KINGTON parish 1587 Worcs 9-3/4 miles e Worcester pop 153
   archd and dioc Worcester
KINGTON, MAGNA parish 1670 Dorset 6-1/2 miles w Shaftesbury
   pop 539 archd Dorset dioc Bristol
KINGTON, WEST parish 1758 Wilts 8-1/2 miles nw Chippenham pop
   298 archd Wilts dioc Salisbury
KINGWATER township parish Lanercost Abbey Cumberland pop 365
KINGWESTON parish 1653 Somerset 3-1/2 miles ne Somerton pop
   122 archd Wells dioc Bath and Wells
KINLET parish 1657 Shrops 5-1/4 miles ne Cleobury Mortimer pop
   532 archd Salop dioc Hereford
KINNERLEY parish 1677 Shrops 6-1/2 miles se Oswestry pop 1,158
   archd and dioc St Asaph
KINNERSLEY parish 1626 Herefs 4-1/2 miles sw Weobley pop 351
   archd and dioc Hereford
KINNERSLEY parish 1691 Shrops 4-3/4 miles ne Wellington pop 295
   archd Salop dioc Lichfield
KINNERTON, LOWER township parish Doddleston Ches pop 104
KINNEYSIDE township parish St Bees, Allerdale Cumberland pop 227
KINOULTON parish 1569 Notts 9 miles se Nottingham pop 389 pec
   of vicar
KINSHAM parish 1594 Herefs 3-1/2 miles e Presteign pop 109 archd
   and dioc Hereford
KINSHAM hamlet parish Bredon Worcs
KINSON Dorset See KINGSTON
KINTBURY parish 1558 Berks 3-1/4 miles se Hungerford pop 1,781
   archd Berks dioc Salisbury Wesl Meth
KINTON township parish Leintwardine Herefs pop 191
KINVASTON township parish Wolverhampton Staffs pop 23
KINVER Staffs See KINFARE
KINWALSEY hamlet parish Hampton in Arden Warws pop 19
KINWARTON parish 1556 Warws 1-1/4 miles ne Alcester pop 40
   archd and dioc Worcester
KIPLIN township parish Catterick N R York pop 103
KIPPAX parish 1539 W R York 6-1/2 miles nw Pontefract comp
   townships Allerton, Bywater, Kippax, Great and Little Preston
   pop 1,901 archd and dioc York Wesl Meth
KIRBY BEDON parish 1558 Norfolk 3-3/4 miles se Norwich pop 245
   archd Norfolk dioc Norwich
KIRBY BELLARS parish 1713 Leics 3-1/2 miles sw Melton Mowbray
   pop 227 archd Leicester dioc Lincoln
KIRBY CANE parish 1538 Norfolk 4 miles nw Beccles pop 385 archd
   Norfolk dioc Norwich
KIRBY, COLD parish 1596 N R York 7-3/4 miles ne Thirsk pop 185
   archd Cleveland dioc York
KIRBY GRINDALYTH parish 1722 E R York 9 miles se New Malton
   comp townships Duggleby, Kirby Grindalyth, Thirkleby pop 414
   archd East Riding dioc York

KIRBY HORTON Kent See HORTON, KIRBY

KIRBY KNOWLE parish 1556 N R York 4-3/4 miles ne Thirsk comp chapelry Bagby, townships Balk, Kirby Knowle pop 507 archd Cleveland dioc York

KIRBY LE SOKEN parish 1681 Essex 11-1/4 miles se Manningtree pop 972 pec of Sokens Wesl Meth

KIRBY, MONKS parish 1678 Warws 7 miles nw Rugby pop 1,637 archd Coventry dioc Lichfield Bapt

KIRBY ON THE MOOR parish 1607 N R York 1-1/4 miles nw Boroughbridge comp townships Kirby on the Moor, Langthorp, portion of Humberton with Milby pop 524 archd Richmond dioc Chester

KIRBY SIGSTON York See SIGSTON, KIRBY

KIRBY UNDERDALE parish 1557 E R York 6-1/2 miles n Pocklington pop 293 archd East Riding dioc York

KIRBY, WEST parish 1692 Ches 7-1/2 miles nw Great Neston comp townships Great and Little Caldey, Frankby, Grange, Greasby, Hoose, Great Meolse, Little Meolse, Newton with Larton, West Kirby pop 1,289 archd and dioc Chester

KIRBY WISK parish 1615 N R York 4-3/4 miles nw Thirsk comp township Newsham with Breckenbrough, Kirby Wisk, Maunby, Newby Wisk pop 872 archd Richmond dioc Chester

KIRDFORD parish 1558 Sussex 4-1/2 miles ne Petworth pop 1,653 archd and dioc Chichester

KIRK ANDREWS, NETHER township parish Kirk Andrews upon Esk Cumberland pop 485

KIRK ANDREWS UPON ENDEN parish 1702 Cumberland 3-1/4 miles nw Carlisle pop 107 archd and dioc Carlisle

KIRK ANDREWS UPON ESK parish 1655 Cumberland 3 miles ne Longtown comp chapelry Nichol Forest, townships Middle Kirk Andrews, Nether Kirk Andrews, Moat pop 2,053 archd and dioc Carlisle

KIRK BAMPTON Cumberland See BAMPTON, KIRK

KIRK BRIDE parish 1662 Cumberland 5-3/4 miles nw Wigton pop 383 archd and dioc Carlisle Soc of Friends

KIRK BRAMWITH York See BRAMWITH, KIRK

KIRK BURN parish 1686 E R York 4 miles sw Great Driffield comp townships East Burn, Kirk Burn, South Burn, Tibthorp pop 489 archd East Riding dioc York

KIRK BURTON Yorks See BURTON, KIRK

KIRKBY chapelry 1678 parish Walton on the Hill Lancs pop 1,190

KIRKBY joint parish with Osgodby 1555 Lincs 4-3/4 miles nw Market Rasen pop 350 archd and dioc Lincoln

KIRKBY township parish Kirby Overblows W R York pop 231 Wesl Meth

KIRKBY, EAST parish 1583 Lincs 5 miles sw Spilsby pop 396 archd and dioc Lincoln

KIRKBY FLEETHAM parish 1591 N R York 4 miles se Catterick pop 625 archd Cleveland dioc Chester

KIRKBY FRITH liberty parish Glenfield Leics pop 32

KIRKBY GREEN parish 1722 Lincs 7-3/4 miles ne Sleaford pop 74 archd and dioc Lincoln

KIRKBY HALL township parish Little Ouseburn W R York pop 50

KIRKBY IN ASHFIELD parish 1620 Notts 5-1/4 miles sw Mansfield pop 2,032 archd Nottingham dioc York

KIRKBY IN CLEVELAND parish 1627 N R York 2 miles se Stokesley comp townships Great and Little Broughton, Kirkby in Cleveland pop 469 archd Cleveland dioc York

KIRKBY IN MALHAM DALE parish 1597 W R York 5-1/2 miles se Settle comp townships Calton, Airton, Hanlith, Kirkby in Malham Dale, Malham, Malham Moor, Otterburn, Scosthorpe pop 1,033 archd and dioc York

KIRKBY IRELETH parish 1607 Lancs 4-1/2 miles nw Ulverstone comp chapelries Broughton in Furness, Dunnerdale, Seathwaite, Woodland with Heathwaite, townships Low Quarter, Middle Quarter pop 3,234 archd Richmond dioc Chester

KIRKBY LE THORPE parish 1660 Lincs 2 miles ne Sleaford pop 170 archd and dioc Lincoln

KIRKBY LONSDALE parish 1538 Westm 30 miles sw Appleby comp town Kirkby Lonsdale, chapelries Barbon, Firbank, Hutton Roof, Killington, Mansergh, Middleton, townships Casterton, Lupton pop 3,949 archd Richmond dioc Chester Indep, Wesl Meth, Glassites, Sandemanians

KIRKBY MALLORY parish 1598 Leics 4-1/2 miles ne Hinckley pop 2,261 archd Leicester dioc Lincoln

KIRKBY MALZEARD parish 1653 W R York 6 miles nw Ripon comp town Kirkby Malzeard, chapelries Hartwith with Winsley, Maddlesmoor, townships Cozenley, Fountains Earth, Gravelthorpe, Laverton, Down Stonebeck, Upper Stonebeck pop 4,707 pec Dean and Chapter of York

KIRKBY MISPERTON parish 1789 N R York 3-3/4 miles sw Pickering comp townships Barugh Ambe, Great Habton, Little Habton, Kirkby Misperton, Ryton pop 864 archd Cleveland dioc York

KIRKBY MOORSIDE parish 1622 N R York 29 miles ne York comp town Kirkby Moorside, townships Bransdale East Side, Fadmore, Farndale Low Quarter, Gillimoor pop 2,324 archd Cleveland dioc York Soc of Friends, Indep, Wesl Meth

KIRKBY MUXLOE chapelry 1639 parish Glenfield Leics 4-1/2 miles w Leicester pop 275

KIRKBY ON THE HILL township parish Kirkby Ravensworth N R York pop 118

KIRKBY OVERBLOWS parish 1647 W R York 6 miles w Wetherby comp chapelry Stainburn, townships Kirkby with Netherby, Kirkby Overblows, Rigton, Sicklinghall, portion of Swindon pop 1,538 archd and dioc York

KIRKBY RAVENSWORTH parish 1599 N R York 4-3/4 miles nw Richmond comp townships Gayles, Kirkby on the Hill, New Forest,

Newsham, Ravensworth, Whashton, portion of Dalton pop 1,727 archd Richmond dioc Chester

KIRKBY, SOUTH parish 1620 W R York 8-1/2 miles s Pontefract comp townships North Elmsall, South Elmsall, South Kirkby, Skelbrooke pop 1,478 archd and dioc York

KIRKBY STEPHEN parish 1647 Westm 11 miles se Appleby comp town Kirkby Stephen, chapelries Mallerstang, Soulby, townships Hartley, Kaber, Nateby, Smardale, Waitby, Wharton, Winton pop 2,798 archd and dioc Carlisle Indep, Wesl Meth

KIRKBY THORE parish 1593 Westm 5-1/4 miles nw Appleby comp chapelries Milburn with Milburn Grange, Temple Sowerby, townships Kirkby Thore pop 1,231 archd and dioc Carlisle Wesl Meth

KIRKBY UNDERWOOD parish 1569 Lincs 5 miles nw Bourne pop 162 archd and dioc Lincoln

KIRKBY UPON BAIN parish 1562 Lincs 6 miles sw Horncastle pop 596 pec Manor Court of Kirkstead Wesl Meth

KIRKBY WHARFE parish 1583 W R York 2-1/4 miles se Tadcaster comp townships Ulleskelf, Grimston, Kirkby Wharfe pop 492 pec of Prebendary of Wetwang

KIRKDALE township parish Walton on the Hill Lancs pop 2,591

KIRKDALE parish 1579 N R York 4-1/4 miles ne Helmsley comp townships Norton Wombleton, Welburn, Beadlam, Bransdale (West Side), Muscoates, Newton, North Holme, Skiplam pop 1,107 archd Cleveland dioc York

KIRK ELLA Yorks See ELLA, KIRK

KIRKHAM parish 1539 Lancs 22 miles sw Lancaster comp town Kirkham, chapelries Goosnargh, Hambleton, Ribby with Wrea, Singleton, Warton, townships Bryning with Kellasnergh, Clifton with Salwick, Little Eccleston with Larbrick, Freckleton, Greenhalgh with Thistleton, Medlar with Wesham, Newsham, Newton with Scales, Treales with Roseacre, Wharles, Weston, Westby with Plumptons, Whittingham pop 11,630 archd Richmond dioc Chester Indep, Swedenborgians, Roman Cath

KIRKHAM extra parochial liberty E R York 5-1/2 miles sw New Malton pop 31

KIRK HAMMERTON Yorks See HAMMERTON, KIRK

KIRKHARLE Northumberland See HARLE, KIRK

KIRKHAUGH parish 1686 Northumberland 2-1/2 miles nw Alston Moor pop 309 archd Northumberland dioc Durham

KIRKHEATON chapelry incl regs of Thockrington parish Kirk Harle Northumberland pop 182

KIRK IRETON Derbys See IRETON, KIRK

KIRKLAND township parish Torpenhow Cumberland

KIRKLAND parish 1620 Cumberland 10-1/2 miles ne Penrith comp chapelry Culgaith, townships Kirkland with Blencarn, Skirwith pop 765 archd and dioc Carlisle

KIRKLAND township parish Garstang Lancs pop 458

KIRKLAND township parish Kendal Westm pop 1,250

KIRK LEATHAM parish 1559 N R York 4-1/2 miles nw Guisborough comp townships Kirk Leatham, Wilton pop 1,074 archd Cleveland dioc York

KIRK LEAVINGTON Yorks See LEAVINGTON, KIRK

KIRK LEES hamlet parish Dewsbury W R York

KIRKLEY township parish Ponteland Northumberland pop 165 Presb

KIRKLEY parish 1751 earlier regs of Pakefield Suffolk 1-1/2 miles sw Lowestoft pop 374 archd Suffolk dioc Norwich

KIRKLINGTON parish 1578 Notts 3-1/2 miles nw Southwell pop 243 pec Chapter of Collegiate Church of Southwell

KIRKLINGTON parish 1568 N R York 6-1/4 miles se Bedale comp townships Kirklington with Upsland, Sutton with Howgrave, East Tanfield pop 486 archd Richmond dioc Chester

KIRK LINTON or KIRK LEVINGTON parish 1650 Cumberland 4-3/4 miles se Longtown comp townships Hethersgill, Middle Quarter, West Linton or Levington pop 1,892 archd and dioc Carlisle Soc of Friends

KIRK OSWALD parish 1575 Cumberland 15-1/2 miles se Carlisle comp town Kirk Oswald, township Staffield or Staffol pop 1,033 archd and dioc Carlisle Wesl Meth, Indep

KIRKSTEAD parish 1739 Lincs 8 miles sw Horncastle pop 179 pec Manor of Kirkstead Unit

KIRKTON parish 1538 Notts 2-3/4 miles ne Ollerton pop 247 pec of Sub Dean of Lincoln

KIRK WHELPINGTON Northumberland See WHELPINGTON, KIRK

KIRMINGTON parish 1698 Lincs 8 miles n Caistor pop 310 archd and dioc Lincoln

KIRMOND LE MIRE parish 1751 Lincs 6-1/4 miles ne Market Rasen pop 74 archd and dioc Lincoln

KIRSTEAD parish 1677 Norfolk 7-1/4 miles nw Bungay pop 261 archd Norfolk dioc Norwich

KIRTLING parish 1585 Cambs 4-1/4 miles se Newmarket pop 735 archd Sudbury dioc Norwich

KIRTLINGTON parish 1558 co Oxford 5 miles ne Woodstock pop 687 archd and dioc Oxford

KIRTON Notts See KIRKTON

KIRTON parish 1562 Lincs 4-1/4 miles sw Boston pop 1,886 archd and dioc Lincoln

KIRTON parish 1689 Suffolk 7-1/2 miles se Ipswich pop 624 archd Suffolk dioc Norwich

KIRTON IN LINDSEY parish 1585 Lincs 18 miles nw Lincoln pop 1,542 pec Sub Dean of Lincoln Cath Bapt, Wesl Meth

KISLINGBURY parish 1538 co Northampton 3-1/2 miles sw Northampton pop 683 archd Northampton dioc Peterborough Bapt

KITTISFORD parish 1694 Somerset 4-3/4 miles nw Wellington pop 171 archd Taunton dioc Bath and Wells

KNAITH parish 1576 Lincs 3-1/2 miles se Gainsborough pop 63 archd Stow dioc Lincoln

KNAPP tything parish North Curry Somerset

KNAPTOFT parish incl in regs of Mowsley Leics 7 miles ne Lutterworth comp chapelry Mowsley, Shearsby, hamlet Walton pop 924 archd Leicester dioc Lincoln

KNAPTON parish 1687 Norfolk 3-1/4 miles ne North Walsham pop 327 archd Norfolk dioc Norwich

KNAPTON township parish Acomb E R York pop 120

KNAPTON chapelry 1760 parish Wintringham pop 242 E R York

KNAPWELL parish 1678 Cambs 4-1/2 miles ne Caxton pop 128 archd and dioc Ely

KNARESBOROUGH parish 1561 borough W R York 18 miles nw York comp manor of Beach Hill, town Knaresborough, chapelry Arkendale, townships Bilton with Harrogate, Brearton, Scriven with Tentergate pop 10,214 pec of honour of Knaresborough Soc of Friends, Indep, Wesl Meth, Roman Cath

KNARESDALE parish 1695 Northumberland 6 miles nw Alston Manor pop 566 archd Northumberland dioc Durham

KNAYTON township parish Leak N R York pop 336 Wesl Meth

KNEBWORTH parish 1606 Herts 4 miles n Welwyn pop 259 archd Huntingdon dioc Lincoln

KNEDLINGTON township parish Howden E R York pop 123

KNEESALL parish 1682 Notts 4 miles se Ollerton comp township Ompton, hamlet Kersall pop 613 archd Nottingham dioc York Wesl Meth

KNEESWORTH hamlet parish Bassingbourne Cambs pop 191

KNEETON parish 1592 Notts 7-3/4 miles sw Newark pop 119 archd Nottingham dioc York

KNEIGHTON township parish Muckleston Staffs pop 156

KNETTISHALL parish 1772 Suffolk 5 miles sw East Harling pop 67 archd Suffolk dioc Norwich

KNIGHTLEY township parish Gnosall Staffs

KNIGHTON chapelry 1695 parish St Margaret Leicester Leics pop 402 Wesl Meth

KNIGHTON UPON TEAME chapelry 1559 parish Lindridge Worcs pop 553

KNIGHTON, WEST parish 1693 Dorset 3-1/2 miles se Dorchester pop 308 archd Dorset dioc Bristol

KNIGHTSBRIDGE chapelry parish St Margaret Westminster Middlesex Bapt

KNIGHTS ENHAM Hamps See ENHAM, KNIGHTS

KNIGHT THORPE township parish Loughborough Leics pop 79

KNIGHTWICK parish 1539 Worcs 5-1/2 miles e Bromyard pop 169 archd and dioc Worcester

KNILL parish 1585 Herefs 2-3/4 miles nw Kington pop 94 archd and dioc Hereford

KNIPTON parish 1562 Leics 7 miles sw Grantham pop 322 archd Leicester dioc Lincoln

KNITSLEY township parish Lanchester Co Durham

KNIVETON parish 1591 Derbys 3-1/2 miles ne Ashbourn pop 342 pec Dean and Chapter of Lichfield

KNOCKHOLT See NOCKHOLT

KNOCKIN parish 1672 Shrops 5-3/4 miles se Oswestry pop 311 archd and dioc St Asaph

KNODDISHALL parish 1566 Suffolk 3 miles se Saxmundham pop 315 archd Suffolk dioc Norwich

KNOOK parish 1687 Wilts 1 mile se Heytesbury pop 282 pec of Dean of Salisbury

KNOSSINGTON parish 1558 Leics 4-1/2 miles sw Oakham pop 240 archd Leicester dioc Lincoln

KNOTTING parish 1592 Beds 4-1/2 miles se Higham Ferrers pop 165 archd Bedford dioc Lincoln

KNOTTINGLY chapelry 1724 parish Pontefract W R York pop 3,666 Indep, Wesl Meth

KNOTT LANES district parish Ashton Under Line Lancs

KNOWLE tything parish Crediton Devon

KNOWLE tything parish Buckland Newton Dorset

KNOWLE parish incl in regs of Long Sutton Somerset 2-3/4 miles sw Ilminster pop 108 archd Taunton dioc Bath and Wells

KNOWLE chapelry 1682 parish Hampton in Arden Warws pop 1,120 pec Manor of Knowle

KNOWLE, CHURCH parish 1547 Dorset 1 mile w Corfe Castle pop 438 archd Dorset dioc Bristol

KNOWL END township parish Audley Staffs pop 282

KNOWLTON parish 1550 Kent 4-1/4 miles se Wingham pop 30 archd and dioc Canterbury

KNOWSLEY township parish Huyton Lancs pop 1,162 Unit

KNOWSTONE parish 1538 Devon 7 miles se South Molton comp East and West Knowstone pop 521 archd Barnstaple dioc Exeter

KNOYLE, EAST parish 1538 Wilts 2-1/4 miles sw Hindon pop 1,028 archd and dioc Salisbury Bapt

KNOYLE, WEST parish 1796 Wilts 3 miles e Mere pop 206 archd and dioc Salisbury

KNUTSFORD parish 1581 Ches 24-3/4 miles ne Chester comp town Knutsford, townships Bexton, Over Knutsford, Ollerton, Toft pop 3,599 archd and dioc Chester Indep, Wesl Meth, Unit

KNUTSFORD, OVER township parish Knutsford Ches pop 217

KNUTTON township parish Wolstanton Staffs pop 933

KYLOE parish 1674 co Durham and Northumberland by Berwick upon Tweed pop 927 archd Northumberland dioc Durham

KYME, NORTH township parish South Kyme Lincs pop 322

KYME, SOUTH parish 1647 Lincs 8-1/2 miles sw Tattershall pop 815 archd and dioc Lincoln

KYNNERSLEY Shrops See KINNERSLEY

KYO township parish Lanchester co Durham pop 412

KYRE, GREAT parish 1694 Worcs 4 miles se Tenbury pop 159 archd Salop dioc Hereford

KYRE, LITTLE chapelry parish Stoke Bliss Worcs pop 169

LACEBY parish 1538 Lincs 4-1/2 miles sw Grimsby pop 616 archd and dioc Lincoln Wesl Meth

LACK DENNIS township parish Great Budworth Ches pop 32

LACKFORD parish 1587 Suffolk 5-1/2 miles nw Bury St Edmund's pop 193 archd Sudbury dioc Norwich

LACKINGTON, WHITE parish 1678 Somerset 1-1/2 miles ne Ilminster pop 254 archd Taunton dioc Bath and Wells

LACOCK Wilts See LAYCOCK

LACON township parish Wem Shrops pop 45

LADBROOKE parish 1559 Warws 1-3/4 miles s Southam pop 268 archd Coventry dioc Lichfield

LADOCK parish 1683 Cornwall 4-1/4 miles nw Grampound pop 761 archd Cornwall dioc Exeter Wesl Meth

LAINDON parish 1653 Essex 3-1/2 miles se Billericay pop 536 Commissary of Essex and Herts, concurrently with Consistorial Court of Bishop of London

LAINSON parish incl in regs of Sparsholt Hamps 3 miles nw Winchester archd and dioc Winchester

LAITH KIRK chapelry parish Romaldkirk N R York

LAKE tything parish Wilsford Wilts

LAKENHAM Norfolk See NORWICH

LAKENHEATH parish 1712 Suffolk 5-3/4 miles n Mildenhall pop 1,209 archd Sudbury dioc Norwich Huntingtonians, Wesl Meth

LALEHAM parish 1538 Middlesex 2 miles se Staines pop 588 archd Middlesex dioc London

LAMARSH parish 1555 Essex 7-1/4 miles ne Halstead pop 323 Commissary of Essex and Herts, concurrently with Consistorial Court of Bishop of London

LAMBCROFT hamlet parish Kelstern Lincs pop 34

LAMBERHURST parish 1563 Kent 15 miles sw Maidstone pop 1,521 archd and dioc Rochester Bapt

LAMBETH St Mary 1539, St John 1824, St Matthew 1824, St Mark 1824, St Luke 1824, borough Surrey comp hamlets Brixton, Kennington, Stockwell, Vauxhall part of Norwood, extra parochial liberty of Lambeth Palace pop 87,856 archd Surrey dioc Winchester Bapt, Indep, Wesl Meth, Welsh Meth, Swedenborgians

LAMBLEY parish 1742 Northumberland 6-1/2 miles sw Haltwhistle comp townships Ash Holm, Lambley pop 252 archd Northumberland dioc Durham

LAMBLEY parish 1560 Notts 5-3/4 miles ne Nottingham pop 824 archd Nottingham dioc York

LAMBOURN parish 1560 Berks 5 miles n Hungerford comp market town Chipping Lambourn, tythings Blagrave with Hadley, Eastbury with Bockhampton, Upper Lambourn pop 2,386 archd Berks dioc Salisbury Wesl Meth

LAMBOURN, UPPER tything parish Lambourn Berks pop 387

LAMBOURNE parish 1582 Essex 5 miles se Epping pop 778 archd

Essex dioc London

LAMBRIGG township parish Kendal Westm pop 176

LAMBROOK, EAST parish 1771 Somerset 6-1/4 miles se Langport
pec of Chancellor in Cathedral Church of Wells Indep

LAMBROOK, WEST tything parish Kingsbury Episcopi Somerset

LAMBTON township parish Chester le Street co Durham pop 256

LAMBERTON parish 1538 Devon 2-1/2 miles nw Tavistock pop 1,209
archd Totnes dioc Exeter

LAMESLEY chapelry parish Chester le Street 1603 co Durham pop
1,920

LAMMAS parish 1538 Norfolk 3 miles nw Coltishall pop 303 archd
and dioc Norwich

LAMONBY township parish Skelton Cumberland pop 544

LAMORRAN parish 1573 Cornwall 4 miles sw Tregoney pop 96 archd
Cornwall dioc Exeter

LAMPLUGH parish 1581 Cumberland 8 miles ne Whitehaven comp
townships Ketton Quarter, Lamplugh, Murton or Moor Town,
Winder pop 624 archd Richmond dioc Chester

LAMPORT parish 1628 co Northampton 8-3/4 miles n Northampton
pop 250 archd Northampton dioc Peterborough

LAMYATT parish 1615 Somerset 2-1/4 miles nw Bruton pop 204
archd Wells dioc Bath and Wells

LANCASTER St Ann 1796, St John 1755, St Mary 1599 parish borough,
port Lancs 240 miles nw London comp market town Lancaster,
chapelries Caton, Gresingham, Overton, Poulton, Over Wyersdale,
townships Aldcliffe, Ashton with Stoday, Bare, Bulk, Heaton with
Oycliffe, Middleton, Quernmoor, Scotforth, Skerton, Thurnham,
Torrisholme, chapelries Bleasdale, Stalmine with Stanall, townships Fulwood, Myerscough, Preesall with Hackersall pop 22,294
sep juris archd Richmond dioc Chester Bapt, Soc of Friends,
Indep, Prim and Wesl Meth, Presb, Roman Cath

LANCAUT chapelry parish Tidenham Gloucs

LANCHESTER parish 1560 co Durham 8 miles nw Durham comp
chapelries Ebchester, Esh, Medomsley, Satley, townships Benfield
side, Burnop with Hamsteels, Butsfield, Collierly, Conside with
Knitsley, Billingside, Greencroft, Heeyfield, Holmside, Ivestone,
Kyo, Lanchester, Langley pop 5,076 archd and dioc Durham
Wesl Meth

LANCING parish 1559 Sussex 2 miles ne Worthing pop 695 archd and
dioc Chichester

LANDBEACH parish 1538 Cambs 4 miles ne Cambridge pop 422
archd and dioc Ely

LANDCROSS parish 1608 Devon 2-1/2 miles se Bideford pop 96 archd
Barnstaple dioc Exeter

LANDEWEDNACK parish 1578 Cornwall 10-1/2 miles se Helston pop
406 archd Cornwall dioc Exeter Wesl Meth

LANDFORD parish 1671 Wilts 10 miles se Salisbury pop 226 archd
and dioc Salisbury

LANDGUARD FORT garrison, chapelry parish Felixtow Suffolk 1761

LANDICAN township parish Woodchurch Ches pop 61

LANDKEY parish 1602 Devon 2-1/4 miles se Barnstaple pop 790 pec of Consistorial Court of Bishop of Exeter Wesl Meth

LANDMOTH township parish Leak N R York pop 53

LANDRAKE parish 1555 Cornwall 4 miles nw Saltash pop 872 pec of Consistorial Court of Bishop of Exeter

LANDULPH parish 1540 Cornwall 5 miles n Saltash pop 570 archd Cornwall dioc Exeter

LANDWADE parish 1700 Cambs 4 miles nw Newmarket pop 25 archd Sudbury dioc Norwich

LANEAST parish 1680 Cornwall 7 miles w Launceston pop 279 archd Cornwall dioc Exeter

LANE END chapelry parish Stoke upon Trent 1764 Staffs pop 1,488 archd Staffs dioc Lichfield Bapt, Indep, Calvinistic and Wesl Meth, Meth of New Connection, Roman Cath

LANEHAM parish 1538 Notts 6-3/4 miles ne Tuxford pop 347 pec of Dean and Chapter of York

LANERCOST ABBEY parish 1684 Cumberland 2-1/2 miles ne Brampton comp townships Askerton, Banks, Burtholme, Kingwater, Waterhead pop 1,550 archd and dioc Carlisle

LANGAR parish 1595 Notts 10 miles se Nottingham pop 274 archd Nottingham dioc York

LANGBAR township parish Ilkley W R York Wesl Meth

LANGCLIFFE township parish Bentham W R York pop 550

LANGDALE chapelry comp Great and Little Langdale parish Grasmere Westm pop 314

LANGDON, EAST parish 1560 Kent 3-3/4 miles ne Dover pop 322 archd and dioc Canterbury

LANGDON HILLS parish 1686 Essex 2-1/2 miles ne Horndon on the Hill pop 224 archd Essex dioc London

LANGDON, WEST parish 1590 Kent 3-1/2 miles n Dover pop 86 archd and dioc Canterbury

LANGENHOE parish 1660 Essex 5-1/4 miles se Colchester pop 146 archd Colchester dioc London

LANGFIELD township parish Halifax W R York pop 2,514

LANGFORD parish 1717 Beds 2-1/4 miles s Biggleswade pop 726 archd Bedford dioc Lincoln

LANGFORD parish 1538 co Oxford 3-1/2 miles ne Lechlade comp tything Little Farringdon, township Grafton, hamlet Radcutt pop 673 pec of Prebendary of Church Langford

LANGFORD parish 1558 Essex 2 miles nw Maldon pop 273 archd Colchester dioc London

LANGFORD parish 1770 Norfolk 6-1/4 miles sw Watton pop 36 archd Norfolk dioc Norwich

LANGFORD parish 1692 Notts 3-3/4 miles ne Newark pop 125 archd Nottingham dioc York

LANGFORD hamlet in parishes Bewrington and Churchill Somerset

LANGFORD BUDVILLE parish 1538 Somerset 3 miles nw Wellington pop 608 pec Archdeacon of Taunton

LANGFORD, LITTLE parish 1699 Wilts 5-1/4 miles nw Wilton pop 39 archd and dioc Salisbury

LANGFORD, STEEPLE parish 1674 Wilts 5-3/4 miles nw Wilton pop 587 archd and dioc Salisbury

LANGHALE parish Norfolk 6 miles nw Bungay archd Norfolk dioc Norwich

LANGHAM parish 1638 Essex 1-3/4 miles nw Dedham pop 821 archd Colchester dioc London Bapt

LANGHAM parish 1559 co Rutland 2 miles nw Oakham pop 608 archd Northampton dioc Peterborough

LANGHAM parish 1561 Suffolk 3-1/4 miles se Ixworth pop 264 archd Suffolk dioc Norwich

LANGHAM GREAT or BISHOPS GREAT parish 1695 Norfolk 4 miles sw Cley pop 375 archd and dioc Norwich

LANGHAM, LITTLE parish regs with Great Langham Norfolk 3 miles sw Cley archd and dioc Norwich

LANGHO or BILLINGTON chapelry 1733 parish Blackburn Lancs 5-1/4 miles sw Clitheroe

LANGLEY chapelry parish Hampstead Norris Berks

LANGLEY township parish Lanchester co Durham pop 75

LANGLEY parish 1678 Essex 7-3/4 miles sw Saffron Walden pop 384 archd Colchester dioc London Bapt

LANGLEY parish 1664 Kent 4 miles se Maidstone pop 244 archd and dioc Canterbury Wesl Meth

LANGLEY parish 1695 Norfolk 7-1/2 miles sw Acle pop 361 archd Norfolk dioc Norwich

LANGLEY chapelry parish Shipton under Whychwood co Oxford pop 67

LANGLEY chapelry parish Acton Burnell Shrops

LANGLEY hamlet parish Claverdon Warws pop 164

LANGLEY tything parish Kington St Michael Wilts pop 560

LANGLEY, ABBOT'S parish 1538 Herts 1-3/4 miles se King's Langley pop 1,980 archd St Albans dioc London

LANGLEY BURRELL parish 1607 Wilts 1-3/4 miles ne Chippenham pop 438 archd Wilts dioc Salisbury

LANGLEY DALE township parish Staindrop co Durham pop 217 Wesl Meth

LANGLEY, KING'S parish 1558 Herts 19 miles sw Hertford pop 1,423 archd Huntingdon dioc Lincoln

LANGLEY KIRK parish 1654 Derbys 4-3/4 miles nw Derby pop 553 archd Derby dioc Lichfield

LANGLEY MARISH parish 1644 Bucks comp portion Colnbrook pop 1,797 archd Buckingham dioc Lincoln Indep

LANGLEY, MEYNELL township parish Kirk Langley Derbys

LANGLEY PRIORY extra parochial liberty 3 miles sw Castle Donnington Leics pop 16

LANGPORT EAST OVER market town parish 1728 borough Somerset
4-1/2 miles sw Somerton pop 1,245 sep juris pec of Archdeacon
of Wells as Prebendary of Huish cum Brent in Cathedral Church
of Wells Indep
LANGRICK VILLE chapelry 1818 5 miles nw Boston Lincs pop 202
not dependent on a parish
LANGRIDGE parish 1756 Somerset 4 miles nw Bath pop 109 archd
Bath dioc Bath and Wells
LANGRIGG township parish Bromfield Cumberland pop 269
LANGRISH tything parish East Meon Hamps
LANGSETT township parish Penistone W R York pop 320
LANGSTONE parish 1757 co Monmouth 4-1/4 miles ne Newport pop
194 archd and dioc Llandaff
LANGTHORNE township parish Bedale N R York pop 136
LANGTHORP township parish Kirby on the Moor N R York pop 196
LANGTHWAITE township parish Doncaster W R York pop 28
LANGTOFT parish 1668 Lincs 2 miles nw Market Deeping pop 606
archd and dioc Lincoln
LANGTOFT parish 1587 E R York 6-1/2 miles nw Great Driffield
comp townships Cotton, Langtoft pop 523 pec of Prebendary of
Langtoft in Cathedral Church of York Wesl Meth
LANGTON township parish Gainford co Durham pop 107
LANGTON by Horncastle Parish 1753 Lincs 1-1/2 miles sw Horn-
castle pop 115 archd and dioc Lincoln
LANGTON juxta Parthey parish 1558 Lincs 3-3/4 miles nw Spilsby
pop 230 archd and dioc Lincoln
LANGTON by Wragby parish 1653 Lincs 1-1/4 miles se Wragby pop
206 archd and dioc Lincoln
LANGTON township parish Appleby St Michael Westm
LANGTON parish 1653 E R York 3-1/2 miles se New Malton comp
townships Kennythorpe, Langton pop 341 archd East Riding dioc
York
LANGTON, CHURCH parish 1559 Leics 4 miles nw Market Harbor-
ough comp chapelries Thorp Langton, Tur Langton, West Langton,
township East Langton pop 868 archd Leicester dioc Lincoln
LANGTON, EAST township parish Church Langton Leics pop 281
LANGTON, GREAT or LANGTON ON SWALE parish 1695 N R York
5-1/2 miles nw North Allerton comp townships Great Langton,
Little Langton pop 230 archd Richmond dioc Chester
LANGTON HERRING parish 1681 Dorset 5 miles nw Weymouth pop
205 archd Dorset dioc Bristol
LANGTON, LITTLE township parish Great Langton N R York pop 97
LANGTON LONG BLANDFORD parish 1591 Dorset 3/4 mile se Bland-
ford Forum pop 187 archd Dorset dioc Bristol
LANGTON MATRAVERS parish 1670 Dorset 4 miles se Corfe Castle
pop 676 archd Dorset dioc Bristol
LANGTON, THORP chapelry 1564 parish Church Langton Leics pop
177

LANGTON, TUR chapelry 1572 parish Church Langton Leics pop 338

LANGTON, WEST chapelry parish Church Langton Leics pop 90

LANGTREE parish 1659 Devon 3-1/4 miles se Great Torrington pop 888 archd Barnstaple dioc Exeter

LANGTREE township parish Standish Lancs

LANGWATHBY chapelry parish Edenhall 1695 Cumberland 4-3/4 miles ne Penrith pop 250

LANGWITH BASSET parish 1685 Derbys 6 miles nw Mansfield pop 165 archd Derby dioc Lichfield

LANGWITH township parish Cuckney Notts pop 437

LANGWITH township parish Wheldrake E R York pop 44

LANHYDROCK parish 1559 Cornwall 2-3/4 miles se Bodmin pop 239 archd Cornwall dioc Exeter

LANIVET parish 1608 Cornwall 2-1/2 miles sw Bodmin pop 922 archd Cornwall dioc Exeter Wesl Meth

LANLIVERY parish 1600 Cornwall 1-1/2 miles sw Lostwithiel pop 1,687 archd Cornwall dioc Exeter Wesl Meth

LANOVER co Monmouth See LLANOVER

LANREATH parish 1555 Cornwall 6 miles nw West Looe pop 651 archd Cornwall dioc Exeter

LANSALLOES parish 1600 Cornwall 6 miles sw West Looe pop 884 archd Cornwall dioc Exeter

LANTEGLOS by Fowey parish 1661 Cornwall 2 miles e Fowey pop 1,208 archd Cornwall dioc Exeter

LANTEGLOS cum CAMELFORD parish 1558 Cornwall 1-1/2 miles sw Camelford pop 1,359 archd Cornwall dioc Exeter Wesl Meth

LANTON township parish Kirk Newton Northumberland pop 78

LAPFORD parish 1567 Devon 5-1/4 miles se Chulmleigh pop 700 archd Barnstaple dioc Exeter

LAPLEY parish 1538 Staffs 3-3/4 miles sw Penkridge pop 1,042 archd Stafford dioc Lichfield

LAPWORTH parish 1561 Warws 3-1/2 miles ne Henley in Arden pop 656 archd and dioc Worcester Indep

LARBRICK township parish Kirkham Lancs

LARK STOKE hamlet parish Ilmington Gloucs pop 23

LARKTON township parish Malpas Ches pop 44

LARLING parish 1678 Norfolk 2 miles nw East Harling pop 227 archd Norfolk dioc Norwich

LARTINGTON township parish Romald Kirk N R York pop 183

LARTON township parish west Kirby Ches

LASBOROUGH parish 1827 Gloucs 4-3/4 miles nw Tetbury archd and dioc Gloucester

LASHAM parish 1560 Hamps 4 miles nw Alton pop 236 archd and dioc Winchester

LASKILL PASTURE township parish Helmsley N R York pop 85

LASSINGTON parish 1661 Gloucs 3-1/4 miles nw Gloucester archd and dioc Gloucester pop 60

LASTINGHAM parish 1559 N R York 7 miles nw Pickering comp
chapelry Rosedale West Side, townships Oppleton le Moors, Farn-
dale East Side, Farndale High Quarter, Hutton le Hole, Lasting-
ham, Spaunton pop 1,766 archd Cleveland dioc York
LATCHFORD chapelry 1777 parish Grapenhall Ches pop 2,166
LATCHFORD hamlet parish Great Haseley co Oxford pop 35
LATCHINGDON parish 1725 Essex 5-1/4 miles nw Burnham pop 451
pec Archbishop of Canterbury
LATHBURY parish 1690 Bucks 3/4 mile n Newport Pagnell pop 172
archd Buckingham dioc Lincoln
LATHOM township parish Ormskirk Lancs pop 3,272
LATTIMERS chapelry 1756 parish Chesham Bucks
LATTON parish 1567 Essex 1-1/2 miles sw Harlow pop 319 Com-
missary of Essex and Herts, concurrently with Consistorial
Court of Bishop of London
LATTON parish 1576 Wilts 1-1/2 miles nw Cricklade pop 360 archd
Wilts dioc Salisbury
LAUGHTON parish 1754 Leics 5-1/4 miles nw Market Harborough
pop 154 archd Leicester dioc Lincoln
LAUGHTON parish no regs Lincs 1-3/4 miles se Falkingham pop
75 archd and dioc Lincoln
LAUGHTON parish 1566 Lincs 6 miles ne Gainsborough comp town-
ship Laughton hamlet Wildsworth pop 441 archd Stow dioc Lin-
coln Wesl Meth
LAUGHTON hamlet parish Kettle Thorpe Lincs
LAUGHTON parish 1561 Sussex 6-1/2 miles ne Lewes pop 804 archd
Lewes dioc Chichester
LAUGHTON EN LE MORTHEN parish 1562 W R York 7-1/2 miles
sw Tickhill comp chapelry Letwell, townships Gilden Wells,
Laughton en le Morthen, Throapham, Woodsetts pop 1,232 pec
Chancellor in Cathedral Church of York Indep
LAUNCELLS parish 1642 Cornwall 1 miles se Stratton pop 848 archd
Cornwall dioc Exeter
LAUNCESTON borough, market town parish 1559 Cornwall 20-1/2
miles ne Bodmin pop 2,231 sep juris archd Cornwall dioc Exe-
ter Indep, Wesl Meth
LAUNCESTON TARRANT Dorset See TARRANT, LAUNCESTON
LAUNDE extra parochial liberty Leics pop 60 6-3/4 miles nw Up-
pingham
LAUNTON parish 1648 co Oxford 1-3/4 miles e Bicester pop 570
archd and dioc Oxford
LAVANT parish 1653 Sussex 2-1/2 miles n Chichester comp East
and West Lavant pop 407 pec of Deanery of Pagham
LAVANT, MID parish 1567 Sussex 2-3/4 miles nw Chichester pop
278 archd and dioc Chichester
LAVENDON parish 1574 Bucks 2-3/4 miles ne Olney pop 664 archd
Buckingham dioc Lincoln
LAVENHAM parish 1558 Suffolk 18-1/2 miles nw Ipswich pop 2,107

archd Sudbury dioc Norwich Indep, Wesl Meth

LAVER, HIGH parish 1553 Essex 4 miles nw Chipping Ongar pop 495 archd Essex dioc London

LAVER, LITTLE parish 1538 Essex 5 miles n Chipping Ongar pop 112 archd Essex dioc London

LAVER MAGDALEN parish 1557 Essex 5-1/4 miles nw Chipping Ongar pop 206 archd Essex dioc London

LAVERSTOCK parish 1726 Wilts 1 mile ne Salisbury comp hamlet Ford, tything Milford pop 817 archd and dioc Salisbury

LAVERSTOKE parish 1657 Hamps 2-3/4 miles ne Whitchurch pop 117 archd and dioc Winchester

LAVERTON hamlet parish Buckland Gloucs

LAVERTON parish 1678 Somerset 3-1/2 miles n Frome pop 196 archd Wells dioc Bath and Wells Bapt

LAVERTON township parish Kirkby Malzeard W R York pop 457

LAVINGTON or LINTON parish 1576 Lincs 6 miles ne Corby comp township Osgodby, hamlets Hanby, Keisby pop 341 archd and dioc Lincoln

LAVINGTON, EAST or MARKET parish 1673 Wilts 6 miles s Devizes comp East Lavington, tything Easterton pop 1,525 archd and dioc Salisbury Indep

LAVINGTON, WEST parish 1598 Wilts 1-1/2 miles sw Lavington pop 1,322 archd and dioc Salisbury

LAWFORD parish 1558 Essex 1-1/2 miles w Manningtree pop 794 archd Colchester dioc London

LAWFORD, CHURCH parish 1575 Warws 4 miles nw Rugby pop 320 archd Coventry dioc Lichfield

LAWFORD, LITTLE hamlet parish Newbold Upon Avon Warws pop 28

LAWFORD, LONG hamlet parish Newbold upon Avon Warws pop 478

LAWHITTON parish 1640 Cornwall 2-1/4 miles se Launceston pop 485 pec Bishop of Exeter

LAWKLAND township parish Clapham W R York pop 351

LAWLING chapelry parish Latchingdon Essex

LAWRENCE, ST Newland parish 1704 Essex 3 miles sw Bradwell near the Sea archd Essex dioc London pop 182

LAWRENCE, ST parish Kent See THANET, ISLE OF

LAWRENCE, ST chapelry parish Preston Lancs

LAWRENCE, ST parish 1746 Hamps 8-3/4 miles se Newport pop 78 archd and dioc Winchester

LAWRENCE ST Ilketshall Suffolk See ILKETSHALL

LAWRENCE WESTON Gloucs See WESTON, LAWRENCE

LAWSHALL parish 1558 Suffolk 7-1/2 miles se Bury St Edmund's pop 885 archd Sudbury dioc Norwich

LAWTON, CHURCH parish 1559 Ches 6 miles se Sandbach pop 516 archd and dioc Chester Wesl Meth

LAXFIELD parish 1579 Suffolk 6 miles ne Famlingham pop 1,158 archd Suffolk dioc Norwich Bapt

LAXTON parish 1689 co Northampton 7-1/4 miles ne Rockingham

pop 188 archd Northampton dioc Peterborough

LAXTON or LEXINGTON parish 1565 Notts 2-3/4 miles sw Tuxford pop 659 archd Nottingham dioc York

LAXTON chapelry parish Howden 1779 E R York pop 281 Wesl Meth

LAYCOCK parish 1559 Wilts 3-3/4 miles s Chippenham pop 1,640 archd Wilts dioc Salisbury Indep

LAYER BRETON parish 1755 Essex 6-1/4 miles sw Colchester pop 262 archd Colchester dioc London Indep

LAYER DE LA HAY parish 1767 Essex 4-1/4 miles sw Colchester pop 637 archd Colchester dioc London

LAYER MARNEY parish 1742 Essex 7 miles sw Colchester pop 275 archd Colchester dioc London

LAYHAM parish 1538 Suffolk 1-1/2 miles se Hadleigh pop 552 archd Sudbury dioc Norwich

LAYSTERS parish 1703 Herefs 4 miles sw Tenbury pop 212 archd Salop dioc Hereford

LAYSTHORPE township parish Stonegrave N R York

LAYSTON parish 1563 Herts 3/4 mile ne Buntingford pop 1,093 archd Middlesex dioc London

LAYTHAM township parish Aughton E R York pop 138

LAYTON township parish Bispham Lancs pop 943

LAYTON, EAST township parish Stanwick St John N R York pop 156

LAYTON, WEST township parish Hutton Magnum N R York pop 94

LAZONBY parish 1538 Cumberland 1 mile sw Kirk Oswald comp chapelry Plumpton Wall, township Lazonby pop 841 archd and dioc Carlisle

LEA township parish Backford Ches pop 92

LEA township parish Wybunbury Ches pop 56

LEA Derbys See DETHWICK LEA

LEA parish 1706 Herefs 4-1/2 miles se Ross pop 161 archd Gloucester dioc Hereford

LEA township parish Freston Lancs pop 687

LEA parish 1603 Linc 2-1/4 miles se Gainsborough pop 197 archd Stow dioc Lincoln

LEA parish 1751 Wilts 1-3/4 miles se Malmesbury pop 419 archd Wilts dioc Salisbury

LEA BAILEY tything parish Newland Gloucs pop 108

LEA HALL hamlet parish Bradborne Derbys pop 26

LEA MARSTON parish 1570 Warws 4 miles n Coleshill pop 269 archd Coventry dioc Lichfield

LEA NEWBOLD township parish St Oswald Ches pop 43

LEACH township parish St Mary Ches

LEACROFT township parish Cannock Staffs

LEADENHAM parish 1558 Lincs 9 miles nw Sleaford pop 565 archd and dioc Lincoln

LEADEN ROOTHING Essex See ROOTHING, LEADEN

LEAD HALL township parish Ryther W R York pop 59

LEADON township parish Bishop's Froome Herefs

LEADON, HIGH hamlet parish Rudford Gloucs pop 100

LEAFIELD chapelry parish Shipton under Whychwood 1784 co Oxford pop 656

LEAGRAM township with Bowland parish Whalley Lancs

LEAK parish 1570 N R York 6 miles n Thirsk comp townships Borrowby, Crosby, Knayton with Brawith, Landmoth with Catto, Leak, chapelry Nether Silton, township Gueldable pop 1,090 pec Bishop of Durham

LEAKE parish 1559 Lincs 7-1/4 miles nw Boston pop 1,744 archd and dioc Lincoln Wesl Meth

LEAKE, EAST parish 1600 Notts 4-3/4 miles e Kegworth pop 975 archd Nottingham dioc York Bapt, Wesl Meth

LEAKE, WEST parish 1580 Notts 2-3/4 miles e Kegworth pop 203 archd Nottingham dioc York

LEAMINGTON HASTINGS parish 1565 Warws 4-1/2 miles ne Southam pop 464 archd Coventry dioc Lichfield

LEAMINGTON PRIORS parish 1702 Warws 2-1/2 miles e Warwick pop 6,209 archd Coventry dioc Lichfield Indep, Wesl Meth, Roman Cath

LEAP tything parish Exbury Hamps

LEARCHILD township parish Edlingham Northumberland pop 20

LEASINGHAM, NORTH or ROXHOLME parish 1695 Lincs 2-3/4 miles nw Sleaford archd and dioc Lincoln

LEASINGHAM, SOUTH parish 1695 Lincs 2 miles nw Sleaford pop 358 archd and dioc Lincoln

LEATHERHEAD parish 1656 Surrey 12 miles ne Guildford pop 1,724 archd Surrey dioc Winchester Indep

LEATHLEY parish 1674 W R York 2-1/2 miles ne Otley comp townships Castley, Leathley pop 413 archd and dioc York

LEATON township parish St Mary, Shrewsbury Shrops

LEAVELAND parish 1553 Kent 4 miles sw Faversham pop 69 archd and dioc Canterbury

LEAVENING township parish Acklam E R York pop 354 Wesl Meth

LEAVINGTON, CASTLE township parish Kirk Leavington N R York pop 45

LEAVINGTON, KIRK parish 1734 N R York 2-1/4 miles se Yarm comp townships Castle Leavington, Kirk Leavington, Pickton, Low Worsall pop 517 archd Cleveland dioc York

LEBTHORPE hamlet parish North Witham Lincs

LECHLADE or LEACHLADE market town, parish 1686 Gloucs 28 miles se Gloucester pop 1,244 archd and dioc Gloucester Bapt

LECK chapelry parish Tunstall 1801 Lancs pop 326

LECKBY township parish Cundall N R York

LECKFORD parish 1757 Hamps 1-3/4 miles ne Stockbridge pop 221 archd and dioc Winchester

LECKHAMPSTEAD chapelry parish Chieveley Berks pop 402

LECKHAMPSTEAD parish 1558 Bucks 3-1/2 miles ne Buckingham pop 499 archd Buckingham dioc Lincoln

LECKHAMPTON parish 1682 Gloucs 2 miles sw Cheltenham pop 929
arched and dioc Gloucester

LECKONFIELD or LECONFIELD parish 1551 E R York 3 miles nw
Beverley pop 301 archd East Riding dioc York

LEDBURN hamlet parish Mentmore Bucks

LEDBURY parish 1538 Herefs 15 miles se Hereford comp market
town Ledbury,township Parkhold pop 3,909 archd and dioc Hereford Bapt,Indep, Wesl Meth

LEDSHAM township parish Neston Ches pop 70

LEDSHAM parish 1539 W R York 4-1/2 miles nw Ferrybridge comp
townships Fairburn, Ledsham, Ledstone pop 944 archd and dioc
York

LEDSTONE township parish Ledsham W R York pop 243

LEDWELL hamlet parish Sanford co Oxford

LEE parish 1679 Bucks 2-1/2 miles n Great Missenden pop 186
archd Buckingham dioc Lincoln

LEE parish 1579 Kent 7 miles se London pop 1,108 archd and dioc
Rochester

LEE parish 1664 Northumberland 1-1/2 miles ne Hexham comp chapelries Bingfield and Wall, townships West Acomb, Anick, Anick
Grange, Cocklaw, Fallowfield, Halington, Portage, Sandhoe pop
1,962 pec of Archbishop of York for pec Court of Hexhamshire

LEE BOTWOOD parish 1547 Shrops 4 miles ne Church Stretton pop
223 archd Salop dioc Lichfield

LEE BROCKHURST parish 1556 Shrops 2-3/4 miles se Wem pop 150
archd Salop dioc Lichfield

LEE, EAST or CHAPEL liberty parish East Tilbury Essex

LEE WARD township parish Rothbury Northumberland pop 103

LEEMAILING township parish Bellingham Northumberland pop 293

LEEDS parish 1557 Kent 5 miles se Maidstone pop 613 archd and
dioc Canterbury

LEEDS parish St Peter 1572, St John 1725, St Paul 1796, Trinity
Church 1730, borough W R York 25 miles sw York comp borough
Leeds, chapelries Armley, Beeston, Bramley, Chapel Allerton,
Farnley, Headingley with Burley, Holbeck, Hunslet or Hunfleet
and Worthley, township Potter Newton pop 123,393 sep juris
archd and dioc York Arians, Bapt, Soc of Friends, Indep, Wesl
Meth, Prim Meth, Female Revivalist, Swedenborgians, Unit, Roman
Cath

LEEK parish 1634 Staffs 23 miles ne Stafford comp market town Leek,
chapelries Endon, Onecote, Rushton Spencer, townships Bradnop,
Longdon, Heaton, Leek Frith, Rushton James, Stanley, Tittisworth,
Rudyard with Caudery pop 10,780 archd Stafford dioc Lichfield
Soc of Friends, Indep, Wesl Meth

LEEK FRITH township parish Leek Staffs pop 873

LEEK WOOTTON Warws See WOOTTON, LEEK

LEEMING chapelry parish Burneston 1581 N R York pop 633

LEES hamlet parish Dalbury Derbys

LEES chapelry parish Ashton under Line 1743 Lancs archd and dioc
Chester
LEESE township parish Sandbach Ches pop 126
LEESTHORPE hamlet parish Pickwell Leics
LEFTWICH township parish Davenham Ches pop 1,799
LEGBOURN parish 1711 Lincs 3 miles se Louth pop 449 archd and
dioc Lincoln Wesl Meth
LEGSBY parish 1562 Lincs 3-1/2 miles se Market Rasen pop 236
archd and dioc Lincoln
LEICESTER borough, market town Leics 97 miles nw London sep
juris comp All Saints 1571, St Marin, 1558, St Nicholas 1560, St
Mary 1600, St Margaret 1615 archd Leicester dioc Lincoln
Bapt, Soc of Friends, Huntingtonians, Indep, Wesl Meth, Prim Meth,
Unit, Roman Cath
LEICESTER ABBEY extra parochial liberty Leics pop 18 1 miles n
Leicester
LEICESTER FOREST extra parochial liberty Leics pop 67
LEIGH tything parish Wimbourne Minster Dorset pop 532
LEIGH chapelry parish Yetminster Dorset pop 400
LEIGH parish 1684 Essex 17-1/2 miles se Chelmsford pop 1,254
archd Essex dioc London Wesl Meth
LEIGH parish 1569 Gloucs 5-1/2 miles ne Gloucester comp hamlet
Evington pop 355 archd and dioc Gloucester
LEIGH parish 1639 Kent 3-3/4 miles w Tonbridge pop 1,011 archd
and dioc Rochester
LEIGH parish 1560 Lancs 46 miles se Lancaster comp chapelries
Astley, Atherton, townships Bedford, Tyldesley, Pennington, West
Leigh pop 20,083 archd and dioc Chester Indep, Wesl Meth,
Swedenborgians, Roman Cath
LEIGH tything parish Pitminster Somerset Wesl Meth
LEIGH parish 1541 Staffs 5-3/4 miles nw Uttoxeter pop 1,038 archd
Stafford dioc Lichfield
LEIGH parish 1579 Surrey 3-1/2 miles sw Reigate pop 483 archd
Surrey dioc Winchester
LEIGH chapelry parish Ashton Keynes Wilts pop 267
LEIGH township parish Westbury Wilts pop 1,420
LEIGH parish 1538 Worcs 5 miles sw Worcester pop 1,933 archd
and dioc Worcester
LEIGH, ABBOT'S parish 1656 Somerset 3-1/4 miles nw Briston pop
360 archd Bath dioc Bath and Wells
LEIGH DE LA MERE parish 1626 Wilts 4-3/4 miles nw Chippenham
pop 128 archd Wilts dioc Salisbury
LEIGH, HIGH chapelry parish Rosthern Ches pop 983
LEIGH, LITTLE chapelry parish Great Budworth 1782 Ches pop
381 Bapt
LEIGH, NORTH parish 1697 Devon 3-3/4 miles nw Colyton pop 240
archd and dioc Exeter
LEIGH, NORTH parish 1573 co Oxford 3-1/4 miles ne Witney pop

591 archd and dioc Oxford

LEIGH, SOUTH parish 1718 Devon 2-3/4 miles sw Colyton pop 320 archd and dioc Exeter

LEIGH, SOUTH chapelry 1612 parish Stanton Harcourt co Oxford pop 339

LEIGH UPON MENDIP parish 1566 Somerset 5-1/2 miles w Frome pop 640 archd Wells dioc Bath and Wells

LEIGH, WEST parish 1561 Devon 2-1/2 miles ne Bideford pop 484 archd Barnstaple dioc Exeter

LEIGH, WEST township parish Leigh Lancs pop 2,780

LEIGH, WOOLEY tything parish Great Bradford Wilts pop 1,680

LEIGHLAND chapelry 1754 parish Old Cleeve Somerset

LEIGHS, GREAT parish 1556 Essex 5-1/2 miles sw Braintree pop 756 archd Essex dioc London

LEIGHS, LITTLE parish 1679 Essex 5-1/4 miles sw Braintree pop 189 archd Essex dioc London

LEIGHTERTON chapelry parish Boxwell Gloucs

LEIGHTON township parish Nantwich Ches pop 261

LEIGHTON township parish Neston Ches pop 333

LEIGHTON parish 1653 Hunts 5-1/2 miles ne Kimbolton pop 452 pec Prebendary of Leighton in Cathedral Church of Lincoln

LEIGHTON parish 1662 Shrops 5-1/4 miles nw Much Wenlock pop 360 archd Salop dioc Lichfield

LEIGHTON BUZZARD parish 1562 Beds 20 miles sw Bedford comp market town Leighton Buzzard, chapelries Billington, Eggington, Heath with Reach, Standbridge pop 5,149 pec of Prebendary of Leighton Buzzard Bapt, Soc of Friends, Wesl Meth

LEINTHALL, EARLS chapelry 1591 parish Aymestrey Herefs 7 miles sw Ludlow archd and dioc Hereford

LEINTHALL STARKES parish 1740 Herefs 6 miles sw Ludlow pop 127 archd and dioc Hereford

LEINTWARDINE parish 1547 Herefs 9 miles sw Ludlow comp townships Adforton, Brakes, Grange, Heath with Jay, Kinton, Leintwardine, Letton, Marlow, Newton, Payton, Walford, Whitton with Trippleton pop 1,358 archd Salop dioc Hereford

LEIRE parish 1559 Leics 4 miles nw Lutterworth pop 485 archd Leicester dioc Lincoln

LEISTON parish 1538 Suffolk 4 miles se Saxmundham pop 1,070 archd Suffolk dioc Norwich

LELANT, UNY parish 1679 Cornwall 3 miles sw St Ives pop 1,602 archd Cornwall dioc Exeter Wesl Meth

LELLEY township parish Preston E R York pop 114

LEMINGTON, LOWER parish 1685 Gloucs 2 miles ne Moreton in the Marsh pop 56 archd and dioc Gloucester

LEMMINGTON township parish Edlingham Northumberland pop 85

LENBOROUGH hamlet parish Buckingham Bucks

LENCH ATCH hamlet parish Church Lench Worcs pop 82

LENCH, CHURCH parish 1696 Worcs 5-3/4 miles nw Evesham comp

hamlets Atch Lench, Sheriff Lench pop 399 archd and dioc Worcester Bapt

LENCH, ROUSE parish 1558 Worcs 7 miles sw Alcester pop 251 archd and dioc Worcester

LENCH, SHERIFF'S hamlet parish Church Lench Worcs pop 76

LENCH WICK chapelry parish Norton Worcs

LENHAM parish 1558 Kent 10 miles se Maidstone pop 2,197 archd and dioc Canterbury Indep

LENTON parish 1540 Notts 1 mile sw Nottingham pop 3,077 archd Nottingham dioc York

LEOMINSTER parish 1559 Herefs 13-1/2 miles n Hereford comp borough of Leominster, chapelry Ivington, township Broadward pop 5,249 sep juris archd and dioc Hereford Bapt, Soc of Friends, Moravians, Unit

LEOMINSTER parish 1566 Sussex 2 miles sw Arundel pop 715 archd and dioc Chichester

LEONARD, ST chapelry parish Aston Clinton Bucks pop 147

LEONARD, ST, SHOREDITCH Middlesex See SHOREDITCH

LEONARD, STANLEY Gloucs See STANLEY LEONARD

LEONARDS, ST ON SEA parish 1636 Sussex 1 mile w Hastings pop 356

LEPPINGTON chapelry parish Scrayingham E R York pop 118

LEPTON township parish Kirk Heaton W R York pop 3,320

LESBURY parish 1689 Northumberland 4 miles se Alnwick comp townships Alemouth, Lesbury with Hawkhill, townships Bilton, Wooden pop 976 archd Northumberland dioc Durham

LESKEARD Cornwall See LISKEARD

LESNEWTH parish 1563 Cornwall 5-3/4 miles nw Camelford pop 123 archd Cornwall dioc Exeter

LESSINGHAM parish 1557 Norfolk 7-3/4 miles se North Walsham pop 191 archd Norfolk dioc Norwich

LESSNESS chapelry parish Erith Kent Bapt

LETCHWORTH parish 1695 Herts 2-1/2 miles ne Hitchin pop 76 archd Huntingdon dioc Lincoln

LETCOMB BASSETT parish 1564 Berks 3 miles sw Wantage pop 288 archd Berks dioc Salisbury Wesl Meth

LETCOMB REGIS parish 1697 Berks 2 miles sw Wantage comp chapelries East Challow, West Challow pop 869 archd Berks dioc Salisbury

LETHERINGHAM parish 1585 Suffolk 3 miles nw Wickham Market pop 174 archd Suffolk dioc Norwich

LETHERINGSETT parish 1653 Norfolk 1-1/2 miles nw Holt pop 251 archd and dioc Norwich

LETTON parish 1673 Herefs 6-3/4 miles sw Weobley comp townships Letton, Hurstley pop 200 archd and dioc Hereford

LETTON township parish Leintwardine Herefs pop 212

LETTON parish Norfolk 5-1/4 miles sw East Dereham pop 133 archd Norfolk dioc Norwich

LETWELL chapelry parish Laughton on le Morthen 1612 W R York
pop 155

LEVAN, ST parish 1694 Cornwall 9 miles sw Penzance pop 515 pec
. of Rector and Dean of St Burian's Wesl Meth

LEVEN parish 1628 E R York 7 miles ne Beverley comp townships
Hempholme, Leven pop 771 archd and dioc York Wesl Meth

LEVENS chapelry parish Heversham Westm pop 789

LEVENSHULME township parish Manchester Lancs pop 1,086

LEVER, DARCH chapelry parish Bolton Lancs pop 1,119

LEVER, GREAT township parish Middleton Lancs pop 637

LEVER, LITTLE chapelry parish Bolton le Moors 1791 Lancs pop
2,231 Wesl Meth

LEVERINGTON parish 1558 Cambs 2 miles nw Wisbeach pop 1,700
pec of Bishop of Ely

LEVERSDALE township parish Irthington Cumberland pop 431

LEVERTON parish 1538 Lincs 5-3/4 miles ne Boston pop 631 archd
and dioc Lincoln Wesl Meth

LEVERTON tything parish Chilton Foliatt Wilts

LEVERTON, NORTH parish 1669 Notts 5-1/4 miles ne East Retford
pop 303 pec of Prebendary of North Leverton in Collegiate
Church of Southwell Wesl Meth

LEVERTON, SOUTH parish 1658 Notts 5-1/2 miles e East Retford
pop 400 archd Nottingham dioc York Wesl Meth

LEVESDON hamlet parish Watford Herts

LEVINGTON Cumberland See LINTON, WEST

LEVINGTON parish 1562 Suffolk 5-1/2 miles se Ipswich pop 228
archd Suffolk dioc Norwich

LEVISHAM parish 1700 N R York 5-1/2 miles ne Pickering pop 168
archd Cleveland dioc York

LEW hamlet parish Witney co Oxford pop 237

LEW, NORTH parish 1689 Devon 4 miles sw Hatherleigh pop 980
archd Totnes dioc Exeter

LEWANNICK parish 1660 Cornwall 5 miles sw Launceston pop 643
archd Cornwall dioc Exeter Bapt, Wesl Meth

LEWES borough, market town Sussex 7 miles ne Brighton St Michael
1589, St Peter and St Mary 1679, St John 1602, All Saints 1561,
St Thomas at Cliffe 1606 pop 8,592 archd Lewes dioc Chichester
Soc of friends, Indep and Wesl Meth, Unit, Bapt, Huntingtonians

LEWISHAM parish 1558 Kent 6-1/2 miles se London pop 9,059 archd
and dioc Rochester Presb, Indep, Wesl Meth

LEWKNOR parish 1666 co Oxford 3-1/2 miles se Tetsworth pop 709
archd and dioc Oxford

LEWSTON extra parochial liberty 4 miles s Sherborne Dorset pop 18

LEWTRENCHARD parish 1706 Devon 8-1/2 miles ne Launceston pop
438 archd Totnes dioc Exeter

LEXDEN parish 1560 Essex 1-1/2 miles w Colchester pop 1,184
Commissary of Essex and Herts, concurrently with Consistorial

Court of Bishop of London

LEXHAM, EAST parish 1538 Norfolk 6-1/2 miles ne Swaffham pop 206 archd and dioc Norwich

LEXHAM, WEST parish 1689 Norfolk 5-3/4 miles ne Swaffham pop 103 archd and dioc Norwich

LEY, UPPER township parish Aymestrey Herefs

LEYBOURN market town parish Wensley N R York pop 1,003 46 miles nw York Indep, Wesl Meth, Roman Cath

LEYBOURNE parish 1560 Kent 5 miles nw Maidstone pop 299 archd and dioc Rochester

LEYLAND parish 1653 Lancs 4-1/2 miles nw Chorley comp chapelries Euxton, Heapey, Hoghton, Whittle le Woods, townships Clayton le Woods, Cuerden, Leyland, Wheelton, Withnell pop 13,871 archd and dioc Chester Wesl Meth

LEYSDOWN parish 1701 Kent 7-3/4 miles se Queenborough pop 191 archd and dioc Canterbury

LEYTON, LOW parish 1575 Essex 6 miles ne London pop 3,323 Commissary of London, concurrently with Consistorial Court of Bishop Indep, Wesl Meth

LEZANT parish 1539 Cornwall 4-1/2 miles se Launceston pop 841 pec of Bishop of Exeter Wesl Meth

LEZIATE parish incl in regs of Ashwicken Norfolk 5 miles e Lynn Regis pop 159 archd and dioc Norwich

LIBBERSTON township parish Filey N R York pop 179

LICHFIELD city Staffs 16-1/2 miles se Stafford pop 6,499 comp parishes St Mary 1566, St Michael 1574, St Chad 1635, Cathedral Church 1660 pec of Dean and Chapter of Lichfield Indep, Wesl Meth, Kilhamites, Roman Cath

LIDBROOK hamlet parish English Bicknor Gloucs Bapt

LIDDIARD MILLICENT parish 1697 Wilts 3 miles ne Wootton Basset pop 406 archd Wilts dioc Salisbury

LIDDIARD TREGOOZE parish 1666 Wilts 4 miles nw Swindon pop 765 archd Wilts dioc Salisbury

LIDDINGTON parish 1561 co Rutland 2-1/2 miles se Uppingham pop 534 pec of Prebendary of Liddington in Cathedral Church of Lincoln Wesl Meth

LIDDINGTON parish 1692 Wilts 4 miles se Swindon pop 407 archd Wilts dioc Salisbury

LIDGATE parish 1547 Suffolk 6-3/4 miles se Newmarket pop 442 archd Sudbury dioc Norwich

LIDDINGTON or LITTLINGTON parish 1705 Beds 3-1/2 miles nw Ampthill pop 814 archd Bedford dioc Lincoln Wesl Meth

LIDNEY or LYDNEY parish 1648 Gloucs 19 miles sw Gloucester pop 1,534 archd Hereford dioc Gloucester

LIDSEY hamlet parish Aldingbourn Sussex

LIDSING or LIDGEN village parish Gillingham Kent pop 51

LIDSTONE hamlet parish Church Enstone co Oxford

LIFTON parish 1653 Devon 4 miles ne Launceston pop 1,535 archd

archd Totnes dioc Exeter

LIGHTCLIFFE chapelry 1704 parish Halifax W R York Indep

LIGHTGRAVE or LEEGRAVE hamlet parish Luton Beds pop 685

LIGHTHORNE parish 1538 Warws 4 miles ne Kington pop 346 archd
and dioc Worcester

LILBOURN parish 1573 co Northampton 4 miles se Rugby pop 274
archd Northampton dioc Peterborough Wesl Meth

LILBURN, EAST township parish Eglingham Northumberland pop 95

LILBURN, WEST township parish Eglingham Northumberland pop 235

LILFORD parish 1560 co Northampton 3 miles sw Oundle pop 127
archd Northampton dioc Peterborough

LILLESHALL parish 1653 Shrops 3 miles sw Newport pop 3,569 archd
Salop dioc Lichfield

LILLEY parish 1711 Herts 5 miles sw Hitchin pop 451 archd Huntingdon dioc Lincoln

LILLIFFEE hamlet parish Hedsor Bucks

LILLINGS AMBO township parish Sheriff Hutton N R York pop 197

LILLINGSTONE DAYRELL parish 1584 Bucks 4-1/2 miles n Buckingham pop 150 archd Buckingham dioc Lincoln

LILLINGSTONE LOVELL parish 1558 Bucks 4-3/4 miles ne Buckingham pop 159 archd and dioc Oxford

LILLINGTON parish 1712 Dorset 3-1/2 miles sw Sherborne pop 205
pec of Dean of Salisbury

LILLINGTON parish 1538 Warws 2-1/2 miles ne Warwick pop 274
archd Coventry dioc Lichfield

LILLISDON tything parish North Curry Somerset

LILLY hamlet parish Catmere Berks

LILSTOCK parish 1654 Somerset 11-1/2 miles nw Bridgewater pop
64 archd Taunton dioc Bath and Wells

LILWALL township parish Kinton Herefs

LIMBER, MAGNA parish 1561 Lincs 5-1/4 miles ne Caistor pop 421
archd and dioc Lincoln

LIMBER, PARVA hamlet parish Brocklesby Lincs

LIMBURY CUM BISCOTT hamlet parish Luton Beds

LIMEHOUSE parish 1730 Middlesex 2 miles se London pop 15,695
Commissary of London, concurrently with Consistorial Court of
Bishop and in Fellows of Brasenose College, Oxford Wesl Meth

LIMINGTON parish 1681 Somerset 1-1/4 miles se Ilchester pop 313
archd Wells dioc Bath and Wells

LIMPENHOE parish 1662 Norfolk 5-1/4 miles s Acle pop 156 archd
and dioc Norwich

LIMPSFIELD parish 1539 Surrey 4 miles ne Godstone pop 1,042
archd Surrey dioc Winchester

LINACRE township parish Walton on the Hill Lancs

LINBRIGGS township parish Allenton Northumberland pop 64

LINBY parish 1692 Notts 7-3/4 miles nw Nottingham pop 352 archd
Nottingham dioc York

LINCH parish 1701 Sussex 5 miles nw Midhurst pop 86 archd and dioc Chichester

LINCHMERE parish 1566 Sussex 7-1/2 miles nw Midhurst pop 301 archd and dioc Chichester

LINCOLN city Lincs 132 miles nw London pop 13,081 comp St Benedict 1645, St Botolph 1561, St John 1708, St Margaret 1538, St Mark 1681, St Martin 1548, St Mary le Wigford 1563, St Mary Magdalene 1665, St Michael 1562, St Nicholas 1736, St Paul 1694, St Peter 1561, St Peter on Eastgate 1662, St Peter at Gowts 1538, St Swithin 1685, and modern parishes of All Saints, Bracebridge, All Saints Branston, All Saints Canwick, St Michael Waddington archd and dioc Lincoln Gen and Part Bapt, Soc of Friends, Countess of Huntingdon's Connection, Indep, Wesl Meth, Unit, Roman Cath

LINDALE chapelry parish Cartmel Lancs

LINDETH township parish Warton Lancs

LINDFIELD parish 1558 Sussex 3-3/4 miles ne Cuckfield pop 1,485 pec of Archbishop of Canterbury Indep

LINDLEY hamlet parish Higham on the Hill Leics

LINDLEY chapelry parish Huddersfield W R York pop 2,306 Wesl Meth

LINDLEY township parish Otley W R York pop 125

LINDON hamlet parish Rock Worcs

LINDRIDGE parish 1648 Worcs 5-1/2 miles e Tenbury comp chapelries Knighton upon Teme, Fensax, hamlet Newham pop 1,802 archd Salop dioc Hereford

LINDSELL parish 1568 Essex 4 miles se Thaxted pop 381 archd Middlesex dioc London

LINDSEY parish 1559 Suffolk 4 miles nw Hadleigh pop 250 archd Sudbury dioc Norwich

LINEHAM parish 1653 Wilts 4-1/4 miles sw Wootton Bassett pop 1,030 archd Wilts dioc Salisbury

LINESIDE township parish Arthuret Cumberland pop 137

LINFORD, GREAT parish 1654 Bucks 1-3/4 miles sw Newport Pagnell pop 420 archd Buckingham dioc Lincoln

LINFORD, LITTLE parish 1757 Bucks 2-1/4 miles nw Newport Pagnell pop 55 archd Buckingham dioc Lincoln

LING parish 1691 Somerset 6-1/4 miles se Bridge Water pop 363 archd Taunton dioc Bath and Wells

LINGARTHS township parish Almondbury W R York pop 758

LINGEN parish 1751 Herefs 4 miles ne Presteigne pop 298 archd and dioc Hereford

LINGFIELD parish 1559 Surrey 6 miles se Godstone pop 1,814 archd Surrey dioc Winchester Bapt

LINGWOOD parish 1560 Norfolk 2-3/4 miles sw Acle pop 294 archd and dioc Norwich

LINKENHOLT parish 1579 Hamps 7-3/4 miles se Great Bedwin pop 87 archd and dioc Winchester

LINKINHORNE parish 1616 Cornwall 4 miles nw Callington pop 1,159 archd Cornwall dioc Exeter

LINLEY parish incl in regs of Broseley Shrops 4-1/4 miles nw
Bridgenorth pop 111 archd Salop dioc Hereford

LINMOUTH township parish Woodhorn Northumberland pop 23

LINOP township parish Ingram Northumberland pop 71

LINSHEELES township parish Hallystone Northumberland pop 114

LINSLADE or LINCHLADE parish 1690 Bucks 2 miles nw Leighton
Buzzard pop 407 archd Buckingham dioc Lincoln

LINSTEAD parish 1654 Kent 3-1/4 miles se Sittingbourne pop 952
archd and dioc Canterbury

LINSTEAD, MAGNA parish 1655 Suffolk 4-3/4 miles sw Halesworth
pop 110 archd Suffolk dioc Norwich

LINSTEAD, PARVA or LOWER parish 1539 Suffolk 3-1/4 miles w
Halesworth pop 186 archd Suffolk dioc Norwich

LINSTOCK township parish Stanwix Cumberland pop 228

LINTHORP township parish Middlesborough N R York pop 229

LINTHWAITE chapelry parish Almondbury W R York pop 2,952
Wesl Meth

LINTON market town and parish 1559 Cambs 10-1/2 miles se Cambridge pop 1,678 archd and dioc Ely Soc of Friends, Indep

LINTON township parish Church Gresley Derbys pop 241 Wesl Meth

LINTON or LYNTON parish 1548 Devon 14 miles ne Ilfracombe pop
792 archd Barnstaple dioc Exeter Indep

LINTON hamlet parish Churcham Gloucs pop 327

LINTON township parish Bromyard Herefs pop 500

LINTON parish 1570 Herefs 5 miles ne Ross pop 636 archd and dioc
Hereford Bapt

LINTON parish 1560 Kent 4 miles s Maidstone pop 723 archd and
dioc Canterbury

LINTON Lincs See LAVINGTON

LINTON hamlet parish Wintringham E R York

LINTON township parish Spofforth W R York pop 166 Wesl Meth

LINTON parish 1562 W R York 9 miles n Skipton comp townships
Grassington, Hebden, Linton, Threshfield pop 2,113 archd and
dioc York

LINTON UPON OUZE township parish Newton upon Ouze N R York
pop 258 Roman Cath

LINTON, WEST or LEVINGTON township parish Kirk Linton or Kirk
Levington Cumberland pop 629

LINTZ GREEN township parish Chester le Street co Durham pop 650

LINWOOD parish 1620 Lincs 2-1/2 miles se Market Rasen pop 169
archd and dioc Lincoln

LINWOOD extra parochial liberty Hamps near Godshill

LIPHOOD hamlet parish Bramshott Hamps

LIPWOOD township parish Warden Northumberland pop 583

LISCARD township parish Wallazey Ches pop 967

LISCOMBE hamlet parish Soulbury Bucks

LISKEARD borough sep juris market town, parish 1539 Cornwall 18 miles sw London pop 4,042 archd Cornwall dioc Exeter Soc of Friends, Indep, Wesl Meth

LISS chapelry 1590 parish Odiham Hamps pop 663

LISSETT chapelry parish Beeford 1661 E R York pop 102

LISSINGTON parish 1562 Lincs 4-1/4 miles s Market Rasen pop 182 archd and dioc Lincoln Wesl Meth

LISTON parish 1599 Essex 2-3/4 miles nw Sudbury pop 88 Commissary of Essex and Herts, concurrently with Consistorial Court of Bishop of London

LITCHAM parish 1550 Norfolk 7-1/4 miles ne Swaffham pop 771 archd and dioc Norwich

LITCHBOROUGH parish 1727 co Northampton 5-1/2 miles nw Towcester pop 415 archd Northampton dioc Peterborough

LITCHFIELD parish 1627 Hamps 4 miles n Whitchurch pop 82 archd and dioc Winchester

LITCHURCH hamlet parish St Peter Derby Derbys pop 516

LITHERLAND township parish Sephton Lancs pop 789

LITCHEWELL or LUDWELL chapelry parish Dawlish Devon

LITLINGTON Cambs See LITTLINGTON

LITTLE ABINGTON Cambs See ABINGTON, LITTLE

LITTLEBOROUGH chapelry 1758 parish Rochdale Lancs Wesl Meth

LITTLEBOROUGH parish 1539 Notts 8-1/2 miles ne East Retford pop 82 archd Nottingham dioc York

LITTLEBOURN parish 1559 Kent 4-1/4 miles e Canterbury pop 733 archd and dioc Canterbury

LITTLEBURY parish 1544 Essex 2 miles nw Saffron Walden pop 875 Commissary of Essex and Herts, concurrently with Consistorial Court of Bishop of London

LITTLECOT chapelry parish Chilton Foliatt Wilts

LITTLECOTE hamlet parish Stewkely Bucks

LITTLEDALE chapelry parish Lancaster Lancs

LITTLEHAM near Exmouth parish 1603 Devon 1-1/2 miles e Exmouth pop 3,189 pec juris of Dean and Chapter of Exeter Wesl Meth

LITTLEHAM parish 1538 Devon 2 miles sw Bideford pop 424 pec juris of Dean and Chapter of Exeter

LITTLEHAMPTON 1573 Sussex

LITTLEMOOR liberty parish St Mary the Virgin co Oxford pop 425

LITTLE OVER chapelry parish 1683 Derbys pop 412

LITTLEPORT parish 1753 Cambs 5-1/4 miles ne Ely pop 2,644 pec juris of Bishop of Ely Wesl Meth

LITTLETHORPE hamlet parish Cosby Leics

LITTLETON township parish Christleton Ches pop 48

LITTLETON farm 1-1/2 miles se Blandford Dorset

LITTLETON parish 1562 Middlesex 3 miles se Staines pop 134 archd Middlesex dioc London

LITTLETON hamlet parish Compton Dundon Somerset

LITTLETON parish 1736 Hamps 3 miles nw Winchester pop 120 pec juris of Littleton

LITTLETON chapelry parish Steeple Ashton Wilts pop 79

LITTLETON DREW parish 1706 Wilts 8 miles nw Chippenham pop 177 archd Wilts dioc Salisbury

LITTLETON, HIGH parish 1658 Somerset 9-1/2 miles sw Bath pop 911 archd Bath dioc Bath and Wells Wesl Meth

LITTLETON, MIDDLE township parish Littleton Worcs

LITTLETON, NORTH parish 1661 Worcs 5 miles ne Evesham pop 360 archd and dioc Worcester

LITTLETON PANNELL tything parish West Lavington Wilts pop 532

LITTLETON, SOUTH parish 1538 Worcs 3-1/2 miles ne Evesham pop 110 archd and dioc Worcester

LITTLETON UPON SEVERN parish 1701 Gloucs 2 miles w Thornbury pop 179 Consistorial Court of Bishop of Bristol

LITTLETON, WEST chapelry parish Tormarton Gloucs pop 128

LITTLEWORTH extra parochial liberty Gloucs pop 615 Wesl Meth

LITTLINGTON parish 1642 Cambs 3-1/2 miles nw Royston pop 622 archd and dioc Ely

LITTLINGTON parish 1695 Sussex 4 miles ne Sleaford pop 143 archd Lewes dioc Chichester

LITTON hamlet parish Tideswell Derbys pop 866

LITTON township parish Presteign Herefs pop 92

LITTON parish 1584 Somerset 6-1/4 miles ne Wells pop 414 archd Wells dioc Bath and Wells

LITTON township parish Arncliffe W R York pop 102

LITTON CHENEY parish 1614 Dorset 6-3/4 miles se Bridgeport pop 420 archd Dorset dioc Bristol

LIVENDEN co Northampton See ALDWINKLE

LIVERMERE, GREAT parish 1538 Suffolk 5-3/4 miles ne Bury St Edmund's pop 336 archd Sudbury dioc Norwich

LIVERMERE, LITTLE parish 1538 Suffolk 6-1/4 miles ne Bury St Edmund's archd Sudbury dioc Norwich

LIVERPOOL sea port, borough, market town Lancs 53 miles sw Lancaster pop 165,175 sep juris comp St Nicholas 1659, St Peters 1704, St George 1734, St Thomas 1750, St Paul's 1769, St Anne's 1773, St John's 1767, St Michael's 1826, St Luke's 1815, St Martin's in Fields 1828, Holy Trinity 1792, Christ Church 1798, St Mark 1815, St Andrew's 1815, St Philip 1817, St David's 1827, St Catherine's 1831, St Bride's 1831, St Stephen's 1792, St Mathew's 1798, St Simon 1831, St Mary's 1829, All Saints 1796 archd and dioc Chester Bapt, Welsh Calvinists, Welsh, Indep, Wesl Meth, Welsh Meth, New Connection, Sandemanians, Swedenborgians, Unit, Scottish Kirks, Seceders, Roman Cath, Jews

LIVERSEDGE chapelry parish Birstall W R York pop 5,265

LIVERTON chapelry parish Easington 1665 N R York pop 239

LIVESLEY township parish Blackburn Lancs pop 1,787

LLANARTH parish 1598 co Monmouth 3-1/4 miles nw Ragland pop 655 archd and dioc Llandaff

LLANBADOCK parish 1710 co Monmouth 1 mile sw Usk pop 374

archd and dioc Llandaff

LLANBEDER chapelry parish Langstone co Monmouth

LLANCILLO parish 1728 Herefs 14-1/2 miles sw Hereford pop 76
arch Brecon dioc St David

LLANDEGVETH parish 1746 co Monmouth 3-1/2 miles ne Caerleon
pop 105 archd and dioc Llandaff

LLANDENNY parish 1714 co Monmouth 4 miles ne Usk pop 404
archd and dioc Llandaff

LLANDEVAND chapelry parish Llanmartin co Monmouth

LLANDEVENNY hamlet parish St Bride Netherwent co Monmouth
pop 37

LLANDINABO parish 1596 Herefs 6-1/2 miles nw Ross pop 53 archd
and dioc Hereford

LLANDOGO parish 1694 co Monmouth 7-1/2 miles se Monmouth pop
646 archd and dioc Llandaff

LLANELLEN parish 1756 co Monmouth 2-1/2 miles s Abergavenny
pop 372 archd and dioc Llandaff

LLANFOIST parish 1736 co Monmouth 1-1/2 miles sw Abergavenny
pop 891 archd and dioc Llandaff

LLANFRECHFA 1727 co Monmouth

LLANGARRAN parish 1569 Herefs 5 miles sw Ross pop 1,125 archd
and dioc Hereford

LLANGATTOCK parish 1597 co Monmouth pop 1,362 archd and dioc
Llandaff

LLANGATTOCK LLINGOED parish 1696 co Monmouth 6 miles ne
Abergavenny pop 191 archd and dioc Llandaff

LLANGATTOCK NIGH USK parish 1695 co Monmouth 3-1/4 miles se
Abergavenny pop 164 archd and dioc Llandaff

LLANGATTOCK VIBON AVEL parish 1683 co Monmouth 6 miles nw
Monmouth pop 449 archd and dioc Llandaff

LLANGEVIEW parish 1709 co Monmouth 1 mile e Usk pop 180 archd
and dioc Llandaff

LLANGIBBY parish 1678 co Monmouth 2-1/4 miles sw Usk pop 515
archd and dioc Llandaff Indep

LLANGOVEN parish 1749 co Monmouth 3-1/4 miles se Ragland pop
136 archd and dioc Llandaff

LLANGUA parish 1714 co Monmouth 11 miles ne Abergavenny pop
76 archd and dioc Llandaff

LLANGWYN parish 1663 co Monmouth 3-1/2 miles e Usk pop 292
archd and dioc Llandaff

LLANHENNOCK parish 1695 co Monmouth 1-3/4 miles ne Caerleon
pop 187 archd and dioc Llandaff

LLANHILETH parish 1753 co Monmouth 11 miles nw Usk pop 545
archd and dioc Llandaff

LLANISHEN parish 1591 co Monmouth 8 miles sw Monmouth pop 296
archd and dioc Llandaff Wesl Meth

LLANITHOG extra parochial liberty Herefs 3-1/2 miles ne Pontrilas

LLANLLOWELL parish 1664 co Monmouth 1-1/2 miles se Usk pop

78 archd and dioc Llandaff

LLANMARTIN parish 1755 co Monmouth 3-3/4 miles se Caerleon pop 158 archd and dioc Llandaff

LLANOVER parish 1661 co Monmouth 3-1/2 miles se Abergavenny pop 2,124 archd and dioc Llandaff

LLANROTHALL parish 1740 Herefs 5 miles nw Monmouth pop 128 archd and dioc Hereford

LLANSAINTFREAD parish 1753 co Monmouth 3-3/4 miles se Abergavenny pop 24 archd and dioc Llandaff

LLANSOY parish 1592 co Monmouth 4-3/4 miles ne Usk pop 148 archd and dioc Llandaff

LLANTHEWY RYTHERCH parish 1733 co Monmouth 4 miles e Abergavenny pop 359 archd and dioc Llandaff

LLANTHEWY SKIRRID parish 1754 co Monmouth 4 miles ne Abergavenny pop 100 archd and dioc Llandaff

LLANTHEWY VACH parish 1741 co Monmouth 3-1/2 miles sw Usk pop 163 archd and dioc Llandaff

LLANTHONY extra parochial liberty near Gloucester city, Gloucs

LLANTHONY ABBEY chapelry parish Owmyoy 1767 co Monmouth

LLANTILLIO GROSSENNY parish 1719 co Monmouth 7-1/2 miles nw Monmouth pop 589 archd and dioc Llandaff

LLANTILLIO PERTHOLEY parish 1591 co Monmouth 1-3/4 miles ne Abergavenny pop 749 archd and dioc Llandaff

LLANTRISSENT parish 1743 co Monmouth 2-1/2 miles se Usk pop 304 archd and dioc Llandaff

LLANVACHES parish 1754 co Monmouth 6 miles e Caerleon pop 327 archd and dioc Llandaff

LLANVAIR DISCOED parish 1680 co Monmouth 6-1/2 miles sw Chepstow pop 206 archd and dioc Llandaff

LLANVAIR KILGEDIN parish 1733 co Monmouth 5-3/4 miles nw Usk pop 261 archd and dioc Llandaff

LLANVAIR WATERDINE parish 1606 Shrops 4-1/2 miles nw Knighton pop 566 archd Salop dioc Hereford

LLANVANAIR chapelry no parish no regs archd and dioc Llandaff

LLANVAPLEY parish 1699 co Monmouth 4 miles e Abergavenny pop 90 archd and dioc Llandaff Indep

LLANVETHERINE parish 1693 co Monmouth 5 miles ne Abergavenny pop 214 archd and dioc Llandaff

LLANVEYNO chapelry 1714 parish Clodock Herefs pop 298

LLANVIHANGEL CRUCORNEY parish 1629 co Monmouth 5 miles ne Abergavenny comp hamlet Penbiddle pop 365 archd and dioc Llandaff

LLANVIHANGEL LLANTARNAM parish 1727 co Monmouth 2 miles nw Caerleon pop 626 archd and dioc Llandaff

LLANVIHAMGEL NEAR ROGGIET parish 1753 co Monmouth 8 miles sw Chepstow pop 46 archd and dioc Llandaff

LLANVIHANGEL NEAR USK parish 1751 co Monmouth 6-1/2 miles nw Usk pop 117 archd and dioc Llandaff

LLANVIHANGEL PONT Y MOILE parish 1742 co Monmouth 5 miles nw Usk pop 149 archd and dioc Llandaff

LLANVIHANGEL TOR Y MYNYDD parish 1592 co Monmouth 6-1/2 miles ne Usk pop 204 archd and dioc Llandaff

LLANVIHANGEL YSTERN LLEWERN parish 1685 co Monmouth 5-1/2 miles nw Monmouth pop 163 archd and dioc Llandaff

LLANVRECHVA parish 1727 co Monmouth 2 miles n Caerleon pop 1,167 archd and dioc Llandaff

LLANWARNE parish 1675 Herefs 7 miles nw Ross pop 390 archd and dioc Hereford

LLANWENARTH parish 1725 co Monmouth 2-1/4 miles nw Abergavenny comp Llanwenarth Citra pop 2,203 archd and dioc Llandaff Bapt

LLANWERN parish 1750 co Monmouth 3-1/4 miles se Caerleon pop 22 archd and dioc Llandaff

LLANYBLODWELL parish 1695 Shrops 6 miles sw Oswestry pop 915 archd and dioc St Asaph

LLANYMYNOCH parish 1668 Shrops 6 miles sw Oswestry pop 525 archd and dioc Llandaff

LLOYNDU hamlet parish Abergavenny co Monmouth pop 163

LLWYNLLANAN township parish Llanymynech Shrops

LOAD, LONG chapelry parish Martock 1711 Somerset

LOAN END township parish Norham or Norhamshire co Durham pop 147

LOBB hamlet parish Great Haseley co Oxford

LOCKERIDGE township parish Overton Wilts

LOCKERLEY parish 1583 Hamps 6 miles nw Romsey pop 560 archd and dioc Winchester Bapt

LOCKHAY or LOCKO chapelry parish Spondon Derbys

LOCKING parish 1750 Somerset 6-1/4 miles nw Axbridge pop 212 archd Wells dioc Bath and Wells

LOCKINGE, EAST and WEST parish 1546 Berks 3-3/4 miles se Wantage pop 363 archd Berks dioc Salisbury

LOCKINGTON parish 1557 Leics 7-1/2 miles nw Loughborough pop 624 archd Leicester dioc Lincoln

LOCKINGTON parish 1565 E R York 6-1/2 miles nw Beverley pop 475 archd and dioc York Wesl Meth

LOCKTON township parish Middleton 1713 N R York pop 312 Wesl Meth

LOCKWOOD chapelry parish Almondbury W R York pop 3,134 Bapt

LODDINGTON parish 1554 Leics 7-1/4 miles nw Uppingham pop 164 archd Leicester dioc Lincoln

LODDINGTON parish 1622 co Northampton 1-3/4 miles s Rothwell pop 218 archd Northampton dioc Peterborough

LODDISWELL or LODDISWELL ARUNDELL parish 1559 Devon 3 miles nw Kingsbridge pop 826 archd Totnes dioc Exeter

LODDON market town and parish 1556 Norfolk 10 miles se Norwich pop 1,175 archd Norfolk dioc Norwich Wesl Meth

LODERS parish 1636 Dorset 2 miles ne Bridgeport pop 812 archd
Dorset dioc Bristol

LODSWORTH chapelry 1563 parish Easebourne Sussex pop 599

LOFTHOUSE township parish Rothwell W R York

LOFTHOUSE parish 1697 N R York 8-1/2 miles ne Guisborough pop
1,038 archd Cleveland dioc York Wesl Meth

LOFTSOME township parish Wressel E R York

LOGASTON township parish Almeley Herefs

LOLWORTH parish 1565 Cambs 6-1/4 miles nw Cambridge pop 129
archd and dioc Ely

LONDESBOROUGH parish 1653 E R York 3 miles n Market Weighton
pop 259 archd and dioc York

LONDON capital of England and co Middlesex pop 1-1/4 million
parishes in the city of London (not including Westminster; see
WESTMINSTER)

Parishes marked (1) in juris Archd London dioc London

Parishes marked (2) in juris Commissary of London dioc London

Parishes marked (3) in pec juris of Archbishop of Canterbury

Parishes marked (4) in pec juris of Dean and Chapter of St Pauls

Parishes marked (5) in pec juris of St Katherine by the Tower

Parishes marked (6) in juris Archd Middlesex

St Alban Wood Street 1566 (2), All Hallows Barking 1558 (2), All
Hallows Bread Street 1539 (3), All Hallows the Great 1654 (1),
All Hallows Honey Lane 1538 (2), All Hallows the Less [Ropery]
1558 (1), All Hallows Lombard Street 1550 (3), All Hallows London Wall 1559 (1), All Hallows Staining 1642 (2), St Alphage London Wall 1613 (1), St Andrew Hubbard [Eastcheap] 1791 (2), St
Andrew Undershaft 1558 (2), St Andrew by the Wardrobe 1558 (1),
St Andrew Holborn 1558 (1), St Anne [see Temple Church], St Anne
and St Agnes Aldersgate 1640 (1), St Antholin 1528 (2), St Augus-
tine Watling Street 1559 (1), St Anne Blackfriars 1560 (2), St Bar-
tholomew Exchange 1558 (1), St Bartholomew the Great 1616 (1),
St Bartholomew the Less 1547 (1), St Benet Fink 1538 (2), St Benet
Gracechurch 1558 (2), St Benet Paul's Wharf 1619 (2), St Benet
Sherehog 1629 (2), St Botolph without Aldgate 1558 (1), St Botolph
Aldersgate 1638 (1), St Botolph Billingsgate 1685 (2), St Botolph
Bishopsgate 1558 (2), St Bride Fleet Street 1653 (2), Bridewell
Hospital [extra parochial] 1666, Christ Church Newgate [Grey-
friars] 1538 (1), St Christopher le Stocks 1558 (2), St Clement
Eastcheap 1539 (2), St Dionis Backchurch 1538 (3), St Dunstan in
the East 1558 (3), St Dunstan in the West 1558 (2), St Edmund the
King [Lombard Street] 1670 (2), St Ethelburga 1671 (1), St Faith
1559 (4), St Gabriel Fenchurch 1571 (2), St George Botolph Lane
1547 (2), St Giles Cripplegate 1561 (4), St Gregory 1559 (4), St
Helen Bishopgate 1575 (4), Holy Trinity the Less 1547 (1), Holy
Trinity Minories 1563 (1), St James Duke Place 1668 (2), St James
Garlickhithe 1538 (2), St John the Baptist [Walbrook] 1686 (1), St
John the Evangelist [Friday Street] 1653 (3), St John Zachary

1693 (1), St Katherine by Tower 1584 (5), St Katherine Coleman
1559 (1), St Katherine Cree 1663 (2), St Lawrence Jewry 1538 (2),
St Lawrence Pountney 1538 (2), St Leonard Eastcheap 1538 (3),
St Leonard Foster [destroyed in fire 1666 after which see Christ-
church Newgate], St Magnus the Martyr 1557 (1), St Margaret
Lothbury 1558 (1), St Margaret Moses 1559 (1), St Margaret New
Fish Street 1712 (2), St Margaret Pattens 1559 (2), St Martin Iron-
monger Lane 1539 (2), St Martin Ludgate 1539 (1), St Martin Or-
gar 1624 (2), St Martin Outwich 1670 (2), St Martin Vintry 1664
(2), St Mary Abchurch 1558 (1), St Mary Aldermanbury 1538 (2),
St Mary Aldermary 1558 (3), St Mary Bothaw 1538 (3), St Mary le
Bow 1538 (3), St Mary Colechurch 1558 (1), St Mary at Hill 1558
(1), St Mary Mounthaw 1711 (1), St Mary Somerset 1711 (1), St
Mary Staining 1673 (1), St Mary Woolchurch 1558 (2), St Mary
Woolnoth 1538 (1), St Mary Magdalen Milk Street 1559 (2), St Mary
Magdalen Old Fish Street 1712 (1), St Michael Bassishaw 1538 (1),
St Michael Cornhill 1546 (2), St Michael Crooked Lane 1538 (3),
St Michael Queenhithe 1653 (1), St Michael le Querne 1669 (1), St
Michael Paternoster 1558 (3), St Michael Wood Street 1559 (2),
St Mildred Bread Street 1658 (2), St Mildred Poultry 1538 (2), St
Nicholas Acons 1539 (2), St Nicholas Cole Abbey 1538 (2) St Nich-
olas Olave 1705 (2), St Olave Hart Street 1563 (1), St Olave Jewry
1558 (2), St Olave Silver Street 1562 (1), St Pancras Soper Lane
1538 (3), St Paul's Cathedral 1697 (4), St Peter Westcheap 1538 (1),
St Peter Cornhill 1538 (1), St Peter Paul's Wharf 1607 (2), St Peter
le Poor 1651 (2), St Peter in Tower [ad Vincula] 1550 (6), St
Sepulchre 1662 (2), St Stephen Coleman Street 1538 (2), St Stephen
Walbrook 1557 (1), St Swithin 1615 (2), St Thomas Apostle 1558
(1), St Vedast Foster Lane 1558 (1)

Parishes adjacent to the city of London: St George the Martyr
1707 (1), St George Bloosbury 1730 (2), St Giles in the Fields 1561
(2), St George in the East 1729 (2), St John Savoy 1680 (1)

47 Baptist chapels, 6 Society of Friends, 100 Independents, 32
Wesl Meth, 4 Swedenborgians, 6 Unit, 4 Welsh Calv Meth, 9 Church
of Scotland, 14 Roman Cath, 7 synagogues, 18 foreign Protestant
and numerous other protestant dissenter chapels
LONDON COLNEY chapelry parishes St Peter and St Albans Herts
LONDONTHORPE parish 1539 Lincs 3-1/2 miles ne Grantham pop
    187 archd and dioc Lincoln
LONG BENTON Northumberland See BENTON LONG
LONGBOROUGH parish 1676 Gloucs 3 miles nw Stow on the Wold pop
    619 archd and dioc Gloucester
LONGBRIDGE DEVERILL Wilts See DEVERILL LONGBRIDGE
LONGBURTON Dorset See BURTON LONG
LONGBURGH township parish Burgh upon the Sands Cumberland pop
    118
LONGCOT chapelry 1667 parish Shrivenham Berks pop 452

LONGDON chapelry parish Pontesbury Shrops

LONGDON parish 1681 Staffs 4 miles nw Lichfield pop 1,147 pec of Prebendary of Longdon Indep, Soc of Friends

LONGDON township parish Leek Staffs pop 398

LONGDON parish 1538 Worcs 3 miles sw Upton upon Severn pop 612 archd and dioc Worcester

LONGDON UPON TERNE parish 1692 Shrops 3-1/2 miles nw Wellington pop 109 pec juris of Manorial Court of Longdon upon Terne

LONGFIELD parish 1558 Kent 5-1/2 miles se Dartford pop 125 archd and dioc Rochester

LONGFLEET tything parish Canford Magna Dorset pop 840

LONGFORD parish 1538 Derbys 6-1/2 miles se Ashbourn comp townships Alkmonton, Hollington, Longford, liberty Hungry Hentley, hamlet Rodsley pop 1,233 archd Derby dioc Lichfield

LONGFORD hamlet parishes St Catherine and St Mary de Lode Gloucs pop 338

LONGFORD parish 1558 Shrops 1-1/4 miles sw Newport pop 206 archd Salop dioc Lichfield

LONGHAM parish 1560 Norfolk 4 miles nw East Dereham pop 333 archd and dioc Norwich

LONGHIRST township parish Bothal Northumberland pop 216

LONGHOPE parish 1742 Gloucs 5 miles sw Newent pop 873 archd and dioc Gloucester Wesl Meth

LONGHOUGHTON Northumberland See HOUGHTON LONG

LONGNEY parish 1660 Gloucs 6-1/2 miles sw Gloucester pop 453 archd and dioc Gloucester

LONGNOR parish 1586 Shrops 8 miles s Shrewsbury pop 244 archd Salop dioc Lichfield

LONGNOR market town and chapelry 1694 parish Allstonefield Staffs pop 429 Wesl Meth

LONGPARISH parish 1654 Hamps 3-1/4 miles sw Whitchurch pop 775 archd and dioc Winchester Bapt

LONGPORT borough parish St Paul Canterbury Kent pop 1,025

LONGPORT manufacturing district within parish and township of Burslem Staffs Wesl Meth

LONGRIDGE township parish Norham co Durham pop 105

LONGRIDGE chapelry 1760 parish Ribchester Lancs

LONGSHAWS township parish Longhorsley Northumberland pop 44

LONG SLEDDALE Westm See SLEDDALE, LONG

LONGSTOCK parish 1718 Hamps 1-1/2 miles n Stockbridge pop 428 archd and dioc Winchester

LONGSTONE, GREAT chapelry 1639 parish Bakewell Derbys pop 506

LONGSTONE, LITTLE hamlet parish Bakewell Derbys pop 146

LONG STOW Cambs See STOW, LONG

LONGTHORPE chapelry parish St John Peterborough co Northampton pop 265

LONGTON chapelry parish Penwortham 1813 Lancs pop 1,744 Wesl Meth

LONGTON township parish Stoke upon Trent Staffs pop 8,120
LONGTOWN market town parish Arthuret Cumberland pop 2,049
  Presb
LONGTOWN chapelry parish Clodock Herefs pop 938
LONGWOOD chapelry 1797 parish Huddersfield W R York pop 2,111
LONGWORTH parish 1559 Berks 7 miles ne Great Farringdon comp
  chapelry Charney, hamlet Draycot Moore pop 1,034 archd Berks
  dioc Salisbury
LONGWORTH township parish Bolton Lancs pop 179
LOOE, EAST sea port market town, chapelry 1710 borough Cornwall
  16 miles w Plymouth pop 865 sep juris archd Cornwall dioc
  Exeter Wesl Meth, Soc of Friends
LOOE, WEST chapelry parish Talland borough Cornwall pop 593
  Indep
LOOSE parish 1559 Kent 1-1/2 miles s Maidstone pop 1,061 pec
  juris of Archbishop of Canterbury
LOPEN parish 1694 Somerset 3-3/4 miles nw Crewkerne pop 502
  archd Taunton dioc Bath and Wells
LOPHAM, NORTH parish 1560 Norfolk 5 miles se East Harling pop
  807 archd Norfolk dioc Norwich Wesl Meth
LOPHAM, SOUTH parish 1558 Norfolk 5-1/2 miles se East Harling
  pop 729 archd Norfolk dioc Norwich
LOPPINGTON parish 1654 Shrops 3 miles w Wem pop 669 archd
  Salop dioc Lichfield Wesl Meth
LORBOTTLE township parish Whittingham Northumberland pop 128
LORTON parish 1538 Cumberland 3-3/4 miles se Cockermouth
  comp chapelry Wythop, townships Brackenthwaite, Lorton pop
  639 archd Richmond dioc Chester
LOSCOW township parish Heanor Derbys Bapt
LOSTOCK hamlet parish Bolton Lancs pop 606
LOSTOCK GRALAM township parish Great Budworth Ches pop 537
LOSTWITHIEL market town, parish 1609 borough Cornwall 6 miles
  s Bodmin sep juris pop 1,548 archd Cornwall dioc Exeter
  Bryanites, Indep, Wesl Meth
LOTHERS Dorset See LODERS
LOTHERTON township parish Sherburn W R York pop 426
LOUDWATER chapelry parish High Wycombe Bucks
LOUGHBOROUGH market town parish 1538 Leics 11 miles n Leices-
  ter comp townships Knight Thorpe, Wood Thorpe pop 10,969
  archd Leicester dioc Lincoln Gen and Part Bapt, Soc of Friends,
  Wesl Meth, Unit
LOUGHRIGG township parish Grasmere Westm
LOUGHTON parish 1707 Bucks 3-3/4 miles nw Fenny Stratford pop
  325 archd Bucks dioc Lincoln
LOUGHTON parish 1706 Essex 14 miles ne London pop 1,269 juris of
  Commissary of London, concurrently with Consistorial Court of
  Bishop of London Bapt
LOUGHTON chapelry parish Chetton Shrops pop 112

LOUND township parish Witham on the Hill Lincs

LOUND township parish Sutton Notts pop 382 Wesl Meth

LOUND parish 1695 Suffolk 5 miles nw Lowestoft pop 425 arch Suffolk dioc Norwich

LOUTH market town, parish 1538 Lincs 28 miles ne Lincoln pop 6,976 sep juris pec of Prebendary of Louth Bapt, Indep, Prim and Wesl Meth, Roman Cath

LOVEDALE township parish Penkridge Staffs

LOVERSALL parish 1703 W R York 3-1/2 miles s Doncaster pop 154 archd and dioc York

LOVINGTON parish 1674 Somerset 2-3/4 miles sw Castle Cary pop 214 pec of Dean and Chapter of Wells

LOW ABBOT SIDE York See ABBOT SIDE, LOW

LOWDHAM parish 1559 Notts 7-3/4 miles ne Nottingham comp townships Caythorpe, Gunthorpe pop 1,463 archd Nottingham dioc York Wesl Meth

LOWE township parish Wem Shrops pop 81

LOWER ALLITHWAITE Lancs See ALLITHWAITE LOWER

LOWESBY parish 1653 Leics 9-3/4 miles ne Leicester pop 231 archd Leicester dioc Lincoln

LOWESTOFT sea port, market town, parish 1561 Suffolk 44 miles ne London pop 4,238 archd Suffolk dioc Norwich Bapt, Indep, Wesl Meth

LOWESWATER chapelry 1626 no parish Cumb pop 454 archd Richmond dioc Chester

LOWICK chapelry 1718 parish Ulverstone Lancs pop 371

LOWICK parish 1542 co Northampton 2-3/4 miles nw Thrapstone pop 394 archd Northampton dioc Peterborough

LOWICK parish 1718 Northumberland 8 miles ne Wooler pop 1,864 archd Northumberland dioc Durham

LOW QUARTER township parish Kirby Ireleth Lancs pop 565

LOWSIDE township parish Whickham co Durham pop 1,184

LOWSIDE QUARTER township parish St Bees, Cumberland pop 229

LOWTHER parish 1539 Westm 4-3/4 miles s Penrith pop 494 archd and dioc Carlisle

LOWTHORPE parish 1546 E R York 4-1/2 miles ne Great Driffield pop 138 archd and dioc York

LOWTON chapelry 1733 parish Winwick Lancs pop 2,374

LOXBEAR parish 1560 Devon 4-1/4 miles nw Tiverton pop 157 archd and dioc Exeter

LOXHORE parish 1652 Devon 6-1/4 miles ne Barnstaple pop 248 archd Barnstaple dioc Exeter

LOXLET liberty parish Uttoxeter Staffs

LOXLEY parish 1540 Warws 4-1/4 miles se Stratford Upon Avon pop 290 archd and dioc Worcester

LOXTON parish 1558 Somerset 3-3/4 miles nw Axbridge pop 148 archd Wells dioc Bath and Wells

LOXWOOD END chapelry parish Wisborough Green Sussex

LOYNTON township parish High Offley Staffs pop 68
LUBBESTHORPE chapelry parish Aylestone Leics pop 70
LUBENHAM parish 1559 Leics 2 miles w Market Harborough pop 542 archd Leicester dioc Lincoln
LUCCOMBE See LUCKHAM
LUCKER chapelry 1769 parish Bambrough Northumberland pop 266
LUCKHAM parish 1690 Somerset 4 miles sw Minehead pop 546 archd Taunton dioc Bath and Wells
LUCKINGTON hamlet parish Kilmersdon Somerset
LUCKINGTON parish 1573 Wilts 7-1/2 miles sw Malmesbury pop 275 archd Wilts dioc Salisbury
LUCTON parish 1711 Herefs 6 miles nw Leominster pop 174 archd and dioc Hereford
LUDBOROUGH parish 1601 Lincs 6-1/2 miles nw Louth pop 322 archd and dioc Lincoln Wesl Meth
LUDDENDEN chapelry parish Halifax 1653 W R York Wesl Meth
LUDDENHAM parish 1547 Kent 2 miles nw Faversham pop 219 archd and dioc Canterbury
LUDDESDOWN parish 1681 Kent 5-1/2 miles sw Rochester pop 258 archd and dioc Rochester
LUDDINGTON parish 1700 Lincs 5 miles ne Crowle pop 905 archd Stow dioc Lincoln Wesl Meth
LUDDINGTON hamlet parish Old Stratford Warws pop 127
LUDDINGTON IN THE BROOK parish 1635 co Northampton 6 miles se Oundle pop 117 archd Northampton dioc Peterborough
LUDFORD parish 1643 Shrops 1/2 mile s Ludlow pop 284 archd Salop dioc Hereford
LUDFORD, MAGNA parish 1696 Lincs 6-1/2 miles e Market Rasen pop 322 archd and dioc Lincoln Wesl Meth
LUDFORD, PARVA parish no regs Lincs 6-1/4 miles e Market Rasen pop 206 archd and dioc Lincoln
LUDGERSHALL parish 1538 Bucks 6 miles se Bicester pop 585 archd Buckingham dioc Lincoln
LUDGERSHALL parish 1609 borough Wilts 16-1/2 miles ne Salisbury pop 535 archd and dioc Salisbury Bapt
LUDGVAN parish 1563 Cornwall 2 miles nw Marazion pop 2,322 archd Cornwall dioc Exeter Wesl Meth
LUDHAM parish 1583 Norfolk 7-1/2 miles n Acle pop 909 archd Norfolk dioc Norwich Bapt, Wesl Meth
LUDLOW borough, market town, parish 1558 Shrops 29 miles se Shrewsbury pop 5,253 sep juris archd Salop dioc Hereford Indep, Wesl Meth
LUDNEY hamlet parish Grainthorpe Lincs
LUDWORTH township parish Glossop Derbys pop 1,734
LUFFENHAM, NORTH parish 1572 co Rutland 6 miles ne Uppingham pop 447 archd Northampton dioc Peterborough
LUFFENHAM, SOUTH parish 1678 co Rutland 5-1/2 miles ne Uppingham pop 273 archd Northampton dioc Peterborough

LUFFIELD ABBEY extra parochial liberty co Northampton and Bucks 5-1/2 miles nw Buckingham pop 10

LUFFINCOTT parish 1653 Devon 7 miles sw Holsworthy pop 92 archd Totnes dioc Exeter

LUFTON parish 1748 Somerset 3 miles w Yeovil pop 20 archd Wells dioc Bath and Wells

LUGWARDINE parish 1538 Herefs 2-3/4 miles ne Hereford pop 662 archd and dioc Hereford

LUKE'S ST OLD ST parish 1653 northern outskirts of London Middlesex comp liberties City road, East Finsbury, West Finsbury, Golden lane, Old street, Whitecross street pop 46,642 archd Middlesex dioc London Bapt, Indep, Wesl and Calvinistic Meth

LULLINGSTONE parish 1578 Kent 7 miles se Foot's Cray pop 40 archd and dioc Rochester

LULLINGTON parish 1560 Derbys 7-1/2 miles s Burton upon Trent Derbys pop 548 archd Derby dioc Lichfield

LULLINGTON parish 1712 Somerset 2-3/4 miles ne Frome pop 145 archd Taunton dioc Bath and Wells

LULLINGTON parish 1721 Sussex 4-1/2 miles ne Seaford pop 49 archd and dioc Chichester

LULLWORTH, EAST parish 1561 Dorset 6 miles sw Wareham pop 345 archd Dorset dioc Bristol

LULLWORTH, WEST parish 1745 Dorset 8 miles sw Wareham pop 360 archd Dorset dioc Bristol

LULSLEY chapelry parish Suckley 1754 Worcs pop 128

LUMBY township parish Sherburn W R York

LUMLEY GREAT chapelry parish Chester le Street co Durham pop 2,301 Wesl Meth

LUMLEY, LITTLE township parish Chester le Street co Durham pop 393

LUND chapelry parish Kirkham Lancs

LUND parish 1597 E R York 7 miles nw Beverley pop 370 archd East Riding dioc York

LUND township parish Hemingbrough E R York

LUNDS or HELBECK LUNDS chapelry 1755 parish Aysgarth N R York

LUNDY ISLAND Devon 10 miles nw Hartland Point

LUNE DALE township parish Romald Kirk N R York pop 308

LUNT township parish Sephton Lancs pop 67

LUPPITT parish 1710 Devon 4-1/2 miles n Honiton pop 702 archd and dioc Exeter

LUPTON township parish Kirkby Lonsdale Westm pop 282

LURGASALL parish 1559 Sussex 4-1/2 miles nw Petworth pop 718 archd and dioc Chichester

LUSBY parish 1691 Lincs 4 miles nw Spilsby pop 104 archd and dioc Lincoln Wesl Meth

LUSTLEIGH parish 1631 Devon 5-3/4 miles nw Chudleigh pop 361 archd Totnes dioc Exeter

LUSTON township parish Eye Herefs pop 421

LUTON parish 1603 Beds 20 miles se Bedford comp market town Luton, hamlets East and West Hyde, Leegrave or Lightgrave, Limbury with Biscott, Stopsley pop 5,693 archd Bedford dioc Lincoln Bapt, Soc of Friends, Wesl Meth

LUTTERWORTH market town parish 1653 Leics 13 miles sw Leicester pop 2,262 archd Leicester dioc Lincoln Indep, Wesl Meth

LUTTLEY hamlet parish Hales Owen Worcs pop 131

LUTTON or LUDDINGTON IN THE WOLD parish 1653 co Northampton 5-1/2 miles e Oundle pop 171 archd Northampton dioc Peterborough Wesl Meth

LUTTON Lincs See SUTTON LONG ST NICHOLAS

LUTTON, EAST and WEST township parish Weaverthorpe E R York pop 350

LUXBOROUGH parish 1557 Somerset 4-1/4 miles sw Dunster pop 391 archd Taunton dioc Bath and Wells

LUXULYON parish 1593 Cornwall 3-1/2 miles sw Lostwithiel pop 1,288 archd Cornwall dioc Exeter

LYDBURY, NORTH 1558 Shrops 2-3/4 miles se Bishop's Castle comp townships Acton, Brockton, Down, Eaton with Choulton, Eyton with Plowden, Lydbury, Totterton pop 955 archd Salop dioc Hereford

LYDD market town and parish 1542 Kent 36 miles se Maidstone pop 1,357 pec of Archbishop of Canterbury Indep

LYDDEN parish 1540 Kent 4-1/2 miles nw Dover pop 224 archd and dioc Canterbury

LYDE township parish Pipe Herefs

LYDEARD, BISHOP'S parish 1674 Somerset 5-1/4 miles nw Taunton pop 1,295 archd Taunton dioc Bath and Wells

LYDEARD parish 1573 Somerset 4-3/4 miles ne Wiveliscombe pop 654 archd Taunton dioc Bath and Wells

LYDFORD parish borough 1716 Devon 7-3/4 miles ne Tavistock pop 830 archd Totnes dioc Exeter

LYDFORD, EAST parish 1730 Somerset 4-3/4 miles w Castle Cary pop 166 archd Wells dioc Bath and Wells

LYDFORD, WEST parish 1733 Somerset 5-1/2 miles w Castle Cary pop 357 pec of West Lydford at Wells

LYDGATE Suffolk See LIDGATE

LYDGATE chapelry 1788 parish Rochdale W R York

LYDHAM parish 1596 Shrops 2 miles ne Bishop's Castle pop 207 archd Salop dioc Hereford

LYDIATE chapelry parish Halsall Lancs pop 770 Roman Cath

LYDLINCH parish 1559 Dorset 3 miles sw Sturminster Newton pop 365 archd Dorset dioc Bristol

LYDNEY Gloucs See LIDNEY

LYE, UPPER township parish Aymestry Herefs

LYE, WASTE chapelry parish Old Swinford Worcs Indep, Wesl Meth, Unit

LYFORD chapelry parish West Hanney Berks pop 131

LYME HANDLEY township parish Prestbury Ches pop 222

LYME REGIS borough market town parish 1543 Dorset 22 miles w Dorchester pop 2,261 sep juris pec of Prebendary of Lyme Regis and Halstock Bapt, Indep, Wesl Meth

LYMINGE parish 1679 Kent 4-1/2 miles n Hythe pop 784 pec of Archbishop of Canterbury

LYMINGTON borough, market town, chapelry 1662 Hamps 18 miles sw Southampton pop 3,361 archd and dioc Winchester Bapt, Indep

LYMINSTER Sussex See LEOMINSTER

LYMN parish 1568 Ches 5-1/2 miles se Warrington pop 2,305 archd and dioc Chester Wesl Meth

LYMPNE parish 1617 Kent 2-3/4 miles w Hythe pop 532 archd and dioc Canterbury

LYMPSHAM parish 1737 Somerset 7 miles w Axbridge pop 521 archd Wells dioc Bath and Wells Wesl Meth

LYMPSTON parish 1654 Devon 2-1/2 miles n Exmouth pop 1,066 archd and dioc Exeter Wesl Meth, Unit

LYNCOMB parish 1574 Somerset pop 8,704 archd Bath dioc Bath and Wells

LYNDHURST parish 1737 Hamps 9-1/2 miles sw Southampton pop 1,236 archd and dioc Winchester

LYNDON parish 1580 co Rutland 5 miles se Oakham pop 102 archd Northampton dioc Peterborough

LYNDON quarter parish Church Bickenhill Warws

LYNEHAM Wilts See LINEHAM

LYNEHAM chapelry parish Shipton under Whychwood co Oxford pop 237

LYNESACK township parish St Andrew Auckland co Durham pop 795

LYNFORD parish Norfolk 5 miles ne Brandon Ferry pop 90 archd Norfolk dioc Norwich

LYNG parish 1538 Norfolk 6 miles ne East Dereham pop 645 archd Norfolk dioc Norwich

LYNG Somerset See LING

LYNN, NORTH parish incl regs West Lynn Norfolk 1-1/2 miles nw Kings Lynn pop 54 archd and dioc Norwich

LYNN KINGS borough, seaport, market town 1558 Norfolk 44 miles nw Norwich pop 13,370 excl juris comp parishes All Saints or South Lynn, St Margaret archd and dioc Norwich Bapt, Soc of Friends, Indep, Wesl Meth, Unit, Roman Cath, Jews

LYNN, WEST parish 1695 Norfolk 3/4 mile w Kings Lynn pop 396 archd and dioc Norwich

LYNT tything parish Coleshill Wilts

LYNTON Devon See LINTON

LYONSHALL parish 1682 Herefs 2-1/2 miles se Kington pop 880 archd and dioc Hereford

LYPEAT hamlet parish Kilmersdon Somerset

LYSS Hamps See LISS

LYSS TURNEY Hamps See LISS

LYTCHETT MATRAVERS parish 1656 Dorset 8 miles ne Wareham pop 680 archd Dorset dioc Bristol Wesl Meth

LYTCHETT MINSTER chapelry 1538 parish Sturminster Marshall 1554 Dorset pop 505 pec of Sturminster Marshall

LYTH hamlet parish Heversham Kendal Westm

LYTHAM parish 1679 Lancs 6 miles sw Kirkham pop 1,523 archd Richmond dioc Chester Roman Cath

LYTHE or MILLAND chapelry Sussex

LYTHE parish 1637 N R York 3-1/2 miles nw Whitby comp townships Barnby, Borrowby, Ellerby, Hutton Mulgrave, Lythe, Nickleby, Mulgrave, Ugthorpe pop 2,110 archd Cleveland dioc York Wesl Meth

MABE parish 1653 Cornwall 4-1/2 miles w Falmouth pop 512 juris Consistorial Court of Bishop of Exeter Wesl Meth

MABLETHORPE parish 1650 Lincs 7 miles ne Alford pop 242 archd and dioc Lincoln

MABYN, ST parish 1562 Cornwall 3-1/4 miles ne Wadebridge pop 793 archd Cornwall dioc Exeter Wesl Meth

MACCLESFIELD market town, parochial chapelry 1572 borough Ches 36 miles ne Chester sep juris pop 23,129 archd and dioc Chester Soc of Friends, Indep, Prim Meth, New Connection, Wesl Meth, Socinians, Roman Cath

MACCLESFIELD FOREST chapelry 1669 parish Prestbury Ches pop 279

MACEFEN township parish Malpas Ches pop 48

MACHEN parish 1670 co Monmouth 5-1/2 miles nw Newport pop 1,173 archd and dioc Llandaff Wesl Meth

MACKWORTH parish 1603 Derbys 2-3/4 miles nw Derby pop 621 archd Derby dioc Lichfield

MADDINGTON parish 1652 Wilts 5-3/4 miles nw Amesbury pop 381 archd and dioc Salisbury

MADEHURST parish 1639 Sussex 3-3/4 miles nw Arundel pop 154 archd and dioc Chichester

MADELEY parish 1678 Staffs 5-1/2 miles sw Newcastle under Lyne pop 1,190 archd Stafford dioc Lichfield

MADELEY HOLME liberty parish Checkley Staffs pop 591

MADELEY MARKET parish 1645 Shrops 4-1/2 miles sw Shiffnall pop 5,822 archd Salop dioc Hereford Wesl Meth, Roman Cath

MADINGLEY parish 1691 Cambs 3-1/2 miles nw Cambridge pop 252 archd and dioc Ely

MADLEY parish 1558 Herefs 7 miles sw Hereford pop 930 Dean of Hereford Bapt

MADRESFIELD parish 1742 Worcs 6 miles nw Upton upon Severn pop 191 archd and dioc Worcester

MADRON parish 1577 Cornwall 2-1/4 miles nw Penzance pop 2,058 archd Cornwall dioc Exeter Wesl Meth

MAER parish 1558 Staffs 7 miles nw Eccleshall comp township Maer, hamlet Maerway Lane pop 505 archd Stafford dioc Lichfield

MAERWAY LANE hamlet parish Maer Staffs pop 266

MAGDALENE STOCKLINCH Somerset See STOCKLINCH, MAGDA-
LENE

MAGHULL chapelry 1729 parish Halsal Lancs 5 miles sw Ormskirk
pop 957

MAGOR parish 1799 co Monmouth 6 miles se Caerleon pop 646 archd
and dioc Llandaff Bapt

MAIDEN BRADLY Wilts See BRADLEY MAIDEN

MAIDENHEAD market town, chapelry parishes Bray and Cookham
Berks 13 miles ne Reading sep juris archd Berks dioc Salisbury
Soc of Friends, Countess of Huntingdon's Connection, Indep

MAIDEN NEWTON parish 1553 Dorset 8-1/4 miles nw Dorchester
pop 538 archd Dorset dioc Bristol

MAIDEN WELL parish no regs Lincs 5-1/2 miles s Louth archd and
dioc Lincoln

MAIDFORD parish 1711 co Northampton 5-3/4 miles nw Towcester
pop 373 archd Northampton dioc Peterborough

MAIDS' MORETON Bucks See MORETON, MAIDS

MAIDSTONE borough, market town, parish 1542 Kent 8 miles s Rochester sep juris pop 15,387 pec Archbishop of Canterbury
Wesl Meth, Bapt, Soc of Friends, Unit

MAIDWELL parish 1708 co Northampton 10 miles n Northampton
pop 278 archd Northampton dioc Peterborough

MAINSFORTH township parish Bishop's Middleham co Durham pop
39

MAIDSTONE parish 1604 Shrops 4-3/4 miles sw Bishop's Castle pop
462 archd Salop dioc Hereford

MAISEY HAMPTON Gloucs See HAMPTON, MAISEY

MAISMORE parish 1538 Gloucs 2-3/4 miles nw Gloucester pop 423
archd and dioc Gloucester

MAKER parish 1630 Cornwall 2-1/4 miles sw Devonport pop 2,637
archd Cornwall dioc Exeter Wesl Meth

MALBOROUGH parish 1558 Devon 4 miles sw Kingsbridge pop 1,604
archd Totnes dioc Exeter

MALDEN parish 1676 Surrey 2-1/2 miles nw Ewell pop 209 archd
Surrey dioc Winchester

MALDON borough, port, market town Essex 10 miles e Chelmsford
pop 3,831 sep juris comp parishes of All Saints 1556, St Peter
1558, St Mary 1558 archd Essex dioc London and pec Dean and
Chapter of Westminster Soc of Friends, Indep, Wesl Meth

MALHAM township parish Kirkby in Malham Dale W R York pop
259 Wesl Meth

MALHAM MOOR township parish Kirkby in Malham Dale W R York
pop 94

MALLERSTANG chapelry 1714 parish Kirkby Stephen Westm pop 256

MALLING, EAST parish 1570 Kent 4-3/4 miles nw Maidstone pop
1,542 pec Archbishop of Canterbury

MALLING, SOUTH parish 1629 Sussex 1 mile n Lewes pop 705 pec

Archbishop of Canterbury

MALLING, WEST parish 1698 Kent 5-3/4 miles nw Maidstone pop 1,369 archd and dioc Rochester

MALMESBURY borough, market town 1590 Wilts 42 miles n Salisbury pop 2,293 sep juris archd Wilts dioc Salisbury Bapt, Indep, Moravians, Wesl Meth

MALPAS parish 1561 Ches 15 miles se Chester comp chapelry Iscoed, townships Agden, Bickerton, Bickley, Bradley, Broxton, Buckley or Bulkeley, Chidlow, Cholmondeley, Chorlton, Duckington, Edge, Egerton, Hampton, Larkton, Macefen Malpas, Newton juxta Malpas, Oldcastle, Overton, Stockton, Tuchingham with Grindley, Wichalgh, Wigland, Cuddington pop 5,127 archd and dioc Chester Bapt, Indep, Wesl Meth

MALPAS parish 1733 co Monmouth 2 miles nw Neport pop 211 archd and dioc Llandaff

MALSWICK tything parish Newent Gloucs pop 225

MALTBY chapelry parish Raithby Lincs

MALTBY township parish Stainton N R York pop 168

MALTBY parish 1597 W R York 4-1/2 miles sw Tickhill comp townships Hooton Levet, Maltby pop 844 archd and dioc York

MALTBY LE MARSH parish 1644 Lincs 3 miles ne Alford pop 209 archd and dioc Lincoln

MALTON, NEW market town 1570 borough W R York 18 miles ne York pop 4,173 archd Cleveland dioc York Bapt, Soc of Friends, Indep, Meth, Unit

MALTON, OLD parish 1606 N R York 1 mile ne New Malton pop 1,204 archd Cleveland dioc York Wesl Meth

MALVERN GREAT parish 1556 Worcs 8 miles w Worcester pop 2,140 archd and dioc Worcester Meth

MALVERN LITTLE parish 1691 Worcs 5-1/2 miles nw Upton upon Severn pop 88 archd and dioc Worcester Roman Cath

MAMBLE parish 1590 Worcs 6 miles sw Bewdley pop 355 archd Salop dioc Hereford

MAMHEAD parish 1556 Devon 4-3/4 miles ne Chudleigh pop 320 archd and dioc Exeter

MAMILAD parish 1682 co Monmouth 5 miles ne Usk pop 237 archd and dioc Llandaff

MAMHOLE hamlet parish Bedwelty co Monmouth pop 3,208

MAN, ISLE OF island annexed to British dominions sep juris pop 40,985 comp 17 parishes towns Castleton, Douglas, Peel, Ramsey, Castleton, parish Kirk Malen considered capital 9-1/2 miles sw Douglas or Kirk Bradan Wesl Meth, Prim Meth, Roman Cath, Indep

MANACCAN or MONATHON parish 1615 Cornwall 9 miles sw Falmouth pop 654 archd Cornwall dioc Exeter Calvinistic Dissenters

MANATON parish 1653 Devon 6 miles s Moreton pop 435 archd Totnes dioc Exeter

MANBY parish 1679 Lincs 5-3/4 miles se Louth pop 207 archd and dioc Lincoln Wesl Meth

MANBY hamlet parish Broughton Lincs

MANCETTER parish Cathedral 1576 Warws 1-1/4 miles se Atherstone comp market town Atherstone, hamlets Hartshill, Oldbury pop 5,200 archd Coventry dioc Lichfield

MANCHESTER parish 1573 Lancs borough 36 miles ne Liverpool comp market town Manchester, chapelries Ardwick, Blackley, Cheetham, Chorlton cum Hardy, Denton, Didsbury, Gorton, Heaton Norris, Newton, Salford, Stretford, townships Beswick, Bradford, Broughton, Burnage, Chorlton, Row, Crumpsall, Droylesden, Failsworth, Harpurhey, Houghton, Hulme, Levenshulme, Moss Side, Moston, Openshaw, Reddish, Rushulme, Withington pop 270,961 archd and dioc Chester St Ann's 1736, Trinity Church, St Mary's 1756, St Paul's 1765, St John 1769, St James 1788, St Michael 1789, St Mark 1734, St Peter 1795, All Saints 1820, St Matthew 1825, St George 1798, St George Hulme 1828, St Andrew 1833, St Clement 1793, St Luke 1804 Bapt, Bible Christians, Soc of Friends, Indep, Welsh Indep, Indep Meth, Meth New Connection, Prim Tent, Wesl, Welsh Meth, Presb, Swedenborgians, Unit, Roman Cath

MANEA chapelry 1708 parish Coveney Cambs pop 822 Wesl Meth

MANEWDEN parish 1561 Essex 2-1/2 miles nw Stansted Mountfitchet pop 695 archd Colchester dioc London

MANFIELD parish 1594 N R York 4-3/4 miles sw Darlington pop 491 archd Richmond dioc Chester

MANGERSBURY hamlet parish Stow on the Wold Gloucs pop 370

MANGOTSFIELD parish 1570 Gloucs 5-1/4 miles ne Bristol pop 3,508 juris Consistory Court Bishop of Bristol Indep, other dissenters

MANLEY township parish Frodsham Ches pop 331

MANNINGFORD ABBOTS or ABBAS parish 1538 Wilts 1-3/4 miles sw Pewsey pop 165 archd Wilts dioc Salisbury

MANNINGFORD BOHUN tything parish Wilsford Wilts pop 242

MANNINGFORD BRUCE parish 1657 Wilts 2 miles sw Pewsey pop 261 archd Wilts dioc Salisbury

MANNINGHAM township parish Bradford W R York pop 3,564

MANNINGTON parish incl regs Itteringham Norfolk 4-3/4 miles nw Aylsham pop 13 archd and dioc Norwich

MANNINGTREE market town, parish 1695 Essex 36 miles ne Chelmsford pop 1,237 archd Colchester dioc London Bapt, Indep, Wesl Meth

MANSELL GAMAGE parish 1664 Herefs 8-1/2 miles nw Hereford pop 171 archd and dioc Hereford

MANSELL LACY parish 1714 Herefs 7 miles nw Hereford pop 318 archd and dioc Hereford

MANSERGH chapelry parish Kirkby Lonsdale Westm pop 232

MANSFIELD market town, parish 1559 Notts 14 miles nw Nottingham comp hamlets Pleasley Hill, Radmansthwaite, Moor Haigh pop

9,426 pec Lord of Manor of Mansfield Gen Bapt, Soc of Friends, Indep, Prim and Wesl Meth, Unit

MANSFIELD WOODHOUSE parish 1653 Notts 1-3/4 miles n Mansfield pop 1,859 pec of Lord of Manor of Mansfield Indep, Wesl Meth

MANSRIGGS township parish Ulverstone Lancs pop 69

MANSTON parish 1620 Dorset 6 miles sw Shaftesbury pop 149 archd Dorset dioc Bristol

MANTHORP township parish Grantham Lincs

MANTHORPE hamlet parish Witham on the Hill Lincs pop 100

MANTON parish 1678 Lincs 5-1/4 miles sw Glandford Bridge comp township Leeatham, hamlet Twigmoor pop 150 archd Stow dioc Lincoln

MANTON parish 1573 co Rutland 3-1/4 miles ne Uppingham pop 229 archd Northampton dioc Peterborough

MANUDEN Essex See MANEWDEN

MAPERTON parish 1559 Somerset 3-1/4 miles sw Wincanton pop 187 archd Wells dioc Bath and Wells

MAPLEBECK parish 1562 Notts 5-3/4 miles se Southwell pop 181 archd Nottingham dioc York

MAPLEDERWELL parish 1618 Hamps 3-1/2 miles se Basingstoke pop 211 archd and dioc Winchester

MAPLE DURHAM parish 1627 co Oxford 4 miles nw Reading pop 536 archd and dioc Oxford

MAPLESCOMBE parish no regs now part of Kingsdown Kent

MAPLESTEAD, GREAT parish 1678 Essex 2-1/4 miles nw Halstead pop 446 archd Middlesex dioc London

MAPLESTEAD, LITTLE parish 1688 Essex 2-1/4 miles ne Halstead pop 373 Commissary of Essex and Herts, concurrently with Consistorial Court of Bishop of London

MAPPERLEY township parish Kirk Hallam Derbys pop 384

MAPPERTON parish 1669 Dorset 2-1/2 miles se Beaminster pop 112 pec Dean of Salisbury

MAPPERTON hamlet parish Almer Dorset

MAPPLETON parish 1704 Derbys 1-3/4 miles nw Ashbourn pop 180 archd Derby dioc Lichfield

MAPPLETON parish 1682 E R York 13-1/2 miles ne Beverley pop 327 archd East Riding dioc York

MAPPOWDER parish 1653 Dorset 6 miles sw Sturminster Newton pop 308 archd Dorset dioc Bristol

MARAZION market town, parish St Hilary Cornwall 63-1/2 miles sw Launceston pop 1,393 archd Cornwall dioc Exeter Bapt, Bryanites, Soc of Friends, Wesl Meth

MARBURY township parish Great Budworth Ches pop 26

MARBURY parish 1538 Ches 3-1/2 miles ne Whitchurch pop 811 archd and dioc Chester

MARCH market town chapelry 1558 parish Doddington 31 miles nw Cambridge Cambs pop 5,117

MARCHAM parish 1658 Berks 2-1/2 miles sw Abingdon pop 1,170

archd Berks dioc Salisbury Wesl Meth

MARCHINGTON chapelry 1612 parish Hanbury Staffs 4 miles se Uttoxeter pop 491

MARCHINTON WOODLANDS township parish Hanbury Staffs pop 193

MARCLE, LITTLE parish 1748 Herefs 3 miles sw Ledbury pop 143 archd and dioc Hereford

MARCLE, MUCH parish 1556 Herefs 5 miles sw Ledbury pop 1,212 archd and dioc Hereford

MARDALE chapelry 1684 parishes Bampton and Shap Westm 11 miles nw Orton pop 49

MARDEN parish 1616 Herefs 5-1/2 miles ne Hereford pop 921 Consistory Court of Dean of Hereford

MARDEN parish 1559 Kent 4-3/4 miles ne Goodhurst pop 2,109 archd and dioc Canterbury Indep

MARDEN parish 1685 Wilts 5-1/2 miles ne East Lavington pop 205 archd and dioc Salisbury

MARDEN, EAST parish 1691 Sussex 8 miles sw Midhurst pop 48 archd and dioc Chichester

MARDEN, NORTH parish 1813 Sussex 7 miles sw Midhurst pop 32 archd and dioc Chichester

MARDEN, UP parish 1714 Sussex 9 miles sw Midhurst pop 364 archd and dioc Chichester

MARFIELD township parish Tilton Leics pop 22

MAREHAM LE FEN parish 1562 Lincs 5-1/2 miles se Horncastle pop 625 archd and dioc Lincoln Wesl Meth

MAREHAM ON THE HILL parish 1715 Lincs 2 miles se Horncastle pop 193 archd and dioc Lincoln

MARESFIELD parish 1538 Sussex 2-1/4 miles nw Uckfield pop 1,650 archd Lewes dioc Chichester

MARFLEET parish 1713 E R York 3 miles e Kingston upon Hill pop 130 archd East Riding dioc York Wesl Meth

MARGARET, ST or STREET hamlet parish Ivinghoe Bucks pop 447

MARGARET, ST parish 1697 Herts 1-1/2 miles ne Hoddesdon pop 107 archd Middlesex dioc London

MARGARET'S ST parish 1702 Herefs 13 miles sw Hereford pop 313 archd and dioc St David

MARGARET ST at CLIFFE parish 1558 Kent 3-1/2 miles ne Dover pop 712 pec Archbishop of Canterbury

MARGARET MARSH parish 1682 Dorset 4 miles sw Shaftesbury pop 86 archd Dorset dioc Bristol

MARGARET ROOTHING Essex See ROOTHING, MARGARET

MARGARETTING parish 1628 Essex 1 mile ne Ingatestone pop 545 archd Essex dioc London

MARGATE seaport, market town, parish 1559 Kent 44 miles ne Maidstone pop 10,339 archd and dioc Canterbury Soc of Friends

MARHAM parish 1562 Norfolk 7-1/2 miles nw Swaffham pop 799 archd Norfolk dioc Norwich

MARHAM CHURCH parish 1558 Cornwall 2 miles sw Stratton pop

659 archd Cornwall dioc Exeter

MARHOLM parish 1566 co Northampton 4-1/2 miles nw Peterborough pop 174 archd Northampton dioc Peterborough

MARI ANSLEIGH parish 1727 Devon 3-1/2 miles se South Molton pop 282 archd Barnstaple dioc Exeter

MARK parish 1647 Somerset 6-1/2 miles sw Axbridge pop 1,289 pec Consistorial Decanal Court of Wells Wesl Meth

MARK EATON township parish Mackworth Derbys pop 233

MARKBY parish 1558 Lincs 2-3/4 miles ne Alford pop 94 archd and dioc Lincoln

MARKET BOSWORTH Leics See BOSWORTH, MARKET

MARKET STREET chapelry within parishes Caddington, Flamstead, Studham Beds Bapt, Wesl Meth

MARKET STREET township parish Wymondham Norfolk pop 1,485

MARKFIELD parish 1571 Leics 7 miles nw Leicester pop 1,088 archd Leicester dioc Lincoln

MARKHAM, EAST parish 1561 Notts 1-1/2 miles n Tuxford pop 805 archd Nottingham dioc York Wesl Meth

MARKHAM, WEST or CLINTON parish 1651 Notts 1-3/4 miles nw Tuxford pop 197 archd Notthingham dioc York

MARKINGTON township parish Ripon W R York pop 487

MARKSBURY parish 1563 Somerset 3-1/2 miles se Pensford pop 371 archd Wells dioc Bath and Wells

MARKSHALL parish 1585 Essex 2 miles nw Great Coggeshall pop 52 archd Colchester dioc London

MARKS TEY Essex See TEY MARKS

MARLAND, PETER'S parish 1696 Devon 4-1/2 miles sw Great Torrington pop 356 archd Barnstaple dioc Exeter

MARLBOROUGH borough, market town Wilts 27 miles ne Salisbury pop 3,426 sep juris comp parishes St Mary 1602, St Peter 1611, St Paul 1611 pec Consistorial Episcopal Court of Salisbury Huntingtonians, Indep, Wesl Meth

MARLCLIFT hamlet parish Bidford Warws

MARLDON parish 1598 Devon 5 miles ne Totnes pop 438 pec Bishop of Exeter

MARLESFORD parish 1661 Suffolk 2 miles ne Wickham Market pop 433 archd Suffolk dioc Norwich

MARLINGFORD parish 1558 Norfolk 5 miles ne Wymondham pop 174 archd Norfolk dioc Norwich

MARLOW township parish Leintwardine Herefs pop 60

MARLOW, GREAT borough, market town, parish 1592 Bucks 35-1/2 miles se Buckingham pop 4,237 archd Buckingham dioc Lincoln Indep, Wesl Meth

MARLOW, LITTLE parish 1559 Bucks 1-1/2 miles ne Great Marlow pop 783 archd Buckingham dioc Lincoln

MARLSTON township parish St Mary Chester Ches pop 130

MARNHAM parish 1601 Notts 4-3/4 miles se Tuxford pop 376 archd Nottingham dioc York

MARNHULL parish 1560 Dorset 6 miles sw Shaftesbury pop 1,309 archd Dorset dioc Bristol Wesl Meth

MARPLE chapelry 1655 parish Stockport Ches pop 2,678 Indep, Wesl Meth

MARR parish 1729 W R York 4 miles nw Doncaster pop 221 archd and dioc York

MARRICK parish 1687 N R York 7-1/2 miles sw Richmond pop 659 archd Richmond dioc Chester

MARRISHES township parish Pickering N R York pop 207

MARSDEN chapelry parishes Huddersfield and Almondbury 1776 W R York pop 2,340 archd and dioc York Indep, Wesl Meth

MARSDEN, GREAT chapelry parish Whalley Lancs pop 1,971

MARSDEN, LITTLE township parish Whalley Lancs pop 2,742

MARSH, CHAPEL parish 1590 Lincs 9 miles ne Louth pop 477 archd and dioc Lincoln Wesl Meth

MARSH GIBBON parish 1577 Bucks 4-1/2 miles ne Bicester pop 812 archd Buckingham dioc Lincoln Wesl Meth

MARSHALL, RED Durham See RED MARSHALL

MARSHAM parish 1538 Norfolk 2 miles s Aylsham pop 692 archd and dioc Norwich

MARSHFIELD market town parish 1562 Gloucs 11-1/2 miles e Bristol pop 1,651 archd and dioc Gloucester Unit

MARSHFIELD parish 1656 co Monmouth 5 miles sw Newport pop 458 archd and dioc Llandaff

MARSHWOOD chapelry 1614 parish Whitchurch Canonicorum Dorset 4-1/4 miles sw Beaminster pop 536

MARSK parish 1569 N R York 5 miles ne Guilsbrough comp townships Marks, Redear pop 1,302 archd Cleveland dioc York Wesl Meth

MARSKE parish 1594 N R York 4-3/4 miles w Richmond pop 290 archd Cleveland dioc York

MARSTON township parish Great Budworth Ches pop 465

MARSTON parish 1707 Lincs 5 miles nw Grantham pop 419 archd and dioc Lincoln

MARSTON, ST LAWRENCE parish 1653 co Northampton 5-3/4 miles nw Brackley pop 440 archd Northampton dioc Peterborough

MARSTON parish 1654 co Oxford 1-3/4 miles ne Oxford pop 364 archd and dioc Oxford

MARSTON township parish Church Eaton Staffs

MARSTON chapelry 1556 parish St Mary Stafford Staffs 2-3/4 miles Stafford pop 119

MARSTON quarter parish Church Bickenhill Warws

MARSTON hamlet parish Wolstan Warws

MARSTON tything parish Potterne Wilts pop 175

MARSTON chapelry 1767 parish Yardley Worcs

MARSTON township parish Ripon W R York pop 202

MARSTON BIGOTT parish 1654 Somerset 2-3/4 miles sw Frome pop 485 archd Wells dioc Bath and Wells

MARSTON, BUTLERS parish 1538 Warws 1-1/2 miles sw Kington

pop 332 archd and dioc Worcester

MARSTON FLEET parish 1630 Bucks 3 miles nw Aylesbury pop 41 archd Buckingham dioc Lincoln

MARSTON JABBETT hamlet parish Bulkington Warws

MARSTON, LEA Warws See LEA MARSTON

MARSTON, LONG chapelry parish Tring Herts

MARSTON, LONG 1648 E R York 6 miles ne Tadcaster comp townships Angram, Hutton, Long Marston pop 584 archd and dioc York

MARSTON, MAGNA parish 1566 Somerset 5-1/4 miles ne Yeovil pop 346 archd Wells dioc Bath and Wells

MARSTON MAISEY or MEYSEY parish 1742 Wilts 3-1/2 miles ne Cricklade pop 240 archd and dioc Gloucester

MARSTON MONTGOMERY parish 1660 Derbys 6-3/4 miles sw Ashbourn pop 457 archd Derby dioc Lichfield

MARSTON MORETAINE or MORTEYNE parish 1703 Beds 4 miles nw Ampthill pop 1,007 archd Bedford dioc Lincoln Wesl Meth

MARSTON, NORTH parish 1724 Bucks 3 miles se Winslow pop 606 archd Buckingham dioc Lincoln

MARSTON, POTTER'S chapelry parish Barwell Leics pop 11

MARSTON, PRIOR'S parish 1689 Warws 5-1/2 miles se Southam pop 655 archd Coventry dioc Lichfield

MARSTON SICCA parish 1680 Gloucs 6-1/2 miles n Chipping Campden pop 264 archd and dioc Gloucester

MARSTON, SOUTH chapelry 1539 parish Highworth 2-1/2 miles sw Highworth Wilts pop 339

MARSTON STANNETT chapelry parish Pencombe Herefs

MARSTON TRUSSEL parish 1561 co Northampton 3-1/4 miles sw Market Harborough pop 223 archd Northampton dioc Peterborough

MARSTON UPON DOVE parish 1654 Derbys 5 miles nw Burton upon Trent pop 985 archd Derby dioc Lichfield

MARSTOW parish 1707 Herefs 5 miles sw Ross pop 125 archd and dioc Hereford

MARSWORTH parish 1720 Bucks 2-1/4 miles sw Ivinghoe pop 427 archd Buckingham dioc Lincoln

MARTALL township parish Rosthern Ches pop 281

MARTHA, ST Sussex See CHILWORTH

MARTHAM parish 1558 Norfolk 6-3/4 miles nw Caistor pop 895 pec Dean and Chapter of Norwich Bapt, Wesl Meth

MARTIN parish 1562 Lincs 2-1/2 miles sw Horncastle pop 60 archd and dioc Lincoln

MARTIN parish 1590 Wilts 4-1/2 miles ne Cranbourne archd and dioc Salisbury

MARTIN hamlet parish Timberland Lincs pop 640

MARTIN or MARTON IN CRAVEN 1548 W R York 5-1/2 miles sw Skipton pop 443 archd York dioc York

MARTIN, ST parish 1653 Cornwall 1-1/4 miles n East Looe pop 1,320 archd Cornwall dioc Exeter Wesl Meth

MARTIN, ST parish 1601 Shrops 5-1/2 miles nw Ellesmere pop 2,099 archd and dioc St Asaph

MARTIN, ST township parish Catterick N R York

MARTIN, ST in MENEAGE parish 1571 Cornwall 6-3/4 miles se Helston archd Cornwall dioc Exeter Wesl Meth

MARTIN'S ST STAMFORD BARON parish 1572 co Northampton 1/2 mile se Stamford pop 1,270 archd Northampton dioc Peterborough

MARTIN HUSSINGTREE parish 1538 Worcs 3 miles sw Droitwich pop 208 archd and dioc Worcester

MARTIN, STOWE chapelry parish Tamerton Foliatt Devon

MARTINDALE chapelry 1633 parish Barton Westm 9-1/2 miles ne Ambegside pop 182

MARTINHOE parish 1632 Devon 14 miles ne Barnstaple pop 235 archd Barnstaple dioc Exeter

MARTINSCROFT township parish Warrington Lancs

MARTINSTHORPE parish no regs co Rutland 3-1/2 miles n Uppingham pop 2 archd Northampton dioc Peterborough

MARTLESHAM parish 1653 Suffolk 2 miles sw Woodbridge pop 440 archd Suffolk dioc Norwich

MARTLEY parish 1625 Worcs 7 miles nw Worcester pop 1,395 archd and dioc Worcester

MARTOCK parish 1558 Somerset 4-1/2 miles sw Ilchester pop 2,841 archd Wells dioc Bath and Wells Indep

MARTON township parish Whitegate Ches pop 711

MARTON chapelry 1563 parish Prestbury Ches pop 354

MARTON chapelry parish Poulton Lancs pop 1,487

MARTON parish 1651 Lincs 5-3/4 miles se Gainsborough pop 494 archd Stow dioc Lincoln Wesl Meth

MARTON parish 1660 Warws 4-3/4 miles nw Southam pop 311 archd and dioc Worcester

MARTON township parish Bridlington E R York

MARTON township parish Swine E R Yock pop 125 Roman Cath

MARTON in CLEVELAND parish 1572 N R York 6 miles n Stokesley pop 397 archd Cleveland dioc York

MARTON township parish Sinnington N R York pop 231

MARTON parish 1648 W R York 3 miles s Aldborough pop 482 archd Richmond dioc Chester

MARTON IN CRAVEN York See MARTIN IN CRAVEN

MARTON IN THE FOREST parish 1539 N R York 5-3/4 miles se Easingwould pop 565 archd Cleveland dioc York

MARTON LE MOOR chapelry parish Topcliffe N R York pop 209

MARTON, LONG parish 1586 Westm 4 miles nw Appleby pop 819 archd and dioc Carlisle Wesl Meth

MARTYR WORTHY Hamps See WORTHY, MARTYR

MARWELL or MEREWELL hamlet parish Carisbrooke Hamps

MARWOOD parish 1602 Devon 4 miles nw Barnstaple pop 944 archd Barnstaple dioc Exeter

MARWOOD township parish Gainford co Durham pop 200

MARY, ST CHURCH parish 1641 Devon 2 miles nw Torbay pop 1,204 archd Totnes dioc Exeter

MARY ST EXTRA or WESTON parish 1681 Hamps by town of Southampton pop 1,068 pec Bishop of Winchester

MARY ST IN ARDEN parish no regs co Northampton 1 mile e Market Harborough archd Leicester dioc Lincoln

MARY ST IN THE MARSH chapelry parish Newton Cambs

MARY LE BONE, ST parish 1679 borough Middlesex pop 122,206 archd Middlesex dioc London comp St Mary 1823, All Saints 1823, Christchurch 1824, Holy Trinity 1827 Bapt, Indep, Wesl and Calvinistic Meth, Seceders from Scottish Church, Greek Church, French and Spanish Roman Cath

MARY'S ST parish 1675 Kent 2-1/4 miles n New Romney pop 111 archd and dioc Canterbury

MARYPORT chapelry 1760 parish Cross Cannonby Cumberland 30 miles sw Carlisle pop 3,877 Bapt, Burghers, Soc of Friends, Presb, Wesl Meth

MARY STOW parish 1654 Devon 6-1/2 miles nw Tavistock pop 508 archd Totnes dioc Exeter

MASHAM parish 1599 N R York 34 miles nw York comp market town Masham, townships Burton upon Ure, Ellingstring, Ellingtons, Fearby, Healey with Sutton, Ilton with Pott, Swinton with Warthermask pop 2,995 pec of Masham or Dean and Chapter of York Bapt, Soc of Friends, Wesl Meth

MASHBURY parish 1539 Essex 6 miles nw Chelmsford pop 86 archd Middlesex dioc London

MASON township parish Ponteland Northumberland pop 134

MASSINGHAM, GREAT parish 1564 Norfolk 9-1/2 miles nw Swaffham pop 850 archd and dioc Norwich

MASSINGHAM, LITTLE parish 1558 Norfolk 10-1/2 miles nw Swaffham pop 165 archd and dioc Norwich

MATCHING parish 1558 Essex 3-1/4 miles ne Harlow pop 621 Commissary of Essex and Herts, concurrently with Consistorial Court of Bishop of London

MATFEN, EAST township parish Stamfordham Northumberland pop 139

MAFTEN, WEST township parish Stamfordham Northumberland pop 319

MATHERN parish 1565 co Monmouth 3-1/4 miles sw Chepstow pop 412 archd and dioc Llandaff

MATHON parish 1631 Worcs 7 miles ne Ledbury pop 690 archd and dioc Worcester

MATLASK parish 1558 Norfolk 6 miles se Holt pop 218 archd Norfolk dioc Norwich

MATLEY township parish Mottram in Longden Dale Ches pop 262

MATLOCK parish 1637 Derbys 17-1/2 miles nw Derby pop 3,262 archd Derby dioc Lichfield Indep

MATSON parish 1553 Gloucs 2 miles se Gloucester pop 55 archd and dioc Gloucester

MATTERDALE chapelry 1645 parish Greystock Cumberland pop 325

MATTERSEY parish 1542 Notts 3-1/2 miles se Bawtry pop 455 archd Nottingham dioc York Wesl Meth

MATTINGLEY chapelry parish Heckfield Hamps pop 266

MATTISHALL parish 1656 Norfolk 5 miles se East Dereham archd Norfolk dioc Norwich Wesl Meth

MATTISHALL, BURCH Norfolk See BURGH MATTISHALL

MATTISHALL HEATH Norfolk See MARKSHALL

MAUGHAN'S ST parish 1733 co Monmouth 6 miles nw Monmouth pop 172 archd and dioc Llandaff

MAULDEN parish 1558 Beds 1-1/2 miles e Ampthill pop 1,231 archd Bedford dioc Lincoln Bapt

MAUNBY township parish Kirby Wisk N R York pop 231

MAUTBY parish 1663 Norfolk 2-3/4 miles nw Caistor pop 61 archd and dioc Norwich

MAWDESLEY township parish Croston Lancs pop 886

MAWES, ST sea port, market town, parish St Just in Roseland Cornwall 3 miles e Falmouth Indep, Wesl Meth

MAWGAN IN MENEAGE parish 1559 Cornwall 4 miles se Helston pop 1,094 archd Cornwall dioc Exeter Bapt, Wesl Meth

MAWGAN IN PYDER parish 1686 Cornwall 3 miles nw St Columb Major pop 745 archd Cornwall dioc Exeter Wesl Meth

MAWNAN parish 1553 Cornwall 5 miles sw Falmouth pop 578 archd Cornwall dioc Exeter Bapt, Wesl Meth

MAWTHORPE township parish Well Lincs

MAXEY parish 1538 co Northampton 1-3/4 miles sw Market Deeping pop 576 archd Northampton dioc Peterborough

MAXSTOKE parish 1653 Warws 2-3/4 miles se Coleshill pop 352 archd Coventry dioc Lichfield

MAYFIELD parish 1576 Staffs 2-1/4 miles sw Ashbourn comp chapelry Butterton, Calton, townships Mayfield, Woodhouses pop 1,366 archd Stafford dioc Lichfield Wesl Meth

MAYFIELD parish 1570 Sussex 5-1/2 miles sw Wadhurst pop 2,738 pec of Archbishop of Canterbury Wesl Meth

MAYLAND parish 1748 Essex 4-1/4 miles sw Burnham pop 226 Commissary of Essex and Herts, concurrently with Consistorial Court of Bishop of London

MEABURN, KING'S township parish Morland Westm pop 203

MEALRIGG township parish Bromfield Cumberland

MEARE parish 1560 Somerset 3-1/4 miles nw Glastonbury pop 1,296 archd Wells dioc Bath and Wells

MEARLEY township parish Whalley Lancs pop 63

MEASAND hamlet parish Bampton Westm

MEASHAM parish 1681 Leics 3-3/4 miles sw Ashby de la Zouch pop 1,535 archd Derby dioc Lichfield Wesl Meth

MEAVY parish 1659 Devon 6-1/4 miles se Tavistock pop 336 archd

Totnes dioc Exeter

MEDBOURNE parish 1588 Leics 5 miles nw Rockingham pop 513 archd Leicester dioc Lincoln Wesl Meth

MEDLAR township parish Kirkham Lancs pop 242

MEDMENHAM parish 1654 Bucks 3 miles sw Great Marlow pop 384 archd Buckingham dioc Lincoln

MEDOMSLEY chapelry 1608 parish Lanchester co Durham pop 466

MEDSTED parish 1560 Hamps 3-3/4 miles sw Alton pop 418 pec of incumbent

MEER Lincs See WADDINGTON

MEER township parish Forton Staffs

MEERBROOK chapelry 1738 parish Leek Staffs

MEESDEN parish 1737 Herts 4-1/2 miles se Barkway pop 158 archd Middlesex dioc London

MEESON township parish Great Bolas Shrops

MEETH parish 1752 Devon 3 miles ne Hatherleigh pop 298 archd Barnstaple dioc Exeter

MELAY township parish Aspatria Cumberland

MELBECKS township parish Grinton N R York pop 1,455

MELBOURNE parish 1558 Cambs 3-3/4 miles ne Royston pop 1,474 archd and dioc Ely Bapt, Indep

MELBOURN parish 1653 Derbys 6 miles ne Ashby de la Zouch pop 2,301 archd Derby dioc Lichfield Gen Bapt, Indep, Wesl Meth

MELBOURN township parish Thornton E R York pop 463 Wesl Meth

MELBURY ABBAS parish 1716 Dorset 2-1/2 miles se Shaftesbury pop 354 archd Dorset dioc Bristol

MELBURY BUBB parish 1678 Dorset 9-1/4 miles sw Sherborne pop 121 archd Dorset dioc Bristol

MELBURY OSMOND parish 1580 Dorset 8-3/4 miles sw Sherborne pop 319 archd Dorset dioc Bristol

MELBURY SAMPFORD parish 1606 Dorset 7-1/2 miles ne Beaminster pop 53 archd Dorset dioc Bristol

MELCHBOURN parish 1706 Beds 5-1/4 miles se Higham Ferrers pop 227 archd Bedford dioc Lincoln

MELCHET PARK extra parochial liberty Wilts 9-1/2 miles se Salisborn pop 27

MELCOMBE HORSEY parish 1690 Dorset 8-1/2 miles sw Blandford Forum pop 172 archd Dorset dioc Bristol

MELCOMBE REGIS Dorset See WEYMOUTH

MELDON parish 1706 Northumberland 6-1/2 miles sw Morpeth pop 114 archd Northumberland dioc Durham

MELDRETH parish 1681 Cambs 5-1/4 miles ne Royston pop 643 archd and dioc Ely

MELFORD, LONG parish 1559 Suffolk 22 miles w Ipswich archd Sudbury dioc Norwich Indep, Wesl Meth

MELKRIDGE township parish Haltwhistle Northumberland pop 347

MELKSHAM market town, parish 1568 Wilts 28 miles nw Salisbury pop 5,866 archd and dioc Salisbury Bapt, Soc of Friends, Indep,

Wesl Meth

MELLING parish 1626 Lancs 6 miles sw Kirby Lonsdale comp chapelries Arkholme, Hornby, townships Farleton, Melling with Wratton, Roburndale, Wennington, Wray, hamlet Cawood pop 1,962 archd Richmond dioc Chester

MELLING chapelry parish Halsall 1680 Lancs pop 559

MELLION, ST parish 1558 Cornwall 3-1/4 miles se Callington pop 330 archd Cornwall dioc Exeter

MELLIS parish 1559 Suffolk 4 miles nw Eye pop 513 archd Sudbury dioc Norwich Wesl Meth

MELLONS, ST parish 1722 co Monmouth 3-1/2 miles ne Cardiff pop 564 archd and dioc Llandaff

MELLOR chapelry parish Glossop 1624 Derby 8-1/4 miles nw Chapel en le Frith pop 2,059 Wesl Meth

MELLOR chapelry parish Blackburn Lancs pop 2,071

MELLS parish 1567 Somerset 3 miles nw Frome pop 1,259 archd Wells dioc Bath and Wells

MELLS hamlet parish Wenhaston Suffolk

MELMERBY parish 1701 Cumberland 8-1/2 miles ne Penrith pop 286 archd and dioc Carlisle

MELMERBY chapelry parish Wath N R York pop 338

MELMERBY township parish Coverham N R York pop 127

MELPLASH tything parish Netherbury Dorset

MELSONBY parish 1573 E R York 5 miles ne Richmond pop 514 archd Richmond dioc Chester

MELTHAM chapelry parish Almondbury 1669 W R York pop 2,746 Bapt, Wesl Meth

MELTHWAITE township parish Ireton Cumberland

MELTON parish 1691 Suffolk 2-1/4 miles ne Woodbridge pop 707 archd Suffolk dioc Norwich

MELTON chapelry parish Welton E R York pop 133

MELTON CONSTABLE parish 1561 Norfolk 5-1/2 miles sw Holt pop 114 archd and dioc Norwich

MELTON, GREAT parish 1558 Norfolk 5-3/4 miles sw Norwich pop 406 archd Norfolk dioc Norwich

MELTON, HIGH parish 1538 W R York 4-3/4 miles sw Doncaster pop 131 archd and dioc York Indep

MELTON, LITTLE parish 1734 Norfolk 5-1/4 miles sw Norwich pop 292 archd Norfolk dioc Norwich

MELTON MOWBRAY market town, parish 1547 Leics 15 miles ne Leicester pop 3,520 archd Leicester dioc Lincoln Indep, Wesl Meth

MELTON ROSS parish 1568 Lincs 5-1/2 miles ne Glandford Bridge pop 158 pec of Dean and Chapter of Lincoln

MELTONBY township parish Pocklington E R York pop 60

MELVERLEY parish 1723 Shrops 11 miles nw Shrewsbury pop 216 archd and dioc St Asaph

MEMBURY parish 1637 Devon 3-1/2 miles nw Axminster pop 870

archd and dioc Exeter

MENDHAM parish 1678 Suffolk 1-1/2 miles se Harleston pop 881
archd Suffolk dioc Norwich Wesl Meth

MENDLESHAM parish 1558 Suffolk 15-1/2 miles nw Ipswich pop
1,233 archd Sudbury dioc Norwich Wesl Meth

MENETHORPE township parish Westow E R York pop 126

MENHENIOT parish 1554 Cornwall 2-1/2 miles se Liskeard pop
1,253 archd Cornwall dioc Exeter

MENSTONE township parish Otley W R York pop 346

MENTHORP township parish Hemingbrough E R York pop 59

MENTMORE parish 1685 Bucks 4 miles nw Ivinghoe comp township
Mentmore, hamlet Ledburn pop 329 archd Buckingham dioc Lincoln

MENWITH township parish Hampsthwaite W R York pop 742

MEOLE BRACE Shrops See BRACE MEOLE

MEOLS, NORTH parish 1594 Lancs 9-1/2 miles nw Ormskirk pop
5,132 archd and dioc Chester Indep

MEOLSE, GREAT township parish West Kirby Ches pop 198

MEOLSE, LITTLE township parish West Kirby Ches pop 126

MEON, EAST parish 1560 Hamps 4-1/2 miles sw Petersfield comp
hamlet Westbury, tythings Bordean, Coombe, East Meon, Langrish,
Riplington pop 1,681 pec of Bishop of Winchester

MEON STOKE parish 1599 Hamps 4 miles ne Bishop's Waltham pop
382 pec of Incumbent

MEON, WEST parish 1538 Hamps 7-1/2 miles ne Bishop's Waltham
pop 711 archd and dioc Winchester Indep

MEOPHAM parish 1573 Kent 7-1/2 miles sw Rochester pop 911 pec
of Archbishop of Canterbury

MEPAL parish 1659 Cambs 8 miles nw Ely pop 433 pec of Bishop of
Ely

MEPPERSHALL parish 1653 Beds 1-3/4 miles s Shefford pop 444
archd Bedford dioc Lincoln

MERCASTON township parish Mugginton Derbys pop 163

MERE township parish Rosthern Ches pop 552

MERE parish 1561 Wilts 21-1/2 miles nw Salisbury comp market
town Mere, tythings Woodlands with Chaddenwicke, Zeals pop
2,708 pec juris and patronage of Dean of Salisbury Indep

MEREVALE parish 1727 Warws 1-1/2 miles sw Atherstone pop 246
pec of Manorial Court of Merevale

MEREWORTH parish 1560 Kent 5 miles se Wrotham pop 782 archd
and dioc Rochester

MERIDEN parish 1646 Warws 6-1/4 miles nw Coventry pop 892
archd Coventry dioc Lichfield

MERING extra parochial liberty Notts 8 miles ne Newark pop 4

MERKSHALL or MATTISHALL HEATH parish no regs Norfolk 3-1/2
miles s Norwich archd Norfolk dioc Norwich

MERRINGTON KIRK parish 1578 co Durham 3-3/4 miles ne Bishop
Auckland comp townships Chilton, Ferry Hill, Hett, Merrington

pop 1,325 archd and dioc Durham

MERRINGTON township parish Preston Gubbals Shrops

MERRIOTT parish 1646 Somerset 2 miles n Crewkerne pop 1,405 archd Taunton dioc Bath and Wells

MERROW parish 1538 Surrey 2 miles ne Guildford pop 249 archd Surrey dioc Winchester

MERRYN, ST parish 1688 Cornwall 2-1/4 miles sw Padstowe pop 576 pec of Bishop of Exeter

MERSEA, EAST parish 1720 Essex 9 miles se Colchester pop 300 archd Colchester dioc London

MERSEA, WEST parish 1625 Essex 9 miles s Colchester pop 847 archd Colchester dioc London Bapt

MERSHAM parish 1558 Kent 3-3/4 miles se Ashford pop 677 archd and dioc Canterbury Wesl Meth

MERSTHAM parish 1538 Surrey 3/4 mile ne Gatton pec of Archbishop of Canterbury

MERSTON parish no regs Kent 4-1/4 miles se Gravesend archd and dioc Canterbury

MERSTON parish 1751 Sussex 3 miles se Chichester pop 129 archd and dioc Chichester

MERTHER parish 1658 Cornwall 5 miles w Tregoney pop 411 archd Cornwall dioc Exeter Wesl Meth

MERTON parish 1687 Devon 5-3/4 miles nw Hatherleigh pop 740 archd Barnstaple dioc Exeter

MERTON parish 1566 Norfolk 2-1/4 miles sw Watton pop 126 archd and dioc Norwich

MERTON parish 1635 co Oxford 4 miles sw Bicester pop 234 archd and dioc Oxford

MERTON parish 1559 Surrey 9 miles sw London pop 1,447 archd Surrey dioc Winchester Indep

MESHAW parish 1581 Devon 5-1/4 miles se South Molton pop 166 archd Barnstaple dioc Exeter

MESSING parish 1538 Essex 5-1/2 miles se Great Coggeshall pop 775 archd Colchester dioc London

MESSINGHAM parish 1562 Lincs 7-1/2 miles sw Glandford Bridge pop 1,250 archd Stow dioc Lincoln Wesl Meth

METFIELD parish 1559 Suffolk 3-3/4 miles se Harleston pop 733 archd Suffolk dioc Norwich

METHAM township parish Howden E R York pop 35

METHERINGHAM parish 1538 Lincs 10-1/2 miles n Sleaford pop 880 archd and dioc Lincoln Wesl Meth

METHLEY parish 1560 W R York 5-1/2 miles ne Wakefield pop 1,593 archd and dioc York Wesl Meth

METHOP township parish Beetham Westm pop 86

METHWOLD parish 1685 Norfolk 4 miles se Stoke Ferry pop 1,266 archd Norfolk dioc Norwich Wesl Meth

METTINGHAM parish 1664 Suffolk 2 miles e Bungay pop 406 archd Suffolk dioc Norwich

METTON parish 1738 Norfolk 3-1/4 miles sw Cromer pop 81 archd Norfolk dioc Norwich

MEUX township parish Waghen or Wawn E R York pop 83

MEVAGISSEY parish 1598 Cornwall 6 miles se Grampound pop 2,169 archd Cornwall dioc Exeter Wesl Meth

MEWAN, ST parish 1693 Cornwall 1 mile sw St Austell pop 1,306 archd Cornwall dioc Exeter

MEXBOROUGH parish 1562 W R York 6-1/4 miles ne Rotherham comp townships Dennaby, Mexborough pop 1,270 pec of Archdeacon of York

MICHAEL, ST or MIDSHALL market town parishes St Enoder and Newlyn Cornwall

MICHAEL ST on WYRE parish 1659 Lancs 3-3/4 miles sw Garstang comp chapelry Wood Plumpton, townships Great Eccleston, Elswick, Inskip with Sowerby, Out Rawcliffe, Upper Rawcliffe with Tarnicar pop 4,708 archd Richmond dioc Chester

MICHAEL ST BEDWARDINE parish 1546 Worcs part of city of Worcester pop 726 archd and dioc Worcester

MICHAEL ST CAERHAYS parish 1580 Cornwall 3-3/4 miles se Tregoney pop 197 archd Cornwall dioc Exeter

MICHAEL'S ST MOUNT extra parochial liberty Cornwall 3/4 mile s Marazion pop 161

MICHAEL ST PENKEVIL parish 1516 Cornwall 5 miles sw Tregoney pop 179 archd Cornwall dioc Exeter

MICHAEL CHURCH chapelry parish Tretire Herefs

MICHAEL CHURST, ST parish 1695 Somerset 5-1/4 miles s Bridgewater pop 32 archd Taunton dioc Bath and Wells

MICHAEL CHURCH ESKLEY parish 1719 Herefs 10 miles se Hay pop 406 archd Brecon dioc St David's

MICHAELSTONE LE VELW parish 1661 co Monmouth 5-1/4 miles sw Newport pop 208 archd and dioc Llandaff

MICHAELSTOW parish 1544 Cornwall 3-1/4 miles sw Camelford pop 215 archd Cornwall dioc Exeter

MICKFIELD parish 1558 Suffolk 2-3/4 miles sw Debenham pop 257 archd Suffolk dioc Norwich

MICKLEFIELD township parish Sherburn W R York pop 228

MICKLEHAM parish 1549 Surrey 2 miles se Leatherhead pop 709 archd Surrey dioc Winchester

MICKLEOVER parish 1607 Derbys 3-1/2 miles sw Derby pop 1,526 archd Derby dioc Lichfield Wesl Meth, Unit

MICKLETHWAITE township parish Bingley W R York

MICKLETON parish 1590 Gloucs 2-1/2 miles ne Chipping Campden pop 679 archd and dioc Gloucester

MICKLETON township parish Romald Kirk N R York pop 500

MICKLEWAITE GRANGE extra parochial liberty W R York

MICKLEY chapelry parish Ovingham Northumberland pop 211

MIDDLE or MYDDLE parish 1541 Shrops 8 miles nw Shrewsbury pop 1,205 archd Salop dioc Lichfield

MIDDLE QUARTER township parish Kirk Linton Cumberland pop 520

MIDDLE QUARTER township parish Kirby Ireleth Lancs pop 654

MIDDLEHAM parish 1604 N R York 44 miles nw York pop 914 peculiar Prim, Wesl Meth

MIDDLEHAM, BISHOP'S parish 1559 co Durham 9 miles se Durham comp townships Bishop's Middleham, Cornforth, Gramondsway Moor, Mainsforth, Thrislington pop 837 archd and dioc Durham

MIDDLEHOPE township parish Diddlebury Shrops

MIDDLEMARSH tything parish Mintern Magna Dorset

MIDDLE MEAD hamlet parish Little Baddow Essex pop 182

MIDDLENEY tything parish Drayton Somerset

MIDDLESBOROUGH parish incl regs of Acklam N R York comp townships Linthorp, Middlesborough pop 383 archd Cleveland dioc York

MIDDLESCEUGH hamlet parish St Mary Cumberland pop 195

MIDDLESMOOR chapelry parish Kirby Malzeard 1700 W R York pec of Dean and Chapter of York

MIDDLESTONE township parish St Andrew co Durham pop 92

MIDDLETHORPE township parish St Mary E R York pop 58

MIDDLETON chapelry parish Youlgrave Derbys pop 302 Indep, Wesl Meth

MIDDLETON St George parish co Durham 6-1/2 miles se Darlington pop 299 archd and dioc Durham

MIDDLETON parish 1700 Essex 1 mile sw Sudbury pop 103 Commissary of Essex and Herts, concurrently with Consistorial Court of Bishop of London

MIDDLETON township parish Lancaster Lancs pop 177

MIDDLETON parish 1541 Lancs 55 miles se Lancaster comp market town Middleton, chapelry Ashworth, townships Ainswirth, Birtle cum Bamford, Hopwood, Great Lever, Pilsworth, Thornham pop 14,379 archd and dioc Chester Countess of Huntingdon's Connection, Indep, Prim and Wesl Meth, Swedenborgians

MIDDLETON township parish Winwick Lancs

MIDDLETON parish 1560 Norfolk 3-1/2 miles se Lynn Regis archd and dioc Norwich

MIDDLETON township parish Cottingham co Northampton pop 433

MIDDLETON township parish Belford Northumberland pop 87

MIDDLETON parish 1653 Suffolk 2-1/4 miles se Yoxford pop 580 archd Suffolk dioc Norwich Wesl Meth

MIDDLETON parish 1551 Sussex 8 miles sw Arundel pop 43 archd and dioc Chichester

MIDDLETON parish 1671 Warws 4-1/2 miles sw Tamworth pop 550 archd Coventry dioc Lichfield

MIDDLETON chapelry parish Kirby Lonsdale 1678 Westm pop 286

MIDDLETON ON THE WOLDS parish 1678 E R York 8-3/4 miles nw Beverley pop 527 archd East Riding dioc York Wesl Meth

MIDDLETON parish 1671 N R York 1-3/4 miles nw Pickering comp townships Cowthorn, Cropton, Hartoft, Lockton, Middleton, Rosedale East Side, Wretton, part of Aislaby pop 1,742 archd Cleveland dioc York

MIDDLETON township parish Rothwell W R York pop 976

MIDDLETON township parish Ilkley W R York pop 166

MIDDLETON BY WIRKSWORTH hamlet parish Wirksworth Derbys pop 1,014

MIDDLETON CHENEY parish 1551 co Northampton 3 miles ne Banbury pop 1,415 archd Northampton dioc Peterborough Bapt, Wesl Meth

MIDDLETON GRANGE township parish Runcorn Ches pop 13

MIDDLETON HALL township parish Ilderton Northumberland pop 56

MIDDLETON IN TEASDALE parish 1578 co Durham 10 miles nw Barnard Castle comp market town Middleton, chapelry Egglestone, townships Forest with Frith, Newbiggin pop 3,714 archd and dioc Durham Bapt, Indep, Meth

MIDDLETON, NORTH township parish Ilderton Northumberland pop 156

MIDDLETON, NORTH township parish Hartburn Northumberland pop 108

MIDDLETON ON THE HILL parish 1650 Herefs 6 miles ne Leominster pop 413 archd and dioc Hereford

MIDDLETON QUERNHOW chapelry parish Wath N R York pop 123

MIDDLETON SCRIVEN parish 1728 Shrops 5-1/2 miles sw Bridgenorth pop 99 archd Salop dioc Hereford

MIDDLETON, SOUTH township parish Ilderton Northumberland pop 69

MIDDLETON, SOUTH township parish Hartburn Northumberland pop 33

MIDDLETON, STONEY parish 1598 co Oxford 3 miles nw Bicester pop 307 archd and dioc Oxford

MIDDLETON, STONY chapelry parish Hathersage 1715 Derbys 5-1/2 miles ne Bakewell pop 479

MIDDLETON TYAS parish 1539 N R York 5-1/2 miles ne Richmond comp townships Middleton Tyas with Kneeton, Moulton pop 811 archd Richmond dioc Chester

MIDDLETON UPON LEVEN chapelry 1614 parish Rudby in Cleveland N R York pop 89

MIDDLEWICH parish 1613 Ches 20 miles e Chester comp township Weever, market town Middlewich, townships Byley with Yatehouse, Clive, Croxton, Kinderton with Hulme, Minshull Vernon, Mooresbarrow with Parme, Newton, Occlestone, Ravenscroft, Sproston, Stublach, Sutton, Wimboldsley pop 4,785 archd and dioc Chester Soc of Friends, Indep, Wesl Meth

MIDDLEZOY parish 1754 Somerset 5-1/2 miles sw Langport pop 679 pec of Glastonbury dioc Bath and Wells

MIDDOP township parish Gisburn W R York pop 62

MIDGHAM chapelry 1622 parish Thatcham Berks pop 347

MIDGLEY township parish Halifax W R York pop 2,409

MIDHOPE chapelry parish Ecclesfield 1772 W R York

MIDHURST borough, market town, parish 1565 Sussex 11-1/2 miles ne Chichester pop 1,478 archd and dioc Chichester

MIDLEY parish no regs Kent 3 miles sw New Romney pop 52 archd and dioc Canterbury

MIDLOE extra parochial liberty Hunts 3 miles nw St Neots pop 36

MIDRIDGE township parish Heighington co Durham pop 307

MIDRIDGE GRANGE township parish St Andrew Auckland co Durham pop 55

MIDSOMER NORTON Somerset See NORTON, MIDSOMER

MID VILLE township Lincs 6 miles sw Spilsby pop 162 indep of any parish

MIDBORNE PORT parish 1539 borough Somerset 2-3/4 miles ne Sherborne pop 2,072 archd Wells dioc Bath and Wells Indep

MILBURN tything parish Malmesbury Wilts pop 163

MILBOURNE parish 1570 Dorset 8 miles sw Blandford Forum pop 240 archd Dorset dioc Bristol

MILBOURNE CHURCHSTONE tything parish Milbourne St Andrew Dorset

MILBOURNE STYLEHAM parish Dorset regs incl with Milbourne St Andrews pop 313

MILBROOK chapelry parish Maker Cornwall Wesl Meth

MILBURN township parish Ponteland Northumberland pop 101

MILBURN chapelry parish Kirby Thore 1678 Westm pop 325

MILBURN GRANGE township parish Ponteland Northumberland pop 44

MILBURN GRANGE hamlet parish Kirby Thore Westm

MILBY township parish Kirby on the Moor W R York

MILCOMBE chapelry parish Bloxham co Oxford pop 230

MILCOTT hamlet parish Weston upon Avon Warws pop 15

MILDEN parish 1558 Suffolk 3 miles sw Bildeston pop 177 archd Sudbury dioc Norwich

MILDENHALL parish 1653 Wilts 1-1/2 miles ne Marlborough pop 427 archd Wilts dioc Salisbury Wesl Meth

MILDENHALL, ST ANDREW'S parish 1559 Suffolk 38-1/2 miles nw Ipswich pop 3,267 archd Sudbury dioc Norwich Bapt, Countess of Huntingdon's Connection, Wesl Meth

MILE END parish 1674 Essex 1 mile n Colchester pop 477 archd Colchester dioc London

MILE END district parish Stepney Middlesex 1 mile e London comp Mile End, Old Town pop 33,898; Mile End, New Town pop 7,384 Calvinistic Meth, Indep, Countess of Huntingdon

MILEHAM parish 1538 Norfolk 6-3/4 miles ne East Dereham pop 566 archd and dioc Norwich

MILFIELD township parish Kirk Newton Northumberland pop 262

MILFORD village in township Belper and hamlet Makeny parish Duffield Derbys Prim, Wesl Meth

MILFORD parish 1594 Hamps 3 miles sw Lymington pop 1,533 archd and dioc Winchester

MILFORD tything parish Laverstock Wilts pop 489

MILFORD township parish Kirby Wharfe W R York

MILFORD, SOUTH township parish Sherburn W R York pop 719 Wesl Meth

MILKHOUSE STREET hamlet parish Cranbrooke Kent Wesl Meth

MILLAND chapelry parish Trotton Sussex

MILLAND VILLE extra parochial liberty Hamps near Winchester pop 149

MILLBROOK parish 1558 Beds 1-1/4 miles nw Ampthill pop 602 archd Bedford dioc Lincoln

MILLBROOK parish 1633 Hamps 2 miles nw Southampton pop 2,735 archd and dioc Winchester

MILLFORD hamlet parish Duffield Derbys Wesl Meth, Unit

MILLINGTON township parish Rosthern Ches pop 330

MILLINGTON parish 1609 E R York 3 miles ne Pocklington pop 255 pec of Dean of York Wesl Meth

MILLO hamlet parish Dunton Beds

MILLOM parish 1598 Cumberland 12 miles se Ravenglass comp chapelries Thwaits, Ulpha, townships Birker with Austhwaite, Chepel Sucken, Lower Millom, Upper Millom pop 2,037 archd Richmond dioc Chester

MILLSHIELDS township parish Bywell St Peter Northumberland

MILNROW chapelry 1722 parish Rochdale Lancs

MILNTHORPE market town township parish Heversham Westm pop 1,509 Indep

MILSON parish 1678 Shrops 3-1/4 miles sw Cleobury Mortimer pop 156 archd Salop dioc Hereford

MILSTEAD parish 1543 Kent 3 miles sw Sittingbourne pop 214 archd and dioc Canterbury

MILSTON parish 1539 Wilts 2-3/4 miles n Amesbury pop 107 archd and dioc Salisbury

MILTHORPE hamlet parish Aslackby Lincs

MILTON parish 1654 Berks 3-1/2 miles sw Abingdon pop 413 archd Berks dioc Salisbury

MILTON parish 1707 Cambs 3-1/2 miles ne Cambridge pop 377 archd and dioc Ely

MILTON township parish Weaverham Ches

MILTON hamlet parish Prittlewell Essex

MILTON parish 1746 earlier regs at Thanington Kent 2-1/2 miles sw Canterbury archd and dioc Canterbury

MILTON or MIDDLETON MALZOR parish 1558 co Northampton 3-1/2 miles sw Northampton pop 541 archd Northampton dioc Peterborough Bapt

MILTON chapelry parish East Adderbury co Oxford pop 205

MILTON chapelry parish Shipton under Whychwood co Oxford pop 568

MILTON parish 1654 Hamps 4-3/4 miles ne Christchurch pop 956 archd and dioc Winchester Indep

MILTON ABBAS or ABBEY parish 1650 Dorset 7 miles sw Blandford

Forum pop 846 pec of Milton Abbas

MILTON ABBOT parish 1653 Devon 6 miles nw Tavistock pop 1,205 archd Totnes dioc Exeter

MILTON BRYANT parish 1559 Beds 2-3/4 miles se Woburn pop 373 archd Bedford dioc Lincoln

MILTON CLEVEDON Somerset See CLEVEDON, MILTON

MILTON DAMERELL parish 1754 Devon 5-1/2 miles ne Holsworthy pop 761 archd Totnes dioc Exeter

MILTON ERNEST parish 1538 Beds 5 miles nw Bedford pop 372 archd Bedford dioc Lincoln

MILTON, GREAT parish 1550 co Oxford 4 miles nw Tetsworth pop 782 pec of Prebendary of Great Milton in Cathedral Church of Lincoln

MILTON KEYNES parish 1559 Bucks 3-1/2 miles se Newport Pagnell pop 334 archd Buckingham dioc Lincoln

MILTON LILBORNE parish 1686 Wilts 1-1/2 miles ne Pewsey pop 660 archd Wilts dioc Salisbury

MILTON, LITTLE chapelry parish Adderbury co Oxford pop 473

MILTON MALZOR co Northampton See MILTON

MILTON NEXT GRAVESEND parish 1558 Kent comp part of town Gravesend pop 4,348 archd and dioc Rochester

MILTON NEXT SITTINGBOURNE parish 1538 Kent 12 miles ne Maidstone pop 2,233 archd and dioc Canterbury Indep, Wesl Meth

MILTON PODIMORE Somerset See PODIMORE, MILTON

MILTON, SOUTH parish 1686 Devon 2-3/4 miles sw Kingsbridge pop 415 archd Totnes dioc Exeter

MILTON UPON STOUR hamlet parish Gillingham Dorset

MILTON, WEST chapelry parish Poorstock Dorset

MILVERTON market town, parish 1538 borough Somerset 26 miles sw Somerton pop 2,344 pec of Archdean of Taunton as Prebendary of Milverton in Cathedral Church of Wells Soc of Friends, Indep

MILVERTON parish 1742 Warws 1-3/4 miles ne Warwick pop 537 archd Coventry dioc Lichfield

MILWICH parish 1573 Staffs 5 miles se Stone pop 551 archd Stafford dioc Lichfield

MIMMS, NORTH parish 1565 Herts 4 miles sw Bishop's Hatfield pop 1,068 archd Huntingdon dioc Lincoln

MIMMS, SOUTH parish 1558 Middlesex 3-1/2 miles nw Chipping Barnet pop 2,010 archd Middlesex dioc London

MINCHINHAMPTON Gloucs See HAMPTON, MINCHIN

MINCHINTON tything parish Handley Dorset

MINDTOWN parish 1607 Shrops 5 miles ne Bishop's Castle pop 36 archd Salop dioc Hereford

MINEHEAD market town, parish 1548 borough Somerset 38-1/2 miles nw Somerton pop 1,481 archd Taunton dioc Bath and Wells Bapt

MINETY parish 1663 Wilts 5-1/2 miles ne Malmesbury pop 585 archd Wilts dioc Salisbury

MININGSBY parish 1695 Lincs 6 miles sw Spilsby pop 354 archd and dioc Lincoln

MINLEY tything parish Yately Hamps

MINSHULL, CHURCH parish 1651 Ches 5-1/2 miles ne Nantwich pop 468 archd and dioc Chester Indep

MINSHULL VERNON township parish Middlewich Ches pop 385

MINSKEP township parish Aldborough W R York pop 267

MINSTEAD parish 1682 Hamps 2-3/4 miles nw Lyndhurst pop 1,074 archd and dioc Winchester

MINSTER parish 1676 Cornwall 3-1/4 miles ne Bossiney pop 497 archd Cornwall dioc Exeter Wesl Meth

MINSTER parish 1557 Kent 4-1/2 miles sw Ramsgate pop 911 archd and dioc Canterbury Wesl Meth

MINSTER IN SHEPPY parish 1703 Kent 3 miles ne Queenborough pop 7,983 archd and dioc Canterbury

MINSTER, LOVELL parish 1754 co Oxford 2-3/4 miles nw Witney pop 355 archd and dioc Oxford

MINSTER, SOUTH parish 1702 Essex 3 miles ne Burnham pop 1,422 archd Essex dioc London Indep

MINSTERLEY chapelry parish Westbury Shrops pop 809 Bapt, Indep

MINSTERWORTH parish 1633 Gloucs 4-1/2 miles sw Gloucester pop 496 archd and dioc Gloucester

MINTERN, MAGNA parish 1635 Dorset 10 miles nw Dorchester pop 331 archd Dorset dioc Bristol

MINTERN, PARVA tything parish Buckland Newton Dorset pop 101

MINTING parish 1561 Lincs 5-3/4 miles nw Horncastle pop 301 archd and dioc Lincoln

MINTLYN parish no regs Norfolk 2-3/4 miles se Lynn Regis pop 31

MINVER, ST parish 1558 Cornwall 3-1/2 miles ne Padstow pop 1,110 archd Cornwall dioc Exeter Wesl Meth, cemetery for Soc of Friends

MINWORTH township parish Curdworth Warws pop 324

MIRFIELD parish 1559 W R York 2-3/4 miles sw Dewsbury pop 6,496 archd and dioc York Wesl Meth

MISERDEN parish 1574 Gloucs 5 miles se Painswick pop 441 archd and dioc Gloucester

MISSENDEN hamlet parish Hitchin Herts

MISSENDEN, GREAT parish 1678 Bucks 26 miles se Buckingham pop 1,827 archd Buckingham dioc Lincoln Bapt

MISSENDEN, LITTLE parish 1559 Bucks 2-1/2 miles nw Amersham pop 937 archd Buckingham dioc Lincoln

MISSON parish 1653 Notts 2-3/4 miles ne Bawtry pop 841 archd Nottingham dioc York Wesl Meth

MISTERTON parish 1558 Leics 1 mile se Lutterworth pop 587 archd Leicester dioc Lincoln

MISTERTON parish 1540 Notts 4-3/4 miles nw Gainsborough pop 1,579 pec of Lord of Manor of Gringley on the Hill Calvinistic, Wesl Meth, Roman Cath

MISTERTON parish 1558 Somerset 1-1/4 miles se Crewkerne pop

460 archd Taunton dioc Bath and Wells

MISTLEY parish 1559 Essex 1/2 mile e Manningtree pop 876 archd Colchester dioc London

MITCHAM parish 1563 Surrey 9 miles sw London pop 4,387 archd Surrey dioc Winchester Indep, Wesl Meth

MITCHELDEVER parish 1538 Hamps 6-1/2 miles ne Winchester pop 936 archd and dioc Winchester

MITCHELL DEAN Gloucs See DEAN MITCHELL

MITCHELMERSH parish 1558 Hamps 3-1/2 miles n Romsey comp hamlets Awbridge, Brashfield, Mitchelmersh pop 962 pec of incumbent

MITCHEL TROY parish 1590 co Monmouth 2-3/4 miles sw Monmouth pop 375 archd and dioc Llandaff

MITFORD parish 1667 Northumberland 1-3/4 miles w Morpeth comp townships Edington, Molesden, Benridge, High and Low Heighley, Mitford, Newton Park, Newton Underwood, Nunridge, Pigdon, Spittle Hill, Thropple pop 701 archd Northumberland dioc Durham

MITMEECE township parish Eccleshall Staffs pop 126

MITTON or MYTTON parish 1611 W R York 3 miles sw Clitheroe comp township Old Laund Booth, Aighton with Bailey, Chaigley, chapelries Grindleton, Waddington, townships Bashall Eaves, West Bradford, Mitton pop 5,277 archd and dioc York

MITTON township parish Penkridge Staffs

MITTON, LITTLE township parish Whalley Lancs pop 70

MITTON LOWER chapelry parish Kidderminster 1693 Worcs pop 2,952

MITTON, UPPER hamlet parish Hartlebury Worcs pop 202

MITTONS hamlet parish Bredon Worcs

MIXBURY parish 1645 co Oxford 8 miles ne Bicester pop 387 archd and dioc Oxford

MOAT township parish Kirk Andrews upon Esk Cumberland pop 170

MOBBERLEY parish 1578 Ches 3 miles ne Nether Knutsford pop 1,271 archd and dioc Chester Indep, Wesl Meth

MOCCAS parish 1673 Herefs 9-1/2 miles nw Hereford pop 217 archd and dioc Hereford

MOCKERKIN hamlet parochial chapelry of Loweswater Cumberland

MODBURY market town, parish 1601 Devon 36 miles sw Exeter pop 2,116 archd Totnes dioc Exeter Bapt, Soc of Friends, Indep, Wesl Meth

MOGGERHANGER hamlet parish Blunham Beds pop 381

MOLDASH parish 1557 Kent 5 miles ne Charing pop 391 archd and dioc Canterbury

MOLESDEN township parish Mitford Northumberland pop 36

MOLESWORTH parish 1564 Hunts 4-1/2 miles se Thrapston pop 222 archd Huntingdon dioc Lincoln

MOLLAND parish 1538 Devon 7 miles ne South Molton pop 531 archd Barnstaple dioc Exeter

MOLLINGTON chapelry parish Cropredy Warws pop 360

MOLLINGTON parish 1562 5 miles n Banbury pec of Banbury
MOLLINGTON, GREAT township parish Backford Ches pop 118
MOLLINGTON, LITTLE township parish St Mary Ches pop 24
MOLSCROFT township parish St John E R York pop 124
MOLTON, NORTH parish 1542 Devon 3 miles ne South Molton pop
    1,937 archd Barnstaple dioc Exeter Wesl Meth, Presb
MOLTON, SOUTH market town, parish 1601 Devon 28 miles nw Exe-
    ter pop 3,826 sep juris archd Barnstaple dioc Exeter Indep,
    Wesl Meth
MONCKTON, BISHOP'S chapelry parish Ripon W R York pop 576
    Wesl Meth
MONCKTON DEVERHILL Wilts See DEVERHILL, MONCKTON
MONCKTON, TARRANT parish 1697 Dorset 4-1/4 miles ne Bland-
    ford Forum pop 220 archd Dorset dioc Bristol
MONCKTON UP WIMBORNE tything parish Cranborne Dorset
MONCTON COMBE Somerset See COMBE, MONCTON
MONEWDEN parish 1705 Suffolk 5 miles nw Wickham Market pop 207
    archd Suffolk dioc Norwich
MONGEHAM, GREAT parish 1685 Kent 2 miles sw Deal pop 310
    archd and dioc Canterbury
MONGEHAM, LITTLE parish no regs Kent 2-1/2 miles sw Deal pop
    96 archd and dioc Canterbury
MONGEWELL parish 1682 co Oxford 1-1/2 miles s Wallingford pop
    162 archd and dioc Oxford
MONINGTON township parish Vow Church Herefs
MONK BRETTON York See BRETTON, MONK
MONKEN HADLEY Middlesex See HADLEY, MONKEN
MONK HESLEDEN See HESLEDEN, MONK
MONK FRYSTON See FRYSTON, MONK
MONKHILL township parish Pontefract W R York pop 39
MONKLAND parish 1582 Herefs 2-1/2 miles sw Leominster pop 180
    archd and dioc Hereford
MONKKEIGH parish 1548 Devon 2-3/4 miles nw Great Torrington
    pop 562 archd Barnstaple dioc Exeter
MONKRIDGE WARD township parish Elsdon Northumberland pop 106
MONKSEATON township parish Tynemouth Northumberland pop 489
    Wesl Meth
MONKS ELEIGH parish 1557 Suffolk 2-1/4 miles sw Bildeston pop
    733 pec of Archbishop of Canterbury Wesl Meth
MONKSILVER parish 1653 Somerset 7 miles nw Wiveliscombe pop
    322 archd Taunton dioc Bath and Wells
MONKS PATH or MONKS RIDING liberty parish Tanworth Warws
    pop 379
MONKSTON parish 1726 Hamps 4 miles w Andover pop 276 archd
    and dioc Winchester
MONKSWOOD extra parochial liberty 1783 co Monmouth pop 193
    archd and dioc Llandaff
MONKTON parish 1737 Devon 2 miles ne Honiton pop 120 pec of

Dean and Chapter of Exeter

MONKTON township parish Jarrow co Durham

MONKTON district, parish Otterden Kent

MONKTON parish 1700 Kent 7 miles w Ramsgate pop 376 pec of
Archbishop of Canterbury

MONKTON DEVERILL Wilts See DEVERILL MONKTON

MONKTON FARLEY parish 1570 Wilts 4 miles nw Bradford pop 396
archd and dioc Salisbury

MONKTON, MOOR parish 1681 E R York 7-3/4 miles nw York comp
townships Hessey, Moor Monkton pop 484 archd and dioc York

MONKTON, NUN parish 1708 W R York 8-1/4 miles nw York pop
398 archd Richmond dioc Chester Wesl Meth

MONKTON, WEST parish 1710 Somerset 3-1/2 miles ne Taunton
pop 1,155 archd Taunton dioc Bath and Wells Bapt, Wesl Meth

MONMOUTH borough, market town, parish 1598 co Monmouth 130
miles nw London pop 4,916 sep juris archd and dioc Hereford
Bapt, Indep, Wesl Meth, Roman Cath

MONNINGTON UPON WYE parish 1584 Herefs 9 miles nw Hereford
pop 104 archd and dioc Hereford

MONTACUTE parish 1558 Somerset 4-1/2 miles nw Yeovil pop 1,028
archd Wells dioc Bath and Wells Bapt, Wesl Meth

MONTEFORD parish 1661 Shrops 5 miles nw Shrewsbury pop 566
archd Salop dioc Lichfield

MONXTON Hamps See MONKSTON

MONYASH chapelry parish Bakewell 1707 Derbys pop 409 Soc of
Friends

MOOR township parish Richard's Castle Shrops

MOOR township parish Fladbury Worcs

MOOR TOWN township parish Bradsburton E R York pop 26

MOOR WEST extra parochial liberty Somerset pop 66

MOORBY parish 1561 Lincs 4-1/2 miles se Horncastle pop 154 archd
and dioc Lincoln Wesl Meth

MOORE township parish Runcorn Ches pop 298

MOORESBARROW township parish Middlewich Ches pop 25

MOORHOUSE township parish Burgh upon the Sands Cumberland pop
277 Soc of Friends

MOORHOUSE township parish Houghton le Spring co Durham pop 30

MOORHOUSE chapelry parish Laxton Notts

MOORLINCH parish 1578 Somerset 7 miles e Bridge Water pop
2,192 archd Wells dioc Bath and Wells

MOORSHAM, GREAT township parish Skelton N R York pop 338

MOORSLEY township parish Houghton le Spring co Durham pop 748

MOORTHWAITE township parish Cumwhitton Cumberland pop 255

MOORTON tything parish Thornbury Gloucs

MOORWINSTOW parish 1558 Cornwall 7-1/4 miles se Stratton pop
1,102 archd Cornwall dioc Exeter Wesl Meth

MORBORN parish 1724 Hunts 2-1/2 miles nw Stilton pop 94 archd
Huntingdon dioc Lincoln

MORCHARD, BISHOP'S parish 1660 Devon 6-1/2 miles nw Crediton pop 2,003 pec Bishop of Exeter

MORCOTT parish 1539 co Rutland 4-1/4 miles ne Uppingham pop 480 archd Northampton dioc Peterborough

MORDEN parish 1575 Dorset 6 miles n Wareham pop 813 archd Dorset dioc Bristol Wesl Meth

MORDEN parish 1634 Surrey 10 miles sw London pop 655 archd Surrey dioc Winchester

MORDEN, GUILDEN parish 1553 Cambs 5-1/2 miles e Biggleswade pop 675 archd and dioc Ely

MORDEN, STEEPLE parish 1675 Cambs 5 miles nw Royston pop 645 archd and dioc Ely

MORDIFORD parish 1621 Herefs 5 miles se Hereford pop 635 archd and dioc Hereford

MORDON township parish Sedgefield co Durham pop 174

MORE parish 1569 Shrops 3 miles ne Bishop's Castle pop 272 archd Salop dioc Hereford

MOREBATH parish 1558 Devon 2-1/4 miles nw Bampton pop 436 archd and dioc Exeter

MOREBY township parish Stillingfleet E R York

MORELEIGH or MORLEY parish 1659 Devon 5-1/2 miles se Totnes pop 182 archd Totnes dioc Exeter

MORESBY parish 1717 Cumberland 2 miles ne Whitehaven pop 983 archd Richmond dioc Chester

MORESTEAD parish 1549 Hamps 3-1/4 miles se Winchester pop 90 pec of incumbent

MORETON liberty parish Dinton Bucks

MORETON township parish Astbury Ches pop 141

MORETON township parish Bidstone Ches pop 247

MORETON parish 1741 Dorset 8 miles se Dorchester pop 304 archd Dorset dioc Bristol

MORETON parish 1558 Essex 3 miles nw Chipping Ongar pop 431 archd Essex dioc London

MORETON chapelry parish Llany Blodwell Shrops

MORETON hamlet parish Gnosall Staffs

MORETON CORBET parish 1580 Shrops 5-1/4 miles se Wem pop 247 archd Salop dioc Lichfield

MORETON HAMPSTEAD market town, parish 1603 Devon 11 miles sw Exeter pop 1,864 archd Totnes dioc Exeter Indep, Wesl Meth, Unit

MORETON IN THE MARSH market town, parish 1643 Gloucs 28-1/2 miles ne Gloucester pop 1,331 archd and dioc Gloucester Indep

MORETON, MAIDS' parish 1558 Bucks 1-1/4 miles ne Buckingham pop 474 archd Buckingham dioc Lincoln

MORETON, NORTH parish 1558 Berks 4-1/4 miles w Wallingford pop 362 archd Berks dioc Salisbury

MORETON SEA or SAY parish 1691 Shrops 3-1/4 miles w Drayton in Hales pop 676 archd Salop dioc Lichfield

MORETON, SOUTH parish 1599 Berks 3 miles sw Wallingford pop 169 archd Berks dioc Salisbury

MORETON VALENCE parish 1681 Gloucs 7-3/4 miles nw Stroud pop 324 archd and dioc Gloucester

MORLAND parish 1539 Westm 6-3/4 miles nw Appleby comp chapelries Bolton, Thrimby, townships King's Meaburn, Morland, Newby, Sleagill, Great Strickland, Little Strickland pop 1,940 archd and dioc Carlisle Wesl Meth, Soc of Friends

MORLEY parish 1543 Derbys 4-1/2 miles ne Derby pop 1,064 archd Derby dioc Lichfield

MORLEY parish 1539 Norfolk 3 miles sw Wymondham pop 339 archd Norfolk dioc Norwich

MORLEY parish 1590 Norfolk 4 miles sw Wymondham pop 172 archd Norfolk dioc Norwich

MORLEY chapelry parish Batley W R York pop 3,819 Presb, Indep, Wesl Meth

MORNING THORPE parish 1557 Norfolk 2 miles e St Mary Stratton pop 164 archd Norfolk dioc Norwich

MORPETH parish 1584 borough Northumberland 15 miles n Newcastle upon Tyne, comp townships Catchburn with Morpeth Castle, Parkhouse Stobhill, Hepscot, New Minster Abbey, Shilvington, Tranwell with Gudgeon, High Church, Twizelland, Buller's Green, borough and market town of Morpeth pop 4,797 archd Northumberland dioc Durham Indep, Presb, Prim and Wesl Meth, Roman Cath

MORRAGE township parish Ipstone Staffs pop 403

MORRELL ROOTHING Essex See ROOTHING, MORRELL

MORRICK township parish Warkworth Northumberland pop 64

MORROWE hamlet parish Wisbeach Cambs

MORSTON parish 1548 Norfolk 3-1/4 miles nw Clay pop 171 archd and dioc Norwich

MORTHOE parish 1726 Devon 4 miles sw Ilfracombe pop 338 archd Barnstaple dioc Exeter

MORTIMER, WEST tything parish Stratfield Mortimer Hamps pop 348

MORTLAKE parish 1599 Surrey 6-1/2 miles sw London pop 2,698 pec Archbishop of Canterbury Indep

MORTON parish 1570 Derbys 3-1/2 miles n Alfreton pop 501 archd Derby dioc Lichfield

MORTON parish 1597 Lincs 2-1/2 miles n Bourne pop 842 archd and dioc Lincoln

MORTON extra parochial liberty Lincs 8 miles sw Lincoln pop 9

MORTON hamlet parish Gainsborough Lincs pop 543 Indep, Wesl Meth

MORTON parish 1640 Notts 2-1/2 miles se Southwell pop 156 pec Chapter of Collegiate Church of Southwell

MORTON extra parochial liberty N R York 2-1/2 miles nw Hemsley

MORTON township parish Ainderby Steeple N R York pop 258 Wesl Meth

MORTON township parish Ormsby N R York pop 26

MORTON, ABBOT'S parish 1728 Worcs 5-1/2 miles sw Alcester pop 233 archd and dioc Worcester

MORTON BAGGOTT parish 1663 Warws 3-1/2 miles sw Henley in Arden pop 170 archd and dioc Worcester

MORTON, EAST township parish Dalton le Dale co Durham pop 98

MORTON, EAST and WEST township parish Bingley W R York pop 1,219 Wesl Meth

MORTON GRANGE township parish Houghton le Spring co Durham pop 295

MORTON, JEFFRIES parish 1711 Herefs 5-1/2 miles sw Bromyard pop 46 archd and dioc Hereford

MORTON MORRELL parish 1538 Warws 3-3/4 miles nw Kington pop 298 archd and dioc Worcester

MORTON ON THE HILL parish 1720 Norfolk 5-3/4 miles se Reepham pop 169 archd Norfolk dioc Norwich

MORTON PINKNEY parish 1641 co Northampton 8 miles nw Towcester pop 581 archd Northampton dioc Peterborough

MORTON TYNEMOUTH township parish Gainford co Durham pop 19

MORTON UPON LUGG parish 1739 Herefs 4-1/4 miles n Hereford pop 69 pec Prebendary of Moreton Magna in Cathedral Church of Hereford

MORVAH parish 1617 Cornwall 6 miles nw Penzance pop 377 archd Cornwall dioc Exeter Bryanites, Wesl Meth

MORVAL parish 1538 Cornwall 2-3/4 miles n East Looe pop 644 archd Cornwall dioc Exeter

MORVILL parish 1562 Shrops 3 miles nw Bridgenorth pop 517 archd Salop dioc Hereford

MORWENSTOW Cornwall See MOORWINSTOW

MORWICK township parish Barwick in Elmett W R York

MOSBOROUGH township parish Eckington Derbys

MOSEBY township parish Ripon W R York

MOSELEY hamlet parish Bushbury Staffs

MOSELEY chapelry 1758 parish King's Norton Worcs

MOSS township parish Campsall W R York pop 269

MOSSER chapelry 1787 parish Brigham Allerdale Cumberland pop 94

MOSSLEY chapelry parish Ashton under Line Lancs Meth, New Connection

MOSS SIDE township parish Manchester Lancs pop 208

MOSTERTON parish 1655 Dorset 4 miles nw Beaminster pop 303 archd Dorset dioc Bristol

MOSTON township parish St Mary Chester Ches pop 17

MOSTON township parish Warmingham Ches pop 372

MOSTON township parish Manchester Lancs pop 615

MOSTON township parish Stanton upon Hine Heath Shrops pop 79

MOTCOMB parish 1676 Dorset 1-1/2 miles nw Shaftesbury pop 1,405 pec of manor of Gillingham Wesl Meth

MOTHERBY township parish Greystock Cumberland pop 115

MOTTINGHAM hamlet, parish Chiselhurst Kent pop 124

MOTTISFONT parish 1701 Hamps 4-3/4 miles nw Romsey pop 505 archd and dioc Winchester

MOTTISTON parish 1680 Hamps 5-3/4 miles se Yarmouth pop 142 archd and dioc Winchester

MOTTRAM, ST ANDREW township parish Prestbury Ches pop 387

MOTTRAM IN LONGDEN DALE parish 1559 Ches 7 miles ne Stockport comp townships Godsley, Hatterleigh, Hollingworth, Mattley, Mottram in Longden Dale, Newton Stayley, Tintwisle pop 15,536 archd and dioc Chester Indep, Wesl Meth

MOULDSWORTH township parish Tarvin Ches pop 180

MOULSEY, EAST parish 1668 Surrey 3 miles ne Walton upon Thames pop 546 archd Surrey dioc Winchester

MOULSEY, WEST parish 1729 Surrey 2-1/2 miles ne Walton upon Thames pop 441 archd Surrey dioc Winchester

MOULSFORD parish 1679 Berks 4 miles sw Wallingford pop 169 archd Berks dioc Salisbury

MOULSHAM hamlet parish Chelmsford Essex

MOULSOE parish 1559 Bucks 3 miles se Newport Pagnell pop 303 archd Buckingham dioc Lincoln

MOULTON township parish Davenham Ches pop 243

MOULTON parish 1558 Lincs 4 miles w Holbeach pop 1,850 archd and dioc Lincoln Wesl Meth

MOULTON ST MICHAEL parish 1557 Norfolk 3 miles s Acle pop 209 archd and dioc Norwich

MOULTON parish 1557 Norfolk 3 miles sw St Mary Stratton pop 447 archd Norfolk dioc Norwich

MOULTON parish 1565 co Northampton 4-1/2 miles nw Northampton pop 1,334 archd Northampton dioc Peterborough Bapt, Wesl Meth

MOULTON parish 1560 Suffolk 3-1/2 miles ne Newmarket pop 366 pec Archbishop of Canterbury

MOULTON township parish Middleton Tyas N R York pop 190

MOULTON, CHAPEL chapelry parish Moulton Lincs

MOULTON, GREAT See MOULTON ST MICHAEL

MOULTON PARK extra parochial liberty co Northampton 2-3/4 miles ne Northampton pop 15

MOUNTFIELD parish 1558 Sussex 2-1/2 miles s Robert's Bridge pop 663 archd Lewes dioc Chichester

MOUNT GRACE parish E Harsley N R York 6 miles ne Northallerton

MOUNTHEALY township parish Rothbury Northumberland pop 47

MOUNTNESSING parish 1654 Essex 2 miles sw Ingatestone pop 796 archd Essex dioc London

MOUNTON parish 1790 co Monmouth 2-3/4 miles sw Chepstow pop 58 archd and dioc Llandaff Wesl Meth

MOUNTSORRELL market town, chapelry parish Rothley 1677 Leics
pop 1,602 Bapt, Presb, Unit, Wesl Meth
MOUSEHOLE hamlet parish Paul Cornwall pop 1,014 Wesl Meth
MOUSON township parish Bambrough Northumberland pop 65
MOWSLEY chapelry parish Knaptoft 1660 Leics pop 283
MOXBY hamlet parish Marton in the Forest N R York pop 202
MOSHALL hamlet parish Whishaw Warws
MOZE parish 1551 Essex 7-1/2 miles se Manningtree archd Col-
chester dioc London
MUCH BIRCH Herefs See BIRCH, MUCH
MUCHELNEY parish 1703 Somerset 2-1/2 miles se Langport pop 310
archd Wells dioc Bath and Wells
MUCKING parish 1558 Essex 2 miles se Horndon on the Hill pop 212
archd Essex dioc London
MUCKLEFORD tything parish Bradford Peverell Dorset
MUCKLESTONE hamlet parish Shawbury 1556 Shrops
MUCKLESTON or MUXON parish 1556 Staffs 4 miles ne Drayton in
Hales comp townships Bearston, Dorrington, Gravenhanger,
Woore, Aston, Kneighton, Muckleston, Oadley, Winnington pop
1,854 archd Stafford dioc Lichfield
MUCKLEWICK township parish Hyssington Shrops pop 69
MUCKTON parish 1695 Lincs 5-1/2 miles se Louth pop 118 archd
and dioc Lincoln
MUDFORD parish 1563 Somerset 3 miles ne Yeovil pop 422 archd
Wells dioc Bath and Wells
MUGGINGTON parish 1674 Derbys 7 miles nw Derby pop 491 archd
Derby dioc Lichfield
MUGGLESWICK parish 1730 co Durham 10 miles nw Walsingham pop
298 archd and dioc Durham Bapt, Wesl Meth
MUKER chapelry 1638 parish Grinton N R York pop 1,247
MULBARTON parish 1547 Norfolk 5-1/2 miles sw Norwich pop 523
archd Norfolk dioc Norwich
MULLION parish 1598 Cornwall 7 miles se Helston pop 733 archd
Cornwall dioc Exeter Wesl Meth
MULWITH township parish Ripon W R York
MUMBY parish 1573 Lincs 4 miles se Alford pop 619 archd and dioc
Lincoln
MUMBY, CHAPEL chapelry parish Mumby Lincs pop 218
MUNCASTER parish 1720 Cumberland comp market town and port
Ravenglass, township Birkby pop 657 archd Richmond dioc
Chester
MUNDEN, GREAT parish 1578 Herts 2 miles nw Puckeridge pop
550 archd Huntingdon dioc Lincoln
MUNDEN, LITTLE parish 1680 Herts 4 miles sw Puckeridge pop
521 archd Huntingdon dioc Lincoln Wesl Meth
MUNDFORD parish 1699 Norfolk 5 miles ne Brandon Ferry pop 414
archd Norfolk dioc Norwich
MUNDHAM parish 1559 Norfolk 5-1/2 miles nw Bungay pop 314

archd Norfolk dioc Norwich

MUNDHAM, NORTH parish 1553 Sussex 2-1/2 miles se Chichester pop 467 archd and dioc Chichester

MUNDON parish 1741 Essex 3-3/4 miles se Maldon pop 273 archd Essex dioc London

MUNDSLEY parish 1756 Norfolk 5 miles ne North Walsham pop 436 archd Norfolk dioc Norwich

MUNGRISDALE chapelry 1745 parish Greystock Cumberland pop 226

MUNSLEY parish 1708 Herefs 4 miles nw Ledbury pop 178 archd and dioc Hereford

MUNSLOW parish 1559 Shrops 11 miles n Ludlow pop 680 archd Salop dioc Hereford

MURCOT hamlet parish Charlton upon Otmore co Oxford

MURCOTT hamlet parish Long Buckby co Northampton

MURRAH township parish Greystock Cumberland

MURRELL GREEN tything parish Odiham Hamps

MURSLEY parish 1578 Bucks 3-3/4 miles ne Winslow pop 495 archd Buckingham dioc Lincoln

MURSTON parish 1561 Kent 1 mile se Milton pop 166 archd and dioc Canterbury

MURTON or MOOR TOWN township parish Lamplugh Cumberland

MURTON or MOOR TOWN township parish Tynemouth Northumberland pop 451 Wesl Meth

MURTON township parish Bongate Westm pop 193

MURTON township parish Osbaldwick E R York pop 156

MUSBURY parish 1653 Devon 2 miles ne Colyton pop 418 archd and dioc Exeter

MUSBURY township parish Bury Lancs pop 1,231

MUSCOATES township parish Kirkdale N R York pop 62

MUSCOTT hamlet parish Norton co Northampton

MUSDEN, GRANGE extra parochial liberty Staffs near Ilam pop 15

MUSGRAVE GREAT parish 1562 Westm 2 miles sw Brough pop 179 archd and dioc Carlisle

MUSGRAVE, LITTLE township parish Crosby Garrett Westm pop 75

MUSKHAM, NORTH parish 1704 Notts 3 miles n Newton pop 681 pec Chapter of Collegiate Church of Southwell Wesl Meth

MUSKHAM, SOUTH parish 1589 Cotts 2-1/4 miles n Newark pop 261 pec Chapter of Collegiate Church of Southwell

MUSTON parish 1561 Leics 5-1/2 miles nw Grantham pop 310 archd Leicester dioc Lincoln Wesl Meth

MUSTON parish 1542 E R York 6-1/2 miles se Scarborough pop 382 archd East Riding dioc York Indep

MUTFORD parish 1554 Suffolk 3-1/2 miles se Beccles pop 373 archd Suffolk dioc Norwich

MYDDLE parish 1541 Shrops

MYERSCOUGH township parish Lancaster Lancs pop 510

MYLAND Essex See MILE END

MYLOR parish 1673 Cornwall 3 miles ne Penryn pop 2,647 pec

Bishop of Exeter Bapt, Bryanites, Indep, Wesl Meth, Unit

MYNYDDMAEN hamlet parish Mynyddyslwyn co Monmouth pop 942

MYNYDDYSLWYN parish 1664 co Monmouth 9-1/4 miles ne Newport pop 5,035 archd and dioc Llandaff

MYTHE extra parochial liberty Leics

MUTON UPON SWALE parish 1654 N R York 3-3/4 miles e Boroughbridge pop 147 archd Cleveland dioc York

MYTTON Yorsk See MITTON

NABURN chapelry 1653 parish Acaster Malbis E R York 4-1/4 miles s York pop 425 Wesl Meth

NACKINGTON parish 1563 Kent 2-1/4 miles s Canterbury pop 159 archd and dioc York

NACTON parish 1562 Suffolk 4 miles se Ipswich pop 555 archd Suffolk dioc Norwich

NAFFERTON township parish Ovingham Northumberland pop 60

NAFFERTON parish 1653 E R York 2-1/4 miles ne Great Driffield comp townships Nafferton, Wansford pop 1,184 archd East Riding dioc York Indep, Wesl Meth

NAFFORD formerly a parish, now parish Eckington Worcs

NAILSEA parish 1554 Somerset 8-1/2 miles nw Bristol pop 2,114 archd Bath dioc Bath and Wells

NAILSTONE parish 1694 Leics 3-1/2 miles ne Market Bosworth pop 637 archd Leicester dioc London

NAILSWORTH chapelry 1794 parish Horsley Gloucs pop 4,602 Bapt, Soc of Friends, Indep, Wesl Meth

NANTWICH parish 1539 Ches 20 miles se Chester comp market town Nantwich, township Alvaston, Leighton, Woolstanwood pop 5,357 archd and dioc Chester Bapt, Soc of Friends, Indep, Prim and Wesl Meth, Unit

NAPPA township parish Gisburn W R York pop 43

NAPTON ON THE HILL parish 1604 Warws 3-1/2 miles se Southam pop 833 archd Coventry dioc Lichfield Bapt

NARBOROUGH parish 1599 Leics 5-1/4 miles se Leicester pop 1,147 archd Leicester dioc Lincoln Indep

NARBURGH parish 1558 Norfolk 5-1/2 miles nw Swaffham pop 300 archd Norfolk dioc Norwich

NARFORD parish 1559 Norfolk 4-3/4 miles nw Swaffham pop 103 archd Norfolk dioc Norwich

NASEBY parish 1563 co Northampton 11-3/4 miles nw Northampton pop 707 archd Northampton dioc Peterborough

NASH hamlet parish Whaddon Bucks pop 377

NASH township parish Presteign Herefs

NASH parish 1733 co Monmouth 3-1/2 miles se Newport pop 213 archd and dioc Llandaff Bapt

NASH chapelry parish Burford Shrops

NASSINGTON parish 1654 co Northampton 2-1/4 miles sw Wansford pop 601 pec of Prebendary of Nassington Wesl Meth

NATEBY township parish Garstang Lancs pop 232

NATEBY township parish Kirby Stephen Westm pop 136

NATELEY SCURES parish 1666 Hamps 4-1/2 miles e Basingstoke pop 245 archd and dioc Winchester

NATELY, UP parish 1692 Hamps 2-1/2 miles nw Odiham pop 153 archd and dioc Winchester

NATLAND chapelry parish Kendal 1735 Westm pop 236

NATTON tything parish Ashchurch Gloucs

NAUGHTON parish 1561 Suffolk 2-1/4 miles e Bildeston pop 184 archd Sudbury dioc Norwich

NAUNTON hamlet parish Winchcombe Gloucs

NAUNTON parish 1540 Gloucs 5 miles sw Stow on the Wold pop 797 archd and dioc Gloucester Bapt

NAUNTON BEAUCHAMP parish 1696 Worcs 4-3/4 miles ne Pershore pop 149 archd and dioc Worcester

NAVENBY parish 1681 Lincs 9-1/2 miles nw Sleaford pop 778 archd and dioc Lincoln Wesl Meth

NAVESTOCK parish 1538 Essex 4-1/4 miles sw Chipping Ongar pop 852 pec Dean and Chapter of St Paul's London

NAWORTH township parish Brampton Cumberland pop 405

NAWTON township parish Kirkdale N R York pop 337 Wesl Meth

NAYLAND parish 1558 Suffolk 17 miles sw Ipswich pop 1,047 archd Sudbury dioc Norwich Indep

NAZEING parish 1559 Essex 5-1/4 miles nw Epping pop 757 Commissary of London, concurrently with Consistorial Court of Bishop of London

NEASHAM or NYSAM township parish Hurworth co Durham pop 331

NEATESHEAD parish 1676 Norfolk 5-1/4 miles se Coltishall pop 646 archd Norfolk dioc Norwich Bapt

NEATHAM extra parochial liberty Hamps 2 miles e Alton pop 107

NECTON parish 1558 Norfolk 3-3/4 miles e Swaffham pop 996 archd Norfolk dioc Norwich Bapt

NEDGING parish 1559 Suffolk 1 mile se Bildeston pop 214 archd Sudbury dioc Norwich

NEEDHAM parish 1643 Norfolk 1-1/4 miles sw Harleston pop 341 archd Norfolk dioc Norwich

NEEDHAM MARKET chapelry parish Barking Suffolk pop 1,466 Soc of Friends, Indep

NEEDINGWORTH chapelry parish Holywell Hunts Bapt

NEEDWOOD FOREST district Staffs comp parishes Hanbury, Tatenhill, Tutbury, Yoxhall archd Stafford dioc Lichfield

NEEN SAVAGE parish 1575 Shrops 1-1/4 miles ne Cleobury Mortimer pop 450 archd Salop dioc Hereford

NEEN SOLLARS parish 1678 Shrops 3-1/4 miles sw Cleobury Mortimer pop 208 archd Salop dioc Hereford

NEENTON parish 1558 Shrops 6-1/2 miles sw Bridgenorth archd Salop dioc Hereford

NEITHROP hamlet parish Banbury co Oxford pop 2,169

NEMPNETT THRUBWELL parish 1556 Somerset 9 miles ne Axbridge

pop 225 archd Bath dioc Bath and Wells

NENT HEAD Cumberland See ALDSTONE or ALSTON, MOOR

NEOT, ST parish 1549 Cornwall 5 miles nw Liskeard pop 1,425
     archd Cornwall dioc Exeter

NEOTS, ST parish 1691 Hunts 9 miles sw Huntingdon pop 2,617
     archd Huntingdon dioc Lincoln Bapt, Wesl Meth

NEPICAR township parish Wrotham Kent

NESBIT township parish Monk Hesleton co Durham pop 10

NESBIT township parish Stamfordham Northumberland pop 37

NESBITT township parish Doddington Northumberland pop 47

NESFIELD township parish Ilkley W R York pop 206

NESS township parish Great Neston Ches pop 480

NESS, EAST township parish Stonegrave N R York pop 38

NESS, GREAT parish 1589 Shrops 7-1/2 miles nw Shrewsbury pop
     850 archd Salop dioc Lichfield

NESS, LITTLE chapelry 1605 parish Great Ness Shrops pop 242

NESS, WEST township parish Stonegrave N R York pop 59

NESTON, GREAT parish 1559 Ches 11 miles nw Chester comp mar-
     ket town Great Neston, townships Ledsham, Leighton, Ness, Little
     Neston, Raby, Thornton Mayow, Willaston pop 3,518 archd and
     dioc Chester Indep, Wesl Meth

NESTON, LITTLE township parish Great Neston Ches pop 412

NESWICK township parish North Dalton E R York pop 57

NETHERAVON parish 1582 Wilts 5-1/4 miles nw Amesbury pop 508
     pec Prebendary of Netheravon

NETHERBURY parish 1592 Dorset 2 miles sw Beaminster comp
     tythings Aish, Bowood, Melplash, Netherbury pop 1,942 pec Pre-
     bendary of Netherbury

NETHERBY township parish Arthuret Cumberland pop 326

NETHERBY township parish Kirby Overblows W R York

NETHER CERNE Dorset See CERNE, NETHER

NETHERCOTE hamlet parish Warkworth co Northampton

NETHER EXE parish 1731 Devon 5 miles ne Exeter pop 99 archd
     and dioc Exeter

NETHERHAMPTON Wilts see HAMPTON, NETHER

NETHERMORE tything parish Chippenham Wilts

NETHERTON township parish Bedlington Northumberland

NETHERTON township parish Sephton Lancs pop 273

NETHERTON chapelry parish Cropthorn Worcs pop 129 Bapt

NETHERTON NORTH SIDE township parish Allenton Northumberland
     pop 53

NETHERTON SOUTH SIDE township parish Allenton Northumberland
     pop 62

NETHERWENT co Monmouth See BRIDE ST NETHERWENT

NETSWELL or NETTLESWELL parish 1558 Essex 2-1/4 miles sw
     Harlow pop 316 Commissary of Essex and Herts, concurrently
     with Consistorial Court of Bishop of London

NETTLEBED parish 1653 co Oxford 4-3/4 miles nw Henley upon

Thames pop 618 pec of Dorchester

NETTLECOMBE tything parish Poorstock Dorset

NETTLECOMBE parish 1540 Somerset 7 miles nw Wiveliscombe
   pop 325 archd Taunton dioc Bath and Wells

NETTLEDEN chapelry parish Pigles Thorne, incl regs Great Gaddesden Bucks pop 142

NETTLEHAM parish 1583 Lincs 3 miles ne Lincoln pop 714 archd
   Stow dioc Lincoln Wesl Meth

NETTLESTEAD parish 1640 Kent 5-1/4 miles sw Maidstone pop 344
   archd and dioc Rochester

NETTLESTEAD parish 1618 Suffolk 4-3/4 miles s Needham Market
   pop 74 archd Suffolk dioc Norwich

NETTLETON parish 1679 Lincs 1 mile sw Caistor pop 385 archd and
   dioc Lincoln Wesl Meth

NETTLETON parish 1556 Wilts 8-1/2 miles nw Chippenham pop 448
   archd Wilts dioc Salisbury Bapt, Wesl Meth

NEVENDON parish 1669 Essex 5-3/4 miles se Billericay pop 181
   archd Essex dioc London

NEW ALRESFORD Hamps See ALRESFORD, NEW

NEWARK chapelry parish St John the Baptist Peterboro co Northampton

NEWARK UPON TRENT borough, market town, parish 1599 Notts 20
   miles ne Nottingham pop 9,557 exc juris archd Nottingham dioc
   York Gen and Part Bapt, Indep, Calvinistic, Prim and Wesl Meth,
   Roman Cath

NEWBALD parish 1600 E R York 4-1/2 miles se Market Weighton
   pop 769 pec Prebendary of North Newbald Wesl Meth

NEWBALL hamlet parish Stainton by Langworth Lincs

NEWBIGGIN township parish Dacre Cumberland

NEWBIGGIN township parish Middleton in Teasdale co Durham pop
   507

NEWBIGGIN chapelry parish Newburn Northumberland pop 64

NEWBIGGIN chapelry parish Woodhorn 1665 Northumberland pop 519

NEWBIGGIN township parish Shotley Northumberland pop 60

NEWBIGGIN parish 1572 Westm 7-1/4 miles nw Appleby pop 140
   archd and dioc Carlisle

NEWBIGGIN hamlet parish Kirby Lonsdale Westm

NEWBIGGIN township parish Aysgarth N R York pop 122

NEWBIGGIN, EAST and WEST township parish Bishopton co Durham
   pop 35

NEWBOLD hamlet parish Chesterfield Derbys pop 1,140

NEWBOLD hamlet parish Ouston Leics

NEWBOLD liberty parish Breedon Leics

NEWBOLD hamlet parish Tredington Warws pop 300

NEWBOLD GROUNDS hamlet parish Catesby Abbey co Northumberland

NEWBOLD, LEA Ches See LEA NEWBOLD

NEWBOLD PACEY parish 1554 Warws 5-3/4 miles nw Kington pop

341 archd and dioc Worcester

NEWBOLD REVEL hamlet parish Monks Kirby Warws

NEWBOLD UPON AVON parish 1558 Warws 2-1/2 miles nw Rugby pop 1,063 archd Coventry dioc Lichfield

NEWBOLD VERDON parish 1542 Leics 2-3/4 miles ne Market Bosworth pop 590 archd Leicester dioc Lincoln

NEWBOROUGH parish 1629 co Northampton 5 miles ne Peterborough pop 340 archd Northampton dioc Peterborough

NEWBOROUGH chapelry 1601 parish Hanbury Staffs pop 757

NEWBOROUGH township parish Coxwold N R York pop 104

NEWBOTTLE township parish Houghton le Spring co Durham pop 2,198 Wesl Meth

NEWBOTTLE parish 1538 co Northampton 4-1/2 miles w Brackley pop 366 archd Northampton dioc Peterborough

NEWBOURN parish 1561 Suffolk 4 miles se Woodbridge pop 176 archd Suffolk dioc Norwich

NEWBROUGH chapelry 1695 4-3/4 miles nw Hexham Northumberland pop 494

NEWBURN parish 1659 Northumberland 5-1/4 miles nw Newcastle upon Tyne comp chapelry Newbiggin, townships Black Callerton, Butterlaw, East Denton, West Denton, North Dissington, South Dissington, Newburn, Newburn Hall, Sugley, Throckley, Wallbottle, East and West Whorlton, Woolsington pop 4,639 archd Northumberland dioc Durham

NEWBURN HALL township parish Newburn Northumberland pop 636

NEWBURY market town, parish 1538 Berks 17 miles sw Reading pop 5,977 sep juris archd Berks dioc Salisbury Bapt, Soc of Friends, Indep, Wesl Meth, Unit

NEWBY township parish Irthington Cumberland pop 110

NEWBY township parish Morland Westm pop 300

NEWBY township parish Topcliffe N R York

NEWBY township parish Stokesley N R York pop 152

NEWBY township parish Scalby N R York pop 55

NEWBY township parish Clapham W R York

NEWBY township parish Ripon W R York pop 39

NEWBY WISK township parish Kirby Wisk N R York pop 254 Wesl Meth

NEWCASTLE township parish Clun Shrops pop 321

NEWCASTLE UNDER LYNE borough, market town, parish 1563 Staffs 16 miles nw Stafford pop 8,192 sep juris archd Stafford dioc Lichfield Bapt, Indep, Meth of New Connection, Prim and Wesl Meth

NEWCASTLE UPON TYNE borough, port, market town Northumberland 276 miles nw London pop 42,760 comp parochial districts St Nicholas 1558, All Saints 1600, St Andrews 1697, St Johns 1587 archd Northumberland dioc Durham Bapt, Soc of Friends, Indep, Wesl, Indep, and Prim Meth, New Connection, Scottish Kirk, Scots relief Congregation, Seceders, Separatists, Burghers, Antiburghers,

Sandemanians, Swedenborgians, Unit, Roman Cath

NEWCHAPEL Staffs See THURSFIELD

NEWCHURCH or WHITEGATE Ches See WHITEGATE

NEWCHURCH township parish Kinnersley Herefs

NEWCHURCH parish 1684 Kent 5 miles n New Romney pop 241 pec of Archbishop of Canterbury

NEWCHURCH chapelry parish Winwick Lancs

NEWCHURCH parish 1710 co Monmouth 6 miles nw Chepstow pop 723 archd and dioc Llandaff

NEWCHURCH parish 1692 Hamps 4-1/2 miles se Newport pop 4,928 archd and dioc Winchester

NEWCHURCH KENYON 1599 Lancs

NEWCHURCH IN PENDLE FOREST chapelry parish Whalley 1574 Lancs Wesl Meth

NEWCHURCH IN ROSSENDALE FOREST chapelry parish Whalley 1654 Lancs pop 9,196 Wesl Meth, Unit

NEWDIGATE parish 1559 Surrey 5-3/4 miles se Dorking pop 519 archd Surrey dioc Winchester

NEWENDEN LIBERTY parish 1559 Kent 5-1/2 miles sw Tenderden pop 158 archd and dioc Canterbury

NEWENT parish 1673 Gloucs 8-1/2 miles nw Gloucester comp liberty and market town Newent, tythings Boulsdon with Killcot, Compton, Cugley, Malswick pop 2,859 archd Hereford dioc Gloucester Dissenters

NEWFIELD township parish St Andrew Auckland co Durham pop 8

NEW FOREST township parish Kirby Ravensworth N R York pop 73

NEWHALL township parish Acton Ches pop 1,011

NEWHALL township parish Davenham Ches pop 22

NEWHALL township parish Stapenhill Derbys Wesl Meth

NEWHALL township parish Otley W R York pop 203

NEWHAM township parish Bambrough Northumberland pop 324

NEWHAM township parish Whalton Northumberland pop 83

NEWHAVEN or MEECHING parish 1553 Sussex 7 miles s Lewes pop 904 archd Lewes dioc Chichester

NEWHOLM township parish Whitby N R York pop 347

NEWICK parish 1558 Sussex 4-3/4 miles w Uckfield pop 724 archd Lewes dioc Chichester

NEWINGTON parish 1558 Kent 3-1/2 miles w Milton pop 730 archd and dioc Canterbury Wesl Meth

NEWINGTON parish 1572 co Oxford 4-3/4 miles ne Wallingford pop 470 pec of Archbishop of Canterbury

NEWINGTON or NEWINGTON BUTTS parish 1707 Surrey 1-3/4 miles s London pop 44,526 pec of Archbishop of Canterbury Bapt, Indep, Wesl Meth

NEWINGTON BAGPATH parish 1686 Gloucs 4-3/4 miles nw Tetbury pop 258 archd and dioc Gloucester

NEWINGTON NEXT HYTHE parish 1559 Kent 2-1/2 miles ne Hythe pop 491 archd and dioc Canterbury

NEWINGTON, NORTH hamlet parish Broughton co Oxford pop 138
NEWINGTON, SOUTH parish 1538 co Oxford 5 miles nw Deddington
  pop 462 archd and dioc Oxford
NEWINGTON, STOKE parish 1559 Middlesex 3 miles ne London pop
  3,480 pec of Dean and Chapter of St Paul's Soc of Friends, Indep,
  Unit
NEWLAND See ST LAWRENCE
NEWLAND liberty parish Hurst Berks pop 252
NEWLAND parish 1560 Gloucs 4 miles se Monmouth comp chapelries
  Breem, Coleford, tythings Clearwell, Lee Bailey, Newland pop
  4,046 archd and dioc Gloucester
NEWLAND township parish Ulverstone Lancs pop 491
NEWLAND chapelry parish Great Malvery 1562 Worcs pop 130
NEWLAND extra parochial liberty W R York 3 miles ne Wakefield
  pop 46
NEWLAND township parish Drax W R York pop 282
NEWLANDS chapelry 1749 parish Crosthwaite Cumberland pop 113
  Wesl Meth
NEWLANDS township parish Bywell St Peter Northumberland pop 161
NEWLAND SIDE township parish Stanhope co Durham pop 847
NEWLYN parish 1559 Cornwall 2-1/4 miles nw St Michael or Midshall
  pop 1,218 archd Cornwall dioc Exeter Wesl Meth
NEWLYN hamlet parish Paul Cornwall pop 2,345
NEWMARKET market town Cambs and Suffolk comp parishes St Mary
  1638 Suffolk, All Staints 1622 Cambs pop 2,548 archd Sudbury
  dioc Norwich Indep
NEW MILLS manufacturing district parish Glossop Derbys 41 miles
  nw Derby pop 5,000 archd Derby dioc Lichfield Prim and Wesl
  Meth
NEWMINSTER ABBEY township parish Morpeth Northumberland
  pop 121
NEWNHAM market town and parish 1547 Gloucs 11-1/2 miles sw
  Gloucester pop 1,074 archd and dioc Gloucester Indep
NEWNHAM parish 1676 Herts 3 miles n Baldock pop 157 archd St
  Albans dioc London
NEWNHAM parish 1722 Kent 4-1/2 miles sw Faversham pop 436
  archd and dioc Canterbury
NEWNHAM parish 1678 co Northampton 2-1/2 miles se Daventry pop
  581 archd Northampton dioc Peterborough
NEWNHAM parish 1754 Hamps 4-1/2 miles ne Basingstoke pop 329
  archd and dioc Winchester
NEWNHAM hamlet parish Lindridge Worcs
NEWNHAM, KINGS parish (incl with Church Lawford) Warws 4-1/2
  miles nw Rugby pop 139 archd Coventry dioc Lichfield
NEWNHAM MURREN parish 1678 co Oxford 1 mile s Wallingford
  pop 249 archd and dioc Oxford
NEWNTON, LONG parish 1648 Wilts 3-1/4 miles nw Malmesbury
  pop 307 archd Wilts dioc Salisbury

NEWPARKS liberty parish Thurlaston Leics pop 25

NEWPORT parish St Stephen Cornwall by Launceston

NEWPORT hamlet parish Bishop's Tawton Devon

NEWPORT parish 1558 Essex 3-1/2 miles sw Saffron Walden pop
914 Commissary of Essex and Herts, concurrently with Consistorial Court of the Bishop of London Indep

NEWPORT sea port, market town, parish Woollos 1702 co Monmouth
25 miles sw Monmouth Bapt, Indep, Wesl Meth, Roman Cath

NEWPORT market town, parish 1569 Shrops 19 miles ne Shrewsbury
pop 2,343 archd Salop dioc Lichfield Indep

NEWPORT borough, market town, parish 1541 Hamps 18 miles se
Southampton pop 4,081 excl juris archd and dioc Winchester
Bapt, Indep, Wesl Meth, Unit, Roman Cath

NEWPORT PAGNELL market town, parish 1558 Bucks 15 miles ne
Buckingham pop 3,385 archd Buckingham dioc Lincoln Bapt,
Indep, Wesl Meth

NEWPORT WALLINGFENN township parish Eastrington E R York
pop 367

NEW QUAY hamlet parish St Columb Minor Cornwall Bryanites,
Wesl Meth

NEWSHAM township parish Eaglescliffe co Durham pop 58

NEWSHAM township parish Kirkham Lancs

NEWSHAM township parish Wressel E R York pop 203

NEWSHAM township parish Kirby Wisk N R York pop 182

NEWSHAM township parish Kirby Ravensworth N R York pop 546

NEWSHOLME township parish Gisburn W R York pop 70

NEWSTEAD township parish Bambrough Northumberland pop 110

NEWSTEAD liberty parish Papplewick Notts pop 159

NEWSTEAD ON ANCOLM extra parochial liberty Lincs 1-1/2 miles
s Glandford Bridge

NEWTHORP township parish Sherburn W R York pop 63

NEW TIMBER parish 1558 Sussex 3 miles sw Hurst Pierrepoint pop
172 archd Lewes dioc Chichester

NEWTON parish 1560 Cambs 6-3/4 miles s Cambridge pop 161 archd
and dioc Ely

NEWTON parish 1653 Cambs 3-3/4 miles nw Wisbeach pop 431 pec
of Bishop of Ely

NEWTON township parish Mottram in Longden Dale Ches pop 5,997

NEWTON township parish Prestbury Ches pop 90

NEWTON township parish Middlewich Ches pop 1,649

NEWTON township parish West Kirby Ches pop 56

NEWTON hamlet parish Ponsonby Cumberland

NEWTON ST PETROCK parish 1578 Devon 7-1/2 miles sw Great
Torrington pop 250 archd Barnstaple dioc Exeter

NEWTON township parish Ashchurch Gloucs

NEWTON township parish Clodock Herefs pop 253

NEWTON township parish Leintwardine Herefs

NEWTON township parish Croft Herefs pop 95

NEWTON township parish Kirkham Lancs pop 381

NEWTON township parish Poulton Lancs

NEWTON chapelry parish Manchester 1723 Lancs comp townships Bradford, Droylesden, Failsworth, Moston, Newton pop 11,821 Wesl Meth, Unit, Morvanians

NEWTON township parish Sweepstone Leics

NEWTON township parish Ratby Leics

NEWTON parish 1612 Lincs 2-1/4 miles nw Falkingham pop 176 archd and dioc Lincoln

NEWTON hamlet parish Trowse Norfolk

NEWTON parish 1687 co Northampton 3-3/4 miles ne Kettering pop 111 a donative

NEWTON township parish Embleton Northumberland pop 271

NEWTON township parish Chillingham Northumberland pop 141

NEWTON township parish Bywell St Peter Northumberland pop 111

NEWTON township parish Bingham and Shelford Notts

NEWTON or NEWTOWN parish Calbourn Hamps 5-1/4 miles nw Newport pop 68

NEWTON liberty parish Blithfield Staffs pop 269

NEWTON or NOWTON parish 1559 Suffolk 2-3/4 miles se Bury St Edmund's pop 137 archd Sudbury dioc Norwich

NEWTON hamlet parish Clifton upon Dunsmoor Warws pop 239

NEWTON township parish Wintringham E R York

NEWTON township parish Burneston N R York

NEWTON parish 1725 N R York 4 miles sw Guilsbrough pop 148 pec of Dean of York

NEWTON township parish Pickering N R York pop 211 Indep

NEWTON township parish Slaidburn W R York pop 544

NEWTON ABBOTT market town, chapelry, parish Woolborough Devon Bapt, Indep

NEWTON, ARCHDEACON township parish Darlington co Durham pop 50

NEWTON ARLOSH hamlet parish Holme Cultram Cumberland

NEWTON, BANK township parish Gargrave W R York pop 125

NEWTON BEWLEY township parish Billingham co Durham pop 92

NEWTON BLOSSOMVILLE parish 1730 Bucks 3 miles e Olney pop 237 archd Buckingham dioc Lincoln

NEWTON BROMSWOLD parish 1749 co Northampton 3-1/4 miles se Higham Ferrers pop 122 archd Northampton dioc Peterborough

NEWTON BUSHELL chapelry parish Highweek Devon Wesl Meth

NEWTON BY CASTLEACRE parish 1771 Norfolk 4-1/4 miles ne Swaffham pop 70 archd Norfolk dioc Norwich

NEWTON BY CHESTER township parish St Oswald Ches pop 213

NEWTON BY DARESBURY township parish Runcorn Ches pop 165

NEWTON BY FRODSHAM township parish Frodsham Ches pop 130

NEWTON BY TATTENHALL township parish Tattenhall Ches pop 67

NEWTON BY TOFT parish 1592 Lincs 4-1/4 miles sw Market Rasen pop 82 archd and dioc Lincoln

NEWTON CAPP township parish St Andrew Auckland co Durham pop
156
NEWTON, COLD chapelry parish Lowesby Leics pop 120
NEWTON ST CYRES parish 1554 Devon 3-1/2 miles se Crediton pop
1,311 archd and dioc Exeter
NEWTON DIXTON co Monmouth See DIXTON, NEWTON
NEWTON, EAST township parish Aldbrough E R York pop 29
NEWTON, EAST township parish Stonegrave N R York pop 79
NEWTON, ST FAITH hamlet parish Horsham St Faith Norfolk
NEWTON FERRERS parish 1600 Devon 2 miles sw Yealmpton pop
767 archd Totnes dioc Exeter
NEWTON FLOTMAN parish 1558 Norfolk 3-1/2 miles ne St Mary
Stratton pop 382 archd Norfolk dioc Norwich
NEWTON GRANGE liberty parish Ashbourn Derbys pop 41
NEWTON HALL township parish By Well St Peter Northumberland
pop 84
NEWTON HARCOURT chapelry parish Wistow Leics pop 279
NEWTON IN MACKERFIELD chapelry 1735 parish Winwick Lancs
borough pop 2,139
NEWTON IN THE THISTLES or NEWTON REGIS parish 1657 Warws
5-3/4 miles ne Tamworth pop 383 archd Coventry dioc Lichfield
NEWTON JUXTA MALPAS township parish Malpas Ches pop 17
NEWTON KIRK parish 1789 Northumberland 5-1/4 miles nw Kirk
Newton comp townships Akeld, Couldsumberland with Thompson's
Walls, Coupland, Crookhouse, Grey Forest, Heathpool, Howtell,
Kilham, Kirk Newton, Lanton, Milfield, West Newton, Paston, Se-
loy's Forest, Yearvering pop 1,674 archd Northumberland dioc
Durham
NEWTON KYME parish 1633 W R York 2-1/4 miles nw Tadcaster
pop 221 archd and dioc York
NEWTON LE WILLOWS township parish Brompton Patrick 1637 N
R York pop 269 Wesl Meth
NEWTON, ST LOE parish 1538 Somerset 3-1/2 miles w Bath pop
477 archd Bath dioc Bath and Wells
NEWTON, LONG parish 1564 co Durham 4-1/2 miles sw Stockton
upon Tees pop 313 archd and dioc Durham Wesl Meth
NEWTON LONGVILLE parish 1560 Bucks 3 miles sw Fenny Strat-
ford pop 473 archd Buckingham dioc Lincoln
NEWTON MORRELL township parish Barton N R York pop 31
NEWTON MULGRAVE township parish Lythe N R York pop 123
NEWTON NEAR SUDBURY parish 1558 Suffolk 3-1/4 miles e Sudbury
pop 432 archd Sudbury dioc Norwich
NEWTON, NORTH chapelry 1778 parish North Petherton Somerset
NEWTON, NORTH parish 1755 Wilts 3-1/4 miles sw Pewsey pop 317
archd Wilts dioc Salisbury
NEWTON, OLD parish 1677 Suffolk 3 miles ne Stow Market pop 679
archd Sudbury dioc Norwich
NEWTON ON THE MOOR township parish Shilbottle Northumberland

pop 265

NEWTON, OUT township parish Easington E R York pop 63

NEWTON PARK township parish Mitford Northumberland pop 16

NEWTON POPPLEFORD chapelry parish Aylesbear Devon pop 588

NEWTON, POTTER township parish St Peter W R York pop 863

NEWTON PURCELL parish 1681 co Oxford 5 miles ne Bicester pop 131 archd and dioc Oxford

NEWTON RIGNY parish 1572 Cumberland 3 miles nw Penrith pop 276 archd and dioc Carlisle

NEWTON SOLNEY parish 1667 Derbys 2-1/4 miles ne Burton upon Trent pop 338 archd Derby dioc Lichfield

NEWTON, SOUTH parish 1695 Wilts 2-1/2 miles nw Wiltons pop 565 archd and dioc Salisbury

NEWTON, ST PETROCK Devon See NEWTON

NEWTON REGIS Warws See NEWTON IN THE THISTLES

NEWTON STACEY tything parish Barton Stacey Hamps

NEWTON TONEY parish 1568 Wilts 4 miles se Amesbury pop 268 archd and dioc Salisbury

NEWTON TRACEY parish 1562 Devon 4-1/2 miles sw Barnstaple pop 111 archd Barnstaple dioc Exeter

NEWTON UNDERWOOD township parish Mitford Northumberland pop 85

NEWTON UPON DERWENT township parish Wilberfoss E R York pop 228 Wesl Meth

NEWTON UPON OUZE parish 1651 N R York 8-1/2 miles nw York comp townships Benningbrough, Linton upon Ouze, Newton upon Ouze pop 844 pec Lord of Manor of Newton Wesl Meth

NEWTON UPON TRENT parish 1658 Lincs 10 miles nw Lincoln pop 310 archd Stow dioc Lincoln Wesl Meth

NEWTON VALENCE parish 1569 Hamps 4 miles s Alton pop 289 archd and dioc Winchester

NEWTON, WATER parish 1687 Hunts 6 miles nw Stilton pop 108 archd Huntingdon dioc Lincoln

NEWTON, WELSH parish 1758 Herefs 4 miles nw Monmouth pop 224 archd and dioc Hereford

NEWTON, WEST township parish Bromfield Cumberland pop 322

NEWTON, WEST parish 1560 Norfolk 3 miles ne Castle Rising pop 232 archd and dioc Norwich

NEWTON, WEST township parish Kirk Newton Northumberland pop 86

NEWTON, WEST township parish Aldbrough E R York pop 173

NEWTON, WOLD or NEWTON UPON THE WOLDS parish 1578 Lincs 9-1/4 miles sw Great Grimsby pop 158 archd and dioc Lincoln

NEWTON, WOLD parish 1709 E R York 11-1/4 miles ne Great Driffield pop 252 archd East Riding dioc York

NEWTON, WOOD parish 1588 co Northampton 4-1/2 miles n Oundle pop 449 pec juris and patronage of Prebendary of Nassington in Cathedral Church of Lincoln

NEWTON township parish Irthington Cumberland pop 215

NEWTON hamlet parish Leominster Herefs

NEWTON township parish Rothbury Northumberland pop 55

NEWTON chapelry parish Wem 1780 Shrops pop 78

NEWTON LINFORD parish 1654 Leics 5-1/2 miles nw Leicester pop 449 pec of Lord of Manor of Groby

NEWTON NEAR NEWBURY parish 1666 Hamps 2 miles se Newbury pop 269 archd and dioc Winchester

NEW VILLAGE extra parochial liberty E R York 2-1/2 miles sw North Cave pop 140

NEYLAND hamlet parish Ashwellthorpe Norfolk

NIBLEY, NORTH parish 1567 Gloucs 2-1/2 miles nw Wotton under Edge pop 1,562 archd and dioc Gloucester Wesl Meth

NIBTHWAITE township parish Coulton Lancs

NICHOL FOREST chapelry 1761 parish Kirk Andrews upon Esk Cumberland pop 907

NICHOLAS, ST parish 1622 Devon 5-1/2 miles se Newton Abbott pop 1,178 archd and dioc Exeter

NICHOLAS, ST chapelry parish Stanford le Hope Essex

NICHOLAS ST AT WADE parish 1653 Kent 6-1/2 miles sw Margate pop 726 pec of Archbishop of Canterbury

NICHOLAS ST CASTLE HOLD parish (regs with Carisbrooke) Hamps by Newport pop 317 archd and dioc Winchester

NICKLEBY township parish Lythe N R York pop 170 Indep

NIDD parish 1678 W R York 1-1/2 miles e Ripley pop 110 archd Richmond dioc Chester

NIGHTON chapelry parish St Winnow Cornwall

NINEBANKS chapelry 1767 parish Allendale Northumberland pec of Archbishop of York

NINEHEAD or NYNEHEAD parish 1670 Somerset 1-1/2 miles nw Wellington pop 311 archd Taunton dioc Bath and Wells

NINFIELD parish 1663 Sussex 5-1/4 miles sw Battle pop 606 archd Lewes dioc Chichester

NITON parish 1559 Hamps 8 miles e Newport pop 573 archd and dioc Winchester

NIXONS township parish Bewcastle Cumberland pop 220

NOCKHOLT parish 1548 Kent 5 miles nw Seven Oaks pop 471 pec of Archbishop of Canterbury Wesl Meth

NOCTON parish 1582 Lincs 7 miles se Lincoln pop 445 archd and dioc Lincoln

NOCTORUM township parish Wood Church Ches pop 28

NOKE parish 1574 co Oxford 5-1/4 miles ne Oxford pop 187 archd and dioc Oxford

NONINGTON parish 1525 Kent 4-1/4 miles se Wingham pop 832 archd and dioc Canterbury

NOOK, THE township parish Bellingham Northumberland pop 99

NORBRECK township parish Bispham Lancs

NORBURY chapelry parish Stockport (incl regs of Poynton) Ches

pop 671

NORBURY township parish Marbury Ches pop 408

NORBURY parish 1686 Derbys 4 miles sw Ashbourn pop 465 archd Derby dioc Lichfield

NORBURY parish 1560 Shrops 4-1/2 miles ne Bishop's Castle pop 382 archd Salop dioc Hereford

NORBURY parish 1538 Staffs 4 miles ne Newport pop 370 archd Stafford dioc Lichfield

NORCOTT township parish St Helen Berks pop 89

NORDLEY, KING'S township parish Alvelev Shrops

NORHAM or NORHAMSHIRE parish 1653 co Durham 7 miles sw Berwick upon Tweek comp chapelry Cornhill, townships Duddo, Felkington, Grindon, Horncliffe, Loan End, Longridge, Norham, Norham Mains, Shoreswood, Thornton, Twizel pop 3,744 archd Northumberland dioc Durham Indep

NORHAM MAINS township parish Norham co Durham pop 119

NORLAND township parish Halifax W R York pop 1,618

NORLEY township parish Frodsham Ches pop 502

NORMANBY parish 1653 Lincs 7 miles sw Market Rasen pop 438 archd Stow dioc Lincoln Wesl Meth

NORMANBY township parish Stow Lincs pop 17

NORMANBY tything parish Ash Surrey

NORMANBY township parish Ormsby N R York pop 138

NORMANBY parish 1699 N R York 5-1/4 miles sw Pickering comp townships Normanby, Thornton Riseb pop 258 archd Cleveland dioc York

NORMANBY ON THE WOLD parish 1561 Lincs 4 miles ne Market Rasen pop 122 archd and dioc Lincoln

NORMANTON parish 1769 (earlier regs at St Peters Derby) Derbys 2 miles s Derby pop 295 archd Derby dioc Lichfield

NORMANTON hamlet parish Bottesford Leics

NORMANTON parish 1669 Lincs 7-1/4 miles ne Grantham pop 204 archd and dioc Lincoln

NORMANTON hamlet parish Southwell Notts

NORMANTON parish 1755 co Rutland 5 miles se Oakham pop 33 archd Northampton dioc Peterborough

NORMANTON parish 1538 W R York 4-1/2 miles ne Wakefield comp townships Altofts, Normanton, Snydale pop 899 archd and dioc York

NORMANTON LE HEATH chapelry parish Nailstone 1695 Leics pop 216 Wesl Meth

NORMANTON ON THE WOLDS township parish Plumtree Notts pop 185

NORMANTON, SOUTH parish 1540 Derbys 2-3/4 miles ne Alfreton pop 1,154 archd Derby dioc Lichfield Wesl Meth

NORMANTON, TEMPLE chapelry parish Chesterfield Derbys pop 146

NORMANTON TURVILLE hamlet parish Thurlaston Leics pop 55

NORMANTON UPON SOAR parish 1559 Notts 4-1/2 miles nw Lough-
borough pop 365 archd Nottingham dioc York Wesl Meth
NORMANTON UPON TRENT parish 1673 Notts 3-3/4 miles se Tux-
ford pop 349 arch Nottingham dioc York Wesl Meth
NORMICOTT liberty parish Stone Staffs pop 890
NORTHALL hamlet parish Eddlesborough Bucks pop 553
NORTHALLERTON N R York See ALLERTON NORTH
NORTHAM parish 1538 Devon 1-1/2 miles nw Bideford pop 2,727
archd Barnstaple dioc Exeter Indep
NORTHAMPTON borough, market town co Northampton 66 miles nw
London pop 15,351 sep juris comp parishes All Saints 1560, St
Giles 1559, St Peter 1578, St Sepulchre 1566 archd Northampton
dioc Peterborough Bapt, Soc of Friends, Huntingtonians, Indep,
Wesl Meth, Roman Cath
NORTHAW parish 1654 Herts 4-1/2 miles ne Chipping Barnet pop
600 archd St Albans dioc London
NORTHBOROUGH parish 1538 co Northampton 1-3/4 miles se Mar-
ket Deeping pop 227 archd Northampton dioc Peterborough
NORTHBOURNE parish 1586 Kent 2-3/4 miles w Deal pop 869 archd
and dioc Canterbury
NORTHBROOK tything parish Mitcheldever Hamps
NORTHCHAPEL parish 1717 Sussex 5 miles nw Petworth pop 845
archd and dioc Chichester
NORTHCHURCH Herts See BERKHAMSTEAD
NORTHCOTT hamlet parish Boyton Devon pop 105
NORTHEN or NORTHENDEN parish 1564 Ches 4-1/2 miles w Stock-
port pop 1,420 archd and dioc Chester
NORTHFIELD parish 1560 Worcs 6 miles sw Birmingham pop 1,870
archd and dioc Worcester
NORTHFLEET parish 1539 Kent 1-1/2 miles w Gravesend pop 2,124
pec of Archbishop of Canterbury Wesl Meth
NORTH FORTY FOOT BANK or FEN CORNER extra parochial lib-
erty Lincs 9 miles nw Boston pop 241
NORTH FORTY FOOT BANK near FOSDYKE extra parochial liberty
Lincs
NORTH FORTY FOOT BANK near PELHAM'S LANDS extra parochial
liberty Lincs pop 20
NORTH HALES or COVERHITHE parish 1575 Suffolk 4-1/4 miles ne
Southwold pop 182 archd Suffolk dioc Norwich
NORTH HILL parish 1555 Cornwall 6-3/4 miles sw Launceston pop
1,155 archd Cornwall dioc Exeter Wesl Meth
NORTH HOLME parish (incl regs of Wainfleet) Lincs 8 miles se
Spilsby archd and dioc Lincoln
NORTHAM parish 1558 Sussex 7-3/4 miles nw Rye pop 1,448 archd
Lewes dioc Chichester
NORTHILL parish 1562 Beds 3 miles nw Biggleswade pop 1,106
archd Bedford dioc Lincoln
NORTHINGTON parish 1579 Hamps 3-3/4 miles nw New Alresford

pop 291 archd and dioc Winchester

NORTHLEACH market town, parish 1556 Gloucs 20 miles se Gloucester pop 795 archd and dioc Gloucester Indep, Wesl Meth

NORTHLEIGH See LEIGH, NORTH

NORTHMOOR parish 1654 co Oxford 6-3/4 miles sw Oxford pop 360
archd and dioc Oxford

NORTHOLT parish 1560 Middlesex 2-3/4 miles sw Harrow on the
Hill pop 447 archd Middlesex dioc London

NORTHORPE hamlet parish Thurlby Lincs

NORTHORPE parish 1594 Lincs 8 miles ne Gainsborough pop 128
archd Stow dioc Lincoln

NORTHOVER parish 1722 Somerset 1/4 mile n Ilchester pop 138
archd Wells dioc Bath and Wells

NORTHSCEUGH township parish Cumwhitton Cumberland

NORTHWAY tything parish Ashchurch Gloucs pop 188

NORTHWICH market town, parochial chapelry Witton parish Great
Budworth Ches 17-1/2 miles ne Chester pop 1,481 Indep, Wesl
Meth

NORTHWICH hamlet parish Blockley Gloucs

NORTHWICK chapelry 1667 parish Henbury Gloucs

NORTHWOLD parish 1656 Norfolk 4-1/4 miles se Stoke Ferry pop
1,094 archd Norfolk dioc Norwich

NORTHWOOD township parish Wem Shrops pop 233

NORTHWOOD parish 1539 Hamps 1-3/4 miles s West Cowes pop
4,491 archd and dioc Winchester

NORTON township parish Runcorn Ches pop 306

NORTON parish 1560 Derbys 3 miles ne Dronfield pop 1,747 archd
Derby dioc Lichfield Unit

NORTON parish 1574 co Durham 2 miles n Stockton upon Tees pop
1,486 archd and dioc Durham Wesl Meth

NORTON parish 1686 Gloucs 4 miles ne Gloucester pop 423 archd
and dioc Gloucester

NORTON township parish Bromyard Herefs pop 554

NORTON parish 1571 Herts 1 mile nw Baldock pop 364 archd St Albans dioc London

NORTON parish 1559 Kent 3-1/4 miles w Faversham pop 111 archd
and dioc Canterbury

NORTON parish 1678 co Northampton 2-1/2 miles ne Daventry pop
541 archd Northampton dioc Peterborough Wesl Meth

NORTON township parish Cuckney Notts pop 324

NORTON parish 1539 Suffolk 3-1/2 miles se Ixworth pop 802 archd
Suffolk dioc Norwich

NORTON parish 1538 Worcs 3 miles ne Evesham pop 397 archd and
dioc Worcester

NORTON parish 1560 E R York 3/4 mile se New Malton comp townships Norton, Sutton, Welham pop 1,425 archd East Riding dioc
York

NORTON township parish Campsall W R York pop 643 Wesl Meth

NORTON BAVANT parish 1616 Wilts 2-3/4 miles se Warminster pop 279 archd and dioc Salisbury

NORTON, BISHOP'S 1587 Lincs 10 miles nw Market Rasen pop 426 pec of Prebendary of Bishop's Norton in Cathedral Church of Lincoln Wesl Meth

NORTON, BRIZE parish 1585 co Oxford 5 miles se Burford pop 627 archd and dioc Oxford

NORTON BY BREDON chapelry parish Bredon Worcs pop 199

NORTON BY KEMPSEY parish 1538 Worcs 3-1/2 miles se Worcester pop 560 pec of Dean and Chapter of Worcester

NORTON CANON parish 1716 Herts 3-1/4 miles sw Weobley pop 338 Consistory Court of Dean of Hereford

NORTON, CHIPPING market town, parish 1563 co Oxford 18 miles nw Oxford pop 2,637 excl juris archd and dioc Oxford Bapt, Soc of Friends, Meth

NORTON, COLD parish 1539 Essex 5 miles s Maldon pop 216 archd Essex dioc London

NORTON, COLD township parish Chebsey Staffs pop 37

NORTON COLEPARLE parish 1663 Wilts 3-3/4 miles sw Malmesbury pop 113 archd Wilts dioc Salisbury

NORTON CONYERS chapelry parish Wath N R York pop 73

NORTON CUCKNEY Notts See CUCKNEY

NORTON DISNEY parish 1578 Lincs 7 miles ne Newark pop 210 archd and dioc Lincoln

NORTON, EAST parish 1721 Leics 6 miles nw Uppingham pop 137 archd Leicester dioc Lincoln

NORTON FALGATE extra parochial liberty Middlesex near Bishopgate London pop 1,918

NORTON FITZWARREN parish 1556 Somerset 2-3/4 miles nw Taunton pop 545 archd Taunton dioc Bath and Wells

NORTON, GREENS co Northampton See GREENS NORTON

NORTON HAWFIELD village Somerset 5-1/2 miles s Bristol pop 40

NORTON, HOOK parish 1566 co Oxford 5-1/4 miles ne Chipping Norton pop 1,506 archd and dioc Oxford Bapt, Wesl Meth

NORTON IN HALES parish 1573 Shrops 3-1/2 miles ne Drayton in Hales pop 311 archd Salop dioc Lichfield

NORTON JUXTA TWYCROSS parish 1686 Leics 6-1/2 miles nw Market Bosworth pop 497 archd Leicester dioc Lincoln

NORTON KING'S parish 1588 Leics 7-1/2 miles se Leicester comp chapelry Stretton Parva, Ilston on the Hill, townships King's Norton pop 161 archd Leicester dioc Lincoln

NORTON, KING'S parish 1546 Worcs 6 miles se Birmingham pop 3,977 archd and dioc Worcester

NORTON LE CLAY township parish Cundall N R York pop 146

NORTON LINDSEY parish 1742 Warws 3-3/4 miles sw Warwick pop 141 archd and dioc Worcester

NORTON MALEREWARD parish 1554 Somerset 2-1/4 miles nw Pensford pop 110 archd Bath dioc Bath and Wells

NORTON MANDEVILLE parish 1783 Essex 3 miles ne Chipping Ongar
   pop 114 archd Essex dioc London
NORTON, MIDSUMMER parish 1677 Somerset 9-1/2 miles sw Bath
   comp tythings Clapton, Downside, Midsummer Norton, Wilton
   pop 2,942 archd Wells dioc Bath and Wells Wesl Meth
NORTON ON THE MOORS parish 1576 Staffs 2-1/2 miles ne Hanley
   pop 2,407 archd Stafford dioc Lichfield
NORTON, OVER hamlet parish Chipping Norton co Oxford pop 375
NORTON, ST PHILLIP parish 1680 Somerset 6-1/2 miles se Bath
   pop 767 archd Wells dioc Bath and Wells Bapt
NORTON, PUDDING parish no regs Norfolk 1-1/2 miles s Faken-
   ham pop 17 archd and dioc Norwich
NORTON SUBCOURSE parish 1560 Norfolk 6 miles nw Beecles pop
   367 archd Norfolk dioc Norwich
NORTON UNDER CANNOCK or CANES parish 1566 Staffs 8-1/2 miles
   sw Lichfield pop 678 pec Prebendary of Hansacre and Harmitage
NORTON UNDER HAMBDON parish 1558 Somerset 4-1/2 miles ne
   Crewkerne pop 513 archd Wells dioc Bath and Wells
NORWELL parish 1685 Notts 6 miles nw Newark pop 939 pec of
   Chapter of Collegiate Church of Southwell
NORWELL WOODHOUSE township parish Norwell Notts pop 141
NORWICH city Norfolk 108 miles ne London pop 61,110 comp par-
   ishes All Saints 1573, St Julian 1589, St Andrew 1557, St Augus-
   tine 1558, St Benedict 1562, St Clement 1538, St Edmund 1550, St
   Ethelred 1665, St George Colegate 1538, St George Tombland
   1538, St Giles 1538, St Gregory 1571, St Helen 1678, St John Mad-
   dermarket 1558, St John Sepulchre 1636, St John Timberhill 1559,
   St James 1556, St Paul 1567, St Lawrence 1558, St Margaret de
   Westwick 1559, St Martin at Palace 1538, St Martin at Oak 1704,
   St Mary Coslany 1557, St Mary 1591, St Michael Coslany 1558,
   St Michael at Plea 1538, St Michael at Thorn 1562, St Peter Hun-
   gate 1596, St Peter Mancroft 1538, St Peter Mountergate 1538,
   St Peter Southgate 1558, St Savior 1555, St Simon 1539, St Jude
   1539, St Stephen 1538, St Swithin 1700, Eaton St Andrew 1568,
   Heigham 1565, Pockthorpe with St James, Lakenham 1568 All
   are archd and dioc Norwich except St Andrew, St Helen, St James,
   St Pauls and Lakenham which are pec of Dean and Chapter of
   Norwich Bapt, Soc of Friends, Indep, Wesl Meth, Countess of
   Huntingdon's Connection, Unit, Jews, Roman Cath
NORWOOD parish 1654 Middlesex 2-1/2 miles nw Hounslow pop
   1,320 pec Archbishop of Canterbury
NORWOOD district parish Lambeth Surrey Indep
NORWOOD township parish Fewston W R York
NOSLEY extra parochial liberty Leics 8-1/2 miles ne Market Har-
   borough pop 11
NOSTAL township parish Wragby W R York
NOTGROVE parish 1660 Gloucs 4-3/4 miles n Northleach pop 166

archd and dioc Gloucester

NOTLEY, BLACK parish 1570 Essex 1-1/2 miles se Braintree pop 486 archd Colchester dioc London

NOTLEY, WHITE parish 1541 Essex 3-1/2 miles nw Witham pop 453 archd Colchester dioc London

NOTTINGHAM borough, market town Notts 124 miles nw London pop 50,680 comp parishes St Mary 1566, St Nicholas 1562, St Paul 1839, St Peter 1572 archd Nottingham dioc York Bapt, Indep, Wesl Meth, Soc of Friends, Huntingtonians, Sabellians, Sandemanians, Unit, Jews, Roman Cath

NOTTINGHAM FEE liberty parish Blewbury Berks

NOTTINGTON hamlet parish Broadway Dorset

NOTTON township parish Royston W R York pop 317

NOWTON Suffolk See NEWTON

NUFFIELD parish 1570 co Oxford 4-1/2 miles se Wallingford pop 197 archd and dioc Oxford

NUN BURNHOLME parish 1586 E R York 3-1/2 miles se Pocklington comp township Thorpe in the Street, Nun Burnholme pop 253 archd East Riding dioc York

NUNEATON market town, parish 1577 Warws 15 miles ne Warwick pop 7,799 archd Coventry dioc Lichfield Indep, Wesl Meth

NUNEHAM COURTNEY parish 1715 co Oxford 5 miles se Oxford pop 314 archd and dioc Oxford

NUNKEELING parish 1559 E R York 11 miles ne Beverley pop 263 archd East Riding dioc York

NUNNEY parish 1547 Somerset 2-3/4 miles sw Frome pop 1,204 archd Wells dioc Bath and Wells Wesl Meth

NUNNIKIRK township parish Nether Witton Northumberland pop 16

NUNNINGTON parish 1539 N R York 4-1/2 miles se Helmsley pop 441 archd Cleveland dioc York Wesl Meth

NUNRIDGE township parish Mitford Northumberland pop 37

NUNTHORPE chapelry parish Ayton E R York pop 125

NUNTON chapelry parish Downton 1672 Wilts

NUNWICK township parish Ripon W R York pop 38

NURSLING or NUTSHALLING parish 1617 Hamps 3 miles s Romsey pop 884 archd and dioc Winchester Wesl Meth

NURSTED parish 1561 Kent 4-1/4 miles sw Gravesend pop 38 archd and dioc Rochester

NURSTED tything parish Buriton Hamps

NUTFIELD parish 1674 Surrey 1-1/4 miles w Bletchingley pop 718 archd Surrey dioc Winchester

NUTHALL or NUTTALL parish 1657 Notts 4-1/2 miles nw Nottingham pop 509 archd Nottingham dioc York

NUTHAMPSTEAD hamlet parish Barkway Herts pop 249

NUTHILL formerly a parish E R York 8-1/2 miles ne Kingston upon Hull archd East Riding dioc York

NUTHURST parish 1563 Sussex 3-3/4 miles se Horsham pop 723 archd and dioc Chichester

NUTHURST hamlet parish Hampton in Arden Warws pop 124

NUTLEY parish 1688 Hamps 5 miles sw Basingstoke pop 138 archd and dioc Winchester

NYLAND formerly a parish Somerset 6-1/4 miles nw Wells pop 52

NYMETT, BROAD parish 1599 Devon 1-1/2 miles sw Bow archd Barnstaple dioc Exeter

NYMETT ROWLAND parish 1719 Devon 4-3/4 miles se Chulmleigh pop 99 archd Barnstaple dioc Exeter

NYMETT TRACEY Devon See BOW

NYMPSFIELD parish 1678 Gloucs 5-1/4 miles ne Dursley pop 434 archd and dioc Gloucester

NYMPTON ST GEORGE 1599 parish Devon 2-1/2 miles se South Molton pop 268 archd Barnstaple dioc Exeter

NYMPTON, BISHOP'S parish 1556 Devon 3 miles se South Molton pop 1,116 archd and dioc Exeter

NYMPTON, KING'S parish 1538 Devon 3-1/2 miles n Chulmleigh pop 699 archd Barnstaple dioc Exeter

OADBY parish 1653 Leics 3-1/2 miles se Leicester pop 1,023 archd Leicester dioc Lincoln

OAKE parish 1630 Somerset 5-3/4 miles w Taunton pop 147 archd Taunton dioc Bath and Wells

OKEN hamlet parish Tettenhall Staffs pop 271

OAKENGALE hamlet parish Shiffnall Shrops

OAKENSHAW hamlet parish Birstall W R York

OAKFORD parish 1568 Devon 3-1/4 miles sw Bampton pop 497 archd Barnstaple dioc Exeter

OAKHAM or OAKHAM LORDSHOLD parish 1564 co Rutland 95 miles nw London pop 2,390 archd Northampton dioc Peterborough Bapt, Soc of Friends, Indep, Wesl Meth

OAKHAMPTON or OKEHAMPTON market town, parish 1634 borough Devon 22 miles nw Exeter pop 2,055 sep juris archd Totnes dioc Exeter Indep

OAKHAMPTON, MONK parish 1653 Devon 2-3/4 miles ne Hatherleigh pop 259 archd Totnes dioc Exeter

OAKINGHAM, Berks See WOKINGHAM

OAKINGTON parish 1561 Cambs 5 miles nw Cambridge pop 532 archd and dioc Ely Bapt

OAKLEY parish 1680 Beds 4 miles nw Bedford pop 516 archd Bedford dioc Lincoln

OAKLEY parish 1704 Bucks 6 miles nw Thame pop 413 archd Buckingham dioc Lincoln

OAKLEY township parish Croxhall Staffs pop 29

OAKLEY township parish Muckleston Staffs pop 85

OAKLEY parish 1538 Suffolk 3 miles ne Eye pop 365 archd Sudbury dioc Norwich

OAKLEY, CHURCH parish 1559 Hamps 4-1/2 miles sw Basingstoke pop 249 archd and dioc Winchester

OAKLEY, GREAT parish 1559 Essex 7 miles se Manningtree pop

1,118 archd Colchester dioc London Wesl Meth

OAKLEY, GREAT parish 1562 co Northampton 5 miles n Kettering pop 204 archd Northampton dioc Peterborough

OAKLEY, LITTLE parish 1558 Essex 4-1/2 miles sw Harwich pop 244 archd Colchester dioc London

OAKLEY, LITTLE parish 1679 co Northampton 5-1/2 miles ne Kettering pop 128 archd Northampton dioc Peterborough

OAKLEY PARVA parish Suffolk 3 miles ne Eye (now with Oakley)

OAKMERE township parish Delamere Ches pop 140

OAKOVER parish 1737 Staffs 2-1/2 miles nw Ashbourn pop 62 dioc Lichfield

OAKSEY parish 1670 Wilts 5-1/2 miles ne Malmesbury pop 494 archd Wilts dioc Salisbury

OAKSHOT hamlet parish Stoke D'Abernon Surrey

OAKTHORPE hamlet parish Measham Derbys pop 757 Bapt, Wesl Meth

OAKWOOD chapelry 1700 parish Wotton Surrey Bapt

OARE chapelry parish Chieveley Berks

OARE parish 1714 Kent 1-1/2 miles nw Faversham pop 176 archd and dioc Canterbury

OARE parish 1674 Somerset 12 miles w Minehead pop 70 archd Taunton dioc Bath and Wells

OATHILL tything parish Wayford Somerset

OBLEY township parish Clunbury Shrops

OBORNE parish 1567 Dorset 1-1/4 miles ne Sherborne pop 83 pec of Dean of Salisbury

OBTHORPE hamlet parish Thurley Lincs

OBY parish (incl in regs Ashby) Norfolk 3-1/2 miles ne Acle archd and dioc Norwich

OCCANEY extra parochial district W R York 3-1/2 miles n Knaresboro

OCCLESTONE township parish Middlewich Ches pop 93

OCCOLD parish 1681 Suffolk 2-1/2 miles se Eye pop 518 archd Sudbury dioc Norwich

OCKBROOK parish 1630 Derbys 5-1/2 miles se Derby pop 1,634 archd Derby dioc Lichfield Wesl Meth

OCKENDON, NORTH parish 1570 Essex 4-1/2 miles se Hornchurch pop 294 archd Essex dioc London

OCKDENDON, SOUTH parish 1538 Essex 4-1/4 miles nw Grays Thurrock pop 816 archd Essex dioc London Wesl Meth

OCKHAM parish 1567 Surrey 1 mile e Ripley pop 590 archd Surrey dioc Winchester

OCKLEY parish 1539 Surrey 6-1/4 miles sw Dorking pop 710 archd Surrey dioc Winchester

OCLE LIVERS extra parochial liberty Herefs 6-1/2 miles ne Hereford

OCLE PITCHARD parish 1773 Herefs 7-1/2 miles ne Hereford pop 236 archd and dioc Hereford

OCTON township parish Thwing E R York

OCTON GRANGE township parish Thwing E R York

ODCOMBE parish 1669 Somerset 3-1/4 miles sw Yeovil pop 616 archd Wells dioc Bath and Wells

ODDINGLEY parish 1661 Worcs 3 miles s Droitwich pop 157 archd and dioc Winchester

ODDINGTON parish 1549 Gloucs 2-1/2 miles e Stow on the Wold pop 539 archd and dioc Gloucester

ODDINGTON parish 1572 co Oxford 7 miles sw Bicester pop 176 archd and dioc Oxford

ODELL parish 1604 Beds 1-1/4 miles ne Harrold pop 475 archd Bedford dioc Lincoln

ODESTONE hamlet parish Shackerstone Leics pop 163

ODIHAM market town, parish 1538 Hamps 26 miles ne Winchester pop 3,310 archd and dioc Winchester Connection of Countess of Huntingdon, Indep

ODSTOCK parish 1541 Wilts 3 miles s Salisbury pop 148 archd and dioc Salisbury

ODSTONE tything parish Ashbury Berks pop 33

OFFCHURCH parish 1669 Warws 5 miles ne Warwick pop 350 archd Coventry dioc Lichfield

OFFCOAT liberty parish Ashbourn Derbys pop 328

OFFENHAM parish 1538 Worcs 2-1/2 miles ne Evesham pop 360 archd and dioc Worcester

OFFERTON township parish Stockport Ches pop 431

OFFERTON hamlet parish Hope Derbys pop 22

OFFERTON township parish Houghton le Spring co Durham pop 190

OFFHAM parish 1538 Kent 3-1/4 miles se Wrotham pop 262 archd and dioc Rochester

OFFHAM tything parish Southstoke Sussex

OFFLEY parish 1653 Herts 3-1/4 miles sw Hitchin pop 967 archd Huntingdon dioc Lincoln

OFFLEY, HIGH parish 1689 Staffs 4-1/4 miles sw Eccleshall comp townships Loynton, High Offley pop 827 pec of Prebendary of Offley and Flixton

OFFLOW, BISHOP'S township parish Abdaston Staffs pop 205

OFFORD CLUNY parish 1598 Hunts 5 miles ne St Neots pop 232 archd Huntingdon dioc Lincoln

OFFORD DARCY parish 1697 Hunts 4-1/2 miles ne St Neots pop 277 archd Huntingdon dioc Lincoln

OFFTON parish 1558 Suffolk 5 miles e Bildeston pop 399 archd Suffolk dioc Norwich

OFFWELL parish 1551 Devon 2-1/2 miles se Honiton pop 385 archd and dioc Exeter

OGBOURN ST ANDREW parish 1664 Wilts 2 miles n Marlborough pop 489 pec of Dean of Sarum

OGBOURN ST GEORGE parish 1538 Wilts 3-1/4 miles n Marlborough pop 548 pec of Dean of Sarum

OGLE or OCLE township parish Whalton Northumberland pop 137

OGLY HAY extra parochial district Staffs 4 miles sw Lichfield Staffs
   pop 24
OGWELL, EAST parish 1674 Devon 1-1/2 miles sw Newton Abbott
   pop 318 archd and dioc Exeter
OGWELL, WEST parish 1681 Devon 2-1/4 miles sw Newton Abbott
   pop 50 archd and dioc Exeter
OKEFORD, CHILD parish 1652 Dorset 6-1/2 miles nw Blandford
   Forum pop 612 archd Dorset dioc Bristol
OKEFORD FITZPAINE parish 1592 Dorset 7-1/2 miles nw Blandford
   Forum pop 620 archd Dorset dioc Bristol
OKENEY CUM PETSOE parish (incl in regs of Emberton) Bucks 2
   miles se Olney archd Buckingham dioc Lincoln
OLD or WOLD parish 1539 co Northampton 6-1/2 miles sw Kettering
   pop 458 archd Northampton dioc Peterborough
OLD ALRESFORD Hamps See ALRESFORD, OLD
OLDBERROW parish 1649 Worcs 2-1/4 miles w Henley in Arden pop
   65 archd and dioc Worcester
OLDBURY parish 1583 Shrops 1 mile sw Bridgenorth pop 126 archd
   Salop dioc Hereford Bapt, Indep, Wesl Meth
OLDBURY hamlet parish Hales Owen Shrops
OLDBURY hamlet parish Mancetter Warws pop 80
OLDBURY chapelry parish Halesowen Worcs
OLDBURY ON THE HILL parish 1567 Gloucs 4-1/4 miles sw Tetbury
   pop 414 archd and dioc Gloucester
OLDBURY UPON SEVERN chapelry parish Thornbury Gloucs
OLDCASTLE township parish Malpas Ches pop 98
OLDCASTLE parish 1783 co Monmouth 8-1/2 miles ne Abergavenny
   pop 62 archd Brecon dioc St David's
OLDCOTT township parish Wolstanton Staffs pop 822
OLDFIELD township parish Heswall Ches
OLDHAM CUM borough, parochial chapelry 1558 Lancs 7 miles ne
   Manchester comp chapelries Chadderton, Royton, townships
   Crompton, Oldham pop 67,579 archd and dioc Chester Bapt,
   Soc of Friends, Indep, Kilhamites, Moravians, Prim, Wesl and
   Indep Meth, Unit
OLDLAND chapelry parish Bitton Gloucs pop 5,233
OLDMOOR township parish Bothall Northumberland pop 66
OLD PARK township parish St Andrew Auckland co Durham pop 67
OLDRIDGE chapelry parish St Thomas Devon
OLDSWINFORD Worcs See SWINFORD, OLD
OLERSET hamlet parish Glossop Derbys pop 304
OLLERTON township parish Knutsford Ches pop 283
OLLERTON market town, chapelry 1592 parish Edwinstow Notts pop
   658 Wesl Meth
OLLERTON township parish Stoke upon Tern Shrops pop 175
OLNEY market town, parish 1665 Bucks 19 miles ne Buckingham
   pop 2,418 archd and dioc Lincoln Bapt, Soc of Friends, Indep,
   Wesl Meth

OLVESTON parish 1560 Gloucs 3-1/4 miles sw Thornbury comp tythings Olveston, Upper Tockington pop 1,523 pec of Bishop of Bristol Wesl Meth, Soc of Friends

OMBERSLEY parish 1574 Worcs 4-1/4 miles w Droitwich pop 2,118 archd and dioc Worcester

OMPTON township parish Kneesall Notts pop 120

ONECOTE chapelry 1755 parish Leek Staffs pop 456

ONE HOUSE parish 1552 Suffolk 2 miles w Stow market pop 169 archd Sudbury dioc Norwich

ONELY hamlet parish Barby co Northampton

ONGAR, CHIPPING market town, parish 1558 Essex 12 miles sw Chelmsford pop 798 archd Essex dioc London Indep

ONGAR, HIGH parish 1538 Essex 3/4 mile ne Chipping Ongar pop 1,205 archd Essex dioc London

ONIBURY parish 1577 Shrops 5-1/2 miles ne Ludlow pop 438 archd Salop dioc Hereford

ONN, HIGH township parish Church Eaton Staffs

ONN, LITTLE township parish Church Eaton Staffs

ONSTON township parish Weaverham Ches pop 92

OPENSHAW township parish Manchester Lancs pop 838

ORBY parish 1725 Lincs 6-1/2 miles ne Spilsby pop 287 archd and dioc Lincoln Bapt

ORCHARD, EAST parish (incl regs Iwerne Minster) Dorset 4 miles sw Shaftesbury pop 211 archd Dorset dioc Bristol

ORCHARD PORTMAN parish 1538 Somerset 2 miles se Taunton pop 112 archd Taunton dioc Bath and Wells

ORCHARD, WEST parish 1754 Dorset 5 miles sw Shaftesbury pop 183 archd Dorset dioc Bristol

ORCHARDLEIGH parish 1623 Somerset 2 miles n Frome pop 27 archd Wells dioc Bath and Wells

ORCHESTON parish 1647 Wilts 6-1/2 miles nw Amesbury pop 219 archd and dioc Salisbury

ORCHESTON parish 1688 Wilts 7 miles nw Amesbury pop 134 archd and dioc Salisbury

ORCOP parish 1672 Herefs 9-1/2 miles nw Ross pop 560 pec of Chancellor of Dioc of Hereford

ORDSALL parish 1538 Notts 1-1/2 miles s East Retford pop 809 archd Nottingham dioc York

ORE parish 1558 Sussex 2-1/2 miles nw Hastings pop 965 archd Lewes dioc Chichester

ORFORD parish 1538 borough Suffolk 20 miles ne Ipswich pop 1,302 sep juris archd Suffolk dioc Norwich

ORFORTH extra parochial district Lincs near Binbrooke St Mary

ORGARSWICK parish Kent 5 miles ne New Romney pop 8 archd and dioc Canterbury

ORGREAVE hamlet parish Alrewas Staffs pop 123

ORGREAVE township parish Rotherham W R York pop 35

ORLESTONE parish 1554 Kent 5-1/2 miles sw Ashford pop 539

archd and dioc Canterbury

ORLETON parish 1565 Herefs 6 miles ne Leominster pop 586 archd
and dioc Hereford

ORLETON chapelry parish Eastham Worcs pop 119

ORLINGBURY parish 1564 co Northampton 3-3/4 miles nw Wellingborough pop 336 archd Northampton dioc Peterborough

ORMSBY parish 1599 N R York 5-1/4 miles nw Guilsbrough pop
901 archd Cleveland dioc York

ORMSBY parish 1675 Norfolk 3 miles nw Caistor pop 720 archd and
dioc Norwich

ORMSBY parish 1568 Norfolk 2-1/4 miles nw Caistor pop 273 archd
and dioc Norwich

ORMSBY, NORTH or NUN parish 1741 Lincs 6-3/4 miles nw Lough
pop 128 archd and dioc Lincoln

ORMSBY, SOUTH parish 1561 Lincs 7-3/4 miles nw Spilsby pop 237
archd and dioc Lincoln

ORMSIDE or ORMSHED parish 1563 Westm 3-1/4 miles se Appleby
pop 190 archd and dioc Carlisle

ORMSKIRK parish 1557 Lancs 13 miles ne Liverpool comp market
town Ormskirk, chapelry Skelmersdale, townships Bickerstaffe,
Birkdale, Burscough, Lathom, Scarisbrick pop 14,503 archd and
dioc Chester Indep, Meth of New Connection, Unit

ORPINGTON parish 1560 Kent 3 miles sw Foot's Cray pop 842 pec
of Archbishop of Canterbury Indep

ORRELL township parish Sephton Lancs pop 244

ORRELL township parish Wigan Lancs pop 2,518 Indep

ORSETT parish 1669 Essex 18-1/2 miles sw Chelmsford pop 1,274
Commissary of Essex and Herts, concurrently with Consistorial
Court of Bishop of London

ORSTON parish 1589 Notts 6-1/4 miles ne Bingham pop 439 archd
Nottingham dioc York Wesl Meth

ORTON GREAT parish 1569 Cumberland 5-1/2 miles sw Carlisle
comp townships Baldwin Holme, Orton pop 445 archd and dioc
Carlisle

ORTON chapelry parish Rothwell co Northampton pop 109

ORTON liberty parish Wombourne Staffs pop 176

ORTON market town, parish 1595 Westm 9 miles sw Appleby pop
1,501 archd and dioc Carlisle

ORTON LONGVILLE parish 1559 Hunts 2-1/4 miles sw Peterborough
pop 286 archd Huntingdon dioc Lincoln

ORTON ON THE HILL parish 1657 Leics 4-3/4 miles n Atherstone
pop 350 archd Leicester dioc Lincoln

ORTON WATERVILLE parish 1539 Hunts 3 miles sw Peterborough
pop 286 archd Huntingdon dioc Lincoln

ORWELL parish 1560 Cambs 7-1/2 miles nw Royston pop 537 archd
and dioc Ely

OSBALDESTON township parish Blackburn Lancs pop 349

OSBALDWICK parish 1581 N R York 2-1/4 miles e York comp townships Murton, Osbaldwick pop 319 pec of Prebendary of Strensall

OSBASTON township parish Market Bosworth Leics pop 186

OSBOURNBY parish 1682 Lincs 2-3/4 miles n Falkingham pop 522 archd and dioc Lincoln

OSGARTHORPE parish 1683 Leics 5-1/4 miles ne Ashby de la Zouch pop 344 archd Leicester dioc Lincoln

OSGODBY township parish Lavington Lincs pop 99

OSGODBY parish incl regs of Kirkby Lincs 4 miles nw Market Rasen pop 350 Wesl Meth

OSGODBY township parish Hemingbrough E R York pop 170

OSGODBY township parish Cayton N R York pop 65

OSGODBY GRANGE hamlet parish Kilburn W R York

OSLESTON township parish Sutton on the Hill Derbys pop 392

OSLOW township parish Church Easton Staffs

OSMASTON parish 1606 Derbys 2-1/4 miles se Ashbourn pop 289 archd Derby dioc Lichfield

OSMINGTON parish 1678 Dorset 4-1/2 miles ne Melcombe Regis pop 421 archd Dorset dioc Bristol

OSMONDISTON Norfolk See SCOLE

OSMOTHERLEY township parish Ulverstone Lancs pop 293 Wesl Meth

OSMOTHERLEY parish 1696 N R York 7-1/2 miles ne North Allerton comp townships Ellerbeck, West Harsley, Osmotherley, Thimbleby pop 1,417 pec juris of Court of Bishop of Durham Soc of Friends, Wesl Meth, Roman Cath

OSPRINGE LIBERTY parish 1561 Kent 3/4 mile sw Faversham pop 1,087 archd and dioc Canterbury

OSSETT chapelry parish Dewsbury 1792 W R York pop 5,325 archd and dioc York Indep, Wesl Meth

OSSINGTON parish 1594 Notts 4-1/4 miles se Tuxford pop 257 archd Nottingham dioc York

OSTENHANGER Kent See WESTEN HANGER

OSWALD, KIRK Cumberland See KIRK OSWALD

OSWALD KIRK parish 1538 N R York 3-1/2 miles s Helmsley pop 209 archd Cleveland dioc York

OSWALD KIRK QUARTER township parish Ampleforth N R York pop 191

OSWALD, ST Northumberland See WALL

OSWALDTWISTLE township parish Whalley Lancs pop 5,897

OSWESTRY market town, parish 1558 sep juris Shrops 17 miles nw Shrewsbury comp townships Llanforda with Trevarclawdd, Pontregaer, Lynymon, Maesbury with Morton, Crickheath, Middleton with Aston, Hisland, Wooton, Weston with Sweeney, Trevach, Trevonnen pop 8,581 archd and dioc St Asaph Bapt, Indep, Wesl Meth

OSYTH ST CHICH parish 1666 Essex 11 miles se Colchester pop 1,583 archd Colchester dioc London

OTFORD parish 1630 Kent 3 miles n Seven Oaks pop 746 pec of Archbishop of Canterbury Wesl Meth

OTHAM parish 1538 Kent 2-3/4 miles se Maidstone pop 344 archd
and dioc Canterbury

OTHERTON township parish Penkridge Staffs

OTHERY parish 1560 Somerset 4-1/2 miles nw Langport pop 581
juris of Glastonbury dioc Bath and Wells

OTLEY parish 1734 Suffolk 5-3/4 miles nw Woodbridge pop 616 archd
Suffolk dioc Norwich Bapt

OTLEY parish 1562 W R York 28 miles sw York comp market town
Otley, chapelries Baildon, Bramhope, Burley, Poole, townships Esholt, Hawksworth, Menstone, Denton, chapelry townships Farnley,
Lindley, Newhall with Clifton, Little Timble pop 10,163 archd
and dioc York Wesl Meth, Soc of Friends, Indep

OTTERBOURNE parish 1648 Hamps 4-1/4 miles sw Winchester pop
583 pec of Vicar of Hursley

OTTERBURN township parish Kirby in Malham Dale W R York pop 66

OTTERBURN WARD township parish Elsdon Northumberland pop 385

OTTERDEN parish 1660 Kent 3-1/2 miles n Charing pop 181 archd
and dioc Canterbury

OTTERFORD parish 1558 regs very incomplete Somerset 7 miles s
Taunton pop 406 archd Taunton dioc Bath and Wells

OTTERHAM parish 1687 Cornwall 6 miles ne Camelford pop 227
archd Cornwall dioc Exeter

OTTERHAMPTON parish 1636 Somerset 5-3/4 miles nw Bridgewater
pop 240 archd Taunton dioc Bath and Wells

OTTERINGTON, NORTH parish 1591 N R York 3-1/2 miles s North
Allerton comp townships North Otterington, Thornton le Beans,
Thornton le Moor pop 617 juris pec Court of Allertonshire

OTTERINGTON, SOUTH parish 1718 N R York 4-1/2 miles se North
Allerton pop 241 archd Cleveland dioc York

OTTERSAY STOCKLINCH Somerset See STOCKLINCH, OTTERSAY

OTTERTON parish 1559 Devon 4 miles sw Sidmouth pop 1,178 archd
and dioc Exeter

OTTERY ST MARY market town, parish 1601 Devon 11 miles ne Exeter pop 3,849 archd and dioc Exeter Indep, Wesl Meth

OTTRINGHAM parish 1566 E R York 6-1/4 miles se Hedon pop 627
archd East Riding dioc York Wesl Meth

OUGHTERBY township parish Kirk Bampton Cumberland pop 118

OULSTON township parish Coxwold N R York pop 215

OULSWICK chapelry parish Monks Risborough Bucks

OULTON township parish Wigton Cumberland pop 379 Bapt

OULTON parish 1706 Norfolk 4 miles nw Aylsham pop 386 archd and
dioc Norwich Indep

OULTON parish 1659 Suffolk 3 miles w Lowestoft pop 588 archd Suffolk dioc Norwich

OULTON, LOW township parish Over Ches pop 55

OUNDLE market town, parish 1625 co Northampton 30 miles ne Northampton pop 2,450 archd Northampton dioc Peterborough Bapt,
Indep, Wesl Meth

OUNELEY or ONNELEY township parish Madeley Staffs pop 186

OUSBY parish 1663 Cumberland 9-1/4 miles ne Penrith pop 291 archd and dioc Carlisle

OUSDEN parish 1675 Suffolk 6-1/4 miles se Newmarket pop 328 archd Sudbury dioc Norwich

OUSEBURN, GREAT parish 1662 W R York 4-1/4 miles se Aldborough pop 534 pec of Honour of Knaresborough Indep

OUSEBURN, LITTLE parish 1564 W R York 5 miles se Aldborough comp townships Kirkby Hall, Thorp Underwoods, Little Ouseburn, Widdington pop 511 archd Richmond dioc Chester Wesl Meth

OUSEFLEET township parish Whitgift W R York pop 243

OUSTON township parish Chester le Street co Durham pop 273

OUSTON parish 1701 Leics 8 miles se Melton Mowbray pop 197 archd Leicester dioc Lincoln

OUSTON township parish Stamfordham Northumberland pop 19

OUTCHESTER township parish Bambrough Northumberland pop 11

OUTERSIDE township parish Aspatria Cumberland pop 381

OUTSEATS hamlet parish Hathersage Derbys pop 202

OUTTON township parish Rothwell W R York pop 1,496

OUTWELL parish 1559 Norfolk 5-1/2 miles se Wisbeach pop 986 archd Norfolk dioc Norwich

OVENDEN township parish Halifax W R York pop 8,871 Wesl Meth

OVER parish 1577 Cambs 4-1/2 miles se St Ives pop 989 archd and dioc Ely Bapt

OVER parish 1558 sep juris Ches 16-1/4 miles e Chester comp town Over, chapelry Wettenhall, township Little Oulton pop 2,928 archd and dioc Chester Indep

OVER hamlet parish Churcham Gloucs

OVER tything parish Almondsbury Gloucs pop 99

OVER, CHURCH Ches See UPTON

OVER, HADDON Derbys See HADDON, OVER

OVERBURY parish 1557 Worcs 5-1/2 miles ne Tewkesbury pop 817 archd and dioc Worcester

OVERSLEY hamlet parish Arrow Warws pop 179

OVERSTONE parish 1680 co Northampton 5 miles nw Northampton pop 203 archd Northampton dioc Peterborough

OVERSTRAND parish 1558 Norfolk 1-3/4 miles se Cromer pop 178 archd Norfolk dioc Norwich

OVERTON township parish Malpas Ches pop 111 Wesl Meth

OVERTON chapelry 1724 parish Lancaster Lancs pop 366

OVERTON township parish Richard's Castle Shrops

OVERTON parish 1645 Hamps 3 miles ne Whitchurch pop 1,507 pec of Rector Indep Borough

OVERTON parish 1682 Wilts 2-1/2 miles sw Marlborough pop 923 archd Wilts dioc Salisbury

OVERTON parish 1593 N R York 4-3/4 miles nw York comp townships Overton, Shipton, Skelton pop 704 archd Cleveland dioc York

OVERTON, COLD parish 1556 Leics 7 miles se Melton Mowbray

pop 123 archd Leicester dioc Lincoln

OVERTON, MARKET parish 1573 co Rutland 6 miles ne Oakham pop 470 archd Northampton dioc Peterborough

OVING parish 1678 Bucks 6 miles nw Aylesbury pop 384 archd Buckingham dioc Lincoln

OVING parish 1561 Sussex 2-3/4 miles e Chichester pop 789 archd and dioc Chichester

OVINGDEAN parish 1719 Sussex 2-3/4 miles se Brighton pop 119 archd and dioc Chichester

OVINGHAM parish 1679 Northumberland 11 miles w Newcastle upon Tyne comp chapelry Mickley, townships Dukeshagg, Eltringham, Harlowhill, Hedley, Hedley Woodside, Horsley, Nafferton, Ovingham, Ovington, Prudhoe Castle, Rouchester, Spittle, Welton, Whittle, Wylam pop 3,028 archd Northumberland dioc Durham Indep

OVINGTON parish 1559 Essex 2-1/4 miles sw Clare pop 179 archd Middlesex dioc London

OVINGTON parish 1654 Norfolk 1-1/2 miles ne Watton pop 230 archd and dioc Norwich

OVINGTON township parish Ovingham Northumberland pop 339

OVINGTON parish 1591 Hamps 2 miles sw New Alresford pop 179 pec juris of incumbent

OVINGTON township parish Forcett N R York pop 164

OWERMOIGNE parish 1569 Dorset 7-1/4 miles se Dorchester pop 379 archd Dorset dioc Bristol

OWERSBY parish 1559 Lincs 5-1/2 miles nw Market Rasen pop 407 archd and dioc Lincoln

OWLPEN parish 1677 Gloucs 3-3/4 miles e Dursley pop 255 archd and dioc Gloucester

OWMBY parish 1700 Lincs 7-1/2 miles sw Market Rasen pop 227 archd Stow dioc Lincoln

OWMBY parish incl reg of Searby Lincs 4-1/2 miles nw Caistor

OWRAM, NORTH township parish Halifax W R York pop 10,184

OWRAM, SOUTH township parish Halifax W R York pop 5,751

OWRE Kent See OARE

OWSLEBURY parish 1678 Hamps 5 miles se Winchester pop 664 pec of Vicar

OWSTHORPE township parish Pocklington E R York pop 20

OWSTON parish 1605 Lincs 7-1/2 miles n Gainsborough pop 2,207 archd Stow dioc Lincoln

OWSTON parish 1683 W R York 5-1/4 miles nw Doncaster comp townships Owston, Skellow pop 473 archd and dioc York

OWSTWICK township parishes Garton and Rooss E R York pop 125

OWTHORNE parish 1574 E R York 18-1/2 miles e Kingston upon Hill comp townships Waxholme, South Frodingham, Owthorne, Rimswell pop 401 archd East Riding dioc York

OWTHORPE parish 1731 Notts 8-1/2 miles se Nottingham pop 144 archd Nottingham dioc York

OXBOROUGH parish 1538 Norfolk 3 miles ne Stoke Ferry pop 427

archd Norfolk dioc Norwich

OXCLIFFE township parish Lancaster Lancs

OXCOMB parish Lincs 7 miles ne Horncastle pop 32 archd and dioc Lincoln

OXENDEN, GREAT parish 1564 co Northampton 3 miles se Market Harborough pop 239 archd Northampton dioc Peterborough

OXENDEN, LITTLE hamlet parish Little Bowden co Northampton pop 2

OXENHALL hamlet parish Darlington co Durham

OXENHALL parish 1665 Gloucs 1 mile nw Newent pop 306 archd Hereford dioc Gloucester

OXENTON parish 1678 Gloucs 5-1/2 miles se Tewkesbury pop 166 archd and dioc Gloucester

OXFORD city co Oxford 55 miles nw London pop 20,434 sep juris comp parishes St Aldage 1678, All Saints 1559, Holywell or St Cross 1653, St Ebge 1557, St Giles 1576, Christ Church Cathedral 1639, St Clements 1666, St John the Baptist 1616, St Martin 1569, St Mary Magdalene 1602, St Mary the Virgin 1599, St Michael 1558, St Peter le Bailey 1585, St Peter in the East 1653, St Thomas 1655 archd and dioc Oxford Bapt, Wesl Meth, Roman Cath

OXHEY hamlet parish Watford Herts

OXHILL parish 1568 Warws 4 miles sw Kington pop 326 archd and dioc Worcester Wesl Meth

OXNEAD parish 1573 Norfolk 4 miles se Aulsham pop 72 archd and dioc Norwich

OXNEY formerly a parish now annexed to St Margaret at Cliffs Kent pop 7

OXSPRING township parish Penistone W R York pop 283

OXTED parish 1603 Surrey 2 miles ne Godstone pop 959 archd Surrey dioc Winchester

OXTON township parish Woodchurch Ches pop 234

OXTON parish 1564 Notts 5 miles sw Southwell pop 778 pec of Chapter of Collegiate Church of Southwell Wesl Meth

OXTON township parish Tadcaster E R York pop 60

OXWICK parish 1538 Norfolk 3-1/4 miles sw Fakenham pop 74 archd and dioc Norwich

OZENDIKE township parish Ryther W R York

OZLEWORTH or WOOSLEWORTH parish 1698 Gloucs 3-1/2 miles se Wotton under Edge pop 152 archd and dioc Gloucester

PACKINGTON parish 1677 Leics 1-3/4 miles se Ashby de la Zouch pop 730 archd Leicester dioc Lincoln

PACKINGTON liberty parish Weeford Staffs pop 44

PACKINGTON, GREAT parish 1538 Warws 4-3/4 miles se Coleshill pop 334 archd Coventry dioc Lichfield

PACKINGTON, LITTLE parish 1628 Warws 3-1/2 miles se Coleshill pop 150 archd Coventry dioc Lichfield

PACKWOOD parish 1668 Warws 4-1/2 miles ne Henley in Arden pop 319 pec of Manorial Court of Packwood

PADBURY parish 1538 Bucks 2-3/4 miles se Buckingham pop 708 archd Buckingham dioc Lincoln Wesl Meth

PADDINGTON parish 1701 Middlesex pop 14,500 Commissary of London, concurrently with Consistorial Court of Bishop Bapt, Wesl Meth

PADDLESWORTH parish 1715 Kent 6-1/4 miles sw Rochester archd and dioc Rochester

PADDLESWORTH parish Kent 3-3/4 miles nw Folkestone pop 54 pec jurisdiction of Archbishop of Canterbury

PADDOCKS extra parochial district Lincs pop 3

PADFIELD township parish Glossop Derbys pop 1,102

PADIHAM chapelry parish Whalley 1573 Lancs pop 3,529 Wesl Meth, Unit

PADLEY, NETHER hamlet parish Hope Derbys pop 31

PADSIDE township parish Hampsthwaite W R York

PADSTOW sea port, market town, parish 1599 Cornwall 14 miles nw Bodmin pop 1,822 pec of Bishop of Exeter Wesl Meth

PADWORTH parish 1693 Berks 9 miles sw Reading pop 234 archd Berks dioc Salisbury

PAGHAM parish 1707 Sussex 6 miles se Chichester pop 958 pec Archbishop of Canterbury

PAGLESHAM parish 1719 Essex 4 miles ne Rochford pop 450 archd Essex dioc London

PAINGTON parish 1559 Devon 5-3/4 miles e Totnes pop 1,960 pec of Bishop of Exeter Indep

PAINSFORD chapelry parish Ashprington Devon

PAINSHAW chapelry 1754 parish Houghton le Spring co Durham pop 2,539 Wesl Meth

PAINSWICK market town, parish 1548 Gloucs 6-1/2 miles se Gloucester comp tythings Edge, Shepscomb, Spoonbed, Stroudend pop 4,099 archd and dioc Gloucester Soc of Friends, Indep, Wesl Meth, Presb

PAITTON hamlet parish Monks Kirby Warws pop 493

PAKEFIELD parish 1678 Suffolk 2-1/4 miles sw Lowestoft pop 472 archd Suffolk dioc Norwich

PAKENHAM parish 1670 Suffolk 5 miles ne Bury St Edmunds pop 979 archd Sudbury dioc Norwich

PALGRAVE hamlet parish Sporle Norfolk

PALGRAVE parish 1559 Suffolk 1-1/4 miles s Diss pop 760 archd Sudbury dioc Norwich Unit

PALLING parish 1616 Norfolk 11-1/4 miles se North Walsham pop 343 archd Norfolk dioc Norwich

PAMBER parish 1661 Hamps 4-1/4 miles nw Basingstoke pop 473 archd and dioc Winchester

PAMINGTON tything parish Ashchurch Gloucs pop 122

PAMPISFORD parish 1565 Cambs 4-1/2 miles nw Linton pop 293 archd and dioc Ely

PANBOROUGH hamlet parish Wedmore Somerset

PANCRAS, ST parish 1660 Middlesex suburb of London pop 103,548
pec of Dean and Chapter of St Paul's Bapt, Huntingtonians, Indep,
Calvinistic, Wesl and other Meth, Scottish Church, Roman Cath

PANCRAS, ST See AXMOUTH, Devon

PANCRASSWEEK or WYKE parish 1694 Devon 3 miles nw Holsworthy
pop 526 archd Totnes dioc Exeter

PANFIELD parish 1569 Essex 2-1/2 miles ne Braintree pop 316
archd Middlesex dioc London

PANGBOURN parish 1556 Berks 5-1/2 miles nw Reading pop 692
archd Berks dioc Salisbury Indep

PANNALL parish 1586 W R York 7 miles nw Wetherby pop 1,261
pec of Honour of Knaresborough Wesl Meth

PANTEAGUE parish 1598 co Monmouth 4 miles sw Usk pop 1,584
archd and dioc Llandaff

PANTON parish 1736 Lincs 3-3/4 miles ne Wragby pop 93 archd
and dioc Lincoln

PANXWORTH parish incl in regs of Ranworth Norfolk 4-1/2 miles
nw Acle archd and dioc Norwich

PAPCASTLE township parish Bridekirk Cumberland pop 461

PAPERHAUGH township parish Rothbury Northumberland pop 79

PAPPLEWICK parish 1661 Notts 7-1/2 miles nw Nottingham pop 518
archd Nottingham dioc York

PAPWORTH ST AGNES parish 1558 Cambs 5 miles nw Caxton pop
106 archd and dioc Ely

PAPWORTH, ST EVERARD parish 1565 Cambs 4 miles nw Caxton
pop 107 archd and dioc Ely

PARACOMBE parish 1687 Devon 12 miles ne Barnstaple pop 409
archd Barnstaple dioc Exeter

PARBOLD township parish Eccleston Lancs pop 382

PARDSEY township parish Dean Cumberland

PARHAM parish 1538 Suffolk 3-1/2 miles ne Wickham market pop
502 archd Suffolk dioc Norwich

PARHAM parish 1538 Sussex 6 miles ne Arundel pop 46 archd and
dioc Chichester

PARK ward parish St Stephen St Albans Herts

PARK END township parish Audley Staffs pop 94

PARKGATE hamlet parish Leighton parish Neston Ches

PARKHAM parish 1538 Devon 6 miles sw Bideford pop 923 archd
Barnstaple dioc Exeter

PARKHOLD township parish Ledbury Herefs pop 57

PARK LEYS extra parochial district Notts near Kelham pop 16

PARK QUARTER township parish Stanhope co Durham pop 1,873

PARKSTON chapelry parish Great Canford Dorset pop 609

PARLEY, WEST parish 1715 Dorset 6-3/4 miles se Wimborne Minster pop 235 archd Dorset dioc Bristol Indep

PARLINGTON township parish Aberford W R York pop 207

PARME township parish Middlewich Ches

PARNDON, GREAT parish 1547 Essex 3-1/2 miles sw Harlow pop

296 Commissary of Essex and Herts, concurrently with Consistorial Court of Bishop of London

PARNDON, LITTLE parish 1660 Essex 2-3/4 miles sw Harlow pop 90 Commissary of Essex and Herts, concurrently with Consistorial Court of Bishop of London

PARR township parish Prescot Lancs pop 1,942

PARSON DROVE chapelry 1657 parish Leverington Cambs pop 755

PARTINGTON township parish Bowdon Ches pop 466

PARTNEY parish 1699 Lincs 1-3/4 miles ne Spilsby pop 389 archd and dioc Lincoln Bapt

PARTON township parish Moresby Cumberland pop 559 Indep

PARTON township parish Thursby Cumberland pop 85

PARWICK parish 1730 Derbys 6 miles ne Ashbourn pop 544 archd Derby dioc Lichfield

PASSENHAM parish 1695 co Northampton 1-1/4 miles sw Stony Stratford pop 828 archd Northampton dioc Peterborough

PASTON parish 1538 Norfolk 4 miles ne North Walsham pop 286 archd Norfolk dioc Norwich

PASTON parish 1644 co Northampton 2-3/4 miles ne Peterborough pop 836 archd Northampton dioc Peterborough

PASTON township parish Kirk Newton Northumberland pop 207

PATCHAM parish 1558 Sussex 3-1/4 miles nw Brighton pop 489 archd Lewes dioc Chichester

PATCHING parish 1560 Sussex 4-3/4 miles se Arundel pop 149 pec of Archbishop of Canterbury

PATCHWAY tything parish Almondsbury Gloucs

PATELEY BRIDGE market town, parochial chapelry 1552 W R York 8 miles nw Ripley pec of Archbishop of York Indep

PATMER hamlet parish Albury and Bishop's Stortford Herts

PATNEY parish 1592 Wilts 4-3/4 miles se Devizes pop 144 archd and dioc Salisbury

PATRINGTON market town, parish 1570 E R York 56 miles se York pop 1,298 archd East Riding dioc York Indep, Prim and Wesl Meth

PATRIXBOURNE parish 1556 Kent 3-1/4 miles se Canterbury pop 280 archd and dioc Canterbury

PATSHULL parish 1559 Staffs 5-3/4 miles se Shiffnall pop 132 archd Stafford dioc Lichfield

PATTERDALE chapelry 1611 parish Barton Westm archd and dioc Carlisle

PATTESLEY parish Norfolk 4 miles sw Fakenham archd and dioc Norwich

PATTINGHAM parish 1559 Staffs 6-1/2 miles w Wolverhampton pop 921 archd Stafford dioc Lichfield

PATTISHALL parish 1556 co Northampton 4 miles nw Towcester pop 742 archd Northampton dioc Peterborough

PATTISWICK parish 1677 Essex 2-3/4 miles nw Great Coggeshall pop 341 archd Colchester dioc London

PATTON township parish Kendal Westm pop 71

PAUL parish 1595 Cornwall 2-3/4 miles sw Penzance pop 4,191 archd Cornwall dioc Exeter Bapt, Indep, Wesl Meth

PAUL parish 1657 E R York 2-1/4 miles sw Hedon comp chapelry Thorn Grumbald, township Paul pop 739 archd East Riding dioc York Wesl Meth

PAULERS PURY parish 1557 co Northampton 3 miles se Towcester pop 1,092 archd Northampton dioc Peterborough Wesl Meth

PAULTON parish 1733 Somerset 9-1/2 miles sw Bath pop 1,784 archd Wells dioc Bath and Wells Bapt, Wesl Meth

PAUNTLEY parish 1538 Gloucs 2-3/4 miles ne Newent pop 263 archd Hereford dioc Gloucester

PAVENHAM parish 1560 Beds 7 miles nw Bedford pop 543 archd Bedford dioc Lincoln

PAWLETT parish 1667 Somerset 5 miles n Bridgewater pop 577 archd Wells dioc Bath and Wells Wesl Meth

PAXFORD hamlet parish Blockley Gloucs

PAXTON, GREAT parish 1583 Hunts 3 miles ne St Neots pop 267 archd Huntingdon dioc Lincoln

PAXTON, LITTLE parish 1567 Hunts 2 miles n St Neots pop 310 archd Huntingdon dioc Lincoln

PAYHEMBURY parish 1559 Devon 5-1/4 miles nw Honiton pop 542 archd and dioc Exeter

PAYTHORNE township parish Gisburn W R York pop 187

PAYTON township parish Leintwardine Herefs pop 218

PEAK hamlet parish East Meon Hamps

PEAK FOREST extra parochial liberty 1678 Derbys 3-1/2 miles nw Tideswell pop 573 pec of Dean and Chapter of Lichfield

PEAKIRK parish 1560 co Northampton 3-1/4 miles se Market Deeping pop 191 archd Northampton dioc Peterborough

PEALS township parish Allenton Northumberland pop 57

PEASEMORE parish 1538 Berks 4-1/4 miles sw East Ilsley pop 298 archd Berks dioc Salisbury Wesl Meth

PEASENHALL parish 1558 Suffolk 2-3/4 miles nw Yoxford pop 773 archd Suffolk dioc Norwich Wesl Meth

PEASMARSH parish 1568 Sussex 3-1/4 miles nw Rye pop 920 archd Lewes dioc Chichester Wesl Meth

PEATLING MAGNA parish 1565 Leics 6-1/2 miles ne Lutterworth pop 267 archd Leicester dioc Lincoln

PEATLING PARVA parish 1711 Leics 4-3/4 miles ne Lutterworth pop 174 archd Leicester dioc Lincoln

PEATON township parish Diddlebury Shrops

PEBMARSH parish 1648 Essex 3-1/2 miles ne Halsted pop 642 archd Middlesex dioc London

PEBWORTH parish 1595 Gloucs 6-1/4 miles nw Chipping Camden pop 578 archd and dioc Gloucester Wesl Meth

PECKFORTON township parish Bunbury Ches pop 331

PECKHAM hamlet parish Camberwell Surrey Bapt, Indep

PECKHAM, EAST parish 1558 Kent 6 miles ne Tonbridge pop 2,018 pec of Archbishop of Canterbury

PECKHAM, WEST parish 1561 Kent 6 miles ne Tonbridge pop 536 archd and dioc Rochester Wesl Meth

PECKLETON parish 1567 Leics 5-1/2 miles ne Hinckley pop 294 archd Leicester dioc Lincoln Wesl Meth

PEDMORE parish 1539 Worcs 1-1/2 miles se Stourbridge pop 394 archd and dioc Worcester

PEDEARDINE township parish Brampton Bryan Herefs

PEEL Lancs See HULTON, LITTLE

PEELE township parish Tarvin Ches

PEERSTON JAGLIN township parish Featherstone W R York pop 260 Wesl Meth

PEGSWORTH township parish Bothall Northumberland pop 189

PELDON parish 1725 Essex 5-1/2 miles sw Colchester pop 424 archd Colchester dioc London

PELHAM, BRENT parish 1539 Herts 5-3/4 miles ne Buntingford pop 271 pec of Dean and Chapter of St Paul's London

PELHAM, FURNEUX parish 1560 Herts 5-1/2 miles se Huntingford pop 619 pec of Dean and Chapter of St Paul's London

PELHAM, STOCKING parish 1695 Herts 6-1/2 miles e Buntingford pop 158 archd Middlesex dioc London

PELHAM'S LAND extra parochial liberty Lincs 10 miles nw Boston pop 41

PELSALL chapelry 1763 parish Wolverhampton Staffs pop 721

PELTON township parish Chester le Street co Durham pop 550

PELYNT parish 1678 Cornwall 4 miles nw West Looe pop 804 archd Cornwall dioc Exeter

PEMBERS OAK township parish Kington Herefs

PEMBERTON chapelry parish Wigan Lancs pop 4,276

PEMBRIDGE parish 1564 Herefs 15-1/2 miles nw Hereford pop 1,293 archd and dioc Hereford Wesl Meth

PEMBURY parish 1561 Kent 3-1/2 miles se Tonbridge pop 1,070 archd and dioc Rochester

PENALTH parish 1765 co Monmouth 1-3/4 miles se Monmouth pop 549 archd and dioc Llandaff

PENBIDDLE hamlet parish Llavihangel Crucorney co Monmouth pop 90

PENCOMBE parish 1543 Herefs 4-1/4 miles sw Bromyard pop 521 archd and dioc Hereford

PENCOYD parish 1564 Herefs 6 miles nw Ross pop 183 archd and dioc Hereford

PENDEFORD township parish Tettenhall Staffs pop 198

PENBLEBURY township parish Eccles Lancs pop 1,556 Indep

PENDLETON chapelry 1776 parish Whalley Lancs pop 1,205

PENDLETON chapelry 1776 parish Eccles Lancs pop 8,435 Indep, Wesl and Meth of New Connection

PENDOCK parish 1558 Worcs 5-1/2 miles sw Upton upon Severn

pop 302 archd and dioc Worcester Wesl Meth

PENDOMER parish 1729 Somerset 4-3/4 miles sw Yeovil pop 98 archd Wells dioc Bath and Wells

PENGE hamlet parish Battersea Surrey pop 229

PENHOW parish 1725 co Monmouth 5-1/2 miles se Caerleon archd and dioc Llandaff

PENHURST parish 1559 Sussex 3-3/4 miles nw Battle pop 102 archd Lewes dioc Chichester

PENISTONE parish 1644 W R York 8 miles sw Barnesly comp market town Penistone, chapelry Denby, townships Gunthwaite, Hunshelf, Ingbirchworth, Langsett, Oxspring, Thurlestone pop 5,201 archd and dioc York Soc of Friends, Indep, Wesl Meth

PENKETH township parish Prescot Lancs pop 548 Wesl Meth

PENKHUL township parish Stoke upon Trent Staffs pop 5,876

PENKRIDGE parish 1572 Staffs 6 miles s Stafford comp town Penkridge, chapelries Coppenhall, Dunston, Stretton, townships Lovedale with Drayton, Mitton, Otterton, Pileton, Water Easton, Rodbaston, Whiston with Bickford pop 2,991 pec of Penkridge

PENMAIN hamlet parish Mynyddslwyn co Monmouth pop 2,175 Indep

PENN parish 1563 Bucks 3 miles ne Beaconsfield pop 1,103 archd Buckingham dioc Lincoln Bapt, Wesl Meth

PENN parish 1569 Staffs 2 miles sw Wolverhampton comp township Lower Penn, liberty Upper Penn pop 863 archd Stafford dioc Lichfield

PENN, LOWER township parish Penn Staffs pop 233

PENNARD, EAST parish 1608 Somerset 5-3/4 miles sw Shepton Mallet pop 726 archd Wells dioc Bath and Wells

PENNARD, WEST parish 1538 Somerset 3-1/4 miles se Glastonbury pop 920 pec of Glastonbury Wesl Meth

PENNINGTON parish 1623 Lancs 2 miles sw Ulverstone pop 355 archd Richmond dioc Chester

PENNINGTON township parish Leigh Lancs pop 3,165

PENNINGTON tything parish Milford Hamps

PENNYCROSS or PANCRAS ST See AXMOUTH DEVON

PENRITH parish 1556 Cumberland 18 miles se Carlisle comp market town Penrith, townships Burrowgate, Dockray, Middlegate with Sandgate, Netherend Bridge with Carleton town with Plumpton Head pop 6,059 archd and dioc Carlisle Soc of Friends, Indep, Prim and Wesl Meth, Scottish Seceders

PENROSE or PENRHOS 1718 co Monmouth 2 miles n Ragland pop 398 archd and dioc Llandaff Bapt

PENRUDDOCK hamlet parish Greystock Cumberland Indep

PENRYN sea port, borough, market town parishes Gluvias and Budock Cornwall 2 miles nw Falmouth pop 3,521 sep juris Bryanites, Indep, Wesl Meth

PENSAX chapelry parish Lindridge 1563 Worcs pop 571

PENSBY township parish Woodchurch Ches pop 22

PENSCELLWOOD parish 1721 Somerset 3-3/4 miles ne Wincanton

pop 361 archd Wells dioc Bath and Wells

PENSFORD, ST THOMAS parish 1651 Somerset 27 miles ne Somerton pop 355 archd Bath dioc Bath and Wells Indep, Wesl Meth

PENSHAM hamlet parish St Andrew Worcs pop 118

PENSHAW co Durham See PAINSHAW

PENSHURST parish 1558 Kent 4-1/4 miles sw Tonbridge pop 1,453 pec of Archbishop of Canterbury Indep

PENSTHORPE parish no regs Norfolk 2 miles se Fakenham pop 30 archd Norfolk dioc Norwich

PENTERRY parish 1721 co Monmouth 3-1/4 miles nw Chepstow pop 55 archd and dioc Llandaff

PENTLOW parish 1539 Essex 2-3/4 miles ne Clare pop 340 Commissary of Essex and Herts, concurrently with Consistorial Court of Bishop of London

PENTNEY parish 1730 Norfolk 7-1/2 miles nw Swaffham pop 480 archd and dioc Norwich

PENTON GRAFTON hamlet parish Weyhill Hamps

PENTON NEWSEY parish 1642 Hamps 2-3/4 miles nw Andover pop 254 archd and dioc Winchester

PENTONVILLE chapelry parish St James, Clerkenwell Middlesex

PENTRICH parish 1653 Derbys 2-3/4 miles sw Alfreton comp townships Pentrich, Ripley pop 2,521 archd Derby dioc Lichfield Indep, Unit

PENTRIDGE parish 1714 Dorset 3-1/2 miles nw Cranborne pop 241 archd Dorset dioc Bristol

PENWORTHAM parish 1586 Lancs 1-3/4 miles sw Preston comp chapelry Longton, townships Farrington, Howick, Hutton, Penwortham pop 4,679 archd and dioc Chester

PENY CLAWDD parish 1727 co Monmouth 4-3/4 miles sw Monmouth pop 46 archd and dioc Llandaff

PENZANCE seaport, market town, chapelry parish Madron 1789 Cornwall 67 miles sw Launceston pop 6,563 excl juris archd Cornwall dioc Exeter Bapt, Soc of Friends, Indep, Prim and Wesl Meth, Jews

PEOPLETON parish 1632 Worcs 3-1/2 miles n Pershore pop 276 archd and dioc Worcester

PEOVER, LITTLE township parish Great Budworth Ches pop 108

PEOVER, NETHER chapelry parish Great Budworth 1570 Ches pop 226

PEOVER, SUPERIOR chapelry 1688 parish Rosthern Ches pop 561

PEPPER HARROW parish 1697 Surrey 3 miles w Godalming pop 144 archd Surrey dioc Winchester

PERLETHORPE chapelry 1538 parish Edwinstow Notts pop 89

PERRAN ARWORTHAL parish 1754 Cornwall 3 miles n Penryn pop 1,504 archd Cornwall dioc Exeter Bryanites, Wesl Meth

PERRAN UTHNOE parish 1562 Cornwall 1-3/4 miles se Marazion pop 1,033 archd Cornwall dioc Exeter

PERRAN WHARF or COVE parishes Perran Arworthal and Mylor

Cornwall 5 miles sw Truro

PERRANZABULOE or PERRAN IN THE SAND parish 1566 Cornwall 7 miles nw St Michael or Midshall pop 2,793 pec of Dean and Chapter of Exeter Wesl Meth

PERRIVALE parish 1707 Middlesex 3-1/4 miles se Harrow on the Hill pop 32 archd Middlesex dioc London

PERROT, NORTH parish 1684 Somerset 3-1/4 miles e Crewkerne pop 454 archd Wells dioc Bath and Wells

PERROT, SOUTH parish 1538 Dorset 4-1/4 miles nw Beaminster pop 381 archd Dorset dioc Bristol

PERRY, EAST hamlet parish Graffham Hunts

PERRY HILL tything parish Worplesdon Surrey

PERSHALL township parish Eccleshall Staffs pop 101

PERSHORE market town, parish St Andrew 1641 Worcs 9 miles se Worcester comp Holy Cross 1540 pop 2,536 archd and dioc Worcester Bapt

PERTENHALL parish 1582 Beds 2 miles sw Kimbolton pop 373 archd Bedford dioc Lincoln

PERTHOLEY chapelry parish Llantrissent co Monmouth

PERTWOOD, UPPER parish 1800 Wilts 2 miles nw Hindon pop 29 archd and dioc Salisbury

PETER ST Kent See THNAET, ISLE OF

PETER CHURCH parish 1711 Herefs 11-1/2 miles w Hereford pop 676 archd and dioc Hereford Bapt

PETERBOROUGH city, Cathedral 1615, St John 1558 co Northampton 42 miles ne Northampton pop 5,553 sep juris archd Northampton dioc Peterborough Bapt, Indep, Wesl and other Meth

PETERSFIELD chapelry parish Buriton 1558 Hamps 24 miles ne Southampton comp borough and market town Petersfield, tything Street pop 1,803 archd and dioc Winchester Indep, Wesl Meth

PETERSHAM parish 1574 Surrey 7 miles sw London pop 610 archd Surrey dioc Winchester

PETERSTONE parish 1707 co Monmouth 6-1/2 miles sw Newport pop 110 archd and dioc Llandaff

PETERS MARLAND See MARLAND PETERS

PETERSTOW parish 1538 Herefs 3 miles nw Ross pop 261 archd and dioc Hereford Wesl Meth

PETHAM parish 1559 Kent 6 miles sw Canterbury pop 582 archd and dioc Canterbury

PETHERICK, LITTLE parish 1706 Cornwall 2-1/2 miles s Padstow pop 224 pec of Bishop of Exeter

PETHERTON, NORTH parish 1558 Somerset 3-1/4 miles sw Bridgewater pop 3,566 archd Taunton dioc Bath and Wells

PETHERTON, SOUTH parish 1574 Somerset 5-1/2 miles nw Crewkerne pop 2,294 archd Taunton dioc Bath and Wells Bapt, Indep, Wesl Meth

PETHERWYN, NORTH parish 1653 Devon 5 miles nw Launceston pop 1,044 archd Cornwall dioc Exeter

PETHERWIN, SOUTH parish 1656 Cornwall 2 miles sw Launceston pop 988 pec of Bishop of Exeter Wesl Meth

PETROCKSTOW parish 1695 Devon 4 miles nw Hatherleigh pop 581 archd Barnstaple dioc Exeter

PETSOE hamlet parish Okeney Bucks

PETT parish 1675 Sussex 3-1/2 miles sw Winchelsea pop 297 archd Lewes dioc Chichester

PETTAUGH parish 1653 Suffolk 2-1/2 miles s Debenham pop 284 archd Suffolk dioc Norwich

PETTERELL CROOKS township parish Hesket the Forest Cumberland pop 544

PETTISTREE parish 1539 Suffolk 3/4 mile sw Wickham Market pop 276 archd Suffolk dioc Norwich

PETTON parish 1677 Shrops 6-1/4 miles se Ellesmere pop 49 archd Salop dioc Lichfield

PETWORTH market town, parish 1559 Sussex 14 miles ne Chichester pop 3,114 archd and dioc Chichester Indep, Wesl Meth

PEVENSEY parish 1565 Sussex 6 miles se Hailsham pop 343 archd Lewes dioc Chichester

PEVINGTON parish no regs Kent 4 miles sw Charing archd and dioc Canterbury

PEWSEY Berks See PUSEY

PEWSEY parish 1568 Wilts 6 miles sw Great Bedwin pop 1,588 archd Wilts dioc Salisbury

PEWSHAM extra parochial liberty Wilts 1-1/2 miles se Chippenham pop 383

PEXALL township parish Prestbury Ches

PEYTON chapelry parish Bampton Devon

PHILLACK parish 1560 Cornwall 9 miles ne Marazion pop 3,053 archd Cornwall dioc Exeter

PHILLEIGH or FILLEY parish 1733 Cornwall 6 miles sw Tregoney pop 442 archd Cornwall dioc Exeter Wesl Meth

PHILLYHOLME tything parish Hawkchurch Dorset pop 570

PHOSIDE liberty parish Glossop Derbys pop 663

PICKBURN township parish Brodsworth W R York

PICKENHAM, NORTH parish 1678 Norfolk 3-1/2 miles se Swaffham pop 245 archd Norfolk dioc Norwich

PICKENHAM, SOUTH parish 1694 Norfolk 4-1/2 miles se Swaffham pop 195 archd Norfolk dioc Norwich

PICKERING parish 1559 N R York 26 miles ne York comp market town Pickering, chapelry Goadland or Goatland, townships Kingthorp, Marrishes, Newton pop 3,346 pec Dean of York Soc of Friends, Indep, Wesl Meth

PICKHILL parish 1567 N R York 7 miles nw Thirsk comp township Holme with Howgrave Ainderby, Quernhow, Howe, Pickhill with Roxby, Sinderby, Swainby with Allarthorp pop 758 archd and dioc York Wesl Meth

PICKMERE township parish Great Budworth Ches pop 228

PICKTON township parish Plemonstall Ches pop 97

PICKTON township parish Kirk Leavington N R York pop 86

PICK UP BANK township parish Whalley Lancs

PICKWELL parish 1572 Leics 5-3/4 miles se Melton Mowbray pop 160 archd Leicester dioc Lincoln

PICKWORTH parish 1538 Lincs 2-3/4 miles w Falkingham pop 187 archd and dioc Lincoln

PICKWORTH parish 1660 co Rutland 4-3/4 miles nw Stamford pop 140 archd Northampton dioc Peterborough

PIDDINGHOE parish 1540 Sussex 5-1/2 miles se Lewes pop 231 archd Lewes dioc Chichester

PIDDINGTON parish 1573 co Northampton 5-3/4 miles se Northampton pop 983 archd Northampton dioc Peterborough

PIDDINGTON parish 1654 co Oxford 5-1/2 miles se Bicester pop 422 archd and dioc Oxford

PIDDLE, NORTH parish 1565 Worcs 8-1/2 miles se Worcester pop 199 archd and dioc Worcester

PIDDLEHINTON parish 1539 Dorset 5-1/4 miles ne Dorchester pop 403 archd Dorset dioc Bristol

PIDDLETOWN parish 1538 Dorset 5 miles ne Dorchester pop 1,223 archd Dorset dioc Bristol

PIDDLETRENTHIDE parish 1646 Dorset 7-1/2 miles ne Dorchester pop 680 archd Dorset dioc Bristol

PIDLEY parish 1558 Hunts 2 miles nw Somersham pop 406 archd Huntingdon dioc Lincoln

PIECOMBE parish 1561 Sussex 3 miles s Hurst Pierrepoint pop 227 archd Lewes dioc Chichester

PIERRE, ST parish 1686 co Monmouth 3 miles sw Chepstow pop 89 archd and dioc Llandaff

PIERSE BRIDGE township parish Gainford co Durham pop 278

PIGDON township parish Mitford Northumberland pop 33

PIGLESTHORNE or PITSTONE parish 1653 Bucks 1 mile sw Ivinghoe pop 578 archd Buckingham dioc Lincoln

PILETON township parish Penkridge Staffs

PILHAM parish 1677 Lincs 4-3/4 miles ne Gainsborough pop 100 archd Stow dioc Lincoln

PILKINGTON township parish Oldham Lancs pop 11,006

PILL, ST GEORGE'S chapelry parish Easton in Gordano Somerset 6 miles nw Bristol pop 2,000 Bapt, Indep, Wesl Meth

PILLATON parish 1557 Cornwall 3-1/2 miles s Callington pop 413 archd Cornwall dioc Exeter

PILLERTON HERSEY parish 1539 Warws 3-1/4 miles sw Kington pop 261 archd and dioc Worcester

PILLERTON PRIORS parish 1604 Warws 4 miles sw Kington pop 217 archd and dioc Worcester church burned 1666

PILLING chapelry 1638 parish Garstang Lancs pop 1,127 Wesl Meth

PILSDON parish 1754 Dorset 4-1/2 miles sw Beaminster pop 99 archd Dorset dioc Bristol

PILSGATE hamlet parish Barnack co Northampton pop 140

PILSLEY hamlet parish Edensor Derbys pop 304

PILSLEY hamlet parish Chesterfield Derbys pop 304

PILSWORTH township parish Middleton Lancs pop 403

PILTON parish 1569 Devon pop 1,819 archd Barnstaple dioc Exeter

PILTON parish 1569 co Northampton 2-3/4 miles sw Oundle pop 131 archd Northampton dioc Peterborough

PILTON parish 1548 co Rutland 4-3/4 miles ne Uppingham pop 69 archd Northampton dioc Peterborough

PILTON parish 1558 Somerset 2-3/4 miles sw Shepton Mallet pop 1,118 pec of Precenter of Cathedral Church of Wells Wesl Meth

PIMLICO parochial district formerly a chapelry parish St George Middlesex

PIMPERNE parish 1559 Dorset 2-1/2 miles ne Blandford Forum pop 489 archd Dorset dioc Bristol

PINCHECK parish 1560 Lincs 2-1/4 miles nw Spalding pop 2,391 archd and dioc Lincoln Indep

PINCHINGTHORPE township parish Guilsbrough N R York pop 57

PINDLEY hamlet parish Claverdon Warws pop 15

PINHOE parish 1561 Devon 3 miles ne Exeter pop 517 archd and dioc Exeter

PINNALS extra parochial liberty Leics 1-1/4 miles n Atherstone

PINNER parish 1654 Middlesex 2-1/2 miles nw Harrow on the Hill pop 1,270 pec of Archbishop of Canterbury

PINNOCK parish (incl regs Didbrooke) Gloucs 3-1/2 miles e Winchcombe pop 47 archd and dioc Gloucester

PINNOCK, ST parish 1566 Cornwall 4 miles sw Liskeard pop 425 archd Cornwall dioc Exeter

PINVIN chapelry 1552 parish St Andrew Worcs pop 179

PINXTON parish 1561 Derbys 4 miles se Alfreton pop 868 archd Derby dioc Lichfield Wesl Meth

PION, CANON Herefs See CANON, PION

PION KING'S parish 1538 Herefs 3 miles se Weobley pop 359 archd and dioc Hereford

PIPE parish 1558 Herefs 3 miles n Hereford pop 131 Consistory Court of Dean of Hereford

PIPE HILL hamlet parish St Michael Staffs pop 111

PIPEWELL hamlet parishes Great Oakey and Wilbarston co Northampton

PIRBRIGHT Surrey See PURBRIGHT

PIRTON parish 1558 Herefs 3-1/2 miles nw Hitchin pop 758 archd Huntingdon dioc Lincoln

PIRTON parish 1598 co Oxford 5 miles s Tetsworth pop 661 archd and dioc Oxford

PIRTON hamlet parish Tettenhall Staffs pop 295

PIRTON parish 1538 Worcs 4-1/2 miles nw Pershore pop 214 archd and dioc Worcester

PISFORD parish 1560 co Northampton pop 539 archd Northampton dioc Peterborough Wesl Meth

PISHILL parish 1765 co Oxford 5-1/2 miles nw Henley upon Thames
pop 170 juris of Pec Court of Dorchester

PITCHCOMB parish 1709 Gloucs 1-3/4 miles sw Painswick pop 224
archd and dioc Gloucester

PITCHCOMB parish 1709 Bucks 5-3/4 miles nw Aylesbury pop 28
archd Buckingham dioc Lincoln

PITCHFORD parish 1558 Shrops 6-1/2 miles se Shrewsbury pop 197
archd Salop dioc Lichfield

PITCHLEY parish 1695 co Northampton 2-3/4 miles sw Kettering
pop 558 archd Northampton dioc Peterborough Wesl Meth

PITCOMB parish 1538 Somerset 1-3/4 miles sw Bruton pop 480
archd Bath dioc Bath and Wells

PITFOLD tything parish Frensham Surrey

PITMINSTER parish 1542 Somerset 4-1/4 miles sw Taunton pop
1,426 archd Taunton dioc Bath and Wells Indep

PITNEY parish 1699 Somerset 2-1/2 miles w Somerton pop 368
archd Wells dioc Bath and Wells

PITSEA parish 1688 Essex 4-1/2 miles sw Rayleigh pop 276 archd
Essex dioc London

PITSTONE Bucks See PIGGLESTHORNE

PITSFORD co Northampton See PISFORD

PITTINGTON parish 1574 co Durham 3-1/2 miles ne Durham comp
townships Hall Garth, Shadforth, Sherburn pop 2,503 archd and
dioc Durham

PITTLEWORTH extra parochial district Hamps near Broughton

PITTON chapelry parish Alderbury Wilts pop 379

PIXLEY parish 1745 Herefs 3-3/4 miles nw Ledbury pop 110 archd
and dioc Hereford

PLAINMELLOR township parish Haltwhistle Northumberland pop 160

PLAISTOW ward 1830 parish West Ham Essex Indep, Wesl Meth

PLAISTOW (incl in regs of Kirdford) Sussex

PLAITFORD parish 1710 Wilts 4-1/2 miles sw Romsey pop 263 arc
archd Wilts dioc Salisbury

PLASHETS township parish Falstone Northumberland pop 249

PLAWSWORTH township parish Chester le Street co Durham pop 149

PLAXTOL chapelry 1648 parish Wrotham Kent pec of Archbishop of
Canterbury

PLAYDEN parish 1714 Sussex 3/4 mile n Rye pop 297 archd Lewes
dioc Chichester

PLAYFORD parish 1660 Suffolk 4-1/4 miles ne Ipswich pop 299
archd Suffolk dioc Norwich

PLEASELEY parish 1553 Derbys 3-1/4 miles nw Mansfield pop 611
archd Derby dioc Lichfield

PLEASINGTON township parish Blackburn Lancs pop 633

PLEDGON hamlet parish Henham Essex pop 160

PLEMONSTALL parish 1558 Ches 4-1/4 miles ne Chester comp
townships Hoole, Pickton, Mickle Trafford, Bridge Trafford pop

413

737 archd and dioc Chester

PLESHEY parish 1656 Essex 6-1/2 miles nw Chelmsford pop 320 Commissary of Essex and Herts, concurrently with Consistorial Court of Bishop of London

PLESSEY township parish Stannington Northumberland

PLOMPTON township parish Spofforth W R York pop 221

PLUCKLEY parish 1560 Kent 3 miles sw Charing pop 714 archd and dioc Canterbury

PLUMBLAND parish 1677 Cumberland 6-1/2 miles ne Cockermouth pop 524 archd and dioc Carlisle

PLUMLEY township parish Great Budworth Ches pop 378

PLUMPTON township parish Kirkham Lancs Wesl Meth

PLUMPTON parish 1682 co Northampton 6-1/2 miles w Towcester pop 75 archd Northampton dioc Peterborough

PLUMPTON parish 1558 Sussex 4-3/4 miles nw Lewes pop 275 archd Lewes dioc Chichester

PLUMPTON STREET township parish Hesket in the Forest Cumberland pop 165

PLUMPTON WALL chapelry parish Laxonby Cumberland pop 297

PLUMPTON WOOD chapelry 1604 parish St Michael on Wyre pop 1,719 Lancs

PLUMSTEAD parish 1654 Kent 10 miles se London pop 2,745 archd and dioc Rochester

PLUMSTEAD parish 1556 Norfolk 5 miles se Holt pop 220 archd and dioc Norwich

PLUMSTEAD, GREAT parish 1558 Norfolk 5-1/4 miles e Norwich pop 305 pec of Dean and Chapter of Norwich

PLUMSTEAD, LITTLE parish 1559 Norfolk 5-3/4 miles ne Norwich pop 312 archd and dioc Norwich

PLUMTREE parish 1558 Notts 5-1/4 miles se Nottingham comp township Clipston, Normanton on the Wolds pop 605 archd Nottingham dioc York Wesl Meth

PLUNGAR parish 1695 Leics 10-1/2 miles ne Melton Mowbray pop 244 archd Leicester dioc Lincoln Wesl Meth

PLUSH tything parish Buckland Newton Dorset pop 154

PLYMOUTH sea port, borough, market town Devon 44 miles sw Exeter pop 31,000 sep juris comp St Andrew 1581, King Charles the Martyr 1653 archd Totnes dioc Exeter Bapt, Soc of Friends, Indep, Wesl Meth, Presb, Unit, Jews

PLYMOUTH DOCK Devon See DEVONPORT

PLYMPTON St Mary parish 1603 Devon 1/2 mile nw Earl's Plympton pop 2,153 archd Totnes dioc Exeter

PLYMPTON EARL'S or PLYMPTON, ST MAURICE market town, parish 1616 Devon 39 miles sw Exeter pop 804 sep juris archd Totnes dioc Exeter Indep, Calvinists

PLYMSTOCK parish 1591 Devon 3 miles sw Earl's Plympton pop 3,088 archd Totnes dioc Exeter Wesl Meth

PLYMTREE parish 1538 Devon 3-3/4 miles se Cullompton pop 439

archd and dioc Exeter

POCKLEY township parish Helmsley N R York pop 217

POCKLINGTON parish 1559 E R York 13 miles se York comp market town Pocklington, chapelry Yapham, townships Meltonby, Owsthorpe pop 2,265 pec of Dean of York Indep, Prim, Wesl Meth, Roman Cath

PODEN hamlet parish Church Honeybourne Worcs

PODIMORE, MILTON parish 1635 Somerset 2 miles ne Ilchester pop 175 archd Wells dioc Bath and Wells

POINTINGTON See POYNTINGTON Sussex

POINTINGTON parish 1618 Somerset 2-1/2 miles ne Sherbourne pop 165 archd Wells dioc Bath and Wells

POINTON chapelry parish Semperingham Lincs pop 409

POLEBROOK parish 1653 co Northampton 2-3/4 miles se Oundle pop 417 archd Northampton dioc Peterborough

POLESWORTH parish 1631 Warws 4-1/4 miles se Tamworth pop 1,870 archd Coventry dioc Lichfield Indep

POLING parish 1653 Sussex 3 miles se Arundel pop 202 archd and dioc Chichester

POLLARDS LANDS township parish St Andrew Auckland co Durham pop 138

POLLECOT hamlet parish Bucks

POLLINGTON township parish Snaith W R York pop 482 Indep

POLPERRO sea port, market town parishes Lansalloes and Talland Cornwall 5 miles e Fowey Indep, Wesl Meth

POLSTEAD parish 1538 Suffolk 3-1/4 miles ne Nayland pop 960 archd Sudbury dioc Norwich

POLTIMORE parish 1718 Devon 4 miles ne Exeter pop 292 archd and dioc Exeter

PONDERS END hamlet parish Enfield Middlesex Indep

PONSNOORTH hamlet parishes Gluvias, Perran Arworthal and Stithians Cornwall Bryanites, Wesl Meth

PONSONBY parish 1723 Cumberland 4-3/4 miles se Egremont pop 180 archd Richmond dioc Chester

PONTEFRACT parish 1585 borough W R York 23 miles sw York comp chapelry Knottingly, townships Carleton, East Hardwick, Monkhill, Tanshelf pop 9,254 sep juris archd and dioc York Soc of Friends, Indep, Prim and Wesl Meth, Roman Cath

PONTEFRACT PARK extra parochial liberty W R York 1/2 mile nw Pontefract pop 51

PONTELAND parish 1602 Northumberland 7-1/2 miles nw Newcastle upon Tyne comp townships Berwick Hill, Brenkley, High Callerton, Little Callerton Coldcoats, Darras Hall, Dinnington, Higham Dykes, Horton Grange, Kirkley, Mason, Milburn, Milburn Grange, Ponteland, Prestwick pop 1,796 archd Northumberland dioc Durham Scotch Presb

PONTESBURY parish 1538 Shrops 7-3/4 miles sw Shrewsbury comp chapelry Longdon, townships Cruckton, Edge, Pontesbury pop

2,936 Bapt

PONTISBRIGHT or CHAPEL parish 1538 Essex 5-1/2 miles ne Great Coggeshall pop 390 archd Colchester dioc London

PONTON, GREAT parish 1622 Lincs 4 miles n Colsterworth pop 446 archd and dioc Lincoln

PONTON, LITTLE parish 1729 Lincs 2-1/2 miles se Grantham pop 200 archd and dioc Lincoln

PONTOP hamlet parish Lanchester co Durham

PONT Y POOL market town, chapelry parish Trevethan co Monmouth Bapt, Wesl Meth, Indep, Soc of Friends, Roman Cath

POOL township parish Brotherton W R York pop 84

POOL, NETHER township parish Eastham Ches pop 19

POOL, OVER township parish Eastham Ches pop 93

POOL, SOUTH parish 1664 Devon 4-3/4 miles se Kingsbridge pop 493 archd and dioc Exeter

POOLE township parish Acton Ches pop 188

POOLE sea port, borough, market town 1538 Dorset 27 miles e Dorchester pop 6,459 pec of Great Canford and Poole Bapt, Soc of Friends, Indep, Wesl Meth, Unit

POOLE chapelry parish Otley W R York pop 315

POOLE KEYNES parish 1632 Wilts 7 miles ne Malmesbury pop 169 archd Wilts dioc Salisbury

POORSTOCK parish 1568 Dorset 4 miles ne Bridport pop 1,024 archd Dorset dioc Bristol

POORTON, NORTH parish 1695 Dorset 5 miles se Beaminster pop 89 archd Dorset dioc Bristol

POORTON, SOUTH tything parish Poorstock Dorset

POPHAM parish 1628 Hamps 7 miles sw Basingstoke pop 104 archd and dioc Winchester

POPLAR parish 1711 Middlesex 3 miles se London pop 16,849 Commissary of London, concurrently with Consistorial Episcopal Court Bapt, Indep, Wesl Meth

POPPLETON, NETHER parish 1640 E R York 4 miles nw York pop 259 archd and dioc York

POPPLETON, UPPER chapelry 1640 parish St Mary Bishopshill E R York pop 319 Wesl Meth

PORCHESTER or PORTCHESTER parish 1607 Hamps 2-1/2 miles se Fareham pop 739 archd and dioc Winchester

PORINGLAND, GREAT or EAST parish 1560 Norfolk 5 miles se Norwich pop 543 archd Norfolk dioc Norwich

PORINGLAND, LITTLE or WEST parish (incl in regs Howe) Norfolk 5-3/4 miles se Norwich archd Norfolk dioc Norwich

PORLOCK parish 1625 Somerset 6 miles w Minehead pop 830 archd Taunton dioc Bath and Wells

PORTBURY parish 1719 Somerset 6 miles nw Bristol pop 621 archd Bath dioc Bath and Wells

PORTCASSEGG hamlet parish St Arvans co Monmouth pop 21

PORTCHESTER Hamps See PORCHESTER

PORT EAST Cornwall See CHAPEL POINT

PORTGATE township parish St John Lee Northumberland pop 29

PORT GAVORN small sea port parish Endellion Cornwall

PORT GUIN or QUIN village small sea port parish Endellion Cornwall

PORT ISAAC village small sea port parish Endellion Cornwall

PORTINGSCALE township parish Crosthwaite Cumberland Wesl Meth

PORTINGTEN township parish Eastrington E R York pop 160

PORTISHAM parish 1573 Dorset 7-3/4 miles sw Dorchester pop 663
    archd Dorset dioc Bristol

PORTISHEAD parish 1554 Somerset 8-1/2 miles nw Bristol pop 800
    archd Bath dioc Bath and Wells Wesl Meth

PORTLAND parish 1591 Dorset 3 miles sw Weymouth pop 2,670 archd
    Dorset dioc Bristol Wesl Meth

PORTLEMOUTH, EAST parish 1563 Devon 6 miles se Kingsbridge
    pop 427 archd Totnes dioc Exeter

PORTON tything parish Idminston Wilts pop 185

PORTREATH small port, parish Illogan Cornwall pop 700 Wesl Meth

PORTSCUETT parish 1593 co Monmouth 5 miles sw Chepstow pop
    190 archd and dioc Llandaff

PORTSEA parish 1653 Hamps 21 miles se Southampton pop 42,306
    archd and dioc Winchester Bapt, Indep, Wesl Meth, Roman Cath,
    Jews

PORTSLADE parish 1666 Sussex 2-1/2 miles ne New Shoreham pop
    615 archd Lewes dioc Chichester

PORTSMOUTH sea port, borough, market town, parish 1653 Hamps
    21 miles se Southampton sep juris pop 8,083 archd and dioc
    Winchester Indep, Wesl Meth, Unit

PORTSWOOD tything parish South Stoneham Hamps pop 654

POSENHALL extra parochial district Shrops 1-1/4 miles w Broseley
    pop 28

POSLINGFORD parish 1678 Suffolk 1-3/4 miles n Clare pop 316
    archd Sudbury dioc Norwich

POSTCOMBE chapelry parish Lewknor co Oxford

POSTERN township parish Duffield Derbys

POSTLING parish 1687 Kent 3-1/4 miles nw Hythe pop 188 archd and
    dioc Canterbury

POSTLIP hamlet parish Winchcombe Gloucs

POSTWICK parish 1570 Norfolk 4-1/4 miles se Norwich pop 237
    archd and dioc Norwich

POTSGROVE parish 1663 Beds 3-1/4 miles se Woburn pop 262 archd
    Bedford dioc Lincoln

POTT township parish Masham N R York

POTT SHRIGLEY chapelry 1630 parish Prestbury Ches pop 334

POTTER HANWORTH parish 1683 Lincs 6-1/4 miles se Lincoln pop
    402 archd and dioc Lincoln

POTTER HEIGHAM See HEIGHAM, POTTER Norfolk

POTTERNE parish 1557 Wilts 1-3/4 miles sw Devizes comp tythings
    Marston, Worthon pop 1,647 pec of Bishop of Salisbury

POTTERS BAR hamlet parish Monken Hadley Middlesex Bapt

POTTERS PURY parish 1671 co Northampton 2-1/2 miles nw Stony Stratford comp hamlet Yardley Gobion, part of Old Stratford pop 1,544 archd Northampton dioc Peterborough Indep

POTTERTON township parish Barwick in Elmett W R York

POTTO township parish Whorlton N R York pop 187

POTTON market town, parish 1614 Beds 11-1/2 miles e Bedford pop 1,768 archd Bedford dioc Lincoln Bapt

POUGHILL parish 1538 Cornwall 1-1/4 miles nw Stratton pop 360 archd Cornwall dioc Exeter

POUGHYLL parish 1567 Devon 6-1/2 miles ne Crediton pop 331 archd and dioc Exeter

POULSHOT parish 1627 Wilts 3-3/4 miles sw Devizes pop 348 archd and dioc Salisbury

POULTNEY hamlet parish Misterton Leics

POULTON township parish Pulford Ches pop 128

POULTON township parish Bebbington Ches pop 120

POULTON township parish Wallazey Ches pop 1,212

POULTON parish no regs Kent 3-1/2 miles w Dover pop 25

POULTON LE SANDS chapelry 1747 parish Lancaster Lancs pop 540

POULTON township parish Warrington Lancs pop 709

POULTON parish 1695 Wilts 4 miles sw Fairford pop 368 archd Wilts dioc Salisbury

POULTON IN THE FYLDE parish 1591 Lancs 21 miles sw Lancaster comp market town Poulton, chapelry Marton, townships Carleton, Hardhorn with Newton, Thornton pop 4,082 archd Richmond dioc Chester Soc of Friends, Indep, Wesl Meth, Roman Cath

POUNDEN hamlet parish Twyford Bucks pop 84

POUNDISFORD tything parish Pitminster Somerset

POUNDSTOCK parish 1615 Cornwall 4-3/4 miles sw Stratton pop 727 archd Cornwall dioc Exeter

POWDERHAM parish 1558 Devon 8-1/4 miles se Exeter pop 275 archd and dioc Exeter

POWERSTOCK See POORSTOCK Dorset

POWICK parish 1662 Worcs 2-3/4 miles sw Worcester comp chapelry Clieveland, hamlet Woodsfield, part of chapelry Bransford pop 1,598 archd and dioc Worcester

POWNAL FEE township parish Wilmslow Ches pop 1,747

POXWELL parish 1674 Dorset 6 miles se Dorchester pop 99 archd Dorset dioc Bristol

POYNINGS parish 1558 Sussex 3-1/2 miles sw Hurst Pierrepoint pop 268 archd Lewes dioc Chichester

POYNTON chapelry 1723 parish Prestbury Ches pop 747

PREBEND END precinct parish Buckingham Bucks

PREEN, CHURCH parish 1680 Shrops 6-1/4 miles sw Much Wenlock pop 75 archd Salop dioc Hereford

PREES parish 1597 Shrops 4-3/4 miles ne Wem comp chapelries Calverhall, Whixhall, townships Prees with Steel, Sandford pop

3,355 pec of Prebendary of Prees or Pipe Minor in Cathedral Church of Lichfield Indep

PREESALL township parish Lancaster Lancs pop 745

PRENDICK township parish Alnham Northumberland pop 61

PRENTON township parish Woodchurch Ches pop 104

PRESCOT extra parochial liberty Gloucs 5-1/4 miles ne Cheltenham pop 51

PRESCOTT parish 1580 Lancs 51 miles s Lancaster comp market town Prescot, chapelries Rainford, Great Sankey, townships Bold, Cronton, Cuerdley, Ditton, Eccleston, Parr, Penketh, Rainhill, Sutton, Whiston, Widness with Appleton, Widdle pop 28,084 archd and dioc Chester Indep, Wesl Meth, Unit

PRESCOTT hamlet parish Cropredy co Oxford pop 15

PRESHUTE parish 1607 Wilts 1-1/4 miles sw Marlborough pop 760 pec of Bishop of Salisbury

PRESTBURY parish 1560 Ches 2-3/4 miles nw Macclesfield comp market town Macclesfield, chapelries Bosley, Capesthorne, Chelford, Macclesfield, Forest, Marton, Poynton, Pott-Shrigley, Rainow, Siddington, Wincell, townships Adlington, Birtles, Bollington, Butley, Easton, Fallybroom, Henbury with Pexall, Hurdsfield, Kettleshulme, Lyme, Hadley, Mottram, St Andrew, Newton, Prestbury, North Rode, Sutton, Tytherington, Upton, Wildboar Clough, Lower Withington, Old Withington, Woodford, Worth pop 47,257 archd and dioc Chester Wesl Meth

PRESTBURY parish 1633 Gloucs 1-1/2 miles ne Cheltenham pop 1,231 archd and dioc Gloucester

PRESTON parish 1693 Dorset 3-1/2 miles ne Melcombe Regis pop 555 pec of Prebendary of Preston in Cathedral Church of Salisbury Wesl Meth

PRESTON parish 1677 Gloucs 1-1/2 miles se Cirencester pop 196 archd and dioc Gloucester

PRESTON parish 1665 Gloucs 3-1/4 miles sw Ledbury pop 79 archd Hereford dioc Gloucester

PRESTON hamlet parish Hitchin Herts

PRESTON parish 1559 Kent 1/2 mile s Faversham pop 673 archd and dioc Canterbury

PRESTON parish 1558 Kent 2 miles n Wingham pop 576 archd and dioc Canterbury

PRESTON parish 1611 borough Lancs 21-3/4 miles se Lancaster comp chapelries Broughton, Grimsargh with Brockholes, townships Barton, Elston, Fishwick, Haighton, Lea with Ashton, Ingol, Cottam, Ribbleton pop 36,336 sep juris archd Richmond dioc Chester comp St George 1723, Holy Trinity 1814, St Paul's 1825, St Peter's in the Fylde Road 1825 Indep, Bapt, Soc of Friends, Prim and Wesl Meth, Unit, Roman Cath

PRESTON township parish Ellingham Northumberland pop 85

PRESTON township parish Tynemouth Northumberland pop 765

PRESTON parish 1560 co Rutland 1-3/4 miles n Uppingham pop 352 archd Northampton dioc Peterborough

PRESTON parish 1741 Somerset 1-1/2 miles w Yeovil pop 347 archd
Bath dioc Bath and Wells

PRESTON parish 1628 Suffolk 2-1/2 miles ne Lavenham pop 321
archd Sudbury dioc Norwich

PRESTON parish 1538 Sussex 1-3/4 miles nw Brighton pop 235 archd
and dioc Chichester

PRESTON parish 1559 E R York 7 miles ne Kingston upon Hull pop
957 pec of Sub Dean of York Prim and Wesl Meth

PRESTON BAGGOTT parish 1677 Warws 2-1/4 miles se Henley in
Arden pop 221 archd and dioc Worcester

PRESTON BISSETT parish 1662 Bucks 4-1/2 miles sw Buckingham
pop 502 archd Buckingham dioc Lincoln

PRESTON BROCKHURST township parishes Shawbur and Moreton
Corbet Shrops

PRESTON CANDOVER Hamps See CANDOVER, PRESTON

PRESTON CAPES parish 1613 co Northampton 5-3/4 miles s Daventry pop 378 archd Northampton dioc Peterborough

PRESTON DEANERY parish 1670 co Northampton 4-1/4 miles se
Northampton pop 64 archd Northampton dioc Peterborough

PRESTON, EAST parish 1573 Sussex 3-1/2 miles e Little Hampton
pop 242 archd and dioc Chichester

PRESTON, GREAT and LITTLE township parish Kippax W R York
pop 398

PRESTON GUBBALS or GOBALDS parish 1602 Shrops 4-3/4 miles
n Shrewsbury pop 385 archd Salop dioc Lichfield

PRESTON LE SKERNE township parish Aycliffe co Durham pop 176

PRESTON, LONG 1563 W R York 4-1/2 miles se Settle comp townships Hellifield, Long Preston, Wigglesworth pop 1,501 archd
and dioc York Wesl Meth

PRESTON ON THE HILL township parish Runcorn Ches pop 461
Wesl Meth

PRESTON PATRICK chapelry 1703 parish Burton in Kendal Westm
pop 418

PRESTON QUARTER township parish St Bees Cumberland pop 4,323

PRESTON RICHARD township parish Heversham Westm pop 395

PRESTON, STAPLETON Dorset See IWERNE STAPLETON

PRESTON, TARRANT tything parish Crawford Tarrant Dorset

PRESTON UNDER SCAR township parish Wensley N R York pop 362
Wesl Meth

PRESTON UPON STOUR parish 1540 Gloucs 4-1/2 miles s Stratford
upon Avon pop 355 archd and dioc Gloucester

PRESTON UPON TEES township parish Stockton upon Tees co Durham pop 76

PRESTON UPON THE WILD MOORS parish 1693 Shrops 3-1/2 miles
ne Wellington pop 218 archd Salop dioc Lichfield

PRESTON UPON WYE parish 1574 Herefs 8-1/2 miles nw Hereford
pop 251 Consistory Court of Dean of Hereford

PRESTON WYNNE chapelry 1730 parish Withington Herefs pop 139
PRESTWICH parish with Oldham 1603 Lancs 4-3/4 miles nw Manches-
ter pop 2,941 archd and dioc Chester
PRESTWICK township parish Ponteland Northumberland pop 168
PRESTWOOD township parish Ellastone Staffs pop 77
PRESTSOULD parish 1560 Leics 3 miles ne Loughborough pop 942
archd Leicester dioc Lincoln
PRIDDY parish 1761 Somerset 4-1/2 miles nw Wells pop 202 pec of
Archidiaconal court of Wells
PRIESTCLIFFE township parish Bakewell Derbys
PRIME THORP township parish Broughton Astley Leics
PRINCE'S RISBOROUGH Bucks See RISBOROUGH, PRINCE'S
PRINCETHORPE hamlet parish Stretton upon Dunsmoor Warws
PRINCETOWN parish 1807 Devon 7 miles e Tavistock
PRINKNASH PARK extra parochial district Gloucs 3-1/4 miles ne
Painswick pop 14
PRIORS ASH Somerset See ASH PRIORS
PRIORS, HARDWICK See HARDWICK PRIORS
PRIOR'S LEE chapelry parish Shiffnall Shrops pop 2,130
PRISTON parish 1764 Somerset 5-1/4 miles sw Bath pop 308 archd
Bath dioc Bath and Wells
PRITTLEWELL parish 1645 Essex 19 miles se Chelmsford pop
2,266 archd Essex dioc London
PRIVETT parish 1538 Hamps 5-3/4 miles nw Petersfield pop 225
pec of Incumbent
PROBUS parish 1641 Cornwall 2-1/4 miles sw Grampount pop 1,350
archd Cornwall dioc Exeter Wesl Meth
PROVOSTS FEE township parish Walkington E R York pop 177
PRUDHOE township parish Ovingham Northumberland pop 341 Wesl
Meth
PRUDHOE CASTLE township parish Ovingham Northumberland pop
71
PUBLOW parish 1569 Somerset 1/4 mile ne Pensford pop 839 archd
Bath dioc Bath and Wells
PUCKERIDGE hamlet parishes Braughin and Standon Herts
PUCKINGTON parish 1693 Somerset 2-3/4 miles ne Ilminster pop
182 archd Taunton dioc Bath and Wells
PUCKLE CHURCH parish 1590 Gloucs 5-1/4 miles sw Chipping Sod-
bury pop 796 archd and dioc Gloucester
PUDDING NORTON Norfolk See NORTON, PUDDING
PUDDINGTON parish 1662 Beds 5 miles nw Harrold pop 563 archd
Bedford dioc Lincoln
PUDDINGTON township parish Burton Ches pop 145
PUDDINGTON parish 1684 Devon 8 miles sw Tiverton pop 186 archd
Barnstaple dioc Exeter
PUDDLESTONE parish 1566 Herefs 5-3/4 miles ne Leominster pop
268 archd and dioc Hereford
PUDLICOTT tything parish Charlbury co Oxford

PUDSEY chapelry parish Calverley W R York pop 7,460 Indep, Wesl Meth

PULBOROUGH parish 1595 Sussex 9 miles ne Arundel pop 1,979 archd and dioc Chichester

PULFORD parish 1559 Ches 5-1/4 miles sw Chester comp townships Poulton and Pulford pop 289 archd and dioc Chester

PULHAM parish 1538 Norfolk 3-1/4 miles nw Harleston pop 1,046 archd Norfolk dioc Norwich

PULHAM parish 1539 Norfolk 2-1/2 miles nw Harleston pop 831 archd Norfolk dioc Norwich

PULHAM, EAST parish 1734 Dorset 7-1/2 miles se Sherborne pop 302 archd Dorset dioc Bristol

PULHAM, WEST manor parish East Pulham Dorset

PULLOXHILL parish 1706 Beds 2-1/4 miles sw Silsoe pop 529 archd Bedford dioc Lincoln

PULVERBATCH, CHURCH parish 1542 Shrops 8 miles sw Shrewsbury pop 557 archd Salop dioc Hereford

PUNCKKOWLE parish 1630 Dorset 6-1/2 miles se Bridport pop 424 archd Dorset dioc Bristol

PURBRIGHT parish 1574 Surrey 6-1/2 miles nw Guildford pop 594 archd Surrey dioc Winchester

PURFLEET township parish West Thurrock Essex

PURITON parish 1558 Somerset 4 miles ne Bridgewater pop 509 archd Wells dioc Bath and Wells

PURLEIGH parish 1592 Essex 4 miles sw Maldon pop 1,044 archd Essex dioc London

PURLEY parish 1662 Berks 4 miles nw Reading pop 172 archd Berks dioc Salisbury

PURSON hamlet parish King's Sutton co Northampton

PURTON parish 1558 Wilts 3-3/4 miles ne Wootton Bassett pop 1,778 archd Wilts dioc Salisbury Wesl Meth

PUSEY parish 1661 Berks 4-1/2 miles ne Great Farrington pop 125 archd Berks dioc Salisbury

PUTFORD, EAST parish 1671 Devon 8-1/2 miles sw Great Torrington pop 209 archd Barnstaple dioc Exeter

PUTFORD, WEST parish 1668 Devon 9 miles sw Great Torrington pop 400 archd Totnes dioc Exeter

PUTLEY parish 1561 Herefs 5-3/4 miles w Ledbury pop 165 Consistory Court of Dean of Hereford

PUTLEY township parish Woolhope Herefs

PUTNEY parish 1620 Surrey 4 miles sw London pop 3,811 pec of Archbishop of Canterbury

PUTTENHAM parish 1678 Herts 3-3/4 miles ne Tring pop 130 archd Huntingdon dioc Lincoln

PUTTENHAM parish 1562 Surrey 4-1/4 miles sw Guildford pop 372 archd Surrey dioc Winchester

PUXTON parish 1542 Somerset 6 miles nw Axbridge pop 145 pec of Banwell in Cathedral Church of Wells

PYLLE parish 1591 Somerset 3-1/2 miles sw Shepton Mallet pop 205 archd Wells dioc Bath and Wells

PYRFORD parish 1666 Surrey 1-3/4 miles nw Ripley pop 307 archd Surrey dioc Winchester

PYWORTHY parish 1653 Devon 2-1/4 miles sw Holsworthy pop 700 archd Totnes dioc Exeter

QUADRING parish 1583 Lincs 8-1/2 miles nw Spalding pop 858 archd and dioc Lincoln

QUAINTON parish 1599 Bucks 6 miles nw Aylesbury pop 1,056 archd Buckingham dioc Lincoln Bapt

QUANTOXHEAD, EAST parish 1654 Somerset 12-1/2 miles nw Bridge Water pop 277 archd Taunton dioc Bath and Wells

QUANTOCHEAD, WEST parish 1558 Somerset 15-1/2 miles nw Bridge Water pop 222 archd Taunton dioc Bath and Wells

QUARLES extra parochial district Norfolk 3-3/4 miles nw New Waisingham pop 33

QUARLEY parish 1559 Hamps 7 miles sw Andover pop 201 archd and dioc Winchester

QUARLTON township parish Bolton Lancs pop 376

QUARNDON parish 1754 Derbys 3 miles nw Derby pop 487 archd Derby dioc Lichfield

QUARNFORD chapelry 1744 parish Allstonefield Staffs pop 783

QUARRENDON parish no regs Bucks 2-1/4 miles nw Aylesbury pop 60 pec of Dean and Chapter of Lincoln

QUARRINGTON township parish Kelloe co Durham pop 173

QUARRINGTON parish 1558 Lincs 1-1/2 miles sw Sleaford pop 184 archd and dioc Lincoln

QUATFORD parish 1577 Shrops 2 miles se Bridgenorth pop 492 Royal pec Court of Bridgenorth

QUATT MALVERN parish 1672 Shrops 4-1/2 miles se Bridgenorth pop 328 archd Salop dioc Lichfield

QUEDGLEY parish 1559 Gloucs 3-1/2 miles sw Gloucester pop 297 archd and dioc Gloucester

QUEENBOROUGH parish 1719 borough Kent 15 miles ne Maidstone pop 786 excl juris archd and dioc Canterbury

QUEEN CAMEL See CAMEL QUEEN Somerset

QUEEN CHARLETON Somerset See CHARLETON, QUEEN

QUEENHILL chapelry 1733 parish Ripple Worcs pop 107

QUEENIBOROUGH parish 1561 Leics 6-1/4 miles ne Leicester pop 518 archd Leicester dioc Lincoln

QUENBY hamlet parish Hungerton Leics pop 17

QUENDON parish 1687 Essex 4-1/2 miles n Stansted Mountfitchet pop 211 Commissary of Essex and Herts, concurrently with Consistorial Court of Bishop of London

QUENNINGTON parish 1653 Gloucs 2 miles n Fairford pop 365 archd and dioc Gloucester

QUERNMOOR township parish Lancaster Lancs pop 605

QUETHIOCK parish 1574 Cornwall 4 miles e Liskeard pop 692 archd

Cornwall dioc Exeter

QUICK W R York See SADDLEWORTH

QUIDDENHAM parish 1538 Norfolk 2 miles ne East Harling pop 84
archd Norfolk dioc Norwich

QUINTON parish 1547 Gloucs 7 miles ne Chipping Campden pop 609
archd and dioc Gloucester

QUINTON parish 1648 co Northampton 4-1/2 miles se Northampton
pop 128 archd Northampton dioc Peterborough

QUOISLEY township parish Marbury Ches

QUORNDON chapelry 1576 parish Barrow upon Soar Leics pop 1,752
Bapt, Prim and Wesl Meth

QUY chapelry parish Stow Cambs

RABY township parish Neston Ches pop 165

RABY township parish Staindrop co Durham pop 247

RACKENFORD parish 1597 Devon 8-1/4 miles nw Tiverton pop 472
archd Barnstaple dioc Exeter

RACKHEATH parish 1660 Norfolk 5 miles ne Norwich pop 262 archd
and dioc Norwich

RACTON parish 1680 Sussex 6-1/2 miles nw Chichester pop 88 archd
and dioc Chichester

RADBOURN parish 1572 Derbys 4-1/2 miles w Derby pop 253 archd
Derby dioc Lichfield

RADBOURN, LOWER extra parochial district Warws 3-3/4 miles
se Southam pop 14

RADBOURN, UPPER extra parochial district Warws 3-1/2 miles se
Southam pop 8

RADCLIFFE parish 1555 Lancs 2-1/2 miles sw Bury pop 3,904 archd
and dioc Chester Wesl Meth

RADCLIFFE ON TRENT Notts See RATCLIFFE ON TRENT

RADCLIFFE UPON SOAR Notts See RATCLIFFE UPON SOAR

RADCLIVE parish 1594 Bucks 1-3/4 miles w Buckingham pop 334
archd Buckingham dioc Lincoln

RADCUTT hamlet parish Langford co Oxford pop 55

RADDINGTON parish 1583 Somerset 4-3/4 miles sw Wiveliscombe
pop 105 archd Taunton dioc Bath and Wells

RADFORD hamlet parish St Michael city of Coventry pop 228

RADFORD parish 1563 Notts 1 miles nw Nottingham pop 9,806 archd
Nottingham dioc York

RADFORD hamlet parish Church Enstone co Oxford

RADFORD SEMELE parish 1565 Warws 4 miles e Warwick pop 478
archd Coventry dioc Lichfield

RADIPOLE parish (incl with Melcombe Regis) Dorset 2-1/2 miles nw
Melcombe Regis pop 382 archd Dorset dioc Bristol

RADLEY parish 1599 Berks 2-1/2 miles ne Abingdon pop 515 archd
Berks dioc Salisbury

RADNAGE parish 1574 Bucks 6 miles nw High Wycombe pop 399
archd Buckingham dioc Lincoln Wesl Meth

RADNOR township parish Astbury Ches pop 20

RADSTOCK parish 1719 Somerset 7-1/2 miles nw Frome pop 1,165 archd Wells dioc Bath and Wells

RADSTON parish 1565 co Northampton 2-1/2 miles n Brackley pop 203 archd Northampton dioc Peterborough

RADWAY parish 1600 Warws 3-1/4 miles se Kington pop 315 archd Coventry dioc Lichfield

RADWELL hamlet parish Felmersham Beds pop 166 Wesl Meth

RADWELL parish 1590 Herts 1-1/2 miles nw Baldock pop 103 archd Huntingdon dioc Lincoln

RADWINTER parish 1638 Essex 4-1/2 miles n Thaxted pop 819 Commissary of Essex and Herts, concurrently with Consistorial Court of Bishop of London

RAFFORD liberty parish Chalgrove co Oxford pop 28

RAGDALE parish 1668 Leics 7 miles nw Melton Mowbray pop 108 archd Leicester dioc Lincoln

RAGLAND parish 1711 co Monmouth 7-1/2 miles sw Monmouth pop 681 archd and dioc Llandaff Bapt

RAGLEY hamlet parish Arrow Warws

RAGNALL chapelry 1700 parish Dunham Notts pop 168

RAINFORD chapelry parish Prescot 1718 Lancs pop 1,642 Indep

RAINHAM Essex See RAYNHAM

RAINHAM parish 1592 Kent 4 miles se Chatham pop 1,222 archd and dioc Canterbury

RAINHAM, EAST parish 1627 Norfolk 4 miles sw Fakenham pop 115 archd and dioc Norwich

RAINHAM, SOUTH parish 1740 Norfolk 5-1/4 miles sw Fakenham pop 122 archd and dioc Norwich

RAINHAM, WEST parish 1539 Norfolk 5-1/2 miles sw Fakenham pop 335 archd and dioc Norwich

RAINHILL township parish Prescot Lancs pop 679

RAINOW chapelry 1765 parish Prestbury Ches pop 1,807 Wesl Meth

RAINSCLIFF township parish Wolstanton Staffs pop 835

RAINSTHORPE Norfolk See TASEBURGH

RAINTON township parish Topcliffe N R York pop 411 Wesl Meth

RAINTON, EAST township parish Houghton le Spring co Durham pop 1,600 Wesl Meth

RAINTON, WEST chapelry parish Houghton le Spring co Durham pop 1,184 Wesl Meth

RAISTHORPE township parish Wharram Percy E R York pop 45

RAITHBY parish 1558 Lincs 2 miles nw Spilsby pop 175 archd and dioc Lincoln Wesl Meth

RAITHBY, SOUTH parish 1654 Lincs 2 miles sw Louth pop 147 archd and dioc Lincoln

RAMBOTTOM hamlet chapelry Lower Tottington parish Bury Lancs Wesl Meth

RAME parish 1653 Cornwall 4-1/2 miles sw Devonport pop 896 archd Cornwall dioc Exeter

RAMPISHAM parish 1576 Dorset 6-1/2 miles e Beaminster pop 416 archd Dorset dioc Bristol

RAMPSIDE Lancs See RAMSYDE

RAMPTON parish 1674 Cambs 6-1/2 miles nw Cambridge pop 191 archd and dioc Ely

RAMPTON parish 1565 Notts 6-3/4 miles se East Retford pop 411 pec of Prebendary of Rampton in Collegiate Church of Southwell

RAMSBURY parish 1678 Wilts 5-1/2 miles nw Hungerford comp tythings Axford, Eastridge, Town tything pop 2,290 pec juris of Dean of Salisbury Wesl Meth

RAMSDEN chapelry parish Skipton under Whychwood co Oxford pop 423

RAMSDON BELLHOUSE parish 1562 Essex 4 miles e Billericay pop 438 archd Essex dioc London

RAMSDON CRAYS parish 1558 Essex 3 miles se Billericay pop 272 archd Essex dioc London

RAMSEY parish 1645 Essex 3 miles sw Harwich pop 708 archd Colchester dioc London Wesl Meth

RAMSEY parish 1559 Hunts 11 miles ne Huntingdon pop 3,006 archd Huntingdon dioc Lincoln Indep

RAMSGATE sea port market town, parish 1827 formerly in parish of St Lawrence Isle of Thanet Kent 4 miles s Margate pop 7,985 archd and dioc Canterbury Bapt, Indep, Wesl Meth

RAMSGRAVE township parish Blackburn Lancs pop 515

RAMSHOLT parish 1706 Suffolk 7 miles se Woodbridge pop 215 archd Suffolk dioc Norwich

RAMSHOPE extra parochial district Northumberland 16-3/4 miles nw Bellingham pop 9

RAMSHORN township parish Ellastone Staffs pop 130

RAMSYDE or RAMPSIDE chapelry parish Dalton in Furness Lancs

RANBY parish 1569 Lincs 6-1/2 miles ne Wragby pop 109 archd and dioc Lincoln

RAND parish 1661 Lincs 2-1/4 miles nw Wragby pop 71 archd and dioc Lincoln

RANDS GRANGE hamlet parish Bedale N R York

RANDWICK parish 1662 Gloucs 2 miles nw Stroud pop 1,031 archd and dioc Gloucester Wesl Meth, Countess of Huntingdon

RANGEWORTHY chapelry 1704 parish Thornbury Gloucs Wesl Meth

RANSKILL township parish Blyth Notts pop 347 Indep

RANWORTH parish 1558 Norfolk 4 miles nw Acle pop 400 archd and dioc Norwich

RASEN, MARKET market town, parish 1561 Lincs 12 miles ne Lincoln pop 1,428 archd and dioc Lincoln Indep, Wesl Meth, Roman Cath

RASEN, MIDDLE parish 1754 Lincs 1-1/2 miles nw Market Rasen pop 685 archd and dioc Lincoln

RASEN MIDDLE TUPHOLME parish 1708 Lincs 2 miles nw Market Rasen archd and dioc Lincoln

RASEN, WEST parish 1683 Lincs 3-1/4 miles w Market Rasen pop

RASKELF chapelry 1754 parish Easingwould N R York pop 459

RASTRICK chapelry 1614 parish Halifax W R York pop 3,021 Indep

RATBY parish 1754 Leics 5 miles nw Leicester comp hamlets Botcheston, Groby, Newton Unthank, Old Hays, Whittington Grange pop 996 pec of Lord of Manor of Groby

RATCHWOOD township parish Bambrough Northumberland pop 20

RATCLIFFE hamlet parish Stepney Middlesex pop 9,741

RATCLIFFE CURLEY chapelry 1585 parish Sheepy Magna Leics pop 212

RATCLIFFE ON THE WREAK parish 1698 Leics 6-3/4 miles ne Leicester pop 144 archd Leicester dioc Lincoln

RATCLIFFE ON TRENT parish 1632 Notts 5-1/2 miles se Nottingham pop 1,125 archd Nottingham dioc York Wesl Meth

RATCLIFFE UPON SOAR parish 1597 Notts 1-1/2 miles ne Kegworth pop 177 archd Nottingham dioc York

RATHMILL township parish Giggleswick W R York pop 347

RATLEY parish 1701 Warws 4-1/4 miles se Kington pop 376 archd Coventry dioc Lichfield Wesl Meth

RATLINGHOPE parish 1702 Shrops 4-1/2 miles nw Church Stretton comp townships Gatton, Ratlinghope pop 252 archd Salop dioc Hereford

RATTERY parish 1654 Devon 4-1/4 miles ne Totnes pop 506 archd Totnes dioc Exeter

RATTLESDEN parish 1558 Suffolk 4-3/4 miles w Stow Market pop 1,113 archd Sudbury dioc Norwich Bapt

RAUCEBY, NORTH parish 1688 Lincs 4 miles w Sleaford pop 262 archd and dioc Lincoln

RAUCEBY, SOUTH parish (incl with North Rauceby) Lincs pop 255

RAUGHTON township parish Dalston Cumberland pop 330

RAUGHTON HEAD chapelry parish Castle Sowerby 1663 Cumberland

RAUNDS parish 1581 co Northampton dioc Peterborough Bapt, Wesl Meth

RAVELEY, GREAT parish (incl regs Upwood) Hunts 3-3/4 miles sw Ramsey pop 275 archd Huntingdon dioc Lincoln Wesl Meth

RAVELEY, LITTLE parish 1576 Hunts 4-1/4 miles sw Ramsey pop 54 archd Huntingdon dioc Lincoln

RAVENDALE, EAST parish 1723 Lincs 7 miles sw Great Grimsby pop 104 archd and dioc Lincoln

RAVENDALE, WEST chapelry parish East Ravendale Lincs pop 26

RAVENFIELD parish 1563 W R York 4 miles ne Rotherham pop 229 pec of Archdeacon of York

RAVENGLASS small sea port, market town, parish Muncaster Cumberland 54 miles sw Carlisle

RAVENINGHAM parish 1691 Norfolk 4-1/2 miles nw Beccles pop 215 archd Norfolk dioc Norwich

RAVENSCROFT township parish Middlewich Ches pop 16

RAVENSDALE PARK hamlet parish Mugginton Derbys pop 65

RAVENSDEN parish 1558 Beds 4 miles ne Bedford pop 258 archd Bedford dioc Lincoln

RAVENSTHORPE parish 1539 co Northampton 9-1/2 miles nw Northampton archd Northampton dioc Peterborough pop 685 Bapt

RAVENSTONE parish 1568 Bucks 3-1/4 miles sw Olney pop 430 archd Buckingham dioc Lincoln

RAVENSTONE parish 1705 Leics 4 miles se Ashby de la Zouch pop 430 archd Derby dioc Lichfield Wesl Meth

RAVENSTONEDALE parish 1571 Westm 4-3/4 miles sw Kirby Stephen pop 1,036 pec of Earl of Lonsdale Indep

RAVENSWORTH township parish Chester le Street co Durham pop 187

RAVENSWORTH township parish Kirby Ravensworth N R York pop 300 Wesl Meth

RAVENSWORTH, KIRBY N R York See KIRBY RAVENSWORTH

RAW township parish Rothbury Northumberland pop 49

RAWCLIFF chapelry 1689 parish Snaith W R York pop 1,450 pec Court of Snaith Wesl Meth

RAWCLIFFE township parishes St Michael le Belfrey and St Olave N R York pop 54

RAWCLIFFE, OUT township parish St Michael Lancs pop 575

RAWCLIFFE, UPPER township parish St Michael Lancs pop 665

RAWDEN or RAWDEON chapelry 1783 parish Guisley W R York pop 2,057 Bapt, Wesl Meth

RAWLEIGH tything parishes Bicton and Rockbear Devon

RAWLEIGH, COLYTON Devon See COLYTON, RAWLEIGH

RAWMARSH parish 1653 W R York pop 1,538 2-1/2 miles ne Rotherham archd and dioc York Indep, Wesl Meth

RAWRETH parish 1539 Essex 3 miles nw Rayleigh pop 321 archd Essex dioc London

RAYDON parish 1562 Suffolk 3-1/4 miles se Hadleigh pop 559 archd Suffolk dioc Norwich

RAYLEIGH parish 1548 Essex 14 miles se Chelmsford pop 1,339 archd Essex dioc London Bapt

RAYNE parish 1558 Essex 1-3/4 miles w Braintree pop 320 archd Middlesex dioc London

RAYNHAM parish 1570 Essex 3-1/4 miles nw Purfleet pop 671 archd Essex dioc London

REACH chapelry parish Leighton Buzzard Beds

REACH hamlet parishes Burwell and Swaffham Prior Cambs

READ township parish Whalley Lancs pop 510

READING borough, market town Berks 26 miles se Abingdon pop 15,595 sep juris comp parishes St Giles 1599, St Lawrence 1605, St Mary 1538 archd Berks dioc Salisbury Bapt, Indep, Soc of Friends, Wesl Meth, Roman Cath

REAGILL hamlet parish Crosby Ravensworth Westm

REARSBY parish 1648 Leics 7-1/4 miles ne Leicester pop 503 archd Leicester dioc Lincoln Wesl Meth

REAVELEY township parish Ingram Northumberland pop 67

RECULVER parish 1602 Kent 10 miles ne Canterbury pop 297 pec of Archbishop of Canterbury

REDBOURN parish 1626 Herts 17 miles w Hertford pop 2,047 archd St Albans dioc London Bapt, Indep, Wesl Meth

REDBOURN parish 1558 Lincs 2-1/2 miles ne Kirton pop 300 archd Stow dioc Lincoln

REDBRIDGE hamlet parish Millbrook Hamps

REDCAR chapelry parish Marsk N R York pop 729 Wesl Meth

REDCLIFFE, St Mary See BRISTOL

REDDENHALL parish (in reg Harleston) Norfolk 1-1/2 miles ne Harleston pop 1,784 archd Norfolk dioc Norwich

REDDISH township parish Manchester Lancs pop 860

REDDITCH chapelry 1770 parish Tardebigge Worcs Indep, Wesl Meth

REDGRAVE parish 1538 Suffolk 2 miles ne Botesdale pop 712 archd Sudbury dioc Norwich

REDISHAM parish 1713 Suffolk 5 miles ne Halesworth pop 179 archd Suffolk dioc Norwich

REDISHAM, LITTLE Suffolk See RINGFIELD

REDLINGFIELD parish 1739 Suffolk 3-1/2 miles se Eye pop 235 archd Sudbury dioc Norwich

REDLYNCH chapelry parish Bruton Somerset pop 64

REDMAIN township parish Isall Cumberland

REDMARLEY hamlet parish Great Witley Worcs

REDMARLEY D'ABITOT parish 1539 Worcs 5-1/2 miles se Ledbury pop 1,028 archd and dioc Worcester

RED MARSHALL parish 1559 co Durham 4-3/4 miles nw Stockton upon Tees comp chapelries Carleton, Stillington, township Red Marshall pop 335 archd and dioc Durham

REDMILE parish 1653 Leics 12-1/4 miles ne Melton Mowbray pop 461 archd Leicester dioc Lincoln

REDMIRE chapelry parish Wensley (incl regs Bolton Castle) N R York pop 344 Wesl Meth

REDRUTH market town, parish 1560 Cornwall 53 miles se Launceston pop 8,191 archd Cornwall dioc Exeter Bapt, Soc of Friends, Prim and Wesl Meth

REDWICK tything parish Henbury Gloucs pop 285

REDWICK chapelry 1787 parish Magor co Monmouth pop 252

REDWORTH township parish Heighinton co Durham pop 370

REED parish 1539 Herts 1-3/4 miles nw Barkway pop 232 archd Middlesex dioc London

REED parish 1558 Suffolk 6-1/2 miles sw Bury St Edmunds pop 231 archd Sudbury dioc Norwich

REEDHAM parish 1754 Norfolk 6 miles se Acle pop 535 archd and dioc Norwich

REEDLY HALLOWS township parish Whalley Lancs pop 468

REEDNESS township parish Whitgift W R York pop 644

REEPHAM parish 1633 Lincs 4-1/4 miles ne Lincoln pop 295 archd

Stow dioc Lincoln

REEPHAM market town, parish 1538 Norfolk 12 miles nw Norwich pop 452 archd and dioc Norwich Bapt, Wesl Meth

REETH market town, parish Grinton N R York pop 1,456 Indep, Wesl Meth

REIGATE borough, market town, parish 1556 Surrey 19 miles e Guildford pop 3,397 archd Surrey dioc Winchester Soc of Friends, Indep

REIGHTON parish 1559 E R York 6-1/4 miles nw Bridlington pop 234 archd East Riding dioc York

REMENHAM parish 1697 Berks 1-1/2 miles ne Henley upon Thames pop 463 archd Berks dioc Salisbury

REMPSTONE parish 1570 Notts 4-3/4 miles ne Loughborough pop 398 archd Nottingham dioc York

REMPTON township parish Glunbury Shrops

RENDCOMBE parish 1566 Gloucs 5-1/2 miles n Cirencester pop 218 archd and dioc Gloucester

RENDHAM parish 1554 Suffolk 2-1/2 miles nw Saxmundham pop 449 archd Suffolk dioc Norwich Indep

RENDLESHAM parish 1722 Suffolk 3 miles se Wickham Market pop 261 archd Suffolk dioc Norwich

RENHOLD parish 1654 Beds 3-3/4 miles ne Bedford pop 453 archd Bedford dioc Lincoln

REINSHAW township parish Eckington Derbys

RENNINGTON chapelry 1768 parish Embleton Northumberland pop 273 archd Northumberland dioc Durham

RENWICK parish 1649 Cumberland 3-1/4 miles ne Kirk Oswald pop 364 archd and dioc Carlisle Wesl Meth

REPPS parish 1563 Norfolk 5-1/4 miles ne Acle pop 255 archd and dioc Norwich

REPPS, NORTH parish 1558 Norfolk 3 miles se Cromer pop 605 archd and dioc Norwich

REPPS, SOUTH parish 1558 Norfolk 4-3/4 miles nw North Walsham pop 733 archd and dioc Norwich

REPTON parish 1580 Derbys 4-1/4 miles ne Burton upon Trent pop 2,083 archd Derby dioc Lichfield Indep, Wesl Meth

RESTON, NORTH parish 1562 Lincs 4-3/4 miles se Louth pop 39 archd and dioc Lincoln Wesl Meth

RESTON, SOUTH parish 1757 Lincs 6-1/4 miles nw Alford pop 139 archd and dioc Lincoln

RETFORD, EAST borough, market town, parish 1573 Notts 32 miles ne Nottingham pop 2,491 archd Nottingham dioc York Gen Bapt, Indep, Wesl Meth

RETFORD, WEST parish 1772 Notts 1/4 mile w East Retford pop 593 archd Nottingham dioc York

RETTENDON parish 1678 Essex 4-1/2 miles nw Rayleigh pop 671 archd Essex dioc London

REVELSTOKE parish 1653 Devon 7-1/2 miles se Earl's Plympton

pop 492 archd Totnes dioc Exeter

REVESBY parish 1595 Lincs 2-1/2 miles nw Bolingbroke pop 646 archd and dioc Lincoln Wesl Meth

REWE parish 1686 Devon 4-1/4 miles ne Exeter pop 286 archd and dioc Exeter

REYDON parish 1712 Suffolk 1-3/4 miles nw Southwold pop 338 archd Suffolk dioc Norwich

REYMERSTON parish 1559 Norfolk 6 miles se East Dereham pop 299 archd Norfolk dioc Norwich

RIBBESFORD parish 1574 Worcs 3/4 miles s Bewdley pop 4,003 archd and dioc Worcester

RIBBY chapelry parish Kirkham Lancs pop 482

RIBBLETON township parish Preston Lancs pop 170

RIBCHESTER parish 1598 Lancs 6 miles nw Blackburn comp townships Alston with Hathersall, Dilworth, Dutton, Ribchester pop 4,283 archd Richmond dioc Chester

RIBSTON, GREAT township parish Hunsingore W R York pop 152 Wesl Meth

RIBSTON, LITTLE township parish Spofforth W R York pop 222

RIBTON township parish Bridekirk Cumberland pop 26

RIBY parish 1559 Lincs 7 miles sw Great Grimsby pop 163 archd and dioc Lincoln

RICCALL parish 1613 E R York 4-1/2 miles ne Selby pop 705 pec Prebendary of Riccall in Cathedral Church of York Wesl Meth

RICHARD'S CASTLE parish 1559 Shrops 4-1/4 miles sw Ludlow pop 586 archd Salop dioc Hereford

RICHBOROUGH Kent See ASH

RICHMOND parish 1582 Surrey 8 miles sw London pop 7,243 archd Surrey dioc Winchester

RICHMOND borough, market town, parish 1556 N R York 44 miles nw York pop 3,900 sep juris archd Richmond dioc Chester Bapt, Roman Cath, Wesl Meth

RICKERBY township parish Stanwix Cumberland pop 74

RICKERSCOTE township parish Castle Church Staffs

RICKINGHALL INFERIOR parish 1652 Suffolk 1/4 mile sw Botesdale pop 465 archd Suffolk dioc Norwich

RICKINGHALL SUPERIOR parish 1557 Suffolk 3/4 mile sw Botesdale pop 774 archd Sudbury dioc Norwich

RICKLING parish 1660 Essex 5-3/4 miles nw Stansted Mountfitchet pop 447 Commissary of Essex and Herts, concurrently with Consistorial Court of Bishop of London

RICKMANSWORTH market town, parish 1653 Herts 24 miles sw Hertford pop 4,574 archd St Albans dioc London Bapt, Indep

RIDDINGS market town, chapelry, parish Alfreton Derbys Bapt, Indep, Wesl Meth

RIDDLES QUARTER township parish Long Horsley Northumberland

RIDDLESWORTH parish 1686 Norfolk 4-1/4 miles sw East Harling pop 76 archd Norfolk dioc Norwich

RIDGE parish 1558 Herts 3-1/2 miles nw Chipping Barnet pop 347 archd St Albans dioc London

RIDGE tything parish Chilmark Wilts

RIDGMONT parish 1539 Beds 3-1/4 miles ne Woburn pop 992 archd Bedford dioc Lincoln Bapt

RIDGWELL parish 1562 Essex 5 miles nw Castle Hedingham pop 713 Commissary of Essex and Herts, concurrently with Consistorial Court of Bishop of London Bapt, Indep

RIDING township parish Bywell St Andrew Northumberland pop 151

RIDLEY township parish Bunbury Ches pop 100

RIDLEY parish 1626 Kent 3-1/4 miles n Wrotham pop 91 archd and dioc Rochester

RIDLEY township parish Haltwhistle Northumberland pop 233

RIDDINGTON parish 1559 Norfolk 4-1/4 miles e North Walsham pop 205 archd Norfolk dioc Norwich

RIDLINGTON parish 1559 co Rutland 2-1/4 miles nw Uppingham pop 262 archd Northampton dioc Peterborough

RIDWARE, HAMSTALL Staffs See HAMSTALL RIDWARE

RIDWARE, MAVESYN parish 1538 Staffs 4-3/4 miles se Rugeley pop 576 pec of Dean of Lichfield

RIDWARE, PIPE parish 1561 Staffs 4-3/4 miles e Rugeley pop 111 pec of Dean of Lichfield

RIGSBY parish 1686 Lincs 1-1/2 miles sw Alford pop 99 archd and dioc Lincoln

RIGTON township parish Kirkby Overblows W R York pop 451 pec of Court of Honour of Knaresborough Wesl Meth

RIGTON township parish Bardse W R York

RILLINGTON parish 1638 E R York 3-3/4 miles ne New Malton comp chapelry Scamptston, township Rillington pop 955 archd East Riding dioc York Wesl Meth, Indep

RILSDON chapelry 1559 parish Burnsall W R York pop 115

RIMMINGTON township parish Gisburn W R York pop 701

RIMPTON parish 1538 Somerset 6-1/4 miles ne Yeovil pop 208 archd Wells dioc Bath and Wells

RIMSWELL township parish Owthorne E R York pop 144

RINGEY chapelry parish Bowdon Ches

RINGLAND parish 1688 Norfolk 7-1/2 miles nw Norwich pop 286 archd Norfolk dioc Norwich

RINGLEY chapelry 1719 parish Oldham Lancs

RINGMER parish 1605 Sussex 2-3/4 miles ne Lewes pop 1,271 pec of Archbishop of Canterbury

RINGMORE parish 1719 Devon 4 miles sw Modbury pop 309 archd Totnes dioc Exeter

RINGSFIELD parish 1751 Suffolk 2 miles sw Beccles pop 315 archd Suffolk dioc Norwich

RINGSHALL parish 1539 Suffolk 3-3/4 miles sw Needham Market pop 337 archd Suffolk dioc Norwich

RINGSTEAD parish 1570 co Northampton 2-3/4 miles sw Thrapston pop 620 archd Northampton dioc Peterborough Bapt, Wesl Meth

RINGSTEAD, GREAT parish 1546 Norfolk 7-3/4 miles sw Burnham Westgate pop 524 archd Norfolk dioc Norwich

RINGSTEAD, LITTLE parish 1546 Norfolk 8 miles sw Burnham Westgate archd Norfolk dioc Norwich

RINGWAY chapelry 1751 parish Bowden Ches

RINGSWOULD parish 1569 Kent 3 miles sw Deal pop 566 archd and dioc Canterbury

RINGWOOD parish 1561 Hamps 20 miles sw Southampton comp market town Ringwood, tything Burley with the Ville of Bistern Closes, extra parochial liberties of Burley, Lodge, Godshill, Linwood and exclusively of extra parochial district of Woodgreen pop 4,382 archd and dioc Winchester Indep, Unit

RIPE parish 1538 Sussex 6 miles nw Hailsham pop 360 archd Lewes dioc Chichester

RIPLEY chapelry 1828 parish Pentrich Derbys pop 1,997 Wesl Meth, Unit

RIPLEY chapelry parish Send Surrey Bapt

RIPLEY parish 1560 W R York 23 miles nw York comp townships Clint, Killinghall, Ripley pop 1,219 archd Richmond dioc Chester

RIPLINGTON township parish Whalton Northumberland pop 17

RIPLINGTON tything parish East Meon Hamps

RIPON parish 1587 W R York 23 miles nw York comp borough, market town Ripon, chapelries Bishop Monckton, Bishop Thornton, Pateley Bridge, Sawley, Skelton, townships Aismunderby with Bondgate, High and Low Bishopside, Bishopton, Clotherholme, Eavendale, Grantley with Skeldin, Hewick Bridge, Hewick Copt, Ingerthorpe, Markington with Wallerthwaite, Marston with Moseby, Newby with Mulwith, Nunwick with Howgrave, Sharrow, North Stanley with Slenningford, Sutton Grange, Warsill, Westwick, Whitcliffe with Thorpe, chapelries Aldfield, Winksley, township Beverley, Dacre, Shelding, Studley Roger, Studley Royal pop 5,080 sep juris pec Archbishop of York Wesl Meth, Indep, Prim Meth

RIPPINGALE parish 1633 Lincs 4-1/4 miles n Bourne pop 658 archd and dioc Lincoln

RIPPLE ward parish Barking Essex pop 387

RIPPLE parish 1560 Kent 2-3/4 miles sw Deal pop 209 archd and dioc Canterbury

RIPPLE parish 1568 Worcs 3 miles se Upon upon Severn pop 972 pec of the Incumbent

RIPPONDEN chapelry 1684 parish Halifax W R York Wesl Meth

RIPTON, ABBOT'S parish 1559 Hunts 4 miles n Huntingdon pop 365 archd Huntingdon dioc Lincoln

RIPTON, KING'S parish 1633 Hunts 3-1/2 miles ne Huntingdon pop 279 archd Huntingdon dioc Lincoln

RISBOROUGH, MONKS' parish 1587 Bucks 6-1/4 miles nw Great Middenden pop 1,018 pec of Archbishop of Canterbury Wesl Meth

RISBOROUGH, PRINCE'S market town, parish 1561 Bucks 6 miles

nw Great Missenden pop 2,122 archd Buckingham dioc Lincoln Bapt, Wesl Meth

RISBRIDGE, MONKS' extra parochial liberty Suffolk 4-3/4 miles nw Clare pop 11

RISBURY township parishes Humber and Stoke Prior Herefs pop 151

RISBY parish (incl with Roxby) Lincs 8 miles nw Glandford Bridge archd Stow dioc Lincoln

RISBY parish 1674 Suffolk 3-3/4 miles nw Bury St Edmunds pop 332 archd Sudbury dioc Norwich

RISCA parish 1736 co Monmouth 5 miles nw Newport pop 742 archd and dioc Llandaff Wesl Meth

RISE parish 1559 E R York 8-1/2 miles ne Beverley pop 164 archd East Riding dioc York

RISEBROUGH, THORNTON township parish Normanby N R York pop 39

RISEHOLME parish no regs Lincs 2-1/2 miles ne Lincoln pop 62 archd Stow dioc Lincoln

RISHANGLES parish 1593 Suffolk 4 miles s Eye pop 242 archd Sudbury dioc Norwich

RISHTON township parish Blackburn Lancs pop 919

RISHWORTH township parish Halifax W R York pop 1,536 Bapt

RISLEY parish 1628 Beds 5-1/4 miles sw Kimbolton pop 871 archd Bedford dioc Lincoln Wesl Meth, Moravian

RISLEY chapelry parish Saniacre and Sawley Derby 1667 pop 252 pec Prebendary of Sawley in Cathedral Church of Lichfield

RISSINGTON, GREAT parish 1538 Gloucs 5-3/4 miles s Stow on the Wold pop 468 archd and dioc Gloucester

RISSINGTON, LITTLE parish 1543 Gloucs 3-3/4 miles s Stow on the Wold pop 231 archd and dioc Gloucester

RISSINGTON, WICK parish 1739 Gloucs 3 miles s Stow on the Wold pop 219 archd and dioc Gloucester

RISTON Norfolk See RYSTON

RISTON township parish Church Stoke Shrops

RISTON, LONG parish 1653 E R York 6-3/4 miles ne Beverley pop 379 archd East Riding dioc York Indep

RITTON COLTPARK township parish Netherwitton Northumberland pop 58

RITTON WHITEHOUSE township parish Netherwitton Northumberland pop 31

RIVAULX township parish Helmsley N R York pop 225

RIVENHALL parish 1639 Essex 2-3/4 miles ne Witham pop 653 archd Colchester dioc London

RIVER parish 1620 Kent 2-1/2 miles nw Dover pop 690 archd and dioc Canterbury

RIVER GREEN extra parochial liberty Northumberland 5 miles sw Morpeth pop 48

RIVERHEAD chapelry parish Seven Oaks Kent

RIVINGTON chapelry 1703 parish Bolton Lancs pop 537 Unit

RIXTON township parish Warrington Lancs pop 906

ROACH or ROCHE parish 1572 Cornwall 7 miles sw Bodmin pop
1,630 archd Cornwall dioc Exeter Wesl Meth, Bryanites

ROAD parish 1587 Somerset 4-1/2 miles ne Frome pop 954 archd
Wells dioc Bath and Wells Bapt, Wesl Meth

ROADE parish 1587 co Northampton 5 miles s Northampton pop 553
archd Northampton dioc Peterborough Bapt

ROBERT'S BRIDGE or ROTHER BRIDGE village parish Salehurst
Sussex

RODBOROUGH parish 1619 Devon 5-1/2 miles se Great Torrington
pop 584 archd Barnstaple dioc Exeter

ROBURNDALE township parish Melling Lancs pop 199

ROBY township parish Huyton Lancs pop 401

ROCESTER parish 1568 Staffs 4-1/2 miles ne Uttoxeter pop 1,040
archd Stafford dioc Lichfield

ROCHDALE parish 1582 W R York 50 miles se Lancaster comp chapelries Blatchinworth, Todmorden, townships Butterworth Castleton, Spotland Further Side, Spotland Nearer Side, Walsden, Wardleworth, Wuerdale with Wardle, chapelry Saddleworth with Quick
pop 74,427 archd and dioc Chester Bapt, Soc of Friends, Prim
and Wesl Meth, Unit, Roman Cath

ROCHESTER city and port 1657 Kent 8-1/2 miles n Maidstone pop
9,891 sep juris comp St Margaret 1640, St Nicholas 1624 archd
and dioc Rochester Soc of Friends, Indep, Wesl Meth, Unit

ROCHESTER WARD township parish Elston Northumberland pop 467

ROCHFORD market town, parish 1678 Essex 19-1/4 miles se Chelmsford pop 1,256 archd Essex dioc London Indep

ROCHFORD parish 1569 Herefs and Worcs 2-1/2 miles ne Tenbury
pop 264 archd Salop dioc Hereford

ROCK chapelry 1768 parish Embleton Northumberland pop 200

ROCK parish 1548 Worcs 4-3/4 miles sw Bewdley pop 1,307 archd
Salop dioc Hereford

ROCK SAVAGE Ches See CLIFTON

ROCKBEARE parish 1645 Devon 6 miles e Exeter pop 530 archd and
dioc Exeter

ROCKBOURNE parish 1561 Hamps 3-1/2 miles nw Fordingbridge
pop 517 a donative

ROCKCLIFF parish 1679 Cumberland 4-3/4 miles nw Carlisle comp
townships Castle Rockcliff, Church Rockcliff pop 885 archd and
dioc Carlisle

ROCKCLIFF, CASTLE township parish Rockcliff 1679 Cumberland
pop 422

ROCKFIELD parish 1696 co Monmouth 2 miles nw Monmouth pop 279
archd and dioc Llandaff

ROCKHAM hamlet parish Amberley Sussex

ROCKHAMPTON parish 1565 Gloucs 2-1/2 miles ne Thornbury pop
220 archd and dioc Gloucester

ROCKINGHAM parish 1562 co Northampton 25 miles ne Northampton

pop 296 archd Northampton dioc Peterborough

ROCKLAND ST MARY parish 1656 Norfolk 6-1/2 miles se Norwich pop 437 archd Norfolk dioc Norwich

ROCKLAND ALL SAINTS parish 1696 Norfolk 3-3/4 miles nw Attleburgh pop 322 archd Norfolk dioc Norwich

ROCKLAND ST ANDREW parish no regs Norfolk 3-1/4 miles w Attleburgh pop 136 archd Norfolk dioc Norwich

ROCKLAND ST PETER parish 1538 Norfolk 4-1/4 miles nw Attleburgh pop 298 archd Norfolk dioc Norwich

ROCLIFFE township parish Aldborough W R York pop 265

ROD township parish Fresteign Herefs pop 157

RODBASTON township parish Penkridge Staffs

RODBORNE chapelry parish Malmesbury Wilts pop 155

RODBORNE CHENEY parish 1663 Wilts 3 miles nw Swindon pop 574 archd Wilts dioc Salisbury

RODBOROUGH chapelry 1692 parish Minchinhampton Gloucs pop 2,141 Indep

RODDAM township parish Ilderton Northumberland pop 118

RODDEN parish 1659 Somerset 2 miles se Frome pop 295 archd Wells dioc Bath and Wells

RODDINGTON parish 1678 Shrops 5 miles nw Wellington pop 423 archd Salop dioc Lichfield

RODE HUISH chapelry parish Carhampton Somerset

RODE, NORTH township parish Prestbury Ches pop 256

RODE, ODD township parish Astbury Ches pop 1,300

RODING See ROOTHING

RODLEY township parish Westbury upon Severn Gloucs

RODMARTON parish 1605 Gloucs 6 miles sw Cirencester pop 369 archd and dioc Gloucester

RODMELL parish 1704 Sussex 3-3/4 miles se Lewes pop 350 archd Lewes dioc Chichester

RODMERSHAM parish 1538 Kent 2 miles se Sittingbourne pop 311 archd and dioc Canterbury

RODNEY STOKE Somerset See STOKE, RODNEY

RODSLEY hamlet parish Longford Derbys pop 183 Wesl Meth

ROEHAMPTON hamlet parish Putney Surrey

ROFFORD liberty parish Chalgrove co Oxford pop 28

ROGATE parish 1558 Sussex 6 miles nw Midhurst pop 901 archd and dioc Chichester Indep

ROGERSTONE hamlet parish Bassaleg co Monmouth pop 870

ROGGIET parish 1750 co Monmouth 6-1/2 miles sw Chepstow pop 40 archd and dioc Llandaff

ROKEBY parish 1598 N R York 2-1/2 miles nw Greta Bridge pop 211 archd Richmond dioc Chester

ROLLESBY parish 1558 Norfolk 5-1/4 miles ne Acle pop 717 archd and dioc Norwich

ROLLESTON chapelry 1599 parish Billesdon Leics pop 41

ROLLESTON parish 1559 Notts 4-1/2 miles sw Newark pop 272

archd Nottingham dioc York

ROLLESTON parish 1589 Staffs 3-1/4 miles nw Burton upon Trent pop 866 archd Stafford dioc Lichfield Wesl Meth

ROLLRIGHT, GREAT parish 1560 co Oxford 3 miles ne Chipping Norton pop 438 archd and dioc Oxford

ROLLRIGHT, LITTLE parish 1754 co Oxford 2-1/4 miles nw Chipping Norton pop 29 archd and dioc Oxford

ROLLESTONE parish 1653 Wilts 5-1/4 miles nw Amesbury pop 39 archd and dioc Salisbury

ROLVENDEN parish 1561 Kent 2-1/2 miles sw Tenterden pop 1,507 archd and dioc Canterbury Wesl Meth

ROMALD KIRK parish 1578 N R York 6 miles nw Barnard Castle comp townships Cotherston, Holwick, Hunderthwaite, Lartingdon, Lune Dale, Mickleton, Romald Kirk pop 2,507 archd Richmond dioc Chester

ROMANBY township parish North Allerton N R York pop 325

ROMANSLEIGH parish 1539 Devon 3-1/4 miles se South Molton pop 217 archd Barnstaple dioc Exeter

ROMFORD market town, parish 1561 Essex 18 miles sw Chelmsford pop 4,294 pec of Warden and Fellows of New College Oxford Indep, Wesl Meth

ROMILY or CHAD KIRK chapelry parish Stockport Ches pop 1,290

ROMNEY MARSH liberty in Lathe of Shepway Kent comp parishes Broomhill, Burmarsh, Dymchurch with Blackmanstone, East Bridge, Hope All Saints, Ivy Church, Lydd, St Mary's Midley, Newchurch, Orgarswick, New Romney, Old Romney, Snargate, Snave, parts of Aldington, Bilsington, Bonnington, Brenzett, Hurst, Lympne, Orlestone

ROMNEY, NEW cinque port, market town, parish 1662 borough Kent 34 miles se Maidstone pop 983 sep juris pec of Archbishop of Canterbury

ROMNEY, OLD parish 1538 Dent 1-3/4 miles nw New Romney pop 113 pec of Archbishop of Canterbury

ROMSEY market town, parish 1569 Hamps 8 miles nw Southampton pop 5,432 sep juris archd and dioc Winchester Bapt, Indep, Wesl Meth, Sandemainians

ROMSLEY parish 1736 Worcs 3 miles s Halesowen

ROMSLEY liberty parish Alveley Shrops pop 113

RONTON parish 1655 Staffs 4 miles se Eccleshall pop 273 archd Stafford dioc Lichfield

RONTON ABBEY extra parochial liberty Staffs 3-1/2 miles se Ecclesall pop 17

ROOKWITH township parish Thornton Watlass N R York pop 78

ROOSDOWN extra parochial liberty Devon 3-1/4 miles sw Lyme Regis pop 10

ROOSS parish 1571 E R York 14 miles e Kingston upon Hull pop 430 archd East Riding dioc York Wesl Meth

ROOTHING, ABBOT'S parish 1560 Essex 5-3/4 miles ne Chipping

Ongar pop 234 archd Middlesex dioc London Indep

ROOTHING, AYTHORPE parish 1559 Essex 5-1/2 miles sw Great
Dunmow pop 259 Commissary of Essex and Herts concurrently
with Consistorial Court of Bishop of London

ROOTHING, BEAUCHAMP parish 1688 Essex 4-1/4 miles ne Chipping Ongar pop 238 archd Middlesex dioc London

ROOTHING, BERNERS parish 1538 Essex 5-3/4 miles ne Chipping
Ongar pop 100 archd Middlesex dioc London

ROOTHING, HIGH parish 1538 Essex 4-1/2 miles sw Great Dunmow
pop 405 archd Middlesex dioc London

ROOTHING, LEADEN parish 1572 Essex 6-1/2 miles sw Great Dunmow pop 147 Commissary of Essex and Herts, concurrently with
Consistorial Court of Bishop of London

ROOTHING, MARGARET parish 1538 Essex 7-1/4 miles ne Chipping
Ongar pop 233 archd Middlesex dioc London

ROOTHING, MORRELL hamlet parish White Roothing Essex

ROOTHING, WHITE parish 1547 Essex 6-3/4 miles sw Great Dunmow pop 479 archd Middlesex dioc London

ROPE township parish Wybunbury Ches pop 119

ROPLEY parish 1538 Hamps 4 miles e New Alresford pop 779 archd
and dioc Winchester

ROPSLEY parish 1558 Lincs 6-1/4 miles w Falkingham pop 578
archd and dioc Lincoln

ROSEACRE township parish Kirkham Lancs

ROSE ASH parish 1591 Devon 5-3/4 miles se South Molton pop 487
archd Barnstaple dioc Exeter

ROSEDALE, EAST SIDE township parish Middleton N R York pop 376

ROSEDALE, WEST SIDE chapelry 1616 parish Lastingham N R York
pop 178

ROSEDON township parish Ilderton Northumberland pop 78

ROSLEY township parish Westward Allerdale Cumberland pop 650

ROSLISTON parish 1768 Derbys 4-1/2 miles sw Burton upon Trent
pop 360 archd Derby dioc Lichfield

ROSS township parish Belford co Durham pop 65

ROSS market town, parish, borough 1671 Herefs 14 miles se Hereford
pop 3,078 archd and dioc Hereford Bapt, Soc of Friends, Indep

ROSSINGTON parish 1538 W R York 4-1/2 miles nw Bawtry pop 325
archd Nottingham dioc York

ROSTHERN parish 1595 Ches 3-1/2 miles nw Nether Knutsford comp
chapelries High Leigh, Peover Superior, townships Agden, Bollington, Martall with Little Warford, Mere, Millington, Rosthern, Tabley Superior, Tatton Snelson pop 3,730 archd and dioc Chester

ROSTON township parish Norbury Derbys

ROTHBURY market town, parish 1658 Northumberland 30 miles nw
Newcastle comp townships Bickerton, Caistron, Cartington, Deb-
don, Fallowless, Flotterton, Hellinghill, Hepple, Hepple Demesne,
Hesley, Hurst, Lee Ward, Mounthealy, Newton, Paperhaugh, Raw,
Rothbury, Rye Hill, Snitter, Thropton, Great Tossen, Little Tossen,

High and Low Trewhitt, Warton, Whitton, Wreigh Hill pop 2,869 archd Northumberland dioc Durham

ROTHERBY parish 1561 Leics 5-1/2 miles sw Melton Mowbray pop 152 archd Leicester dioc Lincoln

ROTHERFIELD tything parish East Tisted Hamps

ROTHERFIELD parish 1539 Sussex 5-3/4 miles sw Wadhurst pop 3,085 archd Lewes dioc Chichester Bapt, Wesl Meth

ROTHERFIELD GRAYS parish 1591 co Oxford 2-1/4 miles w Henley pop 1,145 archd and dioc Oxford

ROTHERFIELD, PEPPARD parish 1571 co Oxford 3-3/4 miles sw Henley upon Thames pop 426 archd and dioc Oxford

ROTHERHAM parish 1556 W R York 49 miles sw York comp market town Rotherham, chapelry Tinsley, townships Brinsworth, Catcliffe, Dalton, Orgreave, chapelry Greasbrough, township Kimberworth pop 10,417 archd and dioc York Bapt, Indep, Wesl Meth, Unit

ROTHERHITHE parish 1556 Surrey 1 mile se London pop 12,875 archd Surrey dioc Winchester Bapt, Indep, Wesl Meth

ROTHERSTHORPE parish 1563 co Northampton 3 miles sw Northampton pop 270 archd Northampton dioc Peterborough

ROTHERWICK parish 1561 Hamps 5 miles sw Hartford Bridge pop 436 archd and dioc Winchester

ROTHLEY parish 1562 Leics 1-1/2 miles se Mountsorrel comp chapelries Keyham, Wartnaby, Wycomb with Chadwell, chapelry Mountsorrel, extra parochial liberty Rothley Temple pop 1,342 pec of Rothley Gen Bapt, Wesl Meth

ROTHLEY township parish Hartburn Northumberland pop 138

ROTHLEY TEMPLE extra parochial liberty Leics 1-1/2 miles s Mountsorrel

ROTHWELL parish 1560 Lincs 2-3/4 miles se Caistor pop 231 archd and dioc Lincoln

ROTHWELL parish 1708 co Northampton 19 miles ne Northampton pop 2,003 archd Northampton dioc Peterborough

ROTHWELL parish 1538 W R York 6 miles ne Wakefield comp townships Carlton, Lofthouse, Middleton, Otton, Rhodes Green, Rothwell, Rothwell Haigh, Thorp, Woodlesford pop 6,635 archd and dioc York Wesl Meth

ROTHWELL HAIGH township parish Rothwell W R York

ROTSEA township parish Hutton Cranswick E R York pop 30

ROTTINGDEAN parish 1558 Sussex 4 miles se Brighton pop 880 archd Lewes dioc Chichester

ROTTINGTON township parish St Bees Cumberland pop 45

ROUDHAM parish 1803 Norfolk 2-3/4 miles w East Harling pop 73 archd and dioc Norwich

ROUGHAM parish 1783 Norfolk 7-1/2 miles ne Swaffham pop 340 archd Norfolk dioc Norwich

ROUGHAM parish 1567 Suffolk 4-1/2 miles se Bury St Edmund's pop 868 archd Sudbury dioc Norwich

ROUGH LEE BOOTH township parish Whalley Lancs pop 949 Wesl Meth

ROUGHTON parish 1564 Lincs 4 miles sw Horncastle pop 118 archd and dioc Lincoln

ROUGHTON parish 1562 Norfolk 3-3/4 miles s Cromer pop 439 archd Norfolk dioc Norwich

ROUGHWAY township parish Wrotham Kent

ROULSTON parish 1561 Lincs 7 miles ne Sleaford pop 156 archd and dioc Lincoln

ROUNCTON, EAST chapelry 1595 parish Rudby in Cleveland N R York pop 127

ROUNCTON, WEST parish 1725 N R York 7-1/2 miles sw Yarm pop 192 pec of Dean and Chapter of Durham Wesl Meth

ROUNDHAY chapelry parish Barwick in Elmett W R York pop 314

ROUSDEN parish 1685 Devon 4 miles s Axminster

ROUSHAM parish 1544 co Oxford 6-1/4 miles ne Woodstock pop 156 archd and dioc Oxford

ROUS LENCH Worcs See LENCH, ROUS

ROUTH parish 1633 E R York 4-1/4 miles ne Beverley pop 119 archd East Riding dioc York

ROWBERROW parish 1723 Somerset 4 miles ne Axbridge pop 392 archd Wells dioc Bath and Wells Bapt

ROW BOUND township parish Castle Sowerby Cumberland pop 101

ROWDE parish 1606 Wilts 2 miles nw Devizes pop 1,016 archd Wilts dioc Salisbury

ROWELL hamlet parish Hawling Gloucs pop 38 Indep

ROWINGTON parish 1638 Warws 6 miles nw Warwick pop 933 archd and dioc Worcester

ROWLAND township parish Bakewell Derbys pop 101

ROWLEY hamlet parish Lanchester co Durham

ROWLEY parish 1653 E R York 4 miles ne South Cave comp townships Rowley, Wauldby pop 501 archd East Riding dioc York

ROWLEY REGIS parish 1539 Staffs 3 miles se Dudley pop 7,438 archd Stafford dioc Worcester Bapt

ROWLSTON township parish Mappleton E R York

ROWLSTONE parish 1723 Herefs 13 miles sw Hereford pop 162 archd Brecon dioc St David

ROWNER parish 1590 Hamps 3 miles s Fareham pop 140 archd and dioc Winchester

ROWSHAM hamlet parish Wingrave Bucks

ROWSLEY, GREAT township parish Bakewell Derbys pop 242

ROWSTON Lincs See ROULSTON

ROWTON township parish Christleton Ches pop 122

ROWTON township parish Abberbury Shrops

ROWTON township parish Swine E R York

ROXBY parish 1689 Lincs 9 miles sw Barton upon Humber pop 373 archd Stow dioc Lincoln

ROXBY township parish Pickhill 1758 N R York

ROXBY township parish Hinderwell N R York pop 183

ROXHAM parish incl regs Royston Norfolk 3-1/4 miles se Downham Market pop 41 archd Norfolk dioc Norwich

ROXHOLME hamlet parish Leasingham Lincs

ROXTON parish 1684 Beds 4-3/4 miles sw St Neots pop 575 archd Bedford dioc Lincoln Indep

ROXWELL parish 1558 Essex 4-1/2 miles nw Chelmsford pop 847 pec of Writtle with Roxwell

ROYDON parish 1567 Essex pop 717 4-1/2 miles sw Harlow archd Middlesex dioc London

ROYDON parish 1559 Norfolk 1-1/2 miles w Diss pop 633 archd Norfolk dioc Norwich

ROYDON parish 1721 Norfolk 2-1/2 miles se Castle Rising pop 174 pec of Castle Rising

ROYSTON market town, parish 1662 Herts 20 miles ne Hertford pop 1,757 Commissary of Essex and Herts, concurrently with Consistorial Court of the Bishop of London Soc of Friends, Indep

ROYSTON parish 1563 W R York 4-1/4 miles ne Barnsley comp chapelries Monk Bretton, Woolley with Emley, townships Carlton, Chevett, Cudworth, Notton, Royston pop 3,690 archd and dioc York Wesl Meth

ROYTON chapelry 1755 parish Oldham Lancs pop 5,652 Soc of Friends, Wesl Meth, Calvinistic Meth

RUAN LANTHORNE parish 1685 Cornwall 3 miles sw Tregoney pop 424 archd Cornwall dioc Exeter Wesl Meth

RUAN, MAJOR parish 1682 Cornwall 8 miles se Helston pop 162 archd Cornwall dioc Exeter

RUAN, MINOR parish 1653 Cornwall 10 miles se Helston pop 269 archd Cornwall dioc Exeter Wesl Meth

RUARDEAN parish 1540 Gloucs 6-1/4 miles nw Newnham pop 858 archd Hereford dioc Gloucester Indep

RUCKINGE parish 1538 Kent 6-1/2 miles se Ashford pop 379 archd and dioc Canterbury Wesl Meth

RUCKLAND parish 1757 Lincs 6-1/4 miles se Louth pop 24 archd and dioc Lincoln

RUCKLEY township parish Acton Burnell Shrops pop 86

RUDBY IN CLEVELAND parish 1584 N R York 3-3/4 miles sw Stokesley comp chapelry Middleton upon Leven, townships Hutton, East Rouncton, Rudby in Cleveland, Skutterskelfe pop 1,397 archd Cleveland dioc York

RUDDINGTON parish 1636 Notts 5 miles s Nottingham pop 1,428 archd Nottingham dioc York Bapt, Wesl Meth

RUDFORD parish 1729 Gloucs 3-1/2 miles nw Gloucester pop 203 archd Hereford dioc Gloucester

RUDGE township parish Pattingham Shrops pop 104

RUDGWICK parish 1558 Sussex 7 miles nw Horsham pop 950 archd and dioc Chichester

RUDHAM, EAST parish 1562 Norfolk 6-3/4 miles sw Fakenham pop

950 archd Norfolk dioc Norwich Wesl Meth

RUDHAM, WEST parish 1565 Norfolk 7-1/4 miles sw Fakenham pop 456 archd Norfolk dioc Norwich

RUDHEATH township parishes Great Budworth and Sandbach Ches pop 367

RUDSTONE parish 1550 E R York 5 miles w Bridlington pop 518 archd East Riding dioc York

RUDYARD township parish Leek Staffs pop 117

RUFFORD parish 1669 Lancs 5-1/2 miles ne Ormskirk pop 869 archd and dioc Chester

RUFFORD extra parochial liberty Notts 2 miles sw Otterton pop 322

RUFFORD parish 1655 E R York 5-1/2 miles w York pop 302 archd and dioc York

RUGBY market town, parish 1620 Warws 16-1/2 miles ne Warwick pop 2,501 archd Coventry dioc Lichfield Bapt, Wesl Meth

RUGELEY market town, parish 1569 Staffs 9 miles se Stafford pop 3,165 pec of Dean and Chapter of Lichfield Indep, Wesl Meth

RUISHTON parish 1754 Somerset 2-1/2 miles e Taunton pop 400 archd Taunton dioc Bath and Wells

RUISLIP parish 1689 Middlesex 3-1/2 miles ne Uxbridge pop 1,197 archd Middlesex dioc London

RUMBOLD'S WYKE parish 1669 Sussex 3/4 mile se Chichester pop 319 archd and dioc Chichester

RUMBURGH parish 1558 Suffolk 4 miles nw Halesworth pop 421 archd Suffolk dioc Norwich

RUMNEY parish 1744 co Monmouth 3 miles ne Cardiff pop 264 archd and dioc Llandaff

RUMWORTH township parish Dean Lancs pop 1,164

RUNCORN parish 1558 Ches 4-1/2 miles nw Frodsham comp chapelries Aston by Sutton, Daresbury, Halton, Thelwall, township Acton, Grange, Clifton, alias Rock Savage, Hatton, Keekwick, Moore, Newton by Daresbury, Norton, Preston on the Hill, Runcorn, Stockham, Sutton, Walton Inferior, Walton Superior, Weston pop 10,326 archd and dioc Chester Wesl Meth

RUNCTON, NORTH parish 1563 Norfolk 3 miles se Lynn Regis pop 307 archd and dioc Norwich

RUNCTON, SOUTH parish (incl in regs Holm) Norfolk 4-1/4 miles ne Downham Market pop 133 archd Norfolk dioc Norwich

RUNFOLD tything parish Farnham Surrey

RUNHALL parish 1566 Norfolk 5-1/4 miles nw Wymondham pop 176 archd Norfolk dioc Norwich

RUNHAM parish 1539 Norfolk 4-3/4 miles sw Caistor pop 249 archd and dioc Norwich

RUNNINGTON parish 1586 Somerset 2 miles nw Wellington pop 127 archd Taunton dioc Bath and Wells

RUNSTON hamlet parish St Pierre co Monmouth

RUNTON parish 1743 Norfolk 2-1/2 miles nw Cromer pop 473 archd Norfolk dioc Norwich

RUNWELL parish 1558 Essex 5 miles nw Rayleigh pop 341 archd Essex dioc London

RUNWICK tything parish Farnham Surrey pop 330

RUSCOMB parish 1559 Berks 5-1/2 miles ne Reading pop 160 pec of Dean of Salisbury Indep

RUSHALL parish 1560 Norfolk 3 miles w Harleston pop 283 archd Norfolk dioc Norwich

RUSHALL parish 1686 Staffs 1 mile ne Walsall pop 693 archd Stafford dioc Lichfield

RUSHALL parish 1651 Wilts 3-1/2 miles sw Pewsey pop 244 archd and dioc Salisbury

RUSHBROOK parish 1568 Suffolk 3 miles se Bury St Edmunds pop 177 archd Sudbury dioc Norwich

RUSHBURY parish 1538 Shrops 4-3/4 miles se Church Stretton pop 507 archd Salop dioc Hereford

RUSHDEN parish 1607 Herts 4-3/4 miles nw Buntingford pop 342 archd Huntingdon dioc Lincoln

RUSHDEN parish 1559 co Northampton 1-1/2 miles s Higham Ferrers pop 1,245 archd Northampton dioc Peterborough Bapt

RUSHFORD parish 1762 Norfolk 4 miles se Thetford pop 138 archd and dioc Norwich

RUSHMERE ALL SAINTS parish 1718 Suffolk 5 miles sw Lowestoft pop 114 archd Suffolk dioc Norwich

RUSHOCK parish 1661 Worcs 5-1/2 miles nw Bromsgrove pop 177 archd and dioc Worcester

RUSHMERE ST ANDREW parish 1582 Suffolk 2 miles ne Ipswich pop 568 archd Suffolk dioc Norwich

RUSHROFT hamlet parish Ainstable Cumberland

RUSHTON township parish Tarporley Ches pop 330

RUSHTON ALL SAINTS AND ST PETER joint parishes 1625 co Northampton pop 405 archd Northampton dioc Peterborough

RUSHTON JAMES township parish Leek Staffs pop 304

RUSHTON SPENCER chapelry 1700 parish Leek Staffs pop 337

RUSHULME township parish Manchester Lancs pop 1,078

RUSKINGTON parish 1668 Lincs 3-3/4 miles ne Sleaford pop 782 archd and dioc Lincoln

RUSLAND chapelry parish Coulton Lancs

RUSPER parish 1560 Sussex 5-1/4 miles ne Horsham pop 531 archd and dioc Chichester

RUSSELS hamlet parish Danbury Essex

RUSTINGTON parish 1568 Sussex 2 miles ne Little Hampton pop 365 archd and dioc Chichester

RUSTON, EAST parish 1558 Norfolk 5-3/4 miles se North Walsham pop 730 archd Norfolk dioc Norwich

RUSTON, PARVA parish 1720 E R York 3-3/4 miles ne Great Driffield pop 152 archd East Riding dioc York

RUSTON, SOUTH parish 1708 Norfolk 1-1/2 miles ne Coltishall pop 105 archd Norfolk dioc Norwich

RUSWARP township parish Whitby N R York pop 1,980

RUTCHESTER township parish Ovingham Northumberland pop 28

RUTHALE township parish Prior's Ditton Shrops

RUYTON IN THE ELEVEN TOWNS parish 1719 Shrops 10-1/2 miles ne Shrewsbury pop 993 archd Salop dioc Lichfield

RYALL chapelry parish Stamfordham Northumberland pop 89

RYALL parish 1674 co Rutland 2-1/2 miles ne Stamford pop 569 archd Northampton dioc Peterborough

RYARSH parish 1539 Kent 6-3/4 miles nw Maidstone pop 414 archd and dioc Rochester

RYBURGH, GREAT parish 1547 Norfolk 4 miles se Fakenhall pop 598 archd Norfolk dioc Norwich

RYBURG, LITTLE parish 1688 Norfolk 3-3/4 miles se Fakenham pop 162 archd Norfolk dioc Norwich

RYCOTE chapelry parish Great Haseley co Oxford pop 35

RYDAL chapelry parish Grasmere Westm

RYDE market town, chapelry, parish Newchurch Isle of Wight Hamps Indep, Wesl Meth

RYE tything parish Odiham Hamps

RYE cinque port, borough, market town, parish 1538 Sussex 76 miles ne Chichester pop 3,715 sep juris archd Lewes dioc Chichester Bapt, Indep, Wesl Meth

RYE HILL township parish Rothbury Northumberland

RYHILL hamlet parish Epping Essex

RYHILL township parish Burstwick E R York pop 263

RYHILL township parish Wragby W R York pop 160

RYHOPE township parish Bishop Wearmouth co Durham pop 365

RYLE, GREAT township parish Whittingham Northumberland pop 94

RYLE, LITTLE township parish Whittingham Northumberland pop 40

RYME INTRINSICA parish 1631 Dorset 6-1/4 miles sw Sherborne pop 171 pec of Dean of Salisbury

RYSTON parish 1687 Norfolk 1-3/4 miles se Downham Market pop 26 archd Norfolk dioc Norwich

RYTHER parish 1550 W R York 6-3/4 miles nw Selby pop 361 archd and dioc York

RYTON parish 1581 co Durham 8-3/4 miles nw Gateshead comp townships Chopwell, Crawcrook, Ryton Woodside, Stella, Winlaton pop 6,568 archd and dioc Durham Meth

RYTON parish 1659 Shrops 4 miles se Shiffnall pop 154 archd Salop dioc Lichfield

RYTON hamlet parish Bulkington Warws

RYTON township parish Kirkby Misperton N R York pop 222

RYTON UPON DUNSMOOR parish 1538 Warws 4-1/2 miles se Coventry pop 510 archd Coventry dioc Lichfield

RYTON WOODSIDE township parish Ryton co Durham pop 951

SABRIDGEWORTH Herts See SAWBRIDGEWORTH

SACOMB parish 1726 Herts 4 miles nw Ware pop 360 archd Huntingdon dioc Lincoln

SADBERGE chapelry 1662 parish Haughton le Skerne Durham 4-1/4 miles ne Darlington pop 403

SADDINGTON parish 1538 Leics 6 miles nw Market Harborough pop 288 archd Leicester dioc Lincoln

SADDLEWOOD tything parish Hawkesbury Gloucs

SADDLEWORTH chapelry 1613 parish Rochdale W R York 12 miles sw Huddersfield pop 15,986 Dissenters

SAFFRON WALDEN Essex See WALDEN, SAFFRON

SAHAM TONEY parish 1547 Norf 1-3/4 miles nw Watton pop 1,060 archd and dioc Norwich Wesl Meth

SAIGHTON township parish St Oswald Chester Ches pop 303

SAINTBURY parish 1585 Gloucs 2-1/4 miles Chipping Campden archd and dioc Gloucester

SALCOMBE chapelry parish Melborough Devon Bapt, Wesl Meth

SALCOMBE REGIS parish 1702 Devon 2 miles ne Sidmouth pop 448 pec Dean and Chapter of Exeter

SALCOTT parish 1587 Essex 8-1/2 miles sw Colchester pop 164 archd Colchester dioc London

SALDEN hamlet parish Mursley Bucks

SALE township parish Ashton upon Mersey Ches pop 1,104

SALEBY parish 1554 Lincs 1-1/2 miles ne Alford pop 220 archd and dioc Lincoln

SALEHURST parish 1575 Sussex 6 miles n Battle pop 2,204 archd Lewes dioc Chichester

SALESBURY chapelry 1807 parish Blackburn Lancs 4-1/2 miles n Blackburn

SALFORD parish 1558 Beds 4-1/2 miles nw Woburn pop 340 united in 1750 Holcutt archd Bedford dioc Lincoln Wesl Meth

SALFORD Trinity chapelry 1635 parish Manchester Lancs

SALFORD chapelry St Stephen 1794 parish Manchester Lancs

SALFORD chapelry St Phillips 1825 parish Manchester Lancs

SALFORD parish 1754 co Oxford 2 miles nw Chipping Norton pop 341 archd and dioc Oxford

SALFORD or SALFORD PRIORS parish 1568 Warws 5-3/4 miles sw Alcester pop 899 archd and dioc Worcs

SALHOUSE parish 1561 Norfolk 4-1/4 miles se Coltishall pop 539 archd and dioc Norwich Bapt

SALING BARDFIELD Essex See BARDFIELD, SALING

SALING, GREAT parish 1715 Essex 5 miles nw Braintree pop 367 Commissary of Essex and Herts, concurrently with Consistorial Bishop of London

SALING, LITTLE See BARDFIELD SALING Essex

SALISBURY city Wilts 82 miles sw London sep juris pop 9,876 comp St Edmund 1560, Cathedral 1564, St Martin 1620, St Thomas 1570 all peculiars of the Sub Dean of Cathedral dioc Salisbury Cathedral Close is extra parochial in juris of Dean of Cathedral

SALKELD, GREAT parish 1583 Cumb 3 miles sw Kirk Oswald pop 447 archd and dioc Carlisle Presb, Prim Meth

SALKELD, LITTLE township parish Addingham Cumb pop 105

SALL parish 1558 Norfolk 1-3/4 miles ne Reepham pop 298 archd Norfolk dioc Norwich

SALMONBY parish 1558 Lincs 5-1/4 miles ne Horncastle pop 90 archd and dioc Lincoln

SALPERTON parish 1629 Gloucs 5 miles nw Northleach pop 216 archd and dioc Gloucester

SALSEY FOREST extra parochial 6-1/2 miles se Northampton

SALT township parish St Mary Lichfield Staffs 4 miles ne Stafford pop 533 Wesl Meth

SALTASH or ESSAY chapelry 1697 borough sep juris parish St Stephen Cornwall 4 miles nw Plymouth pop 1,637 Bapt, Wesl Meth

SALTBY parish 1565 Leics 8-1/4 miles ne Melton Mowbray pop 263 archd Leicester dioc Lincoln

SALTER extra parochial Cumb 8 miles se Whitehaven pop 42

SALTERFORTH township parish Barnoldwick York 8-1/4 miles sw Skipton pop 725

SALTERSFORD chapelry 1770 parish Prestbury Ches 6 miles ne Macclesfield

SALTFLEET HAVEN hamlet parish Skidbrook Lincs

SALTFLEETBY All Saints parish 1558 Lincs 10-1/4 miles ne Louth pop 180 archd and dioc Lincoln

SALTFLEETBY St Clements 1718 Lincs 10-1/2 miles ne Louth pop 110 archd and dioc Lincoln

SALTFLEETBY St Peter parish 1653 Lincs 8-1/2 miles ne Louth pop 200 archd and dioc Lincoln

SALTFORD parish 1712 Somerset 5-1/4 miles nw Bath pop 360 archd Bath dioc Bath and Wells

SALT HILL village parishes Farnham Royal and Upton, Bucks

SALTHOUSE parish 1544 Norfolk 2-1/4 miles e Clay pop 262 archd and dioc Norwich

SALTMARSH township parish Howden Yorks pop 191

SALTON parish 1573 N R York comp townships Brawby, Salton pop 355 6-3/4 miles sw Pickering pec of Impropriator

SALTWICK township parish Stannington Northumberland

SALTWOOD parish 1560 Kent 3/4 mile nw Hythe pop 534 pec Archbishop of Canterbury

SALWARPE parish 1666 Worcs 2-1/2 miles sw Droitwich pop 475 archd and dioc Worcester

SAMBOURN hamlet parish Coughton Warws pop 694

SAMLESBURY chapelry 1722 parish Blackburn Lancs 4 miles ne Preston pop 1,948

SAMPFORD ARUNDEL parish 1695 Somerset 2-3/4 miles sw Wellington pop 427 archd Taunton dioc Bath and Wells

SAMPFORD BRETT parish 1654 Somerset 7-1/4 miles se Dunster pop 197 archd Taunton dioc Bath and Wells

SAMPFORD COURTENEY parish 1558 Devon 5-1/4 miles ne Oakhampton pop 1,217 archd Totnes dioc Exeter

SAMPFORD, GREAT parish 1559 Essex 3-3/4 miles ne Thaxted pop 800 Commissary of Essex and Herts, concurrently with Cons of Bishop of London Bapt

SAMPFORD, LITTLE parish 1563 Essex 3-3/4 miles ne Thaxted pop 423 Commissary of Essex and Herts, concurrently with Cons of Bishop of London

SAMPFORD PEVERELL parish 1672 borough Devon 5 miles ne Tiverton pop 787 archd and dioc Exeter

SAMPFORD SPINEY parish 1659 Devon 4-1/4 miles se Tavistock pop 366 archd Totnes dioc Exeter

SAMPSON'S ST parish 1568 Cornwall 4 miles se Lostwithiel pop 314 archd Cornwall dioc Exeter

SANCREED parish 1559 Cornwall 4 miles sw Penzance pop 1,069 archd Cornwall dioc Exeter Bapt, Wesl Meth

SANCTON parish 1538 E R York comp townships North Cliff, Sancton with Houghton pop 462 2-1/2 miles se Market Weighton archd East Riding dioc York Wesl Meth

SANDALL, GREAT parish 1652 W R York comp townships Crigglestone, Great Sandall, Walton, part of West Bretton pop 2,878 2 miles se Wakefield archd and dioc York

SANDALL, KIRK or SANDAL PARVA parish 1679 W R York 4-1/4 miles ne Doncaster pop 200 archd and dioc York

SANDALL, LONG township parish Doncaster York pop 323

SANDBACH parish 1562 Ches comp market town Sandwich, chapelries Church Hulme, Goostrey with Barnshaw, townships Arclid, Blackden, Bradwell, Cotton, Cranage, Leese, Twemlow, Wheelock, part of Rudheath, townships Bechton, Hassall pop 7,214 26 miles se Chester archd and dioc Chester Indep, Prim Meth, Wesl Meth

SANDERINGHAM parish 1558 Norfolk 3-1/4 miles ne Castle Rising pop 81 archd and dioc Norwich

SANDERSTEAD parish 1564 Surrey 3 miles se Croydon pop 242 archd Surrey dioc Winchester

SANDFORD chapelry parish St Helen Abingdon Berks pop 114

SANDFORD township parish Sonning Berks pop 759

SANDFORD parish 1603 Devon 2 miles nw Crediton pec of Bishop of Exeter pop 2,011

SANDFORD parish 1695 co Oxford 3 miles se Oxford pop 229

SANDFORD ON THAMES parish 1572 co Oxford 3-3/4 miles ne Neat Enstone pop 334 archd and dioc Oxford

SANDFORD township parish Prees Shrops pop 487

SANDFORD hamlet parish Warcop Westm

SANDFORD ORCAS parish 1538 Somerset 6 miles ne Yeovil pop 353 archd Wells dioc Bath and Wells Wesl Meth

SANDGATE chapelry parishes Folkestone, Cheriton, Kent Wesl Meth

SANDHOE township parish St John Lee Northumberland pop 240 Roman Cath

SANDHOLME township parish St John Beverley E R York Wesl Meth

SANDHURST parish 1603 Berks 5-1/4 miles se Wokingham pop 672 pec of Dean of Salisbury

SANDHURST parish 1538 Gloucs 3 miles n Gloucester pop 434 archd and dioc Gloucester

SANDHURST parish 1563 Kent 7 miles sw Tenterden pop 1,307 archd and dioc Canterbury Bapt, Wesl Meth

SAND HUTTON York See HUTTON, SAND

SANDIACRE parish Derbys 1570 9-1/2 miles e Derby pop 758 pec of Prebendary of Sandiacre Cathedral Church of Lichfield Wesl Meth

SANDON parish 1554 Essex 2 miles sw Danbury pop 525 archd Essex dioc London

SANDON parish 1678 Herts 4-3/4 miles nw Buntingford pop 716 archd Huntingdon dioc Lincoln

SANDON parish 1635 Staffs 4-1/2 miles ne Stafford pop 558 archd Stafford dioc Lichfield Meth

SANDON FEE tything parish Hungerford Berks pop 674

SANDRIDGE parish 1559 Herts 2-3/4 miles ne St Albans pop 810 archd St Albans dioc London

SANDRINGHAM parish 1558 Norfolk 6 miles ne Kings Lynn archd and dioc Norwich

SANDWICH market town St Clement 1563, St Mary 1538, St Peter 1538, Kent 39 miles e Maidstone borough sep juris pop 3,136 Indep Wesl Meth

SANDWITH township parish St Bees Cumberland pop 328

SANDY parish 1538 Beds 3-3/4 miles nw Biggleswade pop 1,617 archd Bedford dioc Lincoln

SANKEY, GREAT chapelry 1728 parish Prescot Lancs 2-3/4 miles w Warrington pop 563

SANTON township parish Irton Cumberland

SANTON parish 1770 Norfolk 4 miles nw Thetford pop 18 archd Norfolk dioc Norwich

SAPCOTE parish 1564 Leics 4-1/4 miles se Hinckley pop 871 archd Leicester dioc Lincoln

SAPEY PRITCHARD or SAPEY LOWER parish 1674 Worcs 5-3/4 miles ne Bromyard pop 250 archd Salop dioc Hereford

SAPEY, UPPER parish 1679 Herefs 6-1/2 miles ne Bromyard pop 357 archd and dioc Hereford

SAPISTON parish 1680 Suffolk 3-1/4 miles nw Ixworth pop 234 archd Suffolk dioc Norwich

SAPLEY extra parochial Hunts 2 miles e Huntingdon

SAPPERTON township parish Church Broughton Derbys

SAPPERTON parish 1662 Gloucs comp townships Frampton Marshall, Sapperton 5-1/4 miles nw Cirencester pop 453 archd and dioc Gloucester

SAPPERTON parish 1565 Lincs 4-1/2 miles w Falkingham pop 62 archd and dioc Lincoln

SAREDON, GREAT and LITTLE township parish Shareshill Staffs pop 246

SARK Island 6 miles east Guernsey Channel Islands

SARNESFIELD parish 1755 Herefs 2-1/2 miles sw Weobley pop 98
    archd and dioc Hereford
SARR village parish Sandwich Kent pop 200
SARRATT parish 1560 Herts 3-1/2 miles nw Rickmansworth pop 452
    archd St Albans dioc London
SARSDEN parish 1575 co Oxford 3-3/4 miles sw Chipping Norton
    pop 154 archd and dioc Oxford
SARSON tything parish Amport Hamps
SARUM, OLD parish Stratford sub Castle Wilts borough
SATLEY chapelry 1797 parish Lanchester co Durham 5 miles ne
    Wolsingham pop 112 archd and dioc Durham
SATTERLEIGH parish 1570 Devon 3-3/4 miles sw South Molton pop
    58 archd Barnstaple dioc Exeter
SATTERTHWAITE chapelry 1766 parish Hawkeshead Lancs 4 miles
    sw Hawkeshead pop 403 archd Richmond dioc Chester
SATTHERTHWAITE chapelry parish Ulverstone Lancs 7-1/2 miles
    nw Ulverstone pop 163
SAUGHALL, GREAT township parish Shotwick Ches pop 367
SAUGHALL, LITTLE township parish Shotwick Ches pop 40
SAUGHALL MASSEY township parish Bidstone Ches pop 143
SAUL parish 1720 Gloucs 9 miles nw Stroud pop 443 archd and dioc
    Gloucester Wesl Meth
SAUNDBY parish 1558 Notts 2-1/2 miles sw Gainsboro pop 104
    archd Nottingham dioc York
SAUNDERTON parish 1728 Bucks 1-1/2 miles sw Princes Risboro
    pop 231 archd Buckingham dioc Lincoln
SAUSTHORPE parish 1745 Lincs 3 miles nw Spilsby pop 206 archd
    and dioc Lincoln
SAVERNAKE PARK or NORTH SIDE extra parochial 1-1/2 miles se
    Marlboro Wilts pop 110
SAVERNAKE FOREST or SOUTH SIDE extra parochial 2 miles s
    Marlboro Wilts
SAWBRIDGEWORTH parish 1558 Herts 11-1/2 miles ne Hertford pop
    2,231 archd Middlesex dioc Lincoln Indep, Wesl Meth
SAWDON township parish Brompton N R York pop 146 Wesl Meth
SAWLEY parish 1654 Derbys comp chapelries Breason, Wilne, town-
    ships Long Eaton, Risley, Sawley, liberties Draycott, Hopwell
    pop 3,750 4 miles nw Kegworth pec of Prebendary of Sawley
    Wesl Meth
SAWLEY chapelry parish Ripon W R York 5-1/2 miles sw Ripon
    pop 499 Wesl Meth
SAWLEY extra parochial W R York 4 miles ne Clitheroe pop 588
SAWSTON parish 1640 Cambs 5-1/4 miles nw Linton pop 771 archd
    and dioc Ely Indep
SAWTRY All Saints parish 1591 Hunts 3-1/2 miles s Stilton pop 510
    archd Huntingdon dioc Lincoln Wesl Meth
SAWTRY St Andrew parish 1662 Hunts 3-1/2 miles se Stilton pop 320
    archd Huntingdon dioc Lincoln

SAWTRY St Judith extra parochial 4 miles se Stilton Hunts pop 227
SAXBY parish 1678 Leics 4-1/2 miles ne Melton Mowbray pop 206
    archd Leicester dioc Lincoln
SAXBY St Helen parish 1666 Lincs 7-1/4 miles sw Market Rasen
    archd and dioc Lincoln
SAXBY All Saints parish 1719 Lincs 5 miles sw Barton on Humber
    pop 260 archd and dioc Lincoln
SAXELBY parish 1538 Leics 4 miles nw Melton Mowbray pop 120
    archd Leicester dioc Lincoln
SAXELBY parish 1563 Lincs 6-1/2 miles nw Lincoln pop 719 archd
    Stow dioc Lincoln Wesl Meth
SAXHAM, GREAT parish 1555 Suffolk 5 miles sw Bury St Edmunds
    pop 260 archd Sudbury dioc Norwich
SAXHAM, LITTLE parish 1559 Suffolk 3-3/4 miles w Bury St Ed-
    munds pop 198 archd Sudbury dioc Norwich
SAXLINGHAM parish 1558 Norfolk 3-3/4 miles nw Holt pop 153
    archd and dioc Norwich Wesl Meth
SAXLINGHAM NETHERGATE parish 1556 Norfolk 3-1/2 miles ne St
    Mary Stratton pop 666 archd Norfolk dioc Norwich
SAXLINGHAM THORPE parish Norfolk 3-1/4 miles ne St Mary Strat-
    ton pop 161 archd Norfolk dioc Norwich
SAXMUNDHAM parish 1538 Suffolk 20 miles ne Ipswich pop 1,048
    archd Suffolk dioc Norwich
SAXONDALE township parish Shelford Notts pop 116
SAXTEAD parish 1546 Suffolk 2-1/4 miles nw Framlingham pop 505
    archd Suffolk dioc Norwich
SAXTHORPE parish 1720 Norfolk 5-1/4 miles nw Aylsham archd and
    dioc Norwich
SAXTON parish 1538 W R York comp townships Saxton with Scar-
    thingwell, Towton 4-1/4 miles sw Tadcaster pop 522 archd and
    dioc York
SCACKLETON township parish Hovingham N R York pop 164
SCAFTWORTH township parish Everton Notts pop 78
SCAGGLETHROPE township parish Settrington E R York pop 252
    Prim Meth
SCALBY township parish Blacktoft E R York pop 127
SCALBY parish 1656 N R York comp chapelry Claughton, townships
    Burniston, Newby, Scalby Stainton Dale, Throxenby pop 1,676
    3-1/4 miles nw Scarboro archd and dioc York
SCALDWELL parish 1560 co Northampton 8-1/2 miles ne Northamp-
    ton pop 387 archd Northampton dioc Peterborough
SCALEBY parish 1724 Cumberland comp townships East and West
    Scaleby 6 miles ne Carlisle pop 560 archd and dioc Carlisle
SCALERGATE township parish Appleby St Lawrence Westm pop 179
SCALES township parish Bromfield Cumberland
SCALES township parish Kirkham Lancs
SCALFORD parish 1558 Leics 4 miles ne Melton Mowbray pop 467
    archd Leicester dioc Lincoln

SCAMBLESBY parish 1570 Lincs 6-3/4 miles ne Horncastle pop 413
pec Dean and Chapter of Lincoln
SCAMMONDEN chapelry 1746 parish Huddersfield W R York 7-1/2
miles w Huddersfield pop 912 archd and dioc York
SCAMPSTON chapelry 1756 parish Rillington E R York 5-1/4 miles
ne New Malton pop 231 archd East Riding dioc York
SCAMPTON parish 1548 Lincs 5-3/4 miles nw Lincoln pop 242 archd
Stow dioc Lincoln
SCANSBY township parish Brodsworth W R York
SCARBORO parish 1672 borough sep juris N R York 39 miles ne
York pop 8,760 archd East Riding dioc York Bapt, Soc of Friends,
Indep, Wesl Meth, Roman Cath
SCARCLIFF parish 1680 Derbys 6 miles nw Mansfield pop 524 archd
Derby dioc Lichfield
SCARCROFT township parish Thorner W R York pop 168
SCARGILL township parish Barningham N R York pop 119
SCARISBRICK township parish Ormskirk Lancs pop 1,783
SCARLE, NORTH parish 1571 Lincs 10 miles sw Lincoln pop 479
archd and dioc Lincoln Wesl Meth
SCARLE, SOUTH parish 1684 Notts 7-1/2 miles ne Newark pop 479
archd Nottingham dioc York
SCARNING parish 1538 Norfolk 2 miles sw East Dereham pop 602
archd and dioc Norwich
SCARRINGTON parish 1570 Notts 12-1/2 miles ne Nottingham pop
188 archd Nottingham dioc York Wesl Meth
SCARTHINGWELL township parish Saxton W R York
SCARTHO parish 1560 Lincs 2-1/4 miles s Grimsby pop 147 archd
and dioc Lincoln
SCATHWAITERIGG HAY township parish Kendal Westm pop 380
SCAWBY parish 1558 Lincs 2-1/4 miles se Glandford Brigg pop 942
archd Stow dioc Lincoln Wesl Meth
SCAWTON parish 1721 N R York 5 miles w Helmsley pop 146 archd
Cleveland dioc York
SCHOLES township parish Barwick in Elmet W R York Wesl Meth
SCILLY ISLES St Mary parish 1726 Cornwall off south coast pop
2,465 archd Cornwall dioc Exeter Wesl Meth
SCOLE or OSMONDISTON parish 1561 Norfolk 19-1/2 miles sw Nor-
wich pop 617 archd Norfolk dioc Norwich
SCOPWICK parish 1605 Lincs 8-1/4 miles n Sleaford pop 278 archd
and dioc Lincoln
SCORBOROUGH parish 1543 E R York 4-1/2 miles nw Beverley pop
79 archd East Riding dioc York
SCOREBY township parish Catton E R York
SCORTON township parish Catterick N R York pop 492
SCOSTHORPE township parish Kirkby in Malhamdale W R York pop
95
SCOTBY township parish Wetheral Cumberland pop 397 Soc of
Friends

SCOTFORTH township parish Lancaster Lancs pop 557

SCOTHERN parish 1630 Lincs 5-1/4 miles ne Lincoln pop 366 archd Stow dioc Lincoln

SCOTTER parish 1563 Lincs 9-1/4 miles ne Gainsboro pop 1,043 archd Stow dioc Lincoln

SCOTTLESTHORP hamlet parish Edenham Lincs

SCOTTON parish 1560 Lincs 8-3/4 miles ne Gainsboro pop 494 archd Stow dioc Lincoln Wesl Meth

SCOTTON township parish Catterick N R York

SCOTTON township parish Farnham W R York pop 312

SCOTTON parish 1558 Norfolk 2-1/2 miles n Coltishall pop 460 archd and dioc Norwich

SCOTT WILLOUGHBY Lincs See WILLOUGHBY SCOTT

SCOULTON parish 1550 Norfolk 4-1/4 miles e Watton pop 328 archd and dioc Norwich

SCRAFTON, WEST township parish Coverham N R York pop 146

SCRAPTOFT parish 1538 Leics 4 miles ne Leicester pop 126 archd Leicester dioc Lincoln

SCRATBY parish (incl regs Oremesby St Margaret) Norfolk 2-1/2 miles nw Caistor archd and dioc Norwich

SCRAYFIELD parish (incl regs Hameringham) Lincs 3 miles se Horncastle archd and dioc Lincoln

SCRAYINGHAM parish 1648 E R York comp chapelry Leppington townships Howsham, Scrayingham 9-1/2 miles nw Pocklington pop 522 archd East Riding dioc York

SCREDINGTON parish 1738 Lincs 4-1/4 miles se Sleaford pop 306 pec Dean and Chapter of Lincoln

SCREMBY parish 1716 Lincs 3-1/2 miles ne Spilsby pop 204 archd and dioc Lincoln

SCRENWOOD township parish Alnham Northumberland pop 37

SCREVETON parish 1640 Notts 8-1/2 miles sw Newark pop 312 archd Nottingham dioc York

SCRIVELSBY parish 1565 Lincs 2-1/2 miles s Horncastle pop 129 archd and dioc Lincoln

SCRIVEN township parish Knaresboro W R York pop 1,598

SCROOBY parish 1695 Notts 1-3/4 miles s Bawtry pop 281 archd Nottingham dioc York

SCROPTON parish 1680 Derbys 11-1/2 miles sw Derby pop 500 archd Derby dioc Lichfield

SCRUTON parish 1572 N R York 4-1/4 miles ne Bedale pop 438 archd Richmond dioc Chester

SCULCOATES parish 1576 E R York 1-1/4 miles n Kingston on Hull pop 13,468 archd East Riding dioc York

SCULTHORPE parish 1561 Norfolk 2 miles nw Fakenham pop 619 archd Norfolk dioc Norwich

SCUNTHORPE township parish Frodingham Lincs pop 240 Wesl Meth

SEABOROUGH parish 1562 Somerset 2-1/2 miles sw Crewkerne pop 124 archd Taunton dioc Bath and Wells

SEABRIDGE township parish Swinnerton and Stoke on Trent Staffs pop 120

SEABROOK hamlet parish Ivinghoe Bucks

SEACOMB township parish Wallesey Ches Indep

SEACOURT hamlet parish Wytham Berks pop 25

SEACROFT township parish Whitkirk W R York pop 918 Wesl Meth

SEAFORD parish 1559 borough Sussex 42 miles se Chichester pop 1,098 archd Lewes dioc Chichester

SEAFORTH Lancs in reg Sephton

SEAGRAVE parish 1682 Leics 3-1/2 miles ne Mountsorrel pop 426 archd Leicester dioc Lincoln

SEAGRY, LOWER and UPPER parish 1610 Wilts 4-1/4 miles se Malmesbury pop 234 archd Wilts dioc Salisbury

SEAHAM parish 1646 co Durham comp townships Seaham, Seaton with Slingley pop 264 archd and dioc Durham

SEAL parish 1654 Kent 2-1/4 miles ne Sevenoaks pop 1,454 archd and dioc Rochester

SEAL parish 1539 Surrey 2-1/2 miles ne Farnham pop 366 archd Surrey dioc Winchester

SEAL, NETHER and OVER parish 1566 Leics 5-3/4 miles sw Ashby de la Zouch pop 1,222 archd Leicester dioc Lincoln

SEAMER or SEAMER IN CLEVELAND parish 1588 N R York 2-1/4 miles nw Stokesley pop 224 archd Cleveland dioc York

SEAMER parish 1638 N R York 4-1/4 miles sw Scarborough comp chapelry East Ayton, townships Irton, Seamer pop 981 archd East Riding dioc York Wesl Meth

SEARBY parish 1558 Lincs 4-3/4 miles nw Caistor pop 252 Pec Dean and Chapter of Lincoln

SEASALTER parish 1588 Kent 5-1/4 miles nw Canterbury pop 945 archd and dioc Canterbury

SEASONCOTE parish (incl regs Longborough) Gloucs 2 miles sw Moreton in the Marsh pop 51 archd and dioc Gloucester

SEATHWAITE chapelry 1684 parish Kirkby Ireleth Lancs 8 miles nw Hawkeshead pop 190

SEATON township parish Cammerton Cumberland pop 745

SEATON parish 1583 Devon 2-1/4 miles s Colyton pop 1,803 archd and dioc Exeter Indep, Prim Meth

SEATON township parish Seaham co Durham pop 134

SEATON parish 1538 co Rutland 2-1/2 miles se Uppingham pop 435 archd Northampton dioc Peterborough

SEATON township parish Sigglesthorne E R York pop 288 Wesl Meth

SEATON CAREW township parish Stranton co Durham pop 333 Wesl Meth

SEATON DELAVAL township parish Earsdon Northumberland pop 271

SEATON, HOUSE township parish Long Houghton Northumberland

SEATON, NORTH township parish Woodhorn Northumberland pop 150

SEATON ROSS parish 1653 E R York 7-1/4 miles sw Market Weighton pop 438 archd East Riding dioc York Wesl Meth

SEATON SLUICE or HARTLEY PANS seaport township Hartley parish
Earsdon Northumberland Presb
SEAVINGTON St Mary parish 1718 Somerset 3 miles e Ilminster pop
366 archd Taunton dioc Bath and Wells
SEAVINGTON St Michael parish 1558 Somerset 3-1/2 miles e Ilmin-
ster pop 397 archd Taunton dioc Bath and Wells
SEBERGHAM parish 1694 Cumberland comp townships Church or
Low Sebergham, Castle or High Sebergham 6-1/4 miles se Wigton
pop 840 archd and dioc Carlisle
SECKINGTON parish 1612 Warws 3-3/4 miles ne Tamworth pop 129
archd Coventry dioc Lichfield
SEDBERGH parish 1595 W R York comp chapelries Dent, Garsdale
pop 4,711 77 miles nw York archd Richmond dioc Chester Soc
of Friends, Indep, Wesl Meth
SEDGEBERROW parish 1566 Worcs 4 miles sw Evesham pop 224
archd and dioc Worcester
SEDGEBROOK parish 1559 Lincs 4 miles nw Grantham pop 252
SEDGEFIELD parish 1580 co Durham comp townships Sedgefield,
Bradbury, Butterwick, Embleton, Fishburn, Foxton with Shotton,
Mordon 11 miles se Durham pop 2,179 archd and dioc Durham
Wesl Meth
SEDGEFORD parish 1560 Norfolk 8-1/2 miles ne Castle Rising pop
595 pec Dean and Chapter Norwich
SEDGHILL parish 1758 Wilts 4-1/2 miles sw Hindon pop 235 archd
and dioc Salisbury
SEDGELEY parish 1558 Staffs comp hamlets Coseley, Gornall 3 miles
s Wolverhampton pop 20,577 archd Stafford dioc Lichfield Bapt,
Wesl Meth, Prim Meth, Indep, Presb, Roman Cath
SEDGEWICK township parish Heversham Westm pop 204 Indep
SEDLESCOMB parish 1558 Sussex 3 miles ne Battle pop 732 archd
Lewes dioc Chichester Wesl Meth
SEEND chapelry 1612 parish Melksham Wilts 3-1/2 miles se Melk-
sham pop 1,144 Wesl Meth
SEER GREEN hamlet parish Farnham Royal Bucks pop 245
SEETHING parish 1561 Norfolk 5-3/4 miles nw Bungay pop 438 archd
Norfolk dioc Norwich
SEIGHFORD parish 1560 Staffs 2-3/4 miles nw Stafford pop 898
archd Stafford dioc Lichfield
SEISDON township parish Trysull Staffs
SELATTYN parish 1557 Shrops 3-1/4 miles nw Oswestry pop 1,142
archd and dioc St Asaph
SELBORNE parish 1556 Hamps 4-1/2 miles se Alton pop 924 archd
and dioc Winchester
SELBY parish 1590 W R York 14-1/2 miles se York pop 4,600 pec
Selby Soc of Friends, Indep, Wesl Meth, Unit, Roman Cath
SELBY'S FOREST township parish Kirk Newton Northumberland pop
66
SELE See BEEDING, UPPER Sussex

SELHAM parish 1565 Sussex 3-1/2 miles sw Petworth pop 89 archd and dioc Chichester

SELLACK parish 1566 Herefs 4-1/4 miles nw Ross pop 327 pec Bishop of Hereford

SELLING parish 1558 Kent 4 miles se Faversham pop 539 archd and dioc Canterbury

SELLINGE parish 1559 Kent 5-1/4 miles nw Hythe pop 461 archd and dioc Canterbury

SELMESTON parish 1667 Sussex 6-1/4 miles se Lewes pop 189 archd Lewes dioc Chichester

SELSEY parish 1662 Sussex 8 miles s Chichester pop 821 archd and dioc Chichester

SELSIDE chapelry 1753 parish Kendal Westm 4 miles ne Kendal pop 263

SELSTON parish 1557 Notts 9 miles sw Mansfield pop 1,580 archd Nottingham dioc York

SELWORTHY parish 1672 Somerset 4 miles w Minehead pop 558 archd Taunton dioc Bath and Wells

SEMER parish 1538 Suffolk 2 miles se Bildeston pop 275 archd Sudbury dioc Norwich

SEMINGTON chapelry 1589 Wilts 3 miles ne Trowbridge pop 319 Wesl Meth

SEMLEY parish 1665 Wilts 4-3/4 miles sw Hindon pop 700 archd and dioc Salisbury Bapt

SEMPERINGHAM parish 1558 Lincs 3-1/4 miles se Falkingham pop 490 archd and dioc Lincoln

SEND parish 1653 Surrey 3 miles sw Ripley pop 1,483 archd Surrey dioc Winchester Wesl Meth

SENNEN parish 1700 Cornwall 8-1/4 miles sw Penzance pop 689 pec St Burian Bapt, Wesl Meth

SEPHTON parish 1597 Lancs comp chapelry Great Crosby, townships Aintree, Little Crosby, Ince Blundell, Litherland, Lunt, Netherton, Orrell with Ford, Sephton Thornton 7 miles n Liverpool pop 4,485 archd and dioc Chester

SERLBY township parish Haughton Notts

SESSAY parish 1612 N R York 6-3/4 miles nw Easingwould pop 464 archd Cleveland dioc York

SETCHEY parish (incl regs North Runcton) Norfolk 5 miles s Kings Lynn pop 95 archd and dioc Norwich

SETMURTHEY chapelry 1759 parish Brigham Cumberland pop 182

SETTLE market town parish Giggleswick W R York pop 1,627 Indep, Wesl Meth

SETTRINGTON parish 1559 E R York comp townships Scogglethorpe, Settrington 4 miles se Malton pop 779 archd East Riding dioc York

SEVENHAMPTON parish 1588 Gloucs 4-1/4 miles s Winchcombe pop 465 archd and dioc Gloucester

SEVENHAMPTON chapelry 1538 parish Highworth Wilts 1-1/2 miles se Highworth pop 239

SEVENOAKS township parish Great Budworth Ches pop 149

SEVENOAKS parish 1559 Kent 17-1/2 miles w Maidstone pop 4,709
pec of Archbishop of Canterbury Bapt, Wesl Meth

SEVERN STOKE Worcs See STOKE, SEVERN

SEVINGTON parish 1554 Kent 2-1/4 miles se Ashford pop 111 archd
and dioc Canterbury

SEWARDSTONE hamlet parish Waltham Abbey Essex pop 825 Wesl
Meth

SEWERBY township parish Bridlington E R York pop 352

SEWSTERN chapelry parish Buckminster Leics pop 368 Indep, Wesl
Meth

SEXHOW township parish Rudby in Cleveland N R York pop 35

SHABBINGTON parish 1714 Bucks 3 miles nw Thame pop 298 archd
Buckingham dioc Lincoln

SHACKERSTONE parish 1558 Leics 5 miles nw Market Bosworth
pop 432 archd Leicester dioc Lincoln

SHADFORTH township parish Pittington co Durham pop 236

SHADINGFIELD parish 1538 Suffolk 4-3/4 miles s Beccles archd
Suffolk dioc Norwich

SHADOXHURST parish 1538 Kent 5-1/4 miles sw Ashford pop 239
archd and dioc Canterbury

SHADWELL parish 1670 Middlesex 1-1/2 miles se London pop 9,544
archd Middlesex dioc London Indep, Prim Meth, Wesl Meth

SHADWELL township parish Thorner W R York pop 248 Wesl Meth

SHAFTESBURY or SHASTON town, borough sep juris Dorset 28
miles ne Dorchester comp Holy Trinity 1695, St Peter 1623, St
James 1559 pop 3,061 archd Dorset dioc Bristol Soc of Friends,
Indep, Wesl Meth

SHAFTO, EAST township parish Hartburn Northumberland pop 41

SHAFTO, WEST township parish Hartburn Northumberland pop 68

SHAFTON township parish Felkirk W R York pop 248 Wesl Meth

SHALBOURN parish 1678 Berks 4 miles sw Hungerford pop 922 pec
Dean and Chapter of Windsor

SHALBOURN, WEST township parish Shalbourn Wilts pop 410

SHALDEN parish 1686 Hamps 2-3/4 miles nw Alton pop 167 archd
and dioc Winchester

SHALDON or SHALDON GREEN township parishes Stokeinteignhead,
St Nicholas Devon Bapt, Indep, Wesl Meth

SHALFLEET parish 1695 Hamps 3-3/4 miles se Yarmouth Isle of
Wight pop 1,049 archd and dioc Winchester

SHALFORD parish 1558 Essex 5 miles nw Braintree pop 701 Commissary of Essex and Herts, concurrently with Consistorial Court of
Bishop of London

SHALFORD parish 1564 Surrey 1 mile se Guildford pop 910 archd
Surrey dioc Winchester

SHALSTONE parish 1538 Bucks 4 miles nw Buckingham pop 198
archd Buckingham dioc Lincoln

SHAMBLEHURST tything parish South Stoneham Hamps pop 921

SHANGTON parish 1580 Leics 6-1/4 miles nw Market Harboro pop 39 archd Leicester dioc Lincoln

SHANKLIN parish 1724 Hamps 9-1/2 miles se Newport Isle of Wight archd and dioc Winchester

SHAP parish 1563 Westm 6 miles nw Orton pop 1,084 archd and dioc Carlisle

SHAPWICK parish 1654 Dorset 4-1/2 miles se Blandford Forum pop 462 archd Dorset dioc Bristol

SHAPWICK parish 1590 Somerset 6-3/4 miles sw Glastonbury pop 452 archd Wells dioc Bath and Wells

SHARDLOW township parish Wilne Derbys

SHARESHILL parish 1565 Staffs 5-3/4 miles ne Wolverhampton pop 520 archd Stafford dioc Lichfield

SHARLSTON township parish Warmfield W R York 4-1/4 miles se Wakefield pop 243

SHARNBROOK parish 1596 Beds 4 miles ne Harrold pop 754 archd Bedford dioc Lincoln Bapt

SHARNFORD parish 1671 Leics 4-1/4 miles se Hinckley pop 545 archd Leicester dioc Lincoln

SHARPENHOE hamlet parish Streatley Beds

SHARPERTON township parish Allenton Northumberland pop 105

SHARPLES township parish Bolton Lancs pop 2,589

SHARRINGTON parish 1672 Norfolk 4-1/4 miles sw Holt pop 252 archd and dioc Norwich

SHARROW township parish Ripon W R York pop 103

SHATTON hamlet parish Hope Derbys

SHAUGH or SHAUGH PRIOR parish 1565 Devon 6 miles n Earls Plympton pop 570 archd Totnes dioc Exeter

SHAVINGTON township parish Wyburnbury Ches pop 320

SHAW chapelry 1704 parish Oldham Lancs 5 miles se Rochdale Wesl Meth

SHAW cum DONNINGTON parish 1646 Berks 1-1/4 miles ne Speenhamland pop 620 archd Berks dioc Salisbury

SHAWBURY parish 1561 Shrops comp townships Besford, Preston Brockhurst, Acton Reynold, Edgbolton, Shawbury 7-1/4 miles ne Shrewsbury archd Salop dioc Lichfield

SHAWDON township parish Whittingham Northumberland pop 80

SHAWELL parish 1558 Leics 3 miles s Lutterworth pop 216 archd Leicester dioc Lincoln

SHEARSBY chapelry 1658 parish Knaptoft Leics 7 miles ne Lutterworth pop 354

SHEBBEAR parish 1576 Devon 7-3/4 miles nw Hatherleigh pop 1,179 archd Barnstaple dioc Exeter

SHEEN parish 1595 Staffs 10 miles ne Winster pop 366 archd Stafford dioc Lichfield

SHEEN, EAST hamlet parish Mortlake Surrey

SHEEPSHEAD parish 1538 Leics 4 miles sw Loughboro pop 3,714

archd Leicester dioc Lincoln Bapt, Soc of Friends, Wesl Meth

SHEEPSTOR parish 1691 Devon 7 miles se Tavistock pop 154 archd Totnes dioc Exeter

SHEEPWASH parish 1673 Devon 4 miles nw Hatherleigh pop 436 archd Barnstaple dioc Exeter

SHEEPWASH township parish Bothall Northumberland pop 57

SHEEPY MAGNA parish 1607 Leics 3 miles ne Atherstone pop 627 archd Leicester dioc Lincoln

SHEEPY PARVA parish 1607 Leics 3-1/4 miles ne Atherstone pop 87 archd Leicester dioc Lincoln

SHEERING parish 1558 Essex 3 miles ne Harlow pop 547 archd Middlesex dioc London

SHEERNESS chapelry 1695 parish Minster Kent 21 miles ne Maidstone Bapt, Indep, Prim Meth, Wesl Meth, Unit, Roman Cath, Jews

SHEET tything parish Petersfield Hamps pop 380

SHEFFIELD city Cathedral 1560, St Paul 1720, St James 1788, St George 1824, St Mary 1826, St Philip 1827, borough W R York 55 miles sw York comp chapelries Attercliffe 1719, Eccleshall Brierlow 1784, townships Nether Hallam, Upper Hallam, hamlet Darnall, township Brightside Bierlow pop 91,692 archd and dioc York Indep, Wesl Meth, Bapt, Soc of Friends, Unit, Roman Cath

SHEFFORD chapelry parish Campton Beds pop 763

SHEFFORD, EAST parish 1603 Berks 5-3/4 miles ne Hungerford pop 67 archd Berks dioc Salisbury

SHEFFORD HARDWICKS extra parochial Beds 9 miles se Bedford pop 16

SHEFFORD, WEST or GREAT parish 1571 Berks 5-1/2 miles ne Hungerford pop 559 archd Berks dioc Salisbury Wesl Meth

SHEINTON parish 1658 Shrops 3-1/2 miles nw Much Wenlock pop 133 archd Salop dioc Lichfield

SHELDING township parish Ripon W R York pop 49

SHELDON chapelry 1745 parish Bakewell Derbys 3 miles w Bakewell pop 148

SHELDON parish 1721 Devon 7 miles ne Cullompton pop 185 archd and dioc Exeter

SHELDON parish 1558 Warws 4-3/4 miles sw Coleshill pop 422 archd Coventry dioc Lichfield

SHELDWICK parish 1558 Kent 2-3/4 miles sw Faversham pop 497 archd and dioc Canterbury

SHELF township parish Halifax W R York pop 2,614 Prim Meth

SHELFANGER parish 1686 Norfolk 2-1/2 miles nw Diss pop 435 archd Norfolk dioc Norwich Bapt

SHELFORD parish 1563 Notts 8 miles ne Nottingham pop 704 archd Nottingham dioc York

SHELFORD, GREAT parish 1557 Cambs 4-1/2 miles se Cambridge pop 812 pec of Bishop of Ely

SHELFORD, LITTLE parish 1686 Cambs 5-1/2 miles se Cambridge pop 483 archd and dioc Ely Indep

SHELL hamlet parish Himbleton Worcs pop 43

SHELLAND parish 1721 Suffolk 3-1/2 miles nw Stowmarket pop 126 archd Sudbury dioc Norwich

SHELLEY parish 1687 Essex 1-1/2 miles n Chipping Ongar pop 163 archd Essex dioc London

SHELLEY parish 1747 Suffolk 2-1/2 miles s Hadleigh pop 142 archd Suffolk dioc Norwich

SHELLEY township parish Kirk Burton W R York pop 1,319 Indep, Wesl Meth

SHELLINGFORD Berks See SHILLINGSFORD

SHELLOW BOWELS parish 1555 Essex 6-1/4 miles ne Chipping Ongar pop 143 Commissary of Essex and Herts, concurrently with Cons Court of Bishop of London

SHELSLEY BEAUCHAMP parish 1538 Worcs 8-1/4 miles sw Stourport pop 553 archd and dioc Worcester

SHELSLEY, KINGS hamlet parish Shelsley Beauchamp Worcs pop 282

SHELSLEY WALSH parish Worcs 9 miles se Stourport pop 45 archd and dioc Worcester

SHELSWELL parish (incl regs Newton Purcell) co Oxford 6 miles ne Bicester pop 49 archd and dioc Oxford

SHELTON parish 1565 Beds 4 miles nw Kimbolton pop 132 archd Bedford dioc Lincoln

SHELTON parish 1595 Norfolk 2-1/2 miles se St Mary Stratton pop 253 archd Norfolk dioc Norwich

SHELTON parish 1595 Notts 6-1/2 miles sw Newark pop 113 archd Nottingham dioc York

SHELTON chapelry parish Stoke on Trent Staffs pop 9,267 Bapt, Indep, Wesl Meth, Unit

SHELVE parish 1583 Shrops 7-3/4 miles ne Bishops Castle pop 71 archd Salop dioc Hereford

SHELWICK township parish Holmer Herefs

SHENFIELD parish 1539 Essex 1 mile ne Brentford pop 665 archd Essex dioc London

SHENINGTON parish 1721 co Oxford 6 miles nw Banbury pop 433 archd and dioc Gloucester

SHENLEY parish 1653 Bucks comp hamlets Brook End, Church End 3-1/2 miles nw Fenny Stratford pop 484 archd Buckingham dioc Lincoln

SHENLEY parish 1657 Herts 6 miles nw Chipping Barnet pop 1,167 archd Huntingdon dioc Lincoln

SHENSTONE parish 1579 Staffs 3-1/2 miles sw Lichfield pop 1,827 archd Stafford dioc Lichfield

SHENTON chapelry 1625 parish Market Bosworth Leics 2-1/2 miles sw Stevenage pop 217 archd St Albans dioc London

SHEPHALL parish 1560 Herts 2-1/4 miles se Stevenage pop 217 archd St Albans dioc London

SHEPLEY township parish Kirk Burton W R York pop 593

SHEPPERTON parish 1574 Middlesex 2-1/4 miles se Chartsey pop

847 archd Middlesex dioc London

SHEPRETH parish 1734 Cambs 5-3/4 miles nw Royston pop 320 archd and dioc Ely

SHEPSCOMB chapelry parish Painswick Gloucs pop 803

SHEPTON BEAUCHAMP parish 1558 Somerset 3-3/4 miles nw Ilminster pop 648 archd Taunton dioc Bath and Wells

SHEPTON MALLET parish 1634 Somerset 14 miles ne Somerton pop 5,330 archd Wells dioc Bath and Wells Bapt, Indep, Wesl Meth, Roman Cath

SHEPTON MONTAGUE parish 1560 Somerset 2-1/2 miles s Burton pop 452 archd Wells dioc Bath and Wells

SHERATON township parish Monk Hesleton co Durham pop 110

SHERBORNE parish 1538 Dorset 18 miles nw Dorchester pop 4,075 pec Dean of Salisbury Soc of Friends, Indep, Wesl Meth

SHERBORNE parish 1572 Gloucs 6 miles nw Burford pop 767 archd and dioc Gloucester

SHERBORNE parish 1587 Warws 2-3/4 miles sw Warwick pop 241 archd and dioc Worcester

SHERBORNE ST JOHN parish 1652 Hamps 2-3/4 miles nw Basingstoke pop 702 archd and dioc Winchester

SHERBORNE, MONKS parish 1601 Hamps 3-1/2 miles nw Basingstoke pop 522 archd and dioc Winchester

SHERBURN township parish Pittington co Durham pop 337

SHERBURN parish 1653 E R York 11-1/4 miles ne New Malton pop 536 archd East Riding dioc York Wesl Meth

SHERBURN IN ELMET parish 1639 E R York comp town Sherburn, townships Barkston, Huddleston with Lumby, Lotherton with part of Aberford, Micklefield, South Milford, Newthorp 15 miles sw York pop 3,068 pec of Prebendary of Fenton Wesl Meth

SHERBURN HOUSE or SHERBURN HOSPITAL 1692 extra parochial co Durham 2-1/2 miles se Durham pop 59

SHERE parish 1547 Surrey 6 miles se Guildford pop 1,190 archd Surrey dioc Winchester Wesl Meth

SHEREFORD parish 1721 Norfolk 2-1/4 miles w Fakenham pop 110 archd and dioc Norwich

SHERFIELD ENGLISH parish 1640 Hamps 4-3/4 miles nw Romsey pop 338 archd and dioc Winchester

SHERFIELD UPON LODDON parish 1574 Hamps 3-3/4 miles ne Basingstoke pop 599 archd and dioc Winchester

SHERFORD parish 1713 Devon 3-1/4 miles e Kingsbridge pop 511 archd Totnes dioc Exeter

SHERRIF HALES parish 1557 Staffs 3 miles ne Shifnall pop 1,109 archd Stafford dioc Lichfield Wesl Meth

SHERRIF HUTTON Yorks See HUTTON, SHERIFF

SHERMANBURY parish 1653 Sussex 7-1/2 miles ne Steyning pop 345 archd Lewes dioc Chichester

SHERMANS GROUNDS extra parochial Leics pop 23

SHERNBORNE parish 1749 Norfolk 6-1/4 miles ne Castle Rising pop

140 archd Norfolk dioc Norwich

SHERRINGHAM parish 1670 Norfolk 5-1/4 miles w Cromer pop 899 archd and dioc Norwich

SHERRINGTON parish 1698 Bucks 1-3/4 miles nw Newport Pagnell pop 804 archd Buckingham dioc Lincoln

SHERRINGTON parish 1677 Wilts 5-1/4 miles ne Hindon pop 179 archd and dioc Salisbury

SHERSTON MAGNA parish 1653 Wilts 5-3/4 miles sw Malmesbury pop 1,361 archd and dioc Salisbury

SHERSTON PARVA or SHERSTON PINKNEY (parish regs with Sherston Magna) Wilts 4-3/4 miles w Malmesbury pop 122

SHERWILL parish 1538 Devon 4 miles ne Barnstaple pop 688 archd Barnstaple dioc Exeter

SHEVINGTON township parish Standish Lancs pop 899

SHEVIOCK parish 1666 Cornwall 3 miles se St Germans pop 453 archd Cornwall dioc Exeter

SHIELDS, NORTH sea port, market town parish Tynemouth Northumberland pop 20,000 Meth, New Connection, Soc of Friends, Bapt, Indep, Prim Meth, Wesl Meth, Presb, Roman Cath, Jews

SHIELDS, SOUTH parish 1653 borough co Durham 20 miles ne Durham pop 9,074 archd and dioc Durham Bapt, Wesl Meth, Presb, Indep, Meth New Connection, Prim Meth

SHIFNALL parish 1678 Shrops comp market town Shifnall, chapelry Priors Lee, townships Hatton, Woodside, hamlet Oakengates 17-1/2 miles se Shrewsbury pop 4,779 archd Salop dioc Lichfield Bapt, Indep

SHIFFORD chapelry parish Bampton co Oxford pop 47

SHILBOTTLE parish 1690 Northumberland comp townships Guyson, Haxon, Newton on the Moor, Shilbottle, Whittle, Woodhouse 4-1/2 miles se Alnwick pop 1,195 archd Northumberland dioc Durham

SHILDON township parish St Andrew Auckland co Durham pop 867

SHILLINGFORD or SHELLINGFORD parish 1579 Berks 2-3/4 miles se Great Farringdon pop 246 archd Berks dioc Salisbury

SHILLINGFORD parish 1565 Devon 3-1/2 miles sw Exeter pop 89 archd and dioc Exeter

SHILLINGSTONE or SHILLING OKEFORD parish 1654 Dorset 5-3/4 miles nw Blandford Forum pop 473 archd Dorset dioc Bristol

SHILLINGTON Beds See SHITLINGTON

SHILTON or SHILTON ROAD parish 1662 Berks and co Oxford 2-1/2 miles se Burford pop 290 archd and dioc Oxford

SHILTON parish 1695 Warws 5-3/4 miles ne Coventry pop 460 archd Coventry dioc Lichfield

SHILTON, EARL Leics See EARL SHILTON

SHILVINGTON township parish Morpeth Northumberland pop 101

SHIMPLING parish 1538 Norfolk 3-3/4 miles ne Diss pop 227 archd Norfolk dioc Norwich

SHIMPLINGTHORNE parish 1538 Suffolk 4 miles nw Lavenham pop 496 archd Sudbury dioc Norwich

SHINCLIFFE chapelry parish St Oswald Durham co Durham pop 302

SHINETON Shrops See SHEINTON

SHINFIELD parish 1649 Berks 3 miles se Reading pop 1,100 archd Berks dioc Salisbury Indep

SHINGAY parish (incl regs of Wendy) Cambs 8-1/2 miles nw Royston pop 112 archd and dioc Ely

SHINGHAM parish 1762 Norfolk 4-3/4 miles sw Swaffham pop 61 archd Norfolk dioc Norwich

SHIPBORNE parish 1656 Kent 3-3/4 miles n Tonbridge pop 470 archd and dioc Rochester

SHIPBROOK township parish Davenham Ches pop 83

SHIPDEN formerly a parish near Cromer Norfolk

SHIPDHAM parish 1558 Norfolk 4-3/4 miles sw East Dereham pop 1,889 archd Norfolk dioc Norwich

SHIPHAM parish 1560 Somerset 3 miles ne Axbridge pop 691 archd Wells dioc Bath and Wells

SHIPLAKE parish 1672 co Oxford 2-3/4 miles s Henley on Thames pop 515 archd and dioc Oxford

SHIPLEY township parish Heanor Derbys pop 632

SHIPLEY township parish Ellingham Northumberland pop 95

SHIPLEY parish 1609 Sussex 6 miles sw Horsham pop 1,180 archd and dioc Chichester

SHIPLEY district parish Bradford W R York pop 1,926 Bapt, Wesl Meth

SHIPMEADOW parish 1561 Suffolk 3 miles sw Beccles pop 133 archd Suffolk dioc Norwich

SHIPPON chapelry parish St Helen Abingdon Berks pop 151

SHIPSTON UPON STOUR parish Worcs 16 miles se Warwick pop 1,632 archd and dioc Worcester Bapt, Soc of Friends, Wesl Meth

SHIPTON parish 1538 Shrops 7 miles nw Much Wenlock pop 154 archd Salop dioc Hereford

SHIPTON chapelry 1675 parish Market Weighton E R York 1-1/4 miles nw Market Weighton pop 348

SHIPTON township parish Overton E R York pop 364 Calv Meth, Wesl Meth

SHIPTON BELLINGER parish 1540 Hamps 4-1/4 miles sw Ludgershall pop 287 archd and dioc Winchester

SHIPTON GEORGE chapelry parish Burton Bradstock Dorset pop 316

SHIPTON LEE hamlet parish Quainton Bucks pop 104

SHIPTON MOYNE parish 1570 Gloucs 2-1/4 miles se Tetbury pop 389 archd and dioc Gloucester

SHIPTON CLIFFE parish 1653 Gloucs 6-1/4 miles nw Northleach pop 229 archd and dioc Gloucester

SHIPTON SOLLERS parish (regs incl with Shipton Cliffe) Gloucs 6-1/4 miles nw Northleach pop 98 archd and dioc Gloucester

SHIPTON UNDER WHYCHWOOD parish 1538 co Oxford 4 miles ne Burford comp chapelries Langley, Leafield, Lyneham, Milton, Ramsden pop 2,457 archd and dioc Oxford

SHIPTON UPON CHERWELL parish 1653 co Oxford 2-1/4 miles e
Woodstock pop 148 archd and dioc Oxford
SHIRBURN parish 1587 co Oxford 4 miles se Tetsworth pop 325 archd
and dioc Oxford
SHIREHAMPTON chapelry parish Westbury upon Trym Gloucs pop 420
SHIREHEAD chapelry parish Cockerham Lancs
SHIRE NEWTON parish 1730 co Monmouth 4-1/4 miles w Chepstow
pop 791 archd and dioc Llandaff
SHIRLAND parish 1678 Derbys 2 miles nw Alfreton pop 1,212 archd
Derby dioc Lichfield
SHIRLEY parish 1663 Derbys 4-1/4 miles se Ashbourn comp chapel-
ry Yeaveley, township Stydd pop 602 archd Derby dioc Lichfield
SHITLINGTON parish 1544 Beds 4 miles se Silsoe pop 1,307 archd
Bedford dioc Lincoln
SHITLINGTON township parish Thornhill W R York pop 1,893
SHITLINGTON, HIGH township parish Wark Northumberland pop 108
SHITLINGTON, LOW township parish Wark Northumberland pop 58
SHITTERTON tything parish Beer Regis Dorset
SHOBDON parish 1556 Herefs 5-1/2 miles se Presteign pop 536 archd
and dioc Hereford
SHOBROOKE parish 1538 Devon 2 miles ne Crediton pop 644 archd
and dioc Exeter Indep
SHOBY chapelry parish Saxelby Leics pop 15
SHOCKLACH parish 1538 Ches comp townships Caldecott, Church
Shocklach, Oviatt Shocklach pop 431 4-1/2 miles nw Malpas
archd and dioc Chester
SHOEBURY, NORTH parish 1680 Essex 3-1/4 miles ne Southend pop
226 archd Essex dioc London
SHOEBURY, SOUTH parish 1704 Essex 4 miles e Southend pop 202
archd Essex dioc London
SHOPLAND parish 1741 Essex 2 miles ne Prittlewell pop 48 archd
Essex dioc London
SHOREDITCH ST LEONARD parish 1558 Middlesex with Haggerstone,
Hoxton ne London pop 68,564 archd and dioc London Bapt, Indep,
Wesl Meth
SHOREHAM parish 1558 borough Kent 4-1/2 miles n Sevenoaks pop
1,015 pec Archbishop of Canterbury
SHOREHAM, NEW parish 1566 Sussex 23 miles e Chichester pop
1,503 archd Lewes dioc Chichester Indep, Wesl Meth
SHOREHAM, OLD parish 1566 Sussex 1/2 mile nw New Shoreham
pop 231 archd Lewes dioc Chichester
SHORESWOOD township parish Norham Northumberland pop 279
SHORNCUTT parish 1708 Wilts 5-3/4 miles nw Cricklade pop 29
archd and dioc Salisbury
SHORNE parish 1640 (joined with Marston) Kent 3-3/4 miles se Grave-
send pop 730 archd and dioc Rochester
SHORTFLATT township parish Bolam Northumberland pop 22
SHORTHAMPTON parish 1630 co Oxford 5 miles se Chipping Norton

archd and dioc Oxford

SHORWELL parish 1676 Isle of Wight Hamps 5 miles sw Newport pop 699 archd and dioc Winchester

SHOSTON township parish Bambrough Northumberland pop 89

SHOTFORD hamlet parish Mendham Norfolk

SHOT HAUGH township parish Felton Northumberland

SHOTLEY parish 1670 Northumberland comp chapelry High Blanchland, townships Newbiggin, Shotley 10-1/2 miles se Hexham pop 1,104 archd Northumberland dioc Durham

SHOTLEY parish 1571 Suffolk 8-1/4 miles se Ipswich pop 410 archd Norfolk dioc Norwich

SHOTOVER extra parochial co Oxford 4-3/4 miles ne Oxford pop 149

SHOTTESBROOK parish 1556 Berks 5 miles sw Maidenhead pop 138 archd Berks dioc Salisbury

SHOTTESHAM All Saints parish 1538 Norfolk 4-3/4 miles ne St Mary Stratton pop 558 archd Norfolk dioc Norwich

SHOTTESHAM St Martin parish (regs incl Shottesham St Mary) Norfolk 4-1/2 miles ne St Mary Stratton archd Norfolk dioc Norwich

SHOTTESHAM St Mary parish 1687 Norfolk 4-3/4 miles ne St Mary Stratton pop 367 archd Norfolk dioc Norwich

SHOTTISHAM parish 1618 Suffolk 5-1/2 miles se Woodbridge pop 280 archd Suffolk dioc Norwich

SHOTTLE township parish Duffield Derbys pop 556

SHOTTON township parish Staindrop co Durham

SHOTTON township parish Easington co Durham pop 272

SHOTTON township parish Sedgefield co Durham pop 73

SHOTTON township parish Stannington Northumberland

SHOTTSWELL parish 1564 Warws 4-1/2 miles nw Banbury pop 302 archd Coventry dioc Lichfield Wesl Meth

SHOTWICK parish 1551 Ches comp townships Cappenhurst, Kingswood, Great Saughall, Little Saughall, Shotwick, Woodbank or Rough Shotwick 6 miles nw Chester pop 713 archd and dioc Chester

SHOTWICK PARK extra parochial 4-1/4 miles nw Chester Ches pop 18

SHOULDEN parish 1591 Kent 1-1/2 miles w Deal pop 356 archd and dioc Canterbury

SHOULDHAM parish 1653 Norfolk 6-1/2 miles ne Downham Market pop 725 archd Norfolk dioc Norwich Wesl Meth

SHOULDHAM THORPE parish 1737 Norfolk 5 miles ne Downham Market pop 300 archd Norfolk dioc Norwich

SHOWELL chapelry parish Swerford co Oxford

SHRAWARDINE township parish Abberbury Shrops

SHRAWARDINE parish 1645 Shrops 5-3/4 miles nw Shrewsbury pop 189 archd Salop dioc Hereford

SHRAWLEY parish 1537 Worcs 4-1/4 miles sw Stourport pop 497 archd and dioc Worcester

SHREWLEY chapelry parish Hatton Warws pop 264

SHREWSBURY county town Shrops pop 21,297 comp St Alkmund 1560,

St Chad 1616, Holy Cross 1541, St Julian 1559, St Mary 1584, borough sep juris archd Salop dioc Lichfield St Mary a peculiar Bapt, Soc of Friends, Indep, Wesl Meth, Unit, Roman Cath

SHREWTON parish 1651 Wilts 5-3/4 miles nw Amesbury pop 491 archd and dioc Salisbury Bapt

SHRIGLEY POTT Ches See POTT SHRIGLEY

SHRIPPLE tything parish Idmiston Wilts pop 56

SHRIVENHAM parish 1575 Berks 5 miles sw Great Farringdon comp chapelries Longcot, Watchfield, hamlet Fernham, tythings Beckett, Bourton pop 2,113 archd Berks dioc Salisbury

SHROPHAM parish 1720 Norfolk 4 miles nw East Harling pop 507 archd Norfolk dioc Norwich

SHROTON Dorset See IWERN COURTNAY

SHUCKBURGH, LOWER parish 1678 Warws 5 miles e Southam pop 165 archd Coventry dioc Lichfield

SHUCKBURGH, UPPER parish 1757 Warws 5-1/2 miles e Southam pop 40 archd Coventry dioc Lichfield

SHUDY CAMPS parish 1558 Cambs 4-1/4 miles se Linton pop 418 archd and dioc Ely

SHURDINGTON, GREAT parish 1561 Gloucs 2-3/4 miles sw Cheltenham pop 99 archd and dioc Gloucester

SHURLACH township parish Davenham Ches pop 98

SHUSTOCK parish 1538 Warws 2-3/4 miles ne Coleshill pop 634 archd Coventry dioc Lichfield

SHUTE parish 1561 Devon 2 miles n Colyton pop 617 pec of Dean and Chapter of Exeter

SHUTFORD, EAST chapelry 1698 parish Swalcliffe co Oxford pop 31

SHUTFORD, WEST township parish Swalcliffe co Oxford pop 431

SHUTTINGTON parish 1557 Warws 3-3/4 miles ne Tamworth pop 147 archd Coventry dioc Lichfield

SHUTTLEHANGER chapelry parish Stoke Bruerne co Northampton pop 325

SIBBERTOFT parish 1689 co Northampton 5 miles sw Market Harborough pop 402 archd Northampton dioc Peterborough Wesl Meth

SIBBERSTSOLD parish 1563 Kent 6-1/4 miles nw Dover pop 363 archd and dioc Canterbury

SIBDON CARWOOD parish 1580 Shrops 7 miles se Bishops Castle pop 63 archd Salop dioc Hereford

SIBFORD FERRIS hamlet parish Swalcliffe co Oxford pop 248

SIBFORD GOWER hamlet parish Swalcliffe co Oxford pop 507

SIBSEY parish 1568 Lincs 5-1/4 miles ne Boston pop 1,364 archd and dioc Lincoln Wesl Meth

SIBSON hamlet parish Stibbington Hunts

SIBSON parish 1558 Leics 4 miles sw Market Bosworth pop 427 archd Leicester dioc Lincoln

SIBSTONE Leics See SIBSON

SIBTHORPE parish 1720 Notts 6-3/4 miles sw Newark pop 144 archd

Nottingham dioc York

SIBTON parish 1552 Suffolk 2 miles nw Yoxford pop 498 archd Suffolk dioc Norwich

SICKLINGHALL township parish Kirkby Overblow W R York pop 212 Wesl Meth

SIDBURY parish 1559 Devon 2-1/2 miles ne Sidmouth pop 1,725 pec Dean and Chapter of Exeter Indep

SIDBURY parish 1560 Shrops 5-1/4 miles sw Bridgenorth pop 103 archd and dioc Hereford

SIDDINGTON chapelry 1720 parish Prestbury Ches 5 miles nw Congleton pop 479

SIDDINGTON parish 1606 Gloucs 1-3/4 miles se Cirencester pop 409 archd and dioc Gloucester

SIDE parish 1686 Gloucs 7 miles e Painswick pop 50 archd and dioc Gloucester

SIDESTRANDS parish 1558 Norfolk 3 miles se Cromer pop 146 archd Norfolk dioc Norwich

SIDLESHAM parish 1566 Sussex 4 miles s Chichester pop 1,002 archd and dioc Chichester

SIDMONTON chapelry 1570 parish Kingsclere Hamps pop 170

SIDMOUTH parish 1589 Devon 13-1/2 miles se Exeter pop 3,126 archd and dioc Exeter Bapt, Indep, Unit

SIGGLESTHORNE parish 1562 E R York comp townships Catfoss, Little Hatfield, Seaton, Sigglesthorne pop 578 archd East Riding dioc York

SIGHILL township parish Earsdon Northumberland pop 985

SIGNET hamlet parish Burford co Oxford

SIGSTON, KIRBY parish 1574 N R York comp townships Kirby Sigston, Sowerby under Cotcliffe, Winton pop 343 pec Dean and Chapter of Durham

SILCHESTER parish 1653 Hamps 7-1/2 miles n Basingstoke pop 414 archd and dioc Winchester

SILEBY parish 1568 Leics 1-1/2 miles e Mountsorrel pop 1,491 archd Leicester dioc Lincoln Bapt, Wesl Meth

SILFIELD township parish Wymondham Norfolk pop 593

SILKSTONE parish 1558 W R York comp chapelries Barnsley, Stainboro, part of West Bretton, Cumberworth, township Dodworth, Hoyland, Swaine, Silkstone, Thurgoland pop 16,561 4-1/4 miles se Barnsley archd and dioc York Wesl Meth

SILKSWORTH township parish Bishop Wearmouth co Durham pop 252

SILK WILLOUGHBY See WILLOUGHBY SILK Lincs

SILPHO township parish Hackness N R York

SILSDEN chapelry 1768 parish Kildwick W R York 4 miles nw Keighley pop 2,137 pec manor of Silsden Wesl Meth

SILSOE chapelry parish Flitton Beds

SILTON parish 1653 Dorset 3 miles sw Mere pop 396 archd Dorset dioc Bristol

SILTON, NETHER chapelry parish Leak N R York pop 179 Wesl Meth

SILTON, OVER parish 1678 N R York comp townships Kepwick, Over Silton 8-1/2 miles ne Thirsk pop 263 archd Cleveland dioc York

SILVERDALE chapelry parish Warton Lancs pop 240

SILVERLEY parish Cambs 3-3/4 miles e Newmarket (regs with parish Ashley) archd Sudbury dioc Norwich

SILVERSTONE parish co Northampton 3 miles se Towcester pop 947 regs with Whittlebury archd Northampton dioc Peterborough Wesl Meth

SILVERTON parish 1626 Devon 5-1/4 miles sw Cullompton pop 1,389 archd and dioc Exeter Wesl Meth

SILVINGTON parish 1716 Shrops 6 miles nw Cleobury Mortimer pop 30 archd Salop dioc Hereford

SIMONBURN parish 1681 Northumberland comp chapelry Humshaugh, townships Haughton, Simonburn pop 1,133 archd Northumberland dioc Durham

SIMONDSLEY township parish Glossop Derbys pop 454

SIMONSTONE township parish Whalley Lancs pop 440

SIMONSWOOD township parish Walton on the Hill Lancs pop 411

SIMONWARD Cornwall See BREWARD, ST

SIMPSON parish 1719 Bucks 1-1/2 miles ne Fenny Stratford pop 470 archd Buckingham dioc Lincoln

SINDERBY township parish Pickhill W R York pop 93

SINGLEBORO hamlet parish Great Horwood Bucks pop 110

SINGLETON chapelry parish Kirkham Lancs pop 499

SINGLETON parish 1664 Sussex 5-1/2 miles sw Midhurst pop 563 archd and dioc Chichester

SINNINGTON parish 1517 N R York 4-3/4 miles nw Pickering pop 584 archd Cleveland dioc York Wesl Meth

SINWELL tything parish Wotton under Edge Gloucs

SISLAND parish 1558 Norfolk 6-1/4 miles ne Bungay pop 85 archd Norfolk dioc Norwich

SISTON parish 1576 Gloucs 6-1/2 miles ne Bristol pop 973 archd and dioc Gloucester

SITHNEY parish 1664 Cornwall 2 miles nw Helston pop 2,772 archd Cornwall dioc Exeter Bapt, Wesl Meth

SITTINGBOURNE parish 1561 Kent 10 miles ne Maidstone pop 2,182 archd and dioc Canterbury Wesl Meth

SIXHILLS parish 1672 Lincs 5 miles se Market Rasen pop 169 archd and dioc Lincoln

SIZELAND Norfolk See SISLAND

SIZEWELL hamlet parish Leiston Suffolk

SKECKLING parish 1747 E R York 10-1/2 miles e Kingston upon Hull archd East Riding dioc York

SKEEBY township parish Easby N R York pop 183

SKEFFINGTON parish 1514 Leics 9-1/2 miles nw Uppingham pop 180 archd Leicester dioc Lincoln

SKEFFLING parish 1585 E R York 4-1/2 miles se Patrington pop 204 archd East Riding dioc York Wesl Meth

SKEGBY parish 1569 Notts 3 miles w Mansfield pop 656 archd Nottingham dioc York

SKEGNESS parish 1653 Lincs 3-3/4 miles se Burgh pop 185 archd and dioc Lincoln

SKELBROOKE chapelry 1592 parish South Kirby W R York 7-1/4 miles nw Doncaster pop 113

SKELDIN township parish Ripon W R York

SKELLINGTHORPE parish 1563 Lincs 5-1/2 miles w Lincoln pop 417 archd and dioc Lincoln Wesl Meth

SKELLOW township parish Owston W R York 5-1/2 miles nw Doncaster pop 181

SKELMANTHORPE township parish Emley W R York Wesl Meth

SKELMERSDALE chapelry parish Ormskirk Lancs

SKELSMERGH township parish Kendal Westm pop 263

SKELTON parish 1580 Cumberland comp townships Lamonby, Skelton, Unthank 6-3/4 miles ne Penrith pop 1,127 archd and dioc Carlisle

SKELTON township parish Howden E R York pop 228

SKELTON BY YORK parish 1538 N R York 3-3/4 miles nw York pop 291 pec of Alne and Tollerton

SKELTON in CLEVELAND parish 1698 N R York comp townships Great Moorsham, Skelton, Stranghow pop 1,241 4 miles ne Guisboro archd Cleveland dioc York Wesl Meth

SKELTON chapelry parish Ripon W R York

SKELWITH township parish Hawkeshead Lancs

SKENDLEBY parish 1723 Lincs 4 miles ne Spilsby pop 253 archd and dioc Lincoln Wesl Meth

SKENRITH parish 1662 co Monmouth 6-3/4 miles nw Monmouth pop 609 archd and dioc Llandaff

SKERNE parish 1561 E R York 2-3/4 miles se Driffield pop 201 archd East Riding dioc York

SKERTON township parish Lancaster Lancs pop 1,351

SKETCHLEY hamlet parish Aston Flamville Leics

SKEWSBY township parish Dalby N R York

SKEYTON parish 1706 Norfolk 3-3/4 miles se Aylsham pop 317 archd and dioc Norwich

SKIDBROOKE parish 1558 Lincs 10-1/2 miles ne Louth pop 362 archd and dioc Lincoln

SKIDBY parish 1655 E R York 4 miles sw Beverley pop 315 archd East Riding dioc York

SKILGATE parish 1674 Somerset 6-1/2 miles sw Wiveliscombe pop 227 archd Taunton dioc Bath and Wells

SKILLINGTON parish 1542 Lincs 3 miles nw Colsterworth pop 389 pec Dean and Chapter of Lincoln Wesl Meth

SKINBURNESS village parish Holme Cultram Cumberland

SKINNAND parish 1791 Lincs 11-1/2 miles nw Sleaford archd and dioc Lincoln pop 24

SKINNINGROVE township parish Brotton N R York pop 63

SKIPLAM township parish Kirkdale N R York pop 124

SKIPSEA parish 1720 E R York comp chapelry Ulrome, townships Bonwick, Bringhoe with Skipsea 11-1/4 miles se Driffield pop 726 archd East Riding dioc York Wesl Meth, Indep

SKIPTON township parish Topcliffe N R York pop 114 Wesl Meth

SKIPTON parish 1592 W R York comp chapelry Bolton Abbey, townships Barden, Draughton, Embsay with Eastby, East Halton with Bolton, Stirton with Thorlby 44 miles w York archd and dioc York Soc of Friends, Indep, Wesl Meth

SKIPWITH parish 1718 E R York pop 648 5-1/2 miles ne Selby pec Court of Howdenshire

SKIRBECK parish 1661 Lincs 1 mile se Boston pop 1,578 archd and dioc Lincoln

SKIRBECK QUARTER hamlet parish Skirbeck Lincs pop 323

SKIRCOAT township parish Halifax W R York pop 4,060

SKIRLAUGH, NORTH chapelry 1719 parish Swine E R York 9 miles ne Kingston upon Hull pop 210 Wesl Meth

SKIRLAUGH, SOUTH chapelry 1719 parish Swine E R York pop 228

SKIRLINGTON township parish Atwick E R York

SKIRPENBECK parish 1660 E R York 7-3/4 miles nw Pocklington pop 214 archd East Riding dioc York

SKIRWITH township parish Kirkland Cumberland pop 296 Wesl Meth

SKUTTERSKELFE township parish Rudby in Cleveland N R York pop 38

SLADE hamlet parish Stroud Gloucs church built 1831

SLAIDBURN parish 1653 W R York comp townships High Bowland Forest, Low Bowland Forest, Easington, Newton, Slaidburn 8 miles nw Clitheroe pop 2,409 archd East Riding dioc York Wesl Meth

SLAITHWAITE chapelry 1684 parish Huddersfield W R York 5 miles sw Huddersfield pop 2,892

SLALEY parish 1714 Northumberland 5-1/2 miles se Hexham pop 616 archd Northumberland dioc Durham

SLAPTON parish 1653 Bucks 3-1/4 miles nw Ivinghoe pop 360 archd Buckingham dioc Lincoln Wesl Meth

SLAPTON parish 1634 Devon 6 miles sw Dartmouth pop 665 archd Totnes dioc Exeter

SLAPTON parish 1573 Northampton 3-3/4 miles sw Towcester pop 197 archd Northampton dioc Peterborough Wesl Meth

SLAUGHAM parish 1654 Sussex 4-1/4 miles nw Cuckfield pop 740 archd Lewes dioc Chichester

SLAUGHTER, LOWER parish (incl regs of Bourton on the Water) Gloucs 3 miles sw Stow on the Wold pop 258 archd and dioc Gloucester

SLAUGHTER, UPPER parish 1538 Gloucs 3-1/4 miles sw Stow on the Wold pop 260 archd and dioc Gloucester

SLAUGHTERFORD parish 1702 Wilts 5-1/4 miles nw Chippenham pop 115 archd Wilts dioc Salisbury

SLAWSTON parish 1559 Leics 5-3/4 miles ne Market Harboro pop

243 archd Leicester dioc Lincoln

SLEAFORD, NEW parish 1575 Lincs 18 miles se Lincoln pop 2,857 pec Prebendary of New Sleaford in Cathedral Church of Lincoln Countess of Huntingdon, Indep, Wesl Meth

SLEAFORD, OLD parish (incl regs of Quarrington) Lincs 1 mile se New Sleaford archd and dioc Lincoln

SLEAGILL township parish Morland Westm pop 184

SLECKBURN, EAST township parish Bedlington co Durham

SLECKBURN, WEST township parish Bedlington co Durham

SLEDDALE, LONG chapelry 1670 parish Kendal Westm

SLEDMERE parish 1696 E R York 7-1/2 miles nw Driffield pop 480 archd East Riding dioc York

SLEEP hamlet parish St Peter, St Albans, Herts pop 722

SLENINGFORD township parish Ripon W R York

SLIMBRIDGE parish 1635 Gloucs 4 miles nw Dursley pop 923 archd and dioc Gloucester Indep

SLINDON township parish Eccleshall Staffs pop 133

SLINDON parish 1558 Sussex 4-1/4 miles nw Arundel pop 539 pec of Archbishop of Canterbury

SLINFOLD parish 1558 Sussex 4 miles nw Horsham pop 682 archd and dioc Chichester

SLINGLEY township parish Seaham co Durham

SLINGSBY parish 1687 N R York 6 miles nw New Malton pop 562 archd Cleveland dioc York

SLIPTON parish 1671 co Northampton 3-1/4 miles nw Thrapstone pop 155 archd Northampton dioc Peterborough

SLOLEY parish 1560 Norfolk 3-1/2 miles ne Coltishall pop 267 archd Norfolk dioc Norwich

SLOUGH village parishes Stoke Poges and Upton Bucks

SLYNE township parish Bolton le Sands Lancs pop 286

SMALESMOUTH township parish Gaystead Northumberland pop 173

SMALLBURGH parish 1561 Norfolk 5-1/4 miles ne Coltishall pop 699 archd Norfolk dioc Norwich

SMALLEY chapelry 1624 Derbys parish Morley 7 miles ne Derby pop 792

SMALLFORD ward parishes St Steven and St Peter St Albans Herts

SMALL HYTHE chapelry parish Tenterden Kent

SMALLWOOD township parish Astbury Ches pop 554 Wesl Meth

SMARDALE township parish Kirkby Stephen Westm pop 52

SMARDEN parish 1632 Kent 8 miles ne Cranbrook pop 1,177 archd and dioc Canterbury Wesl Meth

SMEATON, GREAT parish 1650 N R York 6-1/2 miles nw North-allerton pop 510 archd Richmond dioc Chester

SMEATON, KIRK parish 1604 W R York 6-1/2 miles se Pontefract pop 318 archd and dioc York

SMEATON, LITTLE township parish Birkby N R York pop 222

SMEETH parish 1662 Kent 4-3/4 miles se Ashford pec of Archbishop of Canterbury

SMEETON WESTERBY township parish Kibworth Beauchamp Leics pop 475

SMERRILL chapelry parish Youlgreave Derbys

SMETHCOTT or SMETHCOTE parish 1609 Shrops 9-1/2 miles se Shrewsbury pop 366 archd Salop dioc Lichfield

SMETHSICK township parish Brereton Ches

SMETHWICK chapelry 1732 parish Harborne Staffs 4 miles nw Birmingham pop 2,676 Indep, Calv Meth

SMISBY parish 1720 Derbys 2-1/2 miles nw Ashby de la Zouch pop 324 archd Derby dioc Lichfield

SNAILWELL parish 1629 Cambs 2-3/4 miles n Newmarket pop 236 archd Sudbury dioc Norwich

SNAINTON chapelry 1650 parishes Ebberston and Brompton N R York 9-1/2 miles se Scarboro pop 636 Wesl Meth

SNAITH parish 1568 W R York comp chapelries Armin, Hooke, Rawcliffe, townships Balne, Cowick, Goole, Gowdall, Hick, Hensall, Pollington pop 8,530 23 miles se York pec of Snaith Wesl Meth

SNAPE parish 1560 Suffolk 2-3/4 miles se Saxmundham pop 514 archd Suffolk dioc Norwich

SNAPE township parish Wells N R York pop 656 Wesl Meth

SNAREHILL HOUSE extra parochial 1-3/4 miles s Thetford Norfolk

SNARESTON parish 1559 Leics 7 miles nw Market Bosworth pop 353 archd Leicester dioc Lincoln

SNARFORD parish 1718 Lincs 7 miles sw Market Rasen pop 61 archd Stow dioc Lincoln

SNARGATE parish 1553 Kent 5-1/2 miles nw New Romney pop 85 archd and dioc Canterbury

SNAVE parish 1619 Kent 4-1/2 miles nw New Romney pop 91 archd and dioc Canterbury

SNEAD hamlet parish Rock Worcs

SNEATON parish 1581 N R York 2-1/4 miles sw Whitby pop 230 archd Cleveland dioc York

SNELLAND parish 1654 Lincs 5 miles nw Wragby pop 105 archd and dioc Lincoln

SNELSMORE tything parish Chieveley Berks

SNELSON township parish Rosthern Ches pop 136

SNELSTON parish 1574 Derbys 2-1/2 miles sw Ashbourne pop 484 archd Derby dioc Lichfield Wesl Meth

SNENTON or SNEINTON parish 1650 Notts 3/4 mile e Nottingham pop 3,605 archd Nottingham dioc York

SNETTERTON parish 1669 Norfolk 3 miles n East Harling pop 247 archd Norfolk dioc Norwich

SNETTISHAM parish 1682 Norfolk 6-3/4 miles nw Castle Rising pop 926 archd Norfolk dioc Norwich Wesl Meth

SNEYD township parish Burslem Staffs Wesl Meth

SNIBSTON chapelry parish Packington Leics

SNILESBY township parish Hawnby N R York pop 116

SNITTER township parish Rothbury Northumberland pop 165

SNITTERBY parish (incl regs Waddingham) Lincs 11-1/4 miles nw Market Rasen pop 182 archd Stow dioc Lincoln

SNITTERFIELD parish 1561 Warws 4 miles ne Stratford on Avon pop 770 archd and dioc Worcester

SNITTERTON hamlet parish Darley Derbys

SNITTLEGARTH township parish Torpenhow Cumberland

SNODLAND parish 1559 Kent 3-3/4 miles ne West Malling pop 518 archd and dioc Rochester

SNOREHAM parish (incl regs Latchingdon) Essex 5 miles se Waldon archd Essex dioc London

SNORING, GREAT parish 1560 Norfolk 1-3/4 miles se Little Walsingham pop 437 archd and dioc Norwich

SNORING, LITTLE parish 1559 Norfolk 3-1/4 miles ne Fakenham pop 287 archd and dioc Norwich

SNOWSHILL parish 1593 Gloucs 6 miles ne Winchcombe pop 292 archd and dioc Gloucester

SNYDALE township parish Normanton W R York pop 114

SOBERTON parish 1539 Hamps 3-3/4 miles se Bishops Waltham pop 931 pec of Soberton

SOCKBRIDGE township parish Barton Westm pop 263

SOCKBURN parish 1588 co Durham and W R York 7 miles se Darlington pop 191 archd and dioc Durham

SODBURY, CHIPPING parish 1661 Gloucs 28 miles sw Gloucester pop 1,306 archd and dioc Gloucester Bapt, Soc of Friends

SODBURY, LITTLE parish 1703 Gloucs 2-3/4 miles ne Chipping Sodbury pop 126 archd and dioc Gloucester

SODBURY, OLD parish 1684 Gloucs 1-3/4 miles e Chipping Sodbury pop 729 archd and dioc Gloucester

SOFTLEY township parish St Andrew Auckland co Durham

SOHAM parish 1559 Cambs 5-3/4 miles se Ely pop 3,667 archd Sudbury dioc Norwich Bapt, Indep, Wesl Meth, Unit

SOHAM, EARL parish 1558 Suffolk 3-1/2 miles w Framlingham pop 762 archd Suffolk dioc Norwich Bapt

SOHAM, MONK parish 1712 Suffolk 6 miles nw Framlingham pop 433 archd Suffolk dioc Norwich

SOHO hamlet parish Handsworth Staffs

SOKEHOLME township parish Warsop Notts pop 68

SOLIHULL parish 1538 Warws 13 miles nw Warwick pop 2,878 archd Coventry dioc Lichfield Indep, Roman Cath

SOLLERS HOPE parish 1695 Herefs 7-1/2 miles ne Ross pop 187 archd and dioc Hereford

SOLPORT township parish Stapleton Cumberland pop 354

SOMBOURN, KINGS parish 1672 Hamps 3 miles s Stockbridge pop 1,046 archd and dioc Winchester

SOMBOURN, LITTLE parish incl regs Kings Sombourn pop 84

SOMERBY parish 1751 Leics 6 miles se Melton Mowbray pop 377 archd Leicester dioc Lincoln Wesl Meth

SOMERBY chapelry 1661 parish Corringham Lincs 2-3/4 miles e

Gainsboro

SOMERBY parish 1730 Lincs 4 miles se Grantham pop 282 archd and dioc Lincoln

SOMERBY parish 1661 Lincs 4-1/2 miles e Glandford Brigg pop 21 archd and dioc Lincoln

SOMERCOATES, NORTH parish 1558 Lincs 8-1/4 miles ne Louth pop 753 archd and dioc Lincoln Wesl Meth

SOMERCOATES, SOUTH parish 1558 Lincs 7-1/4 miles ne Louth pop 320 archd and dioc Lincoln

SOMERFORD BOOTHS township parish Astbury Ches pop 297

SOMERFORD, GREAT parish 1707 Wilts 4 miles se Malmesbury pop 500 archd Wilts dioc Salisbury

SOMERFORD KEYNES parish 1560 Wilts 6-1/2 miles w Cricklade pop 327 archd Wilts dioc Salisbury

SOMERFORD, LITTLE parish 1708 Wilts 3-1/2 miles se Malmesbury pop 376 archd Wilts dioc Salisbury

SOMERLEYTON parish 1558 Suffolk 4-1/2 miles nw Lowestoft pop 419 archd Suffolk dioc Norwich

SOMERSHALL HERBERT parish 1538 Derbys 3-1/2 miles ne Uttoxeter pop 117 archd Derby dioc Lichfield

SOMERSBY parish 1730 Lincs 7 miles nw Spilsby pop 69 archd and dioc Lincoln

SOMERSHAM parish 1538 Hunts 8-3/4 miles ne Huntingdon pop 1,402 archd Huntingdon dioc Lincoln Bapt

SOMERSHAM parish 1675 Suffolk 6 miles nw Ipswich pop 446 archd Suffolk dioc Norwich Indep

SOMERSTOWN chapelry parish St Pancras Middlesex

SOMERTON parish 1627 co Oxford 3-1/2 miles se Deddington pop 392 archd and dioc Oxford

SOMERTON parish 1697 Somerset 5 miles nw Ilchester pop 1,786 archd Wells dioc Bath and Wells Indep

SOMERTON parish 1538 Suffolk 7 miles ne Clare pop 141 archd Sudbury dioc Norwich

SOMERTON, EAST parish (incl regs of Winterton) Norfolk 6-1/4 miles nw Caistor pop 54 archd and dioc Norwich

SOMERTON, WEST parish 1736 Norfolk 6-1/4 miles nw Caistor pop 243 archd and dioc Norwich

SOMPTING parish 1546 Sussex 2 miles ne Worthing pop 519 archd and dioc Chichester

SONNING parish 1592 co Oxford 3-1/2 miles ne Reading pop 2,588 pec of Dean of Salisbury Indep

SOOTHILL township parish Dewsbury W R York pop 3,849

SOPLEY parish 1678 Hamps 2-3/4 miles n Christchurch pop 1,012 archd and dioc Winchester Bapt

SOPWORTH parish 1697 Wilts 7-1/2 miles sw Malmesbury pop 222 archd Wilts dioc Salisbury

SOTBY parish 1658 Lincs 5 miles ne Wragby pop 157 archd and dioc Lincoln

SOTHERTON parish 1675 Suffolk 4-1/4 miles ne Halesworth pop 196 archd Suffolk dioc Norwich

SOTTERLEY parish 1557 Suffolk 4-1/2 miles se Beccles pop 243 archd Suffolk dioc Norwich

SOTWELL parish 1684 Berks 1-3/4 miles nw Wallingford pop 157 archd Berks dioc Salisbury

SOUGHTON or SYCHDIN township parish Llansillin Shrops pop 247

SOULBURY parish 1674 Bucks 5 miles nw Leighton Buzzard pop 578 archd Bucks dioc Lincoln Wesl Meth

SOULBY township parish Dacre Cumberland

SOULBY chapelry parish Kirkby Stephen Westm pop 256

SOULDERN parish 1668 co Oxford 4 miles se Deddington pop 599 archd and dioc Oxford Wesl Meth

SOULDROP parish 1670 Beds 5-1/2 miles ne Harrold pop 242 archd Bedford dioc Lincoln

SOULTON township parish Wem Shrops pop 31

SOUND township parish Wybunbury Ches pop 255

SOURTON parish 1722 Devon 4-1/2 miles sw Oakhampton pop 625 archd Totnes dioc Exeter

SOUTHACRE parish 1575 Norfolk 3-1/2 miles nw Swaffham pop 96 archd Norfolk dioc Norwich

SOUTHAM hamlet parish Bishops Cleeve Gloucs

SOUTHAM parish 1539 Warws 10 miles se Warwick pop 1,256 archd Coventry dioc Lichfield Bapt

SOUTH AMBERSHAM Hamps See AMBERSHAM, SOUTH

SOUTHAMPTON seaport, town Hamps 75 miles sw London pop 18,670 borough comp All Saints 1650, Holy Rood 1653, St Lawrence 1751, St Mary 1675, St Michael 1552 archd and dioc Winchester St Mary a pec of Rector of St Mary Indep, Wesl Meth, Bapt, Soc of Friends, Roman Cath

SOUTHBROOM parish 1572 Wilts 1 mile s Devizes archd and dioc Salisbury

SOUTHBORO chapelry parish Tonbridge Kent

SOUTH BURN township parish Kirkburn E R York pop 107

SOUTHCHURCH parish 1695 Essex 1 mile ne Southend pop 401 pec of Archbishop of Canterbury

SOUTHCOATES township parish Drypool E R York pop 1,114

SOUTHCOT tything parish St Mary Reading Berks pop 84

SOUTHEASE parish 1538 Sussex 3-3/4 miles se Lewes pop 142 archd Lewes dioc Chichester

SOUTHEND hamlet parish Prittlewell Essex Indep

SOUTHERNBY BOUND township parish Castle Sowerby Cumberland pop 162

SOUTHERY parish 1706 Norfolk 6-1/2 miles s Downham Market pop 739 archd Norfolk dioc Norwich

SOUTHFIELDS liberty Leics pop 1,608

SOUTHFLEET parish 1558 Kent 3-1/2 miles sw Gravesend pop 624 archd and dioc Rochester

SOUTHGATE chapelry parish Edmonton Middlesex Indep
SOUTH HAMLET hamlet parish Hempstead Gloucs pop 834
SOUTH HILL parish 1538 Cornwall 3-1/4 miles nw Callington pop
530 archd Cornwall dioc Exeter
SOUTHILL parish 1538 Beds comp hamlets Broom, Stanford, township
Southill pop 1,267 archd Bedford dioc Lincoln Bapt
SOUTH MEAD extra parochial liberty near Gloucester Gloucs
SOUTHLEIGH See LEIGH SOUTH
SOUTHMERE parish (incl regs Docking) Norfolk 5 miles sw Burnham
Westgate archd Norfolk dioc Norwich
SOUTHMINSTER Essex See MINSTER, SOUTH
SOUTHOE parish 1670 Hunts 3-1/4 miles nw St Neots pop 283 archd
Huntingdon dioc Lincoln
SOUTHOLT parish 1538 Suffolk 5 miles se Eye pop 193 archd Suffolk
dioc Norwich
SOUTHORPE extra parochial 7 miles ne Gainsboro Lincs pop 36
SOUTHORPE hamlet parish Barnack co Northampton pop 137
SOUTHOVER Sussex See LEWES
SOUTHPORT chapelry 1594 parish North Neols Lancs 9 miles nw
Ormskirk Indep, Wesl Meth
SOUTHPORT Hamps See PORTSEA
SOUTHROP parish 1656 Gloucs 3 miles n Lechlade pop 350 archd and
dioc Gloucester
SOUTHROP tything parish Herriard Hamps
SOUTHROPE township parish Hook Norton co Oxford
SOUTHSEA Hamps See PORTSEA
SOUTHTOWN parish (incl regs Gorleston) Suffolk 1 mile sw Yarmouth
pop 1,304 archd Suffolk dioc Norwich
SOUTHWARK See LONDON south bank of river Thames in Surrey
comp Christchurch 1671, St George the Martyr 1602, St John Horl-
seydown 1732, St Olave 1685, St Savior 1570, St Thomas 1614
Consistory Court of Bishop of Winchester for letters of Admin-
istrations, Archd Court of Surrey for Wills
SOUTHWELL parish 1559 Notts 14 miles ne Nottingham pop 3,384
pec Chapter of Collegiate Church of Southwell Bapt, Wesl Meth
SOUTHWELL PARK parish Hargrave Suffolk
SOUTHWICK township parish Monk Wearmouth co Durham Wesl Meth
SOUTHWICK parish 1732 co Northampton 2-3/4 miles nw Oundle pop
154 archd Northampton dioc Peterborough
SOUTHWICK parish 1628 Hamps 3-1/4 miles ne Farsham pop 723
archd and dioc Winchester
SOUTHWICK parish 1653 Sussex 1-1/2 miles e New Shoreham pop
502 archd Lewes dioc Chichester
SOUTHWICK chapelry parish North Bradley Wilts Bapt, Wesl Meth
SOUTHWOLD borough parish 1602 sep juris 36 miles ne Ipswich pop
1,876 archd Suffolk dioc Norwich Bapt, Indep, Wesl Meth
SOUTHWOOD parish 1630 Norfolk 3-3/4 miles sw Acle pop 54 archd
and dioc Norwich

SOUTHWORTH township parish Winwick Lancs

SOWE parish 1538 Warws 3 miles ne Coventry pop 1,414 archd Coventry dioc Lichfield

SOWERBY township parish St Michael Lancs

SOWERBY chapelry 1569 parish Thirsk N R York pop 756 archd Cleveland dioc York

SOWERBY chapelry 1643 parish Halifax W R York 4 miles sw Halifax pop 6,457 archd and dioc York Indep, Wesl Meth

SOWERBY BRIDGE chapelry 1709 parish Halifax W R York 2-3/4 miles sw Halifax archd and dioc York Wesl Meth

SOWERBY, CASTLE parish 1711 Cumberland 3-1/4 miles se Hesket Newmarket pop 961 archd and dioc Carlisle

SOWERBY, TEMPLE chapelry 1669 parish Kirkby Thorne Westm 7 miles nw Appleby pop 438 archd and dioc Carlisle Indep

SOWERBY UNDER COTLIFFE township parish Kirby Sigston N R York pop 67

SOWTON parish 1560 Devon 4 miles e Exeter pop 391 archd and dioc Exeter

SOYLAND township parish Halifax W R York pop 3,589

SPALDING parish 1538 44 miles se Lincoln pop 6,497 archd and dioc Lincoln Bapt, Soc of Friends, Indep, Wesl Meth

SPALDINGTON township parish Bubwith E R York pop 352

SPALDWICK parish 1688 Hunts 3-3/4 miles ne Kimbolton pop 388 pec Prebendary of Longstowe in Cathedral Church of Lincoln Bapt, Indep

SPALFORD hamlet parish North Clifton Notts pop 80

SPANDY parish 1681 Lincs 4-1/4 miles ne Falkingham pop 84 archd and dioc Lincoln

SPARHAM parish 1573 Norfolk 3 miles sw Reepham pop 355 archd Norfolk dioc Norwich

SPARKFORD parish 1729 Somerset 4-1/4 miles sw Castle Cary pop 257 archd Wells dioc Bath and Wells

SPARSHOLT parish 1558 Berks 3-1/4 miles w Wantage pop 874 archd Berks dioc Salisbury

SPARSHOLT parish 1602 Hamps 3-3/4 miles nw Winchester pop 357 archd and dioc Winchester

SPAUNTON township parish Lastingham N R York pop 138

SPAXTON parish 1558 Somerset 5 miles w Bridgewater pop 963 archd Taunton dioc Bath and Wells

SPECTON chapelry parish Bridlington E R York pop 111 incl regs Bridlington

SPEEN parish 1629 Berks comp tythings Speenhamland, Benham, Church Speen, township Wood Speen with Bagnor 1 mile w Newbury pop 3,044 archd Berks dioc Salisbury

SPEEN, CHURCH tything parish Speen Berks

SPEEN, WOOD township parish Speen Berks

SPEENHAMLAND hamlet parish Speen Berks

SPEETON incl regs Bridlington York

SPEKE township parish Childwall Lancs pop 514

SPELDHURST parish 1559 Kent 3 miles nw Tonbridge Wells pop 2,640 archd and dioc Rochester

SPELSBURY parish 1539 co Oxford 5 miles se Chipping Norton pop 609 archd and dioc Oxford

SPENITHORN parish 1573 N R York comp townships Bellerby Harmby Spenithorn pop 848 1 mile ne Middleham archd Richmond dioc Chester

SPERNALL parish 1676 Warws 4 miles n Alcester pop 95 archd and dioc Worcester

SPETCHLEY parish 1539 Worcs 3-3/4 miles se Worcester pop 117 archd and dioc Worcester

SPETISBURY parish 1705 Dorset 3 miles se Blandford Forum pop 667 archd Dorset dioc Bristol

SPEXHALL parish 1538 Suffolk 2 miles nw Halesworth archd Suffolk dioc Norwich

SPILSBY parish 1562 Lincs 31 miles e Lincoln pop 1,384 archd and dioc Lincoln Indep, Wesl Meth

SPINDLESTONE township parish Bambrough Northumberland pop 101

SPITALFIELDS, CHRISTCHURCH parish 1538 Middlesex pop 17,949 ne London Commissary of London Indep, Calv Meth, Wesl Meth

SPITTAL ON THE STREET chapelry parish Glentworth Lincs

SPITTLE township parish Bebbington Ches

SPITTLE or SPITTAL village parish Tweedmouth Northumberland Presb

SPITTLE township parish Ovingham Northumberland pop 7

SPITTLE township parish Fangfoss E R York

SPITTLE HILL township parish Mitford Northumberland pop 11

SPITTLEGATE township parish Grantham Lincs pop 1,063

SPIXWORTH parish 1551 Norfolk 4-3/4 miles ne Norwich pop 54 archd and dioc Norwich

SPOFFORTH parish 1559 W R York comp chapelry Wetherby, townships Follifoot, Linton, Plompton, Little Ribston, Spofforth, Stockeld pop 3,233 3-1/4 miles nw Wetherby archd and dioc York Wesl Meth

SPONDON parish 1653 Derbys 3-1/4 miles se Derby pop 1,867 archd Derby dioc Lichfield Wesl Meth

SPOONBED tything parish Painswick Gloucs pop 899

SPORLE parish 1562 Norfolk 2-1/2 miles ne Swaffham pop 746 archd Norfolk dioc Norwich

SPOTLAND chapelry parish Rochdale Lancs pop 15,325

SPRATTON parish 1536 co Northampton 6-3/4 miles nw Northampton pop 1,012 archd Northampton dioc Peterborough

SPREYTON parish 1563 Devon 8 miles ne Oakhampton pop 623 archd and dioc Exeter

SPRIDLINGTON parish 1556 Lincs 9 miles sw Market Rasen pop 250 archd Stow dioc Lincoln

SPRINGFIELD parish 1653 Essex 1 mile ne Chelmsford pop 1,851 archd Essex dioc London

SPRINGTHORPE parish 1588 Lincs 4-1/2 miles se Gainsboro pop 194 archd Stow dioc Lincoln

SPROATLEY parish 1679 E R York 7 miles ne Hull pop 366 archd East Riding dioc York Wesl Meth

SPROSTON township parish Middlewich Ches pop 128

SPROTBORO parish 1559 W R York pop 500 2-3/4 miles sw Doncaster archd and dioc York

SPROUGHTON parish 1541 Suffolk 3 miles nw Ipswich pop 524 archd and dioc Norwich

SPROWSTON parish 1690 Norfolk 3 miles ne Norwich pop 1,179 pec Dean and Chapter of Norwich

SPROXTON parish 1640 Leics 6 miles ne Melton Mowbray pop 378 archd Leicester dioc Lincoln Wesl Meth

SPROXTON township parish Helmsley N R York pop 195

SPURM HEAD or SPURN HEAD in parish Kilnsea E R York

SPURSTON township parish Bunbury Ches pop 588

STADHAMPTON parish 1567 co Oxford 8 miles se Oxford pop 313 pec of Dorchester

STADMERSLOS township parish Wolstanton Staffs pop 290

STAFFIELD or STAFFOL township parish Kirk Oswald Cumberland pop 265

STAFFORD hamlet parish Barwick Somerset

STAFFORD borough, market town Staffs comp St Mary 1559, St Chad 1636, chapelry Marston, townships Salt with Enson, Tillington, Worston, Whitgreave, liberty Hopton, Coton 136 miles nw London pop 7,065 St Mary in archd Stafford dioc Lichfield, St Chad is pec of Prebendary of Prees in Cathedral Church of Lichfield Soc of Friends, Indep, Wesl Meth, Roman Cath

STAFFORD, WEST parish 1570 Dorset 2-1/2 miles se Dorchester archd Dorset dioc Bristol

STAGBATCH hamlet parish Leominster Herefs

STAGSDEN parish 1670 Beds 5-1/2 miles sw Bedford pop 597 archd Beds dioc Lincoln

STAINBOROUGH chapelry parish Silkston W R York pop 304

STAINBURN township parish Workington Cumberland pop 174

STAINBURN chapelry 1803 parish Kirby Overblow W R York 4-1/4 miles ne Otley pop 289 pec honour of Knaresboro

STAINBY parish 1653 Lincs 2-1/2 miles sw Colsterworth pop 186 archd and dioc Lincoln

STAINDROP parish 1635 co Durham comp townships Hilton, Langley Dale with Shotton, Raby with Keverstone, Wackerfield, Woodland pop 2,395 5-1/2 miles ne Barnard Castle archd and dioc Durham Soc of Friends, Wesl Meth, Presb

STAINES parish 1644 Middlesex 10 miles sw Brentford pop 2,486 archd Middlesex dioc London Bapt, Soc of Friends, Indep

STAINFIELD chapelry parish Hacconby Lincs

STAINFIELD parish 1680 Lincs 4 miles sw Wragby pop 136 archd

and dioc Lincoln

STAINFORTH township parish Giggleswick W R York pop 263

STAINFORTH township parish Hatfield W R York pop 852 Wesl Meth, Unit

STAININGHALL parish Norfolk 2 miles sw Colteshall archd and dioc Norwich

STAININGTON chapelry parish Eccleshall W R York

STAINLAND township 1782 parish Halifax W R York 4-1/2 miles sw Halifax pop 3,037 Indep

STAINLEY SOUTH Yorks See STANLEY, SOUTH

STAINMORE chapelry 1708 parish Brough Westm pop 707

STAINSBY township parish Ault Hucknall co Derbys

STAINSBY hamlet parish Ashby Puerorum Lincs

STAINSILKER or STAINSACRE township parish Whitby N R York

STAINTON township parish Stanwix Cumberland

STAINTON township parish Dacre Cumberland

STAINTON township parish Urswick Lancs

STAINTON chapelry parish Heversham Westm Indep

STAINTON township parish Downholme N R York pop 44

STAINTON parish 1551 N R York comp townships Hemington, Ingleby, Barwick, Maltby, Stainton, Thornaby pop 1,000 archd Cleveland dioc York 5 miles nw Stokesley

STAINTON parish 1566 W R York 7 miles sw Doncaster pop 254 archd and dioc York

STAINTON BY LANGWORTH parish 1720 Lincs 5 miles w Wragby pop 238 archd and dioc Lincoln

STAINTON DALE township parish Scalby N R York

STAINTON, GREAT parish 1561 co Durham 7 miles ne Darlington pop 248 archd and dioc Durham

STAINTON LE VALE parish 1757 Lincs 6 miles ne Market Rasen pop 118 archd and dioc Lincoln

STAINTON, LITTLE township parish Bishopton co Durham pop 54

STAINTON, MARKET parish 1689 Lincs 7 miles ne Wragby pop 132 archd and dioc Lincoln

ST ALBANS See ALBANS, ST Herts

STALBRIDGE parish 1691 Dorset 7-1/2 miles ne Sherborne pop 1,773 archd Dorset dioc Bristol

STALHAM parish 1561 Norfolk 7-1/4 miles se North Walsham pop 613 archd Norfolk dioc Norwich Wesl Meth

STALISFIELD parish 1699 Kent 2-1/4 miles ne Charing pop 342 archd and dioc Canterbury

STALLINGBORO parish 1549 Lincs 7-1/4 miles nw Grimsby pop 366 archd and dioc Lincoln Wesl Meth

STALLING BUSK chapelry 1742 parish Aysgarth N R York archd Richmond dioc Chester

STALMINE chapelry 1593 parish Lancaster Lancs pop 504

STALYBRIDGE chapelry 1776 partly in township Hartshead parish Aston under Lyne Lancs, partly in township Duckingfield parish

Stockport Ches, partly in Stalybridge parish Mottram in Long-
dendale Ches 8 miles ne Stockport pop 12,000 archd and dioc
Chester Bapt, Wesl Meth, New Connection Meth

STAMBORNE parish 1559 Essex 5-1/4 miles nw Castle Hedingham
pop 475 Commissary of Essex and Herts, concurrently with
Consistorial Court of Bishop of London Indep

STAMBRIDGE, GREAT parish 1563 Essex 1-3/4 miles e Rochford
pop 405 archd Essex dioc London

STAMBRIDGE, LITTLE parish 1659 Essex 1-1/2 miles ne Rochford
pop 105 archd Essex dioc London

STAMFORD borough Lincs 46 miles se Lincoln pop 5,837 sep juris
comp All Saints 1560, St George 1560, St John 1561, St Mary 1569,
St Michael 1560 archd and dioc Lincoln Wesl Meth, Roman Cath

STAMFORD township parish Embleton Northumberland pop 94

STAMFORD BARON See MARTIN, ST STAMFORD BARON co Northampton

STAMFORD BRIDGE, EAST township parish Catton E R York pop
385

STAMFORD BRIDGE, WEST township parish Catton E R York pop
161 Wesl Meth

STAMFORD HILL See HACKNEY Middlesex

STAMFORDHAM parish 1662 Northumberland 12-1/2 miles nw Newcastle comp chapelry Ryall, townships Bitchfield, Blackheddon,
Cheeseburn Grange, Fenwick, Hawkwell, Heugh, Ingoe, Kearsley,
East Matsen, West Matsen, Nesbit, Ouston, Walridge pop 1,736
archd Northumberland dioc Durham Presb

STANNALL township parish Lancaster Lancs

STANBRIDGE Dorset See HINTON PARVA

STANCILL township parish Tickhill W R York pop 66

STANDBRIDGE chapelry 1560 Beds 3-1/4 miles se Leighton Buzzard
pop 416 pec of Prebendary of Leighton Buzzard

STANDERWICK parish (incl regs Beckington) Somerset 4 miles ne
Frome pop 97 archd Wells dioc Bath and Wells

STANDFORD parish 1556 Kent 3-1/2 miles nw Hythe pop 243 archd
and dioc Canterbury

STANDGROUND parish 1538 Hunts 1 mile se Peterboro pop 1,242
archd Huntingdon dioc Lincoln

STANDHILL hamlet parish Pirton co Oxford

STANDISH parish 1559 Gloucs 6 miles nw Stroud pop 536 archd and
dioc Gloucester

STANDISH parish 1558 Lancs comp chapelry Coppull, townships Adlington, Anderton, Chanrock Heath, Charnock Richard, Duxbury,
Shevington, Standish with Langtree, Welsh Whittle, Worthington
pop 7,719 archd and dioc Chester

STANDLAKE parish 1560 co Oxford 5-1/2 miles se Witney pop 669
archd and dioc Oxford

STANDLINCH parish Wilts 4-3/4 miles se Salisbury pop 31

STANDON parish 1671 Herts 8 miles ne Hertford pop 2,272 archd

243 pec of Knaresborough

STANLOW HOUSE extra parochial Ches 8 miles ne Chester pop 13

STANMER parish 1558 Sussex 4 miles ne Brighton pop 123 pec of
    Archbishop of Canterbury

STANMORE, GREAT parish 1600 Middlesex 10 miles nw London pop
    1,144 Commissary of London Consistorial Court of the Bishop
    of London Indep

STANMORE, LITTLE parish 1558 Middlesex 1/2 mile nw Edgeward
    pop 867 Commissary of London Consistorial Court of the Bishop
    of London

STANNEY, GREAT township parish Stoke Ches pop 32

STANNEY, LITTLE township parish Stoke Ches pop 201

STANNINGFIELD parish 1561 Suffolk 5-1/4 miles se Bury St Edmunds
    pop 306 archd Sudbury dioc Norwich

STANNINGTON parish 1658 Northumberland 5 miles se Morpeth pop
    1,021 archd Northumberland dioc Durham Wesl Meth, Unit

STANNINGTON chapelry parish Ecclesfield W R York

STANSFIELD parish 1538 Suffolk 5-1/4 miles ne Clare pop 470 archd
    Sudbury dioc Norwich

STANSFIELD township parish Halifax W R York pop 8,262

STANSTEAD parish 1564 Kent 2 miles n Wrotham pop 262 pec of
    Archbishop of Canterbury

STANSTEAD parish 1570 Suffolk 5-1/4 miles ne Clare pop 353 archd
    Sudbury dioc Norwich

STANSTEAD, ABBOTS' parish 1678 Herts 2-3/4 miles ne Hoddesden
    pop 966 archd Middlesex dioc London

STANSTED MOUNTFITCHET parish 1560 Essex 18 miles nw Chelms-
    ford pop 1,560 Commissary of Essex and Herts, Consistorial
    Court of the Bishop of London

STANTHORNE township parish Davenham Ches pop 149

STANTON chapelry parish Youlgrave Derbys pop 744

STANTON township parish Stapenhill Derbys pop 1,182

STANTON parish 1572 Gloucs 4-3/4 miles ne Winchcombe pop 293
    archd and dioc Gloucester

STANTON township parish Longhorsley Northumberland pop 135

STANTON township parish Ellastone Staffs pop 371

STANTON, ALL SAINTS parish 1584 Suffolk 3-1/4 miles ne Ixworth
    pop 1,035 archd Sudbury dioc Norwich

STANTON ST BERNARD parish 1568 Wilts 5-3/4 miles e Devizes pop
    319 archd Wilts dioc Salisbury

STANTON ST JOHN parish 1570 Suffolk 3 miles ne Ixworth archd Sud-
    bury dioc Norwich

STANTON BURY parish 1653 Bucks 3 miles sw Newport Pagnell pop
    51 archd Buckingham dioc Lincoln

STANTON BY BRIDGE parish 1664 Derbys 6-3/4 miles se Derby
    pop 215 archd Derby dioc Lichfield

STANTON BY DALE ABBEY parish 1604 Derbys 9 miles ne Derby
    pop 740 archd Derby dioc Lichfield

Middlesex dioc London Wesl Meth, Bapt

STANDON parish 1558 Staffs 4 miles nw Eccleshall pop 420
  Stafford dioc Lichfield

STANE parish Lincs 6-1/2 miles n Alford archd and dioc Li

STANFIELD parish 1558 Norfolk 6 miles nw East Dereham
  archd and dioc Norwich

STANFORD hamlet parish Southill Beds

STANFORD Kent See STAMFORD

STANFORD parish 1754 Norfolk 6 miles sw Watton pop 153
  Norfolk dioc Norwich

STANFORD ON AVON parish 1607 co Northampton 5 miles s
  worth pop 24 archd Northampton dioc Peterborough

STANFORD ON TEME parish 1595 Worcs 8 miles ne Bromy
  198 archd Salop dioc Hereford

STANFORD, BISHOP'S parish 1699 Herefs 3-1/2 miles se B
  pop 362 archd and dioc Hereford

STANFORD DINGLEY parish 1538 Berks 8-1/2 miles ne Spe
  land pop 139 archd Berks dioc Salisbury

STANFORD IN THE VALE parish 1558 Berks 4 miles se Gre
  ringdon pop 1,016 archd Berks dioc Salisbury

STANFORD, KING'S township parish Bishop's Stanford Here
  miles se Bromyard pop 93

STANFORD LE HOPE parish 1680 Essex 1-1/2 miles se Hor
  Hill pop 330 archd Essex dioc London

STANFORD RIVERS parish 1538 Essex 2 miles sw Chipping
  pop 905 archd Essex dioc London Indep

STANFORD UPON SOAR parish 1635 Notts 2-1/2 miles ne L
  borough pop 129 archd Nottingham dioc York

STANGAGE Essex See STEEPLE

STANHOE parish 1558 Norfolk 4 miles sw Burnham Westgate
  archd Norfolk dioc Norwich

STANHOPE parish 1595 co Durham comp townships Forest
  Newland Side, Park Quarter, Stanhope Quarter pop 9,541
  and dioc Durham Wesl Meth

STANION parish 1703 co Northampton 4-3/4 miles se Rockin
  pop 313 archd Northampton dioc Peterborough Wesl Me

STANLEY chapelry parish Spondon 1675 Derbys pop 391

STANLEY township parish Leek Staffs pop 118

STANLEY chapelry parish Wakefield W R York pop 5,047

STANLEY, KING'S parish 1573 Gloucs 3-1/4 miles sw Strouc
  2,438 archd and dioc Gloucester Bapt

STANLEY, ST LEONARD parish 1570 Gloucs 4-1/4 miles sw
  pop 942 archd and dioc Gloucester

STANLEY, NORTH township with Sleningford parish Ripon W
  pop 407

STANLEY PONTLARGE parish Gloucs 2-3/4 miles nw Winch
  pop 62 archd and dioc Gloucester

STANLEY, SOUTH parish 1658 W R York 2-3/4 miles ne Rip

Middlesex dioc London Wesl Meth, Bapt

STANDON parish 1558 Staffs 4 miles nw Eccleshall pop 420 archd Stafford dioc Lichfield

STANE parish Lincs 6-1/2 miles n Alford archd and dioc Lincoln

STANFIELD parish 1558 Norfolk 6 miles nw East Dereham pop 234 archd and dioc Norwich

STANFORD hamlet parish Southill Beds

STANFORD Kent See STAMFORD

STANFORD parish 1754 Norfolk 6 miles sw Watton pop 153 archd Norfolk dioc Norwich

STANFORD ON AVON parish 1607 co Northampton 5 miles se Lutterworth pop 24 archd Northampton dioc Peterborough

STANFORD ON TEME parish 1595 Worcs 8 miles ne Bromyard pop 198 archd Salop dioc Hereford

STANFORD, BISHOP'S parish 1699 Herefs 3-1/2 miles se Bromyard pop 362 archd and dioc Hereford

STANFORD DINGLEY parish 1538 Berks 8-1/2 miles ne Speenhamaland pop 139 archd Berks dioc Salisbury

STANFORD IN THE VALE parish 1558 Berks 4 miles se Great Farringdon pop 1,016 archd Berks dioc Salisbury

STANFORD, KING'S township parish Bishop's Stanford Herefs 3-1/2 miles se Bromyard pop 93

STANFORD LE HOPE parish 1680 Essex 1-1/2 miles se Horndon on Hill pop 330 archd Essex dioc London

STANFORD RIVERS parish 1538 Essex 2 miles sw Chipping Ongar pop 905 archd Essex dioc London Indep

STANFORD UPON SOAR parish 1635 Notts 2-1/2 miles ne Loughborough pop 129 archd Nottingham dioc York

STANGAGE Essex See STEEPLE

STANHOE parish 1558 Norfolk 4 miles sw Burnham Westgate pop 436 archd Norfolk dioc Norwich

STANHOPE parish 1595 co Durham comp townships Forest Quarter, Newland Side, Park Quarter, Stanhope Quarter pop 9,541 archd and dioc Durham Wesl Meth

STANION parish 1703 co Northampton 4-3/4 miles se Rockingham pop 313 archd Northampton dioc Peterborough Wesl Meth

STANLEY chapelry parish Spondon 1675 Derbys pop 391

STANLEY township parish Leek Staffs pop 118

STANLEY chapelry parish Wakefield W R York pop 5,047

STANLEY, KING'S parish 1573 Gloucs 3-1/4 miles sw Stroud pop 2,438 archd and dioc Gloucester Bapt

STANLEY, ST LEONARD parish 1570 Gloucs 4-1/4 miles sw Stroud pop 942 archd and dioc Gloucester

STANLEY, NORTH township with Sleningford parish Ripon W R York pop 407

STANLEY PONTLARGE parish Gloucs 2-3/4 miles nw Winchcombe pop 62 archd and dioc Gloucester

STANLEY, SOUTH parish 1658 W R York 2-3/4 miles ne Ripley pop

243 pec of Knaresborough

STANLOW HOUSE extra parochial Ches 8 miles ne Chester pop 13

STANMER parish 1558 Sussex 4 miles ne Brighton pop 123 pec of
Archbishop of Canterbury

STANMORE, GREAT parish 1600 Middlesex 10 miles nw London pop
1,144 Commissary of London Consistorial Court of the Bishop
of London Indep

STANMORE, LITTLE parish 1558 Middlesex 1/2 mile nw Edgeward
pop 867 Commissary of London Consistorial Court of the Bishop
of London

STANNEY, GREAT township parish Stoke Ches pop 32

STANNEY, LITTLE township parish Stoke Ches pop 201

STANNINGFIELD parish 1561 Suffolk 5-1/4 miles se Bury St Edmunds
pop 306 archd Sudbury dioc Norwich

STANNINGTON parish 1658 Northumberland 5 miles se Morpeth pop
1,021 archd Northumberland dioc Durham Wesl Meth, Unit

STANNINGTON chapelry parish Ecclesfield W R York

STANSFIELD parish 1538 Suffolk 5-1/4 miles ne Clare pop 470 archd
Sudbury dioc Norwich

STANSFIELD township parish Halifax W R York pop 8,262

STANSTEAD parish 1564 Kent 2 miles n Wrotham pop 262 pec of
Archbishop of Canterbury

STANSTEAD parish 1570 Suffolk 5-1/4 miles ne Clare pop 353 archd
Sudbury dioc Norwich

STANSTEAD, ABBOTS' parish 1678 Herts 2-3/4 miles ne Hoddesden
pop 966 archd Middlesex dioc London

STANSTED MOUNTFITCHET parish 1560 Essex 18 miles nw Chelmsford pop 1,560 Commissary of Essex and Herts, Consistorial
Court of the Bishop of London

STANTHORNE township parish Davenham Ches pop 149

STANTON chapelry parish Youlgrave Derbys pop 744

STANTON township parish Stapenhill Derbys pop 1,182

STANTON parish 1572 Gloucs 4-3/4 miles ne Winchcombe pop 293
archd and dioc Gloucester

STANTON township parish Longhorsley Northumberland pop 135

STANTON township parish Ellastone Staffs pop 371

STANTON, ALL SAINTS parish 1584 Suffolk 3-1/4 miles ne Ixworth
pop 1,035 archd Sudbury dioc Norwich

STANTON ST BERNARD parish 1568 Wilts 5-3/4 miles e Devizes pop
319 archd Wilts dioc Salisbury

STANTON ST JOHN parish 1570 Suffolk 3 miles ne Ixworth archd Sudbury dioc Norwich

STANTON BURY parish 1653 Bucks 3 miles sw Newport Pagnell pop
51 archd Buckingham dioc Lincoln

STANTON BY BRIDGE parish 1664 Derbys 6-3/4 miles se Derby
pop 215 archd Derby dioc Lichfield

STANTON BY DALE ABBEY parish 1604 Derbys 9 miles ne Derby
pop 740 archd Derby dioc Lichfield

STANTON DREW parish 1653 Somerset 1-1/2 miles sw Pensford pop 731 archd Bath dioc Bath and Wells

STANTON FEN Hunts See FEN STANTON

STANTON FITZWARREN parish 1542 Wilts 2-1/4 miles sw Highworth pop 188 archd Wilts dioc Salisbury

STANTON, ST GABRIEL chapelry parish Whitchurch Dorset pop 101

STANTON HARCOURT parish 1568 co Oxford 4-1/2 miles se Witney pop 657 archd and dioc Oxford

STANTON, ST JOHN'S parish 1654 co Oxford 4-1/2 miles ne Oxford pop 470 archd and dioc Oxford

STANTON, LACY parish 1561 Shrops 3 miles nw Ludlow pop 1,467 archd Salop dioc Hereford

STANTON, LONG parish 1672 Cambs 6-1/4 miles nw Cambridge pop 428 archd and dioc Ely Wesl Meth

STANTON, LONG parish 1559 Cambs 5-1/2 miles nw Cambridge pop 127 archd and dioc Ely

STANTON, LONG parish 1568 Shrops 7-3/4 miles sw Much Wenlock pop 278 archd Salop dioc Hereford

STANTON ON THE WOLDS parish 1735 Notts 7-1/2 miles se Nottingham pop 125 archd Nottingham dioc York

STANTON PRIOR parish 1572 Somerset 5 miles sw Bath pop 159 archd Bath dioc Bath and Wells

STANTON, ST QUINTIN parish 1679 Wilts 4-1/4 miles nw Chippenham pop 317 archd Wilts dioc Salisbury

STANTON STONEY parish 1558 Leics 4-1/4 miles ne Hinckley pop 549 archd Leicester dioc Lincoln

STANTON UNDER BARDON chapelry parish Thornton Leics 9 miles nw Leicester pop 295 Wesl Meth

STANTON UPON ARROW parish 1558 Herefs 5-1/2 miles ne Kington pop 393 archd and dioc Hereford

STANTON UPON HINE HEATH parish 1655 Shrops comp townships Booley, Harcourt, High Hatton, Moston, Stanton 5-1/2 miles se Wem pop 722 archd Salop dioc Lichfield

STANWAY parish 1704 Essex 4 miles sw Colchester pop 665 archd Colchester dioc London

STANWAY parish 1573 Gloucs 3-1/2 miles ne Winchcombe pop 401 archd and dioc Gloucester

STANWELL parish 1632 Middlesex 2-3/4 miles ne Staines pop 1,386 archd Middlesex dioc Peterborough

STANWICK parish 1550 co Northampton 2-1/4 miles ne Higham Ferrers pop 503 archd Northampton dioc Peterborough Wesl Meth

STANWICK ST JOHN parish 1693 N R York comp townships Aldbrough, Caldwell, Easy Layton, Stanwick St John, part of Stapleton 7-1/2 miles ne Richmond pop 955 archd Richmond dioc Chester

STANWIX parish 1660 Cumberland comp townships Cargo or Craghow, Stainton in Cumberland, Etterby, Houghton, Linstock, Rickerby, Stanwix, Tarraby pop 1,788 archd and dioc Carlisle

STAPELEY township parish Wybunbury Ches pop 356

STAPLEY tything parish Odiham Hamps

STAPENHILL parish 1680 Derbys 1 mile se Burton upon Trent pop 1,926 archd Derby dioc Lichfield

STAPLE tything parish Tisbury Wilts

STAPLE FITZPAINE parish 1684 Somerset 5 miles se Taunton pop 415 archd Taunton dioc Bath and Wells

STAPLE NEXT WINGHAM parish 1544 Kent 1-3/4 miles se Wingham pop 503 archd and dioc Canterbury

STAPLEFORD parish 1707 Cambs 5-1/4 miles se Cambridge pop 464 archd and dioc Ely

STAPLEFORD parish 1578 Herts 3-1/4 miles nw Hertford pop 237 archd Huntingdon dioc Lincoln

STAPLEFORD parish 1579 Leics 4 miles se Melton Mowbray pop 185 archd Leicester dioc Lincoln

STAPLEFORD parish 1695 Lincs 6-1/2 miles ne Newark pop 185 archd and dioc Lincoln

STAPLEFORD parish 1655 Notts 5-3/4 miles sw Nottingham pop 1,533 archd Nottingham dioc York Wesl Meth

STAPLEFORD parish 1637 Wilts 4-1/2 miles nw Wilton pop 337 archd and dioc Salisbury

STAPLEFORD, ABBOT'S parish 1653 Essex 5-3/4 miles se Epping pop 507 archd Essex dioc London

STAPLEFORD BRUEN township parish Tarvin Ches pop 159

STAPLEFORD FOULK township parish Tarvin Ches pop 244

STAPLEFORD, TAWNEY parish 1558 Essex 3-3/4 miles se Epping pop 297 archd Essex dioc London

STAPLEGATE extra parochial district northern suburb of city of Canterbury Kent pop 247

STAPLEGROVE parish 1558 Somerset 1-3/4 miles nw Taunton pop 457 archd Taunton dioc Bath and Wells

STAPLEHURST parish 1538 Kent 4 miles ne Cranbrook pop 1,484 archd and dioc Canterbury Indep

STAPLETON parish 1725 Cumberland comp townships Belbank, Solport, Stapleton, Trough pop 1,097 archd and dioc Carlisle

STAPLETON parish 1720 Gloucs 2-1/2 miles ne Bristol pop 2,176 pec of Bishop of Bristol

STAPLETON township parish Presteign Herefs pop 156

STAPLETON chapelry parish Barwell Leics 5 miles ne Hinckley pop 249

STAPLETON parish 1630 Shrops 6 miles sw Shrewsbury pop 235 archd Salop dioc Lichfield

STAPLETON township parishes St John Stanwick and Croft N R York pop 121

STAPLETON township parish Darrington W R York pop 107

STARBOTTON township parish Kettlewell W R York

STARCROSS small port parish Kenton Devon Wesl Meth

STARSTON parish 1558 Norfolk 1-1/4 miles nw Harleston pop 449 archd Norfolk dioc Norwich

STARTFORTH parish 1668 N R York 3/4 mile sw Barnard Castle pop 632 archd Richmond dioc Chester

STATFOLD parish Staffs 3-1/4 miles ne Tamworth pop 41 archd Stafford dioc Lichfield

STATH DIVISION tything parish Stoke St Gregory Somerset

STATHERN parish 1567 Leics 8-3/4 miles ne Melton Mowbray pop 481 archd Leicester dioc Lincoln

STAUGHTON, GREAT parish 1540 Hunts 3-1/4 miles se Kimbolton pop 1,191 archd Huntingdon dioc Lincoln

STAUGHTON, LITTLE parish 1598 Beds 4 miles se Kimbolton pop 455 archd Bedford dioc Lincoln

STAUNTON township parish Gainford co Durham pop 324

STAUNTON parish 1653 Gloucs 3-1/2 miles ne Monmouth pop 204 archd and dioc Gloucester

STAUNTON parish 1654 Notts 6-3/4 miles s Newark pop 173 archd Nottingham dioc York

STAUNTON LONG Shrops See STANTON, LONG

STAUNTON ON ARROW Herefs See STANTON UPON ARROW

STAUNTON parish 1559 Worcs 6 miles ne Newent pop 348 archd and dioc Worcester

STAUNTON HARROLD chapelry parish Breedon Leics 3-1/2 miles ne Ashby de la Zouch pop 342

STAUNTON UPON WYE parish 1677 Herefs 8-3/4 miles nw Hereford pop 544 archd and dioc Hereford

STAUNTON WHITE parish Somerset See WHIT STAUNTON

STAVELEY parish 1702 Derbys 4-3/4 miles ne Chesterfield pop 2,920 archd Derby dioc Lichfield

STAVELEY chapelry (incl regs Cartmel) Lancs 9 miles ne Ulverstone pop 326

STAVELEY parish 1558 W R York 3 miles sw Bofroughbridge pop 330 pec of Knaresborough

STAVELEY, NETHER township parish Kendal pop 190

STAVELEY, OVER chapelry 1651 parish Kendal Westm 5 miles nw Kendal pop 412 archd Richmond dioc Chester

STAVERTON parish 1614 Devon 3-1/4 miles nw Totnes pop 1,055 pec Dean and Chapter of Exeter

STAVERTON parish 1542 Gloucs 4-3/4 miles nw Cheltenham pop 245 pec of Deerhurst

STAVERTON parish 1564 co Northampton 2 miles sw Daventry pop 475 archd Northampton dioc Peterborough

STAVERTON chapelry parish Towbridge 1675 Wilts 2-1/2 miles n Trowbridge

STAWELL chapelry 1685 parish Moorlinch Somerset 5 miles ne Bridgewater pop 214

STAWLEY parish 1653 Somerset 3 miles sw Wiveliscombe pop 180 archd Taunton dioc Bath and Wells

STAXTON township parish Willerby E R York pop 260 Wesl Meth

STAYLEY township parish Mottram Longden Dale Ches pop 2,440

STAYTHORPE township parish Averham Notts pop 61

STEAN parish (incl regs Hinton) co Northampton 2-3/4 miles nw Brackley pop 24 archd Northampton dioc Peterborough

STEARSBY hamlet parish Bransby N R York

STEBBING parish 1712 Essex 3-1/4 miles ne Great Dunmow pop 1,434 Commissary of Essex and Herts, Consistorial Court of Bishop of London Indep

STEDHAM parish 1538 Sussex 2-1/4 miles nw Midhurst pop 494 archd and dioc Chichester

STEEL township parish Press Shrops

STEEP parish 1610 Hamps 1-3/4 miles n Petersfield pop 835 archd and dioc Winchester

STEEP HOLMES ISLAND place in parish Uphill Somerset

STEEPING, GREAT parish 1711 Lincs 3 miles se Spilsby pop 2,811 archd and dioc Lincoln Wesl Meth

STEEPING, LITTLE parish 1559 Lincs 3-3/4 miles se Spilsby pop 263 archd and dioc Lincoln

STEEPLE parish 1548 Dorset 4-1/4 miles sw Corfe Castle pop 237 archd Dorset dioc Bristol

STEEPLE parish 1666 Essex 5-1/2 miles sw Bradwell near the sea pop 497 archd Essex dioc London

STEEPLE ASHTON Wilts See ASHTON, STEEPLE

STEEPLE MORDEN Cambs See MORDEN, STEEPLE

STEEPLETON PRESTON parish 1755 Dorset 4-1/4 miles nw Blandford Forum pop 36 archd Dorset dioc Bristol

STEEPLETON IWERNE Dorset See IWERNE STAPLETON

STEETON township parish Bolton Percy E R York pop 85

STEETON township parish Kildwick W R York pop 859 Wesl Meth

STELLA township parish Ryton co Durham pop 482

STELLING parish 1557 Kent 6 miles sw Canterbury pop 313 archd and dioc Canterbury

STELLING township parish Bywell St Peter Northumberland pop 17

STENIGOT parish 1562 Lincs 5-3/4 miles sw Louth pop 89 archd and dioc Lincoln

STENSON township parish Barrow Derbys

STEPHENS ST parish 1569 Cornwall 3/4 mile nw Launceston pop 1,084 archd Cornwall dioc Exeter

STEPHENS ST parish 1552 Herts 1 mile sw St Albans pop 1,746 archd St Albans dioc London

STEPHENS ST Kent See HACKINGTON

STEPHENS BY SALTASH parish 1545 Cornwall 1 mile nw Saltash pop 3,092 archd Cornwall dioc Exeter

STEPHENS ST IN BRANNEL parish 1694 Cornwall 4-1/2 miles nw St Austell pop 2,477 archd Cornwall dioc Exeter Indep

STEPNEY parish 1568 Middlesex 2-1/2 miles e London comp hamlets Mile End, New Town, Mile End, Old Town, Ratcliff pop 51,023 St Paul Shadwell separated Stepney 1666, St Mary's, Whitechapel 1673, St John's Wapping in 1694, St Mary's Stratford le Bow in

1717, parishes Christchurch Spitalfields, St George in the East
1729, St Anne's Limehouse 1730, St Matthew's Bethnal Green 1743,
All Saints', Poplar, Blackwell 1817 pec Commissary of London
Consistorial Court of Bishop Bapt, Soc of Friends, Calv Meth,
Indep

STEPNEY MARSH Middlesex See DOGS, ISLE OF

STEPPINGLEY parish 1562 Beds 2-1/2 miles sw Ampthill pop 348
archd Bedford dioc Lincoln

STERNDALE, EARL chapelry 1765 parish Hartington Derbys 5-1/2
miles se Buxton pop 354

STERNFIELD parish 1558 Suffolk 1-1/2 miles se Saxmundham pop
203 archd Suffolk dioc Norwich

STERSCOTE Staffs See SYERSCOTE

STERT parish 1579 Wilts 2 miles se Devizes pop 185 pec of Bishop
of Salisbury

STETCHWORTH parish 1666 Cambs 2-3/4 miles sw Newmarket pop
545 archd and dioc Ely

STEVENAGE market town, parish 1538 Herts 12 miles nw Hertford
pop 1,589 archd Huntingdon dioc Lincoln Indep, Wesl Meth

STEVENTON parish 1558 Berks 5 miles sw Abingdon pop 691 archd
Berks dioc Salisbury Bapt

STEVENTON parish 1604 Hamps 6-1/4 miles e Whitchurch pop 197
archd and dioc Winchester

STEVINGTON parish 1653 Beds 5-1/2 miles nw Bedford pop 500
archd Bedford dioc Lincoln

STEWKLEY parish 1545 Bucks 6 miles se Winslow pop 1,053 archd
Buckingham dioc Lincoln Wesl Meth

STEWTON parish 1711 Lincs 2-3/4 miles e Louth pop 69 archd and
dioc Lincoln

STEYNING market town, parish 1565 Sussex 24 miles ne Chichester
pop 1,436 archd and dioc Chichester

STIBBARD parish 1733 Norfolk 4-1/4 miles se Fakenham pop 505
archd Norfolk dioc Norwich

STIBBINGTON parish (incl regs Sibson) Hunts 1 mile se Wansford
pop 456 archd Huntingdon dioc Lincoln

STICKFORD parish 1663 Lincs 5-1/2 miles sw Spilsby pop 425 archd
and dioc Lincoln Wesl Meth

STICKNEY parish 1643 Lincs 2-1/2 miles ne Bolingbroke pop 809
archd and dioc Lincoln Wesl Meth

STIDD or STEDE extra parochial Lancs 7 miles nw Blackburn

STIFFKEY parish 1548 Norfolk 3-1/4 miles e Wells pop 460 archd
and dioc Norwich

STIFFORD parish 1568 Essex 1-3/4 miles nw Gray's Thurrock pop
274 archd Essex dioc London

STILLINGFLEET parish 1598 E R York comp townships Acaster
Selby, Kelfield, Stillingfleet with Moreby pop 909 archd Cleveland
dioc York Wesl Meth

STILLINGTON chapelry parish Red Marshall co Durham pop 96

STILLINGTON parish 1666 N R York 4-1/2 miles se Eastingwould pop 717 pec Prebendary of Stillington Cathedral Church of York Wesl Meth

STILTON parish 1660 Hunts 12-1/2 miles nw Huntingdon pop 793 archd Huntingdon dioc Lincoln Wesl Meth

STINCHCOMBLE parish 1582 Gloucs 2 miles nw Dursley pop 352 archd and dioc Gloucester

STINSFORD parish 1579 Dorset 1-1/4 miles ne Dorchester pop 382 archd Dorset dioc Bristol

STIRCHLEY parish 1638 Shrops 3 miles sw Shiffnall pop 271 archd Shropshire dioc Lincoln

STIRTON township parish Kildwick W R York 1-1/4 miles nw Skipton pop 170

STISTED parish 1538 Essex 3-1/2 miles ne Braintree pop 895 pec Archbishop of Canterbury

STITHIANS parish 1623 Cornwall 4 miles nw Penryn pop 1,874 archd Cornwall dioc Exeter Wesl Meth

STITTENHAM township parish Sheriff Hutton N R York pop 86

STIVICHALL parish 1653 Warws 1-3/4 miles sw Coventry pop 103 archd Coventry dioc Lichfield

STIXWOULD parish 1541 Lincs 6-3/4 miles sw Horncastle pop 221 archd and dioc Lincoln

STOBOROUGH liberty parish Wareham Dorset

STOCK or STOCK HARWARD 1563 Essex 3 miles ne Billericay pop 619 archd Essex dioc London

STOCK hamlet parish Fladbury 1562 Worcs

STOCK DENNIS tything parish Tintinhull Somerset pop 13

STOCK GAYLAND parish 1567 Dorset 7 miles se Sherborne pop 63 archd Dorset dioc Bristol

STOCKBRIDGE market town, parish sep juris 1663 borough Hamps 18 miles nw Southampton pop 851 archd and dioc Winchester Indep

STOCKBURY parish 1653 Kent 4-1/2 miles sw Milton pop 618 archd and dioc Canterbury

STOCKELD township parish Spofforth W R York pop 62

STOCKERSTON parish 1574 Leics 2-3/4 miles sw Uppingham pop 60 archd Leicester dioc Lincoln

STOCKHAM township parish Runcorn Ches pop 52

STOCKHILL township parish Ilkley W R York

STOCKHILL township parish St John Beverley E R York pop 34

STOCKINGFORD hamlet parish Nuneaton Warws

STOCKLAND parish 1640 Dorset 6-1/4 miles ne Honiton pop 1,206 archd Dorset dioc Bristol

STOCKLAND BRISTOL parish 1538 Somerset 7 miles nw Bridgewater pop 202 archd Taunton dioc Bath and Wells

STOCKLEWATH BOUND township parish Castle Sowerby Cumberland pop 260

STOCKLEY township parish Brancepeth co Durham pop 57

STOCKLEY ENGLISH parish 1610 Devon 5-1/4 miles ne Crediton pop 144 archd and dioc Exeter

STOCKLEY POMEROY parish 1556 Devon 3-1/2 miles ne Crediton pop 238 archd and dioc Exeter

STOCKLINCH, MAGDALENE parish 1712 Somerset 2-3/4 miles ne Ilminster pop 95 archd Taunton dioc Bath and Wells

STOCKLINCH, OTTERSAY parish 1560 Somerset 2-1/2 miles ne Ilminster pop 120 archd Taunton dioc Bath and Wells

STOCKSFIELD HALL township parish Bywell St Andrew Northumberland pop 35

STOCKPORT parish 1584 Ches comp market town and borough Stockport, chapelries Disley, Marple, Norbury, townships Bramhall, Bredbury, Brinnington, Dukinfield, Hyde, Offerton, Romilly, Torkington, Wernith, part of Etchells pop 66,610 archd and dioc Chester St Peter 1768, St Thomas 1825 Indep, Wesl Meth, Soc of Friends, Prim Meth, Meth of New Connection, Unit, Roman Cath

STOCKTON township parish Malpas Ches pop 30

STOCKTON parish 1561 Norfolk 3 miles nw Beccles pop 110 archd Norfolk dioc Norwich

STOCKTON parish 1558 Shrops 4-3/4 miles ne Bridgenorth pop 459 archd Salop dioc Lichfield

STOCKTON parish 1567 Warws 2-1/4 miles ne Southam pop 380 archd Coventry dioc Lichfield

STOCKTON parish 1589 Wilts 6-1/4 miles ne Hindon pop 274 archd and dioc Salisbury

STOCKTON ON TEME parish 1539 Worcs 7-1/4 miles sw Bewdley pop 113 archd Salop dioc Hereford

STOCKTON ON THE FOREST parish 1653 N R York 5-1/4 miles ne York pop 319 pec Prebendary of Bugthorpe in the Cathedral Church of York Wesl Meth

STOCKTON UPON TEES parish 1621 co Durham comp market town and port of Stockton upon Tees, townships Hartburn, Preston upon Tees pop 7,991 20 miles se Durham archd and dioc Durham Part Bapt, Soc of Friends, Indep, Prim and Wesl Meth, Unit, Roman Cath

STOCKWELL chapelry parish Lambeth Surrey 3 miles sw London Bapt, Indep

STOCKWITH, EAST hamlet parish Gainsborough Lincs pop 269 Wesl Meth

STOCKWITH, WEST chapelry parish Misterton Notts pop 635 Wesl Meth

STOCKWOOD parish Dorset 8 miles sw Sherborne pop 33 pec of Dean of Salisbury

STODDAY township parish Lancaster Lancs

STODMARSH parish 1558 Kent 4-1/2 miles ne Canterbury pop 119 archd and dioc Canterbury

STODY parish 1661 Norfolk 3 miles sw Holt pop 161 archd and dioc

Norwich

STOGUMBER parish 1559 Somerset 7 miles ne Wiveliscombe pop 1,294 archd Taunton dioc Bath and Wells

STOGURSEY or STOKE COURCY parish 1660 Somerset 8-1/2 miles nw Bridgewater pop 1,496 archd Taunton dioc Bath and Wells

STOKE township parish Acton Ches pop 124

STOKE parish 1545 Ches comp townships Great Stanney, Little Stanney, Stoke, part of Whitby pop 334 archd and dioc Chester

STOKE parish 1574 Warws pop 848 archd Coventry dioc Lichfield

STOKE township parish Hope Derbys pop 60

STOKE parish 1666 Kent 8 miles ne Rochester archd and dioc Rochester

STOKE parish 1538 Norfolk 5-1/2 miles ne St Mary Stratton pop 350 archd Norfolk dioc Norwich

STOKE parish 1654 Shrops 7 miles ne Ludlow pop 597 archd Salop dioc Hereford

STOKE parish 1561 Somerset 5 miles nw Langport pop 1,507 pec of Dean and Chapter of Wells

STOKE parish 1676 Somerset 3-1/4 miles se Taunton pop 275 archd Taunton dioc Bath and Wells Indep

STOKE ABBAS parish 1559 Dorset 2 miles sw Beaminster pop 587 archd Dorset dioc Bristol

STOKE ALBANY parish 1575 co Northampton 5 miles sw Rockingham pop 339 archd Northampton dioc Peterborough

STOKE ASH parish 1538 Suffolk 3-1/2 miles sw Eye pop 392 archd Sudbury dioc Norwich Bapt

STOKE BARDOLPH township parish Gedling Notts pop 181

STOKE, BISHOP'S tything parish Westbury upon Trym Gloucs pop 2,328

STOKE, BISHOP'S parish 1558 Hamps 6-1/2 miles nw Bishop's Waltham pop 1,026 archd and dioc Winchester

STOKE BLISS parish 1571 Worcs Herefs 6-1/4 miles n Bromyard pop 344 archd and dioc Hereford

STOKE BRUERNE parish 1560 co Northampton 3-1/2 miles ne Towcester pop 762 archd Northampton dioc Peterborough

STOKE BY CLARE parish 1538 Suffolk 2-1/4 miles sw Clare pop 792 archd Sudbury dioc Norwich

STOKE CANNON parish 1654 Devon 3-1/2 miles ne Exeter pop 446 pec Dean and Chapter of Exeter

STOKE CHARITY parish 1544 Hamps 6-1/2 miles se Whitchurch pop 135 archd and dioc Winchester

STOKE CLIMSLAND parish 1538 Cornwall 3-1/2 miles n Callington pop 1,608 archd Cornwall dioc Exeter Wesl Meth

STOKE D'ABERNON parish 1619 Surrey 1-1/2 miles se Cobham pop 289 archd Surrey dioc Winchester

STOKE DAMERALL parish 1689 Devon pop 34,883 archd Totnes dioc Exeter Indep, Calv Meth, Wesl Meth

STOKE DOYLE parish 1560 co Northampton 1-1/2 miles sw Oundle

pop 165 archd Northampton dioc Peterborough

STOKE, DRY parish 1559 Leics and co Rutland 3-1/2 miles sw Uppingham pop 53 archd Northampton dioc Peterborough

STOKE, EARL wilts See EARL STOKE

STOKE, EAST parish 1742 Dorset 4 miles sw Wareham pop 561 archd Dorset dioc Bristol

STOKE EAST NEWARK parish 1553 Notts 3-3/4 miles sw Newark pop 320 archd Nottingham dioc York

STOKE EDITH parish 1538 Herefs 7-1/4 miles e Hereford pop 505 archd and dioc Hereford

STOKE FERRY market town, parish 1736 Norfolk 38 miles sw Norwich pop 706 archd Norfolk dioc Norwich

STOKE FLEMING parish 1538 Devon 2 miles sw Dartmouth pop 725 archd Totnes dioc Exeter

STOKE GABRIEL parish 1539 Devon 4 miles se Totnes pop 718 pec Bishop of Exeter Bapt

STOKE GIFFORD parish 1556 Gloucs 5 miles ne Bristol pop 441 pec Bishop of Exeter

STOKE GOLDING chapelry 1656 parish Hinckley Leics 2-3/4 miles ne Hinckley pop 543

STOKE GOLDINGTON parish 1538 Bucks 4 miles sw Olney pop 912 archd Buckingham dioc Lincoln

STOKE GUILDFORD parish 1662 Surrey 3/4 mile n Guildford pop 1,327 archd Surrey dioc Winchester

STOKE HAMMOND parish 1538 Bucks 2-3/4 miles s Fenny Stratford pop 323 archd Buckingham dioc Lincoln

STOKE LACY parish 1567 Herefs 4-1/4 miles sw Bromyard pop 381 archd and dioc Hereford

STOKE LANE or STOKE parish 1644 Somerset 4 miles ne Shepton Mallet pop 980 archd Wells dioc Bath and Wells Wesl Meth

STOKE, LIMPLEY chapelry 1707 parish Great Bradford Wilts

STOKE LYNE parish 1665 co Oxford 4-1/4 miles nw Bicester pop 593 archd and dioc Oxford

STOKE MANDEVILLE parish 1699 Bucks 2-3/4 miles nw Wendover pop 461 pec Dean and Chapter of Lincoln

STOKE NEAR NAYLAND parish 1558 Suffolk 2 miles ne Nayland pop 1,447 archd Sudbury dioc Norwich

STOKE, NORTH township parish South Stoke Lincs pop 124

STOKE, NORTH parish 1740 co Oxford 2-1/2 miles s Wallingford pop 199 archd and dioc Oxford

STOKE, NORTH parish 1649 Somerset 4-1/4 miles nw Bath pop 128 archd Bath dioc Bath and Wells

STOKE, NORTH parish 1678 Sussex 3 miles ne Arundel pop 86 archd and dioc Chichester

STOKE ORCHARD chapelry parish Bishop's Cleeve Gloucs pop 229

STOKE PERO parish 1712 Somerset 6-3/4 miles sw Minehead pop 61 archd Taunton dioc Bath and Wells

STOKE POGES parish 1563 Bucks 2 miles n Slough pop 1,252 archd

Buckingham dioc Lincoln Wesl Meth

STOKE PRIOR parish 1678 Herefs comp townships Stoke Prior, Wickton with Risbury 3 miles se Leominster pop 478 archd and dioc Hereford

STOKE PRIOR parish 1557 Worcs 1-3/4 miles s Bromsgrove pop 1,100 archd and dioc Worcester

STOKE RIVERS parish 1553 Devon 5 miles ne Barnstaple pop 270 archd Barnstaple dioc Exeter

STOKE, RODNEY parish 1564 Somerset 5 miles nw Wells pop 333 archd Wells dioc Bath and Wells

STOKE, SEVERN parish 1538 Worcs 3 miles ne Upton upon Severn pop 745 archd and dioc Worcester

STOKE, SOUTH parish 1660 Lincs 2 miles nw Colsterworth pop 438 archd and dioc Lincoln

STOKE, SOUTH parish 1557 co Oxford 4-1/4 miles sw Wallingford pop 751 archd and dioc Oxford Indep

STOKE, SOUTH parish 1691 Somerset 2-1/2 miles s Bath pop 266 archd Bath dioc Bath and Wells

STOKE, SOUTH parish 1553 Sussex 2-1/2 miles ne Arundel pop 101 archd and dioc Chichester

STOKE, TALMAGE parish 1754 co Oxford 2 miles sw Tetsworth pop 107 archd and dioc Oxford

STOKE TRISTER parish 1751 Somerset 2 miles e Wincanton pop 428 archd Wells dioc Bath and Wells

STOKE UNDER HAMDON parish 1558 Somerset 5-3/4 miles nw Yeovil pop 1,365 archd Wells dioc Bath and Wells

STOKE UPON TERN parish 1654 Shrops comp townships Eaton, Ollerton, Stoke, Westanswick pop 1,030 6 miles sw Drayton in Hales archd Salop dioc Lichfield

STOKE UPON TRENT parish 1689 parish borough Staffs 1-3/4 miles e Newcastle under Lyne comp chapelries Hanley, Lane End, Shelton with Cobridge, Etruria, townships Botteslaw, Eaves, Fenton Calvert, Fenton Vivian, Longron, Penkhul with Bootham, part of Seabridge, liberty of Clayton pop 36,340 archd Stafford dioc Lichfield Bapt, Indep, Wesl Meth, Meth New Connection

STOKE WAKE parish 1546 Dorset 10 miles w Blandford Forum pop 147 archd Dorset dioc Bristol

STOKE, WEST parish 1564 Sussex 3-1/2 miles nw Chichester pop 101 archd and dioc Chichester

STOKEHAM parish 1672 Notts 5 miles ne Tuxford pop 48 pec Dean and Chapter of York

STOKINTINHEAD parish 1538 Devon 4 miles se Newton Bushell pop 621 archd and dioc Exeter

STOKENCHURCH parish 1707 co Oxford 6 miles se Tetsworth pop 1,290 archd and dioc Oxford Wesl Meth

STOKENHAM or STOKINGHAM parish 1578 Devon 5-1/4 miles se Kingsbridge pop 1,609 archd Totnes dioc Exeter

STOKESAY parish 1558 Shrops 7 miles nw Ludlow pop 529 archd

Salop dioc Hereford

STOKESBY parish 1560 Norfolk 2-1/4 miles e Acle pop 324 archd and dioc Norwich Wesl Meth

STOKESLEY parish 1571 N R York comp market town Stokesley, townships Great and Little Busby, Essby, Newby pop 2,376 41 miles nw York archd Cleveland dioc York Prim Meth, Wesl Meth

STONALL, OVER chapelry parish Shenstone Staffs

STONAR parish Kent 3/4 mile ne Sandwich pop 52 archd and dioc Canterbury

STONDON, LOWER hamlet parish Shitlington Beds

STONDON MASSEY parish 1708 Essex 2 miles se Chipping Ongar pop 290 archd Essex dioc London

STONDON, UPPER parish 1683 Beds 2-3/4 miles s Shefford pop 37 archd Bedford dioc Lincoln

STONE parish 1538 Bucks 3 miles sw Aylesbury pop 773 archd Buckingham dioc Lincoln Meth

STONE chapelry 1594 parish Berkeley Gloucs 2-3/4 miles sw Berkeley archd and dioc Gloucester

STONE parish 1604 Kent 6-1/2 miles se Tenterden pop 410 archd and dioc Canterbury

STONE parish 1568 Staffs 7 miles nw Stafford comp market town Stone, liberties Beech, Hilderstone, Kibblestone, Normicott pop 7,808 archd Stafford dioc Lichfield Indep, Wesl Meth, Roman Cath

STONE parish 1601 Worcs 2-1/4 miles se Kidderminster archd and dioc Worcester

STONE DELPH township parish Tamworth Warws

STONE EASTON parish 1572 Somerset 6-1/2 miles ne Shepton Mallet pop 386 archd Wells dioc Bath and Wells

STONE parish 1718 Kent 2 miles ne Dartford pop 719 archd and dioc Rochester

STONE NEXT FAVERSHAM parish Kent 2-1/2 miles nw Faversham pop 80 archd and dioc Canterbury

STONEBECK, DOWN township parish Kirkby Malzeard W R York pop 494

STONEBECK, UPPER township parish Kirkby Malzeard W R York pop 332

STONEFERRY township parish Sutton E R York Wesl Meth

STONEGRAVE parish 1584 N R York comp townships East Ness, West Ness, East Newton with Laythorpe, Stonegrave pop 327 4-3/4 miles ne Southampton archd Cleveland dioc York

STONEHAM, NORTH parish 1640 Hamps 4-3/4 miles ne Southampton pop 766 archd and dioc Winchester

STONEHAM, SOUTH parish 1663 Hamps 3 miles ne Southampton pop 2,737 pec of Incumbent

STONEHOUSE parish 1558 Gloucs 3 miles w Stroud pop 2,469 archd and dioc Gloucester Indep, Wesl Meth

STONEHOUSE, EAST parish 1754 Devon pop 9,571 archd Totnes

dioc Exeter   Bapt, Indep, Wesl Meth, Roman Cath

STONELEIGH parish 1634 Warws 3-1/4 miles ne Kenilworth pop 1,298 archd Coventry dioc Lichfield

STONERAISE township parish Westward Cumberland

STONESBY parish 1625 Leics 6 miles ne Melton Mowbray pop 287 archd Leicester dioc Lincoln

STONESFIELD parish 1571 co Oxford 4-1/4 miles w Woodstock pop 535 archd and dioc Oxford

STONEY MIDDLETON Derbys See MIDDLETON, STONEY

STONHAM, ASPEL parish 1558 Suffolk 5 miles ne Needham Market pop 612 archd Suffolk dioc Norwich

STONHAM, EARL parish 1654 Suffolk 3 miles ne Needham Market pop 757 archd Suffolk dioc Norwich

STONHAM, PARVA parish 1542 Suffolk 4 miles ne Needham Market pop 329 archd Suffolk dioc Norwich

STONTON WYVILLE parish 1538 Leics 5-1/2 miles ne Market Harborough pop 106 archd Leicester dioc Lincoln

STOODLEY or STOODLEIGH parish 1597 Devon 4 miles sw Bampton pop 524 archd Barnstaple dioc Exeter

STOPHAM parish 1544 Sussex 4-1/4 miles se Petworth pop 129 archd and dioc Chichester

STOPSLEY hamlet parish Luton Beds pop 510

STORETON township parish Bebbington Ches pop 192

STORITHS township parish Skipton W R York

STORMORE extra parochial liberty Leics near Westrill

STORRINGTON parish 1547 Sussex 8-1/2 miles ne Arundel pop 916 archd and dioc Chichester

STORTFORD, BISHOP parish 1561 borough Herts 14 miles ne Hertford pop 3,958 Commissary of Essex and Herts Consistorial Court of the Bishop of London Bapt, Soc of Friends, Indep, Meth

STORWOOD township parish Thornton E R York pop 119

STOTFOLD parish 1703 Beds 2-1/2 miles nw Baldock pop 833 archd Bedford dioc Lincoln Wesl Meth

STOTFORD township parish Hooton Pagnell W R York pop 9

STOTTESDEN parish 1565 Shrops 5-1/4 miles n Cleobury Mortimer pop 1,579 archd Salop dioc Hereford

STOUGHTON chapelry 1538 parish Thurnby Leics 4 miles se Leicester pop 139

STOUGHTON parish 1675 Sussex 6 miles nw Chichester pop 570 archd and dioc Chichester

STOULTON parish 1542 Worcs 2-3/4 miles nw Pershore pop 312 archd and dioc Worcester

STOURBRIDGE chapelry parish St Andrew the Less Cambridge Cambs

STOURBRIDGE market town parish Old Swinford Worcs 21 miles ne Worcester pop 6,148 Soc of Friends, Indep, Wesl Meth, Presb, Roman Cath

STOURMOUTH parish 1538 Kent 8 miles ne Canterbury pop 257 archd and dioc Canterbury

STOURPAIN parish 1631 Dorset 3 miles nw Blandford Forum pop 594 pec Dean and Chapter of Salisbury

STOURPORT market town chapelry Mitton parish Kidderminster Worcs 4 miles sw Kidderminster Wesl Meth

STOURTON parish 1570 Wilts 2-1/2 miles nw Mere pop 653 archd and dioc Salisbury

STOUTING parish 1539 Kent 8 miles se Ashford pop 254 archd and dioc Canterbury

STOVEN parish 1653 Suffolk 5-1/4 miles ne Halesworth pop 112 archd Suffolk dioc Norwich

STOW hamlet parish Threckingham Lincs

STOW parish 1561 Lincs 7-3/4 miles se Gainsborough pop 808 pec Prebendary of Stow in Lindsey Cathedral Church of Lincoln Wesl Meth

STOW parish 1576 Shrops 1-1/2 miles ne Knighton pop 147 archd Salop dioc Hereford

STOW BARDOLPH parish 1559 Norfolk 2 miles ne Downham Market pop 760 archd Norfolk dioc Norwich

STOW BEDON parish 1722 Norfolk 4-3/4 miles se Watton pop 303 archd and dioc Norwich

STOW cum QUY parish 1650 Cambs 5 miles ne Cambridge pop 400 archd and dioc Ely

STOW LA GTOFT parish 1559 Suffolk 2-1/2 miles se Ixworth pop 204 archd Sudbury dioc Norwich

STOW, LONG parish 1569 Cambs 2-3/4 miles se Caxton pop 231 archd and dioc Ely

STOW, LONG parish 1591 Hunts 2-1/2 miles ne Kimbolton pop 180 archd Huntingdon dioc Lincoln

STOW MARIES parish 1559 Essex 5-1/2 miles sw Maldon pop 242 archd Essex dioc London

STOW MARKET parish 1559 Suffolk 12 miles nw Ipswich pop 2,672 archd Sudbury dioc Norwich Bapt, Indep

STOW MARKET hamlet chapelry Gipping Suffolk

STOW ON THE WOLD parish 1558 Gloucs 25 miles ne Gloucester pop 1,810 archd and dioc Gloucester Bapt

STOW UPLAND parish 1693 Suffolk by Stow Market archd Sudbury dioc Norwich

STOW, WEST parish 1558 Suffolk 5-1/4 miles nw Bury St Edmund's pop 266 archd Sudbury dioc Norwich

STOW WOOD parish co Oxford 4 miles nw Buckingham pop 26

STOWE parish 1568 Bucks 2-1/2 miles nw Buckingham pop 490 archd Buckingham dioc Lincoln Wesl Meth

STOWE parish (incl regs Barholm) Lincs 2-3/4 miles nw Market Deeping pop 25 archd and dioc Lincoln

STOWE parish 1577 Staffs 7 miles ne Stafford pop 1,283 archd Stafford dioc Lichfield

STOW NINE CHURCHES parish 1560 co Northampton 5-1/2 miles se Daventry pop 404 archd Northampton dioc Peterborough

STOWELL parish 1590 Gloucs 2 miles sw Northleach pop 43 archd and dioc Gloucester

STOWELL parish 1745 Somerset 5 miles sw Wincanton pop 123 archd Wells dioc Bath and Wells

STOWELL tything parish Overton Wilts

STOWER, EAST parish 1598 Dorset 4-1/4 miles sw Shaftesbury pop 870 archd Dorset dioc Bristol

STOWER PROVOST parish 1701 Dorset 4-1/2 miles sw Shaftesbury pop 870 archd Dorset dioc Bristol

STOWER, WEST parish 1654 Dorset 5-1/4 miles w Shaftesbury pop 219 archd Dorset dioc Bristol

STOWERTON hamlet parish Whichford Warws

STOWEY parish 1584 Somerset 3-1/2 miles sw Pensford pop 234 archd Bath dioc Bath and Wells

STOWEY, NETHER parish 1640 Somerset 8 miles nw Bridgewater pop 778 pec Consistorial Decanal Court of Wells Indep

STOWEY, OVER parish 1558 Somerset 8 miles nw Bridgewater pop 592 archd Taunton dioc Bath and Wells

STOWFORD parish 1707 Devon 8 miles ne Launceston pop 463 archd Totnes dioc Exeter

STOWICK tything parish Henbury Gloucester pop 568

STRADBROOK parish 1538 Suffolk 5-3/4 miles e Eye pop 1,527 archd Suffolk dioc Norwich Bapt

STRADISHALL parish 1548 Suffolk 5 miles nw Clare pop 393 archd Sudbury dioc Norwich

STRADSETT parish 1559 Norfolk 3-3/4 miles ne Downham Market pop 183 archd Norfolk dioc Norwich

STRAGGLESTHORPE parish 1765 Lincs 8 miles se Newark pop 82 archd and dioc Lincoln

STRAMSHALL township parish Uttoxeter Staffs

STRANGHOW township parish Skelton N R York pop 122

STRANTON parish 1580 co Durham comp townships Brierton, Seaton Carew, Stranton pop 736 5 miles sw Hartlepool archd and dioc Durham Wesl Meth

STRATFIELD MORTIMER parish 1681 Hamps and Berks 7 miles sw Reading pop 1,206 archd Berks dioc Salisbury Indep

STRATFIELD SAYE parish 1539 Hamps 7-3/4 miles ne Basingstoke pop 808 archd and dioc Winchester

STRATFIELD TURGIS parish 1672 Hamps 6-1/2 miles ne Basingstoke pop 232 archd and dioc Winchester

STRATFORD parish 1720 Suffolk 3 miles sw Saxmundham pop 200 archd Suffolk dioc Norwich

STRATFORD parish 1562 Suffolk 5-1/4 miles nw Manningtree pop 630 archd Suffolk dioc Norwich

STRATFORD, ST ANTHONY or STRATFORD TONY parish 1562 Wilts 4 miles sw Salisbury pop 125 archd and dioc Salisbury

STRATFORD FENNY chapelry 1730 parish Bletchley and Simpson Bucks 13-1/2 miles e Buckingham pop 635 archd Buckingham dioc Lincoln Bapt, Wesl Meth

STRATFORD LANGTHORNE ward, parish West Ham Essex 4 miles
ne London Indep, Wesl Meth, Roman Cath

STRATFORD LE BOW Middlesex See BOW

STRATFORD, OLD hamlet parishes Cosgrove, Furtho, Passenham,
Potters Pury co Northampton

STRATFORD, OLD parish 1558 Warws comp town Stratford upon
Avon pop 5,171 See also STRATFORD ON AVON

STRATFORD, STONY 1738 Bucks 8 miles ne Buckingham pop 1,619
archd Buckingham dioc Lincoln Bapt, Indep, Wesl Meth

STRATFORD UNDER THE CASTLE parish 1654 Wilts 1-3/4 miles
nw Salisbury pop 374 archd and dioc Salisbury

STRATFORD UPON AVON market town parish Old Stratford 1558
sep juris Warws 8 miles sw Warwick pop 3,488 Bapt, Indep, Wesl
Meth

STRATFORD, WATER parish 1596 Bucks 2 miles nw Buckingham
pop 186 archd Buckingham dioc Lincoln

STRATTON hamlet parish Biggleswade Beds

STRATTON parish 1687 incl seaport Bude Cornwall 17-1/2 miles nw
Launceston pop 1,613 archd Cornwall dioc Exeter Wesl Meth

STRATTON parish 1560 Dorset 3-1/2 miles nw Dorchester pop 310
pec Dean of Salisbury

STRATTON parish 1600 Gloucs 1-3/4 miles nw Cirencester pop 468
archd and dioc Gloucester

STRATTON parish 1558 Norfolk 1 mile ne St Mary Stratton pop 203
archd Norfolk dioc Norwich

STRATTON extra parochial liberty Suffolk by parish Levington

STRATTON parish 1608 Wilts 2-3/4 miles ne Swindon pop 924 archd
Wilts dioc Salisbury

STRATTON AUDLEY parish 1696 co Oxford 3 miles ne Bicester pop
360 archd and dioc Oxford

STRATTON, EAST parish 1540 Hamps 6 miles nw New Alresford
pop 386 archd and dioc Winchester

STRATTON, LONG parish 1547 Norfolk 10-1/2 miles sw Norwich
pop 721 archd Norfolk dioc Norwich Indep

STRATTON ON THE FOSS parish 1710 Somerset 6 miles ne Shepton
Mallet pop 407 archd Wells dioc Bath and Wells

STRATTON STRAWLESS parish 1562 Norfolk 4-3/4 miles se Aylsham
pop 218 archd and dioc Norwich

STRATTON, UPPER tything parish Stratton St Margaret Wilts

STRATTON, WEST tything parish Mitcheldever Hamps

STREATHAM parish 1538 Surrey 6 miles sw London comp hamlets
Upper Tooting, Balham Hill pop 5,068 archd Surrey dioc Winchester Indep, Wesl Meth

STREATLAM township parish Gainford co Durham

STREATLEY parish 1693 Beds 5 miles nw Luton pop 339 archd Bedford dioc Lincoln

STREATLEY parish 1679 Berks 5-1/2 miles sw Wallingford pop 582 archd Berks dioc Salisbury

STREET parish 1639 Somerset 1-3/4 miles sw Glastonbury pop 899 archd Wells dioc Bath and Wells Bapt, Soc of Friends

STREET tything parish Christchurch Hamps

STREET parish 1560 Sussex 6-1/2 miles nw Lewes pop 168 archd Lewes dioc Chichester

STREETHALL parish 1739 Essex 4 miles nw Saffron Walden pop 41 archd Colchester dioc London

STREETHAY hamlet parish St Michael Lichfield Staffs pop 112

STRELLY parish 1665 Notts 4-1/2 miles nw Nottingham pop 426 archd Nottingham dioc York

STRENSALL parish 1580 N R York 6 miles ne York pop 398 pec Prebendary of Strensall in Cathedral Church of York

STRENSHAM parish 1569 Worcs 4-1/2 miles sw Pershore pop 328 archd and dioc Worcester

STRETFORD parish 1720 Herefs 4-3/4 miles sw Leominster pop 44 archd and dioc Hereford

STRETFORD hamlet parish Leominster Herefs

STRETFORD chapelry 1598 parish Manchester Lancs 4 miles sw Manchester pop 2,463 archd and dioc Chester

STRETHAM parish 1558 Cambs 4-1/4 miles sw Ely pop 1,173 pec Bishop of Ely Bapt, Wesl Meth

STRETTON township parish Tilston Ches pop 105

STRETTON chapelry parish Great Budworth Ches pop 324

STRETTON township parish North Wingfield Derbys pop 439

STRETTON parish 1631 co Rutland 8-1/4 miles ne Oakham pop 208 archd Northampton dioc Peterborough

STRETTON chapelry 1659 parish Penkridge Staffs pop 268

STRETTON township parish Burton upon Trent Staffs pop 373

STRETTON BASKERVILLE parish no regs Warws pop 59 archd Coventry dioc Lichfield

STRETTON, CHURCH parish 1662 Shrops 13 miles sw Shrewsbury pop 1,302 archd Salop dioc Hereford

STRETTON EN LE FIELDS parish 1695 Leics 5 miles sw Ashby de la Zouch pop 109 archd Derby dioc Lichfield

STRETTON GRANDSOME parish 1558 Herefs 7-3/4 miles nw Ledbury pop 168 archd and dioc Hereford

STRETTON, MAGNA parish 1603 Leics 5-1/2 miles se Leicester pop 27 archd Leicester dioc Lincoln

STRETTON ON THE FOSS parish 1538 Warws 3 miles sw Shipston upon Stour pop 455 archd Gloucester dioc Worcester

STRETTON, PARVA chapelry 1592 parish King's Norton Leics

STRETTON SUGWAS parish 1733 Herefs 3-3/4 miles nw Hereford pop 155 archd and dioc Hereford

STRETTON UNDER FOSS hamlet parish Monk's Kirby Warws pop 304

STRETTON UPON DUSNMOOR parish 1681 Warws 5-1/2 miles nw Dunchurch pop 817 archd Coventry dioc Lichfield

STRICKLAND, GREAT township parish Morland Westm Soc of Friends

STRICKLAND KETTLE township parish Kendal Westm pop 366
STRICKLAND, LITTLE township parish Morland Westm pop 121
STRICKLAND ROGER township parish Kendal Westm pop 326
STRINGSTON parish 1623 Somerset 10-/4 miles nw Bridgewater pop
128 archd Taunton dioc Bath and Wells Indep
STRIXTON parish 1730 co Northampton 4-1/4 miles se Wellingborough
pop 69 archd Northampton dioc Peterborough
STROUD tything parish Cumner Berks pop 72
STROUD or STROUDWATER parish 1624 borough Gloucs 10 miles se
Gloucester pop 8,607 archd and dioc Gloucester Part Bapt, In-
dep, Wesl Meth
STROUD or STROOD parish 1565 Kent pop 2,722 1/2 mile nw Roches-
ter archd and dioc Rochester Indep
STROUD END tything parish Painswick Gloucs pop 838
STROXTON parish 1735 Lincs 3-3/4 miles sw Grantham pop 124
archd and dioc Lincoln
STRUBBY parish 1558 Lincs 4 miles n Alford pop 201 pec Dean and
Chapter of Lincoln
STRUMPSHAW parish 1562 Norfolk 3-1/2 miles sw Acle pop 374
archd and dioc Norwich
STUBBS township parish Adwick le Street W R York
STUBBY LANE hamlet parish Hanbury Staffs
STUBLACH township parish Middlewich Ches pop 66
STUBTON parish 1660 Lincs 6-3/4 miles se Newark pop 182 archd
and dioc Lincoln
STUDHAM parish 1570 Herts and Beds comp hamlets Humbershoe,
Studham, part of Market Street pop 821 3-3/4 miles sw Market
Street archd Bedford dioc Lincoln
STUDLAND parish 1581 Dorset 5-1/2 miles ne Corfe Castle pop 435
archd Dorset dioc Bristol
STUDLEY chapelry parish Beckley co Oxford pop 405
STUDLEY parish 1663 Warws 4-3/4 miles nw Alcester pop 1,903
archd and dioc Worcester Wesl Meth
STUDLEY HALL incl regs Aldfield Yorks
STUDLEY ROGER township parish Ripon W R York pop 157
STUDLEY ROYAL hamlet parish Ripon W R York pop 60
STUKELEY, GREAT parish 1569 Hunts 2-1/2 miles nw Huntingdon
pop 397 archd Huntingdon dioc Lincoln
STUKELEY, LITTLE parish 1655 Hunts 3-1/4 miles nw Huntingdon
pop 413 archd Huntingdon dioc Lincoln
STUNTNEY chapelry 1545 parish Holy Trinity Ely Cambs 1-1/2 miles
se Ely
STURBRIDGE Cambs See STOURBRIDGE
STURMER parish 1733 Essex 6 miles sw Clare pop 320 Commissary
of Essex and Herts Consistorial Court of the Bishop of London
STURMINSTER MARSHALL parish 1562 Dorset 5 miles w Wimborne
Minster pop 803 pec Sturminster Marshall
STURMINSTER NEWTON CASTLE parish 1681 Dorset 9 miles nw

Blandford pop 1,831 archd Dorset dioc Bristol Wesl Meth

STURRY parish 1538 Kent 2-1/2 miles ne Canterbury pop 925 archd and dioc Canterbury

STURSTON hamlet parish Ashbourn Derbys pop 578

STURSTON parish incl regs of Tottington Norfolk 5-1/4 miles sw Watton pop 49 archd and dioc Norwich

STURTON township parish Scawby Lincs

STURTON township parish Stow Lincs pop 318 Wesl Meth

STURTON parish 1638 Notts 6 miles ne East Retford pop 638 archd Nottingham dioc York

STURTON GRANGE township parish Warkworth Northumberland pop 88

STURTON GRANGE township parish Aberford W R York pop 74

STURTON, GREAT parish 1679 5-1/2 miles nw Horncastle pop 138 archd and dioc Lincoln

STUSTON parish 1630 Suffolk 3 miles nw Eye pop 212 archd Sudbury dioc Norwich

STUTCHBURY parish (incl regs of Helmdon) co Northampton 5 miles nw Brackley pop 29 archd Northampton dioc Peterborough

STUTTON parish 1665 Suffolk 6-1/4 miles sw Ipswich pop 475 archd Suffolk dioc Norwich

STUTTON township parish Tadcaster W R York pop 330

STYDD township parish Shirley Derbys pop 29

STYFORD township parish Bywell Northumberland pop 65

STYRRUP township parishes Blyth, Narworth, Houghton Notts pop 510

SUCKLEY parish 1695 Worcs 5-1/2 miles se Bromyard pop 1,196 archd and dioc Worcester Wesl Meth

SUDBORNE parish 1661 Suffolk 1-1/2 miles ne Orford pop 631 archd Suffolk dioc Norwich

SUDBOROUGH parish 1660 co Northampton 4-1/4 miles nw Thrapstone pop 346 archd Northampton dioc Peterborough

SUDBROOK parish no regs co Monmouth 5-1/4 miles sw Chepstow archd and dioc Llandaff

SUDBROOKE parish 1579 Lincs 4-3/4 miles ne Lincoln pop 84 archd Stow dioc Lincoln

SUDBURY parish 1673 Derbys 5 miles se Uttoxeter pop 642 archd Derby dioc Lichfield

SUDBURY borough, market town sep juris Suffolk 22 miles sw Ipswich pop 4,677 comp All Saints 1564, St Gregory 1653, St Peter 1593 archd Sudbury dioc Norwich

SUDELEY MANOR parish 1705 Gloucs 1 mile se Winchcombe pop 84 archd and dioc Gloucester

SUDELEY TENEMENTS hamlet parish Winchcombe Gloucs

SUFFIELD parish 1558 Norfolk 3-1/4 miles nw North Walsham pop 272 archd Norfolk dioc Norwich

SUFFIELD township parish Hackness N R York pop 124

SUGLEY township parish Newburn Northumberland pop 255

SUGNALL, MAGNA township parish Eccleshall Staffs pop 130

SUGNALL, PARVA township parish Eccleshall Staffs pop 61

SULBY extra parochial district co Northampton pop 78 5-1/4 miles sw Market Harborough

SULGRAVE parish 1668 co Northampton 8-1/2 miles nw Brackley pop 576 archd Northampton dioc Peterborough

SULHAM parish 1720 Berks 5 miles nw Reading pop 72 archd Berks dioc Salisbury

SULHAMPSTEAD ABBOTS parish 1602 Berks 7 miles sw Reading pop 423 archd Berks dioc Salisbury

SULHAMPSTEAD BANNISTER parish 1654 Berks 6-3/4 miles sw Reading pop 289 archd Berks dioc Salisbury

SULLINGTON parish 1555 Sussex 5-1/2 miles nw Steyning pop 320 archd and dioc Chichester

SUMMERFORD township parish Astbury Ches pop 112

SUMMERHOUSE township parish Gainford co Durham pop 192 Wesl Meth

SUNBURY parish 1565 Middlesex 15 miles sw London pop 1,863 archd Middlesex dioc London

SUNDERLAND township parish Isall Cumberland pop 77

SUNDERLAND parish 1719 borough co Durham 13 miles ne Durham pop 17,000 archd and dioc Durham Bapt, Scotch Burghers, Soc of Friends, Indep, Calv and Prim Meth, Wesl Meth, Meth New Connection, Presb, Unit, Roman Cath, Jews

SUNDERLAND BRIDGE township parish St Andrew Auckland co Durham pop 283

SUNDERLAND, NORTH township parish Bambrough Northumberland pop 860

SUNDERLAND WICK township parish Hutton Cranswick E R York pop 35

SUNDON parish 1582 Beds 4-3/4 miles nw Luton pop 408 archd Bedford dioc Lincoln

SUNDRIDGE parish 1579 Kent 4 miles nw Sevenoaks pop 1,268 pec Archbishop of Canterbury

SUNK ISLAND extra parochial district E R York pop 242 20 miles se Hull Wesl Meth

SUNNINGHILL parish 1560 Berks 6 miles sw New Winder pop 1,520 pec Dean of Salisbury Bapt

SUNNINGWELL parish 1543 Berks 2-1/2 miles n Abingdon pop 339 archd Berks dioc Salisbury

SURFLEET parish 1662 Lincs 4 miles n Spalding pop 871 archd and dioc Lincoln

SURLINGHAM parish 1561 Norfolk 5-1/2 miles se Norwich pop 399 archd Norfolk dioc Norwich

SURRENDRAL tything parish Hullavington Wilts

SUSTEAD parish 1558 Norfolk 4-1/4 miles sw Cromer pop 162 archd Norfolk dioc Norwich

SUTCOMBE parish 1684 Devon 5 miles ne Holsworthy pop 491 archd Totnes dioc Exeter

SUTTERBY parish 1595 Lincs 4-3/4 miles sw Alford pop 34 archd and dioc Lincoln

SUTTERTON parish 1538 Lincs 8-1/4 miles nw Holbeach pop 1,093 archd and dioc Lincoln

SUTTON parish 1538 Beds 1-3/4 miles s Potton pop 386 archd Bedford dioc Lincoln

SUTTON parish 1558 Cambs 6-1/4 miles sw Ely pop 1,362 pec Bishop of Ely Bapt, Wesl Meth

SUTTON township parish Runcorn Ches pop 237

SUTTON township parish Prestbury Ches pop 5,836

SUTTON township parish Middlewich Ches pop 18

SUTTON CUM DUCKMANTON parish 1662 Derbys 4 miles se Chesterfield pop 700 archd Derby dioc Lichfield

SUTTON parish 1741 Essex 1-1/2 miles se Rochford pop 96 archd Essex dioc London

SUTTON St Michael parish 1678 Herefs 4-1/4 miles ne Hereford pop 98 archd and dioc Hereford

SUTTON St Nicholas parish 1586 Herefs 4-1/4 miles ne Hereford pop 234 archd and dioc Hereford

SUTTON township parish Prescot Lancs pop 3,173

SUTTON township parish Wymondham Norfolk pop 739

SUTTON parish 1558 Norfolk 5-1/4 miles ne Coltishall pop 313 archd Norfolk dioc Norwich

SUTTON chapelry 1758 parish Castor co Northampton 1-1/4 miles se Wansford pop 118

SUTTON hamlet parish Granby Notts

SUTTON on Lound parish 1538 Notts 3-1/4 miles nw East Retford pop 801 archd Nottingham dioc York

SUTTON township parish Diddlebury Shrops

SUTTON parish (incl regs of Meole Brace) Shrops 2-1/4 miles se Shrewsbury pop 81 archd Salop dioc Hereford

SUTTON parish 1554 Suffolk 3-1/2 miles se Woodbridge pop 680 archd Suffolk dioc Norwich

SUTTON parish 1636 Surrey 2-3/4 miles ne Ewell pop 1,121 archd Surrey dioc Winchester Indep

SUTTON parish 1656 Sussex 5 miles s Petworth pop 379 archd and dioc Chichester

SUTTON hamlet parish Tenbury Worcs pop 185

SUTTON township parish Norton E R York

SUTTON in Holderness parish 1558 E R York 3-1/2 miles ne Kingston upon Hull pop 4,383 archd East Riding dioc York

SUTTON township parish Kirklington N R York pop 121 Wesl Meth

SUTTON township parish Masham N R York

SUTTON township parish Brotherton W R York pop 37

SUTTON township parish Campsall W R York pop 134

SUTTON township parish Kildwick W R York pop 1,153

SUTTON AT HONE parish 1607 Kent 2-1/2 miles se Dartford pop 1,012 archd and dioc Rochester

SUTTON BASSETT parish 1576 co Northampton 3-1/4 miles ne Market Harborough pop 139 archd Northampton dioc Peterborough

SUTTON BENGER parish 1653 Wilts 5 miles ne Chippenham pop 443 archd Wilts dioc Salisbury

SUTTON BINGHAM parish 1742 Somerset 3-1/2 miles sw Yeovil pop 78 archd Wells dioc Bath and Wells

SUTTON, BISHOP'S parish 1711 Hamps 1-3/4 miles se New Alresford pop 527 archd and dioc Winchester Indep

SUTTON BONNINGTON parish St Anne 1560, St Michael 1558 Notts 2 miles se Kegworth pop 1,136 archd Nottingham dioc York Wesl Meth

SUTTON BOURNE hamlet parish Long Sutton Lincs pop 706

SUTTON BY DOVER parish 1538 Kent 4 miles sw Deal pop 164 archd and dioc Canterbury

SUTTON, CHART Kent See CHART, SUTTON

SUTTON CHENEY chapelry 1674 parish Market Bosworth Leics 2 miles se Market Bosworth pop 335 Wesl Meth

SUTTON COLDFIELD parish 1603 sep juris Warws 26 miles nw Warwick pop 3,684 archd Coventry dioc Lichfield

SUTTON COURTNEY parish 1539 Berks 3 miles se Abingdon pop 1,284 archd Berks dioc Salisbury Indep

SUTTON, EAST parish 1648 Kent 6 miles se Maidstone pop 379 archd and dioc Rochester

SUTTON, ST EDMUND'S chapelry 1706 parish Long Sutton Lincs pop 626

SUTTON, FULL parish 1713 E R York 5-1/4 miles nw Pocklington pop 140 archd East Riding dioc York

SUTTON GRANGE township parish Ripon W R York pop 83

SUTTON, GREAT township parish Eastham Ches pop 162

SUTTON, GUILDEN parish 1595 Ches 3-1/4 miles ne Chester pop 132 archd and dioc Chester

SUTTON IN ASHFIELD parish 1572 Notts 3-1/2 miles sw Mansfield pop 5,476 pec Manorial Court of Mansfield Gen and Part Bapt, Indep, Prim and Wesl Meth

SUTTON IN THE ELMS township parish Broughton Astley Leics Bapt

SUTTON IN THE MARSH parish 1685 Lincs 6-1/2 miles ne Alford pop 183 archd and dioc Lincoln

SUTTON, ST JAMES chapelry 1570 parish Long Sutton Lincs 5-1/2 miles se Holbeach pop 391

SUTTON, KING'S parish 1582 co Northampton 6 miles sw Brackley pop 1,270 pec Banbury Indep, Wesl Meth

SUTTON, LITTLE township parish Eastham Ches pop 367

SUTTON, LONG parish 1672 Lincs 4-3/4 miles se Holbeach pop 5,233 archd and dioc Lincoln Indep

SUTTON, LONG parish 1558 Somerset 2-3/4 miles sw Somerton pop 957 pec Dean and Chapter of Wells

SUTTON, LONG parish 1561 Hamps 2-1/2 miles s Odiham archd and dioc Winchester pop 326

SUTTON MADDOCK parish 1559 Shrops 6 miles n Bridgenorth pop 384 archd Salop dioc Lichfield

SUTTON MALLET chapelry 1683 parish Moorlinch Somerset 5-1/4 miles se Bridgewater pop 153

SUTTON MANDEVILLE parish 1748 Wilts 7 miles sw Wilton pop 256 archd and dioc Salisbury

SUTTON MONTIS or MONTAGUE parish 1701 Somerset 5-1/4 miles s Gastle Cary pop 178 archd Wells dioc Bath and Wells

SUTTON NEAR SEAFORD parish Sussex 3/4 mile ne Seaford archd Lewes dioc Chichester

SUTTON ON THE FOREST parish 1557 N R York comp townships Huby, Sutton on the Forest pop 1,019 8-1/2 miles ne York archd Cleveland dioc York Indep

SUTTON ON THE HILL parish 1575 Derbys 8 miles sw Derby pop 574 archd Derby dioc Lichfield

SUTTON POINTZ tything parish Preston Dorset pop 340

SUTTON SCOTNEY chapelry parish Wonston Hamps

SUTTON St Nicholas 1538 Lincs 4 miles se Holbeach archd and dioc Lincoln

SUTTON UNDER BRAILS parish 1578 Gloucs and Warws 4-3/4 miles se Shipton upon Stour pop 239 archd and dioc Gloucester

SUTTON UNDER WHITESTONE CLIFFE township parish Felixkirk N R York pop 238 Calvin Meth

SUTTON UPON DERWENT parish 1593 E R York 6-1/2 miles sw Pocklington pop 417 archd East Riding dioc York Wesl Meth

SUTTON UPON TRENT parish 1584 Notts 5-1/2 miles se Tuxford pop 1,002 archd Nottingham dioc York Bapt, Wesl Meth

SUTTON VALENCE parish 1576 Kent 4-1/2 miles se Maidstone pop 1,144 archd and dioc Canterbury Indep

SUTTON VENEY parish 1653 Wilts 2 miles sw Heytesbury pop 848 archd and dioc Salisbury

SUTTON WALDRON parish 1678 Dorset 5-1/2 miles s Shaftesbury pop 236 archd Dorset dioc Bristol

SUTTON WICK township parish Sutton Courtney Berks pop 271

SWABY parish 1660 Lincs 5-1/2 miles nw Alford pop 396 archd and dioc Lincoln Wesl Meth

SWADLINCOTE chapelry parish Church Gresley Derbys pop 645 Wesl Meth

SWAFFHAM parish 1559 Norfolk 26 miles nw Norwich pop 3,285 archd Norfolk dioc Norwich Bapt, Wesl Meth

SWAFFHAM BULBECK parish 1558 Cambs 6 miles sw Newmarket pop 727 archd and dioc Ely

SWAFFHAM PRIOR parish 1559 Cambs 5-1/2 miles nw Newmarket pop 1,102 archd and dioc Ely

SWAFIELD parish 1660 Norfolk 1-1/2 miles ne North Walsham pop 155 archd Norfolk dioc Norwich

SWAINBY township parish Pickhill York pop 27 Prim and Wesl Meth

SWAINSCOE township parish Blore Staffs

SWAINSTHORPE parish 1558 Norfolk 4-1/4 miles ne St Mary Stratton pop 180 archd and dioc Norwich

SWAINSWICK parish 1557 Somerset 3 miles ne Bath pop 427 archd Bath dioc Bath and Wells

SWALCLIFFE parish 1558 comp chapelries Epwell, East Shutford, township West Shutford, hamlets Sibford Ferris, Sibford Gower co Oxford 6 miles sw Banbury pop 1,963 archd and dioc Oxford with Sibford pec Manor of Sibford

SWALECLIFFE parish 1558 Kent 6-1/2 miles n Canterbury pop 133 archd and dioc Canterbury

SWALLOW parish 1672 Lincs 3-3/4 miles ne Caistor pop 168 archd and dioc Lincoln

SWALLOWCLIFFE parish 1760 Wilts 6-1/2 miles se Hindon pop 278 pec Dean of Salisbury

SWALLOWFIELD parish 1539 Wilts 6 miles se Reading pop 1,106 archd Berks dioc Salisbury Wesl Meth

SWALWELL township parish Whickham co Durham pop 1,372 Presb, Wesl Meth

SWANAGE Dorset See SWANWICH

SWANBOURNE parish 1566 Bucks 2-1/4 miles e Winslow pop 668 archd Buckingham dioc Lincoln Bapt

SWANLAND township parish North Ferriby co Yorks pop 478 Indep

SWANNINGTON chapelry parish Whitwick Leics pop 549 Wesl Meth

SWANNINGTON parish 1538 Norfolk 3-1/2 miles se Reepham pop 370 archd Norfolk dioc Norwich

SWANSCOMBE parish 1559 Kent 4 miles e Dartford pop 1,166 archd and dioc Rochester

SWANTHORPE tything parish Crondall Hamps

SWANTON ABBOTT parish 1538 Norfolk 3 miles sw North Walsham pop 448 archd and dioc Norwich

SWANTON MORLEY parish 1548 Norfolk 3-3/4 miles ne East Dereham pop 837 archd and dioc Norwich

SWANTON NOVERS parish 1667 Norfolk 6-1/4 miles sw Holt pop 377 archd and dioc Norwich

SWANWICH parish 1563 Dorset 7 miles se Corfe Castle pop 1,734 archd Dorset dioc Bristol Indep, Wesl Meth

SWANWICK hamlet parish Alfreton Derbys Bapt, Wesl Meth

SWARBY parish 1678 Lincs 5-1/2 miles nw Falkingham pop 142 archd and dioc Lincoln

SWARDESTON parish 1538 Norfolk 4-1/2 miles sw Norwich pop 371 archd Norfolk dioc Norwich

SWARKESTONE parish 1604 Derbys 5-3/4 miles se Derby pop 308 archd Derby dioc Lichfield

SWARLAND township parish Felton Northumberland pop 210

SWARRATON parish 1754 Hamps 3 miles nw New Alresford pop 120 archd and dioc Winchester

SWATON parish 1681 Lincs 5-3/4 miles ne Falkingham pop 311 archd and dioc Lincoln

SWAVESEY parish 1576 Cambs 5-1/4 miles se St Ives pop 1,115 archd and dioc Ely Bapt

SWAY hamlet parish Boldre Hamps Bapt

SWAYFIELD parish 1724 Lincs 2 miles sw Corby pop 260 archd and dioc Lincoln

SWEETHOPE township parish Thockrington Northumberland pop 18

SWEFLING parish 1679 Suffolk 2-3/4 miles sw Saxmundham pop 336 archd Suffolk dioc Norwich

SWELL parish 1559 Somerset 4 miles sw Langport pop 87 archd Taunton dioc Bath and Wells

SWELL, LOWER or NETHER parish 1678 Gloucs 1 mile w Stow on the Wold pop 298 archd and dioc Gloucester

SWELL, UPPER parish 1543 Gloucs 1-1/4 miles nw Stow on the Wold pop 95 archd and dioc Gloucester

SWEPSTONE parish 1561 Leics 4-3/4 miles se Ashby de la Zouch pop 627 archd Leicester dioc Lincoln

SWERFORD parish 1577 co Oxford 4-1/4 miles ne Chipping Norton pop 441 archd and dioc Oxford

SWETTENHAM parish 1570 Ches comp townships Kermincham, Swettenham pop 421 5 miles nw Congleton archd and dioc Chester

SWILLAND parish 1678 Suffolk 6 miles ne Ipswich pop 272 archd Suffolk dioc Norwich

SWILLINGTON parish 1553 W R York 6-1/2 miles se Leeds pop 523 archd and dioc York

SWIMBRIDGE parish 1562 Devon 4-1/2 miles se Barnstaple pop 1,511 Consistorial Court of the Bishop of Exeter Wesl Meth

SWINBROOK parish 1684 co Oxford 2-1/2 miles e Burford pop 222 archd and dioc Oxford

SWINBURN township parish Chollerton Northumberland Roman Cath chapel Swinburn Castle

SWINBURN, LITTLE township parish Chollerton Northumberland

SWINCOMB parish 1568 co Oxford 5-1/4 miles ne Wallingford pop 367 archd and dioc Oxford

SWINDALE chapelry parish Shap Westm

SWINDERBY parish 1568 Lincs 8-1/2 miles se Lincoln pop 449 archd and dioc Lincoln Wesl Meth

SWINDON parish 1606 Gloucs 2-1/4 miles nw Cheltenham pop 225 archd and dioc Gloucester

SWINDON parish 1640 Wilts 41 miles n Salisbury archd Wilts dioc Salisbury Indep, Wesl Meth

SWINDEN township parish Gisburn W R York pop 36

SWINE parish 1706 comp chapelries Bilton, South Skirlaugh, townships Benningholme with Grange, Coniston, Ellerby, Ganstead, Marton, Swine, Thirtleby, Wyton, Wyton township of North Skirlaugh with Rowton E R York pop 1,603 6-1/2 miles ne Kingston upon Hull archd East Riding dioc York

SWINEFLEET chapelry parish Whitgift W R York 4-3/4 miles se Howden pop 1,055 Wesl Meth

SWINESHEAD parish 1550 Beds 3-1/2 miles sw Kimbolton pop 262 archd Huntingdon dioc Lincoln

SWINESHEAD parish 1639 Lincs 7 miles sw Boston pop 1,994 archd and dioc Lincoln

SWINETHORP extra parochial liberty Lincs pop 54 7 miles sw Lincoln

SWINFEN hamlet parish Weeford Staffs pop 120

SWINFORD tything parish Cumner Berks pop 38

SWINFORD parish 1559 Leics 3-1/2 miles se Lutterworth pop 438 archd Leicester dioc Lincoln

SWINFORD, KING'S parish 1603 Staffs 3 miles nw Stourbridge pop 15,156 archd Stafford dioc Lichfield

SWINFORD, OLD parish 1602 Worcs 1 mile se Stourbridge pop 13,874 archd and dioc Worcester

SWINGFIELD parish 1698 Kent 5 miles n Folkestone pop 282 archd and dioc Canterbury

SWINHOE township parish Bambrough Northumberland pop 110

SWINHOPE parish 1697 Lincs 7-3/4 miles se Caistor pop 126 archd and dioc Lincoln

SWINNERTON parish 1558 Staffs 3-1/2 miles nw Stone pop 791 archd Stafford dioc Lichfield

SWINSTEAD parish 1648 Lincs 2 miles se Corby pop 402 archd and dioc Lincoln Wesl Meth

SWINTON chapelry 1791 township Worsley parish Eccles Lancs 4-1/2 miles w Manchester

SWINTON township parish Masham N R York pop 207

SWINTON chapelry parish Appleton le Street N R York pop 333 Wesl Meth

SWINTON chapelry parish Wath upon Dearn W R York pop 1,252 archd and dioc York

SWITHLAND parish 1676 Leics 2-1/4 miles sw Mountsorrel pec Grooby

SWYRE parish 1718 Dorset 5-1/2 miles se Bridport pop 226 archd Dorset dioc Bristol

SYDE Gloucs See SIDE

SYDENHAM chapelry parish Lewiston Kent Indep, Wesl Meth

SYDENHAM parish 1705 co Oxford 2-3/4 miles e Tetsworth pop 423 pec Thame to Dean and Chapter of Lincoln

SYDENHAM DAMAREL parish 1639 Devon 5-1/4 miles nw Tavistock pop 296 archd Totnes dioc Exeter

SYDERSTONE parish 1585 Norfolk 6-1/4 miles s Burnham Westgate pop 421 archd Norfolk dioc Norwich

SYDLING parish 1565 Dorset 8 miles nw Dorchester pop 617 archd Dorset dioc Bristol Indep

SYERSCOTE or STERSCOTE liberty parish Tamworth Staffs pop 34

SYERSTON parish 1567 Notts 5-3/4 miles sw Newark pop 138 archd Nottingham dioc York

SYKEHOUSE chapelry 1700 parish Fishlake W R York 5-1/2 miles nw Thorne pop 617

SYLEHAM parish 1539 Suffolk 3-1/2 miles sw Harleston pop 391 archd Suffolk dioc Norwich

SYMONDSBURY parish 1558 Dorset 1-1/2 miles nw Bridport pop 1,147 archd Dorset dioc Bristol

SYMONDS HALL tything parish Wotton Under Edge Gloucs

SYNFIN liberty parish Barrow Derbys pop 71

SYRESHAM parish 1668 co Northampton 4-3/4 miles ne Brackley pop 895 archd Northampton dioc Peterborough Wesl Meth

SYSONBY parish (incl in regs of Melton Mowbray) Leics pop 81 archd Leicester dioc Lincoln

SYSTON parish 1644 Leics 5-1/4 miles ne Leicester pop 1,349 archd Leicester dioc Lincoln

SYSTON parish 1561 Lincs 4 miles ne Grantham pop 203 archd and dioc Lincoln

SYWELL parish 1571 co Northampton 5 miles w Wellingborough pop 216 archd Northampton dioc Peterborough

TABLEY, INFERIOR township parish Great Budworth Ches pop 134

TABLEY, SUPERIOR township parish Rosthern Ches pop 442

TACHBROOK, BISHOP'S parish 1538 Warws 3-3/4 miles se Warwick pop 674 pec Prebendary of Tachbrook Cathedral Church of Lichfield

TACHBROOK MALLORY hamlet parish Bishop's Tachbrook Warws

TACKLEY parish 1559 co Oxford 3-1/4 miles ne Woodstock pop 564 archd and dioc Oxford Wesl Meth

TACOLNESTON parish 1653 Norfolk 4-1/2 miles nw St Mary Stratton pop 486 archd Norfolk dioc Norwich

TADCASTER parish 1570 comp market town Tadcaster, township Stutton with Hazlewood, Catterton, Oxton E R York pop 2,855 archd and dioc York Indep, Inghamites, Prim and Wesl Meth

TADDINGTON chapelry 1643 parish Bakewell Derbys 3-1/2 miles sw Tideswell pop 391 Bapt

TADLEY parish 1683 Hamps 6 miles nw Basingstoke pop 683 pec Incumbent Indep

TADLOW parish 1653 Cambs 4-1/2 miles se Potton pop 176 archd and dioc Ely

TADMARTON parish 1548 co Oxford 4-3/4 miles sw Banbury pop 355 archd and dioc Oxford

TAKELEY parish 1662 Essex 2-3/4 miles se Stansted Mountfitchet pop 1,099 Commissary of Essex and Herts, Consistorial Court of Bishop of London Indep

TALATON parish 1621 Devon 4-1/2 miles nw St Mary Ottery pop 479 archd and dioc Exeter

TALK O' TH' HILL chapelry parish Audley Staffs 5 miles nw Newcastle under Line pop 1,196

TALKIN township parish Hayton Cumberland pop 376

TALLAND parish 1651 Cornwall 2 miles sw West Looe pop 1,434 archd Cornwall dioc Exeter

TALLENTIRE township parish Bridekirk Cumberland pop 237

TALLINGTON parish 1690 Lincs 3-1/2 miles sw Market Deeping pop 220 archd and dioc Lincoln

TALWROTH hamlet parish Long Ditton Surrey pop 264

TAMERTON FOLLIOTT parish 1794 Devon 5 miles nw Plymouth pop 1,061 archd Cornwall dioc Exeter

TAMERTON, NORTH parish 1556 Cornwall 5 miles sw Holsworthy pop 517 archd Cornwall dioc Exeter

TAMHORN hamlet parish Whittington Staffs pop 7

TAMWORTH parish 1558 Warws comp borough Tamworth,chapelry Wiggington, townships Almington with Stone Delph, Biddlescote, Boleshall with Glascote, Bonehill, Fazely, liberties Syerscote or Sterscote, Tamworth Castle, hamlet Wilnecote, Dosthill, extra parochial liberty Hopwas Hayes pop 7,182 22 miles se Stafford archd Stafford dioc Lichfield Bapt, Soc of Friends, Indep, Wesl Meth, Unit

TAMWORTH CASTLE liberty parish Tamworth Warws pop 19

TANDRIDGE parish 1680 Surrey 1-1/2 miles se Godstone pop 478 archd Surrey dioc Winchester

TANFIELD chapelry 1719 parish Chester le Street co Durham 6-3/4 miles sw Gateshead archd and dioc Durham

TANFIELD, EAST township parish Kirklington N R York pop 35

TANFIELD, WEST parish 1653 N R York 6-1/2 miles nw Ripon pop 693 archd Richmond dioc Chester Wesl Meth

TANGLEY parish 1675 Hamps 5-1/2 miles nw Andover pop 283 archd and dioc Winchester Wesl Meth

TANGMERE parish 1539 Sussex 3 miles ne Chichester pop 197 pec Archbishop of Canterbury

TANKERSLEY parish 1598 W R York comp chapelry Wortley, township Tankersley pop 1,596 5-1/4 miles s Barnsley archd and dioc York

TANNINGTON parish 1539 Suffolk 4-3/4 miles nw Framlingham pop 264 archd Suffolk dioc Norwich

TANSHELF township parish Pontefract W R York pop 423

TANSLEY hamlet parish Crich Derbys pop 507 Wesl Meth

TANSOR parish 1639 co Northampton 2-1/4 miles ne Oundle pop 225 archd Northampton dioc Peterborough

TANWORTH parish 1558 Warws 4-1/4 miles nw Hanley in Arden comp liberty Monks Riding pop 2,201 archd and dioc Worcester

TAPLOW parish 1710 Bucks 1 mile ne Maidenhead pop 647 archd Buckingham dioc Lincoln

TAPTON township parish Chesterfield Derbys pop 171

TARBOCK township parish Huyton Lancs pop 755

TARDEBIGG parish 1566 Warws and Worcs 3 miles se Bromsgrove pop 4,145 comp hamlets Bentley, Redditch, Tutnal with Cobley, Wibheath Yeilds archd and dioc Worcester

TARLETON parish 1719 Lancs 8-1/2 miles ne Ormskirk pop 1,886 archd and dioc Chester

TARNICAR township parish St Michael Lancs

TARPORLEY parish 1558 Ches comp market town Tarporley, townships Eaton, Rushton, Utkinton pop 2,391 archd and dioc Chester Wesl Meth

TARRABY township parish Stanwix Cumberland pop 138

TARRANT CRAWFORD Dorset See CRAWFORD TARRANT

TARRANT GUNVILLE parish 1719 Dorset 6 miles ne Blandford Forum pop 502 archd Dorset dioc Bristol

TARRANT HINTON Dorset See HINTON, TARRANT

TARRANT KEYNSTON parish 1737 Dorset 3-1/2 miles se Blandford Forum pop 277 archd Dorset dioc Bristol

TARRANT LAUNCESTON parish (incl with Tarrant Monckton) Dorset 5-1/4 miles ne Blandford Forum pop 72 archd Dorset dioc Bristol

TARRANT MONCKTON Dorset See MONCKTON, TARRANT

TARRANT RAWSTON parish 1749 Dorset 4-1/2 miles ne Blandford Forum pop 48 archd Dorset dioc Bristol

TARRANT RUSHTON parish 1696 Dorset 3-3/4 miles e Blandford Forum pop 226 archd Dorset dioc Bristol

TARRETBURN township parish Bellingham Northumberland pop 266

TARRING NEVILLE parish 1569 Sussex 2-1/2 miles n Newhaven pop 80 archd Lewes dioc Chichester

TARRING, WEST parish 1559 Sussex 1-1/2 miles nw Worthing pop 626 pec Archbishop of Canterbury

TARRINGTON parish 1561 Herefs 7 miles nw Ledbury pop 540 archd and dioc Hereford

TARSET, WEST township parish Thorneyburn Northumberland pop 149

TARVIN parish 1563 Ches comp townships Ashton, Bruen Stapleford, Burton, Clotton,Hoofield, Peele, Kelsall, Mouldsworth, Tarvin pop 3,415 6 miles ne Chester archd and dioc Chester

TASBURGH parish 1558 Norfolk 2 miles n St Mary Stratton pop 479 archd Norfolk dioc Norwich

TASLEY parish 1563 Shrops 1-3/4 miles nw Bridgenorth pop 102 archd Salop dioc Hereford

TATENHILL parish 1563 Staffs 3-3/4 miles sw Burton upon Trent pop 2,180 archd Stafford dioc Lichfield

TATHAM parish 1558 Lancs comp townships Ireby, Tatham pop 853 11 miles ne Lancaster archd Richmond dioc Chester

TATHAM FELL chapelry parish Tatham 1745 Lancs 12-1/2 miles ne Lancaster

TATHWELL parish 1625 Lincs 3-1/4 miles sw Louth pop 338 archd and dioc Lincoln

TATSFIELD parish 1690 Surrey 5-1/2 miles ne Godstone pop 166 archd Surrey dioc Winchester

TATTENHALL parish 1654 Ches comp townships Golborn Bellow, Newton by Tattenhall, Tattenhall pop 1,080 5-3/4 miles sw Tarporley archd and dioc Chester Wesl Meth

TATTENHOE parish 1733 Bucks 3-3/4 miles w Fenny Stratford pop

13 archd Buckingham dioc Lincoln

TATTERFORD parish 1560 Norfolk 4 miles sw Fakenham pop 75 archd Norfolk dioc Norwich

TATTERSET parish 1558 Norfolk 5 miles w Fakenham pop 118 archd Norfolk dioc Norwich

TATTERSHALL parish 1569 Lincs 30 miles se Lincoln pop 599 pec manorial court of Kirstead Wesl Meth

TATTINGSTONE parish 1654 Suffolk 5-1/2 miles sw Ipswich pop 356 archd Suffolk dioc Norwich Wesl Meth

TATTON township parish Rosthern Ches pop 69

TATWORTH tything parish Chard Somerset

TAUNTON borough, market town Somerset 11 miles sw Bridgewater pop 11,139 comp St James parish 1626, St Mary Magdalene parish 1558 Bapt, Soc of Friends, Indep, Unit, Roman Cath

TAVERHAM parish 1713 Norfolk 5-3/4 miles nw Norwich pop 191 archd and dioc Norwich

TAVISTOCK parish 1614 borough Devon 33 miles sw Exeter pop 5,602 archd Totnes dioc Exeter Soc of Friends, Indep, Wesl Meth, Unit

TAVY parish 1560 Devon 4 miles ne Tavistock pop 1,123 archd Totnes dioc Exeter

TAVY parish 1614 Devon 3-1/2 miles ne Tavistock pop 444 archd Totnes dioc Exeter

TAWNEY STAPLEFORD Essex See STAPLEFORD, TAWNEY

TAWSTOCK parish 1538 Devon 2 miles s Barnstaple pop 1,346 archd Barnstaple dioc Exeter Indep

TAWSTOCK Suffolk See TOSTOCK

TAWTON, BISHOP'S parish 1558 Devon 2 miles se Barnstaple pop 1,641 pec Bishop of Exeter

TAWTON, NORTH parish 1538 Devon 12 miles nw Crediton pop 1,788 archd Barnstaple dioc Exeter Indep

TAWTON, SOUTH parish 1540 Devon 2-1/4 miles se Oakhampton pop 1,937 archd and dioc Exeter

TAXALL parish 1612 Ches comp townships Taxall, Whaley with Yeardsley pop 662 archd and dioc Chester

TAYNTON parish 1538 Gloucs 3-1/2 miles se Newent pop 555 archd Hereford dioc Gloucester

TAYNTON parish 1538 co Oxford 1-3/4 miles nw Burford pop 371 archd and dioc Oxford

TEALBY parish 1714 Lincs 4-1/2 miles ne Market R asen pop 824 archd and dioc Lincoln Wesl Meth

TEAN hamlet parish Checkley Staffs Calv and Wesl Meth

TEATH parish 1558 Cornwall 3 miles sw Camelford pop 1,260 archd Cornwall dioc Exeter Bryanites, Wesl Meth

TEDBURN parish 1558 Devon 4-1/2 miles sw Crediton pop 821 archd and dioc Exeter

TEDDINGTON parish 1558 Middlesex 11 miles sw London pop 895 Commissary of London Consistorial Court of the Bishop of London

TEDDINGTON chapelry 1560 parish Overbury Worcs 5 miles ne

Tewkesbury pop 129

TEDSTONE DELAMERE parish 1690 Herefs 4-1/2 miles ne Bromyard pop 230 archd and dioc Hereford

TEDSTONE WAFER parish 1729 Herefs 3-3/4 miles ne Bromyard pop 91 archd and dioc Hereford

TEETON hamlet parish Ravensthorpe co Northampton pop 73

TEFFONT EVIAS parish 1597 Wilts 6-1/2 miles sw Wilton pop 176 archd and dioc Salisbury

TEFFONT MAGNA parish (incl regs of Dinton) Wilts 5-1/4 miles e Hindon pop 213 archd and dioc Salisbury

TEIGH parish 1572 co Rutland 5 miles n Oakham pop 176 archd Northampton dioc Peterborough

TEIGNMOUTH market town parish West Teignmouth 1706,parish East Teignmouth 1665 Devon 15 miles se Exeter pop 4,688 pec Dean and Chapter of Exeter Bapt,Indep,Calv Meth

TEIGNTON, BISHOP'S parish 1558 Devon 1-3/4 miles nw West Teignmouth pop 1,085 pec Bishop of Exeter

TEIGNTON DREWS parish 1653 Devon 4-1/2 miles nw Moreton Hampstead pop 1,313 archd and dioc Exeter

TEIGNTON, KING'S parish 1670 Devon 2 miles ne Newton Bushell pop 1,288 archd Totnes dioc Exeter Indep

TEINGRACE parish 1683 Devon 2-1/4 miles nw Newton Bushell pop 160 archd Totnes dioc Exeter

TELLISFORD parish 1539 Somerset 6 miles ne Frome pop 162 archd Wells dioc Bath and Wells

TELSCOMBE parish 1684 Sussex 3-1/2 miles nw Newhaven pop 121 archd Lewes dioc Chichester

TEMPLE parish no regs Cornwall 6-1/4 miles ne Bodmin pop 29 pec no probate records

TEMPLE BREWER extra parochial liberty Lincs 6-3/4 miles nw Sleaford pop 73

TEMPLE GRAFTON Warws See GRAFTON, TEMPLE

TEMPLE HALL extra parochial liberty Leics 2-1/2 miles sw Market Bosworth pop 28

TEMPLE NEWSOM township parish Whitkirk W R York pop 1,458 pec manorial court of Temple Newsom

TEMPLETON parish 1556 Devon 5 miles nw Tiverton pop 222 archd and dioc Exeter

TEMPSFORD parish 1604 Beds 6-1/2 miles nw Biggleswade pop 535 archd Bedford dioc Lincoln Wesl Meth

TENBURY parish 1653 Worcs comp market town Tenbury, hamlets Berrington, Sutton, Tenbury Foreign pop 1,768 archd Salop dioc Hereford Part Bapt

TENBURY FOREIGN hamlet parish Tenbury Worcs pop 325

TENDRING parish 1538 Essex 6-1/2 miles se Manningtree pop 758 archd Colchester dioc London

TENTERDEN parish 1544 sep juris Kent 18 miles se Maidstone pop 3,177 archd and dioc Canterbury Bapt, Wesl Meth, Unit

TENTERGATE township parish Knaresborough W R York

TERLING parish 1538 Essex 3-3/4 miles w Witham pop 892 archd Colchester dioc London Wesl Meth

TERRINGTON parish 1597 Norfolk 5-1/2 miles nw Lynn Regis pop 1,466 archd and dioc Norwich Wesl Meth

TERRINGTON parish 1538 Norfolk 6 miles sw Lynn Regis pop 595 archd and dioc Norwich

TERRINGTON parish 1599 N R York comp townships Ganthorpe, Terrington with Wigginthorpe pop 759 archd Cleveland dioc York Wesl Meth

TERWICK parish Sussex See TURWICK

TESTERTON parish no regs Norfolk 2-3/4 miles se Fakenham pop 18 archd and dioc Norwich

TESTON parish 1538 Kent 4 miles sw Maidstone pop 255 archd and dioc Rochester

TETBURY parish 1631 Gloucs 20 miles se Gloucester pop 2,939 archd and dioc Gloucester Bapt, Indep

TETCHWORTH hamlet parish Ludgershall Bucks

TETCOTT parish 1599 Devon 5 miles sw Holsworthy pop 293 archd Totnes dioc Exeter

TETFORD parish 1709 Lincs 6 miles ne Horncastle pop 690 archd and dioc Lincoln Wesl Meth

TETNEY parish 1730 Lincs 10-1/2 miles n Louth pop 647 archd and dioc Lincoln Wesl Meth

TETSWORTH parish 1604 co Oxford 11-1/2 miles se Oxford pop 530 pec Dean and Chapter of Lincoln Wesl Meth

TETTENHALL REGIS parish 1602 comp hamlets Oaken, Pirton with Trescott, Tattenhall Clericorum, hamlet Wrottesley Staffs 1-3/4 miles nw Wolverhampton pop 2,889 pec Court of Tattenhall Wesl Meth

TETTON township parish Warmington Ches pop 181

TETWORTH parish Hunts (incl in Everton, Beds) 3 miles nw Potton pop 183

TEVERSALL parish 1571 Notts 5-1/4 miles nw Mansfield archd Nottingham dioc York

TEVERSHAM parish 1592 Cambs 3-1/2 miles e Cambridge pop 197 pec Bishop of Ely

TEW, GREAT parish 1609 co Oxford 3-3/4 miles ne Neat Enstone pop 656 archd and dioc Oxford

TEW, LITTLE chapelry parish Great Tew co Oxford pop 216

TEWIN parish 1559 Herts 3 miles se Welwyn archd Huntingdon dioc Lincoln

TEWKESBURY parish 1559 borough sep juris Gloucs 10 miles ne Gloucester pop 5,780 archd and dioc Gloucester Soc of Friends, Indep, Wesl Meth

TEY, GREAT parish 1559 Essex 4 miles ne Great Coggeshall pop 682 archd Colchester dioc London

TEY, LITTLE parish 1660 Essex 2-3/4 miles ne Great Coggeshall pop 58 archd Colchester dioc London

TEY, MARKS parish 1560 Essex 4 miles nw Great Coggeshall pop 363 archd Colchester dioc London

TEYNHAM parish 1539 Kent 4-1/4 miles e Sittingbourne pop 753 archd and dioc Canterbury

THAKEHAM parish 1628 Sussex 6-1/2 miles nw Steyning pop 597 archd and dioc Chichester

THAME parish 1601 co Oxford 13 miles e Oxford comp townships Old Thame, New Thame, Priestend, North Weston, Moreton, Thame Park pop 2,885 Dean and Chapter of Lincoln

THAMES DITTON Surrey See DITTON, THAMES

THANET, ISLE OF St Lawrence 1560, St Peters 1582 ne extremity of Kent archd and dioc Canterbury Wesl Meth

THANINGTON parish 1558 Kent 1-3/4 miles sw Canterbury pop 316 archd and dioc Canterbury

THARSTON parish 1560 Norfolk 1-1/2 miles nw St Mary Stratton pop 369 archd Norfolk dioc Norwich

THATCHAM parish 1561 borough Berks 3 miles e Newbury pop 3,912 archd Berks dioc Salisbury Indep

THAXTED parish 1558 Essex 19 miles nw Chelmsford pop 2,293 Commissary of Essex and Herts, Consistorial Court of the Bishop of London Bapt, Soc of Friends, Indep

THEAKSTONE township parish Burneston N R York pop 82

THEALE chapelry parish Tilehurst Berks

THEARNE township parish St John Beverley E R York pop 67

THEBARTON parish 1548 Suffolk 4 miles ne Saxmundham pop 537 archd Suffolk dioc Norwich

THEDDINGWORTH parish 1635 Leics 4-1/2 miles sw Market Harborough pop 283 archd Leicester dioc Lincoln

THEDDLETHORPE parish 1561 Lincs 10-1/2 miles ne Alford pop 266 archd and dioc Lincoln

THEDDLETHORPE parish 1716 Lincs 9-3/4 miles ne Alford pop 275 archd and dioc Lincoln Wesl Meth

THELBRIDGE parish 1612 Devon 7-1/4 miles se Chulmleigh pop 219 archd Barnstaple dioc Exeter

THELNETHAM parish 1538 Suffolk 3-1/2 miles nw Botesdale pop 553 archd Sudbury dioc Norwich

THELVETON parish 1538 Norfolk 1-3/4 miles n Scole pop 175 archd Norfolk dioc Norwich

THELWALL chapelry 1782 parish Runcorn Ches 3-1/2 miles se Warrington pop 332 archd and dioc Chester

THEMELTHORPE parish 1715 Norfolk 1-3/4 miles se Foulsham pop 89 archd Norfolk dioc Norwich

THENFORD parish 1562 co Northampton 5-1/2 miles nw Brackley pop 231 archd Northampton dioc Peterborough

THERFIELD parish 1538 Herts 2-1/2 miles sw Royston pop 974 archd Huntingdon dioc Lincoln

THETFORD chapelry 1654 parish Stretham Cambs 2-1/4 miles sw Ely pop 257

THETFORD borough excl juris Suffolk 30 miles sw Norwich pop 3,462 comp St Cuthbert 1672, St Peter 1672, St Mary the Less 1653 archd and dioc Norwich Soc of Friends, Indep, Wesl Meth, Roman Cath

THICKLEY, EAST township parish St Andrew Auckland co Durham pop 35

THIMBLEBY parish 1695 Lincs 1-1/2 miles nw Horncastle pop 364 archd and dioc Lincoln

THIMBLEBY township parish Camotherley N R York pop 185

THINGDON co Northampton See FINEDON

THINGWELL township parish Woodchurch Ches pop 77

THIRKLEBY township parish Kirkby Grindalyth E R York pop 44

THIRKLEBY parish 1611 N R York 4 miles se Thirsk pop 317 archd Cleveland dioc York

THIRLBY township parish Felixkirk N R York pop 131

THIRLWALL township parish Haltwhistle Northumberland pop 328

THIRN township parish Thornton Watlass N R York pop 142

THIRNE parish (incl in regs of Ashby) Norfolk 4-1/2 miles ne Acle pop 138 archd and dioc Norwich

THIRNTOFT township parish Ainderby Steeple N R York pop 170

THIRSK parish 1556 N R York comp borough Thirsk, chapelries Carlton Islebeck or Miniot, Sand Hutton, Somerby pop 3,829 23 miles nw York archd Cleveland dioc York Soc of Friends, Indep, Wesl Meth

THIRTLEBY township parish Swine E R York pop 59

THISTLETON township parish Kirkham Lancs

THISTLETON parish 1574 co Rutland 8 miles ne Oakham pop 151 archd Northampton dioc Peterborough

THIXENDALE township parish Wharram Percy E R York pop 207

THOCKRINGTON parish 1715 Northumberland comp townships Little Savington, Cary Coats, Sweethope, Thockrington pop 203 pec Prebendary of Thockrington Cathedral Church of York

THOLTHORP township parish Alne N R York pop 265

THOMAS CLOSE township parish Hutton in the Forest Cumberland pop 106

THOMAS ST STREET extra parochial hamlet parish St Thomas the Apostle Cornwall pop 37

THOMAS ST THE APOSTLE parish 1673 Cornwall near Launceston pop 626 archd Cornwall dioc Exeter

THOMAS ST THE APOSTLE parish 1554 Devon 1/2 miles s Oldridge pop 3,245 archd and dioc Exeter

THOMPSON parish 1538 Norfolk 3 miles se Watton pop 478 archd and dioc Norwich

THOMPSON'S WALL township parish Kirknewton Northumberland pop 41

THOMSON parish 1802 Dorset 7 miles se Blandford Forum pop 41 pec Dean of Salisbury

THONG, NETHER township parish Almondbury W R York pop 1,004

THONG, UPPER township parish Almondbury W R York pop 1,648
Wesl Meth

THORALNY township parish Aysgarth N R York pop 273

THORESBY, NORTH parish 1546 Lincs 8-1/2 miles nw Louth pop
544 archd and dioc Lincoln Wesl Meth

THORESBY, SOUTH parish 1665 Lincs 4 miles nw Alford pop 142
archd and dioc Lincoln

THORESTHORPE hamlet parish Salaby Lincs

THORESWAY parish 1727 Lincs 5 miles se Caistor pop 158 archd
and dioc Lincoln

THORGANBY parish 1561 Lincs 6-1/4 miles se Caistor pop 108 archd
and dioc Lincoln

THORGANBY parish 1653 E R York 8-1/2 miles ne Selby pop 342
archd Cleveland dioc York Wesl Meth

THORINGTON parish 1561 Suffolk 4 miles se Halesworth pop 159
archd Suffolk dioc Norwich

THORLBY township parish Kildwick W R York

THORLEY parish 1539 Herts 2-1/2 miles sw Bishop's Stortford pop
414 archd Middlesex dioc London

THORLEY parish 1658 Hamps 1 mile se Yarmouth pop 146 archd and
dioc Winchester

THORMANBY parish 1658 N R York 4-1/4 miles nw Easingwould pop
133 archd Cleveland dioc York

THORN parish 1715 Somerset 3 miles w Wellington pop 165 archd
Taunton dioc Bath and Wells

THORNABY chapelry parish Stainton N R York pop 301 archd Cleveland dioc York

THORNAGE parish 1560 Norfolk 2-3/4 miles sw Holt archd and dioc
Norwich pop 332

THORNBOROUGH parish 1602 Bucks 3-1/2 miles e Buckingham pop
673 archd Buckingham dioc Lincoln

THORNBOROUGH township parish Corbridge Northumberland pop 81

THORNBOROUGH township parish South Kilvington N R York pop 21

THORNBURY parish 1652 Devon 4-1/2 miles ne Holsworthy pop 546
archd Totnes dioc Exeter

THORNBURY parish 1538 Gloucs 24 miles sw Gloucester pop 4,375
comp chapelries Falfield, Oldbury upon Severn, Tangeworthy, tythings Kington, Moorton archd and dioc Gloucester Soc of Friends,
Bapt, Indep, Wesl Meth

THORNBURY parish 1538 Herefs 4-1/4 miles nw Bromyard pop 212
archd and dioc Hereford

THORNBY parish 1649 co Northampton pop 198 10-1/2 miles nw
Northampton archd Northampton dioc Peterborough

THORN COFFIN parish 1690 Somerset 2-1/2 miles nw Yeovil pop 101
archd Wells dioc Bath and Wells

THORNCOMBE parish 1551 formerly in Devon now in Dorset 6-1/2
miles sw Axminster pop 1,368 archd and dioc Exeter

THORNCOTE hamlet parish Northill Beds pop 268

THORNDON parish 1538 Suffolk 3-1/4 miles sw Eye pop 696 archd
Sudbury dioc Norwich

THORNE parish 1565 W R York 29 miles se York pop 3,779 archd
and dioc York Soc of Friends, Indep, Prim and Wesl Meth, Unit

THORNE FALCON parish 1725 Somerset 3-1/2 miles se Taunton
pop 273 archd Taunton dioc Bath and Wells

THORNER parish 1622 W R York comp townships Scarcroft, Shadwell,
Thorner pop 1,220 archd and dioc York Wesl Meth

THORNES township parish Wakefield W R York

THORNEY parish 1653 Cambs 35 miles nw Cambridge pop 308 pec
Thorney

THORNEY parish 1562 Notts 6-3/4 miles ne Tuxford pop 308 archd
Nottingham dioc York

THORNEY, WEST parish 1530 Sussex 7-1/2 miles sw Chichester
pop 104 archd and dioc Chichester

THORNEYBURN parish 1819 Northumberland comp townships West
Tarset, Thorneyburn pop 334 archd Northumberland dioc Durham

THORNFORD parish 1676 Dorset 3-1/2 miles sw Sherborne pop 383
pec Dean of Salisbury

THORNGRAFTON township parish Haltwhistle Northumberland pop
263

THORN GUMBALD chapelry parish Paul E R York pop 266 Indep

THORNHAM parish 1625 Kent 4 miles ne Maidstone pop 571 archd
and dioc Canterbury Wesl Meth

THORNHAM township parish Middleton Lancs pop 1,455

THORNHAM parish 1716 Norfolk 6-1/4 miles nw Burnham Westgate
pop 668 archd Norfolk dioc Norwich

THORNHAM MAGNA parish 1555 Suffolk 3-1/4 miles sw Eye pop 380
archd Sudbury dioc Norwich

THORNHAM PARVA parish 1766 Suffolk 2-3/4 miles sw Eye pop 206
archd Sudbury dioc Norwich

THORNHAUGH parish 1562 no Northampton 1-1/4 miles n Wansford
pop 271 archd Northampton dioc Peterborough

THORNHILL hamlet parish Hope Derbys pop 135

THORNHILL tything parish Stalbridge Dorset pop 257

THORNHILL parish 1580 W R York comp chapelry Flockton, townships Shitlington, Thornhill, Lower Whitley pop 6,271 archd and
dioc York Bapt, Wesl Meth

THORNHOLM township parish Burton Agnes E R York pop 93

THORNLEY township parish Kelloe co Durham pop 50

THORNLEY township parish Chipping Lancs pop 516

THORNSETT hamlet parish Glossop Derbys pop 685

THORNTHWAITE chapelry 1775 parish Crosthwaite Cumberland pop
174

THORNTHWAITE chapelry parish Hampsthwaite W R York 7-1/2
miles sw Ripley pop 304

THORNTON parish 1562 Bucks 4-1/4 miles ne Buckingham pop 94
archd Buckingham dioc Lincoln

THORNTON or THORNTON IN THE MOOR parish Ches 1574 comp townships Dunham, Elton, Hapsford, Thornton in the Moor, Wimbold Trafford pop 914 archd and dioc Chester

THORNTON hamlet parish Hope Derbys pop 104

THORNTON tything parish Marnhull Dorset

THORNTON township parish Norham co Durham and Northumberland pop 192

THORNTON township parish Poulton Lancs pop 842 Wesl Meth

THORNTON township parish Sephton Lancs pop 342

THORNTON parish 1559 Leics 6 miles ne Market Bosworth pop 1,078 comp chapelries Bagworth, Stanton under Bardon, township Horsepool, extra parochial liberty Bagworth Park archd Leicester dioc Lincoln

THORNTON parish 1561 Lincs 1-3/4 miles sw Horncastle pop 216 archd and dioc Lincoln

THORNTON parish 1651 E R York 4-1/4 miles sw Pocklington pop 791 pec Dean of York

THORNTON township parish Coxwold N R York pop 67

THORNTON chapelry 1678 parish Bradford W R York 4-1/2 miles w Bradford pop 5,968

THORNTON or THORNTON IN CRAVEN parish 1568 W R York 5-3/4 miles sw Skipton pop 2,246 archd Richmond dioc Chester

THORNTON, BISHOP chapelry parish Ripon W R York pop 614 pec of Ripon

THORNTON BRIDGE township parish Brafferton N R York pop 47

THORNTON CHILDER township parish Eastham Ches pop 296

THORNTON CURTIS parish 1568 Lincs 5 miles se Barton upon Humber pop 362 archd and dioc Lincoln

THORNTON DALE parish 1539 W R York comp townships Farmanby, Thornton Dale pop 1,368 2-1/2 miles se Pickering archd Cleveland dioc York Wesl Meth

THORNTON, EAST township parish Hartburn Northumberland pop 59

THORNTON IN LONSDALE parish 1576 W R York comp chapelry Black Burton, township Thornton pop 1,152 archd Richmond dioc Chester

THORNTON LE BEANS township parish North Otterington N R York pop 219 Wesl Meth

THORNTON LE FEN chapelry no regs 8-1/2 miles nw Boston Lincs pop 156

THORNTON LE MOOR parish 1735 Lincs 5-1/2 miles sw Caistor pop 99 archd and dioc Lincoln

THORNTON LE MOOR township parish North Otterington N R York 5 miles nw Thirsk pop 337

THORNTON LE STREET parish 1600 N R York 3 miles nw Thirsk comp townships North Kilvington, Thornton le Street pop 226 pec of Bishop of Durham

THORNTON MAYOW township parish Neston Ches pop 144

THORNTON RUST township parish Aysgarth N R York pop 158

THORNTON STEWARD parish 1563 N R York 3-1/2 miles se Middle-
ham pop 310 archd Richmond dioc Chester
THORNTON UPON CLAY township parish Foston N R York pop 205
THORNTON WATLASS parish 1574 N R York comp townships Clifton
upon Ure, Rookwith, Thirn, Thornton Watlass pop 448 archd Rich-
mond dioc Chester
THORNTON, WEST township parish Hartburn Northumberland pop 53
THORNVILLE township parish Whixley W R York pop 17
THORNWOOD hamlet parish North Weald Essex
THOROTON parish 1583 Notts 8 miles sw Newark pop 143 archd Not-
tingham dioc York
THORP township parish Rothwell W R York pop 62
THORP ACRE parish (incl in regs of Dishley) Leics 1-1/4 miles nw
Loughborough pop 366 archd Leicester dioc Lincoln
THORP ARCH parish 1595 E R York 2-3/4 miles se Wetherby pop
316 archd and dioc York Wesl Meth
THORP AUDLING township parish Badsworth W R York pop 355
THORP BASSETT parish 1656 E R York 5 miles ne New Malton pop
206 archd East Riding dioc York
THORP MORIEUX parish 1538 Suffolk 4-1/4 miles nw Bildeston pop
412 archd Sudbury dioc Norwich
THORP STAPLETON township parish Whitkirk W R York pop 19
THORP SUB MONTEM township parish Burnsall W R York pop 242
THORP UNDERWOODS township parish Little Ouseburn W R York
pop 144
THORPE parish 1538 Derbys 3-1/2 miles nw Ashbourn pop 189 archd
Derby dioc Lichfield
THORPE hamlet parish Tattershall Lincs pop 284
THORPE parish 1706 Norfolk 2-3/4 miles se Norwich pop 2,151 pec
Bishop of Norwich
THORPE parish 1559 Notts 3-1/4 miles sw Newark pop 105 archd
Nottingham dioc York
THORPE parish Notts 6-3/4 miles ne Loughborough pop 39 archd
Nottingham dioc York
THORPE hamlet parish Aldringham Suffolk
THORPE chapelry parish Ashfield Suffolk archd Suffolk dioc Norwich
THORPE parish 1653 Surrey 2 miles nw Chertsey pop 471 archd Sur-
rey dioc Winchester
THORPE township parish Howden E R York pop 44
THORPE township parish Wycliffe N R York
THORPE township parish Ripon W R York
THORPE ABBOTS parish 1695 Norfolk 2-1/4 miles e Scole pop 272
archd Norfolk dioc Norwich
THORPE ACHURCH parish 1670 co Northampton 4-1/2 miles ne
Thrapstone pop 240 archd Northampton dioc Peterborough
THORPE ARNOLD parish 1558 Leics 1-1/2 miles ne Melton Mowbray
pop 117 archd Leicester dioc Lincoln
THORPE BRANTINGHAM township parish Brantingham E R York

pop 66

THORPE BULMER township parish Monk Mesleton co Durham pop 28

THORPE BY IXWORTH parish 1718 Suffolk 1/2 mile nw Ixworth pop 128 archd Suffolk dioc Norwich

THORPE BY WATER hamlet parish Seaton co Rutland pop 89

THORPE CONSTANTINE parish 1538 Staffs 5 miles ne Tamworth pop 49 archd Stafford dioc Lichfield

THORPE, EAST hamlet parish Londesborough E R York

THORPE IN BALNE township parish Barnby upon Don W R York pop 121

THORPE IN THE STREET township parish Nun Burnholme E R York pop 31

THORPE LE SOKEN parish 1682 Essex 9-1/2 miles se Manningtree pop 1,173 pec Court of the Sokens Bapt

THORPE, LITTLE parish (incl in regs of Billington) Norfolk 1/2 mile e Scole archd Norfolk dioc Norwich

THORPE LANGTON Leics See LANGTON, THORPE

THORPE LUBENHAM township parish Marston Trussel co Northampton pop 3

THORPE MALSOR parish 1683 co Northampton 2 miles nw Kettering pop 297 archd Northampton dioc Peterborough

THORPE MANDERBILLE parish 1576 co Northampton 6 miles ne Banbury pop 175 archd Northampton dioc Peterborough

THORPE, MARKET parish 1538 Norfolk 4-3/4 miles nw North Walsham pop 254 archd Norfolk dioc Norwich

THORPE NEXT HADDISCOE parish 1530 Norfolk 5-3/4 miles ne Beccles pop 79 archd Norfolk dioc Norwich

THORPE ON THE HILL parish 1695 Lincs 6 miles sw Lincoln Wesl Meth

THORPE SALVIN parish 1592 W R York 5-3/4 miles nw Worksop pop 233 pec Chancellor of the Cathedral Church of York Wesl Meth

THORPE SATCHVILLE chapelry parish Twyford Leics pop 163

THORPE TINLEY township parish Timberland Lincs pop 127

THORPE UNDERWOOD hamlet parish Rothwell co Northampton pop 18

THORPE, WEST or THORDE ST PETER parish 1653 Lincs 7-1/2 miles Lincoln archd Stow dioc Lincoln

THORPE WILLOUGHBY township parish Brayton W R York pop 148

THORPELAND hamlet parish Wallington Norfolk

THORPLAND hamlet parish Fakenham Lancaster Norfolk

THORRINGTON parish 1553 Essex 8-1/4 miles se Colchester pop 431 archd Colchester dioc London Wesl Meth

THORROCK hamlet parish Gainsborough Lincs

THORVERTON parish 1725 Devon 7 miles sw Cullompton pop 1,455 archd and dioc Exeter

THOTDON BOIS parish 1717 Essex 3-1/2 miles s Epping pop 676 archd Essex dioc London

THOYDON GARDON or COPPERSHALL parish 1558 Essex 2-1/2 miles

se Epping pop 841 archd Essex dioc London

THOYDON, MOUNT parish 1564 Essex 4 miles se Epping pop 249 archd Essex dioc London

THRANDESTON parish 1558 Suffolk 3 miles nw Eye pop 358 archd Sudbury dioc Norwich

THRAPSTON or THRAPSTONE parish 1560 co Northampton 21 miles ne Northampton archd Northampton dioc Peterborough Bapt

THREAPLAND township parish Torpenhow Cumberland

THRECKINGHAM parish 1572 Lincs 2 miles ne Falkingham pop 191 archd and dioc Lincoln

THREE FARMS township parish Eccleshall Staffs pop 67

THRELKELD chapelry 1573 parish Greystock Cumberland 4 miles ne Keswick pop 320 archd and dioc Carlisle

THRESHFIELD township parish Linton W R York pop 212

THREXTON parish 1731 Norfolk 2-1/4 miles sw Watton pop 29 archd Norfolk dioc Norwich

THRIBERGH parish 1599 W R York 3 miles ne Rotherham pop 332 archd and dioc York

THRIGBY parish 1539 Norfolk 4-1/2 miles w Caistor pop 43 archd and dioc Norwich

THRIMBY chapelry parish Morland Westm 9 miles nw Orton pop 81 archd and dioc Carlisle

THRINGSTONE chapelry parish Whitwick Leics pop 1,267 archd Leicester dioc Lincoln Wesl Meth

THRIPLOW parish 1538 Cambs 5-1/2 miles ne Royston pop 417 pec Bishop of Ely

THRISLINGTON township parish co Durham pop 15

THRISTON, EAST and WEST township parish Felton Northumberland pop 307

THROAPHAM township parish Laughton en le Morthen W R York pop 70

THROCKING parish 1612 Herts 2 miles nw Buntingford pop 76 archd Huntingdon dioc Lincoln

THROCKLEY township parish Newburn Northumberland pop 208

THROCKMORTON chapelry 1546 parish Fladbury Worcs 3-1/4 miles ne Pershore pop 159

THROPPLE township parish Mitford Northumberland pop 78

THROPTON township parish Rothbury Northumberland pop 218 Presb, Roman Cath

THROSTON township parish Hart co Durham pop 70

THROWLEY parish 1653 Devon 6-3/4 miles se Oakhampton pop 460 archd and dioc Exeter

THROWLEY parish 1557 Kent 4-1/2 miles sw Faversham pop 675 archd and dioc Canterbury

THROWLEY hamlet parish Ilam Staffs

THROXENBY township parish Scalby N R York pop 54

THRUMPTON parish 1679 Notts 4 miles ne Kegworth pop 132 archd Nottingham dioc York

THRUP hamlet parish Kidlington co Oxford pop 84

THRUPP tything parish Great Farringdon Berks

THRUPP hamlet parish Stroud Gloucs

THUPPWICK liberty parish Radley Berks pop 31

THRUSSINGTON parish 1660 Leics 8-1/4 miles ne Leicester pop 454 archd Leicester dioc Lincoln

THRUXTON parish 1582 Herefs 6-1/4 miles sw Hereford pop 59 Consistorial Court of Dean of Hereford

THRUXTON parish 1600 Hamps 5 miles w Andover pop 269 archd and dioc Winchester Wesl Meth

THUNDERLEY hamlet parish Wimbish Essex 2 miles se Saffron Waldon

THUNDERSLEY parish 1569 Essex 2-1/4 miles sw Rayleigh pop 526 archd Essex dioc London

THUNDRIDGE parish 1556 Herts 2-1/2 miles ne Ware pop 588 archd Middlesex dioc London

THURCASTON parish 1561 Leicester 3-1/4 miles sw Mountsorrel comp chapelry Anstey, township Cropston pop 1,241 archd Leicester dioc Lincoln

THURCROSS township parish Fewston W R York pop 601

THURGARTON parish 1538 Norfolk 4-3/4 miles sw Cromer pop 247 archd Norfolk dioc Norwich

THURGARTON parish 1721 Notts 3-1/4 miles sw Southwell pop 329 archd Nottingham dioc York

THURGOLAND township parish Silkstone W R York pop 1,147

THURLASTON parish 1588 Leics 6 miles ne Hinckley comp hamlet Normanton Turville, liberty Newparks pop 636 archd Leicester dioc Lincoln

THURLASTON hamlet parish Dunchurch Warws pop 281

THURLBEAR parish 1700 Somerset 3-1/4 miles se Taunton pop 202 archd Taunton dioc Bath and Wells

THURLBY parish 1575 Lincs 9-1/2 miles sw Lincoln pop 145 pec Dean and Chapter of Lincoln

THURLBY hamlet parish Bilsby Lincs

THRULBY parish 1560 Lincs 5-1/4 miles nw Market Deeping pop 632 archd and dioc Lincoln

THURLEIGH parish 1562 Beds 6-1/2 miles n Bedford pop 538 archd Bedford dioc Lincoln

THURLESTONE parish 1558 Devon 4-1/2 miles sw Kingsbridge pop 466 archd Totnes dioc Exeter

THURLESTONE township parish Penistone W R York pop 1,599 Wesl Meth

THURLOW, GREAT parish 1636 Suffolk 5 miles ne Haverhill pop 425 archd Sudbury dioc Norwich

THURLOW, LITTLE parish 1562 Suffolk 5-1/2 miles ne Haverhill pop 464 archd Sudbury dioc Norwich

THURLOXTON parish 1558 Somerset 5 miles sw Bridgewater pop 229 archd Taunton dioc Bath and Wells

THURLSTON parish (incl in regs of Whitton) Suffolk 2-1/2 miles nw Ipswich archd Suffolk dioc Norwich

THURLTON parish 1695 Norfolk 5-1/2 miles n Beccles pop 416 archd Norfolk dioc Norwich

THURMASTON, NORTH chapelry parish Barkby Leics pop 184 Wesl Meth

THURMASTON, SOUTH chapelry 1719 parish Belgrave Leics 3 miles ne Leicester pop 947

THURNBY parish 1538 Leics 4 miles se Leicester comp chapelry Stoughton, hamlet Bushby pop 383 archd Leicester dioc Lincoln

THURNHAM township parish Lancaster Lancs pop 526

THURNING parish 1560 co Northampton and Hunts 4-1/2 miles se Oundle pop 130 archd Huntingdon dioc Lincoln

THURNING parish 1715 Norfolk 4-3/4 miles nw Reepham pop 140 archd Norfolk dioc Norwich

THURNSCOE parish 1619 W R York 8 miles e Barnesley pop 223 archd and dioc York

THURROCK, GRAYS parish 1674 Essex 22 miles sw Chelmsford pop 1,248 archd Essex dioc London

THURROCK, LITTLE parish 1654 Essex 1 mile e Grays Thurrock pop 302 archd Essex dioc London

THURROCK, WEST parish 1668 Essex 1 mile w Grays Thurrock pop 804 Commissary of Essex and Herts, Consistorial Court of the Bishop of London

THURSBY parish 1649 Cumberland comp townships Crofton Quarter, Parton, High Thursby pop 564 6-1/2 miles sw Carlisle archd and dioc Carlisle

THURSFIELD or NEWCHAPEL chapelry 1723 parish Wolstanton Staffs 6-1/2 miles ne Newcastle under Line pop 389

THURSFORD parish 1692 Norfolk 3-1/2 miles se Little Walsingham pop 392 archd and dioc Norwich

THURSHELTON parish 1654 Devon 10 miles sw Oakhampton pop 353 archd Totnes dioc Exeter

THURSLEY parish 1613 Surrey 5-1/2 miles sw Godalming pop 708 archd Surrey dioc Winchester

THURSTASTON parish 1706 Ches 5 miles nw Great Neston pop 92 archd and dioc Chester

THURSTON parish 1707 Suffolk 5-1/2 miles ne Bury St Edmunds pop 462 archd Sudbury dioc Norwich

THURSTONLAND township parish Kirk Burton W R York pop 1,098 Wesl Meth

THURTON parish 1559 Norfolk 8 miles se Norwich pop 193 archd Norfolk dioc Norwich

THURVASTON township parish Sutton on the Hill Derby Wesl Meth

THUXTON parish 1538 Norfolk 4 miles ne Hingham pop 83 archd Norfolk dioc Norwich

THWAITE parish 1562 Norfolk 4-3/4 miles n Aylsham pop 142 archd and dioc Norwich

THWAITE parish 1538 Norfolk 3-1/2 miles n Bungay pop 107 archd Norfolk dioc Norwich

THWAITE parish 1709 Suffolk 4-3/4 miles sw Eye pop 175 archd Sudbury dioc Norwich

THWAITE chapelry 1724 parish Millom Cumberland 10 miles se Ravenglass pop 324

THWING parish 1691 E R York 8-3/4 miles nw Bridlington pop 350 archd East Riding dioc York

TIBBENHAM parish 1560 Norfolk 5 miles sw St Mary Stratton pop 650 archd Norfolk dioc Norwich

TIBBERTON parish 1659 Gloucs 4-1/4 miles se Newent pop 307 archd Hereford dioc Gloucester

TIBBERTON chapelry 1719 parish Edgmond Shrops 4-1/4 miles nw Newport pop 351

TIBBERTON parish 1680 Worcs 4 miles ne Worcester pop 337 pec Dean and Chapter of Worcester

TIBERTON parish 1672 Herefs 9 miles w Hereford pop 118 pec Dean of Hereford

TIBSHELF parish 1626 Derbys 4 miles ne Alfreton pop 759 archd Derby dioc Lichfield

TIBTHORP township parish Kirkburn E R York pop 227 Wesl Meth

TICEHURST parish 1560 Sussex 4 miles se Wadhurst pop 2,314 archd Lewes dioc Chichester

TICHBOURNE Hamps See TITCHBOURNE

TICHENHAM parish 1538 Somerset 9-1/4 miles sw Bristol pop 427 archd Bath dioc Bath and Wells

TICHFIELD Hamps See TITCHFIELD

TICKENCOTE parish 1574 co Rutland 3 miles nw Stamford pop 128 archd Northampton dioc Peterborough

TICKHILL parish 1538 W R York comp town Tickhill, township Stancill with Wellingley Wilsick pop 2,804 45 miles s York archd and dioc York Indep, Wesl Meth

TICKNALL parish 1627 Derbys 5-3/4 miles nw Ashby de la Zouch pop 1,274 archd Derby dioc Lichfield Wesl Meth

TICKTON township parish St John E R York pop 110

TIDCOMBE parish 1639 Wilts 6-1/4 miles ne Ludgershall pop 243 archd Wilts dioc Salisbury

TIDDESLEY HAY extra parochial liberty Staffs 2-1/4 miles ne Penkridge pop 50

TIDDINGTON hamlet parish Albury co Oxford pop 198

TIDENHAM parish 1708 Gloucs 2 miles ne Chepstow pop 1,180 archd and dioc Gloucester

TIDESWELL parish 1635 Derbys comp market town Tideswell, chapelry Wormhill, hamlets Litton, Wheston pop 2,807 pec Dean and Chapter of Lichfield Wesl Meth, Roman Cath

TIDMARSH parish 1730 Berks 6 miles nw Reading pop 143 archd Berks dioc Salisbury

TIDMINGTON parish 1691 Worcs 1-1/2 miles se Shipston upon Stour

pop 76 archd and dioc Worcester

TIDWORTH, NORTH parish 1700 Wilts 2-1/2 miles sw Ludgershall pop 392 archd and dioc Salisbury

TIDWORTH, SOUTH parish 1599 Hamps 2-3/4 miles sw Ludgershall pop 217 archd and dioc Winchester

TIFFIELD parish 1559 co Northampton 2-3/4 miles ne Towcester pop 131 archd Northampton dioc Peterborough

TILBROOK parish 1573 Beds 1-1/2 miles nw Mimbolton pop 295 archd Bedford dioc Lincoln

TILBURY, EAST parish 1627 Essex 5-1/4 miles se Gray's Thurrock pop 245 archd Essex dioc London

TILBURY JUXTA CLARE parish 1561 Essex 4 miles nw Castle Hedingham pop 236 archd Middlesex dioc London

TILBURY, WEST parish 1540 Essex 3-3/4 miles e Gray's Thurrock pop 276 archd Essex dioc London

TILDESLEY Lancs See TYLDERSLEY

TILEHURST parish 1630 Berks 2-3/4 miles w Reading pop 1,878 archd Berks dioc Salisbury Wesl Meth

TILFORD tything parish Farnham Surrey

TILLEY township parish Wem Shrops pop 323

TILLINGHAM parish 1562 Essex 2-1/4 miles sw Bradwell near the Sea pop 970 pec Dean and Chapter of St Paul's London

TILLINGTON township parish Burghill Herefs pop 419

TILLINGTON township parish St Mary Lichfield Staffs pop 42

TILLINGTON parish 1572 Sussex 1-1/4 miles nw Petworth pop 806 archd and dioc Chichester

TILMANSTONE parish 1558 Kent 6 miles sw Deal pop 303 archd and dioc Canterbury

TILNEY parish (incl with Islington) Norfolk 4-1/4 miles sw Lynn Regis

TILNEY parish 1538 Norfolk 4-1/2 miles sw Lynn Regis pop 420 archd and dioc Norwich

TILNEY chapelry 1653 parish Tilney All Saints Norfolk 6 miles sw Lynn Regis pop 552

TILSHEAD parish 1650 Wilts 4 miles se East Lavington pop 465 archd and dioc Salisbury

TILSOP chapelry parish Burford Shrops

TILSTOCK chapelry parish Whitchurch Shrops 2-1/2 miles s Whitchurch archd Salop dioc Lichfield

TILSTON parish 1558 Ches comp townships Carden, Grafton, Horton, Stretton, Tilston pop 873 3 miles nw Malpas archd and dioc Chester

TILSTON FERNALL township parish Bunbury Ches pop 170

TILSWORTH parish 1654 Beds 3-1/2 miles nw Dunstable pop 275 archd Bedford dioc Lincoln

TILTON parish 1610 Leics 8-1/4 miles sw Oakham pop 342 archd Leicester dioc Lincoln

TILTS township parish Doncaster W R York

TILTY parish 1724 Essex 3 miles sw Thaxted pop 82 Commissary
Court of London

TIMBERLAND parish 1563 Lincs 10 miles ne Sleaford pop 1,278 archd
and dioc Lincoln Wesl Meth

TIMBERSCOMBE parish 1656 Somerset 2-1/2 miles sw Dunster pop
453 Prebendary of Timberscombe

TIMBLE, GREAT township parish Fewston W R York pop 218

TIMBLE, LITTLE township parish Otley W R York pop 86

TIMPERLEY township parish Bowdon Ches pop 752

TIMSBURY parish 1561 Somerset 5 miles se Pensford pop 1,367
archd Bath dioc Bath and Wells Wesl Meth

TIMSBURY parish 1564 Hamps 2-1/4 miles nw Romsey pop 165 archd
and dioc Winchester Wesl Meth

TIMWORTH parish 1565 Suffolk 4-1/4 miles ne Bury St Edmund's pop
216 archd Sudbury dioc Norwich

TINGLETON parish 1576 Dorset 5-1/4 miles e Dorchester pop 171
archd Dorset dioc Bristol

TINGEWICK parish 1560 Bucks 2-3/4 miles sw Buckingham pop 866
archd Buckingham dioc Lincoln

TINGRITH parish 1572 Beds 4-1/4 miles se Woburn pop 162 archd
Bedford dioc Lincoln

TINHEAD tything parish Edington Wilts pop 472

TINSLEY chapelry 1715 parish Rotherham W R York 2-3/4 miles sw
Rotherham pop 368

TINTAGEL parish 1546 Cornwall comp borough Bossiney pop 1,006
archd Cornwall dioc Exeter Wesl Meth

TINTERN, LITTLE parish 1694 co Monmouth 4-3/4 miles n Chepstow
pop 313 archd and dioc Llandaff

TINTINHULL parish 1680 Somerset 2-1/4 miles sw Ilchester pop 473
archd Wells dioc Bath and Wells

TINTWISLE township parish Mottram in Longden Dale Ches pop 1,820
Calv Meth borough

TINWELL parish 1561 co Rutland 1-1/2 miles sw Stamford pop 262
archd Northampton dioc Peterborough

TIPTON parish 1573 Staffs 1-1/2 miles ne Dudley pop 14,951 pec
Prebendary of Prees or Pipa Minor in Cathedral Church of Lichfield Wesl Meth

TIRLEY parish 1653 Gloucs 5-1/4 miles sw Tewkesbury pop 498 pec
of Deerhurst Wesl Meth

TISBURY parish 1563 Wilts 3-1/2 miles se Hindon pop 2,259 archd
and dioc Salisbury Indep

TISSINGTON parish 1661 Derbys 3-3/4 miles n Ashbourn pop 459
archd Derby dioc Lichfield

TISTED, EAST parish 1538 Hamps 4-1/2 miles sw Alton pop 278
archd and dioc Winchester

TISTED, WEST parish 1538 Hamps 4-3/4 miles se New Alresford
pop 264 archd and dioc Winchester

TITCHBOURN parish 1667 Hamps 2-1/2 miles sw New Alresford pop

363 pec Incumbent of Cheriton

TITCHFIELD parish 1589 Hamps 2-1/4 miles w Fareham pop 3,712 archd and dioc Winchester Indep

TITCHMARSH parish 1544 co Northampton 2 miles ne Thrapston pop 843 archd Northampton dioc Peterborough

TITCHWELL parish 1559 Norfolk 5 miles nw Burnham Westgate pop 159 dioc Norwich archd Norfolk Wesl Meth

TITLEY parish 1569 Herefs 3 miles ne Kington pop 328 archd and dioc Hereford

TITLINGTON township parish Eglingham Northumberland pop 78

TITSEY parish 1579 Surrey 5 miles ne Godstone pop 202 archd Surrey dioc Winchester

TITTENHANGER hamlet parish St Peter St Albans Herts pop 1,038

TITTENLEY township parish Audlem Ches pop 30

TITTISWORTH township parish Leek Staffs pop 447

TITTLESHALL parish 1538 Norfolk 6-1/4 miles sw Fakenham pop 750 archd and dioc Norwich

TIVERTON township parish Bunbury Ches pop 618

TIVERTON parish 1559 borough excl juris Devon 14 miles ne Exeter pop 9,766 archd and dioc Exeter Bapt, Indep, Wesl Meth

TIVETSHALL parish 1673 Norfolk 5-3/4 miles ne Diss pop 376 archd Norfolk dioc Norwich

TIVETSHALL parish 1672 Norfolk 5-1/4 miles ne Diss pop 313 archd Norfolk dioc Norwich

TIXALL parish 1707 Staffs 3-3/4 miles se Stafford pop 176 archd Stafford dioc Lichfield Roman Cath

TIXOVER parish 1754 co Rutland 7-1/2 miles ne Uppingham pop 108 pec Prebendary of Ketton in Cathedral Church of Lincoln

TOCKENHAM parish 1653 Wilts 2-3/4 miles sw Wootton Bassett pop 164 archd Wilts dioc Salisbury

TOCKETTS township parish Guisbrough N R York pop 35

TOCKHOLES chapelry parish Blackburn Lancs pop 1,124 Indep

TOCKINGTON, LOWER tything parish Almondbury Gloucs pop 327

TOCKINGTON, UPPER tything parish Olveston Gloucs pop 729

TOCKWITH township parish Bilton E R York pop 547 Wesl Meth

TODBERE parish 1750 Dorset 4-1/2 miles sw Shaftesbury pop 119 archd Dorset dioc Bristol

TODBURN township parish Longhorsley Northumberland pop 32

TODDENHAM parish 1721 Gloucs 3-3/4 miles ne Moreton in the Marsh pop 481 archd and dioc Gloucester

TODDINGTON parish 1540 Beds 15 miles s Bedford pop 1,926 archd Bedford dioc Lincoln Wesl Meth

TODDINGTON parish 1666 Gloucs 3 miles ne Winchcombe pop 290 archd and dioc Gloucester

TODMORDEN chapelry 1666 Yorks parish Rochdale Lancs 20 miles ne Manchester pop 6,055 archd and dioc Chester Bapt, Soc of Friends, Indep, Wesl Meth, New Connection, Unit

TODRIDGE township parish Hartburn Northumberland pop 4

TODWICK parish 1577 W R York 8-1/2 miles se Rotherham pop 210 archd and dioc York

TOFT parish 1539 Cambs 5 miles se Caxton pop 279 archd and dioc Ely

TOFT township parish Knutsford Ches pop 200

TOFT hamlet parish Witham on the Hill Lincs pop 194

TOFT hamlet parish Dunchurch co Warws

TOFT, MONKS' parish 1538 Norfolk 3-1/2 miles ne Beccles pop 333 archd Norfolk dioc Norwich

TOFT NEXT NEWTON parish 1653 Lincs 4 miles sw Market Rasen pop 74 archd and dioc Lincoln

TOFT, TREES parish 1763 Norfolk 2-1/2 miles sw Fakenham pop 78 archd and dioc Norwich

TOFT, WEST parish 1733 Norfolk 5-1/4 miles ne Brandon Ferry pop 182 archd Norfolk dioc Norwich

TOGSTON township parish Warkworth Northumberland pop 149

TOLLAND parish 1706 Somerset 3-1/4 miles ne Wiveliscombe pop 121 archd Taunton dioc Bath and Wells

TOLLARD ROYAL parish 1688 Wilts 6-3/4 miles se Shaftesbury pop 286 archd and dioc Salisbury

TOLLER FRATRUM parish 1558 Dorset 9 miles nw Dorchester pop 56 archd Dorset dioc Bristol

TOLLER PORCORUM parish 1654 Dorset 10 miles nw Dorchester pop 540 archd Dorset dioc Bristol

TOLLERTON parish 1558 Notts 4-3/4 miles se Nottingham pop 149 archd Nottingham dioc York

TOLLERTON township parish Alne N R York pop 529

TOLLESBURY parish 1558 Essex 8 miles ne Maldon pop 1,066 archd Colchester dioc London Indep

TOLLESHUNT, D'ARCY parish 1560 Essex 6-1/2 miles ne Maldon pop 690 archd Colchester dioc London

TOLLESHUNT, KNIGHTS' parish 1695 Essex 7-1/2 miles ne Maldon pop 374 archd Colchester dioc London

TOLLESHUNT, MAJOR parish 1559 Essex 5-1/2 miles ne Maldon pop 428 archd Colchester dioc London

TOLPUDDLE parish 1718 Dorset 7 miles ne Dorchester pop 349 archd Dorset dioc Bristol Wesl Meth

TONBRIDGE or TUNBRIDGE parish 1559 Kent 14 miles sw Maidstone pop 10,380 archd and dioc Rochester Calv, Wesl Meth

TONBRIDGE or TUNBRIDGE, WELLS chapelry 1729 parish Tonbridge, Speldhurst Kent and Sussex Indep, Wesl Meth

TONG parish 1717 Kent 2 miles ne Sittingbourne pop 226 archd and dioc Canterbury

TONG parish 1629 Shrops 3-1/4 miles se Shiffnall pop 510 archd Salop dioc Lichfield

TONG chapelry 1550 parish Birstall W R York 4-3/4 miles se Bradford pop 2,067

TONG township parish Bolton Lancs pop 2,201

TONGE township parish Oldham Lancs pop 1,800

TONGHAM hamlet parish Seal Surrey

TOOLEY hamlet parish Peckleton Leics

TOOTING, LOWER or TOOTING GRAVENEY parish 1555 Surrey 7 miles sw London pop 2,063 archd Surrey dioc Winchester Indep, Wesl Meth

TOOTING, UPPER hamlet parish Streatham Surrey

TOPCLIFFE parish 1570 comp townships Catton, Dalton, Elmer with Crakehall, Skipton, Topcliffe, chapelry Dishforth, townships Asenby, Baldersby, Marton le Moor, Rainton with Newby N R York pop 2,592 archd Cleveland dioc York Wesl Meth

TOPCROFT parish 1556 Norfolk 4-3/4 miles se Stratton St Mary pop 463 archd Norfolk dioc Norwich

TOPPESFIELD parish 1559 Essex 4 miles nw Castle Hedingham pop 1,088 Commissary Essex and Herts, Consistorial Court of Bishop of London

TOPSHAM parish 1600 Devon 3-1/2 miles sw Exeter pop 3,194 pec Dean and Chapter of Exeter Indep, Wesl Meth

TORBRIAN parish 1564 Devon 4 miles sw Newton Bushell pop 257 archd Totnes dioc Exeter

TORKINGTON township parish Stockport Ches pop 284

TORKSEY parish 1654 Lincs 8 miles se Gainsborough pop 484 archd Stow dioc Lincoln

TORLETON hamlet parishes Coates and Rodmartan Gloucs

TORMARTON parish 1679 Gloucs 4 miles se Chipping Sodbury pop 402 archd and dioc Gloucester

TOR MOHUN or TOR MOHAM parish 1637 Devon 3/4 mile nw Torquay pop 3,582 archd Totnes dioc Exeter Roman Cath

TORPENHOW parish 1651 Cumberland comp townships Bewaldeth with Snittlegarth, Blennerhasset with Kirkland, Rothel with Threapland, Torpenhow with Whitrigg pop 1,032 2-1/2 miles nw Ireby archd and dioc Carlisle

TORPOINT chapelry parish St Anthony Cornwall Indep, Wesl Meth

TORQUAY chapelry parish Tor Mohun Devon Calv, Wesl Meth

TORRINGTON, BLACK parish 1604 Devon 5-1/4 miles nw Hatherleigh pop 1,083 archd Totnes dioc Exeter Bapt

TORRINGTON, EAST parish 1754 Lincs 4 miles ne Wragby pop 84 archd and dioc Lincoln

TORRINGTON, GREAT parish 1616 sep juris Devon 34 miles nw Exeter pop 3,083 archd Barnstaple dioc Exeter Bapt, Indep, Wesl Meth

TORRINGTON, LITTLE parish 1672 Devon 2 miles s Great Torrington pop 572 archd Barnstaple dioc Exeter

TORRINGTON, WEST parish 1721 Lincs 2-3/4 miles ne Wragby archd and dioc Lincoln

TORRISHOLME township parish Lancaster Lancs pop 188

TORTINGTON parish 1560 Sussex 2-1/2 miles sw Arundel pop 76 archd and dioc Chichester

TORTWORTH parish 1591 Gloucs 4 miles w Wootton under Edge pop 266 archd and dioc Gloucester

TORVER chapelry 1661 parish Ulverstone Lancs 6 miles sw Hawkeshead pop 224 archd Richmond dioc Chester

TORWORTH township parish Blyth Notts pop 205

TOSELAND parish 1702 Hunts 4-3/4 miles ne St Neots pop 161 archd Huntingdon dioc Lincoln

TOSSEN, GREAT township parish Rothbury Northumberland pop 195

TOSSEN, LITTLE township parish Rothbury Northumberland pop 29

TOSSIDE or TOSSET chapelry 1769 parish Gisburn W R York 7-1/2 miles sw Settle

TOSSIDE ROW extra parochial liberty W R York

TOSTOCK parish 1675 Suffolk 7-1/2 miles e Bury St Edmund's pop 283 archd Sudbury dioc Norwich

TOTHAM, GREAT parish 1557 Essex 3 miles ne Maldon pop 696 archd Colchester dioc London

TOTHAM, LITTLE parish 1558 Essex 3-1/2 miles ne Maldon pop 306 archd Colchester dioc London

TOTHILL parish 1608 Lincs 5-1/4 miles nw Alford pop 67 archd and dioc Lincoln

TOTLEY hamlet parish Dronfield Derbys pop 351

TOTNESS parish 1557 borough sep juris Devon 24 miles sw Exeter pop 3,442 archd Totnes dioc Exeter Indep, Wesl Meth

TOTON hamlet parish Attenborough Notts pop 202

TOTTENHAM parish 1558 Middlesex 4 miles ne London comp High Cross, Lower, Middle, Wood Green Warcs pop 6,937 Commissary of London Consistorial Court of Bishop of London Bapt, Soc of Friends, Indep, Wesl Meth, Roman Cath

TOTTENHILL parish 1679 Norfolk 6-1/2 miles ne Downham Market pop 358 archd Norfolk dioc Norwich

TOTTERIDGE parish 1570 Herts 2 miles sw Chipping Barnet pop 595 archd Huntingdon dioc Lincoln Indep

TOTTERNHOE parish 1673 Beds 2 miles sw Dunstable pop 515 archd Bedford dioc Lincoln

TOTTINGTON parish 1711 Norfolk 3-3/4 miles sw Watton pop 313 archd and dioc Norwich

TOTTINGTON, HIGHER township parish Bury Lancs pop 2,572

TOTTINGTON, LOWER chapelry 1799 parish Bury Lancs 3 miles nw Bury pop 9,280

TOUCHEN division parish Bray Berks

TOULSTON township parish Newton Kyme W R York

TOWCESTER parish 1561 co Northampton 8-1/2 miles sw Northampton pop 2,671 archd Northampton dioc Peterborough Bapt, Indep, Wesl Meth

TOWEDNACK parish 1676 Cornwall 3 miles sw St Ives pop 737 archd Cornwall dioc Exeter Wesl Meth

TOWERSEY parish 1733 Bucks 2-1/4 miles se Thame pop 403 pec Dean and Chapter of Lincoln

TOWNGREEN township parish Wymondham Norfolk pop 1,052

TOWNSTALL Devon See DARTMOUTH

TOWNTHORPE township parish Wharram Percy E R York pop 48

TOWTHORPE township parish Strensall E R York and Huntingdon
N R York pop 70

TOWTON township parish Saxton W R York pop 115

TOXTETH PARK chapelry 1775 parish Walton on the Hill Lancs pop
24,007 Unit

TOYNTON parish 1716 Lincs 1-1/2 miles s Spilsby pop 475 archd and
dioc Lincoln

TOYNTON parish 1742 Lincs 2-1/4 miles se Spilsby pop 372 archd
and dioc Lincoln

TOYNTON, HIGH parish 1808 Lincs 1-1/2 miles e Horncastle pop 164
archd and dioc Lincoln Wesl Meth

TOYNTON, LOW parish 1606 Lincs 1-1/4 miles ne Horncastle pop
108 archd and dioc Lincoln Wesl Meth

TRAFFORD, BRIDGE township parish Plemonstall Ches pop 58

TRAFFORD, MICKLE township parish Plemonstall Ches pop 333

TRAFFORD, WIMBOLDS township parish Thornton Ches pop 118

TRANMORE township parish Bebbington Ches pop 1,168

TRANWELL township parish Morpeth Northumberland pop 64

TRAWDEN FOREST township parish Whalley Lancs pop 2,853 Soc of
Friends, Wesl Meth

TRAYFORD parish 1728 Sussex 5-1/2 miles sw Midhurst pop 130
archd and dioc Chichester

TREALES township parish Kirkham Lancs pop 756

TREBOROUGH parish (no regs can be found) Somerset 6-1/4 miles
se Dunster pop 105 archd Taunton dioc Bath and Wells

TREDEGAR mining district parish Bedwelty co Monmouth pop 6,000
Bapt, Wesl Meth

TREDINGTON parish 1514 Gloucs 3 miles se Tewkesbury pop 132
archd and dioc Gloucester

TREDINGTON parish 1541 Worcs 2-1/4 miles ne Shipston upon Stour
pop 1,036 pec of Rector

TREDUNNOCK parish 1695 co Monmouth 4-1/4 miles s Usk pop 158
archd and dioc Llandaff

TREETON parish 1677 W R York comp townships Brampton en le
Morthen, Treeton, Ulley pop 680 4 miles se Rotherham archd and
dioc York

TREGARE parish 1751 co Monmouth 5-1/2 miles sw Monmouth pop
326 archd and dioc Llandaff

TREGAVETHAN manor parish Kea Cornwall pop 59

TREGONEY with Cuby parish 1571 borough comp market town Tregoney Cornwall 41-1/2 miles sw Launceston pop 1,127 archd
Cornwall dioc Exeter Indep, Wesl Meth

TRELLECK parish 1763 comp chapelry Trelleck Grange, township
Trelleck co Monmouth pop 1,110 archd and dioc Llandaff

TRELLECK GRANGE chapelry 1770 parish Trelleck co Monmouth

6 miles nw Chepstow pop 170 archd and dioc Llandaff Bapt, Indep

TREMAYNE parish 1726 Cornwall 6-3/4 miles nw Launceston pop 118 archd Cornwall dioc Exeter

TRENDLE tything parish Pitminster Somerset

TRENEGLOS parish 1686 Cornwall 7-1/2 miles ne Camelford pop 183 archd Cornwall dioc Exeter

TRENT parish 1558 Somerset 3 miles ne Yeovil pop 449 archd Wells dioc Bath and Wells

TRENTHAM parish 1558 Staffs comp chapel of Blurton with Lightwood Forest, townships Butterton, Clayton-Griffith, Hanchurch, Handford and Trentham pop 2,344 3-1/2 miles se Newcastle under Lyne archd Stafford dioc Lichfield

TRENTISHOE parish 1695 Devon 10-1/2 miles ne Ilfracombe pop 128 archd Barnstaple dioc Exeter

TREPRENAL township parish Llanymynech Shrops

TRESCOTT hamlet parish Tettenhall Staffs

TRESHAM chapelry parish Hawkesbury Gloucs

TRESMEER parish 1625 Cornwall 6-1/2 miles nw Launceston pop 171 archd Cornwall dioc Exeter

TRESWELL parish 1563 Notts 5-1/2 miles se East Retford pop 224 archd Nottingham dioc York Wesl Meth

TRETIRE parish 1586 Herefs 5-3/4 miles w Ross pop 120 archd and dioc Hereford

TREVALGA parish 1538 Cornwall 1-1/2 miles ne Bossiney pop 192 archd Cornwall dioc Exeter

TREVENA Cornwall See BOSSINEY with TREVENA

TREVENTHAN parish 1651 co Monmouth 2 miles n Pontypool pop 10,280 archd and dioc Llandaff

TREVILLE extra parochial liberty Herefs 6-1/2 miles nw Ross pop 66

TREWEN parish 1616 Cornwall 5-1/4 miles sw Launceston pop 213 pec of Bishop of Exeter

TREWHITT, HIGH and LOW township parish Rothbury Northumberland

TREWICK township parish Bolam Northumberland

TRIMDON parish 1720 co Durham 9 miles se Durham pop 276 archd and dioc Durham

TRIMINGHAM parish 1748 Norfolk 5 miles se Cromer pop 168 archd Norfolk dioc Norwich

TRIMLEY ST MARTIN parish 1538 Suffolk 8-1/2 miles se Ipswich pop 514 archd Suffolk dioc Norwich

TRIMLEY ST MARY parish 1654 Suffolk 8-3/4 miles se Ipswich pop 401 archd Suffolk dioc Norwich

TRING parish 1566 Herts 30 miles ne Hertford pop 3,488 archd Huntingdon dioc Lincoln Bapt, Indep

TRIPPLETON township parish Leintwardine Herefs pop 63

TRITLINGTON township parish Hebburn Northumberland pop 82

TROSTON parish 1558 Suffolk 7 miles ne Bury St Edmund's pop 399 archd Sudbury dioc Norwich Wesl Meth

TORSTREY parish 1723 co Monmouth 2-1/2 miles nw Usk pop 202
archd and dioc Llandaff

TROTTERSCLIFFE or TROSLEY parish 1540 Kent 2 miles ne Wrotham pop 310 archd and dioc Rochester

TROTTON parish 1581 Sussex 3-1/2 miles nw Midhurst pop 416
archd and dioc Chichester

TROUGH township parish Stapleton Cumberland pop 169

TROUGHEND WARD township parish Elsdon Northumberland pop 327

TROUTBECK chapelry 1592 parish Windermere Westm 5-1/2 miles
se Ambleside pop 349

TROUTSDALE township parish Brompton N R York pop 59

TROWAY township parish Eckington Derbys

TROWBRIDGE parish 1538 Wilts 30 miles nw Salisbury pop 10,863
pec of Bishop of Salisbury Part Bapt, Gen Bapt, Indep, Wesl Meth,
Presb

TROWELL parish 1568 Notts 5-3/4 miles w Nottingham pop 402 archd
Nottingham dioc York

TROWSE parish 1695 Norfolk 1-3/4 miles se Norwich pop 583 pec of
Dean and Chapter of Norwich

TRUDOX HILL hamlet parish Nunney Somerset

TRULL parish 1670 Somerset 2 miles sw Taunton pop 506 archd
Taunton dioc Bath and Wells

TRUMPINGTON parish 1671 Cambs 2-1/2 miles s Cambridge pop 722
archd and dioc Ely

TRUNCH parish 1558 Norfolk 3 miles ne North Walsham pop 441
archd Norfolk dioc Norwich Wesl Meth

TRURO parish 1597 borough Cornwall 43 miles sw Launceston pop
2,468 archd Cornwall dioc Exeter Bapt, Bryanites, Soc of Friends,
Indep, Wesl Meth

TRUSHAM parish 1559 Devon 2-1/4 miles nw Chudleigh pop 207 archd
and dioc Exeter

TRUSLEY parish 1538 Derbys 7 miles w Derby pop 101 archd Derby
dioc Lichfield

TRUSTHORPE parish 1665 Lincs 7 miles ne Alford pop 286 archd and
dioc Lincoln Wesl Meth

TRYSULL parish 1572 Staffs 5 miles sw Wolverhampton pop 562 archd
Stafford dioc Lichfield

TUBNEY parish no regs Berks 4-1/4 miles nw Abingdon pop 167
archd Berks dioc Salisbury

TUDDENHAM parish 1664 Suffolk 3-1/4 miles ne Ipswich pop 369
archd Suffolk dioc Norwich

TUDDENHAM parish 1558 Suffolk 3 miles se Mildenhall pop 388 archd
Sudbury dioc Norwich

TUDDENHAM, EAST parish 1561 Norfolk 6-3/4 miles se East Dereham pop 587 archd Norfolk dioc Norwich

TUDDENHAM, NORTH parish 1560 Norfolk 4-1/4 miles se East Dereham pop 399 archd Norfolk dioc Norwich

TUDELEY parish 1663 Kent 2-1/2 miles se Tonbridge pop 575 archd and dioc Rochester

TUDERLEY, EAST and WEST Southampton See TYTHERLEY

TUDHOE township parochial chapelry Whitworth co Durham pop 237

TUDY, ST parish 1559 Cornwall 6-1/4 miles n Bodmin pop 658 archd
Cornwall dioc Exeter Wesl Meth

TUFFLEY hamlet parish St Mary de Lode Gloucs pop 109

TUFTON or TUCKINGTON parish 1716 Southampton 1/2 mile sw
Whitchurch pop 197 archd and dioc Winchester

TUGBY parish 1668 Leics 7-1/2 miles nw Uppingham pop 226 archd
Leicester dioc Lincoln

TUGFORD parish 1754 Shrops 10 miles ne Ludlow pop 188 archd
Salop dioc Hereford

TUGGAL township parish Bambrough Northumberland pop 102

TUMBY hamlet parish Revesby Lincs pop 6

TUNBRIDGE Kent See TONBRIDGE

TUNSTALL township parish Bishop Wearmouth co Durham pop 75

TUNSTALL parish 1538 Kent 1-1/2 miles sw Sittingbourne pop 171
archd and dioc Canterbury

TUNSTALL parish 1557 Norfolk 2-3/4 miles se Acle pop 101 archd
and dioc Norwich

TUNSTALL chapelry parish Abdaston Staffs pop 98

TUNSTALL parish 1539 Suffolk 4-1/2 miles se Wickham Market pop
733 archd Suffolk dioc Norwich

TUNSTALL parish 1568 E R York 14-1/2 miles ne Kingston upon Hull
pop 172 pec of Succentor of the Cathedral Church of York

TUNSTALL township parish Catterick N R York pop 312

TUNSTALL COURT liberty parish Wolstanton Staffs pop 3,673 Wesl
Meth, Seceders

TUNSTEAD parish 1678 Norfolk 3-1/4 miles ne Coltishall pop 498
archd Norfolk dioc Norwich

TUNWORTH parish 1749 Hamps 3-3/4 miles se Basingstoke pop 126
archd and dioc Winchester

TUPHOLME extra parochial liberty Lincs 9 miles sw Horncastle
pop 68

TUPSLEY township parish Bishop Hampton Herefs pop 512

TUPTON township parish North Wingfield Derbys pop 201

TURKDEAN parish 1572 Gloucs 2-1/4 miles nw Northleach pop 237
archd and dioc Gloucester

TURNASTONE parish 1678 Herefs 10 miles se Hay pop 54 archd and
dioc Hereford

TURNDITCH chapelry 1783 parish Duffield Derbys 3-3/4 miles sw
Belper pop 370

TURNERS PUDDLE parish 1632 Dorset 7-1/2 miles nw Wareham pop
82 pec Dean of Salisbury

TURNHAM GREEN hamlet parish Chiswick Middlesex Wesl Meth

TUR LANGTON parish Leics See LAWGTON TUR

TURNWORTH parish 1577 Dorset 5 miles nw Blandford Forum pop
78 archd Dorset dioc Bristol

TURTON chapelry parish Bolton Lancs pop 2,563 Unit

TURVEY parish 1629 Beds 8 miles nw Bedford pop 988 archd Bedford dioc Lincoln Indep

TURVILLE parish 1582 Bucks 6 miles nw Great Marlow pop 442 archd Buckingham dioc Lincoln

TURWESTON parish 1695 Bucks 3/4 mile e Brackley pop 371 archd Buckingham dioc Lincoln

TURWICK parish 1577 Sussex 5 miles nw Midhurst pop 97 archd and dioc Chichester

TUSHINGHAM township parish Malpas Ches pop 328

TUSMORE parish no regs co Oxford 6 miles nw Bicester archd and dioc Oxford

TUTBURY parish 1668 Staffs 5-1/4 miles nw Burton upon Trent pop 1,553 archd Stafford dioc Lichfield Indep, Calv, Prim, Wesl Meth

TUTNAL hamlet parish Tardebigg Warws and Worcs pop 518

TUTTINGTON parish 1544 Norfolk 2-3/4 miles e Aylsham pop 228 archd and dioc Norwich

TUXFORD parish 1624 Notts 30 miles ne Nottingham pop 1,113 archd Nottingham dioc York Wesl Meth

TWAMBROOK township parish Great Budworth Ches

TWEEDMOUTH parish 1711 Northumberland by Berwick upon Tween pop 4,971 archd Northumberland dioc Durham Scotch Presb

TWEMLOW township parish Sandbach Ches pop 152

TWICKENHAM parish 1538 Middlesex 9 miles sw London pop 4,571 archd Middlesex dioc London Indep, Wesl Meth

TWIGMOOR hamlet parish Manton Lincs pop 25

TWIGWORTH hamlet parish St Mary de Lode Gloucester Gloucs pop 87

TWINEHAM parish 1716 Sussex 5 miles sw Cuckfield pop 337 archd Lewes dioc Chichester

TWINING parish 1648 Gloucs 2-3/4 miles ne Tewkesbury pop 942 archd and dioc Gloucester

TWINSTEAD parish 1567 Essex 5-1/2 miles ne Halstead pop 205 archd Middlesex dioc London

TWISTON township parish Whalley Lancs pop 222

TWITCHEN parish 1715 Devon 6-1/2 miles ne South Melton pop 170 archd Barnstaple\ dioc Exeter

TWIVERTON parish 1538 Somerset 1-3/4 miles sw Bath pop 2,478 archd Bath dioc Bath and Wells Wesl Meth

TWIZELL township parish Norham co Durham Northumberland pop 292

TWIZELL township parish Morpeth Northumberland pop 50

TWYCROSS parish 1585 Leics 4-3/4 miles nw Market Bosworth pop 319 archd Leicester dioc Lincoln

TWYFORD chapelry parish Hurst Wilts 5 miles ne Reading Indep

TWYFORD parish 1558 Bucks 5-1/4 miles sw Buckingham pop 660 archd Buckingham dioc Lincoln

TWYFORD chapelry 1736 parish Barrow Derbys 5-1/2 miles sw

Derby pop 219

TWYFORD parish 1558 Leics 6-1/4 miles sw Melton Mowbray pop 512 archd Leicester dioc Lincoln

TWYFORD township parish Colsterworth Lincs

TWYFORD extra parochial liberty 1722 Middlesex 6 miles nw London pop 43

TWYFORD parish 1558 Norfolk 3/4 mile w Foulsham pop 82 archd and dioc Norwich

TWYFORD parish 1626 Hamps 3 miles s Winchester pop 1,177 pec of Incumbent

TWYWELL parish 1586 co Northampton 3-1/2 miles sw Thrapstone pop 199 archd Northampton dioc Peterborough

TYDD parish 1559 Cambs 5-1/2 miles nw Wisbeach pop 967 pec Bishop of Ely

TYDD parish 1541 Lincs 6 miles sw Wisbeach pop 960 archd and dioc Lincoln

TYLDERSLEY or TILDESLEY parochial district Lancs 2-1/2 miles ne Leigh pop 5,038 archd and dioc Chester Countess of Huntingdon, Wesl Meth

TYNHAM parish 1581 Dorset 6-1/2 miles sw Corfe Castle pop 247 archd Dorset dioc Bristol

TYNEMOUTH parish 1607 Northumberland comp chapelries North Shields, Whitley, townships Chirton, Cullercoats, Monkseaton, Murton or Moortown, Preston, Tynemouth pop 24,778 archd Northumberland dioc Durham

TYRLEY Staffs See BLOORE IN TYRLEY

TYRRINGHAM parish 1629 Bucks 2-1/4 miles nw Newport Pagnell pop 227 archd Buckingham dioc Lincoln

TYSOE parish 1575 Warws 5 miles se Kington pop 1,007 archd and dioc Worcester Wesl Meth

TYTHBY parish 1550 Notts 9 miles se Nottingham pop 695 archd Nottingham dioc York

TYTHERINGTON township parish Prestbury Ches pop 427

TYTHERINGTON parish 1662 Gloucs 3 miles se Thornbury pop 476 archd and dioc Gloucester

TYTHERINGTON hamlet parish Heytesbury Wilts pop 132 pec of Dean of Salisbury

TYTHERLEY or TUDERLEY, EAST parish 1562 Hamps 7 miles sw Stockbridge pop 297 archd and dioc Winchester

TYTHERTON KELLAWAYS tything parish Bremhill Wilts 3-1/4 miles ne Chippenham

TYTHERTON LUCAS chapelry parish Chippenham Wilts

TYTHERTON STANLEY tything parish Chippenham Wilts

TYWARDRETH parish 1642 Cornwall 3-3/4 miles nw Fowey archd Cornwall dioc Exeter Wesl Meth

UBBESTON parish 1558 Suffolk 5-3/4 miles sw Halesworth pop 199 archd Suffolk dioc Norwich

UBLEY or OBLEIGH parish 1671 Somerset 9 miles nw Wells pop

340 archd Bath dioc Bath and Wells Wesl Meth

UCKERBY township parish Catterick N R York pop 50

UCKFIELD parish 1530 Sussex 8 miles ne Lewes pop 1,261 pec Archbishop of Canterbury Bapt

UCKINGTON chapelry parish Elmstone Hardwicke Gloucs pop 175

UDIMORE parish 1558 Sussex 3-1/2 miles nw Winchelsea pop 454 archd Lewes dioc Chichester

UFFCULME parish 1538 Devon 4-3/4 miles ne Cullompton pop 2,082 pec Prebendary of Uffculme, Cathedral Church of Salisbury Bapt, Indep

UFFINGTON parish 1654 Berks 4-1/4 miles se Great Farringdon pop 1,019 archd Berks dioc Salisbury

UFFINGTON parish 1675 Lincs 2-1/4 miles ne Stamford pop 481 archd and dioc Lincoln

UFFINGTON parish 1578 Shrops 3-1/4 miles ne Shrewsbury archd Salop dioc Lichfield

UFFORD parish 1570 co Northampton pop 460 archd Northampton dioc Peterborough

UFFORD parish 1558 Suffolk 2-1/2 miles ne Woodbridge pop 661 archd Suffolk dioc Norwich

UFORD tything parish Crediton Devon

UFTON parish 1636 Berks 7-1/4 miles sw Reading pop 357 archd Berks dioc Salisbury

UFTON parish 1709 Warws 2-1/2 miles nw Southam pop 166 pec Prebendary of Ufton Cathedral Church of Lichfield

UGBOROUGH parish 1538 Devon 3 miles ne Modbury pop 1,467 archd Totnes dioc Exeter

UGGESHALL parish 1558 Suffolk 4-3/4 miles nw Southwold pop 303 archd Suffolk dioc Norwich

UGGLESBARNBY chapelry 1732 parish Whitby N R York 4 miles sw Whitby pop 426 archd Cleveland dioc York

UGLEY parish 1560 Essex 3-1/2 miles n Standsted Mountfitchet pop 318 Commissary of Essex and Herts, Consistorial Court of the Bishop of London

UGTHORPE township parish Lythe N R York pop 260

ULCEBY parish 1749 Lincs 3-1/2 miles sw Alford pop 218 archd and dioc Lincoln Wesl Meth

ULCEBY parish 1567 Lincs 7-1/4 miles se Barton upon Humber pop 694 archd and dioc Lincoln

ULCOMBE parish 1560 Kent 7-1/4 miles se Maidstone pop 761 archd and dioc Canterbury

ULDALE parish 1642 Cumberland 2-1/2 miles se Ireby pop 344 archd and dioc Carlisle

ULEY parish 1668 Gloucs 2-1/2 miles ne Dursley pop 2,641 archd and dioc Gloucester Bapt, Indep, Wesl Meth

ULGHAM chapelry 1602 parish Morpeth Northumberland 5 miles ne Morpeth pop 359 archd Northumberland dioc Durham

ULLENHALL chapelry parish Wootton Waven Warws

ULLESKELF township parish Kirkby Wharfe W R York pop 339

ULLESTHORPE hamlet parish Claybrooke Leics pop 599 Bapt, Indep

ULLEY township parish Aston W R York pop 193

ULLINGSWICK parish 1561 Herefs 5 miles sw Bromyard pop 293 archd and dioc Hereford

ULLOCK township parish Dean Cumberland pop 356

ULNES WALTON township parish Croston Lancs pop 537

ULPHA chapelry 1703 parish Millom Cumberland 9 miles se Ravenglass pop 405 Bapt

ULPHA township parish Beetham Westm

ULROME chapelry 1767 parish Barnston E R York pop 166 6-1/4 miles nw Honnsea

ULTING parish 1723 Essex 4-1/2 miles sw Witham pop 158 archd Colchester dioc London

ULVERCROFT extra parochial liberty Leics 6 miles sw Mountsorrell pop 100

ULVERSTONE parish 1545 Lancs comp market town of Ulverstone, chapelries Slawwith, Church Conistone, Egton cum Torver, Lowick, Satterthwaite, townships Newland, Osmotherley, extra parochial district Mansriggs pop 7,741 archd Richmond dioc Chester Indep, Wesl Meth, Roman Cath

UNDERBARROW chapelry 1735 parish Kendal Westm 2-3/4 miles w Kendal pop 526

UNDERMILBECK township parish Windermere Westm pop 854

UNDER SKIDDAW township parish Crosthwaite Cumberland pop 477

UNDERWOOD liberty parish Ashbourn Derbys

UNDY parish 1760 co Monmouth 7 miles se Newport pop 291 archd and dioc Llandaff

UNERIGG township parish Dearham Cumberland

UNSTONE township parish Dronfield Derbys pop 586

UNSWORTH chapelry 1730 parish Oldham Lancs 3 miles se Bury Wesl Meth

UNTHANK township parish Skelton Cumberland pop 235

UNTHANK township parish Alnham Northumberland pop 34

UPCHURCH parish 1633 Kent 5-1/2 miles se Chatham pop 456 archd and dioc Canterbury

UP EXE tything parish Rewe Devon pop 100

UPHAM parish 1598 Hamps 2-3/4 miles nw Bishop's Waltham pop 511 pec of Incumbent

UPHAVEN parish 1687 Wilts 4 miles sw Pewsey pop 498 archd and dioc Salisbury Part Bapt

UPHILL parish 1704 Somerset 8 miles nw Axbridge pop 306 archd Wells dioc Bath and Wells Bapt

UP HOLLAND Lancs See HOLLAND, UP

UPLEADON parish 1538 Gloucs 3-3/4 miles ne Newent pop 241 archd Hereford dioc Gloucester

UPLEATHAM parish 1654 N R York 3-1/4 miles ne Guilsbrough pop 265 archd Cleveland dioc York Wesl Meth

UPLOWMAN parish 1662 Devon 4-3/4 miles ne Tiverton pop 335
archd and dioc Exeter
UPLYME parish 1691 Devon 1-1/4 miles nw Lyme Regis pop 975
archd and dioc Exeter
UPMINSTER parish 1543 Essex 4 miles se Romford pop 1,033 archd
Essex dioc London Indep
UP OTTERY parish 1560 Devon 5-1/4 miles ne Honiton pop 940
archd and dioc Exeter Bapt, Calv Meth
UPPER ALLITHWAITE Lancs See ALLITHWAITE, UPPER
UPPERBY township parish St Cuthbert Cumberland pop 393
UPPINGHAM parish 1571 co Rutland 6 miles s Oakham pop 1,757
archd Northampton dioc Peterborough Indep, Calv and Wesl Meth
UPPINGTON parish 1650 Shrops 3-1/2 miles sw Wellington pop 117
archd Salop dioc Lichfield
UPSALL township parish South Kilvington N R York pop 114
UPSALL township parish Ormsby N R York
UPSHIRE hamlet parish Waltham Abbey Essex pop 745 Wesl Meth
UPSLAND township parish Kirklington N R York
UPTON chapelry 1588 parish Blewberry Berks 4-3/4 miles ne East
Ilsey pop 254
UPTON parish 1538 Bucks 1/2 mile se Slough pop 1,502 archd Buck-
ingham dioc Lincoln
UTPON township parish St Mary Ches pop 289
UPTON township parish Prestbury Ches pop 64
UPTON or OVER CHURCH parish 1600 Ches 7-3/4 miles nw Great
Neston pop 191 archd and dioc Chester
UPTON tything parish Hawkesbury Gloucs pop 696 Wesl Meth
UPTON parish 1646 Gloucs 3-1/4 miles se Gloucester pop 898 archd
and dioc Gloucester
UPTON parish 1755 Hunts 6-1/2 miles nw Huntingdon dioc Lincoln
UPTON township parish Sibson Leics pop 148
UPTON parish 1563 Lincs 5 miles se Gainsborough pop 460 archd
Stow dioc Lincoln Wesl Meth
UPTON parish 1558 Norfolk 1-3/4 miles n Acle pop 510 archd and
dioc Norwich
UPTON parish 1594 co Northampton 2 miles w Northampton pop 48
archd Northampton dioc Peterborough
UPTON chapelry parish Castor co Northampton 2-1/4 miles ne Wans-
ford pop 122
UPTON parish 1660 Notts 2-3/4 miles e Southwell pop 533 pec of
Chapter of Collegiate Church of Southwell
UPTON hamlet parish Headon Notts
UPTON hamlet parish Burford co Oxford pop 246
UPTON parish 1708 Somerset 4-1/4 miles ne Dulverton pop 344 archd
Taunton dioc Bath and Wells
UPTON township parish Ratley Warws
UPTON township parish Badsworth W R York pop 229
UPTON, BISHOP'S parish 1571 Herefs 4 miles ne Ross pop 626 archd

and dioc Hereford

UPTON CRESSETT parish 1755 Shrops 5 miles sw Bridgenorth pop 43 archd Salop dioc Hereford

UPTON GRAY parish 1561 Hamps 4 miles sw Odiham pop 388 archd and dioc Winchester

UPTON HELLIONS parish 1678 Devon 2-1/2 miles se Crediton pop 152 archd and dioc Exeter

UPTON LOVELL parish 1653 Wilts 2 miles se Heytesbury pop 249 archd and dioc Salisbury

UPTON MAGNA parish 1563 Shrops 5-1/2 miles e Shrewsbury pop 612 archd Salop dioc Lichfield

UPTON NOBLE parish 1677 Somerset 4 miles ne Bruton pop 282 archd Wells dioc Bath and Wells Wesl Meth

UPTON PYNE parish 1673 Devon 3-1/2 miles nw Exeter pop 514 archd and dioc Exeter

UPTON SCUDAMORE parish 1654 Wilts 2 miles n Warminster pop 393 archd and dioc Salisbury

UPTON SNODSBURY parish 1577 Worcs 6-1/2 miles se Worcester pop 316 archd and dioc Worcester

UPTON UPON SEVERN parish 1546 Worcs 10 miles s Worcester pop 2,343 archd and dioc Worcester Bapt

UPTON WARREN parish 1604 Worcs 3-1/2 miles ne Droitwich pop 474 archd and dioc Worcester

UPTON WATERS parish 1563 Shrops 5-1/2 miles nw Wellington pop 193 archd Salop dioc Lichfield

UP WALTHAM Sussex See WALTHAM, UP

UPWAY parish 1654 comp liberty Weybey House, tything Stottingway, Elwell Dorset 4-1/2 miles sw Dorchester pop 618 archd Dorset dioc Bristol

UPWELL parish 1650 Cambs Norfolk 5-3/4 miles se Wisbeach pop 4,176 archd Norfolk dioc Norwich Wesl Meth

UPWOOD parish 1558 Hunts 2-3/4 miles sw Ramsey pop 388 archd Huntingdon dioc Lincoln

URCHFONT parish 1538 Wilts 2-3/4 miles ne East Lavington pop 1,389 archd and dioc Salisbury

URMSTON township parish Flixton Lancs pop 706

URPETH township parish Chester le Street co Durham pop 716

URSWICK parish 1608 Lancs 3 miles sw Ulverstone pop 752 archd Richmond dioc Chester

USHLAWRCOED hamlet parish Bedwelty co Monmouth pop 2,359

USK parish 1742 co Monmouth 13 miles sw Monmouth pop 1,775 archd and dioc Llandaff Indep, Wesl Meth, Roman Cath

USSELBY parish 1564 Lincs 3-1/4 miles nw Market Rasen pop 84 archd and dioc Lincoln

USWORTH, GREAT and LITTLE township parish Washington co Durham pop 1,477 Wesl Meth

UTKINTON township parish Tarporley Ches pop 564

UTON tything parish Crediton Devon

UTTERBY parish 1695 Lincs 4-3/4 miles nw Lough pop 198 archd
and dioc Lincoln

UTTOXETER parish 1596 Staffs 13 miles ne Stafford pop 4,864 archd
Stafford dioc Lichfield Bapt, Indep, Soc of Friends, Wesl Meth

UXBRIDGE chapelry 1538 parish Hillingdon Middlesex 15 miles nw
London pop 3,043 Bapt, Soc of Friends, Indep

VANGE parish 1558 Essex 5 miles ne Bordon on the Hill pop 165
archd Essex dioc London

VAULTERSHOME tything parish Maker Devon pop 1,092

VEEP, ST parish 1538 Cornwall 3 miles ne Fowey pop 697 archd
Cornwall dioc Exeter

VENN OTTERY parish 1681 Devon 3-1/4 miles sw Ottery St Mary
pop 133 archd and dioc Exeter

VERNHAM DEAN parish 1598 Hamps 3 miles nw Andover pop 694
archd and dioc Winchester

VERYAN parish 1683 Cornwall 4 miles sw Tregoney pop 1,525 archd
Cornwall dioc Exeter

VIRGINSTOW parish 1730 Devon 6-1/4 miles ne Launceston pop 136
archd Totnes dioc Exeter

VIRLEY parish 1628 Essex 8-1/4 miles sw Colchester pop 65 archd
Essex dioc London

VOWCHURCH parish 1642 Herefs 11-1/2 miles nw Hereford pop 371
archd and dioc Hereford

VOWMINE township parish Clifford Herefs

WABERTHWAITE parish 1695 Cumberland 1-1/2 miles se Ravenglass
pop 139 archd Richmond dioc Chester

WACKERFIELD township parish Staindrop co Durham pop 112

WACTON parish 1663 Herefs 4-1/2 miles nw Bromyard pop 113 archd
and dioc Hereford

WACTON MAGNA parish 1560 Norfolk 1-1/4 miles sw St Mary Stratton
pop 242 archd Norfolk dioc Norwich

WACTON PARVA parish (incl in Wacton Magna) Norfolk 1-1/2 miles
sw St Mary Stratton archd Norfolk dioc Norwich

WADBOROUGH hamlet parish Holy Cross Pershore Worcs pop 198

WADDESDON parish 1538 Bucks 5-1/2 miles nw Ahlesbury pop 1,734
archd Buckingham dioc Lincoln Wesl Meth

WADDINGTON parish 1675 Lincs 4-1/2 miles s Lincoln pop 768 archd
and dioc Lincoln Wesl Meth

WADDINGTON chapelry 1616 parish Mitton W R York 1-3/4 miles
nw Clitheroe pop 624 Wesl Meth

WADDINGWORTH parish 1640 Lincs 6 miles nw Horncastle pop 63
archd and dioc Lincoln

WADEBRIDGE market town parish St Breock and Egloshayle Cornwall
Indep, Wesl Meth

WADENHOE parish 1559 co Northampton 4 miles sw Oundle pop 243
archd Northampton dioc Peterborough

WADHURST parish 1604 Sussex 5 miles se Tonbridge Wells pop 2,256
pec Archbishop of Canterbury Bapt

WADINGHAM parish 1652 Lincs 3-1/2 miles sw Glandford Bridge pop 523 archd Stow dioc Lincoln Wesl Meth
WADLEY or LITTLEWORTH tything parish Great Farringdon Berks
WADSWORTH township parish Halifax W R York pop 5,198
WADWOTTH parish 1575 W R York 5-1/4 miles s Doncaster pop 690 pec Dean and Chapter of York Wesl Meth
WAGHEN or WAWN parish 1653 E R York comp townships Meux, Waghen pop 338 pec Chancellor of Cathedral Church of York
WAINFLEET All Saints 1677 regs mutilated, St Mary 1611, St Thomas between 1831-38 Lincs 39-1/2 miles se Lincoln archd and dioc Lincoln Soc of Friends, Wesl Meth
WAITBY township parish Kirkby Stephen Westm pop 41
WAITH parish 1698 Lincs 6-3/4 miles se Great Grimsby pop 31 archd and dioc Lincoln
WAKEFIELD parish All Saints 1613, St John 1795 W R York comp market town Wakefield, chapelries Horbury, Stanley, townships Alverthorpe with Thorne, Wrenthorpe pop 24,538 archd and dioc York Indep, Wesl Meth, Soc of Friends, Prim Meth, Unit, Roman Cath
WAKELEY extra parochial liberty Herefs 2 miles sw Buntingford pop 7
WAKERING parish 1685 Essex 4-1/2 miles ne Southend pop 834 archd Essex dioc London Indep
WAKERING, LITTLE parish 1715 Essex 4-1/2 miles ne Southend pop 297 archd Essex dioc London
WAKERLEY parish 1540 co Northampton 6-3/4 miles e Uppingham pop 218 archd Northampton dioc Peterborough
WALBERSWICK parish 1656 Suffolk 1-3/4 miles sw Southwold pop 279 archd Suffolk dioc Norwich
WALBERTON parish 1556 Sussex 3-1/2 miles sw Arundel pop 616 archd and dioc Chichester
WALBURN township parish Downholme N R York pop 26
WALBY township parish Crosby upon Eden pop 52
WALCOT parish 1546 Lincs 1-1/2 miles nw Falkingham pop 183 archd and dioc Lincoln
WALCOTE hamlet parish Misterton Leics
WALCOTT chapelry parish Billinghay Lincs pop 514 archd and dioc Lincoln Wesl Meth
WALCOTT parish 1558 Norfolk 5-1/4 miles ne North Walsham pop 129 archd Norfolk dioc Norwich
WALCOTT parish 1691 Somerset pop 26,023 incl part of town of Bath arch Bath dioc Bath and Wells
WALCOTT hamlet parish Holy Cross Pershore Worcs pop 375
WALDEN township parish Aysgarth N R York
WALDEN, KING'S parish 1558 Herts 4-1/4 miles sw Hitchin pop 1,004 archd Huntingdon dioc Lincoln
WALDEN, ST PAUL'S parish 1653 Herts 5-1/4 miles nw Welwyn pop 1,058 archd St Albans dioc London Bapt, Indep

WALDEN, SAFFRON parish 1558 sep juris Essex 27 miles nw Chelmsford pop 4,762 archd Colchester dioc London Gen Bapt, Soc of
Friends, Indep, Wesl Meth, Unit

WALDEN STUBBS township parish Womersley W R York pop 139

WALDERSHARE parish 1561 Kent 4-1/2 miles nw Dovor pop 67 archd
and dioc Canterbury

WALDINGFIELD, GREAT parish 1539 Suffolk 3-1/4 miles ne Sudbury
pop 679 archd Sudbury dioc Norwich

WALDINGFIELD, LITTLE parish 1566 Suffolk 4-1/2 miles ne Sudbury pop 403 archd Sudbury dioc Norwich Wesl Meth

WALDRIDGE township parish Chester le Street co Durham pop 104

WALDRINGFIELD parish 1695 Suffolk 3-1/2 miles se Woodbridge
pop 166 archd Suffolk dioc Norwich Bapt

WALDRON parish 1564 Sussex 5-3/4 miles se Uckfield pop 997 archd
Lewes dioc Chichester Wesl Meth

WALES parish 1580 W R York 8 miles se Rotherham pop 226 pec
Chancellor of Cathedral Church of York

WALESBY parish 1562 Lincs 3-1/4 miles ne Market Rasen pop 247
archd and dioc Lincoln

WALESBY parish 1579 Notts 3 miles ne Ollerton pop 340 archd Nottingham dioc York

WALFORD parish 1663 Herefs 2-3/4 miles sw Ross pop 1,155 archd
and dioc Hereford

WALFORD township parish Leintwardine Herefs pop 212

WALGHERTON township parish Wybunbury Ches pop 213

WALGRAVE parish 1571 co Northampton 7-1/4 miles nw Wellingborough pop 575 archd Northampton dioc Peterborough Bapt

WALHAM GREEN chapelry parish Fulham Middlesex 3 miles sw
London

WALKER township parish Long Benton Northumberland

WALKERINGHAM parish 1605 Notts 4 miles nw Gainsborough pop 529
pec Manorial Court of Gringley on the Hill Wesl Meth

WALKERITH hamlet parish Gainsborough Lincs pop 65

WALKERN parish 1680 Herts 4-3/4 miles ne Stevenage pop 771 archd
Huntingdon dioc Lincoln Indep

WALKHAMPTON parish 1675 Devon 4-1/2 miles se Tavistock pop
691 archd Totnes dioc Exeter

WALKINGHAM HILL extra parochial liberty W R York 4 miles n
Knaresborough pop 25

WALKINGTON parish 1754 E R York 2-3/4 miles sw Beverley pop
558 pec Court of Howdenshire Wesl Meth

WALKINGSTEAD Surrey See GODSTONE

WALKMILL township parish Warkworth Northumberland pop 7

WALL chapelry parish St John Lee Northumberland pop 495 pec Archbishop of York

WALL hamlet parish St Michael Lichfield Staffs pop 93

WALL TOWN township parish Haltwhistle Northumberland pop 96

WALLASEA, ISLE OF parishes Canewdon, Eastwood, Paglesham,

Great Stambridge, Little Wakering Essex
WALLASEY parish 1574 Ches comp townships Liscard, Poulton with Seacomb, Wallasey pop 2,737 archd and dioc Chester
WALLBOTTLE township parish Newburn Northumberland pop 688
WALLCOTT hamlet parish Charlbury co Oxford pop 9
WALLDITCH parish 1738 Dorset 1-1/2 miles se Bridport pop 164 archd Dorset dioc Bristol
WALLERSCOAT township parish Weaverham Ches pop 10
WALLERTHWAITE township parish Ripon W R York
WALLINGFORD market town 1638 borough excl juris Berks 15 miles nw Reading pop 2,467 comp All Hallows 1638, St Leonard 1711, St Peter 1711 Soc of Friends, Indep, Wesl Meth
WALLINGTON parish 1661 Herts 3 miles e Baldock pop 213 archd Huntingdon dioc Lincoln
WALLINGTON parish (incl in regs Holm) Norfolk 3-1/2 miles ne Downham Market pop 47 archd Norfolk dioc Norwich
WALLINGTON hamlet parish Beddington Surrey pop 933
WALLINGTON DEMESNE township parish Hartburn Northumberland pop 193
WALLINGSWELL extra parochial liberty Notts 3-3/4 miles nw Worksop pop 21
WALLOP, NETHER parish 1631 Hamps 4 miles nw Stockbridge pop 900 archd and dioc Winchester Wesl Meth
WALLOP, OVER parish 1538 Hamps 5 miles nw Stockbridge pop 478 archd and dioc Winchester
WALLSEND parish 1669 Northumberland 3-1/2 miles ne Newcastle upon Tyne comp townships Howden Pans, Wallsend, Wellington archd Northumberland dioc Durham Meth
WALMER parish 1560 Kent 2 miles s Deal pop 1,779 archd and dioc Canterbury
WALMERSLEY township parish Bury Lancs pop 3,456 Indep
WALMSGATE parish (incl regs of Burwell) Lincs 8 miles nw Spilsby pop 72 archd and dioc Lincoln
WALMSLEY chapelry parish Bolton Lancs archd and dioc Chester Unit
WALNEY, ISLE OF chapelry parish Dalton in Furness Lancs archd Richmond dioc Chester
WALPOLE ST ANDREW parish 1654 Norfolk 8-3/4 miles sw Lynn Regis pop 514 archd and dioc Norwich
WALPOLE ST PETER parish 1559 Norfolk 9 miles sw Lynn Regis pop 1,237 archd and dioc Norwich Wesl Meth
WALPOLE parish 1753 Suffolk 2 miles sw Halesworth pop 658 archd Suffolk dioc Norwich Indep
WALDRIDGE township parish Stamfordham Northumberland pop 7
WALSALL parish 1570 Staffs comp market town Walsall, Walsall Foreign a township pop 15,066 18 miles se Stafford archd Stafford dioc Lichfield Indep, Wesl Meth, Unit, Roman Cath
WALSALL FOREIGN township parish Walsall Staffs pop 8,665

WALSDEN township parish Rochdale Lancs

WALSGRAVE ON SOWE Warws See SOWE

WALSHAM LE WILLOWS parish 1539 Suffolk 4-1/2 miles ne Ixworth
pop 1,167 archd Suffolk dioc Norwich Bapt, Wesl Meth

WALSHAM, NORTH parish 1557 Norfolk 15 miles ne Norwich pop
2,615 archd Norfolk dioc Norwich Soc of Friends, Indep, Prim
and Wesl Meth

WALSHAM, SOUTH parish 1551 Norfolk 2-3/4 miles nw Acle archd
and dioc Norwich pop 575

WALSHFORD township parish Hunsingore W R York

WALSINGHAM, GREAT parish 1564 Norfolk 1 mile ne Little Walsingham pop 434 archd Norfolk dioc Norwich

WALSINGHAM, LITTLE parish 1558 Norfolk 28 miles nw Norwich
pop 1,004 archd Norfolk dioc Norwich Wesl Meth

WALSOKEN parish 1558 Norfolk adj town Wisbeach pop 1,356 archd
and dioc Norwich

WALTERSTONE parish 1761 Herefs 15 miles sw Hereford pop 149
archd Brecon dioc St David's

WALTHAM parish 1538 Kent 7 miles sw Canterbury pop 572 archd
and dioc Canterbury

WALTHAM parish 1561 Lincs 3-3/4 miles sw Great Grimsby pop 545
archd and dioc Lincoln

WALTHAM ABBEY or HOLY CROSS parish 1563 Essex comp market
of Waltham Abbey, hamlets Holyfield, Sewardstone, Upshire pop
4,104 23-1/2 miles sw Chelmsford Commissary of London, Consistorial Court of Bishop of London Bapt, Wesl Meth

WALTHAM, BISHOP'S parish 1612 Hamps 10 miles ne Southampton
pop 2,181 pec of incumbent

WALTHAM, BRIGHT parish 1558 Berks 5 miles sw East Ilsley pop
442 archd Berks dioc Salisbury

WALTHAM, COLD parish 1594 Sussex 5-1/2 miles se Petworth pop
449 pec of Bishop of Chichester

WALTHAM CROSS ward parish Cheshunt Herts Indep

WALTHAM, GREAT parish 1703 Essex 4-1/2 miles nw Chelmsford
pop 2,103 archd Essex dioc London

WALTHAM, ST LAWRENCE parish 1559 Berks 5-1/2 miles sw Maidenhead pop 739 archd Berks dioc Salisbury

WALTHAM, LITTLE parish 1540 Essex 4-1/4 miles ne Chelmsford
pop 674 archd Essex dioc London Indep

WALTHAM, NORTH parish 1654 Hamps 6 miles sw Basingstoke pop
458 pec of Incumbent

WALTHAM ON THE WOLDS parish 1565 Leics 5-1/4 miles ne Melton
Mowbray pop 653 archd Leicester dioc Lincoln

WALTHAM, UP parish 1790 Sussex 6-1/2 miles sw Petworth pop 95
archd and dioc Chichester

WALTHAM, WHITE parish 1563 Berks 4 miles sw Maidenhead pop
902 archd Berks dioc Salisbury

WALTHAMSTOW parish 1645 Essex 6 miles ne London pop 4,258

Commissary of London Consistorial Court of Bishop of London Indep, Unit

WALTON parish 1598 Bucks 2 miles ne Fenny Stratford pop 114 archd Buckingham dioc Lincoln

WALTON parish 1684 Cumberland comp townships High, Low Walton pop 481 archd and dioc Carlisle

WALTON chapelry Chesterfield Derbys pop 935

WALTON or DEERHURST WALTON hamlet parish Deerhurst Gloucs

WALTON township parish Bishop's Froome Herefs pop 101

WALTON hamlet parish Knaptoft Leics pop 234

WALTON hamlet parish Paston co Northampton pop 160

WALTON parish 1682 Somerset 3-1/2 miles sw Glastonbury pop 635 archd Wells dioc Bath and Wells Wesl Meth

WALTON township parish Baswick Staffs

WALTON township parish Eccleshall Staffs pop 92

WALTON parish 1554 Suffolk 10 miles se Ipswich pop 887 archd Suffolk dioc Norwich Bapt

WALTON parish 1619 E R York pop 237 2-1/2 miles se Wetherby archd and dioc York Wesl Meth

WALTON township parish Great Sandall W R York pop 376

WALTON CARDIFF parish 1677 Gloucs 1-1/4 miles se Tewkesbury pop 57 archd and dioc Gloucester

WALTON DEIVILE parish (incl with Wellesbourne Hastings) Warws 3-3/4 miles nw Kington archd and dioc Worcester

WALTON, EAST parish 1560 Norfolk 7 miles nw Swaffham pop 220 archd and dioc Norwich

WALTON, INFERIOR township parish Runcorn Ches pop 340

WALTON IN GORDANO parish 1667 Somerset 11-1/2 miles w Bristol pop 297 archd Bath dioc Bath and Wells

WALTON LE DALE chapelry 1653 parish Blackburn Lancs 2 miles se Preston pop 5,767

WALTON LE SOKEN parish 1688 Essex 13-1/2 miles se Manningtree pop 469 pec of Sokens

WALTON ON THE HILL parish 1586 Lancs comp chapelries Everton, Formby, Kirkby, Wesl Derby, townships Bootle with Linacre, Faxakerley, Kirkdale, Simonswood, Walton on the Hill pop 22,575 archd and dioc Chester 3 miles ne Liverpool

WALTON ON THE HILL parish 1581 Surrey 4-1/4 miles se Epsom pop 352 archd Surrey dioc Winchester

WALTON ON THE WOLDS parish 1566 Leics 4 miles e Loughborough pop 289 archd Leicester dioc Lincoln

WALTON ON TRENT parish 1639 Derbys 4-1/4 miles sw Burton upon Trent pop 408 archd Derby dioc Lichfield

WALTON, SUPERIOR township parish Runcorn Ches pop 238

WALTON UPON THAMES parish 1592 Surrey 2 miles ne Weybridge pop 2,035 archd Surrey dioc Winchester Indep

WALTON, WEST parish 1662 Norfolk 2-3/4 miles ne Wisbeach pop 905 archd and dioc Norwich

WALTON, WOOD parish 1754 Hunts 7 miles nw Huntingdon pop 305 archd Huntingdon dioc Lincoln

WALWICK extra parochial liberty parish Warden Northumberland

WALWORTH township parish Heighington co Durham pop 155

WALWORTH chapelry parish St Mary, Newington Surrey

WAMBROOK parish 1653 Dorset 1-3/4 miles sw Chard pop 217 pec Prebendary of Chadstock Cathedral Church of Salisbury

WAMPOOL township parish Aikton Cumberland pop 127

WANBOROUGH chapelry parish Puttenham Surrey 4-1/4 miles w Guildford pop 111

WANBOROUGH parish 1582 Wilts 3-1/2 miles se Swindon pop 1,016 archd Surrey dioc Salisbury Wesl Meth

WANDSWORTH parish 1603 Surrey 6 miles sw London pop 6,879 archd Surrey dioc Winchester Bapt, Soc of Friends, Indep, Wesl Meth

WANGFORD parish 1678 Suffolk 3-1/2 miles nw Southwold pop 792 archd Suffolk dioc Norwich

WANGFORD parish 1660 Suffolk 3 miles sw Brandon Ferry pop 53 archd Suffolk dioc Norwich

WANLIP parish 1561 Leics 3-1/2 miles se Mountsorrel pop 91 archd Leicester dioc Lincoln

WANSFORD parish 1808 co Northampton 36 miles ne Northampton pop 179 archd Northampton dioc Peterborough

WANSFORD township parish Nafferton E R York pop 152

WANSTEAD parish 1640 Essex 7 miles ne London pop 1,403 archd Essex dioc London

WANSTROW parish 1653 Somerset 5 miles ne Bruton pop 410 archd Wells dioc Bath and Wells

WANTAGE parish 1538 Berks comp market town Wantage, hamlets Charlton, Grove, West Lockinge pop 3,282 24 miles ne Reading pec Dean and Canons of Windsor Indep, Wesl Meth, Bapt

WANTISDEN parish 1708 Suffolk 4-3/4 miles nw Orford pop 125 archd Suffolk dioc Norwich

WAPLEY parish 1662 Gloucs 2-1/2 miles sw Chipping Sodbury pop 253 archd and dioc Gloucester

WAPLINGTON township parish Allerthorpe E R York pop 18

WAPPENBURY parish 1753 Warws 6-3/4 miles nw Southam pop 252 archd Coventry dioc Lichfield

WAPPENHAM parish 1675 co Northampton 5 miles sw Towcester pop 568 archd Northampton dioc Peterborough Wesl Meth

WAPPING parish 1617 Middlesex adj East London pop 3,564 archd Middlesex dioc London Roman Cath

WARBLETON parish 1559 Sussex 6-1/2 miles ne Hailsham pop 1,225 archd Lewes dioc Chichester

WARBLINGTON parish 1631 Hamps 3/4 mile se Havant pcp 2,118 archd and dioc Winchester

WARBOROUGH parish 1538 co Oxford 2-3/4 miles n Wallingford pop 681 pec Dorchester

WARBOYS parish 1551 Hunts 4-1/2 miles se Ramsey pop 1,550 archd Huntingdon dioc Lincoln Bapt

WARBRICK township parish Bispham Lancs

WARBSTOW parish 1695 Cornwall 8-1/2 miles ne Camelford pop 481 archd Cornwall dioc Exeter Bryanites, Wesl Meth

WARBURTON parish 1611 Ches 6-1/2 miles ne Warrington pop 510 archd and dioc Chester

WARCOP parish 1597 Westm 3 miles nw Brough comp hamlets Bleatarn, Burton, Sandford, Warcop pop 680 archd and dioc Carlisle Wesl Meth

WARDEN parish 1688 Kent 6-3/4 miles e Queenborough pop 27 archd and dioc Canterbury

WARDEN parish 1695 Northumberland comp chapelry Haydon or Elrington, townships Brokenhaugh, Dean Raw, Lipwood, Warden pop 2,286 2-1/2 miles nw Hexham archd Northumberland dioc Durham

WARDEN CHIPPING parish 1579 co Northampton 7-3/4 miles ne Banbury pop 500 archd Northampton dioc Peterborough

WARDEN LAW township parish Houghton le Spring co Durham pop 54

WARDEN, OLD parish 1576 Beds 3-3/4 miles sw Biggleswade pop 660 archd Bedford dioc Lincoln

WARDINGTON chapelry 1603 parish Cropredy co Oxford 5 miles ne Banbury pop 824

WARDLE township parish Bunbury Ches pop 144

WARDLE township parish Rochdale Lancs Wesl Meth

WARDLEWORTH township parish Rochdale Lancs pop 9,360

WARDLEY parish 1574 co Rutland 2-3/4 miles nw Uppingham pop 50 archd Northampton dioc Peterborough

WARDLOW township parish Hope Bakewell Derbys pop 149

WARE parish 1577 Herts 2-1/4 miles ne Hertford pop 4,214 archd Middlesex dioc London Indep, Wesl Meth, Soc of Friends

WAREHAM market town 1762 borough excl juris Dorset 17 miles se Dorchester pop 2,325 archd Dorset dioc Bristol Indep, Wesl Meth, Unit

WAREHORNE parish 1727 Kent 7-1/4 miles sw Ashford pop 439 archd and dioc Canterbury

WARESLEY parish 1647 Hunts 4-1/4 miles ne Potton pop 241 archd Huntingdon dioc Lincoln

WARFIELD parish 1666 Berks 6 miles ne Wokingham pop 1,207 archd Berks dioc Salisbury

WARFORD, GREAT township parish Alderley Ches pop 349

WARFORD, LITTLE township parish Rosthern Ches

WARGRAVE parish 1538 Berks 6-1/2 miles ne Reading pop 1,423 archd Berks dioc Salisbury

WARHAM parish St Mary 1565, All Saints 1558 Norfolk 2 miles se Wells pop 461 archd and dioc Norwich

WARK parish 1815 Northumberland comp townships High Shitlington, Low Shitlington, Wark, Warksburn pop 861 archd Northumberland dioc Durham Presb

WARKLEY parish 1550 Devon 5-1/2 miles sw South Molton pop 283 archd Barnstaple dioc Exeter

WARKSBURN township parish Wark Northumberland pop 278

WARKTON parish 1558 co Northampton 2-1/4 miles ne Kettering pop 301 archd Northampton dioc Peterborough

WARKWORTH parish incl in regs Marston St Lawrence co Northampton 2 miles e Banbury pop 521 archd Northampton dioc Peterborough

WARKWORTH parish 1677 comp townships Birling, Brotherick, High Buston, Low Buston, Sturton Grange, Walkmill, townships Amble, Acklington, Acklington Park, Bullock's Hall, East Chivington, West Chivington, Glosterhill, Hauxley, Hadston, Morrick, Togston, Warkworth Northumberland pop 2,478 7 miles se Alnwick archd Northumberland dioc Durham Scottish Seceders, Wesl Meth

WARLABY township parish Ainderby Steeple N R York pop 76

WARLEGGON parish 1540 Cornwall 5-3/4 miles ne Bodmin pop 274 archd Cornwall dioc Exeter

WARLEY township parish Halifax W R York pop 5,685 Indep

WARLEY, GREAT parish 1539 Essex 3-3/4 miles s Brentwood pop 424 archd Essex dioc London

WARLEY, LITTLE parish 1539 Essex 3-1/2 miles se Brentwood pop 163 archd Essex dioc London

WARLEY WIGORN hamlet parish Halesowen Worcs

WARLINGHAM parish 1653 Surrey 4-3/4 miles se Croydon pop 454 archd Surrey dioc Winchester

WARMFIELD parish 1652 W R York comp townships Sharlston, Warmfield with Heath pop 995 archd and dioc York

WARMINGHAM parish 1538 Ches comp townships Elton, Moston, Tetton, Warmingham pop 1,831 archd and dioc Chester

WARMINGHURST parish 1714 Sussex 6 miles nw Steyning pop 116 archd and dioc Chichester

WARMINGTON parish 1558 co Northampton 3-1/4 miles ne Oundle pop 617 archd Northampton dioc Peterborough Wesl Meth

WARMINGTON parish 1636 Warws 5 miles nw Banbury pop 470 archd Coventry dioc Lichfield Wesl Meth

WARMINSTER parish 1556 Wilts 21 miles nw Salisbury pop 6,115 archd and dioc Salisbury Bapt, Indep, Wesl Meth, Unit

WARMSWORTH parish 1594 W R York 3-1/4 miles sw Doncaster pop 362 archd and dioc York

WARMWELL parish 1641 Dorset 5-1/2 miles se Dorchester pop 87 archd Dorset dioc Bristol

WARNBOROUGH, NORTH tything parish Odiham Hamps

WARNBOROUGH, SOUTH parish 1538 Hamps 2-3/4 miles sw Odiham pop 374 archd and dioc Winchester

WARNDON parish 1561 Worcs 2-1/2 miles ne Worcester pop 171 archd and dioc Worcester

WARNFORD or WARRINGTON township parish Bambrough Northumberland pop 35 Presb

WARNFORD parish 1541 Hamps 6-1/4 miles ne Bishop's Waltham pop 418 pec Bishop of Winchester Indep

WARNHAM parish 1558 Sussex 3 miles nw Horsham pop 952 archd and dioc Chichester

WARNINGCAMP tything parish Leominster Sussex pop 104

WARPSGROVE parish (incl in regs of Chalgrave) co Oxford pop 36 archd and dioc Oxford

WARRENTON township parish Hambrough Northumberland pop 158

WARRINGTON hamlet parish Olney Bucks

WARRINGTON parish 1591 Lancs comp borough Warrington, chapelry Burtonwood, townships Poulton with Fearnhead, Roxton, Woolston with Martinscroft pop 19,155 archd and dioc Chester Bapt, Soc of Friends, Countess of Huntingdon's Connection, Indep, Indep and Wesl Meth, Unit, Roman Cath

WARSILL township parish Ripon W R York pop 86 Indep

WARSLOW chapelry 1785 parish Allstonefield Staffs 7-1/4 miles ne Leek pop 595 archd Stafford dioc Lichfield

WARSOP parish 1539 Notts 5-1/4 miles ne Mansfield pop 1,281 archd Nottingham dioc York

WARTER parish 1669 E R York 4-1/2 miles ne Pocklington pop 470 archd East Riding dioc York Wesl Meth

WARTHERMASK township parish Masham N R York

WARTHILL parish 1689 E R York pop 162 5-1/2 miles ne York pec of Prebendary of Warthill Cathedral Church of York

WARTLING parish 1538 Sussex 4-1/2 miles se Hailsham pop 948 archd Lewes dioc Chichester

WARTNABY chapelry 1633 parish Rothley Leics 4-1/2 miles nw Melton Mowbray pop 86

WARTON chapelry (incl in regs of Kirkham) parish Kirkham Lancs 3 miles sw Kirkham pop 531 archd Richmond dioc Chester

WARTON parish 1568 Lancs comp chapelry Silverdale, townships Borwick, Carnforth, Hutton, Warton with Lindeth, Yealand Redmayne pop 2,151 archd Richmond dioc Chester

WARTON township parish Rothbury Northumberland pop 59

WARWICK parish 1681 Cumberland comp townships Aglionby, Warwick, Little Corby pop 686 4-3/4 miles ne Carlisle archd and dioc Carlisle

WARWICK borough sep juris Warws 90 miles nw London pop 9,109 comp St Mary 1651, St Nicholas 1538 archd and dioc Worcester Bapt, Soc of Friends, Indep, Wesl Meth, Unit

WARWICK BRIDGE township parish Wetheral Cumberland pop 1,285 Roman Cath

WASDALE or NETHER WASDALE chapelry 1711 parish St Bees Cumberland 7 miles ne Ravenglass pop 185

WASDALE HEAD chapelry 1721 parish St Bees Cumberland 11 miles sw Keswick

WASHAWAY hamlet parish Egloshayle Cornwall

WASHBOURN, GREAT parish 1567 Gloucs 5-1/2 miles sw Winchcombe pop 87 archd and dioc Gloucester

WASHBOURN, LITTLE chapelry 1550 parish Overbury Worcs 6-1/2
miles ne Tewkesbury pop 51

WASHBROOK parish 1559 Suffolk 4 miles sw Ipswich pop 418 archd
Suffolk dioc Norwich

WASHFIELD parish 1556 Devon 2-1/2 miles nw Tiverton pop 453
archd and dioc Exeter

WASHFORD PINE parish 1587 Devon 8-1/2 miles nw Crediton pop
174 archd Barnstaple dioc Exeter

WASHINGBOROUGH parish 1564 Lincs 2 miles ne Lincoln pop 1,124
archd and dioc Lincoln

WASHINGLEY parish (incl in Lutton) Hunts 1-1/2 miles w Stilton
pop 81 archd Northampton dioc Peterborough

WASHINGTON parish 1603 co Durham comp townships Barmston,
Great and Little Usworth, Washington pop 2,673 5-1/2 miles se
Gateshead archd and dioc Durham Wesl Meth

WASHINGTON parish 1558 Sussex 4-1/2 miles nw Steyning pop 793
archd and dioc Chichester

WASING parish 1730 Berks 7-1/2 miles se Newbury pop 79 archd
Berks dioc Salisbury

WASPERTON parish 1538 Warws 4 miles sw Warwick pop 292 archd
and dioc Worcester

WASTE LANDS extra parochial liberty parish Swineshead Lincs 6-1/2
miles sw Boston

WATCHETT market town parish St Decuman Somerset 5 miles e
Dunster Bapt, Wesl Meth

WATCHFIELD township parish Shrivenham Berks pop 341

WATERBEACH parish 1653 Cambs 5-1/4 miles ne Cambridge pop
1,146 archd and dioc Ely

WATERDEN parish 1730 Norfolk 4 miles sw Little Walsingham pop
24 archd Norfolk dioc Norwich

WATER EATON township parish Bletchley Bucks pop 243

WATER EATON township parish Kidlington co Oxford pop 102

WATER EATON township parish Penkridge Staffs

WATER EATON township parish Eisey Wilts pop 68

WATERFALL parish 1712 Staffs 7 miles se Leek pop 531 archd
Stafford dioc Lichfield Wesl Meth

WATERGALL extra parochial liberty Warws 4 miles s Southam pop
13

WATERHEAD township parish Lanercost Abbey Cumberland pop 177

WATERINGBURY parish 1705 Kent 5 miles sw Maidstone pop 1,109
archd and dioc Rochester

WATER MILLOCK chapelry 1579 parish Greystock Cumberland 7
miles sw Penrith pop 429

WATER OAKLEY division parish Bray Berks

WATER OVERTON chapelry parish Aston Warws 2-1/2 miles nw
Coleshill

WATERPERRY parish 1678 co Oxford 5-3/4 miles w Thame pop 243 archd and dioc Oxford

WATERSTOCK parish 1580 co Oxford 5-1/4 miles w Thame pop 142 archd and dioc Oxford

WATFORD parish 1539 Herts comp market town Watford, hamlets Cashio, Levesden, Oxhey pop 5,293 20 miles sw Hertford archd St Albans dioc London Bapt, Connection of Countess of Huntingdon, Wesl Meth

WATFORD parish 1565 co Northampton 4-3/4 miles ne Daventry pop 353 archd Northampton dioc Peterborough

WATH parish 1565 comp chapelry Norton Conyers, chapelries Melmerby, Middleton, Quernhow, township Wath N R York pop 730 4-1/4 miles ne Ripon archd Richmond dioc Chester

WATH township parish Hovingham N R York pop 21

WATH UPON DEARNE parish 1598 W R York comp chapelries Brampton Bierlow, Nether Hoyland, Swinton, Wentworth, township Wath upon Dearne pop 6,927 5-3/4 miles n Rotherham archd and dioc York Wesl Meth

WATLESBOROUGH township parish Cardeston Shrops

WATLINGTON parish 1570 Norfolk 5-1/2 miles n Downham Market pop 500 archd Norfolk dioc Norwich

WATLINGTON parish 1636 co Oxford 15 miles se Oxford pop 1,833 archd and dioc Oxford Bapt, Indep, Wesl Meth

WATTISFIELD parish 1540 Suffolk 2 miles sw Botesdale pop 592 archd Sudbury dioc Norwich Indep

WATTISHAM parish 1538 Suffolk 2 miles ne Bildeston pop 202 archd Sudbury dioc Norwich Bapt

WATTLEFIELD division parish Wymondham Norfolk pop 451

WATTON parish 1560 Herts 4-3/4 miles nw Hertford pop 830 archd Huntingdon dioc Lincoln

WATTON parish 1539 Norfolk 24 miles sw Norwich pop 1,027 archd and dioc Norwich Indep

WATTON parish 1558 E R York 5-1/2 miles s Great Driffield pop 345 archd East Riding dioc York

WAULDBY township parish Rowley E R York pop 50

WAVENDON parish 1567 Bucks 3-1/2 miles ne Fenny Stratford pop 802 archd Buckingham dioc Lincoln Wesl Meth

WAVERLEY extra parochial liberty Surrey 2 miles se Farnham pop 74

WAVERTON parish 1582 Ches comp townships Hatton, Huxley, Waverton pop 720 archd and dioc Chester

WAVERTON, HIGH and LOW township parish Wigton Cumberland

WAVERTREE chapelry 1794 parish Childwall Lancs 2-1/2 miles se Liverpool pop 1,932

WAXHAM parish 1763 Norfolk 12 miles se North Walsham pop 59 archd Norfolk dioc Norwich

WAXHOLME township part of parish Owthorne E R York pop 68

WAYFORD parish 1704 Somerset 2-1/2 miles sw Crewkerne pop 219 archd Taunton dioc Bath and Wells

WEALD chapelry parish Sevenoaks Kent
WEALD hamlet parish Harrow on the Hill Middlesex
WEALD, NORTH parish 1557 Essex 3-1/4 miles ne Epping pop 887
    archd Essex dioc London
WEALD, SOUTH parish 1539 Essex pop 2,825 archd Essex dioc
    London
WEARDALE, ST JOHN or ST JOHN'S CHAPEL chapelry 1788 parish
    Stanhope co Durham 6-1/4 miles nw Stanhope Indep, Prim and
    Wesl Meth
WEARDLEY township parish Harewood W R York pop 169
WEARE parish 1631 Somerset 3-1/2 miles sw Axbridge pop 764
    archd Wells dioc Bath and Wells
WEAR GIFFORD parish 1583 Devon 2-3/4 miles nw Great Torrington
    pop 547 archd Barnstaple dioc Exeter
WEARMOUTH, BISHOP parish 1567 co Durham comp townships
    Bishop Wearmouth, Bishop Wearmouth Pans, Burdon, Ford, Ryhope,
    Silksworth, Tunstall pop 16,590 archd and dioc Durham Meth of
    New Connection
WEARMOUTH, MONK parish 1768 co Durham comp townships Ful-
    well, Hylton, Monk Wearmouth, Monk Wearmouth Shore, Southwick
    pop 9,428 archd and dioc Durham Bapt, Presb, Wesl Meth
WEARMOUTH PANS BISHOP township parish Bishop Wearmouth co
    Durham pop 363
WEARMOUTH SHORE, MONK township parish Monk Wearmouth co
    Durham pop 6,051
WEASENHAM parish 1568 Norfolk 7-3/4 miles sw Fakenham pop
    313 archd and dioc Norwich
WEASENHAM parish 1581 Norfolk 7-1/4 miles sw Fakenham pop
    309 archd and dioc Norwich
WEATHERSFIELD parish 1647 Essex 6-3/4 miles nw Braintree pop
    1,698 archd Middlesex dioc London Indep
WEAVERHAM parish 1576 Ches comp townships Acton, Crowton,
    Cuddington, Onston, Wallerscoat, Weaverham cum Milton, Weaver-
    ham pop 2,321 archd and dioc Chester
WEAVERTHORP parish 1702 E R York comp townships Luttons Ambo,
    Weaverthorp pop 753 pec of Dean and Chapter of York Wesl Meth
WEDDINGTON parish 1663 Warws 1-1/4 miles n Nuneaton pop 69
    archd Coventry dioc Lichfield
WEDGWOOD township parish Wolstanton Staffs pop 125
WEDHAMPTON tything parish Urchfont Wilts pop 221
WEDMORE parish 1561 Somerset 4-3/4 miles se Axbridge pop 3,557
    pec Dean of Wells Bapt, Wesl Meth
WEDNESBURY parish 1562 Staffs 19 miles se Stafford pop 8,437
    archd Stafford dioc Lichfield Indep, Prim and Wesl Meth
WEDNESFIELD chapelry 1751 parish Wolverhampton Staffs 2 miles
    ne Wolverhampton pop 1,879 pec of Wolverhampton Wesl Meth
WEEDON hamlet parish Hardwicke Bucks pop 405
WEEDON or WEEDON BECK parish 1589 co Northampton 4 miles se

Daventry pop 1,439 archd Northampton dioc Peterborough Indep, Wesl Meth

WEEDON LOYS parish 1559 co Northampton 6-1/4 miles sw Towcester pop 528 archd Northampton dioc Peterborough

WEEFORD parish 1563 Staffs 4 miles se Lichfield pop 470 pec Prebendary of Alrewas and Weeford

WEEK parish Devon See GERMANSWEEK

WEEK St Mary parish 1602 Cornwall 7 miles s Stratton pop 769 archd Cornwall dioc Exeter

WEEK parish 1573 Hamps 1 mile nw Winchester pop 182 archd and dioc Winchester

WEEKE CHAMPFLOWER chapelry 1625 parish Bruton Somerset pop 93 archd Wells dioc Bath and Wells

WEEKLEY parish 1550 co Northampton 2-1/4 miles ne Kettering pop 273 archd Northampton dioc Peterborough

WEEL township parish St John Beverley E R York pop 136

WEELEY parish 1562 Essex 9-1/2 miles se Manningtree pop 573 archd Colchester dioc London Wesl Meth

WEETHLEY parish 1572 Warws 3-1/4 miles sw Alcester pop 62 archd and dioc Worcester

WEETING parish 1558 Norfolk 1-1/2 miles n Brandon Ferry pop 357 archd Norfolk dioc Norwich

WEETON township parish Kirkham Lancs pop 477

WEETON township parish Harewood W R York pop 322 Wesl Meth

WEETSTED township parish Long Benton Northumberland

WEEVER township parish Middlewich Ches pop 196

WEIGHTON, MARKET parish 1653 E R York comp market town Market Weighton, chapelry Shipton, hamlet Arras pop 2,169 pec Prebendary of Keighton Indep, Wesl Meth

WELBECK extra parochial liberty co Nottingham 3-1/2 miles sw Worksop pop 63

WELBORNE parish 1695 Norfolk 6-1/2 miles nw Wymondham pop 231 archd Norfolk dioc Norwich

WELBOURN parish 1561 Lincs 9-1/2 miles nw Sleaford pop 494 archd and dioc Lincoln

WELBURN township parish Bulmer W R York pop 391

WELBURN township parish Kirkdale N R York pop 112

WELBURY parish 1682 N R York 6-3/4 miles nw North Allerton pop 233 archd Cleveland dioc York

WELBY township parish Melton Mowbray Leics pop 44

WELBY parish 1569 Lincs 4-1/2 miles ne Grantham pop 399 archd and dioc Lincoln

WELCHES DAM extra parochial liberty Cambs 7 miles nw Ely pop 137

WELDON, GREAT parish 1594 co Northampton 4-1/4 miles se Rockingham pop 778 archd Northampton dioc Peterborough Indep

WELDON, LITTLE hamlet parish Great Weldon co Northampton pop 440

WELFORD parish 1559 Berks 5-1/4 miles nw Speenhamland pop 1,061 pec Dean of Salisbury

WELFORD parish 1562 co Northampton 8-3/4 miles sw Market Harborough pop 1,011 archd Northampton dioc Peterborough Indep, Wesl Meth

WELFORD parish 1561 Gloucs 4-1/4 miles sw Stratford on Avon pop 669 archd and dioc Gloucester Wesl Meth

WELHAM parish 1695 Leics 4-1/4 miles ne Market Harborough pop 73 archd Leicester dioc Lincoln

WELHAM township parish Norton E R York

WELL parish 1649 Lincs 2-1/4 miles sw Alford pop 76 archd and dioc Lincoln

WELL parish 1558 N R York comp townships Snape, Well pop 1,060 4-1/2 miles s Bedale archd Richmond dioc Chester

WELL HAUGH township parish Falstone Northumberland pop 272

WELLAND parish 1670 Worcs 3 miles sw Upton upon Severn pop 400 pec Bishop of Worcester

WELLCOMBE parish 1653 Devon 4-3/4 miles sw Hartland pop 258 archd Barnstaple dioc Exeter

WELLESBOURN HASTINGS parish 1560 Warws 4-3/4 miles nw Kington pop 697 archd and dioc Worcester

WELLESBOURN MONTFORD parish (with Wellesbourne Hastings) Warws 5 miles nw Kington pop 660

WELLINGBOROUGH parish 1586 co Northampton 10 miles ne Northampton pop 4,688 archd Northampton dioc Peterborough Bapt, Soc of Friends, Wesl Meth, Indep

WELLINGHAM parish 1765 Norfolk 6-1/4 miles sw Fakenham pop 165 archd and dioc Norwich

WELLINGLEY township parish Tickhill W R York

WELLINGORE parish 1653 Lincs 9 miles nw Sleaford pop 752 pec Dean and Chapter of Lincoln Wesl Meth

WELLINGTON parish 1559 Herefs 5-1/4 miles n Hereford pop 630 archd and dioc Hereford

WELLINGTON parish 1626 Shrops 11 miles e Shrewsbury pop 9,761 archd Salop dioc Lichfield Wesl Meth, Bapt, Indep

WELLINGTON parish 1683 Somerset 24 miles sw Somerset pop 4,762 archd Taunton dioc Bath and Wells Bapt, Soc of Friends, Indep, Wesl Meth

WELLOW parish 1703 Notts 1-1/2 miles se Ollerton pop 473 archd Nottingham dioc York

WELLOW parish 1561 Somerset 4-1/4 miles s Bath pop 960 archd Wells dioc Bath and Wells Wesl Meth

WELLOW, EAST parish 1570 Hamps 3-3/4 miles w Romsey pop 318 archd and dioc Winchester Wesl Meth

WELLOW, WEST tything parish East Wellow Wilts pop 394

WELLS parish 1549 Norfolk 33 miles nw Norwich pop 3,624 archd and dioc Norwich Soc of Friends, Indep, Wesl Meth

WELLS city sep juris 1608 Somerset 19 miles sw Bath pop 6,649

Bapt, Indep, Wesl Meth

WELNETHAM, GREAT parish 1561 Suffolk 3-1/2 miles se Bury St Edmund's pop 422 archd Sudbury dioc Norwich

WELNETHAM, LITTLE parish 1557 Suffolk 3-1/2 miles se Bury St Edmund's pop 180 archd Sudbury dioc Norwich

WELNEY chapelry 1642 parish Upwell Norfolk 8 miles se March pop 805

WELSHAMPTON parish Shrops See HAMPTON, WELSH

WELTON parish 1568 Lincs 6 miles ne Lincoln pop 516 pec Dean and Chapter of Lincoln Wesl Meth

WELTON parish 1578 co Northampton 2-1/2 miles ne Daventry pop 600 archd Northampton dioc Peterborough

WELTON township parish Ovingham Northumberland pop 69

WELTON parish 1713 E R York comp chapelry Melton, township Welton pop 805 pec of Howdenshire Wesl Meth

WELTON IN THE MARSH parish 1558 Lincs 6 miles ne Spilsby pop 363 archd and dioc Lincoln

WELTON LE WOLD parish 1558 Lincs 3-3/4 miles w Louth pop 241 archd and dioc Lincoln

WELWICK parish 1650 E R York 2 miles se Patrington pop 401 archd East Riding dioc York Soc of Friends, Wesl Meth

WELWYN parish 1558 Herts 8 miles nw Hertford pop 1,369 archd Huntingdon dioc Lincoln Huntingtonians, Wesl Meth

WEM parish 1582 Shrops comp market town Wem, chapelries Ed-staston, Newtown, townships Aston, Cotton, Horton, Lacon, Lowe with Ditches, Northwood, Soulton, Tilley, Wolverley pop 3,967 archd Salop dioc Lichfield Bapt, Presb.

WEMBDON parish 1672 Somerset 1-1/2 miles nw Bridgewater pop 289 archd Taunton dioc Bath and Wells

WEMBURY parish 1611 Devon 5-1/4 miles sw Plympton Earle pop 652 archd Totnes dioc Exeter

WEMSWORTHY parish 1674 Devon 3-1/2 miles sw Chulmleigh pop 378 archd Barnstaple dioc Exeter

WENDLEBURY parish 1589 co Oxford 2-1/2 miles sw Bicester pop 196 archd and dioc Oxford

WENDLING parish 1539 Norfolk 4-1/4 miles w East Dereham pop 347 archd and dioc Norwich

WENDON LOFTS parish 1674 Essex 5-1/4 miles nw Saffron Walden pop 54 Commissary of Essex and Herts, Consistorial Court of the Bishop of London

WENDONS AMBO parish 1540 Essex 2-1/2 miles sw Saffron Walden pop 333 Commissary of Essex and Herts, Consistorial Court of Bishop of London

WENDOVER parish 1626 borough Bucks 23 miles se Buckingham pop 2,008 archd Buckingham dioc Lincoln Bapt, Indep

WENDRON parish 1560 Cornwall pop 8,073 comp borough Helston archd Cornwall dioc Exeter Bapt, Wesl Meth

WENDY parish 1550 Cambs 6-1/4 miles nw Royston pop 125 archd and dioc Ely

WENHAM, GREAT parish 1648 Suffolk 4-1/2 miles se Hadleigh pop 181 archd Suffolk dioc Norwich

WENHAM, LITTLE parish 1558 Suffolk 5 miles se Hadleigh pop 88 archd Suffolk dioc Norwich

WENHASTON parish 1687 Suffolk 2-1/4 miles se Halesworth pop 1,070 archd Suffolk dioc Norwich

WENLOCK, LITTLE parish 1690 Shrops 3-1/4 miles s Wellington pop 1,057 archd Salop dioc Hereford

WENLOCK, MUCH parish 1558 borough sep juris Shrops 12 miles se Shrewsbury pop 2,424 archd Salop dioc Hereford Wesl Meth

WENN, ST parish 1678 Cornwall 4 miles ne St Columb Major archd Cornwall dioc Exeter

WENNINGTON parish 1654 Essex 2 miles nw Purfleet pop 127 archd Essex dioc London

WENNINGTON township parish Melling Lancs pop 155

WENSLEY parish 1538 N R York comp chapelry Bolton Castle, townships Leybourn, Preston upon Scar, Redmire, Wensley pop 2,266 archd Richmond dioc Chester

WENSLEY FOLD township parish Blackburn Lancs pop 1,047

WENTNOR parish 1662 Shrops 5-1/2 miles ne Bishop's Castle pop 707 archd Salop dioc Hereford

WENTWORTH or WINGFORD parish 1754 Cambs 4-1/2 miles sw Ely pop 144 pec Bishop of Ely

WENTWORTH chapelry 1654 parish Wath upon Dearne W R York 5-1/2 miles nw Rotherham pop 1,394 archd and dioc York

WEOBLEY parish 1635 borough Herefs 12 miles nw Hereford pop 819 archd and dioc Hereford

WEONARD'S ST parish 1624 Herefs 7-1/4 miles nw Ross pop 564 archd and dioc Hereford Wesl Meth

WEREHAM parish 1558 Norfolk 1-3/4 miles nw Stoke Ferry pop 575 archd Norfolk dioc Norwich

WERNITH township parish Stockport Ches pop 3,462 Unit

WERRINGTON parish 1653 Devon 2-1/2 miles nw Launceston pop 661 archd Cornwall dioc Exeter

WERRINGTON chapelry parish Paston co Northampton 3-1/2 miles nw Peterborough pop 537

WERVIN township parish St Oswald Chester Ches pop 64

WESHAM township parish Kirkham Lancs

WESSINGTON township parish Crich Derbys pop 465

WESSINGTON hamlet parish Chipping Campden Gloucs pop 128

WEST ACOMB Northumberland See ACOMB, WEST

WEST ACRE parish 1668 Norfolk 5-1/4 miles nw Swaffham pop 415 archd and dioc Norwich

WESTANSWICK township parish Stoke upon Tern Shrops pop 181

WESTBEER parish 1577 Kent 3-1/2 miles ne Canterbury pop 219 archd and dioc Canterbury

WESTBOROUGH parish 1567 Lincs 7 miles nw Grantham pop 215

archd and dioc Lincoln

WESTBOURNE Sussex See BOURNE, WEST

WEST BROMWICH Staffs See BROMWICH, WEST

WESTBROOK tything parish Boxford Berks

WESTBURTON tything parish Bury Sussex

WESTBURY parish 1558 Bucks 4-3/4 miles nw Buckingham pop 391 archd Buckingham dioc Lincoln

WESTBURY parish 1637 Shrops comp chapelry Minsterley, township Westbury pop 2,228 8-3/4 miles sw Shrewsbury archd Salop dioc Hereford

WESTBURY parish 1713 Somerset 4 miles nw Wells pop 681 pec Dean of Wells

WESTBURY hamlet parish East Meon Hamps pop 226

WESTBURY parish 1556 Wilts comp borough Westbury, chapelries Bratton, Dilton, townships Hawkeridge, Haywood, Leigh pop 7,324 pec of Precentor of the Cathedral Church of Salisbury Indep, Bapt, Wesl Meth

WESTBURY UPON SEVERN parish 1538 Gloucs 2-1/2 miles ne Newnham pop 2,032 archd Hereford dioc Gloucester Wesl Meth

WESTBURY UPON TRYM parish 1559 Gloucs 3 miles nw Bristol pop 4,263 pec Bishop of Bristol Wesl Meth

WESTBY parish (with Basingthorpe) Lincs 3-3/4 miles nw Corby

WESTCOTE parish 1630 Gloucs 4 miles se Stow on the Wold pop 188 archd and dioc Gloucester

WESTCOTE township parish Tysoe Warws

WESTCOTT hamlet parish Waddesdon Bucks pop 242

WESTEND township parish Burgh upon the Sands Cumberland pop 457

WESTEND tything parish Worplesdon Surrey

WESTENHANGER or OSTHENHANGER manor parish Standford Kent 3 miles nw Hythe archd and dioc Canterbury

WESTERDALE parish 1562 N R York 7-1/2 miles se Qualsbrough pop 281 pec manorial Court of Westerdale

WESTERFIELD parish 1538 Suffolk 2-1/2 miles ne Ipswich pop 327 archd Suffolk dioc Norwich

WESTERGATE hamlet parish Aldingbourn Sussex

WESTERHAM parish 1559 Kent 22 miles w Maidstone archd and dioc Rochester Soc of Friends, Wesl Meth

WESTERLEIGH parish 1693 Gloucs 3 miles sw Chipping Sodbury pop 1,709 archd and dioc Gloucester

WESTERTON township parish St Andrew Auckland co Durham pop 85

WESTFIELD parish 1706 Norfolk 2-1/2 miles s East Dereham pop 127 archd Norfolk dioc Norwich

WESTFIELD parish 1552 Sussex 4-1/4 miles se Battle pop 938 archd Lewes dioc Chichester

WESTGATE township parish St John Northumberland pop 2,996

WESTHALL parish 1559 Suffolk 4 miles ne Halesworth pop 442 archd Suffolk dioc Norwich

WESTHAM parish 1571 Sussex 5-3/4 miles se Hailsham pop 752

archd Lewes dioc Chichester

WESTHAMPNETT Sussex See HAMPNETT, WEST

WESTHIDE Herefs See HIDE, WEST

WESTHORPE parish 1538 Suffolk 7-3/4 miles n Stow Market pop 263
archd Sudbury dioc Norwich

WESTHOUGHTON Lancs See HOUGHTON, WEST

WESTLETON parish 1545 Suffolk 2-3/4 miles e Yoxford pop 884 archd
Suffolk dioc Norwich

WESTLEY township parish Westbury Shrops

WESTLEY parish 1565 Suffolk 2 miles w Bury St Edmunds pop 132
archd Sudbury dioc Norwich

WESTLEY WATERLESS parish 1557 Cambs 5 miles sw Newmarket
pop 158 archd and dioc Ely

WESTMANCOATE hamlet parish Bredon Worcs Bapt

WESTMESTON parish 1587 Sussex 5-3/4 miles nw Lewes pop 494
archd Lewes dioc Chichester

WESTMILL parish 1565 Herts 1-1/2 miles se Buntingford pop 418
archd Huntingdon dioc Lincoln

WESTMINSTER city adj city of London Middlesex pop 182,000 comp
St Anne Soho 1686, St Clement Danes 1558, Duke Street Chapel
1745, St George Hanover Square 1725, St James Picadilly 1685,
St John the Evangelist 1728, St Margaret 1538, St Martin in the
Fields 1550, St Mary le Strand 1558, St Paul Covent Garden 1653,
Savoy Chapel 1680, Somerset House Chapel 1714, Westminster
Abbey 1606, Whitehall Chapel Royal 1704, Trinity Chapel Knights-
bridge 1658 All are in archd Middlesex dioc London except St
John Evangelist and St Margaret which are pec Dean and Chapter
of Westminster Many nonconformist chapels

WESTOE chapelry parish Jarrow co Durham pop 9,682 archd and
dioc Durham

WESTON township parish Runcorn Ches pop 532

WESTON township parish Wybunbury Ches pop 401

WESTON tything parish Stalbridge Dorset pop 225

WESTON parish 1539 Herts 4-1/2 miles ne Stevenage pop 1,046
archd Huntingdon dioc Lincoln Wesl Meth

WESTON parish 1678 Norfolk 5-1/4 miles s Reepham pop 406 archd
Norfolk dioc Norwich

WESTON hamlet parish Loys Weedon co Northampton

WESTON parish 1559 Notts 3 miles se Tuxford pop 395 archd Nottingham dioc York

WESTON chapelry parish Burford Shrops

WESTON parish 1538 Somerset 1-3/4 miles nw Bath pop 2,560 archd
Bath dioc Bath and Wells Wesl Meth

WESTON hamlet parish Wanstrow Somerset

WESTON tything parish Buriton Hamps

WESTON parish 1538 Suffolk 2-3/4 miles s Beccles pop 233 archd
Suffolk dioc Norwich

WESTON hamlet parish Thames Ditton Surrey

WESTON hamlet parish Bulkington Warws
WESTON parish 1673 W R York comp townships Askwith, Weston
    pop 521 archd and dioc York
WESTON, Hunts See ALCONBURY
WESTON BAMFYLD parish 1632 Somerset 5-3/4 miles sw Castle
    Cary pop 123 archd Wells dioc Bath and Wells
WESTON BEGGARD parish 1587 Herefs 5 miles e Hereford pop 281
    archd and dioc Hereford Wesl Meth
WESTON BIRT parish 1611 Gloucs 3-3/4 miles sw Tetbury pop 138
    archd and dioc Gloucester
WESTON BY WELLAND parish (incl in regs of Sutton Bassett) co
    Northampton 4-1/4 miles ne Market Harborough pop 208 archd
    Northampton dioc Peterborough
WESTON, COLD parish 1690 Shrops 6-3/4 miles ne Ludlow pop 25
    archd Salop dioc Hereford
WESTON COLLEY tything parish Mitcheldever Hamps
WESTON COLVILLE parish 1712 Cambs 6 miles ne Linton pop 444
    archd and dioc Ely
WESTON CONEY parish 1562 Suffolk 6-1/4 miles ne Ixworth pop 257
    archd Suffolk dioc Norwich
WESTON CORBETT extra parochial liberty Hamps 4 miles se Ba-
    singstoke pop 17
WESTON COYNEY township parish Caverswall Staffs pop 619
WESTON, EDITH co Rutland See EDITH WESTON
WESTON FAVELL parish 1540 co Northampton 2-1/2 miles ne North-
    ampton pop 443 archd Northampton dioc Peterborough
WESTON IN GORDANO parish 1684 Somerset 10 miles ne Bristol
    pop 124 archd Bath dioc Bath and Wells
WESTON JONES township parish Norbury Staffs pop 118
WESTON, KING Somerset See KINGWESTON
WESTON, KING'S tything parish Henbury Gloucs pop 107
WESTON, LAWRENCE tything parish Henbury Gloucs pop 329
WESTON, MARKET parish 1563 Suffolk 7 miles s East Harling pop
    312 archd Sudbury dioc Norwich
WESTON, OLD parish 1784 Hunts 7-1/4 miles n Kimbolton pop 356
    archd Huntingdon dioc Lincoln
WESTON ON THE GREEN parish 1591 co Oxford 4-1/2 miles sw
    Bicester pop 494 archd and dioc Oxford
WESTON PATRICK parish 1574 Hamps 4-1/4 miles sw Odiham pop
    210 archd and dioc Winchester
WESTON PEVEREL or PENNY CROSS chapelry 1634 parish St An-
    drew Plymouth Devon 2-3/4 miles nw Plymouth pop 274
WESTON RHYN township parish St Martin Shrops
WESTON, SOUTH parish 1558 co Oxford 2-3/4 miles se Tetsworth
    pop 118 archd and dioc Oxford Wesl Meth
WESTON SUB EDGE parish 1612 Gloucs 1-3/4 miles nw Chipping
    Campden pop 367 archd and dioc Gloucester
WESTON SUPER MARE parish 1668 Somerset 9-3/4 miles nw Ax-

bridge pop 1,310 archd Wells dioc Bath and Wells

WESTON TURVILLE parish 1538 Bucks 2-1/4 miles nw Wendover pop 637 archd Buckingham dioc Lincoln

WESTON UNDER LIZARD parish 1701 Staffs 5-3/4 miles ne Shiffnall pop 257 archd Stafford dioc Lichfield

WESTON UNDER PENYARD parish 1568 Herefs 2-1/4 miles se Ross pop 639 archd and dioc Hereford

WESTON UNDER RED CASTLE chapelry parish Hodnet Shrops pop 328

WESTON UNDER WEATHERLY parish 1661 Warws 6 miles ne Warwick pop 208 archd Coventry dioc Lichfield

WESTON UNDERWOOD parish 1681 Bucks 1-3/4 miles sw Olney pop 441 archd Buckingham dioc Lincoln

WESTON UNDERWOOD township parish Stanton by Dale Derbys pop 272

WESTON UPON AVON parish 1685 Warws and Gloucs 4-1/2 miles sw Stratford on Avon pop 108 archd and dioc Gloucester

WESTON UPON TRENT parish 1565 Derbys 7 miles se Derby pop 367 archd Derby dioc Lichfield

WESTON UPON TRENT parish 1585 Staffs 4-1/2 miles ne Stafford pop 608 archd Stafford dioc Lichfield

WESTON ZOYLAND parish 1558 Somerset 4 miles se Bridgewater pop 937 archd Wells dioc Bath and Wells

WESTONING parish 1560 Beds 4 miles sw Ampthill pop 627 archd Bedford dioc Lincoln Bapt

WESTOVER tything parish Wherwell Hamps

WESTOW parish 1560 E R York comp townships Eddlethorp, Firby, Menethorpe, Westow pop 606 archd East Riding dioc York Wesl Meth

WEST PARK tything parish Malmesbury Wilts

WESTPORT parish 1661 Wilts pop 1,286 archd Wilts dioc Salisbury adj to Malmesbury

WESTRILL extra parochial liberty Leics 5 miles se Lutterworth pop 7

WESTROP tything parish Highworth Wilts pop 644

WEST VILLE township Lincs pop 118

WESTWARD parish 1605 Cumberland comp townships Brocklebank with Stoneraise, Rosley, Woodside 2-3/4 miles se Wigton pop 1,253 archd and dioc Carlisle

WESTWATER tything parish Axminster Devon

WESTWELL parish 1558 Kent 2-1/2 miles se Charing pop 861 pec Archbishop of Canterbury

WESTWELL parish 1602 co Oxford 2 miles sw Burford pop 162 archd and dioc Oxford

WESTWICK hamlet parish Oakington Cambs pop 47

WESTWICK township parish Gainford co Durham pop 98

WESTWICK parish 1642 Norfolk 2-3/4 miles s North Walsham pop 210 archd Norfolk dioc Norwich

WESTWICK township parish Ripon W R York pop 30

WESTWOOD township parish Thornbury Herefs

WESTWOOD parish 1666 Wilts 2 miles sw Bradford pop 390 archd Wilts dioc Salisbury

WESTWOOD extra parochial liberty Worcs 2-1/4 miles nw Droitwich pop 10

WETHERAL parish 1674 Cumberland comp townships Cumwhinton with Coathill, Scotby, Wetheral, townships Great Corby, Warwick Bridge pop 4,149 archd and dioc Carlisle

WETHERBY chapelry 1783 parish Spofforth W R York 12-1/2 miles sw York pop 1,321 archd and dioc York Indep, Wesl Meth

WETHERDEN parish 1538 Suffolk 4-1/4 miles nw Stow Market pop 487 archd Sudbury dioc Norwich

WETHERFIELD Essex See WEATHERSFIELD

WETHERINGSETT parish 1556 Suffolk 2-1/4 miles ne Mendlesham pop 1,001 archd Sudbury dioc Norwich

WETTENHALL chapelry parish Over Ches pop 272

WETTON parish 1657 Staffs 7-1/2 miles nw Ashbourn pop 497 archd Stafford dioc Lichfield

WETWANG parish 1653 E R York comp chapelry Fimber, township Wetwang pop 621 pec Prebendary of Wetwang in Cathedral Church of York Wesl Meth

WEXHAM parish 1606 Bucks 1-1/2 miles ne Slough pop 181 archd Buckingham dioc Lincoln

WEYBOURNE parish 1727 Norfolk 3-3/4 miles ne Holt pop 273 archd and dioc Norwich

WEYBREAD parish 1687 Suffolk 1-3/4 miles sw Harleston pop 708 archd Suffolk dioc Norwich

WEYBRIDGE parish 1625 Surrey 20 miles sw London pop 930 archd Surrey dioc Winchester Bapt

WEYHILL parish 1564 Hamps 3-1/4 miles nw Andover pop 429 archd and dioc Winchester

WEYMOUTH AND MELCOME REGIS borough 1606 sep juris Dorset 8 miles sw Dorchester pop 7,655 Indep, Bapt, Wesl Meth

WHADDON parish 1580 Bucks 4-1/4 miles se Stony Stratford pop 889 archd Buckingham dioc Lincoln

WHADDON parish 1692 Cambs 4-1/4 miles n Royston pop 339 archd and dioc Ely

WHADDON parish 1674 Gloucs 3-1/4 miles sw Gloucester pop 152 archd and dioc Gloucester

WHADDON parish 1653 Wilts 2-3/4 miles ne Trowbridge pop 58 archd and dioc Salisbury

WHALEY township parish Taxall Ches pop 403 Wesl Meth

WHALLEY parish 1538 comp borough Clitheroe, market towns Burnley, Colne, chapelries Old Accrington, Altham, Bacup, Clivinger, Downham, Goldshaw Booth, Great Marsden, Newchurch with Deadwin Clough, Padiham, Pendleton, townships New Accrington, Barley with Whitley Booths, Barrowford, Higher Booths, Lower Booths, Brierscliffe with Extwistle, Chatburn, Dunnockshaw, Foulridge, Habergham, Eves, Hapton, Heyhouses, Higham Booth, Readly Hal-

lows with Filly Close and New Laund Booth, Huncoat, Ightenhill
Parrk, Little Marsden, Mearley, Little Mitton, Read, Rough Lee
Booth, Simonstone, Trawden Forest, Twiston, Whalley, Wheatley
Carr, Wiswell, Worsthorn, Worston, Yate with Pick up Bank,
market town Haslingden, chapelry Church Town, townships Bow-
land with Leagram, Clayton le Moors, Oswaldtwisttle Lancs,
township Wittlington Ches, chapelry Whitewell W R York
pop 97,585 archd and dioc Ches Wesl Meth
WHALTON parish 1661 Northumberland comp townships Newnham,
Ocle or Ogle, Riplington, Whalton pop 548 archd Northumberland
dioc Durham
WHAPLODE parish 1559 Lincs 2 miles w Holbeach pop 1,998 archd
and dioc Lincoln
WHAPLODE DROVE chapelry 1713 parish Whaplode Lincs 5-3/4
miles ne Crowland pop 580
WHARLES township parish Kirkham Lancs pop 756
WHARRAM LE STREET parish 1538 comp township Wharram le
Street W R York 6-3/4 miles se New Malton pop 150 pec of
Dean and Chapter of York
WHARRAM PERCY parish 1554 comp townships Raisthorpe with Bird-
all, Thixendale, Towthorpe, Wharram Percy pop 350 archd East
Riding dioc York
WHARTON township parish Blyton Lincs
WHARTON township parish Kirkby Stephen Westm pop 76
WHARTON township parish Davenham Ches pop 1,060
WHASHTON township parish Kirkby Ravensworth N R York pop 159
WHATBOROUGH liberty parish Tilton and Loddington Leics pop 19
WHATCOMBE tything parish Fawley Berks
WHATCOTT parish 1572 Warws 4-1/4 miles ne Shipton upon Stour
pop 219 archd and dioc Worcester
WHATCROFT township parish Davenham Ches pop 50
WHATFIELD parish 1558 Suffolk 3-1/4 miles se Bildestone pop 377
archd Sudbury dioc Norwich
WHATLEY parish 1672 Somerset 2-3/4 miles sw Frome pop 386
archd Wells dioc Bath and Wells
WHATLINGTON parish 1558 Sussex 2 miles ne Battle pop 286 archd
Lewes dioc Chichester
WHATTON parish 1538 Notts 2-3/4 miles e Bingham pop 677 archd
Nottingham dioc York Wesl Meth
WHATTON, LONG parish 1549 Leics 4-1/4 miles nw Loughborough
pop 855 archd Leicester dioc Lincoln
WHEATACRE parish 1558 Norfolk 4-3/4 miles ne Beccles pop 186
archd Norfolk dioc Norwich
WHEATACRE BURGH or BURGH parish 1538 Norfolk 6-3/4 miles ne
Beccles pop 316 archd Norfolk dioc Norwich
WHEATENHURST or WHITMINSTER parish 1538 Gloucs 7 miles nw
Stroud pop 473 archd and dioc Gloucester
WHEATFIELD parish 1721 co Oxford 2-1/4 miles s Tetsworth pop

105 archd and dioc Oxford

WHEATHAMSTEAD parish 1690 Herts 4-1/4 miles sw Welwyn pop
1,666 archd Huntingdon dioc Lincoln Indep

WHEATHILL parish 1573 Shrops 9-1/2 miles ne Ludlow pop 123
archd Salop dioc Hereford

WHEATHILL parish 1777 Somerset 4 miles sw Castle Cary pop 56
archd Wells dioc Bath and Wells

WHEATLEY township parish Chipping Lancs

WHEATLEY chapelry parish Cuddesden co Oxford pop 976

WHEATLEY township parish Doncaster W R York

WHEATLEY CARR township parish Whalley Lancs pop 58

WHEATLEY, NORTH parish 1649 Notts 5-1/4 miles ne East Retford
pop 435 archd Nottingham dioc York Wesl Meth

WHEATLEY, SOUTH parish 1546 Notts 5-1/2 miles ne East Retford
pop 35 pec Chapter of Collegiate Church of Southwell

WHEATON ASTON chapelry parish Lapley Staffs

WHEDDICAR township parish St Bees Cumberland pop 55

WHEELOCK township parish Sandbach Ches pop 440 Wesl Meth

WHEELTON township parish Leyland Lancs pop 1,519

WHELDRAKE parish 1603 E R York 7-1/2 miles se York pop 619
archd Cleveland dioc York Wesl Meth, Meth New Connection

WHELPINGTON, KIRK parish 1679 Northumberland comp townships
Great Bavington, Capheaton, Catcherside, Coldwell, Crogdean,
Fawns, Little Harle, West Harle, Kirk Whelpington, West Whelp-
ington pop 789 archd Northumberland dioc Durham

WHELPINGTON, WEST township parish Kirk Whelpington Northumberland pop 72

WHENBY parish 1556 N R York 9-1/4 miles e Easingwould pop 115
archd Cleveland dioc York

WHEPSTEAD parish 1540 Suffolk 4-1/4 miles sw Bury St Edmunds
pop 618 archd Sudbury dioc Norwich

WHERSTEAD parish 1590 Suffolk 2-3/4 miles sw Ipswich pop 233
archd Suffolk dioc Norwich

WHERWELL parish 1634 Hamps 3-3/4 miles se Andover pop 686
archd and dioc Winchester

WHESSOE chapelry parish Haughton le Skerne co Durham pop 123

WHESTON hamlet parish Tideswell Derbys pop 47

WHETMORE chapelry parish Burford Shrops

WHETSTONE hamlet parish Tideswell Derbys pop 75

WHETSTONE parish 1560 Leics 5-1/4 miles sw Leicester pop 903
archd Leicester dioc Lincoln

WHETSTONE hamlet parish East Barnet Middlesex

WHICHAM parish 1569 Cumberland 10 miles se Ravenglass pop 285
archd Richmond dioc Chester

WHICHFORD parish 1540 Warws 6 miles se Shipston upon Stour pop
638 archd and dioc Worcester

WHICKHAM parish 1576 co Durham comp townships Fellside, Lowside, Swalwell, Whickham pop 3,848 archd and dioc Durham

WHIDHILL township parish St Sampson Wilts

WHILE parish (incl with Puddlestone) Herefs 5-1/2 miles ne Leominster pop 268 archd and dioc Hereford

WHILLYMOOR township parish Arlecdon Cumberland

WHILTON parish 1570 co Northampton 5 miles ne Daventry pop 397 archd Northampton dioc Peterborough

WHIMPLE parish 1653 Devon 4-1/2 miles nw Ottery St Mary pop 739 archd and dioc Exeter

WHINBERGH parish 1703 Norfolk 3-1/2 miles se East Dereham pop 219 archd Norfolk dioc Norwich

WHINFELL township parish Brigham Cumberland pop 122

WHINFELL township parish Kendal Westm pop 214

WHIPPINGHAM parish 1727 Hamps 3-1/2 miles ne Newport pop 2,229 archd and dioc Winchester

WHIPSNADE parish 1682 Beds 3 miles sw Dunstable pop 204 archd Bedford dioc Lincoln

WHISBY chapelry parish Doddington Lincs pop 58

WHISSENDINE parish 1637 co Rutland 4-1/2 miles nw Oakham pop 800 archd Northampton dioc Peterborough

WHISSONSETT parish 1700 Norfolk 4-3/4 miles s Fakenham pop 628 archd and dioc Norwich

WHISTLEY HURST liberty parish Hurst Berks pop 867

WHISTON township parish Prescot Lancs pop 1,468

WHISTON parish 1700 co Northampton 6-3/4 miles se Northampton pop 64 archd Northampton dioc Peterborough

WHISTON township parish Penkridge Staffs

WHISTON township parish Kingsley Staffs pop 549

WHISTON parish 1592 W R York 2-1/2 miles se Rotherham pop 927 archd and dioc York Wesl Meth

WHISTONS tything parish Claines Worcs pop 2,518

WHITACRE, NETHER parish 1539 Warws 3-1/4 miles ne Coleshill pop 413 archd Coventry dioc Lichfield Wesl Meth

WHITACRE, OVER parish 1653 Warws 3-1/2 miles ne Coleshill pop 288 archd Coventry dioc Lichfield

WHITBECK parish 1597 Cumberland 8-3/4 miles se Ravenglass pop 234 archd Richmond dioc Chester

WHITBOURNE parish 1588 Herefs 6 miles ne Bromyard pop 899 archd and dioc Hereford

WHITBURN parish 1579 co Durham 3-1/2 miles n Sunderland pop 1,001 archd and dioc Durham Wesl Meth

WHITBY township parish Eastham Ches pop 234

WHITBY parish 1608 N R York comp borough Whitby, townships Aislaby, Eskdale Side, Hawsker cum Stainsacre, Newhelm cum Dunsley, Ruswarp, Uggesbarnby pop 11,725 archd Cleveland dioc York Wesl Meth, Soc of Friends, Indep, Presb, Prim Meth, Unit, Roman Cath

WHITCHBURY or WHITSBURY parish 1714 Wilts 3-1/2 miles ne Fordingbridge pop 183 archd and dioc Winchester

WHITCHESTER township parish Heddon on the Wall Northumberland pop 57

WHITCHURCH parish 1653 Bucks 4-3/4 miles nw Aylesbury pop 928 archd Buckingham dioc Lincoln Wesl Meth

WHITCHURCH parish 1559 Devon 1-1/2 miles se Tavistock pop 791 archd Totnes dioc Exeter

WHITCHURCH parish 1675 Herefs 6-1/2 miles sw Ross pop 885 archd and dioc Hereford Wesl Meth

WHITCHURCH parish 1597 co Oxford 6-1/2 miles nw Reading pop 745 archd and dioc Oxford

WHITCHURCH parish 1633 Ches comp market town Whitchurch, townships Alkington, Great Ash, Little Ash, Black Park, Broughall, Chimnell, Dodington, Edgeby, Hinton, Hollyhurst, chapelry Tilstock, Shrops, township Wirsmall 20 miles ne Shrewsbury pop 5,819 archd Salop dioc Lichfield Bapt, Indep, Wesl Meth, Unit

WHITCHURCH or FELTON parish 1565 Somerset 3 miles n Pensford pop 423 archd and dioc Bath and Wells

WHITCHURCH parish 1605 borough Hamps 12 miles ne Winchester pop 1,673 archd and dioc Winchester Bapt, Indep, Wesl Meth

WHITCHURCH parish 1561 Warws 3-1/2 miles se Stratford upon Avon pop 261 archd and dioc Worcester

WHITCHURCH CANONICORUM parish 1558 comp chapelries Marswood, Stanton St Gabriel Dorset 5 miles nw Bridport pop 1,399 archd Dorset dioc Bristol

WHITCLIFF township parish Ripon W R York pop 198

WHITCOMBE parish 1696 Dorset 2-1/4 miles se Dorchester pop 64 archd Dorset dioc Bristol

WHITCOMBE MAGNA parish 1749 Gloucs 3-1/2 miles ne Painswick pop 174 archd and dioc Gloucester

WHITECHAPEL chapelry (incl in regs of Kirkham) Lancs 5-1/2 miles se Garstang archd Richmond dioc Chester

WHITECHAPEL parish Middlesex pop 30,733 adj London pec Commissary of London, Consistorial Court of the Bishop Bapt, Indep, Wesl Meth, other dissenters

WHITEFIELD hamlet parish Deerhurst Gloucs

WHITEGATE or NEWCHURCH parish 1565 Ches 3-1/2 miles sw Northwich comp townships Darnall Marton pop 909 archd and dioc Chester

WHITEHAVEN market town parish St Bees Cumberland 40 miles sw Carlisle pop 11,393 archd Richmond dioc Chester comp St James 1753, St Nicholas 1694, Holy Trinity 1715 Presb, Part Bapt, Soc of Friends, Indep, Prim and Wesl Meth, Roman Cath

WHITEPARISH parish 1559 Wilts 8 miles se Salisbury pop 1,254 archd and dioc Salisbury

WHITE ROOTHING Essex See ROOTHING, WHITE

WHITESIDELAW township parish Chollerton Northumberland

WHITEWELL chapelry 1713 parish Whalley W R York archd and dioc Chester

WHITFIELD township parish Glossop Derbys pop 1734 Wesl Meth
WHITFIELD parish 1585 Kent 3-1/4 miles nw Dovor pop 199 pec of
    Archbishop of Canterbury
WHITFIELD parish 1678 co Northampton 2 miles ne Brackley pop 328
    archd Northampton dioc Peterborough
WHITFIELD parish 1612 Northumberland 11-1/2 miles sw Hexham
    pop 388 archd Northumberland dioc Durham
WHITGIFT parish 1562 W R York comp chapelry Swinefleet, townships
    Ousefleet, Reedness, Whitgift pop 2,252 archd and dioc York
WHITGREAVE township parish St Mary, Lichfield Staffs pop 195
WHITKIRK parish 1603 W R York 4 miles e Leeds comp townships
    Austhorpe, Seacroft, Temple Newsom, Thorp Stapleton pop 2,564
    archd and dioc York
WHITLEY tything parish Cumner Berks pop 38
WHITLEY hamlet parish St Giles Reading Berks pop 363
WHITLEY chapelry 1764 parish Tynemouth Northumberland 2-1/2
    miles ne North Shields pop 632
WHITLEY township parish Kellington W R York pop 310
WHITLEY BOOTHS township parish Whalley Lancs pop 707
WHITLEY, LOWER chapelry 1777 parish Great Budworth Ches 4-3/4
    miles nw Northwich pop 237 archd and dioc Chester Wesl Meth
WHITLEY, LOWER township parish Thornhill W R York pop 1,012
WHITLEY, OVER township parish Great Budworth Ches pop 283
WHITLEY, UPPER township parish Kirk Heaton W R York pop 885
WHITLINGHAM parish (incl in regs of Towse Newton) Norfolk 2-1/2
    miles se Norwich pop 45 archd Norfolk dioc Norwich
WHITMORE parish 1558 Staffs 4 miles sw Newcastle under Lyne pop
    281 archd Stafford dioc Lichfield
WHITNASH parish 1679 Warws 3 miles se Warwick pop 260 archd
    Coventry dioc Lichfield
WHITNEY parish 1616 Herefs 5 miles ne Hay pop 254 archd and dioc
    Hereford
WHITREY tything parish Willand Devon pop 122
WHITRIDGE township parish Hartburn Northumberland pop 11
WHITRIGG township parish Torpenhow Cumberland
WHITSTABLE parish 1556 Kent 5-3/4 miles nw Canterbury pop 1,926
    archd and dioc Canterbury Indep, Wesl Meth
WHIT STAUNTON parish 1606 Somerset 3-1/2 miles se Chard pop
    318 archd Taunton dioc Bath and Wells
WHITSTONE parish 1663 Cornwall 7 miles se Stratton pop 481 archd
    Cornwall dioc Exeter
WHITSTONE parish 1594 Devon 3-3/4 miles nw Exeter pop 643 archd
    and dioc Exeter
WHITTERING parish 1548 co Northampton 2-1/2 miles nw Wansford
    pop 216 archd Northampton dioc Peterborough
WHITTINGHAM township parish Kirkham Lancs pop 710
WHITTINGHAM parish 1658 Northumberland comp townships Calaley
    with Yetlington, Glanton, Lorbottle, Great Ryle, Little Ryle, Shaw-

don, Whittingham pop 1,790 8-1/2 miles sw Alnwick archd Northumberland dioc Durham

WHITTINGTON parish 1644 Derbys 2-1/4 miles n Chesterfield pop 740 archd Derby dioc Lichfield

WHITTINGTON parish 1539 Gloucs 4-1/2 miles se Cheltenham pop 247 archd and dioc Gloucester

WHITTINGTON parish 1538 Lancs pop 542 2 miles sw Kirkby Lonsdale archd Richmond dioc Chester

WHITTINGTON parish 1591 Shrops 3 miles ne Oswestry pop 1,788 archd and dioc St Asaph

WHITTINGTON parish 1538 Staffs 2-1/2 miles se Lichfield pop 773 pec Prebendal Court of Whittington and Baswick

WHITTINGTON hamlet parish Grendon Warws

WHITTINGTON chapelry 1653 parish St Peter Worcs 2-1/2 miles se Worcester pop 279

WHITTINGTON, GREAT township parish Corbridge Northumberland pop 209

WHITTINGTON, LITTLE township parish Corbridge Northumberland pop 11

WHITTLE hamlet parish Glossop Derbys pop 2,266

WHITTLE township parish Shilbottle Northumberland pop 53

WHITTLE township parish Ovingham Northumberland pop 29

WHITTLE LE WOODS township parish Leyland Lancs pop 2,016

WHITTLE, WELSH township parish Standish Lancs pop 147

WHITTLEBURY parish 1653 co Northampton 3-3/4 miles sw Towcester pop 670 archd Northampton dioc Peterborough Wesl Meth

WHITTLESEY parish St Andrew 1653, St Mary 1559 Cambs 6 miles se Peterborough pop 6,019 pec Bishop of Ely Bapt, Indep, Calv and Wesl Meth

WHITTLESFORD parish 1559 Cambs 6-1/4 miles nw Linton pop 523 archd and dioc Ely

WHITTON township parish Grindon co Durham pop 75

WHITTON township parish Leintwardine Herefs pop 63

WHITTON parish 1546 Lincs 11 miles nw Barton upon Humber pop 245 archd Stow dioc Lincoln

WHITTON township parish Rothbury Northumberland pop 104

WHITTON township parish Burford Shrops pop 76

WHITTON parish 1599 Suffolk 2-1/2 miles nw Ipswich pop 343 archd Suffolk dioc Norwich

WHITTONSTALL chapelry 1754 parish Bywell St Peter Northumberland 10 miles se Hexham pop 175 archd Northumberland dioc Durham

WHITWELL parish 1672 Derbys 10-3/4 miles ne Chesterfield pop 1,007 archd Derby dioc Lichfield

WHITWELL parish 1559 Norfolk 1-1/4 miles sw Reepham pop 483 archd Norfolk dioc Norwich

WHITWELL parish 1716 co Rutland 7 miles nw Stamford pop 124 archd Northampton dioc Peterborough

WHITWELL parish 1559 Hamps 8 miles se Newport pop 556 archd
and dioc Winchester

WHITWELL township parish Kendal Westm

WHITWELL chapelry parish Catterick W R York 3 miles e Catterick
pop 86

WHITWELL HOUSE extra parochial liberty co Durham 2-3/4 miles
se Durham pop 32

WHITWELL ON THE HILL township parish Crambe N R York pop
227

WHITWICK parish 1601 Leics 5-1/2 miles se Ashby de la Zouch pop
3,368 archd Leicester dioc Lincoln Wesl Meth

WHITWOOD township parish Featherstone W R York pop 306

WHITWORTH parochial chapelry 1569 co Durham comp townships
Tudhoe, Whitworth pop 337 pec Dean and Chapter of Durham

WHITWORTH chapelry 1763 parish Rochdale Lancs 2-3/4 miles nw
Rochdale archd and dioc Chester

WHIXHALL chapelry 1758 parish Prees Shrops 3-3/4 miles ne Wem
pop 957 pec Prebendary of Prees in Cathedral Church of Lichfield

WHIXLEY parish 1568 W R York comp township Thornville, Green
Hammerton, Whixley pop 968 6-1/2 miles se Aldborough archd
Richmond dioc Chester Wesl Meth

WHIXOE parish 1674 Suffolk 4 miles sw Clare pop 146 archd Sudbury
dioc Norwich

WHORLTON chapelry 1626 parish Gainford co Durham 4 miles se
Barnard Castle pop 311 archd and dioc Durham

WHORLTON township Northumberland comp East and West Whorlton
parish Newbury pop 59

WHORLTON parish 1689 N R York comp townships Faceby, Potto,
Whorlton archd Cleveland dioc York pop 915

WIBSEY chapelry 1640 parish Bradford W R York 2-1/4 miles sw
Bradford archd and dioc York

WIBTOFT chapelry parish Claybrooke Warws pop 104

WICHAUGH township parish Malpas Ches pop 35

WICHENFORD parish 1690 Worcs 6-1/4 miles nw Worcester pop 355
archd and dioc Worcester

WICHNOR chapelry 1735 parish Tatenhill Staffs 6-1/2 miles ne Lichfield pop 157

WICK Gloucester See ABSON

WICK parish 1615 Somerset 8-1/2 miles nw Axbridge pop 281 archd
Wells dioc Bath and Wells

WICK tything parish Kemble Wilts

WICK EPISCOPI township parish St John Bedwardine Worcs

WICK NEAR PERSHORE chapelry 1695 parish St Andrew, Pershore
Worcs 1-1/2 miles se Pershore pop 280

WICKEN parish 1565 Cambs 7 miles se Ely pop 892 archd Sudbury
dioc Norwich

WICKEN parish 1559 co Northampton 3-1/2 miles sw Stony Stratford

pop 536 archd Northampton dioc Peterborough

WICKEN BONANT parish 1588 Essex 4-3/4 miles se Saffron Walden pop 134 pec Commissary of Essex and Herts, Consistorial Court of Bishop of London

WICKENBY parish 1558 Lincs 5-1/2 miles nw Wragby pop 137 archd and dioc Lincoln

WICKERSLEY parish 1567 W R York 3-1/2 miles se Rotherham pop 527 archd and dioc York

WICKFORD parish 1538 Essex 6 miles se Billericay pop 402 archd Essex dioc London Indep

WICKHAM chapelry 1559 parish Welford Berks 5-1/2 miles w Speenhamland

WICKHAM chapelry parish Spalding Lincs

WICKHAM parish 1556 Hamps 4 miles se Bishop's Waltham pop 1,106 archd and dioc Winchester

WICKHAM, BISHOP'S parish 1662 Essex 2-1/2 miles se Witham pop 549 pec Commissary of Essex and Herts, Consistorial Court of the Bishop of London

WICKHAM, CHILDS parish 1560 Gloucs 5-1/4 miles sw Chipping Campden pop 415 archd and dioc Gloucester

WICKHAM, EAST parish 1715 Kent 3-1/2 miles nw Crayford archd and dioc Rochester

WICKHAM MARKET parish 1557 Suffolk 12-1/2 miles ne Ipswich pop 1,202 archd Suffolk dioc Norwich Indep

WICKHAM, St Paul parish 1609 Essex 3-1/4 miles ne Castle Hedingham pop 388 pec Dean and Chapter of St Paul's London

WICKHAM SKEITH parish 1557 Suffolk 2-3/4 miles n Mendlesham pop 556 archd Sudbury dioc Norwich

WICKHAM, WEST parish 1682 Cambs 4-3/4 miles ne Linton pop 529 archd and dioc Ely

WICKHAM, WEST parish 1558 Kent 2-3/4 miles sw Bromley pop 614 archd and dioc Rochester Wesl Meth

WICKHAMBREUX parish 1623 Kent 5 miles ne Canterbury pop 486 archd and dioc Canterbury

WICKHAMBROOK parish 1559 Suffolk 6-1/4 miles nw Clare pop 1,400 archd Sudbury dioc Norwich Indep

WICKHAMFORD parish 1538 Worcs 2-1/4 miles se Evesham pop 136 pec Chancellor of Cathedral Church of Worcester

WICKHAMPTON parish 1561 Norfolk 4-1/2 miles se Acle pop 122 archd and dioc Norwich Wesl Meth

WICKLEWOOD parish 1561 Norfolk 3 miles nw Wymondham pop 787 archd Norfolk dioc Norwich

WICKMERE parish 1559 Norfolk 5 miles nw Aylsham pop 319 archd and dioc Norwich

WICKTON township parish Stoke Prior Herefs pop 143

WICKWAR parish 1689 Gloucs 24 miles sw Gloucester pop 1,000 archd and dioc Gloucester Indep, Wesl Meth

WIDCOMB parish (incl regs Lyncomb) Somerset 1-1/2 miles se Bath pop 8,704 archd Bath dioc Bath and Wells

WIDCOMBE tything parish Chewton Mendip Somerset pop 160

WIDDINGTON parish 1666 Essex 5 miles nw Thaxted pop 386 Commissary of Essex and Herts, Consistorial Court of the Bishop of London

WIDDINGTON township parish Little Ouseburn W R York pop 30

WIDDRINGTON parochial chapelry 1698 Northumberland 8 miles ne Morpeth pop 395 archd Northumberland dioc Durham

WIDECOMBE IN THE MOOR parish 1560 Devon 5-3/4 miles nw Ashburton pop 959 archd Totnes dioc Exeter

WIDFORD parish 1601 Essex 1-1/2 miles sw Chelmsford pop 157 archd Essex dioc London

WIDFORD parish 1751 Gloucs 1-1/2 miles se Burford pop 51 archd and dioc Gloucester

WIDFORD parish 1558 Herts 3-3/4 miles ne Ware pop 506 archd Middlesex dioc London

WIDLEY parish 1611 Hamps 5-1/2 miles ne Fareham pop 512 archd and dioc Winchester

WIDMERPOOL parish 1539 Notts 9 miles se Nottingham pop 180 archd Nottingham dioc York

WIDNESS township parish Prescot Lancs pop 1,986

WIDWORTHY parish 1540 Devon 3-1/2 miles se Honiton pop 278 archd and dioc Exeter

WIELD parish 1538 Hamps 6 miles w Alton pop 248 archd and dioc Winchester

WIGAN parish 1580 Lancs comp borough Wigan sep juris chapelries Billinge, Hindley, Uplolland, townships Abram Billings, Dalton, Haigh, Ince, Orrell, Pemberton, Winstanley Derbys, township Aspull Lancs pop 44,486 archd and dioc Chester All Saints, St George Bapt, Indep, Roman Cath, Presb, Wesl Meth

WIGBOROUGH, GREAT parish 1560 Essex 6-1/2 miles sw Colchester pop 434 archd Colchester dioc London

WIGBOROUGH, LITTLE parish 1586 Essex 7-1/4 miles sw Colchester pop 123 archd Colchester dioc Exeter

WIGGENHALL parish 1653 Norfolk 4-1/4 miles sw Lynn Regis pop 552 archd and dioc Norwich

WIGGENHALL parish 1558 Norfolk 5-3/4 miles sw Lynn Regis pop 206 archd and dioc Norwich

WIGGENHALL parish 1562 Norfolk 6 miles sw Lynn Regis pop 576 archd and dioc Norwich

WIGGENHALL parish 1695 Norfolk 5 miles sw Lynn Regis pop 114 archd and dioc Norwich

WIGGESLEY hamlet parish Thorney Notts pop 86

WIGGINTHORPE township parish Terrington N R York

WIGGINTON parish Herts 1-1/4 miles se Tring pop 536 archd Huntington dioc Lincoln

WIGGINTON parish 1558 co Oxford 5-1/4 miles nw Deddington pop 327 archd and dioc Oxford

WIGGINTON chapelry parish Tamworth Staffs pop 737 archd Stafford dioc Lichfield

WIGGINTON parish 1691 N R York 5 miles n York pop 359 pec of Alne and Tollerton

WIGGLESWORTH township parish Long Preston W R York pop 443

WIGGONBY township parish Aikton Cumberland pop 175

WIGGONHOLT parish 1597 Sussex 7-1/4 miles ne Arundel pop 37 archd and dioc Chichester

WIGHILL parish 1717 E R York 2-1/2 miles nw Tadcaster pop 276 archd and dioc York

WIGHT, ISLE OF Hamps all places on island appear in their alphabetical sequence with the rest of England

WIGHTON parish 1660 Norfolk 2-1/4 miles ne Little Walsingham pop 542 archd and dioc Norwich

WIGLAND township parish Malpas Ches pop 265

WIGMORE parish 1572 Herefs 10 miles nw Leominster pop 429 archd and dioc Hereford

WIGSTHORPE hamlet parish Lilford co Northampton

WIGSTON, MAGNA parish 1572 Leics 3-1/2 miles se Leicester pop 2,174 archd Leicester dioc Lincoln Indep

WIGSTON, PARVA chapelry parish Claybrooke Leics pop 69

WIGTOFT parish 1638 Lincs 3 miles se Swineshead pop 697 archd and dioc Lincoln

WIGTON parish 1613 Cumberland comp market town Wigton, townships Oulton, High and Low Waverton, Woodside Quarter archd and dioc Carlisle Soc of Friends, Indep, Wesl Meth, Roman Cath

WIGTON township parish Harewood W R York pop 168

WIKE township parish Birstall W R York pop 1,916 Indep

WIKE township parish Harewood W R York pop 142

WILBARSTON parish 1746 co Northampton 4-1/2 miles sw Rockingham pop 681 archd Northampton dioc Peterborough Indep

WILBERFOSS parish 1618 E R York comp townships Newton upon Derwent, Wilberfoss pop 580 5-1/2 miles nw Pocklington archd East Riding dioc York

WILBRAHAM, GREAT parish 1561 Cambs 7-1/4 miles se Cambridge pop 510 archd and dioc Ely

WILBRAHAM, LITTLE parish 1538 Cambs 7-1/4 miles e Cambridge pop 315 archd and dioc Ely

WILBURTON parish 1739 Cambs 6-1/2 miles sw Ely pop 471 archd and dioc Ely Bapt

WILBY parish 1541 Norfolk 3-1/2 miles ne East Harling pop 123 archd Norfolk dioc Norwich

WILBY parish 1562 co Northampton 2-1/4 miles sw Wellingborough pop 386 archd Northampton dioc Peterborough

WILBY parish 1538 Suffolk 6 miles se Eye pop 649 archd Suffolk dioc Norwich

WILCOT parish 1564 Wilts 1-3/4 miles nw Pewsey pop 677 archd Wilts dioc Salisbury

WILCOTE parish 1755 co Oxford 4 miles nw Witney pop 10 archd and dioc Oxford

WILDBOAR CLOUGH township parish Prestbury Ches pop 476

WILDEN parish 1545 Beds 5-1/4 miles ne Bedford pop 411 archd Bedford dioc Lincoln

WILDON GRANGE township parish Coxwold N R York pop 27

WILDSWORTH hamlet parish Laughton Lincs pop 132

WILERICK or WILLCRICK parish 1755 co Monmouth 4-1/2 miles se Caerleon pop 33 archd and dioc Llandaff

WILFORD parish 1621 Notts 1-3/4 miles sw Nottingham pop 602 archd Nottingham dioc York

WILKESLEY township parish Audlem Ches

WILKSBY parish 1562 Lincs 5-3/4 miles se Horncastle pop 67 archd and dioc Lincoln

WILLAND parish 1717 Devon 2-1/4 miles ne Cullompton pop 321 archd and dioc Exeter Wesl Meth

WILLASTON township parish Nantwich Ches pop 99

WILLASTON township parish Wybunbury Ches pop 122

WILLASTON township parish Neston Ches pop 276

WILLEN parish 1666 Bucks 1-1/2 miles s Newport Pagnell pop 83 archd Buckingham dioc Lincoln

WILLENHALL chapelry 1642 parish Wolverhampton Staffs 3-1/4 miles e Wolverhampton pop 5,834 Wesl Meth

WILLENHALL hamlet parish Holy Trinity Warws pop 120

WILLERBY parish 1658 E R York comp townships Binnington, Staxton, Willerby pop 356 archd East Riding dioc York

WILLERBY township parish Cottingham and Kirk Ella E R York pop 189

WILLERSEY parish 1721 Gloucs 3 miles w Chipping Campden pop 327 archd and dioc Gloucester

WILLERSLEY parish 1764 Herefs 7-1/2 miles ne Hay pop 13 archd and dioc Hereford

WILLESBOROUGH parish 1538 Kent 2 miles se Ashford pop 472 archd and dioc Canterbury

WILLESDEN or WILSDON parish 1560 Middlesex 5 miles nw London pop 1,876 pec Dean and Chapter of St Paul's London

WILLESLEY parish 1677 Derbys and Leics 2-1/2 miles sw Ashby de la Zouch archd Derby dioc Lichfield

WILLEY township parish Presteign Herefs pop 147

WILLEY parish 1644 Shrops 4-3/4 miles nw Bridgenorth pop 155 archd Salop dioc Hereford

WILLEY parish 1660 Warws 3-1/2 miles w Lutterworth pop 96 archd Coventry dioc Lichfield

WILLIAMSCOTT or WILLSCOT hamlet parish Cropredy co Oxford

WILLIAN parish 1557 Herts 2-3/4 miles ne Hitchin pop 313 archd Huntingdon dioc Lincoln

WILLINGALE DOE parish 1570 Essex 4-1/2 miles ne Chipping Ongar pop 466 pec Commissary of Essex and Herts, Consistorial Court of Bishop of London

WILLINGALE SPAIN parish 1576 Essex 4-1/4 miles ne Chipping Ongar pop 239 archd Middlesex dioc London

WILLINGDON parish 1560 Sussex 2-1/4 miles nw East Bourne pop 603 archd Lewes dioc Chichester

WILLINGHAM parish 1559 Cambs 6-1/4 miles se St Ives pop 1,403 pec Bishop of Ely Bapt

WILLINGHAM chapelry parish Carlton Cambs

WILLINGHAM parish 1562 Lincs 6 miles se Gainsborough pop 392 archd and dioc Lincoln Wesl Meth

WILLINGHAM parish (incl in regs North Cove) Suffolk 4 miles s Beccles pop 158 archd Suffolk dioc Norwich

WILLINGHAM, CHERRY parish 1662 Lincs 4 miles ne Lincoln pop 103 archd Stow dioc Lincoln

WILLINGHAM, NORTH parish 1658 Lincs 4 miles se Market Rasen pop 223 archd and dioc Lincoln

WILLINGHAM, SOUTH parish 1711 Lincs 5-1/4 miles ne Wragby pop 212 archd and dioc Lincoln

WILLINGTON parish 1676 Beds 4 miles e Bedford pop 332 archd Bedford dioc Lincoln

WILLINGTON township parish Whalley Ches pop 115

WILLINGTON parish 1679 Derbys 5 miles ne Burton upon Trent pop 402 archd Derby dioc Lichfield

WILLINGTON township parish Brancepeth co Durham pop 216 Wesl Meth

WILLINGTON township parish Wallsend Northumberland

WILLINGTON hamlet parish Barcheston Warws

WILLISHAM parish 1558 Suffolk 4 miles sw Needham Market pop 224 archd Suffolk dioc Norwich

WILLITOFT township parish Bubwith E R York

WILLITON chapelry 1792 parish St Decuman Somerset 6-1/4 miles se Dunster Bapt, Wesl Meth

WILLOUGHBY parish 1538 Lincs 3-1/2 miles se Alford pop 557 archd and dioc Lincoln Wesl Meth

WILLOUGHBY parish 1625 Warws 3 miles se Dunchurch pop 376 archd Coventry dioc Lichfield Prim Meth

WILLOUGHBY IN THE WOLDS parish 1680 Notts 7-1/2 miles ne Loughborough pop 465 archd Nottingham dioc York Wesl Meth

WILLOUGHBY, SCOTT parish no regs Lincs 4 miles nw Falkingham pop 24 archd and dioc Lincoln

WILLOUGHBY, SILK parish 1561 Lincs 2-1/4 miles sw Sleaford pop 193 archd and dioc Lincoln

WILLOUGHBY WATERLESS parish 1559 Leics 5-3/4 miles ne Lutterworth pop 327 archd Leicester dioc Lincoln

WILLOUGHTON parish 1599 Lincs 8-1/2 miles ne Gainsborough pop 477 archd Stow dioc Lincoln Wesl Meth

WILLSBOROUGH extra parochial liberty Leics 2-1/2 miles sw Market Bosworth

WILLS PASTURES extra parochial liberty Warws 3-1/2 miles s
Southam pop 7

WILLSWORTHY hamlet parish St Peter Tavy Devon

WILMINGTON parish 1683 Kent 1 mile s Dartford pop 724 archd and
dioc Rochester

WILMINGTON parish 1538 Sussex 4-1/2 miles sw Hailsham pop 328
archd Lewes dioc Chichester

WILMSLOW parish 1558 Ches 7 miles nw Macclesfield comp townships Bollen Fee, Chorley, Fulshaw, Pownal Fee pop 4,296 archd
and dioc Chester Indep, Wesl Meth

WILNE, GREAT parish 1540 Derbys 7-3/4 miles se Derby pop 1,091
pec of Prebendal Court of Sawley

WILNE, LITTLE chapelry parish Sawley Derbys

WILNECOTE chapelry parish Tamworth Warws pop 688

WILPSHIRE township parish Blackburn Lancs pop 337

WILSDEN township parish Bradford W R York pop 2,252 Indep, Wesl
Meth

WILSFORD parish 1668 Lincs 4-1/2 miles sw Sleaford pop 393 archd
and dioc Lincoln

WILSFORD parish 1618 Wilts 1-3/4 miles sw Amesbury pop 119 pec
Prebendary of Wilsford, Woodford Cathedral Church of Salisbury

WILSFORD DAUNTSEY parish 1558 Wilts 4-1/2 miles sw Pewsey
pop 512 archd and dioc Salisbury

WILSHAMPSTEAD parish 1594 Beds 4 miles se Bedford pop 753
archd Bedford dioc Lincoln Wesl Meth

WILSICK township parish Tickhill W R York

WILSTHORPE chapelry 1754 parish Greatford Lincs 5 miles nw Market Deeping pop 69

WILSTROP township parish Kirk Hammerton E R York pop 112

WILTON parish 1634 Norfolk 4-1/4 miles w Brandon Ferry archd
Norfolk dioc Norwich Wesl Meth

WILTON tything parish Midsummer Norton Somerset

WILTON parish 1558 Somerset pop 795 archd Taunton dioc Bath and
Wells

WILTON borough parish 1615 excl juris Wilts 3 miles nw Salisbury
pop 1,997 archd and dioc Salisbury Indep, Meth

WILTON chapelry 1719 parish Kirk Leatham N R York 3-1/2 miles
nw Guisborough pop 411

WILTON chapelry parish Ellerburn N R York pop 192

WILTON, BISHOP parish 1603 E R York comp townships Bishop
Wilton with Belthorpe, Bolton, Youlthorpe with Gowthorpe pop 831
pec Dean of York Wesl Meth

WILY parish 1581 Wilts 7 miles ne Hindon pop 476 archd and dioc
Salisbury

WIMBISH parish 1583 Essex 4-1/4 miles se Saffron Walden pop 921
archd Middlesex dioc London

WIMBLEDON parish 1538 Surrey 9 miles sw London pop 2,195 pec
Archbishop of Canterbury Indep, Wesl Meth

WIMBLINGTON hamlet parish Doddington Cambs pop 965 Wesl Meth

WIMBOLDSLEY township parish Middlewich Ches pop 102

WIMBORNE parish Dorset 1/2 mile n Wimborne St Giles archd Dorset dioc Bristol

WIMBORNE parish 1589 Dorset 2-1/2 miles sw Cranborne pop 384 archd Dorset dioc Bristol

WIMBORNE MINSTER parish 1635 Dorset 26 miles ne Dorchester comp market town Wimborne Minster, tythings Abbottstreet, Barnesley, Cowgrove, Leigh, Petersham, Stone, Thornhill, Wimborne Borough pop 4,009 Bapt, Indep, Wesl Meth

WIMBOTSHAM parish 1562 Norfolk 1-1/4 miles ne Downham Market pop 476 archd Norfolk dioc Norwich

WIMESWOULD parish 1560 Leics 5-1/4 miles ne Loughborough pop 1,276 archd Leicester dioc Lincoln Wesl Meth

WIMPOLE parish 1560 Cambs 6 miles se Caxton pop 583 archd and dioc Ely

WINCANTON parish 1636 Somerset 34 miles e Taunton pop 2,123 archd Wells dioc Bath and Wells Indep

WINCEBY parish 1579 Lincs 4 miles se Horncastle pop 65 archd and dioc Lincoln

WINCH, EAST parish 1678 Norfolk 5-1/2 miles se Lynn Regis pop 466 archd and dioc Norwich

WINCH, WEST parish 1559 Norfolk 3 miles se Lynn Regis pop 394 archd and dioc Norwich

WINCHAM township parish Great Budworth Ches pop 589

WINCHCOMB parish 1539 Gloucs 15-1/2 miles ne Gloucester comp chapelries Greet, Gretton, hamlets Coates, Cockbury, Corndean, Langley with Abbey Demesnes, Naunton with Frampton, Postlip, Sudeley Tenements pop 2,514 archd and dioc Gloucester Bapt, Wesl Meth

WINCHELSEA parish 1655 borough sep juris Sussex 74 miles ne Chichester pop 772 archd Lewes dioc Chichester Wesl Meth

WINCHENDON, NETHER parish 1563 Bucks 7 miles sw Aylesbury pop 294 archd Buckingham dioc Lincoln

WINCHENDON, UPPER parish 1672 Bucks 6 miles nw Aylesbury pop 223 archd Buckingham dioc Lincoln

WINCHESTER city sep juris Hamps pop 8,712 comp St Bartholomew 1563, Cathedral Church 1599, St Cross 1676, St John 1595, St Lawrence 1754, St Maurice 1595, St Michael 1632, St Peter 1595, St Swithin 1562, St Thomas 1678 archd and dioc Winchester Bapt, Indep, Wesl Meth, Roman Cath

WINCHFIELD parish 1659 Hamps 2-1/2 miles ne Odiham pop 277 archd and dioc Winchester

WINCHMORE HILL chapelry parish Edmonton Middlesex Soc of Friends, Indep, Wesl Meth

WINCLE chapelry parish Prestbury Ches 5-1/2 miles se Macclesfield pop 453 archd and dioc Chester

WINDER township parish Lamplugh Cumberland

WINDER, LOW township parish Barton Westm pop 19

WINDERMERE parish 1617 Westm 9 miles ne Kendal comp chapelry Troutbeck, townships Applethwaite, Undermilbeck pop 1,632 archd Richmond dioc Chester

WINDFORD parish 1655 Somerset 6-1/2 miles sw Bristol pop 865 archd Bath dioc Bath and Wells

WINDLE township parish Prescot Lancs pop 5,825

WINDLESHAM parish 1677 Surrey 1 mile ne Bagshot pop 1,912 archd Surrey dioc Winchester

WINDLESTON township parish St Andrew co Durham pop 201

WINDLEY township parish Duffield Derbys pop 204

WINDRIDGE ward parish St Stephen town of St Albans Herts

WINDRUSH parish 1586 Gloucs 5-1/4 miles e Northleach pop 291 archd and dioc Gloucester

WINDSOR, NEW parish 1559 borough sep juris Berks 20 miles ne Reading pop 5,650 archd Berks dioc Salisbury Indep, Wesl Meth

WINDSOR, OLD parish 1754 Berks 2 miles se New Windsor pop 1,453 archd Berks dioc Salisbury

WINESTEAD parish 1578 E R York 2 miles nw Patrington pop 145 archd East Riding dioc York

WINFARTHING parish 1614 Norfolk 4-1/4 miles nw Diss pop 703 archd Norfolk dioc Norwich

WINFIELD township parish Wrotham Kent

WINFORD EAGLE parish (incl in regs of Troller Fratrum) Dorset 8-1/2 miles nw Dorchester pop 134 archd Dorset dioc Bristol

WINFORTON parish 1690 Herefs 6 miles ne Hay pop 158 archd and dioc Hereford

WINFRITH NEWBURGH parish 1585 Dorset 9 miles sw Wareham pop 891 archd Dorset dioc Bristol

WING parish 1546 Bucks 3 miles sw Leighton Buzzard pop 1,152 archd Buckingham dioc Lincoln Wesl Meth

WING parish 1625 co Rutland 3 miles ne Uppingham pop 307 archd Northampton dioc Peterborough

WINGATE township parish Kelloe co Durham pop 115

WINGATES township parish Long Horsley Northumberland pop 163

WINGERWORTH parish 1539 Derbys 2-3/4 miles sw Chesterfield pop 471 archd Derby dioc Lichfield

WINGFIELD parish 1538 Suffolk 5-3/4 miles ne Eye pop 668 archd Suffolk dioc Norwich

WINGFIELD, NORTH parish 1567 Derbys 4-1/2 miles se Chesterfield comp townships Claylane, Stretton, Tupton, Woodthorpe pop 1,691 archd Derby dioc Lichfield Wesl Meth

WINGFIELD, SOUTH parish 1585 Derbys 2-1/4 miles w Alfreton pop 1,091 archd Derby dioc Lichfield Wesl Meth

WINGHAM parish 1568 Kent 34 miles e Maidstone pop 1,115 pec Archbishop of Canterbury Indep

WINGRAVE parish 1550 Bucks 5-1/2 miles ne Aylesbury pop 783 archd Buckingham dioc Lincoln Indep

WINKBOURN parish 1727 Notts 3 miles n Southwell pop 134 archd Nottingham dioc York

WINKFIELD parish 1577 Berks 5-1/2 miles sw New Windsor pop 2,009 archd Berks dioc Salisbury

WINKFIELD parish 1654 Wilts 2 miles sw Trowbridge pop 288 archd and dioc Salisbury

WINKLEY or WINKLEIGH parish 1569 Devon 6-1/2 miles sw Chulmleigh pop 1,596 archd Barnstaple dioc Exeter Wesl Meth

WINKSLEY chapelry parish Ripon W R York 4-3/4 miles w Ripon pop 259

WINKTON tything parish Christchurch Hamps

WINLATON parochial district co Durham 6-1/4 miles sw Gateshead pop 3,951 archd and dioc Durham Meth

WINMARLEIGH township parish Garstang Lancs pop 275

WINNALL parish 1680 Hamps 3/4 mile ne Winchester pop 115 pec of Rector

WINNERSH liberty parish Hurst Berks pop 531

WINNINGTON township parish Great Budworth Ches pop 256

WINNINGTON township parish Muckleston Staffs pop 249

WINNOW, ST parish 1622 Cornwall 2-1/2 miles se Lostwithiel pop 1,048 pec Dean and Chapter of Exeter

WINSCALES township parish Workington Cumberland pop 100

WINSCOMBE parish 1662 Somerset 2 miles nw Axbridge pop 1,526 archd Wells dioc Bath and Wells

WINSFORD parish 1660 Somerset 5 miles nw Dulverton pop 524 archd Taunton dioc Bath and Wells Wesl Meth

WINSHAM parish 1559 Somerset 4 miles se Chard pop 932 pec of Consistorial Court of Dean and Chapter of Wells

WINSHILL township parish Burton upon Trent Derbys pop 342

WINSKILL township parish Addingham Cumberland

WINSLADE parish 1723 Hamps 3 miles se Basingstoke pop 134 archd and dioc Winchester

WINSLEY hamlet parish Darley Derbys pop 671

WINSLEY chapelry 1724 parish Great Bradford Wilts 1-1/2 miles w Bradford pop 2,847 Wesl Meth

WINSLEY chapelry parish Kirkby Malzeard W R York pop 943

WINSLOW parish 1560 Bucks 6-1/2 miles se Buckingham pop 1,290 archd St Albans dioc London Bapt, Indep, Wesl Meth

WINSLOW township parish Bromyard Herefs pop 450

WINSON chapelry parish Bibury Gloucs 5 miles sw Northleach pop 176

WINSTANLEY township parish Wigan Lancs pop 731

WINSTER chapelry 1632 parish Youlgrave Derbys 19 miles nw Derby pop 962 Prim and Wesl Meth

WINSTER chapelry 1720 parish Kendal Westm 7 miles w Kendal

WINSTON parish 1572 co Durham 6-1/2 miles e Barnard Castle pop 327 archd and dioc Durham

WINSTON parish 1558 Suffolk 1-1/4 miles se Debenham pop 398

archd Suffolk dioc Norwich

WINSTONE parish 1577 Gloucs 6-1/4 miles nw Cirencester archd and dioc Gloucester Bapt

WINTERBOURNE chapelry parish Chieveley Berks 3-1/2 miles nw Speenhamland pop 326

WINTERBOURNE parish 1653 Dorset 3 miles sw Dorchester pop 369 archd Dorset dioc Bristol

WINTERBOURNE parish 1600 Gloucs 6-1/2 miles ne Bristol pop 2,889 pec of Consistorial Court of Bishop of Bristol Wesl Meth

WINTERBOURNE ABBAS parish 1754 Dorset 4-3/4 miles w Dorchester pop 133 archd Dorset dioc Bristol

WINTERBOURNE BASSETT parish 1709 Wilts 7-3/4 miles nw Marlborough pop 288 archd and dioc Salisbury

WINTERBOURNE CAME parish 1756 Dorset 2-3/4 miles se Dorchester pop 80 archd Dorset dioc Bristol

WINTERBOURNE CLENSTONE parish 1684 Dorset 4-1/4 miles sw Blandford Forum pop 84 archd Dorset dioc Bristol

WINTERBOURNE DANTSEY parish 1560 Wilts 3-3/4 miles ne Salisbury pop 161 pec Prebendary Chute and Chisenbury

WINTERBOURNE, EARLS parish 1557 Wilts 3-1/2 miles ne Salisbury pop 243 pec of Prebendary Chute and Chisenbury Wesl Meth

WINTERBOURNE FARRINGDON or ST GERMAN'S extra parochial Dorset 2-1/2 miles s Dorchester

WINTERBOURNE HERRINGSTONE Dorset See HERRINGSTONE

WINTERBOURNE HOUGHTON parish 1558 Dorset 4-1/2 miles sw Blandford Forum pop 265 archd Dorset dioc Bristol

WINTERBOURNE KINGSTON parish 1588 Dorset 6-1/2 miles sw Blandford Forum pop 564 pec of Dean of Salisbury

WINTERBOURNE MONKTON parish 1756 Dorset 2 miles sw Dorchester pop 101 archd Dorset dioc Bristol

WINTERBOURNE MONKTON parish 1670 Wilts 7 miles ne Marlborough pop 263 archd and dioc Salisbury

WINTERBOURNE STEEPLETON parish 1558 Dorset 4 miles sw Dorchester pop 176 archd Dorset dioc Bristol

WINTERBOURNE STOKE parish 1726 Wilts 5 miles sw Amesbury pop 272 archd and dioc Salisbury

WINTERBOURNE STRICKLAND parish 1615 Dorset 3-3/4 miles sw Blandford Forum pop 401 archd Dorset dioc Bristol

WINTERBOURNE WHITCHURCH parish 1600 Dorset 5-1/2 miles sw Blandford Forum archd Dorset dioc Bristol

WINTERBOURNE ZELSTONE parish 1548 Dorset 6-1/4 miles se Blandford Forum pop 233 archd Dorset dioc Bristol

WINTERBURN township parish Gargrave W R York Indep

WINTERINGHAM parish 1562 Lincs 7-1/2 miles w Barton upon Humber pop 726 archd Stow dioc Lincoln Wesl Meth

WINTERSET township parish Wragby W R York pop 49

WINTERSLOW parish 1598 Wilts pop 749 archd and dioc Salisbury Wesl Meth

WINTERTON parish 1558 Lincs 8-1/4 miles sw Barton upon Humber pop 1,295 archd Stow dioc Lincoln Wesl Meth

WINTERTON parish 1717 Norfolk 5-1/4 miles nw Caistor pop 631 archd and dioc Norwich

WINTHORPE parish 1572 Lincs 11 miles ne Spilsby pop 244 archd and dioc Lincoln

WINTHORPE parish 1687 Notts 1-3/4 miles ne Newark archd Nottingham dioc York

WINTNEY, HARTLEY Hamps See HARTLEY WINTLEY

WINTON township parish Kirkby Stephen Westm pop 267

WINTON township parish Kirkby Sigston W R York pop 145

WINTRINGHAM parish 1690 E R York comp chapelry Knapton townships Linton, Newton, Wintringham pop 589 a donative

WINWICK parish 1538 Hunts and Northampton 6-1/4 miles se Oundle pop 326 archd Huntingdon dioc Lincoln

WINWICK parish 1563 Lancs comp borough Newton in Makerfield, chapelries Ashton in Makerfield, Lowton, Newchurch, townships Culcheth, Golborne, Haydock, Houghton with Middleton, Arbury, Kenyon, Southworth with Croft, Winwick pop 17,691 3 miles ne Warrington archd and dioc Chester Wesl Meth

WINWICK parish 1563 co Northampton 8-3/4 miles ne Daventry pop 159 archd Northampton dioc Peterborough

WIRKSWORTH parish 1608 Derbys comp market town Wirksworth, townships Cromford, Honton, Ible, hamlets Callow, Middleton, townships Alderwasley, Ashleyhay, Biggan, Iridgehay with Allton, hamlet Iron Brock Grange pop 7,754 13 miles nw Derby archd Derby dioc Lichfield Bapt, Indep, Wesl Meth

WIRSWALL township parish Whitchurch Ches pop 83

WISBECH parish 1557 Cambs 2 miles nw Wisbech St Peter pop 1,524 archd and dioc Ely

WISBECH parish 1558 Cambs 44 miles n Cambridge pop 7,253 archd and dioc Ely Bapt, Soc of Friends, Indep, Johnsonians, Wesl Meth, Presb, Unit

WISBOROUGH GREEN parish 1560 Sussex 6-1/4 miles ne Petworth pop 1,782 archd and dioc Ely Indep

WISETON or WYESTON township parish Clayworth Notts pop 118

WISHAW parish 1688 Warws 3-3/4 miles se Sutton Coldfield pop 216 archd Coventry dioc Lichfield

WISHFORD, GREAT parish 1559 Wilts 2-1/2 miles nw Wilton pop 361 archd and dioc Salisbury

WISHFORD, LITTLE tything parish South Newton Wilts

WISLEY parish 1666 Surrey 2-1/2 miles ne Ripley pop 155 archd Surrey dioc Winchester

WISPINGTON parish 1662 Lincs 4-1/4 miles nw Horncastle pop 91 archd and dioc Lincoln

WISSETT parish 1559 Suffolk 2 miles nw Halesworth pop 419 archd Suffolk dioc Norwich

WISTANSTOW parish 1687 Shrops 9-3/4 miles nw Ludlow pop 989

archd Salop dioc Hereford

WISTASTON parish 1572 Ches 2-1/2 miles ne Nantwich pop 350 archd and dioc Chester

WISTESTON chapelry parish Marden Herefs 7 miles ne Hereford

WISTON or WISSINGTON parish 1538 Suffolk 1-1/2 miles sw Nayland pop 249 archd Sudbury dioc Norwich

WISTON parish 1638 Sussex 1-1/2 miles nw Steyning pop 296 archd and dioc Chichester

WISTOW parish 1629 Hunts 3-3/4 miles sw Ramsey pop 404 archd Huntingdon dioc Lincoln

WISTOW parish 1586 Leics 7-1/4 miles se Leicester pop 298 archd Leicester dioc Lincoln

WISTOW parish 1590 W R York 3 miles nw Selby pop 665 pec Prebendary of Wistow in Cathedral Church of York

WISWELL township parish Whalley Lancs pop 724

WITCHAM parish 1633 Cambs 5-1/2 miles w Ely pop 519 archd and dioc Ely Wesl Meth

WITCHAMPTON parish 1656 Dorset 4-1/2 miles nw Wimborne Minster pop 481 archd Dorset dioc Bristol Wesl Meth

WITCHFORD parish 1725 Cambs 3 miles sw Ely pop 461 pec Bishop of Ely

WITCHINGHAM, GREAT parish 1539 Norfolk 2 miles s Reepham pop 582 archd and dioc Norwich

WITCHINGHAM, LITTLE parish 1565 Norfolk 2-1/4 miles se Reepham pop 62 archd and dioc Norwich

WITCHLING parish 1717 Kent 2-1/2 miles ne Lenham pop 128 archd and dioc Canterbury

WITHAM parish 1669 Essex 8 miles ne Chelmsford pop 2,735 archd Colchester dioc London Soc of Friends, Indep, Roman Cath

WITHAM FRIARY parish 1684 Somerset 5-1/2 miles sw Frome pop 574 archd Wells dioc Bath and Wells

WITHAM, NORTH parish 1592 Lincs 1-1/2 miles sw Colsterworth pop 273 archd and dioc Lincoln

WITHAM ON THE HILL parish 1670 Lincs 4-1/4 miles sw Bourne pop 530 archd and dioc Lincoln Wesl Meth

WITHAM, SOUTH parish 1686 Lincs 3-1/4 miles sw Colsterworth pop 410 archd and dioc Lincoln

WITHCALL parish 1576 Lincs 3-3/4 miles sw Louth pop 72 archd and dioc Lincoln

WITHCOTE parish 1679 Leics 9-1/2 miles se Melton Mowbray pop 32 archd Leicester dioc Lincoln

WITHERIDGE parish 1585 Devon 8-1/4 miles e Chulmleigh pop 1,263 archd Barnstaple dioc Exeter

WITHERLEY parish 1564 Leics 1-1/2 miles se Atherstone pop 492 archd Leicester dioc Lincoln

WITHERN parish 1558 Lincs 4-1/2 miles nw Alford pop 390 archd and dioc Lincoln Wesl Meth

WITHERNSEA chapelry parish Hollym E R York 19 miles se Kingston upon Hull pop 130

WITHERNWICK parish 1653 E R York 12 miles e Beverley pop 443 pec Prebendary of Holme Wesl Meth

WITHERSDALE parish 1653 Suffolk 33 miles se Harleston pop 194 archd Suffolk dioc Norwich

WITHERSFIELD parish 1558 Suffolk 2-1/4 miles nw Haverhill pop 545 archd Sudbury dioc Norwich

WITHERSLACK chapelry 1670 parish Beetham Westm 7-1/2 miles nw Milnthorpe pop 488 archd Richmond dioc Chester

WITHERSTONE parish Dorset 5 miles ne Bridport archd Dorset dioc Bristol

WITHIEL parish 1567 Cornwall 5 miles sw Bodmin pop 406 archd Cornwall dioc Exeter

WITHIELL FLOREY parish 1696 Somerset 5-3/4 miles ne Dulverton pop 89 archd Taunton dioc Bath and Wells

WITHINGTON parish 1609 Gloucs 6 miles w Northleach pop 743 pec of Incumbent

WITHINGTON parish 1573 Herefs 4-1/2 miles ne Hereford pop 723 Consistory Court of Dean of Hereford Bapt

WITHINGTON township parish Manchester Lancs pop 1,048

WITHINGTON parish 1591 Shrops 6-1/4 miles e Shrewsbury pop 193 archd Salop dioc Lichfield

WITHINGTON, LOWER township parish Prestbury Ches pop 584 Wesl Meth

WITHINGTON, OLD township parish Prestbury Ches pop 191

WITHNELL township parish Leyland Lancs pop 1,251

WITHYBROOK parish 1653 Warws 8 miles ne Coventry pop 318 archd Coventry dioc Lichfield

WITHYCOMBE parish 1669 Somerset 2-1/2 miles se Dunster pop 332 archd Taunton dioc Bath and Wells

WITHYCOMBE RAWLEIGH parish 1754 Devon pop 1,063 archd and dioc Exeter

WITHYHAM parish 1663 Sussex 7-1/2 miles se East Grimstead pop 1,610 archd Lewes dioc Chichester

WITHYPOOLE parish 1613 Somerset 7 miles nw Dulverton pop 212 archd Taunton dioc Bath and Wells

WITLEY parish 1653 Surrey 3-1/2 miles sw Godalming pop 1,376 archd Surrey dioc Winchester

WITLEY, GREAT parish 1538 Worcs 5 miles sw Stourport pop 386 archd and dioc Worcester

WITLEY, LITTLE chapelry 1680 parish Holt Worcs 6-3/4 miles sw Stourport pop 286

WITNESHAM parish 1538 Suffolk 4-1/2 miles ne Ipswich pop 562 archd Suffolk dioc Norwich

WITNEY parish 1578 co Oxford comp market town Witney, chapelry Hailey, hamlets Crawley, Curbridge pop 5,336 11 miles nw Oxford archd and dioc Oxford Soc of Friends, Indep, Wesl Meth

WITSTON parish 1728 co Monmouth 6-1/2 miles se Newport pop 106

archd and dioc Llandaff

WITTENHAM, LITTLE parish 1538 Berks 4-1/4 miles nw Wallingford pop 113 archd Berks dioc Salisbury

WITTENHAM, LONG parish 1557 Berks 4 miles nw Wallingford pop 547 archd Berks dioc Salisbury Wesl Meth

WITTERING, EAST parish 1658 Sussex 5-3/4 miles sw Chichester pop 226 archd and dioc Chichester

WITTERING, WEST parish 1622 Sussex 7-1/4 miles sw Chichester pop 606 archd and dioc Chichester

WITTERSHAM parish 1550 Kent 45-1/4 miles se Tenterden pop 919 pec Archbishop of Canterbury Wesl Meth

WITTON chapelry 1561 parish Great Budworth Ches 1/4 mile e Northwich pop 2,912

WITTON or WYTTON parish 1633 Hunts 2-1/2 miles nw St Ives pop 277 archd Huntingdon dioc Lincoln

WITTON parish 1571 Norfolk 5-1/2 miles e Norwich pop 144 archd and dioc Norwich

WITTON parish 1721 Norfolk 3-1/2 miles ne North Walsham pop 295 archd Norfolk dioc Norwich

WITTON, EAST parish 1671 N R York 2-1/2 miles se Middleham pop 687 archd Richmond dioc Chester

WITTON, GILBERT parish 1571 co Durham 3-1/2 miles nw Durham pop 517 archd and dioc Durham

WITTON LE WEAR parish 1558 co Durham 4-1/4 miles ne Bishop Auckland pop 502 archd and dioc Durham

WITTON, LONG township parish Hartburn Northumberland pop 143

WITTON, NETHER parish 1696 Northumberland comp townships Coat Yards or Coal Yards, Ewesley, Healy with Comb Hill, Nether Witton, Nunnikirk, Ritton, Colpark, Ritton Whitehouse pop 520 archd Northumberland dioc Durham

WITTON SHIELS township parish Long Horsley Northumberland pop 13 Roman Cath

WITTON, UPPER hamlet parish Aston Warws

WITTON, WEST parish 1570 N R York 4-1/2 miles w Middleham pop 552 archd Richmond dioc Chester

WIVELISCOMBE parish 1558 Somerset 28 miles w Somerton pop 3,047 pec Prebendary of Wiveliscombe Indep

WIVELSFIELD parish 1559 Sussex 4 miles se Cuckfield pop 559 archd Lewes dioc Chichester Wesl Meth, Bapt

WIVENHOE parish 1560 Essex 4-1/2 miles se Colchester pop 1,714 archd Colchester dioc London

WIVETON parish 1558 Norfolk 1/4 mile sw Clay pop 218 archd and dioc Norwich

WIX or WEEKS parish 1686 Essex 4-1/2 miles se Manningtree pop 832 archd Colchester dioc London

WIXFORD parish (incl regs of Exhall) Warws 2 miles s Alcester pop 108 archd and dioc Worcester

WOBURN parish 1558 Beds 15 miles sw Bedford pop 1,827 pec of

Incumbent Indep, Wesl Meth

WOKEFIELD tything parish Stratfield Mortimer Berks pop 160

WOKING parish 1653 Surrey 2-1/2 miles nw Ripley pop 1,975 archd Surrey dioc Winchester

WOKINGHAM parish 1674 sep juris Wilts and Berks 7 miles se Reading pop 3,139 pec of Dean of Salisbury Bapt, Wesl Meth

WOLD co Northampto See OLD

WOLD NEWTON E R York See NEWTON, WOLD

WOLDINGHAM parish 1765 Surrey 3 miles ne Godstone pop 48 archd Surrey dioc Winchester

WOLFERLOW parish 1629 Herefs 5-1/2 miles ne Bromyard pop 134 archd and dioc Hereford

WOLFAMCOTE parish 1558 Warws 3-3/4 miles nw Daventry pop 372 archd Coventry dioc Lichfield

WOLFORD, GREAT parish 1654 Warws 4 miles sw Shipston upon Stour pop 580 archd and dioc Worcester

WOLFORD, LITTLE hamlet parish Great Wolford Warws pop 280

WOLLASTON parish 1663 co Northampton 3 miles se Wellingborough pop 973 archd Northampton dioc Peterborough Indep, Wesl Meth

WOLLASTON chapelry parish Alberbury Shrops 10-1/2 miles w Shrewbury pop 383 archd Salop dioc Hereford

WOLLASTONE parish 1696 Gloucs 5-1/4 miles ne Chepstow pop 880 archd Hereford dioc Gloucester

WOLLATON parish 1576 Notts 3 miles w Nottingham pop 537 archd Nottingham dioc York

WOLLEY parish 1560 Somerset 3 miles n Bath pop 104 archd Bath dioc Bath and Wells

WOLNEY township parish Dalton in Furness Lancs pop 848

WOLSINGHAM parish 1655 co Durham 16 miles sw Durham pop 2,239 archd and dioc Durham Bapt, Prim and Wesl Meth

WOLSTAN parish 1558 Warws 5-1/2 miles se Coventry pop 968 archd Coventry dioc Lichfield Bapt

WOLSTANTON parish 1628 Staffs comp chapelry Thursfield, townships Chatterley, Chell, Chesterton, Knutton, Oldcott, Rainscliff, Stadmerslow, Wedgwood, Wolstanton, hamlet Brerehurst, liberty Sunstall court pop 10,853 archd Stafford dioc Lichfield

WOLSTONE chapelry parish Uffington Berks 5-1/4 miles se Great Farringdon pop 270

WOLTERTON parish 1560 Norfolk 4-1/4 miles nw Aylsham pop 41 archd and dioc Norwich

WOLVERHAMPTON parish 1603 Staffs comp townships Bilston, Wolverhampton, chapelries Pelsall, Wednesfield, Willenhall, township Bentley, Featherstone, Hatherton, Hilton, Kinvaston pop 44,080 16 miles s Stafford pec Wolverhampton Bapt, Soc of Friends, Indep, Wesl Meth, Meth New Connexion,, Unit, Roman Cath

WOLVERLEY township parish Wem Shrops pop 62

WOLVERLEY parish 1539 Worcs 2 miles nw Kidderminster pop 1,840 pec of Dean and Chapter of Worcester Wesl Meth

WOLVERTON parish 1663 Norfolk 2-3/4 miles nw Castle Rising pop
163 archd and dioc Norwich

WOLVERTON parish 1680 Warws 5 miles sw Warwick pop 166 archd
and dioc Worcester

WOLVES NEWTON parish 1680 co Monmouth 5-1/4 miles se Usk
pop 248 archd and dioc Llandaff

WOLVEY parish 1653 Warws 5-1/4 miles se Nuneaton pop 935 pec
Bishop of Lichfield

WOLVISTON chapelry 1739 parish Billingham co Durham 4-1/2 miles
ne Stockton upon Tees pop 582

WOMBLETON township parish Kirkdale N R York 4 miles se Helmsley pop 262 Wesl Meth

WOMBOURNE parish 1570 Staffs 4 miles sw Wolverhampton pop
1,647 archd Stafford dioc Lichfield

WOMBRIDGE parish 1721 Shrops 2-1/4 miles e Wellington pop 1,855
pec of Monkbridge Abbey

WOMBWELL chapelry parish Darfield W R York pop 836

WOMENSWOULD parish 1574 Kent 5 miles sw Wingham pop 263 archd
and dioc Canterbury

WOMERSLEY parish 1564 W R York comp townships Cridling Stubbs,
Little Smeaton, Wladen Stubbs, Womersley 5 miles se Pontefract
pop 843 archd and dioc York

WONASTOW parish 1674 co Monmouth 2 miles sw Monmouth pop 149
archd and dioc Llandaff

WONERSH parish 1539 Surrey 3-1/2 miles se Guildford pop 1,069
archd Surrey dioc Winchester

WONSTON parish 1570 Hamps 5-3/4 miles s Whitchurch pop 740
pec of Incumbent

WOOBURN parish 1653 Bucks 3 miles sw Beaconsfield pop 1,927
archd Buckingham dioc Lincoln Indep, Wesl Meth

WOOD member cinque port liberty of Dover Kent 3 miles sw Margate
pop 292

WOOD DALLING parish 1653 Norfolk 3 miles nw Reepham pop 512
archd Norfolk dioc Norwich

WOOD EATON parish 1539 co Oxford 4 miles ne Oxford pop 86 archd
and dioc Oxford

WOOD NORTON parish 1722 Norfolk 7 miles nw Reepham pop 315
archd Norfolk dioc Norwich

WOOD RISING parish 1561 Norfolk 2-1/2 miles nw Hingham pop 127
archd Norfolk dioc Norwich

WOOD THORPE hamlet parish Loughborough Leics pop 90

WOODBANK or ROUGH SHOTWICK township parish Shotwick Ches
pop 51

WOODBASTWICK parish 1558 Norfolk 5-1/4 miles nw Acle pop 288
archd and dioc Norwich

WOODBOROUGH parish 1547 Notts 7-1/2 miles ne Nottingham pop
774 pec Collegiate Church of Southwell

WOODBOROUGH parish 1567 Wilts 3-1/2 miles w Pewsey pop 372

archd Wilts dioc Salisbury Wesl Meth

WOODBRIDGE parish 1545 Suffolk 7-1/2 miles ne Ipswich pop 4,769 archd Suffolk dioc Norwich Bapt, Soc of Friends, Indep, Wesl Meth

WOODBURY parish 1557 Devon 3 miles se Topsham pop 1,673 pec Custos and College of Vicars Choral, Cathedral Church of Exeter

WOODCHESTER parish 1563 Gloucs 2-1/2 miles sw Stroud pop 887 archd and dioc Gloucester Bapt

WOODCHURCH parish 1572 Ches comp townships Arrow, Barnston, Irby, Landican, Noctorum, Oxton, Pensby, Prenton, Thingwell, Woodchurch pop 929 archd and dioc Chester

WOODCHURCH parish 1538 Kent 4 miles ne Tenterden pop 1,187 pec Archbishop of Canterbury Wesl Meth

WOODCOT township parish Wrenbury Ches pop 30

WOODCOTE liberty parish South Stoke co Oxford

WOODCOTE chapelry parish Sheriff Hales Shrops pop 195

WOODCOTE tything parish Handley Dorset

WOODCUTT parish 1764 Hamps 5 miles nw Whitchurch pop 90 archd and dioc Winchester

WOOD DITTON Cambs See DITTON, WOOD

WOODEN township parish Lesbury Northumberland

WOODEND hamlet parish Blakesley co Northampton pop 302

WOOD ENDERBY Lincs See ENDERBY, WOOD

WOODFORD township parish Prestbury Ches pop 403

WOODFORD parish 1619 co Northampton 7-1/2 miles sw Daventry pop 827 archd Northampton dioc Peterborough Moravians

WOODFORD parish 1680 co Northampton 2-1/2 miles sw Thrapstone pop 639 archd Northampton dioc Peterborough

WOODFORD parish 1538 Wilts 4-1/4 miles nw Salisbury pop 397 pec Prebendary of Wilsford and Woodford

WOODFORD parish 1638 Essex 3 miles ne London pop 2,548 pec Commissary of London, Consistorial Court of Bishop of London Indep, Wesl Meth

WOODFORD GRANGE extra parochial liberty near Trysull Staffs pop 18

WOODGARSTON tything parish Monk's Sherborne Hamps

WOODGREEN extra parochial liberty Hamps 3 miles ne Fordingbridge pop 363

WOODHALL parish 1562 Lincs 2-3/4 miles sw Horncastle pop 196 pec Manorial Court of Kirkstead

WOODHALL township parish Hemingbrough E R York

WOODHALL township parish Harthill W R York

WOODHAM hamlet parish Waddesdon Bucks pop 38

WOODHAM township parish Aycliffe co Durham pop 204

WOODHAM FERRIS parish 1558 Essex 4-1/2 miles se Danbury pop 826 archd Essex dioc London

WOODHAM MORTIMER parish 1664 Essex 2-1/2 miles sw Maldon pop 339 archd Essex dioc London

WOODHAM WALTER parish 1568 Essex 2-1/2 miles ne Danbury pop 538 archd Essex dioc London

WOODHAY, EAST parish 1610 Hamps 10-1/2 miles nw Whitchurch pop 1,269 pec of Incumbent

WOODHAY, WEST parish 1656 Berks 6 miles sw Newbury pop 127 archd and dioc Salisbury

WOODHEAD chapelry 1782 parish Mottram in Longden Dale Ches 13-1/4 miles ne Stockport Calv Meth

WOODHORN parish 1605 Northumberland comp chapelry Newbiggin, townships Cresswell, Ellington, Hurst, Linmouth, North Seaton, Woodhorn pop 1,416 8 miles ne Morpeth archd Northumberland dioc Durham

WOODHORN demesne parish Woodhorn Northumberland pop 9

WOODHOUSE chapelry 1623 parish Barrow upon Soar Leics 3-1/2 miles w Mountsorrel pop 1,262 archd Leicester dioc Lincoln Wesl Meth

WOODHOUSE township parish Shilbottle Northumberland pop 31

WOODHOUSE township parish St Michael, Lichfield Staffs pop 206

WOODHOUSE HALL extra parochial liberty Notts 6-1/2 miles sw Worksop pop 11

WOODHOUSES township parish Mayfield Staffs pop 28

WOODHURST parish 1653 Hunts 4 miles n St Ives pop 408 archd Huntingdon dioc Lincoln

WOODKIRK Yorks See ARDSLEY, WEST

WOODLAND chapelry 1560 parish Ipplepen Devon 2 miles se Ashburton pop 237 archd Totnes dioc Exeter

WOODLAND township parish Staindrop co Durham pop 233 Wesl Meth

WOODLAND chapelry parish Kirkby Ireleth Lancs 8-1/4 miles nw Ulverstone pop 302

WOODLAND EYAM township parish Eyam Derbys pop 213

WOODLAND HOPE hamlet parish Hope Derbys pop 273

WOODLANDS tything parish Horton Dorset pop 423 Wesl Meth

WOODLANDS tything parish Mere Wilts pop 716

WOODLEIGH parish 1663 Devon 3 miles n Kingsbridge pop 297 archd Totnes dioc Exeter

WOODLESFORD township parish Rothwell W R York

WOODLEY township parish Sonning Berks pop 796

WOODMANCOTE tything parish North Cerney Gloucs

WOODMANCOTE parish 1582 Sussex 5 miles ne Steyning pop 342 archd Lewes dioc Chichester

WOODMANCOTT hamlet parish Bishop's Cleeve Gloucs pop 267

WOODMANCOTT parish 1762 Hamps 8 miles sw Basingstoke pop 92 archd and dioc Winchester

WOODMANSEY township parish St John, Beverley E R York pop 360

WOODMANSTERNE parish 1566 Surrey 4-1/2 miles se Ewell pop 184 archd Surrey dioc Winchester

WOODNESBOROUGH parish 1561 Kent 1-3/4 miles sw Sandwich pop 822 archd and dioc Canterbury

WOODPLUMPTON Lancs See PLUMPTON, WOOD
WOODSETTS township parish Laughton en le Morthen W R York pop 146
WOODSFIELD hamlet parish Powick Worcs pop 42
WOODSFORD parish 1695 Dorset 5-1/2 miles e Dorchester pop 182 archd Dorset dioc Bristol
WOODSIDE township parish Westward Cumberland pop 650
WOODSIDE township parish Shiffnall Shrops pop 379
WOODSIDE QUARTER township parish Wigton Cumberland pop 750
WOODSIDE WARD township parish Elsdon Northumberland pop 131
WOODSTOCK, NEW borough 1653 sep juris co Oxford 8 miles nw Oxford pop 1,380 Part Bapt, Wesl Meth
WOODSTONE parish 1559 Hunts 3/4 mile sw Peterborough pop 243 archd Huntingdon dioc Lincoln
WOODTHORPE township parish North Wingfield Derbys pop 231
WOODTON parish 1538 Norfolk 5 miles nw Bungay pop 539 archd Norfolk dioc Norwich
WOODWALTON Hunts See WALTON, WOOD
WOODYATES, WEST extra parochial liberty Dorset 5-1/2 miles nw Cranborne pop 18
WOOKEY parish 1565 Somerset 1-3/4 miles w Wells pop 1,100 pec of Subdean of Wells Cathedral
WOOL parish 1736 Dorset 6 miles sw Warsham pop 467 archd Dorset dioc Bristol
WOOLASCOTT township parish St Mary, Shrewsbury Shrops
WOOLAVINGTON parish 1694 Somerset 4 miles ne Bridgewater pop 412 archd Wells dioc Bath and Wells
WOOLAVINGTON, EAST and WEST parish 1668 Sussex 4-1/2 miles sw Petworth pop 338 archd and dioc Chichester
WOOLBEDING parish 1581 Sussex 1-3/4 miles nw Midhurst pop 307 archd and dioc Chichester
WOOLBOROUGH or WOLBOROUGH parish 1558 Devon 1 mile s Newton Abbott pop 2,194 archd Totnes dioc Exeter
WOOLDALE township parish Kirk Burton W R York pop 3,993
WOOLER parish 1692 Northumberland 46 miles nw Newcastle upon Tyne pop 1,926 archd Northumberland dioc Durham Bapt, Presb, Scotch Relief, Roman Cath
WOOLFARDISWORTHY parish 1723 Devon 9-1/2 miles sw Bideford pop 840 archd Barnstaple dioc Exeter
WOOLFARDISWORTHY parish 1664 Devon 6 miles nw Crediton pop 226 archd Barnstaple dioc Exeter
WOOLFERTON township parish Richard's Castle Shrops
WOOLHAMPTON parish 1636 Berks 7-1/4 miles e Newbury pop 364 archd Berks dioc Salisbury
WOOLHOPE parish 1558 Herefs 7-3/4 miles sw Ledbury pop 880 Consistorial Court of Dean of Hereford
WOOLLAND parish 1726 Dorset 8 miles nw Blandford Forum pop 119 pec of Consistorial Court of Milton Abbas

WOOLLEY tything parish Chaddleworth Berks

WOOLLEY parish 1576 Hunts 5 miles ne Kimbolton pop 58 archd Huntingdon dioc Lincoln

WOOLLEY chapelry 1651 parish Royston W R York 5-3/4 miles nw Barnsley pop 553 archd and dioc York

WOOLLOS, ST parish co Monmouth pop 7,062 archd and dioc Llandaff Indep

WOOLPIT parish 1558 Suffolk 5-3/4 miles nw Stow Market pop 880 archd Sudbury dioc Norwich

WOOLSINGTON township parish Newburn Northumberland pop 57

WOOLSTANWOOD township parish Nantwich Ches pop 70

WOOLSTASTON parish 1601 Shrops 3-1/2 miles n Church Stretton pop 89 archd Salop dioc Hereford

WOOLSTHORPE parish 1688 Lincs 6-1/4 miles sw Grantham pop 650 archd and dioc Lincoln

WOOLSTON hamlet parish North Cadbury Somerset

WOOLSTONE parish 1563 Gloucs 5 miles nw Winchcomb pop 92 archd and dioc Gloucester

WOOLSTONE township parish Warrington Lancs pop 578

WOOLSTONE tything parish Hound Hamps

WOOLSTONE, GREAT parish 1538 Bucks 3-1/2 miles n Fenny Stratford pop 120 archd Buckingham dioc Lincoln

WOOLSTONE, LITTLE parish 1558 Bucks 3-3/4 miles n Fenny Stratford pop 124 archd Buckingham dioc Lincoln

WOOLSTROP hamlet parish Quedgley Gloucs pop 39

WOOLTON, LITTLE township parish Childwall Lancs pop 734

WOOLTON, MUCH chapelry parish Childwall Lancs pop 1,344

WOOLVERCOTT parish 1596 co Oxford 2-3/4 miles nw Oxford pop 524 archd and dioc Oxford

WOOLVERSTONE parish 1539 Suffolk 4-1/2 miles se Ipswich pop 235 archd Suffolk dioc Norwich

WOOLVERTON parish 1599 Bucks 1 mile ne Stony Stratford pop 417 archd Buckingham dioc Lincoln

WOOLVERTON parish 1754 Somerset 4-1/2 miles ne Frome pop 207 archd Wells dioc Bath and Wells

WOOLVERTON parish 1717 Hamps 7-1/2 miles nw Basingstoke pop 229 archd and dioc Winchester

WOOLWICH parish 1669 Kent 8 miles se London pop 17,661 archd and dioc Rochester Bapt, Indep, Arminian Bible Christians, Welsh and Wesl Meth, Scottish, Roman Cath

WOOPERTON township parish Eglingham Northumberland pop 107

WOORE chapelry parish Muckleston Shrops pop 400

WOOTHORPE hamlet parish Stamford Baron co Northampton pop 49

WOOTON hamlet parish St Mary de Lode Gloucester Gloucs pop 804

WOOTON parish 1760 Hamps 4 miles ne Newport archd and dioc Winchester Wesl Meth

WOOTTON parish 1562 Beds 4-1/2 miles sw Bedford pop 1,051 archd Bedford dioc Lincoln Wesl Meth

WOOTTON parish 1657 Berks 3-1/2 miles nw Abingdon pop 340 archd Berks dioc Salisbury

WOOTTON parish 1546 Kent 9-1/2 miles se Canterbury pop 128 archd and dioc Canterbury

WOOTTON parish 1563 Lincs 5-3/4 miles se Barton upon Humber pop 459 archd and dioc Lincoln Wesl Meth

WOOTTON parish 1797 co Northampton 2-1/2 miles se Northampton pop 643 archd Northampton dioc Peterborough

WOOTTON parish 1564 co Oxford 2-1/4 miles nw Woodstock pop 1,060 archd and dioc Oxford

WOOTTON parish 1560 Hamps 4-1/4 miles nw Basingstoke pop 847 archd and dioc Winchester

WOOTTON township parish Eccleshall Staffs pop 150

WOOTTON township parish Ellastone Staffs pop 269

WOOTTON BASSETT parish 1591 borough Wilts 36 miles nw Salisbury archd Wilts dioc Salisbury pop 1,896 Indep

WOOTTON COURTNEY parish 1558 Somerset 3 miles w Dunster pop 426 archd Taunton dioc Bath and Wells

WOOTTON FITZPAIN parish 1678 Dorset 4 miles ne Lyme Regis pop 455 archd Dorset dioc Bristol

WOOTTON GLANVILLE parish 1546 Dorset 7-1/2 miles se Sherborne pop 331 archd Dorset dioc Bristol

WOOTTON, LEEK parish 1581 Warws 2-1/4 miles s Kenilworth pop 433 archd Coventry dioc Lichfield

WOOTTON NEWLAND tything parish Wootton Glanville Dorset

WOOTTON, NORTH parish 1539 Dorset 2 miles se Sherborne pop 78 pec Dean of Salisbury

WOOTTON, NORTH parish 1654 Norfolk 2 miles sw Castle Rising pop 179 pec of Castle Rising

WOOTTON, NORTH parish 1563 Somerset 4 miles sw Shepton Mallet pop 307 pec Precentor of Cathedral Church of Wells

WOOTTON RIVERS parish 1728 Wilts 3 miles ne Pewsey pop 405 archd Wilts dioc Salisbury

WOOTTON, SOUTH parish 1556 Norfolk 2-1/4 miles sw Castle Rising pop 177 pec of Castle Rising

WOOTTON UNDER WOOD parish 1599 Bucks 7 miles nw Thame pop 312 pec Archbishop of Canterbury

WOOTTON WAWEN parish 1547 Warws 1-1/2 miles s Henley in Arden pop 2,271 archd and dioc Worcester Roman Cath

WORCESTER city excl juris Worcs 111 miles nw London pop 18,610 comp St Albans 1630, All Saints 1560, St Andrews 1656, St Clement 1694, St Helen 1538, St Martin 1538, St Nicholas 1563, St Oswald's Hospital 1695, St Peter the Great 1686, St Swithin 1538, Cathedral Church 1693 archd and dioc Worcester Bapt, Soc of Friends, Countess of Huntingdon's Connexion, Indep, Wesl Meth, Roman Cath

WORDWELL parish 1581 Suffolk 6 miles nw Bury St Edmunds pop 69 archd Sudbury dioc Norwich

WORFIELD parish 1562 Shrops 3-3/4 miles ne Bridgenorth pop 1,676 archd Stafford dioc Lichfield

WORGRET tything parish East Stoke Dorset 1 mile w Wareham

WORKINGTON parish 1663 Cumberland comp market town Workington, chapelry Great Clifton, townships Little Clifton, Stainburn, Winscales pop 7,196 34 miles sw Carlisle archd Richmond dioc Chester Indep, Prim and Wesl Meth, Presb, Roman Cath

WORKSOP parish 1558 Notts 26 miles n Nottingham pop 5,566 archd Nottingham dioc York Indep, Wesl Meth, Roman Cath

WORLABY extra parochial liberty Lincs 7 miles s Louth pop 34

WORLABY parish 1559 Lincs 5-1/2 miles ne Glandford Bridge pop 309 archd and dioc Lincoln

WORLDHAM, EAST parish 1690 Hamps 2-1/2 miles se Alton pop 212 archd and dioc Winchester

WORLDHAM, WEST parish 1649 Hamps 2-1/2 miles se Alton pop 96 archd and dioc Winchester

WORLE parish 1712 Somerset 8 miles nw Axbridge pop 770 archd Wells dioc Bath and Wells Wesl Meth

WORLESTON township parish Acton Ches pop 367

WORLINGHAM parish 1538 Suffolk 1-1/4 miles se Beccles pop 202 archd Suffolk dioc Norwich

WORLINGTON parish 1719 Suffolk 1-1/4 miles sw Mildenhall pop 368 archd Sudbury dioc Norwich

WORLINGTON, EAST parish 1725 Devon 6 miles e Chulmleigh pop 292 archd Barnstaple dioc Exeter

WORLINGTON, WEST parish 1681 Devon 5-1/2 miles e Chulmleigh pop 187 archd Barnstaple dioc Exeter

WORLINGWORTH parish 1558 Suffolk 5 miles nw Framlingham pop 729 archd Suffolk dioc Norwich

WORMBRIDGE parish 1753 Herefs 9 miles sw Hereford pop 121 archd and dioc Hereford

WORMEGAY parish 1561 Norfolk 7-1/2 miles ne Downham Market pop 323 archd Norfolk dioc Norwich

WORMHILL chapelry 1674 parish Tideswell Derbys 2-1/4 miles sw Tideswell pop 313 pec Dean and Chapter of Lichfield

WORMINGFORD parish 1557 Essex 3-3/4 miles sw Nayland pop 543 archd Colchester dioc London

WORMINGHALL parish 1538 Bucks 4-3/4 miles nw Thame pop 297 archd Buckingham dioc Lincoln

WORMINGTON parish 1719 Gloucs 9 miles ne Winchcombe archd and dioc Gloucester

WORMLEIGHTON parish 1586 Warws 5-3/4 miles se Southam pop 161 archd Coventry dioc Lichfield

WORMLEY parish 1674 Herts 2-1/4 miles ne Cheshunt pop 471 archd of Middlesex Consistorial Court of Bishop of London

WORMSHILL parish 1717 Kent 5 miles sw Sittingbourne pop 186 archd and dioc Canterbury

WORMSLEY parish 1595 Herefs 3-1/2 miles se Weobley pop 102

archd and dioc Hereford

WORPLESDON parish 1570 Surrey 3-1/2 miles nw Guildford pop 1,360 archd Surrey dioc Winchester

WORSALL, HIGH chapelry 1726 parish North Allerton N R York 4 miles sw Yarm pop 133 pec Dean and Chapter of Durham

WORSALL, LOW township parish Kirk Leavington N R York pop 164

WORSBROUGH chapelry 1559 parish Darfield W R York 2-1/2 miles se Barnesley 2,677 archd and dioc York

WORSLEY chapelry parish Eccles Lancs pop 7,839 archd and dioc Chester Wesl Meth

WORSTEAD parish 1558 Norfolk 2-3/4 miles se North Walsham pop 830 archd Norfolk dioc Norwich Bapt

WORSTHORN township parish Whalley Lancs pop 798

WORSTON township parish Whalley Lancs pop 129

WORSTON township parish St Mary Staffs pop 25

WORTH township parish Prestbury Ches pop 490

WORTH or WORD parish 1720 Kent 1-1/2 miles s Sandwich pop 411 archd and dioc Canterbury

WORTH parish 1600 Sussex 7-1/2 miles n Cuckfield pop 1,859 archd Lewes dioc Chichester Dissenters

WORTH MATRAVERS parish 1762 Dorset 3-1/2 miles se Corfe Castle pop 356 archd Dorset dioc Bristol

WORTHAM parish 1538 Suffolk 5-1/2 miles nw Eye pop 1,016 archd Sudbury dioc Norwich

WORTHEN parish 1558 Shrops pop 2,668 9 miles ne Montgomery archd Salop dioc Hereford

WORTHEN quarter parish Worthen Shrops

WORTHING parish 1653 Norfolk 4 miles ne East Dereham pop 138 archd and dioc Norwich

WORTHING chapelry parish Broadwater Sussex Indep, Wesl Meth

WORTHINGTON township parish Standish Lancs pop 124

WORTHINGTON chapelry 1759 parish Breedon Leics 4-1/4 miles ne Ashby de la Zouch pop 1,211

WORTHY, ABBOTS tything parish King's Worthy Hamps

WORTHY, HEADBOURN parish 1616 Hamps 2 miles ne Winchester pop 190 archd and dioc Winchester

WORTHY, KING'S parish 1538 Hamps 2-1/4 miles ne Winchester pop 345 archd and dioc Winchester

WORTHY, MARTYR parish 1542 Hamps 3 miles ne Winchester pop 219 archd and dioc Winchester

WORTING parish 1604 Hamps 2-1/4 miles w Basingstoke pop 120 archd and dioc Winchester

WORTLEY tything parish Wootton under Edge Gloucs

WORTLEY chapelry 1678 parish St Peter Leeds W R York 2-1/2 miles sw Leeds pop 5,944 Wesl Meth, Indep

WORTLEY chapelry parish Tankersley W R York 5-1/2 miles sw Barnsley pop 918

WORTON hamlet parish Cassington co Oxford pop 75

WORTON tything parish Potterne Wilts pop 302 Wesl Meth

WORTON, NETHER parish 1562 co Oxford 3-3/4 miles sw Deddington pop 94 archd and dioc Oxford

WORTON, OVER parish no regs co Oxford 4 miles sw Deddington pop 56 archd and dioc Oxford

WORTWELL hamlet parish Reddenhall Norfolk pop 537

WOTHERSOME township parish Bardsey W R York pop 21

WOTTON ABBAS liberty parish Whitchurch Canonicorum Dorset 4-3/4 miles ne Lyme Regis

WOTTON LOW HILL and UP HILL parish 1596 Surrey 3 miles sw Dorking pop 651 archd Surrey dioc Winchester

WOTTON UNDER EDGE parish 1571 Gloucs 19 miles sw Gloucester comp tythings Huntingford, Sinwell with Bradley, Symonds Hall with Combe, Wortley pop 5,482 archd and dioc Gloucester Bapt, Indep, Wesl Meth

WOUGHTON ON THE GREEN parish 1558 Bucks 2-1/2 miles sw Fenny Stratford pop 303 archd Buckingham dioc Lincoln

WOULDHAM parish 1538 Kent 2-3/4 miles sw Rochester pop 411 archd and dioc Rochester

WRABNESS parish 1650 Essex 4-3/4 miles e Manningtree pop 248 archd Colchester dioc Essex Wesl Meth

WRAGBY parish 1567 Lincs 10-1/2 miles ne Lincoln pop 601 archd and dioc Lincoln Wesl Meth

WRAGBY parish 1540 W R York comp townships West Hardwick, Hasle, Hill Top, Hurstwick with Nostal 5 miles sw Pontefract pop 756 archd and dioc York

WRAGHOLME hamlet parish Grainthorpe Lincs

WRAMPLINGHAM parish 1566 Norfolk 3 miles ne Wymondham pop 247 archd Norfolk dioc Norwich

WRANGLE parish 1653 Lincs 8-1/4 miles ne Boxton pop 1,030 archd and dioc Lincoln

WRANTAGE tything parish North Curry Somerset

WRATTING, GREAT parish 1593 Suffolk 2-3/4 miles ne Haverhill pop 344 archd Sudbury dioc Norwich

WRATTING, LITTLE parish 1555 Suffolk 5-3/4 miles nw Clare pop 212 archd Sudbury dioc Norwich

WRATTING, WEST parish 1579 Cambs 5-1/4 miles ne Linton pop 763 archd and dioc Ely

WRATTON or WRAYTON township parish Melling Lancs

WRAWBY parish 1715 Lincs 2 miles ne Glandford pop 2,418 archd and dioc Lincoln

WRAXALL parish (incl in regs of Rampisham) Dorset 8 miles se Beaminster pop 70 archd Dorset dioc Bristol

WRAXALL parish 1562 Somerset 6-1/2 miles sw Bristol pop 802 archd Bath dioc Bath and Wells

WRAXALL, NORTH parish 1677 Wilts 7 miles nw Chippenham pop 415 archd Wilts dioc Salisbury

WRAXALL, SOUTH chapelry 1676 parish Great Bradford Wilts 5

miles nw Melksham pop 389

WRAY township parish Melling Lancs pop 586

WREA township parish Kirkham Lancs

WREAY chapelry 1750 parish St Mary, Carlisle Cumberland 5-3/4 miles se Carlisle pop 166

WRECKLESHAM township parish Farnham Surrey pop 770

WREIGH HILL township parish Rothbury Northumberland pop 27

WRELTON township parish Middleton N R York pop 172

WRENBURY parish 1684 Ches comp townships Broomhall, Chorley, Woodcot, Wrenbury with Frith pop 903 4-3/4 miles sw Nantwich archd and dioc Chester

WRENINGHAM, GREAT and LITTLE parish 1656 Norfolk 4-1/4 miles se Wymondham pop 409 archd Norfolk dioc Norwich

WRENTHAM parish 1602 Suffolk 4-1/2 miles nw Southwold pop 1,022 archd Suffolk dioc Norwich Indep

WRENTHORP township parish Wakefield W R York

WRESSEL parish 1724 E R York comp townships Newsham with Brind, Wressel with Loftsome pop 386 3-3/4 miles nw Howden archd East Riding dioc York

WRESTLINGWORTH parish 1578 Beds 6 miles ne Biggleswade pop 448 archd Bedford dioc Lincoln

WRETHAM, EAST parish 1748 Norfolk 5-3/4 miles ne Thetford pop 325 archd Norfolk dioc Norwich

WRETHAM, WEST parish Norfolk 5-1/2 miles ne Thetford archd Norfolk dioc Norwich

WRETTON parish 1693 Norfolk 1 mile w Stoke Ferry pop 523 archd Norfolk dioc Norwich

WRIBBENHALL hamlet parish Kidderminster Worcs

WRIGHTINGTON township parish Eccleston Lancs pop 1,601

WRINEHILL township parish Wybunbury Ches

WRINGTON parish 1538 Somerset 7 miles ne Axbridge pop 1,540 archd Bath dioc Bath and Wells Indep, Wesl Meth

WRITHLINGTON parish 1675 Somerset 7 miles nw Frome pop 245 archd Wells dioc Bath and Wells

WRITTLE parish 1634 Essex 2-1/2 miles sw Chelmsford pec Writtle Indep

WROCKWARDINE parish 1591 Shrops 2 miles nw Wellington pop 2,528 archd Salop dioc Lichfield

WROOT parish 1573 Lincs 8 miles ne Bawtry pop 289 archd Stow dioc Lincoln Wesl Meth

WROTHAM parish 1558 Kent 11 miles nw Maidstone pop 2,469 pec Archbishop of Canterbury

WROTTESLEY hamlet parish Tettenhall Staffs pop 246

WROUGHTON parish 1653 Wilts 3 miles sw Swindon pop 1,545 archd Wilts dioc Salisbury Wesl Meth

WROXETER parish 1613 Shrops 5-3/4 miles se Shrewsbury pop 636 archd Shrops dioc Lichfield

WROXHALL parish 1586 Warws 6 miles nw Warwick pop 181 archd

and dioc Worcester

WROXHAM parish 1558 Norfolk 2-1/2 miles se Coltishall pop 368 archd and dioc Norwich

WROXTON parish 1548 co Oxford 3 miles nw Banbury pop 780 archd and dioc Oxford Wesl Meth

WUERDALE township parish Rochdale Lancs pop 6,754

WYASTON township parish Edlaston Derbys

WYBERTON parish 1538 Lincs 2-1/4 miles s Boston pop 530 archd and dioc Lincoln

WYBUNBURY parish 1558 Ches comp townships Bartherton, Basford, Blakenhall, Bridgemere, Checkley with Wrinehill, Chorlton, Doddington, Hatherton, Hough, Hunterson, Lea, Rope, Shavington with Cresty, Stapeley, Walgherton, Weston, Willaston, Wybunbury pop 4,193 archd and dioc Chester Wesl Meth

WYCLIFFE parish 1681 N R York 2-1/2 miles ne Greta Bridge pop 156 archd Richmond dioc Chester

WYCOMB hamlet 1700 parish Rothwell Leics 4-1/2 miles ne Melton Mowbray

WYCOMBE, HIGH or CHIPPING parish 1674 borough Bucks 31 miles se Buckingham pop 6,299 archd Buckingham dioc Lincoln Indep, Bapt, Soc of Friends

WYCOMBE, WEST parish 1581 Bucks 2-1/2 miles nw High Wycombe pop 1,901 archd Buckingham dioc Lincoln Indep, Wesl Meth

WYDDIALL parish 1666 Herts 1-1/2 miles ne Buntingford pop 243 archd Middlesex dioc London

WYE parish 1538 Kent 4 miles ne Ashford pop 1, 639 archd and dioc Canterbury Wesl Meth

WYERSDALE, NETHER township parish Garstang Lancs pop 770

WYERSDALE, OVER chapelry parish Lancaster Lancs pop 872

WYFORDBY or WYVERBY parish 1557 Leics 3 miles e Melton Mowbray pop 98 archd Leicester dioc Lincoln

WYHAM parish 1695 Lincs 7-1/4 miles nw Louth pop 94 archd and dioc Lincoln

WYKE tything parish Axminster Devon

WYKE HAMON hamlet parish Wicken Co Northampton

WYKE CHAMPFLOWER parish Somerset See WEEKE CHAMPFLOWER

WYKE REGIS parish 1676 Dorset 1-1/4 miles sw Weymouth pop 1,197 archd Dorset dioc Bristol

WYKEHAM parish 1653 N R York 6-1/2 miles sw Scarborough pop 605 archd Cleveland dioc York

WYKEHAM, EAST parish no regs Lincs 7 miles nw Louth pop 31 archd and dioc Lincoln

WYKEHAM, WEST parish no regs Lincs 7-1/2 miles nw Louth archd and dioc Lincoln

WYKEN parish 1600 Warws 3 miles ne Coventry pop 104 archd Coventry dioc Lichfield

WYLAM township parish Ovingham Northumberland pop 887

WYLDECOURT tything parish Hawkchurch Dorset pop 316

WYMERING parish 1738 Hamps 4-1/4 miles w Havant pop 578 archd and dioc Winchester

WYMINGTON parish 1662 Beds 6-1/4 miles n Harrold pop 257 archd Bedford dioc Lincoln

WYMONDHAM parish 1538 Leics 6-1/2 e Melton Mowbray pop 746 archd Leicester dioc Lincoln

WYMONDHAM or WINDHAM parish 1614 Norfolk 9 miles sw Norwich comp market town Wymondham, divisions Downham, Market Street, Silfield, Sutton, Towngreen, Wattlefield pop 5,485 archd Norfolk dioc Norwich Bapt, Soc of Friends, Indep, Wesl Meth

WYMONDLEY, GREAT parish 1561 Herts 2 miles se Hitchin pop 321 archd Huntingdon dioc Lincoln

WYMONDLEY, LITTLE parish 1650 Herts 2-1/4 miles se Hitchin archd Huntingdon dioc Lincoln

WYRARDISBURY or WRAYSBURY parish 1734 Bucks 3 miles sw Colnbrook pop 682 archd Buckingham dioc Lincoln

WYRE PIDDL chapelry 1670 parish Fladbury Worcs pop 175

WYRLEY, GREAT township parish Canoock Staffs pop 531

WYRLEY, LITTLE township parish Norton under Cannock Staffs

WYSALL parish 1654 Notts 8-3/4 miles se Nottingham pop 271 archd Nottingham dioc York

WYTHALL chapelry 1760 parish King's Norton Worcs 8 miles ne Bromsgrove archd and dioc Worcester

WYTHAM parish 1559 Berks 3 miles nw Oxford pop 218 archd Berks dioc Salisbury

WYTHBURN chapelry parish Crosthwaite Cumberland

WYTHOP chapelry 1792 parish Lorton Cumberland 5 miles se Cockermouth pop 121

WYTON township parish Swine E R York pop 93

WYVERSTONE parish 1560 Suffolk 6-3/4 miles n Stow Market pop 316 archd Sudbury dioc Norwich

WYVILL parish no regs Lincs 6 miles nw Colsterworth archd and dioc Lincoln

YADDLETHORPE hamlet parish Bottesford Lincs pop 105

YAFFORTH chapelry 1675 parish Danby Wisk N R York 1-1/2 miles nw North Allerton pop 165

YALDING parish 1559 Kent 5 miles sw Maidstone pop 2,460 archd and dioc Rochester

YANWATH township parish Barton Westm pop 327

YANWORTH chapelry 1695 parish Pocklington E R York 2-1/2 miles nw Pocklington pop 137

YAPTON parish 1539 Sussex 5 miles sw Arundel pop 578 archd and dioc Chichester

YARBOROUGH or YARBURGH parish 1561 Lincs 4-3/4 miles ne Louth pop 175 archd and dioc Lincoln Wesl Meth

YARBOROUGH hamlet parish Croxton Lincs

YARCOMBE parish 1551 Devon 5-1/2 miles w Chard pop 804 archd and dioc Exeter Bapt

YARDLEY parish 1546 Herts 4-1/2 miles sw Buntingford pop 599 archd Huntingdon dioc Lincoln

YARDLEY parish 1539 Worcs 4-1/2 miles e Birmingham pop 2,488 archd and dioc Worcester

YARDLEY GOBION hamlet parish Potters Pury co Northampton pop 594 Indep

YARDLEY HASTINGS parish 1558 co Northampton 8-1/2 miles se Northampton pop 1,051 archd Northampton dioc Peterborough Indep

YARKHILL parish 1559 Herefs 7-1/4 miles ne Hereford pop 409 archd and dioc Hereford

YARLESIDE township parish Dalton in Furness Lancs pop 499

YARLETT liberty parish Weston upon Trent Staffs pop 21

YARLINGTON parish 1654 Somerset 3-1/2 miles sw Wincanton pop 283 archd Wells dioc Bath and Wells

YARLINGTON hamlet parish North Cadbury Somerset

YARM parish 1649 N R York 44 miles nw York pop 1,636 archd Cleveland dioc York Soc of Friends, Indep, Prim and Wesl Meth, Roman Cath

YARMOUTH parish 1614 borough Hamps 10 miles w Newport pop 586 archd and dioc Winchester Bapt, Wesl Meth

YARMOUTH, GREAT parish 1558 borough sep juris Norfolk 23 miles se Norwich pop 21,115 archd and dioc Norwich Part Bapt, Soc of Friends, Indep, Prim and Wesl Meth, Unit, Roman Cath

YARNFIELD hamlet parish Maiden Bradley Somerset pop 91

YARNSCOMBE parish 1653 Devon 6 miles ne Great Torrington pop 498 archd Barnstaple dioc Exeter

YARNTON or YARINGTON parish 1569 co Oxford 4-1/4 miles nw Oxford pop 299 archd and dioc Oxford

YARPOLE parish 1561 Herefs 5 miles nw Leominster pop 651 archd and dioc Hereford

YARWELL parish 1572 co Northampton 1-1/4 miles sw Wansford pop 369 pec Prebendary of Nassington

YATE parish 1660 Gloucs 1 mile w Chipping Sodbury pop 824 archd and dioc Gloucester

YATE township parish Whalley Lancs pop 1,209

YATE, GREAT township parish Croxden Staffs

YATEHOUSE township parish Middlewich Ches

YATELY parish 1636 Hamps 3-3/4 miles ne Hartford Bridge pop 1,874 archd and dioc Winchester

YATESBURY parish 1706 Wilts 4-1/2 miles ne Calne pop 274 archd Wilts dioc Salisbury

YATTENDON parish 1558 Berks 6-1/2 miles se East Ilsey pop 241 archd Berks dioc Salisbury

YATTON chapelry parish Much Marcle Herefs pop 211

YATTON parish 1675 Somerset 6 miles n Axbridge comp East and West Yatton pop 1,865 pec Prebendary of Yatton, Cathedral Church of Wells

YATTON KEYNALL parish 1653 Wilts 4-1/4 miles nw Chippenham pop 419 archd Wilts dioc Salisbury

YAVERLAND parish 1632 Hamps 8 miles se Newport pop 96 archd and dioc Winchester

YAXHAM parish 1686 Norfolk 2-1/2 miles se East Dereham pop 505 archd Norfolk dioc Norwich

YAXLEY parish 1653 Hunts 14 miles nw Huntingdon pop 1,140 archd Huntingdon dioc Lincoln Indep

YAXLEY parish 1684 Suffolk 1-1/2 miles w Eye pop 478 archd Sudbury dioc Norwich

YAZOR parish 1621 Herefs 4-1/2 miles s Weobley pop 196 archd and dioc Hereford

YEADON township parish Guisley W R York pop 2,761 Wesl Meth

YEALAND CONYERS township parish Warton Lancs pop 294

YEALAND REDMAYNE township parish Warton Lancs pop 227

YEALMPTON parish 1600 Devon 3-3/4 miles se Earl's Plympton pop 1,262 archd Totnes dioc Exeter

YEARDSLEY township parish Taxall Ches Wesl Meth

YEARSLEY township parish Coxwold N R York pop 164

YEAVELEY chapelry parish Shirley Derbys pop 271 Indep

YEAVERING township parish Kirk Newton Northumberland pop 68

YEDDINGHAM parish 1717 E R York 8-1/4 miles ne New Malton pop 109 archd East Riding dioc York

YELDERSLEY hamlet parish Ashbourn Derbys pop 226

YELDHAM, GREAT parish 1653 Essex 3 miles nw Castle Hedlingham pop 673 archd Middlesex dioc London

YELDHAM, LITTLE parish 1564 Essex 4-1/4 miles n Castle Hedingham pop 371 Commissary of Essex and Herts, Consistorial Court of Bishop of London

YELFORD parish 1745 co Oxford 3-1/4 miles s Witney pop 17 archd and dioc Oxford

YELLING parish 1583 Hunts 6 miles ne St Neots pop 326 archd Huntingdon dioc Lincoln

YELVERTOFT parish 1573 co Northampton 9-3/4 miles ne Daventry pop 596 archd Northampton dioc Peterborough Indep

YELVERTON parish 1559 Norfolk 5-3/4 miles se Norwich pop 80 archd Norfolk dioc Norwich

YEOVIL parish 1563 Somerset 9-1/2 miles se Somerton pop 5,921 archd Wells dioc Bath and Wells Bapt, Indep, Wesl Meth, Unit

YEOVILTON parish 1658 Somerset 1-1/2 miles e Ilchester pop 275 archd Wells dioc Bath and Wells

YETLINGTON township parish Whitingham Northumberland

YETMINSTER parish 1677 Dorset 5-1/4 miles sw Sherborne pop 1,199 pec of Prebendary of Yetminster

YIELDING or YELDEN parish 1653 Beds 3-3/4 miles e Higham Ferrers pop 276 archd Bedford dioc Lincoln

YOCKLETON township parish Westbury Shrops

YOKEFLEET E R York See YORKFLEET

YORK city excl juris E R York 198 miles nw London pop 25,359
Bapt, Soc of Friends, Indep, Prim and Wesl Meth, Sandemanians,
Unit, Roman Cath comp York Minster 1634, All Saints 1577, All
Saints Pavement 1554, St Crux 1540, St Cuthbert 1581, St Denis
1558, St Helen Stonegate 1568, St John Micklegate 1570, St Law-
rence 1606, St Margaret Walmgate 1558, St Martin Coney St 1557,
St Martin Micklegate 1539, St Mary Hishopshill 1598, St Mary
Bishopshill Jun 1602, St Mary Castlegate 1604, St Maurice 1647,
St Michael le Belfry 1565, St Michael Spurrier Gate 1598, St
Olave, Marygate 1538, St Sampton 1640, St Savior 1567, Holy Trin-
ity Goodramgate 1573, Holy Trinity King's Court 1616, Holy Trin-
ity Micklegate 1586, some parishes in pec of Dean and Chapter of
York others in archd and dioc York Search both
YORKFLEET township parish Howden E R York pop 190
YOULGRAVE parish 1558 comp chapelry Middleton with Smerrill,
township Elton, chapelries Birchover, Stanton, Winster, township
Youlgrave, hamlet Gratton Derbys pop 3,681 3 miles sw Bake-
well archd Derby dioc Lichfield Wesl Meth
YOULTHORPE township parish Bishop Wilton E R York pop 106
YOXFORD parish 1559 Suffolk 23-1/2 miles ne Ipswich pop 1,149
archd Suffolk dioc Norwich
YOXHALL parish 1645 Staffs 7-1/2 miles ne Lichfield pop 1,582
archd Stafford dioc Lichfield
ZEAL MONACHORUM parish 1594 Devon 1-1/4 miles n Bow pop 747
archd Barnstaple dioc Exeter
ZEAL, SOUTH chapelry parish South Tawton Devon
ZEALS tything parish Mere Wilts pop 510
ZENNOR parish 1592 Cornwall 5 miles se St Ives pop 811 archd
Cornwall dioc Exeter Wesl Meth